# THE CRB COMMODITY YEARBOOK 1997

BRIDGE Information Systems America, Inc./
Commodity Research Bureau

John Wiley & Sons, Inc.
New York • Chichester • Weinheim • Brisbane • Singapore • Toronto

Published by John Wiley & Sons, Inc.


ISBN 0-471-17966-3

Printed in the United States of America
10 9 8 7 6 5 4 3 2 1



**BRIDGE** Commodity Research Bureau
30 South Wacker Drive, Suite 1810
Chicago IL 60606
312-454-1801
800-621-5271

# TABLE OF CONTENTS

# ACKNOWLEDGMENTS

*The editors wish to thank the following for source material:*

Aluminum Association
American Bureau of Metal Statistics
American Gas Association
American Iron and Steel Institute
*American Metal Market*
American Paper and Pulp Association
American Petroleum Institute
Atomic Industrial Forum Inc.
Chicago Board of Trade
Chicago Mercantile Exchange
Citrus Associates of the N.Y. Cotton Exchange
Coffee, Sugar & Cocoa Exchange
Commodity Exchange, N.Y.
Commodity Futures Trading Commission
The Conference Board
Edison Electric Institute
F.W. Dodge Corp.
Federal Power Commission
Federal Reserve Board
Florida Department of Citrus
Futures Industry Association
General Services Administration
Gill & Duffus Ltd.
Gold Fields Mineral Services Ltd.
Handy & Harman
International Cotton Advisory Committee
International Monetary Market (Chicago)
International Rubber Study Group
International Tea Committee
Johnson Matthey Ltd.
*The Journal of Commerce*
Kansas City Board of Trade
Leather Industries of America Inc.
London Metal Exchange
MidAmerica Commodity Exchange
Minneapolis Grain Exchange
National Coffee Association of U.S.A., Inc.
New York Cotton Exchange
New York Futures Exchange
New York Mercantile Exchange
Newsprint Service Bureau
Nuclear Exchange Corp.
Nuclear Regulatory Commission
*Oil World*
Organization for Economic Co-operation and Development (OECD)
Portland Cement Association
*Random Lengths*
Rubber Manufacturers Association
Shell Briefing Service
The Silver Institute
Society of the Plastics Industry Inc.
Tea Council Inc.
Textile Economics Bureau Inc.
Textile Organon
U.N. Conference on Trade and Development
U.N. Food and Agriculture Organization
U.S. Bureau of Mines
U.S. Department of Agriculture
U.S. Department of Commerce
U.S. Department of Energy
U.S. Department of the Interior
U.S. Department of Labor
U.S. Department of the Treasury
*The Wall Street Journal*
Winnipeg Commodity Exchange
Wool Services Co.
Zinc Institute

In 1996, the BRIDGE Commodity Research Bureau Futures Price Index[1] declined for the first time since 1992, ending the year at 239.61. The loss for the year was a minimal 3.57 points, or 1.47 percent.

Among the eight sub-indices[2], four were higher and four were lower. Advances in excess of 20 percent were seen in the livestock and energy groups, while grains and orange juice, the lone component of the miscellaneous sub-index, registered losses greater than 20 percent.

### *Livestock*

The 28.09 percent rise in the livestock index was solely due to strong gains in the pork complex as lean hog prices rose 23.45 percent and pork belly prices rose 41.32 percent. These gains balanced out a small 2.18 percent decline in live cattle prices.

The gains in pork prices were a result of rising world consumption with much of the gain attributable to increased demand from China.

### *Energy*

The energy index rose a strong 22.90 percent on the back of a 32.58 percent rise in crude oil prices. Heating oil was up 23.88 percent for the year and unleaded gasoline prices rose 20.06 percent.

In the fourth quarter of 1996, crude oil prices traded to a five-year high of $26.80 based on low stock levels of both crude and its products in the U.S and Europe, strong demand from the U.S. and non-OECD countries, and extensive delays in reaching the U.N.-Iraq oil-for-food deal.

### *Imported*

The imported index rose 9.94 percent in 1996 on a mixed performance from its three components. Coffee prices rose 23.19 percent, cocoa prices rose 9.22 percent, while sugar values dropped 5.17 percent for the year.

Coffee prices began rising in the third quarter and ended the year close to the 1996 highs based on very low stock levels in the U.S. and Europe. Cocoa prices posted small gains but remain far below the long-term average. Sugar prices were retreating at the end of the year due to the availability of a large Brazilian crop.

### *Industrials*

The industrial index rose a slight 2.12 percent as strong gains in lumber and crude oil offset declines in the other four components.

Lumber rose 56.43 percent and crude gained the previously mentioned 32.58 percent. Moving lower were were copper down 16.84 percent, silver down 8.01 percent, cotton down 7.28 percent, and platinum down 7.26 percent.

### *Grains and Oilseeds*

The grains index registered the largest decline among the sub-indices falling 22.91 percent due to large year-on-year increases in production. All four components showed losses for the year led by oats down 37.25 percent, corn down 30.06 percent, wheat down 25.57 percent, and soybean meal down 2.96 percent.

The oilseeds index dropped 5.36 percent for the year due to a 6.09 percent drop in soybeans and an 8.55 percent decline in canola. Flaxseed, the third component of the oilseeds index, was unchanged from 1995.

### *Precious Metals*

The precious metals sub-index fell 6.52 percent for the year as all three component markets registered losses.

Silver was down 8.01 percent, platinum down 7.26 percent, and gold was off 4.87 percent as the lack of volatility and persistent price downtrends diminished investment interest in the three metals.

### *Miscellaneous*

The miscellaneous index, whose only component market is frozen concentrated orange juice, fell 21.19 percent for the year. 1996 closing price levels for orange juice reached three-year lows due to large crops in Florida and Brazil.

---

1 Knight-Ridder Financial and the Commodity Research Bureau were acquired by BRIDGE Information Systems, Inc. in July, 1997.

2 The sub-indices may contain markets that are not included in the BRIDGE CRB Futures Price Index in order to most accurately reflect market movements and situations within the individual sub-index groups.

## Monthly CRB Futures Price Index  High, Low & Close 1967 = 100

| Year | | Jan. | Feb. | Mar. | Apr. | May | June | July | Aug. | Sept. | Oct. | Nov. | Dec. | Range |
|---|---|---|---|---|---|---|---|---|---|---|---|---|---|---|
| 1987 | High | 213.9 | 213.7 | 210.1 | 221.7 | 235.6 | 234.6 | 227.8 | 226.8 | 227.3 | 232.7 | 237.1 | 234.7 | 237.1 |
| | Low | 208.3 | 204.2 | 205.7 | 209.4 | 222.6 | 223.1 | 220.7 | 222.4 | 223.5 | 222.7 | 221.1 | 227.5 | 204.2 |
| | Close | 212.6 | 205.4 | 208.7 | 221.7 | 224.9 | 225.9 | 225.9 | 223.0 | 223.8 | 223.4 | 234.6 | 232.5 | ------ |
| 1988 | High | 239.3 | 232.9 | 233.5 | 236.0 | 248.4 | 270.5 | 265.8 | 251.0 | 248.6 | 246.5 | 247.0 | 252.8 | 270.5 |
| | Low | 230.4 | 224.3 | 224.5 | 232.7 | 232.5 | 249.8 | 242.0 | 243.7 | 237.1 | 237.6 | 236.0 | 244.1 | 224.3 |
| | Close | 230.4 | 225.7 | 233.0 | 234.4 | 248.4 | 265.1 | 246.2 | 246.2 | 238.8 | 243.9 | 244.9 | 251.8 | ------ |
| 1989 | High | 251.6 | 243.3 | 248.1 | 244.6 | 242.8 | 235.4 | 237.0 | 225.5 | 226.8 | 228.1 | 231.7 | 229.9 | 251.6 |
| | Low | 241.1 | 236.6 | 241.7 | 237.7 | 229.4 | 227.9 | 221.2 | 221.5 | 222.9 | 223.0 | 226.0 | 225.6 | 221.2 |
| | Close | 242.4 | 243.2 | 242.1 | 238.0 | 229.4 | 234.4 | 221.2 | 225.5 | 226.8 | 225.7 | 228.8 | 229.9 | ------ |
| 1990 | High | 235.1 | 236.3 | 239.0 | 245.8 | 247.8 | 241.2 | 240.0 | 244.7 | 239.8 | 242.0 | 231.1 | 223.8 | 247.8 |
| | Low | 228.8 | 229.9 | 234.2 | 238.4 | 241.5 | 233.8 | 230.3 | 233.1 | 234.9 | 228.6 | 223.2 | 220.1 | 220.1 |
| | Close | 229.9 | 234.6 | 238.2 | 245.8 | 241.5 | 236.9 | 235.0 | 233.7 | 239.2 | 229.8 | 223.3 | 222.6 | ------ |
| 1991 | High | 222.8 | 215.6 | 221.8 | 222.2 | 217.0 | 217.7 | 214.1 | 216.5 | 217.6 | 219.8 | 218.6 | 213.9 | 222.8 |
| | Low | 214.1 | 209.7 | 217.3 | 216.2 | 214.1 | 208.4 | 205.9 | 204.7 | 211.9 | 216.2 | 213.3 | 207.2 | 204.7 |
| | Close | 214.1 | 215.6 | 218.5 | 216.2 | 215.4 | 208.4 | 214.1 | 211.8 | 215.6 | 218.2 | 213.3 | 208.1 | ------ |
| 1992 | High | 212.2 | 215.3 | 212.9 | 210.3 | 211.7 | 212.9 | 209.1 | 204.9 | 203.5 | 202.9 | 203.6 | 204.3 | 215.3 |
| | Low | 206.9 | 207.2 | 208.6 | 204.5 | 204.9 | 208.0 | 203.0 | 198.2 | 199.3 | 199.1 | 199.2 | 201.2 | 198.2 |
| | Close | 211.2 | 209.6 | 209.8 | 204.8 | 208.0 | 209.3 | 203.1 | 201.0 | 200.4 | 199.9 | 203.1 | 202.8 | ------ |
| 1993 | High | 203.2 | 204.9 | 214.3 | 213.9 | 211.8 | 210.0 | 219.7 | 223.5 | 217.8 | 220.6 | 223.8 | 226.8 | 226.8 |
| | Low | 199.3 | 198.4 | 203.4 | 207.8 | 207.4 | 202.6 | 207.2 | 212.1 | 211.9 | 216.6 | 217.4 | 218.4 | 198.4 |
| | Close | 199.5 | 202.9 | 212.5 | 210.9 | 208.7 | 207.1 | 219.3 | 217.2 | 216.1 | 218.4 | 218.0 | 226.3 | ------ |
| 1994 | High | 229.8 | 229.2 | 231.0 | 227.8 | 239.2 | 239.7 | 234.7 | 235.4 | 234.4 | 235.2 | 234.7 | 237.2 | 239.7 |
| | Low | 226.2 | 225.7 | 227.4 | 227.8 | 225.2 | 235.9 | 230.4 | 228.0 | 228.6 | 227.0 | 228.8 | 227.0 | 225.2 |
| | Close | 225.6 | 227.6 | 227.7 | 225.0 | 235.5 | 230.4 | 233.7 | 231.9 | 229.9 | 233.3 | 229.2 | 236.6 | ------ |
| 1995 | High | 238.0 | 236.2 | 236.9 | 237.7 | 237.1 | 238.0 | 235.9 | 240.3 | 245.8 | 242.7 | 244.5 | 246.5 | 246.5 |
| | Low | 232.6 | 231.0 | 231.1 | 233.2 | 229.6 | 232.2 | 229.3 | 231.7 | 239.4 | 238.3 | 240.9 | 240.9 | 229.3 |
| | Close | 232.8 | 234.3 | 232.9 | 235.3 | 232.7 | 233.4 | 233.2 | 240.0 | 241.7 | 242.2 | 241.8 | 243.2 | ------ |
| 1996 | High | 247.6 | 251.2 | 253.5 | 263.8 | 261.2 | 252.9 | 251.9 | 252.0 | 250.4 | 249.6 | 247.1 | 246.9 | 263.8 |
| | Low | 238.6 | 245.6 | 242.7 | 250.2 | 251.8 | 246.6 | 240.1 | 242.8 | 243.1 | 237.8 | 236.0 | 238.1 | 236.0 |
| | Close | 247.5 | 248.8 | 251.4 | 256.1 | 254.1 | 248.7 | 242.0 | 249.5 | 245.6 | 237.8 | 243.4 | 239.6 | ------ |

*Source: BRIDGE - Commodity Research Bureau*

CRB FUTURES PRICE INDEX
1967 = 100
MONTHLY CASH
AS OF:02/28/97
CRB Futures Price Index
17 Futures Markets
Cattle (Live)
Cocoa
Coffee
Copper
Corn
Cotton
Crude Oil
Gold (N.Y.)
Heating Oil #2
Hogs
Natural Gas
Orange Juice
Platinum
Silver (N.Y.)
Soybeans
Sugar #11 (World)
Wheat (Chi)
INDEX VALUE
340
320
300
280
260
240
220
200
180
160
140
120
73 74 75 76 77 78 79 80 81 82 83 84 85 86 87 88 89 90 91 92 93 94 95 96 97

GOLDMAN SACHS COMMODITY INDEX
CASH
MONTHLY CASH
AS OF:02/28/97
INDEX VALUE
320
300
280
260
240
220
200
180
160
140
120
100
73 74 75 76 77 78 79 80 81 82 83 84 85 86 87 88 89 90 91 92 93 94 95 96 97

KR-CRB INDICES 1967=100 vs CPI 1982=100
MONTHLY CASH
AS OF:02/28/97
CRB FUTURES PRICE INDEX
CRB (BLS) SPOT PRICE INDEX
CONSUMER PRICE INDEX 82-84=100
INDEX VALUE
CRB Futures Price Index
17 Futures Markets
Cattle (Live)
Cocoa
Coffee
Copper
Corn
Cotton
Crude Oil
Gold (N.Y.)
Heating Oil #2
Hogs
Natural Gas
Orange Juice
Platinum
Silver (N.Y.)
Soybeans
Sugar #11 (World)
Wheat (Chi)
CRB (BLS) Commodity Price Index
23 Spot Markets
Burlap
Butter
Cocoa
Copper Scrap
Corn
Cotton
Hides
Hogs
Lard
Lead
Print Cloth
Rosin
Rubber
Soybean Oil
Steel Scrap
Steers
Sugar
Tallow
Tin
Wheat (MPLS)
Wheat (KC)
Wool Tops
Zinc
325
300
275
250
225
200
175
150
125
100
75
50
73
74
75
76
77
78
79
80
81
82
83
84
85
86
87
88
89
90
91
92
93
94
95
96
97

CRB INDEX vs CPI
12-month RATE OF CHANGE
MONTHLY CASH
AS OF:01/31/97
CRB INDEX - RATE OF CHANGE
CPI - RATE OF CHANGE
CRB %
CPI %
80
70
60
50
40
30
20
10
0
-10
-20
-30
16
14
12
10
8
6
4
2
0
-2
-4
-6
73
74
75
76
77
78
79
80
81
82
83
84
85
86
87
88
89
90
91
92
93
94
95
96
97

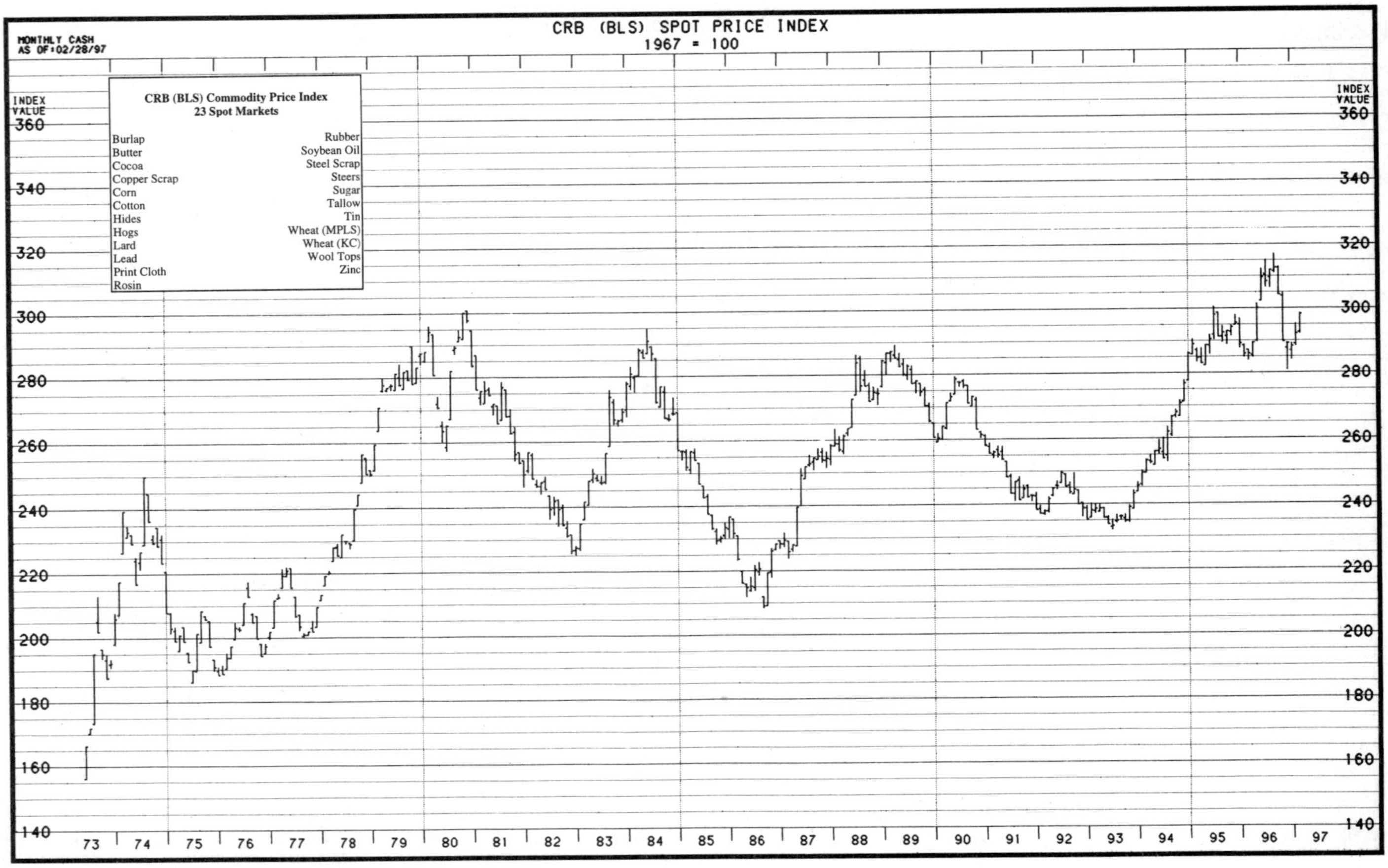
MONTHLY CASH
AS OF:02/28/97
CRB (BLS) SPOT PRICE INDEX
1967 = 100
INDEX VALUE
CRB (BLS) Commodity Price Index
23 Spot Markets
Burlap
Butter
Cocoa
Copper Scrap
Corn
Cotton
Hides
Hogs
Lard
Lead
Print Cloth
Rosin
Rubber
Soybean Oil
Steel Scrap
Steers
Sugar
Tallow
Tin
Wheat (MPLS)
Wheat (KC)
Wool Tops
Zinc
360
340
320
300
280
260
240
220
200
180
160
140
73 74 75 76 77 78 79 80 81 82 83 84 85 86 87 88 89 90 91 92 93 94 95 96 97

WEEKLY CASH
AS OF:03/14/97
CRB (BLS) SPOT PRICE INDEX
1967 = 100
INDEX VALUE
CRB (BLS) Commodity Price Index
23 Spot Markets
Burlap
Butter
Cocoa
Copper Scrap
Corn
Cotton
Hides
Hogs
Lard
Lead
Print Cloth
Rosin
Rubber
Soybean Oil
Steel Scrap
Steers
Sugar
Tallow
Tin
Wheat (MPLS)
Wheat (KC)
Wool Tops
Zinc
320
310
300
290
280
270
260
250
240
230
220
210
1991 1992 1993 1994 1995 1996
M J J A S O N D J F M A M J J A S O N D J F M A M J J A S O N D J F M A M J J A S O N D J F M A M J J A S O N D J F M A M J J A S O N D J F M A M

CRB (BLS) FOODSTUFFS INDEX
WEEKLY CASH
AS OF:03/14/97
CRB (BLS) FoodStuffs Sub-Index
10 Spot Markets
Hogs
Steers
Lard
Butter
Soybean Oil
Cocoa
Corn
Sugar
Wheat (KC)
Wheat (MPLS)
INDEX VALUE
290
280
270
260
250
240
230
220
210
200
190
180
1991
1992
1993
1994
1995
1996


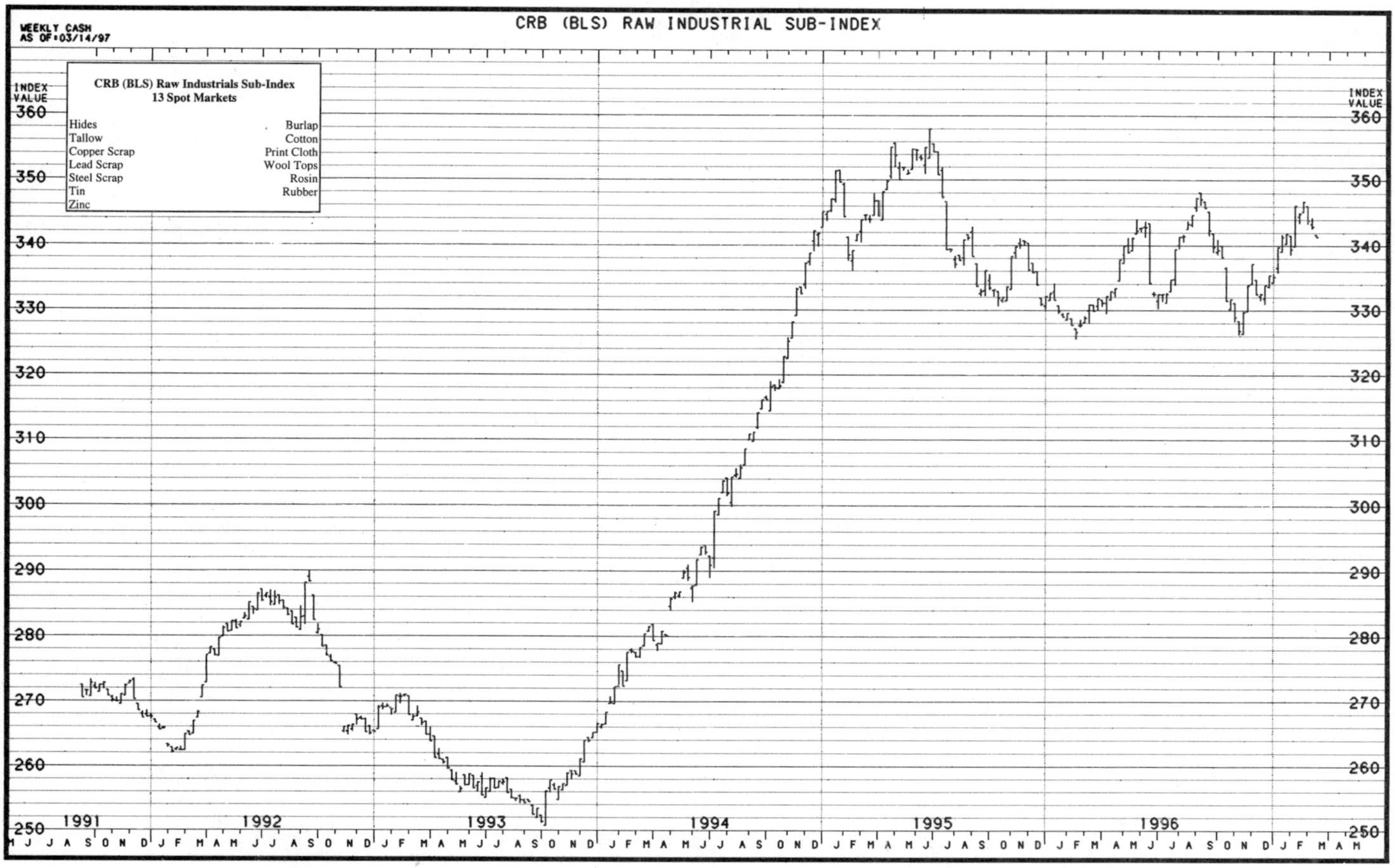

CRB (BLS) RAW INDUSTRIAL SUB-INDEX
WEEKLY CASH
AS OF:03/14/97
CRB (BLS) Raw Industrials Sub-Index
13 Spot Markets
Hides
Tallow
Copper Scrap
Lead Scrap
Steel Scrap
Tin
Zinc
Burlap
Cotton
Print Cloth
Wool Tops
Rosin
Rubber
INDEX VALUE
360
350
340
330
320
310
300
290
280
270
260
250
1991
1992
1993
1994
1995
1996

WEEKLY CASH
AS OF:03/14/97
CRB IMPORTED INDEX
1967 = 100
CRB Imported Index
3 Futures Markets
Cocoa
Coffee
Sugar
INDEX VALUE
450
425
400
375
350
325
300
275
250
225
200
175
1991
1992
1993
1994
1995
1996

WEEKLY CASH
AS OF:03/14/97
CRB INDUSTRIAL SUB-INDEX
1967 = 100
CRB Industrials Index
6 Futures Markets
Cotton
Copper
Crude Oil
Lumber
Platinum
Silver
INDEX VALUE
310
300
290
280
270
260
250
240
230
220
210
200
1991
1992
1993
1994
1995
1996

WEEKLY CASH
AS OF:03/14/97
CRB GRAINS INDEX
1967 = 100
CRB Grains Index
4 Futures Markets
Corn
Oats
Soybean Meal
Wheat (Chi)
INDEX VALUE
1991
1992
1993
1994
1995
1996

WEEKLY CASH
AS OF:03/14/97
CRB OILSEEDS INDEX
1967 = 100
CRB Oilseeds Index
3 Futures Markets
Flaxseed
Canola
Soybean Oil
INDEX VALUE
1991
1992
1993
1994
1995
1996

WEEKLY CASH
AS OF:03/14/97
CRB LIVESTOCK INDEX
1967 = 100
CRB Livestock & Meats Index
3 Futures Markets
Live Cattle
LIve Hogs
Pork Bellies
INDEX VALUE
270
260
250
240
230
220
210
200
190
180
170
160
1991
1992
1993
1994
1995
1996

WEEKLY CASH
AS OF:03/14/97
CRB PRECIOUS METALS INDEX
1967 = 100
CRB Precious Metals Index
3 Futures Markets
Gold (N.Y.)
Platinum
Silver (N.Y.)
INDEX VALUE
310
300
290
280
270
260
250
240
230
220
210
200
1991
1992
1993
1994
1995
1996

WEEKLY CASH
AS OF 03/14/97
CRB ENERGY INDEX
1977 = 100
CRB Energy Index
3 Futures Markets
(1977=100)
Crude Oil
Unleaded Gas
Heating Oil #2
INDEX VALUE
1991
1992
1993
1994
1995
1996

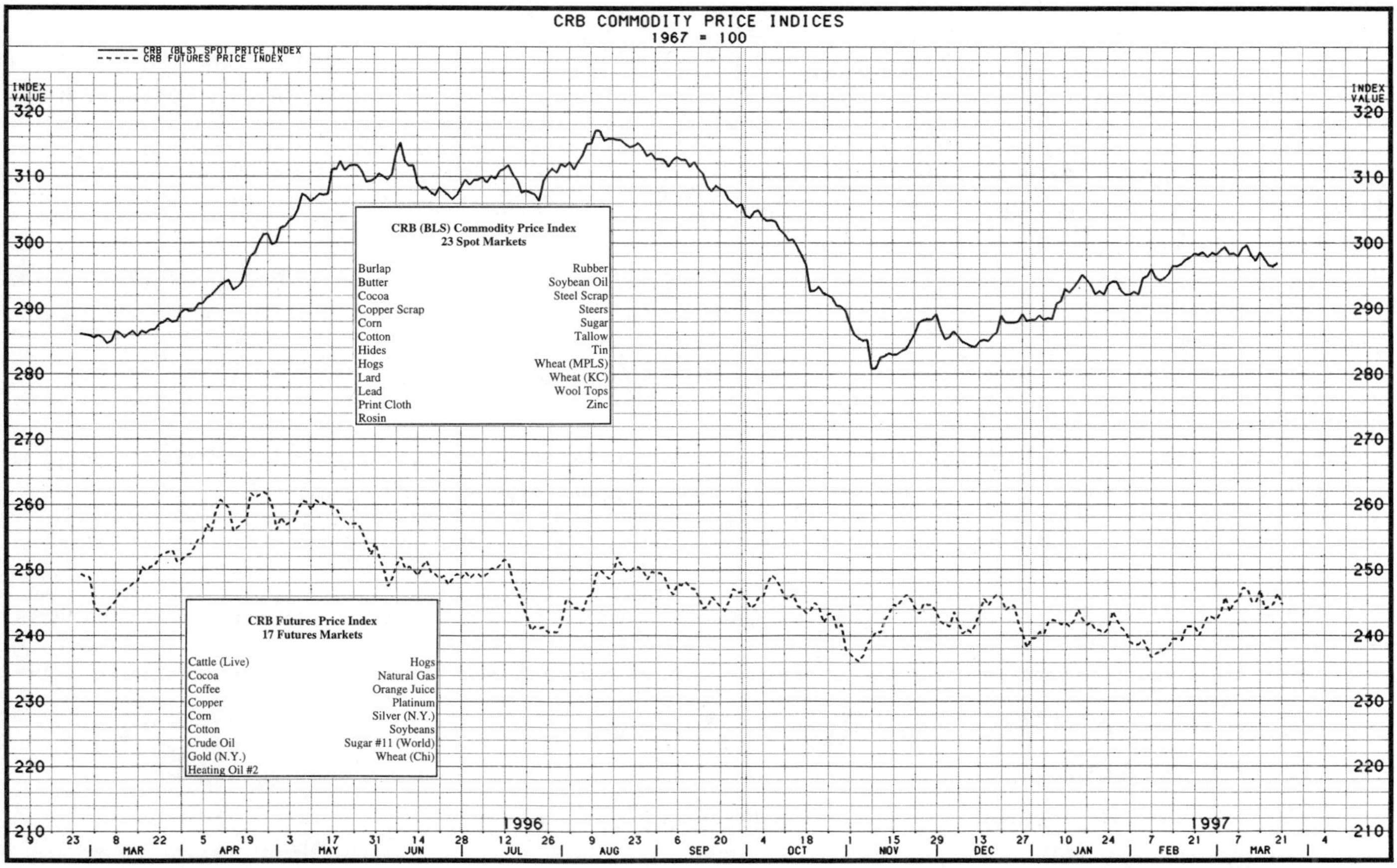
CRB COMMODITY PRICE INDICES
1967 = 100
CRB (BLS) SPOT PRICE INDEX
CRB FUTURES PRICE INDEX
INDEX VALUE
CRB (BLS) Commodity Price Index
23 Spot Markets
Burlap
Butter
Cocoa
Copper Scrap
Corn
Cotton
Hides
Hogs
Lard
Lead
Print Cloth
Rosin
Rubber
Soybean Oil
Steel Scrap
Steers
Sugar
Tallow
Tin
Wheat (MPLS)
Wheat (KC)
Wool Tops
Zinc
CRB Futures Price Index
17 Futures Markets
Cattle (Live)
Cocoa
Coffee
Copper
Corn
Cotton
Crude Oil
Gold (N.Y.)
Heating Oil #2
Hogs
Natural Gas
Orange Juice
Platinum
Silver (N.Y.)
Soybeans
Sugar #11 (World)
Wheat (Chi)
1996
1997

# SEASONALITY OF VOLUME AND OPEN INTEREST

*by Kenneth H. Shaleen*

Classical bar chartists in the futures markets have a general rule for analyzing the interaction of price change, volume, and open interest change to assess the "health" of a price trend:

**Volume and open interest should increase as prices move in the direction of the major price trend**

According to this rule, the most bullish condition is price moving up on increasing volume and increasing open interest; the longs are in control and the price uptrend is expected to continue. On a daily basis, this rule implies that on price-up days (a higher close) in a healthy bull market, volume should expand and open interest should increase. When price is moving downward, the ideal healthy bear market is also categorized by expanding volume and expanding open interest.

Generations of futures technicians have used this general rule. They realized that the ideal interaction of price, volume, and open interest is subject to considerable interpretation. Many idiosyncrasies to the general rule exist. One is the possibility of a seasonal influence.

The BRIDGE Commodity Research Bureau (CRB) has produced seasonal charts of volume and open interest for nineteen U.S. futures contracts covering the 10-year period from January 1986 thru September 1996. This article will examine the seasonality of these futures contracts and discuss the necessity of a secondary level of analysis when applying the general volume and open interest rule for a healthy price trend.

## *Methodology*

The monthly variation in volume and open interest each calendar year is measured by constructing seasonal indexes. These are percentages representing each month's relationship to the average for the year, which is taken as a base equal to 100%. Thus, a Soybean seasonal open interest index of 84% for the month of August indicates that, typically, the average total open interest for August is expected to be below the average monthly open interest by 16%. The 105% figure for U.S. Treasury Bond futures for November means that open interest in this month is usually 5% higher than the monthly average. The arithmetic mean of the 12 monthly index values is 100%.

The Commodity Research Bureau has periodically updated the seasonal charts of the agricultural futures since the mid-1950's. The absolute level of volume and open interest is different from year to year, but the percentage changes do exhibit a regular pattern. There is a distinct difference between the look of seasonal variations of volume and open interest in the agricultural commodity futures versus the financial instrument futures. This is the tendency for the contract specifications of the financial futures to dominate the monthly swings in volume and open interest. The calendar year-end effect is particularly evident.

## *Application of the General Rule*

The change in open interest is the important condition monitored by technical analysts. In its most minute application, the open interest change from one trading day to the next is analyzed in conjunction with the price change that day. If the investigation is expanded to encompass several weeks, a seasonal influence may have to be factored into the analysis.

For example, given a price uptrend on a chart, declining open interest implies that a weak price uptrend is occurring. But what if total open interest normally declines at that time of year? A second step in the analysis is necessary. The following question must be answered: Is the current decline in open interest equal to or greater than what would normally be expected? If so, the same (not bullish) conclusion would be reached. But if the current open interest is only falling slightly in the face of an expected severe seasonal open interest decline, a bullish reading of the current price rally would result.

Volume also exhibits seasonal characteristics but variations in volume are more important in day-to-day comparisons than over extended periods. Thus no seasonal adjustment is necessary. Each day's volume is categorized as "high", "average", or "low." The result is then analyzed in conjunction with the price change to determine the direction of the major price trend. For example, low volume sell-offs are bullish; low volume rallies are bearish.

The historic seasonal variation charts can aid a technician in determining how often to re-calibrate the definitions of high, average, and low volume. In the unusually low volume month of July in T-Bill futures (75%), looking back as far as the month of May for volume comparisons would not be productive. The seasonal volume index in T-Bills declines from above 100% in May, to 90% in June, and bottoms in the lowest volume month of the year, July.

## *Overview of the Seasonal Graphs*

### Year-End Effect

The tendency for December to be a relative low volume and open interest month is general throughout the U.S. futures markets. Since open positions are marked-to-the-market for U.S. taxpayers the tendency is for speculative positions to be reduced by December 31. The main exception to this overview is Heating Oil. The dominant seasonal tendency for the physical product generates high volume in December.

### I. Agricultural Products

**A. Wheat, Corn, and Soybeans**

The Chicago Wheat, Corn, and Soybean futures exhibit strong seasonal tendencies for open interest to increase as the U.S. harvests approach. The move from low to high average monthly open interest occurs in the short time span of two months. The size of the crop becomes more assured and is reflected in the need to place hedges by both the producer and user of the commodity.

The seasonal high in open interest for Soybeans (104%) is in the month of October. Corn open interest reaches its seasonal peak (107.5%) in November. Wheat open interest is bi-modal with a peak in June/July as the big Winter Wheat crop is harvested, and another high in October when the Spring Wheat crop comes in.

Relative lows in open interest in Wheat and Corn (below 95%) are posted in December. A possible reason: Wheat or Corn deliveries against the Dec. future can begin on the first business day in December. Conservative traders have exited from Dec. futures by the end of November. It is apparent from the seasonal open interest graphs that these positions are not automatically rolled into the next (March) contract month. Soybeans do not have a Dec. future listed so open interest holds fairly constant (at above 100%) thru the end of the calendar year.

Volume in the three main Chicago Board of Trade (CBOT) commodity futures tends to build in the early summer months, with a relative peak in June or July. Volume posts a relative low in the month of December for the same reasons discussed above.

**B. Cattle, Hogs, and Pork Bellies**

Cattle and Hog futures record their highest seasonal open interest index in March. The monthly average open interest then drops sharply at the beginning of the summer into a yearly low in August.

Pork Belly futures also exhibit a steep drop in open interest into the month of August. The seasonal decline produces the largest movement in the index readings of any of the 19 markets surveyed. Within a two month period (June - August) the open interest index declines from 117% to 70%. This very strong seasonal tendency must be taken into consideration by technical traders analyzing Pork Belly futures.

Volume in the Chicago Mercantile Exchange's livestock futures is more stable than the well defined variation in seasonal open interest would imply. In fact, Cattle and Hog volume shows less month-to-month variation than grain or oilseed futures. Volume in Pork Bellies coincides with the unusually strong seasonal open interest influence in that market.

### II. Interest Rates: **Treasury Bonds, Treasury-Bills, and Eurodollars**

Relative open interest highs in Treasury Bond futures occur every three months coinciding with the quarterly U.S. Treasury refundings in February, May, August, and November. Options on T-Bond futures (the most active quarterly series) also expire in these months. And physical delivery in T-Bonds can occur beginning on the first business day of the next month so speculative positions are often removed in February, May, August, and November, the months prior to the delivery month. With the U.S. Treasury now reducing the auctions of the 30 year Bonds to less than 4 times per year the seasonal influence may change, but not dramatically.

Open interest in the futures at the short end of the U.S. Dollar yield curve (Eurodollar and T-Bill futures) exhibit peaks at similar three month intervals and in the same months as the T-Bonds.

Volume movements in interest rate futures coincide with the relative monthly highs in open interest with one major exception. T-Bill volume is unusually low in the month of July, down to an index reading of 75%. The 75% figure is only reached on the T-Bonds and Eurodollars in the month of December. This year-end phenomenon, especially in T-Bond futures, has been observed by technical traders since the mid-1980's.

**III. Currencies: Deutsche Mark, Japanese Yen, and British Pound**

The distinct peaks every three months on the D-Mark seasonal open interest graph can be explained by the contract specifications of the Chicago Mercantile Exchange (CME) currency products. Physical delivery takes place on a single day, typically the third Wednesday of the last month of each calendar quarter. Substantial deliveries cause the open interest to drop sharply (on a single day) in the months of March, June, September, and December.

A note on how the seasonal graphs are plotted is in order. The average volume and open interest for the month is plotted at the middle of the month. Total open interest in the CME currency futures usually rises into the delivery month. The method of plotting the monthly averages creates the impression that the relative highs in open interest occurs in the prior months of February, May, August, and November; "on average" it does, but the actual highest number of contracts open will typically occur in the delivery month. This must be taken into consideration when examining the seasonal open interest indexes of the currency futures.

The Japanese Yen and British Pound conform to what would be expected in open interest behavior with one curious deviation. Instead of an open interest peak in the month of August the peak shifts one month later to September. Open interest then returns to posting the expected cyclical highs in November, February, and May. The answer to the question of why this happens remains a mystery.

Volume in the currency futures records spikes in the quarterly expiration months of March, June, and September. This is different from the T-Bond and T-Bill financial futures which record the higher volume one month earlier. This is expected. The CME's foreign exchange deliveries occur in the delivery month but, unlike the physical delivery contracts at the CBOT, the currency deliveries occur two days after the last day of trading. This means there is considerable trading of the expiring future in the delivery month without the threat of delivery.

There are two additional factors that contribute to the unusually high currency futures volume in the months of March, June, September, and December (although December is by far the lowest of the four months.) The Chicago Mercantile Exchange broadened its definition of volume in January of 1994. It now includes expired in-the-money futures options and futures deliveries in reported volume. Both of these anomalies occur on specific days in the quarterly delivery months. For proper day to day comparison of volume a classical bar chartist must remove the exogenous volume associated with those two days every quarter. The serial (monthly) futures options expirations do distort the volume at expiration as well, but to date these option series are not as heavily traded as the quarterly options.

**IV. Metals: Gold and Silver**

One only has to look at the contract months listed for trading in Silver to determine why the open interest hits relative lows in those months. Open interest drops when the lead contract enters the (physical) delivery month. Gold exhibits the same characteristics but to a lesser extent. It can be inferred from this seasonal study that expiring positions are not immediately rolled into the next contract month via a spread or switch order.

A comment on the scale gradients of the Silver and Gold graphs are in order. It "looks" like sizable swings occur in the open interest indexes from month to month. But unlike some of the other seasonal graphs where a 5% differential exists between the index readings the distance between the Silver numbers is 3%, and only 2% on the Gold graph. The overview is that the 16% range from high to low in Silver and (only) 6% high-low range in Gold means that seasonal open interest analysis is not as crucial as in, say, Heating Oil with its large 40% range between the open interest extremes.

Volume variations in these two metal futures are more extreme than monthly open interest fluctuations, with volume indexes often changing 40% from one month to the next in Silver. A distinct pattern exists. Volume peaks in the months prior to futures expiration months. As discussed in the T-Bill comment, a technician establishing the categories for high, average, and low volume must realize these distinct monthly volume traits.

**V. New York Markets: Coffee, Sugar, Cotton, and Heating Oil**

Of all the commodities analyzed in the previous study in the *1991 CRB Year Book,* the change in the Coffee graph is the most pronounced. In the 10 years ending in 1988, Coffee moved within a maximum range of 14% in open interest and even less in volume. In the most recent 10 year study ending in 1996, the open interest range remained the same, but the lowest index readings of both open interest (89%) and volume (80%) occurred in the month of December. A definite year-end effect has developed.

Sugar showed no change in its tendency to build open interest from an October low. But like most of the U.S. futures, the month of December is now a decidedly lower volume month.

Cotton now has a sharper seasonal open interest peak in the month of September whereas the 1988 study showed a three month plateau of high open interest in September thru November. And December is the lowest volume month (80%) both then and now.

Heating Oil futures are the salvation of the futures industry in the otherwise lackluster month of December. Open interest is an above average 112% and volume is robust at 120% of the average month for the year. A futures technician will need to factor the distinct seasonal increase in both volume and open interest into any technical analysis of the internal make-up of Heating Oil futures.

**VI. Stock Index Futures: S&P 500**

Insight into the seasonality of volume and open interest in the S&P 500 futures is new to this CRB study. The graph definitely shows a volume surge into the end of the first calendar quarter (March), summer doldrums (July/August), and steady but below average volume in the last quarter of the year.

A more interesting phenomenon is the clear tendency for open interest to escalate to higher peaks as the year progresses. This is not simply due to the growth curve in open interest over the 10 year period in the study. Each calendar year tends to exhibit the same seasonal increase. For example, total open interest in S&P futures in 1993 increased from 186,253 on March 15, to 206,384 on December 15, a 10.8% expansion. In 1996, open interest over this same time frame increased from 187,367 to 242,828 contracts, a 29.6% expansion.

A possible answer is that fund managers, under increasing pressure to report favorable year-on-year return comparisons, are hedging (some long, some short) as the calendar year-end approaches. In any event, a technical S&P trader must revise high, average, and low volume parameters every quarter to insure they are appropriate. Since open interest changes are the important technical input, the expectation is that larger actual daily changes will occur as the year progresses and incrementally each quarter as the expirations approach.

## *Summary and Conclusion*

Futures technicians have taken seasonal variations in volume and open interest in the traditional agricultural and livestock futures into consideration for many years. This updated analysis shows that the shape of the seasonal graphs of these commodities have not changed. Including the possibility of a seasonal influence on volume and open interest enhances the results of an investigation into the health of a price trend on any futures chart.

Proper analysis of the financial instrument futures requires a knowledge of the contract specifications. These include whether the contract is cash or physical delivery, when delivery takes place, and when options on the futures expire.

Most noticeable in this updated study was the larger month-to-month changes in volume than recorded in the previous CRB study in 1988. This is due to the increase in options volume and especially the expanded definition of volume by the Chicago Mercantile Exchange. The additional volume in CME futures due to the inclusion of in-the-money exercised options and futures deliveries must be removed for proper day-to-day comparisons.

Another ramification of the unequal monthly volumes: the setting of high, average, and low volume categories must take into consideration any distinct seasonal volume peaks and troughs which occur over a very short time period.

The CRB publishes a weekly chart magazine, *CRB Futures Perspective*. The task of analyzing seasonal open interest considerations is made easier by the inclusion of a plot of average open interest for the previous six years on the daily charts. This provides a quick and easy visual comparison to current open interest movements.

* * *

Editor's Note: Additional insights into interpretation of volume and open interest are available in Mr. Shaleen's book, *Volume and Open Interest: Classic Trading Strategies for 24-Hour Markets*, IRWIN Professional Publishing, 1997.

***Kenneth H. Shaleen*** *is President of CHARTWATCH, an international research firm to the futures industry. CHARTWATCH distributes a weekly technical publication and produces a daily telephone market update covering the financial instrument futures. Mr. Shaleen has instructed technical analysis courses for the Chicago Mercantile Exchange since 1978. These courses are also conducted in Singapore, Malaysia, Hong Kong, London, and numerous other locations throughout the world. Mr. Shaleen is the author of Volume and Open Interest: Cutting Edge Trading Strategies in the Futures Markets (Probus 1991); Technical Analysis & Option Strategies (Probus 1992); Volume and Open Interest: Classic Trading Strategies for 24-Hour Markets (IRWIN Professional Publishing 1997); three Chicago Mercantile Exchange course books as well as numerous articles. Mr. Shaleen can be contacted at CHARTWATCH, Fulton House, 345 Canal Street, Chicago, IL 60606, 312-454-1130; or at his website: http://www.chartwatch.com/research.*

## HEATING OIL Seasonal Trends Of Volume & Open Interest

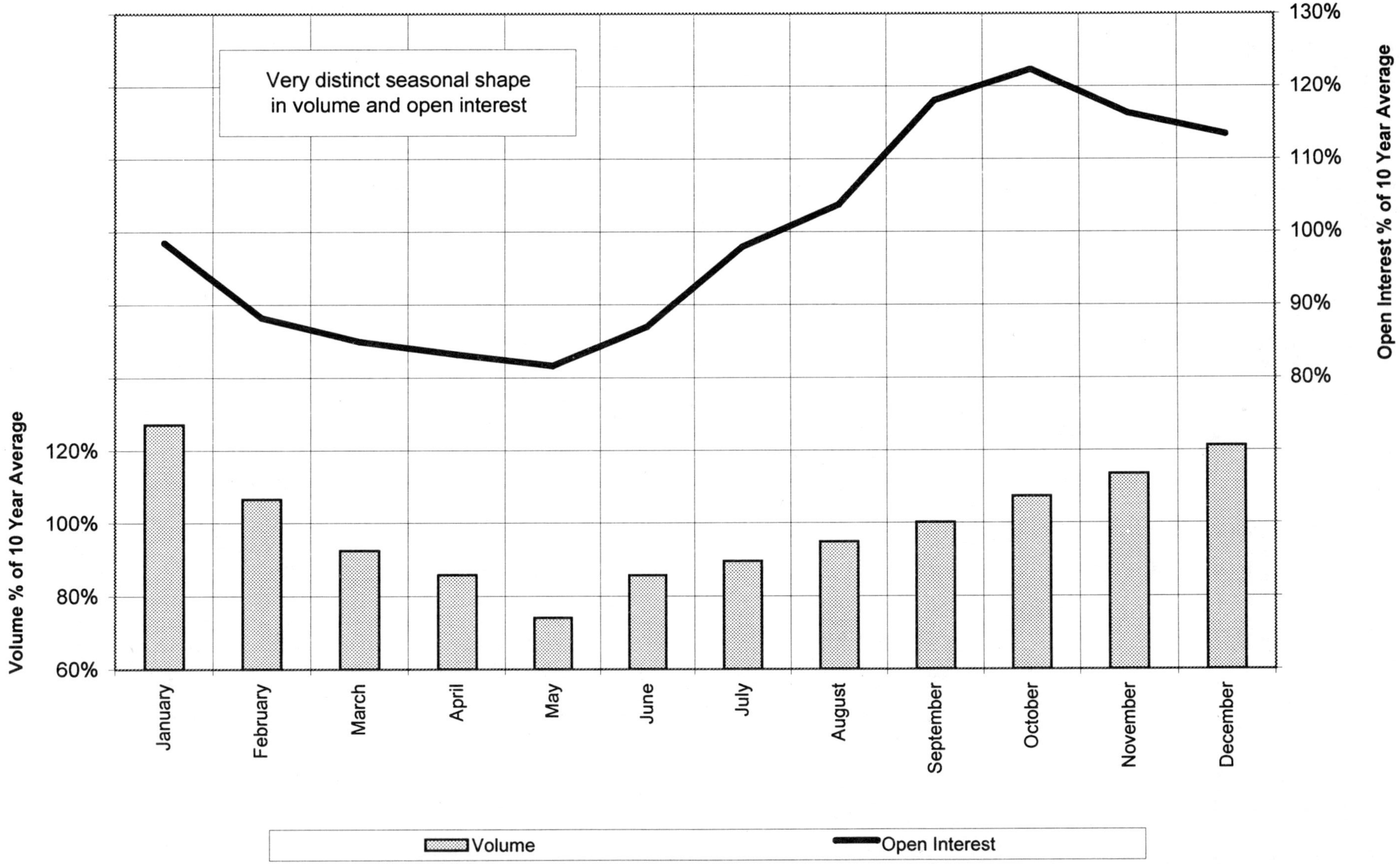

## COTTON Seasonal Trends Of Volume & Open Interest

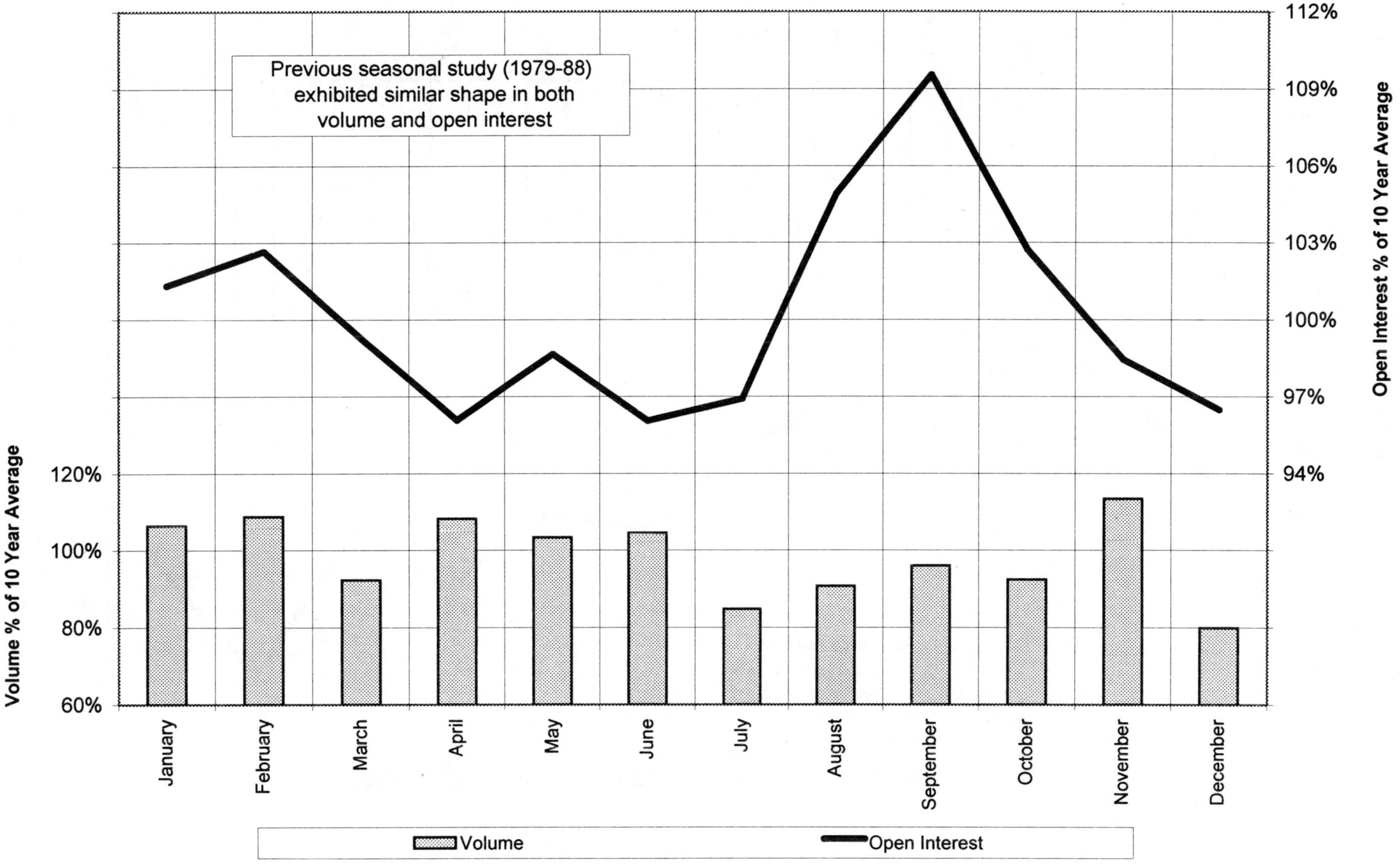

## SUGAR Seasonal Trends Of Volume & Open Interest

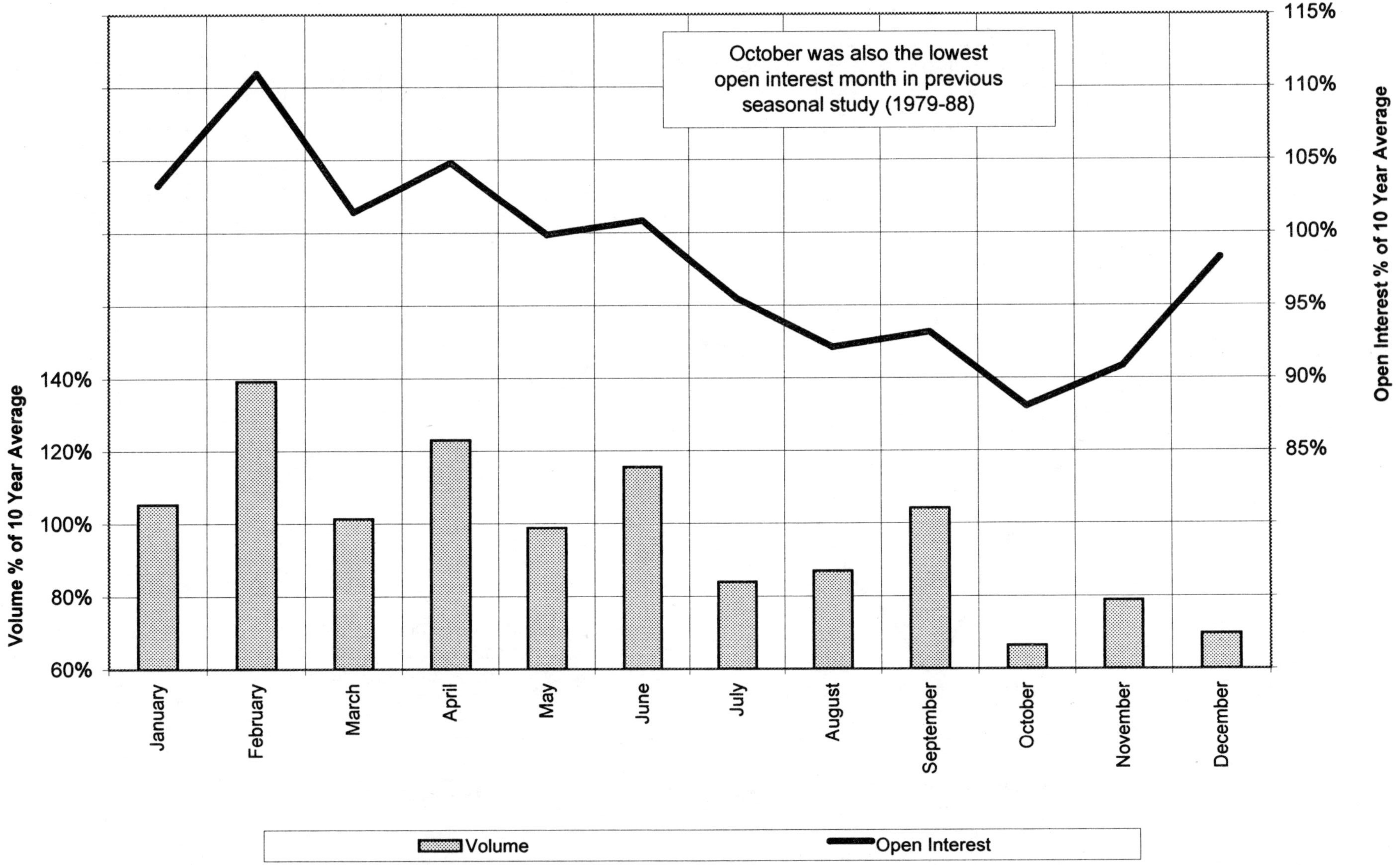

## COFFEE Seasonal Trends Of Volume & Open Interest

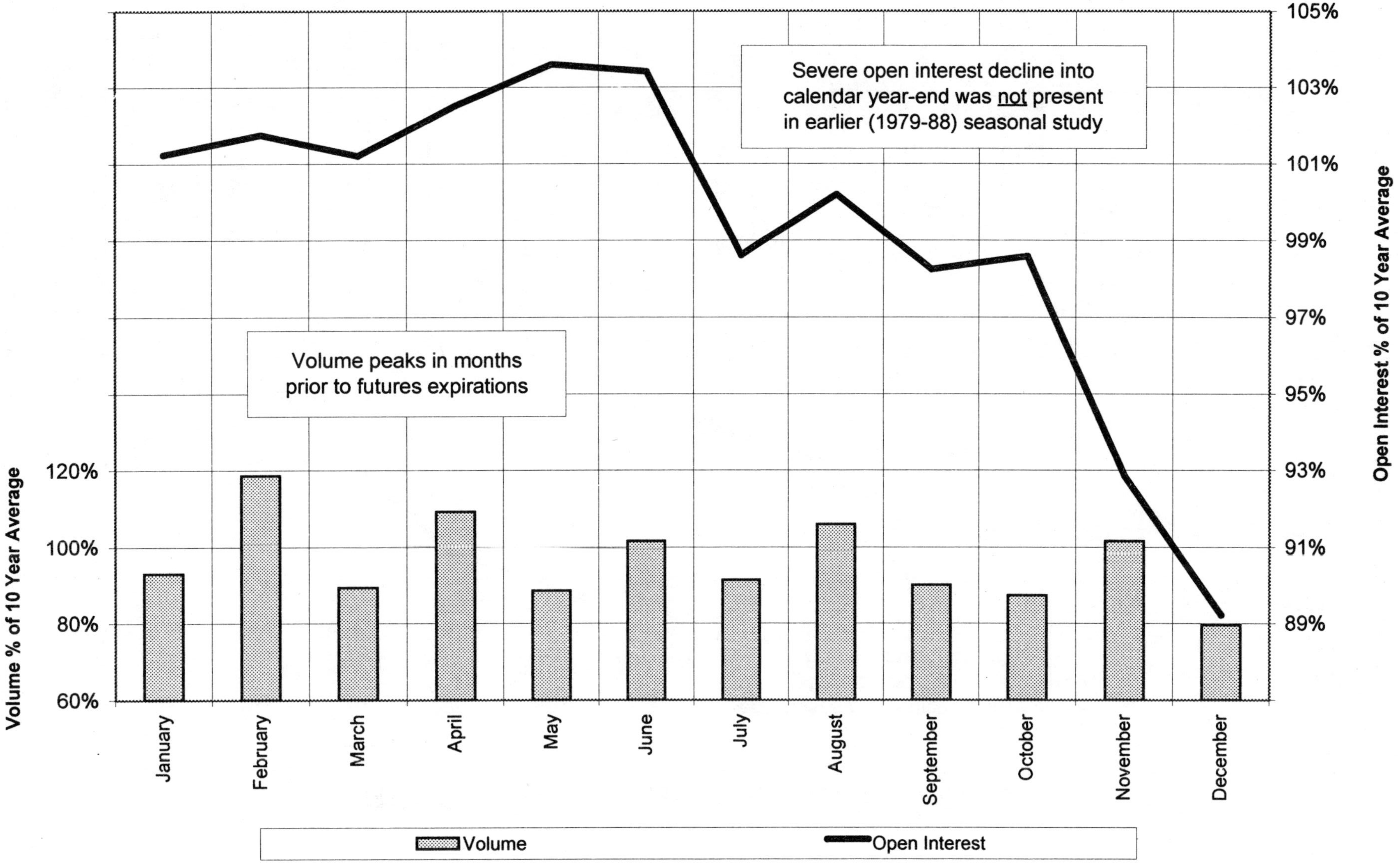

# GOLD Seasonal Trends Of Volume & Open Interest

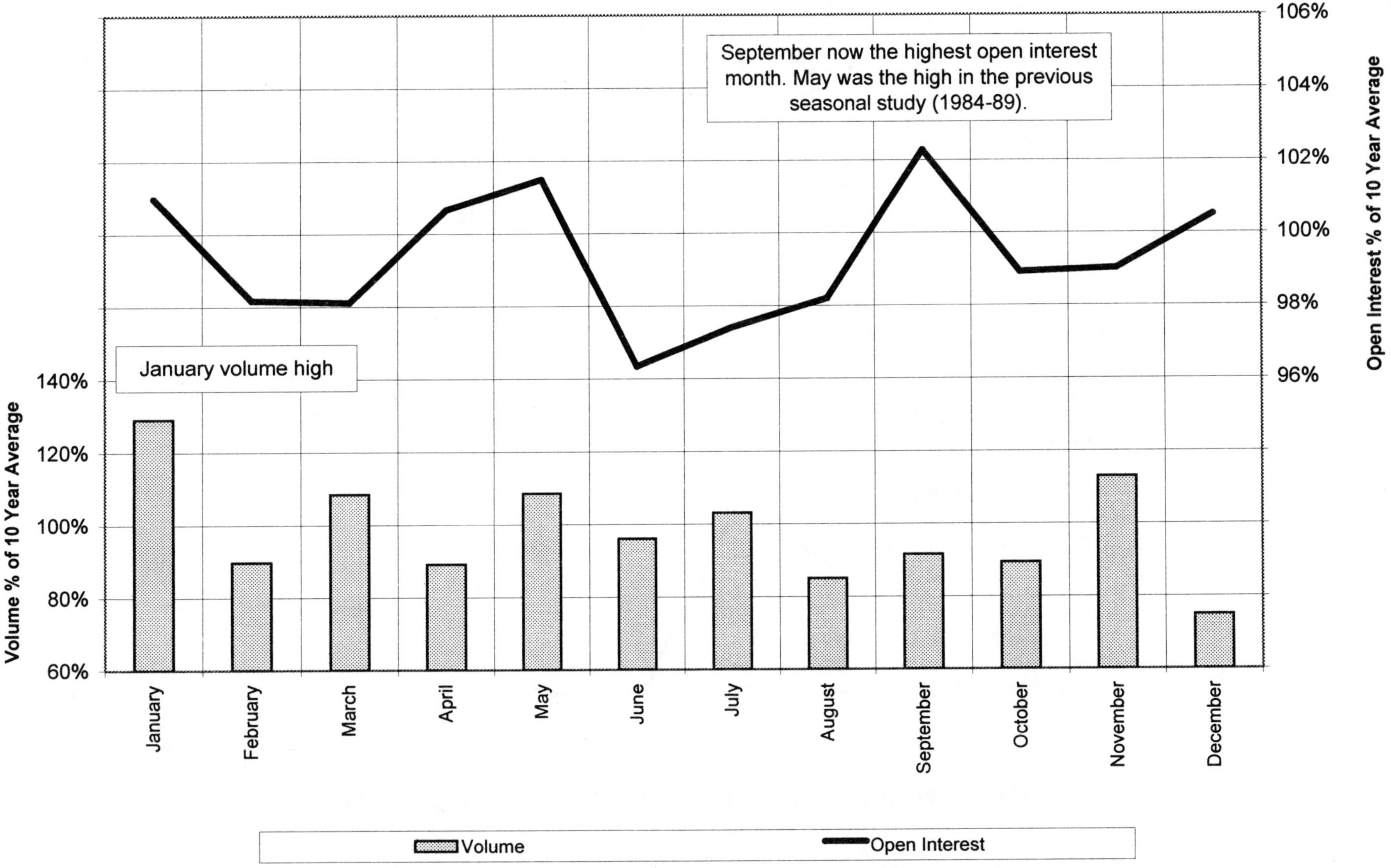

## SILVER Seasonal Trends Of Volume & Open Interest

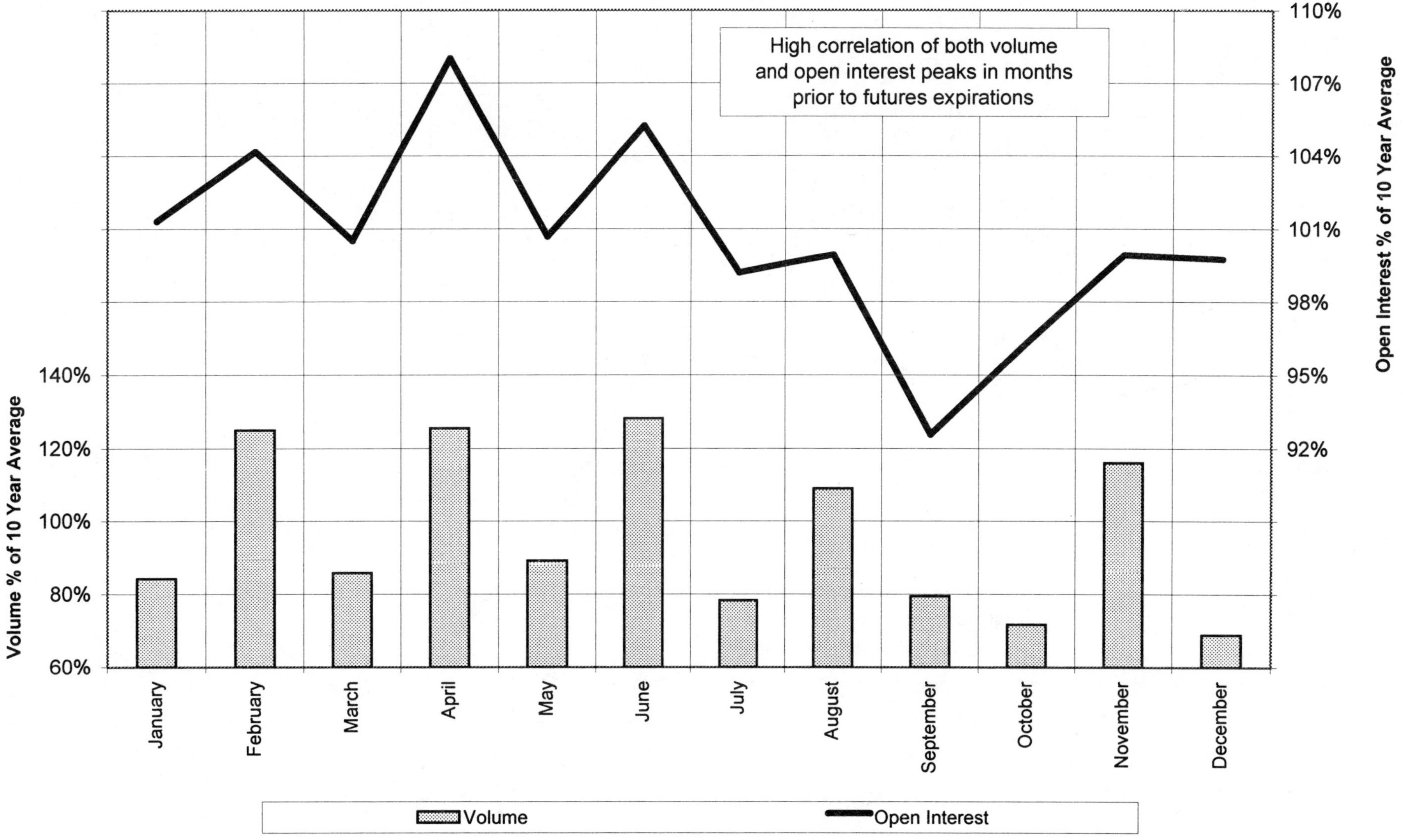

## LIVE CATTLE Seasonal Trends Of Volume & Open Interest

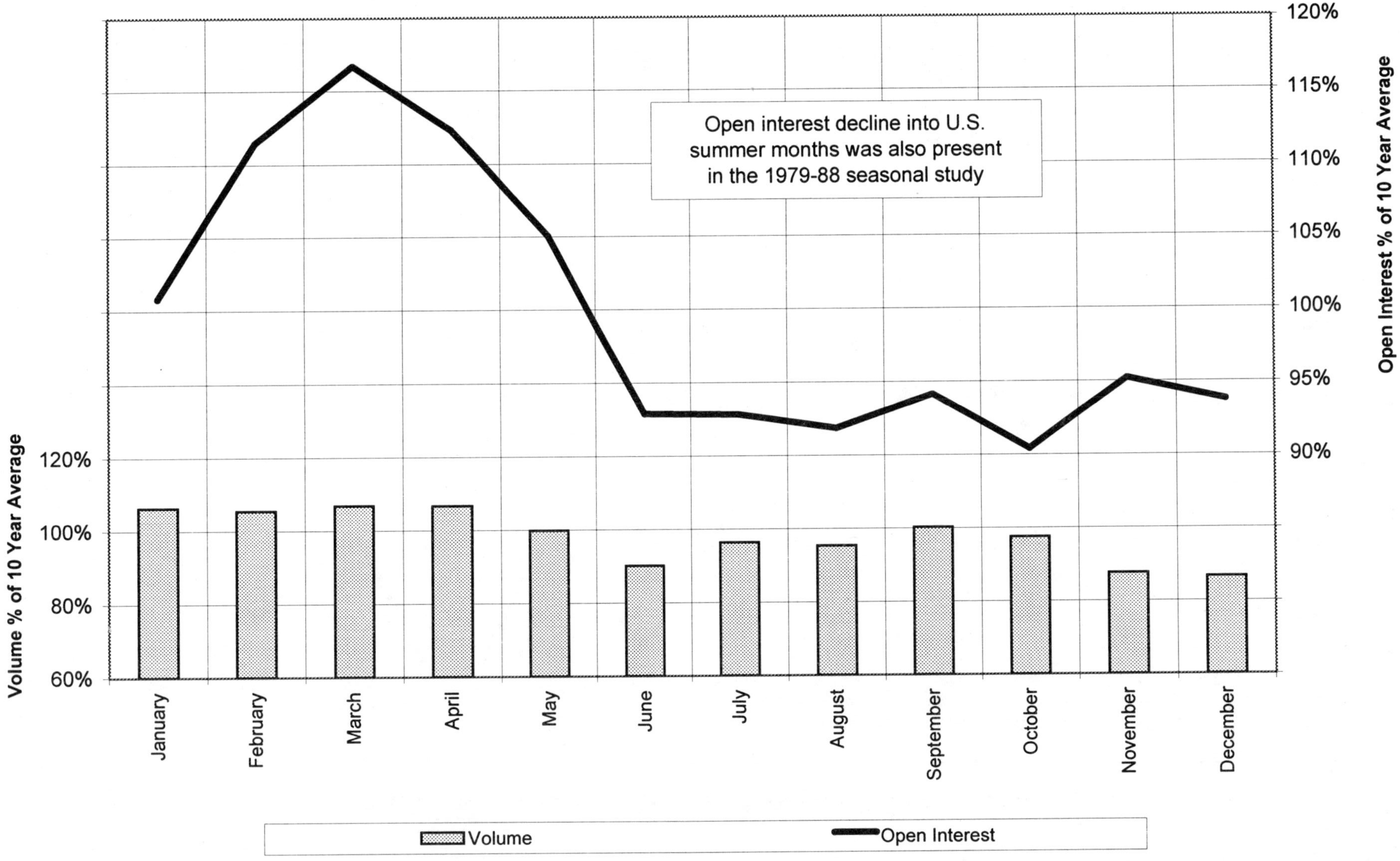

## LIVE HOGS Seasonal Trends Of Volume & Open Interest

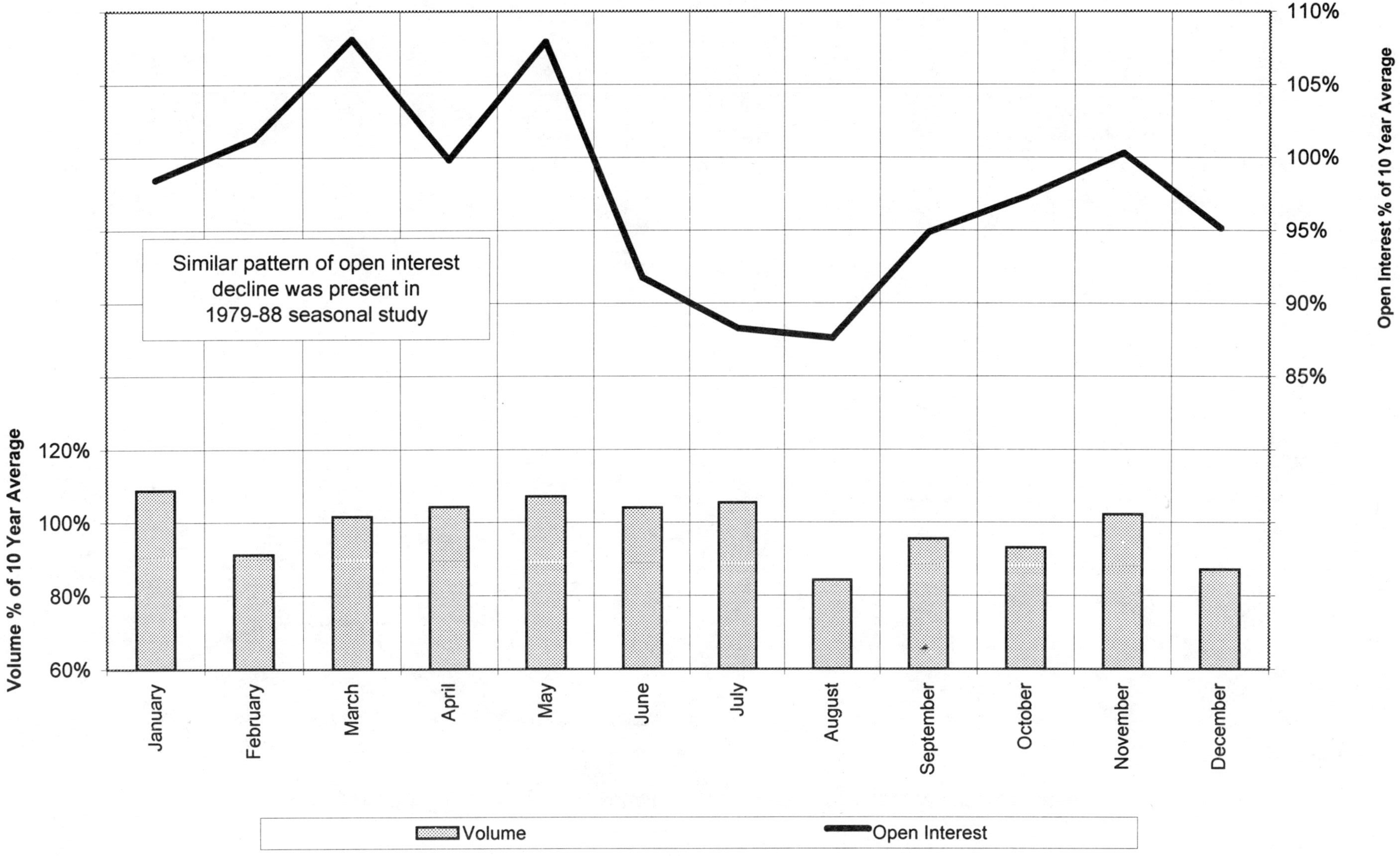

## PORK BELLIES Seasonal Trends Of Volume & Open Interest

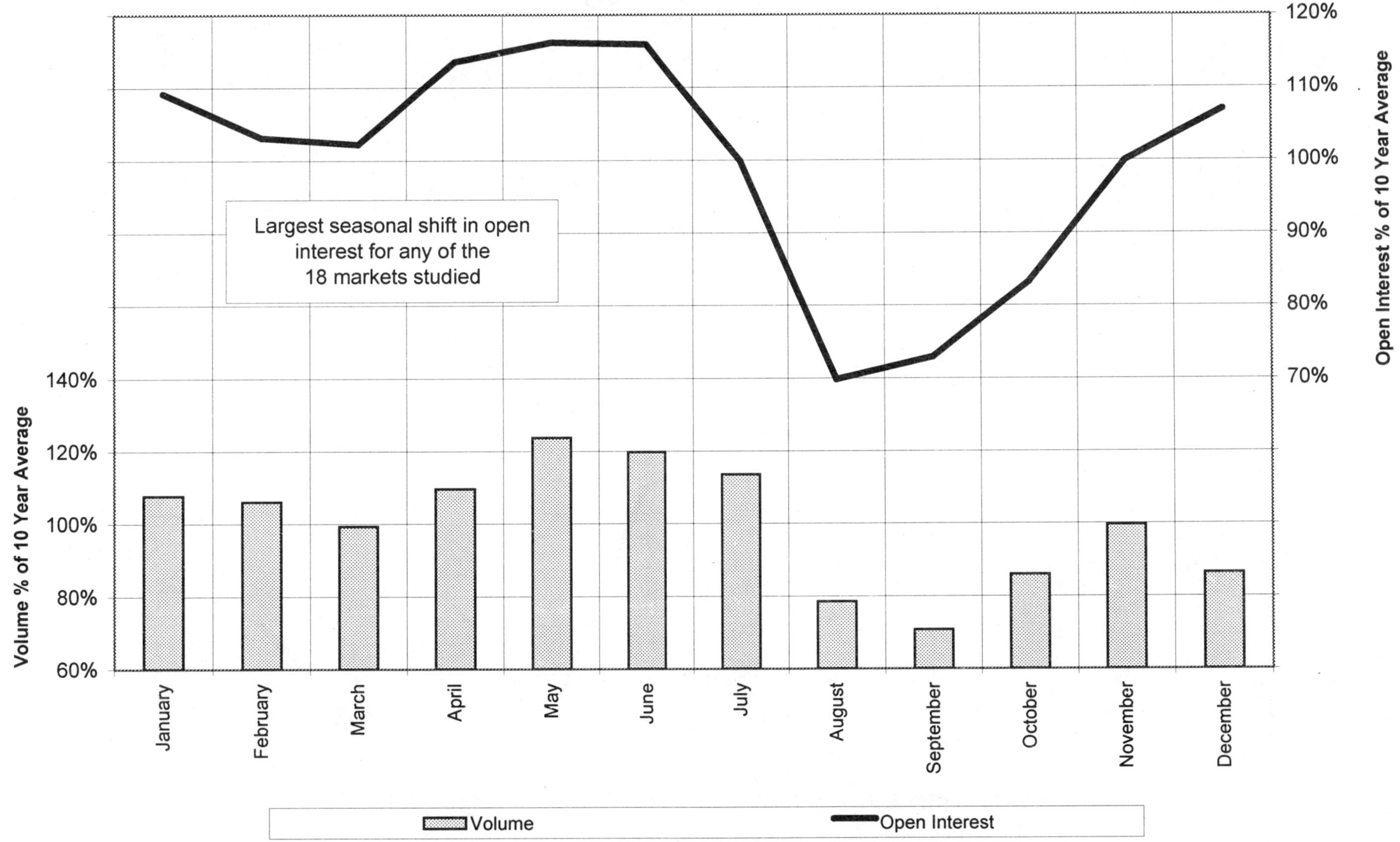

## EURODOLLARS Seasonal Trends Of Volume & Open Interest

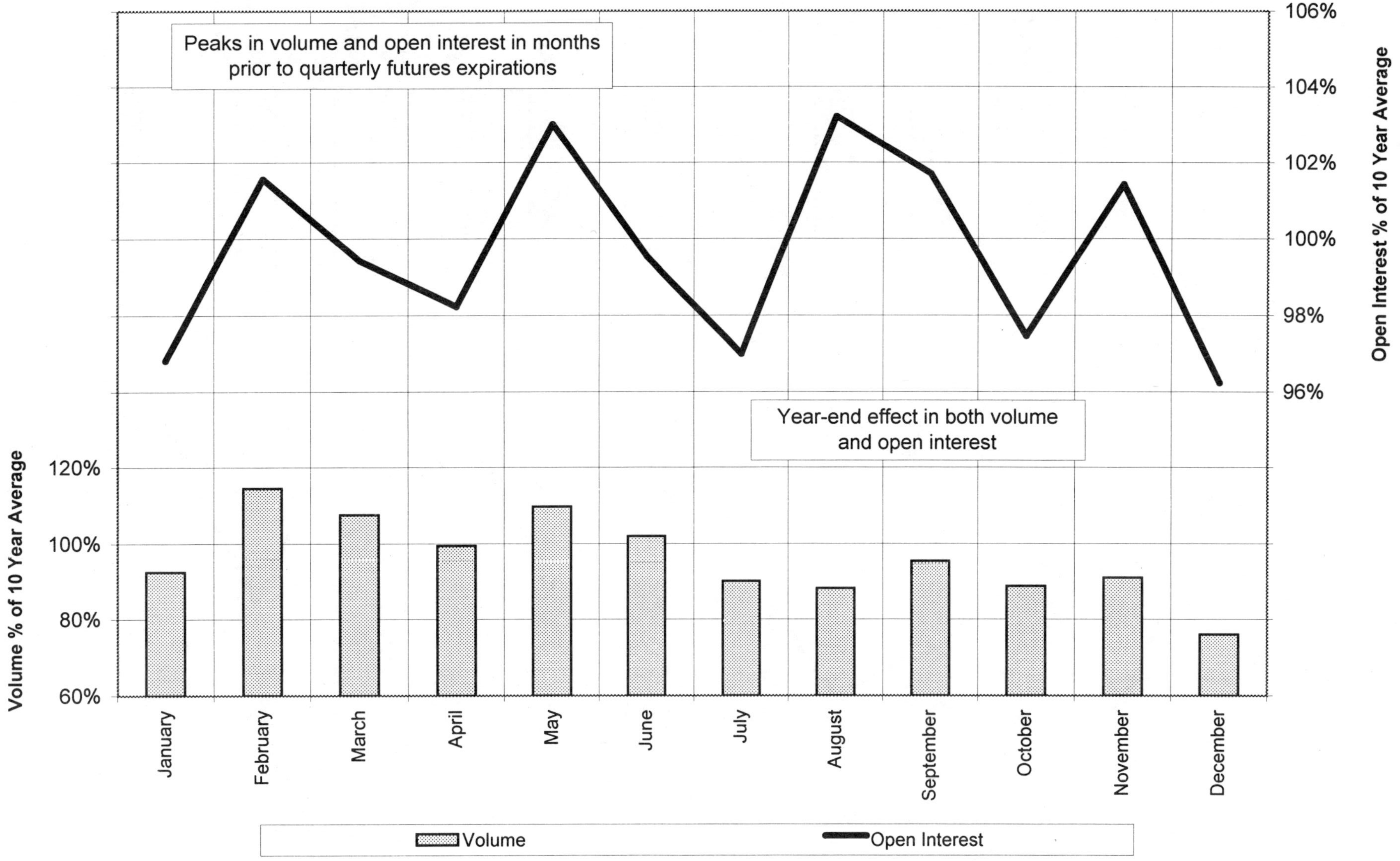

## TREASURY BONDS Seasonal Trends Of Volume & Open Interest

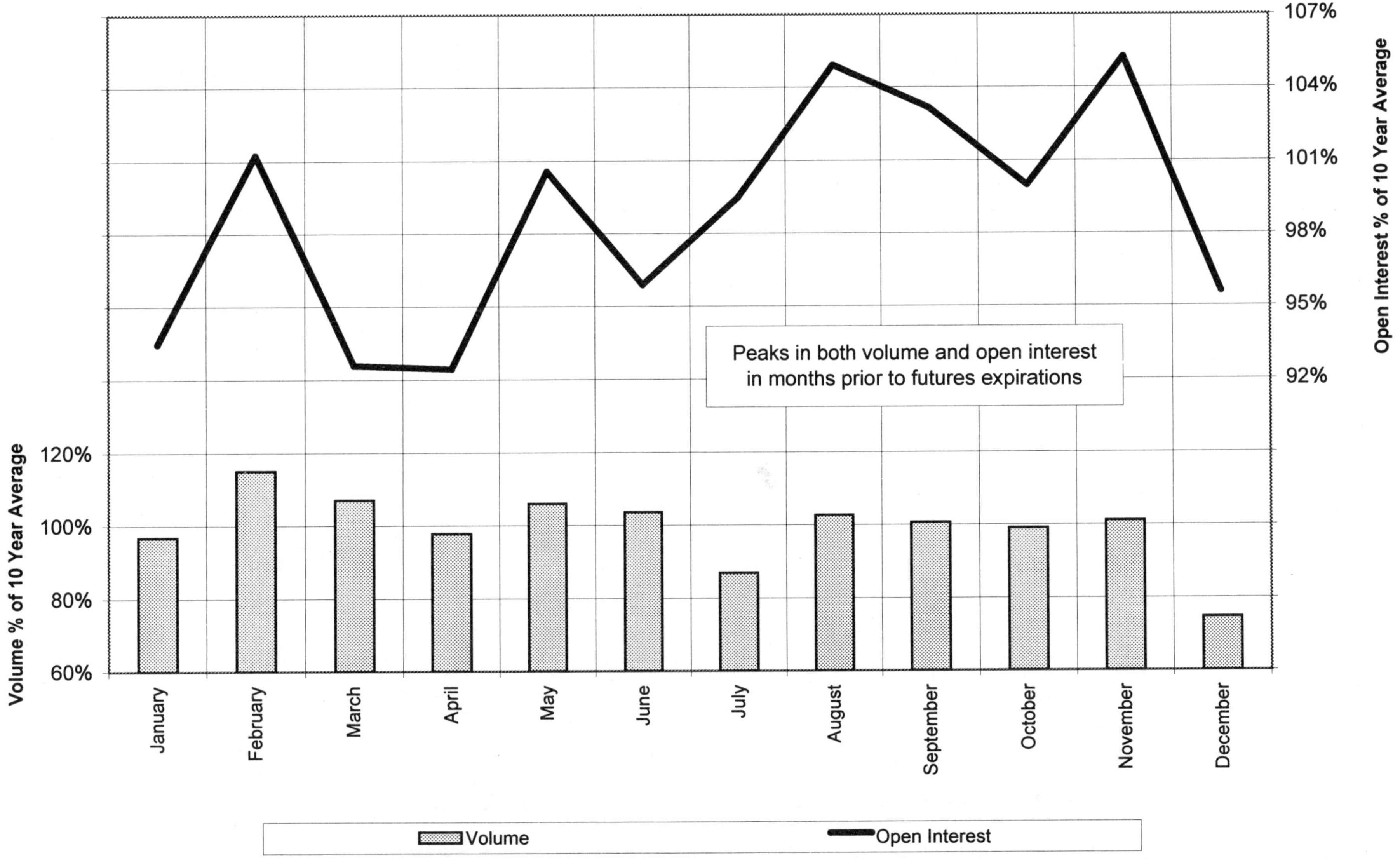

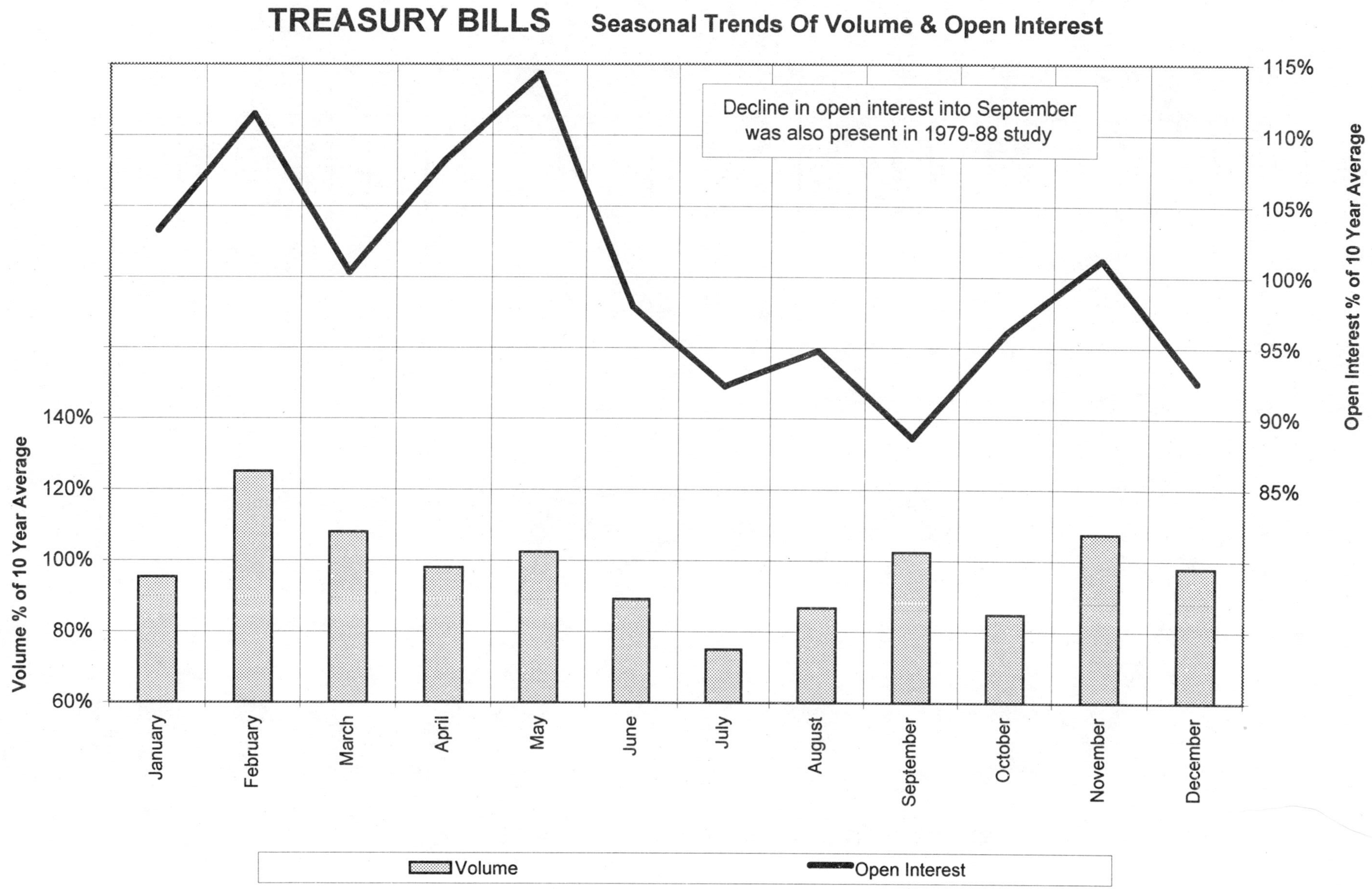

TREASURY BILLS
Seasonal Trends Of Volume & Open Interest
Decline in open interest into September
was also present in 1979-88 study
140%
120%
100%
80%
60%
Volume % of 10 Year Average
115%
110%
105%
100%
95%
90%
85%
Open Interest % of 10 Year Average
January
February
March
April
May
June
July
August
September
October
November
December
Volume
Open Interest

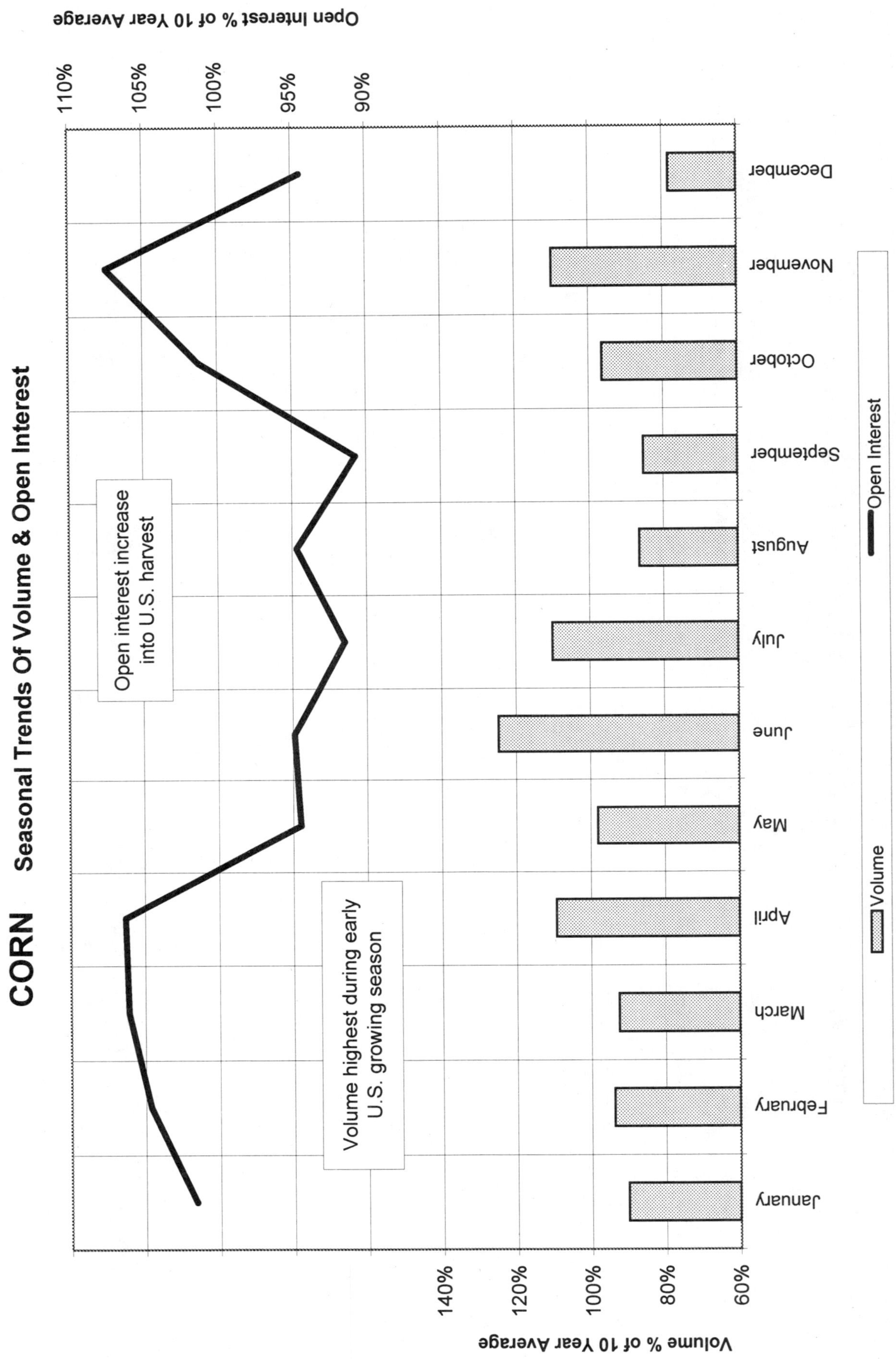
CORN Seasonal Trends Of Volume & Open Interest
Open Interest % of 10 Year Average
110%
105%
100%
95%
90%
Volume % of 10 Year Average
140%
120%
100%
80%
60%
January
February
March
April
May
June
July
August
September
October
November
December
Volume highest during early U.S. growing season
Open interest increase into U.S. harvest
Volume
Open Interest

## SOYBEANS Seasonal Trends Of Volume & Open Interest

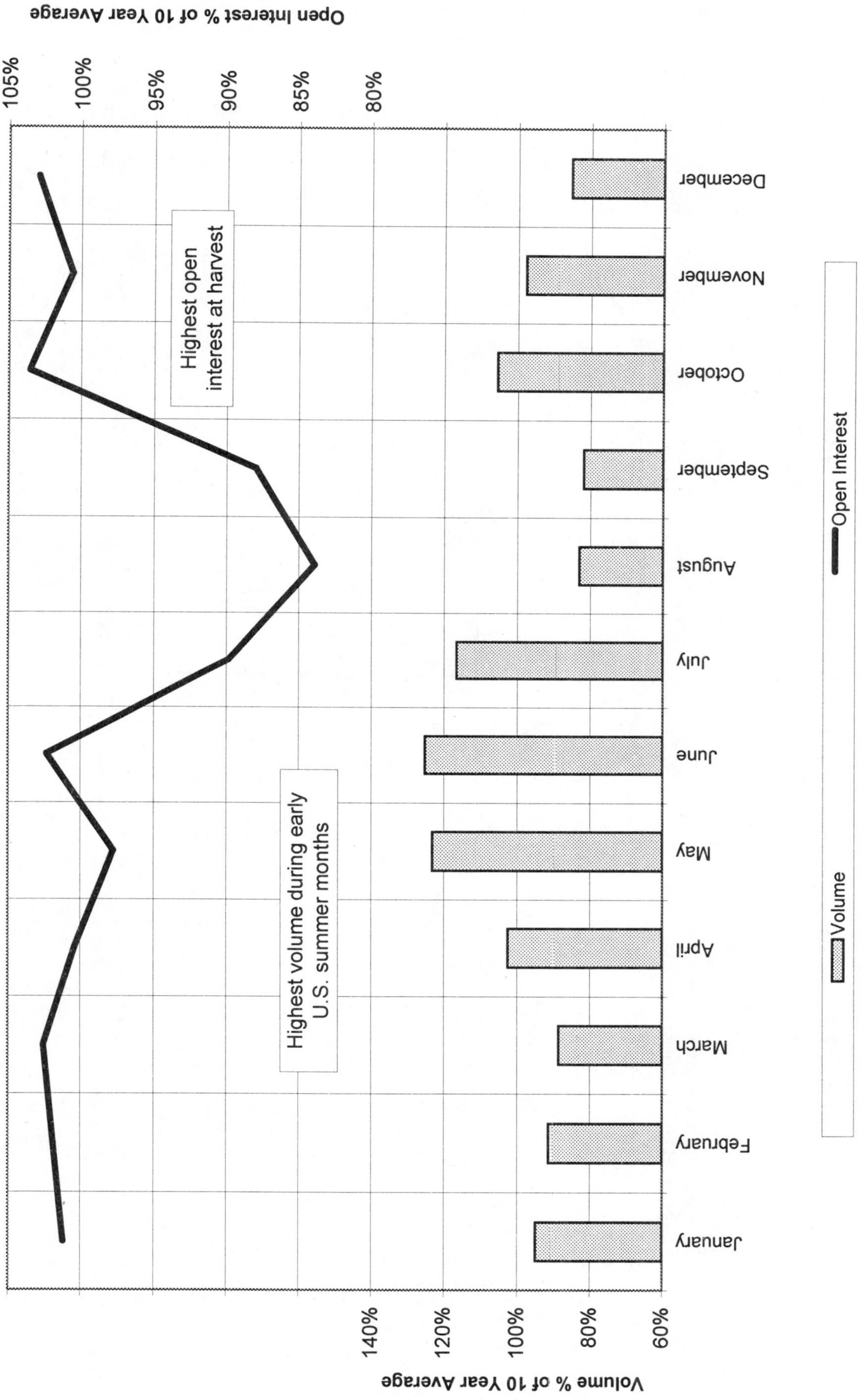

# WHEAT (Chicago) Seasonal Trends Of Volume & Open Interest

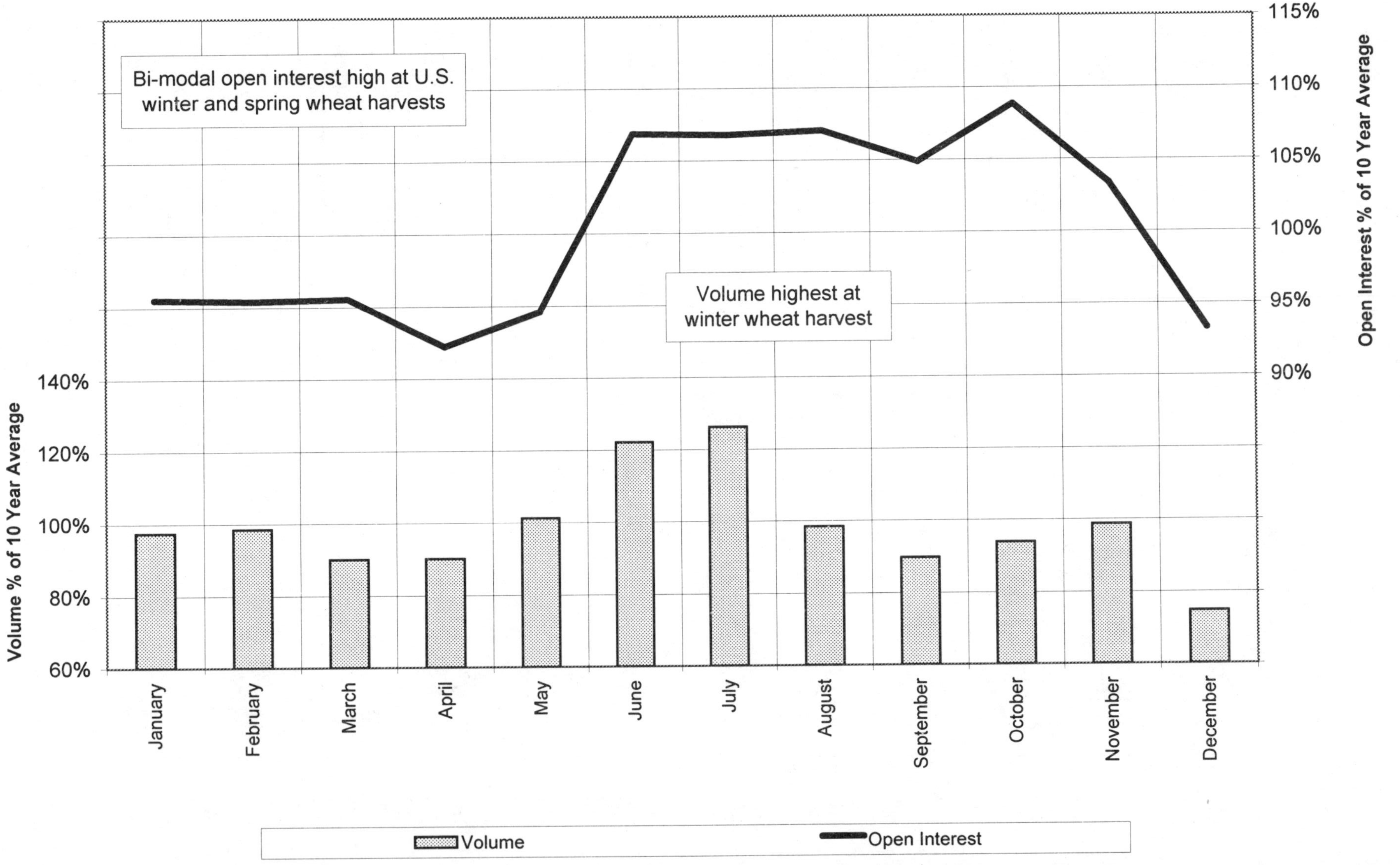

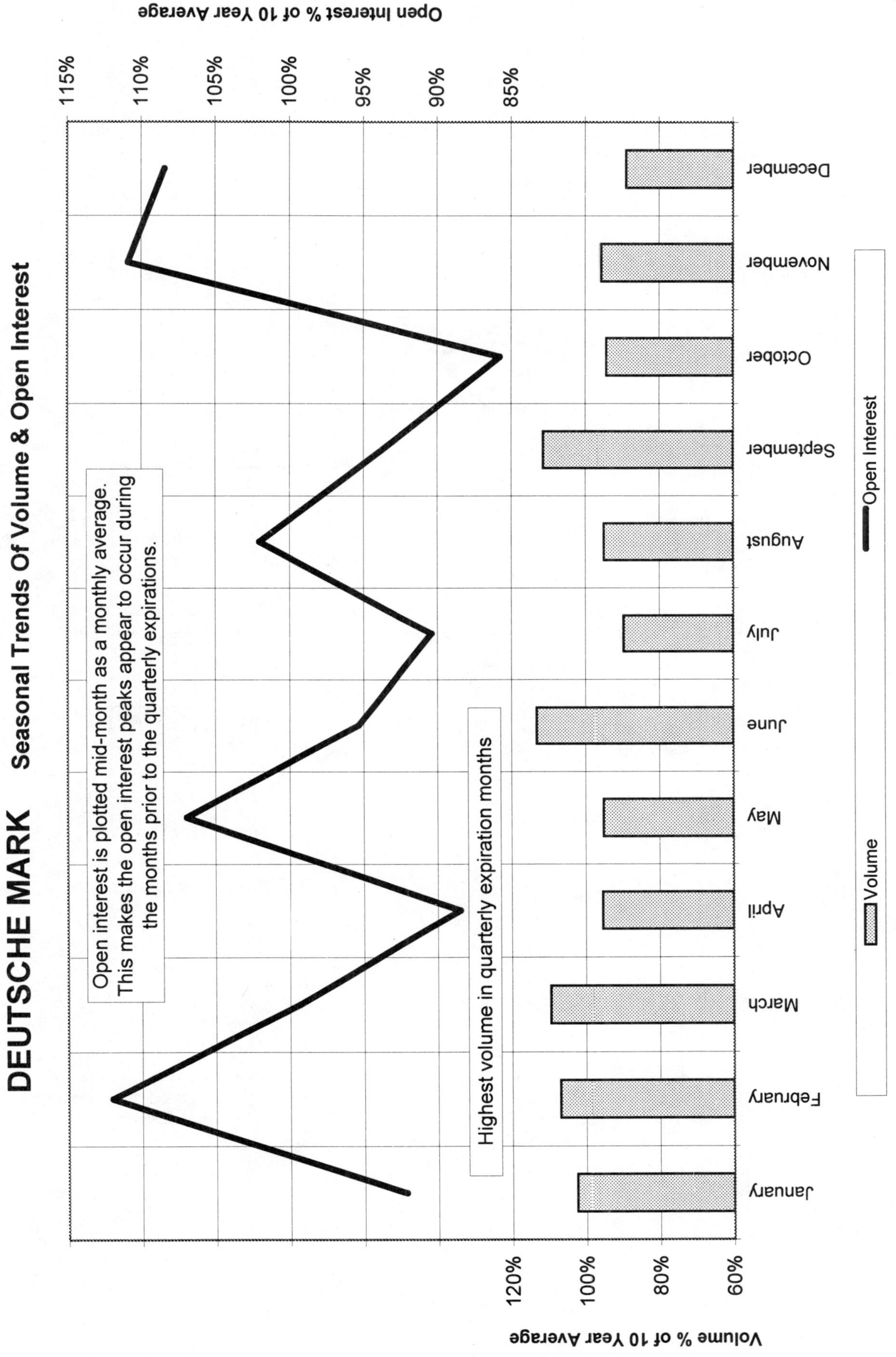
DEUTSCHE MARK
Seasonal Trends Of Volume & Open Interest
Open interest is plotted mid-month as a monthly average.
This makes the open interest peaks appear to occur during
the months prior to the quarterly expirations.
Highest volume in quarterly expiration months
Open Interest % of 10 Year Average
115%
110%
105%
100%
95%
90%
85%
Volume % of 10 Year Average
120%
100%
80%
60%
January
February
March
April
May
June
July
August
September
October
November
December
Volume
Open Interest

## BRITISH POUND Seasonal Trends Of Volume & Open Interest

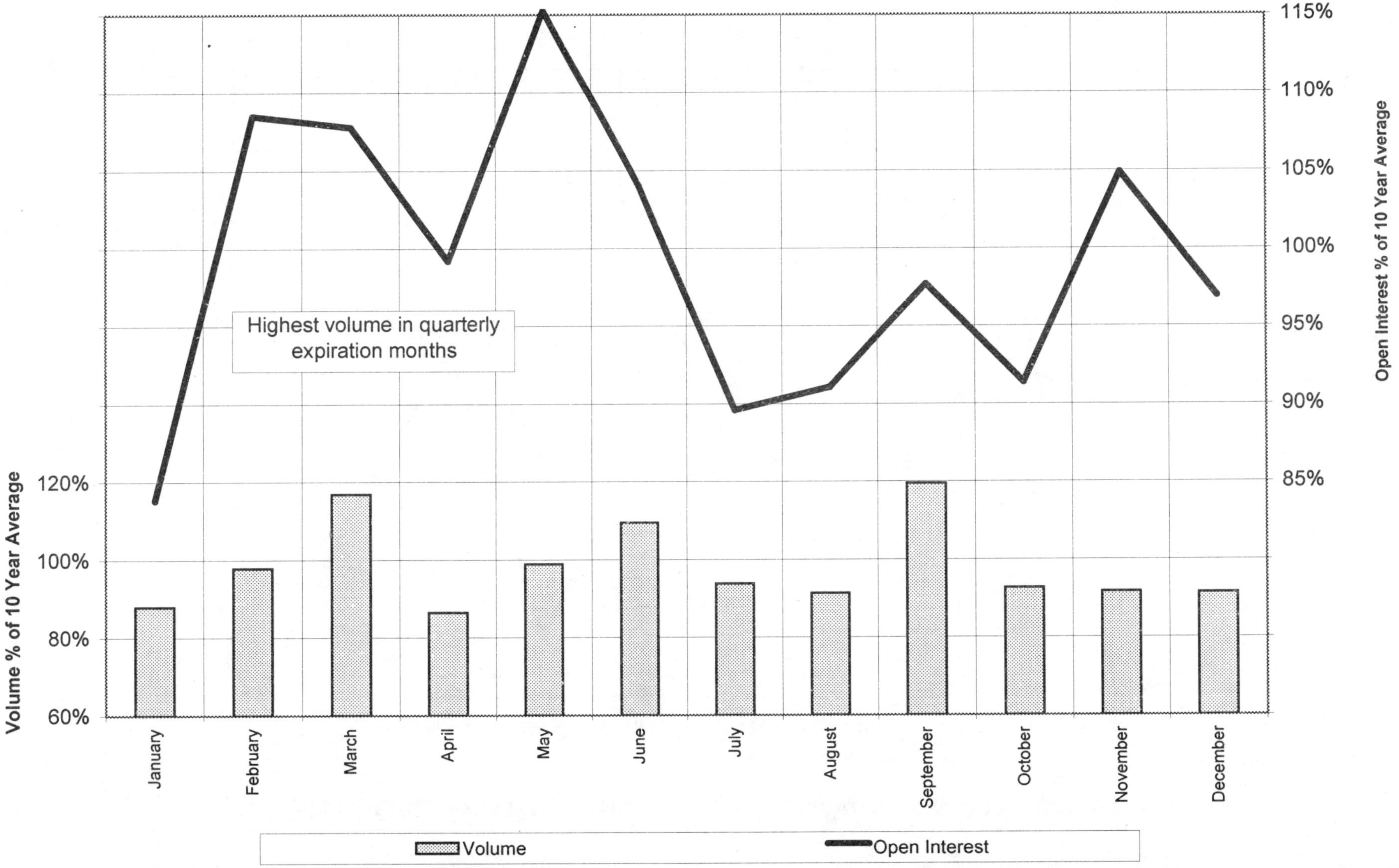

## JAPANESE YEN Seasonal Trends Of Volume & Open Interest

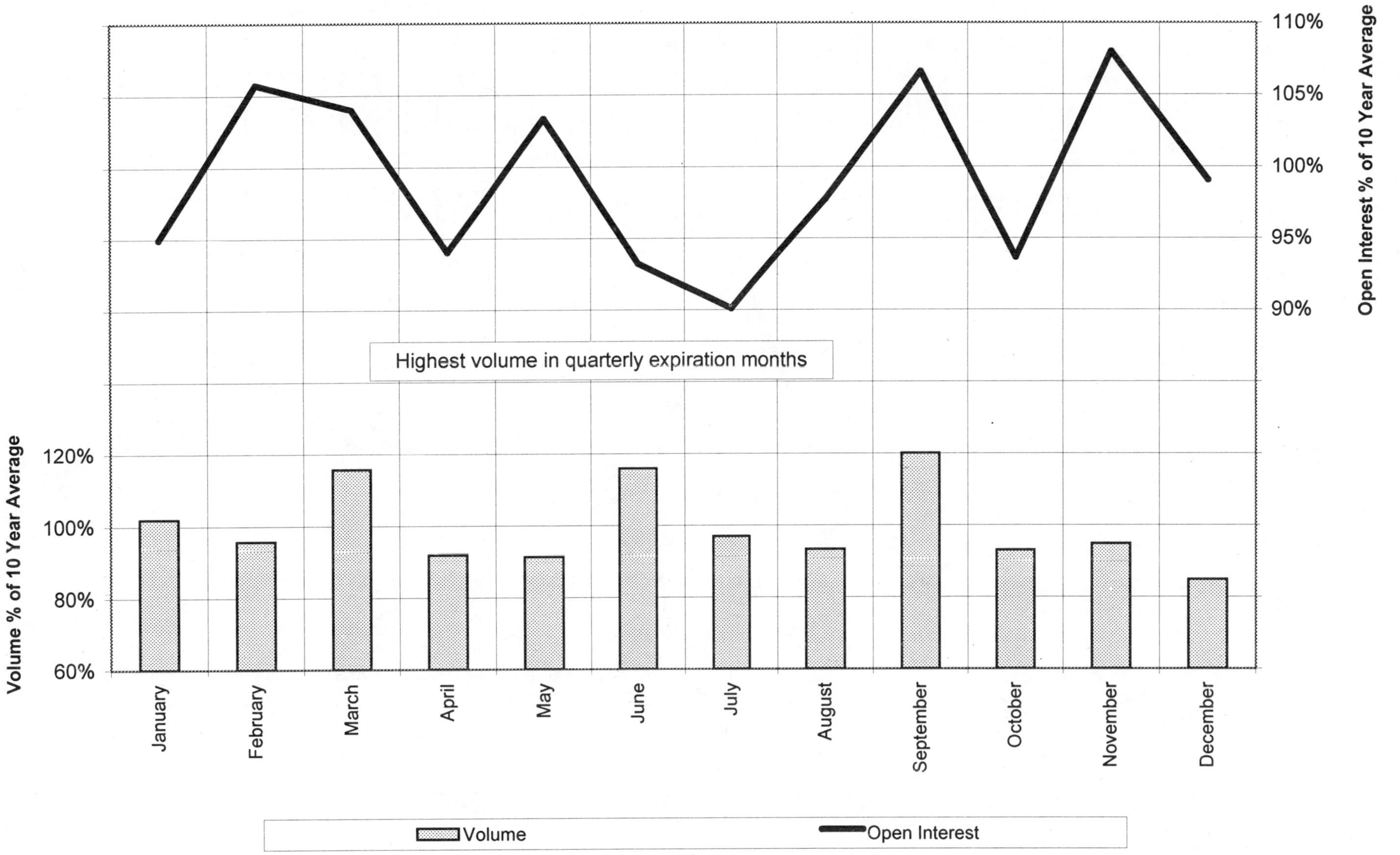

## S & P 500 Seasonal Trends Of Volume & Open Interest

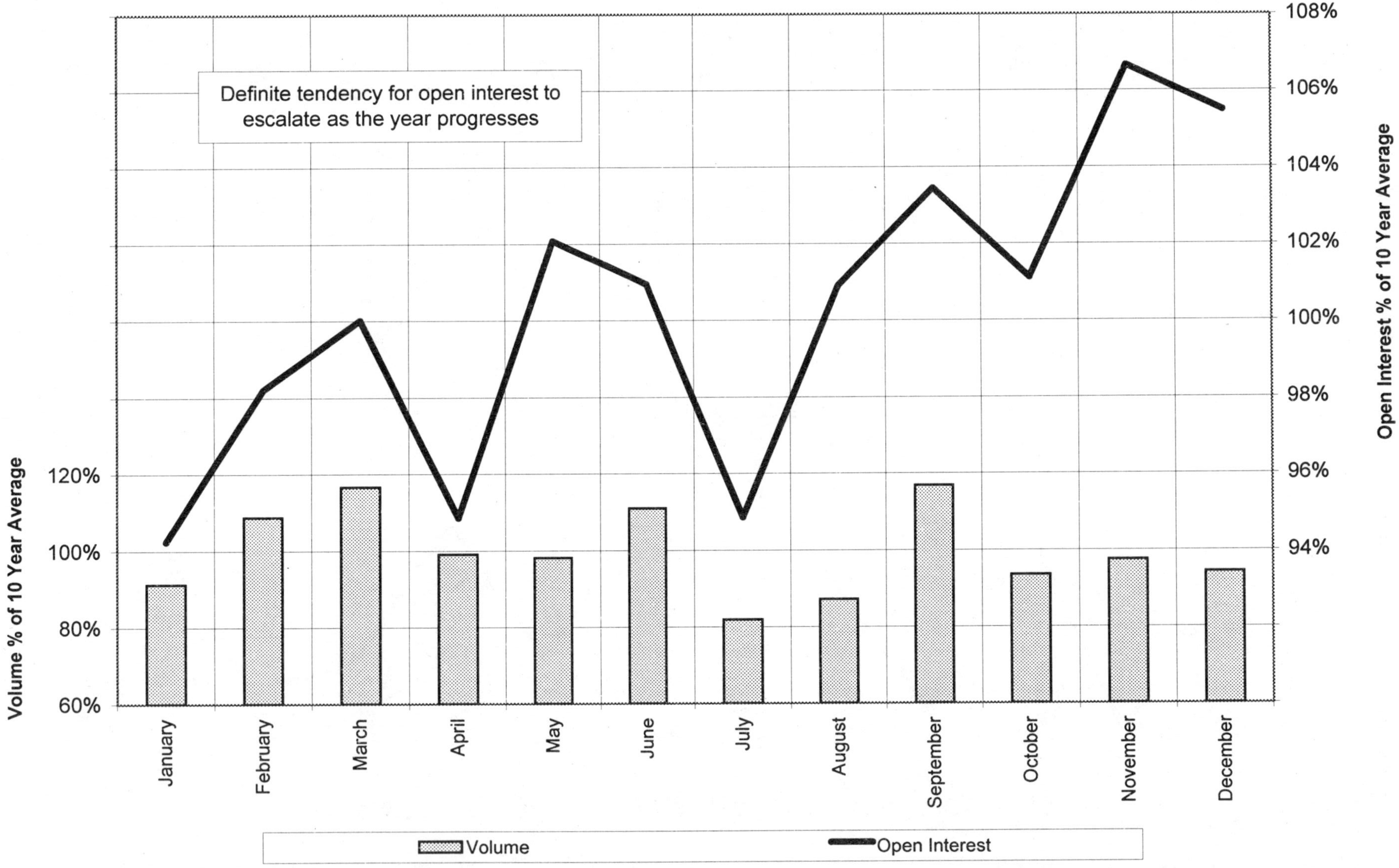

# THE AMBER WAVES OF HISTORY—200 Years of Grain Prices

*by Hugh Ulrich*

## Origins of World Grain Market

They say a picture is worth a thousand words, and that goes double for commodity markets. In their case, the best picture is a price chart. Charts show us at a glance the effects that supply, demand, war, inflation, and changes in society and technology have had on commodities over the years, and over the centuries.

But the story behind these pictures is an important one that deserves to be told. Along with some very long-term charts, we've included a few thousand words: a brief history of the modern world grain markets.

### *The Market Emerges*

There has not always been a world grain market. While various grains have been traded among tribes, city-states, and nations for thousands of years, until the modern era they were individual markets and quite limited in scope. They often fell within the present day borders of a single nation or river system: rice trade in China and wheat in ancient Mesopotamia (Iraq), for example.

There were exceptions when grain moved in quantity across today's international boundaries, such as during the days of the Roman and Ottoman Empires, but they all proved temporary. As these great empires declined, so did the large 'international' grain markets they had sustained. Longer distance wanderers like the Vikings sometimes mixed a bit of grain trading in with their general mayhem, and they ranged all the way from Scandinavia to the Mediterranean Sea in so doing. But they moved minute quantities of grain compared with what was traded and used on a local basis.

The modern world grain market began with the Industrial Revolution in Britain during the last quarter of the 1700s. This revolution started with mechanization of the cotton and woolen industries. It spawned large factory towns inhabited by fast-growing numbers of workers who lost the direct access to food they'd had as peasants and farmers. Factory towns were typically located near the natural resources needed for industry—water to power the mills, protected seaports where imported cotton could be unloaded, navigable rivers so raw materials and finished products could be moved between the factories and the ports—places not necessarily surrounded by a fertile hinterland that could support a booming industrial population.

It became necessary to pull basic foodstuffs from farther afield. Railroads might have done the job with British grain alone during early industrialization, but the first rail line was not opened there until much later, 1825, and it took years longer for a rail network to develop. Some grain was moved overland by cart, or through canals built to connect the industrial centers with coal mines and with one another, but these systems were either too crude in the early stages or they failed to make direct links with areas that produced a consistent surplus of grain.

The obvious solution was to treat grain like any other industrial raw material. Buy it wherever it was produced in surplus and haul it into one of Britain's industrial ports on a ship. While it was possible to accomplish this entirely within the British Isles—to load grain produced in more fertile parts of England or Ireland and then sail it around the coast to Liverpool—once industry made the leap to using ocean freight to supply basic food needs, it was only logical to start looking outside Britain for sources where grain was cheaper and more abundant.

Buyers initially looked no farther than an established regional grain market in Eastern/Central Europe, that of Poland and present day Ukraine. Wheat and barley were pulled westward and northward from these areas to the old German (formerly Hanseatic) trading centers on the Baltic Sea. From there it was a relatively short and uncomplicated journey by sea to Britain. The Industrial Revolution next spread to Holland, and then to Northwestern Germany, which were even shorter hauls via ship from the Baltic Sea. Soon, a fairly liquid super-regional cash grain market was in existence.

### *From Super-Regional to Global*

By the early 1800s, a kind of critical mass had been achieved, and out of this emerged two of the hallmarks of today's world grain market: a) international ports which were liquid markets unto themselves, and b) an international brokerage community that specialized in grain and maintained representation on both ends of the international pipelines.

As the major ports grew and became more organized they produced a by-product that was crucial to market development: "world" prices. The price of wheat delivered to the port of Liverpool, England, became an early barometer. The Liverpool Corn Exchange was founded in 1806 to organize cash grain trade, keep track of prices, and establish minimal contract standards. (In more recent times, great ports such as Rotterdam and Yokohama have played similar roles.)

As demand grew, the supply routes from the Baltic proved inadequate and vulnerable in times of war. Brokers from northwestern Europe shifted all or part of their operations southeast to Black Sea ports, where they tended to supplant Greek merchants whose ancestors had plied those waters on and off for 2,500 years. There, from places like Odessa and Rostov-on-Don, grain brokers could more directly access supplies of wheat from Ukraine (the Russian Empire) without the need to move it through parts of Prussia, or the Austro-Hungarian Empire, to reach the Baltic. Odessa became the world's most important loading and export pricing point—the New Orleans of its day.

*Early 1800s at a Glance*

| | |
|---|---|
| 1800-15 | Napoleonic Wars |
| 1806 | Liverpool Corn Exch. Opens |
| 1815 | Corn Laws Passed |
| 1825 | Erie Canal Completed |
| 1837 | John Deere's Steel Plow |
| 1845-47 | Irish Famine |
| 1846 | Corn Laws Repealed |
| 1848 | CBOT Founded |
| 1848-49 | Revolutions Across Europe |
| 1854-56 | Crimean War |

However, this was far from a seamless process of marketization. The first big roadblock was none other than Napoleon Bonaparte, who came to full power in France in 1799. For the next 15-16 years, he attempted to conquer and rule Continental Europe which placed him between the grain supplies to the east and English consumers to the west. He formalized this interference with a so-called Continental System that attempted to blockade trade with Britain and its colonies. Britain retaliated with a naval blockade, and since it controlled the seas around Europe after the Battle of Trafalgar in 1805, its trade and industrial growth continued.

But Napoleon's power on land was enormous. It extended to present day Poland at various times, and all the way into northwestern Russia in 1812. This greatly interfered with the Baltic to Liverpool routes, but had some positive results in that it hastened the shift to the Black Sea.

### *Protectionism*

Britain's landed aristocracy was the developing market's second early roadblock. They were far more powerful politically than were industrialists during the early stages of the Industrial Revolution. Their wealth was based largely on the ownership of great estates and on marketing the food these estate farms produced. Growth of industrial cities, and disruption of supply routes during the Napoleonic Wars, brought windfall profits to these powerful domestic producers. The end of those wars brought sharply lower prices and increased import competition. The aristocracy was not amused.

Round One of the battle went to the landowners who pushed the so-called Corn Laws through Parliament. The most important of these laws came in 1815, and it instituted high import duties on wheat (called corn by the English.) This caused terrific hardship for the already poverty-stricken industrial workers by making their food scarce and more costly.

The Corn Laws were widely criticized and Parliament amended them to allow more grain imports in 1828. Reformers and Free Traders continued to push for a full repeal which finally occurred in 1846.

Repeal of the Corn Laws was one of the key events in the history of modern world trade. Not only was it one of the major free trade actions in history, but it came not a moment too soon. The second phase of the Industrial Revolution, after 1830, brought the sort of mechanization in iron and steel that had previously occurred in textiles which further accelerated urban population growth.

These forces began to feed on one another during the mid-1800s. The British Fleet added to these growth factors by ensuring relative security throughout a global network of sea lanes. This meant traders could, theoretically, obtain cheap grain from almost any point on the globe where it could be brought to an ocean port. Improved ship design allowed brokers to transport grain in larger ships which, in turn, could carry cargoes over much greater distances in less time and with less spoilage. Ergo, greatly increased market capacity.

The already fierce competition among brokers, combined with the relative safety of major sea lanes, ensured that this could be done on thinner profit margins, another hallmark of the modern world grain market.

These events would not have meant much were it not for similarly momentous events on the supply side. Britons and Northwestern Europeans drove this side of the equation too, with waves of outmigration and the subsequent cultivation of millions of acres of virgin land around the world. In Chile and Argentina, these immigrants produced wheat, barley, and corn in surplus, and by the 1840s that surplus was making its way back to the cities of Britain and NW Europe. The list of major suppliers at that time was rounded out by the fertile Indus River Valley of Greater India (present day Pakistan.)

From this time forward the world market expanded with few interruptions. More and more tonnage moved across a growing menu of international boundaries with more and more countries joining the ranks of chronic grain importers. The United States joined the list of major grain exporters in the 1870s, followed by Australia and Canada in the 1880s.

But while the list of importers has expanded by fits and spurts through the present day, the list of major exporters has changed very little since Australia and Canada joined it. In fact, the list of exporters has been more notable for deletions. Russia, Poland, Chile, Romania, and India/Pakistan dropped out of the grain export business long ago, and the few additions since the late 1800s—South Africa, Thailand, and China—have been either minor exporters, or very temporary ones.

The European Union is the major exception. It emerged as a major net exporter of wheat and some feed grains in the 1970s and 1980s. Brazil became a big exporter too, and we'll address them later, but they export soybeans (an oilseed) and their products.

## The First "World" Prices

Unfortunately, price data are not very consistent or reliable prior to the mid-1800s. Record-keeping at major ports was often poor, and many of the records that did exist have been lost over the years to fires, wars, and overly energetic cleaning ladies.

But price records for English wheat are largely complete. They provide us with our first true snapshot of the world market.

The 1800s start off with a bang, a series of gigantic price spikes caused by the Napoleonic Wars. The first, in 1801, took wheat to $3.63 per bushel in England. This peak was eclipsed in 1812, with a price of $3.85, a level not reached in Chicago for another 162 years!

The Napoleonic Era was followed by 3-4 decades of somewhat lower, but still very volatile, prices. One spike came during the nationalistic revolts which swept across Europe from Hungary to France in 1848-1849. Another came during the Crimean War (1854-1856), and for good reason. This war pitted the largest wheat exporter, Russia, against the largest grain importer, England. Furthermore, hostilities were concentrated in Crimea, located directly between the two Black Sea ports where the majority of Russian grain entered international waters: Odessa and Rostov-on-Don. Other spikes were mainly the result of demand surges or financial panics.

### *Chicago*

In the meantime, a new and ultimately more important market center was emerging: Chicago. The Chicago Board of Trade was founded in 1848 to facilitate grain trade in that growing city, much as The Liverpool Corn Exchange had in England in 1806. We will turn to (wheat) prices generated and recorded by the CBOT at an early date, partly because they are very reliable, and partly because they provide us with both highs and lows from 1859 to the present. But most importantly, because CBOT prices would eventually become the unquestioned world benchmark.

Chicago and Liverpool vied for the role of premier world price barometer through WW I, but Chicago entered the contest with advantages that Liverpool could never hope to match. Most importantly, it sat at the center of a North American grain belt that would soon be the world's most productive. Prices generated there could be said to accurately reflect the world supply side. And like Odessa, Chicago was also a port. In fact, it was a huge export outlet where a growing volume of grain was being loaded for transport by mid-century, destined first for the Eastern United States and later for Europe. Like Liverpool, Chicago was also a major demand destination, both for wheat to feed its rapidly growing human population, and later in the century, for corn to feed the huge populations of cattle and pigs that were fattened up prior to slaughter in the city's giant stockyards.

Our Chicago wheat chart also starts with a bang. The 1860s were yet another period of volatility and high prices caused by war—in this case the American Civil War, fought from 1861 to 1865.

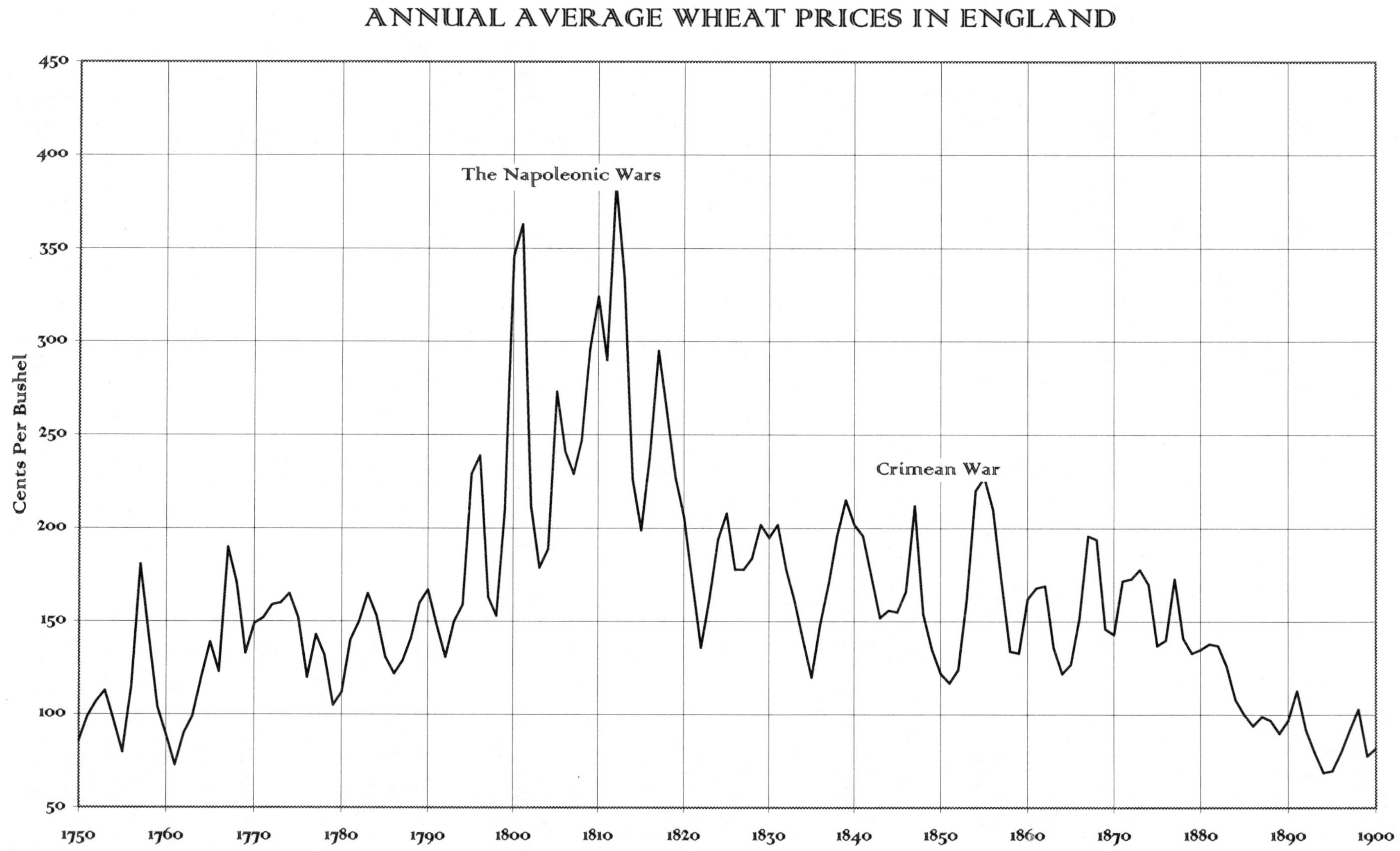


**Wheat, Annual Average Cash Price in England, 1750-1900**

But these rallies do not reflect a grain shortage. Food remained fairly abundant in the North throughout the war, and while there was terrible privation in the South during hostilities, this was not a major market factor. (There were no Southern grain brokers buying grain in Chicago for export to the South during the war.) Nor was there a problem with interrupted trade routes since most Union Army supply lines remained clear throughout the war. For this reason prices at Liverpool, England, remained fairly steady in the 1860s.

In fact, the amount of land under cultivation in the North probably increased during the Civil War. Women took up most of the slack in lost manpower on the farm, and they were bolstered by immigrants who continued to pour into the country. Most remarkably, the Federal Government embarked on a major expansion of land under cultivation with the Homestead Act of 1862. It gave government land away to anyone who settled and cultivated it for a specified period of time.

The price spikes at Chicago in the 1860s came from the demand side. Union Armies were enormously large for the era. Furthermore, there were lots of them and they were often on the move. It was as if dozens of large (at that time) cities had sprung up out of thin air, each of them lacking the hundreds of small-scale sources of supply enjoyed by established cities. For the most part these moving cities had to be supplied through a centralized (governmental) procurement process. This in turn brought a need for much bigger commercial transactions for commodities like grain, and lots of them. Direct governmental involvement added fuel to the fire because money was often thrown at army contractors by federal bureaucrats who asked too few questions about the prices paid and amounts delivered. Still more fuel was added by immigration, an industrial wartime population boom in Northern cities, and the rapid growth of an urban middle class. Vastly more people suddenly needed to be supplied through a large-scale commercial system.

**Late 1800s at a Glance**

| | |
|---|---|
| 1861-65 | American Civil War |
| 1860s | Futures Emerge at CBOT |
| 1862 | Homestead Act |
| 1870 | U.S. Becomes Grain Exporter |
| 1880s | Australia & Canada Become Exporters |
| Mid 1890s | Lows of the Century |

Ergo, the events of the 1860s jolted more than just market prices, they jolted the marketplace. It was during this decade that the CBOT's simple forward contracts proved to be inadequate, and they evolved into something like futures contracts. While these were not exactly like today's futures contracts, they focused on providing what the exploding markets most needed: a) accurate price discovery for a series of dates into the future; b) a financial instrument that gave traders the flexibility they needed to get in and out of the market; and c) the ability to accumulate (and liquidate) large positions quickly. The old system proved inadequate because it was based on grain physically gathered in or headed for Chicago.

The ultimate high in Chicago (cash) wheat during this transitional decade was about $2.85 per bushel in 1867. This would not be exceeded in Chicago for 50 years. Technically, this did not approach the highs in England during the Napoleonic Wars, but it is probably a mistake to directly compare the two markets. England, in 1800-1815, was a deficit center which had to pay up to attract increasing amounts of wheat from up to a thousand miles away, through war zones and blockades. Chicago, during the Civil War, was surrounded by a bountiful surplus that began within a mile or two of downtown.

That's why we need to shift exclusively to Chicago prices at an early date. Price-wise, we need to compare apples with apples through the rest of the story.

### *A Century of Prices*

Despite the problem of comparing charts, it's clear the 19th Century is divided into two segments: high prices and high volatility during the first two thirds of the century, and declining prices and oversupply during the last third.

The most immediate cause for the early volatility was warfare and political instability in Europe. But it might be better to group these together and call them birth pangs. An entirely new system, a global grain market, was struggling to be born. It took high prices and dramatic swings for the rapidly growing demand side to stimulate the changes needed on the supply side: capital investment and specialization in the brokerage community, and the development of exchanges and port facilities on both ends of the international pipeline. Most importantly, high prices were needed to spark diversification of the sources of supply.

These birth pangs set off powerful forces on the supply side that played themselves out through the end of the 19th Century. Starting in about the 1820s, European settlement of previously uncultivated land had started to accelerate around the world. By the time the process finally slowed at the end of the century, several hundred million virgin acres were settled and planted to various grains in Argentina, Chile, the United States, Canada, Australia, South Africa, and even Eastern Europe.

### *Too Much Grain*

The amount of grain that poured from these areas into places like Chicago, Eastern North America, and Northwestern Europe grew at such an astounding rate that world supply consistently exceeded world demand for 40 plus-years, from the late 1860s to about 1910. This despite the fact that by then industrialization was occurring across most of Europe, Japan, and throughout the English-speaking world, producing an explosive expansion of urban populations in these areas.

At Chicago, there were just two quick price spikes in wheat over this long bearish stretch. Each was short-lived and fell well short of the post-Civil War high, topping out at $2.00, and just over $1.80.

But the real story was the lows. They were also successively lower through the end of the century with the ultimate bottom coming in the mid-1990s, the Gay Nineties, at the decidedly not very gay level of about 50 cents per bushel. Corn was under the same pressure, and its prices bottomed just above 20 cents per bushel.

In the U.S., the worst of this long bear market was felt by farmers in the newly settled areas west of the Mississippi, and northwest into Minnesota and the Dakotas. They were far from Chicago and other big urban demand centers as well as from the major ports where grain was gathered for export. And then, as now, their local price per bushel usually traded at a discount to the price at Chicago. The fact that some of the land west of the Mississippi was either less fertile or more drought prone than land to the east meant smaller yields per acre. In a depressed market this made farming in the Western Grain Belt a very tough proposition indeed.

Farmers in these remote regions believed the low prices were caused either by market manipulation by brokers in Chicago and Minneapolis, or by monopolistic wheat millers, railroads, and grain elevators.

The former view was wishful thinking. The attempts at manipulation in Chicago were usually an effort to squeeze the market which, if successful, would have forced prices higher. However, the second accusation, price-fixing by local monopolies, was sometimes legitimate. An area's rail access to major markets was sometimes controlled by a single company, and these monopolists used their control to buy grain at distressed prices.

Populist organizations and farm associations arose to fight railroads, processors, and merchandisers for freer access to markets and higher farm prices. While this resulted in many needed reforms and regulations, in the end prices remained low, reflecting the oversupply. The era left farmers in western areas with a general distrust of the futures markets that was more pronounced than in farming regions to the east. This attitude was still in strong evidence as late as the bear markets of the 1980s!

Internationally, low prices put great pressure on the older producer/exporters such as Russia. Despite their proximity to the biggest importers, they lagged behind the newer exporters with poorer farming methods, a poorly developed transportation system, local corruption, an underdeveloped system of contracts and jurisprudence, and inferior storage facilities. Grain from Russia also developed the reputation of being filled with dirt and other foreign matter.

### CORN TO IRELAND

Wheat was king on world export markets during the 19th Century, but a spectacular exception came during the Irish Famine of 1845-1847.

Millions of Irish farmers had become dependent on subsistence potato farming by the early 1800s. Starting in 1845, a blight appeared that destroyed much of the potato crop, bringing hundreds of thousands, and then millions, to the brink of starvation. Authorities were faced with the need to import a vast amount of nutritious food into a completely primitive infrastructure, then deliver it to hundreds of locations where it had to be quickly prepared and fed to people who literally might die without their next meal. Nothing like it had ever been attempted.

The international wheat market was incapable of meeting the emergency. It was based on the import of raw grain into a modern port where it was unloaded, distributed to commercial flour mills via a system of industrial canals, baked into bread products at a commercial bakery, and then distributed to people who ate it immediately. The problem for Ireland was that there were few good ports, no internal transport, few flour mills, and few commercial bakeries.

The solution turned out to be corn. Corn could be bought on the cheap in large quantities in America, dumped on the ground at dockside in Ireland, ground into a coarse meal with primitive equipment, hauled around on carts, and turned into a nutritious meal by anyone with some water, a pot, and a fire. To this day, some Irish are bitter over British policies that seemed to make things worse. (Furthermore, the gruel made from corn meal was not popular.) A million died from the famine and a million more left for America during and after the ordeal. But corn from the New World did its job, probably preserving more lives than were lost.

Under vastly different circumstances, all of these problems remain prevalent in Eastern Europe to this day.

***A Golden Age***

All trends come to an end, and after the mid-1890s grain prices slowly started trending higher. As a result, both mechanized farming and general prosperity began to spread more quickly across the Midwest and even out onto the Great Plains. Over the next twenty years this growing agricultural prosperity was demonstrated by the fact that most of the remaining thousands of farm cabins and sod houses were replaced by the Victorian frame houses we often associate with rural America.

In particular, the period of 1909 to 1914 came to be viewed as a sort of golden age in American agriculture. During this time supply and demand were in rough balance, as were the overall size of urban and rural economies. Prices for most grains averaged 100% or more above the lows of the late 1800s, and they did so year after year. Most farm operations experienced a consistently positive cash flow.

So attractive did this prosperity and balance seem to farmers and politicians of later years, these golden years (eventually 1910-1914) were actually codified into law during the New Deal of the 1930s. They became the economic standard that the national farm policy sought to recreate from the 1930s onward. To this day, the USDA maintains an index which calculates the price that various commodities need to trade at in order to achieve parity with those five prosperous years. This index remained the basis for certain aspects of USDA support programs until the 1990s.

## PRICE SHOCK!

The balance of the parity years was shattered in August, 1914, when most of the grain market's customers declared war on one another. World War I (1914-1918) magnified the disruption caused by earlier events, such as the Napoleonic Wars, since it was both vastly bigger, and it occurred in a region—Northwestern Europe—that was by then heavily dependent on grain imports from throughout the world.

Wheat doubled in price by the summer of 1915, but a harvest break took the market right back down to the mid-point of the parity years. Then, starting in 1916, the Chicago market began the biggest rally in its history to that point.

By spring 1917, wheat at Chicago had vaulted above the post-Civil War highs to a peak of $3.45 per bushel. A good deal of velocity was added on the way up by a very poor U.S. winter wheat crop. The final stage of the rally came when German U-boats had surrounded Great Britain—still the world's biggest grain importer—cutting off nearly all of its food imports. The market peaked as the blockade was being broken, and while America was scrambling to replace stocks in Britain which had fallen to a scant six-week supply. The peak also roughly coincided with America's own entry into the war, which brought the further need to gather vast quantities of food for millions of American soldiers both in their training camps and in France.

As was the case during the American Civil War, the grain markets were suddenly infused with a large number of huge transactions and government money to pay for them. It took this potent combination to end more than 45 years of ample grain supplies, and produce the 20th Century's first price shock.

By summer 1917, the Federal Government had stepped in to manage domestic markets: buying wheat when prices fell, and selling into areas where domestic shortages occurred. Government also negotiated export sales and eventually guaranteed high prices to farmers to stimulate overall production. (The "high" guarantee for wheat was soon less attractive than the unrestricted market prices for feedgrains. Feedgrain production increased more than wheat. Farmers fed the extra grain to pigs which resulted in a glut of pork and a shortage of wheat for European relief.)

America had an on-going surplus of labor that was able to satisfy manpower needs in Europe without causing severe labor disruption on the farm, so overall production soared. Many farming areas prospered as never before.

For a time wheat prices backed off from the 1917 highs. The true extent of the drop will never be known since government intervention supported wheat at about $2.20 for the last year or so of the war. But when trading resumed in 1918-1919, all of the major trade routes into Northwestern Europe were thrown back open. Shipping that had been tied up for war uses was suddenly available in virtually unlimited amounts and American relief ensured that the market would not lack for money. Wheat prices staged a second huge rally as both private and governmental buy orders flooded in.

The surge was topped off by one more violent European episode. The Russian Revolution had broken out in late 1917 and it was followed by massive turmoil and then Civil War. By 1919-1920, mass starvation in Russia was imminent. Under the direction of Herbert Hoover, the apparatus that had been used to acquire and distribute American grain and foodstuffs during and after the war was extended to feed starving Russians, saving as many as ten million lives by U.S. estimates. This was probably the greatest catalyst for a wheat rally that peaked in Chicago at $3.50 in 1919, taking out the 1917 all-time high by five cents. Months later, a third run at the highs fell just short. That third peak marked the end of widespread prosperity on American farms for more than 20 years.

*Early 1900s at a Glance*

| | |
|---|---|
| 1910-14 | Parity Years |
| 1914-18 | U-Boat Embargo Peaks |
| 1917 (fall) | Russian Revolution |
| 1918-22 | Russian Civil War |

### *Boom and Bust*

By spring planting time in 1920, prices were already collapsing. That year's crops were big throughout most of the world adding relentless pressure. Wheat prices failed to recover for more than four years, plunging large segments of the farm economy in America and other big exporting countries into recession.

A number of supply factors contributed. Planted acreage had grown during the war years in areas not affected by war—places like the U.S., South America, and even Africa. When the war ended in 1918, millions of farmers returned to more or less intact farms in Central, Western, and Southern Europe, adding the labor that was needed to sharply boost European acreage and production. In fairly short order, the areas of Northern France that had been devastated by war also began generating crops.

Eventually, even the Civil War in Russia ended bringing tens of millions of additional acres back into production. At first, Russia's vast potential was stymied by confiscatory Bolshevik policies, but in 1921-1922, Lenin realized that chaos in Russia's farm economy threatened his party's hold on power. He reversed course and allowed peasants to keep and market a substantial amount of their crops. Mussolini got in the act too. When the Fascist Dictator came to power in 1922, he set about to make Italy self-sufficient in basic food production by various means, including the draining of ancient swamps for cropland and a slight modernization of farming methods. By the mid-1920s there was a worldwide glut of grain.

Yet, it was not as bad as the 1890s. There were two small bounces in price during the second half of the decade, and the lows of the early Twenties were actually higher than the lows during the supposedly golden parity years. For most farmers, these prices were plenty good enough, but a large minority had borrowed heavily during the boom to expand land holdings, buy modern equipment, and raise their standards of living. Heavy debt loads carried over from the boom could not be repaid during the bust, and many farmers went bankrupt. It was an old pattern.

### *Big Changes Down on the Farm*

The Twenties were also a time when important social and economic changes accelerated in the American food economy. One change was demographic. The farm labor surplus that was already evident before WW I became overwhelming in the Roaring Twenties. Huge numbers of men and women left recessionary farms for the booming cities. For the first time in the peacetime history of the U.S., the total farm population entered a down trend. Except for a brief interruption in the 1930s, that trend has continued through today.

The Twenties were also the decade when wheat lost some of its luster as the king of the world's grain markets, a role it had played without question since the Industrial Revolution. The end of the war, and the resumption of the growth of the urban middle class, resulted in increased consumption of meat and dairy products by a broader range of America's urban population, and a corresponding decrease in per capita consumption of wheat products. Satisfying the demand for meat and dairy products required feed grains, which in the U.S. generally means corn. It was during this time that corn began to nudge wheat aside to start becoming the core of the human diet in the Developed World. Eventually corn would also become the most heavily traded agricultural commodity at the Chicago Board of Trade.

*The 1920s at a Glance*

| | |
|---|---|
| 1921 | NEP Market Reforms (USSR) |
| 1921 | Futures Trading Act in U.S. |
| 1922 | Grain Futures Act |
| 1922 | 1st U.S. Soy Processing Plant |
| 1925 | CBOT Clearing Corp. Established |
| 1925 | First Commercially Sliced Bread |
| 1929 | New York Stock Market Crash |

But the lost status of the wheat contract was nothing in comparison to what happened to another old standby: oats. Mass production of automobiles during the 1920s, and the development of mechanized mass transit in and between cities, meant the end of the central role of the horse in most cities and towns. This process had begun before WW I, but it was during the 1920s that the mechanization of urban transit was

Wheat, Chicago Cash, 1860-1966

largely completed. As a result the number of horses in the country plunged, and most of those that remained were on or near the farms where they worked. Oats needed to feed farm horses were mostly produced locally, and since the vast majority of oats produced in the U.S. are used for horse feed, there was suddenly far less need to merchandise great quantities of them over long distances.

Ergo, not much need for a heavily traded futures contract. Oats became a minor crop and a minor futures contract at the Chicago Board of Trade. Few traders today realize that oat futures once rivaled wheat for the top spot in interest and activity, and that oats were often the speculator's commodity of choice—the soybeans or pork bellies of their day.

### *A New Deal and a Dust Bowl*

The largely urban prosperity of the Twenties ended with a crash, the New York Stock Exchange crash of October, 1929. The Great Depression followed and this made the existing farm depression far deeper and broader. Wheat prices quickly fell below the lows of the early Twenties, and with barely a pause, continued on down through the lows of the 1890s. (Corn held just above the 1890s lows.) The ultimate lows in many markets occurred right around Election Day in 1932, very bad timing for a beleaguered President Hoover, but pretty good luck for Franklin D. Roosevelt whose election was made inevitable by the deep valley we see on grain charts.

As President, FDR engineered a revolution in U.S. farm policy starting in early 1933. The new farm policies concentrated on raising or supporting farm prices during periods of oversupply. This was attempted by means ranging from acreage reductions, to the slaughter and mass burial of livestock, to removing supplies of wheat from the market and storing them until prices rose. This concept of manipulating the free supply in order to support prices remained the cornerstone of grain programs through the early 1990s.

| The 1930s at a Glance | |
|---|---|
| 1933 | 1st New Deal Farm Legislation |
| 1933-36 | Dust Bowl Droughts |
| 1936 | First CBOT Soybean Futures |
| 1936 | Commodity Exchange Act |
| 1939 | Germany Invades Poland |

Prices began rising from the 1932 lows but this had little to do with the new government programs. More important was the simple exhaustion of a mature downtrend near 100-year lows, combined with the onset of one of the worst series of droughts in U.S. history. From 1933 through 1936, droughts effected many growing areas but were concentrated in the southern Great Plains. Conditions deteriorated to the point where the savage windstorms that regularly broke out in the area stripped large sections of their unprotected topsoil and carried it for miles in great clouds of dust, often blotting out the sun. The area most severely effected by these storms came to be called the Dust Bowl, and this term is often used to represent the entire drought era.

By spring 1937, the last drought of the series ended. So did the bounce. By this time a full-fledged system of price supports were in effect, and with falling prices they constantly kicked in, taking grain off the market whenever prices declined below prescribed support levels. As improved weather brought increased production, this happened a lot. Oversupply turned into yet another glut which, this time around, fell into government hands. Government loans made to farmers to tide them over during a 'temporary' downturn in price were mostly defaulted.

During 1938-1939, commodities from wheat to potatoes dropped back to the lows of 1932-1933, which were also the lows of the century. By mid-1939, it was generally assumed that the glut would overwhelm and bankrupt the new support programs. Since yields were generally rising and weather was mostly good into the 1940s, this would certainly have happened. It did not, however, because on September 1, 1939, Nazi Germany invaded Poland.

## AMERICA TAKES CENTER STAGE

After the initial carnage of the Blitzkrieg, there was a lull in the war: the Sitz-krieg. This was broken to a degree when Germany invaded Denmark, Norway, Belgium, Holland, and France during 1940, but the Allied armies were quickly defeated and relatively little territory was disrupted compared to WW I.

Grain prices moved higher during fall and winter of 1939, but only modestly. Supplies of most crops, especially wheat, were very large in the U.S. Even European supplies were ample since most countries had stockpiled in anticipation of renewed hostilities. As a result, wheat prices broke sharply in May, 1940, when it appeared that Germany's successes in France and the Low Countries would quickly end the war.

The United States' entry into the war at the end of 1941 brought governmental entry into the markets to a greater degree than during WW I. This brought a renewed uptrend in wheat but carryover stocks were at record levels so the move was modest.

Corn was a very different story. Stocks of corn were smaller and the government's needs were huge. Military mobilization would eventually put 12 million men and women in the U.S. armed forces, and the Federal Government was determined to feed them well. Over the preceding generation, well-fed had come to mean meat which, in turn, required feed-grains. So great was the anticipated need for feed corn that the Federal Government seized stocks in all 15 terminal locations during 1942-1943. So ample were the supplies of wheat, that massive amounts of it were shifted into use as animal feed, or for the production of grain alcohol during that crop year. It was a stark illustration of the long term shift in fundamental importance from wheat to corn.

Crop production increased dramatically during the war, especially for corn, continuing a trend that had begun in the 1930s. It was during the war that American farms largely completed their long-term transformation from horse and mule to tractor and truck, leaving mostly just the Amish and poor Southerners as the major groups still engaged in non-mechanical farming after the war.

Wartime governmental involvement included the suspension of futures trading in some markets until the end of the war, and for some time thereafter when military and relief needs were at their highest. When trading was resumed in Chicago in late summer, 1946, wheat stocks were almost entirely depleted. A big 1946-1947 wheat crop produced barely enough to meet the unprecedented military and European relief needs.

### *A Test of Wills*

The crisis in wheat was soon overshadowed by a catastrophe in corn, a drop of nearly 30% in the 1947 U.S. crop vs. a year earlier. As if this were not enough, 1948 was set to be the first year of a longer term relief effort—The Marshall Plan. So acute was the looming shortage that President Truman took to the airwaves in 1947 to beg Americans to eat less. Meatless and poultry/eggless days were urged. Families were even asked to save one slice of bread per day. This turned out to be one of America's finest hours. The country literally risked the first widespread food shortage since the Civil War in order to maintain the frantic export pace needed to prevent starvation in Europe and Eastern Asia.

*The 1940s at a Glance*

| | |
|---|---|
| *1941 (Dec)* | *U.S. Enters WW II* |
| | *CBOT Futures Suspended* |
| *1948-49* | *Berlin Airlift* |
| *1948-52* | *Marshall Plan* |
| *1948* | *CCC Chartered* |

**THE BERLIN AIRLIFT**

For sheer drama, the climax of the post-war relief efforts came in 1948-49. West Berlin was completely surrounded by Soviet controlled territory after the war, except for a narrow land and air corrider that was not much wider than an Autobahn.

Stalin decided this island of freedom was his for the taking. He blockaded the city along the 99% of its periphery that he controlled, in the assumption Berlin would quickly submit. He was gambling that America lacked either the extra food or the will to break the blockade. The U.S. and Britian saw this as a test of their willingness to resist Soviet expansion. They assembled all of the city's food, fuel, and medicine needs in Western Europe and sent it to Berlin via the only available route: that narrow air corrider. Lines of planes flew day and night for the better part of two years before Stalin finally backed down. The affair was a public relations disaster for communism. It defined the goals and aspirations of both sides and cemented a grateful Germany to the Western Alliance.

Corn prices led the resulting advance in Chicago where cash hit a record high of just under $3.00 in 1947. Given the looming shortages, many Americans blamed speculators in the soaring futures markets for the food inflation. Truman requested, and then demanded, higher futures margins and a public clamor arose for the public release of lists of commodity traders to see who was guilty of excess speculation. These lists were made available at the end of 1947.

The day was saved in 1948 with a record large corn crop based on a (then) near miraculously large yield of 42.5 bushels per acre. That year's production total would not be exceeded for more than a decade.

The big crop brought a drop in prices which fell sharply thru the end of 1949. At first, this break looked suspiciously like the one in the early Twenties which had started a worldwide ag recession. But for corn, there would be one more run at the highs. It came in 1952, near the height of the Korean War, taking prices back up to $2.90, just short of the 1947 high.

This time around there would be no new highs for wheat. Its 1947 peak was just over $3.20, well shy of the 1919 high at Chicago, and even farther below the 1811 highs in England. Furthermore, wheat did not join corn in making a second run at the post-WW II highs in 1952. Instead, it gradually chopped its way lower all through the 1950s, as did corn after the 1952 rally. It would be 20 years before any of the grain markets would rally anywhere close to their post-war highs.

Corn, Chicago Cash, 1860-1966

### *The Export Machine*

But the Fifties were not a repeat of the depressed Twenties. After the First War, America had retreated into isolationism, reveled in its urban prosperity, and largely laid aside its preeminent wartime role in the world food markets.

After the Second War, America moved in the opposite direction. It institutionalized and expanded upon its wartime role as the world's granary. Initially, this meant foreign aid via the State Department as a part of The Marshall Plan. State later carved out a subsidiary agency—the U.S. Agency for International Development (USAID)—which handled most long term aid. It set up operations throughout the world, and its offices and projects often provided U.S. commercial food exporters and processors with an entree and a base of operations in brand new markets.

More importantly for grain, the Department of Agriculture (USDA) added serious export promotion to the list of its basic duties. Perhaps the principal example was the passage of Public Law 480 (PL480) in 1954. PL480 channeled domestic food surpluses into foreign aid, sold commodities for foreign currency (which was used for relief), and exchanged commodities for strategic materials. This story does not wander very deeply into the details at USDA—they are utterly endless—but events like the passage of PL480 demonstrate how much more aggressive America became in world markets after WW II, and how these efforts were integrated with government at various levels.

Add to these assistance agencies the worldwide presence of the U.S. Armed Forces and a much more sophisticated international marketing effort by American food companies, and the result is another increase in the size and scope of the international food system that had gotten its start way back during the Industrial Revolution. It also resulted in making America the unquestioned centerpiece of that system.

### *The Americanization of Food*

On the domestic front, several trends that had been building for generations now took deep root. One was the commercialization of the human diet. By the 1950s, large segments of the world's urban population had no direct connection to the farm or to farm food. This was increasingly true in all developed countries, but especially so in the U.S. where a substantial majority of the population was decoupled from food growers by this time.

Furthermore, the food eaten by these consumers started reaching them in a more highly processed state. Packaged foods sold in stores were increasingly designed to be prepared and served quickly and conveniently. These trends in turn added up to more standardization. Big companies introduced the same packaged products across much broader markets. Older local products became regional. Regional products gradually became national. A few became international. Restaurants too started coming in larger chains which generally sold the same menu products at similar quality levels in each restaurant. The most obvious example, and the pioneer in the field, was McDonalds, which appeared on the scene in 1954 in a suburb of Chicago.

Wheat continued to play a major role, but one that was limited to much the same end products as always. Corn increasingly became the basic fuel of the changing world dietary order. The focus of the 'improving' American diet was beef. Americans, and consumers in other developed countries, started eating more beef per capita which translated into huge demand numbers as the population grew.

Feeding cattle on grass takes a long time. The beef industry in the 19th Century had already perfected the process of confining cattle in feedlots and stuffing them with corn to quickly add weight prior to slaughter. The surge in demand in the post-WW II years could not have been satisfied without vast quantities of feedgrains. Corn obliged with increases in yield that outstripped all other major crops, going from 37 bushels/acre in 1946 to over 47 in 1956, to nearly 74 in 1965. Nor did it stop there. The average national yield reached the current record of 138.6 bushels per acre in 1994/1995. No other major grain crop has seen an increase of this magnitude.

### *The Miracle Bean*

But it was a newcomer that became the real glamour crop of the new food order. Soybeans—a.k.a. The Miracle Bean—came from nowhere before WW II to become a fundamental element in what we are calling the world 'grain' market. (Soybeans are actually not a grain, but an oilseed.) Soybeans had been raised in China for thousands of years, but were almost entirely absent on the international market until WW II. Even in the U.S., now the world's largest producer and exporter, the first processing plant for soybeans did not open until 1922. Through the 1930s, soybeans were often planted as a nitrogen-boosting cover crop that was plowed under upon maturation.

All that changed during and after the war. Soybeans are processed into two basic products: a high quality protein meal and a vegetable oil, and these were made to order for the Americanized diet. Soybeans generate about 48 pounds of protein meal per 60 pound bushel, far more than other major oilseeds, and when a bit of this was added to a basic feed like corn it acted like an octane booster that accelerated weight gain by livestock-on-feed.

In addition, soybean oil is ideal for many packaged consumer products. It is nearly tasteless, unlike other major oils such as sunseed or olive oil, and it is relatively colorless at an early stage in its processing, unlike palm oil, rapeseed oil, or olive oil. In short, a generic oil. After the war, it was made available worldwide at a consistent level of quality. U.S. entities marketed it in traditional destinations such as Western Europe and in less traditional areas such as Iran. By the Sixties it was the most heavily exported vegetable oil on the world market.

*The 50s & 60s at a Glance*

| | |
|---|---|
| 1950 | 1st CBOT Soyoil Futures |
| 1951 | 1st CBOT Soymeal Futures |
| 1954 | 1st McDonalds Opens |
| 1954 | PL 480 Passed |
| 1955 | McDonalds Incorporates |
| 1956 | Soil Bank Instituted |
| 1963 | 1st Soviet Grain Purchase |
| 1965 | 2nd Soviet Grain Purchase |

Farmers also loved the Miracle Beans. They were hard to kill, they fetched a higher market price than corn, wheat, or oats, and they required relatively less work to produce than corn. In the South, and a few areas of the Midwest, soybeans could even be planted late enough to be double-cropped with winter wheat which greatly increased the farmer's profit per acre. Planted area soared to nearly 40 million acres in the U.S. in the late Sixties, by which time soybeans were the nation's #1 cash crop.

Since virtually all soybeans need to be processed before they are used, they contributed to social change on the farm itself. One reason farmers had kept livestock around in the old days was as an outlet for their grain when the price at the local grain elevator was too low to return a profit. Cattle or pigs could chew up the cheap and unprofitable corn or sorghum and turn it into a value-added meat product. Unfortunately, feeding animals could also be a money-loser, and taking care of them required far more physical labor than simply raising a field crop. More to the point, caring for animals kept the family tied to the farm on a daily basis all year-round.

Soybeans cut right through these unpleasantries. If a farmer raised only soybeans there was no compelling reason to have a single animal on the farm. It didn't take long for the logic of this to sink in, and even corn producers started to reevaluate the need for animals. Soon it was: goodbye pig sty, hello Florida. By the 1970s, it was common for middle-aged Midwestern farm couples to work their land from April through harvest, and head south by Thanksgiving. This might have been the biggest miracle of all!

Naturally, there were other factors behind the trend toward greater specialization such as a consolidation of the meat-packing industry which lined up better with bigger grocery stores and restaurant chains, but soybeans contributed to the centralization and commercialization of the food system on both ends of the pipeline.

Finally, traders loved soybeans. They were higher-priced than either corn or wheat, and experienced much greater volatility. During the 1950s, corn futures frequently stayed within a 20 cent range in nearby contracts for an entire year. A big price event was when corn fell 30-35 cents. Wheat was only a little better from the trader's perspective, with annual ranges of 40 cents except for the slightly bigger ranges during down years. Oat futures once spent an entire year within a trading range of five cents.

Soybeans, by contrast, were sensational. 1953-1954 saw a soybean rally of over $1.80 per bushel, followed by an equally thrilling drop of over $2.00. 1955-1956 saw a rally of $1.20. Two more soybean rallies of comparable size occurred in the Sixties.

In general, the markets trended lower through the Fifties, and then slowly higher during the Sixties. Soybean futures bottomed in 1959, and corn did so in 1960. Chicago wheat seemed to have bottomed in the late 1950s, but prices collapsed to new lows in 1964, followed by another round of new lows in 1968. Government programs in the U.S. became the dominant market factor during the era, as the USDA worked fiercely to take supplies off the market when prices were low, and to move as much grain as possible into export channels. When this did not work, they paid farmers not to plant millions of acres for periods of up to ten years. All of these efforts were variations on policy themes established during the New Deal.

## THE GREAT GRAIN ROBBERY

During summer 1972, price stability came to an abrupt end. The Soviet Politburo had made an historic decision: to enter the world grain and soy complex markets suddenly and secretly as a massive buyer.

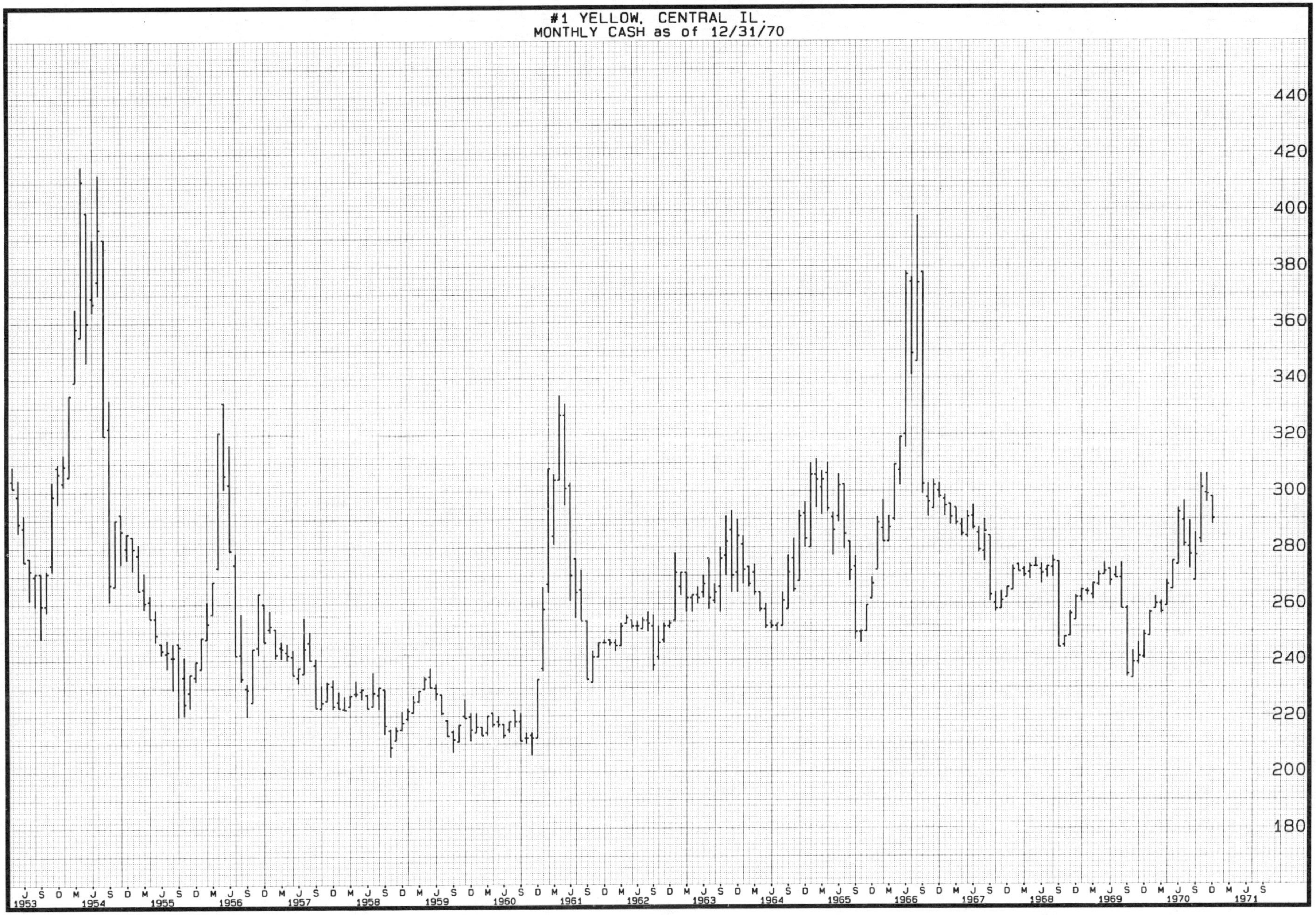


Soybean, Monthly No. 1 Yellow Central Illinois Cash, September 1952-December 1970

For decades, food in the U.S.S.R. had been of abysmal quality and in short supply. In 1962, food riots occurred in Russia after a crop failure. (Rioters in Novocherkassk were said to have shouted for Khrushchev sausage.) The Politburo responded by importing grain—mostly wheat—from the West as a "one-time" measure. They made another large one-time purchase in 1965, but this was followed by several years of good weather and bumper crops in the U.S.S.R.. It seemed their troubles were over.

By 1970, however, the string of good crops had come to an end. This time around, food riots broke out in a Soviet client state—Poland—and they were more widespread. In both cases the unrest had been sparked by food, but the Polish riots of 1970 quickly turned anti-Party and actually forced a death-bed resignation by the Head of State, Wladyslaw Gomulka. The Soviet leadership realized that food problems were a serious threat to their own grip on power, and that they could never be solved within a centralized Soviet economic system. However, they also realized that they could nip the whole problem in the bud by simply swallowing their pride and starting regular, massive imports of grains, oilseeds, protein meal, and other foodstuffs.

Ironically, the U.S.S.R. was forced to turn to its Cold War enemy—the United States—as the only country able to meet their massive need for a quick fix. Over the summer months of 1972 they purchased some 24 million metric tons of wheat, corn, soybeans, and soymeal—mostly from the U.S.—undoubtedly the largest single food purchase by one customer in all history up to that point. In the process they pretty much wiped out the huge U.S. grain surplus that had seemed eternal and inexhaustible, and which the USDA had labored so diligently to get rid of for the previous 20 years.

These transactions were made in secret between the big international grain trading firms on one side, and the Soviet grain trading agency (Exportkhleb) on the other. The CIA later reported that it had sent memos to USDA warning them of the huge transactions, but no one admitted seeing them. Ironically, in 1971, the Nixon Administration had eliminated an obscure, but remarkably useful, regulation that required grain companies to notify the U.S. government whenever they sold large quantities of basic commodities for export.

The drama of the Great Grain Robbery coincided with other events which greatly exacerbated its bullish effect. First came an uptick in inflation in the U.S. in the late 1960s, followed by President Nixon's lifting of the U.S. dollar gold standard in the early 1970s. More importantly, as the Soviet purchases came to light in late 1972, and early 1973, the world began to experience a series of crop failures which dangerously tightened supplies. End users of basic commodities eventually rushed into the cash and futures markets in America to secure their needs at any price.

The secrecy of the affair, combined with the previously bearish environment, meant a delayed reaction. Prices edged slowly higher through the end of summer 1972, by which time virtually all of the buying was completed. As summer turned to autumn, prices continued higher with no real harvest break. While the levels of those months seem very low by today's standards, \$3.00 to \$3.50 for soybeans, for example, they were near the highest levels for the previous 20 years. By early 1973, the secret was out and the markets exploded. Soybean Meal futures led the way, rallying from about 80 dollars per ton in 1972, to just over 450 dollars in mid-1973. (A cool 460% increase.) Soybeans nearly matched that with a surge to just under \$13.00 per bushel. Corn eventually reached \$4.00, but not until late 1974. Wheat also peaked in 1974, finally eclipsing the highs established nearly 50 years earlier. (Wheat also finally eclipsed the 1811 highs of the Napoleonic Wars.)

Every major crop made new all-time highs over this stretch—a true price shock that disrupted food economies all over the world.

**A NIXON EMBARGO**

While the Soviet buying spree in 1972 seriously depleted U.S. grain stocks, it positively wiped out supplies of soybean meal. By winter, 1972-73, it was clear that the U.S. could not process enough soybeans to meet the existing sales of meal before the new crop was harvested the following fall.

President Nixon responded with a partial embargo of soy meal exports that extended across the board. Soviet sales were trimmed, but so were outstanding orders by regular customers who had bought in good faith and thought themselves well-positioned when the big rally began. These customers were faced with the prospect of replacing their embargoed purchases at prices that were 200-400% higher than the original costs. Some disputes arising from the embargo remained in international arbitration until 1977. The event only added to the resentment and suspicion over the secrecy of the whole affair.

This was also a major stimulus toward negotiation of a series of Long Term Agreements (LTAs) between the U.S. and U.S.S.R. These agreements stipulated minimum annual purchases by the U.S.S.R. which had the right to buy additional amounts up to a higher threshold without prior U.S. approval.

The inflationary cocktail was completed following the Arab-Israeli War of October, 1973. Losing Arab nations were bitterly angry with the U.S. and other powers for saving Israel from apparent defeat. They embargoed shipments of oil to the West in retaliation. Non-Arab producers who were members of a nearly moribund group—the Organization of Petroleum Exporting Countries (OPEC)—saw this as an opportunity to strip overall control of world trade in crude oil from Western powers, and to vastly increase their own revenues in the process. The price of a barrel of crude oil was approximately quadrupled, ushering in a decade of world-wide inflation. This would have profound long term implications for grain and oilseed producers.

### *Feed the World!*

As always, the shock of high prices stimulated production. Since there was no general war to disrupt the process of expansion after the century's third price shock, the world's market economies responded very quickly.

Brazil expanded soybean planting in its vast interior savanna. Malaysia boosted palm acreage and invested in improved plant stock and a modernized palm oil processing industry. The European Community (today the European Union) managed to boost production significantly with higher subsidies and more advanced seed, fertilizers, and pesticides. In fact, by the 1980s, the EC (i.e. Western Europe) had actually reversed its historic role during virtually all of the Industrial Age to become a large and consistent exporter of wheat. Canada, Argentina, and Australia stayed within their historic roles as grain and/or oilseed exporters, but at higher tonnage levels. After 1977, largely because of the death of Mao, even China began embarking on a course of market reforms which resulted in vast increases in food production by the early 1980s.

The major exceptions to this expansionary trend were countries and regions which continue to run grain or oilseed deficits to this day. For example, the Former Soviet Union and Eastern Europe, where the main problem was a state-run economy; Japan, South Korea, and Taiwan, which have little additional land for crop production; and sub-Saharan Africa and most of the Islamic World, which suffer from a variety of economic and social problems including rapidly growing populations. (The EC/EU remains a large net importer of oilseeds and their products and it is both a large importer and exporter of feed grains.)

In the U.S., the surge in commodity futures was followed by a sharp run-up in the cost of the consumer food products they went into. Consumer food prices rose 23% from 1970-1973, prompting a Congressional investigation into The Great Grain Robbery.

These events completely ruled out any extension of the big USDA acreage reduction programs of the 1950s and 1960s which just happened to be winding down at this time. In fact, a new Farm Bill was passed in August, 1973, which officially declared that its goal was to expand production to meet an ever-growing demand for food and fiber, a complete policy reversal. Unofficially, the directive went out from the Federal Government to plant fence-row to fence-row so that the U.S. could feed the world. This message was aggressively delivered on the stump by none other than Earl Butz, Nixon's famous and controversial Secretary of Agriculture.

It was an overreaction. Farmers responded with a burst of borrowing to finance the purchase of land and to buy upgraded equipment. Unfortunately, the cost of all these inputs was rising steeply at the time. Most basic was the boom in land prices which caused the price of one acre of high-quality farmland to nearly triple by the end of the Seventies. Also, the larger and more sophisticated farm equipment that had started hitting the market in the late 1960s rose in price through the 1970s at a rate rivaling the increase in land. On top of it all came a sharp increase in the price of commercial fertilizers, insecticides, and pesticides, ingredients which had become an indispensable part of American agriculture in the years since WW II, and which were derived in large part from increasingly costly Mideastern crude oil. Naturally, the price of fuel needed to power the bigger equipment rose as well.

Even so, these cost increases might have been taken in stride by the big borrowers, if not for inflation in the cost of one last input: money. Interest rates also began to rise after the early 1970s, and they too would eventually hit all-time highs near 20% by 1980.

### *Volatility Cuts Both Ways*

Prices trended lower from the price shock highs in most markets as weather improved and world stocks were replenished. This despite the fact that the U.S.S.R. confirmed its new status as importer with additional large purchases in 1975.

The weakening prices sent another signal to American soybean farmers. They reduced soybean plantings in favor of corn during the summer of 1976. (Corn benefited more from USDA price supports then, as it does now, and so was shielded from lower prices in a way that soybeans are not. Soybean farmers were therefore quicker to respond to lower prices with reduced plantings.)

Lower plantings meant a smaller U.S. crop. But demand for soybeans did not drop during 1976, which meant that soybean stocks were likely to be down substantially by the end of the 1976/1977 crop year. During the 1976 harvest, and on into winter, the U.S. crush (soybean processing) rate remained near record levels, and the market's attention shifted to the world's second largest exporter—Brazil. By mid-winter it was clear the 1977 Brazilian crop (which matures during January through March) was also going to be down as much as 20% from the previous year.

This meant that usage was almost certain to exceed supply if one or both sides of the supply/demand equation did not change. In such cases, it's the job of market prices to bring about the needed adjustment.

This occurred by means of an unusual and very powerful mid-winter rally in soybean futures which culminated just prior to planting time in the U.S. Traders in the soybean pit at Chicago tried to cheer the market on with chants of, "Beans in the teens!," in hopes that the futures market would take out the all-time high of just under $13.00 per bushel. But it was not to be. The sharp increase in prices reduced demand enough to leave the market with a workable carryover, and the peak fell short of $11.00. Since the rally occurred just prior to planting, it generated an increase in U.S. soybean acreage. Prices plunged through planting time and on into summer when good weather ensured that there would be ample supplies after harvest.

### *The Soviet Embargo*

Prices for most crops trended slowly higher for about two years from the major lows of mid-1977. The trend was bolstered during the last half of 1979 by another round of Soviet purchases that were every bit as large as those of 1972.

But prices remained far below the all-time highs in all markets. This price restraint was testimony to the vast increases in productive capacity the world set off by the 1973-1974 shocks. Planted acreage remained high, yields per acre edged higher for wheat and soybeans in the U.S., and they positively vaulted higher for corn, continuing the trend that began in the 1930s.

The Soviet Union closed out the decade with another action that roiled grain and oilseed markets. In late 1979, they invaded neighboring Afghanistan to support a Communist government that was near collapse. President Carter decided that this was a major expansion of the Soviet sphere which America had been trying to contain for more than 30 years. He believed the U.S.S.R. should pay a heavy price for their aggression, but unfortunately, he had very few cards to play. The biggest one was the grain card.

Futures markets closed to await the announced retaliation, but everyone knew what it would be. President Carter canceled all but 8 million tons of the previous year's enormous Soviet grain purchases. That left a total of 17 million metric tons of extra corn and wheat supplies hanging ominously over the market. To prevent this new free supply from flooding the market and driving prices sharply lower, much of the embargoed grain was quickly pulled off the free market and deposited in USDA loan and reserve programs. To further calm the markets, provisions were added to existing price support programs which kept this grain off the market for even longer periods, and which required higher prices to trigger release of these supplies.

*The 1970s at a Glance*

| | |
|---|---|
| 1972 | Great Grain Robbery |
| 1973 | Nixon Embargos Meal Sales |
| 1973-74 | Price Shock Rallies |
| 1976 | CFTC Authorized |
| 1979 | USSR Invades Afghanistan |

Over the short term, it worked. The markets reacted very calmly, trending modestly lower through spring, 1980. But the short term is rarely the end of the story, and the Soviet Embargo episode would take a rather perverse turn before the year was out.

It began with the unexpected: summer drought and higher than normal temperatures across a large portion of the grain belt—most severe to the south and west of Central Illinois. While this was a serious weather event, an unfettered market could have taken it in stride. Overall supplies were very large, and the embargoed grain alone would have gone a long way toward covering the losses in yield. A modest rally would have done the rest by pulling supplies out of long term government programs and marginally reducing demand.

Unfortunately, the stricter embargo provisions kept supplies locked away in government programs more securely than in previous years, and a modest rally was not enough to pull them back onto the free market. Even a substantial rally did not do the trick. Corn rallied to about $3.60 by the end of the growing season which was only 40 cents short of the all-time high.

Wheat had traded around $4.60-80 for much of 1979, and into early 1980. This too was toward the upper end of the historic range. After a brief harvest dip in late spring/early summer wheat recovered all of its losses. None of this triggered the release of sorely needed government grain stocks.

Therefore, there was no crash when the drought eased and yield prospects improved mid-summer, as would normally be the case. In fact, prices failed to break during harvest when new crop supplies were pouring in from the fields. During October and November, corn, wheat, and soybeans all pushed into new highs.

The harvest strength attracted more public (non-commercial, speculative) participation in futures trading than at any previous time which helped to extend the rally. Grain elevators kept purchasing the big harvest and hedging their inventories with short positions in futures markets, but still no break. In some pits open interest continued to rise as late as November. Grain elevator managers were scratching their heads and meeting enormous margin calls as the market moved against them. All the while, ample supplies remained locked away in government-controlled stocks.

Unfortunately, if prices remain high enough for long enough and fail to stimulate the supply side, they will effect the demand side. More to the point, high prices will reduce demand to fit the available supply. And that's what happened in 1980.

Around December 1, the markets ran out of the fresh speculative longs needed to prop them up, and the chickens came home to roost. Prices began a two-week drop. Now it was the spec longs' turn to receive daily margin calls from their commission houses, and each morning the market opened lower as they all tried to get out at once.

### *Boom and Bust, Act II*

That two-week plunge is far from the most dramatic one on the charts, but it marked the bitter end of the grain and soybean boom that began eight years earlier. Most markets tried to rally back up to the November-December highs in January, but fell short.

Prices worked their way lower into spring planting season as the markets still tried to attract government stocks onto the free supply. By late spring, however, good weather and the prospect of relatively high U.S. planted acreage ended the game by confronting the markets with the prospect of huge new supplies. Crop reports in August confirmed the bearish outlook. The soybean crop was near record large. Winter wheat had already come in at a record of over two billion bushels by early summer. But corn provided the worst (or best) news of all with a gigantic new record U.S. crop of over 8.2 billion bushels, a figure that looked like a misprint to many analysts when it first crossed the newswires.

This ensured the onset of the second major American farm recession of the 20th Century, a kind of price shock in reverse. It was brought on by overexpansion, increased foreign competition, and terrible miscues on the part of USDA which greatly helped countries like Argentina and Brazil as they sought to capture export market share from America. The recession would be deepened by what would become the greatest glut of grain in human history. The ultimate lows on the charts would not be in place until 1986.

This time around, the "problem" would be corn. It began, in the 1980s, to overwhelm government programs in the way that wheat had during the late 1930s and early '40s. Yet, it was not the huge supply or the lower prices that made the recession of the 1980s so severe for certain farmers. Higher yields per acre meant that most grain and soybean farmers could earn more profit per harvested acre than they had in the 1960s. Nor was it a recession for all farmers. As usual, the problem was indebtedness.

After the 1973-1974 price shocks, many farmers and bankers had assumed that high prices were always around the next bend. They developed huge debt loads in the 1970s that any prudent lender could see were beyond the farmer's ability to ever repay.

After December 1980, the fantasy of higher prices could not be sustained. Bankers who had lent without question in the Seventies started to completely cut lines of credit to the most indebted farmers. This received a great deal of press throughout the Eighties spawning, among other things, a series of so-called save the farm movies as well as Willie Nelson's Farm Aid. Lost amidst much sentimentality was the fact that the farmers in the most trouble were the ones who had piled on outrageous debt levels in a headlong rush to expand land holdings and to buy equipment that was often far larger and more elaborate than what was needed. Few noted that a majority of U.S. farms, large and small, had come through the inflationary boom of the 1970s with little or no long term debt.

Nevertheless, historically high interest rates made the game tougher for everyone. The most basic

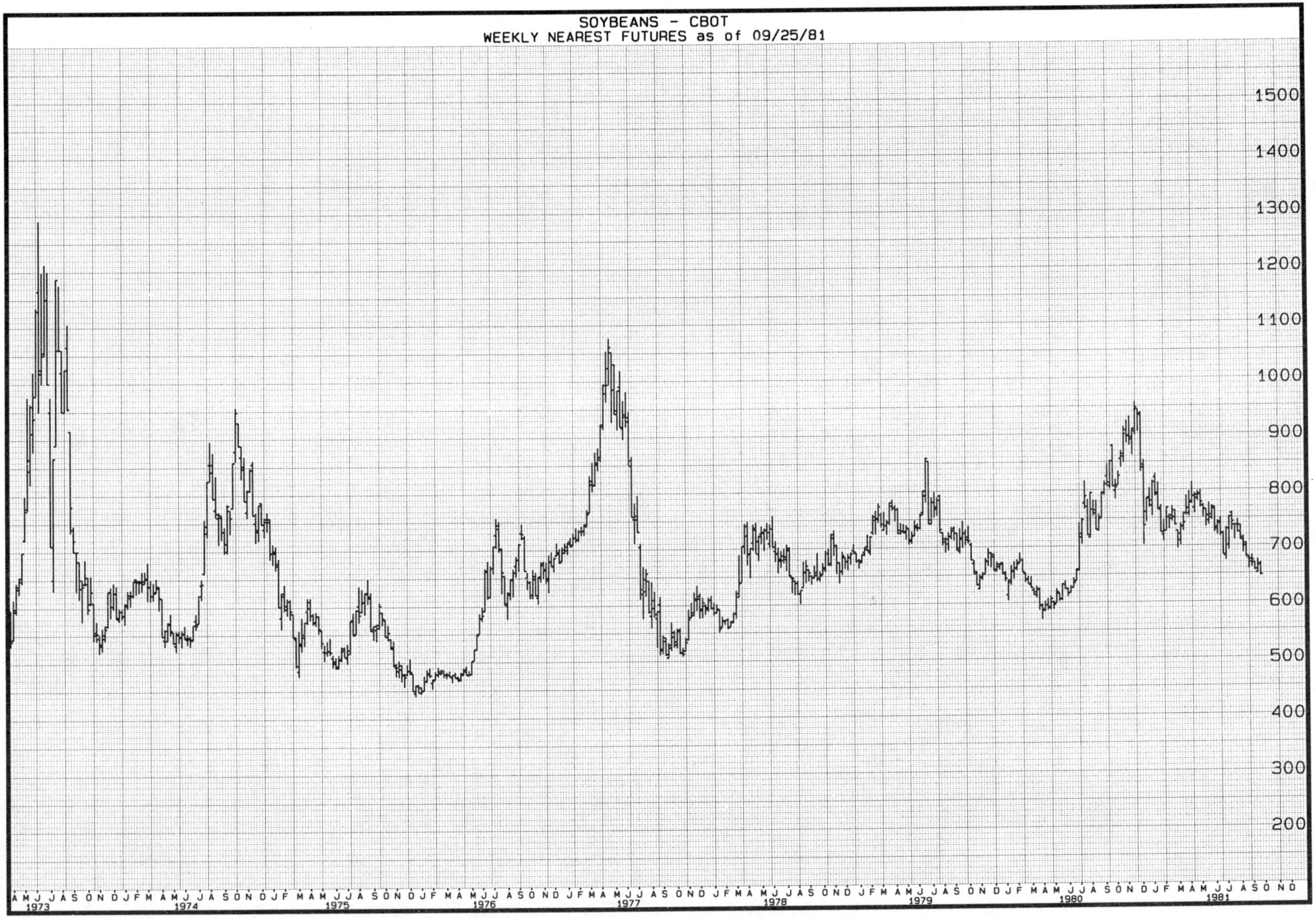


**Soybean, CBOT Weekly Nearest Futures, March 1973 - December 1981**

change came in the attitude toward inventory. From 1973-1980, extra inventory had generally been viewed in a positive light. Farmers with extra grain could hope to sell on the next bounce. Merchandisers and end users tended to view a bit of inventory as a safety cushion against another price surge.

With bear markets and near record interest rates this view changed 180 degrees. The cost of financing holdings of grain came to be seen as a burden that could bathe any balance sheet in red ink, and one which the market might never eliminate via higher prices.

Grain middlemen quickly adopted inventory practices perfected by the Japanese called, *just in time*. All parties learned to keep supply pipelines empty of all but the most immediate needs. This psychological shift created a long term buyer's market that combined with oversupply to generate relentless downward pressure, and thinner profit margins all round.

## Another Drought, Another Big Mistake

In the early-to-mid 1980s, the volume of grains and oilseeds being taken off the market and stored under various support programs threatened to overwhelm the vast grain storage capacity of the United States. The chief culprit was corn. By 1982, its average yield had climbed to 113 bushels per acre. Prices reflected this by falling below $2.20 during early harvest, and they seemed poised to test the ten-year lows or even the pre-Grain Robbery lows of 1972.

The USDA responded with the first big paid acreage reduction program initiated since the 1960s. It paid farmers to reduce plantings in 1983, but did so with commodities (kind) instead of with cash, so the effort was called Payment in Kind, or PIK. The goal was to attract millions of corn and wheat acres into a one-year set-aside—a brief, big, and highly-targeted response to the grain glut. It seemed like such a good idea at the time.

However, PIK turned out to be perhaps the most poorly-timed government program in history. It idled those millions of acres during the 1983 growing season which just happened to coincide with the one of the worst droughts of the century. The 1983 drought was more severe and widespread than the one in 1980. Also, it was accompanied by severe droughts in South Africa, Malaysia, and Australia—developments related by many weather analysts to the so-called El Nino effect in the waters of the Pacific Ocean off Peru.

Corn futures actually took off during the 1982 harvest as PIK was coming onstream. By planting time the next year, nearby contracts were already up about 50%. Wheat rose over this stretch as well, but less dramatically.

Which brings us to the unintended consequences of PIK. Almost no one realized that the program would also sharply reduce soybean acres. As a result, soybean futures rallied very weakly during the PIK sign-up in sympathy with corn, but then turned and fell all through the 1983 planting season and right up to the end of June. This despite the fact that the big drought was already well underway.

On June 29th, the November soybean futures closed on a new low for the recent downward move. Forty-five minutes after the close, USDA released its Planting Intentions Report which pegged U.S. soybean planted acres below even the lowest trade estimate. (Among other things, millions of double-crop wheat acres were enrolled in PIK which made them off limits to other crops, such as soybeans, for the entire season.) Soybeans opened limit up on the 30th. By mid August, nearby beans had rallied $3.50 to over $9.50 per bushel, just nudging through the 1980 drought high.

The summer rally was mainly a soybean affair. Since corn had rallied substantially prior to planting, it only managed to tack on another 55 cents or so during the drought. Wheat barely moved. Unlike 1980, high summer prices quickly reduced demand and the market moved lower into harvest.

Again, a government program had intervened to reduce supplies in a year when drought had done this on its own. Yet this double whammy on the supply side need not have been a serious problem since carryover stocks from previous years were gigantic. PIK's biggest flaw came in the fine print. It managed to manipulate the free supply to do precisely the opposite of what would occur in a free market.

Farmers had been paid not to plant with grain instead of with money. Since the program was designed before any of the markets rallied, the planners' greatest fear was that farmers would dump PIK grain as soon as they received it, further depressing prices. Therefore, they prohibited the sale of PIK grain until late 1983, and spread the bulk of permitted sales well into 1984.

So when the rally was at it's raging peak during the summer of 1983, supplies were withheld. When the market no longer needed increased supply, and was headed lower due to harvest pressure, grain was released.

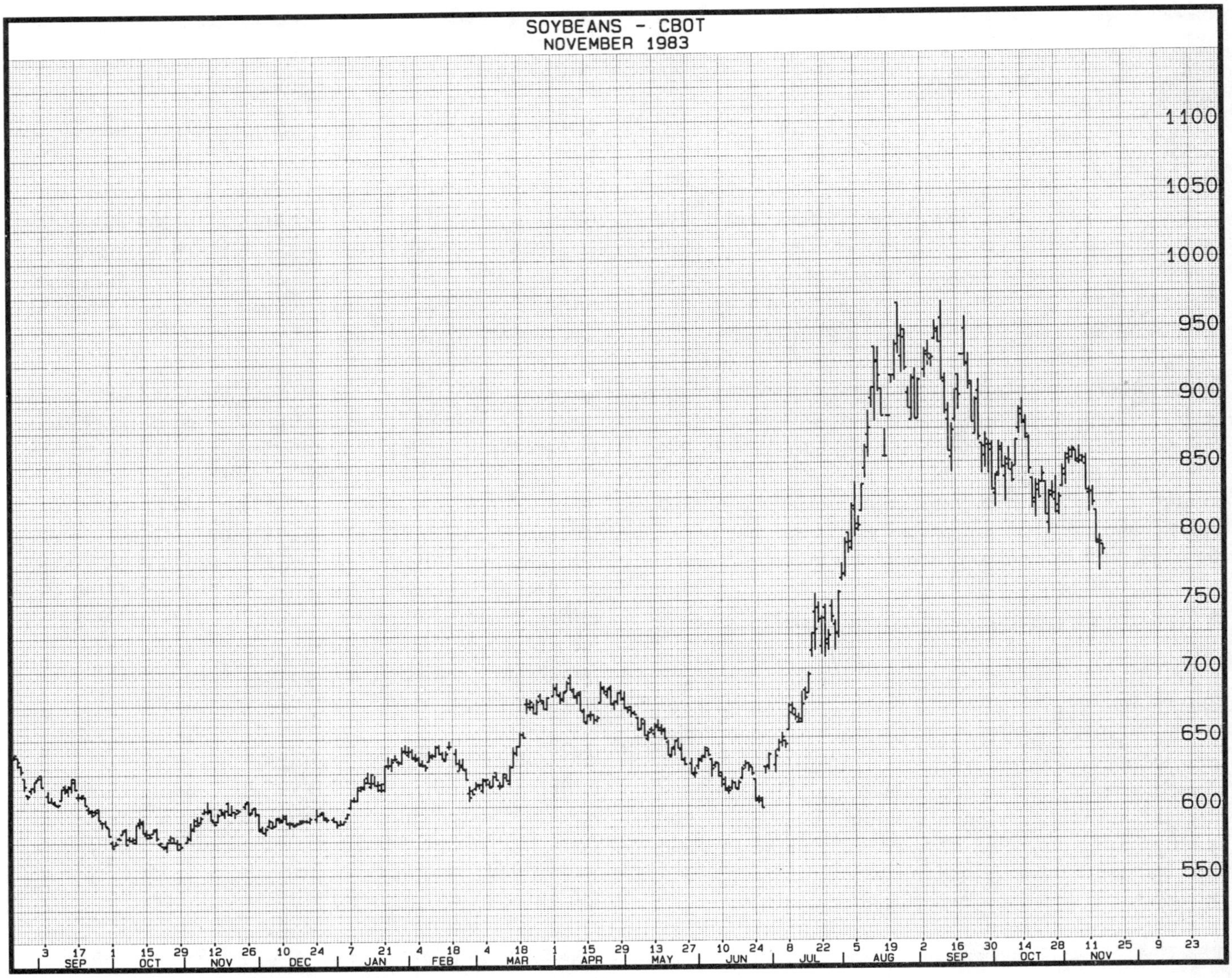


## Soybean, CBOT November 1983 Daily Futures, October 1982 - November 1983

The fact that high summer prices had trimmed demand made the late 1983 oversupply even worse. On top of it all, foreign producers/exporters like Argentina and Brazil had, by then, perfected the art of aggressively marketing to America's export customers at exactly those times when the U.S. was withholding supplies through government intervention. The United States lost export sales and market share. Adding insult to injury was the fact that PIK turned out to be the most expensive program ever for the American taxpayer.

However, America was not alone in adopting unwise farm policies that year. Malaysia had earlier introduced an African insect which was supposed to stress its palm trees into higher output of palm nuts. This coincided with an El-Nino induced drought in the region and it stressed some palm trees into non-production. Palm oil production dropped sharply and importers of palm oil who had been shifting away from the more expensive soybean oil for several years had to quickly shift back to soyoil. This generated an unusual follow-up rally in the soy complex which started in February, 1984, and culminated in May. Soybean oil futures exceeded the previous year's highs, and soybeans and corn were pulled close to their 1983 highs. Wheat prices were again unaffected.

The winter-spring rally in soyoil turned out to be last hurrah for the Miracle Bean. Malaysian palm oil production began to rebound sharply during the second half of 1984 and it has climbed every year since. Palm oil overtook soyoil as the most heavily traded vegetable oil on world export markets by 1985, a ranking soyoil had enjoyed since at least the 1960s.

## Soybean Oil, CBOT July 1984 Daily Futures, July 1983 - July 1984

### Hitting Bottom

The rallies of 1983-1984 were an aberration in the middle of a period of overwhelming oversupply. When they were over, it was back to the main event: the long term bear market/farm recession which dated back to late 1980.

The final leg of the bear market lasted from May 1984, through the end of 1986. These last down years proved to be the final straw for a wide variety of players in grain and oilseed markets. Farmers, elevators, and merchandisers who had survived depressed markets earlier in the decade went bankrupt or were bought out in droves. The last leg down also brought reduced trading activity in the agricultural trading pits at the CBOT which, in turn, brought a major consolidation among commission houses in the futures industry. Famous Chicago brokerage firms and thousands of jobs disappeared along with the last of the debt-laden farmers.

But the end finally came. Wheat bottomed first, in mid-1986, followed by soybean oil that September, soybeans in October, corn in February, and soybean meal in March, 1987.

An important new farm bill was passed in the meantime (1985), and it brought some market-oriented reforms. The Bill boosted demand for U.S. commodities by making it a major policy objective to proactively sell off the huge surplus built up during the first half of the decade.

Congress also reevaluated the disastrously failed policy of trying to put an artificial floor under U.S. and world prices by unilaterally taking supplies off the market at higher and higher price levels each year. The new bill set a new schedule that actually lowered government supports (the loan levels at which supplies started flowing into government programs), on an annual basis. This reversed a trend of higher price supports that could be traced back, on and off, to the New Deal, but which really began in earnest back in 1973.

Adding to the potential for a long term reversal of the down trend was another USDA attempt to reduce production by sharply reducing planted acreage. This reduction was fairly well timed and it idled acreage for ten years, instead of one year like PIK, and the farmer was paid in cash, not in kind. The new effort was called the Conservation Reserve Program (CRP). Soybean and wheat surpluses dropped quickest as a result of these changes, and prices rose gradually from the major lows of 1986, into early 1988.

### *The Drought of the Decade*

By late winter, 1988, the third big drought of the decade was underway across much of the grain belt. It was the most severe and widespread of the three, and was eventually accompanied by the hottest temperatures. This time it started earlier, devastating winter wheat yields before continuing on into spring planting. As a result, it slashed yields for all three major crops: winter wheat, corn, and soybeans.

Starting in May 1988, all of the major grain, oilseed, and product markets began one of the biggest and most rapid rallies ever. The nearby soybean contract surged to about $11.00 by late June, and nearby corn peaked at $3.60 in early July when rainfall boosted yield prospects in many areas. Prices dropped for corn and the soybean complex with the improved weather, reversing perhaps half of the year's gains. In the case of soybeans the drop stalled near $8.00 after August, 1988, and for most of the next year prices slowly ratcheted their way down to $7.00.

Beans failed to collapse all the way down to below $6.00, as was typical for soybeans after a big rally, due to USDA projections of extremely tight ending stocks. A few die-hard bulls assumed that the market would literally run out of soybeans before another crop could be harvested, and that this would cause a final big run-up in 1989. Those bulls bought or stayed long in nearby contracts into 1989, but the trend remained down through the expiration of the January, March, and May contracts. By July, it was clear that the market would not run out of soybeans and the game was up. Prices plunged as the last hopeful specs were forced by the CBOT to liquidate. By harvest, soybeans were back below $5.50.

Wheat continued to rise after the 1988 drought rally, finally peaking in early 1989. By then it was clear that the world wheat crop prospects were excellent, so prices fell through early fall, 1990. When the smoke cleared, futures had once again failed to take out the all-time highs of 1973-1974 in all major crops.

However, in retrospect, important technical changes had occurred. The $11.00 high in nearby soybeans had eclipsed the highs of 1983, 1980, and 1977. In addition, the lowly oat futures, which are still considered a bit of a bellwether by a few traditionalists, broke ranks with the major crops in taking out their all-time CBOT futures highs by a wide margin in 1988. (Oat acres were down more than in other crops that year, and oats were planted and matured before the drought eased in early July.)

**The 1980s at a Glance**

| | |
|---|---|
| 1980 | Soviet Grain Embargo |
| 1980 | Major U.S. Drought |
| 1982-83 | PIK Acreage Program |
| 1983 | 1st Soybean Options |
| 1984 | Major U.S. Drought |
| 1985 | Palm Becomes #1 Veg. Oil Export |
| 1989 | Feruzzi Liquidation |

It was far from being another shock, but it was the first confirmation that a major bottom was now in place.

### *Changing Roles and Dwindling Stocks*

The 1990s started out with less in the way of market news than some earlier decades. The first potentially big market event was the demise of the Soviet Union in late 1991. While this was plenty momentous on the political front, its effect on commodity markets was indirect.

Make that indirect and bearish. Economic conditions there were (and are) so poor that the remnants of the Former Soviet Union (FSU) could no longer afford to make substantial purchases on world markets. Actually, the U.S.S.R. had technically been too poor to import food for some time prior to its demise. They had only been able to afford imports after 1972 by selling gold, crude oil, natural gas, and other commodities which the U.S.S.R. had in abundance. These commodities rallied even more than grains and soybeans in the Seventies, so the U.S.S.R. made money on the spread. (Grain traders often tracked gold sales in Europe for hints of upcoming Soviet grain buying.)

After 1980, however, the prices for these commodities plunged even more than corn, wheat, and soybeans, and the U.S.S.R. started losing money in its international commodity trading. From that time forward, the Soviet Union basically had to borrow to meet import needs, and the Soviet balance sheet deteriorated alarmingly throughout the Eighties as a result.

When the FSU finally unraveled in 1991, the excuse for food imports evaporated. The main reason the Politburo had commenced large-scale imports in the first place was to keep themselves in power and to keep the U.S.S.R. intact. With that excuse gone, the financial sacrifice was no longer worth it to the leaders of the various Republics. The upshot is that the FSU, once the world's largest grain importer, is now a medium-sized player on all the major grain and oilseed import listings.

The most dramatic weather event of the early 1990s came next: the Midwestern flood of 1993. This was called a 500-year flood because it is thought to be the region's worst over that period. Some 16,000 square miles of normally dry Midwestern land was under water at the flood's peak including many millions of acres of cropland which was never planted that summer.

But a much more important story was unfolding behind the scenes. Namely, the fact that world demand for grain, especially corn, grew faster than supply for several years running, leaving world carryover stocks in 1995/1996 near their lowest levels since 1947 in terms of the number of day's supply on hand.

The biggest factor in this incremental story was China's shift from being the world's second largest exporter of corn (after the U.S.), to being a medium large net importer. For three years, from 1991 to 1994, they had exported a net total of 10-12 million metric tons per year. The following year, they suddenly switched to being a net importer of 2-3 million tons. From high to low, this shift amounted to a net change of nearly 15 million metric tons on the world trade balance sheet within just two marketing years. While the net amount purchased (2-3 million tons) was modest, the 15 million ton net shift compares in size with some of the big Soviet (coarse grain) purchases of the 1970s and early 1980s.

China's imports in other major food categories also ballooned. They began the 1990s already the world's largest importer of vegetable oils, and from 1990 to 1994 their total imports nearly doubled. (Totals backed off in 1995/1996, but that year's total still amounted to an increase of about 50% in vegetable oil imports over the decade.) Chinese wheat imports grew as well. China jumped into the #2 spot among customers for U.S. wheat (behind Egypt) in 1994/1995 with 3.3 million tons bought.

While we cannot assume that this growth will continue, it's harder to imagine why it will not. China's population is over 1.2 billion. It is still growing and still relatively young. The country is in the midst of an economic boom and a transformation to capitalism that is deeply entrenched, having begun way back in the late 1970s. The increased prosperity this brings results in growing demand for meat, bread, and higher quality vegetable oils, as has been the case with virtually every other developing nation since the Industrial Revolution began. Given the huge population numbers, and the fact that China is still in the early stages of development by Western standards, the demand potential seems open-ended.

**The 1990s at a Glance**

| | |
|---|---|
| 1991 | U.S.S.R. Disbanded |
| 1993 | Great Midwestern Flood |
| 1994-95 | China Becomes a Net Corn Importer |
| 1996 | New Highs in Chicago Wheat |
| 1996 | New Highs in Chicago Corn |

Having said that, it's worth pointing out that prophecy is well known to be a tough job. The most obvious scenarios—bullish or bearish—seem to never quite happen. (Remember those traders waiting for the U.S. to run out of soybeans in 1989?) It's also worth noting that soaring yields and production have bailed the world out of predicted food shortages countless times since Thomas Robert Malthus wrote his gloomy (Malthusian) treatise on the subject in 1798.

In the middle of the 1990s, this long-term and incremental demand story was capped off with a more standard bullish event: drought in the Great Plains. This drought was centered in the extreme southern Great Plains, notably Texas, and was thought to be that area's worst single drought this century. The hardest hit grain crops were the hard red winter wheat (traded at Kansas City) and sorghum. However, there was little effect on corn and soybeans.

***The 1990s on the Charts***

The decade also began uneventfully from a technical perspective, especially in corn and soybeans. They remained in narrow and low-priced ranges all the way through early 1993.

Wheat was the star performer over this early stretch since its stocks dropped the farthest initially. Chicago

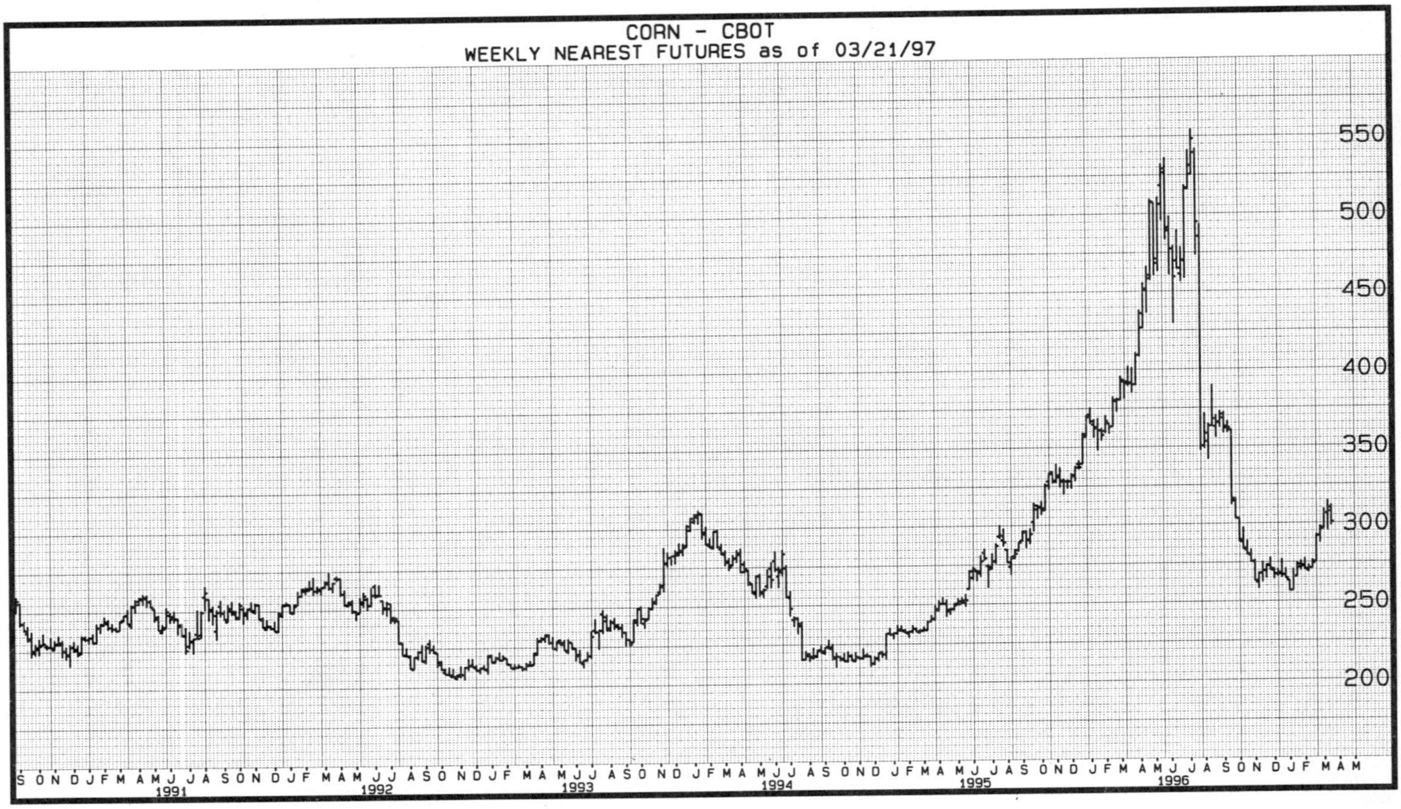


**Corn, CBOT Weekly Nearest Futures, January 1981 - March 1997**

**Wheat, CBOT Weekly Nearest Futures, January 1981 - March 1997**

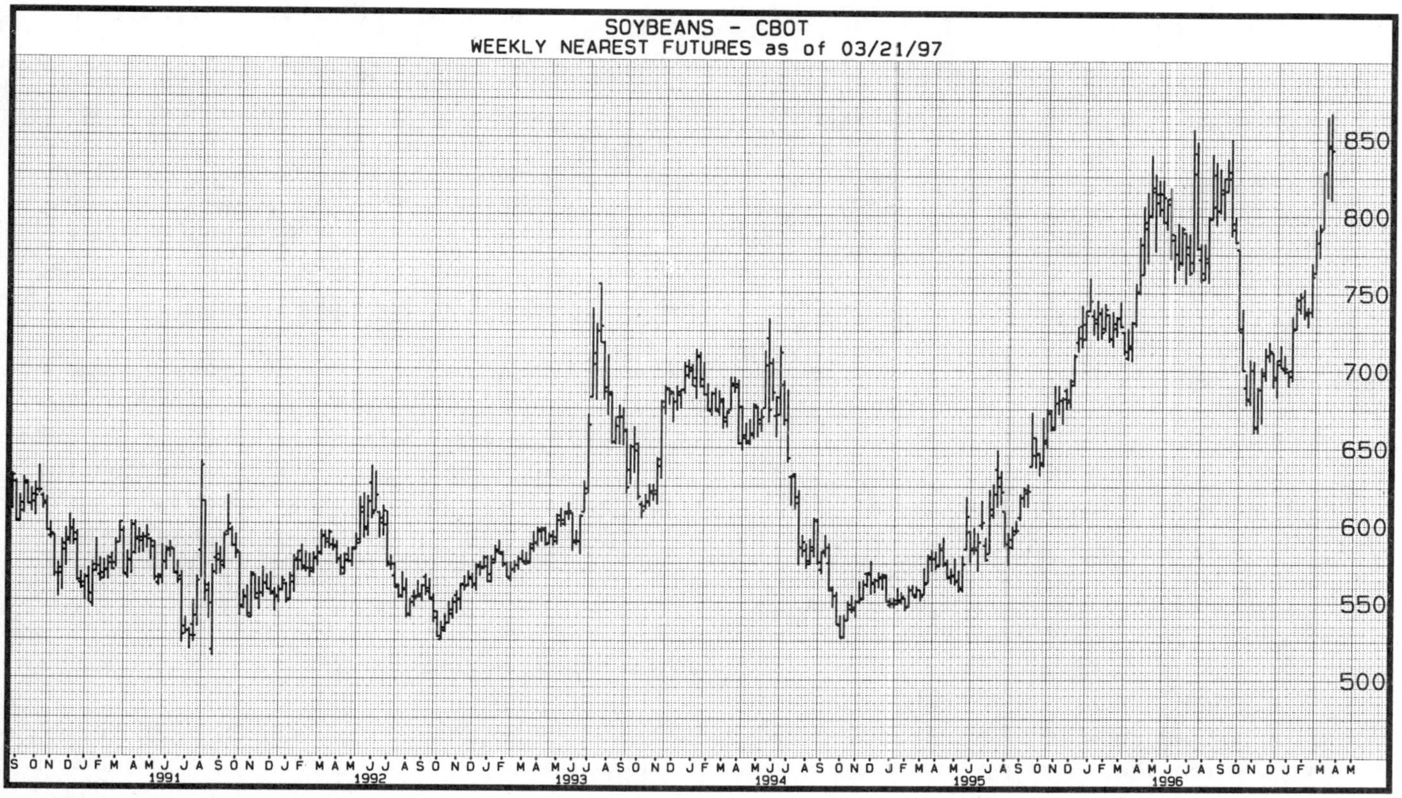


## Soybean, CBOT Weekly Nearest Futures, January 1981 - March 1997

futures responded with a rally of more than $2.00 per bushel beginning around the first of the year in 1991, peaking in February 1992, at just above $4.80. Over the next year and a half the market gradually lost nearly all of this gain—about $2.00—bottoming near $2.80 during the 1993 winter wheat harvest, but holding above the lows of the early 1990s. Following those 1993 harvest lows, Chicago wheat moved back above $3.00, and has remained above that level ever since.

But the major news event of the early 1990s was the Flood of 1993. Throughout the modern history of markets, excitable bulls have tried to make every weather event into a case for rally, including wet spring planting seasons. In the past, all anyone needed to say in reply to these enthusiasts was, "rain makes grain." Eventually, during even the wettest of springs, most acres devoted to corn and soybeans got planted to one or the other of the two crops, and the extra moisture simply resulted in bigger yields.

Not so in 1993. Planted areas dropped sharply for both big summer crops, especially corn, as the extreme wetness stretched into July. In the case of corn prices, the flood started with nearby futures near $2.10, just above the lows established during the 1992 harvest. Through August, corn rallied less than 40 cents. This was not enough to stem the strong demand that had been building both domestically and in export markets. When the USDA made unusually large reductions in late-season carryover estimates this point was driven home to traders. Prices moved higher through harvest and on into January when futures peaked at just over $3.10.

Soybeans made their move during the flood itself, rallying about $1.75 during June and July. Prices broke into early harvest and then staged a secondary and less powerful rally that peaked in January along with corn. While the flood-induced rally was modest by soybean standards, it did manage to finally break the market out of the very low-priced and narrow range it had been stuck in from late 1989 through 1993.

Excellent growing conditions returned during the summer of 1994, along with big summer crops. Both beans and corn tried to hold some of their flood-induced gains, but as the excellent crop prospects became apparent in July and August both markets fell sharply. The nation's average corn yield hit a record 138.6 bushels per acre. Harvest lows in 1994 were only a few cents above the pre-flood lows.

In the past, this would have squeezed the volatility out of corn for a year or more, or at least until a major new crop weather disaster occurred. But not in the

Nineties. Starting in December 1994, corn futures stopped falling and turned on a dime. They began an uninterrupted and historic upward march that finally peaked at $5.54 1/2 in July, 1996. Not only did this top far exceed the previous all-time high near $4.00, but the size of the move, from low to high, was more than $3.40. This was considerably larger than the $2.90 total move of the early Seventies, and it occurred over a shorter period of time.

Wheat futures entered 1994 with a bit more volatility than corn, but the result was the same. New all-time highs were reached in March, 1996, at $7.50.

As usual, the shock of new highs curtailed the growth in overall demand and stimulated increased planted acreage. Good crop weather followed in most major growing areas around the world during 1996, and this helped to replenish the dangerously low world stocks of 1995/1996.

As a result, wheat and corn spent only 2-3 months testing the general areas of their new highs, then commenced a drop that was every bit as fast as the rise. Wheat fell first, then corn. Within 2-3 months of making their highs, both had lost all of the gains of winter-spring 1995/1996, and more.

### *What Happens After a Price Shock?*

It's hard to wrap up a big story, especially when it's still in progress. This is not a technical treatise, so we will not be concluding with price projections or trading recommendations of any kind.

But we've now seen new all-time highs in major crops on four occasions during the 20th Century, and the periods that followed have shared a number of basic characteristics worth noting. Most basic is the fact that each new high was followed by a long stretch, ten or more years, during which price ranges were bigger than before the shock. That means higher highs and higher lows. Even in the recessionary 1920s, prices were substantially higher than they had been for the 20 years or so before the 1917 price shock. More dramatically, after the 1973-1974 shock, highs and lows in many markets were 100% or more above those of any preceding inter-shock era.

With higher price levels comes greater volatility, or at least bigger moves on an absolute basis, and this has been particularly true in the 2-5 years immediately after each new high. In two cases, the first surge was actually followed by a higher high. For example, wheat took out its 1917 high in 1919-1920, and the 1973 price shock was followed by higher highs in both wheat and corn in 1974.

Even when the initial new high has held, there has always been at least one serious test of it before an extended stretch of lower prices set in. After the 1947 peak in corn, there was a second big rally in 1952, which fell only a few cents short of the new high. And after the 1917 price shock, corn tested its new high, not once but twice, in 1919 and again in 1920. (The 1917 high held in both cases.) We could stretch the point a bit and say that the 1977 rallies were a test of the initial price shock highs of 1973-1974.

However, all commodities may not follow the leader into new highs. After WW II, wheat did not follow corn and make a new high at Chicago. It is also clear that markets become seriously depressed after the initial period of volatility is over—as soon as 3-5 years after the new high. In the past, farmers and companies that expanded and borrowed during the boom suffered greatly when it ended.

### *Things to Ponder After All*

It would not be right to finish our big story without returning to some of the great themes and trends we've encountered along the way: a kind of "where are they now." (They follow in no particular order and are not necessarily related.)

*The Twilight of the American Farm Culture.* America began as a predominantly rural culture and economy. Starting in the 1820s, the Federal Government tried to ensure that ownership of land was very broad-based, and that the farm population was largely made up of self-sufficient family businesses. They did this first by selling land in smaller plots at low fixed prices, instead of selling it in huge tracts to the highest bidders. Eventually, starting in 1862, they simply gave the land away. This created a huge, stable, and highly entrepreneurial rural middle class.

Starting just after WW I, the total farm population started to decline. The drop was reversed temporarily during the Great Depression, but has otherwise continued to the present day when less than 2% of the population are still involved in farming and ranching. Furthermore, that small remnant is considerably older on average than the rest of the population. While increased productivity allows for a very small farm population, some sort of new trend will have to emerge as the long term decline comes to its inevitable end.

*The Commercialization of Food.* This trend began in fits and spurts at the very start of our story. Initially, it was the poverty-stricken industrial workers of Northern and Central England and Scotland who became separated from the farm and dependent on a commercial food system. By the middle of the 19th Century, the urban middle classes had also joined the trend.

Food started passing through more hands on its way to these consumers, and middlemen became larger in scale: first the flour mills, slaughterhouses, meatpackers, and commercial bakeries, then packaged food companies, convenience, and fast foods. By the 1990s, even U.S. farmers receive the vast bulk of their food through commercial entities in the U.S.

*Importers and Exporters.* While the list of countries involved in the international food business has grown, the list of grain exporters has seen only one major long term addition—the European Union—since the late 1800s. The list of importers on the other hand, continues to grow. On balance, the world has become increasingly dependent on grain from just one region: North America. While this is good for America's trade balance, it bespeaks an extreme vulnerability and in an unstable world, the potential for extreme volatility.

*Weather.* This subject is complicated and even controversial given the debate over global warming and other issues. But one thing is not debatable, weather has become more volatile during the 1980s and '90s, especially in America. The U.S. saw three big droughts in the 1980s, record drought in Texas in the 1990s, record cold winters in the early 1980s, record or near record hot summers in 1983, 1988, and 1995, a 500-year flood, and record-setting snowfall in the Northeast in the 90s. The combination of a more volatile price environment and more volatile weather raises the odds of a big weather-related rally by early in the 21st Century.

*The Divergence of Major Markets.* Corn, wheat, soybeans, and related markets do not move in tandem. They even tend to have different patterns under similar circumstances. Soybean rallies tend to be spikier, often occurring within a few months, followed by a break that erases most of the gains in an equally short period of time. Corn tends to both rally and fall over a longer period of time (unlike 1996.) Some related markets actually move in opposite directions at the same time. Soymeal and soyoil have often done this. For example, demand sometimes increases only for meal, but the crushing process produces both meal and oil, resulting in a glut of oil (or vice versa). During lower priced periods it is even possible for corn and soybeans, or corn and wheat, to move in opposite directions for short periods of time.

*The Timing of New Highs.* During the 20th Century, the intervals between the big peaks have been a remarkably consistent 22-27 years: 1920 to 1947 to 1973-1974 to 1996. If we look at the initial bursts, we get a consistent but progressively shorter spacing: 1917.

### *What We Know For Sure*

When discussing grain, and its future as an important global foodstuff, there are items which can be defined as certainties.

The world's population will continue to grow, and in so doing will consume ever larger quantities of grain. Already the current inhabitants of economically challenged and third-world countries are demanding higher living standards, equating first and foremost to increased availability of grain and meat.

The amount of land committed to growing crops is currently static. Increases in planted acreage in future years are inevitable, but it will take improved technologies in irrigation to realize large scale increases in available acreage.

The weather, everyone's favorite subject and one especially fond to grain traders, will play its role year after year, with the harsh extremes of the late 20th Century likely becoming the norm in the early 21st Century.

These factors, increased demand and consumption, countered by a stable maximum available supply and the inevitable short-term disruptions to that supply, will lead to higher levels of both raw price and market volatility in the years ahead.

Those who are familiar with the fundamental history of the grain markets through today will not be surprised by unfolding events tomorrow.

*   *   *

*Hugh Ulrich started in the grain and oilseed markets in 1977, first as a runner on the floor of the Chicago Board of Trade, and then as a senior grain and oilseed analyst for one of Chicago's largest commission houses. He also served as a full member of the CBOT. Along the way Mr. Ulrich became a regular grain market commentator on venues ranging from CNN to National Public Radio in Chicago to Maryland Public Television to local Chicago TV. In recent years Mr. Ulrich has shifted to writing and education. His work took him to the Former Soviet Union where he lived and worked for the three years, including the last year of the U.S.S.R.'s existence. While there, he was a popular lecturer and worked with major educational institutions, (Soviet) media and international organizations including World Bank, USAID and PERU (an off-shoot of Harvard's Kennedy School of Government.)*

*The Amber Waves of History is excerpted from Mr. Ulrich's reference book, The Practical Grain Encyclopedia. The Practical Grain Encyclopedia also contains an exhaustive glossary that covers: market terminology, background on major exporters and importers, major crop overviews, the history of US farm programs and much more. It also contains the most complete overview of the grain merchandising process available, as well as detailed grain and oilseed supply/demand data. All of this in an easy-to-understand format that's accessible to everyone from the greenest beginner to the most experienced grain merchandiser. Mr. Ulrich can be reached at Commodity Center Corporation, 8541 N. 600 W., Lake Village, IN 46349.*

Wheat, CBOT Monthly Nearest Futures, July 1958 - March 1997

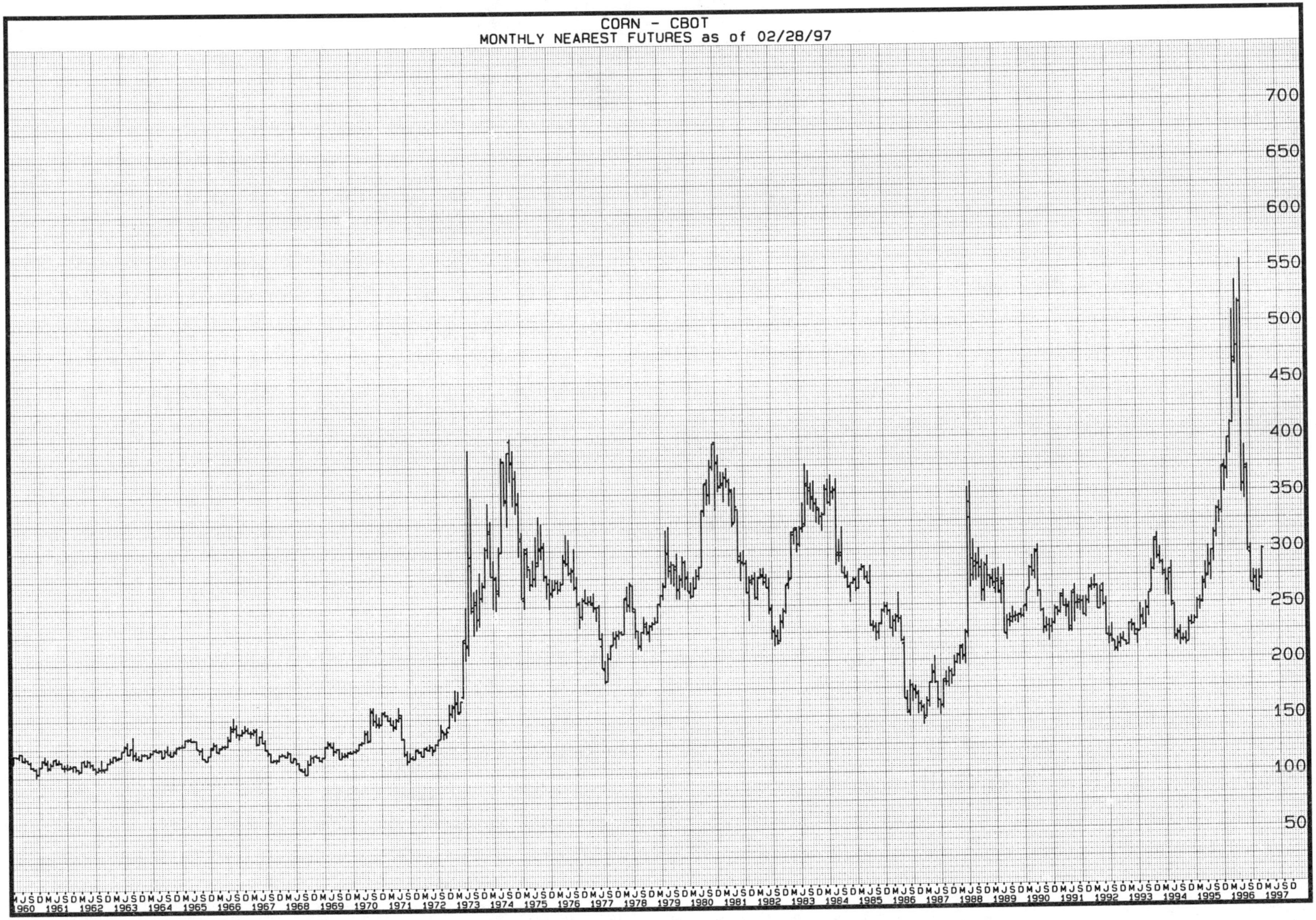


Corn, CBOT Monthly Nearest Futures, July 1958 - March 1997

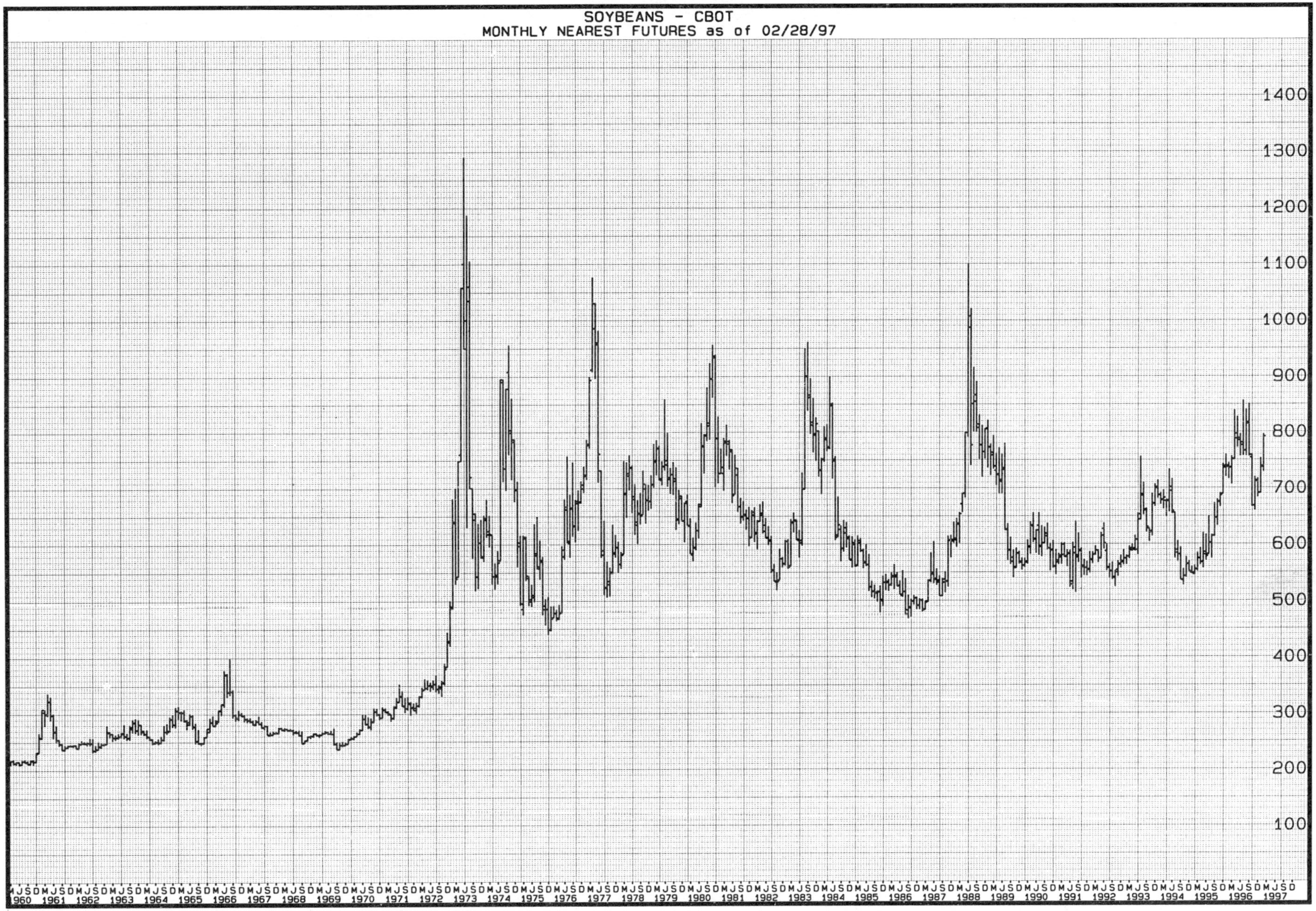


**Soybean, CBOT Monthly Nearest Futures, July 1958 - March 1997**

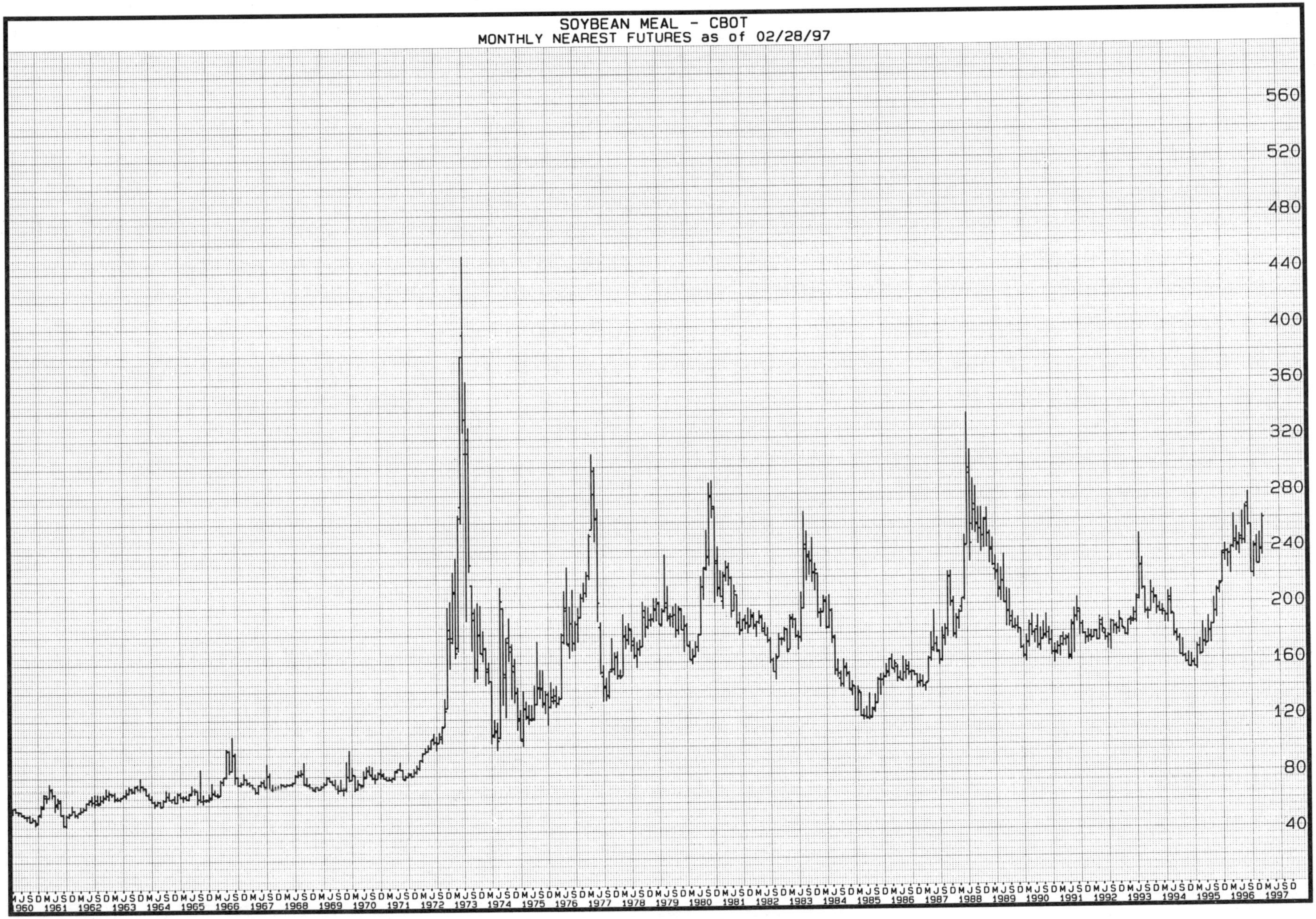


Soybean Meal, CBOT Monthly Nearest Futures, July 1958 - March 1997

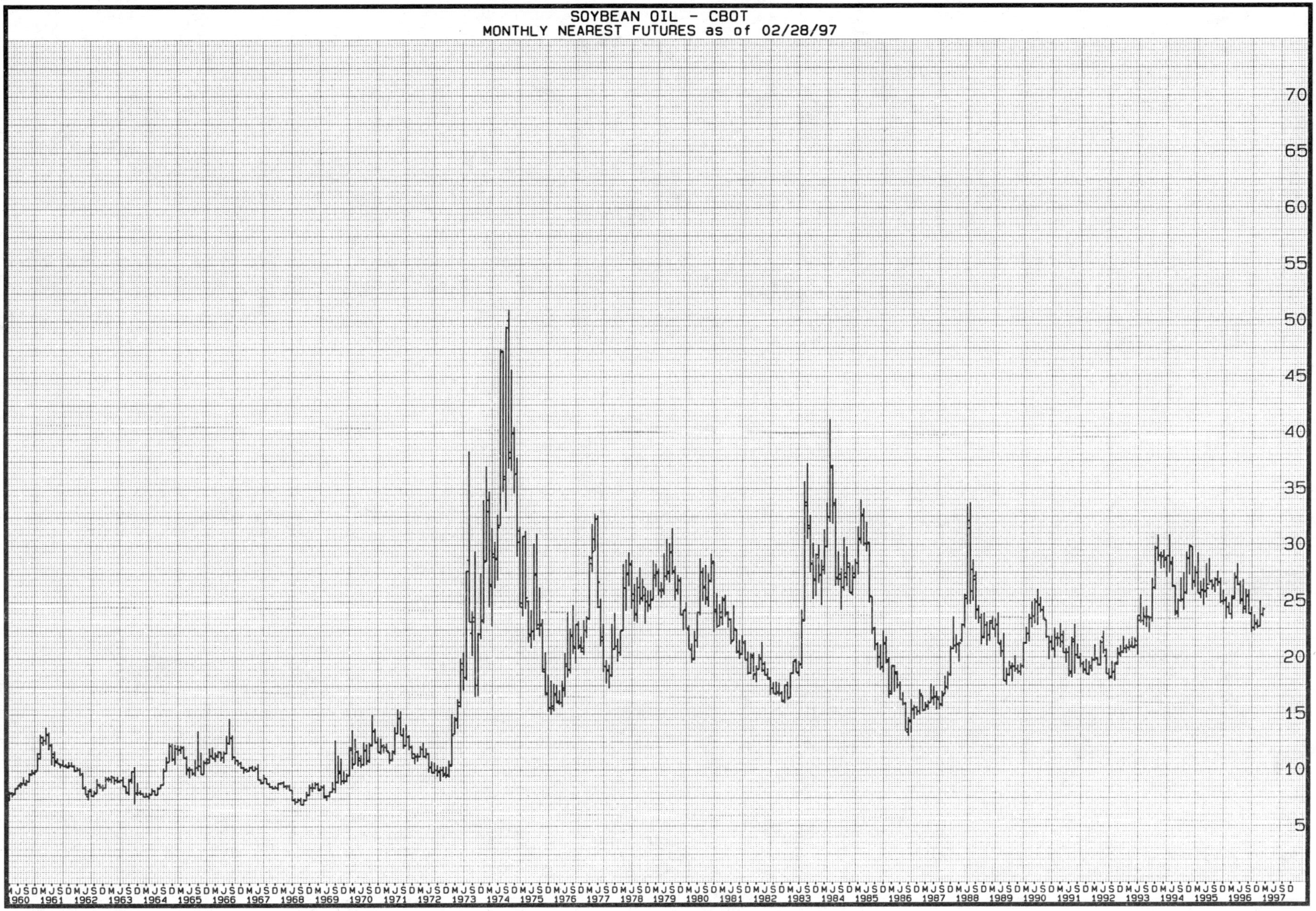


Soybean Oil, CBOT Monthly Nearest Futures, July 1958 - March 1997

# Volume U.S.

## U.S. FUTURES VOLUME HIGHLIGHTS

### 1996 in Comparison with 1995

| 1996 Rank | Top 50 Contracts Traded in 1996 | 1996 Contracts | 1996 % | 1995 Contracts | 1995 % | 1995 Rank |
|---|---|---|---|---|---|---|
| 1 | Eurodollar, CME | 88,883,119 | 22.37% | 95,730,019 | 24.59% | 1 |
| 2 | T-Bonds, CBT | 84,725,128 | 21.32% | 86,375,916 | 23.45% | 2 |
| 3 | Crude Oil, NYMEX | 23,487,821 | 5.91% | 23,613,994 | 6.29% | 3 |
| 4 | T-Notes (10 Year), CBT | 21,939,725 | 5.52% | 22,445,356 | 5.65% | 4 |
| 5 | S&P 500 Index, CME | 19,899,999 | 5.01% | 18,852,149 | 4.39% | 5 |
| 6 | Corn, CBT | 19,620,188 | 4.94% | 15,105,147 | 2.70% | 6 |
| 7 | Soybeans, CBT | 14,236,295 | 3.58% | 10,611,534 | 2.52% | 8 |
| 8 | T-Notes (5 Year), CBT | 11,463,640 | 2.88% | 12,637,054 | 2.92% | 7 |
| 9 | Gold (100 oz.), COMEX Div. of NYMEX | 8,902,179 | 2.24% | 7,781,596 | 1.99% | 11 |
| 10 | Natural Gas, NYMEX | 8,813,867 | 2.22% | 8,086,718 | 1.49% | 10 |
| 11 | #2 Heating Oil, NYMEX | 8,341,877 | 2.10% | 8,266,783 | 2.11% | 9 |
| 12 | Unleaded Regular Gas, NYMEX | 6,312,339 | 1.59% | 7,071,787 | 1.75% | 13 |
| 13 | Deutsche Mark, CME | 5,979,464 | 1.50% | 7,186,476 | 2.57% | 12 |
| 14 | Soybean Meal, CBT | 5,955,977 | 1.50% | 5,601,242 | 1.08% | 15 |
| 15 | Wheat, CBT | 5,385,967 | 1.36% | 4,955,067 | 0.85% | 17 |
| 16 | Japanese Yen, CME | 5,101,819 | 1.28% | 5,630,053 | 1.55% | 14 |
| 17 | Silver (5,000 oz), COMEX Div. of NYMEX | 4,870,808 | 1.23% | 5,183,236 | 1.41% | 16 |
| 18 | Sugar #11, CSC | 4,751,852 | 1.20% | 4,711,082 | 1.11% | 18 |
| 19 | Soybean Oil, CBT | 4,980,277 | 1.25% | 4,611,336 | 1.19% | 19 |
| 20 | Swiss Franc, CME | 3,929,225 | 0.99% | 4,399,932 | 1.22% | 20 |
| 21 | Live Cattle, CME | 3,926,192 | 0.99% | 3,257,105 | 0.84% | 21 |
| 22 | British Pound, CME | 2,961,782 | 0.75% | 2,610,510 | 0.84% | 22 |
| 23 | Cotton, NYCE | 2,373,855 | 0.60% | 2,525,434 | 0.54% | 23 |
| 24 | High Grade Copper, COMEX Div. of NYMEX | 2,311,919 | 0.58% | 2,519,414 | 0.64% | 24 |
| 25 | Cocoa, CSC | 2,121,576 | 0.53% | 2,090,098 | 0.57% | 25 |
| 26 | Coffee "C", CSC | 2,039,576 | 0.51% | 2,003,014 | 0.62% | 26 |
| 27 | Canadian Dollar, CME | 1,932,729 | 0.49% | 1,756,569 | 0.41% | 27 |
| 28 | Wheat, KCBT | 1,830,276 | 0.46% | 1,560,538 | 0.35% | 30 |
| 29 | Live Hogs, CME | 1,784,564 | 0.45% | 1,699,680 | 0.36% | 29 |
| 30 | T-Bonds, MIDAM | 1,281,967 | 0.32% | 1,341,877 | 0.33% | 31 |
| 31 | One Month LIBOR, CME | 1,190,652 | 0.30% | 1,707,062 | 0.45% | 28 |
| 32 | Wheat, MGE | 996,780 | 0.25% | 914,882 | 0.17% | 33 |
| 33 | Soybeans, MIDAM | 976,134 | 0.25% | 868,577 | 0.19% | 34 |
| 34 | Municipal Bond Index, CBT | 883,901 | 0.22% | 1,169,470 | 0.38% | 32 |
| 35 | Mexican Peso, CME | 850,040 | 0.21% | | | |
| 36 | Platinum, NYMEX | 802,468 | 0.20% | 846,693 | 0.21% | 35 |
| 37 | NYSE Composite Index, NYFE | 791,325 | 0.20% | 685,922 | 0.17% | 38 |
| 38 | Feeder Cattle, CME | 772,222 | 0.19% | 511,895 | 0.10% | 43 |
| 39 | Orange Juice (Frozen Conc.), NYCE | 654,937 | 0.16% | 688,932 | 0.15% | 37 |
| 40 | T-Notes (2 Year), CBT | 643,845 | 0.16% | 744,866 | 0.22% | 36 |
| 41 | Pork Bellies, CME | 612,649 | 0.15% | 56,191 | 0.15% | 42 |
| 42 | 30 Day Federal Funds, CBT | 608,308 | 0.15% | 643,717 | 0.10% | 39 |
| 43 | U.S. Dollar Index, NYCE | 509,067 | 0.13% | 456,859 | 0.13% | 45 |
| 44 | Euroyen, CME | 503,104 | 0.13% | | | |
| 45 | Nikkei 225, CME | 502,072 | 0.13% | 609,720 | 0.13% | 41 |
| 46 | Oats, CBT | 501,858 | 0.13% | 475,538 | 0.12% | 44 |
| 47 | Corn, MIDAM | 462,318 | 0.12% | 305,347 | 0.05% | 47 |
| 48 | Australian Dollar, CME | 461,084 | 0.12% | 346,823 | 0.08% | 46 |
| 49 | Goldman Sachs Commodity Index, CME | 446,186 | 0.11% | 270,504 | 0.04% | 48 |
| 50 | NASDAQ 100, CME | 380,963 | 0.10% | | | |
| | Top 50 Contracts | 393,695,915 | | 392,029,436 * | | |
| | Contracts Below the Top 50 | 3,706,238 | 0.93% | 3,284,044 | 0.83% | |
| | **TOTAL** | **397,402,153** | **100.00%** | **395,313,480** | **100.00%** | |

* For 1995 Top 50 contracts totaled 393,082,938 including 3 contracts that are not among 1996's Top 50.

## U.S. FUTURES VOLUME HIGHLIGHTS

### 1996 in Comparison with 1995

| 1996 RANK | EXCHANGE | 1996 CONTRACTS | 1996 % | 1995 CONTRACTS | 1995 % | 1995 RANK |
|---|---|---|---|---|---|---|
| 1 | Chicago Board of Trade (CBT) | 171,134,185 | 43.06% | 165,616,177 | 41.89% | 1 |
| 2 | Chicago Mercantile Exchange (CME) | 141,600,469 | 35.63% | 146,662,764 | 37.10% | 2 |
| 3 | New York Mercantile Exchange (NYMEX) * | 64,223,291 | 16.16% | 63,636,046 | 16.10% | 3 |
| 4 | Coffee, Sugar & Cocoa Exchange (CSCE) | 9,102,029 | 2.29% | 8,925,205 | 2.26% | 4 |
| 5 | New York Cotton Exchange (NYCE) ** | 4,967,176 | 1.25% | 4,702,985 | 1.19% | 5 |
| 6 | MidAmerica Commodity Exchange | 3,229,710 | 0.81% | 3,047,982 | 0.77% | 6 |
| 7 | Kansas City Board of Trade (KCBT) | 2,084,493 | 0.52% | 1,747,664 | 0.44% | 7 |
| 8 | Minneapolis Grain Exchange (MGE) | 1,012,598 | 0.25% | 936,016 | 0.24% | 8 |
| 9 | Philadelphia Board of Trade (PBOT) | 48,202 | 0.01% | 38,641 | 0.01% | 9 |
| | **TOTAL** | **397,402,153** | **100.00%** | **395,313,480** | **100.00%** | |

* In August 1994, the Commodity Exchange and the New York Mercantile Exchange merged and is now listed as one exchange.
** The New York Cotton Exchange volume now includes the New York Futures Exchange volume.

## U.S. FUTURES VOLUME 1992 - 1996

### CHICAGO BOARD OF TRADE (CBT)

| FUTURE | CONTRACT UNIT | 1996 | 1995 | 1994 | 1993 | 1992 |
|---|---|---|---|---|---|---|
| Wheat | 5,000 bu | 5,385,967 | 4,955,067 | 3,620,631 | 3,019,629 | 3,498,814 |
| Corn | 5,000 bu | 19,620,188 | 15,105,147 | 11,529,884 | 11,462,618 | 10,356,632 |
| Oats | 5,000 bu | 501,858 | 475,538 | 492,504 | 455,335 | 459,578 |
| Soybeans | 5,000 bu | 14,236,295 | 10,611,534 | 10,749,109 | 11,649,333 | 9,000,169 |
| Soybean Oil | 60,000 lbs | 4,980,277 | 4,611,336 | 5,063,188 | 4,612,229 | 4,282,678 |
| Soybean Meal | 100 tons | 5,955,977 | 5,601,242 | 4,593,814 | 4,718,095 | 4,145,397 |
| Rice | 200,000 lbs | 119,900 | 121,914 | 16,693 | | |
| Crop Yield | Crop yield est. X 10 | 1,343 | 3,123 | | | |
| Diammonium Phosphate | 100 tons | 3,935 | 6,755 | 15,588 | 45,314 | 34,465 |
| Anhydrous Ammonia | 100 tons | 351 | 1,060 | 2,811 | 9,831 | 5,563 |
| Edible Oil Index | 100 tons | | 21 | 298 | | |
| Barge Freight Index | %BF x $5/ton | | | | 6 | 20 |
| Structural Panel Index | 100,000 sq. ft. | | 885 | 7,033 | | |
| Eastern Catastrophe Insurance | Loss/EP x $25,000 | | | | 4,600 | 133 |
| Midwest Catastrophe Insurance | Loss/EP x $25,000 | | | | 74 | |
| National Catastrophe Insurance | Loss/EP x $25,000 | | | 4 | 4,782 | 79 |
| Silver | 5,000 oz | 110 | 8,617 | 10,278 | 1,022 | 472 |
| Silver | 1,000 oz | 41,575 | 76,667 | 88,663 | 89,141 | 52,658 |
| Gold | 100 oz | 335 | 647 | 984 | 778 | 56 |
| Gold | Kilo | 17,687 | 20,245 | 22,712 | 22,220 | 10,362 |
| T-Bonds | $100,000 | 84,725,128 | 86,375,916 | 99,959,881 | 79,428,444 | 70,003,894 |
| T-Notes (6 1/1-10 Year) | $100,000 | 21,939,725 | 22,445,356 | 24,077,828 | 16,601,258 | 11,217,938 |
| T-Notes (5 Year) | $100,000 | 11,463,640 | 12,637,054 | 12,462,838 | 8,123,939 | 6,441,193 |
| T-Notes (2 Year) | $200,000 | 643,845 | 744,866 | 939,043 | 532,203 | 445,394 |
| 30-Day Federal Funds | $5,000,000 | 608,308 | 643,717 | 416,200 | 182,319 | 233,727 |
| Mortgage Backed 7.5% | $100,000 | | | | | 44 |
| Mortgage Backed 8.0% | $100,000 | | | | | 96 |
| Municipal Bond Index | $1,000 x Index | 883,901 | 1,169,470 | 1,600,533 | 1,120,510 | 776,205 |
| Canadian Government Bonds | $100,000 C$ | | | 27,163 | | |
| Brady Bond Index | $1,000 x Index | 69 | | | | |
| Yield Curve Spread | $25,000 x 100YC | 3,771 | | | | |
| 5 Year Swap | 25 million | | | | | 2,389 |
| US Dollar Index | $1,250 x Index | | | | 733 | |
| MMI Maxi | $500 x Index | | | | 155,338 | 360,879 |
| Wilshire Small Cap Index | $500 x Index | | | | 1,626 | |
| **Total** | | **171,134,185** | **165,616,177** | **175,697,680** | **142,241,377** | **121,328,835** |

# Volume U.S.

## CHICAGO MERCANTILE EXCHANGE (CME)

| FUTURE | CONTRACT UNIT | 1996 | 1995 | 1994 | 1993 | 1992 |
|---|---|---|---|---|---|---|
| Live Hogs | 40,000 lbs | 1,784,564 | 1,669,680 | 1,554,022 | 1,401,754 | 1,556,092 |
| Lean Hogs | 40,000 lbs | 311,347 | 984 | | | |
| Pork Bellies, Frozen | 40,000 lbs | 612,649 | 561,913 | 633,646 | 698,799 | 784,152 |
| Butter | 40,000 lbs | 273 | | | | |
| Fluid Milk | 50,000 lbs | 2,336 | | | | |
| Broilers | 40,000 lbs | | | | | 1,312 |
| Live Cattle | 40,000 lbs | 3,926,192 | 3,257,105 | 3,580,896 | 3,306,952 | 3,319,618 |
| Feeder Cattle | 44,000 lbs | 772,222 | 511,895 | 446,639 | 419,888 | 369,042 |
| Lumber | 160,000 bd ft | 26,293 | 179,538 | 172,963 | 178,184 | 170,534 |
| Orient Strand Board Lumber | 100,000 bd ft | | | | | |
| Random Lumber | 80,000 bd ft | 277,781 | 3,148 | | | |
| T-Bills (90-day) | $1,000,000 | 251,353 | 620,223 | 1,020,491 | 1,017,350 | 1,337,061 |
| T-Bills (1 Year) | $500,000 | | | 586 | | |
| Eurodollar (3-month) | $1,000,000 | 88,883,119 | 95,730,019 | 104,823,245 | 64,411,394 | 60,531,066 |
| Euroyen | $1,000,000,000 xy | 503,104 | | | | |
| Euromark (3-month) | $1,000,000 | | | 566 | 26,058 | |
| Federal Funds Rate | $3,000,000 | 47,495 | 52,412 | | | |
| One Month LIBOR | $3,000,000 | 1,190,652 | 1,707,062 | 1,911,184 | 1,128,321 | 918,593 |
| Argentine FRB Bond | $1,000 X Bond | 9,610 | | | | |
| Brazilian C Bond | $500 x Bond | 10,198 | | | | |
| Brazilian EL Bond | $500 x Bond | 253 | | | | |
| Mexican PAR Bond | $500 x Bond | 1,926 | | | | |
| BP/DM Cross | 50,000 x bp/dm X | | | | | 15 |
| DM/JY Cross (Old) | 125,000 x dm/jy X | | | | | 718 |
| DM/JY Cross (New) | 125,000 x dm/jy X | | 106 | | 175 | 10,005 |
| DM/SF Cross | 125,000 x dm/sf X | | | | | 41 |
| British Pound | 62,500 | 2,961,782 | 2,610,510 | 3,562,865 | 3,701,427 | 3,053,428 |
| Brazilian Real | 100,000 | 87,323 | 20,364 | | | |
| Canadian Dollar | 100,000 | 1,932,729 | 1,756,569 | 1,740,205 | 1,410,818 | 1,171,640 |
| Deutschemark | 125,000 | 5,979,464 | 7,186,476 | 10,956,479 | 12,866,451 | 11,593,174 |
| Japanese Yen | 12,500,000 | 5,101,819 | 5,630,053 | 6,612,993 | 6,023,132 | 4,520,356 |
| Mexican Peso | 500,000 | 850,040 | 133,791 | | | |
| Swiss Franc | 125,000 | 3,929,225 | 4,399,932 | 5,217,236 | 5,604,841 | 5,134,717 |
| Australian Dollar | 100,000 | 461,084 | 346,823 | 355,183 | 198,954 | 89,784 |
| French Franc | 250,000 | 67,835 | 48,621 | 49,005 | 19,343 | |
| Deutschemark Forward | $250,000 | | 38,582 | 46,979 | | |
| Japanes Yen Forward | $250,000 | | 16,898 | | | |
| British Pound Rolling Spot | 250,000 sterling | | | | 1,729 | |
| Japanese Yen Rolling Spot | 250,000 U.S. | | 15,310 | | | |
| Deutschemark Rolling Spot | 250,000 U.S. | | 44,013 | 126,994 | 28,936 | |
| Nikkei 225 | $5 x Index | 502,072 | 609,720 | 548,233 | 356,523 | 383,755 |
| Mexican IPC Index | $25 x Index | 4,481 | | | | |
| S&P 500 Index | $500 x 500 Index | 19,899,999 | 18,852,149 | 18,708,599 | 13,204,413 | 12,414,157 |
| S&P 500 Barra Growth Index | $500 x 500 Index | 3,400 | 1,240 | | | |
| S&P 500 Barra Value Index | $500 x 500 Index | 7,531 | 1,478 | | | |
| S&P MidCap 400 Index | $500 x 400 Index | 289,989 | 253,741 | 285,962 | 218,531 | 102,708 |
| FT-SE 100 | 50 x FTSE Index | | | | 94 | 1,057 |
| Major Market | $500 x Index | 4,592 | 58,048 | 150,308 | 49,286 | |
| NASDAQ 100 Index | $500 x Index | 380,963 | | | | |
| Russell 2000 | $500 x Index | 78,353 | 43,857 | 36,239 | 19,479 | |
| Goldman Sachs Commodity Index | $250 x GSCI | 446,186 | 270,504 | 154,511 | 122,281 | 36,320 |
| **Total** | | **141,600,469** | **146,662,764** | **162,696,029** | **116,415,113** | **107,499,345** |

## COFFEE, SUGAR & COCOA EXCHANGE (CSCE)

| FUTURE | CONTRACT UNIT | 1996 | 1995 | 1994 | 1993 | 1992 |
|---|---|---|---|---|---|---|
| Coffee "C" | 37,500 lbs | 2,039,576 | 2,003,014 | 2,658,073 | 2,489,223 | 2,152,383 |
| Sugar #11 | 112,000 lbs | 4,751,852 | 4,711,082 | 4,719,218 | 4,285,945 | 3,667,481 |
| Sugar #14 | 112,000 lbs | 182,393 | 119,508 | 150,472 | 133,898 | 138,609 |
| White Sugar | 50 metric tons | 333 | | | | 10 |
| Cocoa | 10 metric tons | 2,121,576 | 2,090,098 | 2,417,006 | 2,128,384 | 1,397,235 |
| Brazil-Diff Coffee | 37,500 lbs | | | | 11 | 359 |
| Cheddar Cheese | 40,000 lbs | 980 | 977 | 1,366 | 669 | |
| Non Fat Dry Milk | 44,000 lbs | 282 | 90 | 905 | 1,276 | |
| Butter | 10,000 lbs. | 93 | | | | |
| Milk | 50,000 lbs | 4,944 | 436 | | | |
| **Total** | | **9,102,029** | **8,925,205** | **9,947,040** | **9,039,406** | **7,356,077** |

## KANSAS CITY BOARD OF TRADE (KCBT)

| FUTURE | CONTRACT UNIT | 1996 | 1995 | 1994 | 1993 | 1992 |
|---|---|---|---|---|---|---|
| Wheat | 5,000 bu | 1,830,276 | 1,560,538 | 1,502,348 | 1,348,500 | 1,339,842 |
| Western Natural Gas | 10,000 MMBtu | 89,706 | 77,595 | | | |
| Value Line Index | $500 x Index | 28,663 | 35,185 | 50,259 | 45,806 | 46,195 |
| Mini Value Line | $100 x Index | 135,848 | 74,346 | 51,901 | 40,662 | 34,454 |
| **Total** | | **2,084,493** | **1,747,664** | **1,604,508** | **1,434,968** | **1,420,491** |

## MIDAMERICA COMMODITY EXCHANGE (MidAm)

| FUTURE | CONTRACT UNIT | 1996 | 1995 | 1994 | 1993 | 1992 |
|---|---|---|---|---|---|---|
| Wheat | 1,000 bu | 151,755 | 137,573 | 102,145 | 101,353 | 239,180 |
| Corn | 1,000 bu | 462,318 | 305,347 | 232,855 | 276,502 | 458,772 |
| Oats | 1,000 bu | 8,449 | 5,846 | 5,208 | 4,555 | 8,008 |
| Soybeans | 1,000 bu | 976,134 | 863,577 | 797,803 | 966,244 | 1,130,629 |
| Soybean Meal New | 20 tons | 11,638 | 4,060 | 3,757 | 3,800 | 2,201 |
| Soybean Oil | 30,000 lbs | 14,248 | 6,658 | | | |
| Live Cattle | 20,000 lbs | 20,983 | 18,811 | 15,895 | 16,314 | 15,366 |
| Live Hogs | 20,000 lbs | 21,118 | 24,059 | 19,614 | 17,841 | 17,597 |
| Rice, Rough New | 200,000 lbs | | | 68,379 | 65,970 | 25,291 |
| New York Silver | 1,000 oz | 8,398 | 13,320 | 17,170 | 10,986 | 8,888 |
| New York Gold | 33.2 oz | 15,876 | 18,964 | 24,926 | 19,803 | 6,813 |
| Platinum | 25 oz | 6,949 | 3,055 | 2,841 | 1,750 | 861 |
| T-Bonds | $50,000 | 1,281,967 | 1,341,877 | 1,385,904 | 1,125,645 | 1,342,251 |
| T-Bills | $500,000 | 753 | 754 | 826 | 1,129 | 2,017 |
| T-Notes (10 Year) | $50,000 | 41,849 | 38,494 | 35,303 | 11,615 | |
| T-Notes (5 Year) | $50,000 | 383 | 37 | 4 | 39 | |
| Eurodollars | $500,000 | 8,893 | 23,550 | 8,987 | 7,229 | 2,885 |
| U.S. Dollar Index | $1,250 x USDI | | | | 7 | 1,755 |
| Australian Dollar | 50,000 | 266 | 221 | | | |
| British Pound | 12,500 | 21,424 | 23,620 | 66,162 | 67,208 | 44,120 |
| Swiss Franc | 62,500 | 48,027 | 50,201 | 64,501 | 73,532 | 62,788 |
| Deutschemark | 62,500 | 79,093 | 95,775 | 113,166 | 123,573 | 105,543 |
| Japanese Yen | 6,250,000 | 42,085 | 55,213 | 67,641 | 62,874 | 39,293 |
| Canadian Dollar | 50,000 | 7,104 | 11,970 | 9,522 | 8,505 | 4,802 |
| **Total** | | **3,229,710** | **3,047,982** | **3,042,609** | **2,966,474** | **3,519,060** |

## MINNEAPOLIS GRAIN EXCHANGE (MGE)

| FUTURE | CONTRACT UNIT | 1996 | 1995 | 1994 | 1993 | 1992 |
|---|---|---|---|---|---|---|
| Wheat | 5,000 bu | 996,780 | 914,882 | 737,089 | 822,898 | 742,703 |
| White Wheat | 5,000 bu | 14,602 | 20,411 | 27,446 | 10,895 | 6,077 |
| Oats | 5,000 bu | | | | 4,025 | 118 |
| Barley | 180,000 lbs. | 631 | | | | |
| White Shrimp | 5,000 lbs | 56 | 336 | 854 | 1,437 | |
| Black Tiger Shrimp | 5,000 lbs | 529 | 387 | 119 | | |
| **Total** | | **1,012,598** | **936,016** | **765,508** | **839,255** | **748,898** |

## NEW YORK COTTON EXCHANGE (NYCE)*

| FUTURE | CONTRACT UNIT | 1996 | 1995 | 1994 | 1993 | 1992 |
|---|---|---|---|---|---|---|
| Cotton #2 | 50,000 lbs | 2,373,855 | 2,525,434 | 2,289,998 | 1,603,027 | 1,701,258 |
| Potato | 85,000 lbs. | 744 | | | | |
| Cotlook World Cotton | 50,000 lbs X CWC | | | 79 | 3,363 | 12,098 |
| Orange Juice Frozen Concentrate | 15,000 lbs | 654,937 | 688,932 | 653,824 | 640,131 | 339,230 |
| European Currency Unit | $100,000 | | | | | 972 |
| Mark Pound | $125,000 BP | 87,757 | 32,804 | 12,351 | | |
| Mark Paris | $500,000 DM | 77,263 | 36,649 | 10,295 | | |
| Dollar Mark | $125,000 DM | 32,441 | 29,441 | 30,385 | | |
| Mark Yen | $125,000 DM | 167,093 | 66,405 | 30,566 | | |
| Mark Lira | $250,000 DM | 74,997 | 31,604 | 3,572 | | |
| Mark Swiss Franc | $125,000 DM | 37,566 | 1,209 | | | |
| Swedish Krona | $125,000 DM | 8,378 | | | | |
| U.S. Dollar/Swiss France | $125,000 SF | 4,098 | 1,586 | 10 | | |
| U.S. Dollar/Japanese Yen | $12,500,000 JY | 9,037 | 4,943 | 2 | | |
| U.S. Dollar/British Pound | $62,500 BP | 2,290 | 3,021 | 2 | | |
| U.S. Dollar Index | $1,000 x Index | 509,067 | 456,859 | 558,439 | 599,112 | 678,329 |
| Emerging Markets Debt Index | $1,000 x Index | 341 | 732 | | | |

# Volume U.S.

## NEW YORK COTTON EXCHANGE (NYCE)* (continued)

| FUTURE | CONTRACT UNIT | 1996 | 1995 | 1994 | 1993 | 1992 |
|---|---|---|---|---|---|---|
| T-Note (5 Year) | $100,000 | 45,064 | 44,959 | 69,858 | 50,200 | 80,186 |
| T-Note (2 Year) | $200,000 | 1,147 | 11,072 | 3,233 | 734 | 892 |
| NYSE Composite Index | $500 x Index | 791,325 | 685,922 | 729,231 | 848,522 | 1,315,438 |
| NYSE Utility Index | $500 x Index | | | 11 | 10 | |
| PSE Tech 100 | $500 x Index | 8,663 | | | | |
| Commodity Research Bureau Index | $500 x Index | 81,113 | 81,413 | 109,986 | 91,908 | 56,255 |
| **Total*** | | **4,967,176** | **4,702,985** | **4,501,842** | **3,837,007** | **4,184,658** |

## NEW YORK MERCANTILE EXCHANGE (NYMEX)**

### COMEX DIVISION

| FUTURE | CONTRACT UNIT | 1996 | 1995 | 1994 | 1993 | 1992 |
|---|---|---|---|---|---|---|
| High Grade Copper | 25,000 lbs | 2,311,919 | 2,519,414 | 2,737,967 | 2,064,629 | 1,674,163 |
| Silver | 5,000 oz | 4,870,808 | 5,183,236 | 5,994,345 | 4,855,924 | 3,016,339 |
| Gold | 100 oz | 8,902,179 | 7,781,596 | 8,503,366 | 8,916,195 | 6,002,009 |
| Platinum | 50 oz | | | | 342 | 9,963 |
| Paladium | 100 oz | | | | 2 | 333 |
| Eurotop 100 Index | $100 x Price | 38,925 | 49,328 | 62,231 | 56,497 | 26,453 |
| **Total** | | **16,123,831** | **15,533,574** | **17,297,909** | **15,893,589** | **10,729,260** |

### NYMEX DIVISION

| FUTURE | CONTRACT UNIT | 1996 | 1995 | 1994 | 1993 | 1992 |
|---|---|---|---|---|---|---|
| Palladium | 100 oz | 205,610 | 166,713 | 143,773 | 113,681 | 68,209 |
| Platinum | 50 oz | 802,468 | 846,693 | 895,805 | 651,222 | 577,253 |
| No. 2 Heating Oil, NY | 1,000 bbl | 8,341,877 | 8,266,783 | 8,986,835 | 8,625,061 | 8,005,462 |
| Unleaded Gasoline, NY | 1,000 bbl | 6,312,339 | 7,071,787 | 7,470,836 | 7,407,809 | 6,674,757 |
| Natural Gas | 10,000 MMBTU | 8,813,867 | 8,086,718 | 6,357,560 | 4,671,533 | 1,920,986 |
| Gulf Coast Unleaded Gas | 42,000 gal | | 252 | 300 | 510 | 4,902 |
| Alberta Natural Gas | 10,000 MMBTU | 2,876 | | | | |
| Palo Verde Electricity | 736 Mwh | 17,548 | | | | |
| California Oregon Border Electricity | 737 Mwh | 52,340 | | | | |
| Permian Basin Natural Gas | 10,000 MMBTU | 8,811 | | | | |
| Propane | 42,000 gal | 53,903 | 49,532 | 45,100 | 44,923 | 50,601 |
| Crude Oil | 1,000 bbl | 23,487,821 | 23,613,994 | 26,812,262 | 24,868,602 | 21,109,562 |
| Sour Crude Oil | 1,000 bbl | | | | | 10,331 |
| **Total** | | **48,099,460** | **48,102,472** | **50,712,471** | **46,383,341** | **38,422,063** |
| **Total**** | | **64,223,291** | **63,636,046** | **68,010,380** | **62,276,930** | **49,151,323** |

## PHILADELPHIA BOARD OF TRADE (PBOT)

| FUTURE | CONTRACT UNIT | 1996 | 1995 | 1994 | 1993 | 1992 |
|---|---|---|---|---|---|---|
| Australian Dollar | 100,000 | 2,532 | 1,716 | 265 | 142 | 132 |
| British Pound | 62,500 | 1,761 | 4,147 | 2,485 | 1,493 | 234 |
| Canadian Dollar | 100,000 | 91 | 208 | 639 | | |
| ECU | 125,000 | 616 | | 1,768 | | |
| Deutschemark | 125,000 | 23,904 | 17,121 | 21,661 | 11,469 | 60,647 |
| Swiss Franc | 125,000 | 4,723 | 3,915 | 3,038 | 614 | 130 |
| French Franc | 500,000 | 3,704 | 4,162 | 7,167 | 8,814 | 16,432 |
| Japanese Yen | 12,500,000 | 10,871 | 7,372 | 5,323 | 2,564 | 5,780 |
| **Total** | | **48,202** | **38,641** | **42,346** | **25,096** | **83,355** |

| | | 1996 | 1995 | 1994 | 1993 | 1992 |
|---|---|---|---|---|---|---|
| **TOTAL FUTURES** | | **397,402,153** | **395,313,480** | **426,307,942** | **339,075,626** | **295,292,042** |
| **PERCENT CHANGE** | | **0.53%** | **-7.27%** | **25.73%** | **14.83%** | **12.32%** |

* The New York Cotton Exchange volume now includes the New York Futures Exchange.

** In August 1994, the Commodity Exchange and the New York Mercantile Exchange merged and is now listed as one exchange.

## OPTIONS TRADED ON U.S. FUTURES EXCHANGES VOLUME HIGHLIGHTS

### 1996 in Comparison with 1995

| 1996 RANK | EXCHANGE | 1996 CONTRACTS | 1996 % | 1995 CONTRACTS | 1995 % | 1995 RANK |
|---|---|---|---|---|---|---|
| 1 | Chicago Board of Trade (CBT) | 51,304,320 | 50.31% | 45,056,867 | 47.83% | 1 |
| 2 | Chicago Mercantile Exchange (CME) | 35,421,726 | 34.74% | 35,142,349 | 37.30% | 2 |
| 3 | New York Mercantile Exchange (NYMEX) * | 11,576,001 | 11.35% | 9,836,294 | 10.44% | 3 |
| 4 | Coffee, Sugar & Cocoa Exchange (CSCE) | 2,287,750 | 2.24% | 2,390,774 | 2.54% | 4 |
| 5 | New York Cotton Exchange (NYCE) ** | 1,261,109 | 1.24% | 1,645,324 | 1.75% | 5 |
| 6 | Kansas City Board of Trade (KCBT) | 68,479 | 0.07% | 81,409 | 0.09% | 6 |
| 7 | MidAmerica Commodity Exchange (MidAm) | 27,531 | 0.03% | 23,127 | 0.02% | 8 |
| 8 | Minneapolis Grain Exchange (MGE) | 26,891 | 0.03% | 32,666 | 0.03% | 7 |
| | **TOTAL** | **101,973,807** | **100.00%** | **94,208,810** | **100.00%** | |

* In August 1994, the Commodity Exchange and the New York Mercantile Exchange merged and is now listed as one exchange.
** The New York Cotton Exchange volume now includes the New York Futures Exchange volume.

## OPTIONS VOLUME ON U.S. FUTURES EXCHANGES 1992 - 1996

### CHICAGO BOARD OF TRADE (CBT)

| OPTION | CONTRACT UNIT | 1996 | 1995 | 1994 | 1993 | 1992 |
|---|---|---|---|---|---|---|
| Corn | 5000 bu | 6,602,010 | 3,783,446 | 2,144,461 | 2,031,284 | 1,833,816 |
| Soybeans | 5000 bu | 5,135,124 | 3,149,635 | 2,710,656 | 2,927,072 | 1,930,334 |
| Oats | 5000 bu | 45,037 | 35,250 | 20,495 | 17,373 | 15,307 |
| Wheat | 5000 bu | 1,886,909 | 1,243,567 | 827,930 | 713,670 | 1,108,840 |
| Soybean Oil | 60,000 lbs | 285,274 | 232,635 | 287,905 | 181,938 | 104,704 |
| Soybean Meal | 100 tons | 593,165 | 304,835 | 263,734 | 306,523 | 152,394 |
| Rice | 200,000 lbs | 14,658 | 14,336 | 1,750 | | |
| Diammonium Phosphate | 100 tons | 50 | | | | |
| Crop Yield | Crop yield est. X 10 | 1,061 | 3,519 | | | |
| Silver | 1,000 oz | 515 | 1,476 | 5,952 | 12,423 | 20,105 |
| Eastern Catastrophe Insurance | Loss/EP x $25,000 | 66 | 3,274 | 7,742 | 2,482 | 28 |
| Midwest Catastrophe Insurance | Loss/EP x $25,000 | | 50 | 44 | | |
| National Catastrophe Insurance | Loss/EP x $25,000 | | | 1,590 | 4,102 | 22 |
| Westerm Insurance-Annual | Loss/EP x $25,000 | | | 44 | | |
| PCS Castastrophe Insurance | | 14,688 | 1,064 | | | |
| T-Bonds | $100,000 | 25,930,661 | 25,639,950 | 28,142,549 | 23,435,164 | 20,258,740 |
| T-Notes (10 Year) | $100,000 | 7,907,650 | 6,887,102 | 6,437,215 | 4,844,272 | 2,564,191 |
| T-Notes (5 Year) | $100,000 | 2,723,525 | 3,619,462 | 2,675,097 | 1,976,924 | 665,587 |
| T-Notes (2 Year) | $200,000 | 2,806 | 13,189 | 12,862 | 8,235 | 6,677 |
| Mortgage Backed 7.5% | $100,000 | | | | | 20 |
| Mortgage Backed 8.0% | $100,000 | | | | | 45 |
| 5 Year Swap | 25 million | | | | | 400 |
| Muni Bonds | $1,000 x Index | 43,219 | 13,018 | 24,772 | 68,816 | 38,200 |
| Brady Bond Index | $1,000 x Index | 440 | | | | |
| Yield Curve Spread | $25,000 x 100 YCS | 3,284 | | | | |
| Canadian Government Bonds | $100,000 C$ | | | 1,385 | | |
| Flexible U.S. T-Bonds | | 94,453 | 59,804 | 174,295 | | |
| Flexible T-Notes (10 Year) | | 12,735 | 36,425 | 46,606 | | |
| Flexible T-Notes (5 Year) | | 6,990 | 14,730 | 19,060 | | |
| Flexible T-Notes (2 Year) | | | 100 | 250 | | |
| Major Market Index | $500 x Index | | | | 1,368 | 2,215 |
| Wilshire Small Cap Index | $500 x Index | | | | 52 | |
| **Total** | | **51,304,320** | **45,056,867** | **43,806,394** | **36,531,698** | **28,701,625** |

# Volume U.S.

## CHICAGO MERCANTILE EXCHANGE (CME)

| OPTION | CONTRACT UNIT | 1996 | 1995 | 1994 | 1993 | 1992 |
|---|---|---|---|---|---|---|
| Live Hogs | 40,000 lbs | 169,214 | 137,435 | 109,448 | 79,046 | 82,341 |
| Lean Hogs | 40,000 lbs | 35,831 | | | | |
| Live Cattle | 40,000 lbs | 539,523 | 463,455 | 519,813 | 500,664 | 561,058 |
| Fluid Milk | 40,000 lbs | 307 | | | | |
| Butter | 50,000 lbs | 92 | | | | |
| Broilers | 40,000 lbs | | | | | 733 |
| Pork Bellies, Frozen | 40,000 lbs | 52,040 | 21,156 | 24,173 | 32,698 | 32,507 |
| Feeder Cattle | 44,000 lbs | 174,518 | 109,096 | 95,845 | 79,264 | 85,807 |
| Lumber | 160,000 bd ft | 1,753 | 14,433 | 17,603 | 25,934 | 5,278 |
| Orient Strand Board | 100,000 bd ft | 86 | | | | |
| Random Lumber | 80,000 bd ft | 26,922 | 491 | | | |
| One Month LIBOR | $3,000,000 | 16,031 | 54,219 | 79,172 | 90,604 | 98,839 |
| Brazilian C Bond | $500 x Index | 30 | | | | |
| Mexican PAR Bond | $500 x Index | 130 | | | | |
| Euromark (3-month) | $1,000,000 | | | | 8,923 | |
| Eurodollar (3-month) | $1,000,000 | 22,234,888 | 22,363,853 | 28,145,929 | 17,008,764 | 13,762,628 |
| T-Bill (90-day) | $1,000,000 | 80 | 3,594 | 5,269 | 14,485 | 29,670 |
| BP/DM Cross | 50,000 x bp/dm X | | | | | 1 |
| DM/JY Cross (New) | 125,000 x dm/jy X | | | | 82 | 29,106 |
| British Pound | 62,500 | 2,886,041 | 1,668,624 | 920,109 | 528,239 | 597,352 |
| Brazilian Real | 100,000 | 74,106 | 3,700 | | | |
| Deutschemark | 125,000 | 1,822,649 | 2,642,904 | 4,793,639 | 5,916,463 | 6,354,248 |
| Mexican Peso | 500,000 | 13,466 | 1,114 | | | |
| Swiss Franc | 125,000 | 753,418 | 630,016 | 767,583 | 627,923 | 1,026,974 |
| Japanese Yen | 12,500,000 | 1,734,186 | 2,141,043 | 2,946,432 | 2,261,977 | 1,518,409 |
| Canadian Dollar | 100,000 | 197,741 | 259,857 | 185,652 | 176,930 | 306,528 |
| Australian Dollar | 100,000 | 5,785 | 9,892 | 7,800 | 3,482 | 13,132 |
| French Franc | 250,000 | 2,149 | 4,935 | 1,064 | 5,562 | |
| British Pound Rolling Spot | 250,000 sterling | | | | 286 | |
| Deutschemark Rolling Spot | 250,000 U.S. | | | | 420 | |
| Nikkei 225 | $5 x Index | 5,722 | 8,986 | 7,982 | 9,684 | 13,971 |
| Mexican IPC Index | $25 x Index | 75 | | | | |
| S&P 500 Index | $500 x Index | 4,636,236 | 4,568,232 | 3,820,893 | 2,916,047 | 2,209,529 |
| S&P 500 Barra Value Index | $500 x Index | 4,765 | 30 | | | |
| S&P 500 Barra Growth Index | $500 x Index | 2,960 | | | | |
| S&P MidCap 400 Index | $500 x Index | 2,201 | 5,435 | 3,622 | 5,129 | 2,933 |
| FT-SE 100 | $50 x FTSE Index | | | | 2 | 73 |
| Major Market | $500 x Index | 729 | 289 | 804 | 251 | |
| NASDAQ 100 Index | $500 x Index | 23,992 | | | | |
| Russell 2000 | $500 x Index | 2,089 | 1,532 | 2,793 | 1,428 | |
| Goldman Sachs Commodity Index | $250 x GSCI | 1,971 | 28,028 | 33,949 | 37,590 | 8,093 |
| **Total** | | **35,421,726** | **35,142,349** | **42,489,574** | **30,331,877** | **26,739,210** |

## COFFEE, SUGAR & COCOA EXCHANGE (CSCE)

| OPTION | CONTRACT UNIT | 1996 | 1995 | 1994 | 1993 | 1992 |
|---|---|---|---|---|---|---|
| Sugar | 112,000 lbs | 1,094,879 | 1,203,779 | 1,166,748 | 916,170 | 848,750 |
| Coffee | 37,500 lbs | 856,710 | 867,303 | 1,208,925 | 1,022,017 | 860,943 |
| Cocoa | 10 metric tons | 335,173 | 319,513 | 341,131 | 326,760 | 209,938 |
| Cheddar Cheese | 40,000 lbs | 4 | 76 | 150 | 174 | |
| Non Fat Dry Milk | 44,000 lbs | 21 | | 58 | 296 | |
| Milk | 50,000 lbs | 963 | 103 | | | |
| **Total** | | **2,287,750** | **2,390,774** | **2,717,012** | **2,265,417** | **1,919,631** |

## NEW YORK MERCANTILE EXCHANGE (NYMEX)*

### COMEX DIVISION

| OPTION | CONTRACT UNIT | 1996 | 1995 | 1994 | 1993 | 1992 |
|---|---|---|---|---|---|---|
| Gold | 100 oz | 2,079,663 | 2,006,695 | 1,589,065 | 1,717,015 | 1,152,854 |
| 5 Day Gold | 100 oz | 150 | 688 | 911 | 418 | 17,233 |
| Silver | 5,000 oz | 949,239 | 1,146,513 | 1,316,650 | 1,094,702 | 676,543 |
| 5 Day Silver | 5,000 oz | 96 | 221 | 368 | 1,262 | 9,606 |
| Platinum | 50 oz | | | | | 359 |
| High Grade Copper | 25,000 lbs | 150,339 | 134,212 | 184,125 | 146,060 | 87,324 |
| 5 Day Copper | 25,000 lbs | | 34 | 41 | 534 | |
| Eurotop 100 Index | $100 x Price | | | | 533 | |
| **Total** | | **3,179,487** | **3,288,363** | **3,091,160** | **2,960,524** | **1,943,919** |

### NYMEX DIVISION

| OPTION | CONTRACT UNIT | 1996 | 1995 | 1994 | 1993 | 1992 |
|---|---|---|---|---|---|---|
| Heating Oil | 42,000 gal | 1,108,935 | 703,388 | 699,325 | 803,216 | 1,247,891 |
| Crude Oil | 1,000 bbl | 5,271,456 | 3,975,611 | 5,675,072 | 7,156,518 | 6,562,163 |
| Unleaded Gasoline | 1,000 bbl | 655,965 | 766,557 | 573,502 | 660,886 | 860,086 |
| Natural Gas | 10,000 MMBTU | 1,234,691 | 921,520 | 493,491 | 345,814 | 80,756 |
| Alberta Natural Gas | 10,000 MMBTU | 15 | | | | |
| Gas-Crude Oil Spread | 1,000 bbl | 31,743 | 64,285 | 13,932 | | |
| Heating Oil-Crude Oil Spread | 1,000 bbl | 45,920 | 72,969 | 13,965 | | |
| Palo Verde Electricity | 736 Mwh | 3,964 | | | | |
| California Oregon Border Electricity | 737 Mwh | 7,650 | | | | |
| Platinum | 50 oz | 36,175 | 43,601 | 90,556 | 62,661 | 39,458 |
| **Total** | | **8,396,514** | **6,547,931** | **7,559,843** | **9,029,095** | **8,790,354** |
| **Total*** | | **11,576,001** | **9,836,294** | **10,651,003** | **11,989,619** | **10,734,273** |

## KANSAS CITY BOARD OF TRADE (KCBT)

| OPTION | CONTRACT UNIT | 1996 | 1995 | 1994 | 1993 | 1992 |
|---|---|---|---|---|---|---|
| Wheat | 5,000 bu | 65,190 | 75,849 | 89,960 | 87,214 | 85,565 |
| Western Natural Gas | 10,000 MMBtu | 1,850 | 2,546 | | | |
| Mini Value Line | $100 x Index | 1,439 | 3,014 | 3,404 | 1,797 | 918 |
| **Total** | | **68,479** | **81,409** | **93,364** | **89,011** | **86,483** |

## MIDAMERICA COMMODITY EXCHANGE (MidAm)

| OPTION | CONTRACT UNIT | 1996 | 1995 | 1994 | 1993 | 1992 |
|---|---|---|---|---|---|---|
| Soybeans | 1,000 bu | 13,689 | 11,908 | 13,498 | 19,062 | 15,786 |
| Soybean Oil | 30,000 lbs | | 5 | | | |
| Soft Red Winter Wheat | 5,000 bu | 3,422 | 2,425 | 3,536 | 2,652 | 4,038 |
| Corn | 1,000 bu | 9,753 | 7,296 | 5,765 | 6,274 | 8,333 |
| Rough Rice | 200,000 lbs | | | 5,588 | 6,013 | 6,121 |
| T-Bonds | $50,000 | 530 | 721 | 3,149 | 1,966 | 3,657 |
| Gold | 33.2 oz | 137 | 772 | 417 | 39 | 289 |
| **Total** | | **27,531** | **23,127** | **31,953** | **36,006** | **38,224** |

## MINNEAPOLIS GRAIN EXCHANGE (MGE)

| OPTION | CONTRACT UNIT | 1996 | 1995 | 1994 | 1993 | 1992 |
|---|---|---|---|---|---|---|
| American Spring Wheat | 5,000 bu | 21,126 | 26,893 | 26,441 | 27,822 | 13,556 |
| European Spring Wheat | 5,000 bu | 44 | 184 | 284 | 48 | |
| Oats | 5,000 bu | | | | 177 | |
| White Wheat | 5,000 bu | 5,175 | 5,333 | 13,556 | 9,009 | 3,273 |
| Barley | 180,000 lbs. | 8 | | | | |
| White Shrimp | 5,000 lbs | 7 | 118 | 102 | 465 | |
| Black Tiger Shrimp | 5,000 lbs | 531 | 138 | 28 | | |
| **Total** | | **26,891** | **32,666** | **40,411** | **37,521** | **16,829** |

# Volume U.S.

## NEW YORK COTTON EXCHANGE (NYCE)**

| OPTION | CONTRACT UNIT | 1996 | 1995 | 1994 | 1993 | 1992 |
|---|---|---|---|---|---|---|
| Cotton | 50,000 lbs | 816,550 | 1,416,054 | 816,031 | 372,074 | 413,091 |
| Cotlook World Cotton | 50,000 lbs X CWC | | | | 206 | 1,188 |
| Orange Juice Frozen Concentrate | 15,000 lbs | 316,469 | 171,209 | 159,365 | 101,214 | 72,446 |
| Potato | 85,000 lbs. | 26 | | | | |
| European Currency Unit | $100,000 | | | | | 4,570 |
| U.S. Dollar Index | $500 x Index | 50,461 | 23,987 | 42,268 | 67,603 | 470,230 |
| Mark Pound | $125,000 BP | 9,247 | 116 | | | |
| Mark Paris | $500,000 DM | 1,473 | 570 | | | |
| Dollar Mark | $125,000 DM | 266 | | | | |
| Mark Yen | $125,000 DM | 2,010 | 160 | | | |
| Mark Swiss Franc | $125,000 DM | 7,313 | 33 | | | |
| Mark Lira | $250,000 DM | 367 | 354 | | | |
| U.S. Dollar / British Pound | $125,000 BP | 22 | | | | |
| U.S. Dollar / Japanese Yen | $12,500,000 JY | 1,209 | | | | |
| NYSE Composite Index | $500 x Index | 48,714 | 26,457 | 26,636 | 29,571 | 43,386 |
| PSE Tech 100 | $500 x Index | 2,211 | | | | |
| Commodity Research Bureau Index | $500 x Index | 4,771 | 6,384 | 7,495 | 6,818 | 3,589 |
| **Total**** | | **1,261,109** | **1,645,324** | **1,051,795** | **577,486** | **1,008,500** |

| | | | | | |
|---|---|---|---|---|---|
| **TOTAL OPTIONS** | **101,973,807** | **94,208,810** | **100,881,506** | **81,858,635** | **69,244,775** |
| **PERCENT CHANGE** | **8.24%** | **-6.61%** | **23.24%** | **18.22%** | **11.32%** |

* In August 1994, the Commodity Exchange and the New York Mercantile Exchange merged and is now listed as one exchange.
** The New York Cotton Exchange volume now includes the New York Futures Exchange volume.

# Volume Worldwide

## Agricultural Futures Markets (AFM), Netherlands

| | 1996 | 1995 | 1994 | 1993 | 1992 |
|---|---|---|---|---|---|
| Live Hogs | 49,986 | 30,877 | 41,382 | 46,117 | |
| Piglets | 2,529 | 1,047 | 3,417 | 3,358 | |
| Wheat | 536 | | | | |
| Potatoes | 75,046 | 165,313 | 229,071 | 154,832 | |
| **Total** | **128,097** | **197,237** | **273,870** | **204,307** | |

## Austrian Futures & Options Exchange (OTOB), Austria

| | 1996 | 1995 | 1994 | 1993 | 1992 |
|---|---|---|---|---|---|
| Austrian Government Bond | 151,633 | 176,527 | 124,070 | 43,410 | |
| ATX Index | 412,047 | 498,234 | 348,291 | 174,095 | 66,898 |
| Austrian Government Bond Options | 6,835 | | | | |
| ATX Index Options | 960,513 | 1,748,567 | 1,252,782 | 672,985 | 176,219 |
| ATX LEOs (Long-term Equity Options) | 43,990 | 71,555 | 9,077 | | |
| **Total** | **1,575,018** | **2,494,883** | **1,734,220** | **890,490** | **243,117** |

## Belgian Futures and Options Exchange (BELFOX), Belgium

| | 1996 | 1995 | 1994 | 1993 | 1992 |
|---|---|---|---|---|---|
| Belgian Government Bonds | 390,013 | 507,254 | 687,987 | 584,970 | 263,832 |
| BIBOR 3 Months | 157,909 | 175,082 | 150,238 | 190,936 | 51,547 |
| Bel 20 Index | 326,542 | 187,686 | 154,574 | 12,281 | |
| Belgian Government Bonds Options | 1,509 | 4,504 | 51,989 | | |
| Bel 20 Index Options | 1,170,948 | 862,492 | 561,012 | 345,510 | |
| USO (Dollar/Belgian Franc) | 128,548 | 108,471 | 29,546 | | |
| Gold Index Options | 82,442 | 81,897 | | | |
| **Total** | **2,257,911** | **1,927,386** | **1,635,346** | **1,133,697** | **315,379** |

## Bolsa Brasileira de Futuros (BBF), Brazil

| | 1996 | 1995 | 1994 | 1993 | 1992 |
|---|---|---|---|---|---|
| R$/US$ Exchange Rate | 41,130 | 22,948 | | | |
| U.S. Denominated Arabica Coffee | 7,308 | 6,733 | | | |
| Stock Price Future Return Index | 189,773 | | | | |
| Long Term Interest Rate | 15,985 | 20,422 | | | |
| Average Interest Rate on Interbank Deposits | 58,325 | 78,662 | 999,617 | | |
| R$ (Brazilian Real)/US$ Exchange Rate Options | 1,819,120 | 89,700 | | | |
| U.S. Denominated Arabica Coffee Options | 14,628 | 591,752 | | | |
| Average Interest Rate on Interbank Deposits Options | 48,213,690 | 127,924,464 | 2,049,380 | | |
| **Total** | **50,047,438** | **128,734,681** | **3,048,997** | | |

## Budapest Commodity Exchange (BCE), Hungary

| | 1996 | 1995 | 1994 | 1993 | 1992 |
|---|---|---|---|---|---|
| Milling Wheat | 65,454 | 18,065 | | | |
| Corn | 44,253 | 16,954 | | | |
| Feed Wheat | 6,179 | 1,790 | | | |
| Feed Barley | 5,982 | 767 | | | |
| Black Seed | 2,580 | 2,933 | | | |
| BL-55 Flour | 10 | 39 | | | |
| Europe I Live Hogs | 191 | 150 | | | |
| Europe II Live Hogs | 322 | 358 | | | |
| Deutsche Mark | 751,130 | 697,200 | | | |
| U.S. Dollar | 871,174 | 357,610 | | | |
| Japanese Yen | 916,857 | 269,826 | | | |
| European Currency Unit | 1,303,920 | 31,435 | | | |
| British Pound | 304,872 | | | | |
| Swiss Franc | 419,885 | | | | |
| Italian Lira | 710,455 | | | | |
| 3 Month BUBOR | 22,333 | | | | |
| 1 Month BUBOR | 135 | | | | |
| 3 Month Hungarian Interbank Deposit Rate | 1,661 | 2,016 | | | |
| **Total** | **5,427,393** | **1,399,143** | | | |

## Beijing Commodity Exchange (BCE), China

| | 1996 | 1995 | 1994 | 1993 | 1992 |
|---|---|---|---|---|---|
| Peanuts | 18,875 | 1,957 | | | |
| Greenbean | 81,081,235 | 141,662,184 | | | |
| **Total** | **81,100,110** | **141,664,141** | | | |

# Volume Worldwide

## Bolsa de Mercadorias & Futuros (BM&F), Brazil

| | 1996 | 1995 | 1994 | 1993 | 1992 |
|---|---|---|---|---|---|
| Arabica Coffee | 116,071 | 76,206 | 79,220 | 87,753 | 50,873 |
| Live Cattle | 117,395 | 39,174 | 5,687 | 7,438 | 7,046 |
| Sugar Crystal | 6,212 | 4,301 | | | |
| Cotton | 2,339 | | | | 2 |
| Corn | 3,696 | | | | |
| Soybean Futures | 20,274 | 3,750 | 11 | 375 | |
| Gold Futures | 219,567 | 607,288 | 132,240 | 11,720 | |
| Gold Spot | 278,476 | | | | |
| Bovespa Stock Index Futures | 15,122,751 | 15,304,666 | 10,583,594 | 10,374,860 | 7,287,054 |
| Interest Rate | 49,541,598 | 35,152,630 | 28,474,764 | 18,996,117 | 14,072,749 |
| Interest Rate Swap | 6,313,852 | 3,592,277 | 6,002,555 | 1,860,847 | |
| Interest Rate x Exchange Rate Swap | 2,069,329 | 1,500,685 | 3,666,097 | 17,474 | |
| Interest Rate x Reference Rate Swap | 161,159 | 127,796 | 119,229 | | |
| Interest Rate x Inflation Index Swap (formerly Inflation) | 6,486 | 7,601 | | | |
| Interest Rate x Ibovespa Swap | 1 | | | | |
| ID x U.S. Dollar Spread Futures | 99,631 | | | | |
| C-Bond | 608,798 | | | | |
| El-Bond | 1,850 | | | | |
| U.S. Dollar | 45,132,135 | 74,241,367 | 39,231,744 | 7,608,631 | 4,501,952 |
| Exchange Rate Swap | 58,885 | 174,177 | 170,662 | | |
| Reference Rtae x Price Index swap | 1,022 | | | | |
| Reference Rate x Exchange Rate Swap | 328 | 813 | | | |
| Price Index x Exchange Rate | 564 | | | | |
| Robusta Coffee | | | | 36 | 992 |
| Calf Futures | | | | | 916 |
| Interest Rate x Gold Price Variation Swap (Not Guaranteed) Futures | | | 737 | | |
| Inflation Rate Future | | | 75,513 | 258,352 | |
| Interest Rate x Basic Financial Rate Swap | | 2 | | | |
| Interest Rate Options Exercise | | | 120 | | |
| Central Bank Bills | | | 10 | | |
| Gold Options on Actuals | 363,089 | 1,882,502 | 6,772,894 | 9,406,163 | 7,932,576 |
| Gold Options Exercise | 150,144 | 1,124,792 | 2,246,674 | 1,401,370 | 802,402 |
| U.S. $ Denominated Arabica Coffee Options | 14,767 | 2,810,322 | 3,290,667 | 1,504,776 | 2,491 |
| U.S. $ Denominated Arabica Coffee Options Exercise | 29,249 | 1,375,756 | 1,359,128 | 268,159 | 476 |
| Live Cattle Options | 5,882 | 34,240 | 88,428 | | |
| Live Cattle Options Exercise | 1,500 | 38,504 | | | |
| Bovespa Stock Options | 201,757 | 74,469 | 11,875 | | |
| Bovespa Stock Options Exercise | 15,722 | 1,765 | | | |
| Interest Rate Options | 761,541 | 42,200 | 320 | | |
| Interest Rate Options Exercise | 30,550 | | | | |
| Fexible Bovespa Stock Index Options | 167,918 | | | | |
| U.S. Dollar Options on Actuals | 5,180,578 | 3,338,020 | 588,911 | 359,411 | 374,441 |
| U.S. Dollar Options Exercise | 142,710 | 403,456 | 80,703 | 50,190 | 38,176 |
| Flexible Currency Options | 7,662,050 | 6,097,019 | | | |
| **Total** | **134,609,876** | **148,055,778** | **102,981,783** | **52,213,672** | **35,072,146** |

## Budapest Stock Exchange (BSE), Hungary

| | 1996 | 1995 | 1994 | 1993 | 1992 |
|---|---|---|---|---|---|
| 3 Month Hungarian T-Bills | 30,933 | 6,333 | | | |
| 1 Month BUBOR | 4,585 | | | | |
| 3 Month BUBOR | 161 | | | | |
| Budapest Stock Index (BUX) Futures | 136,920 | 3,207 | | | |
| DEM/HUF | 25,429 | 1,407 | | | |
| USD/HUF | 20,439 | 940 | | | |
| ECU/HUF | 24,299 | 494 | | | |
| **Total** | **242,766** | **12,381** | | | |

## Deutsche Terminborse (DTB), Germany

| | 1996 | 1995 | 1994 | 1993 | 1992 |
|---|---|---|---|---|---|
| DAX | 5,452,505 | 4,788,661 | 5,140,803 | 3,976,882 | 3,271,055 |
| MDAX | 47,865 | | | | |
| BUND | 16,496,809 | 12,525,264 | 14,160,460 | 7,624,604 | 5,327,846 |
| Medium Term Notional Bond (BOBL) | 18,269,169 | 7,351,783 | 5,647,859 | 4,533,543 | 1,667,799 |
| 1 Month Euromark | 85,519 | | | | |
| FIBOR | 2,414 | 99,809 | 428,516 | | |
| BUXL | | 4,584 | 89,150 | | |
| DAX Options | 26,042,463 | 24,299,078 | 23,499,552 | 21,419,890 | 13,944,986 |
| BUND Options | 205,520 | 194,036 | 261,110 | 251,859 | 498,324 |
| Medium Term Notional Bond (BOBL) Options | 663,502 | 123,019 | 46,145 | 54,373 | |
| Options on DAX Futures | 24,544 | 21,073 | 49,642 | 62,976 | 136,439 |
| Stock Options | | | | | 9,996,329 |
| **Total** | **67,290,310** | **49,407,307** | **49,323,237** | **37,924,127** | **34,842,778** |

## European Options Exchange (EOE), Netherlands

| | 1996 | 1995 | 1994 | 1993 | 1992 |
|---|---|---|---|---|---|
| EOE Stock Index (FTI) | 2,426,699 | 1,004,005 | 1,031,333 | 811,882 | 510,517 |
| Dutch Top 5 Index (FT5) | 70,873 | 63,751 | 61,957 | 58,483 | 51,896 |
| Eurotop 100 Index | 31 | 233 | 435 | 1,102 | 2,003 |
| U.S. Dollar/Guilder (FUS) | 7,955 | 14,663 | 13,395 | 22,000 | 11,101 |
| Guilder Bond (FTO) | 21,368 | 8,051 | 14,132 | 70,388 | 21,230 |
| Gold Options | 89,779 | 45,283 | 133,412 | 284,040 | 72,815 |
| Silver Options | 7,799 | 5,704 | 5,100 | | |
| Dollar/Guilder Options | 539,799 | 552,452 | 482,961 | 672,632 | 537,892 |
| Dutch Government Bond Options | 474,525 | 406,500 | 449,511 | 436,199 | 270,442 |
| EOE Stock Index Options | 6,039,984 | 3,681,781 | 2,851,170 | 2,694,680 | 2,452,238 |
| Eurotop 100 Options | 5,090 | 5,204 | 853 | 2,647 | 10,424 |
| Dutch Top 5 Index Options | 861,025 | 561,611 | 393,584 | 411,757 | 493,466 |
| Major Market Index Options | | | 1,563 | 6,227 | 18,970 |
| **Total** | **10,544,927** | **6,349,238** | **5,439,406** | **5,472,037** | **4,452,994** |

## Finnish Options Market Exchange (FOM), Finland

| | 1996 | 1995 | 1994 | 1993 | 1992 |
|---|---|---|---|---|---|
| Finnish Government Bond | 291,658 | 125,298 | | | |
| STOBOR-FRA Interest Rate | 4,600 | | | | |
| FRA Interest Rate | 1,167,155 | 4,375 | | | |
| STOX Stock Future | 275,172 | | | | |
| FOX Index | 203,138 | 181,428 | | | |
| FRX Currency Options | | 9,669 | | | |
| FOX Index Options | | 521,008 | | | |
| **Total** | **2,347,684** | **841,778** | | | |

## FUTOP Clearing Centre, Denmark

| | 1996 | 1995 | 1994 | 1993 | 1992 |
|---|---|---|---|---|---|
| Danish Government Bonds 9% 2000 | 16,351 | 14,520 | | 1,250 | 396,181 |
| Danish Government Bonds 8% 2001 | 271,262 | | | | |
| Danish Government Bonds 8% 2006 | 194,430 | 7,679 | | | |
| Danish Government Bonds 7% 2004 | 4,789 | 159,778 | 74,220 | | |
| 6% 2026 Mortgage Bonds | 58,590 | 54,885 | 172,239 | 28,618 | |
| 3 Month CIBOR | 6,843 | 14,260 | 32,718 | 34,727 | |
| KFX Stock Index | 303,856 | 263,537 | 429,466 | 339,024 | 406,694 |
| Danish Government Bonds 9% 1995 | | | | 480 | 117,684 |
| Danish Government Bonds 9% 1998 | | 8,395 | 103,103 | 185,953 | 7,356 |
| Danish Government Bonds 8% 2003 | | | 343,101 | 391,969 | 27,235 |
| 9% 2022 Mortgage Bonds | | | | 1,408 | 23,948 |
| 9% 2006 Mortgage Bonds | | | | | 9,889 |
| 9% 2006 Mortgage Bonds Options | | | | | 120 |
| Danish Government Bonds 8% 2006 Options | 40,923 | 1,204 | | | |
| Danish Government Bonds 7% 2004 Options | 794 | 77,767 | 24,045 | | |
| Danish Government Bonds 9% 2000 Options | | | | 170 | 144,962 |
| Danish Government Bonds 8% 2003 Options | | | 76,548 | 85,580 | 8,100 |
| KFX Stock Index Options | | 51,053 | 79,952 | 87,246 | 193,598 |
| Stock Options | | | | | 186,992 |
| **Total** | **696,288** | **653,078** | **1,335,392** | **1,156,425** | **1,522,759** |

# Volume Worldwide

## International Petroleum Exchange (IPE), United Kingdom

| | 1996 | 1995 | 1994 | 1993 | 1992 |
|---|---|---|---|---|---|
| Crude Oil | 10,675,389 | 9,773,146 | 10,082,761 | 8,852,549 | 6,172,156 |
| Gasoil | 4,361,062 | 4,491,463 | 3,779,064 | 3,608,637 | 3,452,643 |
| Unleaded Gasoline | | 3,030 | 3,977 | 32,062 | |
| Crude Oil Options | 374,233 | 571,308 | 531,742 | 1,059,222 | 791,810 |
| Gasoil Options | 110,226 | 116,424 | 136,859 | 217,508 | 199,256 |
| Unleaded Gasoline Options | | | | | 58,938 |
| **Total** | **15,520,910** | **14,955,371** | **14,534,403** | **13,769,978** | **10,674,803** |

## Irish Futures & Options Exchange, Ireland/1

| | 1996 | 1995 | 1994 | 1993 | 1992 |
|---|---|---|---|---|---|
| DIBOR | 4,389 | 630 | 3,099 | 3,819 | 28,405 |
| Long Gilt | | 1,717 | 12,123 | 9,888 | 3,900 |
| Short Gilt | | | 1,140 | 100 | 2,040 |
| Medium Gilt | | 4,300 | | | |
| **Total** | **4,389** | **6,647** | **16,362** | **13,807** | **34,345** |

## Italian Derivatives Market of the Italian Stock Exchange, Italy

| | 1996 | 1995 | 1994 | 1993 | 1992 |
|---|---|---|---|---|---|
| MIB 30 Index | 2,675,238 | 1,140,636 | | | |
| MIB 30 Index Options | 476,138 | 12,464 | | | |
| **Total** | **3,151,376** | **1,153,100** | | | |

## Kuala Lumpur Commodity Exchange (KLCE), Malaysia

| | 1996 | 1995 | 1994 | 1993 | 1992 |
|---|---|---|---|---|---|
| Crude Palm Oil | 498,118 | 524,665 | 567,902 | 355,743 | 252,731 |
| Crude Palm Kernel Oil (15 tonne) | | | | 4,474 | |
| Crude Palm Kernel Oil (25 tonne) | | | 230 | 2,741 | 2,721 |
| Tin | | | | | 18 |
| Cocoa | | | | | 519 |
| **Total** | **498,118** | **524,665** | **568,132** | **362,958** | **255,989** |

## Kuala Lumpur Options & Financial Futures Exchange, Malaysia

| | 1996 | 1995 | 1994 | 1993 | 1992 |
|---|---|---|---|---|---|
| KLSE Composite Index | 71,278 | | | | |
| **Total** | **71,278** | | | | |

## London Commodity Exchange (LCE), United Kingdom/2

| | 1996 | 1995 | 1994 | 1993 | 1992 |
|---|---|---|---|---|---|
| Barley | 17,892 | 18,088 | 8,072 | 13,479 | 21,516 |
| BIFFEX (Baltic Freight Index) | 60,577 | 74,696 | 47,805 | 43,105 | 52,155 |
| Cocoa | 1,688,921 | 1,653,790 | 1,600,746 | 1,908,136 | 1,397,966 |
| U.S. Dollar Coffee | 1,182,528 | 1,062,744 | 1,269,477 | 908,963 | 876,687 |
| Potatoes in Bulk | 21,330 | 27,268 | 36,672 | 23,073 | 25,384 |
| Wheat | 115,869 | 101,025 | 84,212 | 62,546 | 63,202 |
| White Sugar | 579,463 | 575,734 | 480,973 | 329,414 | 303,377 |
| Hi Pro Soy | | | | 7,020 | 18,142 |
| Lamb | | | | 110 | 650 |
| Raw Sugar | | 34,219 | 30,959 | 14,898 | |
| Pigs | | | | 2,291 | 8,749 |
| Sugar (FOB) | | | 1,104 | | 75,052 |
| Barley Options | 22 | 103 | 64 | 110 | 885 |
| BIFFEX (Baltic Freight Index) Options | 728 | 447 | 94 | 10 | 96 |
| Cocoa Options | 57,094 | 48,196 | 87,215 | 107,102 | 51,219 |
| U.S. Dollar Coffee Options | 129,844 | 169,130 | 204,945 | 282,263 | 108,493 |
| Potatoes Options | 35 | | | | |
| Wheat Options | 8,758 | 12,907 | 6,866 | 1,769 | 2,081 |
| White Sugar Options | 13,268 | 23,016 | 8,196 | | |
| Hi Pro Soy Options | | | | 1 | 3,630 |
| Pigs Options | | | | 25 | |
| **Total** | **3,875,329** | **3,801,363** | **3,867,400** | **3,704,315** | **3,009,284** |

## London International Financial Futures Exchange (LIFFE), United Kingdom

| | 1996 | 1995 | 1994 | 1993 | 1992 |
|---|---|---|---|---|---|
| 3 Month Short Sterling | 15,793,775 | 15,314,576 | 16,603,152 | 12,135,981 | 11,296,327 |
| 3 Month Euromark | 36,231,178 | 25,737,379 | 29,312,222 | 21,318,942 | 12,173,431 |
| 1 Month Euromark | 48,644 | | | | |
| 3 Month Eurolira | 6,936,873 | 4,005,125 | 3,456,437 | 1,479,012 | 375,514 |
| 3 Month Euroswiss | 3,299,058 | 1,749,774 | 1,698,736 | 1,846,376 | 1,970,438 |
| 3 Month ECU | 602,518 | 693,526 | 622,457 | 720,788 | 316,781 |
| 3 Month Euroyen | 242,413 | | | | |
| Long Gilt | 15,408,010 | 13,796,555 | 19,048,097 | 11,808,998 | 8,804,639 |
| German Government Bund | 39,801,928 | 32,231,210 | 37,335,437 | 20,440,442 | 13,604,523 |
| Italian Government Bond | 12,603,754 | 9,612,899 | 11,823,741 | 6,344,233 | 3,773,105 |
| Japanese Government Bond | 816,059 | 845,329 | 610,925 | 421,454 | 221,370 |
| Financial Time Index (FT-SE 100) | 3,627,044 | 3,373,259 | 4,227,490 | 3,119,971 | 2,618,629 |
| Financial Time Index (FT-SE Mid 250 Index) | 34,068 | 35,068 | 40,674 | | |
| 3 Month Eurodollar | | 2,720 | 91,738 | 244,728 | 709,305 |
| U.S. T-Bond | | | | 4,660 | 272,077 |
| Eurotrack 100 | | | | | 81 |
| Spanish Government Bond | | | | 28,318 | |
| ECU Bond | | | | | 7,434 |
| German BOBL | | | 73,043 | 1,049,640 | |
| 3 Month Short Sterling Options | 2,213,494 | 3,348,945 | 4,057,878 | 2,666,711 | 2,648,009 |
| 3 Month Euromark Options | 4,888,942 | 3,427,376 | 2,943,936 | 2,906,476 | 1,964,405 |
| German Government Bond Options | 8,462,806 | 6,988,655 | 8,574,137 | 4,416,480 | 2,749,670 |
| Italian Government Bond Options | 2,456,177 | 1,130,762 | 1,030,672 | 602,096 | 395,354 |
| 3 Month Euroswiss Options | 45,568 | 33,781 | 19,245 | 32,163 | 17,412 |
| 3 Month Eurolira Options | 953,558 | 100,129 | | | |
| Long Gilt Options | 1,361,344 | 1,756,533 | 2,357,348 | 2,059,142 | 1,812,576 |
| Financial Times Index Options (FT-SE 100) | 6,738,955 | 4,434,086 | 4,786,656 | 3,439,460 | 2,571,640 |
| Financial Times FLEX Index Options (FT-SE 100) | 65,701 | 60,699 | | | |
| 3 Month Eurodollar Options | | 2 | 12,400 | 20,015 | 72,906 |
| U.S. T-Bond Options | | | | 2,626 | 68,369 |
| Equity (individual) options | | | | | 3,533,030 |
| **Total** | **162,631,867** | **128,678,388** | **148,726,421** | **97,108,712** | **71,977,025** |

## London Metal Exchange (LME), United Kingdom

| | 1996 | 1995 | 1994 | 1993 | 1992 |
|---|---|---|---|---|---|
| High Grade Primary Aluminum | 14,552,878 | 14,060,243 | 14,604,218 | 10,083,342 | 9,256,740 |
| Aluminum Alloy | 292,429 | 210,787 | 148,685 | 111,450 | 2,394 |
| Copper - Grade A | 18,484,367 | 17,530,263 | 17,236,317 | 14,855,430 | 7,945,054 |
| Standard Lead | 2,202,864 | 1,758,742 | 1,942,234 | 1,020,579 | 986,000 |
| Primary Nickel | 3,104,514 | 3,319,697 | 3,404,942 | 2,118,710 | 1,485,064 |
| Special High Grade Zinc | 4,852,942 | 5,241,931 | 5,303,060 | 4,167,832 | 4,527,594 |
| Tin | 1,121,836 | 1,275,718 | 1,192,735 | 613,952 | 534,074 |
| High Grade Primary Aluminum Options | 1,030,703 | 1,241,596 | 1,231,794 | 900,266 | |
| Aluminum Alloy Options | 242 | 96 | | | |
| Copper - Grade A Options | 1,623,575 | 2,212,821 | 2,155,587 | 1,156,352 | |
| Standard Lead Options | 30,992 | 22,262 | 45,769 | 17,299 | |
| Primary Nickel Options | 54,646 | 83,637 | 142,107 | 70,607 | |
| Special High Grade Zinc Options | 126,094 | 177,005 | 253,782 | 163,475 | |
| Tin Options | 8,925 | 15,532 | 26,487 | 10,638 | |
| **Total** | **47,487,007** | **47,150,330** | **47,687,717** | **35,289,932** | **24,736,920** |

# Volume Worldwide

## Manila International Futures Exchange(MIFE), Philippines/3

| | 1996 | 1995 | 1994 | 1993 | 1992 |
|---|---|---|---|---|---|
| Copra | 38,482 | 82,258 | 544,992 | | |
| Sugar | 37,358 | 115,404 | 496,686 | | |
| Coffee | 35,052 | 132,272 | 516,010 | | |
| Soybean | 40,158 | 86,664 | 615,968 | | |
| Dry Cocoon | 42,758 | 106,228 | 524,544 | | |
| US Dollar - Deutschemark | 12,084 | 95,554 | 43,280 | | |
| US Dollar - Yen | 42,812 | 180,200 | 163,542 | | |
| British Pound - US Dollar | 7,610 | 54,892 | 97,004 | | |
| US Dollar - Swiss Franc | 28,350 | 98,772 | 79,840 | | |
| Interest Rate | | | 7,672 | | |
| US Dollar - Peso | | | 2,356 | | |
| **Total** | **284,664** | **952,244** | **3,091,894** | | |

## Marche a Terme International de France (MATIF), France

| | 1996 | 1995 | 1994 | 1993 | 1992 |
|---|---|---|---|---|---|
| CAC 40 Index | 5,853,172 | 6,549,953 | 7,464,449 | 5,908,739 | 3,601,476 |
| ECU Bond | 579,493 | 657,152 | 618,715 | 873,002 | 1,354,012 |
| Notional Bond | 35,321,843 | 33,610,221 | 50,153,150 | 36,804,824 | 31,062,844 |
| 3 Month Pibor | 14,133,278 | 15,488,076 | 13,176,354 | 11,863,798 | 6,436,765 |
| Potatoes | 11,663 | 29,619 | 33,302 | 11,029 | 10,437 |
| Sugar | 193,024 | 305,598 | 297,940 | 262,940 | 218,250 |
| Wheat | 7,236 | | | | |
| Rapeseed | 60,148 | 51,135 | 7,026 | | |
| French Treasury Bond | | | | 29,213 | |
| French Medium Term | | | 63 | 99,260 | |
| Coffee | | | 170 | 490 | 608 |
| Notional Bond Options | 8,894,196 | 9,517,932 | 18,024,502 | 11,572,671 | 10,047,391 |
| 3 Month Pibor Options | 3,107,113 | 4,615,434 | 3,361,277 | 4,830,198 | 2,659,534 |
| U.S. Dollar/French Franc Options | 32,364 | 67,286 | 75,436 | | |
| U.S. Dollar/Deutschemark Options | 31,637 | 116,127 | 225,497 | | |
| Sterling/Deutschemark Options | 3,244 | 35,734 | | | |
| Deutschemark/Italian Lira Options | 12,652 | 11,249 | | | |
| Deutschemark/French Franc Options | 46,751 | 34,491 | | | |
| Sugar Options | 5,424 | 505 | | | |
| ECU Bond Options | | | 790 | 7,797 | 82,820 |
| **Total** | **68,293,238** | **71,090,512** | **93,438,671** | **72,263,961** | **55,474,137** |

## MEFF RENTA FIJA (RF), Spain

| | 1996 | 1995 | 1994 | 1993 | 1992 |
|---|---|---|---|---|---|
| 90 Day MIBOR Plus | 1,275,222 | 302,681 | | | |
| 360 Day MIBOR Plus | 61,702 | 15,403 | | | |
| German Diff | 123,311 | | | | |
| French Diff | 5,229 | | | | |
| Italian Diff | 8,269 | | | | |
| 3 Year Notional Bond | 212,933 | 456 | 12,112 | 15,585 | 235,804 |
| 10 Year Notional Bond | 18,535,566 | 13,035,805 | 13,191,835 | 4,537,765 | 770,480 |
| 90 Day MIBOR | 7 | 3,153,112 | 3,730,008 | 2,319,132 | 747,191 |
| 360 Day MIBOR | | 177,964 | 446,160 | 44,130 | |
| 5 Year Notional Bond | | | | | 8,291 |
| Spanish Peseta/U.S. Dollar | | | | 26 | 12,215 |
| Spanish Peseta/Deutschemark | | | | 3,172 | 54,635 |
| 3 Year Notional Bond Options | 11,440 | | | | 41,900 |
| 10 Year Notional Bond Options | 3,372,235 | 1,888,547 | 2,047,754 | 1,087,972 | 339,877 |
| 90 Day MIBOR Plus Options | 249,806 | 58,297 | | | |
| 90 Day MIBOR Options | 75,288 | 450,310 | 307,460 | 139,550 | 8,300 |
| **Total** | **23,931,008** | **19,082,575** | **19,735,329** | **8,147,332** | **2,218,693** |

## MEFF RENTA VARIABLE (RV), Spain

| | 1996 | 1995 | 1994 | 1993 | 1992 |
|---|---|---|---|---|---|
| IBEX 35 | 29,243,670 | 28,096,699 | 27,020,886 | 10,856,012 | |
| IBEX 35 Options | 8,639,605 | 8,179,599 | 7,541,551 | 3,563,485 | |
| **Total** | **37,883,275** | **36,276,298** | **34,562,437** | **14,419,497** | |

## Mercato Italiano Futures (MIF), Italy

| | 1996 | 1995 | 1994 | 1993 | 1992 |
|---|---|---|---|---|---|
| 10 Year BTP | 2,240,085 | 2,636,161 | 3,702,802 | 2,776,992 | |
| 5 Year BTP | 68,697 | 166,002 | 667,115 | 1,637,256 | |
| 10 Year BTP Options | 130,307 | 113,665 | | | |
| **Total** | **2,439,089** | **2,915,828** | **4,369,917** | **4,414,248** | |

## Marche des Options Negociables de Paris (MONEP), France

| | 1996 | 1995 | 1994 | 1993 | 1992 |
|---|---|---|---|---|---|
| CAC 40 Index (Short Term) Options | 2,465,497 | 2,425,363 | 2,755,289 | 2,451,512 | 3,170,782 |
| CAC 40 Index (Long Term) Options | 2,126,001 | 3,013,926 | 2,996,181 | 1,760,763 | 547,495 |
| **Total** | **4,591,498** | **5,439,289** | **5,751,470** | **4,212,275** | **3,718,277** |

## Montreal Exchange (ME), Canada

| | 1996 | 1995 | 1994 | 1993 | 1992 |
|---|---|---|---|---|---|
| 3 Month Bankers Acceptance | 2,415,563 | 2,326,709 | 1,918,976 | 724,158 | 419,765 |
| 1 Month Bankers Acceptance | 314 | 7,225 | 12,172 | 24,552 | 23,502 |
| 10 Year Canadian Government Bond | 1,072,111 | 1,026,854 | 1,496,543 | 895,047 | 515,732 |
| 5 Year Canadian Government Bond | 35,649 | 63,842 | | | |
| 5 Year Canadian Government Bond Options | 703 | 2,191 | 6,363 | 9,489 | 5,195 |
| 3 Month Bankers Acceptance Options | 75,224 | 51,855 | 29,464 | | |
| 10 Year Canadian Government Bond Options | 30,159 | 40,147 | 51,305 | 61,455 | 50,955 |
| Equity Options | | | | | 669,190 |
| **Total** | **3,629,723** | **3,518,823** | **3,514,823** | **1,714,701** | **1,684,339** |

## New Zealand Futures Exchange (NZFOE), New Zealand

| | 1996 | 1995 | 1994 | 1993 | 1992 |
|---|---|---|---|---|---|
| 3 Year Government Stock | 14,356 | 26,912 | 101,229 | 74,128 | |
| 10 Year Government Stock | 8,315 | 8,456 | 42,541 | 20,996 | 5 |
| 90 Day Bank Bill | 655,270 | 478,806 | 608,460 | 463,141 | 393,172 |
| NZSE-10 Captial Share Price Index | 5,686 | 2,971 | | | |
| 5 Year Government Stock | | | | 50,836 | 209,232 |
| U.S. Dollar | | 19 | 21 | 9 | 6 |
| New Zealand Wool | | | | | 56 |
| NZSE-40 Captial Share Price Index | | 3,936 | 7,397 | 3,633 | 4,620 |
| 3 Year Government Stock Options | 30 | | 80 | 1,000 | |
| 90 Day Bank Bill Options | 8,845 | 16,321 | 6,870 | 8,193 | 38,258 |
| NZSE-10 Captial Share Price Index Options | 23 | 24 | | | |
| 5 Year Government Stock Options | | | | 1,652 | 28,048 |
| 10 Year Government Stock Options | | 200 | 4,200 | 120 | |
| NZSE-40 Captial Share Price Index Options | | 2,194 | 1,985 | 596 | 760 |
| **Total** | **692,525** | **539,839** | **772,783** | **624,304** | **674,157** |

## Oslo Stock Exchange (OSE), Norway

| | 1996 | 1995 | 1994 | 1993 | 1992 |
|---|---|---|---|---|---|
| OBr10 | 55,376 | 52,001 | 165,443 | 28,245 | |
| OBr5 | 50,673 | 49,187 | 43,745 | | |
| OBX | 36,366 | 18,615 | 4,151 | 16,650 | |
| OBX Options | 512,460 | 481,865 | 422,430 | 385,540 | |
| OBX Long Options | | 12,100 | 1,370 | | |
| **Total** | **654,875** | **613,768** | **637,139** | **430,435** | |

## Swiss Options and Financial Futures Exchange (SOFFEX), Switzerland

| | 1996 | 1995 | 1994 | 1993 | 1992 |
|---|---|---|---|---|---|
| Swiss Market Index | 1,720,053 | 1,457,108 | 1,694,260 | 914,021 | 847,157 |
| Swiss Government Bond (CONF) | 913,466 | 955,895 | 949,657 | 270,653 | 233,761 |
| Medium Term Swiss Government Bond (COMI) | 42,007 | | | | |
| EUROTOP 100 Index | | | | | 4 |
| 3 Month Euro Swiss Franc | | | | 353 | 184,084 |
| 5 Year Swiss Franc | | | | 28,548 | 199,829 |
| Swiss Market Index Options | 8,018,333 | 6,027,308 | 6,678,779 | 5,595,388 | 7,793,949 |
| Swiss Government Bond Options | 26,446 | 35,695 | 49,749 | | |
| EUROTOP 100 Index Options | | | | | 75 |
| **Total** | **10,720,305** | **8,476,006** | **9,372,445** | **6,808,963** | **9,258,859** |

# Volume Worldwide

## Singapore International Monetary Exchange (SIMEX), Singapore

| | 1996 | 1995 | 1994 | 1993 | 1992 |
|---|---|---|---|---|---|
| Eurodollar | 8,184,887 | 8,394,933 | 8,687,969 | 5,535,806 | 5,617,972 |
| Deutschemark | | 66 | 8,727 | 16,368 | 44,990 |
| Japanese Yen | | 106 | 16,825 | 21,009 | 19,921 |
| British Pound | | 8 | 1,741 | 3,912 | 4,111 |
| Deferred Spot US$/JY | 86,833 | 58,922 | 68,605 | 13,182 | |
| Deferred Spot US$/DM | 70,651 | 109,181 | 131,210 | 26,298 | |
| Nikkei 225 Index | 4,887,912 | 6,456,984 | 5,801,098 | 5,162,199 | 3,349,243 |
| Nikkei 300 Index | 156,482 | 174,234 | | | |
| Gold | 133 | | 26 | 436 | 667 |
| High Sulfur Fuel Oil | 42 | 19,421 | 171,896 | 300,201 | 278,205 |
| Brent Crude | 63,535 | 73,445 | | | |
| Euroyen | 8,162,548 | 6,549,295 | 6,820,673 | 3,532,998 | 2,472,931 |
| Euromark | | 1,800 | 231,068 | 23,127 | 4,940 |
| Japanese Government Bond | 138,471 | 297,426 | 443,564 | 29,253 | |
| MSCI Hong Kong Index | | | 317 | 80,245 | |
| Gasoil | | | | 23,288 | 25,806 |
| Eurodollar Options | 3,319 | 5,247 | 13,545 | 6,525 | 11,534 |
| Euroyen Options | 208,363 | 128,944 | 126,280 | 57,395 | 80,815 |
| Japanese Government Bond Options | 18,709 | 35,071 | 39,808 | | |
| Nikkei 225 Index Options | 58,660 | 1,943,096 | 1,496,922 | 897,545 | 269,039 |
| Nikkei 300 Index Options | | 3,160 | | | |
| **Total** | **22,568,545** | **24,251,339** | **24,060,274** | **15,729,787** | **12,180,174** |

## South African Futures Exchange (SAFEX), Africa

| | 1996 | 1995 | 1994 | 1993 | 1992 |
|---|---|---|---|---|---|
| All Share Index | 1,943,973 | 1,816,846 | 2,185,672 | 1,670,540 | |
| Industrial Index | 1,493,987 | 1,030,714 | 920,786 | 422,203 | |
| Financial Index | 10,080 | 4,290 | | | |
| Gold Index | 603,205 | 656,696 | 933,591 | 895,772 | |
| Krugerrand | 4,586 | 5,901 | 5,664 | | |
| 3 Month Bank Bill | 1,360 | 5,154 | 3,901 | 2,135 | |
| R 150 | 39,640 | 30,472 | 1,750 | | |
| R 153 | 101 | | | | |
| E168 (Long Bond) | | 530 | 8,495 | 6,903 | |
| All Share Index Options | 3,759,424 | 2,932,564 | 2,804,855 | 1,236,263 | |
| Industrial Index Options | 912,482 | 481,053 | 377,593 | 148,101 | |
| Financial Index Options | 7,948 | | | | |
| Gold Index Options | 491,075 | 195,720 | 132,230 | 102,136 | |
| Krugerrand Options | | 203 | 3,300 | | |
| R 150 Options | 26,464 | 29,683 | | | |
| R 153 Options | 2,060 | | | | |
| 3 Month Bank Bill Options | | 820 | | | |
| E168 (Long Bond) Options | | 60 | 100 | 920 | |
| **Total** | **9,296,745** | **7,218,914** | **7,377,937** | **4,484,973** | |

## OM Stockholm (OMS), Sweden

| | 1996 | 1995 | 1994 | 1993 | 1992 |
|---|---|---|---|---|---|
| Interest Rate | 15,642,920 | 10,949,860 | 14,123,881 | 11,272,285 | 7,420,164 |
| Interest Rate Index | 3,434 | | | | |
| OMSX Index | 130 | | | | |
| OMX Index | 1,625,391 | 1,593,408 | 1,706,984 | 627,706 | 450,031 |
| Financial Times Index (FT-SE Mid 250) | | | 9,565 | | |
| Interest Rate Options | 32,825 | 42,783 | 86,410 | | 19,584 |
| OMSX Index Options | 274 | | | | |
| OMX Index Options | 5,399,227 | 6,067,268 | 5,812,435 | 4,073,852 | 5,605,059 |
| Financial Times Index (FT-SE Mid 250) Options | | | 2,140 | | |
| **Total** | **22,704,201** | **18,653,319** | **21,741,415** | **15,973,843** | **17,147,096** |

## Sydney Futures Exchange (SFE), Australia

| | 1996 | 1995 | 1994 | 1993 | 1992 |
|---|---|---|---|---|---|
| All Ordinaries Share Price Index | 2,675,754 | 2,476,331 | 2,552,546 | 980,866 | 342,013 |
| 90 Day Bank Bills | 4,977,945 | 6,172,512 | 9,369,008 | 6,415,394 | 5,697,786 |
| 3 Year Treasury Bonds | 9,209,228 | 8,820,651 | 9,709,791 | 6,939,811 | 5,434,795 |
| 10 Year Treasury Bonds | 5,315,845 | 5,740,870 | 6,814,733 | 4,781,905 | 4,253,374 |
| Wool (Cash Set) | | 1,221 | 4,833 | 3,271 | 1,259 |
| Wheat | 6,482 | | | | |
| Greasy Wool | 7,554 | 4,799 | | | |
| Fifty Leaders Share Price Index | | | 1 | 1 | 203 |
| All Ordinaries Share Price Index Options | 896,880 | 652,607 | 833,667 | 466,896 | 154,149 |
| 90 Day Bank Bills Options | 911,005 | 712,834 | 943,749 | 663,317 | 610,458 |
| 3 Year Treasury Bond Options | 457,808 | 426,836 | 507,252 | 514,539 | 317,356 |
| Overnight 3 Year Treasury Bond Options | 42,461 | 7,443 | 2,078 | 320 | |
| 10 Year Treasury Bonds Options | 845,571 | 580,091 | 800,263 | 712,686 | 745,994 |
| Overnight 10 Year Treasury Bond Options | 128,426 | 24,419 | 18,656 | 2,082 | |
| Wheat Options | 788 | | | | |
| Greasy Wool Options | 41 | | | | |
| **Total** | **25,475,788** | **25,620,614** | **31,556,584** | **21,481,096** | **17,557,685** |

## Toronto Futures Exchange (TFE), Canada

| | 1996 | 1995 | 1994 | 1993 | 1992 |
|---|---|---|---|---|---|
| TSE 35 Index | 155,652 | 110,011 | 104,209 | 69,058 | 59,049 |
| TSE 100 Index | 8,135 | 2,963 | 10,819 | | |
| TSE 35 Options | 254,199 | 337,764 | 247,482 | 221,232 | 302,444 |
| TSE 100 Index Options | 845 | 7,824 | 13,200 | | |
| Silver Options | | 656 | 8,300 | 4,583 | 331 |
| **Total** | **418,831** | **459,218** | **384,010** | **294,877** | **361,824** |

## Winnipeg Commodity Exchange (WCE), Canada

| | 1996 | 1995 | 1994 | 1993 | 1992 |
|---|---|---|---|---|---|
| Wheat | 206,120 | 155,699 | 191,696 | 210,074 | 199,060 |
| Oats | 3,496 | 32,761 | 52,550 | 59,244 | 45,913 |
| Canadian Barley | | 18,523 | 31,600 | 4,150 | |
| Rye | | 104 | 1,022 | 7,829 | 26,273 |
| Flaxseed | 99,889 | 132,525 | 105,338 | 104,110 | 144,581 |
| Canola (Rapeseed) | 1,345,952 | 1,075,683 | 1,167,447 | 972,354 | 839,715 |
| Feed Peas | 17,979 | 7,802 | | | |
| Western Barley | 334,809 | 172,733 | 115,376 | 40,248 | 22,655 |
| Thunder Bay Barley | | | 5,378 | 63,643 | 88,150 |
| Wheat Options | 355 | 734 | 3,145 | 5,274 | 2,225 |
| Flaxseed Options | 466 | 1,567 | 1,692 | 4,907 | |
| Canadian Barley Options | | 435 | | 80 | |
| Western Barley Options | 3,166 | 274 | 1,716 | 10 | |
| Canola Options | 61,233 | 71,197 | 82,565 | 44,121 | 50,262 |
| **Total** | **2,073,465** | **1,670,037** | **1,759,525** | **1,615,044** | **1,418,834** |

## Hong Kong Futures Exchange (HKFE), Hong Kong

| | 1996 | 1995 | 1994 | 1993 | 1992 |
|---|---|---|---|---|---|
| Hang Seng Index | 4,656,084 | 4,546,613 | 4,192,574 | 2,415,739 | 1,089,037 |
| Deutschemark Rolling Forex | 76,075 | 12,633 | | | |
| Japanes Yen Rolling Forex | 106,888 | 8,688 | | | |
| British Pound Rolling Forex | 12,392 | | | | |
| 3 Month HIBOR | | | | | 205 |
| Soybeans | | | | | 4,688 |
| Sugar | | | | | 8,598 |
| Gold | | | 490 | 972 | 1,000 |
| Hang Seng Comm. & Ind. Sub-Index | | | | | 205 |
| Hang Seng Properties Sub-Index | | | | | 205 |
| Hang Seng Finance Sub-Index | | | | | 205 |
| Hang Seng Utilities Sub-Index | | | | | 205 |
| Hang Seng Index Options | 1,093,871 | 645,538 | 606,674 | 282,283 | |
| **Total** | **5,945,310** | **5,213,472** | **4,799,738** | **2,698,994** | **1,104,348** |

# Volume Worldwide

## Hokkaido Grain Exchange (HGE), Japan/4

| | 1996 | 1995 | 1994 | 1993 | 1992 |
|---|---|---|---|---|---|
| Red Beans | | 75,501 | 241,555 | 182,611 | 220,096 |
| Imported Soybeans | | 24,912 | 89,916 | 106,152 | 255,198 |
| Domestic Soybeans | | | 18 | 24 | 24 |
| White Beans | | | 18 | 24 | 24 |
| Potato Starch | | | 18 | 24 | 24 |
| **Total** | | **100,413** | **331,525** | **288,835** | **475,366** |

## Kanmon Commodity Exchange (KCE), Japan

| | 1996 | 1995 | 1994 | 1993 | 1992 |
|---|---|---|---|---|---|
| Red Beans | 118,438 | 237,745 | 492,294 | 579,751 | 488,167 |
| Imported Soybeans | 496,376 | 130,520 | 213,271 | 486,850 | 438,817 |
| Refined Sugar | 1,438 | 1,449 | 1,432 | 1,437 | 1,443 |
| Corn | 4,346,586 | 2,890,258 | 1,709,248 | 1,077,057 | 270,809 |
| **Total** | **4,962,838** | **3,259,972** | **2,416,245** | **2,145,095** | **1,199,236** |

## Kansai Agricultural Commodities Exchange (KANEX), Japan

| | 1996 | 1995 | 1994 | 1993 | 1992 |
|---|---|---|---|---|---|
| Red Beans | 877,474 | 1,723,230 | 2,931,256 | 3,092,743 | 4,051,785 |
| Imported Soybeans | 2,656,174 | 1,695,414 | 1,298,180 | 2,113,812 | 2,340,144 |
| Refined Sugar | 2,876 | 2,886 | 2,864 | 2,874 | 2,880 |
| Raw Sugar | 577,641 | 730,582 | 664,683 | 1,063,480 | 648,833 |
| Raw Sugar Options | 71,145 | 79,365 | 63,789 | 26,793 | 95,802 |
| **Total** | **4,185,310** | **4,231,477** | **4,960,772** | **6,299,702** | **7,139,444** |

## KOBE Raw Silk Exchange (KSE), Japan

| | 1996 | 1995 | 1994 | 1993 | 1992 |
|---|---|---|---|---|---|
| Raw Silk | 458,243 | 591,922 | 695,172 | 687,723 | 195,037 |
| **Total** | **458,243** | **591,922** | **695,172** | **687,723** | **195,037** |

## KOBE Rubber Exchange (KRE), Japan

| | 1996 | 1995 | 1994 | 1993 | 1992 |
|---|---|---|---|---|---|
| Rubber (RSS3) | 2,232,827 | 3,810,938 | 2,933,883 | 1,275,051 | 791,948 |
| Rubber Index | 373,879 | 173,409 | | | |
| **Total** | **2,606,706** | **3,984,347** | **2,933,883** | **1,275,051** | **791,948** |

## Maebashi Dried Cocoon Exchange (MDCE), Japan

| | 1996 | 1995 | 1994 | 1993 | 1992 |
|---|---|---|---|---|---|
| Dried Cocoon | 864,703 | 443,411 | 475,978 | 1,782,394 | 492,494 |
| **Total** | **864,703** | **443,411** | **475,978** | **1,782,394** | **492,494** |

## Nagoya Grain & Sugar Exchange, Japan

| | 1996 | 1995 | 1994 | 1993 | 1992 |
|---|---|---|---|---|---|
| Red Beans | 287,220 | 502,369 | 919,371 | 1,217,337 | 1,376,017 |
| Sweet Potato Starch | 48 | 48 | 48 | 48 | 48 |
| Imported Soybeans | 620,703 | 307,451 | 177,513 | 287,612 | 348,733 |
| Refined Sugar | 1,438 | 1,449 | 1,789 | 2,874 | 2,886 |
| **Total** | **909,409** | **811,317** | **1,098,721** | **1,507,871** | **1,727,684** |

## Nagoya Textile Exchange, Japan

| | 1996 | 1995 | 1994 | 1993 | 1992 |
|---|---|---|---|---|---|
| Cotton Yarn (40S) | 296,455 | 755,844 | 1,100,388 | 822,683 | 1,145,017 |
| Staple Fiber Yarn (Dull) | 10,001 | 9,967 | 13,114 | 18,279 | 29,614 |
| Wool Yarn | 27,277 | 53,811 | 87,240 | 79,114 | 123,570 |
| **Total** | **333,733** | **819,622** | **1,200,742** | **920,076** | **1,298,201** |

## Osaka Securities Exchange(OSE), Japan

| | 1996 | 1995 | 1994 | 1993 | 1992 |
|---|---|---|---|---|---|
| Nikkei 225 Index | 7,043,977 | 7,220,900 | 6,208,754 | 8,461,458 | 11,927,329 |
| Nikkei 300 Index | 1,872,983 | 2,318,652 | 4,184,480 | | |
| Nikkei 225 Index Options | 3,924,543 | 5,174,571 | 4,273,641 | 6,090,375 | 9,256,981 |
| Nikkei 300 Index Options | 44,254 | 122,084 | 269,067 | | |
| **Total** | **12,885,757** | **14,836,207** | **14,935,942** | **14,551,833** | **21,184,310** |

## Osaka Textile Exchange (OTE), Japan

| | 1996 | 1995 | 1994 | 1993 | 1992 |
|---|---|---|---|---|---|
| Staple Fiber Yarn (Bright) | 3,109 | 4,128 | 3,507 | 2,928 | 2,940 |
| Staple Fiber Yarn (Dull) | 2,928 | 2,940 | 2,910 | 2,928 | 4,715 |
| Wool Yarn | 18,624 | 64,073 | 266,974 | 524,699 | 258,487 |
| Cotton Yarn (20S) | 1,109,607 | 2,151,580 | 2,000,530 | 648,345 | 652,535 |
| Cotton Yarn (40S) | 254,828 | 659,110 | 833,307 | 574,724 | 644,897 |
| **Total** | **1,389,096** | **2,881,831** | **3,107,228** | **1,753,624** | **1,563,574** |

## Tokyo Commodity Exchange (TOCOM), Japan

| | 1996 | 1995 | 1994 | 1993 | 1992 |
|---|---|---|---|---|---|
| Gold | 9,510,941 | 10,945,134 | 12,481,095 | 8,764,441 | 4,193,775 |
| Silver | 752,995 | 1,440,297 | 1,042,185 | 661,452 | 231,864 |
| Platinum | 6,895,464 | 5,975,872 | 4,551,406 | 4,984,480 | 4,631,724 |
| Palladium | 434,163 | 629,034 | 774,284 | 2,275,843 | 404,091 |
| Rubber | 9,085,709 | 14,287,783 | 9,021,881 | 2,973,241 | 1,726,487 |
| Cotton Yarn | 874,052 | 1,838,448 | 2,573,963 | 1,865,469 | 2,330,029 |
| Woolen Yarn | 6,830 | 8,859 | 36,499 | 32,869 | 67,409 |
| **Total** | **27,560,154** | **35,125,427** | **30,481,313** | **21,557,795** | **13,585,379** |

## Tokyo Grain Exchange (TGE), Japan

| | 1996 | 1995 | 1994 | 1993 | 1992 |
|---|---|---|---|---|---|
| American Soybeans | 7,120,741 | 2,699,926 | 2,559,288 | 3,750,291 | 4,000,410 |
| Red Beans | 2,847,511 | 3,384,267 | 5,122,015 | 6,353,667 | 7,804,868 |
| Corn | 16,034,716 | 6,899,593 | 3,053,244 | 1,263,357 | 556,501 |
| Refined Sugar | 2,876 | 2,898 | 2,864 | 2,874 | 2,886 |
| Raw Sugar | 1,045,438 | 1,291,441 | 1,220,931 | 2,218,688 | 1,279,354 |
| Chinese Soybeans | | | | | 208 |
| American Soybean Options | 275,269 | 206,993 | 96,505 | 60,420 | 54,684 |
| Raw Sugar Options | 182,724 | 158,044 | 67,636 | 38,450 | 43,203 |
| **Total** | **27,509,275** | **14,643,162** | **12,122,483** | **13,687,747** | **13,742,114** |

## Tokyo International Financial Futures Exchange (TIFFE), Japan

| | 1996 | 1995 | 1994 | 1993 | 1992 |
|---|---|---|---|---|---|
| 3 Month Euroyen | 29,334,830 | 36,329,959 | 37,425,846 | 23,386,958 | 14,959,373 |
| 1 Year Euroyen | 23,200 | 25,300 | 25,100 | 4,434 | 9,379 |
| U.S. Dollar /Japanese Yen | 44,194 | 5,037 | 13,770 | 48,241 | 86,008 |
| Euroyen Options | 567,793 | 361,920 | 570,237 | 686,514 | 485,727 |
| **Total** | **29,970,017** | **36,722,216** | **38,034,953** | **24,126,147** | **15,540,487** |

## Tokyo Stock Exchange (TSE), Japan

| | 1996 | 1995 | 1994 | 1993 | 1992 |
|---|---|---|---|---|---|
| 5 Year Government Yen Bond | 220,955 | | | | |
| 10 Year Government Yen Bond | 12,450,925 | 14,010,374 | 12,999,698 | 15,162,159 | 11,868,414 |
| 20 Year Government Yen Bond | 2,242 | 2,734 | 3,194 | 3,106 | 3,972 |
| TOPIX Stock Index | 2,857,272 | 2,745,614 | 2,623,067 | 2,156,960 | 1,358,723 |
| 30 Year U.S. T-Bond | 31,030 | 102,340 | 115,750 | 112,600 | 118,491 |
| TOPIX Options | 13,444 | 16,742 | 20,078 | 37,831 | 48,576 |
| 10 Year Government Yen Bond Options | 1,975,274 | 2,017,031 | 1,691,834 | 1,506,836 | 1,140,541 |
| **Total** | **17,551,142** | **16,877,804** | **15,761,787** | **17,472,656** | **13,398,176** |

## Toyahashi Dried Cocoon Exchange, Japan

| | 1996 | 1995 | 1994 | 1993 | 1992 |
|---|---|---|---|---|---|
| Dried Cocoon | 1,202,536 | 488,709 | 488,558 | 1,066,374 | 519,045 |
| **Total** | **1,202,536** | **488,709** | **488,558** | **1,066,374** | **519,045** |

## Yokohama Raw Silk Exchange, Japan

| | 1996 | 1995 | 1994 | 1993 | 1992 |
|---|---|---|---|---|---|
| Raw Silk | 1,083,386 | 1,256,094 | 998,686 | 1,512,132 | 410,028 |
| **Total** | **1,083,386** | **1,256,094** | **998,686** | **1,512,132** | **410,028** |

1/ Exchange has gone into liquidation.
2/ LCE merged with LIFFE in 1996. LCE contracts will be listed under LIFFE in 1997.
3/ Exchange no longer actively trades.
4/ Merged with TGE in 1995.

# Conversion Factors

## Commonly Used Agricultural Weights and Measurements

**Bushel Weights:**
wheat and soybeans = 60 lbs.
corn, sorghum and rye = 56 lbs.
barley grain = 48 lbs.
barley malt = 34 lbs.
oats = 32 lbs.

**Bushels to tonnes:**
wheat and soybeans = bushels X 0.027216
barley grain = bushels X 0.021772
corn, sorghum and rye = bushels X 0.0254
oats = bushels X 0.014515

**1 tonne (metric ton) equals:**
2204.622 lbs.
1,000 kilograms
22.046 hundredweight
10 quintals

**1 tonne (metric ton) equals:**
36.7437 bushels of wheat or soybeans
39.3679 bushels of corn, sorghum or rye
45.9296 bushels of barley grain
68.8944 bushels of oats
4.5929 cotton bales (the statistical bale used by the USDA and ICAC contains a net weight of 480 pounds of lint)

**Area Measurements:**
1 acre = 43,560 square feet = 0.040694 hectare
1 hectare = 2.4710 acres = 10,000 square meters
640 acres = 1 square mile = 259 hectares

**Yields:**
wheat: bushels per acre X 0.6725 = quintals per hectare
rye, corn: bushels per acre X 0.6277 = quintals per hectare
barley grain: bushels per acre X 0.538 = quintals per hectare
oats: bushels per acre X 0.3587 = quintals per hectare

## Commonly Used Weights

The troy, avoirdupois and apothecaries' grains are identical in U.S. and British weight systems, equal to 0.0648 gram in the metric system. One avoirdupois ounce equals 437.5 grains. The troy and apothecaries' ounces equal 480 grains, and their pounds contain 12 ounces.

**Troy weights and conversions:**
24 grains = 1 pennyweight
20 pennyweights = 1 ounce
12 ounces = 1 pound
1 troy ounce = 31.103 grams
1 troy ounce = 0.0311033 kilogram
1 troy pound = 0.37224 kilogram
1 kilogram = 32.1507 troy ounces
1 tonne = 32,151 troy ounces

**Avoirdupois weights and conversions:**
27 11/32 grains = 1 dram
16 drams = 1 ounce
16 ounces = 1 lb.
1 lb. = 7,000 grains
14 lbs. = 1 stone (British)
100 lbs. = 1 hundredweight (U.S.)
112 lbs. = 8 stone = 1 hundredweight (British)
2,000 lbs. = 1 short ton (U.S. ton)
2,240 lbs. = 1 long ton (British ton)
160 stone = 1 long ton
20 hundredweight = 1 ton
1 lb. = 0.4536 kilogram
1 hundredweight (cwt.) = 45.359 kilograms
1 short ton = 907.18 kilograms
1 long ton = 1,016.05 kilograms

**Metric weights and conversions:**
1,000 grams = 1 kilogram
100 kilograms = 1 quintal
1 tonne = 1,000 kilograms = 10 quintals
1 kilogram = 2.204622 lbs.
1 quintal = 220.462 lbs.
1 tonne = 2204.6 lbs.
1 tonne = 1.102 short tons
1 tonne = 0.9842 long ton

**U.S. dry volumes and conversions:**
1 pint = 33.6 cubic inches = 0.5506 liter
2 pints = 1 quart = 1.1012 liters
8 quarts = 1 peck = 8.8098 liters
4 pecks = 1 bushel = 35.2391 liters
1 cubic foot = 28.3169 liters

**U.S. liquid volumes and conversions:**
1 ounce = 1.8047 cubic inches = 29.6 milliliters
1 cup = 8 ounces = 0.24 liter = 237 milliliters
1 pint = 16 ounces = 0.48 liter = 473 milliliters
1 quart = 2 pints = 0.946 liter = 946 milliliters
1 gallon = 4 quarts = 231 cubic inches = 3.785 liters
1 milliliter = 0.033815 fluid ounce
1 liter = 1.0567 quarts = 1,000 milliliters
1 liter = 33.815 fluid ounces
1 imperial gallon = 277.42 cubic inches = 1.2 U.S. gallons = 4.546 liters

# ENERGY CONVERSION FACTORS

**U.S. Crude Oll (average gravity)**
1 U.S. barrel = 42 U.S. gallons
1 short ton = 6.65 barrels
1 tonne = 7.33 barrels

**Barrels per tonne for various origins**

| | |
|---|---|
| Abu Dhabi | 7.624 |
| Algeria | 7.661 |
| Angola | 7.206 |
| Australia | 7.775 |
| Bahrain | 7.335 |
| Brunei | 7.334 |
| Canada | 7.428 |
| Dubai | 7.295 |
| Ecuador | 7.58 |
| Gabon | 7.245 |
| Indonesia | 7.348 |
| Iran | 7.37 |
| Iraq | 7.453 |
| Kuwait | 7.261 |
| Libya | 7.615 |
| Mexico | 7.104 |
| Neutral Zone | 6.825 |
| Nigeria | 7.41 |
| Norway | 7.444 |
| Oman | 7.39 |
| Qatar | 7.573 |
| Romania | 7.453 |
| Saudi Arabia | 7.338 |
| Trinidad | 6.989 |
| Tunisia | 7.709 |
| United Arab Emirates | 7.522 |
| United Kingdom | 7.279 |
| United States | 7.418 |
| Former Soviet Union | 7.35 |
| Venezuela | 7.005 |
| Zaire | 7.206 |

**Barrels per tonne of refined products:**

| | |
|---|---|
| aviation gasoline | 8.9 |
| motor gasoline | 8.5 |
| kerosene | 7.75 |
| jet fuel | 8 |
| distillate, including diesel | 7.46 |

(continued above)

| | |
|---|---|
| residual feul oil | 6.45 |
| lubricating oil | 7 |
| grease | 6.3 |
| white spirits | 8.5 |
| paraffin oil | 7.14 |
| paraffin wax | 7.87 |
| petrolatum | 7.87 |
| asphalt and road oil | 6.06 |
| petroleum coke | 5.5 |
| bitumen | 6.06 |
| LPG | 11.6 |

**Approximate heat content of refined products:**
(Million Btu per barrel, 1 British thermal unit is the amount of heat required to raise the temperature of 1 pound of water 1 degree F.)

| **Petroleum Product** | **Heat Content** |
|---|---|
| asphalt | 6.636 |
| aviation gasoline | 5.048 |
| butane | 4.326 |
| distillate fuel oil | 5.825 |
| ethane | 3.082 |
| isobutane | 3.974 |
| jet fuel, kerosene | 5.67 |
| jet fuel, naptha | 5.355 |
| kerosene | 5.67 |
| lubricants | 6.065 |
| motor gasoline | 5.253 |
| natural gasoline | 4.62 |
| pentanes plus | 4.62 |

**Petrochemical feedstocks:**

| | |
|---|---|
| naptha less than 401*F | 5.248 |
| other oils equal to or greater than 401*F | 5.825 |
| still gas | 6 |
| petroleum coke | 6.024 |
| plant condensate | 5.418 |
| propane | 3.836 |
| residual fuel oil | 6.287 |
| special napthas | 5.248 |
| unfinished oils | 5.825 |
| unfractionated steam | 5.418 |
| waxes | 5.537 |

*Source: U.S. Department of Energy*

## Natural Gas Conversions

Although there are approximately 1,031 Btu in a cubic foot of gas, for most applications, the following conversions are sufficient:

| **Cubic Feet** | | | | | **MMBtu** |
|---|---|---|---|---|---|
| 1,000 | (one thousand cubic feet) | = | 1 Mcf | = | 1 |
| 1,000,000 | (one million cubic feet) | = | 1 MMcf | = | 1,000 |
| 10,000,000 | (ten million cubic feet) | = | 10 MMcf | = | 10,000 |
| 1,000,000,000 | (one billion cubic feet) | = | 1 Bcf | = | 1,000,000 |
| 1,000,000,000,000 | (one trillion cubic feet) | = | 1 Tcf | = | 1,000,000,000 |

# Cash Market Description for Monthly Charts

**Aluminum**
- Pig Ingots - New York from 1910 thru 1986
- Pig Ingots - Midwest from 11/14/86 to Date
- Cast Scrap - New York 1929 thru 1984
- Cast Scrap - Midwest (Chicago) 1985 to Date
- Clippings - New York 1929 thru 1984 (1950-1951 N/A)
- Clippings - Midwest (Chicago) 1985 to Date

**Barley**
- No. 2 Minneapolis 08/09 thru 06/25
- No. 3 Minneapolis (straight or better) 07/26 thru 06/76
- No. 2 Feed Minneapolis 07/26 thru 12/86
- No. 2 Feed Duluth 03/87 to Date

**Beef Steers**
- Chicago All Grades 1909 thru 1934
- Chicago Good 1935 thru 1939
- Chicago All Grades 1940 thru 1962
- Chicago Good - 1/2/48 to 12/31/64
- Chicago Choice - 1/2/65 to 7/30/71
- Omaha Choice Average - 8/2/71 to 8/25/87
- Texas-Oklahoma Cattle Average - 8/26/87 to Date

**Cocoa**
- Santos No. 4 NY - 1920 to 7/17/75
- Brazilian NY - 1/6/76 to Date
- Colombian Maniz NY - 1/2/48 to 7/6/53
- Colombian Medellin NY - 1/4/54 to 6/8/76; 10/8/76 to 12/27/77
- Colombian NY - 1/10/78 to 12/30/82; 1/2/83 to 7/1/83; 11/14/83 to 2/4/85; 8/29/85 to 10/15/87; 3/1/90 to Date

**Copper**
- Electrolytic NY - 1910 thru 1983
- Electrolytic US - 1984 to Date
- Scrap No. 1 NY - 1927 thru 1955
- Scrap No. 2 NY - 1956 thru 04/88
- Scrap No. 2 Chicago - 5/88 to Date

**Corn**
- No. 3 Yellow Chicago - 1901 to 04/47
- No. 2 Yellow Chicago - 5/5/47 to 3/28/82
- No. 2 Yellow Central Illinois - 3/29/82 to Date

**Corn Oil**
- FOB Midwestern Mills (Decatur) - 07/24 thru 06/85
- Wet Mill at Chicago - 10/85 to Date

**Corporate AAA Bonds**
- Federal Reserve Bank of St. Louis - 1919 to Date

**Cotton**
- 7/8" at Designated Mkts Middling - 08/15 thru 07/30
- 15/16" at Designated Mkts Middling - 08/30 thru 07/73
- 11/16" at Designated Mkts Middling - 08/73 to Date

**Cottonseed Meal**
- 36% Protein Memphis - 08/10 thru 09/20
- 41% Protein Memphis - 10/21 thru 09/46
- 41% Protein (Expeller) Memphis - 10/46 thru 12/81
- 41% Protein (Solvent) Memphis - 01/82 to Date

**Cottonseed Oil**
- FOB Southeastern Mills - 08/90 to Date

**Discount Rate**
- Federal Reserve Bank of St. Louis - 1934 to Date

**Eggs**
- NY Fresh Firsts - 1910 thru 1926
- Chicago Fresh Firsts - 1927 thru 06/43
- Chicago US Standards - 07/43 thru 1947
- Chicago Large - 1948 to Date

**Feeder Cattle**
- Oklahoma City - 1970 to Date

**Five Year T-Bond Yield**
- Federal Reserve Bank of St. Louis - 1953 to Date

**Flaxseed**
- No. 1 Minneapolis - 1901 thru 01/86
- US Farm Price - 1980 to Date

**Gold**
- NY Handy & Harman - 1968 to 05/1990
- BRIDGE composite - 06/1990 to Date

**Hides**
- Chicago (Paker's Heavy Native Steers) - 1920 to Date
- Chicago (Light Native Steers) 1920 thru 1943

**Hogs**
- Top Chicago - 1909 to 4/1/68
- Live Hogs Farrowing Chicago - 4/2/68 to 5/15/70
- Live Hogs Average Omaha - 5/18/70 to Date

**Lard**
- Chicago - 1910 to Date

**Lead**
- Raw - 1910 to Date
- Scrap - 1985 to Date

# Cash Market Description for Monthly Charts

**Lumber**
- White-Fir 2x4 - 1959 thru 1970
- Hem-Fir 2x4 - 1971 thru 03/80
- Spruce-Pine-Fir 2x4 - 03/80 to Date

**Mercury**
- N.Y. 75 pound Flask - 1920 thru 1931
- N.Y. 76 pound Flask - 1932 to Date

**Molasses**
- Blackstrap N.Y. - 1920 thru 1967
- Blackstrap (cane) New Orleans - 1968 to Date

**Municipal Bonds**
- Federal Reserve Bank of St. Louis - 1919 to Date

**Oats**
- No. 3 White Chicago - 1901 thru 1947
- Oats No. 2 White Chicago - 1/2/48 to 11/25/48
- Oats No. 1 White Hvy Chicago - 11/26/48 to 12/15/74
- Oats No. 2 White Hvy Chicago - 12/16/74 to Date

**Pepper**
- Black at N.Y. - 1920 to Date

**Platinum**
- N.Y. Producer Price - 1910 thru 1977
- N.Y. Merchants Price - 1978 to Date

**Pork Bellies**
- 12-14 Lbs Chicago - 1/2/49 to 10/3/75
- Pork Bellies 12-14 Lbs Midwest - 10/6/75 to Date

**Potatoes**
- N.Y. - U.S. No. 1 White - 1913 thru 1960
- U.S. Farmers Price - 1961 to Date

**Prime Rate**
- Federal Reserve Bank of St. Louis - 1930 to Date

**Rice**
- New Orleans Fancy (Honduras Grade) - 8/9 thru 1924
- New Orleans Fancy (Blue Rose Grade) - 1925-1933
- New Orleans Medium to Good (Blue Rose Grade) - 1934 thru 07/47
- New Orleans Fancy No. 2 Zenith Milled - 8/47-4/72
- Southwest Lousiana No. 2 Medium Grain - 5/72 to Date

**Rubber**
- N.Y. Plantation Smoked Sheets - 1908 to Date

**Rye**
- No. 2 Minneapolis - 07/09 to Date
- Winnipeg - 1950 thru 1982

**Silver**
- N.Y. Handy & Harman - 1910 to Date

**Soybeans**
- U.S. Farmers Price - 1913 thru 09/47
- No. 2 Yellow Chicago - 11/30/47 to 12/31/56
- No. 1 Yellow Chicago - 1/2/57 to 3/26/82
- No. 1 Yellow Central Il - 3/29/82 to Date

**Soybean Meal**
- Chicago (Protein no specified) - 10/29 thru 10/36
- Chicago 41% Protein - 11/36 thru 06/50
- Chicago 44% Protein - 07/50 thru 09/65
- Decatur 44% Protein - 10/65 thru 11/16/92
- Decatur 48% Protein - 11/17/92 to Date

**Soybean Oil**
- N.Y. Crude (imported) - 1910 thru 09/29
- Decatur Crude - 10/29 to Date

**Steel Scrap**
- Chicago - 1929 to Date
- Pittsburg - 1910 to Date

**Sugar**
- N.Y. Raw-96 Centrifugal - 1980 to Date
- Raw (cif) NY Duty Pd #7 - 1/2/47 to 11/2/77
- #12 Raw New York - 8/20/79 to 12/30/82
- Spot Raw (cif) New York - 1/3/49 to 2/1/61
- No. 8 World Raw New York - 2/2/61 to 12/31/70
- No. 11 World Raw New York - 1/4/71 to 11/2/77
- No. 11 World Raw New York - 8/20/79 to Date
- Midwest Refined-Wholesale Beet - 1975 to Date

**Tallow**
- Chicago Inedible Prime - 1910 thru 1948
- Chicago Bleachable - 1949 to Date

**Tin**
- Staights - 1910 to Date

**Wheat**
- No. 2 Red Chicago - 1901 to 3/26/82
- No. 2 Red Spot St. Louis - 3/29/82 to Date

**Wool**
- Boston Territory Fine Scoured Staple - 1910 to 1971
- U.S. Mills Territory Fine Scoured Staple - 1972 to Date

**Zinc**
- East St. Louis Prime Western - 1910 to 1970
- U.S. Basis Prime Western - 1971 to Date

# Aluminum

The U.S. Geological Survey reported that U.S. domestic primary aluminum production increased slightly in 1995 to 3.4 million tonnes. There were thirteen companies that operated 22 primary aluminum reduction plants and one plant that remained temporarily closed. Oregon, Washington, and Montana accounted for 36 percent of production, Kentucky, North and South Carolina, and Tennessee were 21 percent, and other states 43 percent. As the year was ending some domestic producers announced the reopening of smelter capacity that had been closed.

At the end of 1995, the aluminum industry reported that stocks of aluminum ingot, semifabricated material, and scrap was 2 million tonnes, down 3 percent from 1994. There were minor stocks at the London Metal Exchange and in the National Defense Stockpile.

Secondary recovery of aluminum from scrap in 1995 was 3.2 million tonnes, an increase of 3 percent from 1994. Secondary recovery from new scrap was 1.68 million tonnes while from old scrap it was 1.51 million tonnes. Exports of aluminum, crude and semicrude, in 1995 were 1.61 million tonnes, up 18 percent while imports for consumption (crude and semicrude) were 2.97 million tonnes, down 12 percent. The apparent U.S. aluminum supply was just over 8 million tonnes, down 5 percent. U.S. apparent consumption of aluminum in 1995 was 6.32 million tonnes, down 8 percent. World production of primary aluminum in 1995 was 19.4 million tonnes, up 1 percent from 1994. The U.S. was the largest producer followed by Russia, Canada, China, and Australia.

U.S. domestic production of primary aluminum in July 1996 was 301,000 tonnes, up from 293,000 tonnes in June 1996. Primary aluminum production over the first seven months of 1996 was 2.08 million tonnes, an increase of 7 percent from the same period of 1995.

U.S. secondary recovery of aluminum from scrap in July 1996 was 277,000 tonnes, up 4 percent from May, and 2 percent from a year ago. For the first seven months of 1996, secondary recovery of aluminum was 1.92 million tonnes. Approximately 1.05 million tonnes came from new scrap and 874,000 tonnes from old. In the same period of 1995, secondary recovery was 1.97 million tonnes with 1.03 million tonnes from new scrap and 943,000 tonnes from old. For all of 1995, secondary recovery of aluminum from scrap was 3.19 million tonnes with 1.68 million from new and 1.51 million from old scrap.

U.S. imports of aluminum for consumption in June 1996 were 210,000 tonnes. 169,000 tonnes came from metals and alloys while 40,000 tonnes came from plate, sheets, and bars. For the January-June 1996 period, imports for consumption were 1.23 million tonnes. For all of 1995, U.S. aluminum imports for consumption were 2.56 million tonnes with 1.93 million tonnes in the form of metals and alloys and 622,000 tonnes in the form of plates, sheets, and bars. Total stocks of aluminum from primary production, secondary recovery, and imports for consumption at the end of May 1996 were 1.96 million tonnes. At the end of 1995, stocks were 2 million tonnes.

U.S. exports of aluminum in June 1996 were 148,000 tonnes. For the first six months of 1996, exports were 768,000 tonnes. The major markets were Canada with 263,000 tones, Japan with 152,000 tonnes, and Mexico with 80,000 tonnes.

***Futures Markets***

Aluminum futures and options are listed on the London Metals Exchange (LME).

**World Production of Primary Aluminum** In Thousands of Metric Tons

| Year | Australia | Austria | Brazil | Canada | China | France | Germany | Italy | Japan | Norway | Russia[3] | Spain | Switzerland | United Kingdom | United States | Venezuela | World Total |
|---|---|---|---|---|---|---|---|---|---|---|---|---|---|---|---|---|---|
| 1987 | 1,004 | 93 | 843 | 1,540 | 615 | 323 | 793 | 233 | 41 | 853 | 2,400 | 341 | 73 | 294 | 3,343 | 428 | 16,514 |
| 1988 | 1,150 | 95 | 874 | 1,534 | 710 | 328 | 753 | 226 | 35 | 864 | 2,400 | 323 | 72 | 300 | 3,944 | 437 | 17,548 |
| 1989 | 1,244 | 93 | 890 | 1,555 | 750 | 335 | 796 | 219 | 35 | 863 | 3,300 | 352 | 71 | 297 | 4,030 | 540 | 19,010 |
| 1990 | 1,230 | 89 | 931 | 1,570 | 850 | 326 | 740 | 232 | 34 | 845 | 3,523 | 353 | 72 | 294 | 4,050 | 590 | 19,300 |
| 1991 | 1,228 | 80 | 1,140 | 1,822 | 963 | 286 | 690 | 206 | 32 | 833 | 3,251 | 355 | 66 | 294 | 4,121 | 601 | 19,700 |
| 1992 | 1,236 | 33 | 1,193 | 1,972 | 1,100 | 418 | 603 | 161 | 19 | 813 | 2,700 | 359 | 52 | 244 | 4,042 | 561 | 19,500 |
| 1993 | 1,380 | ---- | 1,170 | 2,310 | 1,220 | 426 | 552 | 156 | 18 | 887 | 2,820 | 356 | 36 | 239 | 3,700 | 570 | 19,700 |
| 1994[1] | 1,320 | ---- | 1,200 | 2,250 | 1,450 | 400 | 503 | 160 | 17 | 857 | 2,670 | 340 | 31 | 230 | 3,300 | 580 | 19,100 |
| 1995[2] | 1,293 | ---- | 1,188 | 2,172 | 1,658 | 364 | 575 | 178 | 18 | 847 | 2,722 | 361 | 19 | 238 | 3,375 | 626 | 19,453 |

[1] Preliminary. [2] Estimate. [3] Formerly part of the U.S.S.R.; data not reported separately until 1992. *Source: U.S. Geological Survey*

**U.S. Production of Primary Aluminum (Domestic & Foreign Ores)** In Thousands of Metric Tons

| Year | Jan. | Feb. | Mar. | Apr. | May | June | July | Aug. | Sept. | Oct. | Nov. | Dec. | Total |
|---|---|---|---|---|---|---|---|---|---|---|---|---|---|
| 1987 | 262 | 238 | 266 | 263 | 275 | 272 | 282 | 286 | 286 | 301 | 301 | 316 | 3,343 |
| 1988 | 320 | 304 | 330 | 324 | 336 | 323 | 334 | 333 | 327 | 339 | 332 | 344 | 3,944 |
| 1989 | 346 | 312 | 347 | 334 | 347 | 335 | 346 | 341 | 323 | 328 | 328 | 343 | 4,030 |
| 1990 | 345 | 311 | 345 | 331 | 342 | 330 | 340 | 341 | 332 | 347 | 337 | 347 | 4,048 |
| 1991 | 349 | 317 | 352 | 340 | 353 | 343 | 354 | 350 | 336 | 347 | 337 | 343 | 4,121 |
| 1992 | 344 | 320 | 343 | 330 | 342 | 330 | 339 | 340 | 330 | 343 | 335 | 347 | 4,043 |
| 1993 | 335 | 292 | 323 | 313 | 325 | 315 | 316 | 302 | 291 | 303 | 287 | 294 | 3,696 |
| 1994 | 292 | 261 | 286 | 269 | 277 | 268 | 275 | 274 | 267 | 277 | 270 | 280 | 3,296 |
| 1995[1] | 281 | 253 | 280 | 272 | 285 | 277 | 288 | 286 | 280 | 289 | 285 | 299 | 3,375 |
| 1996[1] | 301 | 283 | 303 | 293 | 303 | 293 | 301 | 302 | 292 | 304 | 295 | 305 | 3,575 |

[1] Preliminary. *Source: U.S. Geological Survey*

# ALUMINUM

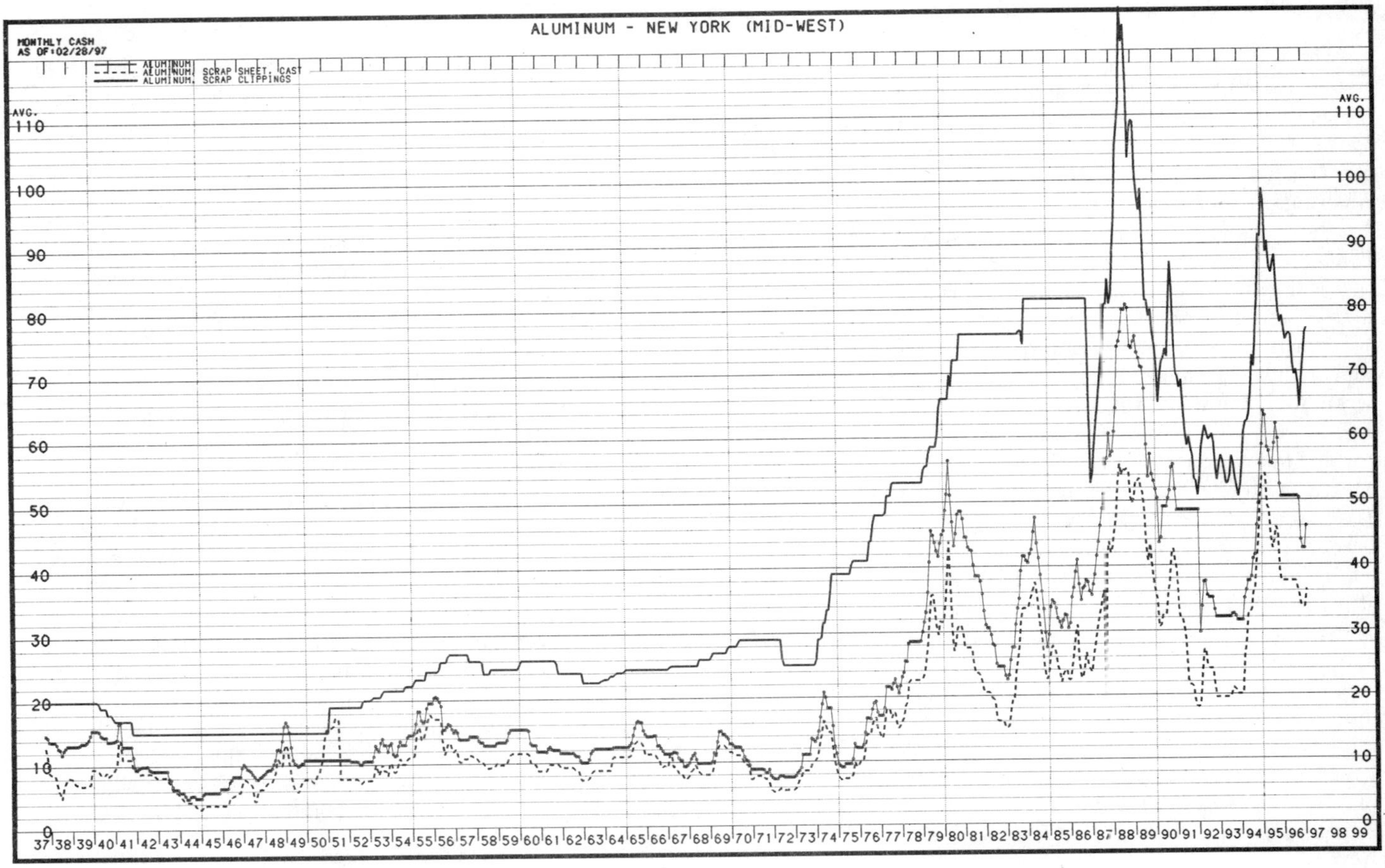


## Salient Statistics of Aluminum in the U.S. In Thousands of Metric Tons

| | Net Import Reliance as a % of Apparent Consumption | --- Production --- | | Primary Shipments[2] | Recovery from ----- Scrap ------- | | Apparent Consumption | Net Shipments[5] by Producers: Wrought Products | | | | Castings | | | | Total All Net Shipments |
|---|---|---|---|---|---|---|---|---|---|---|---|---|---|---|---|---|
| Year | | Primary | Secondary | | Old | New | | Plate Sheet, Foil | Rolled Structural Shapes[3] | Extruded Shapes[4] | All | Permanent Mold | Die | Sand | All | |
| 1986 | 26 | 3,037 | 1,773 | 6,545 | 784 | 989 | 5,143 | 3,397 | 337 | 1,335 | 5,179 | 155 | 749 | 77 | 1,032 | 6,211 |
| 1987 | 23 | 3,343 | 1,986 | 6,813 | 852 | 1,134 | 5,469 | 3,740 | 346 | 1,351 | 5,549 | 181 | 685 | 113 | 1,012 | 6,562 |
| 1988 | 7 | 3,944 | 2,122 | 6,851 | 1,045 | 1,077 | 5,373 | 3,787 | 343 | 1,341 | 5,589 | 201 | 700 | 115 | 1,055 | 6,621 |
| 1989 | E | 4,030 | 2,054 | 6,751 | 1,011 | 1,043 | 4,957 | 3,900 | 339 | 1,280 | 5,633 | 210 | 740 | 110 | 1,096 | 6,728 |
| 1990 | E | 4,048 | 2,390 | 6,590 | 1,360 | 1,030 | 5,260 | 3,799 | 301 | 1,211 | 5,425 | 208 | 620 | 103 | 968 | 6,393 |
| 1991 | E | 4,121 | 2,290 | 6,400 | 1,320 | 969 | 5,040 | 3,787 | 311 | 1,096 | 5,300 | 168 | 575 | 97 | 864 | 6,156 |
| 1992 | 1 | 4,042 | 2,760 | 6,810 | 1,610 | 1,140 | 5,730 | 4,097 | 303 | 1,186 | 5,691 | 198 | 595 | 99 | 804 | 6,609 |
| 1993 | 19 | 3,695 | 2,940 | 7,300 | 1,630 | 1,310 | 6,600 | 4,030 | 297 | 1,300 | 5,770 | 225 | 645 | 103 | 994 | 6,770 |
| 1994[1] | 30 | 3,299 | 3,090 | 8,160 | 1,500 | 1,580 | 6,880 | 4,810 | 296 | 1,420 | 6,690 | 247 | 551 | 208 | 1,050 | 7,740 |
| 1995[1] | 22 | 3,375 | 3,190 | 8,250 | 1,510 | 1,680 | 6,320 | 4,540 | 352 | 1,480 | 6,540 | NA | NA | NA | NA | NA |

[1] Preliminary. [2] To domestic industry. [3] Also rod, bar & wire. [4] Also rod, bar, tube blooms & tubing. [5] Consists of total shipments less shipments to other mills for further fabrication. NA = Not available. E = Net exporter. *Source: U.S. Geological Survey*

## U.S. Supply and Distribution of Aluminum In Thousands of Metric Tons

| Year | Apparent Consumption | ---- Production ---- Primary | From Old Scrap | Imports | Exports | Inventories -- December 31 -- Private | Government[3] |
|---|---|---|---|---|---|---|---|
| 1984 | 5,279 | 4,099 | 825 | 1,477 | 734 | 2,653 | 2 |
| 1985 | 5,174 | 3,500 | 850 | 1,420 | 908 | 2,343 | 2 |
| 1986 | 5,143 | 3,037 | 784 | 1,967 | 753 | 2,235 | 2 |
| 1987 | 5,469 | 3,343 | 852 | 1,850 | 917 | 2,000 | 2 |
| 1988 | 5,373 | 3,944 | 1,045 | 1,620 | 1,247 | 1,883 | 2 |
| 1989 | 4,957 | 4,030 | 1,011 | 1,470 | 1,615 | 1,822 | 2 |
| 1990 | 5,260 | 4,048 | 1,360 | 1,514 | 1,659 | 1,820 | 2 |
| 1991 | 5,040 | 4,121 | 1,320 | 1,490 | 1,762 | 1,780 | 2 |
| 1992 | 5,730 | 4,042 | 1,610 | 1,725 | 1,453 | 1,880 | 57 |
| 1993 | 6,600 | 3,695 | 1,630 | 2,540 | 1,210 | 1,980 | 57 |
| 1994[1] | 6,880 | 3,299 | 1,500 | 3,380 | 1,370 | 2,070 | 57 |
| 1995[2] | 6,320 | 3,375 | 1,510 | 2,970 | 1,610 | 2,000 | 57 |

[1] Preliminary. [2] Estimate. *Source: U.S. Geological Survey*

## U.S. Aluminum Products Distribution of End-Use Shipments In Thousands of Metric Tons

| Year | Building & Construction | Consumer Durables | Containers & Packaging | Electrical | Exports | Machinery & Equipment | Trans-portation | Other | Total |
|---|---|---|---|---|---|---|---|---|---|
| 1985 | 1,375 | 484 | 1,862 | 642 | 546 | 377 | 1,383 | 264 | 6,928 |
| 1986 | 1,432 | 540 | 1,926 | 626 | 413 | 383 | 1,372 | 252 | 6,958 |
| 1987 | 1,441 | 576 | 2,052 | 620 | 569 | 401 | 1,500 | 223 | 7,382 |
| 1988 | 1,316 | 588 | 2,036 | 671 | 787 | 435 | 1,536 | 269 | 7,638 |
| 1989 | 1,294 | 544 | 2,112 | 663 | 1,060 | 436 | 1,448 | 264 | 7,821 |
| 1990 | 1,208 | 509 | 2,157 | 594 | 1,131 | 452 | 1,388 | 261 | 7,700 |
| 1991 | 1,052 | 472 | 2,210 | 579 | 1,357 | 426 | 1,414 | 241 | 7,752 |
| 1992 | 1,144 | 523 | 2,259 | 587 | 1,236 | 448 | 1,591 | 256 | 8,045 |
| 1993 | 1,240 | 563 | 2,180 | 609 | 1,090 | 477 | 1,970 | 259 | 8,390 |
| 1994 | 1,400 | 647 | 2,270 | 682 | 1,200 | 572 | 2,310 | 276 | 9,360 |
| 1995[1] | 1,220 | 621 | 2,310 | 657 | 1,310 | 569 | 2,600 | 279 | 9,560 |

[1] Preliminary. *Source: U.S. Geological Survey (USGS)*

## World Consumption of Primary Aluminum In Thousands of Metric Tons

| Year | Aust-ralia | Belgium | Brazil | Canada | China | France | Ger-many | India | Italy | Japan | Rep. of Korea | Russia | Spain | United Kingdom | United States | World Total |
|---|---|---|---|---|---|---|---|---|---|---|---|---|---|---|---|---|
| 1985 | 288.4 | 267.7 | 323.1 | 345.0 | 720.0 | 586.1 | 1,160.9 | 297.6 | 470.0 | 1,694.8 | 145.6 | 2,700.0 | 211.0 | 350.4 | 4,282.0 | 16,919.2 |
| 1986 | 287.0 | 273.3 | 439.7 | 312.9 | 836.0 | 592.6 | 1,186.4 | 310.0 | 510.0 | 1,624.2 | 196.8 | 2,700.0 | 240.0 | 389.1 | 4,318.9 | 17,391.4 |
| 1987 | 318.7 | 284.7 | 430.3 | 423.1 | 727.0 | 615.6 | 1,185.7 | 326.0 | 548.0 | 1,696.8 | 207.9 | 2,830.0 | 25.7 | 383.6 | 4,546.2 | 18,137.5 |
| 1988 | 327.5 | 302.2 | 324.2 | 437.1 | 658.0 | 660.6 | 1,232.6 | 327.0 | 581.0 | 2,123.2 | 268.0 | 2,900.0 | 268.0 | 427.4 | 4,601.9 | 18,877.9 |
| 1989 | 323.9 | 302.1 | 420.1 | 450.2 | 920.0 | 685.5 | 1,289.1 | 420.0 | 607.0 | 2,211.6 | 287.6 | 2,700.0 | 273.4 | 454.7 | 4,381.4 | 19,281.1 |
| 1990 | 287.8 | 317.8 | 341.2 | 387.2 | 861.0 | 720.9 | 1,295.4 | 433.3 | 652.0 | 2,415.2 | 368.9 | 2,790.0 | 288.0 | 453.7 | 4,330.4 | 19,275.4 |
| 1991 | 298.0 | 323.0 | 354.2 | 408.2 | 938.0 | 734.2 | 1,360.9 | 430.2 | 670.0 | 2,431.6 | 383.5 | 2,409.0 | 297.0 | 412.4 | 4,137.2 | 18,778.2 |
| 1992 | 308.5 | 291.8 | 377.1 | 420.4 | 1,253.8 | 722.8 | 1,457.1 | 414.3 | 660.0 | 2,271.6 | 397.0 | 1,352.0 | 309.0 | 483.3 | 4,616.9 | 18,475.4 |
| 1993 | 339.5 | 275.0 | 378.9 | 486.6 | 1,318.0 | 665.0 | 1,300.0 | 475.3 | 554.0 | 2,138.3 | 524.8 | 767.0 | 310.0 | 475.0 | 4,877.1 | 18,278.7 |
| 1994 | 352.8 | 328.7 | 413.8 | 532.8 | 1,484.0 | 735.0 | 1,501.5 | 415.0 | 660.0 | 2,345.8 | 603.9 | 585.9 | 333.0 | 500.0 | 5,407.1 | 19,723.9 |
| 1995[1] | 344.1 | 328.7 | 413.8 | 532.4 | 1,859.9 | 635.7 | 1,715.6 | 469.1 | 668.2 | 2,443.5 | 692.6 | 590.0 | 387.3 | 500.0 | 5,054.9 | 20,505.6 |

[1] Preliminary. *Source: American Metal Market (AMM)*

## Salient Statistics of Recycling Aluminum in the U.S.

| Year | Percent Recycled | New Scrap[1] | Old Scrap[2] | Recycled Metal[3] | Apparent Supply | New Scrap | Old Scrap | Recycled Metal | Apparent Supply |
|---|---|---|---|---|---|---|---|---|---|
| | | In Thousands of Metric Tons | | | | Value in Millions of Dollars | | | |
| 1987 | 30 | 1,134 | 852 | 1,986 | 6,603 | 1,807 | 1,358 | 3,165 | 10,524 |
| 1988 | 33 | 1,077 | 1,045 | 2,122 | 6,450 | 2,614 | 2,536 | 5,150 | 15,654 |
| 1989 | 34 | 1,043 | 1,011 | 2,054 | 6,000 | 2,020 | 1,958 | 3,978 | 11,620 |
| 1990 | 38 | 1,034 | 1,359 | 2,393 | 6,298 | 1,688 | 2,218 | 3,906 | 10,280 |
| 1991 | 38 | 969 | 1,320 | 2,290 | 6,010 | 1,270 | 1,730 | 3,000 | 7,880 |
| 1992 | 40 | 1,140 | 1,610 | 2,760 | 6,870 | 1,450 | 2,040 | 3,500 | 8,710 |
| 1993 | 37 | 1,310 | 1,630 | 2,940 | 7,920 | 1,540 | 1,920 | 3,460 | 9,300 |
| 1994 | 36 | 1,580 | 1,500 | 3,090 | 8,460 | 2,480 | 2,360 | 4,840 | 13,300 |
| 1995 | 40 | 1,680 | 1,510 | 3,190 | 8,010 | 3,190 | 2,850 | 6,040 | 15,200 |

[1] Scrap that results from the manufacturing process. [2] Scrap that results from consumer products. [3] Metal recovered from new plus old scrap.
*Source: U.S. Geological Survey (USGS)*

## Producer Prices for Aluminum Used Beverage Can Scrap In Cents Per Pound

| Year | Jan. | Feb. | Mar. | Apr. | May | June | July | Aug. | Sept. | Oct. | Nov. | Dec. | Average |
|---|---|---|---|---|---|---|---|---|---|---|---|---|---|
| 1985 | 37.50 | 37.50 | 37.50 | 37.50 | 37.50 | 34.18 | 30.50 | 30.50 | 30.50 | 30.50 | 30.50 | 31.64 | 33.82 |
| 1986 | 34.96 | 38.13 | 41.69 | 42.86 | 39.79 | 38.26 | 37.50 | 37.50 | 37.50 | 37.50 | 35.72 | 35.50 | 38.08 |
| 1987 | 37.15 | 39.93 | 42.59 | 44.50 | 47.40 | 50.55 | 52.73 | 54.50 | 54.36 | 57.14 | 55.50 | 59.45 | 49.65 |
| 1988 | 65.80 | 70.50 | 72.93 | 72.50 | 72.50 | 72.50 | 72.50 | 71.63 | 66.21 | 63.92 | 61.50 | 64.93 | 68.95 |
| 1989 | 72.64 | 73.76 | 73.15 | 69.50 | 71.55 | 66.59 | 57.92 | 55.50 | 54.68 | 55.50 | 54.30 | 51.50 | 63.05 |
| 1990 | 48.50 | 45.50 | 47.55 | 50.50 | 50.77 | 50.50 | 49.71 | 51.13 | 57.53 | 52.15 | 48.00 | 44.67 | 49.71 |
| 1991 | 49.00 | 49.11 | 48.67 | 42.09 | 37.86 | 37.00 | 39.79 | 37.50 | 37.50 | 35.76 | 35.18 | 34.50 | 40.33 |
| 1992 | 35.38 | 38.32 | 40.73 | 43.91 | 44.40 | 41.50 | 41.50 | 41.69 | 39.93 | 38.07 | 38.00 | 38.68 | 40.18 |
| 1993 | 41.00 | 41.00 | 38.04 | 36.63 | 35.00 | 35.00 | 37.52 | 37.59 | 36.50 | 34.19 | 33.60 | 34.78 | 36.74 |
| 1994 | 38.45 | 43.08 | 42.50 | 46.60 | 45.50 | 48.98 | 56.40 | 56.00 | 56.00 | 62.64 | 70.40 | 71.00 | 53.13 |
| 1995 | 74.85 | 72.24 | 65.00 | 65.00 | 65.00 | 65.00 | 65.00 | 67.98 | 64.80 | 58.45 | 57.00 | 58.50 | 64.91 |

*Source: American Metal Market (AMM)*

# ALUMINUM

## Average Price of Cast Aluminum Scrap (Crank Cases) in Chicago Area In Cents Per Pound

| Year | Jan. | Feb. | Mar. | Apr. | May | June | July | Aug. | Sept. | Oct. | Nov. | Dec. | Average |
|---|---|---|---|---|---|---|---|---|---|---|---|---|---|
| 1989 | 53.02 | 52.97 | 53.41 | 51.90 | 51.14 | 47.59 | 42.97 | 40.63 | 43.30 | 40.14 | 37.75 | 35.65 | 45.87 |
| 1990 | 34.68 | 30.50 | 30.77 | 32.50 | 32.50 | 32.50 | 35.93 | 37.50 | 41.97 | 42.50 | 40.58 | 39.00 | 35.91 |
| 1991 | 33.50 | 32.00 | 32.00 | 30.64 | 28.45 | 22.40 | 21.50 | 21.50 | 21.13 | 19.00 | 18.11 | 18.00 | 24.85 |
| 1992 | 18.71 | 23.00 | 26.91 | 27.00 | 24.45 | 24.00 | 24.00 | 24.00 | 21.21 | 19.50 | 19.50 | 19.50 | 22.65 |
| 1993 | 19.50 | 19.50 | 19.50 | 19.50 | 19.50 | 19.50 | 20.79 | 21.00 | 20.62 | 20.00 | 20.00 | 20.00 | 19.95 |
| 1994 | 20.00 | 25.79 | 28.33 | 32.50 | 32.50 | 33.18 | 35.90 | 36.50 | 41.07 | 44.45 | 50.50 | 53.50 | 36.19 |
| 1995 | 53.53 | 54.08 | 49.02 | 48.50 | 44.41 | 42.50 | 43.76 | 45.80 | 45.05 | 39.27 | 37.50 | 37.50 | 45.08 |
| 1996 | 37.50 | 37.50 | 37.50 | 37.50 | 37.50 | 37.50 | 37.50 | 36.50 | 35.40 | 33.80 | 33.50 | 33.50 | 36.27 |

*Source: American Metal Market*

## Aluminum Products (Ingot & Mill Products) Shipments[1] in the U.S. In Million Pounds

| Year | Jan. | Feb. | Mar. | Apr. | May | June | July | Aug. | Sept. | Oct. | Nov. | Dec. | Total |
|---|---|---|---|---|---|---|---|---|---|---|---|---|---|
| 1989 | 1,266 | 1,232 | 1,419 | 1,246 | 1,306 | 1,365 | 1,205 | 1,369 | 1,299 | 1,278 | 1,169 | 1,071 | 15,405 |
| 1990 | 1,234 | 1,154 | 1,313 | 1,224 | 1,355 | 1,318 | 1,257 | 1,272 | 1,224 | 1,247 | 1,098 | 1,120 | 14,761 |
| 1991 | 1,177 | 1,087 | 1,261 | 1,244 | 1,313 | 1,287 | 1,387 | 1,389 | 1,276 | 1,371 | 1,265 | 1,241 | 15,298 |
| 1992 | 1,324 | 1,280 | 1,376 | 1,298 | 1,277 | 1,339 | 1,330 | 1,333 | 1,361 | 1,453 | 1,333 | 1,360 | 16,081 |
| 1993 | 1,251 | 1,291 | 1,486 | 1,408 | 1,377 | 1,440 | 1,296 | 1,410 | 1,382 | 1,306 | 1,364 | 1,284 | 16,294 |
| 1994 | 1,584 | 1,620 | 2,007 | 1,679 | 1,895 | 1,758 | 1,679 | 1,934 | 1,744 | 1,760 | 1,868 | 1,811 | 20,295 |
| 1995 | 1,632 | 1,472 | 1,704 | 1,594 | 1,605 | 1,576 | 1,368 | 1,493 | 1,533 | 1,571 | 1,469 | 1,404 | 18,422 |
| 1996[2] | 1,467 | 1,506 | 1,613 | 1,693 | 1,795 | 1,609 | 1,558 | 1,705 | 1,553 | 1,682 | 1,514 | 1,488 | 19,184 |

[1] Mills products & pig & ingot (net shipments). [2] Preliminary. *Source: Bureau of Census, U.S. Department of Commerce*

## U.S. Aluminum Inventories, Total (Ingot, Mill Products & Scrap) In Million Pounds

| Year | Jan. 1 | Feb. 1 | Mar. 1 | Apr. 1 | May 1 | June 1 | July 1 | Aug. 1 | Sept. 1 | Oct. 1 | Nov. 1 | Dec. 1 |
|---|---|---|---|---|---|---|---|---|---|---|---|---|
| 1989 | 4,151 | 4,189 | 4,163 | 4,160 | 4,246 | 4,224 | 4,289 | 4,373 | 4,253 | 4,158 | 4,064 | 3,991 |
| 1990 | 4,016 | 4,019 | 4,035 | 3,914 | 3,974 | 3,808 | 3,916 | 4,070 | 3,980 | 4,040 | 4,119 | 4,013 |
| 1991 | 4,013 | 4,068 | 4,169 | 4,256 | 4,212 | 4,135 | 4,044 | 3,990 | 4,028 | 4,008 | 3,992 | 3,923 |
| 1992 | 3,913 | 4,321 | 4,346 | 4,375 | 4,411 | 4,486 | 4,482 | 4,333 | 4,376 | 4,418 | 4,336 | 4,263 |
| 1993 | 4,093 | 4,124 | 4,179 | 4,250 | 4,274 | 4,327 | 4,398 | 4,417 | 4,387 | 4,360 | 4,294 | 3,020 |
| 1994 | 4,646 | 4,759 | 4,778 | 4,785 | 4,791 | 4,725 | 4,660 | 4,637 | 4,606 | 4,540 | 4,552 | 3,070 |
| 1995 | 4,710 | 4,845 | 4,691 | 4,743 | 4,745 | 4,639 | 4,691 | 4,594 | 4,494 | 4,366 | 4,346 | 4,403 |
| 1996[1] | 4,382 | 4,481 | 4,433 | 4,451 | 4,327 | 4,358 | 4,318 | 4,216 | 4,174 | 4,061 | 4,030 | 4,041 |

[1] Preliminary. *Source: Bureau of Census, U.S. Department of Commerce*

## Aluminum Exports (Metal & Alloys, Crude) from the U.S. In Cents Per Pound

| Year | Jan. | Feb. | Mar. | Apr. | May | June | July | Aug. | Sept. | Oct. | Nov. | Dec. | Total |
|---|---|---|---|---|---|---|---|---|---|---|---|---|---|
| 1989 | 34.8 | 41.8 | 40.2 | 33.3 | 34.1 | 44.6 | 46.2 | 52.0 | 46.1 | 68.8 | 72.7 | 80.0 | 593.0 |
| 1990 | 79.0 | 65.1 | 55.3 | 61.4 | 41.4 | 48.6 | 41.5 | 39.0 | 53.6 | 59.6 | 62.2 | 76.0 | 679.8 |
| 1991 | 61.1 | 54.8 | 46.7 | 82.8 | 56.4 | 71.3 | 69.0 | 80.1 | 54.6 | 68.0 | 80.7 | 67.3 | 792.8 |
| 1992 | 50.8 | 43.8 | 49.7 | 38.6 | 33.6 | 39.8 | 50.0 | 50.3 | 40.4 | 82.1 | 50.5 | 73.5 | 603.1 |
| 1993 | 54.8 | 38.6 | 41.7 | 26.3 | 38.6 | 30.7 | 33.9 | 24.5 | 27.9 | 31.7 | 24.1 | 27.6 | 400.4 |
| 1994 | 22.1 | 18.3 | 28.3 | 17.9 | 37.5 | 30.5 | 30.6 | 38.3 | 40.3 | 24.8 | 26.1 | 24.1 | 338.9 |
| 1995 | 26.1 | 32.7 | 25.4 | 31.1 | 31.4 | 20.7 | 26.6 | 39.2 | 38.9 | 33.0 | 30.4 | 33.6 | 369.1 |
| 1996[1] | 23.1 | 27.9 | 31.2 | 34.3 | 46.2 | 54.3 | 36.3 | 33.7 | 30.2 | 40.3 | 33.2 | | 390.7 |

[1] Preliminary. *Source: U.S. Geological Survey*

## Aluminum General Imports (Metal & Alloys, Crude) from the U.S. In Cents Per Pound

| Year | Jan. | Feb. | Mar. | Apr. | May | June | July | Aug. | Sept. | Oct. | Nov. | Dec. | Total |
|---|---|---|---|---|---|---|---|---|---|---|---|---|---|
| 1989 | 99.4 | 78.6 | 83.3 | 92.4 | 75.5 | 73.9 | 71.8 | 91.9 | 83.6 | 65.2 | 53.9 | 54.2 | 923.0 |
| 1990 | 84.4 | 73.4 | 85.4 | 85.1 | 90.4 | 94.0 | 102.6 | 82.1 | 76.4 | 66.8 | 58.7 | 60.6 | 959.6 |
| 1991 | 79.5 | 79.4 | 84.3 | 88.2 | 85.1 | 75.9 | 97.3 | 89.0 | 86.6 | 90.4 | 81.0 | 88.0 | 1,024.7 |
| 1992 | 100.7 | 93.1 | 97.1 | 94.6 | 96.3 | 87.8 | 82.4 | 103.4 | 94.3 | 108.4 | 100.5 | 96.8 | 1,155.4 |
| 1993 | 120.8 | 123.9 | 165.8 | 172.0 | 152.1 | 152.6 | 125.1 | 162.7 | 173.5 | 149.4 | 182.9 | 155.6 | 1,836.4 |
| 1994 | 200.2 | 157.8 | 282.0 | 206.9 | 251.9 | 179.3 | 202.8 | 198.3 | 160.0 | 183.4 | 240.1 | 222.2 | 2,484.9 |
| 1995 | 214.0 | 168.0 | 204.0 | 195.0 | 184.0 | 172.0 | 136.0 | 134.0 | 117.0 | 137.0 | 139.0 | 133.0 | 1,933.0 |
| 1996[1] | 158.0 | 150.0 | 148.0 | 188.0 | 176.0 | 169.0 | 139.0 | 149.0 | 136.0 | 170.0 | 147.0 | | 1,730.0 |

[1] Preliminary. *Source: U.S. Geological Survey*

# Antimony

Antimony is a byproduct of mining, smelting and refining of other metals, usually lead and silver-copper ores. It is used in flame retardants, fabrics, plastics and ammunition. Reductions in the use of antimonial lead indicate that demand for antimony is shifting away from metal products and into plastics and pigments. Most antimony is found in Idaho, Alaska, and Montana.

Industrial consumption of primary antimony in the U.S. in 1995 fell 3 percent from the very substantial total posted in 1994. In 1994, primary antimony consumption was 14,800 tonnes, a significant increase from the 1993 total of 12,400 tonnes. For 1995, industrial consumption fell back to about 14,300 tonnes. Of the total, 2,910 tonnes of antimony in metal were used, 11,400 tonnes of oxide with a minor amount of sulfide and residues.

In terms of the distribution of consumption, in 1995, antimonial lead took 1,780 tonnes. Bearing metal and bearings took 30 tonnes while other uses, which include ammunition, cable coverings, castings, sheet and pipe and solder, used 1,230 tonnes. Nonmetal products consumed a total of 2,130 tonnes. Ceramics and glass used 940 tonnes while ammunition primers, pigments and plastics took 1,190 tonnes. Flame retardants consume most of the primary antimony. In 1995, flame-retardant plastics used 6,170 tonnes. Rubber took 252 tonnes while other materials like adhesives and textiles used 334 tonnes.

In the first quarter of 1996, 3,270 tonnes of primary antimony were consumed with 690 tonnes of metal and 2,570 tonnes of oxide. For the second quarter of 1996, 3,300 tonnes of antimony were consumed with 633 tonnes of metal and 2,660 tonnes of oxide.

U.S. antimony imports for consumption in 1995 were 36,600 tonnes, antimony content. Ore and concentrate imports were 4,260 tonnes supplied mostly by Bolivia and China. Over the January-May 1996 period, imports of ore and concentrate were 597 tonnes. In 1995, metal imports were 16,900 tonnes with China supplying 12,100 tonnes. Over the first five months of 1996, metal imports were 9,150 tonnes. Oxide imports for 1995 were 15,400 tonnes with the major suppliers being China, Mexico, South Africa, and Bolivia. In the January-May 1996 period, U.S. imports of metal were 8,200 tonnes. In the second quarter of 1996, U.S. stocks of primary antimony were 11,000 tonnes compared to 10,700 tonnes at the end of 1995.

## World Mine Production of Antimony (Content of Ore) In Metric Tons

| Year | Australia | Bolivia | Canada | China[2] | Czech Republic[3] | Guatemala | Kyrgyzstan[4] | Mexico[5] | Morocco | Peru[6] | Russia[4] | South Africa | Thailand | Turkey | United States | World Total |
|---|---|---|---|---|---|---|---|---|---|---|---|---|---|---|---|---|
| 1992 | 1,701 | 6,022 | 948 | 45,000 | 1,000 | 582 | 3,000 | 1,200 | 197 | 339 | 10,000 | 3,779 | 270 | 309 | 232 | 76,100 |
| 1993 | 1,700 | 5,556 | 673 | 60,000 | 250 | 600 | 2,500 | 1,469 | 180 | 240 | 8,000 | 4,111 | 620 | 111 | 232 | 87,800 |
| 1994[1] | 1,700 | 7,050 | 750 | 80,000 | 5 | 600 | 2,500 | 1,500 | 175 | 460 | 7,000 | 4,534 | 500 | 75 | 232 | 108,000 |
| 1995[2] | 1,700 | 6,500 | 665 | 75,000 | ----- | 610 | 2,500 | 1,500 | 175 | 460 | 7,000 | 4,500 | 500 | 100 | 500 | 103,000 |

[1] Preliminary. [2] Estimate. [3] Formerly part of Czechoslovakia, data not reported separately until 1993. [4] Formerly part of the USSR; data not reported separately until 1992. [5] Includes antimony content of miscellaneous smelter products. [6] Recoverable W=Withheld proprietary data. *Source: U.S. Geological Survey*

## Salient Statistics of Antimony in the United States In Metric Tons

| | Avg. Price ¢ per lb. | Production[3] | | | Imports for Consumption | | | | Industry Stocks, December 31[3] | | | | |
|---|---|---|---|---|---|---|---|---|---|---|---|---|---|
| | | Primary[2] | | | Ore | | Oxide | | | | | | |
| Year | CIF U.S. Ports | Mine | Smelter | Secondary (Alloys)[2] | Gross Weight | Antimony Content | (Gross Weight) | Exports (Oxide) | Metallic | Oxide | Sulfide | Residues & Slag | Total[4] |
| 1993 | 76.9 | W | 22,000 | 20,700 | 1,720 | 543 | 19,322 | 3,896 | 2,790 | 3,320 | 20 | W | 9,080 |
| 1994[1] | 177.7 | W | 25,500 | 24,300 | 7,680 | 5,640 | 21,300 | 6,500 | 2,770 | 5,000 | W | W | 10,900 |
| 1995[2] | 227.8 | W | 23,500 | ----- | 6,140 | 4,260 | 18,600 | 6,950 | 2,450 | 4,450 | W | W | 10,600 |

[1] Preliminary. [2] Estimate. [3] Antimony content. [4] Including primary antimony residues & slag. W = Withheld proprietary data. *Source: U.S. Geological Survey*

## Industrial Consumption of Primary Antimony in the United States In Metric Tons (Antimony Content)

| | Metal Products | | | | | | | | | Non-Metal Products | | | | | |
|---|---|---|---|---|---|---|---|---|---|---|---|---|---|---|---|
| | | | | | | | | Flame Retardents | | | | | | | |
| Year | Ammunition | Antimonial Lead | Sheet & Pipe | Bearing Metal & Bearings | Solder | Type Metal | Total All Metal Products | Plastics | Total | Ceramics & Glass | Rubber Products | Pigments | Plastics | Total | Grand Total |
| 1993 | W | 1,110 | W | 44 | 242 | W | 2,810 | 5,440 | 7,250 | 848 | W | 489 | 786 | 2,310 | 12,400 |
| 1994 | W | 1,990 | W | 36 | 183 | W | 3,740 | 6,690 | 8,570 | 980 | W | 369 | 1,030 | 2,490 | 14,800 |
| 1995[1] | W | 1,780 | W | 30 | 192 | W | 3,040 | 6,170 | 6,760 | 940 | W | 492 | 1,090 | 2,130 | 14,300 |

[1] Preliminary. [2] Estimated coverage based on 77% of the industry. W=Withheld proprietary data. *Source: U.S. Geological Survey*

## United States Prices of Antimony[1] In Cents Per Pound

| Year | Jan. | Feb. | Mar. | Apr. | May | June | July | Aug. | Sept. | Oct. | Nov. | Dec. | Average |
|---|---|---|---|---|---|---|---|---|---|---|---|---|---|
| 1994 | 73.00 | 73.00 | 78.04 | 87.50 | 111.07 | 153.75 | 182.50 | 235.00 | 250.00 | 260.00 | 288.00 | 293.00 | 173.74 |
| 1995 | 293.00 | 293.00 | 284.00 | 284.00 | 201.00 | 142.00 | 188.00 | 240.00 | 244.00 | 213.00 | 170.00 | 170.00 | 226.83 |
| 1996 | 153.00 | 152.50 | 152.50 | 150.12 | 142.50 | 142.50 | 132.50 | 127.50 | 127.50 | 127.50 | 127.50 | 127.50 | 138.59 |

[1] Prices are for antimony metal (99.65%) merchants, minimum 18-ton containers, c.i.f. U.S. Ports. *Source: American Metal Market*

# Apples

## World Production of Apples, Fresh (Dessert & Cooking) In Thousands of Metric Tons

| Year | Argen-tina | Aus-tralia | Canada | France | Ger-many | Hun-gary | Italy | Japan | Mex-ico | Nether-lands | Slo-vakia[4] | South Africa | Spain | Tur-key | United States | World Total |
|---|---|---|---|---|---|---|---|---|---|---|---|---|---|---|---|---|
| 1982 | 817 | 301 | 478 | 1,978 | 2,637 | 1,278 | 2,642 | 924 | 394 | 490 | 746 | 519 | 860 | 1,600 | 3,684 | 21,626 |
| 1983 | 872 | 267 | 485 | 1,575 | 1,313 | 1,141 | 2,057 | 1,048 | 302 | 403 | 557 | 513 | 1,012 | 1,750 | 3,800 | 19,205 |
| 1984 | 922 | 352 | 434 | 2,005 | 1,799 | 1,088 | 2,241 | 812 | 486 | 431 | 584 | 557 | 970 | 1,900 | 3,776 | 20,701 |
| 1985 | 594 | 288 | 479 | 1,793 | 1,410 | 954 | 2,012 | 910 | 443 | 300 | 368 | 517 | 988 | 1,900 | 3,590 | 18,775 |
| 1986 | 1,078 | 362 | 388 | 1,867 | 2,180 | 1,253 | 2,020 | 986 | 629 | 445 | 637 | 470 | 829 | 1,860 | 3,565 | 21,098 |
| 1987 | 925 | 309 | 506 | 1,985 | 1,077 | 1,064 | 2,273 | 998 | 615 | 340 | 423 | 526 | 971 | 1,680 | 4,873 | 20,922 |
| 1988-9 | 1,030 | 350 | 501 | 1,935 | 2,467 | 1,131 | 2,443 | 1,042 | 624 | 383 | 518 | 534 | 845 | 1,950 | 4,140 | 22,662 |
| 1989-90 | 1,050 | 333 | 538 | 1,818 | 1,727 | 959 | 2,162 | 1,045 | 545 | 417 | 546 | 557 | 747 | 1,850 | 4,519 | 21,654 |
| 1990-1 | 950 | 292 | 540 | 1,895 | 2,222 | 945 | 2,102 | 1,053 | 520 | 431 | 523 | 542 | 635 | 1,900 | 4,398 | 21,224 |
| 1991-2 | 1,043 | 289 | 513 | 1,236 | 1,165 | 859 | 1,869 | 760 | 550 | 223 | 480 | 605 | 517 | 1,900 | 4,413 | 18,250 |
| 1992-3 | 947 | 336 | 564 | 2,398 | 3,228 | 666 | 2,394 | 1,039 | 580 | 640 | 112 | 633 | 1,095 | 2,100 | 4,798 | 35,443 |
| 1993-4 | 1,006 | 307 | 488 | 2,079 | 1,719 | 819 | 2,145 | 1,011 | 538 | 670 | 112 | 638 | 891 | 2,080 | 4,847 | 36,505 |
| 1994-5 | 1,146 | 345 | 554 | 2,166 | 2,080 | 610 | 2,153 | 989 | 488 | 590 | 57 | 577 | 739 | 2,095 | 5,217 | 37,712 |
| 1995-6[1] | 986 | 279 | 591 | 2,089 | 1,373 | 353 | 1,889 | 963 | 427 | 595 | 38 | 645 | 842 | 2,100 | 4,870 | 38,572 |
| 1996-7[2] | NA | NA | 560 | 2,055 | 1,717 | 475 | 1,964 | 936 | 465 | 490 | 54 | NA | 811 | 2,100 | 4,812 | 37,049 |

[1] Preliminary. [2] Estimate. [3] Commercial crop. [4] Formerly part of Yugoslavia; data not reported separately until 1992. NA = Not available.
*Source: Foreign Agicultural Service, U.S. Department of Agriculture*

## Salient Statistics of Apples[2] in the United States

| Year | --- Production --- Total | Util-ized | --Growers Prices-- Fresh ¢ Lb. | Pro-cessing $ Ton | Utilization of Quantities Sold: Fresh | Processed[5]: Canned | Dried | Frozen | Juice & Cider | Other[3] | Avg. Farm Price ¢ Per Lb. | Farm Value Million $ | Foreign Trade[4]: Domestic Exports Fresh | Domestic Exports Dried[5] | Imports Fresh & Dried[5] | Fresh Per Capita Con-sump-tion Lbs. |
|---|---|---|---|---|---|---|---|---|---|---|---|---|---|---|---|---|
| | Millions of Pounds | | | | | | | | | | | | Metric Tons | | | |
| 1982 | 8,122 | 8,110 | 13.2 | 118.0 | 4,537 | 1,249 | 210 | 191 | 1,808 | 116 | 10.0 | 809.0 | 261.8 | 16.1 | 98.7 | 17.5 |
| 1983 | 8,379 | 8,358 | 14.8 | 104.0 | 4,621 | 1,204 | 283 | 170 | 1,985 | 95 | 10.5 | 879.0 | 228.7 | 12.0 | 126.0 | 18.3 |
| 1984 | 8,324 | 8,309 | 15.5 | 112.0 | 4,655 | 1,177 | 289 | 198 | 1,889 | 102 | 11.2 | 927.6 | 205.2 | 9.3 | 132.6 | 18.4 |
| 1985 | 7,915 | 7,827 | 17.3 | 103.0 | 4,222 | 1,255 | 242 | 194 | 1,839 | 74 | 11.7 | 914.3 | 147.1 | 5.5 | 152.6 | 17.3 |
| 1986 | 7,859 | 7,833 | 19.1 | 116.0 | 4,464 | 1,179 | 199 | 257 | 1,643 | 91 | 13.4 | 1,046.8 | 175.1 | 10.5 | 149.4 | 17.8 |
| 1987 | 10,742 | 10,451 | 12.7 | 79.3 | 5,610 | 1,306 | 284 | 249 | 2,929 | 74 | 8.6 | 903.1 | 296.2 | 7.7 | 132.7 | 20.8 |
| 1988 | 9,120 | 9,070 | 17.4 | 123.0 | 5,230 | 1,399 | 285 | 266 | 1,824 | 67 | 12.7 | 1,147.8 | 254.5 | 12.0 | 133.0 | 19.9 |
| 1989 | 9,917 | 9,871 | 13.9 | 107.0 | 5,822 | 1,320 | 282 | 322 | 2,068 | 57 | 10.4 | 1,024.6 | 357.4 | 23.7 | 119.7 | 21.2 |
| 1990 | 9,657 | 9,618 | 20.9 | 144.0 | 5,515 | 1,378 | 270 | 304 | 2,077 | 74 | 15.1 | 1,447.7 | 371.3 | 55.5 | 122.0 | 19.6 |
| 1991 | 9,707 | 9,637 | 25.1 | 171.0 | 5,447 | 1,311 | 299 | 286 | 2,194 | 100 | 17.9 | 1,727.0 | 530.1 | 44.2 | 143.9 | 18.2 |
| 1992 | 10,569 | 10,463 | 19.5 | 130.0 | 5,767 | 1,498 | 324 | 247 | 2,472 | 155 | 13.6 | 1,428.0 | 487.8 | 22.1 | 139.3 | 19.2 |
| 1993 | 10,685 | 10,574 | 18.4 | 107.0 | 6,124 | 1,335 | 366 | 282 | 2,382 | 85 | 12.9 | 1,363.9 | 662.9 | 19.2 | 114.0 | 19.2 |
| 1994 | 11,501 | 11,331 | 18.6 | 114.0 | 6,366 | 1,406 | 415 | 304 | 2,707 | 133 | 12.9 | 1,467.1 | 719.6 | ---- | 115.8 | 19.6 |
| 1995[1] | 10,736 | 10,541 | 23.8 | 158.0 | 5,836 | 1,354 | 333 | 276 | 2,664 | 77 | 16.7 | 1,761.5 | 611.3 | ---- | 154.4 | 18.9 |

[1] Preliminary. [2] Commercial crop. [3] Mostly crushed for vinegar, jam, etc. [4] Year beginning July. [5] Fresh weight basis. *Source: Economic Research Service, U.S. Department of Agriculture*

## U.S. Prices of Apples Received by Growers (for Fresh Use) In Cents Per Pound

| Year | Jan. | Feb. | Mar. | Apr. | May | June | July | Aug. | Sept. | Oct. | Nov. | Dec. | Average |
|---|---|---|---|---|---|---|---|---|---|---|---|---|---|
| 1982 | 14.1 | 15.7 | 16.0 | 14.5 | 16.2 | 17.7 | 15.3 | 12.8 | 16.3 | 14.5 | 13.9 | 13.0 | 15.0 |
| 1983 | 11.0 | 12.2 | 12.0 | 11.3 | 11.9 | 11.1 | 12.0 | 16.0 | 15.9 | 14.9 | 14.6 | 14.0 | 13.1 |
| 1984 | 14.3 | 15.1 | 15.2 | 14.8 | 15.0 | 14.6 | 14.9 | 16.5 | 18.5 | 17.4 | 16.4 | 15.6 | 15.7 |
| 1985 | 14.0 | 14.3 | 15.7 | 15.1 | 14.1 | 13.1 | 12.6 | 12.1 | 16.4 | 15.4 | 16.4 | 16.6 | 14.7 |
| 1986 | 16.6 | 17.2 | 17.2 | 17.2 | 20.7 | 21.0 | 28.5 | 27.6 | 20.9 | 18.0 | 17.3 | 16.5 | 19.9 |
| 1987 | 18.3 | 19.0 | 18.0 | 19.1 | 22.4 | 24.6 | 25.5 | 15.2 | 14.8 | 12.1 | 11.3 | 10.4 | 17.6 |
| 1988 | 11.1 | 12.9 | 12.5 | 11.0 | 10.9 | 10.4 | 22.8 | 27.7 | 23.7 | 18.5 | 17.5 | 17.4 | 16.4 |
| 1989 | 18.1 | 17.9 | 16.5 | 14.4 | 13.5 | 10.8 | 11.5 | 15.9 | 16.7 | 14.3 | 13.3 | 12.1 | 14.6 |
| 1990 | 12.2 | 12.4 | 12.3 | 12.0 | 12.6 | 13.7 | 20.3 | 22.3 | 22.2 | 19.3 | 19.6 | 20.9 | 16.7 |
| 1991 | 20.1 | 20.5 | 20.3 | 20.2 | 22.5 | 23.2 | 24.6 | 23.2 | 26.4 | 23.8 | 25.1 | 25.7 | 23.0 |
| 1992 | 24.6 | 24.8 | 24.3 | 24.1 | 25.0 | 25.2 | 28.6 | 33.3 | 27.1 | 21.2 | 19.4 | 19.9 | 24.8 |
| 1993 | 18.3 | 16.7 | 14.5 | 14.3 | 14.9 | 16.1 | 17.8 | 24.4 | 24.1 | 21.1 | 19.3 | 18.6 | 18.3 |
| 1994 | 18.7 | 17.8 | 16.6 | 15.5 | 14.3 | 13.5 | 19.4 | 29.0 | 20.8 | 19.2 | 16.4 | 19.2 | 18.4 |
| 1995 | 19.5 | 18.3 | 18.2 | 16.6 | 15.4 | 15.6 | 17.5 | 24.5 | 26.0 | 25.1 | 23.5 | 24.0 | 20.4 |
| 1996[1] | 25.8 | 25.0 | 25.2 | 23.6 | 22.2 | 22.3 | 22.5 | 24.6 | 31.6 | 25.9 | 24.1 | 23.5 | 24.7 |

[1] Preliminary. *Source: Economic Research Service, U.S. Department of Agriculture*

# Arsenic

According to the U.S. Geological Survey, the United States was the world's largest consumer of arsenic in 1995, accounting for about one half of world demand. For the second year in a row, domestic apparent demand for arsenic metals and compounds appeared to be unchanged. All U.S. domestic arsenic requirements are met by imports. Arsenic production was last reported in the U.S. in 1985. On a contained metal basis, arsenic trioxide accounted for 97 percent of imports. China is the largest producer of both arsenic trioxide and arsenic metal and was the leading source of U.S. imports of both products.

Arsenic is a by-product of copper, lead, gold, and zinc mining. With substantial quantities of these metals found worldwide, the availability and supply of arsenic is ample. Arsenic is employed in a variety of products including laser materials, and as a doping agent in the manufacturing of various solid state devices. Arsenic trioxide is imported and converted to arsenic acid for use in producing wood preservatives. In addition to chromated copper arsenate being the most common arsenic-based wood preservative, ammoniacal copper arsenate and fluor chrome arsenate phenol are also used.

Agricultural uses of arsenic were as herbicides for weed control; arsenic acid is used in the mechanical harvesting of cotton and in glassmaking. Arsenal acid is an arsenical drug used for growth, pigmentation, and disease control. Commercial grade arsenic metal, 99 percent pure, is used in lead and copper-based alloys to increase strength in the posts and grids of lead-acid batteries and to increase corrosion resistance in copper alloys. Very high purity arsenic metal is utilized in the manufacturing of crystalline gallium arsenide. This semiconduction material, which is faster but more costly than silicon products, is used in optoelectronic circuitry and high-speed computers.

The U.S. supply of arsenic in 1995 was 22,700 tonnes (arsenic content), an increase of 5 percent from the 1994 supply of 21,600 tonnes. All of the arsenic was imported. Arsenic metal imports were 557 tonnes in 1995, down from 1,330 tonnes in 1994. Imports of arsenic compounds were 22,100 tonnes, up from 20,300 tonnes the year before.

U.S. imports for consumption of arsenic trioxide in 1995 were 29,000 tonnes , some 8 percent above the 1994 level. The major supplier was China with 15,000 tonnes followed by Mexico, Chile, and France. There were very minor amounts of arsenic acid imported. Imports of arsenic metal were 557 tonnes, down sharply from the 1994 total of 1,330 tonnes. China was the major supplier.

Of the U.S. arsenic supply in 1995 of 22,700 tonnes, wood preservatives used 19,600 tonnes while agricultural chemicals took 1,000 tonnes. Glass production used 700 tonnes with nonferrous alloys and electronics taking 600 tonnes and other uses consuming 400 tonnes. The major market for arsenic is in the production of wood preservatives and demand for arsenic is directly related to the home construction market.

World production of arsenic trioxide in 1995 was estimated at 41,300 tonnes, down 2 percent from 1994. The major producer was China with 13,000 tonnes or about a third of the market. Chile was the next largest producer with 6,400 tonnes followed by France with 5,000 tonnes and Mexico with 4,500 tonnes. Other important producers are Namibia, Belgium, and the Philippines. In 1995, Mexican arsenic trioxide averaged 33 cents per pound, while Chinese arsenic metal averaged 66 cents per pound.

## World Production of White Arsenic (Arsenic Trioxide) In Metric Tons

| Year | Belgium | Bolivia | Canada[4] | Chile | China | France | Germany | Japan | Mexico | Namibia[3] | Peru | Phillippines | Russia[5] | Sweden | World Total |
|---|---|---|---|---|---|---|---|---|---|---|---|---|---|---|---|
| 1987 | 3,500 | 132 | 3,000 | 3,616 | ---- | 10,000 | 360 | 500 | 5,304 | 1,864 | 1,757 | 5,000 | 8,100 | 10,000 | 52,351 |
| 1988 | 3,500 | 191 | 2,825 | 3,207 | 7,000 | 10,000 | 360 | 500 | 5,164 | 2,983 | 828 | 5,046 | 8,100 | 10,000 | 60,335 |
| 1989 | 3,500 | 338 | 1,825 | 5,000 | 7,000 | 10,000 | 360 | 500 | 5,551 | 2,399 | 563 | 4,652 | 8,100 | 10,000 | 61,026 |
| 1990 | 3,000 | 300 | 485 | 5,830 | 9,000 | 6,480 | 360 | 500 | 4,810 | 1,640 | 500 | 5,090 | 7,800 | 7,000 | 53,400 |
| 1991 | 2,500 | 463 | 236 | 6,820 | 10,000 | 2,000 | 300 | 500 | 4,920 | 1,800 | 661 | 5,000 | 7,000 | 2,500 | 46,000 |
| 1992 | 2,000 | 633 | 250 | 6,020 | 14,000 | 2,000 | 300 | 50 | 4,290 | 2,460 | 607 | 5,000 | 2,500 | ---- | 44,800 |
| 1993 | 2,000 | 663 | 250 | 6,200 | 13,000 | 3,000 | 300 | 40 | 4,450 | 2,290 | 610 | 2,000 | 2,000 | ---- | 41,000 |
| 1994[1] | 2,000 | 341 | 250 | 6,300 | 13,000 | 6,000 | 300 | 40 | 4,400 | 2,300 | 610 | 2,000 | 1,500 | ---- | 42,200 |
| 1995[2] | 2,000 | 400 | 250 | 6,400 | 13,000 | 5,000 | 300 | 40 | 4,500 | 2,300 | 610 | 2,000 | 1,500 | ---- | 41,300 |

[1] Preliminary. [2] Estimate. [3] Output of Tsumeb Corp. Ltd. only. [4] Includes low-grade dusts that were exported to the U.S. for further refining. [5] Formerly part of the U.S.S.R.; reported seperately until 1992. *Source: U.S. Geological Survey*

## U.S. Arsenic Supply--Demand Relationships In Metric Tons (Arsenic Content)

| | Supply | | | | Distribution | | Estimated Demand Pattern | | | | | | Average Price | | | |
|---|---|---|---|---|---|---|---|---|---|---|---|---|---|---|---|---|
| | Imports | | Industry | | | Industry | Agricul- | | Wood | Non-Ferrous | | | Trioxide | Metal | | |
| | | Com- | Stocks | | Apparent | Stocks | tural | | Preserv- | Alloys | | | Mexican | Chinese | Imports | |
| Year | Metal | pounds | Jan. 1 | Total | Demand | Dec. 31 | Chemicals | Glass | atives | & Electric | Other | Total | ¢ Per Pound | | Trioxide[3] | Exports |
| 1989 | 928 | 21,498 | 100 | 22,526 | 22,300 | 100 | 4,900 | 900 | 15,600 | 700 | 200 | 22,300 | 27 | 47 | 28,348 | 126 |
| 1990 | 796 | 19,900 | 100 | 20,796 | 20,500 | 100 | 4,200 | 800 | 14,400 | 800 | 300 | 20,500 | 23 | 180 | 26,256 | 149 |
| 1991 | 1,010 | 20,700 | 100 | 21,810 | 21,600 | ---- | 5,000 | 900 | 14,300 | 1,000 | 400 | 21,600 | 25 | 68 | 27,142 | 233 |
| 1992 | 740 | 23,300 | ---- | 24,040 | 23,900 | ---- | 3,900 | 900 | 17,900 | 800 | 400 | 23,900 | 29 | 56 | 30,671 | 94 |
| 1993 | 767 | 20,900 | ---- | 21,667 | 21,300 | ---- | 3,000 | 900 | 16,200 | 800 | 400 | 21,300 | 33 | 44 | 27,500 | 364 |
| 1994[1] | 1,330 | 20,300 | ---- | 21,630 | 21,500 | ---- | 1,200 | 700 | 18,000 | 1,300 | 300 | 21,500 | 32 | 40 | 26,800 | 79 |
| 1995[2] | 557 | 22,100 | ---- | 22,657 | 22,300 | ---- | 1,000 | 700 | 19,600 | 600 | 400 | 22,300 | 33 | 66 | 29,000 | 430 |

[1] Preliminary. [2] Estimate. [3] For Consumption. *Source: U.S. Geological Survey*

# Barley

More than half of the world's barley is produced in Europe. World production rose in 1996/97 to 155 million metric tons from 142 million in 1995/96, and average production in the early 1990's of 165 million tons. Collectively, the EU is the largest producing area with 53 million tons in 1996/97 vs. 44 million in 1995/96, and a recent five year average of 45 million. Russia, once the world's largest producer, has seen production drop steadily from 27 million tons in 1992/93, to 15.8 million in 1995/96, and 15.5 million in 1996/97. Canada is now the largest single producer with 16 million tons in 1996/97, vs. 13 million in 1995/96, and 11 million in 1992/93. In the U.S. barley is the third largest produced feed grain, but on a worldwide basis U.S. production accounts for only 5 percent of the total. World barley usage has slipped, averaging in both 1996/97 and 1995/96 a little under 149 million tons vs. more than 165 million early in the 1990's. The 1996/97 supply/demand imbalance, which depressed prices in late 1996, will boost ending world carryover to 23.2 million tons from the 17.8 million carryin; in recent years world stocks averaged over 30 million tons.

The U.S. barley crop year begins June 1. Production peaked in the 1980's and has since declined about a third as producers found returns more favorable from wheat and sunflower crops. Barley production in 1996/97 of 397 million bushels compares with the 1995/96 record low of 360 million, the moderate increase reflecting larger planted acreage, 2.9 million hectares, and a higher average yield, 3.15 tons per hectare vs 3.08 in 1995/96. North Dakota is usually the largest producing state.

U.S. disappearance in 1996/97 of 436 million bushels compares with a recent low of only 413 million in 1995/96; in 1991/92 total usage neared 500 million bushels. Feed and residual usage were estimated at 235 million bushels, up 50 million from 1995/96. Industrial usage, mostly for beer and alcohol, is unchanged at 166 million bushels. Exports fell to 35 million vs. 62 million in 1995/96, the lowest total of the 1990's. Imports are estimated at 45 million bushels, mostly of malting quality barley from Canada. Carryover stocks on May 31, 1997 are estimated at 105 million bushels, the same as a year earlier.

World barley trade was forecast at 13.5 million bushels in 1996/97 vs. 12 million in 1995/96. The European Union exports about a third of the total with Canada and Australia much of the balance. Importing countries are more numerous, but Saudi Arabia, China, Japan, and the U.S. are likely to take a combined 8.5 million bushels in 1996/97. Since the early 1990's, the U.S. has shown the greatest percentage growth in export demand, with China second.

Barley prices paid to U.S. farmers were forecast to average between $2.45-2.85 per bushel in 1996/97, vs. $2.89 in 1995/96, $2.03 in 1994/95, and $1.99 in 1993/94.

### *Futures Markets*

Barley futures and options are traded on the Winnipeg Commodity Exchange (WCE) and the London Commodity Exchange (LCE). Futures are traded on the Budapest Commodity Exchange.

## World Barley Supply and Demand In Thousands of Metric Tons

| | Exports | | | | | | Imports | | | Utilization | | | | Ending Stocks | | |
|---|---|---|---|---|---|---|---|---|---|---|---|---|---|---|---|---|
| Crop Year | Australia | Canada | EC-12 | Total Non-U.S. | U.S. | Total Exports | Saudi Arabia | Unaccounted | Total Imports | Production | Russia[3] | U.S. | Total Utilization | Canada | U.S. | Total Stocks |
| 1987-8 | 1,600 | 3,500 | 7,000 | 13,100 | 2,900 | 16,000 | 4,800 | NA | 16,000 | 181,300 | 60,900 | 9,300 | 183,100 | 25,200 | 7,000 | 32,200 |
| 1988-9 | 1,364 | 3,419 | 8,349 | 14,137 | 1,718 | 15,855 | 4,714 | -12 | 15,855 | 162,722 | 44,245 | 7,540 | 162,536 | 2,800 | 4,276 | 30,674 |
| 1989-90 | 2,447 | 3,773 | 7,905 | 15,905 | 1,798 | 17,703 | 4,146 | 467 | 17,703 | 164,761 | 22,433 | 8,030 | 167,440 | 2,056 | 3,501 | 28,789 |
| 1990-1 | 2,683 | 4,460 | 7,053 | 17,016 | 1,507 | 18,523 | 4,342 | 742 | 18,523 | 178,056 | 29,156 | 8,283 | 174,898 | 2,646 | 2,948 | 32,317 |
| 1991-2 | 1,951 | 3,379 | 9,459 | 16,929 | 2,090 | 19,019 | 6,873 | 77 | 19,019 | 169,136 | 25,635 | 8,735 | 165,833 | 2,615 | 2,800 | 32,471 |
| 1992-3 | 2,600 | 2,859 | 5,816 | 15,084 | 1,611 | 16,695 | 3,917 | 807 | 16,695 | 165,767 | 28,368 | 7,916 | 166,065 | 3,271 | 3,292 | 31,923 |
| 1993-4 | 4,232 | 3,789 | 6,793 | 16,986 | 1,553 | 18,539 | 4,497 | 415 | 18,539 | 169,962 | 27,041 | 9,053 | 169,633 | 3,376 | 3,023 | 32,252 |
| 1994-5 | 1,356 | 2,556 | 5,061 | 13,339 | 1,355 | 14,694 | 3,002 | 382 | 14,694 | 160,586 | 25,211 | 8,726 | 166,755 | 1,820 | 2,451 | 26,083 |
| 1995-6[1] | 3,700 | 2,600 | 2,750 | 11,310 | 1,100 | 12,410 | 2,750 | 290 | 12,410 | 141,638 | 18,202 | 7,640 | 149,981 | 1,807 | 2,168 | 17,740 |
| 1996-7[2] | 3,300 | 3,600 | 4,000 | 12,930 | 750 | 13,680 | 4,000 | 349 | 13,680 | 154,629 | 15,500 | 8,730 | 149,195 | 3,217 | 2,296 | 23,174 |

[1] Preliminary. [2] Estimate. [3] Formerly part of the U.S.S.R.; data not reported separately until 1989-90. NA = Not available.
*Source: Foreign Agricultural Service, U.S. Department of Agriculture*

## World Production of Barley In Thousands of Metric Tons

| Year | Australia | Canada | China | Denmark | France | Germany | India | Japan | Kazakhstan[3] | Morocco | Saudi Arabia | Spain | Turkey | United Kingdom | United States | World Total |
|---|---|---|---|---|---|---|---|---|---|---|---|---|---|---|---|---|
| 1987-8 | 3,477 | 13,957 | 6,041 | 4,292 | 10,528 | 8,571 | 1,669 | 353 | 58,409 | 1,543 | 80 | 9,282 | 6,000 | 9,225 | 11,354 | 181,511 |
| 1988-9 | 3,306 | 10,212 | 6,041 | 5,419 | 9,800 | 9,587 | 1,577 | 399 | 44,500 | 3,454 | 200 | 12,070 | 6,000 | 8,775 | 6,314 | 167,302 |
| 1989-90 | 4,044 | 11,666 | 6,180 | 4,982 | 9,840 | 9,716 | 1,721 | 371 | 48,500 | 2,999 | 331 | 9,100 | 4,900 | 8,025 | 8,784 | 169,680 |
| 1990-1 | 4,184 | 13,441 | 3,930 | 4,990 | 10,150 | 13,990 | 1,490 | 346 | 8,500 | 2,138 | 372 | 9,410 | 6,600 | 7,900 | 9,192 | 178,056 |
| 1991-2 | 4,606 | 11,617 | 3,928 | 5,041 | 10,789 | 14,494 | 1,640 | 268 | 3,085 | 3,253 | 394 | 9,140 | 6,800 | 7,700 | 10,110 | 169,136 |
| 1992-3 | 5,460 | 11,032 | 4,000 | 2,974 | 10,580 | 12,196 | 1,700 | 286 | 8,511 | 1,081 | 406 | 6,105 | 6,500 | 7,350 | 9,908 | 165,767 |
| 1993-4 | 6,956 | 12,972 | 4,200 | 3,369 | 8,981 | 11,000 | 1,510 | 271 | 7,149 | 1,019 | 1,100 | 9,520 | 7,300 | 6,040 | 8,666 | 169,962 |
| 1994-5 | 2,791 | 11,690 | 3,800 | 3,450 | 7,650 | 10,900 | 1,310 | 225 | 5,100 | 3,720 | 2,025 | 7,600 | 6,500 | 5,950 | 8,162 | 160,586 |
| 1995-6[1] | 5,498 | 13,035 | 4,000 | 3,860 | 7,740 | 11,890 | 1,580 | 218 | 2,407 | 600 | 1,200 | 5,200 | 6,900 | 6,850 | 7,829 | 141,638 |
| 1996-7[2] | 6,000 | 16,000 | 4,000 | 3,700 | 9,500 | 12,000 | 1,600 | 200 | 1,750 | 3,800 | 450 | 10,500 | 7,500 | 7,000 | 8,640 | 154,629 |

[1] Preliminary. [2] Estimate. [3] Formerly part of the U.S.S.R.; data not reported separately until 1990-91. *Source: Foreign Agricultural Service, U.S. Department of Agriculture*

## U.S. Barley Acreage and Prices

| Year Beginning- June 1 | Acreage: 1,000 Acres: Planted | Acreage: 1,000 Acres: Harvested for Grain | Yield Per Harvested Acre -- Bushels -- | Received by Farmers[3] | Seasonal Prices: Minneapolis[4] or Better: Feed (No. 2) | Seasonal Prices: Minneapolis[4] or Better: Malting (No. 3) | Seasonal Prices: Portland No. 2 Western | Government Price Support Operations: National Average Loan Rate | Government Price Support Operations: Target Price | Government Price Support Operations: Put Under Support (Mil. Bu.) | Government Price Support Operations: % of Production |
|---|---|---|---|---|---|---|---|---|---|---|---|
| | | | | Dollars per Bushel | | | | | | | |
| 1989-90 | 3,125 | 8,313 | 48.6 | 2.42 | 2.20 | 3.28 | 2.61 | 1.34 | 2.43 | 24.0 | 5.9 |
| 1990-1 | 8,221 | 7,529 | 56.1 | 2.14 | 2.13 | 2.42 | 2.65 | 1.28 | 2.36 | 33.8 | 8.0 |
| 1991-2 | 8,941 | 8,413 | 55.2 | 2.10 | 2.17 | 2.38 | 2.66 | 1.32 | 2.36 | 38.0 | 8.2 |
| 1992-3 | 7,762 | 7,285 | 62.5 | 2.04 | 2.11 | 2.37 | 2.57 | 1.40 | 2.36 | 42.9 | 9.4 |
| 1993-4 | 7,786 | 6,753 | 58.9 | 1.99 | 2.05 | 2.48 | 2.40 | 1.40 | 2.36 | 37.7 | 9.5 |
| 1994-5 | 7,159 | 6,667 | 56.2 | 2.03 | 2.02 | 2.75 | 2.51 | 1.54 | 2.36 | 28.2 | 7.5 |
| 1995-6[1] | 6,689 | 6,277 | 57.6 | 2.89 | 2.68 | 3.52 | 2.97 | 1.54 | 2.36 | 14.9 | 4.1 |
| 1996-7[2] | 6,689 | 6,277 | 57.6 | 2.70-2.80 | 2.49 | 3.39 | 2.97 | 1.54 | 2.36 | 14.9 | 4.1 |

[1] Preliminary. [2] Estimate. [3] Excludes support payments. [4] Duluth beginning March 1987. [5] Available for total feed grains only.
*Source: Economic Research Service, U.S. Department of Agriculture*

## Salient Statistics of Barley in the United States In Millions of Bushels

| Year Beginning- June 1 | Supply: Beginning Stocks | Supply: Production | Supply: Imports | Supply: Total Supply | Disappearance: Domestic Use: Food & Alcohol Beverages | Disappearance: Domestic Use: Seed | Disappearance: Domestic Use: Feed & Residual | Disappearance: Domestic Use: Total | Disappearance: Exports | Disappearance: Total Disappearance | Ending Stocks: Gov't Owned | Ending Stocks: Privately Owned[3] | Ending Stocks: Total Stocks |
|---|---|---|---|---|---|---|---|---|---|---|---|---|---|
| 1989-90 | 196.4 | 404.2 | 13.1 | 613.7 | 162.0 | 13.5 | 193.3 | 368.8 | 84.0 | 452.9 | 19.3 | 141.5 | 160.8 |
| 1990-1 | 160.8 | 422.2 | 13.5 | 596.5 | 161.1 | 14.6 | 204.8 | 380.5 | 80.6 | 461.1 | 8.4 | 127.0 | 135.4 |
| 1991-2 | 135.4 | 464.3 | 24.5 | 624.2 | 163.3 | 12.9 | 224.9 | 401.1 | 94.5 | 495.6 | 6.5 | 122.1 | 128.6 |
| 1992-3 | 128.6 | 455.1 | 11.4 | 595.1 | 158.4 | 13.1 | 192.1 | 363.6 | 80.3 | 443.9 | 5.4 | 145.8 | 151.2 |
| 1993-4 | 151.2 | 398.0 | 71.5 | 620.7 | 162.9 | 11.8 | 241.1 | 415.8 | 66.1 | 481.8 | 5.2 | 133.7 | 138.9 |
| 1994-5 | 138.9 | 374.9 | 65.9 | 579.6 | 163.8 | 11.2 | 225.8 | 400.8 | 66.2 | 467.0 | 5.8 | 107.6 | 112.6 |
| 1995-6[1] | 113.0 | 360.0 | 41.0 | 513.0 | 163.2 | 11.8 | 185.0 | 360.0 | 62.0 | 413.0 | 5.0 | 83.9 | 88.9 |
| 1996-7[2] | 100.0 | 397.0 | 40.0 | 536.0 | ---- | ---- | 235.0 | 235.0 | 35.0 | 436.0 | ---- | ---- | 100.0 |

[1] Preliminary. [2] Estimate. [3] Uncommitted inventory. [4] Includes quantity under loan & farmer-owned reserves. *Source: Economic Research Service, U.S. Department of Agriculture*

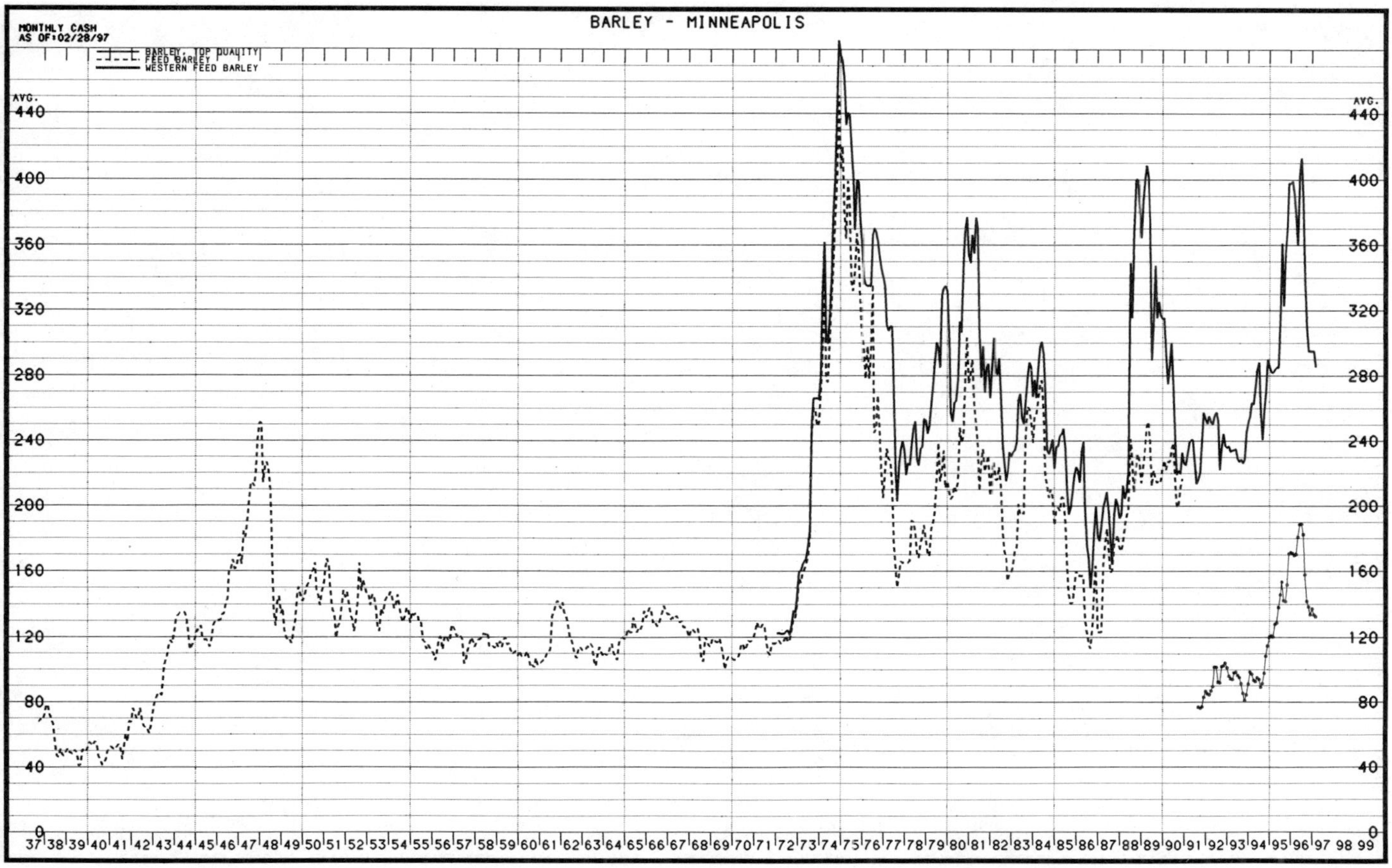

# BARLEY

**Average Cash Prices of No. 2 (or Better) Feed Barley, in Duluth** In Cents Per Bushel

| Year | June | July | Aug. | Sept. | Oct. | Nov. | Dec. | Jan. | Feb. | Mar. | Apr. | May | Average |
|---|---|---|---|---|---|---|---|---|---|---|---|---|---|
| 1988-9 | 241 | 238 | 208 | 224 | 232 | 227 | 214 | 224 | 233 | 249 | 252 | 241 | 232 |
| 1989-90 | 212 | 211 | 217 | 213 | 216 | 215 | 223 | 228 | 220 | 227 | 227 | 233 | 220 |
| 1990-1 | 239 | 217 | 199 | 201 | 211 | 216 | 207 | 209 | 215 | 214 | 212 | 213 | 213 |
| 1991-2 | 202 | 189 | 192 | 208 | 218 | 223 | 218 | 220 | 228 | 230 | 235 | 238 | 217 |
| 1992-3 | 230 | 215 | 203 | 212 | 211 | 208 | 206 | 206 | 208 | 210 | 212 | 205 | 211 |
| 1993-4 | 199 | 196 | 189 | 189 | 201 | 216 | 214 | 215 | 216 | 207 | 208 | 211 | 205 |
| 1994-5 | 205 | 202 | 199 | 204 | 195 | 204 | 200 | 202 | 206 | 202 | 197 | 211 | 202 |
| 1995-6 | 222 | 225 | 209 | 206 | 258 | 298 | 292 | 294 | 300 | 286 | 299 | 320 | 267 |
| 1996-7[1] | 322 | 279 | 260 | 234 | 210 | 190 | 196 | 195 | | | | | 236 |

[1] Preliminary. NQ = No quote. *Source: Economic Research Service, U.S. Department of Agriculture*

**Average Prices Received by Farmers for All Barley in the U.S.** In Cents Per Bushel

| Year | June | July | Aug. | Sept. | Oct. | Nov. | Dec. | Jan. | February | Mar. | Apr. | May | Average |
|---|---|---|---|---|---|---|---|---|---|---|---|---|---|
| 1990-1 | 229 | 216 | 213 | 213 | 204 | 216 | 213 | 214 | 213 | 215 | 210 | 205 | 213 |
| 1991-2 | 190 | 173 | 206 | 206 | 210 | 220 | 224 | 221 | 215 | 212 | 214 | 222 | 209 |
| 1992-3 | 209 | 226 | 216 | 184 | 192 | 205 | 195 | 207 | 200 | 200 | 209 | 197 | 203 |
| 1993-4 | 195 | 190 | 202 | 187 | 182 | 201 | 202 | 215 | 207 | 201 | 202 | 206 | 199 |
| 1994-5 | 191 | 192 | 207 | 193 | 193 | 209 | 199 | 205 | 213 | 213 | 215 | 221 | 204 |
| 1995-6 | 225 | 241 | 262 | 257 | 288 | 309 | 315 | 315 | 328 | 324 | 324 | 342 | 294 |
| 1996-7[1] | 355 | 318 | 299 | 279 | 273 | 265 | 273 | 253 | 247 | | | | 285 |

[1] Preliminary. *Source: National Agricultural Statistics Service, U.S. Department of Agriculture*

**Average Open Interest of Western Feed Barley Futures in Winnipeg** In Contracts -- 20 Tonnes

| Year | Jan. | Feb. | Mar. | Apr. | May | June | July | Aug. | Sept. | Oct. | Nov. | Dec. |
|---|---|---|---|---|---|---|---|---|---|---|---|---|
| 1991 | ------- | 869 | 997 | 1,242 | 1,156 | 1,027 | 1,234 | 1,158 | 1,371 | 1,514 | 919 | 1,065 |
| 1992 | 940 | 662 | 1,060 | 1,572 | 2,025 | 2,692 | 3,168 | 2,605 | 2,994 | 2,746 | 1,519 | 1,685 |
| 1993 | 1,471 | 1,000 | 1,369 | 2,318 | 2,818 | 3,500 | 2,287 | 2,016 | 2,580 | 3,643 | 4,743 | 5,946 |
| 1994 | 7,600 | 8,164 | 7,650 | 8,212 | 8,153 | 9,019 | 8,511 | 8,558 | 9,633 | 12,340 | 10,802 | 9,457 |
| 1995 | 8,900 | 9,295 | 9,965 | 8,657 | 7,279 | 8,731 | 9,297 | 9,770 | 10,704 | 12,043 | 10,324 | 12,089 |
| 1996 | 13,803 | 12,979 | 15,746 | 18,022 | 19,045 | 18,502 | 15,504 | 14,190 | 16,647 | 20,143 | 21,233 | 24,590 |

*Source: Winnipeg Commodity Exchange (WCE)*

# Bauxite

Bauxite is the only raw material used in the production of alumina on a commercial scale in the U.S. However, production data for bauxite in the U.S. is withheld for proprietary reasons. U.S. bauxite production has increased in recent years though it is still less than 1 percent of world production and was used in nonmetal products such as abrasives, chemicals, proppants and refractories. The only active bauxite mines in the U.S. are in Alabama and Georgia and they produce bauxite materials, a natural mixture of bauxite clay and bauxite with very low iron ore content. These materials are use to produce alumina calcines.

U.S. imports for consumption of crude and dried bauxite during April-May 1996 were 1.61 million tonnes. In January-March 1996, U.S. imports of crude and dried bauxite were 2.47 million tonnes, taking the total for the first five months of 1996 to 4.08 million tonnes. Of the total, Jamaica supplied 1.65 million tonnes. The next major supplier was Guinea at 1.42 million tonnes. Brazil provided 708,000 tonnes while Guyana supplied 258,000 tonnes. Other countries supplied 47,700 tonnes. For all of 1995, imports of bauxite were 10.1 million tonnes. Guinea supplied 39 percent while Jamaica supplied 35 percent. Brazil provided 17 percent with Guyana supplying 8 percent.

The U.S. exported small amounts of bauxite. For the April-May period, there were 17,000 tonnes exported while over the first five months of 1996 exports were 43,000 tonnes. The major market for these exports was Canada with 35,600 tonnes. For all of 1995, U.S. bauxite exports were 85,900 tonnes.

U.S. imports of calcined bauxite in April-May 1996 were 30,210 tonnes. In the first quarter 1996, imports were 153,300 tonnes. For all of 1995, U.S. imports of calcined bauxite were 482,000 tonnes. The major suppliers were China at 27 percent, Guyana at 15 percent, with Brazil supplying smaller amounts. U.S. exports of calcined bauxite in April-May 1996 were 3,132 tonnes. For all of 1995, exports were 22,080 tonnes.

U.S. imports for consumption of alumina in April-May 1996 were 806,000 tonnes. In the first five months of 1996, imports were 1.72 million tonnes. Australia supplied 1.29 million tonnes. For all of 1995, imports were 4 million tonnes. For January-May 1996, U.S. exports of alumina were 402,000 tonnes with Canada the major market. For 1995, U.S. alumina exports were 1.04 million tonnes.

**World Production of Bauxite** In Thousands of Metric Tons

| Year | Australia | Brazil | China | Ghana | Greece | Guinea | Guyana[2] | Hungary | India | Indonesia | Jamaica[3] | Russia[3/4] | Sierra Leone | Suriname | United States[3] | World Total |
|---|---|---|---|---|---|---|---|---|---|---|---|---|---|---|---|---|
| 1984 | 31,537 | 6,433 | 2,500 | 49 | 2,296 | 14,738 | 2,485 | 2,994 | 2,078 | 1,003 | 8,735 | 6,200 | 1,041 | 3,375 | 856 | 92,502 |
| 1985 | 31,839 | 5,846 | 2,800 | 170 | 2,435 | 13,956 | 2,206 | 2,815 | 2,341 | 830 | 6,239 | 6,400 | 1,185 | 3,738 | 674 | 89,747 |
| 1986 | 32,384 | 6,446 | 2,900 | 204 | 2,231 | 14,835 | 2,600 | 3,022 | 2,322 | 650 | 6,964 | 6,275 | 1,242 | 3,731 | 510 | 92,534 |
| 1987 | 34,102 | 6,567 | 3,200 | 196 | 2,467 | 16,282 | 2,785 | 3,101 | 2,816 | 635 | 7,660 | 5,700 | 1,391 | 2,581 | 576 | 96,517 |
| 1988 | 36,192 | 8,083 | 2,300 | 285 | 2,433 | 15,624 | 1,339 | 2,593 | 3,961 | 513 | 7,305 | 5,500 | 1,403 | 3,434 | 588 | 103,105 |
| 1989 | 38,584 | 8,665 | 2,388 | 347 | 2,550 | 15,792 | 1,321 | 2,644 | 4,471 | 862 | 9,601 | 5,500 | 1,548 | 3,530 | 670 | 103,722 |
| 1990 | 41,391 | 9,678 | 2,400 | 381 | 2,496 | 15,772 | 1,424 | 2,559 | 4,852 | 1,206 | 10,921 | 5,500 | 1,430 | 3,283 | 495 | 113,000 |
| 1991 | 40,510 | 10,365 | 2,600 | 353 | 2,133 | 15,466 | 2,204 | 2,037 | 4,735 | 1,406 | 11,552 | 5,000 | 1,288 | 3,198 | 50 | 111,000 |
| 1992 | 39,746 | 9,366 | 2,700 | 338 | 2,078 | 13,800 | 2,376 | 1,721 | 4,898 | 804 | 11,302 | 4,578 | 1,250 | 3,250 | 50 | 105,000 |
| 1993 | 41,320 | 9,669 | 3,500 | 424 | 2,205 | 14,100 | 2,130 | 1,561 | 5,277 | 1,320 | 11,391 | 4,260 | 1,165 | 3,412 | 40 | 109,000 |
| 1994[1] | 41,733 | 8,673 | 3,700 | 426 | 2,196 | 14,400 | 2,100 | 830 | 4,809 | 1,342 | 11,564 | 3,000 | 735 | 3,772 | 40 | 107,000 |
| 1995[2] | 42,655 | 8,761 | 5,000 | 490 | 1,916 | 14,400 | 2,100 | 1,100 | 4,800 | 899 | 10,857 | 3,100 | 280 | 3,300 | 35 | 109,000 |

[1] Preliminary. [2] Estimate. [3] Dry Bauxite equivalent of ore processed. [4] Formerly part of the U.S.S.R.; data not reported separetely until 1992.
*Source: U.S. Geological Survey*

**U.S. Salient Statistics of Bauxite** In Thousands of Metric Tons

| Year | Net Import Reliance as a % of Apparent Consumption | Average Price FOB Mine $ per Ton | Mine Production: Crude | Mine Production: Dried Equivalent | Consumption by Industry: Total | Alumina | Abrasive | Chemical | Refractory | Dry Equivalent: Imports[3] (for Consumption) | Dry Equivalent: Exports[3] | Dry Equivalent: Consumption | Stocks, December 31: Producers & Consumers | Government | Total |
|---|---|---|---|---|---|---|---|---|---|---|---|---|---|---|---|
| 1984 | 96 | 13-20 | 1,054 | 856 | 10,519 | 9,465 | 328 | 251 | 420 | 9,435 | 110 | 10,519 | 4,881 | 17,338 | 22,219 |
| 1985 | 96 | 13-20 | 787 | 674 | 8,206 | 7,219 | 305 | 219 | 408 | 7,158 | 69 | 8,206 | 3,643 | 18,357 | 22,000 |
| 1986 | 96 | 13-17 | 617 | 510 | 6,901 | 5,980 | 259 | 231 | 372 | 6,456 | 85 | 6,901 | 3,319 | 18,472 | 21,791 |
| 1987 | 96 | 13-17 | 689 | 576 | 9,548 | 8,601 | 224 | 243 | 422 | 9,156 | 231 | 9,548 | 3,019 | 18,472 | 21,491 |
| 1988 | 97 | 13-17 | 714 | 588 | 10,074 | 8,970 | 274 | 236 | 524 | 9,944 | 71 | 10,074 | 3,021 | 18,474 | 21,495 |
| 1989 | 96 | 15-20 | W | 670 | 11,810 | 10,782 | 275 | 223 | 407 | 10,893 | 44 | 11,810 | 2,891 | 18,474 | 21,365 |
| 1990 | 98 | 15-20 | W | 495 | 12,042 | 11,064 | 276 | 212 | 387 | 12,144 | 74 | 12,042 | 2,318 | 18,477 | 20,795 |
| 1991 | 100 | 15-18 | W | 50 | 12,204 | 11,383 | 204 | 218 | 328 | 11,871 | 51 | 12,204 | 2,620 | 18,477 | 21,097 |
| 1992 | 100 | 15-18 | W | 50 | 11,873 | 11,066 | 223 | 190 | 334 | 10,939 | 63 | 11,873 | 2,319 | 17,805 | 20,124 |
| 1993 | 100 | 15-24 | W | 45 | 11,917 | 11,002 | 203 | 225 | 429 | 11,621 | 90 | 12,200 | 1,590 | 16,938 | 18,500 |
| 19941 | 99 | 15-24 | W | W | 11,200 | 10,400 | 197 | 192 | 350 | 10,700 | 129 | 11,200 | 1,560 | 17,200 | 18,800 |
| 19952 | 99 | 15-18 | W | W | 10,900 | 10,100 | 133 | 201 | 394 | 10,100 | 108 | 10,900 | 1,730 | 16,300 | 18,100 |

[1] Preliminary. [2] Estimate. [3] Including concentrates. W = Withheld proprietary data. *Source: U.S. Geological Survey*

# Bismuth

Bismuth has a wide variety of uses ranging from glass ceramics to pharmaceutical compounds to chemicals and pigments. Bismuth is used for treating stomach ulcers and is found in household pharmaceuticals like Pepto Bismol. In recent years, bismuth has been of interest as a non-toxic substitute for lead in many metallurgical and chemical applications. Bismuth is being tested as an additive to brass for plumbing fixtures, and there has been research into using it as a substitute for lead in shotgun pellets. Because of the limited supply of bismuth, use of it as a substitute in any widespread application such as plumbing is not likely.

In another area, there has been some production of lead-free ceramic glazes containing bismuth for use in china and tableware. Glazes and enamels were also in use for decorative glass coatings for buildings and automobiles. Bismuth glazes have proven to have the same durability as lead without the manufacturing waste being treated as hazardous.

In market developments, on April 15, 1996, Asarco Incorporated announced that it had reached an agreement with the city of Omaha, Nebraska to cease all operations at its Omaha refinery by February 1, 1998, and remediate the property for use as a park. The company ceased lead refining at Omaha on June 1, 1996, but plans to continue processing other materials, including bismuth, at the plant. The U.S. Geological Survey indicated that the anticipated supply of bismuth appears adequate to meet expected demand despite the forthcoming shutdown of the only domestic primary source of bismuth, Asarco's Omaha, Nebraska plant.

No bismuth was sold from the Defense National Stockpile during the second quarter of 1996. The Defense Logistics Agency (DLA) announced its intention to change from a sealed bid auction to negotiated sales for the disposition of bismuth contained in the stockpile. There were reported to be 83,500 kilograms of bismuth available.

U.S. consumption of bismuth in the second quarter of 1996 was 333,000 kilograms (bismuth content), down 18 percent from the first quarter of 1996 and 19 percent lower than the second quarter of 1995. Chemicals and other uses including cosmetics, pharmaceuticals, and experimental took 218,000 kilograms compared to 255,000 kilograms in the first quarter. Fusile alloys and metallurgical additives used 115,000 kilograms in the second quarter, down from 150,000 in the first quarter.

Bismuth imports for consumption in the first quarter 1996 were 441,000 kilograms. For the first five months of 1995, they were 748,000 kilograms. For all of 1995, U.S. imports were 1.45 million kilograms. The major suppliers were Belgium with 636,000 kilograms, Mexico with 444,000, and the United Kingdom with 131,000.

The U.S. exports smaller amounts of bismuth in the form of metal, alloys, waste, and scrap. Over the January-May 1996 period, exports were 55,600 kilograms (metal content). For 1995, U.S. exports of bismuth were 261,000 kilograms. The major markets were Belgium with 157,000 kilograms, followed by Canada, China, and France.

Consumer stocks of bismuth at the end of the second quarter 1996 were 126,000 kilograms, down from stocks at the end of the first quarter of 192,000 kilograms. At the end of 1995, bismuth stocks were 359,000 kilograms.

The outlook for bismuth is optimistic in the area of non-toxic replacements for lead even though demand has decreased in recent years. Since bismuth is a byproduct of lead, a rapid increase in supply is not likely.

**World Production of Bismuth** In Metric Tons

| | Mine Output, Metal Content | | | | | | | | Refined Metal | | | | | | | |
|---|---|---|---|---|---|---|---|---|---|---|---|---|---|---|---|---|
| Year | Australia | Canada | China | Japan | Rep. of Korea | Mexico | Peru | Total | Belgium | China | Kazakhstan[3] | Japan | Mexico | Peru | U.K. | Total |
| 1989 | 500 | 205 | 850 | 150 | 96 | 883 | 687 | 3,750 | 800 | 850 | 85 | 502 | 597 | 646 | 200 | 3,970 |
| 1990 | 400 | 87 | 1,060 | 133 | 79 | 733 | 555 | 3,440 | 1,000 | 1,060 | 80 | 442 | 549 | 521 | 125 | 4,190 |
| 1991 | 400 | 65 | 1,040 | 138 | 42 | 651 | 610 | 3,230 | 800 | 1,260 | 70 | 461 | 500 | 576 | 100 | 4,010 |
| 1992 | 300 | 224 | 820 | 159 | 9 | 807 | 550 | 2,740 | 800 | 1,060 | 45 | 530 | 550 | 418 | 100 | 3,670 |
| 1993 | ---- | 144 | 740 | 149 | 5 | 908 | 1,000 | 3,090 | 950 | 1,050 | 40 | 497 | 650 | 937 | ---- | 4,240 |
| 1994[1] | ---- | 129 | 700 | 152 | ---- | 900 | 1,000 | 3,020 | 900 | 1,000 | 35 | 505 | 650 | 871 | ---- | 4,100 |
| 1995[2] | ---- | 126 | 700 | 177 | ---- | 900 | 1,000 | 3,040 | 800 | 1,100 | 35 | 591 | 700 | 870 | ---- | 4,320 |

[1] Preliminary. [2] Estimate. [3] Formerly part of the U.S.S.R.; data not reported separately until 1992. *Source: U.S. Geological Survey*

**U.S. Salient Statistics of Bismuth** In Metric Tons

| | Bismuth Consumed, By Uses | | | | | | | Imports of Metallic Bismuth from | | | | |
|---|---|---|---|---|---|---|---|---|---|---|---|---|
| Year | Metal-lurgical Additives | Other Alloys & Uses | Fusible Alloys | Chemicals[3] | Total Con-sumption | Consumer Stocks Dec. 31 | Exports of Metal & Alloys | Belgium | Mexico | Peru | Total | Dealer Price $ Per Pound |
| 1986 | 350 | 21 | 290 | 663 | 1,324 | 346 | 42 | 384.4 | 362.9 | 107.0 | 1,129 | 3.25 |
| 1987 | 494 | 22 | 334 | 748 | 1,597 | 294 | 38 | 435.0 | 391.3 | 440.4 | 1,581 | 3.65 |
| 1988 | 493 | 27 | 332 | 679 | 1,531 | 433 | 147 | 340.2 | 448.5 | 188.9 | 1,641 | 5.78 |
| 1989 | 396 | 25 | 272 | 659 | 1,352 | 440 | 122 | 835.7 | 390.8 | 271.4 | 1,880 | 5.76 |
| 1990 | 424 | 24 | 249 | 577 | 1,274 | 331 | 122 | 668.1 | 404.8 | 262.7 | 1,612 | 3.56 |
| 1991 | 341 | 26 | 271 | 789 | 1,427 | 247 | 75 | 345.1 | 535.0 | 169.8 | 1,411 | 3.00 |
| 1992 | 381 | 33 | 278 | 758 | 1,450 | 272 | 90 | 467.4 | 550.5 | 75.7 | 1,621 | 2.66 |
| 1993 | 232 | 59 | 256 | 750 | 1,300 | 323 | 70 | 275.1 | 479.1 | 117.2 | 1,330 | 2.50 |
| 1994[1] | 306 | 26 | 276 | 841 | 1,450 | 402 | 160 | 512.0 | 665.0 | 114.9 | 1,660 | 3.25 |
| 1995[2] | 247 | 29 | 442 | 877 | 2,030 | 390 | 261 | 636.0 | 444.0 | 10.9 | 1,450 | 3.85 |

[1] Preliminary. [2] Estimate. [3] Includes pharmaceuticals. *Source: U.S. Geological Survey*

# Broilers

U.S. broiler production set a new record high in 1996 of more than 26 billion pounds; initial forecasts for 1997 point to yet another record of 27.9 billion pounds. Production of ready-to-cook (RTC) broiler meat was up almost 6 percent in the first half of 1996, but the increases in bird numbers were significantly lower than in recent years at 2 percent vs. a 4 percent gain in 1995, and a long term average annual increase of about 5 percent. However, average liveweight gains of almost 3 percent were much higher than in 1995 (1 percent) and a long term average of almost 2 percent. Net returns for broiler processors strengthened in the second half of 1996 as wholesale prices increased, running about 5 cents per pound of meat during the summer vs. a near breakeven during the first quarter. Towards yearend 1996, the 12-City average wholesale price averaged near 63 cents per pound; a year earlier it was below 60 cents. Retail prices were averaging 85 cents a pound vs. 80 cents in late 1995.

U.S. per capita broiler consumption in 1996 set a new high: 71.3 pounds retail weight in 1996, with 1997's total projected at 74.2 pounds. However, a key factor for the increased production was the record pace of broiler exports. Export growth continues to be stimulated by attractive prices of U.S. broilers, notably leg quarters, and the development of foreign markets. Export forecasts for 1996 and 1997 were forecast at 4.7 billion pounds and 5.1 billion respectively; reflecting strength in shipments to Russia and Hong Kong, the largest markets for U.S. broiler products. Hong Kong, however, is a transshipment site for China. Exports to Mexico rebounded in 1996 in line with their strengthening economy, and Ukraine demand increased to more than 18 million pounds from less than 200,000 pounds in 1995. The Middle East and South Africa are seen as significant markets for U.S. broiler exports in the years ahead.

## Broiler Supply and Prices in the United States

| | Federally Inspected Slaughter | | | | Total | Per Capita | Prices | |
|---|---|---|---|---|---|---|---|---|
| Year & Quarters | Number (Millions) | Average Weight (Pounds) | Liveweight Pounds (Mil. Lbs.) | Certified RTC Weight (Mil. Lbs.) | Production RTC[3] (Mil. Lbs.) | Consumption RTC Basis (Pounds) | Farm (Cents per Pound) | Georgia Dock[4] (Cents per Pound) |
| 1991 | 6,140 | 4.43 | 27,171 | 19,728 | 19,591 | 72.3 | 30.91 | 49.15 |
| 1992 | 6,425 | 4.51 | 28,998 | 21,052 | 20,904 | 75.7 | 31.85 | 50.21 |
| 1993 | 6,681 | 4.56 | 30,474 | 22,178 | 22,015 | 77.7 | 34.40 | 53.65 |
| 1994 | 7,270 | 4.64 | 33,595 | 23,846 | 23,666 | 79.4 | 35.06 | 54.40 |
| 1995[1] | 7,371 | 4.66 | 34,348 | 25,021 | 24,827 | 79.2 | 34.68 | 54.73 |
| 1996[2] | 7,516 | 4.78 | 35,886 | 26,249 | 26,249 | 81.3 | 38.69 | 61.07 |
| I | 1,879 | 4.81 | 9,038 | 6,609 | 6,557 | 20.2 | 35.47 | 55.76 |
| II | 1,895 | 4.76 | 9,014 | 6,607 | 6,554 | 20.9 | 37.40 | 59.06 |
| III | 1,912 | 4.71 | 9,008 | 6,592 | 6,541 | 20.4 | 41.30 | 65.04 |
| IV | 1,831 | 4.82 | 8,826 | 6,486 | 6,597 | 19.8 | 40.60 | 64.42 |

[1] Preliminary. [2] Estimate. [3] Total production equals federally inspected slaughter plus other slaughter minus cut-up and futher processing condemnation. [4] Ready-to-cook-basis. *Source: Economic Research Service, U.S. Department of Agriculture*

## Salient Broiler Statistics in the United States

| | Commercial Production | | Average | | | Total Chickens[3] Supply and Distribution | | | | | | | |
|---|---|---|---|---|---|---|---|---|---|---|---|---|---|
| | | | | | | Production | | | Storage | | | Consumption | |
| Year | Number (Millions) | Liveweight (Mil. Lbs.) | Liveweight Per Bird (Pounds) | Average Price (¢/Pound) | Value of Production (Mil. $) | Federally Inspected (In Millions of Pounds) | Other Chickens (In Millions of Pounds) | Total (In Millions of Pounds) | Stocks January 1 (In Millions of Pounds) | Exports (In Millions of Pounds) | Broiler Feed Ratio in Pounds | Total (Mil. Lbs.) | Per Capita[4] (in Lbs.) |
| 1990 | 5,864 | 25,631 | 4.37 | 32.6 | 8,365 | 18,555 | 29 | 18,583 | 221 | 1,143 | 4.9 | 17,266 | 60.91 |
| 1991 | 6,137 | 27,203 | 4.43 | 30.8 | 8,383 | 19,728 | 32 | 19,760 | 242 | 1,261 | 4.9 | 18,271 | 63.55 |
| 1992 | 6,402 | 28,829 | 4.51 | 31.8 | 9,174 | 21,052 | 36 | 21,088 | 300 | 1,489 | 5.1 | 19,347 | 66.57 |
| 1993 | 6,694 | 30,618 | 4.56 | 34.0 | 10,417 | 22,178 | 36 | 22,015 | 368 | 1,966 | 5.3 | 20,059 | 68.50 |
| 1994 | 7,018 | 32,529 | 4.64 | 35.0 | 11,372 | 23,846 | 38 | 23,666 | 358 | 2,876 | 5.2 | 20,690 | 69.50 |
| 1995[1] | 7,326 | 34,222 | 4.66 | 34.4 | 11,763 | 25,021 | 39 | 24,827 | 458 | 3,894 | 5.2 | 20,831 | 68.80 |
| 1996[2] | | | 4.74 | | | 26,460 | 41 | 26,250 | 560 | 4,607 | 4.5 | 21,603 | 70.70 |

[1] Preliminary. [2] Estimate. [3] Ready-to-cook. [4] Retail weight basis. *Source: Economic Research Service, U.S. Department of Agriculture*

## Average Wholesale Broiler Prices RTC (Ready-to-Cook)

| Year | Jan. | Feb. | Mar. | Apr. | May | June | July | Aug. | Sept. | Oct. | Nov. | Dec. | Average |
|---|---|---|---|---|---|---|---|---|---|---|---|---|---|
| 1990 | 51.70 | 57.37 | 60.39 | 55.28 | 57.93 | 56.44 | 59.47 | 54.89 | 57.35 | 48.79 | 48.02 | 49.63 | 54.77 |
| 1991 | 51.72 | 50.63 | 51.41 | 51.96 | 52.03 | 52.66 | 54.25 | 54.61 | 53.61 | 51.61 | 50.30 | 49.54 | 52.03 |
| 1992 | 50.14 | 50.28 | 50.24 | 49.45 | 55.06 | 52.38 | 56.04 | 56.13 | 51.29 | 53.67 | 54.98 | 51.17 | 52.57 |
| 1993 | 52.14 | 53.01 | 54.02 | 54.66 | 57.86 | 55.04 | 55.36 | 57.77 | 57.59 | 55.72 | 55.82 | 53.17 | 55.18 |
| 1994 | 52.67 | 55.22 | 57.56 | 57.80 | 61.39 | 60.71 | 57.36 | 54.65 | 55.80 | 54.02 | 50.50 | 50.87 | 55.71 |
| 1995 | 51.14 | 51.73 | 52.32 | 51.51 | 52.94 | 55.88 | 58.76 | 61.74 | 61.48 | 58.79 | 61.08 | 58.87 | 56.35 |
| 1996[2] | 59.00 | 55.31 | 54.31 | 56.01 | 61.71 | 65.52 | 64.58 | 64.07 | 64.01 | 62.64 | 64.37 | 63.50 | 61.25 |

[1] Preliminary. *Source: Economic Research Service, U.S. Department of Agriculture*

# Butter

The slide in U.S. butter production accelerated in 1996 as only 540,000 metric tons were produced, down 32,000 tons from 1995 and 79,000 tons below the 1992 record high. U.S. consumption also dropped, but the downward trend is less pronounced. Disappearance in 1996 of 519,000 tons compares with 537,000 tons in 1995 and 525,000 in 1992. Since the late 1980's new supply has consistently outpaced domestic demand; a trend that seems likely to persist. There is a monthly seasonality to production: January is generally the highest producing month and August the smallest. U.S. butter stocks, much of which had been government owned in the early 1990's, have since dropped sharply, from a high in late 1991 of 249,000 tons to only an estimated 8,000 tons at yearend 1996. Annual U.S. per capita butter use has recently averaged about 4.4 pounds vs 4.6 pounds in the 1980's.

Butter production is derived directly from milk production. Butter manufacture is the third largest use of milk production, the first being milk as a fluid and second the conversion into cheese. California is the largest producing state with nearly a third of total U.S. production.

World butter production in 1996 of 5.3 million metric tons was a shade lower than in 1995 and compares with the annual 1991-93 average of nearly 5.6 million tons. Russia and the Ukraine are the world's largest producers with a combined 13 percent of global output, 680,000 tons in 1996. Yet their combined year-to-year-total continues to drop sharply; from 1.1 million tons in 1991 to 808,000 tons by 1994. The U.S. generally produces 10 percent of the world total. Statistically India is the largest producer with a record 1.35 million tons in 1996 vs. 1.3 million in 1995, but their product is mostly Ghee, a butterlike substance which is consumed almost entirely in India. World consumption almost mirrors production: India is first, Russia and the Ukraine second, but Germany's use during 1995 and 1996 at 563,000 tons each has bested the U.S. for the third position. Global foreign trade in butter is small. U.S. imports are insignificant, 3,000 tons in 1996 and slightly above average; exports, however, show sharp variance, reaching 145,000 tons in 1993, sliding to 64,000 tons by 1995 and to 25.000 tons in 1996. New Zealand was the largest exporter with 270,000 tons in 1996, 44 percent of the world total. Russia was the largest importer taking 210,000 of a world import total of 365,000 tons. World stocks are relatively low, only 430,000 tons at yearend 1995 and 1996 vs. ending stocks in excess of 800,000 tons in the early 1990's, suggesting that world trade could yet quicken, but whether the U.S. would benefit is questionable. The key to increased world demand continues to rest largely on Russia and how much more they can afford to import.

International dairy prices generally trended lower during the first half of 1996 with butter making the sharpest decline, reflecting in part sharp increases in Australian and New Zealand production. Butter prices, basis North Europe FOB, fell from $2,225 per ton at the start of 1996 to $1,675 by midyear. Perhaps more importantly, U.S. prices rebounded during the first half of the year owing to reduced supplies of manufacturing milk. Wholesale Grade A butter averaged 75.59 cents per pound in 1995, by mid-year 1996 prices were averaging near $1.45 per pound and the strength was expected to persist into 1997 in line with tight domestic milk supplies.

## Supply and Distribution of Butter in the United States In Millions of Pounds

| | Supply | | | | Distribution | | | | | | | | | 93 Score AA Wholesale Price | |
|---|---|---|---|---|---|---|---|---|---|---|---|---|---|---|---|
| | | | | | Domestic Disapparance | | | | | Department of Agriculture | | | | | |
| Year | Production | Cold Storage Stocks[3] Jan. 1[6] | Imports | Total Supply | Total | Donated | Per Capita (Pounds) | Exports | Shipments[4] | Jan 1. Stocks[5] | Dec. 31 Stocks[5] | Removed by USDA Programs | Total Use | California $ per Pound | Chicago $ per Pound |
| 1987 | 1,104 | 193 | 5 | 1,361 | 1,198 | 231 | 4.7 | 16 | 1 | 220 | 96 | 187.3 | 1,215 | 1.6748 | 1.4172 |
| 1988 | 1,208 | 143 | 5 | 1,359 | 1,131 | 195 | 4.5 | 15 | 1 | 96 | 173 | 312.6 | 1,147 | 1.6097 | 1.3412 |
| 1989 | 1,295 | 215 | 5 | 1,515 | 1,127 | 214 | 4.4 | 112 | 4 | 173 | 223 | 413.4 | 1,243 | 1.5660 | 1.2951 |
| 1990 | 1,302 | 256 | 5 | 1,582 | 1,039 | 182 | 4.4 | 126 | 2 | 223 | 373 | 400.3 | 1,167 | 1.3050 | 1.0346 |
| 1991 | 1,336 | 416 | 5 | 1,759 | 1,181 | 132 | 4.4 | 26 | 1 | 373 | 511 | 442.8 | 1,208 | 1.2856 | 1.0182 |
| 1992 | 1,365 | 539 | 4 | 1,919 | 1,323 | 119 | 4.4 | 142 | 1 | 511 | 430 | 439.5 | 1,466 | 1.1386 | .8427 |
| 1993 | 1,315 | 448 | 4 | 1,774 | 1,327 | 149 | 4.7 | 204 | 1 | 430 | 229 | 288.8 | 1,532 | 1.0612 | .7693 |
| 1994[1] | 1,296 | 235 | 3 | 1,543 | 1,362 | ---- | 4.8 | 101 | ---- | 229 | 67 | 204.3 | 1,464 | .9581 | .7068 |
| 1995[2] | 1,261 | 79 | ---- | 1,340 | ---- | ---- | 4.5 | ---- | ---- | 67 | ---- | 78.5 | ---- | ---- | ---- |

[1] Preliminary. [2] Estimates. [3] Includes butter equivalent. [4] Includes USDA shipments to territories. [5] Includes butteroil. [6] Includes stocks held by USDA.
*Source: Economic Research Service, U.S. Department of Agriculture*

## Commercial Disappearance of Creamery Butter in the U.S. In Millions of Pounds

| Year | First Quarter | Second Quarter | Third Quarter | Fourth Quarter | Total | Year | First Quarter | Second Quarter | Third Quarter | Fourth Quarter | Total |
|---|---|---|---|---|---|---|---|---|---|---|---|
| 1985 | 200.0 | 203.9 | 241.5 | 272.9 | 918.2 | 1991 | 186.8 | 184.0 | 255.6 | 276.5 | 903.5 |
| 1986 | 198.6 | 220.1 | 234.4 | 269.8 | 922.9 | 1992 | 214.6 | 216.6 | 236.8 | 276.2 | 944.3 |
| 1987 | 222.7 | 222.1 | 218.4 | 239.3 | 902.5 | 1993 | 224.6 | 231.5 | 271.9 | 312.7 | 1,040.6 |
| 1988 | 194.5 | 221.6 | 219.7 | 274.0 | 909.8 | 1994 | 261.7 | 254.9 | 285.0 | 298.3 | 1,097.3 |
| 1989 | 188.3 | 145.6 | 228.8 | 291.3 | 854.1 | 1995 | 329.0 | 286.8 | 255.1 | 304.9 | 1,175.8 |
| 1990 | 197.5 | 218.1 | 218.1 | 281.8 | 915.2 | 1996[1] | 327.0 | 300.3 | 234.7 | | 862.0 |

[1] Preliminary. *Source: Economic Research Service, U.S. Department of Agriculture*

## World (Total) Butter[3] Production    In Thousands of Metric Tons

| Year | Argentina | Australia | Brazil | Canada | Former Czechoslovakia | Denmark | France | Germany[4] | India | Ireland | Japan | Netherland | New Zealand | Poland | Russia[5] | Ukraine[5] | U.K. | United States |
|---|---|---|---|---|---|---|---|---|---|---|---|---|---|---|---|---|---|---|
| 1986 | 32 | 105 | 65 | 109 | 156 | 112 | 633 | 567 | 720 | 160 | 88 | 377 | 299 | 289 | ---- | 1,700 | 222 | 545 |
| 1987 | 34 | 104 | 65 | 95 | 149 | 96 | 569 | 553 | 750 | 150 | 69 | 234 | 248 | 293 | ---- | 1,742 | 174 | 501 |
| 1988 | 35 | 98 | 65 | 105 | 148 | 94 | 521 | 585 | 850 | 139 | 68 | 214 | 276 | 293 | ---- | 1,724 | 140 | 547 |
| 1989 | 45 | 96 | 65 | 99 | 156 | 92 | 525 | 711 | 880 | 156 | 78 | 213 | 246 | 325 | 820 | 441 | 130 | 588 |
| 1990 | 40 | 111 | 75 | 100 | 159 | 93 | 514 | 640 | 970 | 159 | 76 | 209 | 276 | 300 | 833 | 444 | 138 | 591 |
| 1991 | 38 | 111 | 70 | 97 | 136 | 71 | 496 | 555 | 1,020 | 146 | 76 | 196 | 269 | 220 | 729 | 376 | 132 | 606 |
| 1992 | 37 | 116 | 65 | 86 | 118 | 62 | 454 | 474 | 1,060 | 142 | 95 | 191 | 268 | 180 | 762 | 303 | 127 | 619 |
| 1993 | 36 | 131 | 65 | 83 | 115 | 59 | 444 | 480 | 1,110 | 135 | 108 | 184 | 276 | 180 | 732 | 312 | 152 | 596 |
| 1994 | 43 | 147 | 60 | 88 | ---- | 59 | 444 | 461 | 1,200 | 136 | 80 | 159 | 297 | 160 | 488 | 320 | 154 | 588 |
| 1995[1] | 46 | 142 | 65 | 92 | ---- | 54 | 455 | 486 | 1,280 | 148 | 80 | 158 | 301 | 162 | 419 | 310 | 114 | 572 |
| 1996[2] | 50 | 149 | 70 | 90 | ---- | 52 | 460 | 480 | 1,350 | 140 | 85 | 148 | 310 | 150 | 380 | 300 | 120 | 540 |

[1] Preliminary. [2] Forecast. [3] Factory (including creameries and dairies) and farm. [4] Includes the former East Germany after 1988. [5] Formerly part of the U.S.S.R.; data not reported seperately until 1989. *Source: Foreign Agricultural Service, U.S. Department of Agriculture*

## Production of Creamery Butter in Factories in the United States    In Millions of Pounds

| Year | Jan. | Feb. | Mar. | Apr. | May | June | July | Aug. | Sept. | Oct. | Nov. | Dec. | Total |
|---|---|---|---|---|---|---|---|---|---|---|---|---|---|
| 1986 | 136.7 | 119.3 | 119.2 | 122.7 | 114.7 | 93.0 | 79.7 | 69.9 | 80.2 | 85.3 | 80.3 | 101.3 | 1,202.3 |
| 1987 | 111.9 | 97.4 | 105.4 | 102.6 | 98.2 | 81.5 | 75.2 | 66.4 | 77.9 | 91.2 | 87.9 | 108.5 | 1,104.1 |
| 1988 | 126.1 | 119.7 | 115.5 | 113.8 | 108.0 | 90.8 | 76.3 | 74.1 | 83.3 | 92.3 | 95.6 | 112.0 | 1,207.5 |
| 1989 | 129.0 | 124.7 | 135.7 | 124.7 | 122.5 | 95.3 | 72.2 | 80.1 | 81.6 | 95.1 | 94.4 | 107.4 | 1,262.7 |
| 1990 | 134.0 | 127.3 | 136.2 | 125.6 | 118.6 | 96.7 | 84.6 | 84.2 | 83.4 | 106.7 | 110.1 | 112.2 | 1,319.6 |
| 1991 | 142.1 | 126.3 | 131.6 | 133.7 | 126.0 | 98.3 | 88.9 | 85.0 | 84.7 | 105.2 | 108.5 | 130.1 | 1,360.4 |
| 1992 | 156.0 | 132.0 | 129.9 | 119.7 | 118.2 | 103.0 | 97.8 | 86.7 | 96.6 | 101.6 | 98.3 | 119.8 | 1,365.2 |
| 1993 | 147.3 | 127.2 | 131.6 | 121.8 | 116.4 | 102.3 | 86.2 | 80.7 | 86.3 | 97.8 | 97.3 | 120.3 | 1,315.2 |
| 1994 | 135.3 | 118.4 | 118.0 | 119.4 | 118.2 | 99.2 | 84.2 | 88.2 | 91.2 | 101.8 | 100.7 | 121.4 | 1,295.9 |
| 1995[1] | 132.0 | 121.7 | 127.3 | 120.6 | 119.4 | 98.4 | 85.0 | 76.0 | 80.2 | 93.5 | 90.5 | 112.4 | 1,260.7 |
| 1996[2] | 125.4 | 118.1 | 113.2 | 107.9 | 100.7 | 72.9 | 72.1 | 73.2 | 81.0 | 95.5 | 94.3 | 111.2 | 1,054.3 |

[1] Preliminary. [2] Estimate. *Source: Economic Research Service, U.S. Department of Agriculture*

## Cold Storage Holdings of Creamery Butter in the U.S. on First of Month    In Millions of Pounds

| Year | Jan. | Feb. | Mar. | Apr. | May | June | July | Aug. | Sept. | Oct. | Nov. | Dec. |
|---|---|---|---|---|---|---|---|---|---|---|---|---|
| 1986 | 205.5 | 206.3 | 242.4 | 283.3 | 305.0 | 330.8 | 342.8 | 337.6 | 304.4 | 279.6 | 253.3 | 218.5 |
| 1987 | 193.0 | 206.6 | 231.6 | 254.0 | 247.9 | 251.1 | 237.9 | 211.2 | 187.3 | 176.2 | 165.6 | 158.5 |
| 1988 | 143.2 | 157.3 | 198.9 | 221.1 | 240.4 | 280.5 | 293.4 | 295.8 | 294.4 | 253.4 | 237.3 | 226.2 |
| 1989 | 214.7 | 246.6 | 314.4 | 341.9 | 377.2 | 438.3 | 464.1 | 461.3 | 439.7 | 407.9 | 370.6 | 294.1 |
| 1990 | 256.2 | 269.7 | 293.8 | 335.4 | 358.8 | 399.6 | 420.0 | 420.8 | 427.9 | 412.3 | 413.6 | 407.6 |
| 1991 | 416.1 | 470.8 | 524.8 | 555.9 | 620.5 | 646.7 | 662.7 | 659.8 | 629.4 | 597.2 | 567.1 | 539.4 |
| 1992 | 539.4 | 565.4 | 624.8 | 645.3 | 678.7 | 712.6 | 747.0 | 755.8 | 705.7 | 608.1 | 541.7 | 487.6 |
| 1993 | 447.7 | 489.1 | 492.5 | 515.6 | 552.7 | 559.0 | 569.0 | 516.4 | 473.3 | 395.4 | 341.1 | 276.3 |
| 1994 | 234.7 | 251.0 | 243.2 | 253.5 | 265.7 | 281.4 | 275.1 | 245.9 | 206.6 | 163.4 | 124.6 | 84.5 |
| 1995 | 79.5 | 89.9 | 88.3 | 74.8 | 79.1 | 81.3 | 79.2 | 68.3 | 50.2 | 32.8 | 23.6 | 15.7 |
| 1996[1] | 18.6 | 25.5 | 33.7 | 48.7 | 39.8 | 34.0 | 29.7 | 31.7 | 27.3 | 21.4 | 20.6 | 17.7 |

[1] Preliminary. *Source: Agricultural Statistics Board, U.S.Department of Agriculture*

## Wholesale Price of 92 Score Creamery (Grade A) Butter in Chicago    In Cents Per Pound

| Year | Jan. | Feb. | March | April | May | June | July | Aug. | Sept. | Oct. | Nov. | Dec. | Average |
|---|---|---|---|---|---|---|---|---|---|---|---|---|---|
| 1986 | 138.8 | 138.8 | 137.5 | 138.8 | 138.8 | 139.1 | 143.7 | 153.9 | 154.2 | 153.5 | 151.9 | 145.5 | 144.5 |
| 1987 | 137.3 | 136.8 | 137.8 | 138.8 | 138.4 | 144.6 | 149.0 | 148.1 | 145.3 | 136.8 | 135.6 | 134.0 | 140.2 |
| 1988 | 131.9 | 131.0 | 131.0 | 131.0 | 131.0 | 133.5 | 135.9 | 135.6 | 134.3 | 132.0 | 131.3 | 131.3 | 132.5 |
| 1989 | 131.0 | 131.0 | 131.0 | 131.0 | 131.0 | 131.0 | 130.3 | 132.8 | 125.1 | 120.5 | 120.5 | 120.0 | 127.9 |
| 1990 | 110.9 | 108.3 | 108.3 | 106.9 | 99.0 | 98.4 | 100.3 | 98.9 | 98.9 | 98.9 | 98.9 | 98.0 | 102.1 |
| 1991 | 97.3 | 97.3 | 97.3 | 97.3 | 97.3 | 98.6 | 98.9 | 98.9 | 100.7 | 106.3 | 104.6 | 98.4 | 99.3 |
| 1992 | 94.9 | 86.3 | 86.3 | 86.3 | 83.8 | 76.6 | 76.6 | 76.6 | 81.7 | 82.2 | 80.7 | 78.6 | 82.5 |
| 1993 | 75.3 | 75.3 | 75.3 | 75.3 | 75.3 | 76.2 | 73.5 | 74.6 | 74.3 | 74.2 | 73.6 | 69.7 | 74.4 |
| 1994 | 64.0 | 64.0 | 65.5 | 65.5 | 64.5 | 65.1 | 66.9 | 71.5 | 71.5 | 71.5 | 71.5 | 67.0 | 67.4 |
| 1995 | 64.0 | 65.5 | 66.5 | 66.5 | 66.5 | 69.9 | 74.5 | 79.5 | 80.9 | 95.4 | 103.5 | 74.4 | 75.6 |
| 1996 | 75.4 | 66.4 | 65.5 | 69.0 | 87.8 | 129.3 | 145.3 | 145.5 | 145.5 | 128.6 | 74.1 | 71.9 | 100.4 |

*Source: Economic Research Service, U.S. Department of Agriculture*

# Cadmium

Cadmium is a rare chemical element that is the by-product of the smelting and refining of zinc ores. It is used primarily for the plating of iron and steel to protect them from corrosion. Due to the cost of waste disposal and assorted problems with its toxicity, the use of cadmium in electroplating has decreased. Due to environmental concerns, the outlook for increased cadmium use is not very positive. Cadmium is highly toxic and its disposal represents a problem for users.

For 1995, two companies in the U.S. recovered cadmium as a by-product of the smelting and refining of zinc concentrates. A third company recovers cadmium from other nonferrous sources, such as lead smelter baghouse dust, but these operations were halted in 1993. The estimated consumption pattern for cadmium includes batteries 65 per cent; pigments 14 per cent; coatings and platings 9 per cent; stabilizers for engineering plastics and similar synthetic products 9 per cent; nonferrous alloys 2 per cent; and other including electrooptics 1 per cent.

Cadmium recycling has proved to be feasible only for nickel-cadmium batteries, some alloys, and dust from electric arc furnaces operated by the steel industry. The exact amounts of cadmium that are recycled are not known. In 1994, the U.S. steel industry generated more than 500,000 tonnes of electric furnace dust, typically containing .003 per cent to .07 per cent cadmium. Seventeen states were reported to be setting up collection networks for recycling nickel-cadmium batteries. The U.S. imports cadmium metal from a number of countries. These include Canada, Mexico, Belgium, and Germany among others.

U.S. refinery production of cadmium in 1995 was estimated at 1,300 tonnes, up 29 per cent from 1994. Imports of cadmium metal for consumption in 1995 were 1,040 tonnes, down 6 per cent from the previous year. U.S. exports of cadmium metal, alloys, and scrap in 1995 were 1,050 tonnes, down 28 per cent from the previous year. Shipments of cadmium from the government stockpile in 1995 were 450 tonnes, up from 209 tonnes the previous year and 185 tonnes in 1993. As of September 30, 1995, the government stockpile of cadmium showed 2,020 tonnes of uncommitted inventory, 243 tonnes of committed inventory, and 2,020 tonnes authorized for disposal. U.S. apparent consumption of cadmium in 1995 was estimated at 1,600 tonnes, up 57 per cent from 1994. Stocks at year end 1995 that were held by producers and distributors were 540 tonnes, up from 439 tonnes the previous year.

World production of cadmium in 1995 was estimated at 18,900 tonnes, up over 4 per cent from the previous year. The major producer of cadmium was Japan with 2,800 tonnes, followed by Canada with 2,300 tonnes, and Belgium with 1,600 tonnes. Other important producers include Germany, Australia, and Mexico. Estimated world resources of cadmium were about 6 million tonnes based on zinc resources containing about .3 per cent cadmium.

**World Refinery Production of Cadmium** In Metric Tons

| Year | Australia | Belgium | Canada | China | Finland | France | Germany | Italy | Japan | Kazakhstan[4] | Mexico | Norway | Poland | United Kingdom | United States[3] | Zaire | World Total |
|---|---|---|---|---|---|---|---|---|---|---|---|---|---|---|---|---|---|
| 1986 | 915 | 1,374 | 1,484 | 650 | 522 | 431 | 1,218 | 411 | 2,489 | 3,000 | 1,016 | 154 | 600 | 379 | 1,486 | 364 | 19,070 |
| 1987 | 944 | 1,308 | 1,481 | 680 | 690 | 457 | 1,125 | 320 | 2,450 | 3,000 | 935 | 147 | 600 | 498 | 1,515 | 299 | 19,066 |
| 1988 | 855 | 1,836 | 1,694 | 750 | 703 | 558 | 1,186 | 686 | 2,614 | 3,000 | 1,117 | 169 | 642 | 399 | 1,885 | 281 | 21,869 |
| 1989 | 696 | 1,764 | 1,620 | 800 | 612 | 170 | 1,234 | 776 | 2,694 | 3,000 | 976 | 207 | 555 | 395 | 1,550 | 224 | 20,873 |
| 1990 | 638 | 1,960 | 1,470 | 1,100 | 569 | 187 | 990 | 691 | 2,450 | 2,800 | 882 | 286 | 373 | 438 | 1,680 | 127 | 20,200 |
| 1991 | 1,076 | 1,807 | 1,829 | 1,200 | 593 | 271 | 1,048 | 658 | 2,889 | 2,500 | 688 | 227 | 364 | 449 | 1,680 | 65 | 20,900 |
| 1992 | 1,001 | 1,550 | 1,963 | 1,150 | 590 | 252 | 961 | 742 | 2,986 | 1,000 | 602 | 247 | 132 | 383 | 1,620 | 84 | 19,600 |
| 1993 | 951 | 1,573 | 1,944 | 1,160 | 785 | 137 | 1,056 | 517 | 2,832 | 1,000 | 797 | 213 | 149 | 458 | 1,090 | 12 | 18,700 |
| 1994[1] | 910 | 1,556 | 2,173 | 1,150 | 876 | 6 | 1,145 | 475 | 2,629 | 995 | 646 | 288 | 61 | 469 | 1,010 | 1 | 18,100 |
| 1995[2] | 842 | 1,710 | 2,360 | 1,200 | 850 | ---- | 1,150 | 308 | 2,652 | 1,000 | 689 | 250 | 60 | 549 | 1,270 | ---- | 18,500 |

[1] Preliminary. [2] Estimate. [3] Primary and secondary metal. [4] Formerly part of the U.S.S.R.; data not reported separately until 1992.
*Source: U.S. Geological Survey*

**Salient Statistics of Cadmium in the United States** In Metric Tons of Contained Cadmium

| Year | Net Import Reliance as a % of Apparent Consumption | Production (Metal) | Producer Shipments | Cadmium Sulfide Production | Production Other Compounds | Imports of Cadmium Metal[3] | Exports[4] | Apparent Consumption | Industry Stocks Dec. 31[5] | N.Y. Dealer Price $ per Pound[6] |
|---|---|---|---|---|---|---|---|---|---|---|
| 1986 | 72 | 1,486 | 2,030 | 645 | 1,511 | 3,174 | 38 | 4,385 | 923 | 1.07 |
| 1987 | 61 | 1,515 | 1,916 | 540 | 1,497 | 2,701 | 241 | 4,178 | 720 | 1.60 |
| 1988 | 59 | 1,885 | 2,074 | 345 | 1,451 | 2,482 | 613 | 3,620 | 854 | 6.91 |
| 1989 | 62 | 1,550 | 2,015 | 267 | 1,451 | 2,787 | 369 | 4,096 | 726 | 6.28 |
| 1990 | 55 | 1,680 | 1,860 | 228 | 1,144 | 1,740 | 385 | 2,800 | 653 | 3.38 |
| 1991 | 58 | 1,680 | 1,740 | 263 | 1,089 | 2,040 | 448 | 3,080 | 835 | 2.01 |
| 1992 | 55 | 1,620 | 2,080 | 270 | 1,073 | 1,960 | 213 | 3,330 | 868 | .91 |
| 1993 | 48 | 1,090 | 1,320 | 303 | 731 | 1,420 | 38 | 2,940 | 579 | .45 |
| 1994[1] | E | 1,010 | 1,290 | 170 | 898 | 1,110 | 1,450 | 1,040 | 423 | 1.13 |
| 1995[2] | E | 1,270 | 1,280 | 105 | 936 | 848 | 1,050 | 1,160 | 542 | 1.84 |

[1] Preliminary. [2] Estimate. [3] For Consumption. [4] Cadmium Metal, alloys, dross, flue dust. [5] Metallic, Compounds, Distributors (including in compounds from 1985). [6] Sticks and Balls in 1 to 5 short ton lots. E = Net exporter. *Source: U.S. Geological Survey*

# Canola (Rapeseed)

Canola (or Rapeseed) is the world's third largest oilseed crop behind soybeans and cottonseed, accounting for about 12 percent of total production. In 1996/97, about 29.7 million metric tons were produced vs. the 1995/96 record high 34.5 million. In the mid 1980's, the crop averaged 17 million tons; if the trend persists rapeseed could soon be the world's second largest oilseed crop as almost occurred in 1995/96 when the difference between cottonseed and rapeseed was less than a half million tons. Total 1996/97 world supplies of 31.7 million tons includes a carryover of 2.0 million tons; the world 1996/97 (July/June) crush of 28.1 million tons compares with the previous year's record 30.3 million tons.

China now produces about a third of total production, 9 million tons in 1996/97 vs. the previous year's record high of 9.8 million as more acreage has been allocated to rapeseed. Canada and India generally produce more than 5 million tons each. Collectively, the European Union is the second largest producing area with 6.9 million tons in 1996/97 vs. 8.3 million in 1995/96. EU rapeseed production, with Germany the largest producer is generally twice that of sunflowerseed, the region's second largest oilseed crop, but in terms of protein meal consumption EU rapeseed usage at 6.5 million tons in 1996/97 is about one-fourth that of soybean meal. EU rapeseed oil usage, however, holds the top spot with 2.1 million tons in 1996/97 vs. 1.9 million for soybean oil. Although world rape/canola oil consumption eased in 1996/97 to 10.5 million tons from a record high 11 million in 1995/96, consumption is still nearly twice that of the mid-1980's. In foreign trade, rapeseed is second only to soybeans. Exports totaled 4.7 million tons in 1996/97 vs. 5.5 million in 1995/96. Carryin for the 1996/97 crop year of 2 million tons is forecast to drop to 830,000 tons at yearend. Meal and oil stocks, which generally total about a million tons, were also expected to decline during 1996/97.

U.S. production of canola seed is small, totaling less than 1 percent of world production at 220,000 tons in 1996/97 (June/May) vs. 250,000 tons in 1995/96, the slippage reflecting a dip in acreage to 150,000 hectares while yield held steady at 1.44 tons per hectare. The crop is grown mostly in the northern plains states. Although rapeseed and canola are used interchangeably, USDA data shows both although rapeseed statistics pale relative to canola. In either case, the total U.S. crop fails to cover disappearance, estimated at 930 million pounds in 1996/97 vs. 1.1 billion in 1995/96. Canolaseed imports, mostly from Canada, bridge the domestic supply/demand imbalance. Imports of 441 million pounds in 1996/97 compare with 558 million in 1995/96 and the record high 773 million in 1993/94. The U.S. also exports canola seed, 132 million pounds in 1996/97 vs. 138 million in 1995/96. The U.S. crush in 1996/97 was forecast at 784 million pounds, down from 899 the year prior. Production of canola oil in 1996/97 (October/September) of 307 million pounds compares with 355 million in 1995/96, while canola oil imports, mostly from Canada, of 1.1 billion pounds compares with 1 billion in 1995/96. A decade earlier, oil production totaled about 14 million pounds and imports about 250 million pounds. Domestic oil demand was forecast at a record high 1.2 billion pounds in 1996/97.

Contributing to the sharp gains in U.S. canola supply/demand data since the mid-1980's include Government enticements to increase canola acreage, development of low-erucic canola varieties that can be grown in the U.S., and wider acceptance of canola oil in cooking due to its lower content of saturated fats. Canola oil is said to be 94 percent saturated fat free, the lowest of any oil. Demand for canola meal as a livestock feed has also grown impressively; domestic usage of meal in 1995/96 of 1.2 million short tons was marginally under the 1995/96 record high.

The average price received by farmers for canola seed in 1996/97 was forecast to range between $11.35-13.45 per cwt. vs. $11.85 in 1995/96. Canola oil's price was forecast at $0.265-.275 per pound while meal's price of $158 to $188 per short ton compares with $156 in 1995/96.

### *Futures Market*

Canola futures and options are traded on the Winnipeg Commodity Exchange (WCE) and quoted in Canadian dollars per ton. Rapeseed futures are traded on the Marche a Terme International de France (MATIF).

**World Production of Canola (Rapeseed)** In Thousands of Metric Tons

| Year | Australia | Bangladesh | Canada | China | Czechoslovakia | Denmark | France | Germany | India | Pakistan | Poland | Sweden | United Kingdom | former U.S.S.R. | World Total |
|---|---|---|---|---|---|---|---|---|---|---|---|---|---|---|---|
| 1983-4 | 17 | 131 | 2,609 | 4,287 | 314 | 309 | 906 | 859 | 2,608 | 217 | 554 | 318 | 565 | 69 | 14,259 |
| 1984-5 | 32 | 140 | 3,412 | 4,205 | 300 | 474 | 1,305 | 1,017 | 3,073 | 234 | 911 | 327 | 925 | 55 | 16,935 |
| 1985-6 | 87 | 261 | 3,498 | 5,607 | 285 | 544 | 1,340 | 1,184 | 2,681 | 250 | 1,073 | 320 | 895 | 74 | 18,699 |
| 1986-7 | 77 | 229 | 3,787 | 5,881 | 306 | 618 | 1,071 | 1,472 | 2,605 | 217 | 1,298 | 321 | 940 | 144 | 19,550 |
| 1987-8 | 66 | 222 | 3,847 | 6,605 | 337 | 556 | 2,645 | 1,723 | 3,455 | 204 | 1,192 | 250 | 1,353 | 296 | 23,435 |
| 1988-9 | 58 | 207 | 4,218 | 5,044 | 380 | 504 | 2,303 | 1,642 | 4,377 | 249 | 1,199 | 250 | 1,040 | 420 | 22,646 |
| 1989-90 | 78 | 217 | 3,209 | 5,436 | 387 | 655 | 1,748 | 1,908 | 4,125 | 233 | 1,586 | 370 | 976 | 424 | 22,096 |
| 1990-1 | 98 | 228 | 3,266 | 6,958 | 380 | 793 | 1,926 | 2,155 | 5,152 | 228 | 1,206 | 367 | 1,258 | 506 | 25,321 |
| 1991-2 | 170 | 243 | 4,224 | 7,436 | 446 | 726 | 2,270 | 3,030 | 5,863 | 219 | 1,043 | 252 | 1,308 | 409 | 28,489 |
| 1992-3 | 179 | 244 | 3,872 | 7,653 | 430 | 406 | 1,810 | 2,617 | 4,872 | 207 | 758 | 247 | 1,159 | 388 | 25,588 |
| 1993-4 | 294 | 252 | 5,480 | 6,939 | 466 | 417 | 1,550 | 2,848 | 5,390 | 215 | 594 | 313 | 1,256 | 325 | 27,039 |
| 1994-5[1] | 309 | 250 | 7,228 | 7,436 | 452 | 366 | 1,800 | 2,896 | 5,370 | 220 | 756 | 214 | 1,254 | 363 | 30,036 |
| 1995-6[2] | 584 | 255 | 6,436 | 9,740 | 662 | 322 | 2,782 | 3,103 | 5,700 | 225 | 1,377 | 216 | 1,235 | 415 | 34,480 |
| 1996-7[3] | 597 | | 5,037 | 8,820 | 531 | 250 | 2,890 | 1,949 | 5,750 | | 438 | 122 | 1,491 | 425 | 30,122 |

[1] Preliminary. [2] Estimate. [3] Forecast. *Source: The Oil World*

# CANOLA

**World Supply and Distribution of Rapeseed & Products** In Thousands of Metric Tons

| Crop Year | Rapeseed Production | Rapeseed Exports | Rapeseed Imports | Rapeseed Crush | Rapeseed Ending Stocks | Rapeseed Meal Production | Rapeseed Meal Exports | Rapeseed Meal Imports | Rapeseed Meal Consumption | Rapeseed Meal Ending Stocks | Rapeseed Oil Production | Rapeseed Oil Exports | Rapeseed Oil Imports | Rapeseed Oil Consumption | Rapeseed Oil Ending Stocks |
|---|---|---|---|---|---|---|---|---|---|---|---|---|---|---|---|
| 1980-1 | 11,104 | 2,305 | 2,366 | 10,477 | 1,489 | 6,297 | 808 | 636 | 6,075 | 199 | 3,933 | 814 | 756 | 3,914 | 210 |
| 1981-2 | 12,345 | 2,142 | 2,216 | 11,959 | 911 | 7,331 | 845 | 683 | 7,182 | 186 | 4,383 | 824 | 775 | 4,404 | 140 |
| 1982-3 | 14,804 | 2,469 | 2,540 | 13,826 | 740 | 8,449 | 768 | 871 | 8,500 | 238 | 4,991 | 841 | 790 | 4,925 | 155 |
| 1983-4 | 14,263 | 2,537 | 2,704 | 13,312 | 647 | 8,130 | 1,198 | 1,303 | 8,206 | 267 | 4,856 | 984 | 980 | 4,827 | 180 |
| 1984-5 | 16,935 | 3,153 | 3,291 | 15,369 | 1,033 | 9,419 | 1,463 | 1,451 | 9,454 | 220 | 5,602 | 1,298 | 1,199 | 5,497 | 186 |
| 1985-6 | 18,699 | 3,632 | 3,648 | 16,986 | 1,267 | 10,260 | 1,823 | 1,734 | 10,109 | 282 | 6,233 | 1,313 | 1,203 | 5,978 | 331 |
| 1986-7 | 19,550 | 4,577 | 4,923 | 18,439 | 1,037 | 11,112 | 1,692 | 2,225 | 11,568 | 359 | 6,849 | 1,662 | 1,409 | 6,540 | 387 |
| 1987-8 | 23,383 | 4,456 | 4,296 | 20,370 | 1,250 | 12,264 | 2,113 | 2,088 | 12,139 | 169 | 7,701 | 1,852 | 1,806 | 7,461 | 922 |
| 1988-9 | 22,646 | 4,417 | 4,610 | 20,252 | 3,760 | 12,160 | 2,709 | 2,675 | 12,213 | 81 | 7,671 | 1,939 | 1,807 | 7,775 | 687 |
| 1989-90 | 22,096 | 2,831 | 2,891 | 21,075 | 3,240 | 12,709 | 1,681 | 1,773 | 12,721 | 160 | 7,944 | 1,624 | 1,730 | 8,000 | 743 |
| 1990-1 | 25,321 | 2,433 | 2,474 | 23,318 | 3,130 | 14,083 | 1,950 | 1,877 | 14,056 | 114 | 8,786 | 1,577 | 1,550 | 8,697 | 781 |
| 1991-2 | 28,489 | 2,674 | 2,645 | 25,111 | 3,700 | 15,203 | 2,527 | 2,507 | 15,169 | 128 | 9,469 | 1,529 | 1,633 | 9,518 | 836 |
| 1992-3 | 25,588 | 3,058 | 3,003 | 23,634 | 780 | 14,304 | 2,705 | 2,626 | 14,206 | 147 | 8,990 | 1,129 | 1,134 | 9,120 | 742 |
| 1993-4 | 27,039 | 4,104 | 4,050 | 25,252 | 790 | 15,147 | 2,620 | 2,732 | 15,282 | 124 | 9,720 | 1,594 | 1,526 | 9,527 | 836 |
| 1994-5[1] | 30,036 | 4,512 | 4,588 | 27,190 | 1,040 | 16,328 | 2,642 | 2,556 | 16,200 | 167 | 10,526 | 2,047 | 2,070 | 10,200 | 1,204 |
| 1995-6[2] | 34,480 | 4,178 | 4,156 | 30,055 | 1,120 | 18,107 | 2,940 | 2,993 | 18,154 | 173 | 11,613 | 1,898 | 1,940 | 11,439 | 1,420 |
| 1996-7[3] | 30,122 | 3,378 | 3,384 | 28,520 | | 17,137 | 2,845 | 2,875 | 17,182 | 159 | 10,918 | 1,672 | 1,648 | 11,263 | 1,052 |

[1] Preliminary. [2] Estimate. [3] Forecast. *Source: The Oil World*

## Salient Statistics of Canola seed and Canola Oil in the United States — In Millions of Pounds

| Crop Year Beginning June 1 | Canola Seed: Supply: Stocks June 1 | Production | Imports | Total | Canola Seed: Disappearance: Crush | Exports | Total[3] | Canola Oil: Supply: Stocks June 1 | Production | Imports | Total | Canola Oil: Disappearance: Domestic | Exports | Total |
|---|---|---|---|---|---|---|---|---|---|---|---|---|---|---|
| 1987-8 | 3 | 27 | 2 | 32 | 30 | 0 | 30 | 4 | 14 | 273 | 291 | 263 | 0 | 263 |
| 1988-9 | 2 | 39 | 37 | 78 | 71 | 4 | 75 | 29 | 54 | 430 | 513 | 486 | 8 | 494 |
| 1989-90 | 3 | 95 | 231 | 329 | 298 | 10 | 308 | 20 | 130 | 391 | 541 | 510 | 6 | 516 |
| 1990-1 | 21 | 97 | 141 | 259 | 195 | 32 | 227 | 24 | 18 | 583 | 625 | 577 | 7 | 584 |
| 1991-2 | 32 | 191 | 2 | 225 | 109 | 97 | 212 | 41 | 32 | 815 | 888 | 801 | 15 | 816 |
| 1992-3 | 13 | 144 | 27 | 184 | 59 | 104 | 174 | 71 | 49 | 861 | 981 | 898 | 16 | 914 |
| 1993-4 | 10 | 252 | 773 | 1,036 | 850 | 78 | 941 | 67 | 406 | 902 | 1,375 | 1,228 | 76 | 1,304 |
| 1994-5 | 95 | 447 | 630 | 1,173 | 899 | 227 | 1,139 | 137 | 299 | 938 | 1,374 | 1,165 | 153 | 1,318 |
| 1995-6[1] | 34 | 547 | 558 | 1,139 | 899 | 138 | 1,051 | 54 | 355 | 1,086 | 1,496 | 1,270 | 147 | 1,417 |
| 1996-7[2] | 88 | 474 | 441 | 1,003 | 784 | 132 | 930 | 79 | 307 | 1,103 | 1,488 | 1,279 | 132 | 1,411 |

[1] Preliminary. [2] Estimate. [3] Forecast. *Source: Economic Research Service, U.S. Department of Agriculture*

## Wholesale Price of Canola Oil, Refined (Denatured), in Tanks in New York — In Cents Per Pound

| Year | Jan. | Feb. | Mar. | Apr. | May | June | July | Aug. | Sept. | Oct. | Nov. | Dec. | Average |
|---|---|---|---|---|---|---|---|---|---|---|---|---|---|
| 1987 | 60.50 | 62.00 | 62.50 | 62.50 | 64.25 | 69.50 | 69.50 | 65.00 | 63.50 | 63.50 | 63.50 | 63.50 | 64.15 |
| 1988 | 63.56 | 63.50 | 63.50 | 63.50 | 63.50 | 63.50 | 63.50 | 63.50 | 63.50 | 64.63 | 66.25 | 70.00 | 64.37 |
| 1989 | 70.00 | 70.00 | 80.25 | 80.25 | 80.25 | 80.75 | 80.25 | 80.25 | 80.25 | 80.25 | 80.25 | 80.25 | 78.58 |
| 1990 | 81.75 | 82.25 | 82.23 | 82.25 | 82.25 | 82.25 | 82.25 | 82.25 | 79.25 | 77.25 | 77.25 | 81.00 | 81.02 |
| 1991 | 82.25 | 82.25 | 82.25 | 82.25 | 82.25 | 82.25 | 82.25 | 82.25 | 82.25 | 82.25 | 82.25 | 82.25 | 82.25 |
| 1992 | 82.25 | 82.25 | 82.25 | 82.25 | 82.25 | 82.25 | 82.25 | 82.25 | 67.25 | 62.25 | 62.25 | 62.25 | 76.00 |
| 1993 | 62.25 | 62.25 | 62.25 | 62.25 | 55.88 | 53.75 | 53.25 | 53.00 | 53.00 | 52.00 | 52.50 | 50.00 | 56.03 |
| 1994 | 53.75 | 53.75 | 53.75 | 53.75 | 53.75 | 53.75 | 53.75 | 53.75 | 53.75 | 53.75 | 53.75 | 53.75 | 53.75 |
| 1995 | 53.75 | 53.75 | 53.75 | 53.75 | 53.15 | 50.75 | 50.75 | 50.75 | 50.75 | 50.75 | 50.75 | 50.75 | 51.95 |
| 1996[1] | 50.75 | 50.75 | 50.75 | 50.75 | 50.75 | 50.75 | 50.75 | 50.75 | 50.75 | | | | 50.75 |

[1] Preliminary. *Source: Economic Research Service, U.S. Department of Agriculture*

## Average Open Interest of Canola Futures in Winnipeg — In 20 Metric Ton Units

| Year | Jan. | Feb. | Mar. | Apr. | May | June | July | Aug. | Sept. | Oct. | Nov. | Dec. |
|---|---|---|---|---|---|---|---|---|---|---|---|---|
| 1986 | 15,553 | 18,146 | 19,741 | 20,435 | 22,262 | 19,193 | 17,192 | 20,594 | 22,570 | 26,838 | 28,391 | 28,972 |
| 1987 | 25,143 | 32,141 | 34,152 | 31,564 | 30,761 | 28,903 | 26,599 | 24,083 | 25,075 | 25,893 | 23,049 | 26,576 |
| 1988 | 28,875 | 33,387 | 31,798 | 34,056 | 34,587 | 31,318 | 30,224 | 29,509 | 26,289 | 29,510 | 28,974 | 29,221 |
| 1989 | 22,435 | 20,889 | 18,591 | 22,690 | 24,587 | 21,025 | 22,280 | 22,027 | 16,153 | 21,556 | 20,981 | 21,749 |
| 1990 | 18,431 | 20,340 | 17,599 | 19,825 | 24,718 | 22,546 | 23,073 | 24,353 | 24,872 | 25,688 | 18,706 | 22,057 |
| 1991 | 22,000 | 22,829 | 24,815 | 26,637 | 30,072 | 28,240 | 28,288 | 27,547 | 27,558 | 29,079 | 23,880 | 20,117 |
| 1992 | 15,943 | 17,556 | 20,559 | 21,410 | 23,727 | 28,885 | 26,013 | 25,674 | 28,049 | 32,724 | 35,693 | 37,375 |
| 1993 | 34,098 | 37,658 | 36,715 | 38,210 | 38,231 | 29,743 | 39,763 | 43,844 | 50,616 | 55,107 | 54,998 | 54,475 |
| 1994 | 50,335 | 55,280 | 54,899 | 58,012 | 60,567 | 55,434 | 54,733 | 57,044 | 57,049 | 54,375 | 55,045 | 49,475 |
| 1995 | 47,579 | 43,662 | 36,530 | 32,580 | 38,361 | 42,961 | 43,607 | 42,828 | 51,067 | 57,638 | 46,640 | 45,444 |
| 1996 | 42,646 | 43,808 | 45,126 | 47,989 | 54,228 | 52,176 | 49,387 | 40,619 | 42,242 | 52,273 | 53,121 | 54,323 |

*Source: Winnipeg Commodity Exchange (WCE)*

## Average Price of Cash Canola in Vancouver — In Canadian Dollars Per Tonne

| Year | Jan. | Feb. | Mar. | Apr. | May | June | July | Aug. | Sept. | Oct. | Nov. | Dec. | Average |
|---|---|---|---|---|---|---|---|---|---|---|---|---|---|
| 1986 | 321.49 | 304.19 | 294.97 | 283.29 | 282.19 | 267.79 | 252.73 | 234.95 | 239.20 | 246.00 | 252.73 | 244.59 | 268.68 |
| 1987 | 242.61 | 227.73 | 219.03 | 221.67 | 243.97 | 256.27 | 247.85 | 235.66 | 243.24 | 257.22 | 267.19 | 281.15 | 245.30 |
| 1988 | 302.56 | 303.16 | 294.22 | 305.27 | 336.31 | 413.98 | 395.28 | 381.19 | 379.83 | 349.68 | 333.96 | 344.35 | 344.98 |
| 1989 | 329.54 | 321.64 | 333.29 | 331.44 | 335.18 | 306.10 | 300.49 | 289.44 | 297.10 | 293.79 | 303.10 | 302.54 | 311.97 |
| 1990 | 300.01 | 301.45 | 311.00 | 318.78 | 322.24 | 303.89 | 300.83 | 299.43 | 292.74 | 295.23 | 290.08 | 290.01 | 302.14 |
| 1991 | 285.01 | 280.36 | 291.50 | 298.57 | 293.83 | 277.25 | 258.12 | 269.40 | 275.00 | 270.30 | 262.90 | 261.60 | 276.99 |
| 1992 | 264.15 | 273.35 | 282.70 | 276.85 | 288.08 | 292.35 | 272.20 | 282.26 | 320.62 | 302.10 | 327.22 | 331.57 | 292.79 |
| 1993 | 344.22 | 329.26 | 328.67 | 325.06 | 318.85 | 319.23 | 331.29 | 322.85 | 311.29 | 311.66 | 331.44 | 366.37 | 328.35 |
| 1994 | 408.60 | 413.10 | 422.23 | 454.90 | 481.44 | 484.95 | 388.63 | 382.54 | 381.70 | 379.99 | 401.38 | 432.35 | 419.32 |
| 1995 | 431.85 | 440.41 | 456.13 | 425.40 | 404.27 | 414.31 | 426.49 | 405.94 | 405.89 | 413.29 | 416.03 | 423.77 | 421.98 |
| 1996 | 424.07 | 422.60 | 417.55 | 443.94 | 473.04 | 469.28 | 470.38 | 453.86 | 453.53 | 444.01 | 432.30 | 439.79 | 445.36 |

*Source: Winnipeg Commodity Exchange (WCE)*

# Cassava

Cassava, or tapioca root, is used primarily as an animal feed and as a foodstuff in tropical countries. For some time, cassava has been looked upon as a possible solution to world hunger problems. Technology advances have held forth the promise of increasing yields substantially. New strains of cassava root are being developed in Africa and they could eventually be used in the fight against hunger.

The major producers of cassava are scattered around the world. For 1994, the Food and Agricultural Organization of the United Nations reported that world production of cassava was 152.4 million tonnes. This was down about 1 per cent from the previous year. For the five year period of 1990-1994, world cassava production averaged 152.7 million tonnes per year. Cassava production has been fairly steady in recent years. Among the major producers of cassava are Brazil, Nigeria, Zaire and Thailand. Other major producers include Indonesia, Tanzania, Ghana and China. In 1994, Brazil was the largest producer of cassava. Production was estimated at just over 24 million tonnes or almost 16 per cent of the world total. Over the most recent five year period, average cassava production was 23.3 million tonnes. The next largest producer is Nigeria with 1994 output at 21 million tonnes or almost 14 per cent of the world total. Average production over the last five years was 20.5 million tonnes. Production of cassava in Zaire was estimated at 19.6 million tonnes, down 6 per cent from the previous year. Production over the last five years averaged 19.5 million tonnes.

Thailand is both a major producer and exporter of tapioca root. For 1994, Thailand produced 19.1 million tonnes or almost 13 per cent of the world total. About 25 per cent of Thailand's production is exported making Thailand by far the world's largest exporter of cassava.

World exports of tapioca root in 1995 were estimated at 3.7 million tonnes, down 36 per cent from the previous year. One strong trend has been that world exports of cassava have been declining. In 1990, world cassava exports were 9.1 million tonnes. This appears to be the result of the exporting countries consuming their own production. Thailand is the world's largest exporter of cassava with over 90 per cent of the market. Indonesia exports smaller amounts of cassava.

World imports of cassava in 1995 were estimated at 3.7 million tonnes, down 26 per cent from the previous year. World imports of cassava have been on the decline. By far the world's largest importer is the 12 nation European Community. Imports in 1995 were 3.3 million tonnes or 90 per cent of the world total. China is a smaller importer of cassava. In part, the decline in imports of cassava may be due to the fact that other animal feeds are being substituted for tapioca root.

## World Cassava Production  In Thousands of Metric Tons

| Year | Brazil | China | Columbia | Ghana | India | Indonesia | Madagascar | Mozambique | Nigeria | Paraguay | Phillippines | Tanzania | Thailand | Uganda | Viet Nam | Zaire | World Total |
|---|---|---|---|---|---|---|---|---|---|---|---|---|---|---|---|---|---|
| 1989 | 23,668 | 3,320 | 1,509 | 3,327 | 4,833 | 17,117 | 2,277 | 4,000 | 15,425 | 3,978 | 1,873 | 7,792 | 15,128 | 3,568 | 2,585 | 17,400 | 151,773 |
| 1990 | 24,322 | 3,216 | 1,939 | 2,717 | 4,962 | 15,830 | 2,292 | 4,056 | 19,043 | 3,550 | 1,854 | 6,922 | 20,701 | 3,339 | 2,276 | 17,600 | 149,844 |
| 1991 | 24,538 | 3,310 | 1,645 | 3,600 | 5,416 | 15,954 | 2,307 | 3,690 | 20,000 | 2,585 | 1,816 | 7,460 | 20,356 | 3,229 | 2,455 | 19,500 | 153,562 |
| 1992 | 21,919 | 3,357 | 1,651 | 4,000 | 5,469 | 16,516 | 2,280 | 3,239 | 21,320 | 2,591 | 1,798 | 7,112 | 20,356 | 2,896 | 2,568 | 20,210 | 153,058 |
| 1993 | 21,865 | 3,403 | 1,723 | 4,200 | 5,340 | 16,799 | 2,350 | 3,511 | 21,000 | 2,680 | 1,844 | 6,833 | 20,203 | 3,137 | 2,631 | 20,835 | 154,328 |
| 1994[1] | 24,009 | 3,503 | 2,000 | 4,378 | 5,340 | 15,000 | 2,260 | 3,294 | 21,000 | 2,550 | 1,850 | 7,209 | 19,091 | 3,420 | 2,631 | 19,600 | 152,473 |

[1] Estimate. *Source: Food and Agricultural Organization of the United Nations*

## Prices of Tapioca, Hard Pellets, F.O.B. Rotterdam  U.S. Dollars Per Metric Ton

| Year | Jan. | Feb. | Mar. | Apr. | May | June | July | Aug. | Sept. | Oct. | Nov. | Dec. | Average |
|---|---|---|---|---|---|---|---|---|---|---|---|---|---|
| 1991 | 187 | 186 | 163 | 160 | 168 | 158 | 158 | 177 | 187 | 187 | 202 | 197 | 178 |
| 1992 | 197 | 184 | 179 | 177 | 179 | 181 | 184 | 192 | 195 | 187 | 172 | 170 | 183 |
| 1993 | 160 | 150 | 140 | 149 | 145 | 133 | 130 | 131 | 136 | 127 | 120 | 125 | 137 |
| 1994 | 122 | 123 | 128 | 133 | 138 | 141 | 147 | 154 | 158 | 161 | 161 | 161 | 144 |
| 1995 | 164 | 170 | 180 | 178 | 174 | 176 | 183 | 176 | 178 | 184 | 182 | 178 | 177 |
| 1996 | 167 | 160 | 155 | 158 | 163 | 154 | 149 | 154 | 146 | 139 | 140 | 133 | 152 |

*Source: Oil World*

## World Trade in Tapioca  In Thousands of Metric Tons

| | Exports | | | | | Imports | | | | | | |
|---|---|---|---|---|---|---|---|---|---|---|---|---|
| Year | China | Indonesia | Thailand | Viet Nam | Total World Exports | China | EC-12[2] | Japan | Rep. of Korea | United States | Former U.S.S.R. | Total World Imports |
| 1990 | 198 | 1,271 | 7,556 | 20 | 9,135 | 573 | 4,947 | 221 | 763 | 179 | 855 | 8,598 |
| 1991 | 410 | 859 | 6,187 | 3 | 7,571 | 175 | 5,692 | 162 | 444 | 127 | ---- | 7,353 |
| 1992 | 316 | 873 | 8,045 | 32 | 9,422 | 230 | 6,128 | 181 | 876 | 217 | 22 | 8,951 |
| 1993 | 269 | 936 | 6,707 | 29 | 8,089 | 149 | 6,449 | 151 | 658 | 60 | 8 | 8,417 |
| 1994 | 77 | 686 | 4,703 | 28 | 5,642 | 92 | 5,441 | 94 | 132 | 18 | ---- | 6,076 |
| 1995[1] | 10 | 481 | 3,297 | 1 | 3,864 | 362 | 2,932 | 16 | 141 | ---- | ---- | 3,553 |
| 1996[1] | 10 | 540 | 3,479 | 1 | 4,085 | 234 | 3,190 | 20 | 520 | ---- | ---- | 4,083 |

[1] Estimate. [2] Excluding trade between the EEC members. *Source: Oil World*

# Castor Beans

India is the world's largest producer of castor beans with about 60 percent of the world's crop. China has been expanding acreage and has some of the highest yields and is now the second largest producer. China produces about 25 percent of the world's castor beans. Brazil is the world's third largest producer though it's output has been falling. Brazil now produces less than 10 percent of the world's supply of castor beans. Among the smaller producers are Pakistan, Paraguay, and Thailand. Production in the former Soviet Union has fallen substantially. World castor bean production has averaged about 1.2 million tonnes per year.

From castor beans, castor oil is produced. As the largest producer of castor beans, India is also the largest producer of castor oil as well as the largest exporter. Additionally, India is also the largest consumer of castor oil. The U.S. is also a major user of castor oil.

The USDA reported that U.S. imports of castor oil in June 1996 were 36 tonnes, a substantial decline from the June 1995 figure of 4,652 tonnes. Over the period of October 1995 to June 1996, U.S. castor oil imports were 36,900 tonnes. This represented an increase of 21 percent from the comparable period of 1994/95 (October-June) when U.S. imports were 30,478 tonnes. The USDA reported that the risk value of the October-June 1995/96 castor oil imports were $28 million. This was some 25 percent above the value of castor oil imports in the October-June 1994/95 period.

## World Production of Castorseed Beans    In Thousands of Metric Tons

| Crop Year | Brazil | China | Ecuador | Ethiopia | India | Mexico | Paraguay | Pakistan | Philip-pines | Romania | Sudan | Tanzania | Thailand | Former U.S.S.R. | World Total |
|---|---|---|---|---|---|---|---|---|---|---|---|---|---|---|---|
| 1990-1 | 148 | 315 | 7 | 1 | 716 | ---- | 37 | 12 | 7 | 2 | 7 | 3 | 15 | 36 | 1,336 |
| 1991-2 | 133 | 310 | 5 | 1 | 575 | 1 | 33 | 13 | 7 | 1 | 6 | 3 | 13 | 32 | 1,163 |
| 1992-3 | 102 | 291 | 12 | 1 | 617 | 1 | 20 | 6 | 7 | 1 | 8 | 3 | 24 | 20 | 1,140 |
| 1993-4 | 45 | 280 | 13 | 1 | 700 | 1 | 15 | 7 | 7 | ---- | 6 | 3 | 22 | 4 | 1,135 |
| 1994-5[1] | 53 | 230 | 7 | 1 | 850 | 1 | 10 | 5 | 7 | ---- | 6 | 3 | 15 | 8 | 1,226 |
| 1995-6[2] | 41 | 180 | 6 | 1 | 930 | 1 | 9 | 5 | 7 | 1 | 6 | 3 | 14 | 8 | 1,239 |
| 1996-7[3] | 35 | 200 | 5 | | 850 | | 8 | 5 | 7 | | | | 9 | 8 | 1,165 |

[1] Preliminary. [2] Estimate. [3] Forecast. *Sources: Foreign Agricultural Service, U.S. Department of Agriculture; Oil World*

## Castor Oil Consumption[2] in the United States    In Thousands of Pounds

| Crop Year | Oct. | Nov. | Dec. | Jan. | Feb. | Mar. | Apr. | May | June | July | Aug. | Sept. | Total |
|---|---|---|---|---|---|---|---|---|---|---|---|---|---|
| 1990-1 | 3,334 | 2,815 | 3,507 | ----------- | 11,787 | ----------- | ----------- | 10,958 | ----------- | ----------- | 11,096 | ----------- | 44,030 |
| 1991-2 | ----------- | 12,073 | ----------- | 3,877 | 2,914 | 3,766 | 2,806 | 3,516 | 3,606 | 3,203 | 3,708 | 3,019 | 42,488 |
| 1992-3 | 4,712 | 3,250 | 3,100 | 3,287 | 4,271 | 3,924 | 4,098 | 3,965 | 4,496 | 4,902 | 5,073 | 4,400 | 49,478 |
| 1993-4 | 5,046 | 5,649 | 5,092 | 5,510 | 4,982 | 5,766 | 4,548 | 6,335 | 5,258 | 4,603 | 4,929 | 4,543 | 62,261 |
| 1994-5 | 5,032 | 4,204 | 5,092 | 6,001 | 5,179 | 4,911 | 4,722 | 3,740 | 5,067 | 4,891 | 6,452 | 4,834 | 60,125 |
| 1995-6[1] | 5,228 | 5,463 | 6,232 | 5,794 | 6,979 | 5,545 | 3,369 | 5,864 | 5,469 | 5,439 | 4,332 | 3,818 | 63,532 |
| 1996-7[1] | 3,921 | 4,460 | 4,555 | 3,744 | | | | | | | | | 16,680 |

[1] Preliminary. [2] In inedible products (Resins, Plastics, etc.). *Source: Bureau of the Census, U.S. Department of Commerce*

## Castor Oil Stocks in the United States    In Thousands of Pounds

| Crop Year | Oct. 1 | Nov. 1 | Dec. 1 | Jan. 1 | Feb. 1 | Mar. 1 | Apr. 1 | May 1 | June 1 | July 1 | Aug. 1 | Sept. 1 |
|---|---|---|---|---|---|---|---|---|---|---|---|---|
| 1990-1 | 18,819 | 18,118 | 25,245 | ----------- | 17,198 | ----------- | ----------- | 21,714 | ----------- | ----------- | 14,417 | ----------- |
| 1991-2 | ----------- | 22,921 | ----------- | 20,382 | 23,499 | 17,293 | 21,511 | 19,429 | 13,036 | 20,383 | 16,066 | 11,346 |
| 1992-3 | 7,158 | 5,383 | 5,364 | 4,124 | 10,076 | 13,154 | 19,345 | 14,983 | 17,094 | 24,652 | 20,616 | 25,070 |
| 1993-4 | 22,981 | 21,275 | 23,482 | 21,132 | 29,871 | 9,946 | 18,394 | 25,249 | 22,550 | 21,795 | 27,911 | 20,950 |
| 1994-5 | 21,066 | 23,484 | 23,357 | 21,132 | 29,245 | 20,986 | 10,387 | 5,492 | 22,765 | 33,557 | 37,542 | 42,516 |
| 1995-6[1] | 27,143 | 35,329 | 43,189 | 51,713 | 45,746 | 37,210 | 29,718 | 36,829 | 55,687 | 43,954 | 37,802 | 25,535 |
| 1996-7[1] | 23,831 | 38,785 | 41,016 | 31,755 | 23,703 | | | | | | | |

[1] Preliminary. NA = Not available. *Source: Bureau of the Census, U.S. Department of Commerce*

## Monthly Average Wholesale Prices of Castor Oil No. 1, Brazilian Tanks at New York    In Cents Per Pound

| Year | Jan. | Feb. | Mar. | Apr. | May | June | July | Aug. | Sept. | Oct. | Nov. | Dec. | Average |
|---|---|---|---|---|---|---|---|---|---|---|---|---|---|
| 1990 | 54.50 | 53.50 | 52.60 | 52.00 | 51.20 | 51.00 | 51.00 | 51.00 | 45.00 | 43.40 | 39.63 | 39.63 | 48.70 |
| 1991 | 39.30 | 36.00 | 36.75 | 37.00 | 37.00 | 36.50 | 35.50 | 35.00 | 35.00 | 35.40 | 35.00 | 37.50 | 36.33 |
| 1992 | 37.50 | 37.50 | 37.50 | 36.00 | 34.50 | 34.50 | 34.50 | 34.50 | 34.50 | 34.00 | 34.00 | 34.00 | 35.21 |
| 1993 | 34.00 | 32.00 | 32.00 | 32.00 | 37.00 | 37.00 | 37.00 | 37.00 | 38.50 | 41.50 | 44.00 | 44.00 | 37.17 |
| 1994 | 44.00 | 41.75 | 41.00 | 41.00 | 46.00 | 45.00 | 45.00 | 45.00 | 45.00 | 45.00 | 45.00 | 45.00 | 44.06 |
| 1995 | 45.00 | 45.00 | 45.00 | 45.00 | 45.00 | 45.00 | 45.00 | 45.00 | 45.00 | 45.00 | 45.00 | 45.00 | 45.00 |
| 1996 | 43.50 | 41.50 | 41.50 | 41.50 | 41.50 | 41.50 | 41.50 | 41.50 | 41.50 | | | | 41.72 |

*Source: Foreign Agricultural Service, U.S.D.A.*

# Cattle and Calves

There has been little net change in the world cattle inventory for several years; the January 1, 1996 total of 1,044 million head was unchanged from a year earlier and compares with the January 1, 1997 estimate of 1,041 million. Despite the steadiness in the world total, some large changes have occurred in selected areas, notably the decline in the Russian Federation and the rise in China. Cattle inventory in the former USSR were placed at 64 million head in early 1966 vs. 71 million a year earlier and nearly 90 million five years earlier; and the estimate for early 1997 was still lower at 57 million head. China's January 1, 1996 inventory of 124 million head compares with 123 million a year earlier, 105 million in early 1992, and a forecast of 128 million in early 1997. The U.S. cattle inventory peaked in the 1980's at 110 million head. The January 1, 1996 total of 104 million head compares with 103 million in early 1995, and is forecast to dip to 102 million in early 1997.

Meat safety concerns were a major global issue in 1996 leading to a 1 percent decline in world beef consumption. Most notable was the outbreak of "mad cow" disease in the European Union where total usage dropped by 13 percent to 6.5 billion metric tons. World total consumption of 45.6 billion tons compares with 46.2 billion in 1995. Beef safety fears are expected to dissipate in 1997, but little recovery in consumption is forecast due to continuing usage declines in the Russian republics; from 4.5 billion tons in 1996 to 4.2 billion in 1997. On the other hand, Asian beef consumption, led by China, has steadily increased, from 3.6 billion tons in 1992, to 6.7 billion in 1996, and 7.1 billion in 1997.

U.S. cattle slaughter in 1996 of 38.5 million head compares to 37.3 million in 1995 and a forecast of 38.5 million in 1997. U.S. slaughter generally accounts for 15-20 percent of world slaughter but yields 25 percent of world beef production, estimated at 47 billion tons in 1996, unchanged from 1995. 1997 world production is estimated at 47.7 billion tons with 12 billion tons from the U.S., vs. 11.8 billion in 1996, and 11.6 billion in 1995. U.S. per capita beef consumption, however, has shown little growth in recent years, holding near 44.5 kilograms, still among the world's highest and surpassed only by some South American countries.

World beef exports fell 5 percent in 1996 to 4.9 million tons primarily due to a 37 percent slide in EU exports although U.S. exports gained 8 percent to .9 million tons from .8 million. Japan is the largest market for U.S. beef. For 1997, world exports are forecast up 3 percent to 5.2 million tons, with the U.S. total at 1 million tons.

The U.S., however, lost its position as the world's largest beef importer to Japan in 1996. The U.S. total of 950,000 metric tons, generally manufacturing grade grass fed beef, compares with Japan's 957,000, while the 1997 totals are forecast at 919,000 and 985,000 tons, respectively. 1996 U.S. beef imports from Australia, generally the largest supplier, dropped 30 percent from 1995 due to competitive U.S. prices, enabling Canada and New Zealand to be the largest exporters to the U.S. Live cattle imports to the U.S. also fell in 1996, to 2 million head from 2.8 million in 1995, due to a drop in Mexican exports to the U.S. Canadian live cattle exports reached a record high 1.5 million head in 1996 and are forecast at 1.1 million head in 1997.

U.S. live cattle prices trended lower in early 1996, but tighter fed cattle supplies in mid-spring firmed prices through late summer, but then weakened again in the wake of seasonal gains in hog and beef cow supplies. For the calendar year of 1996, live cattle prices, basis nearly futures, traded in a $0.20 cent per pound range vs. $0.15 in 1995; in late 1996 prices were pivoting in the low $0.60 per pound range. The 1996 average for Nebraska cash steers of $63-64.00/cwt. compares with $66.26 in 1995. The highest 1997 prices are expected in the first quarter, with the projected average for the year approximately unchanged from 1996. Retail choice beef prices peaked near $2.90 per pound in late 1996, bringing the year's average to $2.80 vs $2.84 in 1995. Prices in 1997 are forecast to average about $2.85 per pound.

### *Futures Markets*

Live cattle futures and options are traded on the Chicago Mercantile Exchange (CME), the Bolsa de Mercadorias & Futuros (BM&F), and the MidAmerica Commodity Exchange (MidAm). Feeder cattle futures are traded on the CME and the BM&F, and feeder cattle options are traded on the CME.

**World Cattle and Buffalo Numbers as of January 1** In Thousands of Head

| Year | Agren-tina | Aust-ralia | Brazil | Canada | China | Colom-bia | France | Ger-many[3] | India | Mexico | Russia[4] | South Africa | Turkey | Ukraine[4] | United Kingdom | United States | World Total (Mil Head) |
|---|---|---|---|---|---|---|---|---|---|---|---|---|---|---|---|---|---|
| 1986 | 53,484 | 23,436 | 122,463 | 10,956 | 86,820 | 19,904 | 22,803 | 15,627 | 275,340 | 32,167 | ---- | 11,750 | 15,000 | 120,888 | 12,695 | 105,378 | 1,067 |
| 1987 | 51,683 | 23,540 | 128,000 | 10,802 | 91,670 | 18,819 | 22,171 | 21,109 | 274,822 | 33,603 | ---- | 12,002 | 14,450 | 122,103 | 12,476 | 102,118 | 1,073 |
| 1988 | 56,482 | 23,469 | 130,000 | 10,756 | 94,650 | 18,400 | 21,053 | 20,608 | 268,720 | 35,378 | ---- | 12,187 | 14,000 | 115,824 | 11,849 | 99,622 | 1,070 |
| 1989 | 56,482 | 23,938 | 130,500 | 10,984 | 97,948 | 17,627 | 21,340 | 20,369 | 268,470 | 34,999 | 59,300 | 12,675 | 13,400 | 25,621 | 11,902 | 98,065 | 1,037 |
| 1990 | 56,482 | 24,673 | 140,400 | 11,220 | 100,752 | 16,835 | 21,394 | 20,287 | 270,070 | 31,747 | 58,800 | 13,398 | 12,700 | 25,195 | 11,922 | 95,816 | 1,035 |
| 1991 | 56,982 | 25,026 | 142,900 | 11,289 | 102,884 | 16,225 | 21,446 | 19,488 | 272,300 | 29,847 | 57,000 | 13,512 | 12,200 | 24,623 | 11,843 | 96,393 | 1,036 |
| 1992 | 55,229 | 25,857 | 141,800 | 11,713 | 104,592 | 16,008 | 20,970 | 17,134 | 271,200 | 30,232 | 54,677 | 13,311 | 12,000 | 23,728 | 11,623 | 97,556 | 1,032 |
| 1993 | 55,577 | 25,182 | 143,700 | 11,786 | 107,840 | 16,391 | 20,383 | 16,207 | 271,255 | 30,649 | 52,226 | 13,239 | 11,900 | 22,457 | 11,620 | 99,176 | 1,032 |
| 1994 | 54,875 | 25,758 | 144,900 | 12,254 | 113,157 | 16,614 | 20,112 | 15,897 | 272,655 | 30,702 | 48,914 | 12,506 | 11,800 | 21,607 | 11,709 | 100,988 | 1,036 |
| 1995 | 54,207 | 25,736 | 148,278 | 12,849 | 123,317 | 16,725 | 20,524 | 15,962 | 274,155 | 30,191 | 43,296 | 12,632 | 11,700 | 19,580 | 11,868 | 102,755 | 1,044 |
| 1996[1] | 53,569 | 26,500 | 151,544 | 13,374 | 124,281 | 16,768 | 20,662 | 15,890 | 276,105 | 28,141 | 39,694 | 13,334 | 11,700 | 17,526 | 11,619 | 103,819 | 1,045 |
| 1997[2] | 51,691 | 26,600 | 153,200 | 13,144 | 128,161 | 16,852 | 20,800 | 15,700 | 277,045 | 27,286 | 36,500 | 13,850 | 11,700 | 15,800 | 11,350 | 102,083 | 1,041 |

[1] Preliminary. [2] Forecast. [3] Prior to 1987, data only reported for the Federal Republic of Germany. [4] Formerly part of the U.S.S.R.; country data not shown seperately prior to 1989. *Source: Foreign Agricultural Service, U.S. Department of Agriculture*

## Cattle Supply and Distribution in the United States In Thousands of Head

| Year | Cattle & Calves on Farms January 1 | Imports | Calves Born | Total Supply | Livestock Slaughter - Cattle and Calves: Commercial: Federally Inspected | Other[3] | All Commercial | Farm | Total Slaughter | Deaths on Farms | Exports | Total Disap-pearance |
|---|---|---|---|---|---|---|---|---|---|---|---|---|
| 1985 | 109,582 | 836 | 41,050 | 151,468 | 37,933 | 1,745 | 39,678 | 370 | 40,048 | 5,046 | 125 | 45,219 |
| 1986 | 105,378 | 1,407 | 41,182 | 147,967 | 39,108 | 1,588 | 40,696 | 350 | 41,046 | 4,992 | 108 | 46,146 |
| 1987 | 102,118 | 1,200 | 40,152 | 143,470 | 37,148 | 1,314 | 38,462 | 330 | 38,792 | 4,800 | 131 | 43,723 |
| 1988 | 99,622 | 1,332 | 39,318 | 141,247 | 36,459 | 1,126 | 37,585 | 295 | 37,889 | 4,573 | 321 | 42,774 |
| 1989 | 96,740 | 1,459 | 38,817 | 139,626 | 35,110 | 980 | 36,089 | 240 | 36,329 | 4,361 | 169 | 40,859 |
| 1990 | 95,816 | 2,135 | 38,613 | 139,546 | 34,133 | 800 | 35,032 | 245 | 35,277 | 4,327 | 120 | 39,724 |
| 1991 | 96,393 | 1,939 | 38,583 | 139,861 | 33,285 | 841 | 34,126 | 242 | 34,368 | 4,247 | 311 | 38,927 |
| 1992 | 97,556 | 2,255 | 38,933 | 141,104 | 33,428 | 817 | 34,245 | 244 | 34,489 | 4,366 | 322 | 39,177 |
| 1993 | 99,176 | 2,499 | 39,448 | 142,750 | 33,752 | 767 | 34,519 | 227 | 34,746 | 4,630 | 153 | 39,529 |
| 1994 | 100,988 | 2,082 | 40,059 | 143,799 | 34,719 | 745 | 35,465 | 227 | 35,700 | 4,268 | 231 | 40,190 |
| 1995[1] | 102,755 | 2,694 | 40,251 | 145,700 | 36,128 | 785 | 36,913 | 187 | 37,100 | 4,500 | 88 | 41,700 |
| 1996[2] | 103,487 | 1,965 | | | 35,719 | 855 | 36,577 | | | | 174 | |

[1] Preliminary. [2] Estimate. [3] Wholesale and retail. *Source: Economic Research Service, U.S. Department of Agriculture*

## United States Beef Supply and Utilization

| Year/Quarter | Beginning Stocks | Production: Commercial | Production: Total | Imports | Total Supply | Exports | Ending Stocks | Total Disap-pearance | Per Capita Disappearance: Carcass Weight | Retail Weight |
|---|---|---|---|---|---|---|---|---|---|---|
| | Million Pounds | | | | | | | | Pounds | |
| 1993 | 360 | 22,942 | 23,049 | 2,401 | 25,810 | 1,275 | 529 | 24,006 | 93.0 | 65.1 |
| I | 360 | 5,357 | 5,394 | 741 | 6,495 | 267 | 390 | 5,838 | 22.7 | 15.9 |
| II | 390 | 5,690 | 5,706 | 580 | 6,676 | 346 | 362 | 5,968 | 23.1 | 16.2 |
| III | 362 | 6,076 | 6,092 | 607 | 7,061 | 334 | 433 | 6,294 | 24.3 | 17.0 |
| IV | 433 | 5,819 | 5,857 | 473 | 6,763 | 328 | 529 | 5,906 | 22.8 | 15.9 |
| 1994 | 529 | 24,278 | 24,386 | 2,368 | 27,283 | 1,611 | 548 | 25,124 | 96.4 | 67.0 |
| I | 529 | 5,745 | 5,783 | 682 | 6,994 | 359 | 562 | 6,073 | 23.4 | 16.4 |
| II | 562 | 6,042 | 6,058 | 603 | 7,223 | 391 | 506 | 6,326 | 24.3 | 17.0 |
| III | 506 | 6,377 | 6,393 | 587 | 7,486 | 416 | 543 | 6,527 | 25.0 | 17.5 |
| IV | 543 | 6,114 | 6,152 | 499 | 7,194 | 445 | 548 | 6,201 | 23.7 | 16.6 |
| 1995[1] | 548 | 25,115 | 25,222 | 2,104 | 27,874 | 1,821 | 519 | 25,534 | 97.0 | 67.4 |
| I | 548 | 5,888 | 5,925 | 572 | 7,045 | 368 | 514 | 6,163 | 23.5 | 16.3 |
| II | 514 | 6,325 | 6,341 | 540 | 7,395 | 452 | 471 | 6,472 | 24.6 | 17.1 |
| III | 471 | 6,625 | 6,641 | 539 | 7,651 | 499 | 464 | 6,688 | 25.4 | 17.6 |
| IV | 464 | 6,277 | 6,315 | 453 | 7,232 | 502 | 519 | 6,211 | 23.5 | 16.4 |
| 1996[2] | 519 | 25,435 | 25,542 | 2,089 | 28,150 | 1,857 | 450 | 25,843 | 97.3 | 67.5 |
| I | 519 | 6,302 | 6,339 | 508 | 7,366 | 452 | 461 | 6,453 | 24.4 | 16.9 |
| II | 461 | 6,642 | 6,658 | 526 | 7,645 | 544 | 406 | 6,695 | 25.2 | 17.5 |
| III | 406 | 6,391 | 6,407 | 555 | 7,368 | 436 | 414 | 6,518 | 24.5 | 17.0 |
| IV | 414 | 6,100 | 6,138 | 500 | 7,052 | 425 | 450 | 6,177 | 23.2 | 16.1 |
| 1997[3] | 450 | 25,375 | 25,482 | 2,050 | 27,982 | 2,185 | 450 | 25,347 | 94.6 | 65.7 |
| I | 450 | 6,300 | 6,337 | 525 | 7,312 | 450 | 450 | 6,412 | 24.0 | 16.7 |
| II | 450 | 6,500 | 6,516 | 525 | 7,491 | 575 | 425 | 6,491 | 24.2 | 16.8 |
| III | 425 | 6,500 | 6,516 | 500 | 7,441 | 560 | 425 | 6,456 | 24.1 | 16.7 |
| IV | 450 | 6,075 | 6,138 | 500 | 7,038 | 600 | 450 | 5,988 | 22.3 | 15.5 |

[1] Preliminary. [2] Estimate. [3] Forecast. *Source: Economic Research Service, U.S. Department of Agriculture*

## U.S. Cattle on Feed in 13 States, Quarterly In Thousands of Head

| Year/Quarter | Number on Feed[3] | Placed on Feed | Marketings | Other Disappearance | Year/Quarter | Number on Feed[3] | Placed on Feed | Marketings | Other Disappearance |
|---|---|---|---|---|---|---|---|---|---|
| 1993 | 10,974 | 24,102 | 22,376 | 1,504 | 1994 | 11,196 | 23,449 | 22,979 | 1,060 |
| I | 10,974 | 5,351 | 5,354 | 439 | I | 11,196 | 5,372 | 5,559 | 275 |
| II | 10,532 | 5,334 | 5,858 | 465 | II | 10,734 | 4,675 | 5,951 | 334 |
| III | 9,543 | 6,341 | 5,918 | 275 | III | 9,124 | 6,315 | 5,996 | 191 |
| IV | 9,691 | 7,076 | 5,246 | 325 | IV | 9,252 | 7,087 | 5,473 | 260 |
| 1995[1] | 9,117 | 22,576 | 21,111 | 732 | 1996[2] | 10,346 | 23,210 | 22,085 | 913 |
| I | 9,117 | 5,455 | 4,956 | 197 | I | 10,346 | 5,270 | 5,591 | 213 |
| II | 9,409 | 4,982 | 5,493 | 199 | II | 9,812 | 4,226 | 5,937 | 261 |
| III | 8,699 | 5,904 | 5,685 | 152 | III | 7,840 | 6,664 | 5,481 | 182 |
| IV | 8,766 | 6,235 | 4,977 | 184 | IV | 8,841 | 7,050 | 5,076 | 257 |

[1] Preliminary. [2] Estimate. [3] Beginning of Period. *Source: Economic Research Service, U.S.D.A.*

# CATTLE AND CALVES

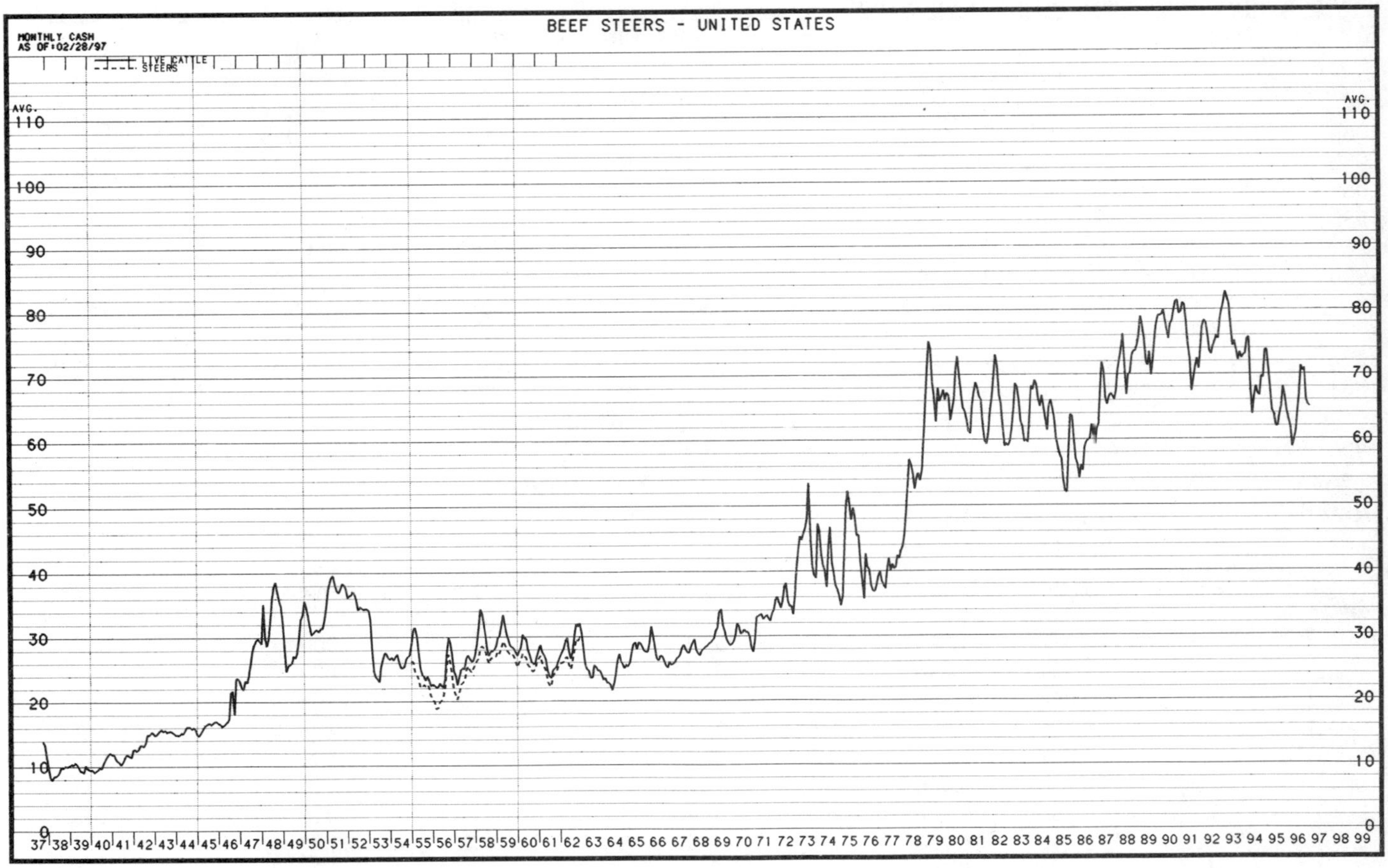


**U.S. Cattle on Feed in 7 States** In Thousands of Head

| Year | Jan. 1 | Feb. 1 | Mar. 1 | Apr. 1 | May 1 | June 1 | July 1 | Aug. 1 | Sept. 1 | Oct. 1 | Nov.1 | Dec.1 |
|---|---|---|---|---|---|---|---|---|---|---|---|---|
| 1985 | 8,635 | 8,184 | 7,891 | 7,826 | 7,526 | 7,490 | 7,127 | 6,509 | 6,270 | 6,591 | 7,732 | 8,062 |
| 1986 | 8,150 | 7,894 | 7,552 | 7,523 | 7,337 | 7,326 | 6,773 | 6,561 | 6,619 | 7,031 | 7,796 | 8,101 |
| 1987 | 7,953 | 7,614 | 7,473 | 7,527 | 7,548 | 7,875 | 7,488 | 6,983 | 7,098 | 7,830 | 8,659 | 8,752 |
| 1988 | 8,411 | 8,204 | 7,912 | 8,056 | 7,829 | 8,134 | 7,736 | 7,140 | 6,944 | 7,404 | 8,194 | 8,255 |
| 1989 | 8,045 | 7,970 | 7,931 | 8,252 | 8,087 | 7,795 | 7,235 | 6,763 | 6,631 | 6,958 | 7,911 | 8,331 |
| 1990 | 8,378 | 8,526 | 8,319 | 8,483 | 8,181 | 7,867 | 7,310 | 6,998 | 6,975 | 7,635 | 8,669 | 9,039 |
| 1991 | 8,992 | 8,963 | 8,874 | 8,941 | 8,590 | 8,570 | 7,877 | 7,388 | 7,064 | 7,216 | 8,013 | 8,477 |
| 1992 | 8,397 | 8,223 | 8,195 | 8,058 | 7,868 | 7,876 | 7,377 | 7,050 | 7,018 | 7,565 | 8,704 | 8,984 |
| 1993 | 9,163 | 9,140 | 8,851 | 8,781 | 8,409 | 8,393 | 7,973 | 7,703 | 7,794 | 8,224 | 8,219 | 8,418 |
| 1994 | 8,256 | 8,139 | 7,981 | 7,960 | 7,772 | 7,511 | 6,910 | 6,841 | 6,949 | 7,295 | 7,988 | 8,198 |
| 1995 | 8,031 | 8,119 | 8,227 | 8,328 | 8,233 | 8,182 | 7,734 | 7,391 | 7,189 | 7,722 | 8,420 | 8,685 |
| 1996[1] | 8,667 | 8,304 | 8,152 | 8,286 | 7,758 | 7,253 | 6,578 | 6,337 | 6,612 | 7,486 | 8,534 | 9,003 |

[1] Preliminary. *Source: Economic Research Service, U.S. Department of Agriculture*

**U.S. Cattle Placed on Feedlots in 7 States** In Thousands of Head

| Year | Jan. | Feb. | Mar. | Apr. | May | June | July | Aug. | Sept. | Oct. | Nov. | Dec. | Total |
|---|---|---|---|---|---|---|---|---|---|---|---|---|---|
| 1985 | 1,449 | 1,341 | 1,592 | 1,436 | 1,691 | 1,296 | 1,098 | 1,520 | 2,000 | 2,829 | 1,801 | 1,590 | 19,643 |
| 1986 | 1,581 | 1,220 | 1,650 | 1,565 | 1,756 | 1,162 | 1,544 | 1,822 | 2,123 | 2,433 | 1,854 | 1,515 | 20,225 |
| 1987 | 1,581 | 1,442 | 1,719 | 1,701 | 1,984 | 1,432 | 1,289 | 1,915 | 2,474 | 2,614 | 1,676 | 1,390 | 21,217 |
| 1988 | 1,663 | 1,379 | 1,848 | 1,521 | 2,175 | 1,387 | 1,251 | 1,660 | 2,209 | 2,450 | 1,690 | 1,421 | 20,654 |
| 1989 | 1,706 | 1,610 | 1,975 | 1,539 | 1,624 | 1,293 | 1,291 | 1,638 | 1,953 | 2,652 | 2,001 | 1,537 | 20,819 |
| 1990 | 1,881 | 1,383 | 1,862 | 1,362 | 1,597 | 1,325 | 1,530 | 1,745 | 2,199 | 2,726 | 1,987 | 1,433 | 21,030 |
| 1991 | 1,721 | 1,455 | 1,703 | 1,427 | 1,772 | 1,102 | 1,327 | 1,459 | 1,826 | 2,539 | 1,917 | 1,456 | 19,704 |
| 1992 | 1,565 | 1,502 | 1,516 | 1,425 | 1,724 | 1,319 | 1,432 | 1,641 | 2,189 | 2,688 | 1,813 | 1,694 | 20,508 |
| 1993 | 1,641 | 1,262 | 1,626 | 1,326 | 1,801 | 1,430 | 1,513 | 1,865 | 2,148 | 2,494 | 1,610 | 1,215 | 19,931 |
| 1994 | 1,416 | 1,256 | 1,518 | 1,310 | 1,359 | 1,113 | 1,520 | 1,761 | 1,915 | 2,244 | 1,642 | 1,345 | 18,863 |
| 1995 | 1,631 | 1,532 | 1,681 | 1,403 | 1,673 | 1,356 | 1,404 | 1,653 | 2,173 | 2,278 | 1,804 | 1,446 | 20,353 |
| 1996[1] | 1,372 | 1,441 | 1,666 | 1,085 | 1,242 | 1,068 | 1,483 | 1,965 | 2,267 | 2,536 | 1,953 | 1,423 | 19,501 |

[1] Preliminary. *Source: Economic Research Service, U.S. Department of Agriculture*

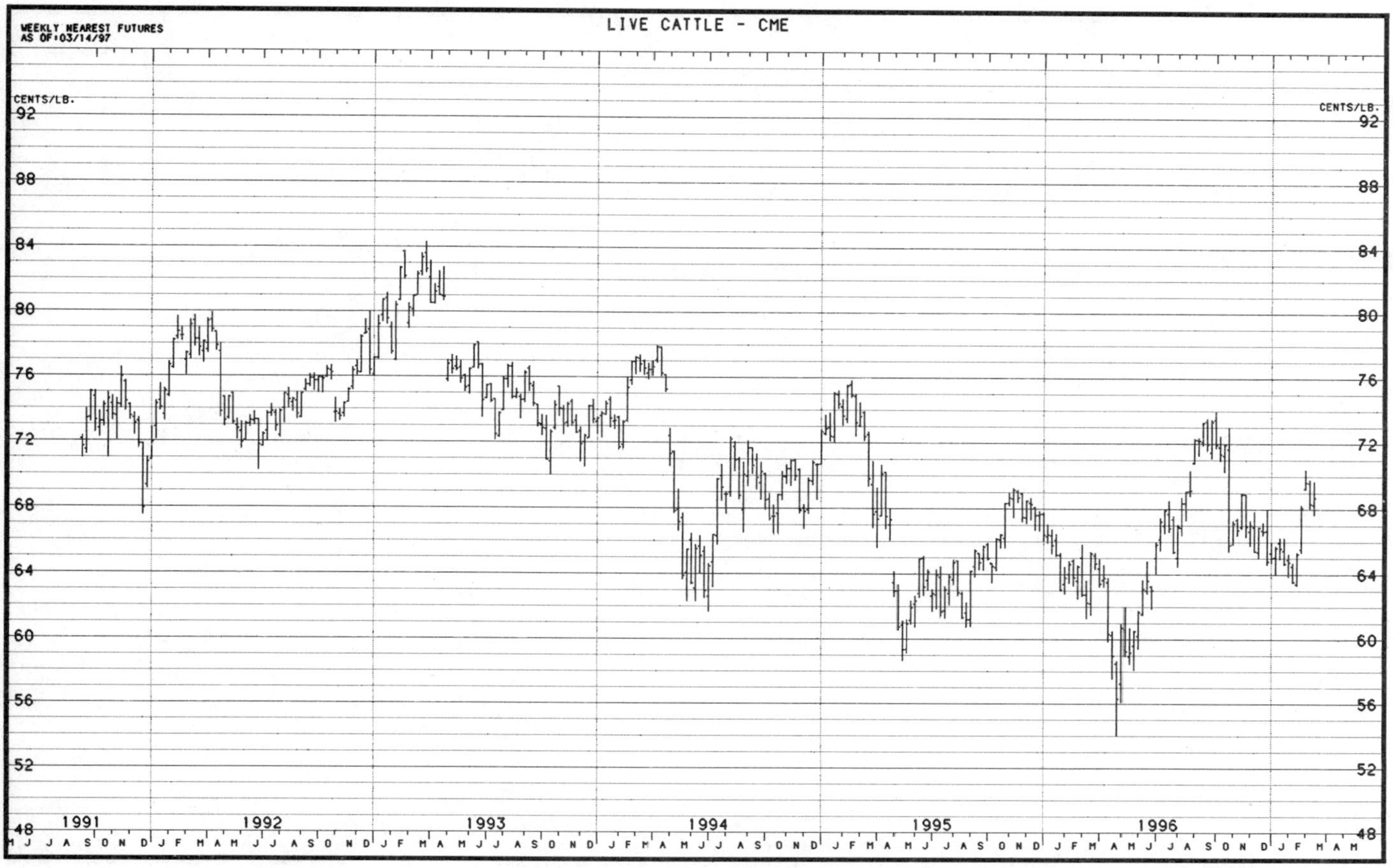


## U.S. Cattle Marketings in 7 States In Thousands of Head

| Year | Jan. | Feb. | Mar. | Apr. | May | June | July | Aug. | Sept. | Oct. | Nov. | Dec. | Total |
|---|---|---|---|---|---|---|---|---|---|---|---|---|---|
| 1986 | 1,750 | 1,470 | 1,593 | 1,631 | 1,635 | 1,648 | 1,692 | 1,694 | 1,652 | 1,587 | 1,462 | 1,559 | 19,373 |
| 1987 | 1,793 | 1,478 | 1,571 | 1,541 | 1,514 | 1,732 | 1,723 | 1,732 | 1,671 | 1,700 | 1,478 | 1,612 | 19,545 |
| 1988 | 1,764 | 1,545 | 1,593 | 1,609 | 1,724 | 1,717 | 1,785 | 1,790 | 1,682 | 1,576 | 1,517 | 1,516 | 19,818 |
| 1989 | 1,677 | 1,534 | 1,579 | 1,580 | 1,752 | 1,791 | 1,700 | 1,694 | 1,579 | 1,628 | 1,490 | 1,403 | 19,407 |
| 1990 | 1,619 | 1,495 | 1,578 | 1,539 | 1,761 | 1,809 | 1,765 | 1,686 | 1,460 | 1,605 | 1,522 | 1,359 | 19,198 |
| 1991 | 1,632 | 1,431 | 1,499 | 1,650 | 1,651 | 1,681 | 1,724 | 1,716 | 1,598 | 1,665 | 1,376 | 1,443 | 19,066 |
| 1992 | 1,640 | 1,410 | 1,536 | 1,490 | 1,594 | 1,702 | 1,674 | 1,592 | 1,581 | 1,473 | 1,442 | 1,414 | 18,548 |
| 1993 | 1,534 | 1,441 | 1,585 | 1,572 | 1,681 | 1,743 | 1,702 | 1,692 | 1,652 | 1,546 | 1,322 | 1,305 | 18,775 |
| 1994 | 1,481 | 1,357 | 1,467 | 1,430 | 1,542 | 1,632 | 1,550 | 1,602 | 1,525 | 1,504 | 1,370 | 1,432 | 18,317 |
| 1995 | 1,484 | 1,372 | 1,513 | 1,437 | 1,667 | 1,754 | 1,698 | 1,815 | 1,594 | 1,529 | 1,478 | 1,412 | 19,038 |
| 1996[1] | 1,681 | 1,541 | 1,476 | 1,613 | 1,747 | 1,696 | 1,678 | 1,653 | 1,342 | 1,431 | 1,418 | 1,415 | 18,691 |

[1] Preliminary. *Source: Economic Research Service, U.S. Department of Agriculture*

## Quarterly Trade of Live Cattle in the U.S. In Head

| | Imports | | | | | Exports | | | | |
|---|---|---|---|---|---|---|---|---|---|---|
| Year | First Quarter | Second Quarter | Third Quarter | Fourth Quarter | Annual | First Quarter | Second Quarter | Third Quarter | Fourth Quarter | Annual |
| 1986 | 375,446 | 265,978 | 174,834 | 590,266 | 1,406,524 | 20,054 | 23,377 | 28,558 | 35,858 | 107,847 |
| 1987 | 433,872 | 334,037 | 75,635 | 356,940 | 1,200,484 | 27,096 | 25,861 | 33,194 | 44,547 | 130,698 |
| 1988 | 731,806 | 216,269 | 131,503 | 252,628 | 1,332,206 | 22,563 | 28,008 | 157,642 | 113,236 | 321,449 |
| 1989 | 515,682 | 287,158 | 132,072 | 524,503 | 1,459,415 | 72,822 | 37,867 | 24,117 | 34,334 | 169,140 |
| 1990 | 566,516 | 577,328 | 301,668 | 689,488 | 2,135,000 | 33,929 | 28,384 | 23,335 | 34,266 | 119,914 |
| 1991 | 599,398 | 551,390 | 225,710 | 562,556 | 1,939,054 | 49,497 | 62,134 | 103,866 | 95,465 | 310,962 |
| 1992 | 599,255 | 505,568 | 389,417 | 801,025 | 2,255,265 | 97,683 | 100,282 | 74,827 | 48,998 | 321,790 |
| 1993 | 672,447 | 635,341 | 469,439 | 721,819 | 2,499,046 | 50,733 | 33,286 | 22,049 | 47,348 | 153,416 |
| 1994 | 569,466 | 540,845 | 386,596 | 585,597 | 2,082,504 | 51,803 | 43,115 | 62,729 | 73,144 | 230,791 |
| 1995[1] | 868,694 | 804,686 | 488,515 | 624,350 | 2,786,245 | 26,597 | 18,441 | 19,794 | 29,716 | 94,548 |
| 1996[1] | 605,648 | 467,059 | 391,633 | 501,108 | 1,965,448 | 33,906 | 42,796 | 42,757 | 54,848 | 174,307 |

[1] Preliminary. *Source: Economic Research Service, U.S. Department of Agriculture*

## CATTLE AND CALVES

### Average Wholesale Prices of Slaughter Steers at Texas, Choice 2-4 (1100-1300 Lbs.) In Dollars Per 100 Lbs.

| Year | Jan. | Feb. | Mar. | Apr. | May | June | July | Aug. | Sept. | Oct. | Nov. | Dec. | Average |
|---|---|---|---|---|---|---|---|---|---|---|---|---|---|
| 1990 | 79.02 | 78.62 | 79.31 | 80.00 | 78.14 | 76.73 | 75.07 | 77.61 | 78.05 | 79.82 | 81.12 | 81.26 | 78.73 |
| 1991 | 79.42 | 79.56 | 80.90 | 80.73 | 78.22 | 74.29 | 72.44 | 67.38 | 69.19 | 71.16 | 72.16 | 70.68 | 74.68 |
| 1992 | 73.88 | 77.21 | 78.18 | 77.83 | 75.98 | 73.55 | 73.02 | 74.26 | 75.04 | 75.97 | 75.29 | 78.35 | 75.71 |
| 1993 | 80.05 | 80.91 | 82.66 | 81.78 | 80.84 | 77.31 | 74.32 | 75.09 | 73.46 | 72.13 | 73.23 | 72.42 | 77.02 |
| 1994 | 72.88 | 73.03 | 75.41 | 75.48 | 68.12 | 63.60 | 66.58 | 68.04 | 66.79 | 66.51 | 69.43 | 69.35 | 69.60 |
| 1995 | 73.60 | 73.79 | 70.64 | 67.54 | 64.27 | 63.08 | 61.81 | 61.95 | 63.80 | 64.89 | 67.94 | 66.14 | 66.62 |
| 1996 | 64.63 | 63.00 | 61.77 | 59.85 | 59.78 | 61.37 | 64.07 | 67.15 | 71.12 | 70.95 | 70.70 | 66.25 | 65.05 |

*Source: Economic Research Service, U.S.Department of Agriculture.*

### Average Prices of Steers (Feeder) Oklahoma City In Dollars Per 100 Pounds

| Year | Jan. | Feb. | Mar. | Apr. | May | June | July | Aug. | Sept. | Oct. | Nov. | Dec. | Average |
|---|---|---|---|---|---|---|---|---|---|---|---|---|---|
| 1990 | 90.32 | 90.81 | 92.32 | 95.21 | 96.90 | 97.90 | 97.12 | 100.35 | 97.54 | 94.13 | 97.82 | 100.42 | 95.90 |
| 1991 | 99.22 | 101.01 | 101.50 | 103.00 | 101.22 | 104.05 | 102.32 | 96.09 | 94.62 | 92.90 | 89.93 | 86.69 | 97.71 |
| 1992 | 86.63 | 88.90 | 90.43 | 89.48 | 88.96 | 89.27 | 90.43 | 91.30 | 90.87 | 86.65 | 90.12 | 89.83 | 89.41 |
| 1993 | 93.59 | 93.80 | 95.82 | 97.65 | 96.85 | 100.09 | 98.58 | 96.48 | 94.78 | 91.82 | 90.57 | 91.04 | 95.09 |
| 1994 | 90.90 | 91.88 | 94.34 | 93.18 | 87.21 | 83.45 | 85.48 | 85.97 | 79.77 | 77.88 | 80.99 | 82.58 | 86.14 |
| 1995 | 83.41 | 83.05 | 79.50 | 76.62 | 73.69 | 72.89 | 70.09 | 69.62 | 66.71 | 68.60 | 63.45 | 64.44 | 72.67 |
| 1996 | 61.38 | 60.16 | 60.03 | 57.20 | 57.06 | 61.66 | 60.56 | 64.79 | 64.33 | 63.45 | 66.33 | 68.26 | 62.10 |

*Source: Wall Street Journal*

### Federally Inspected Slaughter of Cattle in the United States In Thousands of Head

| Year | Jan. | Feb. | Mar. | Apr. | May | June | July | Aug. | Sept. | Oct. | Nov. | Dec. | Total |
|---|---|---|---|---|---|---|---|---|---|---|---|---|---|
| 1990 | 2,775 | 2,437 | 2,690 | 2,550 | 2,920 | 2,873 | 2,796 | 2,918 | 2,553 | 2,877 | 2,622 | 2,380 | 32,391 |
| 1991 | 2,809 | 2,408 | 2,444 | 2,674 | 2,786 | 2,650 | 2,784 | 2,843 | 2,634 | 2,855 | 2,508 | 2,491 | 31,887 |
| 1992 | 2,856 | 2,377 | 2,599 | 2,525 | 2,688 | 2,863 | 2,802 | 2,721 | 2,748 | 2,793 | 2,490 | 2,632 | 32,094 |
| 1993 | 2,601 | 2,411 | 2,712 | 2,623 | 2,720 | 2,957 | 2,811 | 2,883 | 2,810 | 2,729 | 2,632 | 2,706 | 32,593 |
| 1994 | 2,679 | 2,501 | 2,799 | 2,656 | 2,780 | 2,984 | 2,770 | 3,001 | 2,885 | 2,878 | 2,744 | 2,806 | 33,483 |
| 1995 | 2,802 | 2,524 | 2,890 | 2,591 | 3,064 | 3,187 | 2,878 | 3,160 | 3,019 | 2,982 | 2,897 | 2,741 | 34,735 |
| 1996[1] | 3,046 | 2,855 | 2,834 | 3,039 | 3,258 | 3,078 | 3,080 | 3,143 | 2,693 | 3,074 | 2,801 | 2,800 | 35,700 |

[1] Preliminary. *Source: Agricultural Statistics Board, U.S. Department of Agriculture*

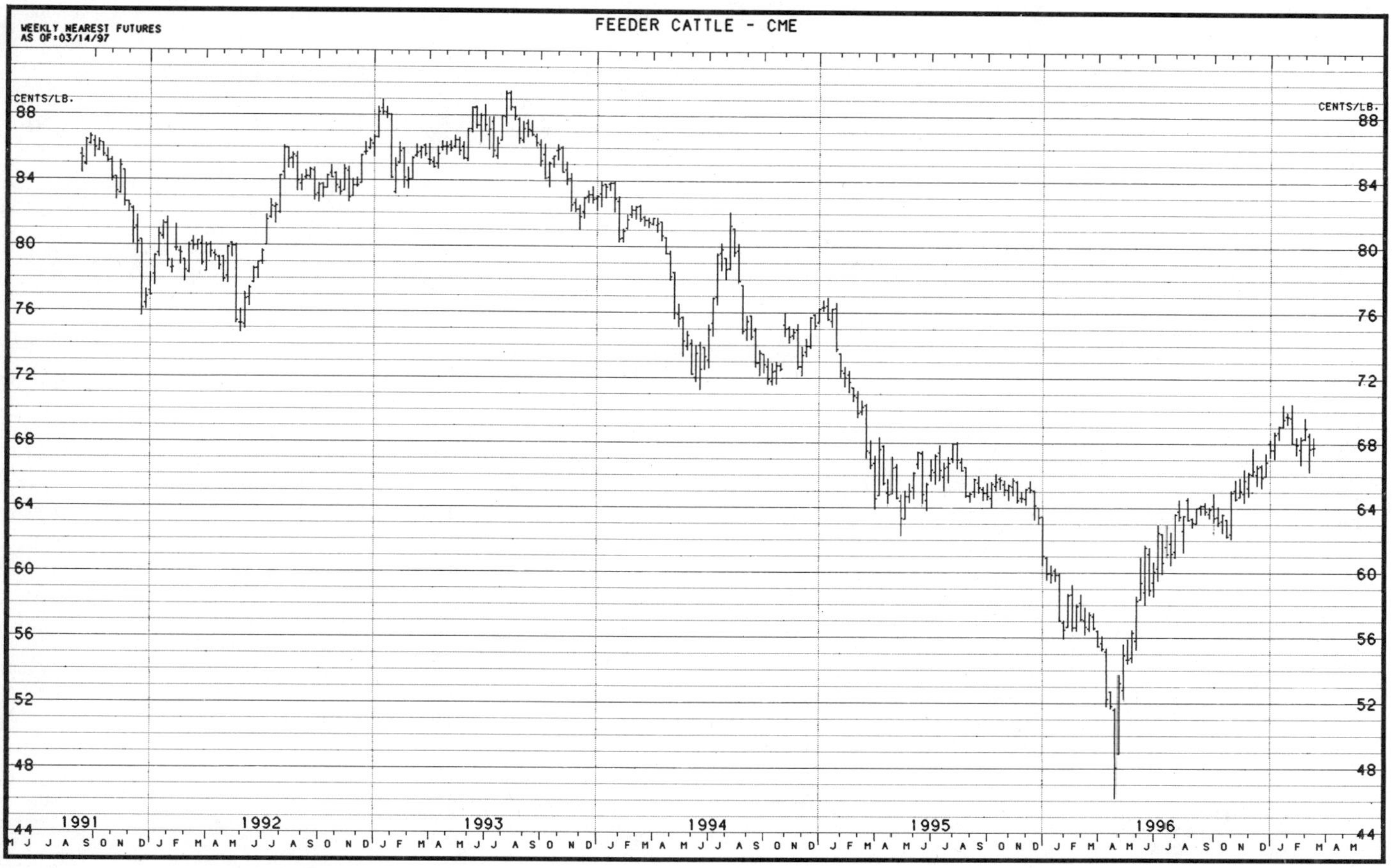


## Average Open Interest of Live Cattle Futures in Chicago    In Contracts

| Year | Jan. | Feb. | Mar. | Apr. | May | June | July | Aug. | Sept. | Oct. | Nov. | Dec. |
|---|---|---|---|---|---|---|---|---|---|---|---|---|
| 1985 | 58,544 | 57,763 | 60,999 | 59,309 | 53,332 | 48,603 | 49,092 | 43,730 | 49,443 | 55,616 | 67,849 | 63,076 |
| 1986 | 57,943 | 54,947 | 55,427 | 49,185 | 56,179 | 55,018 | 64,385 | 63,170 | 64,401 | 56,402 | 62,751 | 58,561 |
| 1987 | 62,770 | 83,958 | 91,018 | 89,818 | 98,350 | 86,144 | 81,399 | 81,315 | 90,915 | 80,156 | 75,379 | 74,839 |
| 1988 | 77,436 | 92,363 | 105,307 | 97,582 | 91,480 | 85,257 | 82,080 | 81,025 | 80,935 | 80,356 | 82,790 | 76,683 |
| 1989 | 80,464 | 84,909 | 93,240 | 82,267 | 81,588 | 69,981 | 78,045 | 76,582 | 73,530 | 65,807 | 73,962 | 71,508 |
| 1990 | 95,515 | 108,149 | 104,647 | 95,709 | 86,875 | 76,130 | 70,462 | 68,375 | 69,611 | 67,122 | 70,576 | 69,647 |
| 1991 | 74,392 | 79,695 | 84,574 | 83,322 | 78,284 | 70,107 | 67,868 | 68,359 | 74,483 | 70,395 | 75,788 | 74,687 |
| 1992 | 79,638 | 97,500 | 97,222 | 90,823 | 83,112 | 68,135 | 67,828 | 62,656 | 61,783 | 60,761 | 63,945 | 67,125 |
| 1993 | 78,481 | 79,256 | 88,113 | 78,144 | 72,183 | 68,287 | 66,617 | 66,560 | 70,275 | 70,559 | 73,571 | 76,042 |
| 1994 | 87,923 | 87,578 | 83,949 | 70,287 | 72,851 | 75,470 | 76,663 | 72,988 | 73,391 | 67,924 | 74,152 | 68,600 |
| 1995 | 80,306 | 78,793 | 76,821 | 64,763 | 61,460 | 56,783 | 58,077 | 55,511 | 58,319 | 62,222 | 69,495 | 69,065 |
| 1996 | 72,870 | 83,064 | 91,348 | 97,315 | 97,911 | 96,320 | 96,547 | 93,557 | 92,804 | 88,467 | 88,062 | 87,305 |

*Source: Chicago Mercantile Exchange (CME)*

## Volume of Trading of Live Cattle Futures in Chicago    In Thousands of Contracts

| Year | Jan. | Feb. | Mar. | Apr. | May | June | July | Aug. | Sept. | Oct. | Nov. | Dec. | Total |
|---|---|---|---|---|---|---|---|---|---|---|---|---|---|
| 1985 | 340.7 | 290.3 | 327.9 | 304.3 | 412.0 | 317.2 | 440.5 | 370.2 | 400.2 | 445.3 | 405.0 | 383.8 | 4,437.3 |
| 1986 | 492.6 | 381.0 | 408.2 | 462.1 | 424.2 | 374.5 | 448.7 | 373.0 | 387.1 | 376.9 | 289.4 | 273.0 | 4,690.5 |
| 1987 | 376.6 | 426.7 | 474.2 | 456.6 | 523.7 | 357.8 | 394.8 | 412.7 | 485.8 | 580.4 | 363.1 | 377.0 | 5,229.3 |
| 1988 | 425.1 | 455.6 | 543.9 | 468.0 | 467.8 | 571.3 | 463.4 | 511.8 | 415.0 | 417.5 | 383.9 | 353.9 | 5,477.2 |
| 1989 | 452.9 | 357.7 | 409.0 | 404.2 | 382.9 | 370.3 | 327.9 | 331.9 | 376.9 | 345.4 | 266.2 | 240.2 | 4,265.7 |
| 1990 | 400.5 | 350.0 | 354.1 | 327.6 | 372.2 | 263.9 | 298.5 | 327.7 | 273.3 | 320.3 | 268.4 | 240.8 | 3,797.4 |
| 1991 | 344.2 | 252.1 | 288.9 | 300.4 | 247.2 | 254.8 | 311.2 | 406.1 | 321.2 | 386.3 | 327.7 | 352.8 | 3,792.9 |
| 1992 | 375.6 | 322.5 | 353.8 | 319.1 | 275.9 | 263.9 | 268.9 | 231.0 | 196.0 | 227.9 | 203.8 | 246.7 | 3,319.6 |
| 1993 | 328.8 | 294.2 | 363.4 | 263.5 | 199.7 | 255.4 | 269.3 | 226.0 | 269.5 | 297.6 | 248.4 | 291.1 | 3,307.0 |
| 1994 | 280.8 | 291.8 | 262.4 | 264.2 | 372.9 | 363.9 | 318.2 | 317.1 | 270.0 | 308.9 | 275.9 | 254.6 | 3,580.9 |
| 1995 | 289.7 | 259.2 | 391.7 | 287.2 | 285.7 | 290.2 | 245.3 | 266.8 | 233.4 | 220.1 | 246.7 | 241.1 | 3,257.1 |
| 1996 | 312.0 | 275.4 | 333.2 | 457.5 | 385.9 | 303.1 | 319.8 | 299.5 | 278.1 | 339.4 | 312.6 | 309.7 | 3,926.2 |

*Source: Chicago Mercantile Exchange (CME)*

# CATTLE AND CALVES

## Beef Steer-Corn Price Ratio in the U.S.[1]

| Year | Jan. | Feb. | Mar. | Apr. | May | June | July | Aug. | Sept. | Oct. | Nov. | Dec. | Average |
|---|---|---|---|---|---|---|---|---|---|---|---|---|---|
| 1989 | 29.2 | 29.2 | 29.7 | 29.4 | 28.7 | 28.5 | 29.0 | 32.6 | 31.4 | 33.1 | 33.8 | 33.4 | 30.67 |
| 1990 | 34.1 | 33.8 | 32.9 | 31.5 | 29.9 | 29.4 | 29.2 | 31.5 | 34.0 | 36.6 | 37.6 | 36.6 | 33.09 |
| 1991 | 36.0 | 35.0 | 34.5 | 33.9 | 33.4 | 33.2 | 32.9 | 30.6 | 30.7 | 32.2 | 31.6 | 30.7 | 32.89 |
| 1992 | 30.3 | 31.0 | 30.7 | 30.8 | 30.2 | 29.8 | 31.7 | 34.7 | 35.0 | 37.3 | 38.2 | 38.7 | 33.20 |
| 1993 | 38.8 | 39.8 | 38.8 | 37.8 | 37.8 | 37.1 | 33.8 | 33.4 | 33.7 | 31.8 | 29.8 | 27.0 | 34.97 |
| 1994 | 27.1 | 26.3 | 27.5 | 28.5 | 26.8 | 24.0 | 28.4 | 31.6 | 30.2 | 32.1 | 34.4 | 31.9 | 29.07 |
| 1995 | 32.6 | 32.4 | 30.5 | 28.4 | 26.3 | 25.2 | 23.5 | 23.5 | 23.0 | 22.3 | 22.7 | 21.1 | 25.96 |
| 1996[2] | 20.3 | 18.1 | 17.2 | 15.1 | 13.9 | 14.1 | 14.0 | 14.8 | 19.1 | 23.6 | 25.8 | 24.9 | 18.41 |

[1] Bushels of corn equal in value to 100 pounds of steers and heifers. [2] Preliminary. *Source: Agricultural Statistics Board, U.S. Department of Agriculture.*

## U.S. Farm Value, Income and Wholesale Prices of Cattle and Calves

| Year | January 1: Per Head Dollars | January 1: Total Million $ | Gross Income From C. & C.[2] Million $ | At Omaha[3]: Steers[3] Choice | Steers[3] Select | Heifers Select | Heifers Choice | Feeder Heifers at Oklahoma City[5] | Cows, Boning Utility Sioux Falls[6] | Vealer, Choice Albany, New York | Cows, Commercial Sioux Falls | Wholesale Prices, Central U.S.: Choice, 700-850 lb. | Select, 700-850 lb. | Cow[6], Canner[7] |
|---|---|---|---|---|---|---|---|---|---|---|---|---|---|---|
| | | | | Dollars per 100 Pounds | | | | | | | | | | |
| 1989 | 581 | 56,211 | 36,429 | 72.52 | 70.28 | 69.52 | 71.93 | 80.00 | 48.98 | 97.57 | 52.14 | 107.80 | 107.70 | 94.43 |
| 1990 | 616 | 58,990 | 39,192 | 77.40 | 75.24 | 73.94 | 76.82 | 85.31 | 53.60 | 97.61 | 57.13 | 123.11 | 116.49 | 99.96 |
| 1991 | 655 | 63,090 | 38,697 | 74.03 | 72.46 | 71.44 | 73.86 | 86.04 | 50.66 | 94.66 | 56.08 | 117.24 | 112.73 | 99.42 |
| 1992 | 630 | 61,451 | 37,272 | 75.17 | 73.65 | 72.88 | 74.95 | 78.41 | 44.84 | 87.01 | 51.22 | 116.02 | 111.66 | 93.85 |
| 1993 | 649 | 64,436 | 39,362 | 76.23 | 74.09 | 73.77 | 76.01 | 82.79 | 47.52 | 89.11 | 56.47 | 117.71 | 113.53 | 95.43 |
| 1994[1] | 659 | 66,490 | 36,445 | 67.60 | 66.33 | 66.14 | 67.93 | 74.55 | 42.51 | 88.01 | 48.28 | 106.73 | 102.08 | 84.39 |
| 1995[1] | 615 | 63,157 | | | | | | 64.43 | 35.58 | NA | 39.03 | 106.09 | 98.45 | 68.67 |

[1] Preliminary. [2] Excludes interfarm sales and Government payments. Cash receipts from farm marketings and value of farm consumption. [3] 1,000 to 1,100 pound weight range. [4] 1,000 to 1,200 pound weight range. [5] 700 to 750 pound weight range. Prior to 1992, 600 to 700 pound weight range. [6] All weights. [7] & cutter. NA=Not available. *Source: Economic Research Service, U.S. Department of Agriculture*

## Average Price Received by Farmers for Beef Cattle In Dollars Per 100 Pounds

| Year | Jan. | Feb. | Mar. | Apr. | May | June | July | Aug. | Sept. | Oct. | Nov. | Dec. | Average |
|---|---|---|---|---|---|---|---|---|---|---|---|---|---|
| 1989 | 70.60 | 71.60 | 72.00 | 70.10 | 68.80 | 67.60 | 68.00 | 69.70 | 68.20 | 68.70 | 69.80 | 71.00 | 69.68 |
| 1990 | 73.70 | 74.60 | 74.20 | 74.60 | 74.60 | 74.20 | 73.60 | 76.00 | 75.00 | 75.50 | 75.30 | 77.10 | 74.87 |
| 1991 | 76.60 | 77.00 | 78.50 | 78.20 | 75.90 | 73.60 | 71.60 | 68.80 | 68.70 | 70.40 | 67.90 | 67.40 | 72.88 |
| 1992 | 68.90 | 72.50 | 72.80 | 72.60 | 71.90 | 70.20 | 70.60 | 71.80 | 71.80 | 71.80 | 70.20 | 70.80 | 71.33 |
| 1993 | 75.10 | 75.80 | 77.20 | 77.30 | 77.10 | 74.50 | 72.50 | 72.70 | 71.40 | 69.10 | 69.30 | 68.50 | 73.38 |
| 1994 | 69.90 | 70.10 | 72.30 | 72.00 | 67.20 | 62.70 | 62.90 | 65.90 | 63.50 | 62.90 | 64.40 | 64.40 | 66.52 |
| 1995 | 67.50 | 68.70 | 66.90 | 63.80 | 60.80 | 60.90 | 59.50 | 59.40 | 59.10 | 58.80 | 60.70 | 60.60 | 62.23 |
| 1996[1] | 59.10 | 57.90 | 56.70 | 54.80 | 54.60 | 56.10 | 58.90 | 60.30 | 63.70 | 63.10 | 63.20 | 60.70 | 59.09 |

[1] Preliminary. *Source: Crop Reporting Board, U.S. Department of Agriculture*

## Average Price Received by Farmers for Calves In Dollars Per 100 Pounds

| Year | Jan. | Feb. | Mar | Apr. | May | June | July | Aug. | Sept. | Oct. | Nov. | Dec. | Average |
|---|---|---|---|---|---|---|---|---|---|---|---|---|---|
| 1989 | 92.80 | 95.90 | 94.00 | 90.40 | 91.10 | 94.10 | 94.60 | 94.20 | 91.10 | 88.10 | 86.70 | 89.10 | 91.84 |
| 1990 | 90.80 | 95.80 | 98.80 | 100.00 | 101.00 | 98.10 | 95.90 | 98.90 | 95.40 | 92.80 | 93.80 | 96.80 | 96.51 |
| 1991 | 98.00 | 104.00 | 106.00 | 109.00 | 107.00 | 106.00 | 103.00 | 98.30 | 96.20 | 93.90 | 90.20 | 87.60 | 99.93 |
| 1992 | 88.30 | 92.80 | 94.10 | 92.00 | 89.60 | 88.50 | 90.10 | 90.40 | 87.40 | 86.00 | 86.50 | 87.00 | 89.39 |
| 1993 | 94.70 | 96.00 | 98.60 | 99.60 | 99.20 | 99.10 | 96.90 | 95.10 | 93.50 | 93.90 | 91.60 | 92.80 | 95.92 |
| 1994 | 93.90 | 94.90 | 97.60 | 95.80 | 89.40 | 84.80 | 83.80 | 84.40 | 80.00 | 78.20 | 81.00 | 81.90 | 87.14 |
| 1995 | 85.00 | 86.90 | 84.40 | 81.80 | 77.00 | 76.90 | 72.00 | 70.90 | 68.50 | 66.20 | 64.00 | 63.30 | 74.74 |
| 1996[1] | 61.80 | 60.00 | 59.40 | 55.20 | 54.40 | 55.20 | 56.80 | 59.20 | 61.00 | 60.10 | 61.20 | 61.80 | 58.84 |

[1] Preliminary. *Source: Crop Reporting Board, U.S. Department of Agriculture*

## Federally Inspected Slaughter of Calves and Vealers in the U.S. In Thousands of Head

| Year | Jan. | Feb. | Mar. | Apr. | May | June | July | Aug. | Sept. | Oct. | Nov. | Dec. | Total |
|---|---|---|---|---|---|---|---|---|---|---|---|---|---|
| 1989 | 196 | 175 | 194 | 152 | 157 | 161 | 169 | 189 | 173 | 191 | 175 | 167 | 2,137 |
| 1990 | 175 | 145 | 165 | 128 | 137 | 131 | 139 | 147 | 132 | 158 | 149 | 136 | 1,743 |
| 1991 | 150 | 120 | 119 | 105 | 102 | 90 | 108 | 108 | 115 | 127 | 125 | 131 | 1,408 |
| 1992 | 128 | 111 | 120 | 108 | 103 | 105 | 106 | 107 | 107 | 111 | 109 | 121 | 1,328 |
| 1993 | 101 | 97 | 116 | 96 | 82 | 91 | 90 | 95 | 94 | 94 | 101 | 103 | 1,159 |
| 1994 | 99 | 94 | 112 | 92 | 90 | 98 | 93 | 106 | 106 | 112 | 114 | 121 | 1,237 |
| 1995 | 121 | 104 | 118 | 96 | 114 | 115 | 111 | 121 | 119 | 124 | 125 | 125 | 1,393 |
| 1996[1] | 140 | 140 | 141 | 128 | 134 | 131 | 156 | 153 | 145 | 159 | 139 | 149 | 1,714 |

[1] Preliminary. *Source: Crop Reporting Board, U.S. Department of Agriculture*

# Cement

Use of cement in the U.S. is directly related to areas where construction activity is the greatest. Based on cement shipments by destination for July 1996, California received almost 771,000 tonnes of finished portland cement. For the first seven months of 1996, California received 4.8 million tonnes of portland cement. Southern California is the most active area receiving 3.02 million tonnes of cement in the January-July 1996 period, with northern California getting 1.79 million tonnes. Another active construction area was Florida. In July 1996, Florida received 531,531 tonnes and for the first seven months of 1996 had received 3.57 million tonnes. The most active area in July 1996 was Texas which received 779,170 tonnes of portland cement. For the January-July 1996 period, northern Texas was destination for 2.63 million tonnes of cement and southern Texas took 2.66 million tones. In July 1996, for the U.S. as a whole, there were 9.1 million tonnes of cement shipped and for the first seven months of 1996, 49.5 million tonnes were shipped. Prepared masonry cement shipments in July 1996 for the U.S. were 346,791 tonnes while for January-July 1996 masonry shipments were 1.99 million tonnes.

Cumulative portland cement shipments for the January-July 1996 period were 7 percent above the same period of 1995. The leading portland cement producing states were California, Michigan, Texas, Pennsylvania, and Missouri. They shipped 37 percent of the July 1996 total. The leading consuming states were Texas, California, Florida, Ohio, and Illinois, with 32 percent of total shipments.

Masonry cement shipments in the first seven months of 1996 were 7 percent higher than in the like period of 1995. The leading producing states were Florida, Indiana, Michigan, Pennsylvania, and Alabama, shipping 49 percent of the total. The leading consuming states were Florida, North Carolina, Texas, Georgia, and Tennessee, taking 42 percent of all shipments.

White cement imports in the first half of 1996 were 206,036 tonnes with the major suppliers being Canada, Denmark, and Mexico. Clinker cement imports in the first half 1996 were 1.14 million tonnes supplied by Canada, Venezuela, and Colombia.

## World Production of Hydraulic Cement by Selected Countries In Thousands of Short Tons

| Year | Brazil | Canada | China | France | Germany | India | Italy | Japan | Poland | Rep. of Korea | Russia[3] | Spain | Turkey | United Kingdom | United States | World Total |
|---|---|---|---|---|---|---|---|---|---|---|---|---|---|---|---|---|
| 1989 | 25,926 | 12,591 | 207,000 | 26,835 | 40,763 | 46,000 | 39,385 | 79,717 | 17,125 | 30,474 | 154,804 | 27,374 | 23,796 | 16,849 | 71,268 | 1,148,912 |
| 1990 | 25,800 | 11,700 | 210,000 | 26,400 | 37,700 | 49,000 | 40,000 | 84,400 | 12,500 | 33,600 | 151,371 | 28,100 | 24,500 | 14,700 | 71,400 | 1,160,000 |
| 1991 | 27,490 | 9,396 | 252,610 | 26,507 | 34,396 | 51,000 | 40,806 | 89,564 | 12,012 | 34,999 | 140,000 | 25,119 | 26,091 | 12,297 | 68,465 | 1,181,793 |
| 1992 | 23,903 | 5,698 | 308,220 | 21,165 | 37,529 | 50,000 | 41,347 | 88,253 | 11,908 | 44,444 | 61,700 | 24,615 | 28,607 | 11,006 | 70,883 | 1,239,683 |
| 1993 | 24,843 | 6,672 | 367,880 | 20,464 | 36,649 | 53,812 | 34,771 | 88,046 | 12,228 | 47,313 | 49,900 | 22,878 | 31,241 | 11,039 | 75,117 | 1,301,527 |
| 1994[1] | 25,229 | 10,584 | 421,180 | 21,296 | 40,380 | 60,000 | 33,192 | 91,624 | 13,834 | 50,730 | 37,200 | 25,150 | 29,493 | 12,493 | 79,353 | 1,380,052 |
| 1995[2] | 25,500 | 10,722 | 445,610 | 21,000 | 40,000 | 70,000 | 35,000 | 90,474 | 13,884 | 55,130 | 36,400 | 25,000 | 33,153 | 12,500 | 78,320 | 1,421,342 |

[1] Preliminary. [2] Estimate. [3] Formerly part of the U.S.S.R.; data not reported separately until 1992. *Source: U.S. Geological Survey*

## Salient Statistics of Cement in the United States

| Year | Net Import Reliance as a % of Apparent Consumption | Production: Portland | Production: Others[3] | Production: Total | Capacity Used at (Portland Mills) % | Shipments From Mills: Total Mil. Tons | Shipments From Mills: Value[4] Mil. $ | Average Value (F.O.B. Mill) $ per ton | Stocks at Mills Dec. 31 | Exports[5] | Apparent Consumption | Imports for Consumption[5] by Country: Canada | Japan | Mexico | Spain | Total |
|---|---|---|---|---|---|---|---|---|---|---|---|---|---|---|---|---|
| | | ----- Thousand Tons ------- | | | % | Mil. Tons | Mil. $ | $ per ton | -------- Million Tons --------- | | | ------------ Thousands of Short Tons ---------- | | | | |
| 1989 | 19 | 67,038 | 2,988 | 70,026 | 75.3 | 70,974 | 4,243 | 54.23 | 5,185 | 421 | 74,626 | 3,103 | 2,191 | 4,002 | 1,417 | 14,280 |
| 1990 | 15 | 67,044 | 2,911 | 69,955 | 76.3 | 78,199 | 4,280 | 54.73 | 5,637 | 503 | 81,305 | 2,918 | 1,906 | 2,093 | 1,188 | 12,041 |
| 1991 | 11 | 64,165 | 3,028 | 67,193 | 72.2 | 68,999 | 3,832 | 55.54 | 6,009 | 633 | 72,413 | 2,837 | 300 | 947 | 634 | 7,893 |
| 1992 | 8 | 66,841 | 2,744 | 69,585 | 76.0 | 69,203 | 3,779 | 54.61 | 5,272 | 746 | 74,124 | 2,997 | 278 | 825 | 446 | 6,166 |
| 1993 | 9 | 70,845 | 2,962 | 73,807 | 79.1 | 74,079 | 4,175 | 56.36 | 4,788 | 625 | 79,198 | 3,629 | 43 | 783 | 597 | 7,060 |
| 1994[1] | 13 | 74,335 | 3,613 | 77,948 | 82.3 | 80,490 | 4,981 | 61.88 | 4,805 | 633 | 86,370 | 4,268 | 14 | 640 | 1,342 | 11,303 |
| 1995[2] | 15 | 73,303 | 3,603 | 76,906 | 81.2 | 79,924 | 5,471 | 68.46 | 5,813 | 759 | 86,612 | 4,886 | [6] | 850 | 1,501 | 13,848 |

[1] Preliminary. [2] Estimate. [3] Masonry, natural & pozzolan (slag-line). [4] Value received F.O.B. mill, excluding cost of containers. [5] Hydraulic & clinker cement. [6] Less than 1/2 unit. NA = Not available. *Source: U.S. Geological Survey*

## Shipments of Finished Portland Cement from Mills in the U.S. In Thousands of Short Tons

| Year | Jan. | Feb. | Mar. | Apr. | May | June | July | Aug. | Sept. | Oct. | Nov. | Dec. | Total |
|---|---|---|---|---|---|---|---|---|---|---|---|---|---|
| 1991 | ---------- | ---------- | ---------- | 38,750.1 | ---------- | ---------- | ---------- | 7,382.0 | 6,780.3 | 7,586.8 | 5,310.9 | 4,434.4 | 70,245.0 |
| 1992 | 4,121.8 | 4,204.5 | 5,258.7 | 6,577.3 | 7,061.2 | 7,675.4 | 7,668.1 | 7,652.7 | 7,732.9 | 8,285.3 | 5,531.8 | 4,817.7 | 76,829.2 |
| 1993 | 3,715.7 | 4,039.0 | 5,381.5 | 6,375.9 | 7,294.4 | 8,079.0 | 7,936.4 | 8,330.6 | 8,747.2 | 8,920.2 | 7,463.4 | 5,968.1 | 86,385.7 |
| 1994 | 4,112.0 | 4,551.6 | 7,033.3 | 7,566.9 | 8,859.2 | 9,465.7 | 8,567.6 | 9,896.7 | 9,338.5 | 9,255.6 | 7,703.6 | 6,347.0 | 92,593.3 |
| 1995 | 4,736.3 | 5,046.2 | 7,077.5 | 7,147.5 | 8,610.7 | 9,521.3 | 8,718.5 | 9,883.6 | 9,108.8 | 9,709.1 | 7,832.4 | 5,907.0 | 93,366.1 |
| 1996[1] | 4,986.2 | 5,444.1 | 6,686.8 | 8,489.0 | 9,599.4 | 9,359.8 | 10,040.7 | 10,488.7 | 9,273.0 | 10,603.8 | | | 84,971.6 |

[1] Preliminary. *Source: U.S. Geological Survey*

# Cheese

Worldwide supply/demand for cheese set new highs in each year of the 1990's. World production in 1996 totaled 11.9 million metric tons vs. 11.7 million in 1995; U.S. production totaled 3.3 million vs. 3.1 million in 1995. France, the second largest producer, turns out about half the U.S. total. World consumption of 11.5 million tons in 1996 compares with 11.3 million in 1995; the U.S. totals were 3.4 million and 3.3 million. France and Italy consumed 2.3 million tons combined in both 1995 and 1996. Most of the world's cheese is consumed where produced. Per capita cheese consumption in the U.S. of a record high 12.79 kilograms compares with 12.45 kg. in 1995. Per capita use in Europe is much higher; France averages more than 21 kg. and Greece 23 kg.

Total world exports dipped slightly in 1996 to 964,000 tons, two-thirds originating in Europe, notably Denmark and France. The world's largest single exporter was New Zealand with 180,000 tons. U.S. exports are small, averaging 25,000 tons during 1994-96. The U.S. and Japan are the largest importers at 155,000 tons each in both 1995 and 1996. World stocks at the end of 1996 of 1.87 million tons were fractionally lower than a year earlier.

American cheese, mostly cheddar, accounts for the largest individual variety of U.S. production and consumption with per capita in 1995 of 11.93 pounds vs the record high of 12.41 in 1987. Since the late 1980's other varieties, primarily Italian, have had a combined production that exceeds American cheese. Per capita consumption of Italian cheeses of 10.28 pounds compares with less than 6.5 pounds in the mid 1980's. Mozzarella makes up the bulk of Italian cheese use. For most dairy products, statistical data is a product of the fat or skim solids content. Not so for cheese. Making cheese exhausts virtually all the value of the skim component of raw milk, even though most of the solids-not-fat are left in the liquid whey. To account for this, the factors used for cheese reflect the total skim solids needed to produce a pound, not just the casein and minerals actually in the cheese.

U.S. cheese prices generally follow a seasonal pattern of low prices in spring and high prices in autumn. Wholesale American cheese prices (40-pound blocks, Wisconsin) averaged $1.33 per pound in 1995. Prices in 1996 strengthened, averaging $1.60 per pound by mid-summer.

***Futures Markets***

Cheddar Cheese futures and options are traded on the Coffee, Sugar & Cocoa Exchange, Inc. (CSCE).

**World Cheese (Total[1]) Production** In Millions of Metric Tons

| Year | Agrentina | Australia | Brazil | Canada | Denmark | France | Germany | Italy | Mexico | Netherlands | New Zealand | Russia[3] | Sweden | Switzerland | Ukraine | United Kingdom | United States |
|---|---|---|---|---|---|---|---|---|---|---|---|---|---|---|---|---|---|
| 1986 | 256 | 170 | 185 | 226 | 252 | 1,320 | 530 | 694 | 262 | 534 | 127 | ---- | 106 | 131 | 844 | 256 | 2,363 |
| 1987 | 277 | 177 | 195 | 246 | 271 | 1,342 | 817 | 704 | 298 | 552 | 113 | ---- | 107 | 128 | 861 | 263 | 2,424 |
| 1988 | 265 | 176 | 200 | 252 | 258 | 1,378 | 849 | 737 | 370 | 559 | 128 | ---- | 115 | 134 | 895 | 299 | 2,527 |
| 1989 | 260 | 190 | 220 | 247 | 275 | 1,485 | 885 | 760 | 373 | 568 | 128 | 460 | 109 | 137 | 184 | 280 | 2,546 |
| 1990 | 270 | 175 | 245 | 255 | 293 | 1,471 | 749 | 811 | 384 | 593 | 122 | 458 | 108 | 138 | 184 | 316 | 2,749 |
| 1991 | 290 | 178 | 290 | 262 | 285 | 1,500 | 777 | 885 | 395 | 610 | 125 | 394 | 107 | 142 | 162 | 303 | 2,747 |
| 1992 | 310 | 197 | 296 | 262 | 290 | 1,489 | 783 | 890 | 390 | 634 | 142 | 299 | 117 | 141 | 113 | 324 | 2,943 |
| 1993 | 350 | 211 | 310 | 271 | 321 | 1,509 | 821 | 885 | 395 | 637 | 145 | 313 | 126 | 138 | 102 | 331 | 2,961 |
| 1994 | 385 | 234 | 330 | 282 | 286 | 1,541 | 855 | 913 | 410 | 648 | 192 | 285 | 133 | 137 | 100 | 326 | 3,054 |
| 1995[1] | 400 | 235 | 360 | 277 | 309 | 1,576 | 890 | 922 | 400 | 680 | 200 | 215 | 130 | 137 | 90 | 342 | 3,148 |
| 1996[2] | 410 | 250 | 375 | 285 | 303 | 1,580 | 900 | 930 | 405 | 680 | 215 | 200 | 134 | 138 | 85 | 340 | 3,280 |

[1] Preliminary. [2] Estimate. [3] Formerly part of the U.S.S.R.; data not reported seperately prior to 1989. *Source: Foreign Agricultural Service, U.S. Department of Agriculture*

**Supply and Distribution of All Cheese in the United States** In Millions of Pounds

| | Supply | | | | | Cheese 40-Lb. Blocks Wisconsin Assembly Points | Distribution | | | | | | | |
|---|---|---|---|---|---|---|---|---|---|---|---|---|---|---|
| | --- Production --- | | January 1 Commercial | | | | Exports | --- Government --- | | American Cheese Removed | Total | --- Domestic Disapparence --- | | |
| Year | Whole Milk[2] | All Cheese[3] | Stocks | Imports[4] | Total Supply | ¢ per lb. | & Shipments[5] | January 1 Stocks | Dec. 31 Stocks | by USDA Programs | Disappearance | American Cheese Donated | Total | Per Capita |
| 1985 | 2,855 | 5,081 | 1,062 | 303 | 6,446 | 127.72 | 125 | 621.0 | 543.7 | 629.0 | 5,501 | 636 | 5,437 | 22.54 |
| 1986 | 2,798 | 5,209 | 945 | 295 | 6,449 | 127.30 | 97 | 543.7 | 420.1 | 468.4 | 5,660 | 560 | 5,602 | 23.11 |
| 1987 | 2,717 | 5,344 | 789 | 265 | 6,399 | 123.19 | 88 | 420.1 | 81.2 | 282.0 | 5,939 | 607 | 5,861 | 24.09 |
| 1988 | 2,757 | 5,572 | 460 | 253 | 6,284 | 123.80 | 76 | 81.2 | 36.7 | 238.1 | 5,886 | 257 | 5,801 | 23.70 |
| 1989 | 2,674 | 5,615 | 361 | 279 | 6,289 | 138.79 | 74 | 36.7 | 6.6 | 37.4 | 5,959 | 67 | 5,901 | 23.81 |
| 1990 | 2,894 | 6,059 | 323 | 302 | 6,689 | 136.69 | 75 | 6.6 | 8.2 | 21.5 | 6,231 | 21 | 6,168 | 24.64 |
| 1991 | 2,769 | 6,055 | 450 | 301 | 6,810 | 124.41 | 72 | 8.2 | 23.1 | 76.9 | 6,393 | 60 | 6,337 | 25.01 |
| 1992 | 2,937 | 6,488 | 393 | 285 | 7,191 | 131.91 | 78 | 23.1 | 16.5 | 14.4 | 6,720 | 0 | 6,661 | 26.01 |
| 1993 | 2,957 | 6,528 | 454 | 320 | 6,719 | 131.52 | 87 | 16.5 | 2.2 | 8.3 | 6,853 | 0 | 6,789 | 26.24 |
| 1994 | 2,974 | 6,735 | 464 | 332 | 7,526 | 131.45 | 55 | 2.2 | .9 | 6.9 | 7,091 | 0 | 7,010 | 26.82 |
| 1995[1] | 3,128 | 6,940 | 436 | | | 132.77 | | .9 | | 6.1 | 6,298 | 0 | | 27.30 |

[1] Preliminary. [2] Whole milk American cheddar. [3] All types of cheese except cottage, pot and baker's cheese. [4] Imports for consumption. [5] Commercial.
*Source: Economic Research Service, U.S. Department of Agriculture*

## Cheese Production in the United States In Millions of Pounds

| Year | American Whole Milk | American Part Skim | American Total | Swiss, Including Block | Munster | Brick | Limburger | Cream & Neufchatel Cheese | Italian Varieties | Blue Mond | All Other Varieties | Total of All Cheese[2] | Cottage Cheese Lowfat | Cottage Cheese Curd[3] | Cottage Cheese Creamed[4] |
|---|---|---|---|---|---|---|---|---|---|---|---|---|---|---|---|
| 1985 | 2,855 | 2.4 | 2,858 | 222.9 | 82.1 | 20.1 | 1.0 | 293.8 | 1,491.3 | 33.4 | 77.7 | 5,081 | 244.4 | 598.8 | 715.6 |
| 1986 | 2,798 | 2.1 | 2,800 | 227.3 | 88.5 | 20.4 | 1.1 | 321.5 | 1,632.9 | 34.2 | 82.1 | 5,209 | 265.5 | 600.1 | 704.8 |
| 1987 | 2,717 | .9 | 2,718 | 227.2 | 92.6 | 28.9 | 1.1 | 342.2 | 1,799.8 | 35.9 | 99.1 | 5,344 | 270.5 | 573.8 | 674.8 |
| 1988 | 2,757 | 1.1 | 2,758 | 250.1 | 83.3 | 24.8 | 1.0 | 375.9 | 1,937.1 | 37.8 | 104.3 | 5,572 | 290.9 | 556.7 | 647.1 |
| 1989 | 2,674 | .8 | 2,675 | 231.2 | 91.1 | 17.5 | .9 | 401.0 | 2,042.9 | 34.6 | 121.2 | 5,615 | 300.9 | 526.9 | 572.3 |
| 1990 | 2,894 | .8 | 2,895 | 261.1 | 100.2 | 17.3 | .8 | 430.8 | 2,207.0 | 36.4 | 110.7 | 6,059 | 301.8 | 493.5 | 530.6 |
| 1991 | 2,769 | .8 | 2,770 | 234.5 | 106.4 | 15.3 | .7 | 446.7 | 2,328.6 | 34.3 | 118.5 | 6,055 | 321.1 | 490.9 | 497.9 |
| 1992 | 2,937 | 1.2 | 2,938 | 237.3 | 116.4 | 15.5 | 1.0 | 516.7 | 2,508.6 | 33.3 | 121.9 | 6,488 | 329.5 | 502.4 | 457.3 |
| 1993 | 2,957 | 3.7 | 2,961 | 231.4 | 117.5 | 12.5 | .9 | 539.9 | 2,494.5 | 33.3 | 137.2 | 6,528 | 317.0 | 471.4 | 430.5 |
| 1994 | 2,974 | 24.7 | 2,999 | 221.2 | 113.6 | 12.2 | .8 | 573.4 | 2,625.7 | 36.5 | 152.1 | 6,735 | 321.1 | 463.3 | 410.0 |
| 1995[1] | 3,129 | 24.0 | 3,153 | 221.7 | 221.7 | 10.4 | .9 | 602.2 | 2,642.0 | 36.6 | 164.7 | 6,940 | 318.3 | 451.1 | 380.4 |

[1] Preliminary. [2] Excludes full-skim cheddar and cottage cheese. [3] Includes cottage, pot, and baker's cheese with a butterfat content of less than 4%. [4] Includes cheese with a butterfat content of 4 to 19%. *Source: Economic Research Service, U.S. Department of Agriculture*

## Wholesale Price of Cheese, 40-lb. Blocks, Wisconsin Assembly Points In Cents Per Pound

| Year | Jan. | Feb. | Mar. | Apr. | May | June | July | Aug. | Sept. | Oct. | Nov. | Dec. | Average |
|---|---|---|---|---|---|---|---|---|---|---|---|---|---|
| 1986 | 123.8 | 124.5 | 123.2 | 125.0 | 126.0 | 125.4 | 126.7 | 129.5 | 129.7 | 130.2 | 133.4 | 130.4 | 127.3 |
| 1987 | 127.8 | 122.5 | 122.3 | 122.4 | 122.0 | 122.0 | 123.2 | 125.5 | 126.6 | 121.9 | 121.3 | 120.8 | 123.2 |
| 1988 | 118.4 | 116.1 | 115.6 | 115.1 | 115.0 | 116.2 | 118.3 | 127.6 | 134.6 | 136.4 | 136.3 | 136.0 | 123.8 |
| 1989 | 129.1 | 117.6 | 117.9 | 120.4 | 123.9 | 130.8 | 140.6 | 143.3 | 155.8 | 160.3 | 163.6 | 162.2 | 138.8 |
| 1990 | 152.3 | 131.6 | 130.7 | 140.5 | 145.8 | 149.5 | 151.0 | 150.3 | 142.6 | 114.9 | 112.0 | 112.7 | 136.2 |
| 1991 | 111.4 | 111.5 | 111.5 | 111.7 | 115.0 | 121.4 | 128.4 | 136.1 | 139.7 | 140.2 | 135.8 | 130.2 | 124.4 |
| 1992 | 125.4 | 119.0 | 119.8 | 131.9 | 140.0 | 141.3 | 141.8 | 142.0 | 136.9 | 132.4 | 129.4 | 123.2 | 131.9 |
| 1993 | 119.3 | 118.6 | 124.3 | 140.8 | 141.8 | 133.7 | 126.3 | 124.8 | 137.4 | 138.9 | 138.7 | 133.7 | 131.5 |
| 1994 | 132.2 | 134.2 | 140.0 | 143.3 | 125.7 | 120.2 | 129.1 | 132.2 | 135.6 | 135.4 | 127.9 | 121.3 | 131.5 |
| 1995 | 124.5 | 130.4 | 131.1 | 122.8 | 122.1 | 126.9 | 126.7 | 132.2 | 141.3 | 145.0 | 145.8 | 144.6 | 132.8 |
| 1996[1] | 139.3 | 139.3 | 140.9 | 145.1 | 151.8 | 151.5 | 158.2 | 167.6 | 145.5 | 162.3 | 133.9 | 126.0 | 146.8 |

[1] Preliminary. *Source: Economic Research Service, U.S. Department of Agriculture*

## United States Total Cheese Production[1] In Millions of Pounds

| Year | Jan. | Feb. | Mar. | Apr. | May | June | July | Aug. | Sept. | Oct. | Nov. | Dec. | Total |
|---|---|---|---|---|---|---|---|---|---|---|---|---|---|
| 1986 | 433.9 | 400.0 | 457.1 | 459.5 | 482.5 | 457.4 | 436.6 | 421.8 | 410.1 | 410.2 | 401.0 | 439.4 | 5,209 |
| 1987 | 422.0 | 398.6 | 457.4 | 462.1 | 477.8 | 465.6 | 453.8 | 426.0 | 430.7 | 448.6 | 431.8 | 469.7 | 5,344 |
| 1988 | 439.5 | 436.2 | 491.6 | 475.3 | 488.2 | 473.7 | 454.9 | 442.0 | 451.9 | 470.0 | 458.9 | 486.5 | 5,572 |
| 1989 | 456.6 | 419.5 | 488.4 | 472.6 | 494.9 | 485.5 | 464.6 | 460.4 | 448.5 | 464.0 | 453.0 | 489.5 | 5,614 |
| 1990 | 483.7 | 471.9 | 531.7 | 521.1 | 542.8 | 522.8 | 502.2 | 495.0 | 472.6 | 505.9 | 495.5 | 522.1 | 6,061 |
| 1991 | 501.7 | 458.0 | 530.1 | 515.4 | 532.3 | 509.0 | 499.5 | 498.2 | 485.0 | 521.0 | 502.3 | 533.7 | 6,061 |
| 1992 | 514.1 | 497.1 | 542.7 | 534.7 | 550.9 | 549.8 | 541.8 | 534.6 | 528.3 | 558.2 | 547.5 | 571.6 | 6,488 |
| 1993 | 517.3 | 492.5 | 563.2 | 561.4 | 576.9 | 563.2 | 537.9 | 525.8 | 531.1 | 560.0 | 540.1 | 558.9 | 6,528 |
| 1994 | 538.3 | 505.8 | 591.8 | 554.3 | 590.4 | 558.7 | 550.7 | 562.4 | 565.5 | 574.5 | 559.3 | 578.3 | 6,730 |
| 1995 | 559.3 | 523.3 | 596.0 | 559.6 | 595.3 | 579.2 | 556.5 | 550.8 | 571.3 | 588.6 | 584.7 | 618.4 | 6,883 |
| 1996[2] | 585.5 | 576.7 | 621.9 | 601.5 | 628.4 | 595.9 | 571.4 | 581.8 | 585.1 | 608.2 | 586.9 | 628.3 | 7,172 |

[1] Excludes cottage and full skim American. [2] Preliminary. *Source: National Agricultural Statistics Service, U.S. Department of Agriculture*

## Cold Storage Holdings of All Varieties of Cheese in the U.S., on First of Month In Millions of Pounds

| Year | Jan. | Feb. | Mar. | Apr. | May | June | July | Aug. | Sept. | Oct. | Nov. | Dec. |
|---|---|---|---|---|---|---|---|---|---|---|---|---|
| 1986 | 852.9 | 835.8 | 813.2 | 815.7 | 838.4 | 873.3 | 892.8 | 915.6 | 916.2 | 859.0 | 805.0 | 757.0 |
| 1987 | 693.6 | 683.9 | 652.4 | 646.5 | 645.1 | 666.8 | 659.0 | 642.5 | 606.6 | 580.8 | 538.0 | 495.9 |
| 1988 | 457.1 | 455.1 | 448.3 | 443.8 | 451.9 | 460.1 | 480.9 | 496.1 | 460.8 | 421.3 | 400.7 | 366.7 |
| 1989 | 388.1 | 395.3 | 404.4 | 396.6 | 412.1 | 431.9 | 429.6 | 430.4 | 419.8 | 370.2 | 331.4 | 330.6 |
| 1990 | 328.0 | 358.4 | 374.9 | 395.8 | 413.4 | 441.6 | 465.0 | 484.6 | 475.7 | 459.9 | 445.4 | 437.3 |
| 1991 | 457.8 | 483.9 | 475.1 | 492.4 | 510.3 | 512.1 | 521.5 | 511.5 | 494.1 | 477.9 | 429.3 | 409.0 |
| 1992 | 415.4 | 440.9 | 445.9 | 449.0 | 449.7 | 455.9 | 465.2 | 496.2 | 487.3 | 449.7 | 441.1 | 462.0 |
| 1993 | 462.0 | 476.1 | 454.4 | 460.0 | 453.6 | 480.5 | 541.2 | 533.3 | 517.7 | 500.1 | 471.9 | 462.4 |
| 1994 | 465.2 | 495.2 | 473.6 | 473.3 | 487.9 | 513.4 | 521.4 | 506.3 | 474.7 | 453.0 | 448.3 | 434.2 |
| 1995 | 436.9 | 449.7 | 448.7 | 458.8 | 466.1 | 465.8 | 473.6 | 482.4 | 458.1 | 428.5 | 418.7 | 393.6 |
| 1996[1] | 412.1 | 441.3 | 466.4 | 490.9 | 517.4 | 533.3 | 535.7 | 526.0 | 490.3 | 485.9 | 485.4 | 480.2 |

[1] Preliminary. [2] Quantities are given in "net weight." *Source: National Agricultural Statistics Service, U.S.Department of Agriculture*

# Chromite

Chromite is the ore mineral of chromium. It is used in making stainless steel and other alloys for which resistance to oxidation and corrosion is important. Chromium is used for plating and as a tanning agent. The mineral chromite is made in refractory linings for steel-making furnaces. Chromium is an essential trade element for human health. However, some chromium compounds are acutely toxic, chronically toxic or carcinogenic. The U.S. has no chromite ore reserves and a limited reserve base. As a result, domestic supply has been a concern during every national military emergency since the first World War.

World chromite resources, mining capacity, and ferrochromium production capacity are concentrated in the Eastern Hemisphere. World chromite ore reserves are more than adequate to meet anticipated world demand. Since the U.S. mines no chromite ore, imports are essential. Recycling is the only domestic supply source of chromium.

South Africa is the leading producer of ferrochromium and its exports to the U.S. are used in the defense industry. Other large chromite producers are Kazakhstan and Albania. In the Western Hemisphere, Brazil and Cuba produce smaller amounts.

U.S. production of ferroalloys and metal in the January-July 1996 period were 23,900 tonnes, chromium content. Total 1995 U.S. production was 49,500 tonnes. Total 1995 U.S. production of stainless steel was 203 million tonnes.

In terms of the components of the U.S. supply, stainless steel scrap receipts were 663,000 tonnes in 1995. For January-July 1996 they were 357,000 tonnes. Chromite ore imports for the first seven months of 1996 were 107,000 tonnes while for all of 1995, ore imports were 253,000 tonnes. Imports of chromium ferroalloys, including high-, medium-, and low-carbon ferrochromium and ferrochromium-silicon were 260,000 tonnes in the first seven months of 1996. For 1995 they were 495,000 tonnes. Chromium metal imports, including waste and scrap, were 4,830 tonnes in January-July 1996 and 7,040 tonnes for all of 1995.

U.S. consumption of chromite ore over the first seven months of 1996 was 193,000 tonnes while for all of 1995 it was 356,000 tonnes. Consumption of chromium ferroalloys and metal were 166,000 tonnes in 1996 while for all of 1995 they were 283,000 tonnes.

The U.S. exports smaller amounts of chromium. Chromite ore exports in January-June 1996 were 62,000 tonnes. In June alone exports were 37,900 tonnes. For all of 1995, exports were only 17,800 tonnes. Chromium ferroalloy exports in the first half of 1996 were 4,170 tonnes while for all of 1995 they were 9,360 tonnes. Chromium metal exports in January-June 1996 were 638 tonnes compared to 714 tonnes for 1995.

At the end of July 1996, industry stocks of chromite ore were 162,000 tonnes. Stocks of chromium ferroalloys and metal were 31,790 tonnes at the end of July. Government stocks in July 1996 were 1.2 million tonnes of chromite ore, 1.07 million tonnes of chromium ferroalloys and 7,690 tonnes of chromium metal.

**World Mine Production of Chromite** In Thousands of Metric Tons (Gross Weight)

| Year | Albania | Brazil | China | Cuba | Finland | Greece | India | Iran | Kazakhstan[3] | Madagascar | Philippines | South Africa | Sudan | Turkey | Zimbabwe | World Total |
|---|---|---|---|---|---|---|---|---|---|---|---|---|---|---|---|---|
| 1986 | 850 | 223 | 50 | 50 | 678 | 62 | 638 | 56 | 3,640 | 83 | 174 | 3,907 | 9 | 543 | 533 | 11,555 |
| 1987 | 1,075 | 338 | 32 | 52 | 543 | 64 | 624 | 92 | 3,570 | 107 | 188 | 3,789 | 13 | 762 | 570 | 11,919 |
| 1988 | 1,109 | 410 | 26 | 52 | 700 | 50 | 821 | 60 | 3,700 | 64 | 129 | 4,245 | 8 | 851 | 561 | 12,896 |
| 1989 | 900 | 476 | 25 | 51 | 513 | 62 | 1,003 | 73 | 3,800 | 63 | 217 | 4,951 | 25 | 1,077 | 627 | 14,006 |
| 1990 | 950 | 263 | 25 | 50 | 504 | 35 | 1,050 | 77 | 3,800 | 151 | 183 | 4,620 | 13 | 836 | 573 | 13,200 |
| 1991 | 587 | 340 | 25 | 50 | 473 | 37 | 940 | 90 | 3,800 | 149 | 191 | 5,100 | 10 | 940 | 564 | 13,300 |
| 1992 | 322 | 449 | 25 | 50 | 499 | 4 | 1,158 | 130 | 3,500 | 161 | 81 | 3,363 | 10 | 531 | 522 | 11,000 |
| 1993 | 282 | 308 | 54 | 50 | 511 | 3 | 1,026 | 130 | 2,900 | 144 | 58 | 2,827 | 12 | 642 | 252 | 9,390 |
| 1994[1] | 223 | 260 | 62 | 50 | 573 | ----- | 1,022 | 129 | 2,020 | 90 | 75 | 3,642 | 25 | 502 | 517 | 9,490 |
| 1995[2] | 250 | 360 | 70 | 50 | 610 | ----- | 1,230 | 129 | 2,400 | 90 | 95 | 5,104 | 25 | 800 | 631 | 12,100 |

[1] Estimate. [2] Preliminary. [3] Formerly part of the U.S.S.R.; data not reported seperately until 1992. *Source: U.S. Geological Survey*

**U.S. Salient Statistics of Chromite** In Thousands of Metric Tons (Gross Weight)

| | | | | | | Consumption by --- Primary Consumer Groups --- | | | -- Consumer Stocks, Dec. 31 -- | | | -- $ per Metric Ton -- | |
|---|---|---|---|---|---|---|---|---|---|---|---|---|---|
| Year | % Net Import Reliance of Apparent Consumption | Production of Ferrochromium | Exports | Imports for Consumption | Reexports | Total | Metallurgical & Chemical | Refractory | Metallurgical & Chemical | Refractory | Total Stocks | South Africa[3] | Turkish[4] |
| 1986 | 79 | 95 | 84 | 443 | 1 | 388 | 342 | 45 | 249 | 35 | 285 | 42 | 125 |
| 1987 | 75 | 107 | 1 | 490 | 5 | 506 | 459 | 48 | 309 | 23 | 332 | 46 | 115 |
| 1988 | 78 | 120 | 4 | 615 | 1 | 551 | 495 | 56 | 366 | 23 | 390 | 56 | 180 |
| 1989 | 78 | 147 | 40 | 525 | 2 | 561 | 517 | 44 | 368 | 24 | 392 | 65 | 185 |
| 1990 | 80 | 109 | 6 | 347 | 4 | 405 | 361 | 44 | 333 | 21 | 355 | 55 | 135 |
| 1991 | 75 | 68 | 9 | 310 | ----- | 375 | 339 | 36 | 310 | 11 | 321 | 50 | 130 |
| 1992 | 86 | 61 | 7 | 324 | ----- | 362 | 335 | 27 | 308 | 13 | 321 | 60 | 110 |
| 1993 | 68 | 63 | 10 | 329 | 2 | 337 | 314 | 23 | 259 | 16 | 275 | 60 | 110 |
| 1994[1] | 70 | 67 | 47 | 273 | ----- | 322 | 302 | 20 | 250 | 17 | 266 | 60 | 110 |
| 1995[2] | 73 | 73 | 18 | 416 | ----- | W | W | W | 194 | 11 | 205 | 61 | 144 |

[1] Preliminary. [2] Estimate. [3] $Cr_2O_3$, 44% (Transvaal). *Source: U.S. Geological Survey*

# Coal

U.S. coal production in the first quarter of 1996 was 258 million short tons. This was down 3 percent from the first quarter of 1995 when coal production reached a record 266 million tons. Coal production in the Interior region rose to 44 million short tons, up 4 percent from the comparable quarter of 1995. The Appalachian Region saw production decline 3 percent while the Western region fell 6 percent from the first quarter 1995 levels. Wyoming is by far the largest producing state followed by West Virginia and Kentucky. For all of 1995, U.S. coal production was 1.03 billion tons.

U.S. coal exports in the January-March 1996 period were 20.5 million tons, up close to 8 percent from the comparable quarter of 1995. Of the total, 12.5 million tons were shipped to Europe. Major markets for U.S. coal include Germany and Italy with metallurgical coal going to Canada, Japan and South Korea.

U.S. coal imports in the first quarter of 1996 were 1.7 million tons, down 5 percent from the first quarter in 1995. For all of 1995, coal imports were 7.2 million tons.

Domestic coal consumption in the first quarter 1996 was 243 million short tons, up almost 7 percent from the first quarter of 1995. The electric utility sector used 8 percent more coal than the year before and accounted for over 88 percent of the first quarter consumption.

Stockpiles of coal at consuming plants at the end of March 1996 were 124 million short tons, down 14 percent from a year earlier. Producer and distributor stocks were almost 37 million short tons, down 13 percent from the year before.

## World Coal Production (Monthly Average)[3] In Thousands of Metric Tons

| Year | Australia | Canada | China | Czech Rep.[4] | France | Germany | India | Indonesia | Kazakhstan[5] | Rep. of Korea | Poland | Romania | Russia[5] | Ukraine[5] | United Kingdom | United States |
|---|---|---|---|---|---|---|---|---|---|---|---|---|---|---|---|---|
| 1988 | 11,234 | 3,215 | 78,872 | 2,159 | 1,012 | 6,610 | 15,692 | 238 | ---- | 1,889 | 16,085 | 742 | 43,587 | ---- | 8,649 | 65,405 |
| 1989 | 12,317 | 3,233 | 87,833 | 2,089 | 1,025 | 6,454 | 16,569 | 380 | ---- | 1,583 | 14,830 | 691 | 48,083 | ---- | 8,190 | 67,608 |
| 1990 | 13,236 | 3,139 | 90,000 | 1,842 | 879 | 6,363 | 16,819 | 611 | ---- | 1,328 | 12,306 | 319 | 39,300 | ---- | 7,442 | 71,137 |
| 1991 | 13,720 | 3,326 | 88,212 | 1,623 | 842 | 6,063 | 18,905 | 1,143 | ---- | 1,148 | 11,698 | 270 | 33,769 | ---- | 8,028 | 68,755 |
| 1992 | 14,594 | 2,693 | 91,278 | NA | 790 | 6,013 | 19,490 | 1,760 | 10,546 | 928 | 10,960 | 292 | 16,123 | ---- | 7,273 | 75,413 |
| 1993 | 14,711 | 2,943 | 96,177 | 1,574 | 715 | 5,347 | 20,503 | 2,299 | 9,323 | 737 | 10,873 | 331 | 16,200 | 9,545 | 5,683 | 71,473 |
| 1994 | 18,912 | 3,664 | 100,508 | 1,530 | 628 | 4,802 | 20,974 | 2,379 | 8,696 | 595 | 11,136 | 377 | 14,622 | 7,650 | 3,976 | 78,102 |
| 1995[1] | 20,255 | 3,215 | 107,624 | 1,563 | NA | 4,905 | 22,121 | 3,165 | 6,933 | 467 | 11,347 | 352 | 13,866 | 7,341 | 4,282 | 80,941 |
| 1996[2] | NA | 3,190 | 114,057 | NA | NA | 4,341 | 26,661 | 3,176 | 6,761 | 427 | 11,673 | 358 | 14,360 | 5,982 | 3,335 | NA |

[1] Preliminary. [2] Estimate. [3] All grades of anthracite and bituminous coal, but excludes recovered slurries, lignite and brown coal. [4] Formerly part of Czechoslovakia; data not reported separately until 1993. [5] Formerly part of the U.S.S.R.; data not reported separately until 1992. NA = Not available.
*Source: United Nations*

## United States Production of Coal by Principal States In Thousands of Short Tons

| Year | Bituminous & Lignite: Alabama | Colorado | Illinois | Indiana | Kentucky | Montana | Ohio | Pennsylvania | Texas | Virgina | West Virgina | Wyoming | Total | Total U.S. |
|---|---|---|---|---|---|---|---|---|---|---|---|---|---|---|
| 1987 | 25,540 | 14,420 | 59,155 | 34,208 | 165,192 | 34,399 | 35,788 | 66,863 | 50,529 | 44,543 | 136,676 | 146,850 | 814,163 | 918,762 |
| 1988 | 26,518 | 15,913 | 58,594 | 31,271 | 157,852 | 38,881 | 34,043 | 67,091 | 52,281 | 45,886 | 145,005 | 164,014 | 837,349 | 950,265 |
| 1989 | 27,992 | 17,123 | 59,267 | 33,641 | 167,389 | 37,742 | 33,689 | 67,248 | 53,854 | 43,006 | 153,580 | 171,558 | 866,089 | 980,729 |
| 1990 | 29,030 | 18,910 | 60,393 | 35,907 | 128,396 | 37,616 | 35,252 | 67,008 | 55,755 | 46,917 | 169,205 | 184,249 | 868,638 | 1,029,076 |
| 1991 | 27,269 | 17,834 | 60,258 | 31,468 | 158,980 | 38,237 | 30,569 | 61,936 | 53,825 | 41,954 | 167,352 | 193,854 | 883,536 | 995,984 |
| 1992 | 25,796 | 19,226 | 59,857 | 30,466 | 161,068 | 38,889 | 30,403 | 65,498 | 55,071 | 43,024 | 162,164 | 190,172 | 881,634 | 997,545 |
| 1993 | 24,768 | 21,886 | 41,098 | 29,295 | 156,299 | 35,917 | 28,816 | 55,394 | 54,567 | 39,317 | 130,525 | 210,129 | 828,011 | 945,424 |
| 1994 | 23,266 | 25,304 | 52,797 | 30,927 | 161,642 | 41,640 | 29,897 | 62,237 | 52,346 | 37,129 | 161,776 | 237,092 | 916,053 | 1,033,504 |
| 1995[1] | 24,640 | 25,710 | 48,180 | 26,007 | 153,739 | 39,451 | 26,118 | 61,576 | 52,684 | 34,099 | 162,997 | 263,822 | 919,023 | 1,032,974 |
| 1996[2] | 24,691 | 24,158 | 49,144 | 28,630 | 151,563 | 37,262 | 27,843 | 57,476 | 57,497 | 34,975 | 165,604 | 278,578 | 937,421 | 1,062,888 |

[1] Preliminary. [2] Estimate. *Source: Energy Information Administration, U.S. Department of Energy*

## Bituminous Coal Production[1] in the United States In Thousands of Short Tons

| Year | Jan. | Feb. | Mar. | Apr. | May. | June | July | Aug. | Sept. | Oct. | Nov. | Dec. | Total |
|---|---|---|---|---|---|---|---|---|---|---|---|---|---|
| 1987 | 74,256 | 71,253 | 75,396 | 70,524 | 70,256 | 76,555 | 69,207 | 80,087 | 81,854 | 85,335 | 78,677 | 79,275 | 912,675 |
| 1988 | 75,325 | 76,757 | 83,943 | 75,324 | 73,981 | 76,443 | 69,176 | 88,175 | 83,196 | 80,799 | 82,925 | 80,260 | 946,304 |
| 1989 | 81,969 | 75,040 | 88,981 | 77,233 | 82,486 | 78,544 | 66,269 | 90,824 | 84,618 | 87,657 | 85,043 | 72,554 | 971,218 |
| 1990 | 90,304 | 81,796 | 91,357 | 83,350 | 86,615 | 84,720 | 79,585 | 91,558 | 83,107 | 93,418 | 86,772 | 75,676 | 1,028,258 |
| 1991 | 85,810 | 82,592 | 85,012 | 79,324 | 79,917 | 76,896 | 79,745 | 88,851 | 81,533 | 90,307 | 81,730 | 79,383 | 991,100 |
| 1992 | 87,979 | 82,102 | 85,835 | 82,364 | 80,197 | 79,968 | 80,768 | 84,401 | 83,555 | 86,265 | 80,240 | 83,021 | 996,695 |
| 1993 | 80,508 | 76,341 | 84,782 | 79,329 | 73,759 | 80,949 | 70,771 | 76,209 | 79,705 | 80,628 | 79,404 | 79,905 | 942,290 |
| 1994 | 76,578 | 81,569 | 95,969 | 87,534 | 82,105 | 86,223 | 77,421 | 93,881 | 88,346 | 85,085 | 86,317 | 87,856 | 1,028,884 |
| 1995 | 88,351 | 83,893 | 93,020 | 80,092 | 83,291 | 84,210 | 79,511 | 88,035 | 89,052 | 90,573 | 86,779 | 81,292 | 1,032,974 |
| 1996[2] | 83,013 | 83,671 | 90,392 | 88,158 | 88,562 | 83,824 | 88,331 | 94,038 | 86,818 | 93,571 | 85,844 | 85,943 | 1,052,166 |

[1] Includes small amounts of lignite. [2] Preliminary. *Source: Energy Information Administration, U.S. Department of Energy*

# COAL

## Pennsylvania Anthracite Coal Production[1] In Thousands of Short Tons

| Year | Jan. | Feb. | Mar. | Apr. | May | June | July | Aug. | Sept. | Oct. | Nov. | Dec. | Total |
|---|---|---|---|---|---|---|---|---|---|---|---|---|---|
| 1987 | 256 | 264 | 305 | 339 | 333 | 359 | 426 | 441 | 441 | 371 | 331 | 310 | 4,176 |
| 1988 | 215 | 268 | 279 | 265 | 296 | 282 | 246 | 360 | 315 | 377 | 302 | 253 | 3,458 |
| 1989 | 281 | 282 | 337 | 273 | 280 | 256 | 197 | 311 | 299 | 373 | 339 | 291 | 3,519 |
| 1990 | 237 | 221 | 259 | 297 | 329 | 327 | 225 | 280 | 323 | 354 | 310 | 183 | 3,345 |
| 1991 | 248 | 243 | 259 | 230 | 224 | 235 | 253 | 313 | 285 | 346 | 299 | 238 | 3,173 |
| 1992 | 247 | 257 | 279 | 296 | 274 | 287 | 305 | 337 | 311 | 322 | 321 | 306 | 3,542 |
| 1993 | 272 | 266 | 290 | 175 | 305 | 358 | 222 | 277 | 351 | 603 | 315 | 271 | 3,705 |
| 1994 | 318 | 335 | 415 | 380 | 375 | 379 | 346 | 457 | 412 | 453 | 452 | 395 | 4,717 |
| 1995 | 304 | 304 | 372 | 332 | 335 | 353 | 307 | 396 | 428 | 445 | 388 | 347 | 4,682 |
| 1996[2] | 290 | 336 | 353 | 357 | 347 | 323 | 348 | 407 | 337 | 385 | 344 | 296 | 4,151 |

[1] Represents production in Pennsylvania only.. [2] Preliminary. *Source: Energy Information Administration, U.S. Department of Energy*

## Salient Statistics of Coal in the United States In Thousands of Short Tons

| Year | Production | Imports | Consumption | Exports: Brazil | Exports: Canada | Exports: Europe | Exports: Asia | Exports: Total | Total Ending Stocks[2] | Losses & Unaccounted For[3] |
|---|---|---|---|---|---|---|---|---|---|---|
| 1987 | 918,762 | 1,747 | 836,941 | 5,830 | 16,464 | 34,159 | 20,206 | 79,607 | 213,780 | -2,499 |
| 1988 | 950,265 | 2,134 | 883,642 | 5,252 | 19,232 | 45,137 | 23,075 | 95,023 | 188,831 | -1,316 |
| 1989 | 980,729 | 2,851 | 889,699 | 5,681 | 16,777 | 51,604 | 22,734 | 100,815 | 178,087 | 6,811 |
| 1990 | 1,029,076 | 2,699 | 895,480 | 5,847 | 15,511 | 58,382 | 22,725 | 105,804 | 201,629 | 3,949 |
| 1991 | 995,984 | 3,390 | 887,621 | 7,052 | 11,178 | 65,520 | 21,788 | 108,969 | 200,682 | 3,731 |
| 1992 | 997,545 | 3,803 | 892,421 | 6,370 | 15,140 | 57,255 | 20,540 | 102,516 | 197,685 | 9,407 |
| 1993 | 945,424 | 7,309 | 925,944 | 5,197 | 8,889 | 37,575 | 19,500 | 74,519 | 145,742 | 4,213 |
| 1994 | 1,033,504 | 7,584 | 930,201 | 5,482 | 9,193 | 35,825 | 17,957 | 71,359 | 169,358 | 15,912 |
| 1995 | 1,032,974 | 7,201 | 940,638 | 6,351 | 9,427 | 48,620 | 19,095 | 88,547 | 169,083 | 8,028 |
| 1996[1] | 1,062,888 | 7,179 | 811,445 | 3,105 | 3,268 | 24,757 | 9,103 | 43,555 | 163,870 | 4,826 |

[1] Preliminary. [2] Producer & distributor and consumer stocks, excludes stocks held by retail dealers for consumption by the residential and commercial secor. [3] Equals production plus imports minus the change in producer & distributor and consumer stocks minus consumption minus exports.
*Source: Energy Information Administration, U.S. Department of Energy*

## U.S. Consumption and Stocks of Total Coal In Thousands of Short Tons

| Year | Consumption: Electric Utilities: Anthracite | Electric Utilities: Bituminous | Electric Utilities: Lignite | Electric Utilities: Total | Industrial: Coke Plants | Industrial: Other Industrial[2] | Residential and Commercial | Total | Stocks, Dec. 31[3]: Consumer: Electric Utilities | Consumer: Coke Plants | Consumer: Other Industrials | Producers and Distributors |
|---|---|---|---|---|---|---|---|---|---|---|---|---|
| 1987 | 972 | 647,824 | 69,098 | 717,894 | 36,957 | 75,175 | 6,914 | 836,941 | 170,797 | 3,884 | 10,777 | 28,321 |
| 1988 | 1,063 | 681,048 | 76,260 | 758,372 | 41,888 | 76,252 | 7,130 | 883,642 | 146,507 | 3,137 | 8,768 | 30,418 |
| 1989 | 1,049 | 688,504 | 77,335 | 766,888 | 40,508 | 76,134 | 6,167 | 889,699 | 135,860 | 2,864 | 7,363 | 29,000 |
| 1990 | 1,031 | 694,317 | 78,201 | 773,549 | 38,877 | 76,330 | 6,724 | 895,480 | 156,166 | 3,329 | 8,716 | 33,418 |
| 1991 | 994 | 691,275 | 79,999 | 772,268 | 33,854 | 75,405 | 6,094 | 887,621 | 157,876 | 2,773 | 7,061 | 32,971 |
| 1992 | 986 | 698,626 | 80,248 | 779,860 | 32,366 | 74,042 | 6,153 | 892,421 | 154,130 | 2,597 | 6,965 | 33,993 |
| 1993 | 951 | 732,736 | 79,821 | 813,508 | 31,323 | 74,892 | 6,221 | 925,944 | 111,341 | 2,401 | 6,716 | 25,284 |
| 1994 | 1,123 | 737,102 | 79,045 | 817,270 | 31,740 | 75,179 | 6,013 | 930,201 | 126,897 | 2,657 | 6,585 | 33,219 |
| 1995 | 978 | 749,951 | 78,078 | 829,007 | 33,011 | 72,796 | 5,824 | 940,638 | 126,304 | 2,632 | 5,702 | 34,444 |
| 1996[1] | 855 | 656,990 | 64,507 | 722,352 | 25,792 | 58,563 | 4,740 | 811,445 | 123,749 | 2,069 | 5,052 | 33,000 |

[1] Preliminary. [2] Including transportation. [3] Excludes stocks held at retail dealers for consumption by the residential and commercial sector.
Source: *Energy Information Administration, U.S. Department of Energy*

## Average U.S. Price of Coal In Dollars Per Short Ton

| Year | End-Use Sector: Electric Utilities | End-Use Sector: Coke Plants | End-Use Sector: Other Industrial[3] | Imports[4] | Exports: Steam | Exports: Metal-lurgical | Exports: Total Average[4] |
|---|---|---|---|---|---|---|---|
| 1987 | 31.83 | 46.55 | 33.71 | 32.04 | 39.22 | 44.49 | 42.77 |
| 1988 | 30.64 | 47.70 | 33.43 | 29.96 | 38.59 | 44.17 | 42.23 |
| 1989 | 30.15 | 47.50 | 33.03 | 34.14 | 37.64 | 45.19 | 42.52 |
| 1990 | 30.45 | 47.73 | 33.59 | 34.45 | 36.81 | 46.51 | 42.63 |
| 1991 | 30.02 | 48.88 | 33.54 | 33.12 | 36.91 | 46.15 | 42.39 |
| 1992 | 29.36 | 47.92 | 32.78 | 33.46 | 35.73 | 45.41 | 41.34 |
| 1993 | 28.58 | 47.44 | 32.23 | 29.89 | 36.03 | 44.11 | 41.41 |
| 1994 | 28.03 | 46.56 | 32.55 | 30.21 | 34.34 | 42.77 | 39.93 |
| 1995[1] | 27.01 | 47.34 | 32.42 | 34.25 | 34.51 | 44.30 | 40.27 |
| 1996[2] | 26.89 | 47.60 | 32.35 | 33.01 | 34.60 | 46.00 | 41.25 |

[1] Preliminary. [2] Estimate. [3] Manufacturing plants only. [4] Based on the free alongside ship (F.A.S) value. NA = Not available.
*Source: Energy Information Administration, U.S. Department of Energy*

## U.S. Trends in Bituminous Coal, Lignite and Pennsylvania Anthracite In Thousands of Short Tons

| | Bituminous Coal and Lignite | | | | | | | Pennsylvania Anthracite | | | | | All Mines |
|---|---|---|---|---|---|---|---|---|---|---|---|---|---|
| | Production | | | | Labor Productivity | | | | | | | | |
| Year | Underground | Surface | Total | Miners[1] Employed | Underground | Surface | Average | Underground | Surface | Total | Miners[1] Employed | Labor Product. Short Tons Miner/Hr. | Labor Product. Short Tons Miner/Hr. |
| | | | | | Short Tons Per Miner Per Hour | | | | | | | | |
| 1980 | 336,925 | 486,719 | 823,644 | 224,938 | 1.21 | 3.27 | 1.94 | 583 | 5,473 | 6,056 | 3,631 | 1.11 | 1.93 |
| 1981 | 315,875 | 502,477 | 818,352 | 226,250 | 1.29 | 3.50 | 2.11 | 621 | 4,802 | 5,423 | 3,052 | .92 | 2.10 |
| 1982 | 338,572 | 494,951 | 833,523 | 214,400 | 1.37 | 3.48 | 2.14 | 579 | 4,009 | 4,588 | 2,717 | .59 | 2.11 |
| 1983 | 299,882 | 478,111 | 778,003 | 173,543 | 1.62 | 3.87 | 2.52 | 487 | 3,602 | 4,089 | 2,099 | 1.01 | 2.50 |
| 1984 | 351,474 | 540,285 | 891,759 | 175,746 | 1.72 | 4.10 | 2.65 | 576 | 3,586 | 4,162 | 2,102 | 1.02 | 2.64 |
| 1985 | 350,073 | 528,856 | 878,930 | 167,009 | 1.79 | 4.32 | 2.76 | 727 | 3,982 | 4,708 | 2,272 | 1.05 | 2.74 |
| 1986 | 359,800 | 526,223 | 886,023 | 152,668 | 2.00 | 4.69 | 3.04 | 638 | 3,654 | 4,292 | 1,977 | 1.03 | 3.01 |
| 1987 | 372,238 | 542,963 | 915,202 | 141,065 | 2.21 | 5.06 | 3.32 | 636 | 2,925 | 3,560 | 1,602 | 1.13 | 3.30 |
| 1988 | 381,546 | 565,164 | 946,710 | 133,913 | 2.38 | 5.41 | 3.58 | 610 | 2,945 | 3,555 | 1,453 | 1.21 | 3.55 |
| 1989 | 393,322 | 584,058 | 977,381 | 130,103 | 2.46 | 5.70 | 3.73 | 513 | 2,835 | 3,348 | 1,394 | 1.12 | 3.70 |
| 1990 | 424,119 | 601,449 | 1,025,570 | 129,619 | 2.54 | 6.07 | 3.86 | 427 | 3,080 | 3,506 | 1,687 | 1.03 | 3.83 |
| 1991 | 406,901 | 585,638 | 992,539 | 119,441 | 2.70 | 6.51 | 4.12 | 324 | 3,121 | 3,445 | 1,161 | 1.39 | 4.09 |
| 1992 | 406,815 | 587,248 | 994,062 | 108,979 | 2.95 | 6.73 | 4.41 | 424 | 3,058 | 3,483 | 1,217 | 1.33 | 4.36 |
| 1993 | 350,637 | 590,482 | 941,119 | 100,099 | 3.24 | 7.84 | 4.74 | 416 | 3,889 | 4,306 | 1,124 | 1.85 | 4.70 |

[1] Excludes miners employed at mines producing less than 10,000 tons. *Source: Energy Information Adminstration, U.S. Department of Energy*

## U.S. Average Mine Prices of Coal In Dollars Per Short Ton

| | Average Mine Price by Method | | | Average Mine Prices by Rank | | | | | | All Coal |
|---|---|---|---|---|---|---|---|---|---|---|
| Year | Underground | Surface | Total | Lignite | Subbituminous | Bituminous | Anthracite[1] | Bituminous & Lignite FOB Mines[2] | Anthracite FOB Mines[2] | CIF[3] Electric Utility Plants |
| 1980 | 33.50 | 18.78 | 24.65 | W | 11.08 | 29.17 | 42.51 | 24.52 | 42.51 | 28.76 |
| 1981 | 35.78 | 20.60 | 26.40 | W | 12.18 | 31.51 | 44.28 | 26.29 | 44.28 | 32.32 |
| 1982 | 35.78 | 21.46 | 27.25 | W | 13.37 | 32.15 | 49.85 | 27.14 | 49.85 | 34.91 |
| 1983 | 34.47 | 20.68 | 25.98 | W | 13.03 | 31.11 | 59.29 | 25.85 | 52.29 | 34.99 |
| 1984 | 33.36 | 20.59 | 25.61 | 10.45 | 12.41 | 30.63 | 48.22 | 25.51 | 48.22 | 35.12 |
| 1985 | 32.91 | 20.13 | 25.20 | 10.68 | 12.57 | 30.78 | 45.80 | 25.10 | 45.80 | 34.53 |
| 1986 | 30.33 | 19.34 | 23.79 | 10.64 | 12.26 | 28.84 | 44.12 | 23.70 | 44.12 | 33.30 |
| 1987 | 29.63 | 18.58 | 23.07 | 10.85 | 11.32 | 28.19 | 43.65 | 23.00 | 43.65 | 31.83 |
| 1988 | 28.97 | 17.43 | 22.07 | 10.06 | 10.45 | 27.66 | 44.16 | 22.00 | 44.16 | 30.64 |
| 1989 | 28.44 | 17.38 | 21.82 | 9.91 | 10.16 | 27.40 | 42.93 | 21.76 | 42.93 | 30.15 |
| 1990 | 28.58 | 16.98 | 21.76 | 10.13 | 9.70 | 27.43 | 39.40 | 21.71 | 39.40 | 30.45 |
| 1991 | 28.56 | 16.60 | 21.49 | 10.89 | 9.68 | 27.49 | 36.34 | 21.45 | 36.34 | 30.02 |
| 1992 | 27.83 | 16.34 | 21.03 | 10.81 | 9.68 | 26.78 | 34.24 | 20.98 | 34.24 | 29.36 |
| 1993 | 26.92 | 15.67 | 19.85 | 11.11 | 9.33 | 26.15 | 32.94 | 20.56 | 37.80 | 28.64 |

[1] Produced in Pennsylvania. [2] FOB = free on board. [3] CIF = cost, insurance and freight. W = Withheld data. *Source: Energy Information Administration, U.S. Department of Energy*

# Cobalt

Cobalt is a strategic metal used in many diverse industrial and military applications. It is found widely in the ores of iron and copper. The largest use of cobalt is in superalloys, which are alloys designed to resist stress and corrosion at high temperatures. Superalloys are used in turbine engine parts for aircraft jet engines and industrial gas turbines. Cobalt, because of its properties, is used in heavy-wear, high-temperature and magnetic applications. It is used to make magnets for a wide range of motors, meters, and devices; corrosion and wear-resistant alloys for hard facing and castings; and high speed steels for cutting tools. Cobalt metal powder acts as a binder in cemented carbides and diamond tools, which are used for metal cutting and forming, mining, and oil and gas drilling. Cobalt compounds are used in catalysts for the petroleum and chemical industries; drying agents for paints, varnishes, and inks; pigments for ceramics, paints, and plastics; battery electrodes; steel-belted radial tires; and magnetic recording media. Cobalt salt is used for electroplating baths and the radioactive isotope of cobalt has medical uses.

Late in 1996 there was considerable unrest in Zaire, one of the world's largest producers of cobalt. Zaire produces 4,000-6,000 tonnes of cobalt a year. The unrest and fighting in that country took place 1,500 miles from the cobalt producing areas so there was no discernible impact on prices.

The U.S. is the world's largest consumer of cobalt, but has no domestic production and relies on imports. There are significant stocks of cobalt metal in the National Defense Stockpile for use in a national emergency.

U.S. reported consumption of cobalt materials in the January-May 1996 period were 2,720 tonnes (contained cobalt). This was 3 percent higher than the same period of 1995. Consumption of cobalt metal, including metal powder, was 1,400 tonnes, up 8 percent from 1995. Consumption of cobalt oxide and other chemical compounds was 715 tonnes, down 1 percent from 1995. Cobalt scrap consumption was 611 tonnes, down 2 percent. For all of 1995, cobalt material consumption was 6,920 tonnes, with 3,650 tonnes of metal, 1,810 tonnes of oxide, and 1,470 tonnes of scrap.

In terms of end use for 1995, stainless and heat resisting steel took 38 tonnes with tool steel using 146 tonnes. Cobalt used in superalloys was 2,870 tonnes. Use of cobalt for magnetic alloys was 755 tonnes, welding material alloys 269 tonnes, and other alloys 80 tonnes. Cemented carbides consumed 752 tonnes. Chemical catalysts took 732 tonnes, with paint driers 770 tonnes, and pigments 168 tonnes.

U.S. industry stocks of cobalt materials at the end of May 1996 were 1,190 tonnes. Of the total, metal stocks were 257 tonnes, oxide and other chemical compounds 835 tonnes, and scrap 99 tonnes. Cobalt stocks at the end of 1995 were 803 tonnes. U.S. government stocks of cobalt metal at the end of May 1996 were 19,800 tonnes. Metal stocks at the end of 1995 were 20,700 tonnes.

U.S. imports of unwrought cobalt alloys over the first four months of 1996 were 16,710 kilograms. For all of 1995 they were 98,200 kilograms. The major suppliers were Canada, Japan, and France. Imports of other cobalt, which includes matte waste and scrap, in the January-April 1996 period were 245,000 kilograms. In 1995 imports were 880,000 kilograms. The major suppliers were Germany and Japan. Imports of wrought cobalt and cobalt articles were 66,900 kilograms. For all of 1995 they were 155,000 kilograms. The major supplier was Japan.

### World Mine Production of Cobalt In Metric Tons (Cobalt Content)

| Year | Albania | Australia | Botswana | Brazil | Canada | Cuba | Finland (Refinery) | France (Refinery) | Japan (Refinery) | Morocco | New Caledonia | Norway (Refinery) | Russia[3] | South Africa | Zaire | Zambia | World Total |
|---|---|---|---|---|---|---|---|---|---|---|---|---|---|---|---|---|---|
| 1987 | 600 | 1,261 | 181 | 150 | 2,490 | 1,566 | 1,234 | 136 | 124 | 224 | 750 | 1,576 | 2,800 | 380 | 23,200 | 7,365 | 41,245 |
| 1988 | 600 | 1,200 | 291 | 150 | 2,398 | 1,783 | 1,132 | 176 | 109 | 253 | 800 | 1,951 | 2,850 | 300 | 26,000 | 7,090 | 43,819 |
| 1989 | 600 | 1,100 | 215 | 300 | 6,167 | 1,825 | 1,295 | 165 | 99 | 121 | 800 | 1,946 | 5,700 | 300 | 18,400 | 7,255 | 42,873 |
| 1990 | 600 | 1,200 | 205 | 400 | 5,470 | 1,460 | 1,300 | 150 | 199 | 194 | 800 | 1,830 | 5,500 | 350 | 19,000 | 7,000 | 42,300 |
| 1991 | 600 | 1,400 | 208 | 400 | 5,274 | 1,100 | 1,503 | 123 | 185 | 325 | 800 | 1,983 | 5,800 | 350 | 9,900 | 6,994 | 33,300 |
| 1992 | 20 | 1,600 | 208 | 400 | 5,102 | 1,150 | 2,100 | 150 | 105 | 461 | 800 | 2,293 | 4,000 | 350 | 5,700 | 6,910 | 27,800 |
| 1993 | 10 | 1,800 | 205 | 400 | 5,108 | 1,060 | 2,200 | 150 | 190 | 397 | 800 | 2,414 | 3,500 | 350 | 2,459 | 4,840 | 21,600 |
| 1994[1] | 10 | 2,200 | 225 | 400 | 4,265 | 972 | 3,000 | 600 | 480 | 440 | 800 | 2,900 | 3,000 | 345 | 826 | 3,711 | 17,600 |
| 1995[2] | ----- | 2,500 | 280 | 400 | 5,266 | 1,561 | 4,000 | 600 | 480 | 450 | 800 | 2,900 | 3,500 | 280 | 1,650 | 5,000 | 22,100 |

[1] Preliminary. [2] Estimate. [3] Formerly part of the U.S.S.R.; data not reported seperately until 1992. *Source: U.S. Geological Survey*

### U.S. Salient Statistics of Cobalt In Metric Tons (Cobalt Content)

| | | | | | Consumption by End Uses | | | | | | | | | | | |
|---|---|---|---|---|---|---|---|---|---|---|---|---|---|---|---|---|
| Year | Net Import Reliance as a % of Apparent Consumption | Cobalt Secondary Production | Processors and Consumer Stocks Dec. 31 | Imports for Consumption | Ground Coat Frit | Stainless & Heat Resisting | Catalysts | Super-Alloys | Tool Steel | Magnetic Alloys | Pigments | Drier in Paints, etc.[3] | Cutting & Wear-Resistant Material | Welding Materials | Total Apparent Uses | Price $ Per Pound[4] |
| 1988 | 87 | 1,018 | 1,766 | 7,051 | 332 | 26 | 617 | 2,865 | 180 | 878 | 378 | 892 | 522 | 206 | 7,824 | 7.09 |
| 1989 | 83 | 1,184 | 1,456 | 5,793 | 366 | 74 | 819 | 2,860 | 219 | 870 | 319 | 718 | 538 | 136 | 7,172 | 7.64 |
| 1990 | 84 | 1,225 | 1,853 | 6,530 | 357 | 41 | W | 3,345 | 123 | 710 | W | 751 | 541 | 180 | 7,512 | 10.09 |
| 1991 | 80 | 1,578 | 1,622 | 6,920 | W | 51 | W | 3,066 | W | 713 | W | 781 | 525 | 135 | 7,240 | 16.92 |
| 1992 | 76 | 1,613 | 840 | 5,760 | 257 | 26 | 949 | 2,697 | 47 | 670 | 197 | 745 | 522 | 128 | 6,471 | 22.93 |
| 1993 | 79 | 1,566 | 819 | 5,950 | W | 41 | 935 | 2,530 | 59 | 569 | 193 | 732 | 569 | 171 | 6,420 | 13.79 |
| 1994[1] | 82 | 1,570 | 914 | 6,780 | W | 41 | 871 | 2,810 | 84 | 698 | 198 | 809 | 723 | 312 | 6,990 | 24.66 |
| 1995[2] | 82 | 1,540 | 802 | 6,440 | 172 | 38 | 732 | 2,940 | 146 | 757 | 172 | 770 | 748 | 287 | 7,000 | 29.21 |

[1] Preliminary. [2] Estimate. [3] Or related usage. [4] Annual spot for cathodes. W = Witheld proprietary data. *Source: U.S. Geological Survey*

# Cocoa

Cocoa is a tropical crop found mostly in a zone that extends approximately 15 degrees north and 15 degrees south from the equator. Growing to a height of 30-35 feet, the cocoa tree produces fruits, called pods, that often grow at ground level. Mature pods are usually yellow, 6-10 inches in length and depending on variety, can contain 20-50 seeds or beans. In the course of a year, the cocoa tree will produce thousands of flowers, but only a very small number will actually produce a mature pod. Flowers and pods are present on the tree throughout the year, though at times they will appear in large concentrations. When successfully pollinated, the flowers lose their petals and the pod begins to grow. The period between fruit-setting and actual maturity is about 5-6 months, followed by the harvest. The trees become productive after 4-5 years, reach peak productivity in 10-11 years, and can remain productive for 50 years.

In addition to the main harvest/crop, most cocoa crops produce a second smaller midcrop. The main crops in West Africa are normally harvested from October through March, with the smaller midcrops harvested from April until August. After the cocoa beans are harvested and dried, they are cleaned and roasted for the development of flavor. The beans separated from the shell are ground into a liquor. The liquor is then passed through a hydraulic press, removing some of the butter and producing cocoa cake. The butter is filtered to remove past particles while the cake is crushed into cocoa powder. These cocoa bean products form the basis of the chocolate industry.

World cocoa production for 1996/97 is forecast at 2.7 million tonnes, down 8 percent from the record 1995/96 crop of 2.9 million tonnes. The smaller production is due to declines in the Ivory Coast, Ghana, Cameroon, Malaysia, and Brazil. Larger crops were expected in Indonesia and Nigeria. The Ivory Coast (Cote d'Ivoire) is by far the world's largest producer of cocoa with about 40 percent of the world total. The 1996/97 crop is forecast at 1.05 million tonnes, down 12 percent from the record 1995/96 crop of 1.2 million tonnes. Heavy rains early in the growing season hampered flowering and the pod set was reported to be poor. It could be expected that following the record crop, the trees would be somewhat less productive and large crops are often followed by smaller ones. The Ivory Coast officially opened it's season October 24, about three weeks late. The producer price was left unchanged from the previous season. The main crop is estimated at 900,000 tonnes with a midcrop of about 150,000 tonnes. There could be some 50,000 tonnes of 1995/96 season midcrop cocoa that will be blended with the 1996/97 main crop. Despite the Ivory Coast government's attempts to control production, cocoa output looks like it will continue to increase.

Ghana is the next largest producer with about 15 percent of world production. The 1996/97 crop is forecast at 390,000 tonnes or about 7 percent less than the 1995/96 crop of 420,000 tonnes. The Ghana season officially opened October 11. The decline looks to be cyclical. Ghana has planted early-maturing high-yielding trees that should mean increased output in the years ahead.

Indonesia's crop is forecast at 280,000 tonnes, up about 2 percent from the previous year. Indonesian cocoa production is on a strong upward trend as the number of bearing trees is increasing. Despite insect infestations and other problems, the government continues to support the industry and Indonesia looks poised to become the second largest producer in the next few years.

Brazil's 1996/97 production is forecast at just under 200,000 tonnes, down 12 percent from the 1995/96 crop of 225,000 tonnes. Brazil's cocoa production has been trending lower as a result of the spread of witches broom fungus, a disease which attacks young shoots, flower buds, and young pods. Despite efforts to halt its spread, the disease threatens the viability of the entire cocoa industry. As a result of the reduced production, Brazil is not likely to export cocoa beans though it will ship cocoa products. Virtually all production is used by the local industry.

The world cocoa grind is forecast at 2.8 million tonnes, up 5 percent from the previous season. The major grinders of cocoa are the Netherlands, Germany, the U.K., and the U.S.. The cocoa producing countries are gradually increasing their grind capacity. World cocoa consumption is trending higher as a result of increased population, income growth, and increased consumption in countries like China and Eastern Europe.

***Futures Markets***

Cocoa futures and options are traded on the Coffee, Sugar and Cocoa Exchange (CSCE) in New York, and in London on the LIFFE. Futures are traded on the Kuala Lumpur Commodity Exchange (KLCE).

**World Cocoa Supply and Demand** In Thousands of Metric Tons

| Crop Year Beginning October | Stock Oct. 1 | Net World Production[4] | Total Availability | Seasonal Grindings | Closing Stocks | Stock Change | Crop Year Beginning October | Stock Oct. 1 | Net World Crop[4] | Total Availability | Seasonal Grindings | Closing Stocks | Stock Change |
|---|---|---|---|---|---|---|---|---|---|---|---|---|---|
| 1981-2 | 643 | 1,712 | 2,355 | 1,606 | 749 | 106 | 1989-90 | 1,124 | 2,394 | 3,518 | 2,217 | 1,300 | 177 |
| 1982-3 | 749 | 1,533 | 2,282 | 1,635 | 647 | -102 | 1990-1 | 1,300 | 2,496 | 3,796 | 2,339 | 1,457 | 156 |
| 1983-4 | 647 | 1,524 | 2,170 | 1,726 | 444 | -202 | 1991-2 | 1,457 | 2,228 | 3,685 | 2,291 | 1,394 | -63 |
| 1984-5 | 444 | 1,920 | 2,364 | 1,862 | 502 | 58 | 1992-3 | 1,394 | 2,322 | 3,716 | 2,439 | 1,277 | -117 |
| 1985-6 | 502 | 1,942 | 2,444 | 1,877 | 567 | 65 | 1993-4 | 1,277 | 2,429 | 3,706 | 2,483 | 1,224 | -53 |
| 1986-7 | 567 | 1,968 | 2,535 | 1,896 | 639 | 72 | 1994-5[1] | 1,224 | 2,347 | 3,571 | 2,544 | 1,027 | -197 |
| 1987-8 | 639 | 2,172 | 2,811 | 2,003 | 808 | 169 | 1995-6[2] | 1,027 | 2,848 | 3,875 | 2,688 | 1,187 | 160 |
| 1988-9 | 808 | 2,436 | 3,245 | 2,121 | 1,124 | 316 | 1996-7[3] | 1,187 | 2,560 | 3,747 | 2,762 | 985 | -202 |

[1] Preliminary. [2] Estimate. [3] Forecast. [4] Obtained by adjusting the Gross World Crop for one percent loss in weight. *Source: E D & F Man Cocoa, Ltd.*

# COCOA

## World Production of Cocoa Beans in Principal Producing Countries — In Thousands of Metric Tons

| Crop Year Beginning October | Brazil | Cameroon | Colombia | Dominican Republic | Ecuador | Ghana | Indonesia | Ivory Coast | Malaysia | Mexico | Nigeria | Papua New Guinea | Peru | Philippines | Togo | Venezuela | World Total |
|---|---|---|---|---|---|---|---|---|---|---|---|---|---|---|---|---|---|
| 1986-7 | 365 | 123 | 52.0 | 45.2 | 77.0 | 228 | 167.0 | 620 | 167 | 37.9 | 100 | 34.0 | 10 | 6.6 | 15.7 | 13.9 | 2,013.5 |
| 1987-8 | 400 | 133 | 53.8 | 50.0 | 76.0 | 188 | 70.0 | 674 | 227 | 47.5 | 145 | 35.0 | 10 | 7.2 | 12.0 | 12.5 | 2,214.2 |
| 1988-9 | 334 | 124 | 56.3 | 44.3 | 82.0 | 300 | 98.0 | 849 | 225 | 41.0 | 160 | 48.0 | 10 | 7.8 | 10.0 | 11.5 | 2,471.3 |
| 1989-90 | 356 | 122 | 58.0 | 57.0 | 102.0 | 295 | 135.0 | 710 | 240 | 38.5 | 155 | 41.0 | 10 | 9.0 | 7.6 | 14.4 | 2,419.1 |
| 1990-1 | 375 | 100 | 60.0 | 42.3 | 104.0 | 293 | 165.0 | 804 | 235 | 38.9 | 160 | 34.0 | 10 | 9.0 | 6.8 | 16.5 | 2,525.5 |
| 1991-2 | 301 | 107 | 60.5 | 48.8 | 82.4 | 243 | 200.0 | 747 | 217 | 41.5 | 110 | 41.0 | 10 | 9.0 | 8.0 | 16.0 | 2,301.0 |
| 1992-3 | 330 | 100 | 60.0 | 50.8 | 76.0 | 312 | 240.0 | 700 | 225 | 43.5 | 140 | 39.0 | 10 | 6.0 | 6.0 | 16.5 | 2,415.5 |
| 1993-4 | 281 | 105 | 60.0 | 58.7 | 80.0 | 312 | 280.0 | 850 | 204 | 34.0 | 130 | 31.0 | 10 | 7.0 | 4.0 | 16.0 | 2,519.2 |
| 1994-5[1] | 228 | 107 | 60.0 | 56.8 | 82.0 | 315 | 255.0 | 873 | 134 | 38.5 | 130 | 29.0 | 10 | 7.9 | 4.0 | 11.0 | 2,398.2 |
| 1995-6[2] | 225 | 130 | 60.0 | 57.7 | 81.5 | 420 | 275.0 | 1,200 | 125 | 42.1 | 140 | 30.0 | 10 | 7.3 | 2.0 | 14.0 | 2,876.3 |
| 1996-7[3] | 198 | 110 | 60.0 | 57.0 | 82.5 | 390 | 280.0 | 1,050 | 120 | 43.0 | 150 | 30.0 | 10 | 7.0 | 2.0 | 14.0 | 2,660.2 |

[1] Preliminary. [2] Estimate. [3] Forecast. *Source: Foreign Agricultural Service, U.S. Department of Agriculture*

## World Absorption (Consumption) of Cocoa[1] — In Thousands of Metric Tons

| Crop Year Beginning October | Belgium | Brazil | Canada | Colombia | Cote d'Ivoire | France | Germany | Italy | Japan | Malaysia | Netherlands | Singapore | Spain | United Kingdom | United States | Former USSR | World Total |
|---|---|---|---|---|---|---|---|---|---|---|---|---|---|---|---|---|---|
| 1986-7 | 34 | 233 | 19 | 48 | 89 | 35 | 205 | 43 | 36 | 36 | 190 | 33 | 33 | 94 | 228 | 164 | 1,896 |
| 1987-8 | 35 | 241 | 21 | 46 | 102 | 40 | 245 | 46 | 40 | 40 | 215 | 40 | 43 | 100 | 241 | 132 | 1,998 |
| 1988-9 | 41 | 210 | 22 | 41 | 110 | 44 | 265 | 46 | 40 | 47 | 234 | 46 | 40 | 112 | 237 | 201 | 2,121 |
| 1989-90 | 47 | 239 | 24 | 45 | 111 | 59 | 287 | 51 | 47 | 72 | 241 | 52 | 42 | 120 | 270 | 106 | 2,217 |
| 1990-1 | 45 | 275 | 25 | 47 | 115 | 70 | 295 | 56 | 52 | 77 | 268 | 51 | 45 | 145 | 272 | 83 | 2,339 |
| 1991-2 | 46 | 216 | 31 | 44 | 108 | 67 | 306 | 62 | 49 | 87 | 294 | 50 | 46 | 153 | 307 | 25 | 2,291 |
| 1992-3 | 47 | 218 | 41 | 45 | 100 | 80 | 331 | 58 | 39 | 99 | 309 | 46 | 46 | 169 | 326 | 95 | 2,439 |
| 1993-4 | 50 | 224 | 32 | 42 | 110 | 95 | 319 | 65 | 38 | 103 | 331 | 51 | 49 | 170 | 317 | 90 | 2,483 |
| 1994-5[2] | 53 | 194 | 35 | 50 | 108 | 108 | 318 | 69 | 39 | 101 | 350 | 51 | 46 | 154 | 331 | 80 | 2,544 |
| 1995-6[3] | 54 | 205 | 39 | 50 | 135 | 111 | 289 | 69 | 49 | 96 | 385 | 54 | 50 | 191 | 345 | 80 | 2,688 |
| 1996-7[4] | 55 | 205 | 40 | 50 | 165 | 111 | 268 | 70 | 50 | 93 | 400 | 55 | 50 | 180 | 365 | 85 | 2,762 |

[1] Figures represent the "grindings" of cocca beans in each country. [2] Preliminary. [3] Estimate. [4] Forecast. *Source: Foreign Agricultural Service, U.S. Department of Agriculture*

## Raw Cocoa Grindings in Selected Countries — In Metric Tons

| Year | Total | First Quarter | Second Quarter | Third Quarter | Fourth Quarter | Total | First Quarter | Second Quarter | Third Quarter | Fourth Quarter |
|---|---|---|---|---|---|---|---|---|---|---|
| | Germany[2] | | | | | Netherlands | | | | |
| 1986 | 201,037 | 53,643 | 50,641 | 42,589 | 54,164 | 182,570 | 46,200 | 45,050 | 40,290 | 51,030 |
| 1987 | 208,684 | 55,190 | 49,224 | 46,424 | 57,846 | 195,627 | 49,141 | 47,399 | 42,772 | 56,315 |
| 1988 | 232,794 | 60,039 | 53,990 | 53,008 | 65,757 | 216,499 | 56,074 | 51,712 | 50,539 | 58,174 |
| 1989 | 245,997 | 61,960 | 59,211 | 56,994 | 67,832 | 233,529 | 61,071 | 56,392 | 55,129 | 60,937 |
| 1990 | 281,855 | 69,125 | 64,613 | 70,994 | 77,123 | 247,590 | 62,243 | 58,817 | 58,702 | 67,828 |
| 1991 | 290,703 | 73,172 | 72,396 | 70,934 | 73,661 | 274,741 | 64,299 | 71,643 | 63,973 | 74,826 |
| 1992 | 319,251 | 78,661 | 73,797 | 80,111 | 86,682 | 293,157 | 77,954 | 71,537 | 69,871 | 73,795 |
| 1993 | 298,681 | 74,119 | 69,805 | 74,010 | 80,747 | 320,060 | 78,338 | 75,548 | 81,183 | 84,991 |
| 1994 | 296,219 | 80,242 | 68,033 | 67,706 | 80,238 | 334,384 | 83,963 | 78,055 | 84,249 | 88,117 |
| 1995 | 258,817 | 69,441 | 56,478 | 61,523 | 71,375 | 355,492 | 91,314 | 85,248 | 85,311 | 93,619 |
| 1996[1] | 194,815 | 69,520 | 59,471 | 65,824 | | 291,139 | 100,866 | 90,724 | 99,549 | |
| | United Kingdom | | | | | United States[3] | | | | |
| 1986 | 87,243 | 21,109 | 21,998 | 20,088 | 24,048 | 153,621 | 33,761 | 37,014 | 42,264 | 40,582 |
| 1987 | 95,396 | 24,469 | 22,941 | 22,405 | 25,581 | 180,811 | 39,665 | 45,930 | 49,864 | 45,352 |
| 1988 | 100,507 | 26,309 | 24,997 | 22,407 | 26,794 | 186,885 | 45,197 | 47,327 | 48,376 | 45,985 |
| 1989 | 114,669 | 28,506 | 30,113 | 26,873 | 29,177 | 192,837 | 43,802 | 49,185 | 47,071 | 52,779 |
| 1990 | 124,791 | 32,116 | 29,322 | 29,419 | 33,934 | 216,740 | 51,559 | 51,683 | 58,278 | 55,220 |
| 1991 | 148,191 | 32,902 | 36,016 | 41,863 | 37,410 | 255,781 | 51,191 | 64,365 | 66,544 | 73,681 |
| 1992 | 159,284 | 39,831 | 37,903 | 37,120 | 44,430 | 313,921 | 70,335 | 74,515 | 84,109 | 84,962 |
| 1993 | 171,343 | 44,575 | 41,975 | 37,496 | 47,297 | 321,905 | 78,968 | 77,720 | 84,593 | 80,624 |
| 1994 | 163,170 | 44,131 | 39,063 | 39,591 | 40,385 | 322,629 | 71,398 | 78,805 | 86,247 | 86,179 |
| 1995 | 159,877 | 43,410 | 35,348 | 34,431 | 46,688 | 338,401 | 78,835 | 78,886 | 87,360 | 93,320 |
| 1996[1] | 143,890 | 50,500 | 44,535 | 48,855 | | 255,690 | 79,044 | 82,713 | 93,933 | |

[1] Preliminary. [2] Beginning October 1990, includes former East Germany. [3] Data incomplete January 1984-March 1991, excludes one major processor. *Source: Foreign Agricultural Service, U.S. Department of Agriculture*

## Imports of Cocoa Butter--Selected Countries In Metric Tons

| Year | Australia | Austria | Belgium | Canada | Finland | France | Germany | Greece | Italy | Japan | Netherlands | Norway | Russia[2] | Sweden | Switzerland | United Kingdom | United States |
|---|---|---|---|---|---|---|---|---|---|---|---|---|---|---|---|---|---|
| 1985 | 8,538 | 3,682 | 15,416 | 5,535 | 2,039 | 19,908 | 33,378 | 1,225 | 3,056 | 8,632 | 24,595 | 1,957 | 7,150 | 4,920 | 11,175 | 31,372 | 70,146 |
| 1986 | 8,204 | 4,387 | 13,795 | 5,377 | 1,966 | 19,397 | 25,513 | 1,557 | 3,246 | 8,474 | 14,925 | 2,295 | 3,450 | 4,866 | 11,369 | 32,669 | 70,264 |
| 1987 | 8,370 | 3,879 | 14,312 | 5,833 | 1,971 | 23,704 | 27,436 | 1,860 | 3,509 | 9,330 | 16,152 | 2,734 | 1,000 | 5,272 | 11,932 | 29,689 | 79,773 |
| 1988 | 9,405 | 4,315 | 12,869 | 7,371 | 2,246 | 24,562 | 33,590 | 2,812 | 4,731 | 12,497 | 20,431 | 2,523 | 1,008 | 5,596 | 12,821 | 34,329 | 78,285 |
| 1989 | 10,291 | 4,599 | 17,748 | 8,224 | 2,469 | 26,597 | 41,765 | 2,806 | 5,932 | 15,280 | 22,924 | 2,706 | 2,500 | 5,735 | 16,276 | 35,045 | 64,353 |
| 1990 | 10,025 | 6,047 | 22,125 | 8,830 | 2,536 | 28,539 | 49,999 | 2,891 | 6,187 | 15,686 | 34,529 | 2,897 | 4,750 | 5,855 | 16,306 | 34,604 | 92,165 |
| 1991 | 11,218 | 5,171 | 24,795 | 8,682 | 2,744 | 28,628 | 54,452 | 3,203 | 7,813 | 15,245 | 29,729 | 3,027 | 610 | 6,299 | 16,544 | 26,876 | 90,004 |
| 1992 | 10,697 | 5,249 | 31,836 | 10,706 | 3,451 | 28,560 | 44,906 | 2,284 | 8,431 | 15,835 | 29,999 | 2,962 | 870 | 5,885 | 17,422 | 26,300 | 99,509 |
| 1993 | 13,129 | 5,417 | 28,989 | 10,225 | 4,530 | 30,611 | 37,269 | 2,448 | 9,851 | 16,422 | 51,559 | 3,566 | 1,308 | 6,390 | 16,711 | 25,941 | 85,400 |
| 1994 | 13,030 | 5,410 | 34,061 | 11,551 | 4,563 | 36,698 | 59,170 | NA | 9,173 | 15,937 | 43,192 | 2,799 | NA | 7,079 | 17,242 | 35,453 | 54,550 |
| 1995[1] | 2,600 | 54 | 26,185 | 11,146 | 4,144 | 40,245 | 69,928 | NA | 12,027 | 12,898 | 38,300 | 3,245 | NA | 7,078 | 17,835 | 30,654 | 57,210 |

[1] Preliminary. [2] Formerly part of the U.S.S.R.; data not reported separately until 1992. NA = Not available. *Source: Food and Agricultural Organization of the United Nations*

## Imports of Cocoa Liquor and Cocoa Powder (Selected Countries) In Metric Tons

| | Cocoa Liquor | | | | | | | Cocoa Powder | | | | | | | | |
|---|---|---|---|---|---|---|---|---|---|---|---|---|---|---|---|---|
| Year | France | Germany | Netherlands | Japan | United Kingdom | United States | Former U.S.S.R. | Belgium | France | Germany | Italy | Japan | Netherlands | Sweden | United Kingdom | United States |
| 1985 | 24,031 | 3,570 | 14,822 | 2,792 | 3,400 | 53,042 | 37,510 | 4,586 | 8,269 | 16,624 | 8,313 | 3,841 | 4,669 | 3,928 | 2,591 | 81,775 |
| 1986 | 28,426 | 2,006 | 10,915 | 3,346 | 4,091 | 50,705 | 30,110 | 4,844 | 8,984 | 15,654 | 9,059 | 4,844 | 4,669 | 3,980 | 3,258 | 89,454 |
| 1987 | 31,171 | 391 | 8,805 | 3,402 | 1,870 | 38,105 | 21,680 | 5,229 | 8,967 | 16,989 | 9,330 | 5,517 | 3,624 | 3,982 | 3,897 | 103,455 |
| 1988 | 31,157 | 793 | 9,014 | 3,445 | 3,022 | 34,454 | 21,000 | 5,572 | 9,750 | 16,455 | 9,498 | 6,470 | 3,432 | 4,330 | 3,576 | 91,337 |
| 1989 | 29,257 | 1,040 | 9,315 | 3,451 | 2,524 | 27,556 | 31,504 | 6,138 | 10,920 | 18,470 | 10,233 | 6,033 | 5,862 | 4,125 | 3,255 | 53,736 |
| 1990 | 35,146 | 1,860 | 9,875 | 3,123 | 1,713 | 25,047 | 18,580 | 6,235 | 12,244 | 21,294 | 11,418 | 6,284 | 6,446 | 4,357 | 3,619 | 58,280 |
| 1991 | 40,251 | 3,242 | 7,443 | 2,057 | 1,918 | 25,320 | NA | 6,665 | 12,215 | 25,315 | 12,189 | 6,557 | 6,239 | 4,314 | 4,315 | 55,636 |
| 1992 | 45,056 | 2,540 | 7,130 | 2,246 | 3,611 | 24,255 | NA | 6,700 | 14,896 | 27,745 | 14,469 | 6,067 | 9,412 | 3,533 | 3,548 | 56,089 |
| 1993 | 41,999 | 1,694 | 15,543 | 2,468 | 1,490 | 31,641 | NA | 6,600 | 16,773 | 25,732 | 13,221 | 5,771 | 5,626 | 4,292 | 2,882 | 66,533 |
| 1994 | 42,392 | 2,682 | 14,913 | 2,312 | 4,443 | 26,846 | NA | 8,748 | 19,215 | 28,806 | 12,884 | 6,461 | 10,078 | 5,015 | 2,661 | 67,207 |
| 1995[1] | 46,570 | 5,083 | 6,822 | 1,832 | 5,030 | 19,192 | NA | NA | 17,081 | 32,247 | 15,265 | 6,310 | 10,048 | 4,866 | 3,077 | 66,075 |

[1] Preliminary. NA = Not available. *Source: E D & F Man Cococa, Ltd.*

## United States Imports of Cocoa and Products In Thousands of Metric Tons

| Year | Jan. | Feb. | Mar. | Apr. | May | June | July | Aug. | Sept. | Oct. | Nov. | Dec. | Total |
|---|---|---|---|---|---|---|---|---|---|---|---|---|---|
| 1985 | 43 | 44 | 40 | 10 | 31 | 16 | 14 | 13 | 11 | 10 | 13 | 25 | 270 |
| 1986 | 30 | 17 | 15 | 9 | 19 | 16 | 22 | 23 | 12 | 8 | 15 | 18 | 209 |
| 1987 | 27 | 28 | 23 | 31 | 21 | 10 | 11 | 14 | 6 | 23 | 24 | 45 | 263 |
| 1988 | 27 | 31 | 27 | 19 | 15 | 21 | 15 | 20 | 9 | 9 | 14 | 31 | 237 |
| 1989 | 44 | 24 | 30 | 29 | 25 | 18 | 18 | 23 | 14 | 20 | 10 | 10 | 266 |
| 1990[2] | 72 | 53 | 70 | 110 | 83 | 60 | NA | 61 | 41 | NA | 72 | 49 | 716 |
| 1991 | 70 | 53 | 51 | 74 | 62 | 66 | 65 | 59 | 53 | NA | NA | 73 | 761 |
| 1992 | 83 | 66 | 62 | 55 | 50 | 60 | 52 | 60 | 67 | 67 | 64 | 69 | 755 |
| 1993 | 67 | 57 | 56 | 61 | 58 | 61 | 77 | 58 | 59 | 71 | 71 | 98 | 801 |
| 1994 | 67 | 68 | 56 | 61 | 49 | 51 | 49 | 58 | 58 | 61 | 45 | 48 | 672 |
| 1995 | 68 | 54 | 44 | 48 | 47 | 48 | 48 | 51 | 53 | 49 | NA | 79 | 643 |
| 1996[1] | NA | NA | 92 | NA | NA | 51 | NA | NA | 55 | NA | NA | | 198 |

[1] Preliminary. [2] Prior to 1990, data for cocoa bean imports only. NA = Not available.
*Source: Foreign Agricultural Service, U.S. Department of Agriculture*

## Visible Stocks of Cocoa at Port of Hampton Road Warehouses[1], End of Month In Thousands of Bags

| Year | Jan. | Feb. | Mar. | Apr. | May | June | July | Aug. | Sept. | Oct. | Nov. | Dec. |
|---|---|---|---|---|---|---|---|---|---|---|---|---|
| 1988 | 140.8 | 274.8 | 347.3 | 434.9 | 480.8 | 474.3 | 511.2 | 464.1 | 486.4 | 465.8 | 442.1 | 419.6 |
| 1989 | 528.4 | 653.3 | 777.7 | 775.0 | 875.0 | 741.6 | 655.8 | 583.2 | 509.1 | 594.2 | 567.0 | 552.3 |
| 1990 | 403.6 | 445.9 | 583.2 | 674.3 | 807.4 | 1,064.7 | 917.2 | 67.2 | 1,046.5 | 19.0 | 996.5 | 958.2 |
| 1991 | 946.5 | 953.3 | 910.1 | 946.0 | 906.1 | 1,036.6 | 1,174.5 | 1,291.2 | 1,386.2 | 1,429.0 | 1,426.0 | 1,502.9 |
| 1992 | 1,588.3 | 1,892.1 | 2,233.1 | 2,236.2 | 2,236.9 | 2,204.8 | 2,150.8 | 2,087.4 | 1,982.4 | 2,018.6 | 2,043.9 | 2,188.5 |
| 1993 | 2,209.9 | 2,497.3 | 2,443.9 | 2,676.8 | 2,771.8 | 2,689.7 | 2,920.0 | 2,708.6 | 2,740.1 | 2,418.7 | 2,328.3 | 2,356.9 |
| 1994 | 2,329.6 | 2,441.1 | 2,443.9 | 2,522.9 | 2,533.1 | 2,460.2 | 2,445.4 | 2,335.0 | 2,308.4 | 2,360.2 | 2,306.9 | 2,253.7 |
| 1995 | 2,152.7 | 2,098.6 | 2,195.7 | 2,212.3 | 2,120.2 | 2,016.0 | 1,919.8 | 1,786.6 | 1,713.1 | 1,598.2 | 1,463.9 | 1,470.3 |
| 1996 | 1,439.8 | 1,492.8 | 1,458.0 | 1,549.6 | 1,561.7 | 1,493.9 | 1,412.3 | 1,315.4 | 1,239.6 | 1,338.9 | 1,108.1 | 1,116.2 |

[1] Licensed and unlicensed warehouses approved by the CSCE. *Source: Coffee, Sugar & Cocoa Exchange, Inc. (CSCE)*

# COCOA

**Visible Stocks of Cocoa in Philadelphia (Delaware River) Warehouses[1], End of Month** In Thousands of Bags

| Year | Jan. | Feb. | Mar. | Apr. | May | June | July | Aug. | Sept. | Oct. | Nov. | Dec. |
|---|---|---|---|---|---|---|---|---|---|---|---|---|
| 1986 | 281.3 | 276.4 | 258.8 | 255.8 | 237.9 | 201.3 | 208.7 | 182.0 | 209.5 | 137.1 | 136.7 | 188.5 |
| 1987 | 209.8 | 210.8 | 228.9 | 224.1 | 243.6 | 276.2 | 291.4 | 259.7 | 236.6 | 177.9 | 189.6 | 206.3 |
| 1988 | 164.6 | 149.2 | 154.9 | 211.1 | 227.3 | 232.0 | 238.1 | 193.3 | 185.5 | 157.6 | 123.4 | 112.0 |
| 1989 | 86.0 | 67.5 | 88.7 | 96.2 | 114.0 | 112.5 | 100.3 | 100.0 | 54.6 | 46.1 | 51.9 | 53.5 |
| 1990 | 35.1 | 61.1 | 87.5 | 107.9 | 120.5 | 204.4 | 297.1 | 231.2 | 185.9 | 193.0 | 195.3 | 215.1 |
| 1991 | 216.2 | 226.9 | 249.3 | 254.9 | 309.2 | 376.8 | 382.8 | 376.8 | 375.5 | 355.1 | 280.5 | 282.7 |
| 1992 | 344.6 | 345.5 | 412.1 | 547.6 | 576.7 | 632.0 | 637.7 | 654.0 | 616.4 | 606.0 | 565.8 | 612.4 |
| 1993 | 562.2 | 589.8 | 603.9 | 606.0 | 653.1 | 678.0 | 665.7 | 648.9 | 600.6 | 611.5 | 685.2 | 781.8 |
| 1994 | 831.5 | 937.7 | 1,004.2 | 1,010.9 | 1,055.4 | 1,095.2 | 1,076.0 | 1,029.8 | 968.5 | 857.1 | 843.9 | 818.9 |
| 1995 | 807.5 | 1,034.3 | 1,038.9 | 1,020.2 | 963.7 | 924.3 | 860.7 | 759.2 | 852.2 | 727.0 | 666.0 | 735.6 |
| 1996 | 960.2 | 1,005.2 | 1,205.6 | 1,658.8 | 1,871.3 | 1,851.7 | 1,969.1 | 1,816.2 | 1,851.1 | 1,705.1 | 1,671.7 | 1,696.5 |

[1] Licensed and unlicensed warehouses approved by the CSCE. *Source: Coffee, Sugar & Cocoa Exchange, Inc. (CSCE)*

**Visible Stocks of Cocoa in New York Warehouses[1], End of Month** In Thousands of Bags

| Year | Jan. | Feb. | Mar. | Apr. | May | June | July | Aug. | Sept. | Oct. | Nov. | Dec. |
|---|---|---|---|---|---|---|---|---|---|---|---|---|
| 1986 | 99.2 | 96.9 | 95.6 | 89.7 | 87.4 | 90.3 | 88.9 | 103.6 | 102.1 | 87.5 | 70.6 | 59.9 |
| 1987 | 51.9 | 43.5 | 40.0 | 39.4 | 55.2 | 46.1 | 58.7 | 43.5 | 49.4 | 44.8 | 107.7 | 149.1 |
| 1988 | 138.7 | 115.4 | 100.1 | 96.8 | 102.8 | 135.4 | 140.8 | 146.8 | 114.3 | 105.8 | 73.7 | 59.8 |
| 1989 | 65.0 | 81.9 | 47.3 | 82.2 | 214.8 | 245.3 | 274.2 | 215.6 | 181.3 | 247.7 | 313.6 | 293.5 |
| 1990 | 288.4 | 267.5 | 311.9 | 335.3 | 294.8 | 359.2 | 431.3 | 409.0 | 442.2 | 406.3 | 413.4 | 397.2 |
| 1991 | 355.6 | 219.6 | 295.9 | 294.1 | 250.4 | 292.6 | 313.3 | 317.1 | 271.5 | 253.9 | 292.9 | 282.4 |
| 1992 | 321.2 | 303.7 | 278.7 | 302.6 | 273.4 | 287.8 | 329.7 | 301.5 | 280.5 | 252.3 | 212.7 | 183.3 |
| 1993 | 150.9 | 144.1 | 122.0 | 125.0 | 119.8 | 119.8 | 119.8 | 119.8 | 119.8 | 118.6 | 132.4 | 187.7 |
| 1994 | 271.0 | 275.0 | 280.8 | 296.6 | 358.6 | 394.1 | 447.5 | 447.5 | 467.3 | 427.3 | 407.2 | 556.1 |
| 1995 | 560.5 | 634.5 | 559.2 | 539.4 | 510.4 | 561.1 | 579.3 | 595.4 | 459.9 | 598.7 | 679.7 | 598.7 |
| 1996 | 667.6 | 646.1 | 632.7 | 627.2 | 656.1 | 633.5 | 1,191.7 | 1,154.2 | 1,121.4 | 973.2 | 950.1 | 919.0 |

[1] Licensed and unlicensed warehouses approved by the CSCE. *Source: Coffee, Sugar & Cocoa Exchange, Inc. (CSCE)*

## U.S. Spot Cocoa Prices[1] for Selected Origins of Cocoa Beans and Products    Dollars Per Metric Ton

| Crop Year Beginning October | Cocoa Beans Brazil | Cocoa Beans Cote d'Ivoire | Cocoa Beans Dominican Republic | Cocoa Beans Ecuador | Cocoa Beans Malaysia | Chocolate Liquor Brazil | Chocolate Liquor Ecuador | Cocoa Butter African | Cocoa Butter Other | Cocoa Cake 10-12% Fat |
|---|---|---|---|---|---|---|---|---|---|---|
| 1986-7 | 2,087 | 2,155 | 1,942 | 1,975 | NA | 2,634 | 2,554 | 4,643 | 4,608 | 965 |
| 1987-8 | 1,807 | 1,952 | 1,664 | 1,700 | NA | 2,280 | 2,216 | 4,001 | 3,919 | 916 |
| 1988-9 | 1,669 | 1,773 | 1,442 | 1,466 | 1,364 | 2,136 | 1,912 | 3,543 | 3,515 | 945 |
| 1989-90 | 1,259 | 1,307 | 1,142 | 1,250 | 1,162 | 1,775 | 1,640 | 3,176 | 3,151 | 666 |
| 1990-1 | 1,222 | 1,289 | 1,091 | 1,168 | 1,131 | 1,704 | 1,646 | 3,232 | 3,199 | 394 |
| 1991-2 | 1,234 | 1,262 | 1,051 | 1,136 | 1,111 | 1,656 | 1,540 | 2,763 | 2,815 | 393 |
| 1992-3 | 1,109 | 1,199 | 969 | 1,123 | 1,020 | 1,571 | 1,513 | 2,517 | 2,572 | 539 |
| 1993-4 | 1,378 | 1,560 | 1,277 | 1,393 | 1,326 | 2,076 | 2,028 | 3,348 | 3,393 | 649 |
| 1994-5 | 1,547 | 1,596 | 1,347 | 1,436 | 1,434 | 2,202 | 2,105 | 3,730 | 3,737 | 560 |
| 1995-6 | 1,539 | 1,522 | 1,387 | 1,390 | 1,449 | 2,167 | 2,023 | 3,780 | 3,795 | 519 |

[1] All prices are nominal and are net ex-dock or ex-warehouse, U.S. eastern seaboard north of Hatteras, for merchandise physically available in interstate commerce, in truckload and regular commercial quantities. NA = Not available. *Source: Foreign Agricultural Service, U.S. Department of Agriculture*

## Average Open Interest of Cocoa Futures in New York    In Contracts

| Year | Jan. | Feb. | Mar. | Apr. | May | June | July | Aug. | Sept. | Oct. | Nov. | Dec. |
|---|---|---|---|---|---|---|---|---|---|---|---|---|
| 1987 | 25,412 | 23,578 | 24,541 | 23,372 | 24,869 | 26,115 | 32,859 | 32,063 | 30,946 | 32,643 | 29,666 | 27,674 |
| 1988 | 27,704 | 28,713 | 32,178 | 33,589 | 35,239 | 36,444 | 37,772 | 38,841 | 38,762 | 38,222 | 37,834 | 36,697 |
| 1989 | 36,747 | 35,492 | 32,917 | 36,597 | 41,341 | 45,016 | 47,222 | 45,700 | 42,731 | 46,366 | 48,062 | 49,553 |
| 1990 | 52,094 | 52,599 | 55,796 | 51,299 | 51,076 | 50,385 | 49,603 | 49,083 | 47,332 | 50,084 | 44,944 | 41,955 |
| 1991 | 42,446 | 38,205 | 40,198 | 45,250 | 47,764 | 49,111 | 53,153 | 53,886 | 53,974 | 54,854 | 53,390 | 53,412 |
| 1992 | 54,464 | 54,797 | 52,110 | 49,904 | 48,076 | 47,690 | 49,924 | 50,532 | 51,706 | 56,101 | 57,426 | 60,521 |
| 1993 | 64,886 | 68,307 | 69,464 | 68,533 | 71,802 | 71,792 | 87,011 | 83,057 | 88,000 | 94,844 | 96,507 | 91,573 |
| 1994 | 89,174 | 87,349 | 91,715 | 82,500 | 82,970 | 72,288 | 72,249 | 69,614 | 73,436 | 74,163 | 72,232 | 75,995 |
| 1995 | 78,873 | 80,786 | 82,299 | 78,435 | 80,547 | 75,496 | 74,975 | 65,794 | 68,547 | 72,758 | 76,680 | 79,844 |
| 1996 | 90,478 | 93,533 | 98,049 | 95,390 | 96,346 | 88,232 | 80,873 | 77,134 | 77,942 | 79,572 | 77,139 | 78,592 |

*Source: Coffee, Sugar & Cocoa Exchange, Inc. (CSCE)*

## Volume of Trading of Cocoa Futures in New York    In Contracts

| Year | Jan. | Feb. | Mar. | Apr. | May | June | July | Aug. | Sept. | Oct. | Nov. | Dec. | Total |
|---|---|---|---|---|---|---|---|---|---|---|---|---|---|
| 1987 | 67,268 | 61,641 | 73,341 | 67,954 | 68,521 | 93,849 | 111,728 | 66,990 | 71,591 | 70,164 | 81,605 | 60,813 | 895,465 |
| 1988 | 84,590 | 83,826 | 92,644 | 85,144 | 111,277 | 121,184 | 128,859 | 106,031 | 87,684 | 137,635 | 142,016 | 87,160 | 1,268,050 |
| 1989 | 138,883 | 122,374 | 116,082 | 132,208 | 135,783 | 129,943 | 98,922 | 137,879 | 73,741 | 95,531 | 101,152 | 59,352 | 1,341,850 |
| 1990 | 121,610 | 128,357 | 166,277 | 191,007 | 194,759 | 181,377 | 126,596 | 143,323 | 75,757 | 120,689 | 116,175 | 69,990 | 1,635,917 |
| 1991 | 94,609 | 92,450 | 104,973 | 99,176 | 76,435 | 104,327 | 96,840 | 146,379 | 104,136 | 135,677 | 106,888 | 72,629 | 1,234,519 |
| 1992 | 122,576 | 119,375 | 94,131 | 116,804 | 66,185 | 135,373 | 104,660 | 145,815 | 113,589 | 109,888 | 137,815 | 95,024 | 1,397,235 |
| 1993 | 145,378 | 139,932 | 111,751 | 149,771 | 82,961 | 189,474 | 225,901 | 215,044 | 240,371 | 217,697 | 229,752 | 183,352 | 2,128,384 |
| 1994 | 178,303 | 190,804 | 205,623 | 188,004 | 267,188 | 251,300 | 193,883 | 241,340 | 142,589 | 183,975 | 210,635 | 164,917 | 2,417,006 |
| 1995 | 197,032 | 183,784 | 191,328 | 208,707 | 169,061 | 199,211 | 140,789 | 205,169 | 120,433 | 149,810 | 211,171 | 113,603 | 2,090,098 |
| 1996 | 177,720 | 226,701 | 213,189 | 242,988 | 164,749 | 183,544 | 159,070 | 164,719 | 107,634 | 167,227 | 185,226 | 128,809 | 2,121,576 |

*Source: Coffee, Sugar & Cocoa Exchange, Inc. (CSCE)*

# Coconut Oil and Copra

Copra, dried coconut meat, is crushed or processed to yield coconut oil and copra meal. Coconut oil is an important ingredient in cosmetics and soap, and is also used as a food ingredient. However, its use as an edible oil is diminishing, particularly in the U.S., as the oil has a high level of saturated fats (92%). U.S. coconut oil imports are mostly processed into inedible products. Coconut oil use in U.S. food products has dropped from about 300,000 tons in the mid-1980's to an average of 200,000 tons in the 1990's; its use in inedible products, soap for example, has increased from about 700,000 tons to near 800,000 tons, respectively.

World copra production is small as most of the crop is processed into oil. 1996/97 production totaled 3.25 million metric tons compared with 3.1 million in 1995/96. Percentagewise, coconut oil accounts for less than 5 percent of the world's vegetable and marine oils. Copra meal production totaled 1.8 million tons in 1996/97 vs. 1.7 million in 1995/96. The Philippines and Indonesia account for two-thirds of world copra output. Copra production is not only dependent on the weather, but also appears to have a biological cycle that historically triggers relatively sharp fluctuations in output although the swings seemed to have stabilized in the 1990's. Foreign trade in copra products is small with coconut oil exports in 1996/97 estimated at 1.6 million tons, approximately equal to 1995/96's total; copra meal exports were placed at 1.05 million tons vs. 1.09 million in 1995/96. The world's carryover stocks of coconut oil and copra are also small with oil at 160,000 tons at the end of 1996/97, and copra stocks totaling about 7,000 tons.

U.S. imports of coconut oil in 1995/96 (October/July) totaled 352,446 metric tons vs. 419,304 in the year earlier period, although the dollar value of $245 million vs. $250 million remained much the same due to price fluctuations. Manufacturers are not adverse to switching to palm oil when coconut oil's premium to palm oil widens too far.

Crude coconut oil prices, basis New Orleans, moved higher in 1996, trading in the high $0.40 per pound area towards yearend vs. the high $0.30's a year earlier. World prices, basis Rotterdam, traversed a wide range during 1995/96 averaging $746 per metric ton vs. $656 in 1994/95; Rotterdam copra prices averaged $487 per ton vs $432, respectively.

### World Copra Production by Principal Countries In Thousands of Metric Tons

| Year | India | Indonesia | Ivory Coast | Malaysia | Mexico | Mozambique | New Guinea | Philippines | Solomon Islands | Sri Lanka | Thailand | Vanuatu | Vietnam | World Total |
|---|---|---|---|---|---|---|---|---|---|---|---|---|---|---|
| 1984 | 360 | 1,260 | 60 | 166 | 100 | 55 | 176 | 1,813 | 45 | 240 | 93 | 39 | 65 | 4,681 |
| 1985 | 380 | 1,250 | 53 | 162 | 100 | 55 | 160 | 2,500 | 31 | 242 | 65 | 41 | 70 | 5,306 |
| 1986 | 320 | 1,270 | 48 | 97 | 115 | 65 | 149 | 2,100 | 28 | 125 | 74 | 36 | 70 | 4,709 |
| 1987 | 434 | 1,195 | 64 | 81 | 201 | 68 | 136 | 1,700 | 29 | 62 | 49 | 30 | 118 | 4,450 |
| 1988 | 487 | 1,021 | 52 | 97 | 203 | 70 | 134 | 1,710 | 35 | 130 | 62 | 24 | 139 | 4,444 |
| 1989 | 470 | 1,381 | 70 | 96 | 202 | 70 | 117 | 2,345 | 30 | 128 | 59 | 45 | 188 | 5,488 |
| 1990 | 450 | 1,392 | 75 | 76 | 175 | 72 | 91 | 1,950 | 24 | 61 | 62 | 28 | 192 | 4,933 |
| 1991 | 440 | 1,110 | 79 | 82 | 175 | 72 | 110 | 1,845 | 29 | 70 | 65 | 27 | 220 | 4,612 |
| 1992 | 440 | 1,110 | 65 | 82 | 200 | 72 | 117 | 1,845 | 23 | 70 | 65 | 24 | 220 | 4,624 |
| 1993 | 445 | 1,100 | 60 | 65 | 173 | 73 | 120 | 1,950 | 23 | 60 | 68 | 26 | 200 | 4,648 |
| 1994 | 455 | 1,270 | 65 | 60 | 170 | 74 | 101 | 1,930 | 25 | 60 | 69 | 27 | 200 | 4,801 |
| 1995[1] | 610 | 1,070 | 72 | 55 | 160 | 74 | 120 | 2,500 | 30 | 55 | 67 | 28 | 208 | 5,347 |
| 1996[2] | 635 | 1,150 | 75 | 52 | 155 | 75 | 127 | 1,800 | 30 | 58 | 70 | 28 | 205 | 4,761 |
| 1997[3] | 650 | 1,220 | 75 | 52 | 150 | 76 | 125 | 2,200 | 30 | 58 | 70 | NA | 205 | 5,240 |

[1] Preliminary. [2] Estimate. [3] Forecast. *Source: The Oil World*

### World Coconut Oil Supply and Distribution In Thousands of Metric Tons

| | Production | | | | | | | Consumption | | | | | | Ending Stocks | | |
|---|---|---|---|---|---|---|---|---|---|---|---|---|---|---|---|---|
| Year | India | Indonesia | Malaysia | Philippines | Total | Exports | Imports | European Union | India | Indonesia | Philippines | United States | Total | Philippines | United States | Total |
| 1985-6 | 236 | 720 | 86 | 1,587 | 3,296 | 1,613 | 1,523 | 575 | 236 | 710 | 286 | 461 | 3,040 | 178 | 140 | 389 |
| 1986-7 | 198 | 731 | 56 | 1,320 | 2,934 | 1,487 | 1,340 | 553 | 198 | 610 | 257 | 488 | 2,800 | 187 | 123 | 375 |
| 1987-8 | 253 | 721 | 38 | 1,141 | 2,851 | 1,451 | 1,490 | 535 | 246 | 479 | 304 | 416 | 2,891 | 122 | 151 | 589 |
| 1988-9 | 285 | 669 | 40 | 957 | 2,685 | 1,219 | 1,287 | 473 | 282 | 517 | 297 | 396 | 2,911 | 100 | 68 | 432 |
| 1989-90 | 284 | 782 | 34 | 1,314 | 3,217 | 1,506 | 1,490 | 535 | 284 | 576 | 278 | 386 | 3,061 | 115 | 128 | 571 |
| 1990-1 | 272 | 843 | 34 | 1,283 | 3,192 | 1,450 | 1,490 | 664 | 279 | 682 | 279 | 402 | 3,332 | 51 | 127 | 473 |
| 1991-2 | 267 | 701 | 33 | 1,110 | 2,852 | 1,343 | 1,321 | 513 | 278 | 380 | 257 | 409 | 2,833 | 115 | 85 | 420 |
| 1992-3 | 267 | 681 | 29 | 1,294 | 3,004 | 1,655 | 1,270 | 516 | 279 | 430 | 249 | 491 | 2,960 | 38 | 114 | 379 |
| 1993-4 | 272 | 746 | 24 | 1,051 | 2,804 | 1,354 | 1,443 | 547 | 275 | 379 | 266 | 483 | 2,950 | 50 | 74 | 322 |
| 1994-5[1] | 363 | 666 | 28 | 1,664 | 3,420 | 1,765 | 1,750 | 666 | 367 | 520 | 269 | 491 | 3,300 | 109 | 74 | 428 |
| 1995-6[2] | 377 | 681 | 28 | 1,172 | 2,957 | 1,393 | 1,394 | 599 | 377 | 455 | 297 | 427 | 3,049 | 85 | 38 | 336 |
| 1996-7[3] | 388 | 729 | 27 | 1,339 | 3,175 | 1,489 | 1,496 | 578 | 389 | 500 | 314 | 447 | 3,162 | 90 | 60 | 357 |

[1] Preliminary. [2] Estimate. [3] Forecast. *Source: The Oil World*

## Supply and Distribution of Coconut Oil in the United States In Millions of Pounds

| Year | Rotterdam Copra Tonne ($ U.S.) | Rotterdam Coconut Oil, CIF ($ U.S.) | Imports For Consumption | Stocks Oct. 1 | Total Supply | Exports | Disappearance Total Domestic | Disappearance Edible Products | Disappearance Inedible Products | Production of Coconut Oil (Refined) Total | Oct. - Dec. | Jan. - March | April - June | July - Sept. |
|---|---|---|---|---|---|---|---|---|---|---|---|---|---|---|
| 1984-5 | 476 | 746 | 891 | 112 | 1,001 | 20 | 851 | 275 | 376 | 658.5 | 176.4 | 161.3 | 175.7 | 145.1 |
| 1985-6 | 200 | 304 | 1,217 | 132 | 1,347 | 22 | 1,019 | 333 | 683 | 546.3 | 134.1 | 130.7 | 133.9 | 147.6 |
| 1986-7 | 285 | 413 | 1,087 | 308 | 1,395 | 49 | 1,076 | 319 | 720 | 685.5 | 151.8 | 197.9 | 180.4 | 155.4 |
| 1987-8 | 385 | 547 | 1,074 | 271 | 1,344 | 77 | 935 | 233 | 700 | 786.1 | 181.7 | 194.2 | 214.9 | 195.3 |
| 1988-9 | 371 | 545 | 778 | 332 | 1,110 | 55 | 904 | 211 | 713 | 712.7 | 199.3 | 165.1 | 182.0 | 166.3 |
| 1989-90 | 251 | 371 | 1,038 | 152 | 1,190 | 44 | 866 | 161 | 705 | 703.1 | 195.4 | 163.8 | 187.3 | 156.6 |
| 1990-1 | 247 | 364 | 946 | 279 | 1,225 | 51 | 897 | 169 | 742 | 754.6 | 196.8 | 150.8 | 141.8 | 265.2 |
| 1991-2 | 397 | 605 | 838 | 277 | 1,115 | 22 | 906 | 164 | 699 | 733.9 | 145.3 | 158.8 | 159.3 | 270.5 |
| 1992-3 | 292 | 446 | 1,162 | 187 | 1,349 | 15 | 1,082 | 202 | 692 | 650.5 | 156.0 | 158.8 | 166.6 | 169.1 |
| 1993-4 | 388 | 564 | 999 | 251 | 1,250 | 20 | 1,067 | 234 | 716 | 536.2 | 155.6 | 129.0 | 131.8 | 119.8 |
| 1994-5 | 432 | 656 | 1,100 | 163 | 1,263 | 18 | 1,082 | 247 | 694 | 546.8 | 137.5 | 142.7 | 144.3 | 122.3 |
| 1995-6[1] | 469 | 726 | 948 | 163 | 1,111 | 18 | 999 | 221 | 453 | 445.0 | 127.5 | 118.4 | 132.8 | 66.4 |

[1] Preliminary. NA = Not available. *Source: Bureau of Census, U.S. Department of Commerce*

## U.S. Consumption of Coconut Oil in End Products (Edible and Inedible) In Millions of Pounds

| Year | Jan. | Feb. | Mar. | Apr. | May | June | July | Aug. | Sept. | Oct. | Nov. | Dec. | Total |
|---|---|---|---|---|---|---|---|---|---|---|---|---|---|
| 1986 | 67.7 | 43.8 | 44.7 | 52.5 | 45.7 | 50.0 | 49.5 | 67.2 | 52.8 | 78.7 | 65.9 | 52.2 | 670.7 |
| 1987 | 63.7 | 58.0 | 76.2 | 74.1 | 72.8 | 81.4 | 73.8 | 79.1 | 82.5 | 89.6 | 70.0 | 72.8 | 894.0 |
| 1988 | 76.1 | 71.2 | 59.1 | 59.6 | 66.8 | 65.8 | 55.1 | 53.8 | 48.7 | 65.2 | 57.8 | 57.9 | 737.1 |
| 1989 | 52.6 | 51.6 | 64.3 | 55.0 | 65.9 | 58.0 | 60.5 | 51.3 | 48.7 | 55.1 | 49.7 | 39.6 | 652.3 |
| 1990 | 45.4 | 44.9 | 44.3 | 44.6 | 43.2 | 39.4 | 39.8 | 39.5 | 39.2 | 49.7 | 41.0 | 43.9 | 514.9 |
| 1991 | | 137.6 | | | 150.6 | | | 134.4 | | | 122.1 | | 544.7 |
| 1992 | 72.5 | 70.6 | 76.5 | 70.7 | 78.7 | 74.8 | 65.2 | 70.6 | 77.4 | 75.8 | 76.2 | 66.4 | 875.4 |
| 1993 | 74.4 | 75.9 | 81.3 | 77.6 | 72.1 | 71.0 | 73.6 | 78.2 | 72.6 | 85.9 | 90.9 | 84.6 | 938.1 |
| 1994 | 74.4 | 77.4 | 77.5 | 80.4 | 86.6 | 88.8 | 76.0 | 88.4 | 65.1 | 74.6 | 85.1 | 95.0 | 969.3 |
| 1995 | 78.2 | 79.5 | 86.5 | 81.0 | 79.7 | 82.0 | 76.5 | 71.4 | 61.6 | 62.1 | 59.8 | 59.9 | 878.0 |
| 1996[1] | 47.0 | 54.3 | 60.1 | 60.2 | 68.6 | 54.6 | 55.1 | 47.9 | 44.9 | 49.6 | 50.3 | 47.9 | 640.7 |

[1]Preliminary. *Source: Bureau of Census, U.S. Department of Commerce*

## Stocks of Coconut Oil (Crude and Refined) in the United States In Millions of Pounds

| Year | Jan. 1 | Feb. 1 | Mar. 1 | Apr. 1 | May 1 | June 1 | July 1 | Aug.1 | Sept.1 | Oct. 1 | Nov. 1 | Dec. 1 |
|---|---|---|---|---|---|---|---|---|---|---|---|---|
| 1986 | 206.5 | 259.0 | 262.1 | 285.1 | 247.4 | 289.3 | 275.0 | 273.4 | 273.8 | 308.0 | 295.5 | 320.5 |
| 1987 | 323.3 | 323.6 | 355.7 | 318.1 | 336.9 | 271.2 | 203.6 | 243.9 | 240.8 | 270.2 | 288.5 | 370.9 |
| 1988 | 367.7 | 358.8 | 370.7 | 371.1 | 356.0 | 353.6 | 336.6 | 290.2 | 287.5 | 335.0 | 332.7 | 307.0 |
| 1989 | 275.7 | 278.9 | 247.4 | 205.3 | 167.7 | 134.7 | 189.9 | 177.5 | 149.8 | 150.8 | 218.6 | 238.5 |
| 1990 | 297.3 | 304.4 | 307.0 | 348.0 | 305.6 | 306.6 | 292.2 | 264.3 | 315.4 | 281.1 | 309.3 | 304.6 |
| 1991 | NA | NA | 359.0 | NA | NA | 364.3 | NA | NA | 279.3 | NA | NA | 298.0 |
| 1992 | NA | 266.3 | 274.2 | 239.7 | 211.2 | 173.7 | 178.3 | 141.1 | 187.1 | 187.7 | 225.1 | 278.8 |
| 1993 | 355.7 | 406.7 | 418.9 | 348.7 | 338.3 | 305.2 | 257.2 | 233.8 | 321.4 | 250.8 | 335.0 | 299.1 |
| 1994 | 291.7 | 316.5 | 284.5 | 251.5 | 237.6 | 199.9 | 151.4 | 163.7 | 156.0 | 164.1 | 166.2 | 152.9 |
| 1995 | 155.6 | 173.6 | 168.1 | 163.7 | 148.5 | 183.5 | 163.8 | 136.9 | 124.1 | 162.9 | 199.7 | 187.7 |
| 1996[1] | 164.7 | 229.1 | 200.4 | 217.7 | 173.6 | 175.9 | 171.5 | 116.7 | 113.8 | 84.0 | 78.6 | 65.1 |

[1] Preliminary. NA = Not avaliable. *Source: U.S. Department of Commerce*

## Average Price of Coconut Oil (Crude) Tank Cars in New York In Cents Per Pound

| Year | Jan. | Feb. | Mar. | Apr. | May | June | July | Aug. | Sept. | Oct. | Nov. | Dec. | Average |
|---|---|---|---|---|---|---|---|---|---|---|---|---|---|
| 1986 | 20.60 | 18.00 | 15.60 | 15.50 | 13.80 | 13.90 | 13.80 | 13.00 | 13.30 | 16.80 | 19.80 | 20.70 | 16.23 |
| 1987 | 21.40 | 20.88 | 19.30 | 20.38 | 21.44 | 24.25 | 25.75 | 25.13 | 24.40 | 24.69 | 24.50 | 27.15 | 23.27 |
| 1988 | 28.81 | 26.06 | 25.45 | 25.25 | 26.50 | 30.45 | 31.88 | 28.30 | 27.38 | 27.44 | 28.06 | 27.81 | 27.78 |
| 1989 | 26.75 | 27.63 | 27.90 | 28.94 | 29.90 | 29.56 | 28.94 | 27.75 | 28.63 | 27.25 | 26.35 | 24.75 | 27.86 |
| 1990 | 24.31 | 23.69 | 22.10 | 21.63 | 21.15 | 20.31 | 19.16 | 18.58 | 18.26 | 18.18 | 20.45 | 20.13 | 20.66 |
| 1991 | 20.22 | 20.31 | 20.50 | 19.38 | 19.69 | 21.69 | 26.19 | 25.63 | 25.63 | 28.50 | 31.50 | 32.38 | 24.30 |
| 1992 | 39.33 | 36.00 | 34.57 | 34.63 | 33.56 | 32.13 | 29.63 | 27.31 | 27.88 | 26.95 | 27.00 | 25.50 | 31.21 |
| 1993 | 24.94 | 24.37 | 23.65 | 23.13 | 24.13 | 24.95 | 25.35 | 25.61 | 24.44 | 23.88 | 26.69 | 34.25 | 25.45 |
| 1994 | 30.30 | 29.69 | 27.31 | 28.19 | 29.45 | 30.25 | 29.56 | 30.35 | 30.63 | 30.60 | 34.19 | 33.69 | 30.35 |
| 1995 | 32.50 | 32.00 | 31.13 | 31.00 | 30.50 | 35.00 | 37.90 | 35.63 | 35.00 | 36.00 | 37.88 | 33.69 | 34.02 |
| 1996[1] | 35.80 | 36.63 | 36.75 | 38.75 | 39.50 | 42.25 | 41.80 | 42.80 | 47.00 | | | | 40.14 |

[1] Preliminary. NA = Not available. *Source: Economic Research Service, U.S. Department of Agriculture*

# Coffee

Coffee in commercial qualities is produced by many nations. Several dominate in terms of production and exports. Brazil itself represents about a third of the market. The coffee tree grows best in tropical highlands, although lowland coffee is grown in abundance. The range of production is near the equator, roughly some 20 degrees north and 20 degrees south in latitude. The main production areas are South America (Brazil and Colombia), Central America, Southeast Asia (Indonesia and Vietnam), and Africa (Ivory Coast, Uganda, Kenya, and Ethiopia).

Coffee has many varieties with the type and quality of coffee produced dependent in part on tree species, management practices, and climate. There are two primary species of coffee trees: robusta and arabica. Arabica production accounts for about two-thirds of world output with robusta the remainder. Arabica coffees are grown mostly in highland regions and are considered more susceptible to weather variations like drought and cold. Arabicas are considered mild in taste. The major producers are Brazil, Colombia, Central America, along with Kenya and Mexico. Robusta coffee is produced mostly in lowlands, which tend to be hotter in Asia and Africa. The taste of robusta is more pungent than arabica and is often used in soluble or instant coffee as well as expresso. The major producer countries are in Africa, except for Kenya and Ethiopia, as well as Indonesia and Vietnam.

World green coffee production in 1996/97 (October-September) is forecast at 99 million bags, a sharp increase from the 1995/96 season which included the severely damaged Brazilian coffee crop. This would be the highest production since the 1991/92 season when the world coffee crop exceeded 102 million bags. Coffee production is extremely difficult to estimate with any accuracy. One major problem is that many producer countries make only minimal efforts to estimate their own crops. A case in point is Brazil, by far the world's largest producer. Brazil does not currently have a central agency to estimate the crop forcing the coffee trade to rely on wide ranging estimates from organizations such as the USDA, trade houses, and exporters. Brazil was struck by two successive frosts in the summer of 1994 causing prices to stage an enormous rally. Over the course of that season production estimates ranged from a low of 12 million bags to a high of 18 million bags. There is still no conclusive estimate with some trade houses at 15.8 million bags and USDA at 16.8 million bags.

For the 1996/97 season, Brazil's crop rebounded aided by excellent weather. The crop is forecast to be between 25-27 million bags. Of that total, Brazil is expected to export about 15 million bags of green coffee with another 2.5 million bags processed for soluble or instant coffee. Domestic consumption in Brazil is growing and is expected to absorb 10 million bags leaving very little coffee to rebuild stocks. To help the domestic roasting industry, the Brazilian government has been conducting monthly auctions of its stockpile which is estimated at 14 million bags. While much of this coffee is older, the auctions so far have proven successful in getting supplies into the hands of domestic roasters. The government has indicated that it will increase the size of the auctions to 200,000 bags and continue to hold them through June 1997. Because of Brazil's dominant production, much of the market focus is on crop prospects in that country. Already there are ideas that the 1997/98 crop will be about 25 million bags. Many in the trade believe that Brazil has larger potential and the coming seasons will see crops closer to 30 million bags.

Colombia is the second largest producer of coffee. Very heavy rains early in the season hurt flowerings and production prospects look less than they initially had. For 1996/97 production is forecast at 12 million bags, down from 12.5 million bags in 1995/96. Colombia has experienced a host of problems apart from the weather. Social unrest and instability culminated in a truck strike that delayed movement of coffee to export locations. The National Coffee Fund, which purchases coffee from producers, has had financial difficulties. This could result in producers having less to spend on their crops.

Two countries that have become important producers by rapidly expanding production are Indonesia and Vietnam. Indonesia is forecast to produce 8 million bags in 1996/97, while Vietnam is expected to produce 4.5 million bags. Both countries produce robusta.

Global 1996/97 coffee consumption is forecast at 100 million bags. Following the dramatic price increases in 1994, coffee consumption appears to have fallen in virtually every country. How much it fell is difficult to estimate but it appears to have been about 6 percent. A major question facing the coffee industry is whether consumers would return to coffee when prices retreated. Based on import data, it appears that has been the case. U.S. coffee roastings in 1996 were running about 3 percent ahead of 1995. Stocks of coffee in consuming countries in Europe and the U.S. were drawn down to very low levels in late 1996. Coffee producers had agreed to reduce their exports in an attempt to increase prices and that effort appeared to be paying off.

### *Futures Markets*

Coffee futures are traded on the Bolsa de Mercadorias & Futuros (BM&F), the Manila International Futures Exchange Inc. (MIFE), the Singapore Commodity Exchange Ltd., the London International Financial Futures and Options Exchange (LIFFE), and the Coffee, Sugar and Cocoa Exchange Inc. (CSCE) in New York. Options are traded on the BM&F, the LIFFE and the CSCE.

## World Coffee Supply and Distribution In Thousands of 60 Kilogram Bags (132.276 Lbs. Per Bag)

| Crop Year | Beginning Stocks | Production | Imports | Supply | Total Exports | Bean Exports | Rst/Grn Exports | Soluble Exports | Domestic Use | Ending Stocks |
|---|---|---|---|---|---|---|---|---|---|---|
| 1982-3 | 43,842 | 81,904 | 733 | 126,479 | 66,059 | 63,344 | 220 | 2,495 | 20,450 | 40,199 |
| 1983-4 | 40,199 | 88,801 | 606 | 129,606 | 68,191 | 65,069 | 351 | 2,771 | 20,897 | 40,838 |
| 1984-5 | 40,838 | 90,362 | 456 | 131,656 | 72,322 | 68,675 | 306 | 3,341 | 22,828 | 37,366 |
| 1985-6 | 37,366 | 95,750 | 397 | 133,513 | 70,478 | 67,724 | 248 | 2,506 | 21,250 | 41,815 |
| 1986-7 | 41,815 | 79,394 | 262 | 121,471 | 66,982 | 64,351 | 298 | 2,333 | 21,372 | 33,287 |
| 1987-8 | 33,287 | 103,170 | 296 | 136,753 | 67,504 | 64,838 | 337 | 2,329 | 21,275 | 48,174 |
| 1988-9 | 48,174 | 94,165 | 415 | 142,754 | 71,371 | 68,108 | 162 | 3,101 | 21,280 | 50,193 |
| 1989-90 | 50,193 | 96,958 | 258 | 147,409 | 83,402 | 80,034 | 129 | 3,239 | 21,065 | 43,012 |
| 1990-1 | 43,012 | 100,181 | 352 | 143,545 | 76,319 | 73,434 | 83 | 2,802 | 22,489 | 44,997 |
| 1991-2 | 44,997 | 103,731 | 349 | 149,077 | 81,387 | 78,341 | 53 | 2,993 | 22,198 | 45,492 |
| 1992-3 | 45,492 | 92,888 | 770 | 139,150 | 77,772 | 73,615 | 113 | 4,044 | 21,650 | 39,728 |
| 1993-4 | 39,728 | 93,303 | 1,002 | 134,033 | 77,332 | 72,610 | 108 | 4,614 | 23,340 | 33,361 |
| 1994-5[1] | 33,361 | 98,178 | 987 | 132,526 | 69,957 | 65,460 | 228 | 4,269 | 22,931 | 39,638 |
| 1995-6[2] | 39,638 | 89,907 | 705 | 130,250 | 74,338 | 69,508 | 209 | 4,621 | 24,203 | 31,709 |
| 1996-7[3] | 31,709 | 100,923 | 651 | 133,283 | 79,573 | 74,937 | 175 | 4,461 | 24,958 | 28,752 |

[1] Preliminary. [2] Estimate. [3] Forecast. *Source: Foreign Agricutural Service, U.S. Department of Agriculture*

## World Green Coffee (Total) Production In Thousands of 60 Kilogram Bags (132.276 Lbs. Per Bag)

| Crop Year | Brazil | Cameroon | Colombia | Costa Rica | El Salvador | Ethiopia | Guatemala | India | Indonesia | Ivory Coast | Mexico | Papua New Guinea | Uganda | Zaire | World Total |
|---|---|---|---|---|---|---|---|---|---|---|---|---|---|---|---|
| 1982-3 | 17,750 | 1,830 | 13,300 | 2,300 | 3,100 | 3,670 | 2,530 | 2,170 | 4,750 | 4,510 | 4,530 | 640 | 3,000 | 1,354 | 82,778 |
| 1983-4 | 30,000 | 1,000 | 13,000 | 2,070 | 2,400 | 3,300 | 2,340 | 1,667 | 5,515 | 4,120 | 4,530 | 925 | 2,700 | 1,350 | 88,595 |
| 1984-5 | 27,000 | 2,316 | 11,000 | 2,516 | 2,680 | 2,587 | 2,703 | 3,250 | 5,600 | 4,609 | 4,250 | 775 | 2,800 | 1,540 | 90,266 |
| 1985-6 | 33,000 | 2,067 | 12,000 | 1,514 | 2,300 | 2,833 | 2,650 | 2,033 | 5,800 | 4,420 | 4,826 | 860 | 2,700 | 1,610 | 95,934 |
| 1986-7 | 13,900 | 2,191 | 11,000 | 2,566 | 2,275 | 2,700 | 2,843 | 3,350 | 5,900 | 4,405 | 5,297 | 756 | 2,700 | 1,875 | 79,549 |
| 1987-8 | 38,000 | 1,251 | 13,000 | 2,375 | 2,538 | 3,200 | 3,020 | 2,050 | 5,965 | 3,103 | 4,717 | 1,100 | 2,600 | 2,000 | 103,231 |
| 1988-9 | 25,000 | 1,760 | 10,700 | 2,758 | 1,492 | 3,400 | 3,022 | 3,590 | 6,750 | 3,989 | 5,500 | 1,175 | 3,300 | 1,750 | 94,363 |
| 1989-90 | 26,000 | 1,440 | 13,300 | 2,453 | 2,787 | 3,400 | 3,472 | 2,150 | 7,100 | 4,734 | 5,100 | 1,092 | 2,500 | 2,000 | 97,286 |
| 1990-1 | 31,000 | 1,450 | 14,500 | 2,565 | 2,603 | 3,500 | 3,282 | 2,970 | 7,480 | 3,300 | 4,550 | 964 | 2,700 | 1,695 | 100,417 |
| 1991-2 | 28,500 | 1,920 | 17,980 | 2,530 | 2,357 | 3,000 | 3,549 | 3,200 | 7,100 | 3,967 | 4,620 | 841 | 2,900 | 1,500 | 103,731 |
| 1992-3 | 24,000 | 837 | 14,950 | 2,620 | 2,894 | 3,500 | 3,584 | 2,700 | 7,350 | 2,500 | 4,180 | 1,030 | 2,800 | 1,790 | 92,888 |
| 1993-4 | 28,500 | 1,250 | 11,400 | 2,475 | 2,361 | 3,700 | 3,078 | 3,465 | 7,400 | 2,700 | 4,200 | 1,080 | 2,700 | 900 | 93,303 |
| 1994-5[1] | 28,000 | 1,000 | 13,000 | 2,492 | 2,314 | 3,800 | 3,500 | 3,060 | 6,400 | 3,733 | 4,030 | 1,050 | 3,100 | 1,300 | 98,178 |
| 1995-6[2] | 16,800 | 1,200 | 12,900 | 2,595 | 2,325 | 3,800 | 3,827 | 3,700 | 6,000 | 2,900 | 5,400 | 1,000 | 4,200 | 1,000 | 89,907 |
| 1996-7[3] | 27,000 | 1,000 | 12,500 | 2,500 | 2,220 | 3,900 | 3,927 | 3,200 | 7,500 | 4,000 | 5,400 | 1,000 | 3,700 | 1,000 | 100,923 |

[1] Preliminary. [2] Estimate. [3] Forecast. *Source: Foreign Agricultural Service, U.S. Department of Agriculture*

## World Green Coffee (Exportable)[4] Production In Thousands of 60 Kilogram Bags (132.276 Lbs. Per Bag)

| Crop Year | Brazil | Cameroon | Colombia | Costa Rica | El Salvador | Ethiopia | Guatemala | Indonesia | Ivory Coast | Kenya | Mexico | Papua New Guinea | Uganda | Zaire | World Total |
|---|---|---|---|---|---|---|---|---|---|---|---|---|---|---|---|
| 1982-3 | 9,750 | 1,785 | 11,445 | 2,077 | 2,900 | 2,108 | 2,195 | 3,636 | 4,445 | 1,501 | 2,830 | 631 | 2,954 | 1,159 | 62,366 |
| 1983-4 | 21,500 | 945 | 11,140 | 1,837 | 2,200 | 1,728 | 2,000 | 4,375 | 1,395 | 1,938 | 3,030 | 923 | 2,653 | 1,150 | 67,676 |
| 1984-5 | 16,500 | 2,261 | 9,135 | 2,281 | 2,480 | 1,087 | 2,373 | 4,590 | 4,582 | 1,488 | 2,635 | 762 | 2,752 | 1,340 | 67,449 |
| 1985-6 | 24,000 | 1,987 | 10,130 | 1,276 | 2,120 | 1,293 | 2,350 | 4,800 | 4,391 | 1,951 | 3,326 | 842 | 2,650 | 1,410 | 74,841 |
| 1986-7 | 4,900 | 2,058 | 9,000 | 2,324 | 2,095 | 1,034 | 2,543 | 4,950 | 4,375 | 1,591 | 3,797 | 738 | 2,649 | 1,670 | 57,786 |
| 1987-8 | 28,000 | 1,206 | 10,980 | 2,140 | 2,369 | 1,756 | 2,720 | 4,915 | 3,071 | 1,985 | 3,137 | 1,087 | 2,547 | 1,791 | 80,390 |
| 1988-9 | 15,500 | 1,725 | 8,891 | 2,508 | 1,332 | 1,767 | 2,717 | 5,478 | 3,957 | 1,787 | 3,880 | 1,160 | 3,250 | 1,530 | 71,891 |
| 1989-90 | 17,000 | 1,405 | 11,538 | 2,198 | 2,607 | 2,239 | 3,162 | 5,820 | 4,700 | 1,665 | 3,650 | 1,081 | 2,450 | 1,780 | 75,944 |
| 1990-1 | 21,500 | 1,420 | 12,885 | 2,305 | 2,423 | 1,800 | 2,972 | 6,185 | 3,264 | 1,433 | 3,150 | 954 | 2,650 | 1,480 | 78,271 |
| 1991-2 | 19,500 | 1,895 | 16,580 | 2,270 | 2,173 | 1,400 | 3,239 | 5,550 | 3,929 | 1,483 | 3,170 | 832 | 2,845 | 1,300 | 81,729 |
| 1992-3 | 15,500 | 812 | 13,647 | 2,365 | 2,677 | 2,000 | 3,274 | 5,570 | 2,461 | 1,195 | 2,880 | 1,021 | 2,745 | 1,615 | 71,631 |
| 1993-4 | 19,100 | 1,225 | 9,700 | 2,225 | 2,131 | 2,200 | 2,777 | 5,535 | 2,661 | 1,208 | 3,000 | 1,071 | 2,640 | 725 | 70,315 |
| 1994-5[1] | 18,300 | 975 | 11,564 | 2,252 | 2,079 | 2,300 | 3,220 | 4,040 | 3,687 | 1,562 | 3,130 | 1,041 | 3,040 | 1,125 | 75,625 |
| 1995-6[2] | 6,300 | 1,175 | 11,439 | 2,360 | 2,055 | 2,300 | 3,527 | 3,950 | 2,852 | 1,558 | 4,340 | 991 | 4,140 | 825 | 66,114 |
| 1996-7[3] | 16,000 | 970 | 10,950 | 2,270 | 1,950 | 2,400 | 3,617 | 5,360 | 3,949 | 1,399 | 4,290 | 991 | 3,640 | 825 | 76,340 |

[1] Preliminary. [2] Estimate. [3] Forecast. [4] Marketing year begins in October in some countries and April or July in others. Exportable production represents total harvested production minus estimated domestic consumption. *Source: Foreign Agricultural Service, U.S. Department of Agriculture*

## Origin of Green Coffee Imports (for Consumption) into the U.S. In Thousands of 60 Kilogram Bags[2]

| Year | Brazil | Colombia | Costa Rica | Domin. Republic | Ecuador | El Salvador | Ethiopia | Guate-mata | Indonesia | Ivory Coast | Mexico | Peru | Philip-pines | Uganda | Vene-zuela | Grand Total |
|---|---|---|---|---|---|---|---|---|---|---|---|---|---|---|---|---|
| 1982 | 3,372 | 1,710 | 248 | 500 | 773 | 919 | 578 | 844 | 1,118 | 998 | 1,377 | 513 | 308 | 1,229 | 16 | 17,416 |
| 1983 | 3,417 | 1,755 | 226 | 430 | 857 | 1,214 | 519 | 887 | 1,079 | 674 | 1,495 | 439 | 276 | 729 | 26 | 16,449 |
| 1984 | 3,866 | 2,170 | 258 | 447 | 961 | 1,052 | 423 | 1,118 | 1,030 | 1,144 | 1,553 | 557 | 296 | 570 | 88 | 17,734 |
| 1985 | 4,148 | 2,554 | 360 | 438 | 974 | 1,366 | 195 | 1,054 | 1,041 | 951 | 1,812 | 543 | 407 | 739 | 107 | 18,698 |
| 1986 | 2,200 | 2,629 | 413 | 488 | 1,371 | 1,108 | 243 | 1,658 | 1,346 | 694 | 2,125 | 675 | 440 | 739 | 224 | 19,483 |
| 1987 | 3,928 | 2,549 | 551 | 446 | 1,285 | 1,117 | 421 | 1,439 | 911 | 476 | 2,764 | 573 | 105 | 587 | 163 | 19,906 |
| 1988 | 4,213 | 2,235 | 233 | 366 | 811 | 829 | 218 | 609 | 731 | 654 | 1,719 | 436 | 298 | 481 | 72 | 15,348 |
| 1989 | 4,155 | 2,413 | 393 | 402 | 1,137 | 790 | 432 | 1,404 | 635 | 335 | 3,937 | 673 | 362 | 458 | 87 | 19,377 |
| 1990 | 3,633 | 2,771 | 403 | 445 | 876 | 843 | 234 | 1,871 | 830 | 54 | 3,305 | 473 | 107 | 246 | 222 | 19,566 |
| 1991 | 5,335 | 3,048 | 603 | 343 | 785 | 868 | 31 | 1,489 | 536 | 54 | 2,993 | 610 | 61 | 287 | 108 | 18,849 |
| 1992 | 4,253 | 4,852 | 662 | 254 | 753 | 1,344 | 23 | 1,812 | 581 | 407 | 3,042 | 526 | 13 | 223 | 104 | 21,673 |
| 1993 | 3,376 | 2,957 | 437 | 213 | 671 | 1,274 | 192 | 1,815 | 542 | 273 | 2,947 | 158 | 6 | 163 | 444 | 18,023 |
| 1994 | 2,850 | 2,372 | 325 | 207 | 969 | 376 | 215 | 1,403 | 558 | 114 | 2,516 | 249 | 78 | 191 | 295 | 14,913 |
| 1995[1] | 2,302 | 2,485 | 388 | 266 | 745 | 284 | 109 | 1,637 | 513 | 129 | 2,887 | 621 | 3 | 61 | 89 | 15,886 |
| 1996[1] | 1,515 | 2,966 | 507 | 306 | 709 | 411 | 81 | 1,644 | 1,092 | 27 | 3,755 | 618 | ----- | 123 | 410 | 17,732 |

[1] Preliminary. [2] 132.276 pounds per bag. *Source: Bureau of Census, U.S. Department of Commerce*

## Total Coffee (Green) Imports (for Consumption) into the U.S. In Thousands of 60 Kilogram Bags[2]

| Year | Jan. | Feb. | Mar. | Apr. | May | June | July | Aug. | Sept. | Oct. | Nov. | Dec. | Total |
|---|---|---|---|---|---|---|---|---|---|---|---|---|---|
| 1982 | 1,287 | 1,195 | 1,490 | 1,147 | 1,476 | 1,335 | 1,282 | 1,602 | 1,640 | 2,005 | 1,356 | 1,602 | 17,416 |
| 1983 | 1,556 | 1,332 | 1,373 | 1,253 | 1,502 | 1,034 | 1,319 | 1,230 | 1,532 | 1,685 | 1,380 | 1,253 | 16,449 |
| 1984 | 1,598 | 1,299 | 1,440 | 1,905 | 1,615 | 1,059 | 1,722 | 1,735 | 1,432 | 1,614 | 1,127 | 1,187 | 17,734 |
| 1985 | 1,622 | 1,681 | 1,702 | 1,430 | 1,324 | 1,751 | 1,217 | 1,757 | 1,773 | 1,385 | 1,272 | 1,785 | 18,698 |
| 1986 | 2,360 | 1,836 | 1,645 | 1,667 | 1,810 | 1,286 | 1,549 | 1,513 | 1,641 | 1,535 | 1,449 | 1,192 | 19,483 |
| 1987 | 1,092 | 1,218 | 1,841 | 1,789 | 1,883 | 2,181 | 1,717 | 1,481 | 1,770 | 2,631 | 1,246 | 1,056 | 19,906 |
| 1988 | 1,175 | 1,683 | 1,427 | 1,179 | 1,141 | 832 | 1,543 | 1,621 | 1,238 | 1,272 | 1,195 | 1,040 | 15,348 |
| 1989 | 1,646 | 1,323 | 1,368 | 1,398 | 1,296 | 1,199 | 1,634 | 1,974 | 1,951 | 2,180 | 1,748 | 1,660 | 19,337 |
| 1990 | 1,950 | 1,989 | 2,358 | 1,783 | 1,658 | 1,548 | 1,451 | 1,261 | 1,229 | 1,611 | 1,140 | 1,591 | 19,566 |
| 1991 | 2,106 | 1,946 | 1,590 | 1,748 | 1,556 | 984 | 1,056 | 1,335 | 1,424 | 1,368 | 1,616 | 2,122 | 18,849 |
| 1992 | 2,262 | 1,944 | 2,125 | 1,698 | 1,534 | 1,795 | 1,806 | 1,692 | 1,644 | 1,615 | 1,508 | 2,050 | 21,673 |
| 1993 | 1,782 | 1,663 | 2,012 | 1,481 | 1,631 | 1,253 | 1,442 | 1,344 | 1,374 | 1,464 | 1,018 | 1,561 | 18,023 |
| 1994 | 1,538 | 1,152 | 1,409 | 1,077 | 1,082 | 1,151 | 1,195 | 1,560 | 1,266 | 1,127 | 1,103 | 1,213 | 14,872 |
| 1995 | 1,469 | 1,253 | 1,702 | 1,221 | 1,190 | 1,240 | 1,117 | 1,094 | 1,220 | 1,326 | 1,492 | 1,563 | 15,886 |
| 1996[1] | 1,824 | 1,657 | 1,753 | 1,395 | 1,444 | 1,236 | 1,329 | 1,341 | 1,364 | 1,279 | 1,485 | 1,828 | 17,936 |

[1] Preliminary. [2] 132.276 pounds per bag. *Source: Bureau of Census, U.S. Department of Commerce*

## Average Spot Price of Coffee (Brazilian[1]) at New York In Cents Per Pound

| Year | Jan. | Feb. | Mar. | Apr. | May | June | July | Aug. | Sept. | Oct. | Nov. | Dec. | Average |
|---|---|---|---|---|---|---|---|---|---|---|---|---|---|
| 1982 | 148.95 | 153.11 | 143.70 | 143.86 | 141.33 | 144.42 | 138.17 | 142.05 | 142.92 | 141.31 | 141.63 | 142.69 | 143.68 |
| 1983 | 140.73 | 142.29 | 142.02 | 140.86 | 141.51 | 142.81 | 142.51 | 138.70 | 136.65 | 145.31 | 146.88 | 152.76 | 142.75 |
| 1984 | 155.15 | 155.38 | 152.82 | 149.80 | 145.91 | 149.45 | 146.99 | 150.62 | 151.55 | 147.63 | 144.93 | 145.59 | 149.65 |
| 1985 | 152.10 | 157.25 | 155.56 | 146.33 | 143.84 | 136.71 | 130.81 | 133.25 | 139.03 | 150.27 | 174.28 | 201.70 | 151.76 |
| 1986 | 303.42 | 276.26 | 286.68 | 288.55 | 280.24 | 229.10 | 183.40 | 190.43 | 210.36 | 187.89 | 175.58 | 162.40 | 231.19 |
| 1987 | 119.75 | 114.42 | 97.41 | 101.68 | 111.96 | 98.34 | 89.95 | 91.40 | 100.67 | 111.68 | 122.05 | 117.09 | 106.37 |
| 1988 | 117.35 | 130.40 | 126.21 | 123.30 | 121.02 | 122.81 | 120.01 | 111.89 | 118.79 | 115.65 | 118.53 | 136.10 | 121.84 |
| 1989 | 145.29 | 128.72 | 128.06 | 131.45 | 128.94 | 115.02 | 78.75 | 67.32 | 67.75 | 60.32 | 65.53 | 67.93 | 98.76 |
| 1990 | 70.36 | 77.59 | 86.17 | 87.45 | 86.31 | 82.94 | 78.94 | 90.25 | 92.20 | 85.78 | 77.46 | 80.17 | 82.97 |
| 1991 | 75.59 | 79.39 | 83.83 | 81.58 | 75.56 | 72.44 | 69.24 | 68.15 | 75.08 | 65.91 | 66.03 | 62.14 | 72.91 |
| 1992 | 62.03 | 58.05 | 59.60 | 54.94 | 51.11 | 49.08 | 48.53 | 46.40 | 49.43 | 59.64 | 64.64 | 74.39 | 56.49 |
| 1993 | 67.13 | 66.34 | 62.60 | 54.92 | 57.26 | 55.70 | 65.76 | 73.25 | 75.58 | 71.65 | 74.20 | 74.51 | 66.58 |
| 1994 | 71.42 | 80.14 | 84.72 | 87.14 | 118.37 | 136.43 | 211.81 | 192.38 | 212.73 | 191.21 | 172.83 | 159.73 | 143.24 |
| 1995 | 162.81 | 161.07 | 171.48 | 166.54 | 161.72 | 145.22 | 139.68 | 149.54 | 130.26 | 127.23 | 125.33 | 110.46 | 145.95 |
| 1996 | 127.54 | 144.05 | 140.99 | 132.92 | 134.76 | 125.44 | 106.93 | 108.28 | 103.10 | 105.77 | 103.76 | 103.71 | 119.77 |

[1] And other Arabicas. NA = Not available. *Source: Foreign Agricultural Service, U.S. Department of Agriculture (FAS-USDA)*

## U.S. Prices of Coffee In Cents Per Pound

| Year | Jan. | Feb. | Mar. | Apr. | May | June | July | Aug. | Sept. | Oct. | Nov. | Dec. | Average |
|---|---|---|---|---|---|---|---|---|---|---|---|---|---|
| Average Monthly Retail[1] | | | | | | | | | | | | | |
| 1992 | 266.8 | 268.8 | 263.1 | 261.2 | 266.0 | 262.5 | 265.2 | 261.3 | 253.7 | 249.2 | 239.1 | 236.4 | 257.8 |
| 1993 | 235.2 | 245.2 | 246.2 | 247.7 | 251.4 | 253.3 | 254.8 | 250.0 | 249.3 | 241.5 | 243.3 | 248.0 | 247.2 |
| 1994 | 253.0 | 252.9 | 251.5 | 251.6 | 253.5 | 259.8 | 334.1 | 448.0 | 445.8 | 445.0 | 448.2 | 438.2 | 340.1 |
| 1995 | 439.8 | 423.4 | 410.8 | 408.4 | 406.7 | 405.9 | 402.7 | 405.1 | 399.6 | 386.5 | 381.4 | 375.2 | 401.8 |
| 1996 | 357.7 | 359.0 | 355.0 | 352.7 | 344.4 | 343.8 | 380.0 | 339.0 | 333.3 | 334.4 | 328.3 | 330.7 | 346.5 |
| Colombian Mild Arabicas[2] | | | | | | | | | | | | | |
| 1992 | 78.40 | 71.75 | 73.67 | 69.55 | 64.93 | 64.10 | 62.50 | 56.49 | 56.18 | 64.77 | 71.72 | 81.52 | 67.97 |
| 1993 | 71.61 | 72.45 | 67.07 | 59.77 | 67.35 | 68.13 | 76.40 | 84.18 | 86.58 | 83.02 | 85.56 | 87.33 | 75.79 |
| 1994 | 85.85 | 93.04 | 93.23 | 97.53 | 133.90 | 151.85 | 222.75 | 210.57 | 231.52 | 206.07 | 186.96 | 173.94 | 157.27 |
| 1995 | 177.23 | 175.07 | 185.75 | 180.30 | 177.18 | 170.87 | 157.22 | 163.21 | 141.49 | 132.08 | 129.09 | 110.47 | 158.33 |
| 1996 | 119.08 | 134.94 | 160.60 | 134.31 | 142.56 | 133.25 | 135.39 | 137.68 | 123.30 | 127.77 | 129.41 | 126.41 | 133.73 |
| Other Mild Arabicas[2] | | | | | | | | | | | | | |
| 1992 | 72.99 | 67.88 | 69.96 | 65.23 | 60.14 | 58.38 | 57.68 | 52.42 | 52.73 | 61.40 | 67.36 | 77.46 | 63.64 |
| 1993 | 68.66 | 67.46 | 62.77 | 56.88 | 61.48 | 61.61 | 71.46 | 76.56 | 79.87 | 75.05 | 77.07 | 80.00 | 69.91 |
| 1994 | 77.21 | 82.69 | 85.57 | 89.23 | 121.97 | 142.57 | 217.67 | 198.07 | 220.10 | 199.06 | 180.76 | 167.47 | 148.53 |
| 1995 | 171.74 | 168.71 | 178.22 | 172.81 | 168.63 | 151.56 | 143.83 | 151.41 | 131.87 | 125.38 | 123.23 | 103.99 | 149.28 |
| 1996 | 109.38 | 122.71 | 119.05 | 122.01 | 128.56 | 124.46 | 120.47 | 122.49 | 114.05 | 120.62 | 119.90 | 115.01 | 119.89 |
| Robustas 1976[2] | | | | | | | | | | | | | |
| 1992 | 49.44 | 43.22 | 43.08 | 42.32 | 38.79 | 38.07 | 39.60 | 39.92 | 42.39 | 45.50 | 49.08 | 52.09 | 43.63 |
| 1993 | 48.13 | 48.25 | 46.86 | 45.51 | 46.91 | 47.65 | 50.39 | 59.29 | 63.44 | 60.05 | 62.53 | 62.90 | 53.49 |
| 1994 | 60.91 | 62.25 | 66.46 | 72.64 | 96.05 | 113.31 | 164.65 | 162.68 | 182.95 | 170.09 | 154.19 | 130.48 | 119.72 |
| 1995 | 132.26 | 135.22 | 146.83 | 145.47 | 141.89 | 129.53 | 120.89 | 131.28 | 116.41 | 114.15 | 112.79 | 94.72 | 126.79 |
| 1996 | 91.99 | 98.99 | 91.99 | 91.45 | 92.10 | 86.46 | 78.14 | 80.16 | 74.83 | 72.97 | 70.51 | 63.08 | 82.72 |
| Composite 1979 ICA[2] | | | | | | | | | | | | | |
| 1992 | 61.12 | 55.51 | 56.48 | 53.64 | 49.27 | 48.13 | 48.70 | 45.89 | 47.11 | 52.88 | 57.49 | 64.00 | 53.35 |
| 1993 | 58.14 | 57.32 | 54.76 | 51.38 | 54.18 | 54.54 | 60.61 | 67.69 | 71.64 | 67.78 | 70.03 | 71.53 | 61.63 |
| 1994 | 69.17 | 72.37 | 76.11 | 81.19 | 108.42 | 127.91 | 191.44 | 181.53 | 202.39 | 185.64 | 168.12 | 149.14 | 134.45 |
| 1995 | 152.08 | 152.24 | 162.73 | 159.59 | 155.96 | 141.66 | 132.71 | 141.70 | 124.75 | 120.02 | 117.99 | 99.57 | 138.42 |
| 1996 | 100.33 | 110.50 | 105.89 | 107.09 | 110.24 | 105.79 | 99.97 | 102.73 | 96.52 | 98.56 | 97.14 | 90.04 | 102.07 |

[1] Roasted in 13.1 to 20 ounce cans. [2] ICO monthly and composite indicator prices on the New York Market, 1979 ICA Agreement basis.

*Source: Foreign Agricultural Service, U.S. Department of Agriculture*

# COFFEE

## Average Open Interest of Coffee Futures at New York In Contracts

| Year | Jan. | Feb. | Mar. | Apr. | May | June | July | Aug. | Sept. | Oct. | Nov. | Dec. |
|---|---|---|---|---|---|---|---|---|---|---|---|---|
| 1985 | 13,493 | 13,291 | 12,952 | 12,885 | 12,811 | 12,393 | 11,722 | 11,015 | 10,198 | 10,504 | 11,652 | 13,287 |
| 1986 | 13,104 | 14,391 | 15,714 | 15,972 | 16,684 | 15,712 | 15,917 | 16,374 | 16,798 | 18,079 | 16,995 | 14,905 |
| 1987 | 15,317 | 16,034 | 17,415 | 20,445 | 22,455 | 21,160 | 22,536 | 23,943 | 25,857 | 26,418 | 22,757 | 21,064 |
| 1988 | 22,581 | 26,100 | 24,591 | 21,413 | 22,228 | 23,346 | 21,570 | 24,525 | 22,460 | 21,961 | 19,424 | 20,356 |
| 1989 | 24,544 | 23,684 | 23,246 | 25,870 | 23,663 | 24,716 | 27,184 | 31,410 | 32,404 | 35,019 | 32,687 | 32,096 |
| 1990 | 37,352 | 43,516 | 46,187 | 43,978 | 41,756 | 40,464 | 39,856 | 41,428 | 39,278 | 39,523 | 43,750 | 41,365 |
| 1991 | 42,320 | 41,326 | 39,948 | 39,410 | 41,726 | 43,717 | 42,037 | 40,661 | 42,126 | 43,940 | 41,819 | 40,628 |
| 1992 | 47,042 | 51,183 | 48,961 | 51,979 | 59,275 | 58,304 | 59,096 | 58,401 | 56,446 | 59,808 | 57,527 | 58,257 |
| 1993 | 59,193 | 54,249 | 53,618 | 55,578 | 51,797 | 50,918 | 53,871 | 48,541 | 47,649 | 49,809 | 46,901 | 48,812 |
| 1994 | 54,796 | 50,230 | 53,713 | 57,226 | 58,574 | 54,589 | 43,056 | 35,052 | 35,800 | 34,258 | 31,046 | 31,134 |
| 1995 | 34,455 | 35,391 | 36,925 | 34,387 | 34,615 | 34,462 | 30,156 | 27,448 | 27,800 | 28,408 | 24,505 | 26,412 |
| 1996 | 28,430 | 28,224 | 28,127 | 28,793 | 28,394 | 25,096 | 26,188 | 25,799 | 23,929 | 26,202 | 27,599 | 27,201 |

*Source: Coffee, Sugar & Cocoa Exchange, Inc. (CSCE)*

## Volume of Trading of Coffee "C" Futures at New York In Contracts

| Year | Jan. | Feb. | Mar. | Apr. | May | June | July | Aug. | Sept. | Oct. | Nov. | Dec. | Total |
|---|---|---|---|---|---|---|---|---|---|---|---|---|---|
| 1985 | 48,733 | 54,809 | 52,365 | 58,531 | 38,755 | 54,725 | 42,222 | 39,425 | 23,615 | 58,870 | 83,845 | 94,671 | 650,768 |
| 1986 | 113,305 | 95,509 | 76,787 | 82,308 | 75,176 | 87,323 | 78,670 | 106,366 | 93,465 | 112,685 | 89,713 | 61,835 | 1,073,142 |
| 1987 | 69,564 | 81,427 | 78,671 | 104,350 | 71,189 | 86,564 | 77,621 | 106,182 | 77,207 | 85,315 | 72,846 | 53,650 | 964,586 |
| 1988 | 67,955 | 119,075 | 85,154 | 80,772 | 73,379 | 125,684 | 91,569 | 118,956 | 88,460 | 83,713 | 85,366 | 129,627 | 1,149,710 |
| 1989 | 141,903 | 106,019 | 102,594 | 129,018 | 95,902 | 134,848 | 100,700 | 122,207 | 97,744 | 104,100 | 111,434 | 82,484 | 1,328,953 |
| 1990 | 130,223 | 174,115 | 211,105 | 144,641 | 128,121 | 147,605 | 127,767 | 172,947 | 119,088 | 113,569 | 175,067 | 119,802 | 1,774,050 |
| 1991 | 138,642 | 174,688 | 188,842 | 153,436 | 103,344 | 135,887 | 107,058 | 170,113 | 180,017 | 148,640 | 159,099 | 112,882 | 1,772,648 |
| 1992 | 153,332 | 199,420 | 174,662 | 188,232 | 156,944 | 164,586 | 177,493 | 182,741 | 163,214 | 108,707 | 211,678 | 199,374 | 2,152,383 |
| 1993 | 290,120 | 214,771 | 183,354 | 209,607 | 176,559 | 197,761 | 193,002 | 233,479 | 202,363 | 187,763 | 217,947 | 182,486 | 2,489,223 |
| 1994 | 188,508 | 219,455 | 208,113 | 284,734 | 380,119 | 304,542 | 210,479 | 196,685 | 159,574 | 177,424 | 184,172 | 142,713 | 2,658,073 |
| 1995 | 169,250 | 191,352 | 213,326 | 156,191 | 163,248 | 186,550 | 162,562 | 161,076 | 165,337 | 152,959 | 157,240 | 123,923 | 2,003,014 |
| 1996 | 203,369 | 186,526 | 152,797 | 197,442 | 137,454 | 158,929 | 171,800 | 196,991 | 136,054 | 196,696 | 135,305 | 166,213 | 2,039,576 |

*Source: Coffee, Sugar & Cocoa Exchange, Inc. (CSCE)*

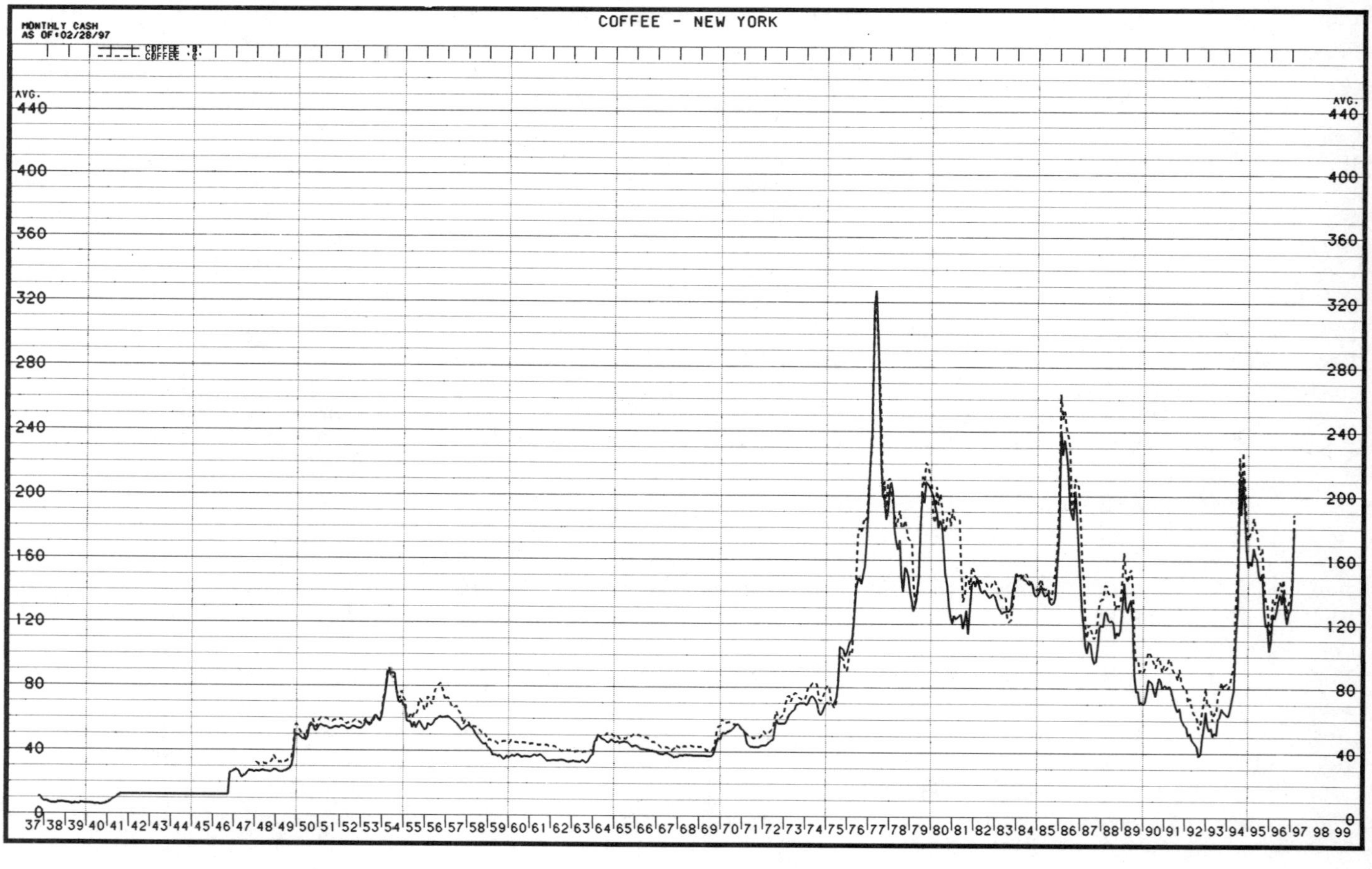

# Coke

## U.S. Salient Statistics of Coke In Thousands of Short Tons

| | Production at Coke Plants | | | | | | Exports | | | | |
|---|---|---|---|---|---|---|---|---|---|---|---|
| Year | Merchant Coke Plants | Furance Coke Plants | Total Coke | Breeze | Imports | Consumption[2] | Total | Canada | Mexico | Producer & Distributor Ending Stocks | Avg. Price of Coal Receipts at Coke Plants |
| 1988 | 3,868 | 28,536 | 28,945 | 2,478 | 2,688 | 30,021 | 1,093 | 348 | 101 | 1,583 | 47.70 |
| 1989 | NA | 28,045 | 28,045 | 2,342 | 2,311 | 28,935 | 1,085 | 644 | 157 | 1,919 | 47.50 |
| 1990 | 3,724 | 23,892 | 27,617 | 1,736 | 765 | 27,811 | 572 | 376 | 94 | 1,918 | 47.73 |
| 1991 | 3,251 | 20,795 | 24,046 | 1,734 | 1,099 | 24,216 | 740 | 239 | 98 | 2,107 | 48.95 |
| 1992 | 3,248 | 20,162 | 23,410 | 1,721 | 1,739 | 24,731 | 642 | 310 | 76 | 1,883 | 47.92 |
| 1993 | 3,209 | 19,973 | 23,182 | 3,424 | 1,534 | 24,303 | 835 | 417 | 92 | 1,461 | 47.44 |
| 1994 | 3,244 | 19,443 | 22,686 | 1,392 | 1,612 | 24,163 | 660 | 371 | 94 | 986 | 46.56 |
| 1995[1] | 3,239 | 20,509 | 23,749 | 1,463 | 1,816 | 24,500 | 750 | 579 | 60 | 1,302 | 47.34 |

[1] Preliminary. [2] Equal to production plus imports minus the change in producer and distributor stocks minus exports.
*Source: Energy Information Administration, U.S. Department of Energy*

## Petroleum Coke Production in the United States In Thousands of Barrels[2]

| Year | Jan. | Feb. | Mar. | Apr. | May | June | July | Aug. | Sept. | Oct. | Nov. | Dec. | Total |
|---|---|---|---|---|---|---|---|---|---|---|---|---|---|
| 1987 | 16,140 | 14,800 | 15,170 | 13,970 | 15,435 | 15,605 | 15,950 | 15,690 | 15,235 | 15,300 | 3,158 | 16,920 | 186,900 |
| 1988 | 17,180 | 15,855 | 17,075 | 15,820 | 16,835 | 16,410 | 16,665 | 16,735 | 16,025 | 16,405 | 3,347 | 17,310 | 199,055 |
| 1989 | 17,525 | 14,655 | 16,005 | 16,000 | 16,685 | 17,030 | 17,545 | 17,235 | 16,275 | 16,260 | 3,104 | 16,135 | 197,665 |
| 1990 | 16,680 | 15,710 | 16,645 | 16,390 | 16,785 | 16,455 | 17,185 | 18,085 | 16,520 | 16,830 | 3,351 | 17,510 | 201,660 |
| 1991 | 17,590 | 15,280 | 16,380 | 16,515 | 17,635 | 17,020 | 17,685 | 17,875 | 17,050 | 17,505 | 3,505 | 19,040 | 207,465 |
| 1992 | 18,550 | 16,330 | 17,825 | 17,615 | 18,460 | 18,685 | 19,330 | 18,280 | 17,845 | 17,665 | 3,540 | 19,385 | 217,995 |
| 1993 | 18,551 | 17,289 | 19,226 | 18,200 | 18,587 | 18,715 | 20,196 | 19,319 | 18,547 | 18,695 | 18,954 | 19,737 | 226,016 |
| 1994 | 19,170 | 16,873 | 18,695 | 18,454 | 19,748 | 19,325 | 20,008 | 19,473 | 17,868 | 18,753 | 18,995 | 19,697 | 227,059 |
| 1995 | 19,079 | 17,117 | 18,556 | 18,519 | 19,774 | 19,949 | 19,527 | 19,722 | 19,184 | 19,292 | 19,349 | 19,887 | 229,955 |
| 1996[1] | 19,536 | 18,706 | 21,015 | 20,663 | 20,426 | 19,927 | 19,836 | 20,328 | 20,124 | 20,558 | 20,447 | 21,389 | 242,955 |

[1] Preliminary. [2] Prior to 1993, data converted from thousands of short tons (5 barrels = 1 short ton). *Source: Energy Information Administration, U.S. Department of Energy*

## Coal Receipts and Carbonization at Coke Plants in the U.S. In Thousands of Short Tons

| | Coal Receipts at Coke Plants | | | | | | | Coal Carbonized at Coke Plants | | | | | | |
|---|---|---|---|---|---|---|---|---|---|---|---|---|---|---|
| | By State | | | | | By Plant Type | | By State | | | | | By Plant Type | |
| Year | Alabama | Indiana | Ohio | Pennsylvania | Total | Merchant Coke Plants | Furance Coke Plants | Alabama | Indiana | Ohio | Pennsylvania | Total | Merchant Coke Plants | Furance Coke Plants |
| 1988 | 3,313 | 11,251 | 5,041 | 10,179 | 41,115 | 5,008 | 36,107 | 3,383 | 11,287 | 5,448 | 10,146 | 41,910 | 5,034 | 36,876 |
| 1989 | 3,330 | 10,558 | 5,143 | 9,822 | 41,019 | 4,959 | 36,060 | 3,314 | 10,568 | 5,265 | 9,877 | 41,369 | 5,010 | 36,876 |
| 1990 | 3,304 | 10,497 | 5,021 | 10,604 | 40,736 | 4,988 | 35,749 | 3,288 | 8,867 | 4,949 | 10,456 | 38,877 | 4,950 | 33,927 |
| 1991 | 3,114 | 8,141 | 3,595 | 8,912 | 33,090 | 4,399 | 28,692 | 3,166 | 8,234 | 3,698 | 8,812 | 33,854 | 4,482 | 29,371 |
| 1992 | 3,334 | 6,894 | 3,717 | 9,761 | 32,027 | 4,295 | 27,732 | 3,297 | 7,153 | 3,755 | 9,868 | 32,366 | 4,316 | 28,050 |
| 1993 | 3,184 | 6,515 | 2,853 | 10,424 | 31,104 | 4,184 | 26,921 | 3,206 | 6,591 | 2,892 | 10,333 | 31,323 | 4,267 | 27,056 |
| 1994 | 3,242 | 5,023 | 3,064 | 10,776 | 31,719 | 4,205 | 27,514 | 3,253 | 4,841 | 3,092 | 10,849 | 31,740 | 4,218 | 27,522 |
| 1995[1] | 3,183 | 5,731 | 2,758 | 10,959 | 33,036 | 4,189 | 28,848 | 3,257 | 5,883 | 2,777 | 10,858 | 33,011 | 4,248 | 28,763 |

[1] Preliminary. *Source: Energy Information Administration, U.S. Department of Energy*

## United States Coke Distribution and Stocks In Thousands of Short Tons

| | Distribution | | | | | | | Coke Plant Stocks, Dec. 31 | | | |
|---|---|---|---|---|---|---|---|---|---|---|---|
| | By Plant Type | | By Consumer Category | | | | | | By Plant Type | | |
| Year | Merchant Coke Plants | Furance Coke Plants | Blast Furance | Foundries | Other Industrial Plants | Total Coke | Breeze | Total Coke | Merchant Coke Plants | Furance Coke Plants | Breeze |
| 1988 | 3,953 | 29,758 | 30,499 | 1,630 | 1,581 | 33,710 | 2,448 | 1,583 | 163 | 1,420 | 189 |
| 1989 | 3,755 | 30,286 | 30,676 | 1,535 | 1,830 | 34,041 | 2,251 | 1,919 | 216 | 1,703 | 179 |
| 1990 | 3,724 | 29,564 | 30,877 | 1,437 | 974 | 33,289 | 1,882 | 1,918 | 244 | 1,674 | 228 |
| 1991 | 3,246 | 24,267 | 25,669 | 1,213 | 630 | 27,513 | 2,057 | 2,107 | 252 | 1,856 | 259 |
| 1992 | 3,253 | 26,718 | 28,075 | 1,290 | 606 | 29,971 | 2,255 | 1,883 | 267 | 1,616 | 215 |
| 1993 | 3,226 | 27,009 | 28,295 | 1,373 | 567 | 30,235 | 3,563 | 1,461 | 272 | 1,189 | 486 |
| 1994 | 3,400 | 25,949 | 27,248 | 1,480 | 621 | 29,349 | 1,735 | 986 | 122 | 864 | 105 |
| 1995[1] | 3,284 | 25,103 | 26,346 | 1,401 | 639 | 28,386 | 1,638 | 1,302 | 112 | 1,189 | 136 |

[1] Preliminary. *Source: Energy Information Administration, U.S. Department of Energy*

# Copper

Copper metal and copper alloy have considerable commercial importance due to their electrical, mechanical, and physical properties. Copper for commercial purposes is obtained by the reduction of copper compounds in ores, followed by electrolytic refining. Copper is used largely in alloys such as brass, which is composed of copper and zinc.

The world's largest producer of copper is Chile with about a quarter of the world's output followed by the U.S., Canada, Australia, Peru, and Zambia. In the U.S., the principal mining states are Arizona, New Mexico, Utah, Michigan, and Montana. Fourteen mines account for 95 percent of U.S. copper production.

The International Copper Study Group (ICSG) reported that world consumption of refined copper in the January-July 1996 period averaged 937,000 tonnes per month. This was less than 1 percent higher than the comparable period of 1995. For the first seven months of 1996, world consumption of refined copper was 7.1 million tonnes compared to 7 million tonnes in the same period of 1995. For all of 1995, world consumption was 11.9 million tonnes. World copper mine capacity in the first seven months of 1996 was 6.9 million tonnes, up close to 6 percent from 1995. For 1995, mine capacity was 11.2 million tonnes. Global copper mine production in January-July 1996 was 6.2 million tonnes compared to 5.7 million tonnes in 1995. For all of 1995, mine production was just over 10 million tonnes, according to the ICSG. Mine capacity utilization was just over 89 percent in the January-July 1996 period compared to just over 87 percent in 1995.

The ICSG reported that primary refined copper production in the first seven months of 1996 was 6 million tonnes, up over 10 percent from the comparable period of 1995. For all of 1995 it was 9.6 million tonnes. Secondary refined copper production was 1.1 million tonnes, down 9 percent from the like period in 1995. For all of 1995 it was just over 2 million tonnes. In January-July 1996, there was 15.4 percent scrap in total production, compared to 18.1 percent in the same period of 1995 and 17.6 percent for all of 1995. Refined copper stocks at the end of July 1996, which include those held by exchanges, producers, consumers, merchants, and governments in western economies were just over a million tonnes, up 16 percent from a year earlier. At the end of 1995, refined copper stocks were 1.1 million tonnes.

The U.S. Geological Survey reported that U.S. production of recoverable mine copper in June 1996 was 161,000 tonnes, up from 157,000 tonnes in May. For January-June 1996 mine production was 922,000 tonnes while for all of 1995 it was 1.85 million tonnes. Smelter production in June 1996 was 107,000 tonnes, up 13 percent from May. For January-June 1996, smelter production was 628,000 tonnes and for all of 1995 it was 1.24 million tonnes. Refinery production of copper in June 1996 was 153,000 tonnes, down 11 percent from May. For January-June 1996 refinery production was 1 million tonnes while for all of 1995 it was 1.92 million tonnes.

### *Futures Markets*

Copper futures and options are traded on the London Metals Exchange (LME) and the New York Mercantile Exchange, COMEX division. Copper futures are traded on the Beijing Commodity Exchange (BCE).

**World Mine Production of Copper (Content of Ore)** In Thousands of Metric Tons

| Year | Australia | Canada[3] | Chile | China | Indonesia | Mexico | Mongolia | Peru | Philippines | Poland | Russia[4] | South Africa | United States[3] | Zaire | Zambia | World Total[2] |
|---|---|---|---|---|---|---|---|---|---|---|---|---|---|---|---|---|
| 1986 | 248.4 | 698.6 | 1,398.8 | 185 | 95.8 | 189.1 | 136.0 | 399.9 | 222.6 | 434.0 | 620 | 184.2 | 1,144.2 | 527.8 | 462.4 | 7,939 |
| 1987 | 232.7 | 802.2 | 1,418.1 | 250 | 102.1 | 252.7 | 120.8 | 417.6 | 216.1 | 438.0 | 630 | 188.1 | 1,243.6 | 515.6 | 463.2 | 8,243 |
| 1988 | 238.3 | 776.5 | 1,451.0 | 282 | 121.5 | 284.9 | 121.7 | 337.5 | 218.1 | 437.0 | 1,000 | 168.5 | 1,419.7 | 495.8 | 456.6 | 8,727 |
| 1989 | 296.0 | 723.1 | 1,609.3 | 276 | 144.0 | 264.2 | 123.6 | 387.9 | 193.0 | 384.0 | 1,000 | 181.9 | 1,507.3 | 466.2 | 466.3 | 9,058 |
| 1990 | 330.0 | 793.7 | 1,588.4 | 285 | 164.1 | 293.9 | 123.9 | 339.3 | 182.1 | 330.0 | 950 | 178.7 | 1,587.8 | 356.0 | 421.0 | 8,950 |
| 1991 | 320.0 | 811.1 | 1,814.3 | 304 | 211.7 | 292.1 | 90.1 | 357.2 | 148.3 | 320.0 | 900 | 184.6 | 1,531.0 | 237.5 | 390.6 | 9,090 |
| 1992 | 371.0 | 766.6 | 1,932.7 | 334 | 280.8 | 279.0 | 105.1 | 345.6 | 123.5 | 331.9 | 699 | 176.1 | 1,762.0 | 132.9 | 429.5 | 9,490 |
| 1993 | 360.0 | 732.6 | 2,055.4 | 345 | 298.6 | 301.1 | 96.9 | 348.3 | 136.3 | 383.6 | 584 | 166.3 | 1,801.0 | 40.3 | 396.2 | 9,420 |
| 1994[1] | 391.0 | 617.3 | 2,219.9 | 396 | 322.2 | 305.5 | 99.6 | 333.6 | 112.1 | 378.0 | 573 | 183.9 | 1,813.0 | 46.3 | 384.4 | 9,490 |
| 1995[2] | 437.0 | 728.7 | 2,488.0 | 370 | 443.6 | 331.9 | 100.4 | 380.7 | 105.7 | 383.6 | 591 | 199.6 | 1,849.0 | 28.8 | 329.2 | 10,000 |

[1] Preliminary. [2] Estimate. [3] Recoverable. [4] Formerly part of the U.S.S.R.; data not reported separately until 1992. *Source: U.S. Geological Survey*

**Commodity Exchange, Inc. (COMEX) Warehouse Stocks of Copper** In Thousands of Short Tons

| Year | Jan. 1 | Feb. 1 | Mar. 1 | Apr. 1 | May 1 | June 1 | July 1 | Aug. 1 | Sept. 1 | Oct. 1 | Nov. 1 | Dec. 1 |
|---|---|---|---|---|---|---|---|---|---|---|---|---|
| 1987 | 93.3 | 102.8 | 108.9 | 97.5 | 88.4 | 71.4 | 65.3 | 69.0 | 73.5 | 89.2 | 66.2 | 33.7 |
| 1988 | 18.5 | 16.9 | 16.8 | 11.8 | 10.2 | 19.0 | 16.9 | 24.6 | 22.3 | 13.6 | 9.5 | 5.9 |
| 1989 | 13.4 | 14.9 | 17.3 | 29.7 | 21.2 | 25.2 | 23.0 | 20.4 | 15.2 | 11.4 | 10.4 | 9.1 |
| 1990 | 16.3 | 7.2 | 4.1 | 4.5 | 6.0 | 14.7 | 18.1 | 11.5 | 8.9 | 6.7 | 8.3 | 9.3 |
| 1991 | 20.2 | 14.7 | 16.4 | 30.2 | 30.9 | 25.0 | 25.1 | 35.9 | 33.6 | 24.4 | 26.8 | 29.3 |
| 1992 | 33.7 | 34.8 | 29.5 | 28.2 | 30.3 | 32.4 | 31.8 | 36.0 | 40.4 | 51.7 | 70.1 | 73.8 |
| 1993 | 105.9 | 124.0 | 114.8 | 107.6 | 110.8 | 108.3 | 105.5 | 113.8 | 100.1 | 94.1 | 96.6 | 80.5 |
| 1994 | 74.0 | 56.7 | 49.8 | 37.2 | 31.6 | 30.4 | 36.0 | 37.4 | 28.5 | 17.9 | 20.3 | 21.5 |
| 1995 | 26.7 | 18.7 | 17.7 | 9.0 | 11.5 | 7.0 | 13.1 | 16.7 | 16.5 | 11.2 | 6.0 | 5.0 |
| 1996 | 23.7 | 12.1 | 12.4 | 13.9 | 20.7 | 13.2 | 7.6 | 17.7 | 22.1 | 21.7 | 30.8 | 36.2 |

*Source: New York Mercantile Exchange, COMEX division*

## U.S. Salient Statistics of Copper In Thousands of Metric Tons

| | New Copper Produced | | | | | | Imports[3] | | Exports | | Stocks, Dec. 31 | | | Apparent Consumption | |
|---|---|---|---|---|---|---|---|---|---|---|---|---|---|---|---|
| | From Domestic Ores | | | | | | | | | | | | | | |
| Year | Mines | Smelters | Refineries | From Foreign Ores[3] | Total New | Secondary Recovered[4] | Unmanufactured | Refined | Ore, Concentrate[6] | Refined[7] | COMEX | Primary Producers (Refined) | Blister & Material in Solution | Refined Copper (Reported) | Primary & Old Copper[8] |
| 1985 | 1,105 | 939 | 1,004 | 54 | 1,057 | 503 | 444 | 378 | 116 | 38 | 109 | 320 | 146 | 1,976 | 2,144 |
| 1986 | 1,144 | 908 | 1,033 | 41 | 1,074 | 479 | 597 | 502 | 174 | 12 | 84 | 225 | 136 | 2,097 | 2,138 |
| 1987 | 1,244 | 972 | 1,127 | W | 1,127 | 498 | 568 | 469 | 125 | 9 | 17 | 113 | 150 | 2,127 | 2,197 |
| 1988 | 1,417 | 1,043 | 1,282 | 124 | 1,406 | 518 | 513 | 332 | 211 | 58 | 12 | 97 | 121 | 2,210 | 2,214 |
| 1989 | 1,498 | 1,120 | 1,352 | 125 | 1,477 | 548 | 515 | 300 | 267 | 130 | 15 | 107 | 132 | 2,203 | 2,185 |
| 1990 | 1,588 | 1,158 | 1,502 | 75 | 1,577 | 537 | 512 | 262 | 258 | 211 | 18 | 101 | 119 | 2,150 | 2,168 |
| 1991 | 1,631 | 1,123 | 1,501 | 77 | 1,577 | 518 | 512 | 289 | 253 | 263 | 31 | 132 | 135 | 2,048 | 2,105 |
| 1992 | 1,765 | 1,180 | 1,615 | 96 | 1,711 | 555 | 593 | 289 | 266 | 177 | 96 | 205 | 166 | 2,178 | 2,311 |
| 1993 | 1,801 | 1,265 | 1,214 | 89 | 1,793 | 543 | 637 | 343 | 227 | 217 | 67 | 153 | 146 | 2,364 | 2,510 |
| 1994[1] | 1,850 | 1,310 | 1,280 | 64 | 1,840 | 500 | 763 | 470 | 261 | 157 | 24 | 119 | 171 | 2,680 | 2,680 |
| 1995[2] | 1,850 | 1,240 | 1,310 | 77 | 1,930 | 442 | 808 | 429 | 239 | 217 | 22 | 163 | 174 | 2,530 | 2,540 |

[1] Preliminary. [2] Estimate. [3] Also from matte, etc., refinery reports. [4] From scrap only. [5] For consumption. [6] Blister (copper content). [7] Ingots, bars, etc. [8] Old scrap only. *Source: U.S. Geological Survey*

## Consumption of Refined Copper[3] in the United States In Thousands of Metric Tons

| | By-Products | | | | | | By Class of Consumer | | | | | | | Total |
|---|---|---|---|---|---|---|---|---|---|---|---|---|---|
| Year | Cathodes | Wire Bars | Ingot & Ingot Bars | Cakes & Slabs | Billets | Other[4] | Wire Rod Mills | Brass Mills | Chemical Plants | Ingot Makers | Foundries | Miscellaneous | Consumption |
| 1985 | 1,563.4 | 70.3 | 64.2 | 115.8 | 139.6 | 22.8 | 1,401.7 | 564.9 | .9 | 1.4 | 20.6 | 22.9 | 2,101.5 |
| 1986 | 1,717.7 | 52.5 | 105.9 | 81.6 | 127.9 | 16.9 | 1,491.9 | 564.9 | .9 | 1.4 | 20.6 | 22.9 | 2,102.6 |
| 1987 | 1,852.9 | 13.8 | 74.0 | 71.9 | 92.7 | 20.3 | 1,593.9 | 488.6 | 1.1 | 1.4 | 14.2 | 26.4 | 2,125.7 |
| 1988 | 1,967.4 | 14.0 | 54.2 | 63.0 | 99.0 | 12.7 | 1,667.2 | 493.2 | 1.0 | 2.6 | 14.5 | 31.9 | 2,210.4 |
| 1989 | 1,981.6 | 6.1 | 34.4 | 64.9 | 104.9 | 11.2 | 1,698.4 | 461.0 | .9 | 1.3 | 14.9 | 26.5 | 2,203.1 |
| 1990 | 1,922.4 | 6.6 | 50.5 | 57.9 | W | 113.0 | 1,653.5 | 445.2 | 1.1 | 4.5 | 14.6 | 31.6 | 2,150.4 |
| 1991 | 1,854.9 | W | 24.7 | 33.3 | W | 135.4 | 1,591.8 | 458.5 | .9 | 3.4 | 12.7 | 25.3 | 2,048.3 |
| 1992 | 1,974.9 | W | 20.0 | 43.7 | W | 139.6 | 1,675.0 | 458.5 | .9 | 3.0 | 15.0 | 25.8 | 2,178.2 |
| 1993 | 2,130.0 | W | 37.7 | 55.5 | W | 136.0 | 1,819.1 | 503.0 | .9 | 2.2 | 10.2 | 27.6 | 2,360.0 |
| 1994[1] | 2,410.0 | W | 37.3 | 73.2 | W | 164.0 | 2,060.0 | 568.0 | 1.1 | 4.5 | 11.1 | 30.4 | 2,680.0 |
| 1995[2] | 2,250.0 | W | 31.3 | 75.9 | W | 180.0 | 1,950.0 | 533.0 | W | W | W | 55.9 | 2,530.0 |

[1] Preliminary. [2] Estimate. [3] Primary & secondary. [4] Data 1991 to date include Wire Bars and Billets. *Source: U.S. Geological Survey*

## London Metals Exchange (LME) Warehouse Stocks of Copper (End of Period) In Thousands of Metric Tons

| Year | Jan. | Feb. | Mar. | Apr. | May | June | July | Aug. | Sept. | Oct. | Nov. | Dec. |
|---|---|---|---|---|---|---|---|---|---|---|---|---|
| 1988 | 59.6 | 74.4 | 69.4 | 54.8 | 86.8 | 109.1 | 145.8 | 148.4 | 122.4 | 86.2 | 78.3 | 79.9 |
| 1989 | 96.6 | 104.2 | 117.4 | 138.7 | 125.2 | 99.2 | 96.1 | 100.8 | 126.7 | 117.8 | 142.2 | 131.2 |
| 1990 | 121.5 | 106.8 | 71.9 | 67.0 | 92.8 | 67.7 | 126.8 | 161.1 | 227.1 | 221.1 | 199.9 | 220.6 |
| 1991 | 189.0 | 202.8 | 213.9 | 237.9 | 275.0 | 264.9 | 266.5 | 307.1 | 308.4 | 291.7 | 308.3 | 332.3 |
| 1992 | 308.6 | 302.7 | 296.4 | 279.7 | 265.4 | 259.1 | 246.8 | 275.2 | 299.7 | 317.8 | 327.0 | 315.8 |
| 1993 | 313.5 | 333.1 | 365.8 | 403.5 | 429.1 | 446.9 | 464.3 | 521.7 | 600.7 | 612.3 | 590.9 | 599.5 |
| 1994 | 597.6 | 554.5 | 504.3 | 446.4 | 379.0 | 350.9 | 338.9 | 367.8 | 359.3 | 333.1 | 318.4 | 301.8 |
| 1995 | 309.9 | 280.9 | 239.9 | 204.9 | 197.9 | 166.5 | 151.5 | 163.1 | 178.2 | 193.6 | 222.2 | 364.8 |
| 1996[1] | 355.1 | 348.4 | 322.3 | 303.9 | 313.7 | 263.0 | 227.6 | 275.5 | 239.6 | 123.4 | 92.6 | 125.4 |

[1] Preliminary. *Source: American Bureau of Metal Statistics*

## U.S. Copper Refined from Scrap In Thousands of Metric Tons

| Year | Jan. | Feb. | Mar. | Apr. | May | June | July | Aug. | Sept. | Oct. | Nov. | Dec. | Total |
|---|---|---|---|---|---|---|---|---|---|---|---|---|---|
| 1986 | 42.5 | 44.9 | 45.2 | 42.6 | 42.4 | 40.8 | 39.1 | 37.4 | 43.9 | 43.5 | 36.0 | 36.7 | 405.9 |
| 1987 | 28.7 | 31.6 | 40.1 | 44.3 | 34.0 | 35.1 | 39.5 | 33.2 | 34.5 | 35.8 | 30.8 | 37.1 | 414.7 |
| 1988 | 34.2 | 35.2 | 42.9 | 38.1 | 38.0 | 38.4 | 30.4 | 37.9 | 42.3 | 37.0 | 37.5 | 40.2 | 453.3 |
| 1989 | 37.4 | 40.8 | 47.0 | 40.1 | 40.8 | 41.1 | 36.6 | 41.4 | 40.6 | 41.3 | 35.9 | 37.1 | 479.9 |
| 1990 | 37.3 | 35.2 | 37.1 | 38.5 | 39.3 | 38.1 | 34.6 | 39.2 | 29.9 | 34.3 | 31.9 | 32.0 | 440.8 |
| 1991 | 35.4 | 32.8 | 40.5 | 39.6 | 38.2 | 35.7 | 32.6 | 33.0 | 28.5 | 37.3 | 32.1 | 32.6 | 417.7 |
| 1992 | 27.8 | 34.1 | 39.8 | 34.8 | 36.7 | 39.4 | 27.8 | 35.4 | 39.8 | 40.0 | 34.3 | 35.8 | 433.2 |
| 1993 | 38.1 | 45.9 | 38.9 | 37.8 | 36.4 | 41.1 | 35.0 | 37.6 | 37.4 | 43.0 | 35.4 | 32.2 | 459.8 |
| 1994 | 33.3 | 28.3 | 37.9 | 30.7 | 37.1 | 28.7 | 26.9 | 33.0 | 38.7 | 27.0 | 34.3 | 37.3 | 391.7 |
| 1995 | 30.9 | 30.6 | 36.0 | 32.7 | 33.7 | 28.2 | 18.7 | 25.1 | 25.4 | 25.0 | 26.2 | 24.4 | 319.0 |
| 1996[1] | 25.0 | 23.7 | 25.5 | 22.5 | 26.8 | 30.9 | 24.4 | 25.0 | 26.8 | 30.6 | 25.9 | 26.3 | 313.4 |

[1] Preliminary. *Source: U.S. Geological Survey*

# COPPER

## Average Open Interest of Copper Futures[1] in New York   In Contracts

| Year | Jan. | Feb. | Mar. | Apr. | May | June | July | Aug. | Sept. | Oct. | Nov. | Dec. |
|---|---|---|---|---|---|---|---|---|---|---|---|---|
| 1986 | 87,280 | 83,713 | 86,713 | 79,370 | 71,169 | 68,505 | 63,529 | 61,827 | 62,779 | 65,073 | 73,414 | 78,164 |
| 1987 | 77,851 | 77,433 | 76,967 | 70,108 | 74,628 | 84,725 | 85,391 | 75,725 | 65,678 | 59,073 | 47,279 | 41,781 |
| 1988 | 43,177 | 41,220 | 35,505 | 34,787 | 31,410 | 35,949 | 31,750 | 29,563 | 35,094 | 35,998 | 37,039 | 33,510 |
| 1989 | 33,819 | 34,199 | 35,058 | 36,021 | 30,901 | 28,527 | 26,534 | 28,420 | 28,849 | 27,287 | 31,240 | 32,343 |
| 1990 | 31,466 | 33,908 | 34,654 | 34,405 | 31,552 | 30,113 | 32,780 | 31,515 | 32,578 | 36,145 | 35,088 | 30,128 |
| 1991 | 34,927 | 35,978 | 35,026 | 34,096 | 44,153 | 39,879 | 33,100 | 33,333 | 40,347 | 42,028 | 41,618 | 44,283 |
| 1992 | 47,109 | 47,929 | 48,700 | 45,114 | 39,986 | 48,129 | 47,065 | 38,397 | 37,041 | 41,658 | 44,927 | 45,541 |
| 1993 | 47,433 | 48,707 | 48,220 | 51,217 | 52,762 | 56,856 | 54,861 | 54,571 | 54,929 | 57,406 | 63,632 | 69,311 |
| 1994 | 65,518 | 65,446 | 66,177 | 59,346 | 63,825 | 60,383 | 51,616 | 46,855 | 56,344 | 59,060 | 59,158 | 51,078 |
| 1995 | 52,632 | 50,770 | 47,267 | 47,793 | 50,089 | 48,200 | 40,968 | 37,744 | 33,709 | 36,476 | 38,475 | 35,996 |
| 1996 | 47,771 | 45,706 | 42,732 | 46,771 | 47,284 | 52,558 | 56,564 | 56,549 | 55,408 | 58,124 | 61,031 | 55,807 |

[1] Data for May 1988 thru December 1989 include Old copper and High Grade copper contracts. *Source: New York Mercantile Exchange, COMEX Division*

## Volume of Trading of Copper Futures[1] in New York   In Contracts

| Year | Jan. | Feb. | Mar. | Apr. | May | June | July | Aug. | Sept. | Oct. | Nov. | Dec. | Total |
|---|---|---|---|---|---|---|---|---|---|---|---|---|---|
| 1985 | 254,052 | 261,784 | 167,686 | 310,487 | 215,079 | 209,506 | 146,396 | 195,882 | 138,803 | 178,728 | 200,142 | 166,007 | 2,444,552 |
| 1986 | 190,983 | 206,513 | 197,818 | 240,770 | 106,750 | 200,547 | 89,818 | 145,468 | 123,779 | 121,361 | 162,963 | 85,439 | 1,872,209 |
| 1987 | 124,845 | 178,598 | 165,216 | 170,827 | 208,696 | 306,029 | 272,794 | 214,181 | 193,035 | 276,491 | 278,985 | 179,481 | 2,569,178 |
| 1988 | 210,209 | 222,625 | 194,722 | 151,177 | 130,289 | 179,991 | 120,108 | 143,103 | 142,041 | 186,479 | 258,834 | 173,805 | 2,113,383 |
| 1989 | 216,528 | 201,132 | 219,910 | 201,997 | 193,956 | 174,055 | 132,793 | 173,273 | 151,097 | 176,822 | 154,241 | 93,243 | 2,089,047 |
| 1990 | 152,156 | 148,766 | 179,445 | 181,726 | 164,489 | 163,372 | 141,602 | 154,383 | 156,924 | 161,814 | 133,718 | 114,790 | 1,853,185 |
| 1991 | 159,621 | 131,044 | 108,191 | 150,390 | 148,777 | 139,207 | 110,025 | 149,702 | 132,354 | 125,757 | 153,910 | 135,132 | 1,643,310 |
| 1992 | 145,245 | 168,015 | 105,003 | 157,473 | 77,722 | 182,091 | 138,225 | 177,581 | 137,423 | 121,392 | 146,062 | 117,931 | 1,674,163 |
| 1993 | 152,387 | 148,388 | 132,705 | 212,086 | 160,751 | 181,427 | 165,727 | 169,428 | 222,099 | 133,364 | 203,729 | 182,538 | 2,064,629 |
| 1994 | 197,959 | 233,016 | 231,239 | 207,963 | 247,143 | 297,393 | 188,644 | 242,393 | 219,788 | 208,957 | 290,585 | 178,887 | 2,737,967 |
| 1995 | 242,760 | 267,883 | 232,229 | 242,302 | 195,554 | 274,587 | 167,836 | 213,110 | 169,689 | 181,945 | 185,141 | 146,378 | 2,519,414 |
| 1996 | 184,431 | 173,689 | 157,553 | 210,836 | 200,469 | 255,172 | 150,445 | 174,351 | 166,537 | 250,420 | 227,800 | 160,216 | 2,311,919 |

[1] Data for May 1988 thru December 1989 include Old copper and High Grade copper contracts. *Source: New York Mercantile Exchange, COMEX Division*

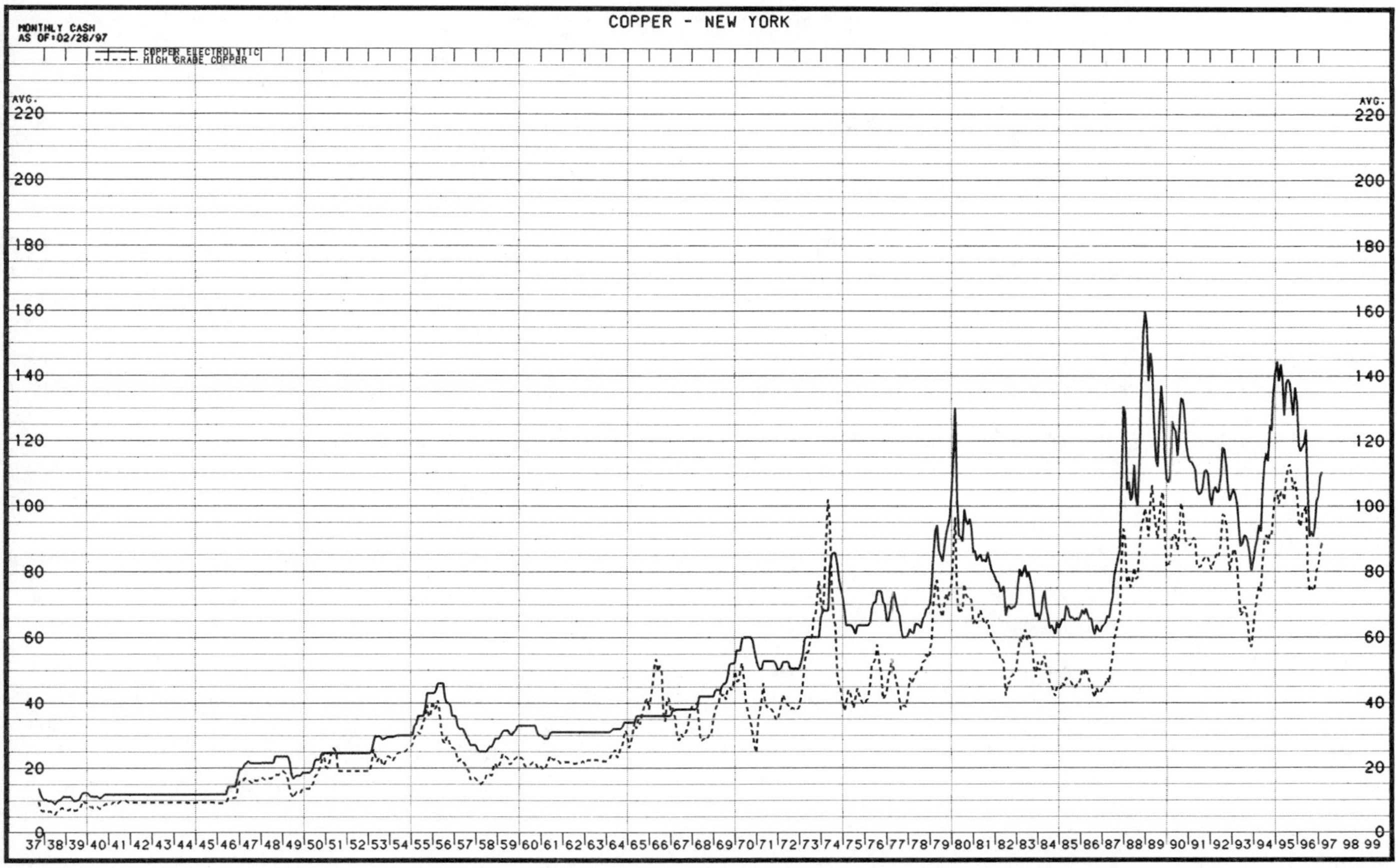


## Producers' Prices of Electrolytic (Wirebar) Copper, Delivered U.S. Destinations In Cents Per Pound

| Year | Jan. | Feb. | Mar. | Apr. | May | June | July | Aug. | Sept. | Oct. | Nov. | Dec. | Average |
|---|---|---|---|---|---|---|---|---|---|---|---|---|---|
| 1986 | 71.57 | 70.21 | 71.78 | 70.55 | 68.69 | 69.15 | 65.47 | 64.12 | 66.82 | 65.61 | 65.06 | 65.91 | 67.91 |
| 1987 | 67.29 | 67.87 | 70.50 | 69.83 | 73.54 | 76.71 | 83.10 | 84.94 | 88.04 | 91.52 | 109.59 | 134.71 | 84.80 |
| 1988 | 135.63 | 110.58 | 111.99 | 107.51 | 106.91 | 116.46 | 107.90 | 103.62 | 118.04 | 126.38 | 159.08 | 167.80 | 122.66 |
| 1989 | 164.21 | 146.17 | 154.89 | 150.26 | 132.72 | 121.45 | 119.27 | 133.75 | 143.60 | 137.61 | 123.59 | 115.64 | 136.93 |
| 1990 | 116.36 | 119.35 | 136.22 | 134.38 | 132.32 | 124.93 | 133.91 | 142.53 | 142.45 | 138.41 | 127.76 | 124.39 | 131.08 |
| 1991 | 122.59 | 122.73 | 121.24 | 120.35 | 133.11 | 111.72 | 111.90 | 113.48 | 118.92 | 118.90 | 117.26 | 110.33 | 118.54 |
| 1992 | 108.16 | 112.52 | 113.56 | 112.35 | 112.56 | 116.74 | 125.66 | 124.30 | 119.39 | 112.09 | 108.23 | 111.13 | 114.72 |
| 1993 | 112.57 | 110.26 | 107.80 | 99.03 | 92.35 | 94.98 | 93.41 | 97.06 | 92.36 | 81.69 | 86.07 | 91.08 | 96.56 |
| 1994 | 95.65 | 99.13 | 101.76 | 99.87 | 112.30 | 120.58 | 123.68 | 121.38 | 132.53 | 130.91 | 141.92 | 148.86 | 119.05 |
| 1995 | 152.02 | 146.00 | 151.14 | 146.03 | 139.80 | 149.51 | 150.00 | 149.77 | 144.14 | 140.00 | 148.48 | 143.78 | 146.72 |
| 1996 | 130.09 | 128.75 | 130.20 | 131.29 | 135.33 | 116.33 | 102.68 | 104.14 | 102.51 | 105.46 | 112.78 | 114.78 | 117.86 |

*Source: American Metal Market*

## Dealers' Buying Price of No. 2 Heavy Copper Scrap In the Chicago Area[1] In Cents Per Pound

| Year | Jan. | Feb. | Mar. | Apr. | May | June | July | Aug. | Sept. | Oct. | Nov. | Dec. | Average |
|---|---|---|---|---|---|---|---|---|---|---|---|---|---|
| 1984 | 41.17 | 40.60 | 43.59 | 44.50 | 43.30 | 42.21 | 39.36 | 38.50 | 38.08 | 36.20 | 34.50 | 35.67 | 39.81 |
| 1985 | 37.50 | 37.50 | 37.50 | 37.50 | 37.50 | 37.50 | 37.50 | 37.50 | 37.50 | 37.50 | 37.50 | 37.50 | 37.50 |
| 1986 | 38.23 | 39.50 | 39.50 | 39.50 | 39.50 | 39.50 | 39.50 | 37.79 | 37.50 | 37.50 | 37.50 | 37.50 | 38.59 |
| 1987 | 37.50 | 37.50 | 37.86 | 39.50 | 41.15 | 42.50 | 44.68 | 49.07 | 49.50 | 53.32 | 55.39 | 64.73 | 46.06 |
| 1988[1] | 77.10 | 68.00 | 63.50 | 63.12 | 70.07 | 70.59 | 69.80 | 69.54 | 72.36 | 78.93 | 83.66 | 85.50 | 72.68 |
| 1989 | 89.83 | 87.13 | 95.33 | 95.95 | 91.14 | 80.27 | 74.45 | 75.54 | 86.50 | 90.32 | 86.00 | 80.25 | 86.06 |
| 1990 | 78.27 | 71.00 | 78.73 | 88.00 | 88.00 | 84.38 | 84.00 | 85.50 | 91.84 | 89.50 | 86.48 | 83.00 | 84.06 |
| 1991 | 83.00 | 79.50 | 82.21 | 82.50 | 78.66 | 72.40 | 71.00 | 71.00 | 72.05 | 75.39 | 75.08 | 74.50 | 76.44 |
| 1992 | 73.21 | 73.37 | 75.23 | 75.16 | 74.00 | 74.27 | 77.18 | 78.38 | 75.38 | 70.27 | 69.00 | 67.18 | 73.55 |
| 1993 | 67.95 | 67.00 | 67.00 | 62.95 | 55.12 | 53.59 | 56.33 | 54.18 | 52.67 | 49.10 | 47.00 | 48.00 | 56.74 |
| 1994 | 50.80 | 56.11 | 59.61 | 62.00 | 64.86 | 72.32 | 76.40 | 74.30 | 75.69 | 76.45 | 78.10 | 82.95 | 69.13 |
| 1995 | 89.48 | 90.79 | 89.39 | 91.75 | 85.91 | 88.73 | 92.32 | 92.65 | 92.70 | 90.64 | 92.00 | 92.00 | 90.70 |
| 1996 | 87.17 | 82.90 | 83.24 | 83.29 | 82.95 | 71.48 | 61.43 | 62.00 | 62.00 | 63.00 | 64.84 | 66.00 | 72.53 |

[1] Data prior to May 1988 are for the New York area. *Source: American Metal Market*

# COPPER

## U.S. Foreign Trade of Refined Copper   In Thousands of Metric Tons

| Year | | Jan. | Feb. | Mar. | Apr. | May | June | July | Aug. | Sept. | Oct. | Nov. | Dec. | Total |
|---|---|---|---|---|---|---|---|---|---|---|---|---|---|---|
| 1988 | Imports | 49.4 | 38.0 | 39.0 | 33.7 | 25.9 | 25.1 | 22.3 | 27.7 | 25.7 | 44.2 | 39.2 | 20.2 | 390.4 |
| | Exports | 4.9 | 2.0 | 3.8 | 5.7 | 7.7 | 9.5 | 3.5 | 4.4 | 14.3 | 2.3 | 4.0 | 4.5 | 66.5 |
| 1989 | Imports | 32.7 | 24.8 | 18.7 | 20.9 | 24.1 | 25.9 | 20.9 | 24.4 | 28.1 | 30.5 | 32.3 | 16.9 | 300.1 |
| | Exports | 6.2 | 4.8 | 5.9 | 13.5 | 4.3 | 6.6 | 21.4 | 15.8 | 23.4 | 13.7 | 6.3 | 12.1 | 130.2 |
| 1990 | Imports | 24.7 | 15.8 | 26.5 | 25.3 | 31.3 | 24.0 | 20.6 | 18.0 | 21.4 | 18.4 | 20.8 | 16.7 | 263.6 |
| | Exports | 18.1 | 20.8 | 12.2 | 7.6 | 15.6 | 12.2 | 23.9 | 20.1 | 22.4 | 21.5 | 17.2 | 19.8 | 211.3 |
| 1991 | Imports | 22.7 | 27.1 | 21.7 | 30.9 | 17.5 | 23.6 | 23.7 | 17.4 | 22.9 | 36.3 | 26.8 | 18.0 | 288.6 |
| | Exports | 33.6 | 21.4 | 37.4 | 16.8 | 31.5 | 23.9 | 20.6 | 20.9 | 17.9 | 13.4 | 15.4 | 17.9 | 270.7 |
| 1992 | Imports | 22.6 | 24.5 | 31.9 | 25.2 | 25.3 | 26.1 | 24.7 | 25.3 | 24.0 | 19.6 | 20.3 | 20.8 | 289.1 |
| | Exports | 21.7 | 18.4 | 10.8 | 12.3 | 11.7 | 12.0 | 9.3 | 13.0 | 13.6 | 24.1 | 14.1 | 16.1 | 176.9 |
| 1993 | Imports | 21.8 | 25.6 | 28.2 | 35.9 | 29.5 | 26.9 | 30.6 | 28.3 | 22.5 | 31.6 | 32.2 | 30.5 | 343.4 |
| | Exports | 14.0 | 24.9 | 23.6 | 16.3 | 15.4 | 13.1 | 10.7 | 10.1 | 19.5 | 19.5 | 14.9 | 14.5 | 216.7 |
| 1994 | Imports | 28.7 | 33.6 | 49.8 | 36.8 | 36.1 | 46.8 | 35.6 | 34.4 | 34.7 | 62.4 | 35.9 | 36.2 | 470.0 |
| | Exports | 13.0 | 10.2 | 10.7 | 6.8 | 14.8 | 9.1 | 15.6 | 10.9 | 15.4 | 15.9 | 13.1 | 21.1 | 157.0 |
| 1995[1] | Imports | 34.9 | 30.0 | 37.1 | 36.9 | 36.5 | 37.9 | 31.5 | 31.8 | 28.7 | 38.7 | 44.4 | 40.3 | 429.0 |
| | Exports | 11.1 | 24.0 | 25.6 | 18.2 | 23.4 | 38.9 | 16.3 | 16.6 | 12.1 | 9.0 | 12.5 | 9.5 | 217.0 |
| 1996[1] | Imports | 43.1 | 41.2 | 48.2 | 49.6 | 56.8 | 44.6 | 53.8 | 64.8 | 62.3 | 46.1 | 61.8 | | 572.3 |
| | Exports | 13.7 | 16.5 | 12.7 | 12.3 | 10.8 | 10.7 | 15.7 | 17.7 | 14.5 | 16.4 | 12.8 | | 153.8 |

[1] Preliminary. *Source: U.S. Geological Survey*

## Refined Copper Stocks in the U.S.A.   In Thousands of Short Tons (Recoverable Copper Content)

| Year | Jan. 1 | Feb. 1 | Mar. 1 | Apr. 1 | May 1 | June 1 | July 1 | Aug. 1 | Sept. 1 | Oct. 1 | Nov. 1 | Dec. 1 |
|---|---|---|---|---|---|---|---|---|---|---|---|---|
| 1981 | 253.0 | 261.6 | 249.4 | 236.8 | 245.5 | 243.4 | 264.7 | 276.9 | 276.0 | 275.5 | 281.6 | 301.2 |
| 1982 | 338.6 | 351.9 | 375.9 | 387.3 | 409.8 | 422.5 | 448.1 | 463.7 | 449.9 | 436.2 | 438.2 | 470.8 |
| 1983 | 484.5 | 489.6 | 501.6 | 508.9 | 524.1 | 519.4 | 498.7 | 509.0 | 522.7 | 509.1 | 514.2 | 505.2 |
| 1984 | 475.3 | 497.8 | 499.6 | 483.3 | 478.3 | 463.4 | 483.2 | 493.4 | 490.7 | 467.1 | 475.2 | 457.3 |
| 1985 | 469.7 | 452.9 | 380.9 | 368.2 | 358.4 | 363.2 | 344.1 | 331.4 | 310.9 | 275.7 | 257.3 | 264.1 |
| 1986 | 270.7 | 271.0 | 261.6 | 242.0 | 231.1 | 201.4 | 188.0 | 209.6 | 214.4 | 188.1 | 189.0 | 211.3 |
| 1987 | 238.4 | 211.5 | 206.8 | 170.1 | 175.7 | 161.6 | 136.4 | 141.0 | 140.4 | 151.3 | 121.1 | 86.7 |
| 1988 | 81.4 | 79.8 | 81.6 | 89.0 | 83.1 | 75.7 | 42.0 | 48.8 | 52.5 | 42.9 | 40.6 | 39.8 |
| 1989 | 56.3 | 67.5 | 56.3 | 60.6 | 54.3 | 54.4 | 49.1 | 61.8 | 66.1 | 42.3 | 48.1 | 48.2 |
| 1990 | 72.7 | 42.4 | 38.6 | 45.2 | 55.9 | 60.2 | 67.5 | 67.2 | 67.6 | 27.4 | 27.9 | 45.4 |
| 1991 | 72.3 | 72.8 | 53.2 | 68.6 | 63.2 | 52.8 | 52.4 | 71.4 | 64.4 | 48.5 | 48.3 | 63.1 |
| 1992 | 75.3 | 76.3 | 67.2 | 69.7 | 75.9 | 65.0 | 62.2 | 71.2 | 87.1 | 99.5 | 110.3 | 107.1 |
| 1993 | 135.4 | 152.7 | 144.3 | 132.3 | 146.0 | 153.6 | 137.1 | 151.0 | 128.4 | 117.2 | 124.6 | 107.1 |
| 1994 | 103.0 | 87.7 | 83.6 | 72.8 | 70.7 | 70.4 | 73.3 | 81.1 | 74.6 | 66.5 | 52.7 | 53.6 |
| 1995[2] | 55.8 | 39.6 | 37.0 | 22.6 | 33.1 | 30.8 | 27.0 | 50.0 | 60.6 | 71.1 | 69.4 | 73.4 |
| 1996[1] | 120.0 | 131.4 | 125.5 | 123.1 | 126.3 | 107.9 | 102.8 | 106.2 | 104.7 | 96.4 | 77.8 | 65.8 |

[1] Preliminary. [2] New reporting method beginning January 1995. *Source: American Bureau of Metal Statistics*

## Refined Copper Stocks Outside the U.S.A.   In Thousands of Short Tons (Recoverable Copper Content)

| Year | Jan. 1 | Feb. 1 | Mar. 1 | Apr. 1 | May 1 | June 1 | July 1 | Aug. 1 | Sept. 1 | Oct. 1 | Nov. 1 | Dec. 1 |
|---|---|---|---|---|---|---|---|---|---|---|---|---|
| 1981 | 476.2 | 485.2 | 471.0 | 463.0 | 458.8 | 449.8 | 446.0 | 454.9 | 454.7 | 433.4 | 419.4 | 403.0 |
| 1982 | 432.5 | 466.3 | 448.4 | 459.6 | 452.0 | 458.7 | 479.3 | 492.0 | 503.6 | 522.7 | 575.1 | 642.9 |
| 1983 | 699.9 | 760.8 | 766.4 | 759.1 | 795.5 | 780.0 | 722.2 | 683.0 | 757.4 | 767.2 | 765.2 | 810.4 |
| 1984 | 832.8 | 817.5 | 730.0 | 653.0 | 618.5 | 519.3 | 551.9 | 526.5 | 516.0 | 493.9 | 483.9 | 430.0 |
| 1985 | 425.0 | 420.7 | 385.7 | 361.9 | 364.6 | 380.4 | 368.8 | 464.0 | 546.7 | 558.4 | 533.6 | 486.6 |
| 1986 | 502.8 | 501.5 | 451.8 | 435.7 | 422.6 | 418.7 | 396.8 | 430.4 | 455.1 | 455.4 | 458.5 | 464.8 |
| 1987 | 473.7 | 467.5 | 410.5 | 397.5 | 387.4 | 348.5 | 337.8 | 336.8 | 341.1 | 314.7 | 254.9 | 269.6 |
| 1988 | 260.9 | 292.1 | 301.1 | 290.2 | 277.4 | 317.9 | 329.9 | 374.7 | 348.7 | 310.9 | 282.8 | 272.2 |
| 1989 | 337.5 | 325.7 | 341.0 | 350.3 | 406.5 | 385.7 | 374.2 | 389.8 | 335.8 | 368.7 | 348.1 | 358.3 |
| 1990 | 362.3 | 382.0 | 335.6 | 320.0 | 332.6 | 356.3 | 291.8 | 370.9 | 417.9 | 484.6 | 483.0 | 447.6 |
| 1991 | 439.5 | 464.2 | 447.1 | 501.1 | 559.5 | 595.4 | 593.1 | 605.4 | 664.7 | 653.5 | 644.9 | 676.9 |
| 1992 | 640.4 | 718.1 | 704.2 | 715.7 | 714.9 | 723.2 | 726.4 | 737.9 | 816.5 | 822.5 | 873.8 | 896.1 |
| 1993 | 757.1 | 765.9 | 789.6 | 817.2 | 885.1 | 912.2 | 910.4 | 943.8 | 1,040.3 | 1,124.3 | 1,133.9 | 1,106.1 |
| 1994 | 1,075.0 | 1,095.5 | 1,046.8 | 984.9 | 913.7 | 859.5 | 843.7 | 839.7 | 874.6 | 870.7 | 835.1 | 818.4 |
| 1995[2] | 506.8 | 516.9 | 483.3 | 439.0 | 398.1 | 386.8 | 356.0 | 325.8 | 326.8 | 328.8 | 342.5 | 364.6 |
| 1996[1] | 421.3 | 427.1 | 413.6 | 378.6 | 359.8 | 425.0 | 369.1 | 337.7 | 404.1 | 360.9 | 254.9 | 232.1 |

[1] Preliminary. [2] New reporting method beginning January 1995. *Source: American Bureau of Metal Statistics*

## Refined Copper Production in the U.S.A. In Thousands of Short Tons (Recoverable Copper Content)

| Year | Refined | | | | | | | | | | | | Crude |
|---|---|---|---|---|---|---|---|---|---|---|---|---|---|
| | Jan. | Feb. | Mar. | Apr. | May | June | July | Aug. | Sept. | Oct. | Nov. | Dec. | Total | |
| 1986 | 109.5 | 98.3 | 103.5 | 115.0 | 122.4 | 112.1 | 109.3 | 108.9 | 106.7 | 114.4 | 116.6 | 138.1 | 1,355 | 1,323 |
| 1987 | 118.0 | 110.5 | 105.4 | 127.7 | 118.5 | 95.5 | 107.7 | 106.4 | 121.8 | 131.3 | 123.3 | 127.7 | 1,394 | 1,308 |
| 1988 | 124.5 | 127.2 | 145.6 | 122.5 | 133.7 | 116.7 | 112.7 | 146.0 | 133.8 | 121.1 | 137.7 | 131.8 | 1,553 | 1,527 |
| 1989 | 129.5 | 128.1 | 137.2 | 118.3 | 132.2 | 142.6 | 121.3 | 150.8 | 116.5 | 137.0 | 127.4 | 130.7 | 1,572 | 1,555 |
| 1990 | 136.0 | 122.0 | 150.4 | 140.1 | 147.5 | 136.1 | 125.5 | 132.5 | 130.1 | 141.6 | 141.0 | 125.5 | 1,628 | 1,630 |
| 1991 | 129.0 | 127.7 | 134.9 | 119.7 | 137.1 | 124.8 | 136.8 | 142.7 | 135.6 | 153.1 | 141.0 | 149.7 | 1,632 | 1,393 |
| 1992 | 139.9 | 135.6 | 150.6 | 142.8 | 123.0 | 138.5 | 140.3 | 150.1 | 146.9 | 155.3 | 156.8 | 153.7 | 1,734 | 1,503 |
| 1993 | 153.9 | 153.8 | 173.2 | 166.0 | 160.3 | 177.0 | 151.4 | 153.7 | 160.2 | 157.3 | 157.2 | 166.2 | 1,930 | 1,269 |
| 1994 | 160.9 | 150.0 | 167.8 | 157.2 | 165.5 | 160.4 | 148.9 | 165.6 | 162.1 | 157.3 | 153.3 | 159.8 | 1,909 | 1,473 |
| 1995[2] | 202.7 | 185.5 | 204.8 | 194.6 | 210.0 | 198.3 | 193.8 | 208.8 | 199.0 | 206.5 | 211.3 | 208.1 | 2,423 | 1,572 |
| 1996[1] | 210.8 | 197.6 | 207.3 | 209.0 | 212.7 | 191.6 | 204.1 | 196.7 | 196.9 | 223.1 | 199.3 | 212.0 | 2,461 | |

[1] Preliminary. [2] New Reporting method beginning January 1995. *Source: American Bureau of Metal Statistics*

## Refined Copper Production Outside the U.S.A. In Thousands of Short Tons (Recoverable Copper Content)

| Year | Refined | | | | | | | | | | | | | Crude |
|---|---|---|---|---|---|---|---|---|---|---|---|---|---|---|
| | Jan. | Feb. | Mar. | Apr. | May | June | July | Aug. | Sept. | Oct. | Nov. | Dec. | Total | |
| 1986 | 366.5 | 351.5 | 401.7 | 409.7 | 373.1 | 361.2 | 361.7 | 374.8 | 400.3 | 407.4 | 396.4 | 403.6 | 4,608 | 5,132 |
| 1987 | 385.8 | 375.4 | 410.6 | 412.2 | 399.9 | 403.6 | 393.3 | 370.6 | 391.2 | 402.7 | 402.5 | 407.5 | 4,755 | 5,233 |
| 1988 | 397.7 | 387.8 | 434.2 | 370.6 | 389.4 | 391.5 | 366.6 | 386.9 | 365.9 | 412.8 | 417.0 | 414.9 | 4,735 | 5,210 |
| 1989 | 387.8 | 372.7 | 411.9 | 404.3 | 430.1 | 388.7 | 409.5 | 413.5 | 421.7 | 436.1 | 434.0 | 402.7 | 4,913 | 5,439 |
| 1990 | 423.7 | 396.7 | 424.6 | 412.8 | 414.1 | 395.6 | 372.6 | 407.1 | 404.6 | 422.6 | 417.4 | 411.0 | 4,902 | 5,278 |
| 1991 | 416.5 | 381.1 | 427.7 | 405.5 | 425.3 | 404.5 | 375.1 | 378.7 | 411.4 | 411.8 | 409.2 | 424.5 | 4,871 | 5,533 |
| 1992 | 441.2 | 412.6 | 447.0 | 418.0 | 438.7 | 449.5 | 418.5 | 425.8 | 418.7 | 438.9 | 431.3 | 426.1 | 5,166 | 5,730 |
| 1993 | 429.2 | 405.6 | 475.1 | 426.2 | 440.9 | 447.5 | 421.6 | 449.4 | 448.0 | 425.9 | 447.2 | 436.5 | 5,253 | 5,378 |
| 1994 | 432.5 | 390.8 | 432.7 | 400.6 | 432.9 | 421.1 | 387.8 | 413.8 | 421.5 | 416.3 | 437.4 | 428.8 | 5,016 | 5,970 |
| 1995[2] | 817.5 | 797.6 | 868.4 | 858.2 | 859.4 | 844.8 | 849.7 | 825.7 | 819.8 | 865.2 | 833.8 | 872.2 | 10,112 | 6,410 |
| 1996[1] | 903.2 | 869.3 | 929.3 | 922.2 | 916.3 | 918.3 | 908.3 | 929.3 | 931.7 | 972.4 | 944.1 | 948.4 | 11,093 | |

[1] Preliminary. [2] New Reporting method beginning January 1995. *Source: American Bureau of Metal Statistics*

## Refined Copper Deliveries to Fabricators in the U.S.A. In Thousands of Short Tons[2]

| Year | Jan. | Feb. | Mar. | Apr. | May | June | July | Aug. | Sept. | Oct. | Nov. | Dec. | Total |
|---|---|---|---|---|---|---|---|---|---|---|---|---|---|
| 1986 | 123.8 | 120.1 | 150.5 | 155.3 | 164.5 | 131.5 | 113.1 | 127.1 | 106.7 | 141.1 | 114.7 | 128.4 | 1,631 |
| 1987 | 160.2 | 138.7 | 166.9 | 152.3 | 165.6 | 152.3 | 131.6 | 127.2 | 121.8 | 188.3 | 192.7 | 168.2 | 1,885 |
| 1988 | 152.0 | 151.5 | 162.5 | 149.6 | 150.1 | 161.2 | 116.5 | 164.7 | 133.8 | 148.2 | 159.1 | 139.0 | 1,824 |
| 1989 | 127.8 | 147.7 | 148.4 | 141.1 | 153.2 | 168.4 | 131.4 | 173.2 | 116.5 | 156.8 | 149.2 | 121.9 | 1,781 |
| 1990 | 167.4 | 132.8 | 163.3 | 156.6 | 153.3 | 144.5 | 129.5 | 132.5 | 130.1 | 140.9 | 130.7 | 108.6 | 1,733 |
| 1991 | 128.4 | 153.3 | 125.3 | 126.7 | 152.7 | 115.0 | 125.4 | 152.8 | 135.6 | 167.7 | 130.4 | 132.9 | 1,684 |
| 1992 | 144.9 | 159.0 | 165.9 | 155.5 | 149.4 | 161.4 | 145.8 | 144.1 | 146.9 | 150.4 | 166.2 | 130.0 | 1,813 |
| 1993 | 142.9 | 165.3 | 201.6 | 170.4 | 162.5 | 209.6 | 144.8 | 191.4 | 178.9 | 164.3 | 194.8 | 182.7 | 2,109 |
| 1994 | 193.3 | 168.6 | 204.6 | 178.3 | 187.8 | 171.9 | 154.3 | 194.6 | 188.2 | 188.7 | 167.5 | 175.1 | 2,173 |
| 1995[3] | 233.8 | 209.2 | 239.1 | 200.9 | 230.0 | 210.5 | 187.1 | 208.8 | 202.9 | 224.7 | 222.4 | 175.6 | 2,545 |
| 1996[1] | 221.6 | 227.2 | 240.0 | 240.0 | 269.5 | 220.7 | 232.1 | 243.7 | 246.6 | 264.3 | 253.9 | 207.3 | 2,867 |

[1] Preliminary. [2] Recoverable copper content. [3] New reporting method beginning January 1995. *Source: American Bureau of Metal Statistics*

## Refined Copper Deliveries to Fabricators Outside the U.S.A. In Thousands of Short Tons[2]

| Year | Jan. | Feb. | Mar. | Apr. | May | June | July | Aug. | Sept. | Oct. | Nov. | Dec. | Total |
|---|---|---|---|---|---|---|---|---|---|---|---|---|---|
| 1986 | 364.5 | 396.9 | 403.4 | 403.2 | 375.6 | 387.9 | 331.0 | 334.1 | 376.2 | 384.9 | 380.9 | 380.8 | 4,519 |
| 1987 | 386.0 | 413.0 | 413.9 | 406.8 | 426.7 | 401.8 | 384.1 | 359.4 | 416.4 | 468.8 | 377.1 | 396.8 | 4,851 |
| 1988 | 359.6 | 375.2 | 448.7 | 385.1 | 366.8 | 403.2 | 340.9 | 405.9 | 401.8 | 437.4 | 455.6 | 356.6 | 4,737 |
| 1989 | 426.0 | 369.9 | 411.8 | 360.9 | 459.0 | 398.0 | 386.8 | 464.2 | 393.2 | 456.9 | 423.0 | 399.1 | 4,949 |
| 1990 | 419.9 | 466.3 | 436.7 | 392.9 | 408.3 | 466.7 | 303.7 | 373.5 | 370.8 | 448.9 | 469.1 | 420.7 | 4,972 |
| 1991 | 405.0 | 404.4 | 391.5 | 361.2 | 406.3 | 433.5 | 368.5 | 323.4 | 420.7 | 499.1 | 391.4 | 483.4 | 4,807 |
| 1992 | 453.7 | 408.9 | 441.8 | 416.4 | 413.4 | 432.4 | 410.4 | 364.7 | 432.6 | 403.5 | 406.1 | 461.3 | 5,045 |
| 1993 | 427.9 | 392.9 | 452.3 | 361.7 | 422.2 | 442.6 | 384.4 | 347.9 | 387.5 | 414.8 | 463.4 | 458.5 | 4,956 |
| 1994 | 399.8 | 429.5 | 481.2 | 466.5 | 468.9 | 428.1 | 387.9 | 369.2 | 423.5 | 448.9 | 457.1 | 436.0 | 5,197 |
| 1995[3] | 792.6 | 810.1 | 892.8 | 882.2 | 852.9 | 867.4 | 863.7 | 814.1 | 803.4 | 835.1 | 796.6 | 726.3 | 9,937 |
| 1996[1] | 875.2 | 859.3 | 933.9 | 906.9 | 812.7 | 950.2 | 908.3 | 817.2 | 933.4 | 1,055.8 | 924.3 | 903.7 | 10,881 |

[1] Preliminary. [2] Recoverable copper content. [3] New reporting method beginning January 1995. *Source: American Bureau of Metal Statistics*

# Corn

The 1996/97 U.S. corn crop of 9.27 billion bushels, the third largest on record, topped by 26 percent the 1995/96 crop of 7.4 billion bushels. The record high 10.1 billion bushel crop was realized in 1994/95. Both harvested acreage and average yield jumped in 1996; acreage of 73.2 million acres was the highest since 1985 and compared with 65 million acres in 1995, while yield of 123 bushels per acre was up from 113.5 bushels in 1995. In the key producing midwestern states a record ear count per acre was realized, helping boost the final overall crop from initial spring estimates of 8.8 billion bushels. Due to the large crop, and moderate dip in 1996/97 exports from initial forecasts, the carryover as of August 31, 1997 was expected to top 1 billion bushels, vs. the year earlier carryin of 426 million, although still well below the 1994/95 carryover of 1.56 billion bushels. The stock-to-use ratio in 1996/97 was forecast at about 10.6 percent vs. the previous season's very low 5 percent.

The 1996/97 supply/demand imbalance was quickly manifested in futures values as prices declined $1.00 per bushel during the second half of calendar 1996, from $3.60/bushel in mid-summer to almost $2.60 at yearend. Although the price weakness was in part seasonal, the magnitude of the break largely reflected the anticipated buildup in carryover. In 1996/97, the average price received by farmers was initially forecast to range between $3.00-3.40 per bushel vs. the 1995/96 average of a record high $3.24, but as the crop's size increased the average farm price was lowered to a range of $2.80-3.20 which, if realized, would still be the second highest average of the 1990s.

Corn is far and away the leading U.S. feed grain with 4.9 billion bushels to be so used in 1996/97 vs. 4.7 billion in 1995/96, and the 1994/95 record high 5.5 billion. Food, seed, and industrial usage (FSI) was estimated at 1.7 billion bushels, marginally higher than in 1995/96, but still below the record 1.7 billion used in 1994/95. The relative steadiness in FSI use during the past few years is somewhat surprising considering that industrial demand for corn as a fuel alcohol and sweetener (High Fructose corn syrup, HFCS) was expected to quicken. Cost factors, however, have apparently placed an indefinite hold some new ethanol producing plants.

The U.S. is the world's largest corn exporter with Argentina a distant second. Importers are numerous, but the leaders are generally in Asia, paced by Japan, South Korea, and Taiwan. 1996/97 U.S. exports of 1.95 billion bushels compares with 2.2 billion in 1995/96, with Japan the primary destination. U.S. corn imports are minimal, on average about 15 million bushels. World foreign trade in corn in 1996/97 of 62 million metric tons compares with 65 million in 1995/96, of which the U.S. accounted for about 80 percent in both years. Argentina exported about 10 percent of the world total. Japan's import needs have hovered around 16 million tons for some time, but Mexico's needs have climbed and are forecast at 4 million tons in 1996/97. Chinese imports have varied widely in the 1990s; from nothing early in the decade, to 4.3 million tons in 1994/95, and back to a half million tons in 1996/97.

The record 1996/97 world corn production of 563 million tons compares with 514 million in 1995/96, with the U.S. accounting for much of the gain. China, since 1987/88 the second largest grower, produced a record 117 million tons in 1996/97 vs. 112 million in 1995/96. The U.S. and China together produced 61 percent of the world's corn in 1996/97; Brazil and Mexico combined to produce 10 percent. The gains in China's production so far in the 1990s reflects increases in per capita income and meat consumption, resulting in the need for more corn as a livestock feed. Global usage in 1996/97 of a record 552 million tons compares with the previous high of 543 million in 1995/96. China's use of 117 million tons places them second in overall usage and compares with 110 million in 1995/96, the first year that China's use topped 100 million tons. The U.S. is the world's largest consumer with almost a third of the total, 168 million tons in 1996/97. Brazil is in third place with about 37 million tons. World corn stocks are forecast to increase in 1996/97 by at least 10 million tons, ending the season near 73 million tons.

U.S. #2 yellow corn prices vary by location. Typically, Gulf port prices are about $0.30 per bushel higher than prices in Central Illinois, while quotes at St. Louis run about $0.10-0.12 higher than Illinois prices. In late 1996, #2 yellow corn in Central Illinois was trading around $2.60/bushel, down about $0.70 from a year earlier.

***Futures Markets***

Corn futures are traded on the Beijing Commodity Exchange (BCE), the Budapest Commodity Exchange, the Tokyo Grain Exchange (TGE), the Chicago Board of Trade (CBOT), and the Mid-American Commodity Exchange (MidAm). Corn options are traded on the CBOT and the MidAm.

The CBOT also trades Iowa Corn Yield Insurance futures and options. Trading in U.S. corn yield insurance futures and options for other key producing states was pending in late 1996.

## World Production of Corn or Maize In Thousands of Metric Tons

| Crop Year | Argentina | Brazil | Canada | China | France | Hungry | India | Indo-nesia | Italy | Mexico | Romania | South Africa | Ukraine[4] | United States | Yugo-slavia | World Total |
|---|---|---|---|---|---|---|---|---|---|---|---|---|---|---|---|---|
| 1982-3 | 9,000 | 19,500 | 6,513 | 60,295 | 10,400 | 7,800 | 6,594 | 3,235 | 6,847 | 7,000 | 12,620 | 4,083 | 13,500 | 209,181 | 11,126 | 438,354 |
| 1983-4 | 9,200 | 21,000 | 5,933 | 68,210 | 10,400 | 6,426 | 7,922 | 5,087 | 6,669 | 9,300 | 11,982 | 4,405 | 12,000 | 106,042 | 10,719 | 345,817 |
| 1984-5 | 11,500 | 22,000 | 7,024 | 73,410 | 10,384 | 6,686 | 8,356 | 5,288 | 6,776 | 9,900 | 13,274 | 7,755 | 12,500 | 194,929 | 11,293 | 456,959 |
| 1985-6 | 12,400 | 21,000 | 6,970 | 63,830 | 12,567 | 8,818 | 6,643 | 4,330 | 6,357 | 10,500 | 11,000 | 8,078 | 14,400 | 225,479 | 9,896 | 479,797 |
| 1986-7 | 9,250 | 26,500 | 5,912 | 70,856 | 11,470 | 7,261 | 7,457 | 5,000 | 6,401 | 10,000 | 15,000 | 7,150 | 12,479 | 209,556 | 12,526 | 477,912 |
| 1987-8 | 9,000 | 24,790 | 7,015 | 79,150 | 12,454 | 7,234 | 5,721 | 4,800 | 5,762 | 9,900 | 10,500 | 7,075 | 14,808 | 181,143 | 8,863 | 448,762 |
| 1988-9 | 5,000 | 26,050 | 5,369 | 77,350 | 14,578 | 6,028 | 8,229 | 5,200 | 6,318 | 10,100 | 10,000 | 12,384 | 16,030 | 125,194 | 7,697 | 401,962 |
| 1989-90 | 5,200 | 22,300 | 6,571 | 78,928 | 13,400 | 6,747 | 9,409 | 5,000 | 6,359 | 9,750 | 6,760 | 8,900 | 7,026 | 191,156 | 9,415 | 460,484 |
| 1990-1 | 7,600 | 24,330 | 7,067 | 96,820 | 9,500 | 4,317 | 8,962 | 5,000 | 5,864 | 14,100 | 6,800 | 8,300 | 4,737 | 201,534 | 6,724 | 477,855 |
| 1991-2 | 10,600 | 30,800 | 7,413 | 98,770 | 12,930 | 7,745 | 8,060 | 5,400 | 6,240 | 14,689 | 10,500 | 3,125 | 4,747 | 189,868 | 11,500 | 487,307 |
| 1992-3 | 10,200 | 29,200 | 4,883 | 95,380 | 14,870 | 4,301 | 9,992 | 5,650 | 7,410 | 18,631 | 6,829 | 9,990 | 2,851 | 240,719 | 6,650 | 538,552 |
| 1993-4 | 10,000 | 32,934 | 6,501 | 102,700 | 14,840 | 4,012 | 9,600 | 5,400 | 8,030 | 19,141 | 8,000 | 13,275 | 3,786 | 160,954 | 5,912 | 475,471 |
| 1994-5[1] | 11,100 | 37,440 | 7,043 | 99,280 | 12,640 | 4,300 | 9,120 | 5,500 | 7,480 | 17,005 | 8,500 | 4,845 | 1,537 | 256,621 | 7,500 | 560,225 |
| 1995-6[2] | 10,700 | 32,480 | 7,271 | 112,000 | 12,500 | 4,600 | 9,800 | 6,200 | 8,500 | 16,000 | 9,923 | 10,200 | 3,392 | 187,305 | 8,300 | 514,069 |
| 1996-7[3] | 13,500 | 34,000 | 7,200 | 117,000 | NA | 5,600 | 10,000 | 6,000 | NA | 17,500 | 9,500 | 9,500 | 820 | 236,064 | 8,200 | 573,154 |

[1] Preliminary. [2] Estimate. [3] Forecast. [4] Formerly part of the U.S.S.R.; data not reported separately until 1989.
*Source: Foreign Agricultural Service, U.S. Department of Agriculture*

## World Course Grains Supply & Demand In Millions of Metric Tons/Hectares

| Crop Year Beginning Oct. 1 | Area Harvested | Yield | Pro-duction | World Trade | Total Con-sumption | Ending Stocks | Stocks as % of Consump-tion[3] |
|---|---|---|---|---|---|---|---|
| 1982-3 | 337.8 | 2.29 | 775.2 | 89.8 | 744.0 | 182.3 | 24.5 |
| 1983-4 | 332.7 | 2.04 | 677.5 | 93.1 | 748.8 | 111.1 | 14.8 |
| 1984-5 | 334.3 | 2.41 | 806.2 | 100.0 | 772.5 | 144.7 | 18.7 |
| 1985-6 | 339.8 | 2.45 | 832.8 | 82.7 | 768.3 | 209.3 | 27.3 |
| 1986-7 | 336.0 | 2.45 | 823.1 | 82.9 | 797.2 | 235.2 | 29.5 |
| 1987-8 | 323.2 | 2.43 | 784.7 | 89.6 | 808.0 | 212.0 | 26.2 |
| 1988-9 | 323.1 | 2.23 | 720.8 | 98.0 | 786.2 | 146.6 | 18.7 |
| 1989-90 | 320.8 | 2.47 | 791.1 | 104.5 | 815.4 | 122.3 | 15.0 |
| 1990-1 | 315.1 | 2.62 | 826.5 | 89.5 | 814.3 | 134.5 | 16.5 |
| 1991-2 | 320.4 | 2.52 | 808.4 | 96.0 | 808.4 | 134.5 | 16.6 |
| 1992-3 | 322.0 | 2.70 | 869.1 | 91.7 | 840.8 | 162.7 | 19.4 |
| 1993-4 | 315.7 | 2.53 | 798.0 | 85.6 | 837.5 | 123.2 | 14.7 |
| 1994-5 | 320.3 | 2.71 | 869.4 | 97.0 | 858.3 | 134.3 | 15.6 |
| 1995-6[1] | 310.5 | 2.56 | 795.8 | 88.6 | 839.4 | 90.7 | 10.8 |
| 1996-7[2] | 317.3 | 2.79 | 884.7 | 88.3 | 866.8 | 108.5 | 12.5 |

[1] Preliminary. [2] Estimate. [3] Represents the ratio of marketing year ending stocks to total consumption. *Source: Foreign Agricultural Service, U.S. Department of Agriculture*

## Acreage and Supply of Corn in the United States In Millions of Bushels

| Crop Year Beginning Sept. 1[3] | Planted | Harvested: For Grain | Harvested: For Silage | Yield Per Harvested Acre | Carry-over, Sept. 1: On Farms[3] | Carry-over, Sept. 1: Off Farms[3] | Supply: Beginning Stocks | Supply: Pro-duction | Supply: Imports | Supply: Total Supply |
|---|---|---|---|---|---|---|---|---|---|---|
| | In Thousands of Acres | | | Bushels | | | | | | |
| 1985-6 | 83,398 | 75,209 | 7,155 | 118.0 | 678.9 | 701.8 | 1,648 | 8,875 | 11 | 10,534 |
| 1986-7 | 76,580 | 68,907 | 6,418 | 119.4 | NA | NA | 4,040 | 8,226 | 2 | 12,267 |
| 1987-8 | 66,200 | 59,505 | 5,994 | 119.8 | 2,284.5 | 2,597.2 | 4,882 | 7,131 | 3 | 12,016 |
| 1988-9 | 67,717 | 58,250 | 8,294 | 84.6 | 2,002.8 | 2,256.3 | 4,259 | 4,929 | 3 | 9,191 |
| 1989-90 | 72,322 | 64,783 | 6,606 | 116.3 | 967.5 | 962.9 | 1,930 | 7,525 | 2 | 9,458 |
| 1990-1 | 74,166 | 66,952 | 6,124 | 118.5 | 754.8 | 589.7 | 1,344 | 7,934 | 3 | 9,282 |
| 1991-2 | 75,957 | 68,822 | 6,101 | 108.6 | 691.2 | 830.0 | 1,521 | 7,475 | 20 | 9,016 |
| 1992-3 | 79,311 | 72,077 | 6,069 | 131.5 | 605.0 | 494.8 | 1,100 | 9,477 | 7 | 10,584 |
| 1993-4 | 73,235 | 62,921 | 6,831 | 100.7 | 1,070.7 | 1,042.0 | 2,113 | 6,336 | 21 | 8,470 |
| 1994-5 | 79,175 | 72,887 | 5,601 | 138.6 | 395.4 | 454.7 | 850 | 10,103 | 10 | 10,962 |
| 1995-6[1] | 71,245 | 64,995 | 5,295 | 113.5 | 740.9 | 816.9 | 1,558 | 7,374 | 16 | 8,948 |
| 1996-7[2] | 79,487 | 73,147 | 5,395 | 127.1 | 196.6 | 229.3 | 426 | 9,293 | 10 | 9,729 |

[1] Preliminary. [2] Estimate. [3] Data prior to 1986-87 are as of October 1. NA = Not available. *Source: Economic Research Service, U.S. Department of Agriculture*

# CORN

## U.S. Corn Supply and Disappearance In Millions of Bushels

| Crop Year Beginning Sept. 1 | Supply: Beginning Stocks | Supply: Production | Supply: Imports | Supply: Total Supply | Disappearance – Domestic Use: Food, Alcohol & Industrial | Disappearance – Domestic Use: Seed | Disappearance – Domestic Use: Feed & Residual | Disappearance – Domestic Use: Total | Disappearance: Exports | Disappearance: Total Disappearance | Ending Stocks: Gov't Owned[3] | Ending Stocks: Privately Owned[4] | Ending Stocks: Total |
|---|---|---|---|---|---|---|---|---|---|---|---|---|---|
| 1993-4 | 2,113 | 6,337 | 20.8 | 8,470 | 1,591 | 20.1 | 4,700 | 6,311 | 1,328 | 7,620 | 45 | 805 | 850 |
| Sept.-Nov. | 2,113 | 6,337 | 5.2 | 8,455 | 380 | 0 | 1,703 | 2,083 | 435 | 2,518 | 53 | 5,884 | 5,937 |
| Dec.-Feb. | 5,937 | ------ | 8.0 | 5,945 | 376 | 0 | 1,243 | 1,619 | 330 | 1,949 | 50 | 3,946 | 3,996 |
| Mar.-May | 3,996 | ------ | 6.3 | 4,002 | 418 | 19.5 | 955 | 1,372 | 270 | 1,642 | 48 | 2,312 | 2,360 |
| June-Aug. | 2,360 | ------ | 1.4 | 2,361 | 418 | .6 | 800 | 1,218 | 293 | 1,511 | 45 | 805 | 850 |
| 1994-5[1] | 850 | 10,103 | 9.6 | 10,962 | 1,690 | 18.4 | 5,537 | 7,227 | 2,177 | 9,405 | 42 | 1,516 | 1,558 |
| Sept.-Nov. | 850 | 10,103 | 2.1 | 10,955 | 406 | 0 | 2,019 | 2,425 | 449 | 2,874 | 55 | 8,026 | 8,080 |
| Dec.-Feb. | 8,080 | ------ | 3.7 | 8,084 | 406 | 0 | 1,497 | 1,903 | 590 | 2,493 | 50 | 5,542 | 5,592 |
| Mar.-May | 5,592 | ------ | 3.0 | 5,595 | 445 | 16.0 | 1,167 | 1,628 | 568 | 2,180 | 50 | 3,365 | 3,415 |
| June-Aug. | 3,415 | ------ | 1.0 | 3,416 | 434 | 2.4 | 854 | 1,290 | 570 | 1,858 | 42 | 1,516 | 1,558 |
| 1995-6[2] | 1,558 | 7,374 | 16.0 | 8,948 | 1,583 | 20.2 | 4,711 | 6,314 | 2,228 | 8,522 | 42 | 575 | 426 |
| Sept.-Nov. | 1,558 | 7,374 | 4.0 | 8,935 | 409 | 0 | 1,760 | 2,169 | 660 | 2,830 | | | 6,106 |
| Dec.-Feb. | 6,106 | ------ | 5.0 | 6,111 | 397 | | 1,352 | 1,749 | 562 | 2,311 | | | 3,800 |
| Mar.-May | 3,800 | ------ | 5.0 | 3,805 | 411 | | 1,066 | 1,477 | 610 | 2,087 | | | 1,718 |
| June-Aug. | 1,718 | ------ | 3.0 | 1,721 | 366 | | 533 | 899 | 396 | 1,295 | | | 426 |
| 1996-7[2] | 426 | 9,293 | 10.0 | 9,729 | 1,670 | | 5,200 | 6,870 | 1,900 | 8,770 | | | 959 |
| Sept.-Nov. | 426 | 9,293 | 4.0 | 9,723 | 383 | | 1,964 | 2,347 | 470 | 2,817 | | | 6,906 |

[1] Preliminary. [2] Estimate. [3] Uncommitted inventory. [4] Includes quantity under loan and farmer-owned reserves. *Source: Economic Research Service, U.S. Department of Agriculture*

## Corn Production Estimates and Cash Prices in the U.S.

| Crop Year | Corn for Grain Production Estimates (In Thousands of Bushels): Aug. 1 | Sept. 1 | Oct. 1 | Nov. 1 | Final | St. Louis No. 2 Yellow (Dollar Per Bushel) | Omaha No. 2 Yellow | Gulf Ports No. 2 Yellow | Kansas City No. 2 White | Chicago No. 2 Yellow | Average Farm Price[2] | Value of Production (Million Dollars) |
|---|---|---|---|---|---|---|---|---|---|---|---|---|
| 1991-2 | 7,474,480 | 7,295,071 | 7,479,421 | 7,485,901 | 7,475,480 | 2.53 | 2.36 | 2.74 | 3.06 | 2.52 | 2.37 | 17,864 |
| 1992-3 | 8,762,060 | 7,873,436 | 8,592,821 | 9,328,850 | 9,476,698 | 2.25 | 2.10 | 2.46 | 2.49 | 2.22 | 2.07 | 19,723 |
| 1993-4 | 7,423,142 | 7,229,427 | 6,961,902 | 6,503,237 | 6,336,470 | 2.67 | 2.56 | 2.85 | NA | 2.68 | 2.50 | 16,032 |
| 1994-5 | 9,214,420 | 9,257,170 | 9,602,340 | 10,010,310 | 10,102,735 | 2.51 | 2.33 | 2.78 | NA | 2.43 | 2.26 | 22,992 |
| 1995-6[1] | 8,121,520 | 7,832,140 | 7,541,400 | 7,373,700 | 7,373,876 | | | | | | 2.95-3.35 | 24,118 |
| 1996-7[1] | 8,694,628 | 8,803,928 | 9,012,148 | 9,265,288 | 9,293,435 | | | | | | | 24,853 |

[1] Preliminary. [2] Season-average price based on monthly weighted by monthly marketings. *Source: Economic Research Service, U.S. Department of Agriculture*

## Production of Corn (for Grain) in the United States In Millions of Bushels

| Year | Colorado | Illinois | Indiana | Iowa | Kansas | Michigan | Minnesota | Missouri | Nebraska | Ohio | Pennsylvania | South Dakota | Texas | Wisconsin |
|---|---|---|---|---|---|---|---|---|---|---|---|---|---|---|
| 1990 | 128.7 | 1,320.8 | 703.1 | 1,562.4 | 188.5 | 238.1 | 762.6 | 205.8 | 934.4 | 417.5 | 109.6 | 234.0 | 130.5 | 354.0 |
| 1991 | 128.5 | 1,177.0 | 510.6 | 1,427.4 | 206.3 | 253.0 | 720.0 | 213.4 | 999.6 | 326.4 | 68.4 | 240.5 | 165.0 | 380.8 |
| 1992 | 130.2 | 1,646.5 | 877.6 | 1,903.7 | 259.5 | 241.5 | 741.0 | 324.0 | 1,066.5 | 507.7 | 118.8 | 277.2 | 202.5 | 306.8 |
| 1993 | 106.8 | 1,300.0 | 712.8 | 880.0 | 216.0 | 225.5 | 322.0 | 166.5 | 785.2 | 360.8 | 93.1 | 160.7 | 212.8 | 216.2 |
| 1994 | 133.5 | 1,786.2 | 858.2 | 1,930.4 | 304.6 | 260.9 | 915.9 | 273.7 | 1,153.7 | 486.5 | 123.6 | 367.2 | 238.7 | 437.1 |
| 1995 | 92.1 | 1,130.0 | 598.9 | 1,402.2 | 244.3 | 249.6 | 731.9 | 149.9 | 854.7 | 375.1 | 94.1 | 193.6 | 216.6 | 347.7 |
| 1996[1] | 131.6 | 1,479.6 | 675.8 | 1,736.0 | 364.3 | 220.9 | 847.0 | 351.0 | 1,188.0 | 313.5 | 129.2 | 346.8 | 183.6 | 348.8 |

[1] Preliminary. *Source: National Agricultural Statistics Service, U.S. Department of Agriculture*

## Distribution of Corn in the United States In Millions of Bushels

| Year Crop Beginning Sept. 1 | Food, Seed and Industrial Use: HFCS | Glucose & Dextrose | Starch | Alcohol: Fuel | Alcohol: Beverage[3] | Seed | Cereal & Other Products | Total | Livestock Feed[4] | Exports (Including Grain Equiv. of Products) | Domestic Disappearance | Total Utilization |
|---|---|---|---|---|---|---|---|---|---|---|---|---|
| 1990-1 | 379 | 200 | 232 | 349 | 80 | 19 | 114 | 1,373 | 4,663 | 1,725 | 6,036 | 7,761 |
| 1991-2 | 392 | 210 | 237 | 398 | 81 | 20 | 116 | 1,454 | 4,878 | 1,584 | 6,332 | 7,916 |
| 1992-3 | 414 | 214 | 238 | 426 | 83 | 19 | 117 | 1,493 | 5,296 | 1,663 | 6,808 | 8,471 |
| 1993-4 | 444 | 223 | 223 | 458 | 106 | 20 | 118 | 1,571 | 4,704 | 1,328 | 6,292 | 7,620 |
| 1994-5[1] | 465 | 231 | 226 | 533 | 100 | 18 | 118 | 1,672 | 5,534 | 2,178 | 7,227 | 9,404 |
| 1995-6[2] | 482 | 237 | 219 | 396 | 110 | 20 | 118 | 1,563 | 4,575 | 2,050 | 6,275 | 8,325 |
| 1996-7[2] | 515 | 240 | 225 | 450 | 100 | | 120 | 1,650 | | | | |

[1] Preliminary. [2] Estimate. [3] Also includes nonfuel industrial alcohol. [4] Feed and waste (residual, mostly feed). *Source: Economic Research Service, U.S. Department of Agriculture*

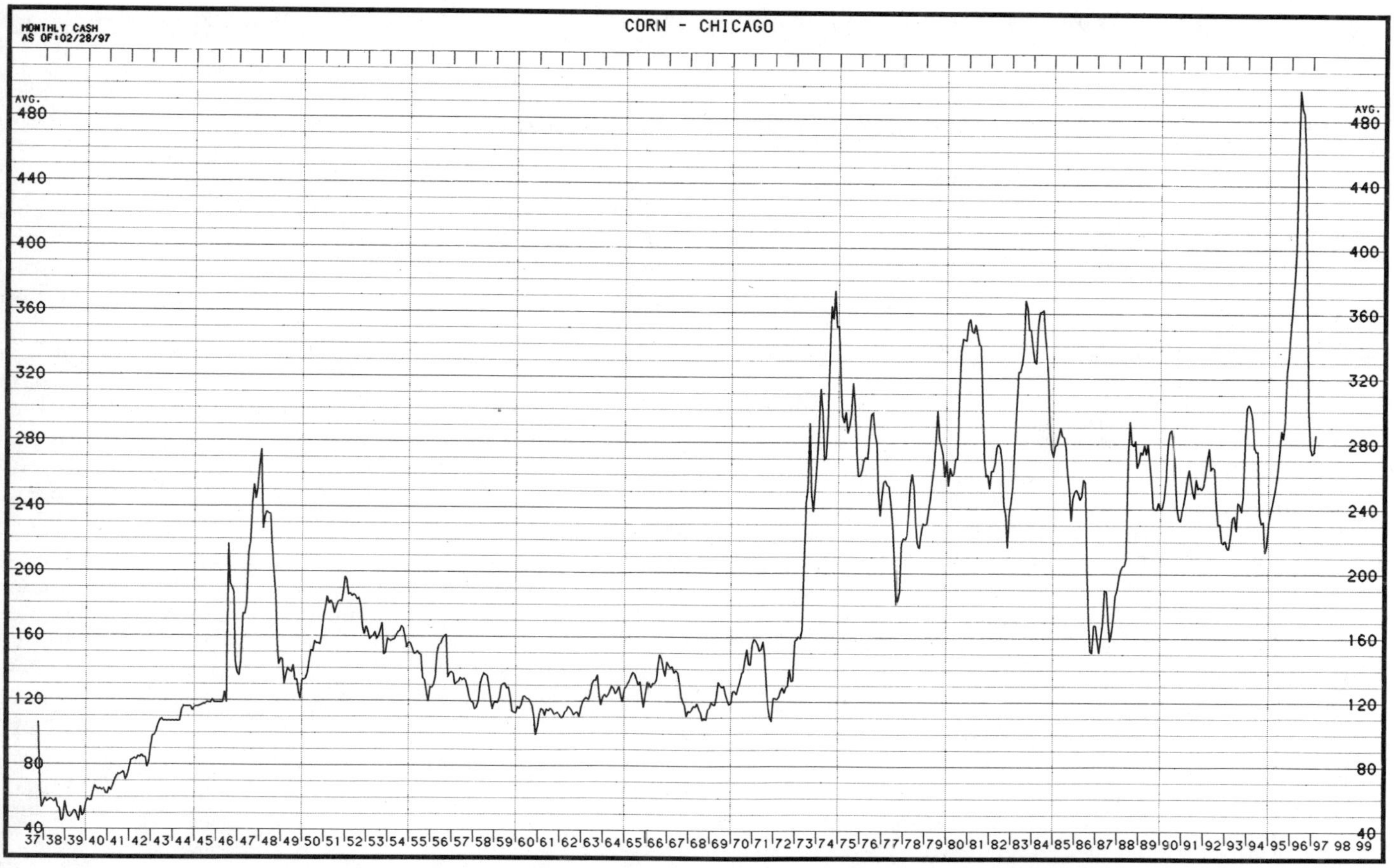


## Average Cash Price of Corn, No. 2 Yellow in Central Illinois[2] In Dollars Per Bushel

| Crop Year | Sept. | Oct. | Nov. | Dec. | Jan. | Feb. | Mar. | Apr. | May | June | July | Aug. | Average |
|---|---|---|---|---|---|---|---|---|---|---|---|---|---|
| 1985-6 | 2.28 | 2.10 | 2.32 | 2.38 | 2.36 | 2.33 | 2.29 | 2.31 | 2.42 | 2.41 | 1.93 | 1.52 | 2.22 |
| 1986-7 | 1.34 | 1.34 | 1.55 | 1.52 | 1.44 | 1.38 | 1.46 | 1.56 | 1.75 | 1.74 | 1.60 | 1.46 | 1.51 |
| 1987-8 | 1.50 | 1.64 | 1.74 | 1.78 | 1.84 | 1.90 | 1.92 | 1.92 | 1.97 | 2.66 | 2.85 | 2.70 | 2.04 |
| 1988-9 | 2.68 | 2.70 | 2.54 | 2.56 | 2.62 | 2.60 | 2.64 | 2.58 | 2.64 | 2.53 | 2.44 | 2.30 | 2.57 |
| 1989-90 | 2.35 | 2.25 | 2.29 | 2.29 | 2.29 | 2.34 | 2.44 | 2.64 | 2.73 | 2.70 | 2.68 | 2.54 | 2.46 |
| 1990-1 | 2.25 | 2.18 | 2.20 | 2.27 | 2.31 | 2.36 | 2.45 | 2.50 | 2.41 | 2.34 | 2.34 | 2.45 | 2.34 |
| 1991-2 | 2.39 | 2.41 | 2.41 | 2.42 | 2.49 | 2.58 | 2.64 | 2.50 | 2.51 | 2.51 | 2.31 | 2.17 | 2.45 |
| 1992-3 | 2.13 | 1.97 | 1.99 | 2.05 | 2.07 | 2.05 | 2.16 | 2.23 | 2.20 | 2.09 | 2.25 | 2.27 | 2.12 |
| 1993-4 | 2.22 | 2.27 | 2.63 | 2.81 | 2.89 | 2.83 | 2.76 | 2.61 | 2.58 | 2.61 | 2.19 | 2.13 | 2.54 |
| 1994-5 | 2.08 | 1.92 | 2.03 | 2.16 | 2.22 | 2.27 | 2.36 | 2.41 | 2.50 | 2.65 | 2.79 | 2.68 | 2.34 |
| 1995-6[1] | 2.83 | 3.12 | 3.22 | 3.36 | 3.53 | 3.71 | 3.92 | 4.47 | 4.86 | 4.74 | 4.70 | 4.48 | 3.91 |
| 1996-7[1] | 3.39 | 2.81 | 2.63 | 2.62 | 2.62 | | | | | | | | 2.81 |

[1] Preliminary. [2] Data prior to 1985-86 are for Omaha. *Source: Economic Research Service, U.S. Department of Agriculture*

## Average Cash Price of Corn, No. 2 Yellow at Gulf Ports[2] In Dollars Per Bushel

| Crop Year | Sept. | Oct. | Nov. | Dec. | Jan. | Feb. | Mar. | Apr. | May | June | July | Aug. | Average |
|---|---|---|---|---|---|---|---|---|---|---|---|---|---|
| 1985-6 | 2.59 | 2.50 | 2.69 | 2.75 | 2.72 | 2.63 | 2.56 | 2.57 | 2.68 | 2.63 | 2.12 | 1.85 | 2.52 |
| 1986-7 | 1.68 | 1.66 | 1.83 | 1.81 | 1.73 | 1.70 | 1.83 | 1.89 | 2.06 | 2.06 | 1.95 | 1.81 | 1.83 |
| 1987-8 | 1.86 | 1.99 | 2.08 | 2.11 | 2.20 | 2.23 | 2.29 | 2.28 | 2.29 | 3.05 | 3.22 | 3.02 | 2.39 |
| 1988-9 | 3.08 | 3.07 | 2.89 | 2.99 | 3.01 | 2.99 | 3.02 | 2.93 | 2.99 | 2.87 | 2.73 | 2.57 | 2.93 |
| 1989-90 | 2.60 | 2.40 | 2.75 | 2.75 | 2.69 | 2.70 | 2.72 | 3.01 | 3.08 | 3.05 | 2.92 | 2.79 | 2.79 |
| 1990-1 | 2.59 | 2.55 | 2.54 | 2.60 | 2.68 | 2.70 | 2.77 | 2.80 | 2.69 | 2.65 | 2.67 | 2.79 | 2.67 |
| 1991-2 | 2.76 | 2.76 | 2.72 | 2.71 | 2.70 | 2.89 | 2.96 | 2.77 | 2.77 | 2.80 | 2.61 | 2.48 | 2.74 |
| 1992-3 | 2.50 | 2.40 | 2.42 | 2.39 | 2.39 | 2.40 | 2.48 | 2.55 | 2.50 | 2.36 | 2.59 | 2.55 | 2.46 |
| 1993-4 | 2.57 | 2.68 | 2.94 | 3.08 | 3.22 | 3.14 | 3.05 | 2.88 | 2.81 | 2.85 | 2.51 | 2.44 | 2.85 |
| 1994-5 | 2.48 | 2.44 | 2.43 | 2.61 | 2.72 | 2.72 | 2.79 | 2.79 | 2.84 | 3.04 | 3.23 | 3.21 | 2.78 |
| 1995-6 | 3.32 | 3.57 | 3.63 | 3.76 | 4.00 | 4.18 | 4.34 | 4.80 | 5.17 | 4.99 | 5.07 | 4.73 | 4.30 |
| 1996-7[1] | 3.69 | 3.27 | 2.97 | 2.97 | 3.02 | | | | | | | | 3.18 |

[1] Preliminary. [2] Barge delivered to Louisiana Gulf. *Source: Economic Research Service, U.S. Department of Agriculture*

# CORN

## Weekly Outstanding Export Sales & Cumulative Exports -- U.S. Corn

In Thousands of Metric Tons

| 1994/95 | | | 1995/96 | | | 1996/97 | | |
|---|---|---|---|---|---|---|---|---|
| Marketing Year 1994/95 Week Ending | Out-standing Sales | Cumu-lative Exports | Marketing Year 1995/96 Week Ending | Out-standing Sales | Cumu-lative Exports | Marketing Year 1996/97 Week Ending | Out-standing Sales | Cumu-lative Exports |
| Sept. 1, 1994 | 5,728 | 53 | Sept. 7, 1995 | 16,892 | 985 | Sept. 5, 1996 | 14,289 | 169 |
| 8 | 6,210 | 510 | 14 | 16,576 | 2,354 | 12 | 14,671 | 557 |
| 15 | 6,370 | 1,162 | 21 | 16,456 | 3,898 | 19 | 14,851 | 1,163 |
| 22 | 6,681 | 1,805 | 28 | 16,176 | 5,244 | 26 | 14,714 | 1,860 |
| 29 | 6,923 | 2,622 | Oct. 5 | 15,798 | 6,510 | Oct. 3 | 14,778 | 2,590 |
| Oct. 6 | 7,460 | 3,151 | 12 | 15,721 | 7,720 | 10 | 15,080 | 3,145 |
| 13 | 7,974 | 3,840 | 19 | 16,208 | 8,956 | 17 | 14,555 | 3,890 |
| 20 | 8,053 | 4,522 | 26 | 16,757 | 9,979 | 24 | 14,487 | 4,727 |
| 27 | 8,350 | 5,308 | Nov. 2 | 3,548 | 17,182 | 31 | 14,298 | 5,776 |
| Nov. 3 | 8,164 | 6,332 | 9 | 17,351 | 12,478 | Nov. 7 | 14,082 | 6,789 |
| 10 | 7,955 | 7,453 | 16 | 17,785 | 13,428 | 14 | 13,921 | 8,117 |
| 17 | 8,745 | 8,317 | 23 | 17,387 | 14,508 | 21 | 13,279 | 9,340 |
| 24 | 9,147 | 9,478 | 30 | 16,881 | 15,973 | 28 | 12,222 | 10,626 |
| Dec. 1 | 10,437 | 10,991 | Dec. 7 | 16,754 | 17,103 | Dec. 5 | 11,447 | 11,908 |
| 8 | 10,953 | 12,089 | 14 | 16,717 | 17,910 | 12 | 10,573 | 13,481 |
| 15 | 10,669 | 13,218 | 21 | 17,474 | 18,962 | 19 | 10,708 | 14,340 |
| 22 | 13,065 | 14,097 | 28 | 17,362 | 20,299 | 26 | 10,175 | 15,319 |
| 29 | 13,403 | 15,185 | Jan. 4, 1996 | 17,975 | 21,154 | Jan. 2, 1997 | 9,344 | 16,367 |
| Jan. 5, 1995 | 13,278 | 16,408 | 11 | 18,538 | 22,389 | 9 | 9,371 | 17,249 |
| 12 | 13,973 | 17,460 | 18 | 19,142 | 23,649 | 16 | 9,297 | 18,568 |
| 19 | 13,531 | 18,815 | 25 | 18,811 | 24,973 | 23 | 9,490 | 19,661 |
| 26 | 13,347 | 19,938 | Feb. 1 | 18,541 | 26,252 | 30 | 9,434 | 20,574 |
| Feb. 2 | 12,613 | 21,330 | 8 | 18,370 | 27,398 | Feb. 6 | 9,236 | 21,656 |
| 9 | 11,853 | 22,750 | 15 | 18,713 | 28,201 | 13 | 9,342 | 22,365 |
| 16 | 11,409 | 23,896 | 22 | 18,119 | 29,367 | 20 | 8,729 | 23,471 |
| 23 | 11,190 | 24,789 | 29 | 18,264 | 30,667 | 27 | 9,224 | 24,482 |
| Mar. 2 | 10,699 | 26,039 | Mar. 7 | 18,289 | 31,784 | Mar. 6 | 9,274 | 25,440 |
| 9 | 10,305 | 27,263 | 14 | 17,669 | 33,217 | 13 | | |
| 16 | 10,639 | 28,335 | 21 | 17,202 | 34,391 | 20 | | |
| 23 | 11,670 | 30,483 | 28 | 16,664 | 35,621 | 27 | | |
| 30 | 11,670 | 30,454 | Apr. 4 | 16,732 | 36,628 | Apr. 3 | | |
| Apr. 6 | 11,223 | 31,342 | 11 | 16,204 | 37,678 | 10 | | |
| 13 | 11,325 | 32,644 | 18 | 15,411 | 39,216 | 17 | | |
| 20 | 11,337 | 33,647 | 25 | 15,283 | 40,284 | 24 | | |
| 27 | 11,409 | 34,430 | May 2 | 14,778 | 41,642 | May 1 | | |
| May 4 | 11,251 | 35,469 | 9 | 14,795 | 42,579 | 8 | | |
| 11 | 10,531 | 36,642 | 16 | 14,054 | 43,695 | 15 | | |
| 18 | 9,971 | 37,669 | 23 | 12,941 | 44,681 | 22 | | |
| 25 | 9,499 | 38,866 | 30 | 11,980 | 45,715 | 29 | | |
| June 1 | 9,272 | 40,109 | June 6 | 11,287 | 46,776 | June 5 | | |
| 8 | 10,061 | 40,867 | 13 | 10,466 | 47,440 | 12 | | |
| 15 | 10,374 | 41,562 | 20 | 9,724 | 48,060 | 19 | | |
| 22 | 10,848 | 42,584 | 27 | 8,694 | 49,010 | 26 | | |
| 29 | 10,265 | 43,832 | July 4 | 7,661 | 50,075 | July 3 | | |
| July 6 | 9,617 | 44,737 | 11 | 6,678 | 50,897 | 10 | | |
| 13 | 8,807 | 46,220 | 18 | 6,005 | 51,506 | 17 | | |
| 20 | 8,133 | 47,295 | 25 | 5,419 | 52,163 | 24 | | |
| 27 | 7,373 | 48,328 | Aug. 1 | 4,608 | 52,976 | 31 | | |
| Aug. 3 | 6,290 | 49,649 | 8 | 3,411 | 53,780 | Aug. 7 | | |
| 10 | 5,123 | 50,993 | 15 | 2,320 | 54,532 | 14 | | |
| 17 | 4,245 | 52,180 | 22 | 1,883 | 54,970 | 21 | | |
| 24 | 3,263 | 53,446 | 29 | 1,163 | 55,623 | 28 | | |
| 31 | 2,023 | 54,742 | | | | | | |

*Source: Foreign Agricultural Service, U.S. Department of Agriculture*

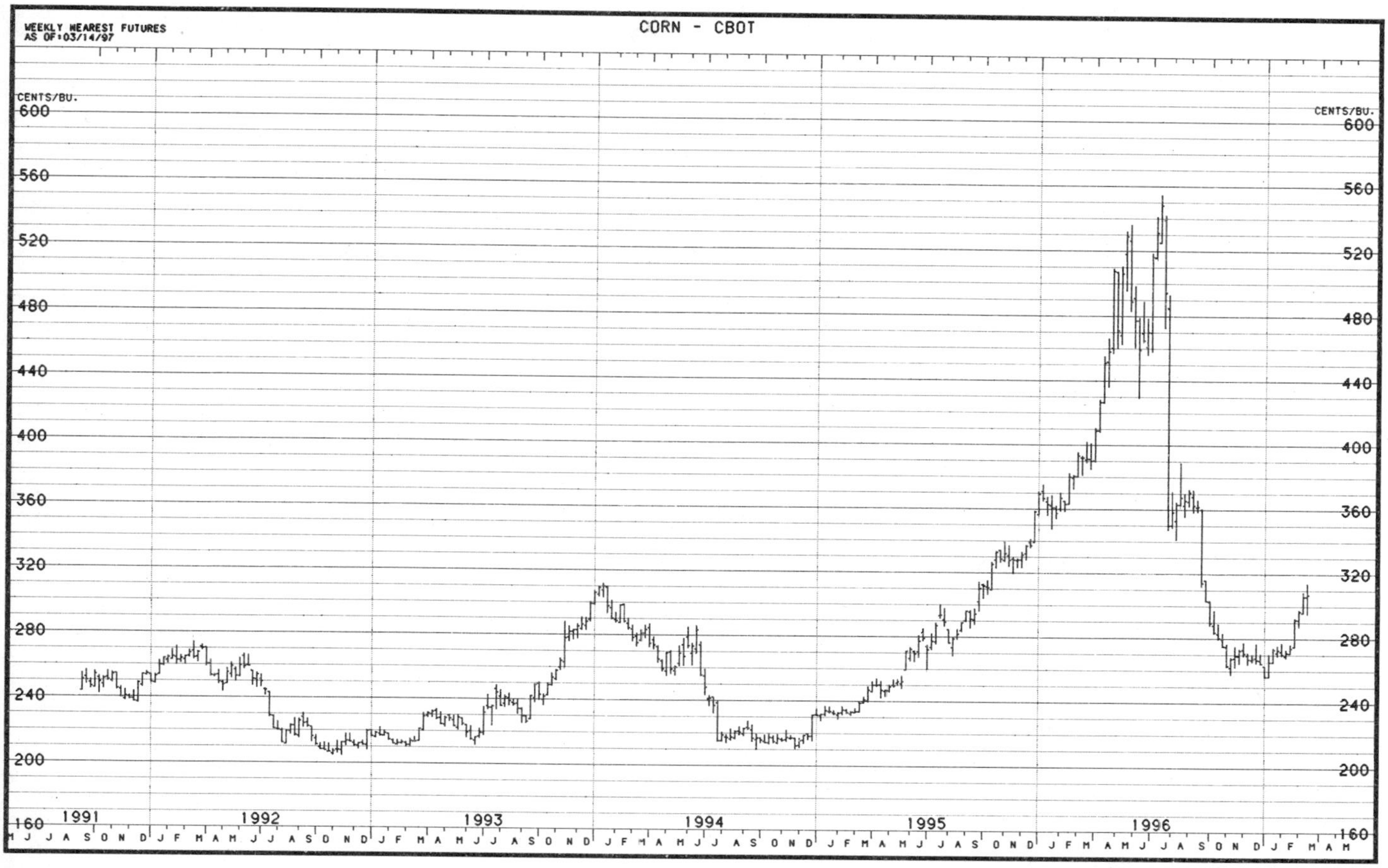


## U.S. Exports[1] of Corn (Including Seed), by Country of Destination In Thousands of Metric Tons

| Year Beginning Oct. | Algeria | Brazil | Canada | Dominican Republic | Egypt | Israel | Japan | Mexico | Rep. of Korea | Russia[3] | Saudi Arabia | Spain | Taiwan | Vene-zuela | Total |
|---|---|---|---|---|---|---|---|---|---|---|---|---|---|---|---|
| 1987-8 | 1,113 | 0 | 158 | 394 | 1,078 | 415 | 14,816 | 2,900 | 4,411 | 5,585 | 545 | 1,836 | 4,169 | 0 | 43,955 |
| 1988-9 | 973 | 20 | 896 | 392 | 1,014 | 304 | 13,016 | 3,113 | 4,591 | 15,573 | 616 | 1,280 | 3,625 | 0 | 50,676 |
| 1989-90 | 1,146 | 12 | 637 | 421 | 1,135 | 250 | 13,885 | 4,585 | 5,680 | 16,371 | 707 | 1,712 | 5,009 | 593 | 59,854 |
| 1990-1 | 1,328 | 393 | 302 | 442 | 1,756 | 299 | 13,639 | 1,901 | 1,982 | 9,077 | 725 | 1,434 | 5,086 | 321 | 44,497 |
| 1991-2 | 827 | 148 | 314 | 531 | 1,058 | 369 | 13,481 | 1,041 | 1,508 | 6,533 | 602 | 1,273 | 4,998 | 552 | 40,693 |
| 1992-3 | 1,224 | 71 | 1,189 | 614 | 1,543 | 539 | 14,235 | 396 | 1,021 | 3,380 | 787 | 1,075 | 5,450 | 777 | 41,766 |
| 1993-4 | 1,182 | 0 | 640 | 604 | 1,437 | 268 | 12,032 | 1,678 | 631 | 2,337 | 851 | 1,116 | 4,955 | 751 | 33,057 |
| 1994-5 | 846 | 0 | 1,135 | 633 | 2,608 | 671 | 16,107 | 3,166 | 8,921 | 9 | 864 | 2,497 | 6,210 | 886 | 58,645 |
| 1995-6[2] | 0 | 0 | 751 | 645 | 2,106 | 625 | 14,900 | 6,268 | 7,426 | 58 | 844 | 1,156 | 5,600 | 479 | 52,681 |

[1] Excludes exports of corn by-products. [2] Preliminary. [3] Formerly part of the U.S.S.R.; data not reported separately until 1992.
*Source: Economic Research Service, U.S. Department of Agriculture*

## Corn (Shelled & Ear) Stocks in the United States In Millions of Bushels

| Year | On Farms | | | | Off Farms | | | | Total Stocks | | | |
|---|---|---|---|---|---|---|---|---|---|---|---|---|
| | Mar. 1 | June 1 | Sept. 1 | Dec. 1 | Mar. 1 | June 1 | Sept. 1 | Dec. 1 | Mar. 1 | June 1 | Sept. 1 | Dec. 1 |
| 1986 | NA | 3,143.1 | 2,049.4 | 6,795.5 | NA | 1,847.0 | 1,990.1 | 3,510.0 | 6,587.1 | 4,990.0 | 4,039.5 | 10,305.5 |
| 1987 | 5,024.0 | 3,491.8 | 2,284.5 | 6,100.0 | 3,224.2 | 2,840.4 | 2,597.2 | 3,668.5 | 8,248.2 | 6,332.2 | 4,881.7 | 9,768.5 |
| 1988 | 4,421.0 | 3,241.0 | 2,002.8 | 4,280.2 | 3,214.6 | 2,594.5 | 2,256.3 | 2,791.4 | 7,635.6 | 5,835.5 | 4,259.1 | 7,071.6 |
| 1989 | 3,021.0 | 2,022.0 | 967.5 | 4,698.8 | 2,182.9 | 1,397.3 | 962.9 | 2,383.3 | 5,203.9 | 3,419.3 | 1,930.4 | 7,082.1 |
| 1990 | 2,910.5 | 1,623.5 | 754.8 | 4,874.0 | 1,901.9 | 1,219.7 | 589.7 | 2,066.3 | 4,812.4 | 2,843.2 | 1,344.5 | 6,940.3 |
| 1991 | 3,064.5 | 1,755.0 | 691.2 | 4,294.5 | 1,724.5 | 1,237.0 | 830.0 | 2,246.6 | 4,789.0 | 2,992.0 | 1,521.2 | 6,541.1 |
| 1992 | 2,610.2 | 1,517.5 | 605.5 | 5,736.9 | 1,950.8 | 1,221.1 | 494.8 | 2,169.5 | 4,561.0 | 2,738.6 | 1,100.3 | 7,906.4 |
| 1993 | 3,630.0 | 2,216.5 | 1,070.7 | 3,803.0 | 2,048.2 | 1,492.9 | 1,042.3 | 2,133.5 | 5,678.2 | 3,709.4 | 2,113.0 | 5,936.5 |
| 1994 | 2,210.0 | 1,203.0 | 395.4 | 5,417.5 | 1,785.5 | 1,156.9 | 454.7 | 2,663.0 | 3,995.7 | 2,359.9 | 850.1 | 8,080.5 |
| 1995 | 3,502.0 | 2,072.0 | 740.9 | 3,960.0 | 2,089.7 | 1,342.9 | 816.9 | 2,145.8 | 5,591.7 | 3,414.9 | 1,557.8 | 6,105.8 |
| 1996[1] | 2,000.2 | 780.1 | 196.6 | 4,800.0 | 1,799.3 | 937.8 | 229.3 | 2,105.5 | 3,799.5 | 1,717.9 | 425.9 | 6,905.5 |

[1] Preliminary. NA = Not available. *Source: National Agricultural Statistics Service, U.S. Department of Agriculture*

# CORN

## Volume of Trading of Corn Futures at Chicago In Millions of Bushels

| Year | Jan. | Feb. | Mar. | Apr | May | June | July | Aug. | Sept. | Oct. | Nov. | Dec. | Total |
|---|---|---|---|---|---|---|---|---|---|---|---|---|---|
| 1986 | 2,629 | 2,153 | 2,203 | 2,840 | 3,029 | 2,390 | 2,605 | 2,217 | 2,486 | 3,103 | 2,591 | 2,555 | 30,801 |
| 1987 | 2,343 | 2,901 | 3,088 | 3,646 | 3,579 | 3,984 | 2,978 | 2,498 | 2,620 | 3,380 | 2,923 | 2,327 | 36,266 |
| 1988 | 3,040 | 3,333 | 3,212 | 3,478 | 4,235 | 7,898 | 6,818 | 5,352 | 4,353 | 4,661 | 5,597 | 3,549 | 55,528 |
| 1989 | 4,170 | 3,384 | 3,818 | 4,138 | 3,930 | 4,485 | 4,323 | 3,433 | 2,827 | 4,702 | 4,352 | 2,793 | 46,354 |
| 1990 | 3,248 | 3,991 | 4,623 | 5,742 | 7,146 | 6,767 | 5,509 | 4,541 | 3,028 | 3,939 | 5,682 | 2,899 | 57,114 |
| 1991 | 4,284 | 3,484 | 4,663 | 5,205 | 4,227 | 5,064 | 6,268 | 5,486 | 3,462 | 4,420 | 4,539 | 3,161 | 54,264 |
| 1992 | 4,506 | 5,013 | 4,761 | 4,343 | 4,691 | 5,076 | 4,328 | 3,975 | 3,443 | 3,442 | 4,981 | 3,222 | 51,783 |
| 1993 | 2,588 | 3,182 | 3,870 | 4,474 | 3,440 | 5,237 | 6,978 | 5,071 | 4,480 | 5,180 | 7,872 | 4,941 | 57,313 |
| 1994 | 6,257 | 5,178 | 5,228 | 5,544 | 5,396 | 7,275 | 3,738 | 3,009 | 3,075 | 3,515 | 5,127 | 4,307 | 57,649 |
| 1995 | 3,936 | 4,162 | 4,868 | 4,939 | 6,069 | 8,798 | 6,469 | 6,593 | 6,101 | 8,066 | 8,716 | 6,780 | 75,526 |
| 1996 | 9,961 | 9,098 | 8,038 | 13,276 | 10,426 | 7,725 | 7,953 | 5,723 | 5,917 | 7,178 | 7,574 | 5,232 | 98,101 |

*Source: Chicago Board of Trade (CBT)*

## Average Open Interest of Corn Futures at Chicago In Thousands of Bushels

| Year | Jan. | Feb. | Mar. | Apr. | May | June | July | Aug. | Sept. | Oct. | Nov. | Dec. |
|---|---|---|---|---|---|---|---|---|---|---|---|---|
| 1986 | 603,350 | 562,749 | 545,073 | 572,669 | 548,970 | 586,031 | 574,077 | 607,718 | 621,703 | 712,114 | 773,156 | 590,845 |
| 1987 | 651,105 | 708,597 | 692,102 | 706,486 | 650,705 | 632,792 | 568,933 | 591,430 | 593,557 | 689,305 | 690,809 | 631,781 |
| 1988 | 728,517 | 759,008 | 787,238 | 813,253 | 826,970 | 1,072,313 | 1,229,357 | 1,174,962 | 1,164,763 | 1,236,846 | 1,211,708 | 1,112,098 |
| 1989 | 1,081,102 | 994,058 | 963,200 | 917,720 | 819,439 | 783,908 | 719,030 | 727,027 | 706,896 | 857,567 | 971,254 | 839,719 |
| 1990 | 890,470 | 1,014,224 | 1,149,729 | 1,260,776 | 1,250,101 | 1,212,310 | 1,063,743 | 1,039,755 | 1,033,015 | 1,056,112 | 1,151,665 | 1,019,404 |
| 1991 | 1,050,031 | 1,096,179 | 1,145,049 | 1,147,020 | 1,024,140 | 1,010,500 | 992,637 | 1,098,500 | 1,077,634 | 1,212,331 | 1,285,325 | 1,141,737 |
| 1992 | 1,270,977 | 1,474,784 | 1,427,144 | 1,302,633 | 1,151,794 | 1,160,944 | 1,056,106 | 1,098,981 | 1,043,064 | 1,199,439 | 1,311,724 | 1,224,013 |
| 1993 | 1,280,564 | 1,304,929 | 1,243,192 | 1,249,999 | 1,145,079 | 1,162,948 | 1,328,361 | 1,324,688 | 1,219,460 | 1,378,962 | 1,662,225 | 1,636,129 |
| 1994 | 1,730,383 | 1,681,711 | 1,637,696 | 1,528,608 | 1,313,103 | 1,231,541 | 1,075,406 | 1,044,950 | 1,064,915 | 1,218,389 | 1,314,246 | 1,253,229 |
| 1995 | 1,460,450 | 1,556,861 | 1,682,163 | 1,777,215 | 1,841,903 | 2,138,722 | 2,069,193 | 2,092,251 | 2,195,849 | 2,368,488 | 2,454,850 | 2,439,887 |
| 1996 | 2,504,187 | 2,542,482 | 2,348,483 | 2,268,535 | 2,015,589 | 1,750,332 | 1,521,323 | 1,494,471 | 1,510,851 | 1,631,866 | 1,664,047 | 1,531,280 |

*Source: Chicago Board of Trade (CBT)*

## Corn Price Support Data in the United States

| Crop Year Beginning Sept. 1 | National Average Loan Rate[3] | Target Price | Placed Under Loan | % of Production | Acquired by CCC | Owned by CCC Aug. 31 | CCC Inventory As of Dec. 31: CCC Owned | CCC Inventory As of Dec. 31: Under CCC Loan | Quantity Pledged | Face Amount |
|---|---|---|---|---|---|---|---|---|---|---|
| | $ Per Bushel | $ Per Bushel | Millions of Bushels | | Millions of Bushels | Millions of Bushels | Millions of Bushels | Millions of Bushels | Ths. Bu | Ths. $ |
| 1985-6 | 2.55 | 3.03 | 3,163 | 35.6 | 580 | 546 | 477 | 2,811 | 56,868 | 156,478 |
| 1986-7 | 1.92 | 3.03 | 4,894 | 59.5 | 1,332 | 1,443 | 1,265 | 4,905 | 59,188 | 114,611 |
| 1987-8 | 1.82 | 3.03 | 4,186 | 58.7 | 787 | 835 | 1,843 | 4,436 | 4,186,077 | 7,514,145 |
| 1988-9 | 1.77 | 2.93 | 756 | 15.3 | 151 | 363 | 679 | 982 | 755,895 | 1,313,581 |
| 1989-90 | 1.65 | 2.84 | 920 | 12.2 | 361 | 233 | 676 | 1,110 | 920,068 | 1,487,026 |
| 1990-1 | 1.57 | 2.75 | 1,071 | 13.5 | 285 | 371 | 214 | 1,071 | 1,071,040 | 1,616,948 |
| 1991-2 | 1.62 | 2.75 | 1,006 | 13.5 | 291 | 113 | 265 | 678 | 26,636 | 45,609 |
| 1992-3 | 1.72 | 2.75 | 1,646 | 17.4 | 0 | 56 | 125 | 1,021 | 15,245 | 28,947 |
| 1993-4 | 1.72 | 2.75 | 618 | 9.7 | 0 | 45 | 54 | 812 | 13,697 | 26,052 |
| 1994-5[1] | 1.89 | 2.75 | 2,002 | 19.8 | NA | NA | 44 | 1,598 | NA | NA |
| 1995-6[2] | 1.89 | 2.75 | 676 | 9.2 | NA | NA | 42 | 579 | NA | NA |
| 1996-7[2] | | | | | | | | | | |

[1] Preliminary. [2] Estimate. [3] Finley or announced loan rate. *Source: National Agricultural Statistics Service, U.S. Department of Agriculture*

## Average Price Received by Farmers for Corn in the U.S. In Dollars Per Bushel

| Crop Year | Sept. | Oct. | Nov. | Dec. | Jan. | Feb. | Mar. | Apr. | May | June | July | Aug. | Average |
|---|---|---|---|---|---|---|---|---|---|---|---|---|---|
| 1986-7 | 1.45 | 1.40 | 1.47 | 1.50 | 1.48 | 1.42 | 1.47 | 1.52 | 1.66 | 1.69 | 1.60 | 1.47 | 1.50 |
| 1987-8 | 1.49 | 1.55 | 1.61 | 1.72 | 1.77 | 1.83 | 1.86 | 1.88 | 1.94 | 2.41 | 2.72 | 2.65 | 1.94 |
| 1988-9 | 2.60 | 2.58 | 2.51 | 2.53 | 2.60 | 2.59 | 2.60 | 2.56 | 2.58 | 2.52 | 2.47 | 2.27 | 2.54 |
| 1989-90 | 2.29 | 2.22 | 2.24 | 2.27 | 2.31 | 2.32 | 2.37 | 2.51 | 2.62 | 2.63 | 2.62 | 2.51 | 2.36 |
| 1990-1 | 2.32 | 2.19 | 2.16 | 2.22 | 2.27 | 2.32 | 2.39 | 2.42 | 2.38 | 2.31 | 2.27 | 2.33 | 2.28 |
| 1991-2 | 2.33 | 2.31 | 2.29 | 2.33 | 2.40 | 2.46 | 2.49 | 2.48 | 2.49 | 2.47 | 2.33 | 2.15 | 2.37 |
| 1992-3 | 2.16 | 2.05 | 1.98 | 1.97 | 2.03 | 2.00 | 2.10 | 2.16 | 2.14 | 2.09 | 2.22 | 2.25 | 2.07 |
| 1993-4 | 2.21 | 2.28 | 2.45 | 2.67 | 2.70 | 2.79 | 2.74 | 2.65 | 2.60 | 2.61 | 2.29 | 2.16 | 2.50 |
| 1994-5 | 2.19 | 2.06 | 1.99 | 2.13 | 2.19 | 2.23 | 2.30 | 2.36 | 2.41 | 2.51 | 2.63 | 2.63 | 2.26 |
| 1995-6[1] | 2.69 | 2.79 | 2.87 | 3.07 | 3.09 | 3.37 | 3.51 | 3.85 | 4.14 | 4.22 | 4.43 | 4.80 | 3.15 |
| 1996-7[1] | 3.56 | 2.89 | 2.64 | 2.63 | 2.63 | | | | | | | | 2.87 |

[1] Preliminary. *Source: Economic Research Service, U.S. Department of Agriculture*

# Corn Oil

## Supply & Distribution of Corn Oil In Millions of Pounds

| Crop Year Beginning Oct. 1 | Supply: Stocks Oct. 1 | Supply: Pro-duction | Supply: Imports | Supply: Total Supply | Disappearance: Baking and Frying Fats | Disappearance: Salad and Cooking Oil | Disappearance: Marg-arine | Disappearance: Total Edible Products | Disappearance: Domestic Disap-pearance | Disappearance: Exports | Disappearance: Total Disap-pearance |
|---|---|---|---|---|---|---|---|---|---|---|---|
| 1986-7 | 120 | 1,400 | ---- | 1,520 | W | 491 | 248 | 934 | 1,143 | 268 | 1,411 |
| 1987-8 | 109 | 1,435 | 2.0 | 1,546 | W | 555 | 212 | 946 | 1,065 | 370 | 1,435 |
| 1988-9 | 111 | 1,415 | 2.0 | 1,528 | 227 | 615 | 218 | 1,060 | 1,073 | 356 | 1,429 |
| 1989-90 | 99 | 1,470 | ---- | 1,569 | W | 659 | 218 | 1,129 | 1,028 | 414 | 1,442 |
| 1990-1 | 127 | 1,656 | 2.0 | 1,785 | 304 | 589 | 195 | 1,143 | 1,149 | 498 | 1,647 |
| 1991-2 | 138 | 1,821 | 5.0 | 1,965 | 411 | 565 | 185 | 1,085 | 1,202 | 566 | 1,768 |
| 1992-3 | 196 | 1,878 | 7.0 | 2,081 | 241 | 547 | W | 945 | 1,220 | 712 | 1,931 |
| 1993-4 | 150 | 1,906 | 7.0 | 2,062 | 86 | 413 | W | 649 | 1,228 | 717 | 1,944 |
| 1994-5[1] | 118 | 2,217 | 10.0 | 2,356 | 100 | 446 | W | 636 | 1,250 | 865 | 2,115 |
| 1995-6[1] | 241 | 2,096 | 10.0 | 2,349 | 82 | 434 | W | 594 | 1,257 | 977 | 2,233 |
| 1996-7[2] | 116 | 2,190 | 10.0 | 2,316 | | | | | 1,285 | 925 | 2,210 |

[1] Preliminary. [2] Estimate. W = Withheld proprietary data. *Source: Economic Research Service, U.S. Department of Agriculture*

## Crude Corn Oil Production in the United States[2] In Millions of Pounds

| Year | Oct. | Nov. | Dec. | Jan. | Feb. | Mar. | Apr. | May | June | July | Aug. | Sept. | Total |
|---|---|---|---|---|---|---|---|---|---|---|---|---|---|
| 1985-6 | 114.2 | 101.5 | 97.1 | 72.8 | 97.9 | 102.2 | 109.8 | 118.4 | 106.3 | 108.6 | 119.9 | 104.1 | 1,253 |
| 1986-7 | 134.6 | 120.2 | 114.0 | 100.1 | 102.2 | 119.3 | 111.2 | 123.8 | 117.5 | 123.0 | 114.7 | 119.5 | 1,400 |
| 1987-8 | 121.5 | 115.9 | 110.6 | 107.1 | 110.2 | 113.4 | 117.3 | 125.6 | 125.4 | 131.7 | 132.1 | 124.5 | 1,435 |
| 1988-9 | 123.8 | 107.5 | 127.8 | 125.5 | 108.6 | 128.9 | 122.0 | 125.1 | 119.9 | 118.6 | 98.7 | 108.5 | 1,415 |
| 1989-90 | 130.2 | 106.1 | 128.6 | 127.7 | 122.0 | 131.4 | 135.6 | 115.5 | 140.7 | 150.4 | 145.2 | 132.2 | 1,566 |
| 1990-1 | 142.0 | 129.4 | 129.3 | | ----------- 405.0 ----------- | | | ----------- 422.3 ----------- | | | ----------- 427.6 ----------- | | 1,656 |
| 1991-2 | | ----------- 436.7 ----------- | | 138.1 | 137.5 | 164.5 | 153.3 | 150.2 | 160.0 | 165.0 | 162.4 | 153.6 | 1,821 |
| 1992-3 | 168.1 | 151.8 | 151.6 | 135.5 | 139.0 | 165.6 | 153.5 | 161.6 | 164.5 | 163.0 | 158.5 | 165.1 | 1,878 |
| 1993-4 | 160.8 | 153.4 | 162.5 | 140.6 | 138.6 | 166.9 | 155.3 | 164.2 | 171.8 | 164.8 | 162.3 | 165.1 | 1,906 |
| 1994-5 | 175.5 | 165.3 | 180.9 | 163.2 | 161.8 | 232.7 | 188.4 | 191.2 | 193.6 | 193.5 | 180.3 | 188.5 | 2,215 |
| 1995-6[1] | 179.5 | 173.8 | 184.5 | 180.6 | 160.4 | 192.9 | 192.1 | 175.9 | 178.4 | 147.1 | 162.2 | 171.2 | 2,099 |

[1] Preliminary. [2] Not seasonally adjusted. *Source: Bureau of Census, U.S. Department of Commerce*

## U.S. Corn Oil Consumption in Refining In Millions of Pounds

| Year | Oct. | Nov. | Dec. | Jan. | Feb. | Mar. | Apr. | May | June | July | Aug. | Sept. | Total |
|---|---|---|---|---|---|---|---|---|---|---|---|---|---|
| 1985-6 | 106.0 | 95.8 | 87.1 | 94.1 | 87.8 | 100.9 | 95.1 | 103.4 | 91.2 | 105.2 | 97.4 | 98.1 | 1,162 |
| 1986-7 | 101.2 | 98.9 | 98.3 | 95.7 | 98.4 | 104.0 | 88.7 | 83.1 | 90.9 | 82.6 | 77.1 | 92.3 | 1,111 |
| 1987-8 | 99.2 | 90.5 | 78.3 | 77.7 | 93.4 | 90.0 | 91.7 | 103.6 | 104.1 | 100.6 | 119.0 | 110.6 | 1,159 |
| 1988-9 | 100.8 | 101.2 | 107.9 | 116.5 | 98.6 | 118.0 | 89.5 | 110.1 | 106.2 | 100.1 | 107.5 | 98.0 | 1,254 |
| 1989-90 | 119.8 | 99.2 | 105.2 | 109.1 | 94.3 | 96.9 | 99.8 | 102.2 | 105.6 | 118.3 | 107.6 | 102.2 | 1,260 |
| 1990-1 | 115.4 | 100.0 | 108.2 | | ----------- 330.2 ----------- | | | ----------- 287.2 ----------- | | | ----------- 293.5 ----------- | | 1,235 |
| 1991-2 | | ----------- 287.2 ----------- | | 138.1 | 137.5 | 164.5 | 153.3 | 150.2 | 160.0 | 165.0 | 162.4 | 153.6 | 1,672 |
| 1992-3 | 168.1 | 151.8 | 151.6 | 81.2 | 93.6 | 110.5 | 102.4 | 85.8 | 99.9 | 88.0 | 90.9 | 96.4 | 1,320 |
| 1993-4 | 106.7 | 101.7 | 114.3 | 71.8 | 76.5 | 92.6 | 79.4 | 91.5 | 91.7 | 90.6 | 106.4 | 109.1 | 1,132 |
| 1994-5 | 103.5 | 107.2 | 116.9 | 100.7 | 92.3 | 109.9 | 97.3 | 95.6 | 108.9 | 97.2 | 78.2 | 95.5 | 1,203 |
| 1995-6[1] | 82.9 | 97.9 | 102.0 | 78.6 | 91.6 | 100.0 | 84.8 | 90.0 | 90.5 | 74.5 | 66.5 | 90.2 | 1,050 |

[1] Preliminary. *Source: Bureau of Census, U.S. Department of Commerce*

## Corn Oil Spot Price, Wet Mill at Chicago In Cents Per Pound

| Year | Oct. | Nov. | Dec. | Jan. | Feb. | Mar. | Apr. | May | June | July | Aug. | Sept. | Average |
|---|---|---|---|---|---|---|---|---|---|---|---|---|---|
| 1986-7 | 19.60 | 20.47 | 21.48 | 22.45 | 24.61 | 22.65 | 20.94 | 21.43 | 22.90 | 21.48 | 20.00 | 19.14 | 21.43 |
| 1987-8 | 20.68 | 20.69 | 21.49 | 23.09 | 22.46 | 21.26 | 20.44 | 21.61 | 26.43 | 29.56 | 26.58 | 24.94 | 23.27 |
| 1988-9 | 23.35 | 21.78 | 21.22 | 20.65 | 20.30 | 21.61 | 21.40 | 21.75 | 21.44 | 20.05 | 19.21 | 19.39 | 21.01 |
| 1989-90 | 20.84 | 22.67 | 23.25 | 22.61 | 23.57 | 24.96 | 26.05 | 24.99 | 26.56 | 25.09 | 28.49 | 28.00 | 24.76 |
| 1990-1 | 26.61 | 24.24 | 22.15 | 25.89 | 27.29 | 28.50 | 29.98 | 28.87 | 29.61 | 29.76 | 29.55 | 28.50 | 27.58 |
| 1991-2 | 27.75 | 27.25 | 28.75 | 29.00 | 28.45 | 27.19 | 26.75 | 26.04 | 24.75 | 22.48 | 20.40 | 21.00 | 25.82 |
| 1992-3 | 20.43 | 20.60 | 20.75 | 20.75 | 20.87 | 20.79 | 20.80 | 20.75 | 20.60 | 20.67 | 21.50 | 22.23 | 20.90 |
| 1993-4 | 22.25 | 23.06 | 26.93 | 28.00 | 29.89 | 30.30 | 29.63 | 29.48 | 29.43 | 27.20 | 25.02 | 24.87 | 27.17 |
| 1994-5 | 24.73 | 24.75 | 24.75 | 28.01 | 27.26 | 28.17 | 27.30 | 26.42 | 26.61 | 27.38 | 26.35 | 25.93 | 26.47 |
| 1995-6[1] | 26.05 | 25.54 | 24.99 | 24.52 | 24.30 | 24.34 | 25.60 | 27.98 | 25.66 | 25.46 | 24.33 | 24.14 | 25.24 |

[1] Preliminary. *Source: Economic Research Service, U.S. Department of Agriculture*

# Cotton

World cotton production in the 1996/97 season (August-July) is projected to reach 87 million bales (480 pounds per bale), a decline of 5 percent from the 1995/96 season. The 1994/95 season world production was 85.5 million bales. The decline in the 1996/97 season was due to production decreases in a number of the major producers including India which was expecting a crop of 12.2 million bales, down less than 1 percent from the year before, Pakistan's crop of 7.1 million bales which was down 13 percent and Uzbekistan's output of 5.1 million bales which was off about 11 million bales. China, the most important producer outside of the U.S., was adversely impacted by severe flooding and the crop was downgraded to 17.5 million bales, a significant decline from the 1995/96 crop of 21.9 million bales.

While cotton production was expected to be lower in all the major northern hemisphere producers except for the U.S., the opposite was true for the southern hemisphere. Australia's crop was estimated at 2.7 million bales compared to 1.93 million in 1995/96 while Argentina's crop of 1.95 million bales was up from 1.8 million bales the prior year. One exception was Brazil which turned out 1.6 million bales, down from 1.79 million bales the previous year. Production of cotton outside the U.S. or foreign production was put at 68.4 million bales or 7 percent less than in 1995/96. With the smaller outturn, foreign exports were 20.5 million bales. Among the larger foreign exporters was Pakistan at 600,000 bales, India with 900,000, Uzbekistan with 4.6 million, and Turkmenistan with 900,000 bales. Australia exported 2.15 million bales while Argentina shipped 1.5 million.

World consumption of cotton was 85.7 million bales in 1996/97, up 1 percent from the previous season. World consumption continued to grow spurred on by population increases, rising incomes, and consumer preferences for the natural fiber. China is the largest user of cotton by far with consumption of 19.8 million bales. Other major users are India with 11.8 million bales and Pakistan with 6.7 million.

U.S. production of cotton in 1996/97 was estimated at 18.6 million bales. It had been a difficult season to estimate the crop. Drought conditions had existed in Texas since the beginning of the year though the rest of the Cotton Belt had seen favorable growing conditions. The first estimate of the crop had been too high but rains in Texas proved to be beneficial and production estimates were raised. In 1995/96 the U.S. cotton crop had been 17.9 million bales. For 1996/97, cotton producers seeded 14.24 million acres and harvested 12.7 million. The national average yield was 698 pounds per acre. The previous year plantings were 16.93 million acres with 16.01 million harvested and an average yield of 537 pounds. The Texas crop improved to 4.1 million bales, down from 4.5 million in 1995/96. California's crop of 2.9 million bales was better than 2.5 million bales the previous season.

U.S. cotton stocks at the start of the season on August 1 were 2.6 million bales. What was interesting were imports of cotton. Because U.S. prices remained persistently higher than foreign growths, imports of cotton were allowed in an attempt to lower domestic prices. Imports were 500,000 bales, a very large amount. The total supply of cotton was 21.7 million bales, about 4 percent more than in 1995/96.

On the usage side of the equation, domestic mill use of cotton was 11 million bales. This was 400,000 bales more than in 1995/96. Domestic consumption continues to trend higher as a result of continued consumer preference for cotton textiles, especially clothing. The situation in the export sector was not as sanguine. U.S. cotton exports were 5.8 million bales, a steep 24 percent decline from the previous season. High U.S. prices took a toll on exporters. Total use of cotton was 16.8 million bales, down 8 percent from the previous year. Carryout or ending stocks of cotton were 4.9 million bales, much above the 2.6 million bales of 1995/96.

### *U.S. Government Programs*

The USDA set the marketing assistance loan rate for 1997-crop upland cotton at 51.92 cents per pound and for extra-long staple cotton at 79.65 cents. USDA said that the upland and ELS cotton prices are at their maximum levels under requirements of the 1996 farm bill.

### *Futures Markets*

Cotton futures and options are traded on the New York Cotton Exchange (NYCE). Cotton futures are traded on the Bolsa de Mercadorias & Futuros (BM&F). Cotton Yarn futures are traded on the Nagoya Textile Exchange, the Osaka Textile Exchange, and the Tokyo Commodity Exchange (TOCOM).

**Supply and Distribution of All Cotton in the United States** In Thousands of 480-Pound Bales

| Crop Year Beginning Aug. 1 | Area: Planted (1,000 acres) | Area: Harveste (1,000 acres) | Yield Lbs./acre | Supply: Beginning Stocks[3] | Supply: Production[4] | Supply: Imports | Supply: Total | Disappearance: Mill Use | Disappearance: Exports | Disappearance: Total | Unaccounted | Ending Stocks | Farm Price[5] (Cents Per Lb.) | "A" Index Price[6] (Cents Per Lb.) | Value of Production Million $ |
|---|---|---|---|---|---|---|---|---|---|---|---|---|---|---|---|
| 1987-8 | 10,397 | 10,030 | 706 | 5,026 | 14,760 | 2 | 19,788 | 7,617 | 6,582 | 14,199 | 182 | 5,771 | 64.3 | 72.26 | 4,555.0 |
| 1988-9 | 12,515 | 11,948 | 619 | 5,771 | 15,412 | 5 | 21,187 | 7,785 | 6,148 | 13,930 | -165 | 7,092 | 56.6 | 66.42 | 4,190.5 |
| 1989-90 | 10,587 | 9,538 | 614 | 7,092 | 12,196 | 2 | 19,290 | 8,759 | 7,694 | 16,453 | 163 | 3,000 | 66.2 | 82.34 | 3,877.9 |
| 1990-1 | 12,348 | 11,732 | 634 | 3,000 | 15,505 | 4 | 18,509 | 8,657 | 7,793 | 16,450 | 285 | 2,344 | 67.1 | 82.87 | 5,075.8 |
| 1991-2 | 14,052 | 12,960 | 652 | 2,344 | 17,614 | 13 | 19,971 | 9,613 | 6,646 | 16,259 | -8 | 3,704 | 58.1 | 62.90 | 4,913.2 |
| 1992-3 | 13,240 | 11,143 | 699 | 3,704 | 16,219 | 1 | 19,923 | 10,250 | 5,201 | 15,451 | 190 | 4,662 | 54.9 | 56.87 | 4,273.9 |
| 1993-4 | 13,438 | 12,783 | 606 | 4,662 | 16,134 | 6 | 20,802 | 10,418 | 6,862 | 17,280 | 8 | 3,530 | 58.4 | 70.75 | 4,520.9 |
| 1994-5 | 13,720 | 13,322 | 708 | 3,530 | 19,662 | 20 | 23,212 | 11,198 | 9,402 | 20,600 | 38 | 2,650 | 72.0 | 92.66 | 6,796.7 |
| 1995-6[1] | 16,931 | 16,007 | 537 | 2,650 | 17,900 | 408 | 20,958 | 10,604 | 7,675 | 18,279 | -70 | 2,609 | 75.4 | 85.61 | 6,550.7 |
| 1996-7[2] | 14,243 | 12,780 | 698 | 2,609 | 18,951 | 500 | 21,703 | 11,000 | 5,800 | 16,800 | -3 | 4,900 | | 76.99 | |

[1] Preliminary. [2] Estimate. [3] Excludes preseason ginnings (adjusted to 480-lb. bale net weight basis). [4] Includes preseason ginnings. [5] Marketing year

## World Production of Cotton (All Types) In Thousands of 480-Lb. Bales

| Crop Year Beginning Aug. 1 | Argentina | Brazil | China | Colombia | Egypt | India | Iran | Israel | Mexico | Pakistan | Sudan | Turkey | United States | Uzbekistan[3] | World Total |
|---|---|---|---|---|---|---|---|---|---|---|---|---|---|---|---|
| 1982-3 | 515 | 2,976 | 16,526 | 151 | 2,115 | 6,755 | 431 | 400 | 840 | 3,783 | 944 | 2,246 | 11,963 | 10,380 | 66,472 |
| 1983-4 | 826 | 3,423 | 21,298 | 352 | 1,838 | 6,122 | 420 | 427 | 1,038 | 2,271 | 1,021 | 2,398 | 7,771 | 9,976 | 66,460 |
| 1984-5 | 786 | 4,423 | 28,700 | 575 | 1,840 | 7,925 | 512 | 402 | 1,240 | 4,628 | 945 | 2,664 | 12,982 | 11,876 | 88,146 |
| 1985-6 | 547 | 3,812 | 19,000 | 531 | 1,999 | 8,355 | 482 | 455 | 970 | 5,669 | 652 | 2,379 | 13,432 | 12,777 | 79,613 |
| 1986-7 | 482 | 3,008 | 16,300 | 493 | 1,822 | 7,418 | 510 | 308 | 630 | 6,060 | 757 | 2,376 | 9,731 | 12,157 | 70,447 |
| 1987-8 | 1,295 | 3,514 | 19,500 | 614 | 1,614 | 7,388 | 487 | 271 | 1,010 | 6,741 | 612 | 2,465 | 15,411 | 11,491 | 81,349 |
| 1988-9 | 896 | 3,376 | 19,100 | 554 | 1,405 | 8,276 | 551 | 285 | 1,416 | 6,547 | 700 | 2,985 | 12,196 | 12,621 | 84,774 |
| 1989-90 | 1,272 | 3,030 | 17,400 | 481 | 1,324 | 10,599 | 524 | 212 | 769 | 6,687 | 584 | 2,835 | 12,196 | 7,605 | 79,780 |
| 1990-1 | 1,355 | 3,215 | 20,700 | 581 | 1,378 | 9,135 | 553 | 236 | 813 | 7,522 | 380 | 3,007 | 15,505 | 7,317 | 86,980 |
| 1991-2 | 1,148 | 3,445 | 26,100 | 724 | 1,338 | 9,291 | 543 | 101 | 831 | 10,000 | 386 | 2,578 | 17,614 | 6,628 | 95,992 |
| 1992-3 | 666 | 2,113 | 20,700 | 290 | 1,620 | 10,775 | 465 | 133 | 138 | 7,073 | 276 | 2,635 | 16,218 | 5,851 | 82,709 |
| 1993-4 | 1,075 | 1,860 | 17,200 | 244 | 1,882 | 9,487 | 310 | 120 | 110 | 6,282 | 250 | 2,666 | 16,134 | 6,067 | 76,049 |
| 1994-5 | 1,608 | 2,526 | 19,900 | 230 | 1,225 | 10,814 | 542 | 142 | 458 | 6,250 | 400 | 2,886 | 19,662 | 5,778 | 85,610 |
| 1995-6[1] | 1,800 | 1,791 | 21,900 | 324 | 1,088 | 12,493 | 800 | 200 | 860 | 8,200 | 490 | 3,845 | 17,900 | 5,740 | 91,822 |
| 1996-7[2] | 1,950 | 1,400 | 17,500 | 230 | 1,680 | 12,300 | 700 | 175 | 1,100 | 6,800 | 650 | 3,500 | 18,951 | 4,800 | 86,367 |

[1] Preliminary. [2] Estimate. [3] Formerly part of the U.S.S.R.; data not reported separately until 1989. *Source: Foreign Agricultural Service, U.S. Department of Agriculture*

## Cotton World Supply and Demand In Thousands of 480-Lb. Bales

| Crop Year | Beginning Stocks | | | | Production | | | | Consumption | | | | Exports | | | |
|---|---|---|---|---|---|---|---|---|---|---|---|---|---|---|---|---|
| Beginning Aug. 1 | United States | Uzbekistan[3] | China | World Total | United States | Uzbekistan[3] | China | World Total | United States | Russia[3] | China | World Total | United States | Uzbekistan[3] | China | World Total |
| 1982-3 | 6,632 | 2,527 | 1,892 | 25,181 | 11,963 | 10,380 | 16,526 | 66,472 | 5,513 | 7,600 | 16,822 | 66,412 | 5,207 | 3,890 | 75 | 19,452 |
| 1983-4 | 7,937 | 1,900 | 3,101 | 25,198 | 7,771 | 9,976 | 21,298 | 66,460 | 5,926 | 7,900 | 15,714 | 67,353 | 6,786 | 3,202 | 760 | 19,166 |
| 1984-5 | 2,775 | 707 | 8,305 | 23,952 | 12,982 | 11,928 | 28,720 | 88,364 | 5,540 | 8,630 | 16,002 | 69,392 | 6,215 | 2,994 | 944 | 20,206 |
| 1985-6 | 4,102 | 1,460 | 20,146 | 43,246 | 13,432 | 12,778 | 19,046 | 79,863 | 6,399 | 9,200 | 18,909 | 76,070 | 1,960 | 3,170 | 2,799 | 20,299 |
| 1986-7 | 9,348 | 2,260 | 16,848 | 47,026 | 9,731 | 12,217 | 16,261 | 70,107 | 7,452 | 9,400 | 20,976 | 83,793 | 6,684 | 3,462 | 3,169 | 26,014 |
| 1987-8 | 5,026 | 2,031 | 10,795 | 35,926 | 14,760 | 11,345 | 19,500 | 81,109 | 7,617 | 9,000 | 20,065 | 83,500 | 6,582 | 3,457 | 2,322 | 23,227 |
| 1988-9 | 5,771 | 1,302 | 7,559 | 32,850 | 15,412 | 12,704 | 19,056 | 84,423 | 7,782 | 9,200 | 20,533 | 85,352 | 6,148 | 3,656 | 1,636 | 25,869 |
| 1989-90 | 7,092 | 473 | 5,971 | 31,423 | 12,196 | 7,605 | 17,400 | 79,741 | 8,759 | 5,831 | 20,000 | 86,579 | 7,694 | 6,810 | 865 | 31,275 |
| 1990-1 | 3,000 | 460 | 4,379 | 25,771 | 15,505 | 7,317 | 20,700 | 86,968 | 8,657 | 5,469 | 20,000 | 85,677 | 7,793 | 5,393 | 928 | 29,656 |
| 1991-2 | 2,344 | 1,555 | 5,956 | 27,073 | 17,614 | 6,628 | 26,100 | 95,659 | 9,613 | 4,539 | 20,500 | 86,045 | 6,646 | 5,200 | 602 | 28,196 |
| 1992-3 | 3,704 | 2,295 | 12,284 | 37,403 | 16,218 | 5,851 | 20,700 | 82,445 | 10,250 | 2,200 | 21,500 | 85,765 | 5,201 | 5,500 | 684 | 25,583 |
| 1993-4 | 4,662 | 1,845 | 10,442 | 35,121 | 16,134 | 6,067 | 17,200 | 76,697 | 10,418 | 2,200 | 21,300 | 85,353 | 6,862 | 5,800 | 749 | 26,731 |
| 1994-5 | 3,530 | 737 | 6,101 | 26,507 | 19,662 | 5,778 | 19,900 | 85,534 | 11,198 | 1,263 | 20,200 | 84,688 | 9,402 | 5,006 | 183 | 28,476 |
| 1995-6[1] | 2,650 | 956 | 9,678 | 29,299 | 17,900 | 5,740 | 21,900 | 91,822 | 10,604 | 1,150 | 19,500 | 84,304 | 7,675 | 4,500 | 21 | 27,156 |
| 1996-7[2] | 2,609 | 1,326 | 15,102 | 36,169 | 18,951 | 4,800 | 17,500 | 86,367 | 11,000 | 1,050 | 19,000 | 85,345 | 6,300 | 4,300 | 100 | 26,887 |

[1] Preliminary. [2] Estimate. [3] Formerly part of the U.S.S.R.; data not reported separately until 1989. *Source: Foreign Agricultural Service, U.S. Department of Agriculture*

## World Consumption of All Cottons in Specific Countries In Thousands of 480-Lb. Bales

| Crop Year Beginning Aug. 1 | Agrentina | Brazil | China | Egypt | France | Germany | India | Italy | Japan | Mexico | Pakistan | Poland | United Kingdom | United States | Uzbekistan[3] | World Total |
|---|---|---|---|---|---|---|---|---|---|---|---|---|---|---|---|---|
| 1982-3 | 460 | 2,600 | 16,400 | 1,370 | 765 | 928 | 6,250 | 1,030 | 3,290 | 625 | 2,450 | 650 | 230 | 5,513 | 9,200 | 67,862 |
| 1983-4 | 514 | 2,435 | 16,000 | 1,310 | 745 | 976 | 6,531 | 1,170 | 3,300 | 528 | 2,030 | 650 | 234 | 5,921 | 9,300 | 68,612 |
| 1984-5 | 464 | 2,665 | 15,500 | 1,367 | 724 | 1,000 | 7,117 | 1,200 | 3,187 | 550 | 2,264 | 712 | 248 | 5,538 | 9,500 | 69,401 |
| 1985-6 | 551 | 3,100 | 19,500 | 1,550 | 672 | 1,000 | 7,191 | 1,170 | 3,146 | 670 | 2,342 | 750 | 248 | 6,413 | 9,600 | 76,888 |
| 1986-7 | 575 | 3,285 | 20,200 | 1,290 | 710 | 1,100 | 7,847 | 1,419 | 3,445 | 580 | 2,990 | 600 | 225 | 7,452 | 9,350 | 82,239 |
| 1987-8 | 575 | 3,399 | 20,000 | 1,334 | 690 | 1,110 | 7,612 | 1,381 | 3,477 | 600 | 3,600 | 715 | 216 | 7,617 | 9,300 | 83,499 |
| 1988-9 | 551 | 3,766 | 20,500 | 1,300 | 640 | 910 | 8,139 | 1,424 | 3,408 | 650 | 3,904 | 725 | 193 | 7,782 | 9,100 | 85,565 |
| 1989-90 | 533 | 3,445 | 20,000 | 1,352 | 600 | 1,435 | 8,667 | 1,450 | 3,229 | 725 | 4,801 | 650 | 170 | 8,759 | 9,200 | 86,579 |
| 1990-1 | 597 | 3,215 | 20,000 | 1,457 | 530 | 955 | 9,018 | 1,470 | 3,027 | 712 | 5,648 | 410 | 140 | 8,657 | 8,700 | 85,677 |
| 1991-2 | 606 | 3,215 | 19,000 | 1,465 | 484 | 830 | 8,674 | 1,447 | 2,783 | 772 | 6,482 | 275 | 100 | 9,613 | 860 | 86,136 |
| 1992-3 | 588 | 3,445 | 21,500 | 1,640 | 470 | 680 | 9,761 | 1,400 | 2,301 | 740 | 6,634 | 390 | 85 | 10,250 | 950 | 85,770 |
| 1993-4 | 550 | 3,675 | 20,900 | 1,530 | 500 | 750 | 9,950 | 1,375 | 2,060 | 825 | 6,500 | 400 | 85 | 10,418 | 925 | 85,325 |
| 1994-5 | 459 | 4,000 | 20,200 | 1,350 | 500 | 660 | 10,334 | 1,525 | 1,800 | 800 | 6,750 | 400 | 90 | 11,198 | 750 | 84,574 |
| 1995-6[1] | 460 | 3,900 | 19,500 | 1,010 | 450 | 610 | 11,400 | 1,470 | 1,520 | 1,000 | 7,000 | 415 | 90 | 10,604 | 875 | 84,304 |
| 1996-7[2] | 460 | 4,000 | 19,000 | 1,150 | 450 | 590 | 11,800 | 1,470 | 1,425 | 1,200 | 7,100 | 425 | 90 | 11,000 | 920 | 85,345 |

[1] Preliminary. [2] Estimate. [3] Formerly part of the U.S.S.R.; data not reported separately until 1991. *Source: Foreign Agricultural Service, U.S. Department of Agriculture*

# COTTON

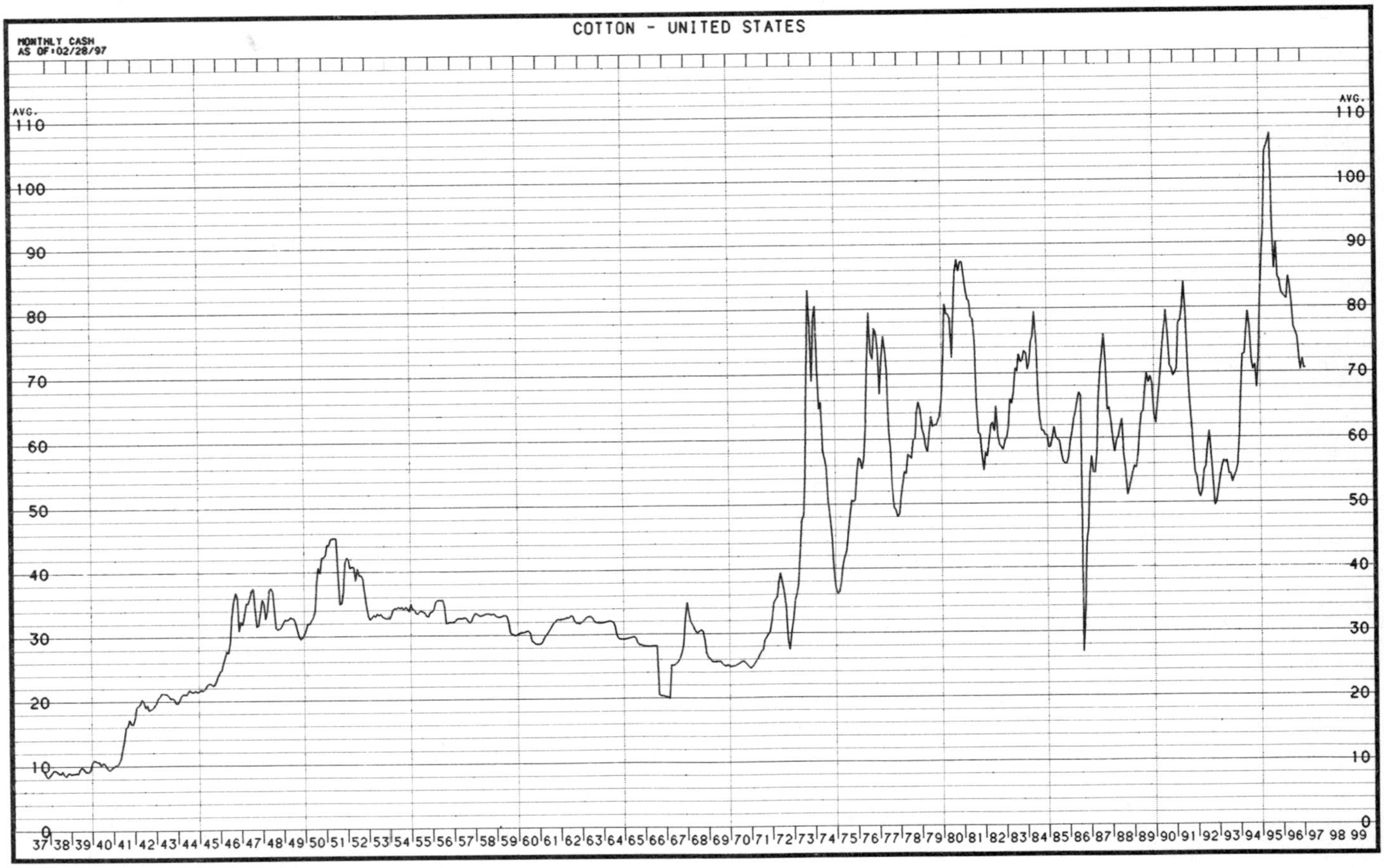


## Average Spot Cotton Prices[2], C.I.F. Northern Europe In U.S. Cents Per Pound

| Crop Year Beginning Aug. 1 | Argentina "C"[3] 1 1/16" | Australia M 1 3/32" | Central America[4] M 1 3/32" | China Type 329 | Cotlook Index A | Cotlook Index B | Egypt Giza[5] 81 | Greece M 1 3/32" | Mexico M 1 3/32" | Pakistan Sind/ Punjab[6] | Tanzania AR[7] Type 3 | Turkey Izmir[8] 1 3/32" | U.S. Calif. ACALA SJV[9] | U.S. Memphis Terr.[10] M 1 3/32" | U.S. Orleans/ Texas[11] M 1 1/32" |
|---|---|---|---|---|---|---|---|---|---|---|---|---|---|---|---|
| | M & SM 1" - 1 3/32" | | | | | | | | | | | | | | |
| 1979-80 | 75.04 | ------ | 83.46 | ------ | 85.40 | 74.55 | 136.37 | 84.00 | 77.87 | 75.45 | 84.01 | ------ | 90.69 | 78.47 | 75.36 |
| 1980-1 | 82.06 | ------ | 98.25 | ------ | 94.20 | 84.20 | 137.66 | 100.41 | 95.48 | 85.11 | 103.78 | 97.43 | 101.85 | 99.99 | 89.14 |
| 1981-2 | 63.55 | ------ | 72.99 | ------ | 73.80 | 64.40 | 115.73 | 81.06 | 75.36 | 65.56 | 87.92 | 77.65 | 79.79 | 75.87 | 66.76 |
| 1982-3 | 62.63 | ------ | 76.13 | ------ | 76.65 | 66.60 | 110.07 | 85.25 | 76.37 | 65.58 | 87.19 | 83.28 | 84.94 | 77.95 | 68.11 |
| 1983-4 | 83.32 | 90.83 | 86.86 | ------ | 87.65 | 80.40 | 134.07 | 94.42 | 87.54 | 75.51 | 95.23 | 92.64 | 94.90 | 87.23 | 78.41 |
| 1984-5 | 60.95 | 60.33 | 67.22 | 62.50 | 69.15 | 59.55 | 134.01 | 76.14 | 70.10 | 56.20 | 77.29 | 75.92 | 76.20 | 73.88 | 65.95 |
| 1985-6 | 49.42 | 50.05 | 42.39 | 42.39 | 49.00 | 40.95 | 111.40 | 50.98 | 53.16 | 37.92 | 55.81 | 57.06 | 59.43 | 65.01 | 52.26 |
| 1986-7 | 68.97 | 66.59 | 62.76 | 62.11 | 62.05 | 55.05 | 112.59 | 63.53 | 64.64 | 55.11 | 67.41 | 64.63 | 74.27 | 61.96 | 56.38 |
| 1987-8 | 64.13 | 76.14 | 71.94 | 71.94 | 72.30 | 67.50 | 145.11 | 83.85 | 73.75 | 65.88 | 87.96 | 86.43 | 81.17 | 74.24 | 72.07 |
| 1988-9 | 64.11 | 72.14 | 60.69 | 60.69 | 66.35 | 61.30 | 176.85 | 63.07 | 61.54 | 56.98 | 69.09 | 68.98 | 77.13 | 69.00 | 63.92 |
| 1989-90 | 77.05 | 84.16 | 80.63 | 85.92 | 82.40 | 77.40 | 189.54 | 83.76 | 82.50 | 76.75 | 86.68 | 90.49 | 88.59 | 83.90 | 78.93 |
| 1990-1 | 77.06 | 85.58 | 83.28 | 87.45 | 82.90 | 77.80 | 177.43 | 84.24 | 84.46 | 77.19 | 89.62 | 81.32 | 92.84 | 88.13 | 80.35 |
| 1991-2 | 55.08 | 65.97 | 68.40 | 71.72 | 63.05 | 58.50 | 128.10 | 65.90 | 68.19 | 58.14 | 68.90 | 74.66 | 74.47 | 66.35 | 63.41 |
| 1992-3 | 64.31 | 64.01 | ------ | 61.59 | 57.70 | 53.70 | 99.24 | 56.92 | ------ | 52.66 | 62.24 | ------ | 68.37 | 63.08 | 58.89 |
| 1993-4 | 80.20 | 72.81 | ------ | 73.49 | 70.60 | 67.30 | 88.35 | 58.81 | ------ | 54.42 | 69.83 | 59.80 | 77.55 | 72.80 | 69.78 |
| 1994-5 | 101.88 | 81.05 | ------ | ------ | 92.75 | 92.40 | 93.70 | 88.64 | 82.65 | 73.75 | ------ | ------ | 106.40 | 98.67 | 95.70 |
| 1995-6[1] | 82.98 | 93.75 | ------ | ------ | 85.61 | 81.06 | ------ | 84.95 | 94.94 | 81.86 | 96.20 | 90.38 | 103.49 | 94.71 | 90.37 |

[1] Preliminary. [2] Generally for prompt shipment. [3] 1 1/32 inches prior to January 20, 1984; 1 1/16 inches since. [4] Guatemala SM 1 1/16 inches 1971/72 through 1985/86; Central American Middling 1 3/32 inches since. [5] Giza 67 1969/70 until December 1983; Giza 69/75/81 until November 1990; Giza 81 since. [6] Punjab until 1979/80; Sind SG until June 1984; Sind/Punjab SG until January 1985; Afzal 1 inch until January 1986; Afzal 1 1/32 inches since. [7] No. 1 until 1978/79; No. 1/2 until January 1987; Izmir/Antalya ST 1 White 1 3/32 inches RG since. [9] SM 1 1/8 inches. [10] SM 1 1/16 inches prior to 1981-82; Middling 1 3/32 inches since. [11] Middling 1 inch prior to 1988/89; Middling 1 1/32 inches since. NA = Not available. *Source: International Cotton Advisory Committee*

## Average Price of Strict Low Middling 1 1/16", Cotton at Designated U.S. Markets ¢ Per Pound (Net Weight)

| Year | Aug. | Sept. | Oct. | Nov. | Dec. | Jan. | Feb. | Mar. | Apr. | May | June | July | Average |
|---|---|---|---|---|---|---|---|---|---|---|---|---|---|
| 1986-7 | 26.81 | 33.56 | 43.95 | 45.74 | 54.19 | 57.17 | 54.75 | 54.60 | 57.72 | 65.94 | 70.42 | 73.07 | 53.16 |
| 1987-8 | 75.89 | 71.41 | 64.30 | 64.66 | 62.26 | 59.69 | 57.83 | 59.64 | 60.07 | 61.55 | 62.86 | 57.40 | 63.13 |
| 1988-9 | 55.20 | 51.25 | 52.20 | 53.40 | 54.80 | 55.67 | 55.37 | 57.59 | 61.43 | 63.70 | 64.06 | 67.39 | 57.67 |
| 1989-90 | 69.88 | 68.46 | 69.40 | 68.33 | 63.56 | 62.21 | 64.95 | 68.06 | 71.31 | 74.61 | 77.06 | 79.53 | 69.78 |
| 1990-1 | 76.27 | 71.01 | 70.54 | 69.48 | 69.92 | 70.50 | 77.69 | 77.92 | 79.94 | 83.94 | 79.05 | 71.33 | 74.80 |
| 1991-2 | 66.44 | 62.39 | 58.28 | 54.70 | 53.89 | 51.54 | 50.76 | 52.01 | 54.97 | 55.45 | 58.82 | 60.93 | 56.68 |
| 1992-3 | 57.56 | 53.49 | 49.47 | 49.98 | 51.85 | 53.72 | 55.38 | 56.45 | 56.17 | 56.37 | 54.38 | 54.35 | 54.10 |
| 1993-4 | 53.04 | 54.01 | 54.58 | 55.61 | 60.29 | 66.53 | 72.69 | 72.74 | 76.12 | 79.30 | 76.85 | 71.71 | 66.12 |
| 1994-5 | 70.32 | 71.10 | 67.58 | 72.00 | 81.92 | 88.11 | 91.89 | 104.20 | 104.94 | 105.38 | 106.96 | 93.26 | 88.14 |
| 1995-6 | 85.90 | 90.00 | 84.65 | 84.16 | 82.18 | 81.81 | 81.56 | 81.13 | 84.69 | 83.22 | 80.23 | 76.84 | 83.03 |
| 1996-7[1] | 76.15 | 75.24 | 72.21 | 70.12 | 71.98 | 70.53 | 70.53 | | | | | | 72.39 |

[1] Preliminary. Note: Grade 41, staple 34 cotton. *Source: Agricultural Marketing Service, U.S Department of Agriculture*

## Average Spot Cotton, 1 3/32", Price (SLM) at Designated U.S. Markets In Cents Per Pound (Net Weight)

| Year | Aug. | Sept. | Oct. | Nov. | Dec. | Jan. | Feb. | Mar. | Apr. | May | June | July | Average | 1 1/32" | 1" |
|---|---|---|---|---|---|---|---|---|---|---|---|---|---|---|---|
| 1986-7 | 28.44 | 35.56 | 46.29 | 48.13 | 56.97 | 59.73 | 57.16 | 56.97 | 60.03 | 68.45 | 73.01 | 75.11 | 55.49 | 50.78 | 47.77 |
| 1987-8 | 78.02 | 73.59 | 66.12 | 66.19 | 64.12 | 61.79 | 60.36 | 62.35 | 63.00 | 64.43 | 65.90 | 60.71 | 65.55 | 60.81 | 59.33 |
| 1988-9 | 58.64 | 54.52 | 54.26 | 54.91 | 56.55 | 57.81 | 57.80 | 59.75 | 63.49 | 66.07 | 66.53 | 69.90 | 60.02 | 53.99 | 52.32 |
| 1989-90 | 72.45 | 71.24 | 71.55 | 70.23 | 65.61 | 63.83 | 66.39 | 69.55 | 72.85 | 76.32 | 78.73 | 81.34 | 71.67 | 66.02 | 64.89 |
| 1990-1 | 78.06 | 72.87 | 72.19 | 70.97 | 71.61 | 72.14 | 79.38 | 79.86 | 81.99 | 85.94 | 81.02 | 73.28 | 76.61 | 71.52 | 69.15 |
| 1991-2 | 68.24 | 64.18 | 59.74 | 55.57 | 54.62 | 52.39 | 51.84 | 53.11 | 56.30 | 56.90 | 60.26 | 62.35 | 57.96 | 54.15 | 53.23 |
| 1992-3 | 59.08 | 54.99 | 50.96 | 51.41 | 53.37 | 55.24 | 56.86 | 58.30 | 58.03 | 58.23 | 56.24 | 56.22 | 55.74 | 52.42 | 52.46 |
| 1993-4 | 54.89 | 55.90 | 56.46 | 57.34 | 61.76 | 67.97 | 73.99 | 74.15 | 77.55 | 80.42 | 78.01 | 72.97 | 67.62 | 64.28 | 63.91 |
| 1994-5 | 71.46 | 72.42 | 68.82 | 73.38 | 83.41 | 89.92 | 94.25 | 106.66 | 107.50 | 107.93 | 109.52 | 96.31 | 90.13 | 85.13 | 84.47 |
| 1995-6 | 88.31 | 92.71 | 87.06 | 86.43 | 84.25 | 84.32 | 84.04 | 83.65 | 87.25 | 85.90 | 82.71 | 78.86 | 85.46 | 80.33 | 77.72 |
| 1996-7 | 77.97 | 76.92 | 73.90 | 71.74 | 75.75 | 72.53 | 72.86 | | | | | | 74.52 | | |

[1] Preliminary. *Source: Economic Research Service, U.S. Department of Agriculture*

## Average Spot Prices of U.S. Cotton,[1] Base Quality--(SLM) at Designated Markets In Cents Per Pound

| Crop Year Beginning Aug. 1 | Dallas (East Tex.-Okl.) | Fresno (San Joaquin Valley) | Greenville (South-east) | Green-wood (South Delta) | Lubbock (West Texas) | Memphis (North Delta) | Phoenix Desert (South-west) | Average |
|---|---|---|---|---|---|---|---|---|
| 1986-7 | 51.03 | 60.97 | 51.66 | 51.99 | 51.20 | 51.70 | 55.38 | 53.16 |
| 1987-8 | 61.14 | 66.02 | 63.37 | 62.41 | 61.09 | 62.54 | 65.69 | 63.13 |
| 1988-9 | 55.88 | 63.30 | 57.26 | 56.67 | 55.77 | 56.71 | 59.67 | 57.90 |
| 1989-90 | 67.11 | 73.47 | 70.64 | 69.50 | 67.06 | 69.51 | 71.19 | 69.78 |
| 1990-1 | 71.40 | 78.30 | 75.90 | 75.53 | 71.09 | 75.49 | 75.90 | 74.80 |
| 1991-2 | 55.63 | 57.50 | 57.70 | 56.21 | 55.79 | 56.18 | 57.77 | 56.68 |
| 1992-3 | 53.78 | 52.84 | 56.73 | 55.03 | 53.53 | 55.03 | 51.61 | 54.10 |
| 1993-4[2] | 66.22 | 65.04 | 67.46 | 67.04 | 65.92 | 67.04 | 64.16 | 66.12 |
| 1994-5 | 86.96 | 93.73 | 87.17 | 87.25 | 86.66 | 87.25 | 87.96 | 88.14 |
| 1995-6 | 80.89 | 87.40 | 83.86 | 83.76 | 80.64 | 83.76 | 80.90 | 83.03 |

[1] Prices are for mixed lots, net weight, uncompressed in warehouse. [2] 1993/94 prices are for mixed lots, net weight, compressed, F.O.B. car/truck.
*Source: Agricultural Marketing Service, U.S. Department of Agriculture*

## Average Price[1] Received by Farmers for Upland Cotton in the U.S. In Cents Per Pound

| Year | Aug. | Sept. | Oct. | Nov. | Dec. | Jan. | Feb. | Mar | Apr. | May | June | July | Average |
|---|---|---|---|---|---|---|---|---|---|---|---|---|---|
| 1986-7 | 46.8 | 48.6 | 50.0 | 52.6 | 52.7 | 52.1 | 46.4 | 47.5 | 50.4 | 60.0 | 66.2 | 68.3 | 51.5 |
| 1987-8 | 63.8 | 65.4 | 65.1 | 65.6 | 64.6 | 61.7 | 57.0 | 57.9 | 59.9 | 58.3 | 62.0 | 59.5 | 63.7 |
| 1988-9 | 53.9 | 51.9 | 55.1 | 57.5 | 55.3 | 54.7 | 52.8 | 55.6 | 58.7 | 58.3 | 57.2 | 59.5 | 55.6 |
| 1989-90 | 60.4 | 63.8 | 65.8 | 65.6 | 61.9 | 60.2 | 61.0 | 63.9 | 65.8 | 66.2 | 64.0 | 63.9 | 63.6 |
| 1990-1 | 64.6 | 65.1 | 67.7 | 68.4 | 67.1 | 64.9 | 67.9 | 68.9 | 69.5 | 70.1 | 67.5 | 66.3 | 67.1 |
| 1991-2 | 66.3 | 64.9 | 62.9 | 61.2 | 55.7 | 51.7 | 49.8 | 50.3 | 53.1 | 53.2 | 58.0 | 56.3 | 56.8 |
| 1992-3 | 52.7 | 52.8 | 53.9 | 52.7 | 54.3 | 53.0 | 53.8 | 56.3 | 55.1 | 54.4 | 53.6 | 53.7 | 53.7 |
| 1993-4 | 52.4 | 51.4 | 52.4 | 53.3 | 56.5 | 62.7 | 65.7 | 66.6 | 67.5 | 69.0 | 63.3 | 58.7 | 58.1 |
| 1994-5 | 66.8 | 65.9 | 66.2 | 68.5 | 73.3 | 78.7 | 80.2 | 82.6 | 77.6 | 76.2 | 86.5 | 80.1 | 72.0 |
| 1995-6 | 72.2 | 74.8 | 74.2 | 75.0 | 75.7 | 76.4 | 75.7 | 76.8 | 78.9 | 76.7 | 76.9 | 73.6 | 75.4 |
| 1996-7[2] | 71.9 | 71.7 | 71.5 | 69.7 | 69.4 | 67.8 | 66.7 | | | | | | 69.8 |

[1] Weighted average by sales. [2] Preliminary. *Source: Agricultural Marketing Service, U.S. Department of Agriculture*

# COTTON

## Purchases Reported by Exchanges in Designated U.S. Spot Markets[1] In Running Bales

| Year Beginning Aug. 1 | Aug. | Sept. | Oct. | Nov. | Dec. | Jan. | Feb. | Mar. | Apr. | May | June | July | Market Total |
|---|---|---|---|---|---|---|---|---|---|---|---|---|---|
| 1986-7 | 585,628 | 638,356 | 392,451 | 422,542 | 1,353,241 | 1,055,081 | 633,852 | 354,643 | 501,265 | 354,008 | 163,307 | 160,474 | 6,614,848 |
| 1987-8 | 152,935 | 252,669 | 650,349 | 718,829 | 1,065,457 | 622,727 | 571,851 | 463,739 | 266,545 | 572,702 | 336,191 | 117,645 | 5,791,639 |
| 1988-9 | 288,187 | 166,692 | 230,724 | 163,642 | 323,025 | 383,699 | 811,630 | 388,169 | 307,937 | 282,564 | 261,958 | 282,288 | 3,890,515 |
| 1989-90 | 119,516 | 49,237 | 89,853 | 214,910 | 258,849 | 388,519 | 333,417 | 206,528 | 157,187 | 86,966 | 42,299 | 46,312 | 1,993,593 |
| 1990-1 | 36,735 | 53,948 | 154,499 | 376,790 | 600,752 | 516,421 | 180,949 | 66,869 | 138,503 | 101,180 | 45,731 | 40,551 | 2,312,928 |
| 1991-2 | 50,469 | 55,637 | 179,671 | 347,393 | 776,233 | 1,043,190 | 1,063,959 | 699,026 | 302,102 | 110,764 | 134,500 | 105,795 | 4,868,739 |
| 1992-3 | 81,778 | 233,424 | 325,600 | 853,846 | 1,049,780 | 1,321,861 | 317,451 | 330,381 | 224,874 | 208,962 | 189,401 | 231,390 | 5,368,748 |
| 1993-4 | 143,237 | 173,896 | 321,119 | 1,071,518 | 1,213,655 | 500,246 | 602,766 | 318,008 | 234,331 | 318,244 | 83,083 | 40,699 | 5,020,802 |
| 1994-5 | 92,401 | 98,251 | 426,371 | 1,075,829 | 1,491,429 | 608,701 | 233,159 | 149,762 | 49,192 | 44,228 | 43,821 | 13,244 | 4,326,388 |
| 1995-6 | 60,442 | 38,855 | 73,857 | 209,279 | 381,943 | 765,502 | 153,758 | 241,197 | 225,797 | 73,459 | 59,042 | 31,324 | 2,314,455 |
| 1996-7 | 62,884 | 73,925 | 148,337 | 477,331 | 613,430 | 696,494 | 412,095 | | | | | | 2,484,496 |

[1] Commencing March 28, 1983, spot transactions are for eight markets; and commencing September 1, 1988, spot transactions are for seven markets.
*Source: Agricultural Marketing Service, U.S. Department of Agriculture*

## Average Open Interest of Cotton Futures in New York In Contracts

| Year | Jan. | Feb. | Mar. | Apr. | May | June | July | Aug. | Sept. | Oct. | Nov. | Dec. |
|---|---|---|---|---|---|---|---|---|---|---|---|---|
| 1987 | 25,196 | 25,048 | 22,482 | 23,760 | 26,074 | 27,996 | 32,012 | 37,426 | 39,204 | 39,912 | 38,017 | 33,888 |
| 1988 | 35,240 | 35,974 | 30,507 | 29,933 | 29,753 | 31,804 | 28,307 | 34,637 | 38,453 | 37,162 | 33,210 | 30,682 |
| 1989 | 31,415 | 30,978 | 36,725 | 36,657 | 40,761 | 38,693 | 40,059 | 45,894 | 49,629 | 49,072 | 48,136 | 42,349 |
| 1990 | 40,237 | 36,291 | 36,073 | 37,829 | 37,908 | 38,556 | 36,083 | 34,042 | 35,250 | 40,431 | 43,997 | 40,241 |
| 1991 | 43,003 | 46,793 | 44,001 | 43,957 | 50,086 | 46,637 | 40,924 | 39,616 | 38,252 | 39,772 | 39,295 | 36,066 |
| 1992 | 38,097 | 40,095 | 38,592 | 36,228 | 37,839 | 36,861 | 35,891 | 42,241 | 46,168 | 46,577 | 40,425 | 38,487 |
| 1993 | 41,946 | 38,657 | 38,576 | 33,641 | 33,012 | 34,057 | 32,118 | 33,872 | 37,393 | 36,479 | 38,567 | 45,975 |
| 1994 | 54,424 | 55,558 | 53,724 | 54,670 | 52,830 | 51,001 | 52,357 | 50,597 | 50,955 | 51,561 | 53,563 | 59,065 |
| 1995 | 71,353 | 75,100 | 79,090 | 71,488 | 71,714 | 68,159 | 65,656 | 69,653 | 69,528 | 65,768 | 38,475 | 35,996 |
| 1996 | 58,001 | 60,231 | 57,542 | 61,795 | 64,555 | 62,342 | 61,921 | 60,182 | 58,168 | 58,415 | 57,397 | 47,652 |

*Source: New York Cotton Exchange (NYCE)*

## Volume of Trading of Cotton Futures in New York In Contracts

| Year | Jan. | Feb. | Mar. | Apr. | May | June | July | Aug. | Sept. | Oct. | Nov. | Dec. | Total |
|---|---|---|---|---|---|---|---|---|---|---|---|---|---|
| 1987 | 110,165 | 106,520 | 88,621 | 106,620 | 110,303 | 132,180 | 98,339 | 127,048 | 131,214 | 124,319 | 126,582 | 107,124 | 1,395,980 |
| 1988 | 114,672 | 119,832 | 97,533 | 118,614 | 127,880 | 149,303 | 89,907 | 100,447 | 108,285 | 135,221 | 124,221 | 84,334 | 1,370,249 |
| 1989 | 124,764 | 135,963 | 113,028 | 118,573 | 135,044 | 167,442 | 91,381 | 151,034 | 165,255 | 143,713 | 178,889 | 124,034 | 1,649,120 |
| 1990 | 135,260 | 116,806 | 126,820 | 121,203 | 139,489 | 135,040 | 132,329 | 129,081 | 103,936 | 142,670 | 150,958 | 98,895 | 1,534,611 |
| 1991 | 133,415 | 179,656 | 148,918 | 156,978 | 174,690 | 122,242 | 116,458 | 115,175 | 107,742 | 125,558 | 150,545 | 82,867 | 1,614,244 |
| 1992 | 134,531 | 134,184 | 149,711 | 167,778 | 173,128 | 153,194 | 105,534 | 142,323 | 144,844 | 129,680 | 161,194 | 105,157 | 1,701,258 |
| 1993 | 171,180 | 135,400 | 136,965 | 135,300 | 105,920 | 128,985 | 130,886 | 122,280 | 110,989 | 107,571 | 178,350 | 139,344 | 1,603,027 |
| 1994 | 210,011 | 207,421 | 210,363 | 252,614 | 179,591 | 208,945 | 161,688 | 128,879 | 140,574 | 179,604 | 205,936 | 203,021 | 2,289,998 |
| 1995 | 223,073 | 290,600 | 286,098 | 219,187 | 214,052 | 185,276 | 183,171 | 199,050 | 191,534 | 196,676 | 195,601 | 141,116 | 2,525,434 |
| 1996 | 215,882 | 196,225 | 147,393 | 251,786 | 236,684 | 264,047 | 131,183 | 177,430 | 166,629 | 229,305 | 229,281 | 128,010 | 2,373,855 |

*Source: New York Cotton Exchange (NYCE)*

## United States Government Crop Forecasts and Actual Cotton Crops

| | Forecast of Production (1,000 Bales of 480 Lbs.[1]) | | | | | | Actual | Forecasts of Yields (Lbs. Per Harvested Acre) | | | | | | Actual |
|---|---|---|---|---|---|---|---|---|---|---|---|---|---|---|
| Year | Aug.1 | Sept.1 | Oct. 1 | Nov. 1 | Dec. 1 | Jan. 1 | Crop | Aug.1 | Sept.1 | Oct. 1 | Nov. 1 | Dec. 1 | Jan. 1 | Yield |
| 1982 | 11,143 | 11,029 | 11,365 | 11,947 | 12,102 | ------ | 11,963 | 563 | 569 | 587 | 605 | 613 | ------ | 590 |
| 1983 | 7,810 | 7,776 | 7,550 | 7,497 | 7,725 | ------ | 7,771 | 503 | 501 | 487 | 504 | 506 | ------ | 508 |
| 1984 | 12,569 | 13,276 | 13,272 | 13,271 | 13,292 | ------ | 12,982 | 583 | 615 | 620 | 613 | 610 | ------ | 600 |
| 1985 | 13,780 | 13,655 | 13,638 | 13,875 | 13,810 | 13,534 | 13,432 | 638 | 632 | 633 | 644 | 644 | 630 | 630 |
| 1986 | 10,676 | 10,506 | 10,006 | 9,875 | 9,792 | 9,785 | 9,731 | 573 | 565 | 539 | 546 | 539 | 553 | 552 |
| 1987 | 12,907 | 12,846 | 13,336 | 13,936 | 14,281 | 14,724 | 14,760 | 615 | 616 | 640 | 671 | 695 | 703 | 706 |
| 1988 | 14,934 | 14,709 | 14,714 | 14,837 | 15,197 | 15,446 | 15,411 | 616 | 605 | 605 | 612 | 627 | 623 | 619 |
| 1989 | 11,834 | 12,279 | 11,991 | 12,102 | 12,083 | 11,233 | 12,196 | 618 | 603 | 607 | 608 | 619 | 619 | 614 |
| 1990 | 14,864 | 14,722 | 14,540 | 14,905 | 15,399 | 15,617 | 15,499 | 622 | 616 | 609 | 622 | 640 | 640 | 634 |
| 1991 | 17,648 | 17,868 | 17,614 | 13,429 | 14,052 | 17,542 | 17,614 | 630 | 638 | 620 | 635 | 630 | 656 | 652 |
| 1992 | 16,533 | 17,943 | 15,885 | 16,204 | 16,259 | 16,260 | 16,219 | 696 | 685 | 694 | 698 | 696 | 700 | 699 |
| 1993 | 18,545 | 17,867 | 17,014 | 16,297 | 16,284 | 16,176 | 16,134 | 668 | 645 | 614 | 594 | 597 | 607 | 606 |
| 1994 | 19,195 | 19,025 | 19,303 | 19,453 | 19,573 | 19,728 | 19,662 | 690 | 690 | 690 | 695 | 699 | 710 | 708 |
| 1995 | 21,811 | 20,266 | 18,771 | 18,838 | 18,236 | 17,971 | 17,900 | 663 | 615 | 574 | 567 | 551 | 540 | 537 |
| 1996 | 18,577 | 17,900 | 18,189 | 18,594 | 18,738 | 18,951 | 18,951 | 686 | 661 | 673 | 698 | 704 | 709 | 709 |

[1] Net weight bales. *Source: Agricultural Statistics Board, U.S. Department of Agriculture*

## U.S. Production of Cotton (Upland) & American-Pima In Thousands of 480-Pound Bales

| Year | Alabama | Arizona | Arkansas | California | Georgia | Louisiana | Mississippi | Missouri | New Mexico | North Carolina | Oklahoma | South Carolina | Tennessee | Texas | Total American-Pima |
|---|---|---|---|---|---|---|---|---|---|---|---|---|---|---|---|
| | Upland | | | | | | | | | | | | | | |
| 1979 | 324 | 1,280 | 606 | 3,408 | 152 | 690 | 1,437 | 157 | 104 | 43 | 522 | 116 | 171 | 5,515 | 98.6 |
| 1980 | 275 | 1,354 | 444 | 3,109 | 86 | 460 | 1,143 | 177 | 107 | 52 | 205 | 77 | 200 | 3,320 | 104.2 |
| 1981 | 422 | 1,556 | 604 | 3,535 | 159 | 742 | 1,565 | 168 | 141 | 95 | 440 | 164 | 315 | 5,663 | 79.6 |
| 1982 | 460 | 1,095 | 534 | 3,073 | 235 | 870 | 1,760 | 204 | 78 | 102 | 238 | 155 | 339 | 2,700 | 98.7 |
| 1983 | 183 | 725 | 323 | 1,971 | 112 | 532 | 900 | 73 | 70 | 43 | 145 | 53 | 151 | 2,380 | 94.7 |
| 1984 | 447 | 1,097 | 612 | 2,913 | 281 | 1,056 | 1,650 | 187 | 87 | 120 | 183 | 170 | 337 | 3,680 | 130.4 |
| 1985 | 545 | 928 | 703 | 3,114 | 370 | 742 | 1,655 | 204 | 71 | 117 | 285 | 180 | 419 | 3,910 | 155.1 |
| 1986 | 330 | 675 | 602 | 2,245 | 185 | 673 | 1,190 | 196 | 62 | 109 | 210 | 87 | 396 | 2,535 | 205.9 |
| 1987 | 397 | 849 | 901 | 2,989 | 338 | 977 | 1,745 | 330 | 89 | 98 | 346 | 106 | 634 | 4,635 | 284.6 |
| 1988 | 380 | 865 | 1,044 | 2,824 | 370 | 948 | 1,825 | 306 | 102 | 133 | 303 | 140 | 584 | 5,215 | 334.2 |
| 1989 | 383 | 649 | 851 | 2,661 | 342 | 868 | 1,555 | 269 | 80 | 141 | 173 | 154 | 476 | 2,870 | 691.7 |
| 1990 | 375 | 811 | 1,081 | 2,734 | 405 | 1,177 | 1,850 | 314 | 95 | 263 | 382 | 145 | 495 | 4,965 | 358.5 |
| 1991 | 553 | 898 | 1,576 | 2,548 | 722 | 1,414 | 2,275 | 429 | 63 | 640 | 240 | 344 | 701 | 4,710 | 398.4 |
| 1992 | 621 | 725 | 1,681 | 2,817 | 744 | 1,299 | 2,131 | 541 | 48 | 468 | 210 | 226 | 834 | 3,265 | 508.3 |
| 1993 | 469 | 790 | 1,094 | 2,918 | 733 | 1,105 | 1,550 | 376 | 78 | 429 | 270 | 204 | 545 | 5,095 | 369.3 |
| 1994 | 726 | 862 | 1,772 | 2,902 | 1,537 | 1,512 | 2,132 | 615 | 95 | 829 | 247 | 393 | 885 | 4,968 | 337.7 |
| 1995[1] | 492 | 793 | 1,468 | 2,312 | 1,941 | 1,375 | 1,841 | 513 | 71 | 798 | 123 | 376 | 724 | 4,460 | 367.6 |
| 1996[2] | 810 | 770 | 1,600 | 2,400 | 2,100 | 1,300 | 1,850 | 600 | 96 | 990 | | 130 | 465 | 674 | 4,350 |

[1] Preliminary. *Source: Agricultural Statistics Board, U.S. Department of Agriculture*

# COTTON

## Supply and Distribution of Upland Cotton in the United States
In Thousands of 480-Pound Bales

| Crop Year Beginning Aug. 1 | Area: Planted (1,000 Acres) | Area: Harvested (1,000 Acres) | Yield Lbs./Acre | Supply: Beginning Stocks[3] | Supply: Production[4] | Supply: Imports | Supply: Total | Disappearance: Mill Use | Disappearance: Exports | Disappearance: Total | Ending Stocks | Farm Price[5] Cents/Lb. |
|---|---|---|---|---|---|---|---|---|---|---|---|---|
| 1983-4 | 7,863 | 7,285 | 506 | 7,844 | 7,676 | 8 | 15,528 | 5,853 | 6,750 | 12,603 | 2,693 | 65.3 |
| 1984-5 | 11,065 | 10,300 | 599 | 2,693 | 12,851 | 21 | 15,566 | 5,490 | 6,125 | 11,615 | 4,024 | 58.7 |
| 1985-6 | 10,601 | 10,145 | 628 | 4,024 | 13,277 | 33 | 17,334 | 6,352 | 1,855 | 8,207 | 9,289 | 56.8 |
| 1986-7 | 9,933 | 8,357 | 547 | 9,289 | 9,525 | 3 | 18,817 | 7,385 | 6,570 | 13,955 | 4,942 | 51.5 |
| 1987-8 | 10,259 | 9,894 | 702 | 4,942 | 14,475 | 2 | 19,419 | 7,565 | 6,345 | 13,910 | 5,718 | 63.7 |
| 1988-9 | 12,325 | 11,759 | 615 | 5,718 | 15,077 | 5 | 20,800 | 7,711 | 5,883 | 13,594 | 7,026 | 55.6 |
| 1989-90 | 10,210 | 9,166 | 602 | 7,026 | 11,504 | 2 | 18,532 | 8,686 | 7,242 | 15,928 | 2,798 | 63.6 |
| 1990-1 | 12,117 | 11,505 | 632 | 2,798 | 15,147 | 4 | 17,949 | 8,592 | 7,378 | 15,970 | 2,262 | 67.1 |
| 1991-2 | 13,802 | 12,716 | 650 | 2,262 | 17,216 | 13 | 19,491 | 9,548 | 6,348 | 15,896 | 3,583 | 56.8 |
| 1992-3 | 12,977 | 10,863 | 694 | 3,583 | 15,710 | 1 | 19,294 | 10,190 | 4,869 | 15,059 | 4,456 | 53.7 |
| 1993-4 | 13,248 | 12,594 | 601 | 4,456 | 15,764 | 6 | 20,226 | 10,346 | 6,555 | 16,901 | 3,303 | 58.1 |
| 1994-5 | 13,552 | 13,156 | 705 | 3,303 | 19,324 | 18 | 22,645 | 11,109 | 8,978 | 20,087 | 2,588 | 72.0 |
| 1995-6[1] | 16,717 | 15,796 | 533 | 2,588 | 17,532 | 400 | 20,520 | 10,502 | 7,375 | 17,877 | 2,541 | 75.4 |
| 1996-7[2] | 13,979 | 12,518 | 691 | 2,541 | 18,027 | 495 | 21,063 | 10,895 | 5,375 | 16,270 | 4,790 | |

[1] Preliminary. [2] Estimate. [3] Excludes preseason ginnings (adjusted to 480-lb. bale net weight basis). [4] Includes preseason ginnings. [5] Marketing year

## U.S. Daily Rate of Upland Cotton Mill Consumption[2] on Cotton-System Spinning Spindles
In Thousands of Running Bales

| Crop Year Beginning Aug. 1 | Aug. | Sept. | Oct. | Nov. | Dec. | Jan. | Feb. | Mar. | Apr. | May. | June | July | Average |
|---|---|---|---|---|---|---|---|---|---|---|---|---|---|
| 1982-3 | 19.3 | 19.0 | 20.8 | 19.5 | 17.0 | 20.2 | 21.5 | 22.0 | 21.5 | 22.0 | 21.7 | 18.4 | 20.3 |
| 1983-4 | 22.6 | 22.4 | 22.9 | 22.3 | 18.7 | 23.5 | 22.4 | 21.9 | 21.5 | 22.1 | 20.1 | 17.7 | 21.6 |
| 1984-5 | 21.4 | 20.4 | 21.4 | 19.5 | 16.9 | 20.0 | 20.9 | 20.8 | 21.0 | 21.9 | 21.0 | 18.5 | 20.3 |
| 1985-6 | 22.9 | 22.5 | 24.6 | 23.9 | 19.5 | 23.8 | 24.9 | 24.6 | 24.8 | 25.2 | 24.4 | 20.9 | 23.4 |
| 1986-7 | 26.7 | 26.2 | 27.3 | 26.5 | 23.1 | 27.3 | 28.1 | 29.4 | 28.7 | 29.3 | 28.3 | 27.0 | 27.3 |
| 1987-8 | 30.3 | 30.1 | 31.0 | 30.3 | 24.4 | 28.4 | 29.5 | 29.5 | 27.8 | 27.6 | 26.5 | 21.7 | 28.1 |
| 1988-9 | 28.8 | 27.7 | 27.6 | 26.1 | 22.9 | 28.3 | 29.2 | 30.0 | 31.2 | 32.2 | 31.9 | 27.9 | 28.6 |
| 1989-90 | 32.9 | 32.8 | 33.0 | 30.6 | 25.9 | 29.9 | 31.4 | 31.5 | 30.9 | 31.8 | 32.8 | 27.8 | 30.9 |
| 1990-1 | 33.8 | 41.4 | 33.2 | 30.2 | 29.7 | ------------ | 32.3 | ------------ | ------------ | 34.0 | ------------ | ------------ | 33.5 |
| 1991-2 | 33.6 | ---------- | ------------ | 33.1 | ------------ | 34.6 | 36.3 | 35.7 | 35.6 | 37.3 | 35.2 | 33.9 | 35.0 |
| 1992-3 | 38.5 | 37.8 | 39.7 | 37.6 | 31.5 | 39.1 | 39.5 | 38.8 | 38.7 | 39.4 | 37.8 | 34.5 | 37.8 |
| 1993-4 | 39.8 | 38.4 | 39.4 | 36.4 | 31.4 | 36.9 | 37.9 | 39.0 | 39.3 | 39.5 | 40.4 | 40.3 | 38.2 |
| 1994-5 | 41.0 | 41.4 | 41.1 | 41.8 | 41.7 | 42.6 | 42.1 | 42.4 | 41.1 | 40.2 | 39.2 | 37.2 | 41.0 |
| 1995-6[1] | 38.8 | 39.4 | 37.6 | 38.1 | 37.9 | 37.5 | 38.1 | 39.5 | 39.4 | 39.6 | 40.6 | 39.8 | 38.9 |
| 1996-7[1] | 39.7 | 39.8 | 39.7 | 40.8 | 40.4 | 40.6 | | | | | | | 40.2 |

[1] Preliminary. [2] Not seasonally adjusted. *Source: Bureau of Census, U.S. Department of Commerce*

## Consumption of American and Foreign Cotton in the United States
In Thousands of Running Bales

| Year | Aug. | Sept. | Oct. | Nov. | Dec. | Jan. | Feb. | Mar. | Apr. | May | June | July | Total |
|---|---|---|---|---|---|---|---|---|---|---|---|---|---|
| 1982-3 | 386 | 474 | 416 | 391 | 425 | 404 | 430 | 549 | 431 | 441 | 543 | 369 | 5,259 |
| 1983-4 | 453 | 560 | 459 | 446 | 468 | 469 | 448 | 548 | 430 | 442 | 503 | 354 | 5,628 |
| 1984-5 | 428 | 509 | 428 | 390 | 423 | 399 | 418 | 519 | 419 | 439 | 525 | 369 | 5,268 |
| 1985-6 | 458 | 562 | 493 | 477 | 486 | 595 | 499 | 492 | 620 | 503 | 489 | 522 | 6,198 |
| 1986-7 | 534 | 523 | 683 | 529 | 576 | 546 | 562 | 734 | 573 | 586 | 708 | 540 | 7,096 |
| 1987-8 | 606 | 753 | 621 | 606 | 610 | 568 | 590 | 738 | 556 | 551 | 662 | 433 | 7,294 |
| 1988-9 | 577 | 693 | 552 | 523 | 572 | 568 | 584 | 751 | 623 | 645 | 798 | 559 | 7,444 |
| 1989-90 | 689 | 860 | 690 | 642 | 685 | 630 | 658 | 826 | 650 | 667 | 826 | 559 | 8,383 |
| 1990-1 | 680 | 835 | 671 | 610 | 601 | ------------ | 2,068 | ------------ | ------------ | 2,212 | ------------ | ---------- | 8,367 |
| 1991-2 | 2,215 | ---------- | ------------ | 2,199 | ------------ | 870 | 730 | 898 | 718 | 752 | 885 | 682 | 9,949 |
| 1992-3 | 776 | 950 | 799 | 756 | 792 | 788 | 796 | 976 | 778 | 792 | 951 | 694 | 9,846 |
| 1993-4 | 801 | 965 | 792 | 731 | 790 | 743 | 785 | 999 | 806 | 830 | 1,032 | 744 | 10,019 |
| 1994-5 | 870 | 1,070 | 873 | 838 | 897 | 858 | 878 | 1,097 | 847 | 842 | 999 | 681 | 10,750 |
| 1995-6[1] | 829 | 1,020 | 798 | 761 | 801 | 744 | 787 | 1,029 | 810 | 824 | 1,040 | 731 | 10,174 |
| 1996-7[1] | 847 | 1,028 | 829 | 816 | 858 | 812 | | | | | | | 5,190 |

[1] Preliminary. *Source: Bureau of Census, U.S. Department of Commerce*

## Exports of All Cotton[2] from the United States In Thousands of Running Bales

| Year | Aug. | Sept. | Oct. | Nov. | Dec. | Jan. | Feb. | Mar. | Apr. | May | June | July | Total |
|---|---|---|---|---|---|---|---|---|---|---|---|---|---|
| 1982-3 | 348 | 304 | 248 | 442 | 357 | 472 | 355 | 435 | 557 | 511 | 381 | 467 | 4,877 |
| 1983-4 | 369 | 329 | 308 | 438 | 566 | 821 | 737 | 783 | 839 | 494 | 429 | 370 | 6,483 |
| 1984-5 | 454 | 249 | 340 | 472 | 712 | 755 | 705 | 692 | 556 | 435 | 359 | 299 | 6,028 |
| 1985-6 | 166 | 218 | 180 | 198 | 236 | 189 | 202 | 206 | 125 | 69 | 68 | 19 | 1,876 |
| 1986-7[2] | 374 | 496 | 489 | 525 | 664 | 591 | 518 | 750 | 500 | 465 | 554 | 439 | 6,365 |
| 1987-8 | 355 | 304 | 316 | 612 | 536 | 698 | 879 | 649 | 565 | 537 | 486 | 359 | 6,296 |
| 1988-9 | 248 | 173 | 292 | 352 | 524 | 756 | 514 | 597 | 575 | 795 | 515 | 649 | 5,990 |
| 1989-90 | 431 | 384 | 507 | 469 | 516 | 909 | 840 | 882 | 818 | 495 | 510 | 550 | 7,311 |
| 1990-1 | 480 | 355 | 433 | 591 | 639 | 1,112 | 950 | 804 | 960 | 488 | 404 | 273 | 7,489 |
| 1991-2 | 219 | 126 | 239 | 396 | 674 | 961 | 725 | 791 | 787 | 535 | 430 | 466 | 6,349 |
| 1992-3 | 252 | 263 | 277 | 342 | 528 | 501 | 502 | 533 | 639 | 401 | 317 | 395 | 4,950 |
| 1993-4 | 287 | 248 | 345 | 405 | 571 | 738 | 512 | 743 | 761 | 854 | 770 | 626 | 6,860 |
| 1994-5 | 531 | 333 | 341 | 710 | 1,098 | 1,115 | 1,383 | 1,392 | 1,104 | 684 | 410 | 300 | 9,402 |
| 1995-6[1] | 315 | 245 | 452 | 733 | 1,230 | 1,262 | 1,295 | 777 | 576 | 343 | 263 | 183 | 7,675 |
| 1996-7[1] | 257 | 171 | 277 | 573 | | | | | | | | | 1,278 |

[1] Preliminary. [2] Data prior to 1986-7 are for American Cotton only. *Source: Foreign Agricultural Service, U.S. Department of Agriculture*

## U.S. Exports of American Cotton to Countries of Destination In Thousands of 480-Pound Bales

| Crop Year Beginning Aug. 1 | Canada | China | Egypt | Germany | Hong Kong | Indonesia | Italy | Japan | Rep. of Korea | Mexico | Philippines | Sweden | Taiwan | Thailand | United Kingdom | Former USSR | Total |
|---|---|---|---|---|---|---|---|---|---|---|---|---|---|---|---|---|---|
| 1982-3 | 238 | 20 | ------ | 163 | 158 | 268 | 105 | 1,286 | 1,322 | ------ | 72 | 23 | 378 | 197 | 50 | 192 | 5,207 |
| 1983-4 | 227 | 12 | ------ | 195 | 283 | 320 | 252 | 1,709 | 1,269 | ------ | 59 | 28 | 495 | 244 | 67 | 351 | 6,785 |
| 1984-5 | 195 | 6 | 126 | 195 | 125 | 258 | 301 | 1,464 | 1,257 | ------ | 58 | 22 | 513 | 139 | 72 | 329 | 6,211 |
| 1985-6 | 98 | ------ | 120 | 85 | 1 | 105 | 91 | 520 | 513 | ------ | 8 | 15 | 46 | 17 | 35 | ------ | 1,958 |
| 1986-7 | 70 | ------ | 68 | 263 | 52 | 324 | 263 | 1,723 | 1,330 | ------ | 153 | 15 | 907 | 239 | 56 | ------ | 6,685 |
| 1987-8 | 153 | ------ | 93 | 376 | 88 | 287 | 406 | 1,569 | 1,450 | ------ | 135 | 19 | 424 | 248 | 69 | 98 | 6,582 |
| 1988-9 | 148 | 793 | 102 | 255 | 108 | 307 | 239 | 1,381 | 1,302 | ------ | 50 | 16 | 254 | 172 | 37 | 2 | 6,147 |
| 1989-90 | 197 | 670 | 242 | 368 | 244 | 499 | 431 | 1,594 | 1,365 | 117 | 134 | 22 | 320 | 375 | 74 | 5 | 7,694 |
| 1990-1 | 191 | 1,233 | 243 | 214 | 306 | 561 | 425 | 1,437 | 1,168 | 202 | 132 | 22 | 358 | 317 | 36 | 5 | 7,793 |
| 1991-2 | 181 | 792 | 339 | 101 | 335 | 739 | 240 | 1,107 | 1,024 | 213 | 181 | 18 | 380 | 368 | 60 | 0 | 6,646 |
| 1992-3 | 154 | 1 | 170 | 74 | 100 | 429 | 144 | 839 | 1,031 | 557 | 117 | 20 | 279 | 150 | 65 | 0 | 5,201 |
| 1993-4 | 165 | 1,183 | ------ | 50 | 314 | 653 | 96 | 790 | 976 | 653 | 168 | 12 | 356 | 277 | 65 | 0 | 6,862 |
| 1994-5[1] | 253 | 2,257 | 162 | 30 | 347 | 925 | 83 | 1,061 | 951 | 558 | 173 | 25 | 352 | 441 | 89 | 0 | 9,402 |
| 1995-6[2] | 294 | 1,847 | 95 | 40 | 223 | 794 | 115 | 940 | 769 | 618 | 144 | 17 | 255 | 331 | 85 | 0 | 7,675 |

[1] Preliminary. [2] Estimate. *Source: Foreign Agricultural Service, U.S. Department of Agriculture*

## Cotton[1] Government Loan Program in the United States

| Crop Year Beginning Aug. 1 | Support Price (¢ per Pound) | Target Price (¢ per Pound) | Put Under Support (Ths Bales) | % of Production | Acquired (Ths. Bales) | Owned July 31 (Ths. Bales) | Crop Year Beginning Aug. 1 | Support Price (¢ per Pound) | Target Price (¢ per Pound) | Put Under Support (Ths Bales) | % of Production | Acquired (Ths. Bales) | Owned July 31 (Ths. Bales) |
|---|---|---|---|---|---|---|---|---|---|---|---|---|---|
| 1984-5 | 55.00 | 81.00 | 2,957 | 23.0 | 649 | 123 | 1990-1 | 50.27 | 72.90 | 3,205 | 21.1 | 1 | 4 |
| 1985-6 | 57.30 | 81.00 | 7,287 | 54.9 | 161 | 792 | 1991-2 | 50.77 | 72.90 | 6,312 | 36.6 | 8 | (3) |
| 1986-7 | 55.00 | 81.00 | 6,170 | 64.8 | 12 | 24 | 1992-3 | 52.35 | 72.90 | 8,302 | 52.9 | [3] | 8 |
| 1987-8 | 52.25 | 79.40 | 5,362 | 37.0 | 131 | 3 | 1993-4 | 52.35 | 72.90 | 7,721 | 49.0 | [3] | 14 |
| 1988-9 | 51.80 | 75.90 | 11,231 | 74.5 | 66 | 35 | 1994-5 | 50.00 | 72.90 | 4,716 | 24.4 | [3] | (3) |
| 1989-90 | 50.00 | 73.40 | 3,732 | 32.4 | 2 | 27 | 1995-6 | 51.92 | 72.90 | 2,640 | 15.1 | 0 | NA |

[1] Upland. [2] Preliminary. [3] Less than 500 bales. NA = Not available. *Source: Economic Research Service, U.S. Department of Agriculture*

## Cotton Cloth[1] Production in the United States In Millions of Square Yards

| Year | First Quarter | Second Quarter | Third Quarter | Fourth Quarter | Total Year | Year | First Quarter | Second Quarter | Third Quarter | Fourth Quarter | Total Year |
|---|---|---|---|---|---|---|---|---|---|---|---|
| 1985 | 1,030 | 1,002 | 933 | 955 | 3,921 | 1991 | 1,081 | 1,148 | 1,082 | 1,093 | 4,404 |
| 1986 | 1,037 | 1,103 | 1,095 | 1,129 | 4,364 | 1992 | 1,154 | 1,172 | 1,130 | 1,144 | 4,600 |
| 1987 | 1,158 | 1,217 | 1,219 | 1,178 | 4,772 | 1993 | 1,150 | 1,144 | 1,071 | 1,039 | 4,403 |
| 1988 | 1,252 | 1,255 | 1,072 | 1,052 | 5,632 | 1994 | 1,073 | 1,125 | 1,131 | 1,143 | 4,473 |
| 1989 | 1,157 | 1,192 | 1,134 | 1,106 | 4,589 | 1995[2] | 1,169 | 1,137 | 1,090 | 1,093 | 4,488 |
| 1990 | 1,202 | 1,127 | 1,087 | 1,048 | 4,463 | 1996[2] | 1,069 | 1,108 | 1,071 | 1,075 | 4,322 |

[1] Cotton broadwoven goods over 12 inches in width. [2] Preliminary. *Source: Bureau of Census, U.S. Department of Commerce*

## United States Cotton Ginnings[1] To: In Thousands of Running Bales

| Crop Year | Aug. 1 | Aug. 15 | Sept. 1 | Sept. 15 | Oct. 1 | Oct. 15 | Nov. 1 | Nov. 15 | Dec. 1 | Dec. 15 | Jan. 1 | Jan. 15 | Feb. 1 | Total Crop |
|---|---|---|---|---|---|---|---|---|---|---|---|---|---|---|
| 1984-5 | 163 | NA | 634 | 780 | 1,175 | 2,277 | 4,321 | 7,025 | 8,972 | 10,478 | 11,079 | 11,682 | 12,319 | 12,452 |
| 1985-6 | 70 | NA | 681 | 1,073 | 2,431 | 4,342 | 6,246 | 8,216 | 10,052 | 11,372 | 12,365 | 12,776 | 12,948 | 13,063 |
| 1986-7 | 145 | NA | 624 | 1,022 | 2,407 | 3,618 | 5,292 | 6,369 | 7,491 | 8,263 | 8,588 | 9,093 | 9,270 | 9,294 |
| 1987-8 | 1 | NA | 429 | 1,242 | 3,196 | 5,359 | 7,531 | 9,135 | 11,082 | 12,588 | 13,276 | 13,733 | 14,177 | 14,493 |
| 1988-9 | 136 | NA | 804 | 1,147 | 2,279 | 4,116 | 6,922 | 9,535 | 11,845 | 13,257 | 14,248 | 14,686 | 14,904 | 14,939 |
| 1989-90 | 90 | NA | 382 | 523 | 981 | 2,772 | 5,948 | 8,388 | 10,353 | 11,246 | 11,548 | 11,681 | 11,771 | 11,913 |
| 1990-1 | 120 | NA | 583 | 1,090 | 2,616 | 4,739 | 7,955 | 10,207 | 12,428 | 13,863 | 14,516 | 14,809 | 14,963 | 15,082 |
| 1991-2 | NA | NA | 699 | 983 | 2,467 | 4,955 | 8,351 | 10,752 | 13,260 | 15,067 | 15,888 | 16,402 | 16,765 | 17,146 |
| 1992-3 | 14 | NA | 446 | 740 | 1,664 | 4,046 | 7,584 | 10,296 | 12,597 | 14,083 | 14,944 | 15,311 | 15,527 | 15,786 |
| 1993-4 | 9 | NA | 435 | 748 | 1,846 | 4,471 | 7,975 | 10,952 | 13,244 | 14,695 | 15,321 | 15,517 | 15,590 | 15,675 |
| 1994-5 | 113 | NA | 680 | 943 | 2,324 | 5,002 | 8,878 | 12,479 | 15,587 | 17,465 | 18,438 | 18,842 | 19,028 | 19,127 |
| 1995-6[2] | 17 | NA | 472 | 898 | 2,455 | 4,795 | 8,430 | 11,262 | 14,199 | 16,102 | 17,011 | 17,292 | 17,416 | 17,499 |
| 1996-7[2] | 48 | NA | 343 | 637 | 2,144 | 4,788 | 8,876 | 11,943 | 14,659 | 16,664 | 17,685 | 18,110 | 18,321 | |

[1] Excluding linters. [2] Preliminary. NA = Not available. *Source: National Agricultural Statistics Service, U.S. Department of Agriculture*

## U.S. Fiber Prices In Cents Per Pound

| Year | Cotton[1] Actual | Cotton[1] Raw[5] Equivalent | Rayon[2] Actual | Rayon[2] Raw[5] Equivalent | Polyester[3] Actual | Polyester[3] Raw[5] Equivalent | Price Ratios[4] in Percent Cotton/ Rayon | Price Ratios[4] in Percent Cotton/ Polyester |
|---|---|---|---|---|---|---|---|---|
| 1984 | 76.06 | 84.51 | 84.00 | 87.50 | 78.83 | 82.12 | .97 | 1.03 |
| 1985 | 65.83 | 73.15 | 78.83 | 82.12 | 66.33 | 69.10 | .89 | 1.06 |
| 1986 | 60.99 | 67.77 | 75.75 | 78.91 | 62.33 | 64.93 | .86 | 1.04 |
| 1987 | 72.71 | 80.79 | 81.00 | 84.38 | 65.75 | 68.49 | .96 | 1.18 |
| 1988 | 64.89 | 72.10 | 90.67 | 94.44 | 73.83 | 76.91 | .77 | .94 |
| 1989 | 71.99 | 79.99 | 109.75 | 114.32 | 85.67 | 89.24 | .70 | .90 |
| 1990 | 79.29 | 88.10 | 119.92 | 124.91 | 82.58 | 86.02 | .71 | 1.03 |
| 1991 | 79.05 | 87.83 | 122.00 | 127.08 | 73.50 | 76.56 | .69 | 1.15 |
| 1992 | 61.92 | 68.80 | 114.08 | 118.84 | 73.50 | 76.56 | .58 | .90 |
| 1993 | 62.43 | 69.37 | 111.42 | 116.06 | 72.50 | 75.52 | .60 | .92 |
| 1994 | 78.69 | 87.43 | 103.00 | 107.29 | 74.92 | 78.04 | .82 | 1.12 |
| 1995 | 100.76 | 111.95 | 118.67 | 123.61 | 88.83 | 92.53 | .91 | 1.21 |
| 1996 Jan. | 88.86 | 98.73 | 125.00 | 130.21 | 92.00 | 95.83 | .76 | 1.03 |
| Feb. | 89.76 | 99.73 | 125.00 | 130.21 | 88.00 | 91.67 | .77 | 1.09 |
| Mar. | 88.79 | 98.66 | 125.00 | 130.21 | 88.00 | 91.00 | .76 | 1.08 |
| Apr. | 92.10 | 102.33 | 120.00 | 125.00 | 84.00 | 87.50 | .82 | 1.17 |
| May | 90.20 | 100.22 | 115.00 | 119.79 | 80.00 | 83.33 | .84 | 1.20 |
| June | 85.99 | 95.54 | 115.00 | 119.79 | 78.00 | 81.25 | .80 | 1.18 |
| July | 82.18 | 91.31 | 115.00 | 119.79 | 78.00 | 81.13 | .76 | 1.12 |
| Aug. | 82.61 | 91.79 | 115.00 | 119.79 | 78.00 | 81.25 | .77 | 1.13 |
| Sept. | 82.99 | 92.21 | 115.00 | 119.79 | 76.00 | 79.17 | .77 | 1.17 |
| Oct. | 78.96 | 87.73 | 115.00 | 119.79 | 73.00 | 76.04 | .73 | 1.15 |
| Nov. | 76.89 | 85.43 | 115.00 | 119.79 | 72.00 | 75.00 | .71 | 1.14 |

[1] SLM-1 1/16" at group B Mill points, net weight. [2] 1.5 and 3.0 denier, regular rayon staples. [3] Reported average market price for 1.5 denier polyester staple for cotton blending. [4] Raw fiber equivalent. [5] Actual prices converted to estimated raw fiber equivalent as follows: cotton, divided by 0.90, rayon and polyester, divided by 0.96. *Source: Economic Research Service, U.S. Department of Agriculture*

## Average Producer Price Index of Gray Cotton Broadwovens Index 1982=100

| Year | Jan. | Feb. | Mar. | Apr. | May | June | July | Aug. | Sept. | Oct. | Nov. | Dec. | Average |
|---|---|---|---|---|---|---|---|---|---|---|---|---|---|
| 1986 | 101.6 | 101.2 | 100.8 | 100.7 | 101.0 | 101.0 | 101.2 | 101.0 | 101.3 | 101.2 | 101.5 | 101.2 | 101.1 |
| 1987 | 101.8 | 101.8 | 101.9 | 102.5 | 103.0 | 103.3 | 106.0 | 103.9 | 107.1 | 109.5 | 110.6 | 111.5 | 105.2 |
| 1988 | 112.7 | 114.3 | 114.5 | 115.9 | 116.2 | 116.1 | 115.9 | 115.6 | 114.8 | 111.9 | 112.5 | 112.3 | 114.4 |
| 1989 | 112.4 | 111.3 | 110.9 | 110.9 | 110.5 | 110.1 | 109.4 | 109.8 | 109.8 | 110.8 | 110.9 | 113.5 | 110.9 |
| 1990 | 113.7 | 113.8 | 113.8 | 114.0 | 114.1 | 109.9 | 115.1 | 115.1 | 112.3 | 112.5 | 116.1 | 116.4 | 113.8 |
| 1991 | 113.3 | 113.6 | 114.1 | 114.5 | 114.9 | 115.2 | 115.3 | 115.3 | 115.3 | 115.4 | 115.7 | 115.6 | 114.9 |
| 1992 | 116.9 | 116.8 | 116.7 | 116.7 | 116.8 | 117.5 | 117.3 | 117.3 | 117.2 | 116.9 | 117.1 | 117.2 | 117.0 |
| 1993 | 117.0 | 116.8 | 115.9 | 116.3 | 115.7 | 115.7 | 115.2 | 115.2 | 112.5 | 114.1 | 114.1 | 114.9 | 115.3 |
| 1994 | 109.9 | 110.8 | 115.4 | 115.7 | 114.9 | 114.9 | 115.0 | 117.5 | 117.6 | 118.9 | 117.2 | 118.0 | 115.5 |
| 1995 | 117.8 | 120.2 | 120.7 | 121.6 | 123.4 | 123.6 | 124.1 | 125.4 | 125.3 | 123.7 | 123.7 | 123.8 | 122.8 |
| 1996[1] | 123.6 | 123.7 | 122.0 | 122.0 | 121.1 | 120.7 | 120.7 | 119.9 | 119.7 | 117.9 | 118.2 | 120.4 | 120.8 |

[1] Preliminary. *Source: Bureau of Labor Statistics (0337-01), U.S. Department of Commerce*

# Cottonseed and Products

Cottonseed production is directly related to the amount of cotton produced. China and the U.S. are the world's largest cotton producers followed by India. For the U.S., in the 1996/97 marketing year, planted cotton acreage was 14.2 million acres, down 16 percent from 1995/96. The season got off to a poor start in Texas as there were drought conditions resulting in the loss of cotton planted on dry land. Rains about halfway through the season helped considerably and prospects for the crop improved. Harvested acreage was estimated by the USDA at 12.78 million acres. While acreage was less than the previous season, improved weather and the abandonment of marginal acreage resulted in an increase in the national average yield to 698 pounds per acre, up 30 percent from 1995/96. As a result, the 1996/97 cotton crop was forecast by the USDA to be 18.6 million bales, up 4 percent from the previous season.

USDA estimated cottonseed production for 1996/97 at 7 million short tons, up almost 2 percent from the previous season. Cottonseed stocks at the beginning of the season were 495,000 tonnes, down 10 percent from the previous year. The total cottonseed supply was 7.5 million tons.

In terms of use, the cottonseed crush was estimated at 3.9 million tons, up 1 percent from 1995/96. Exports were estimated at 125,000 tons, up 10 percent from the year before while other uses were 3.1 million tons, up 5 percent. Projected ending stocks were 375,000 tons.

Cottonseed oil production was 1.25 billion pounds, up 3 percent from 1995/96. Stocks were 100 million pounds. Domestic use was forecast at 1 billion pounds, up 3 percent. Cottonseed oil exports were projected at 225 million pounds, up 9 percent. Ending stocks were 110 million lbs.

Cottonseed meal production was forecast at 1.8 million tons, up 2 percent from 1995/96. Domestic use was put at 1.7 million tons, up 3 percent. Exports were 80,000 tons, down 24 percent from 1995/96. Projected ending stocks of cottonseed meal were 40,000 tonnes, unchanged.

## World Production of Cottonseed In Thousands of Metric Tons

| Crop Year | Agrentina | Australia | Brazil | China | Colombia | Egypt | Greece | India | Mexico | Pakistan | South Africa | Spain | Turkey | United States | Former U.S.S.R. | World Total |
|---|---|---|---|---|---|---|---|---|---|---|---|---|---|---|---|---|
| 1988-9 | 367 | 449 | 1,338 | 7,676 | 229 | 532 | 390 | 3,600 | 491 | 2,852 | 119 | 195 | 920 | 5,499 | 4,779 | 32,699 |
| 1989-90 | 495 | 493 | 1,255 | 7,008 | 201 | 498 | 440 | 4,610 | 255 | 2,911 | 99 | 100 | 987 | 4,243 | 4,600 | 31,242 |
| 1990-1 | 538 | 686 | 1,352 | 8,340 | 265 | 504 | 365 | 3,980 | 294 | 3,275 | 108 | 139 | 977 | 5,415 | 4,550 | 33,919 |
| 1991-2 | 435 | 724 | 1,313 | 10,499 | 298 | 491 | 355 | 4,090 | 307 | 4,352 | 87 | 137 | 878 | 6,283 | 4,283 | 37,691 |
| 1992-3 | 275 | 528 | 800 | 8,340 | 178 | 571 | 410 | 4,740 | 52 | 3,080 | 36 | 104 | 905 | 5,652 | 3,557 | 32,196 |
| 1993-4 | 390 | 466 | 920 | 6,655 | 107 | 655 | 460 | 4,120 | 31 | 2,740 | 26 | 47 | 892 | 5,754 | 3,600 | 29,688 |
| 1994-5 | 631 | 474 | 980 | 7,727 | 95 | 411 | 565 | 4,693 | 155 | 2,959 | 47 | 60 | 930 | 6,898 | 3,360 | 33,023 |
| 1995-6[1] | 780 | 562 | 820 | 8,200 | 133 | 400 | 680 | 5,150 | 305 | 3,550 | 39 | 48 | 1,250 | 6,213 | 3,320 | 34,887 |
| 1996-7[2] | 650 | 755 | 950 | 7,100 | NA | 540 | 650 | 4,900 | 350 | 3,550 | 72 | 140 | 1,180 | 6,600 | 3,300 | 34,520 |

[1] Preliminary. [2] Estimate. *Source: Oil World*

## Salient Statistics of Cottonseed in the United States

| Crop Year Beginning Aug. 1 | Supply: Stocks | Supply: Production | Supply: Total Supply | Disappearance: Crush | Disappearance: Exports | Disappearance: Other | Disappearance: Total Disappearance | Farm Price $/Ton | Value of Production Mil. $ | Products Produced: Oil Millions Lbs. | Products Produced: Meal Thousand Sh. Tons |
|---|---|---|---|---|---|---|---|---|---|---|---|
| | In Thousands of Short Tons | | | | | | | | | | |
| 1988-9 | 359 | 6,062 | 6,421 | 3,730 | 39 | 1,987 | 5,756 | 118 | 718.3 | 1,243 | 1,689 |
| 1989-90 | 665 | 4,677 | 5,342 | 2,974 | 46 | 1,957 | 4,977 | 105 | 492.7 | 1,039 | 1,327 |
| 1990-1 | 366 | 5,969 | 6,337 | 3,369 | 53 | 2,264 | 5,686 | 121 | 722.3 | 1,154 | 1,691 |
| 1991-2 | 651 | 6,926 | 7,579 | 3,981 | 161 | 2,977 | 7,119 | 71 | 492.3 | 1,279 | 1,765 |
| 1992-3 | 460 | 6,230 | 6,690 | 3,629 | 192 | 2,504 | 6,325 | 98 | 608.4 | 1,137 | 1,533 |
| 1993-4 | 365 | 6,343 | 6,708 | 3,470 | 157 | 2,649 | 6,276 | 113 | 714.4 | 1,119 | 1,563 |
| 1994-5 | 432 | 7,604 | 8,036 | 3,947 | 232 | 3,306 | 7,485 | 101 | 771.3 | 1,312 | 1,830 |
| 1995-6[1] | 551 | 6,849 | 7,399 | 3,861 | 114 | 2,929 | 6,904 | 106 | 730.4 | 1,218 | 1,732 |
| 1996-7[2] | 495 | 7,271 | 7,766 | 3,900 | 140 | 3,151 | 7,191 | 110-120 | NA | 1,250 | 1,755 |

[1] Preliminary. [2] Estimate. *Source: Economic Research Service, U.S. Department of Agriculture*

## Average Wholesale Price of Cottonseed Meal (41% Solvent) at Memphis In Dollars Per Short Ton

| Year | Jan. | Feb. | Mar. | Apr. | May | June | July | Aug. | Sept. | Oct. | Nov. | Dec. | Average |
|---|---|---|---|---|---|---|---|---|---|---|---|---|---|
| 1988 | 187.50 | 160.00 | 141.00 | 143.10 | 147.50 | 230.00 | 223.75 | 181.00 | 205.00 | 212.50 | 293.00 | 199.40 | 193.65 |
| 1989 | 200.50 | 191.25 | 196.25 | 184.40 | 161.50 | 163.30 | 157.50 | 172.00 | 190.00 | 181.25 | 180.00 | 180.00 | 179.83 |
| 1990 | 160.00 | 150.00 | 146.25 | 150.00 | 155.00 | 147.50 | 161.50 | 169.50 | 178.75 | 163.00 | 147.50 | 141.25 | 155.85 |
| 1991 | 125.00 | 118.10 | 125.00 | 122.50 | 118.10 | 117.20 | 127.50 | 130.90 | 133.10 | 131.00 | 144.40 | 162.00 | 129.57 |
| 1992 | 156.25 | 140.10 | 124.25 | 121.25 | 127.50 | 132.50 | 133.75 | 146.90 | 163.00 | 154.40 | 157.50 | 174.50 | 144.33 |
| 1993 | 164.40 | 149.40 | 153.50 | 149.00 | 143.10 | 153.00 | 170.30 | 178.50 | 193.75 | 173.10 | 181.00 | 180.00 | 165.75 |
| 1994 | 170.30 | 173.10 | 174.00 | 166.25 | 157.75 | 154.10 | 152.50 | 144.50 | 145.00 | 134.40 | 120.50 | 114.20 | 150.55 |
| 1995 | 106.75 | 97.50 | 100.30 | 98.10 | 92.75 | 108.75 | 116.90 | 116.50 | 137.60 | 153.25 | 165.00 | 185.80 | 123.27 |
| 1996[1] | 208.80 | 202.80 | 195.60 | 220.00 | 191.25 | 192.20 | 201.56 | 193.10 | 193.10 | 183.25 | 196.60 | 224.50 | 200.23 |

[1] Preliminary. *Source: Economic Research Service, U.S. Department of Agriculture*

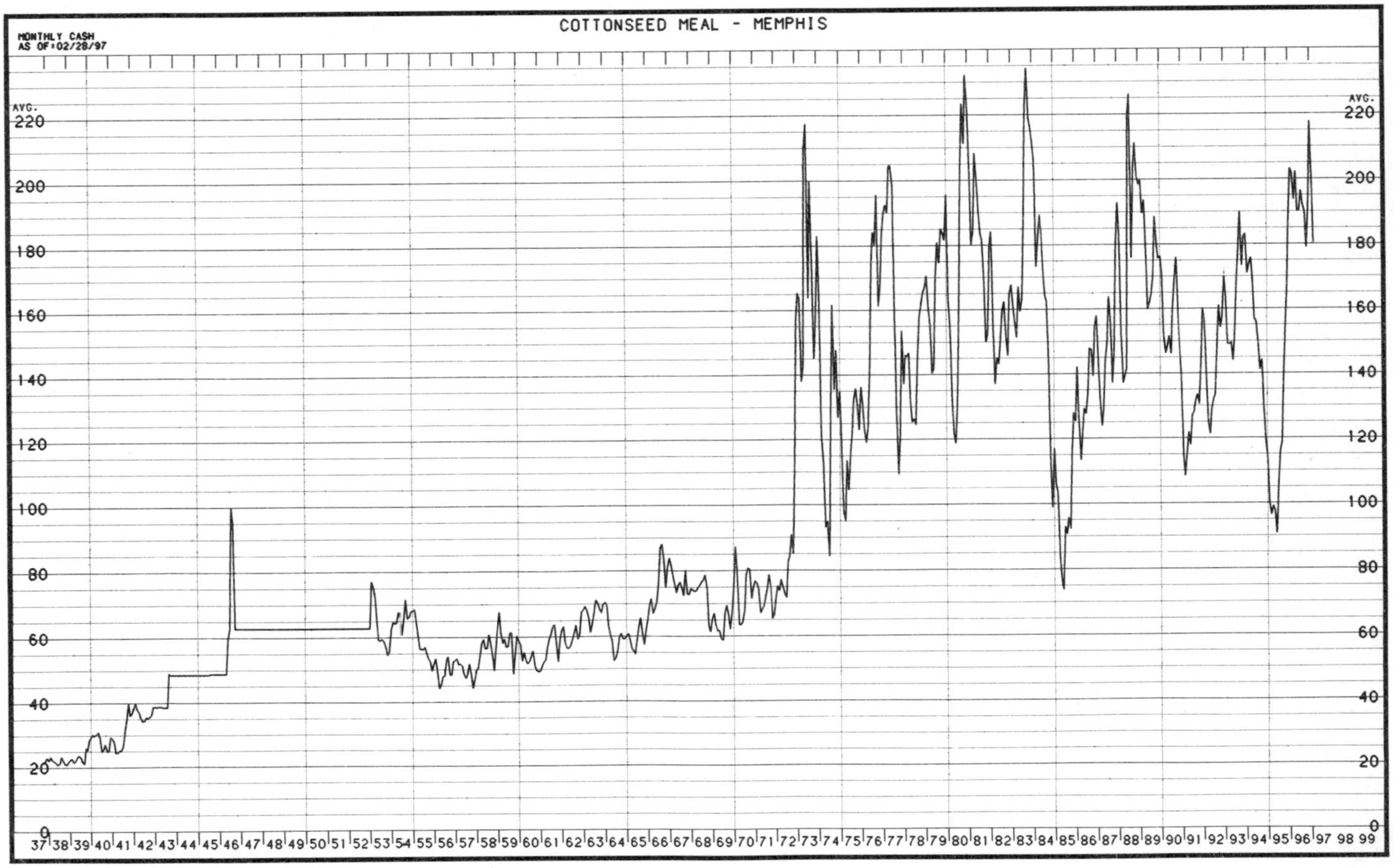


## Supply & Distribution of Cottonseed Oil in the United States — In Millions of Pounds

| Crop Year Beginning Oct. 1 | Supply: Stocks | Supply: Production | Supply: Imports | Supply: Total Supply | Disappearance: Domestic | Disappearance: Exports | Disappearance: Total | Per Capita Consump. of Salad & Ck. Oils -- In Lbs.-- | Utilization Food Uses: Shortening | Utilization Food Uses: Salad & Cooking Oils | Utilization Food Uses: Total | Prices ($/Tonne): U.S.[3] (Crude) | Prices ($/Tonne): Rott[4] (Cif) |
|---|---|---|---|---|---|---|---|---|---|---|---|---|---|
| 1990-1 | 80 | 1,154 | 3 | 1,237 | 851 | 249 | 1,100 | 24 | 272 | 438 | 777 | 492 | 614 |
| 1991-2 | 137 | 1,279 | 18 | 1,434 | 1,075 | 281 | 1,356 | 25 | 247 | 375 | 685 | 443 | 545 |
| 1992-3 | 78 | 1,137 | 38 | 1,253 | 995 | 177 | 1,172 | 26 | 238 | 353 | 640 | 551 | 688 |
| 1993-4 | 81 | 1,119 | 26 | 1,226 | 873 | 248 | 1,121 | 25 | 217 | 289 | 558 | 684 | 750 |
| 1994-5 | 106 | 1,312 | 0 | 1,417 | 1,006 | 329 | 1,335 | 24 | 217 | 262 | 532 | 683 | 671 |
| 1995-6[1] | 82 | 1,218 | 0 | 1,301 | 985 | 221 | 1,207 | 25 | 218 | 235 | 497 | 575 | 613 |
| 1996-7[2] | 94 | 1,250 | 0 | 1,344 | 1,015 | 215 | 1,230 | | | | | | |

[1] Preliminary. [2] Estimate. [3] F.O.B.; Greenwood, MS. (Tank Cars). [4] Rotterdam;U.S. PBSY *Source: Economic Research Service, U.S. Department of Agriculture.*

## U.S. Consumption of Crude Cottonseed Oil in Refining — In Millions of Pounds

| Year | Oct. | Nov. | Dec. | Jan. | Feb | Mar. | Apr. | May | June | July | Aug. | Sept. | Total |
|---|---|---|---|---|---|---|---|---|---|---|---|---|---|
| 1990-1 | 79.4 | 99.7 | 92.8 | | ------------ 264.7 ------------ | | | ------------ 265.9 ------------ | | | ------------ 227.7 ------------ | | 1,030.2 |
| 1991-2 | | ------------ 265.0 ------------ | | 104.6 | 108.9 | 101.3 | 88.7 | 76.0 | 84.2 | 84.6 | 72.7 | 48.6 | 1,034.6 |
| 1992-3 | 75.7 | 93.3 | 95.5 | 107.3 | 85.1 | 77.5 | 92.8 | 79.3 | 74.7 | 65.1 | 68.6 | 57.6 | 972.5 |
| 1993-4 | 82.7 | 113.0 | 103.8 | 110.8 | 96.7 | 111.5 | 69.6 | 74.8 | 73.2 | 74.6 | 88.4 | 64.2 | 1,063.3 |
| 1994-5 | 81.9 | 97.2 | 109.8 | 107.7 | 87.1 | 96.2 | 87.2 | 72.8 | 73.4 | 76.0 | 83.3 | 71.6 | 1,044.4 |
| 1995-6 | 76.1 | 91.8 | 89.7 | 94.5 | 87.2 | 92.2 | 83.4 | 77.3 | 55.5 | 56.2 | 64.3 | 54.4 | 922.5 |
| 1996-7[1] | 67.2 | 85.1 | 85.6 | | | | | | | | | | 237.9 |

[1] Preliminary. *Source: Bureau of Census, U.S. Department of Commerce*

## U.S. Exports of Cottonseed Oil (Crude & Refined) — In Thousands of Pounds

| Year | Jan. | Feb. | Mar. | Apr. | May | June | July | Aug. | Sept. | Oct. | Nov. | Dec | Total |
|---|---|---|---|---|---|---|---|---|---|---|---|---|---|
| 1990 | 34,922 | 37,220 | 39,152 | 14,018 | 39,665 | 35,560 | 16,860 | 21,412 | 8,721 | 18,285 | 9,452 | 46,463 | 321,730 |
| 1991 | | ------------ 55,378 ------------ | | | ------------ 67,155 ------------ | | | ------------ 52,469 ------------ | | | ------------ 38,291 ------------ | | 213,293 |
| 1992 | 68,977 | 69,631 | 19,704 | 19,753 | 13,071 | 13,443 | 16,027 | 7,947 | 13,090 | 8,101 | 4,625 | 17,308 | 271,677 |
| 1993 | 23,904 | 14,238 | 6,294 | 27,370 | 25,849 | 17,685 | 5,066 | 7,065 | 19,246 | 7,079 | 15,103 | 14,075 | 182,974 |
| 1994 | 32,011 | 11,093 | 21,156 | 26,595 | 34,921 | 11,583 | 24,303 | 24,644 | 25,265 | 17,487 | 33,385 | 36,613 | 299,056 |
| 1995 | 18,808 | 43,454 | 48,471 | 34,500 | 28,775 | 22,692 | 18,490 | 11,973 | NA | 9,896 | 30,268 | 13,223 | 280,550 |
| 1996[1] | 26,407 | 8,103 | 38,597 | 24,628 | 16,052 | 14,135 | 7,827 | 21,197 | 10,903 | 12,526 | | | 180,375 |

[1] Preliminary. NA = Not available. *Source: Economic Research Service, U.S. Department of Agriculture*

## Cottonseed Crushed (Consumption) in the United States In Thousands of Short Tons

| Year | Aug. | Sept. | Oct. | Nov. | Dec. | Jan. | Feb. | Mar. | Apr. | May | June | July | Total |
|---|---|---|---|---|---|---|---|---|---|---|---|---|---|
| 1988-9 | 216.8 | 179.5 | 299.3 | 375.3 | 376.7 | 399.7 | 325.4 | 383.3 | 336.6 | 321.7 | 287.0 | 228.9 | 3,730 |
| 1989-90 | 218.8 | 150.6 | 273.4 | 338.3 | 335.1 | 346.6 | 285.1 | 254.8 | 245.5 | 201.5 | 194.9 | 129.3 | 2,974 |
| 1990-1 | 157.3 | 176.1 | 274.9 | 339.4 | 320.8 | ----------- | 973.0 | ----------- | ----------- | 864.5 | ----------- | ------ | 3,106 |
| 1991-2 | 813.6 | ----------- | ----------- | 1,145.2 | ----------- | 420.6 | 378.3 | 381.3 | 297.8 | 245.4 | 292.1 | 270.2 | 4,245 |
| 1992-3 | 245.7 | 162.9 | 323.2 | 353.3 | 372.1 | 413.3 | 334.6 | 324.1 | 323.8 | 296.4 | 242.7 | 237.2 | 3,629 |
| 1993-4 | 182.9 | 162.6 | 300.4 | 391.4 | 375.0 | 391.0 | 335.2 | 358.6 | 265.7 | 257.7 | 239.4 | 210.2 | 3,470 |
| 1994-5 | 192.1 | 195.5 | 343.9 | 386.2 | 397.5 | 404.6 | 360.5 | 391.0 | 345.4 | 304.0 | 316.5 | 310.0 | 3,947 |
| 1995-6 | 264.4 | 245.5 | 337.1 | 386.7 | 362.4 | 402.3 | 373.5 | 381.4 | 349.6 | 325.2 | 223.7 | 209.2 | 3,861 |
| 1996-7[1] | 222.2 | 213.8 | 327.1 | 349.0 | | | | | | | | | 1,112 |

[1] Preliminary. *Source: Economic Research Service, U.S. Department of Agriculture*

## Production of Cottonseed Cake and Meal in the United States In Thousands of Short Tons

| Year | Aug. | Sept. | Oct. | Nov. | Dec. | Jan. | Feb. | Mar. | Apr. | May | June | July | Total |
|---|---|---|---|---|---|---|---|---|---|---|---|---|---|
| 1987-8 | 32.2 | 58.3 | 121.7 | 156.9 | 169.3 | 169.4 | 160.2 | 155.7 | 144.0 | 144.0 | 124.7 | 120.6 | 1,557 |
| 1988-9 | 100.7 | 80.1 | 135.4 | 170.0 | 172.5 | 183.2 | 151.6 | 175.3 | 152.7 | 157.6 | 126.7 | 106.1 | 1,712 |
| 1990-1 | 68.7 | 77.4 | 128.2 | 160.1 | 148.8 | ----------- | 456.2 | ----------- | ----------- | 409.1 | ----------- | ------- | 1,449 |
| 1991-2 | 388.6 | ----------- | ----------- | 533.9 | ----------- | 192.6 | 170.5 | 173.5 | 138.2 | 111.7 | 129.9 | 127.8 | 1,967 |
| 1992-3 | 111.2 | 76.0 | 143.7 | 150.2 | 160.5 | 176.2 | 146.6 | 136.4 | 140.9 | 126.1 | 103.0 | 101.0 | 1,572 |
| 1993-4 | 76.7 | 71.5 | 130.1 | 172.2 | 166.6 | 161.8 | 151.8 | 164.0 | 119.6 | 116.1 | 106.9 | 93.4 | 1,531 |
| 1994-5 | 90.6 | 89.4 | 154.2 | 171.5 | 176.9 | 184.1 | 162.2 | 174.3 | 154.2 | 137.4 | 143.9 | 137.2 | 1,776 |
| 1995-6 | 120.1 | 113.6 | 159.9 | 178.2 | 161.0 | 183.8 | 169.8 | 168.3 | 158.7 | 147.1 | 102.4 | 102.7 | 1,766 |
| 1996-7[1] | 100.9 | 99.1 | 144.5 | 158.8 | 157.2 | | | | | | | | 661 |

[1] Preliminary. *Source: Bureau of Census, U.S. Department of Commerce*

## U.S. Production of Crude Cottonseed Oil[2] In Millions of Pounds

| Year | Aug. | Sept. | Oct. | Nov. | Dec. | Jan. | Feb. | Mar. | Apr. | May | June | July | Total |
|---|---|---|---|---|---|---|---|---|---|---|---|---|---|
| 1988-9 | 72.7 | 56.9 | 98.6 | 125.3 | 125.0 | 129.3 | 106.0 | 127.1 | 111.7 | 109.7 | 94.5 | 76.6 | 1,233 |
| 1989-90 | 81.9 | 56.8 | 97.6 | 115.3 | 117.4 | 118.4 | 98.2 | 89.4 | 88.8 | 74.7 | 75.4 | 48.0 | 1,062 |
| 1990-1 | 58.7 | 57.6 | 86.2 | 104.0 | 102.3 | ----------- | 309.9 | ----------- | ----------- | 283.0 | ----------- | ------ | 1,002 |
| 1991-2 | 263.7 | ----------- | ----------- | 398.9 | ----------- | 137.4 | 127.2 | 121.5 | 97.5 | 79.3 | 91.8 | 91.3 | 1,409 |
| 1992-3 | 77.8 | 56.8 | 99.5 | 110.2 | 117.6 | 134.7 | 107.2 | 104.9 | 101.7 | 96.1 | 77.7 | 76.5 | 1,161 |
| 1993-4 | 59.1 | 51.7 | 93.5 | 122.2 | 117.5 | 124.7 | 99.9 | 119.6 | 85.3 | 85.2 | 78.4 | 69.8 | 1,107 |
| 1994-5 | 61.7 | 61.0 | 109.8 | 122.6 | 125.6 | 133.4 | 115.6 | 125.2 | 110.4 | 97.7 | 102.4 | 96.6 | 1,262 |
| 1995-6 | 87.8 | 84.3 | 105.2 | 121.6 | 111.6 | 130.9 | 121.4 | 125.6 | 110.4 | 101.9 | 73.3 | 76.7 | 1,251 |
| 1996-7[1] | 70.3 | 69.4 | 98.0 | 113.1 | 115.2 | | | | | | | | 466 |

[1] Preliminary. [2] Not seasonally adjusted. *Source: Bureau of Census, U.S. Department of Commerce*

## United States Production of Refined Cottonseed Oil In Millions of Pounds

| Year | Aug. | Sept. | Oct. | Nov. | Dec. | Jan. | Feb. | Mar. | Apr. | May | June | July | Total |
|---|---|---|---|---|---|---|---|---|---|---|---|---|---|
| 1988-9 | 83.2 | 61.7 | 94.1 | 124.8 | 127.8 | 139.7 | 121.9 | 137.0 | 116.3 | 119.1 | 102.8 | 71.6 | 1,300 |
| 1989-90 | 86.6 | 69.1 | 79.8 | 111.8 | 111.6 | 122.3 | 94.4 | 109.7 | 80.4 | 74.8 | 65.0 | 50.8 | 1,056 |
| 1990-1 | 57.8 | 53.7 | 75.4 | 96.0 | 90.0 | ----------- | 253.9 | ----------- | ----------- | 256.3 | ----------- | ------- | 883 |
| 1991-2 | 209.3 | ----------- | ----------- | 205.0 | ----------- | 103.2 | 105.6 | 97.9 | 85.6 | 73.4 | 82.1 | 81.1 | 1,043 |
| 1992-3 | 69.3 | 46.3 | 72.6 | 90.2 | 91.9 | 103.1 | 82.0 | 74.5 | 88.8 | 75.6 | 70.8 | 62.4 | 928 |
| 1993-4 | 65.1 | 54.6 | 79.4 | 109.1 | 100.6 | 107.2 | 93.4 | 107.8 | 66.9 | 71.6 | 70.0 | 72.2 | 998 |
| 1994-5 | 86.3 | 62.9 | 80.0 | 94.4 | 106.2 | 104.2 | 94.4 | 92.6 | 84.2 | 70.1 | 70.7 | 72.6 | 1,019 |
| 1995-6 | 80.5 | 69.0 | 74.0 | 89.5 | 86.9 | 91.7 | 84.6 | 89.8 | 81.7 | 75.0 | 53.8 | 54.5 | 931 |
| 1996-7[1] | 62.4 | 53.0 | 64.9 | 82.8 | 83.3 | | | | | | | | 346 |

[1] Preliminary. *Source: Bureau of Census, U.S. Department of Commerce*

## U.S. Stocks of Cottonseed Oil (Crude & Refined) at End of Month In Millions of Pounds

| Year | Aug. | Sept. | Oct. | Nov. | Dec. | Jan. | Feb. | Mar. | Apr. | May | June | July |
|---|---|---|---|---|---|---|---|---|---|---|---|---|
| 1988-9 | 172.9 | 160.4 | 163.9 | 188.6 | 206.1 | 266.3 | 274.0 | 276.6 | 263.7 | 249.2 | 266.7 | 247.6 |
| 1989-90 | 191.4 | 147.3 | 138.3 | 163.2 | 189.6 | 186.8 | 180.9 | 174.8 | 168.8 | 156.1 | 135.6 | 111.8 |
| 1990-1 | 75.9 | 80.4 | 83.0 | 93.5 | 102.7 | ----------- | 145.8 | ------------ | ----------- | 124.3 | ------------ | ------- |
| 1991-2 | 136.3 | ------------ | ----------- | 163.3 | ------------ | 193.1 | 183.6 | 180.3 | 171.5 | 154.0 | 139.9 | 119.8 |
| 1992-3 | 94.3 | 81.0 | 93.1 | 101.7 | 123.2 | 148.4 | 152.6 | 167.1 | 157.0 | 159.2 | 144.8 | 143.8 |
| 1993-4 | 85.8 | 54.6 | 79.4 | 109.1 | 100.6 | 107.2 | 93.4 | 107.8 | 66.9 | 71.6 | 70.0 | 72.1 |
| 1994-5 | 112.4 | 105.6 | 103.5 | 117.0 | 114.7 | 122.2 | 150.5 | 129.9 | 120.8 | 95.7 | 96.9 | 92.2 |
| 1995-6 | 87.8 | 82.1 | 82.6 | 89.3 | 94.8 | 118.2 | 147.2 | 151.2 | 155.6 | 143.3 | 128.1 | 125.4 |
| 1996-7[1] | 101.2 | 94.1 | 97.5 | 102.5 | 106.1 | | | | | | | |

[1] Preliminary. *Source:Bureau of Census, U.S. Department of Commerce*

## COTTONSEED AND PRODUCTS

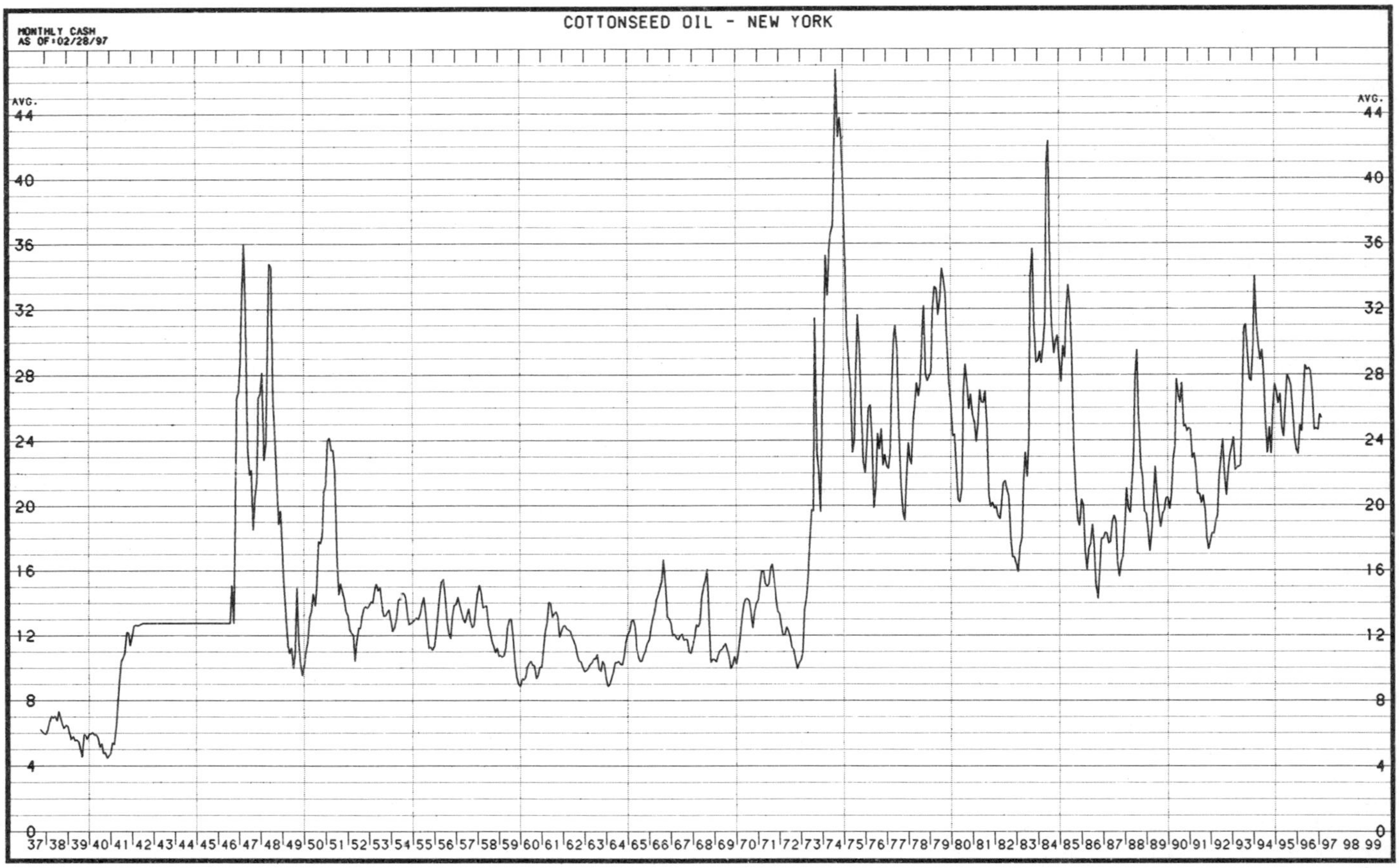


**Average Price of Crude Cottonseed Oil, PBSY, Greenwood, MS.[1] (Tank Cars)** In Cents Per Pound

| Year | Jan. | Feb. | Mar. | Apr. | May | June | July | Aug. | Sept. | Oct. | Nov. | Dec. | Average |
|---|---|---|---|---|---|---|---|---|---|---|---|---|---|
| 1986 | 19.88 | 17.63 | 15.75 | 17.50 | 17.69 | 17.90 | 15.38 | 17.44 | 14.25 | 15.38 | 17.44 | 17.75 | 17.00 |
| 1987 | 18.38 | 18.56 | 17.85 | 17.88 | 18.94 | 19.25 | 19.00 | 16.70 | 15.44 | 16.75 | 17.00 | 18.35 | 17.84 |
| 1988 | 21.31 | 20.19 | 19.60 | 21.00 | 22.88 | 26.65 | 30.25 | 15.00 | 23.00 | 21.44 | 19.70 | 19.94 | 21.75 |
| 1989 | 19.19 | 17.56 | 20.25 | 21.06 | 21.80 | 20.25 | 19.63 | 18.60 | 19.75 | 19.95 | 20.81 | 20.50 | 19.95 |
| 1990 | 19.95 | 20.19 | 22.88 | 22.83 | 26.90 | 26.94 | 26.00 | 24.60 | 24.88 | 24.80 | 24.19 | 24.75 | 24.08 |
| 1991 | 23.75 | 22.88 | 23.00 | 22.13 | 20.67 | 20.31 | 20.50 | 21.00 | 19.88 | 17.98 | 17.41 | 18.07 | 20.63 |
| 1992 | 18.50 | 18.13 | 19.25 | 19.38 | 21.38 | 22.58 | 24.45 | 21.86 | 21.04 | 22.17 | 22.96 | 23.91 | 21.30 |
| 1993 | 24.09 | 22.03 | 22.24 | 22.55 | 22.70 | 26.76 | 30.74 | 30.45 | 28.98 | 24.79 | 26.69 | 30.39 | 26.03 |
| 1994 | 33.16 | 29.96 | 29.60 | 29.06 | 29.66 | 27.55 | 24.20 | 23.71 | 24.51 | 23.64 | 24.85 | 25.50 | 27.12 |
| 1995 | 28.70 | 29.95 | 27.14 | 27.61 | 27.51 | 30.04 | 30.63 | 30.26 | 28.61 | 27.61 | 26.27 | 26.10 | 26.36 |
| 1996 | 24.45 | 24.35 | 24.25 | 26.77 | 28.46 | 27.94 | 28.25 | 27.81 | 26.13 | 24.55 | 24.28 | 24.29 | 25.96 |

[1] Data prior to 1995 are F.O.B. Valley Points, Southeastern mills. *Source: Economic Research Service, U.S Department of Agriculture*

**U.S. Exports of Cottonseed Oil to Important Countries** In Thousands of Metric Tons

| Year | Canada | Dominican Republic | Egypt | Guat-emala | Japan | Mexico | Nether-lands | Salvador | South Korea | Turkey | Venez-uela | Total |
|---|---|---|---|---|---|---|---|---|---|---|---|---|
| 1985 | 2.5 | 7.6 | 57.1 | 9.8 | 24.9 | .3 | 5.8 | 19.4 | 2.3 | ----- | 51.9 | 191.4 |
| 1986 | 2.9 | 2.2 | 16.5 | 11.6 | 27.3 | 9.3 | 8.0 | 25.9 | 5.7 | ----- | 50.9 | 173.7 |
| 1987 | 3.2 | 5.0 | 1.9 | 2.4 | 15.7 | 3.1 | 2.9 | 15.6 | 7.8 | ----- | 47.3 | 109.9 |
| 1988 | 4.8 | 3.1 | 29.6 | .5 | 21.5 | 8.2 | 2.7 | 26.3 | 7.7 | 13.5 | 46.2 | 167.8 |
| 1989 | 6.6 | 5.1 | 39.4 | 6.0 | 34.3 | 3.2 | 3.4 | 30.5 | 21.0 | 2.0 | 53.7 | 209.4 |
| 1990 | 6.8 | 6.0 | 14.7 | .4 | 36.7 | 1.4 | 2.9 | 21.0 | 36.0 | ----- | 9.2 | 136.3 |
| 1991 | 7.8 | 2.1 | 14.7 | ----- | 24.1 | 4.8 | 3.4 | 13.0 | 13.0 | 5.5 | 4.2 | 97.0 |
| 1992 | 11.3 | 1.0 | 8.2 | 3.2 | 15.3 | 8.5 | 17.4 | 26.5 | 10.9 | 7.0 | 3.7 | 123.3 |
| 1993 | 10.9 | ----- | ----- | .5 | 17.6 | 5.8 | .2 | 30.8 | 6.6 | .5 | 1.5 | 83.1 |
| 1994 | 10.8 | ----- | ----- | 12.3 | 29.8 | 10.3 | 1.9 | 26.1 | 16.9 | ----- | 4.5 | 135.7 |
| 1995[1] | 12.0 | ----- | 10.3 | 1.9 | 17.9 | 5.7 | 1.5 | 37.8 | 19.2 | ----- | 2.8 | 133.7 |

[1] Prelminary. *Source: Oil World*

# CRB Futures Index

The Commodity Research Bureau Futures Price Index was first calculated by Commodity Research Bureau, Inc. in 1957 and made its innaugural appearance in the 1958 CRB Commodity Year Book.

The Index was originally comprised of two cash markets and 26 futures markets which were traded on exchanges in the U.S. and Canada. It included barley and flaxseed from the Winnipeg exchange; cocoa, coffee "B", copper, cotton, cottonseed oil, grease wool, hides, lead, potatoes, rubber, sugar #4, sugar #6, wool tops and zinc from New York exchanges; and corn, oats, wheat, rye, soybeans, soybean oil, soybean meal, lard, onions, and eggs from Chicago exchanges. In addition to those 26, the Index also included the spot New Orleans cotton and Minneapolis wheat markets.

Like the Bureau of Labor Statistics spot index, the CRB Futures Price Index is calculated to produce an unweighted geometric mean of the individual commodity price relatives. In other words, a ratio of the current price to the base year average price. Currently, 1967 is the base year the Index is calculated against (1967 = 100).

The formula considers all future delivery contracts which expire on or before the end of the sixth calendar month from the current date, up to a maximum of five delivery months per commodity. However, a minimum of two delivery months must be used to calculate the current price, even if the second contract is outside of the six month window. Contracts are excluded from the calculation when in their delivery period.

The 1996 closing Index value of 239.61 was 1.47 percent lower than 1995's close of 243.18 and marked the first lower close in the last four years. Among the eight CRB Index subindices, four were up and four were down.

***Futures Markets***

Futures and options on the CRB Futures Index are traded on the New York Futures Exchange (NYFE).

## CRB Futures Price Index Component Commodities by Group

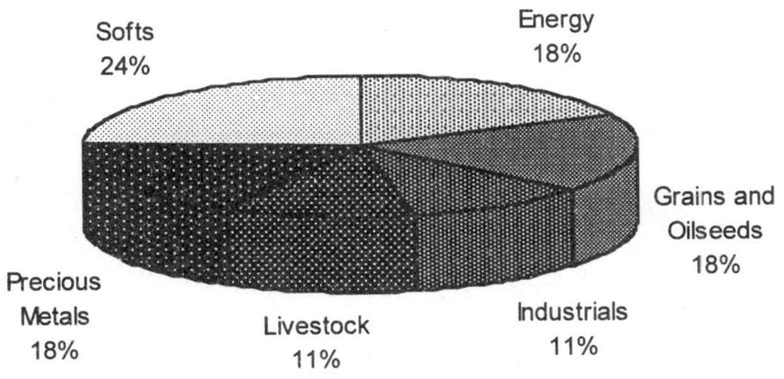


| *Groups:* | *Components:* |
|---|---|
| Energy - | Crude Oil, Heating Oil, Natural Gas |
| Grains and Oilseeds- | Corn, Soybeans, Wheat |
| Industrials - | Copper, Cotton |
| Livestock - | Live Cattle, Live Hogs |
| Precious Metals - | Gold, Platinum. Silver |
| Softs - | Cocoa, Coffee, Orange Juice, Sugar |

**The CRB Futures Price Index is computed using a three-step process:**

**1)** Each of the Index's 17 component commodities is arithmetically averaged using the prices for all of the designated contract months which expire on or before the end of the sixth calendar month from the current date, except that: a) no contract shall be included in the calculation while in delivery; b) there shall be a minimum of two contract months for each component commodity (adding contracts beyond the six month window, if necessary); c) there shall be a maximum of five contract months for each commodity (dropping the most deferred contracts to remain at five, if necessary). The result is that the Index extends six to seven months into the future depending on where one is in the current month. For example, live cattle's average price on October 30, 1995 would be computed as follows:

$$\text{Cattle Average} = \frac{\text{Dec. '96 + Feb. '97}}{2}$$

**2)** These 17 component averages are then geometrically averaged by multiplying all of the numbers together and taking the 17th root.

$$\text{Geometric Average} = \sqrt[17]{\text{Crude Avg. x Heating Avg. x ...Sugar Avg.}}$$

**3)** The resulting average is divided by 30.7766, the 1967 base-year average for these 17 commodities. That result is then multiplied by an adjustment factor of .8486. This adjustment factor is necessitated by the nine revisions to the Index since its inception in 1957. Finally, that result is multiplied by 100 in order to convert the Index into percentage terms:

$$\text{CRB Futures Index} = \frac{\text{Current Geometric Average}}{\text{1967 Geometric Avg. (30.7766)}} \text{ x .8486 x 100}$$

# CRB FUTURES INDEX

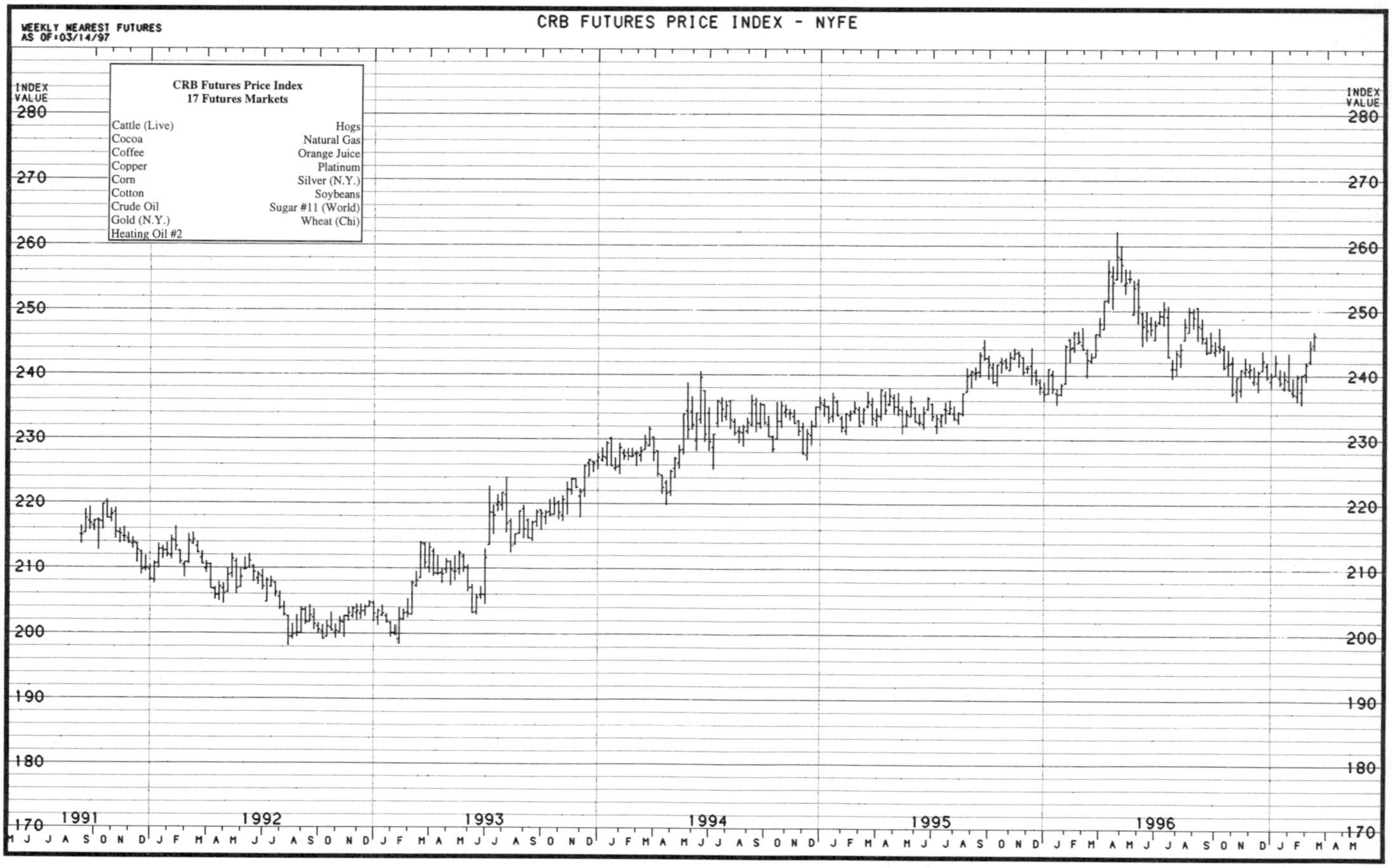


**Average Open Interest of CRB Futures Index in New York** In Contracts

| Year | Jan. | Feb. | Mar. | Apr. | May | June | July | Aug. | Sept. | Oct. | Nov. | Dec. |
|---|---|---|---|---|---|---|---|---|---|---|---|---|
| 1986 | ----- | ----- | ----- | ----- | ----- | 491 | 590 | 813 | 1,121 | 1,102 | 1,750 | 2,158 |
| 1987 | 2,649 | 2,840 | 2,425 | 2,483 | 3,281 | 4,010 | 5,686 | 5,196 | 4,903 | 4,091 | 4,255 | 3,889 |
| 1988 | 2,597 | 2,607 | 2,682 | 2,819 | 3,592 | 3,934 | 2,846 | 2,795 | 2,659 | 2,419 | 2,529 | 2,556 |
| 1989 | 2,679 | 3,008 | 2,491 | 2,274 | 2,117 | 2,104 | 1,891 | 1,992 | 1,861 | 1,907 | 2,215 | 2,209 |
| 1990 | 1,889 | 1,229 | 1,476 | 1,858 | 1,499 | 1,459 | 1,289 | 1,286 | 1,181 | 1,247 | 1,505 | 1,530 |
| 1991 | 1,443 | 1,593 | 1,524 | 1,620 | 1,511 | 1,524 | 1,168 | 1,071 | 1,045 | 1,172 | 1,357 | 1,383 |
| 1992 | 1,435 | 1,472 | 1,185 | 1,347 | 1,311 | 1,087 | 951 | 1,179 | 1,075 | 1,226 | 1,283 | 1,406 |
| 1993 | 1,969 | 1,984 | 1,842 | 2,201 | 2,564 | 2,947 | 2,616 | 2,409 | 2,128 | 2,383 | 2,432 | 2,351 |
| 1994 | 2,607 | 3,146 | 2,680 | 2,691 | 2,339 | 2,698 | 3,838 | 5,146 | 4,562 | 4,942 | 4,535 | 2,800 |
| 1995 | 2,144 | 2,164 | 2,147 | 2,370 | 2,016 | 2,144 | 2,053 | 2,070 | 2,062 | 1,942 | 2,003 | 1,640 |
| 1996 | 1,934 | 1,826 | 1,753 | 2,355 | 1,881 | 1,890 | 1,562 | 1,345 | 1,596 | 1,853 | 1,861 | 1,866 |

*Source: New York Futures Exchange (NYFE)*

**Volume of Trading of CRB Futures Index in New York** In Contracts

| Year | Jan. | Feb. | Mar. | Apr. | May | June | July | Aug. | Sept. | Oct. | Nov. | Dec. | Total |
|---|---|---|---|---|---|---|---|---|---|---|---|---|---|
| 1986 | ----- | ----- | ----- | ----- | ----- | 10,739 | 9,012 | 8,766 | 8,040 | 5,344 | 8,182 | 8,842 | 58,925 |
| 1987 | 3,360 | 7,143 | 8,261 | 10,313 | 15,510 | 16,995 | 13,271 | 13,107 | 9,237 | 14,744 | 13,200 | 11,686 | 136,827 |
| 1988 | 9,557 | 10,726 | 13,841 | 9,480 | 20,299 | 43,591 | 31,043 | 22,020 | 15,615 | 9,044 | 9,691 | 11,044 | 205,951 |
| 1989 | 8,805 | 10,045 | 12,035 | 11,437 | 13,145 | 13,824 | 11,917 | 9,846 | 7,918 | 7,412 | 9,613 | 8,551 | 124,548 |
| 1990 | 6,505 | 5,829 | 7,042 | 6,670 | 7,191 | 6,687 | 6,477 | 6,415 | 4,096 | 4,744 | 4,409 | 3,842 | 69,907 |
| 1991 | 5,835 | 5,391 | 6,715 | 6,432 | 3,671 | 5,557 | 4,853 | 5,876 | 4,414 | 3,766 | 4,132 | 4,543 | 61,185 |
| 1992 | 4,895 | 6,031 | 4,136 | 5,697 | 5,496 | 4,487 | 4,162 | 4,617 | 3,874 | 3,183 | 5,277 | 4,400 | 56,255 |
| 1993 | 3,620 | 5,720 | 8,050 | 7,340 | 8,680 | 10,722 | 12,418 | 8,590 | 6,192 | 4,350 | 8,535 | 6,954 | 91,908 |
| 1994 | 6,956 | 7,473 | 10,085 | 10,274 | 11,298 | 14,652 | 10,560 | 8,967 | 7,445 | 6,575 | 10,186 | 5,515 | 109,986 |
| 1995 | 6,151 | 5,545 | 5,763 | 7,955 | 7,877 | 7,573 | 6,875 | 10,094 | 7,376 | 5,030 | 5,865 | 5,309 | 81,413 |
| 1996 | 7,490 | 6,041 | 6,428 | 10,784 | 9,526 | 5,543 | 7,476 | 5,816 | 6,311 | 6,527 | 5,990 | 3,181 | 81,113 |

*Source: New York Futures Exchange (NYFE)*

# Currencies

There was considerable variance in the world's major currencies against U.S. dollar during 1996. On balance, the dollar's value firmed which apparently was the objective of the U.S. Administration and the Federal Reserve.

The German Deutsche Mark slipped against the dollar, starting the year at $0.70 (about 1.42 dm) and falling to $0.645 (about $1.55 dm) by yearend. The J-Yen showed a parallel trend; falling from $.0095 to a yearend value near $.0087 (equal to 115 yen per dollar). The B-Pound and C-Dollar showed considerably more volatility. The pound rose from the low $1.50 area to a high near $1.70 in late 1996. The C-Dollar drifted in a tight range during much of 1996 then bolted higher in the fall, rising from $0.73 to $0.755, only to lose the entire gain by yearend. When viewed against a basket of currencies the dollar slowly appreciated during the first half of 1996, slipped during mid-summer, then regained its strength in the fourth quarter. The U.S. Dollar Index rose from 84.78 in January to 89.04 in May, dropped to 85.63 in late July and closed the year at 88.18; a range of less than 4 points vs. a 1995 range of 10 points.

Fundamental factors which supported the dollar included an expanding U.S. economy and unemployment near 5.5 percent which was low relative to most nations; the European Union averaged 11 percent, Germany 11.2 percent, Spain 22 percent, and Canada 9.8 percent.

In the July-September quarter the U.S. current account trade deficit swelled to a record large $48 billion; it was the first quarterly setback in export growth since mid-1993 and reflected the dollar's strength, notably the 30 percent rise against the J-Yen since the spring of 1995. Although the trade deficit narrowed in the fourth quarter, the consensus view for 1997 suggested continued problems for U.S. exports due to the dollar's strength.

The core issue for the dollar in 1996 was the Administration's policy. Since mid-1995 the U.S., with the help of Germany's and Japan's central banks, actively pushed for a stronger dollar. The reasons: the strong U.S. economy did not need a cheaper dollar, quite the contrary, the dollar's strength could have the effect of redistributing strong U.S. economic growth to the stagnant economies of Japan and Europe. However, in late 1996 it appears U.S. policy shifted toward establishing a floor under the dollar rather than pushing it higher, probably due to signs of strengthening economies abroad and to prevent any sharp decline in the dollar's value that could trigger a flight of capital away from the U.S.

Germany's economic data in 1996 was generally poor. Unemployment was at a record high, consumer buying weak, and the nation's budget deficit on the rise. Export growth slowed dramatically with little improvement expected in 1997. For Switzerland the setting was even worse in 1996 as the economy was virtually stagnant.

In the United Kingdom the economy was improving in 1996. Unemployment was low compared to most of Europe. The nation's political setting was in flux, but for the first time in years the FOREX market did not appear overly disturbed by a possible Labour party takeover in 1997, the rational being it might bring closer ties with Continental Europe and easier entry into the EMU.

Japan's economy was in flux during 1996; consumer spending was weak and unemployment at a record high, but by late 1996 there were signs of a rebound taking hold. Less certain was the Bank of Japan's position on its exchange rate policy, but it was believed that in 1997 policy may shift from one that advocated a weaker currency to one that desired a more stable, if not higher, currency. What actually emerges is apt to pivot on whether Japan's economic recovery is real or just a bounce that lacks substance. In either case, a good recovery in the J-Yen's value against the key currencies was not likely in the first half of 1997.

***Futures Markets***

The Chicago Mercantile Exchange's International Monetary Market (IMM) trades futures and options on the British Pound, Swiss Franc, Deutsche Mark, Japanese Yen, Canadian Dollar, Australian Dollar, and the Mexican Peso. The exchange also lists a D-Mark rolling spot contract and a D-Mark forward contract. Additional currency futures are likely to begin trading there in 1996. Chicago's MidAmerica Commodity Exchange (MidAm) trades smaller futures contracts on many of the IMM's currencies. The FINEX division of the New York Cotton Exchange (NYCE) trades futures and options on a composite Dollar Index and also offers crossrate futures contracts: D-Mark/J-Yen, D-Mark/French Franc and D-Mark/B-Pound. Currency futures and options are also traded on the Philadelphia Board of Trade (PBOT).

**Monthly Close of the CRB Currency Futures Index** 1977 = 100

| Year | January | February | March | April | May | June | July | August | September | October | November | December |
|---|---|---|---|---|---|---|---|---|---|---|---|---|
| 1986 | 99.50 | 103.90 | 103.30 | 108.50 | 104.30 | 109.60 | 112.40 | 113.20 | 112.30 | 109.20 | 112.00 | 114.40 |
| 1987 | 118.50 | 119.50 | 123.30 | 125.70 | 123.40 | 122.90 | 120.60 | 123.80 | 122.60 | 128.70 | 134.80 | 141.30 |
| 1988 | 134.00 | 133.60 | 138.30 | 137.00 | 134.50 | 129.20 | 127.10 | 125.10 | 126.70 | 131.30 | 136.30 | 133.70 |
| 1989 | 128.20 | 130.00 | 126.00 | 125.50 | 119.30 | 120.20 | 125.20 | 119.70 | 123.60 | 122.60 | 123.90 | 126.10 |
| 1990 | 127.30 | 126.30 | 124.90 | 125.80 | 127.50 | 129.10 | 134.80 | 136.60 | 137.40 | 141.50 | 141.80 | 140.80 |
| 1991 | 142.80 | 139.80 | 129.30 | 130.60 | 129.00 | 125.50 | 128.00 | 128.30 | 132.40 | 132.50 | 134.50 | 138.80 |
| 1992 | 134.40 | 132.00 | 129.80 | 130.20 | 134.00 | 137.90 | 140.60 | 145.60 | 141.10 | 132.70 | 128.90 | 127.60 |
| 1993 | 199.50 | 202.90 | 212.50 | 210.90 | 208.70 | 207.10 | 129.60 | 130.70 | 131.80 | 129.30 | 128.60 | 127.70 |
| 1994 | 129.60 | 131.00 | 131.80 | 133.20 | 132.30 | 137.10 | 136.30 | 136.90 | 140.20 | 143.21 | 138.22 | 138.74 |
| 1995 | 139.40 | 142.82 | 151.42 | 152.26 | 150.15 | 151.44 | 150.29 | 143.92 | 146.19 | 146.32 | 142.94 | 144.09 |
| 1996 | 139.48 | 140.77 | 141.17 | 138.88 | 138.43 | 138.69 | 141.36 | 140.53 | 138.72 | 139.02 | 138.36 | 137.78 |

*Source: BRIDGE - Commodity Research Bureau*

WEEKLY NEAREST FUTURES
AS OF:03/14/97
BRITISH POUND - IMM
USD/GBP
2.2
2.1
2.0
1.9
1.8
1.7
1.6
1.5
1.4
1.3
1.2
1.1
1991
1992
1993
1994
1995
1996
M J J A S O N D J F M A M J J A S O N D J F M A M J J A S O N D J F M A M J J A S O N D J F M A M J J A S O N D J F M A M J J A S O N D J F M A M

WEEKLY NEAREST FUTURES
AS OF:03/14/97
CANADIAN DOLLAR - IMM
USD/CAD
.88
.86
.84
.82
.80
.78
.76
.74
.72
.70
.68
.66
1991
1992
1993
1994
1995
1996
M J J A S O N D J F M A M J J A S O N D J F M A M J J A S O N D J F M A M J J A S O N D J F M A M J J A S O N D J F M A M J J A S O N D J F M A M

DEUTSCHE MARK - IMM
WEEKLY NEAREST FUTURES
AS OF:03/14/97
USD/DEM
.76
.74
.72
.70
.68
.66
.64
.62
.60
.58
.56
.54
1991
1992
1993
1994
1995
1996
M J J A S O N D J F M A M J J A S O N D J F M A M J J A S O N D J F M A M J J A S O N D J F M A M J J A S O N D J F M A M J J A S O N D J F M A M

JAPANESE YEN - IMM
WEEKLY NEAREST FUTURES
AS OF:03/14/97
USD/JPY
1.25
1.20
1.15
1.10
1.05
1.00
.95
.90
.85
.80
.75
.70
1991
1992
1993
1994
1995
1996
M J J A S O N D J F M A M J J A S O N D J F M A M J J A S O N D J F M A M J J A S O N D J F M A M J J A S O N D J F M A M J J A S O N D J F M A M

## CURRENCIES

SWISS FRANC - IMM
WEEKLY NEAREST FUTURES
AS OF:03/14/97
USD/CHF
1.00
.96
.92
.88
.84
.80
.76
.72
.68
.64
.60
.56
1991
1992
1993
1994
1995
1996
M J J A S O N D J F M A M J J A S O N D J F M A M J J A S O N D J F M A M J J A S O N D J F M A M J J A S O N D J F M A M J J A S O N D J F M A M

CRB CURRENCY INDEX
(1977 = 100)
WEEKLY CASH
AS OF:03/14/97
INDEX VALUE
CRB Currencies Index
5 Futures Markets
(1977=100)
British Pound
Canadian Dollar
Deutsche Mark
Japanese Yen
Swiss Franc
165
160
155
150
145
140
135
130
125
120
115
110
1991
1992
1993
1994
1995
1996
M J J A S O N D J F M A M J J A S O N D J F M A M J J A S O N D J F M A M J J A S O N D J F M A M J J A S O N D J F M A M J J A S O N D J F M A M

## Canadian Dollars per U.S. Dollar

| Year | January | February | March | April | May | June | July | August | September | October | November | December | Average |
|---|---|---|---|---|---|---|---|---|---|---|---|---|---|
| 1988 | 1.2840 | 1.2680 | 1.2490 | 1.2350 | 1.2370 | 1.2170 | 1.2080 | 1.2240 | 1.2270 | 1.2060 | 1.2180 | 1.1960 | 1.2308 |
| 1989 | 1.1910 | 1.1890 | 1.1950 | 1.1890 | 1.1930 | 1.1990 | 1.1890 | 1.1760 | 1.1920 | 1.2020 | 1.1690 | 1.1610 | 1.1871 |
| 1990 | 1.1720 | 1.1970 | 1.1800 | 1.1680 | 1.1700 | 1.1700 | 1.1600 | 1.1500 | 1.1600 | 1.1600 | 1.1640 | 1.1600 | 1.1676 |
| 1991 | 1.1560 | 1.1550 | 1.1570 | 1.1540 | 1.1500 | 1.1440 | 1.1240 | 1.1450 | 1.1390 | 1.1210 | 1.1310 | 1.1450 | 1.1434 |
| 1992 | 1.1570 | 1.2180 | 1.1920 | 1.1870 | 1.1990 | 1.1960 | 1.1920 | 1.1910 | 1.2210 | 1.2440 | 1.2680 | 1.2710 | 1.2113 |
| 1993 | 1.2770 | 1.2600 | 1.2470 | 1.2620 | 1.2690 | 1.2790 | 1.2820 | 1.3080 | 1.3210 | 1.3250 | 1.3160 | 1.3310 | 1.2898 |
| 1994 | 1.3175 | 1.3419 | 1.3645 | 1.3821 | 1.3805 | 1.3831 | 1.3818 | 1.3777 | 1.3536 | 1.3495 | 1.3649 | 1.3896 | 1.3656 |
| 1995 | 1.4120 | 1.3995 | 1.4065 | 1.3749 | 1.3607 | 1.3772 | 1.3609 | 1.3550 | 1.3495 | 1.3449 | 1.3525 | 1.3685 | 1.3718 |
| 1996 | 1.3664 | 1.3753 | 1.3651 | 1.3591 | 1.3690 | 1.3649 | 1.3687 | 1.3717 | 1.3691 | 1.3501 | 1.3382 | 1.3621 | 1.3633 |

*Source: BRIDGE Information Systems*

## German (Deutsche) Marks per U.S. Dollar

| Year | January | February | March | April | May | June | July | August | September | October | November | December | Average |
|---|---|---|---|---|---|---|---|---|---|---|---|---|---|
| 1988 | 1.6540 | 1.6970 | 1.6760 | 1.6710 | 1.6930 | 1.7570 | 1.8460 | 1.8880 | 1.8670 | 1.8170 | 1.7480 | 1.7560 | 1.7558 |
| 1989 | 1.8360 | 1.8510 | 1.8690 | 1.8690 | 1.9460 | 1.9790 | 1.8890 | 1.9270 | 1.9490 | 1.8660 | 1.7660 | 1.7360 | 1.8736 |
| 1990 | 1.6920 | 1.6770 | 1.7040 | 1.6880 | 1.6600 | 1.6800 | 1.6400 | 1.5700 | 1.5700 | 1.5400 | 1.4860 | 1.4980 | 1.6171 |
| 1991 | 1.5090 | 1.4810 | 1.6120 | 1.7030 | 1.7180 | 1.7820 | 1.7830 | 1.7430 | 2.1220 | 1.6860 | 1.6200 | 1.5610 | 1.6933 |
| 1992 | 1.5800 | 1.6190 | 1.6590 | 1.6490 | 1.6210 | 1.5720 | 1.4890 | 1.4460 | 1.4490 | 1.4860 | 1.5870 | 1.5830 | 1.5617 |
| 1993 | 1.6140 | 1.6430 | 1.6460 | 1.5940 | 1.6050 | 1.6540 | 1.7140 | 1.6930 | 1.6200 | 1.6400 | 1.7000 | 1.7110 | 1.6528 |
| 1994 | 1.7422 | 1.7340 | 1.6907 | 1.6969 | 1.6557 | 1.6269 | 1.5705 | 1.5637 | 1.5488 | 1.5188 | 1.5410 | 1.5705 | 1.6216 |
| 1995 | 1.5312 | 1.4996 | 1.4044 | 1.3792 | 1.4085 | 1.3988 | 1.3874 | 1.4457 | 1.4599 | 1.4133 | 1.4178 | 1.4397 | 1.4321 |
| 1996 | 1.4627 | 1.4644 | 1.4763 | 1.5053 | 1.5329 | 1.5274 | 1.5026 | 1.4819 | 1.5068 | 1.5277 | 1.5124 | 1.5517 | 1.5043 |

*Source: BRIDGE Information Systems*

## Japanese Yen per U.S. Dollar

| Year | January | February | March | April | May | June | July | August | September | October | November | December | Average |
|---|---|---|---|---|---|---|---|---|---|---|---|---|---|
| 1988 | 127.60 | 129.10 | 127.00 | 124.90 | 124.70 | 127.40 | 133.00 | 133.80 | 134.30 | 128.70 | 123.20 | 123.60 | 128.11 |
| 1989 | 127.40 | 127.70 | 130.60 | 132.00 | 137.90 | 144.00 | 140.40 | 141.40 | 144.90 | 141.40 | 143.40 | 143.70 | 137.90 |
| 1990 | 145.00 | 145.70 | 153.20 | 158.40 | 156.20 | 153.80 | 149.00 | 147.40 | 138.50 | 129.60 | 128.20 | 133.90 | 144.91 |
| 1991 | 133.70 | 130.50 | 137.40 | 137.10 | 138.00 | 139.60 | 137.60 | 136.90 | 134.80 | 130.50 | 129.70 | 128.00 | 134.48 |
| 1992 | 125.30 | 127.70 | 132.80 | 133.50 | 130.70 | 126.70 | 125.70 | 126.10 | 122.60 | 121.20 | 123.80 | 123.90 | 126.67 |
| 1993 | 124.94 | 120.77 | 116.99 | 112.22 | 110.10 | 107.29 | 107.57 | 103.74 | 105.41 | 107.00 | 107.78 | 109.89 | 111.14 |
| 1994 | 111.33 | 106.22 | 105.00 | 103.36 | 103.76 | 102.37 | 98.65 | 99.88 | 98.78 | 98.36 | 98.08 | 100.08 | 102.16 |
| 1995 | 99.67 | 98.14 | 90.40 | 83.59 | 84.96 | 84.55 | 87.22 | 94.72 | 100.49 | 100.76 | 101.93 | 101.84 | 94.02 |
| 1996 | 105.66 | 105.57 | 105.90 | 107.23 | 106.42 | 108.91 | 109.21 | 107.84 | 109.87 | 112.40 | 112.35 | 114.01 | 108.78 |

*Source: BRIDGE Information Systems*

## Swiss Francs per U.S. Dollar

| Year | January | February | March | April | May | June | July | August | September | October | November | December | Average |
|---|---|---|---|---|---|---|---|---|---|---|---|---|---|
| 1988 | 1.3490 | 1.3930 | 1.3870 | 1.3830 | 1.4130 | 1.4630 | 1.5340 | 1.5840 | 1.5750 | 1.5390 | 1.4630 | 1.4800 | 1.4636 |
| 1989 | 1.5620 | 1.5740 | 1.6110 | 1.6470 | 1.7290 | 1.7060 | 1.6290 | 1.6630 | 1.6870 | 1.6320 | 1.6180 | 1.5670 | 1.6354 |
| 1990 | 1.5180 | 1.4890 | 1.5130 | 1.4850 | 1.4200 | 1.4250 | 1.3910 | 1.3090 | 1.3060 | 1.2810 | 1.2560 | 1.2800 | 1.3894 |
| 1991 | 1.2710 | 1.2690 | 1.3890 | 1.4380 | 1.4560 | 1.5300 | 1.5510 | 1.5200 | 1.4820 | 1.4800 | 1.4360 | 1.3830 | 1.4338 |
| 1992 | 1.4030 | 1.4570 | 1.5070 | 1.5180 | 1.4900 | 1.4230 | 1.3320 | 1.2950 | 1.2760 | 1.3190 | 1.4280 | 1.4230 | 1.4059 |
| 1993 | 1.4775 | 1.5197 | 1.5199 | 1.4572 | 1.4471 | 1.4767 | 1.5138 | 1.4947 | 1.4158 | 1.4421 | 1.4966 | 1.4629 | 1.4770 |
| 1994 | 1.4707 | 1.4558 | 1.4295 | 1.4363 | 1.4120 | 1.3723 | 1.3256 | 1.3176 | 1.2895 | 1.2636 | 1.2974 | 1.3275 | 1.3665 |
| 1995 | 1.2865 | 1.2694 | 1.1691 | 1.1362 | 1.1678 | 1.1564 | 1.1542 | 1.1958 | 1.1868 | 1.1444 | 1.1440 | 1.1624 | 1.1811 |
| 1996 | 1.1810 | 1.1942 | 1.1945 | 1.2194 | 1.2546 | 1.2574 | 1.2324 | 1.2022 | 1.2333 | 1.2583 | 1.2757 | 1.3296 | 1.2361 |

*Source: BRIDGE Information Systems*

## British Pounds per U.S. Dollar

| Year | January | February | March | April | May | June | July | August | September | October | November | December | Average |
|---|---|---|---|---|---|---|---|---|---|---|---|---|---|
| 1988 | 1.7990 | 1.7570 | 1.8340 | 1.8770 | 1.8680 | 1.7770 | 1.7040 | 1.6960 | 1.6840 | 1.7380 | 1.8120 | 1.8240 | 1.7808 |
| 1989 | 1.7740 | 1.7530 | 1.7130 | 1.7010 | 1.6280 | 1.5540 | 1.6260 | 1.5930 | 1.5720 | 1.5860 | 1.5730 | 1.5970 | 1.6392 |
| 1990 | 1.6510 | 1.6960 | 1.6250 | 1.6380 | 1.6780 | 1.7110 | 1.8100 | 1.9010 | 1.8800 | 1.9480 | 1.9640 | 1.9210 | 1.7853 |
| 1991 | 1.9350 | 1.9640 | 1.8210 | 1.7510 | 1.7260 | 1.6490 | 1.6480 | 1.6840 | 1.7250 | 1.7210 | 1.7780 | 1.8310 | 1.7694 |
| 1992 | 1.8110 | 1.7780 | 1.7250 | 1.7560 | 1.8100 | 1.8560 | 1.9190 | 1.9450 | 1.8510 | 1.6550 | 1.5270 | 1.5500 | 1.7653 |
| 1993 | 1.5330 | 1.4383 | 1.4621 | 1.5465 | 1.5492 | 1.5090 | 1.4973 | 1.4928 | 1.5251 | 1.5027 | 1.4808 | 1.4904 | 1.5023 |
| 1994 | 1.4933 | 1.4787 | 1.4921 | 1.4832 | 1.5038 | 1.5261 | 1.5446 | 1.5421 | 1.5647 | 1.6073 | 1.5864 | 1.5582 | 1.5317 |
| 1995 | 1.5742 | 1.5727 | 1.6004 | 1.6087 | 1.5886 | 1.5960 | 1.5955 | 1.5668 | 1.5595 | 1.5782 | 1.5612 | 1.5411 | 1.5786 |
| 1996 | 1.5289 | 1.5376 | 1.5278 | 1.5159 | 1.5154 | 1.5417 | 1.5538 | 1.5501 | 1.5595 | 1.5863 | 1.6629 | 1.6660 | 1.5622 |

*Source: BRIDGE Information Systems*

# CURRENCIES

## Average Open Interest of Canadian Dollar Futures in Chicago In Contracts

| Year | January | February | March | April | May | June | July | August | September | October | November | December |
|---|---|---|---|---|---|---|---|---|---|---|---|---|
| 1988 | 22,411 | 24,244 | 22,965 | 24,095 | 27,747 | 35,787 | 33,207 | 28,513 | 22,645 | 23,138 | 19,548 | 24,844 |
| 1989 | 24,221 | 27,726 | 23,102 | 21,146 | 24,900 | 24,807 | 20,007 | 31,041 | 27,206 | 25,903 | 29,645 | 29,116 |
| 1990 | 26,426 | 29,204 | 23,848 | 24,048 | 33,823 | 30,809 | 39,843 | 42,092 | 34,998 | 29,434 | 31,250 | 25,272 |
| 1991 | 29,072 | 28,214 | 25,550 | 24,894 | 29,310 | 33,136 | 25,113 | 25,310 | 30,909 | 28,805 | 27,453 | 22,311 |
| 1992 | 19,724 | 24,020 | 24,118 | 21,354 | 24,020 | 22,860 | 24,773 | 27,665 | 28,221 | 27,827 | 28,025 | 24,923 |
| 1993 | 20,410 | 24,376 | 25,877 | 23,639 | 27,438 | 29,784 | 29,385 | 45,397 | 40,639 | 43,476 | 32,469 | 28,879 |
| 1994 | 28,277 | 38,157 | 48,411 | 42,730 | 44,363 | 42,845 | 35,370 | 39,582 | 49,312 | 40,706 | 42,353 | 59,763 |
| 1995 | 55,863 | 44,677 | 33,706 | 45,394 | 47,832 | 36,677 | 44,930 | 42,629 | 49,526 | 43,032 | 40,047 | 40,592 |
| 1996 | 31,028 | 37,674 | 38,551 | 41,411 | 46,470 | 37,141 | 37,522 | 42,063 | 44,014 | 68,674 | 82,817 | 72,586 |

*Source: International Monetary Market (IOM) division of the Chicago Mercantile Exchange (CME)*

## Average Open Interest of Deutsche Mark Futures in Chicago In Contracts

| Year | January | February | March | April | May | June | July | August | September | October | November | December |
|---|---|---|---|---|---|---|---|---|---|---|---|---|
| 1988 | 32,849 | 45,974 | 42,134 | 37,759 | 53,511 | 60,575 | 48,574 | 60,803 | 48,777 | 46,456 | 53,695 | 46,461 |
| 1989 | 51,439 | 65,251 | 52,869 | 52,693 | 70,062 | 72,766 | 62,365 | 66,520 | 65,666 | 70,976 | 91,393 | 93,491 |
| 1990 | 63,745 | 73,216 | 72,357 | 63,058 | 70,475 | 65,113 | 64,765 | 72,684 | 58,241 | 61,839 | 76,650 | 67,322 |
| 1991 | 51,211 | 73,463 | 72,824 | 71,737 | 79,162 | 80,318 | 68,046 | 73,860 | 70,525 | 59,236 | 85,248 | 77,632 |
| 1992 | 60,390 | 69,246 | 76,614 | 74,945 | 85,123 | 74,761 | 79,297 | 93,027 | 82,287 | 87,679 | 126,380 | 132,676 |
| 1993 | 134,432 | 140,184 | 126,046 | 118,747 | 131,816 | 159,334 | 165,356 | 147,140 | 108,958 | 103,720 | 135,960 | 145,414 |
| 1994 | 146,742 | 144,594 | 118,301 | 99,177 | 125,321 | 108,586 | 94,767 | 106,647 | 108,742 | 88,784 | 101,376 | 101,548 |
| 1995 | 79,425 | 92,975 | 79,700 | 61,954 | 71,050 | 60,698 | 46,832 | 63,789 | 63,820 | 53,300 | 59,123 | 70,267 |
| 1996 | 74,553 | 79,549 | 70,804 | 75,370 | 86,672 | 71,984 | 65,130 | 73,623 | 74,561 | 71,361 | 70,936 | 72,887 |

*Source: International Monetary Market (IOM) division of the Chicago Mercantile Exchange (CME)*

## Average Open Interest of Japanese Yen Futures in Chicago In Contracts

| Year | January | February | March | April | May | June | July | August | September | October | November | December |
|---|---|---|---|---|---|---|---|---|---|---|---|---|
| 1988 | 48,680 | 54,426 | 54,728 | 45,399 | 49,150 | 45,113 | 49,300 | 51,337 | 49,228 | 45,162 | 54,522 | 47,509 |
| 1989 | 39,467 | 48,400 | 53,654 | 52,013 | 67,213 | 73,355 | 48,261 | 30,235 | 71,230 | 50,594 | 60,283 | 57,748 |
| 1990 | 60,012 | 67,723 | 82,783 | 71,709 | 79,850 | 62,252 | 62,760 | 65,050 | 77,686 | 74,890 | 77,115 | 65,365 |
| 1991 | 43,552 | 64,694 | 57,115 | 49,060 | 52,964 | 55,727 | 53,045 | 56,496 | 66,174 | 74,353 | 74,585 | 64,219 |
| 1992 | 63,856 | 67,714 | 71,702 | 63,938 | 63,079 | 64,596 | 56,465 | 58,353 | 53,462 | 44,488 | 45,941 | 46,887 |
| 1993 | 50,066 | 70,195 | 81,979 | 76,696 | 82,028 | 81,103 | 72,186 | 80,780 | 73,002 | 83,097 | 84,812 | 95,817 |
| 1994 | 101,792 | 94,470 | 73,286 | 57,281 | 65,835 | 70,759 | 73,734 | 72,798 | 63,419 | 63,091 | 80,053 | 92,834 |
| 1995 | 86,569 | 86,852 | 77,649 | 63,379 | 67,644 | 56,285 | 48,680 | 63,463 | 73,830 | 67,336 | 73,335 | 70,268 |
| 1996 | 80,645 | 78,915 | 71,643 | 76,655 | 73,832 | 85,398 | 77,941 | 73,535 | 86,723 | 76,620 | 72,130 | 67,301 |

*Source: International Monetary Market (IOM) division of the Chicago Mercantile Exchange (CME)*

## Average Open Interest of Swiss Franc Futures in Chicago In Contracts

| Year | January | February | March | April | May | June | July | August | September | October | November | December |
|---|---|---|---|---|---|---|---|---|---|---|---|---|
| 1988 | 25,852 | 32,781 | 26,245 | 25,640 | 36,244 | 33,748 | 28,750 | 33,839 | 29,886 | 25,733 | 37,820 | 29,276 |
| 1989 | 27,442 | 31,287 | 34,749 | 34,074 | 42,256 | 36,445 | 35,625 | 41,613 | 38,429 | 31,432 | 39,757 | 47,927 |
| 1990 | 36,339 | 42,435 | 34,953 | 32,853 | 45,464 | 42,862 | 39,769 | 48,544 | 40,269 | 37,216 | 44,166 | 37,220 |
| 1991 | 31,489 | 36,483 | 49,061 | 40,026 | 38,601 | 43,476 | 36,031 | 35,881 | 29,833 | 24,949 | 32,342 | 32,439 |
| 1992 | 24,653 | 33,640 | 42,825 | 36,230 | 38,269 | 36,668 | 30,159 | 33,707 | 33,167 | 34,767 | 45,428 | 44,901 |
| 1993 | 52,713 | 49,472 | 48,002 | 43,514 | 47,832 | 42,343 | 40,703 | 44,329 | 60,446 | 49,320 | 58,406 | 49,670 |
| 1994 | 41,914 | 46,280 | 44,134 | 37,450 | 42,071 | 49,162 | 45,223 | 43,746 | 44,495 | 39,587 | 51,539 | 55,424 |
| 1995 | 39,726 | 44,364 | 39,358 | 30,270 | 30,586 | 26,766 | 23,121 | 30,267 | 34,228 | 34,889 | 38,033 | 44,741 |
| 1996 | 42,280 | 42,902 | 36,924 | 39,233 | 46,810 | 44,848 | 38,300 | 40,298 | 43,695 | 47,613 | 53,581 | 59,405 |

*Source: International Monetary Market (IOM) division of the Chicago Mercantile Exchange (CME)*

## Average Open Interest of British Pound Futures in Chicago In Contracts

| Year | January | February | March | April | May | June | July | August | September | October | November | December |
|---|---|---|---|---|---|---|---|---|---|---|---|---|
| 1988 | 29,433 | 40,278 | 41,665 | 43,291 | 45,745 | 29,892 | 18,052 | 18,917 | 18,149 | 17,930 | 21,850 | 23,829 |
| 1989 | 22,870 | 24,705 | 27,436 | 21,170 | 25,871 | 26,512 | 22,899 | 22,559 | 27,661 | 21,971 | 24,850 | 26,124 |
| 1990 | 23,272 | 30,729 | 26,219 | 23,909 | 33,355 | 35,528 | 37,898 | 41,820 | 33,458 | 32,213 | 39,623 | 32,790 |
| 1991 | 23,686 | 34,680 | 33,558 | 29,900 | 30,697 | 33,792 | 26,443 | 21,578 | 28,215 | 22,882 | 31,792 | 26,443 |
| 1992 | 21,578 | 28,215 | 22,882 | 31,595 | 36,426 | 35,529 | 27,160 | 28,041 | 30,137 | 30,330 | 33,121 | 27,935 |
| 1993 | 26,614 | 41,752 | 40,238 | 38,544 | 39,654 | 34,953 | 26,056 | 32,446 | 33,560 | 29,733 | 37,246 | 33,606 |
| 1994 | 39,223 | 43,878 | 35,554 | 44,725 | 46,577 | 41,801 | 37,633 | 34,988 | 40,751 | 42,648 | 49,684 | 65,834 |
| 1995 | 47,740 | 44,935 | 36,805 | 23,161 | 26,571 | 28,402 | 22,662 | 34,932 | 38,900 | 34,485 | 43,634 | 49,804 |
| 1996 | 40,315 | 50,106 | 52,349 | 54,954 | 52,573 | 61,461 | 55,080 | 50,862 | 53,868 | 51,934 | 62,128 | 47,652 |

*Source: International Monetary Market (IOM) division of the Chicago Mercantile Exchange (CME)*

## United States Merchandise Trade Balance[1] In Millions of Dollars

| Year | January | February | March | April | May | June | July | August | September | October | November | December | Total |
|---|---|---|---|---|---|---|---|---|---|---|---|---|---|
| 1987 | -13,453 | -10,956 | -10,628 | -11,613 | -12,410 | -13,721 | -14,431 | -13,747 | -12,484 | -15,298 | -11,932 | -11,445 | -159,557 |
| 1988 | -9,874 | -11,179 | -7,656 | -8,233 | -7,915 | -11,738 | -10,211 | -11,006 | -9,237 | -10,251 | -10,824 | -10,402 | -126,959 |
| 1989 | -8,639 | -8,622 | -6,954 | -7,191 | -9,463 | -8,724 | -10,582 | -11,034 | -8,971 | -11,780 | -10,754 | -6,687 | -115,245 |
| 1990 | -9,640 | -6,150 | -6,369 | -6,527 | -7,308 | -6,476 | -10,759 | -10,509 | -9,157 | -12,805 | -10,529 | -6,211 | -109,030 |
| 1991 | -7,079 | -4,201 | -1,889 | -3,411 | -4,158 | -3,948 | -7,894 | -7,450 | -7,111 | -8,735 | -4,942 | -5,908 | -74,068 |
| 1992 | -5,470 | -2,178 | -3,527 | -5,772 | -5,409 | -6,718 | -9,893 | -10,218 | -9,693 | -9,706 | -8,644 | -7,276 | -96,106 |
| 1993 | -6,113 | -5,905 | -8,886 | -8,428 | -6,542 | -11,749 | -12,609 | -11,949 | -12,516 | -12,638 | -11,120 | -7,322 | -132,609 |
| 1994 | ---------- | -31,545 | ---------- | ---------- | -38,164 | ---------- | ---------- | -49,949 | ---------- | ---------- | -46,463 | ---------- | -166,121 |
| 1995[2] | ---------- | -38,412 | ---------- | ---------- | -45,227 | ---------- | ---------- | -49,234 | ---------- | ---------- | -40,551 | ---------- | -173,424 |
| 1996[2] | ---------- | -36,363 | ---------- | ---------- | -44,560 | ---------- | ---------- | -58,929 | ---------- | ---------- | | ---------- | -139,852 |

[1] Not seasonally adjusted. [2] Preliminary. *Source: Bureau of Economic Analysis, U.S. Department of Commerce*

## Index of Real Trade-Weighted Dollar Exchange Rates for Total Agricultural[2] 1985 = 100

| Year | | January | February | March | April | May | June | July | August | Sept. | October | Nov. | Dec. |
|---|---|---|---|---|---|---|---|---|---|---|---|---|---|
| 1989 | U.S. Markets | 77.2 | 77.5 | 79.4 | 79.1 | 81.0 | 82.1 | 79.5 | 80.6 | 81.4 | 79.5 | 79.5 | 78.5 |
| | U.S. Competitors | 82.1 | 81.4 | 81.9 | 85.0 | 88.7 | 88.7 | 86.8 | 85.7 | 85.2 | 83.7 | 82.4 | 83.9 |
| 1990 | U.S. Markets | 78.3 | 78.1 | 79.3 | 79.4 | 78.5 | 78.9 | 79.2 | 79.1 | 78.5 | 76.6 | 74.7 | 75.3 |
| | U.S. Competitors | 80.1 | 81.2 | 79.6 | 79.2 | 77.8 | 77.5 | 76.4 | 76.1 | 76.3 | 75.0 | 75.3 | 73.5 |
| 1991 | U.S. Markets | 75.8 | 75.0 | 78.4 | 79.4 | 79.7 | 80.8 | 80.5 | 79.8 | 78.4 | 78.3 | 77.1 | 76.3 |
| | U.S. Competitors | 75.3 | 75.1 | 76.4 | 77.0 | 77.3 | 77.8 | 77.8 | 76.9 | 75.8 | 77.0 | 76.4 | 76.2 |
| 1992 | U.S. Markets | 75.5 | 76.4 | 80.9 | 78.2 | 76.5 | 76.0 | 74.7 | 74.2 | 74.2 | 75.2 | 77.6 | 77.3 |
| | U.S. Competitors | 76.2 | 76.8 | 81.1 | 76.6 | 77.4 | 76.6 | 75.6 | 75.1 | 77.2 | 75.7 | 77.7 | 77.4 |
| 1993 | U.S. Markets | 78.2 | 78.4 | 78.3 | 77.0 | 77.3 | 76.0 | 77.1 | 76.8 | 76.0 | 76.6 | 77.4 | 77.9 |
| | U.S. Competitors | 78.3 | 78.6 | 79.1 | 78.4 | 78.9 | 77.7 | 78.5 | 78.7 | 78.0 | 78.3 | 78.6 | 78.1 |
| 1994 | U.S. Markets | 77.0 | 77.0 | 97.1 | 97.4 | 97.0 | 96.9 | 95.3 | 95.2 | 94.3 | 93.8 | 94.2 | 96.7 |
| | U.S. Competitors | 78.3 | 78.3 | 107.3 | 107.6 | 105.7 | 104.5 | 101.5 | 101.2 | 100.1 | 98.4 | 99.1 | 100.5 |
| 1995[1] | U.S. Markets | 99.2 | 98.6 | 96.7 | 92.5 | 92.0 | 92.0 | 92.2 | 94.8 | 96.6 | 96.7 | 98.3 | 98.3 |
| | U.S. Competitors | 98.9 | 98.0 | 95.3 | 93.9 | 94.5 | 93.8 | 92.7 | 94.5 | 95.6 | 94.4 | 94.4 | 95.2 |
| 1996[1] | U.S. Markets | 99.5 | 99.3 | 99.4 | 99.4 | 99.4 | 100.1 | 100.3 | 99.3 | 99.9 | 100.9 | | |
| | U.S. Competitors | 96.0 | 95.9 | 96.2 | 96.9 | 97.8 | 97.5 | 96.7 | 96.2 | 96.7 | 97.3 | | |

[1] Preliminary. [2] Real indexes adjust nominal exchange rates for differences in rates of inflation to avoid the distortion caused by high-inflation countries. A higher value means the dollar has appreciated. Federal Reserve Board Index of trade-weighted value of the U.S. Dollar against ten major currencies. Weights are based on relative importance in world financial markets. *Source: Economic Research Service, U.S.D.A.*

## United States Balance on Current Account[1] In Millions of Dollars

| Year | 1st Quarter | 2nd Quarter | 3rd Quarter | 4th Quarter | Annual |
|---|---|---|---|---|---|
| 1987 | -35,750 | -42,031 | -46,310 | -43,302 | -167,392 |
| 1988 | -29,145 | -30,998 | -34,670 | -33,623 | -128,436 |
| 1989 | -22,132 | -25,670 | -31,115 | -26,659 | -105,575 |
| 1990 | -17,433 | -20,023 | -31,333 | -25,869 | -94,657 |
| 1991 | 14,997 | 2,611 | -17,526 | -9,600 | -9,518 |
| 1992 | -2,017 | -13,755 | -22,961 | -23,851 | -62,583 |
| 1993 | -11,404 | -23,406 | -33,159 | -31,967 | -99,936 |
| 1994 | -23,026 | -34,789 | -45,760 | -44,830 | -148,405 |
| 1995 | -31,094 | -40,098 | -44,694 | -32,269 | -148,154 |
| 1996[2] | -27,037 | -39,619 | -55,652 | | -122,308 |

[1] Not seasonally adjusted. [2] Preliminary. *Source: Bureau of Economic Analysis, U.S. Department of Commerce*

## Merchandise Trade and Account Balances In Billions of Dollars

| | Merchandise Trade Balance | | | | | Current Account Balance | | | | |
|---|---|---|---|---|---|---|---|---|---|---|
| Year | Canada | Germany | Japan | Switzerland | U.K. | Canada | Germany | Japan | Switzerland | U.K. |
| 1988 | 8.1 | 76.7 | 95.0 | -3.2 | -38.2 | -17.1 | 50.1 | 79.6 | 10.4 | -29.6 |
| 1989 | 6.0 | 75.3 | 76.9 | -4.4 | -40.4 | -22.8 | 56.6 | 57.2 | 7.0 | -36.8 |
| 1990 | 8.3 | 69.7 | 63.5 | -3.5 | -33.4 | -21.6 | 48.7 | 35.8 | 8.6 | -33.8 |
| 1991 | 3.9 | 19.5 | 96.1 | -2.5 | -18.1 | -23.6 | -18.1 | 68.2 | 10.6 | -14.4 |
| 1992 | 5.1 | 28.4 | 124.5 | 2.4 | -23.0 | -21.4 | -19.4 | 112.4 | 15.1 | -16.6 |
| 1993 | 7.2 | 41.8 | 139.3 | 4.9 | -20.1 | -22.3 | -13.5 | 131.9 | 19.4 | -16.6 |
| 1994 | 12.3 | 51.6 | 144.1 | 5.2 | -16.6 | -16.2 | -19.6 | 130.5 | 18.4 | -3.7 |
| 1995 | 22.3 | 70.3 | 131.2 | 4.3 | -18.3 | -8.2 | -16.8 | 110.4 | 19.8 | -4.5 |
| 1996[1] | 28.8 | 73.5 | 86.8 | 3.9 | -21.2 | -14.1 | -15.6 | 63.2 | 19.0 | -.9 |
| 1997[2] | 33.2 | 86.3 | 98.0 | 4.4 | -21.6 | 2.3 | -5.2 | 64.0 | 17.6 | -2.9 |

[1] Estimate. [2] Projection. *Source: Organization for Economic Cooperation and Development*

WEEKLY CASH
AS OF:03/14/97
DEUTSCHE MARK / SWISS FRANC
CASH
CHF/DEM
.96
.94
.92
.90
.88
.86
.84
.82
.80
.78
.76
.74
1994
1995
1996
1997
M A M J J A S O N D J F M A M J J A S O N D J F M A M J J A S O N D J F M A M J J

WEEKLY CASH
AS OF:03/14/97
BRITISH POUND / DEUTSCHE MARK
CASH
DEM/GBP
3.0
2.9
2.8
2.7
2.6
2.5
2.4
2.3
2.2
2.1
2.0
1.9
1994
1995
1996
1997
M A M J J A S O N D J F M A M J J A S O N D J F M A M J J A S O N D J F M A M J J

WEEKLY CASH
AS OF:03/14/97
JAPANESE YEN / BRITISH POUND
CASH
JPY/GBP
230
220
210
200
190
180
170
160
150
140
130
120
1994
1995
1996
1997
M A M J J A S O N D J F M A M J J A S O N D J F M A M J J A S O N D J F M A M J J

WEEKLY CASH
AS OF:03/14/97
DEUTSCHE MARK / JAPANESE YEN
CASH
JPY/DEM
78
76
74
72
70
68
66
64
62
60
58
56
1994
1995
1996
1997
M A M J J A S O N D J F M A M J J A S O N D J F M A M J J A S O N D J F M A M J J

# Diamonds

## World Production of Natural Gem Diamonds In Thousands of Carats

| Year | Angola | Australia | Botswana | Brazil | Central African Republic | China | Ghana | Guinea | Namibia | Russia[3] | Sierra Leone | South Africa | Tanzania | Zaire | World Total |
|---|---|---|---|---|---|---|---|---|---|---|---|---|---|---|---|
| 1986 | 240 | 13,145 | 9,590 | 310 | 259 | 200 | 88 | 190 | 970 | 7,400 | 215 | 4,473 | 133 | 4,661 | 42,038 |
| 1987 | 180 | 13,650 | 9,368 | 300 | 304 | 200 | 65 | 163 | 971 | 7,400 | 150 | 4,063 | 87 | 3,885 | 41,024 |
| 1988 | 950 | 17,413 | 10,660 | 350 | 284 | 200 | 55 | 136 | 925 | 11,000 | 12 | 3,800 | 105 | 2,724 | 49,206 |
| 1989 | 1,165 | 17,540 | 10,680 | 350 | 334 | 200 | 395 | 137 | 910 | 11,500 | 90 | 4,000 | 105 | 2,663 | 50,665 |
| 1990 | 1,060 | 17,331 | 12,150 | 600 | 303 | 200 | 520 | 119 | 750 | 12,000 | 66 | 3,900 | 60 | 2,914 | 52,600 |
| 1991 | 899 | 17,978 | 11,550 | 600 | 296 | 200 | 560 | 91 | 1,170 | 10,000 | 160 | 3,800 | 70 | 3,000 | 51,090 |
| 1992 | 1,100 | 18,078 | 11,160 | 653 | 307 | 200 | 570 | 90 | 1,520 | 9,000 | 180 | 4,600 | 48 | 8,934 | 57,300 |
| 1993 | 130 | 18,844 | 10,310 | 600 | 370 | 230 | 570 | 90 | 1,120 | 8,000 | 90 | 4,600 | 48 | 2,006 | 47,700 |
| 1994[1] | 270 | 19,485 | 10,550 | 600 | 400 | 230 | 580 | ----- | 1,312 | 8,500 | 155 | 4,340 | ----- | 4,000 | 51,400 |
| 1995[2] | 450 | 18,312 | 11,502 | 600 | 400 | 230 | 580 | ----- | 1,382 | 9,000 | 113 | 4,300 | ----- | 4,000 | 51,900 |

[1] Preliminary. [2] Estimate. [3] Formerly part of the U.S.S.R.; data not reported separately until 1992. *Source: U.S. Geological Survey*

## World Production of Natural Industrial Diamonds In Thousands of Carats

| Year | Angola | Australia | Botswana | Brazil | Central African Republic | China | Ghana | Liberia | Russia[3] | Sierra Leone | South Africa | Tanzania | Venezuela | Zaire | World Total |
|---|---|---|---|---|---|---|---|---|---|---|---|---|---|---|---|
| 1986 | 10 | 16,066 | 3,500 | 315 | 99 | 800 | 498 | 189 | 7,400 | 100 | 5,755 | 57 | 165 | 18,643 | 53,702 |
| 1987 | 10 | 16,683 | 3,840 | 200 | 108 | 800 | 400 | 183 | 7,400 | 75 | 4,990 | 37 | 68 | 15,540 | 50,464 |
| 1988 | 50 | 17,413 | 4,570 | 180 | 59 | 800 | 465 | 100 | 11,000 | 6 | 4,700 | 45 | 75 | 15,439 | 55,122 |
| 1989 | 80 | 17,540 | 4,570 | 150 | 81 | 800 | 99 | 93 | 11,500 | 39 | 5,100 | 45 | 185 | 15,092 | 55,562 |
| 1990 | 73 | 17,331 | 5,200 | 900 | 78 | 800 | 130 | 60 | 12,000 | 12 | 4,800 | 25 | 248 | 16,513 | 58,452 |
| 1991 | 62 | 17,978 | 4,950 | 900 | 82 | 800 | 140 | 60 | 10,000 | 83 | 4,600 | 30 | 112 | 14,814 | 54,737 |
| 1992 | 80 | 22,095 | 4,790 | 665 | 107 | 800 | 140 | 93 | 9,000 | 116 | 5,600 | 20 | 176 | 4,567 | 48,500 |
| 1993 | 15 | 23,032 | 4,420 | 900 | 125 | 850 | 140 | 90 | 8,000 | 68 | 5,700 | 20 | 155 | 13,620 | 57,400 |
| 1994[1] | 30 | 23,815 | 5,000 | 900 | 131 | 850 | 145 | ----- | 8,500 | 100 | 5,343 | ----- | 214 | 13,000 | 58,300 |
| 1995[2] | 50 | 22,381 | 5,300 | 900 | 130 | 900 | 145 | ----- | 9,000 | 100 | 5,383 | ----- | 64 | 13,000 | 57,700 |

[1] Preliminary. [2] Estimate. [3] Formerly part of the U.S.S.R.; data not reported separately until 1992. *Source: U.S. Geological Survey*

## World Production of Synthetic Diamonds In Thousands of Carats

| Year | Belarus[3] | China | Czech Republic[4] | France | Greece | Ireland | Japan | Russia[3] | South Africa | Sweden | Ukraine[3] | United States | World Total |
|---|---|---|---|---|---|---|---|---|---|---|---|---|---|
| 1988 | ------ | 15,000 | 5,000 | 4,000 | 1,000 | 60,000 | 25,000 | 41,500 | 55,000 | 25,000 | ------ | W | 241,500 |
| 1989 | ------ | 15,000 | 10,000 | 4,000 | 1,000 | 60,000 | 25,000 | 120,000 | 60,000 | 25,000 | ------ | W | 325,000 |
| 1990 | ------ | 15,000 | 10,000 | 5,000 | 1,000 | 60,000 | 25,000 | 120,000 | 60,000 | 25,000 | ------ | W | 329,000 |
| 1991 | ------ | 15,000 | 10,000 | 4,000 | 1,000 | 60,000 | 30,000 | 120,000 | 60,000 | 25,000 | ------ | 90,000 | 423,000 |
| 1992 | 30,000 | 15,000 | 10,000 | 3,500 | 750 | 60,000 | 30,000 | 80,000 | 60,000 | 25,000 | 10,000 | 90,000 | 422,000 |
| 1993 | 30,000 | 15,500 | 5,000 | 3,500 | 1,000 | 65,000 | 32,000 | 80,000 | 60,000 | 25,000 | 10,000 | 103,000 | 445,000 |
| 1994[1] | 25,000 | 15,500 | 5,000 | 3,500 | 1,000 | 65,000 | 32,000 | 80,000 | 60,000 | 25,000 | 8,000 | 104,000 | 439,000 |
| 1995[2] | 25,000 | 15,500 | 5,000 | 3,000 | 1,000 | 60,000 | 32,000 | 80,000 | 60,000 | 25,000 | 8,000 | 115,000 | 445,000 |

[1] Preliminary. [2] Estimate. [3] Formerly part of the U.S.S.R.; data not reported separately until 1992. [4] Formerly part of Czechoslovakia; data not reported separately until 1993. W = Withheld proprietary data. *Source: U.S. Geological Survey*

## U.S. Salient Statistics of Industrial Diamonds In Millions of Carats

| | Bort, Grit & Powder & Dust Natural and Synthetic | | | | | | | | Stones (Natural) | | | | | | |
|---|---|---|---|---|---|---|---|---|---|---|---|---|---|---|---|
| | Production | | | | | | | | | | | | | | |
| Year | Manufactured Diamond | Secondary | Imports for Consumption | Exports & Reexports | In Manufactured Products | Gov't Sales | Apparent Consumption | Price Value of Imports $ Per Carat | Secondary Production | Imports for Consumption | Exports & Reexports | Gov't Sales | Apparent Consumption | Price Value of Imports $ Per Carat | Net Import Reliance % of Consumption |
| 1988 | W | 6.6 | 64.3 | 74.5 | .6 | ----- | W | 1.03 | .6 | 6.9 | 3.0 | 1.8 | 4.5 | 9.31 | 87 |
| 1989 | W | 3.0 | 61.6 | 78.2 | .6 | ----- | 75.8 | .72 | .6 | 8.8 | 2.8 | ----- | 6.6 | 6.94 | 91 |
| 1990 | 90.0 | 5.9 | 85.4 | 71.0 | .6 | 3.0 | 112.7 | .76 | .5 | 11.0 | 1.7 | ----- | 9.8 | 6.57 | 95 |
| 1991 | 90.0 | 3.5 | 70.0 | 78.8 | .6 | 5.0 | 89.1 | .83 | .3 | 7.6 | 2.9 | ----- | 5.0 | 6.68 | 94 |
| 1992 | 95.0 | 3.4 | 97.3 | 83.6 | .6 | 10.4 | 121.9 | .70 | .1 | 9.8 | 5.6 | ----- | 4.3 | 4.56 | 98 |
| 1993 | 105.0 | 15.9 | 133.0 | 107.0 | .6 | ----- | 146.0 | .61 | .1 | 5.2 | 3.4 | 1.3 | 1.9 | 6.85 | 95 |
| 1994[1] | 104.0 | 16.0 | 174.0 | 153.0 | .4 | 2.0 | 141.0 | .51 | .1 | 2.8 | 4.4 | 3.1 | NA | 9.41 | NA |
| 1995[2] | 115.0 | 26.1 | 188.0 | 101.0 | NA | .2 | 228.0 | .43 | .3 | 4.1 | 5.2 | .3 | NA | 6.62 | NA |

[1] Preliminary. [2] Estimate. NA = Not avaliable. W = Withheld proprietary data. *Source: U.S. Geological Survey*

# Eggs

U.S. egg and egg product exports increased more than 30 percent during the first half of 1996 from a year earlier; for the year exports were estimated at a record 258 million dozen, the highest total since 1982. A further gain, to 265 million dozen, is forecast for 1997. Of note was the increase in U.S. egg product exports due to strong Japanese demand; shipments to Mexico and the European Union (EU) also increased. First half exports of table eggs of 26 million dozen to Hong Kong, the destination of more than 60 percent of U.S. table egg exports, jumped 23 percent, and the year's total was forecast at a record high 55 million dozen. Contributing to the rise in foreign demand for U.S. eggs and products was the fall in European egg exports due to decreasing EU export restitutions, and the strength of the Dutch guilder, the primary exchange currency for EU egg exports.

Production in the U.S., the world's second largest producer, lags well behind China, both the largest producer and consumer of eggs. China's production has doubled since the early 1990s; the 300 million dozen eggs produced in 1996 vs. 279 million in 1995 account for half of the world's total. World production in 1997 is forecast at a record high 606 million dozen; China's output is placed at 321 million dozen and the U.S. total at 65 million. However, a major difference persists between the two nations in respect to usage. Much of China's production is directly consumed as fresh brown eggs, whereas in the U.S. about a third of production is processed and white eggs are favored for table use. U.S. per capita table egg consumption in 1996 was forecast at 166 vs. 167 in 1995, and is forecast at 165 for 1997. In recent years, U.S. consumer preference has shifted to egg products relative to table eggs although per capita use is skewed towards tablestock. Per capita egg usage remains much higher abroad than in the U.S. Japan's white egg usage was the world's highest in 1996 at 266 eggs, with 269 forecast for 1997.

Foreign trade in eggs is small. The net totals favor exports. The EC accounts for about a third of world exports while Asia, paced by Japan, imports about 75 percent of the total. Japan's import breakdown includes hatched, table, dried, and preserved eggs as well as egg albumen, and Japan is generally the largest buyer of U.S. egg yolks.

There are definitive seasonal swings in U.S. egg production and table consumption. The table egg flocks typically reach a low in mid-summer and then increase throughout the year with monthly production peaking during the winter. Table egg consumption tends to be highest when consumers have more time for leisurely meals, generally in the summer. Wholesale prices lack a clear seasonality, but on balance are highest during the winter months. U.S. egg production in 1996 of 76.6 billion eggs compares with 74.3 billion in 1995 and forecasts of 78.6 billion in 1997.

The monthly average 12-city metro wholesale price of large grade A eggs in mid-1996 was $0.83 per dozen, 5 cents higher than a year earlier.

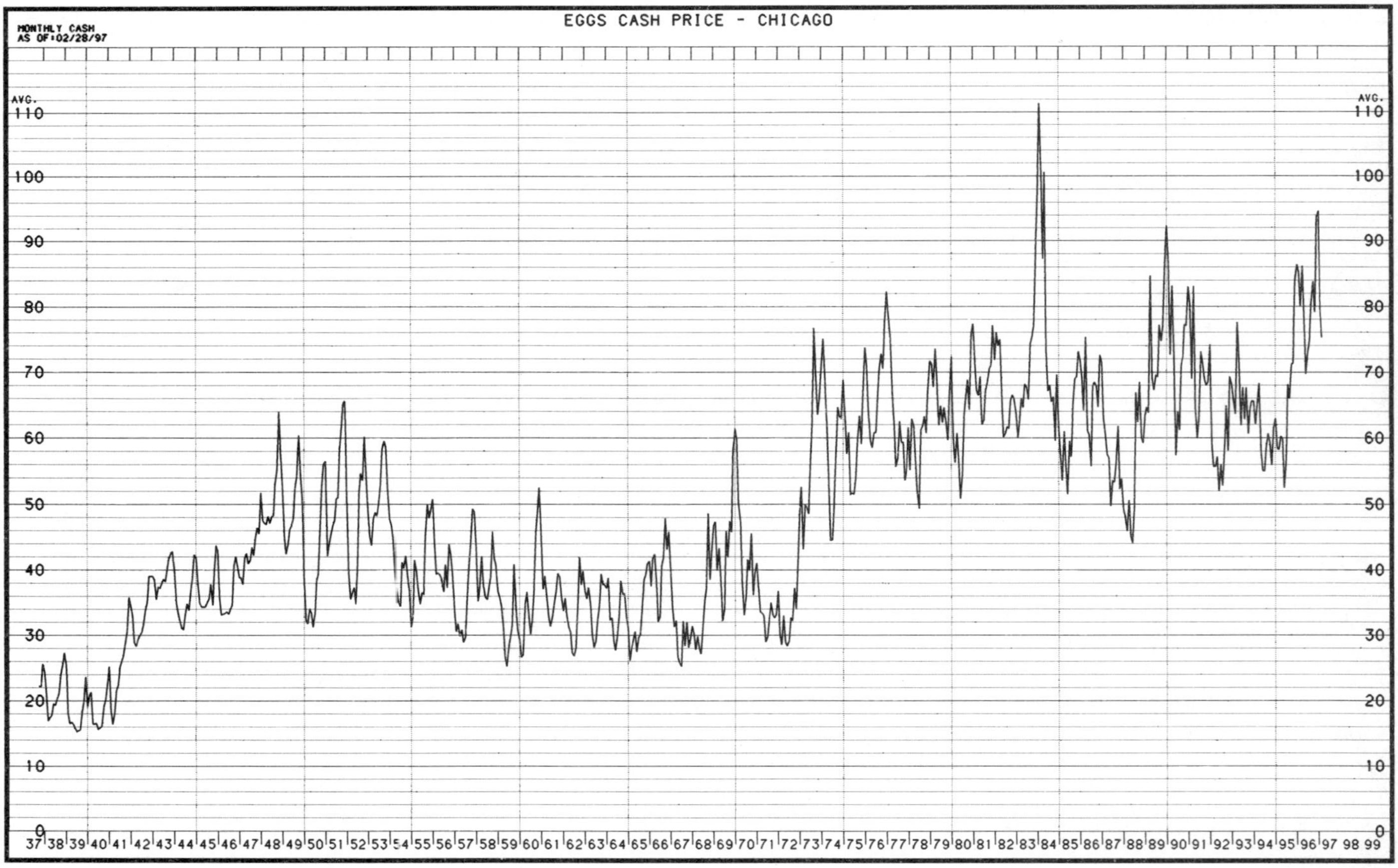

## World Production of Eggs    In Millions of Eggs

| Year | Brazil | Canada | China | France | Germany | Italy | Japan | Rep. of Korea | Mexico | Netherlands | Poland | Russia[4] | Spain | Ukraine[4] | United Kingdom | United States |
|---|---|---|---|---|---|---|---|---|---|---|---|---|---|---|---|---|
| 1987 | 15,400 | 5,706 | 118,000 | 14,540 | 17,995 | 10,743 | 39,567 | 6,574 | 18,039 | 10,930 | 7,966 | 47,447 | 10,500 | 17,425 | 13,300 | 70,418 |
| 1988 | 12,174 | 5,719 | 139,100 | 15,050 | 17,960 | 11,234 | 40,383 | 7,204 | 17,950 | 10,660 | 8,220 | 49,144 | 10,856 | 17,672 | 13,500 | 67,174 |
| 1989 | 12,174 | 5,719 | 140,900 | 15,050 | 17,794 | 11,223 | 40,356 | 6,919 | 17,950 | 10,660 | 8,200 | 49,042 | 10,140 | 17,393 | 10,547 | 67,178 |
| 1990 | 13,454 | 5,661 | 158,920 | 14,629 | 16,800 | 11,454 | 40,318 | 7,145 | 18,040 | 10,801 | 7,649 | 47,470 | 10,659 | 16,287 | 10,658 | 67,987 |
| 1991 | 13,655 | 5,666 | 184,400 | 15,300 | 15,525 | 11,568 | 41,638 | 7,770 | 19,840 | 10,762 | 6,500 | 46,900 | 10,184 | 15,188 | 12,485 | 69,612 |
| 1992 | 14,190 | 5,670 | 230,980 | 15,375 | 15,165 | 11,454 | 42,911 | 8,205 | 19,650 | 10,458 | 6,300 | 42,900 | 8,675 | 13,445 | 10,699 | 70,860 |
| 1993 | 12,700 | 5,689 | 235,960 | 15,355 | 13,678 | 11,502 | 43,252 | 8,196 | 20,140 | 10,019 | 5,450 | 40,300 | 8,454 | 11,766 | 10,645 | 72,072 |
| 1994 | 13,460 | 5,736 | 295,800 | 16,370 | 13,960 | 11,599 | 43,047 | 8,094 | 22,150 | 10,306 | 6,100 | 37,400 | 9,670 | 10,145 | 10,620 | 74,136 |
| 1995[1] | 16,065 | 5,792 | 335,340 | 16,911 | 13,847 | 12,017 | 42,167 | 8,317 | 21,200 | 9,970 | 6,500 | 33,720 | 9,983 | 9,500 | 10,644 | 74,280 |
| 1996[2] | 16,870 | 5,800 | 360,000 | 16,650 | 13,700 | 11,800 | 41,900 | 8,565 | 20,700 | 10,200 | 6,700 | 32,000 | 9,984 | 9,000 | 10,580 | 76,560 |
| 1997[3] | 18,220 | 5,815 | 385,000 | 16,960 | 13,700 | 11,900 | 42,500 | 8,770 | 21,000 | 10,100 | 6,800 | 31,500 | 9,984 | 9,000 | 10,565 | 78,600 |

[1] Preliminary. [2] Estimate. [3] Forecast. [4] Formerly part of the U.S.S.R.; data not reported separately until 1987. *Source: Foreign Agricultural Service, U.S. Department of Agriculture*

## Salient Egg Statistics in the United States

| Year | Hens & Pullets: On Farm Dec. 1[3] (Thousands) | Hens & Pullets: Average Number During Year (Thousands) | Rate of Lay Per Layer During Year[4] (Number) | Eggs: Total Produced (Millions) | Eggs: Price in ¢ Per Dozen | Value of Production[5] Million $ | Total Egg Production (Million Dozen) | Imports[6] (Million Dozen) | Exports[6] (Million Dozen) | Used for Hatching (Million Dozen) | Consumption: Total (Million Dozen) | Consumption: Per Capita Eggs[6] (Number) |
|---|---|---|---|---|---|---|---|---|---|---|---|---|
| 1987 | 288,320 | 283,872 | 248 | 70,356 | 54.7 | 3,209 | 5,868 | 5.6 | 111.2 | 599.1 | 5,160 | 255.0 |
| 1988 | 275,447 | 278,587 | 251 | 69,878 | 52.8 | 2,073 | 5,784 | 5.3 | 141.8 | 606.0 | 5,060 | 247.8 |
| 1989 | 271,064 | 270,415 | 250 | 67,503 | 68.9 | 3,877 | 5,598 | 25.2 | 91.6 | 641.8 | 4,917 | 238.6 |
| 1990 | 271,963 | 270,946 | 251 | 68,134 | 70.8 | 4,021 | 5,666 | 9.1 | 100.8 | 678.5 | 4,916 | 236.0 |
| 1991 | 279,325 | 275,451 | 252 | 69,465 | 67.6 | 3,915 | 5,779 | 2.3 | 154.5 | 708.6 | 4,938 | 234.6 |
| 1992 | 282,034 | 278,824 | 254 | 70,749 | 57.6 | 3,397 | 5,885 | 4.3 | 157.0 | 732.0 | 5,020 | 235.9 |
| 1993 | 290,626 | 284,770 | 253 | 71,936 | 63.4 | 3,800 | 5,960 | 4.7 | 158.9 | 769.6 | 5,082 | 236.2 |
| 1994 | 298,509 | 291,018 | 254 | 73,911 | 61.4 | 3,780 | 6,177 | 3.7 | 187.6 | 803.0 | 5,186 | 238.7 |
| 1995[1] | 298,753 | 293,854 | 253 | 74,591 | 64.0 | 3,959 | 6,190 | 4.1 | 209.0 | 846.8 | 5,142 | 234.6 |
| 1996[2] | 303,248 | 297,483 | 255 | 76,148 | | | 6,376 | 5.2 | 260.0 | 862.8 | 5,258 | 237.6 |

[1] Preliminary. [2] Estimate. [3] All layers of laying age. [4] Number of eggs produced during the year divided by the average number of all layers of laying age on hand during the year. [5] Value of sales plus value of eggs consumed in households of producers. [6] Shell-egg equivalent of eggs and egg products. *Source: National Agricultural Statistics Service, U.S. Department of Agriculture*

## Average Wholesale Prices of Shell Eggs (Large) Delivered, Chicago    In Cents Per Dozen

| Year | Jan. | Feb. | Mar. | Apr. | May | June | July | Aug. | Sept. | Oct. | Nov. | Dec. | Average |
|---|---|---|---|---|---|---|---|---|---|---|---|---|---|
| 1987 | 64.4 | 62.0 | 59.2 | 59.0 | 51.8 | 55.6 | 55.4 | 58.7 | 64.8 | 55.5 | 56.3 | 52.1 | 57.9 |
| 1988 | 51.2 | 48.9 | 53.6 | 47.9 | 47.1 | 52.8 | 69.8 | 65.4 | 71.4 | 63.1 | 62.2 | 66.1 | 58.3 |
| 1989 | 67.8 | 66.6 | 91.0 | 71.6 | 69.8 | 72.0 | 71.8 | 79.6 | 77.2 | 79.4 | 89.1 | 94.3 | 77.5 |
| 1990 | 88.6 | 75.1 | 86.1 | 78.6 | 60.3 | 66.9 | 64.2 | 73.9 | 75.4 | 80.0 | 80.0 | 83.1 | 76.0 |
| 1991 | 86.0 | 72.0 | 85.8 | 67.6 | 60.9 | 63.4 | 73.1 | 71.3 | 68.8 | 67.9 | 68.7 | 73.9 | 71.6 |
| 1992 | 59.1 | 55.7 | 55.7 | 57.4 | 52.0 | 56.0 | 53.0 | 57.9 | 64.9 | 58.2 | 69.4 | 68.0 | 58.9 |
| 1993 | 65.7 | 63.6 | 77.5 | 70.9 | 61.9 | 67.6 | 62.8 | 67.6 | 60.6 | 64.2 | 65.6 | 65.5 | 66.1 |
| 1994 | 62.1 | 64.9 | 68.3 | 58.3 | 55.1 | 55.1 | 58.8 | 60.6 | 59.2 | 55.9 | 61.5 | 62.9 | 60.2 |
| 1995 | 58.6 | 58.2 | 60.2 | 59.9 | 52.5 | 56.8 | 68.1 | 65.9 | 71.1 | 71.3 | 83.9 | 86.4 | 66.1 |
| 1996[1] | 85.3 | 80.0 | 86.1 | 78.9 | 69.8 | 73.0 | 74.7 | 80.6 | 83.8 | 79.1 | 93.7 | 94.6 | 81.6 |

[1] Preliminary. *Source: National Agricultural Statistics Service, U.S. Department of Agriculture*

## Total Egg Production in the United States    In Cents Per Dozen

| Year | Jan. | Feb. | Mar. | Apr. | May | June | July | Aug. | Sept. | Oct. | Nov. | Dec. | Total |
|---|---|---|---|---|---|---|---|---|---|---|---|---|---|
| 1987 | 5,989 | 5,417 | 6,093 | 5,864 | 5,925 | 5,685 | 5,863 | 5,861 | 5,756 | 6,008 | 5,873 | 6,084 | 70,418 |
| 1988 | 6,047 | 5,667 | 6,050 | 5,767 | 5,839 | 5,575 | 5,740 | 5,762 | 5,589 | 5,838 | 5,697 | 5,839 | 69,410 |
| 1989 | 5,758 | 5,182 | 5,782 | 5,569 | 5,696 | 5,498 | 5,648 | 5,613 | 5,450 | 5,658 | 5,543 | 5,781 | 67,178 |
| 1990 | 5,708 | 5,172 | 5,838 | 5,655 | 5,769 | 5,533 | 5,703 | 5,718 | 5,533 | 5,783 | 5,696 | 5,879 | 67,987 |
| 1991 | 5,865 | 5,316 | 5,935 | 5,666 | 5,796 | 5,643 | 5,840 | 5,855 | 5,675 | 5,915 | 5,811 | 6,035 | 69,352 |
| 1992 | 5,951 | 5,558 | 6,042 | 5,832 | 5,918 | 5,693 | 5,908 | 5,919 | 5,753 | 6,019 | 5,913 | 6,112 | 70,618 |
| 1993 | 6,030 | 5,432 | 6,067 | 5,861 | 6,009 | 5,816 | 5,992 | 6,015 | 5,876 | 6,144 | 6,085 | 6,296 | 71,623 |
| 1994 | 6,186 | 5,598 | 6,320 | 6,073 | 6,189 | 5,992 | 6,205 | 6,272 | 6,125 | 6,377 | 6,265 | 6,516 | 74,121 |
| 1995[1] | 6,369 | 5,714 | 6,448 | 6,177 | 6,251 | 6,010 | 6,145 | 6,146 | 5,990 | 6,260 | 6,232 | 6,523 | 74,265 |
| 1996[2] | 6,398 | 5,954 | 6,495 | 6,243 | 6,340 | 6,169 | 6,440 | 6,447 | 6,235 | 6,495 | 6,409 | 6,676 | 76,301 |

[1] Preliminary. [2] Estimate. *Source: National Agricultural Statistics Service, U.S. Department of Agriculture*

# EGGS

## Shell Eggs: Per Capita Disappearance in the United States In Number of Eggs

| Year | Jan. | Feb. | Mar. | Apr. | May | June | July | Aug. | Sept. | Oct. | Nov. | Dec. | Total | Total Consumption (Million Dozen) |
|---|---|---|---|---|---|---|---|---|---|---|---|---|---|---|
| 1985 | 19.5 | 17.0 | 19.5 | 17.9 | 17.7 | 17.4 | 17.6 | 18.0 | 17.6 | 18.1 | 18.3 | 19.2 | 217.9 | 4,331 |
| 1986 | 18.9 | 17.0 | 19.3 | 17.5 | 18.0 | 17.2 | 17.5 | 17.8 | 17.3 | 17.9 | 18.5 | 18.8 | 215.8 | 4,327 |
| 1987 | 18.6 | 16.5 | 18.5 | 17.8 | 17.8 | 16.6 | 17.3 | 17.6 | 17.3 | 18.1 | 17.5 | 18.1 | 211.6 | 4,282 |
| 1988 | 18.4 | 16.8 | 18.0 | 17.0 | 16.7 | 15.6 | 16.9 | 16.4 | 16.1 | 16.8 | 16.6 | 17.3 | 202.6 | 4,138 |
| 1989 | 16.8 | 15.1 | 17.3 | 16.1 | 15.9 | 15.2 | 16.2 | 15.8 | 15.5 | 16.0 | 15.9 | 17.1 | 192.2 | 3,978 |
| 1990 | 16.2 | 14.5 | 16.3 | 15.9 | 15.5 | 14.9 | 15.4 | 15.3 | 15.3 | 15.6 | 15.5 | 16.6 | 186.8 | 3,891 |
| 1991 | 15.9 | 14.4 | 16.4 | 14.6 | 14.8 | 14.4 | 15.0 | 15.2 | 14.9 | 15.1 | 15.7 | 16.2 | 182.6 | 3,844 |
| 1992 | 15.4 | 14.3 | 15.4 | 15.1 | 15.0 | 14.0 | 14.7 | 15.2 | 14.5 | 15.3 | 15.5 | 15.9 | 180.3 | 3,838 |
| 1993 | 16.1 | 14.2 | 15.8 | 15.0 | 14.9 | 14.1 | 14.8 | 14.8 | 14.2 | 15.1 | 15.2 | 15.7 | 179.7 | 3,825 |
| 1994 | 15.5 | 13.9 | 15.6 | 14.5 | 14.7 | 13.8 | 14.9 | 14.6 | 14.4 | 15.2 | 14.9 | 15.9 | 177.9 | 3,864 |
| 1995[1] | --------- | 43.8 | --------- | -------- | 42.7 | -------- | -------- | 42.2 | -------- | -------- | 44.9 | -------- | 173.7 | 3,809 |
| 1996[2] | --------- | 44.7 | --------- | -------- | 42.3 | -------- | -------- | 43.6 | -------- | -------- | | -------- | 175.1 | 3,822 |

[1] Preliminary. [2] Estimate. *Source: Economic Research Service, U.S. Department of Agriculture*

## Egg-Feed Ratio[1] in the United States

| Year | Jan. | Feb. | Mar. | Apr. | May | June | July | Aug. | Sept. | Oct. | Nov. | Dec. | Average |
|---|---|---|---|---|---|---|---|---|---|---|---|---|---|
| 1985 | 7.2 | 7.5 | 8.4 | 7.4 | 7.0 | 7.8 | 7.9 | 9.4 | 10.8 | 11.8 | 12.0 | 11.6 | 9.1 |
| 1986 | 11.1 | 10.3 | 11.7 | 9.4 | 9.1 | 8.0 | 10.8 | 12.6 | 14.0 | 13.3 | 15.4 | 14.6 | 11.7 |
| 1987 | 13.1 | 13.0 | 11.7 | 11.2 | 9.0 | 9.0 | 9.4 | 10.0 | 12.2 | 9.8 | 10.3 | 8.3 | 10.6 |
| 1988 | 8.2 | 7.5 | 8.0 | 6.9 | 6.0 | 5.5 | 6.9 | 7.1 | 8.3 | 7.7 | 8.0 | 8.2 | 7.3 |
| 1989 | 8.3 | 8.2 | 11.1 | 9.0 | 8.4 | 8.8 | 9.2 | 11.6 | 11.8 | 12.1 | 13.6 | 14.3 | 10.5 |
| 1990 | 14.3 | 11.5 | 13.0 | 11.0 | 8.5 | 9.0 | 7.9 | 9.9 | 10.9 | 12.1 | 12.4 | 12.3 | 11.1 |
| 1991 | 13.2 | 11.1 | 12.6 | 10.0 | 8.6 | 8.8 | 10.4 | 9.8 | 9.4 | 9.7 | 9.9 | 11.2 | 10.4 |
| 1992 | 8.4 | 7.8 | 7.4 | 7.6 | 6.7 | 7.0 | 7.3 | 8.1 | 9.6 | 9.3 | 11.2 | 11.1 | 8.5 |
| 1993 | 10.5 | 10.3 | 11.7 | 10.6 | 9.2 | 9.8 | 8.2 | 8.9 | 8.1 | 8.8 | 8.8 | 8.3 | 9.4 |
| 1994 | 7.9 | 8.0 | 8.6 | 7.9 | 7.2 | 7.1 | 7.9 | 9.0 | 9.2 | 9.0 | 10.3 | 10.2 | 8.5 |
| 1995 | 9.7 | 9.6 | 9.2 | 9.2 | 7.8 | 7.8 | 8.0 | 8.7 | 9.2 | 8.9 | 10.4 | 10.6 | 9.1 |
| 1996[2] | 10.1 | 8.9 | 9.3 | 8.1 | 6.6 | 6.9 | 6.5 | 7.1 | 8.3 | 9.5 | 11.5 | 12.5 | 8.8 |

[1] Pounds of laying feed equivalent in value to one dozen eggs. [2] Preliminary. *Source: Economic Research Service, U.S. Department of Agriculture*

## Total Eggs -- U.S. Supply and Distribution In Millions of Dozen

| | Supply | | | | Utilization | | | Consumption | |
|---|---|---|---|---|---|---|---|---|---|
| Year & Quarters | Beginning Stocks | Production | Imports[4] | Total Supply | Exports[4] | Eggs Used for Hatching | Ending Stocks | Total | Per Capita (Number) |
| 1992 I | 13.0 | 1,464 | .8 | 1,477 | 40.5 | 180.0 | 15.8 | 1,241 | 58.5 |
| II | 15.8 | 1,454 | 1.0 | 1,471 | 36.1 | 186.9 | 17.0 | 1,231 | 57.9 |
| III | 17.0 | 1,464 | 1.3 | 1,482 | 34.5 | 180.6 | 15.8 | 1,251 | 58.7 |
| IV | 15.8 | 1,501 | 1.2 | 1,518 | 45.9 | 178.9 | 13.5 | 1,280 | 59.8 |
| 1993 I | 13.5 | 1,461 | .9 | 1,475 | 37.1 | 187.3 | 11.9 | 1,237 | 57.7 |
| II | 11.9 | 1,474 | 1.5 | 1,487 | 34.5 | 196.6 | 11.7 | 1,244 | 57.9 |
| III | 11.7 | 1,490 | 1.4 | 1,503 | 42.0 | 192.4 | 11.4 | 1,258 | 58.4 |
| IV | 11.4 | 1,535 | .9 | 1,548 | 45.3 | 191.4 | 10.7 | 1,300 | 60.2 |
| 1994 I | 10.7 | 1,509 | 1.0 | 1,520 | 40.2 | 195.3 | 12.1 | 1,273 | 58.8 |
| II | 12.1 | 1,521 | 1.1 | 1,535 | 45.5 | 205.3 | 11.9 | 1,272 | 58.6 |
| III | 11.9 | 1,550 | 1.0 | 1,563 | 49.3 | 202.8 | 13.8 | 1,297 | 59.6 |
| IV | 13.8 | 1,597 | .6 | 1,611 | 52.6 | 199.6 | 14.9 | 1,344 | 61.6 |
| 1995[1] I | 14.9 | 1,544 | 1.1 | 1,560 | 45.5 | 207.1 | 14.9 | 1,293 | 59.2 |
| II | 14.9 | 1,537 | 1.2 | 1,553 | 50.1 | 214.1 | 17.9 | 1,271 | 58.0 |
| III | 17.9 | 1,523 | 1.0 | 1,542 | 47.0 | 213.1 | 13.0 | 1,269 | 57.8 |
| IV | 13.0 | 1,586 | .8 | 1,599 | 66.4 | 212.5 | 11.2 | 1,309 | 59.5 |
| 1996[2] I | 11.2 | 1,575 | 1.5 | 1,587 | 59.3 | 216.9 | 9.8 | 1,301 | 59.0 |
| II | 9.8 | 1,566 | 1.6 | 1,577 | 65.6 | 216.3 | 9.6 | 1,286 | 58.2 |
| III | 9.6 | 1,596 | 1.0 | 1,607 | 66.0 | 214.5 | 11.6 | 1,315 | 59.3 |
| IV | 11.6 | 1,640 | 1.0 | 1,653 | 69.0 | 215.0 | 12.0 | 1,357 | 61.1 |
| 1997[3] I | 12.0 | 1,625 | 1.0 | 1,638 | 65.0 | 225.0 | 12.0 | 1,336 | 60.0 |
| II | 12.0 | 1,635 | 1.0 | 1,648 | 70.0 | 235.0 | 12.0 | 1,331 | 59.7 |
| III | 12.0 | 1,660 | 1.0 | 1,673 | 70.0 | 225.0 | 12.0 | 1,366 | 61.1 |

[1] Preliminary. [2] Estimate. [3] Forecast. [4] Shell-egg equivalent of eggs and egg products. *Source: Economic Research Service, U.S. Department of Agriculture*

## Hens and Pullets of Laying Age (Layers) in the U.S., First of Month In Thousands

| Year | Jan. 1 | Feb. 1 | Mar. 1 | Apr. 1 | May 1 | June 1 | July 1 | Aug. 1 | Sept. 1 | Oct. 1 | Nov. 1 | Dec. 1 |
|---|---|---|---|---|---|---|---|---|---|---|---|---|
| 1988 | 286,470 | 285,670 | 283,225 | 279,221 | 277,449 | 272,482 | 270,282 | 271,220 | 273,136 | 275,191 | 276,415 | 275,447 |
| 1989 | 272,243 | 272,780 | 271,590 | 269,278 | 267,269 | 267,239 | 267,088 | 266,253 | 267,656 | 267,919 | 270,006 | 271,064 |
| 1990 | 271,164 | 272,826 | 271,921 | 272,813 | 270,664 | 269,040 | 265,647 | 266,767 | 267,004 | 268,835 | 270,274 | 271,963 |
| 1991 | 273,917 | 275,533 | 274,446 | 272,541 | 272,150 | 272,944 | 272,779 | 272,998 | 274,277 | 276,187 | 278,433 | 279,325 |
| 1992 | 280,697 | 279,274 | 279,117 | 279,009 | 276,757 | 275,645 | 275,179 | 275,091 | 274,010 | 279,233 | 280,183 | 282,034 |
| 1993 | 281,639 | 282,933 | 282,005 | 282,480 | 281,468 | 280,795 | 280,517 | 282,201 | 282,341 | 284,771 | 285,298 | 290,626 |
| 1994 | 290,413 | 289,625 | 290,416 | 290,979 | 289,125 | 288,398 | 287,454 | 288,484 | 292,116 | 294,576 | 295,719 | 298,509 |
| 1995 | 300,331 | 298,202 | 297,689 | 296,290 | 294,697 | 290,806 | 289,018 | 286,519 | 289,595 | 290,889 | 294,486 | 298,293 |
| 1996[1] | 299,261 | 299,180 | 299,219 | 298,871 | 295,805 | 294,408 | 294,616 | 297,166 | 297,450 | 298,801 | 299,729 | 303,248 |

[1] Preliminary. *Source: National Agricultural Statistics Service, U.S. Department of Agriculture*

## Eggs Laid Per Hundred Layers in the United States In Number of Eggs

| Year | Jan. | Feb. | Mar. | Apr. | May | June | July | Aug. | Sept. | Oct. | Nov. | Dec. | Average |
|---|---|---|---|---|---|---|---|---|---|---|---|---|---|
| 1988 | 2,154 | 2,027 | 2,189 | 2,103 | 2,150 | 2,081 | 2,150 | 2,150 | 2,073 | 2,152 | 2,105 | 2,179 | 2,126 |
| 1989 | 2,154 | 1,937 | 2,178 | 2,111 | 2,165 | 2,089 | 2,148 | 2,135 | 2,071 | 2,142 | 2,098 | 2,181 | 2,117 |
| 1990 | 2,149 | 1,940 | 2,185 | 2,120 | 2,171 | 2,105 | 2,179 | 2,181 | 2,104 | 2,189 | 2,140 | 2,208 | 2,139 |
| 1991 | 2,186 | 1,977 | 2,217 | 2,124 | 2,168 | 2,108 | 2,186 | 2,190 | 2,106 | 2,175 | 2,124 | 2,208 | 2,147 |
| 1992 | 2,176 | 2,036 | 2,216 | 2,148 | 2,186 | 2,110 | 2,196 | 2,204 | 2,125 | 2,200 | 2,140 | 2,226 | 2,164 |
| 1993 | 2,192 | 1,970 | 2,209 | 2,132 | 2,182 | 2,112 | 2,175 | 2,183 | 2,124 | 2,209 | 2,167 | 2,237 | 2,158 |
| 1994 | 2,199 | 1,987 | 2,246 | 2,160 | 2,204 | 2,142 | 2,222 | 2,230 | 2,152 | 2,227 | 2,180 | 2,176 | 2,177 |
| 1995 | 2,130 | 1,919 | 2,173 | 2,092 | 2,137 | 2,075 | 2,137 | 2,135 | 2,065 | 2,140 | 2,108 | 2,183 | 2,108 |
| 1996[1] | 2,140 | 1,996 | 2,177 | 2,103 | 2,152 | 2,099 | 2,180 | 2,172 | 2,094 | 2,171 | 2,125 | 2,198 | 2,134 |

[1] Preliminary. *Source: National Agricultural Statistics Service, U.S. Department of Agriculture*

## Egg-Type Chicks Hatched by Commercial Hatcheries in the United States In Thousands

| Year | Jan. | Feb. | Mar. | Apr. | May | June | July | Aug. | Sept. | Oct. | Nov. | Dec. | Total |
|---|---|---|---|---|---|---|---|---|---|---|---|---|---|
| 1988 | 29,274 | 28,433 | 35,615 | 34,749 | 35,984 | 33,049 | 24,876 | 27,838 | 30,918 | 31,007 | 27,181 | 27,311 | 366,235 |
| 1989 | 26,602 | 27,271 | 32,597 | 36,135 | 38,376 | 34,708 | 29,828 | 32,217 | 32,862 | 33,456 | 29,666 | 29,284 | 383,002 |
| 1990 | 32,004 | 32,107 | 36,509 | 36,915 | 37,895 | 34,471 | 31,582 | 32,949 | 31,219 | 32,926 | 29,809 | 31,046 | 398,432 |
| 1991 | 34,487 | 34,837 | 37,041 | 39,775 | 38,404 | 36,227 | 33,696 | 33,656 | 34,007 | 34,307 | 30,400 | 32,717 | 419,554 |
| 1992 | 32,496 | 31,950 | 36,490 | 35,755 | 38,513 | 34,568 | 32,265 | 28,349 | 28,760 | 32,843 | 27,718 | 31,612 | 391,319 |
| 1993 | 34,885 | 34,009 | 38,264 | 37,163 | 36,742 | 35,587 | 33,980 | 31,455 | 31,775 | 31,634 | 30,074 | 30,448 | 405,986 |
| 1994 | 33,236 | 31,086 | 33,489 | 35,657 | 35,322 | 31,985 | 29,613 | 31,295 | 31,587 | 32,066 | 26,075 | 30,166 | 381,577 |
| 1995 | 32,375 | 32,745 | 36,021 | 35,020 | 37,482 | 34,948 | 29,554 | 31,434 | 33,578 | 33,384 | 29,130 | 30,797 | 396,468 |
| 1996[1] | 31,547 | 34,652 | 37,687 | 35,553 | 38,477 | 33,998 | 33,828 | 32,474 | 31,956 | 33,176 | 31,495 | 33,161 | 408,004 |

[1] Preliminary. *Source: National Agricultural Statistics Service, U.S. Department of Agriculture*

## U.S. Cold Storage Holdings of Shell Eggs, First of Month In Thousands Cases (One Case = 30 Dozen)

| Year | Jan. | Feb. | Mar. | Apr. | May | June | July | Aug. | Sept. | Oct. | Nov. | Dec. |
|---|---|---|---|---|---|---|---|---|---|---|---|---|
| 1988 | 43 | 67 | 53 | 32 | 14 | 21 | 30 | 28 | 25 | 23 | 24 | 26 |
| 1989 | 9 | 12 | 7 | 33 | 18 | 26 | 27 | 12 | 17 | 23 | 6 | 11 |
| 1990 | 12 | 22 | 16 | 16 | 12 | 21 | 22 | 29 | 19 | 18 | 11 | 16 |
| 1991 | 15 | 17 | 9 | 23 | 12 | 15 | 13 | 13 | 10 | 13 | 12 | 13 |
| 1992 | 21 | 20 | 25 | 14 | 27 | 34 | 30 | 29 | 23 | 22 | 17 | 15 |
| 1993 | 15 | 12 | 12 | 15 | 6 | 6 | 7 | 6 | 6 | 15 | 13 | 6 |
| 1994 | 10 | 7 | 8 | 9 | 8 | 8 | 8 | 14 | 14 | 9 | 7 | 3 |
| 1995 | 4 | 29 | 40 | 28 | 20 | 22 | 18 | 23 | 19 | 24 | 28 | 13 |
| 1996[1] | 26 | 13 | 64 | 15 | 6 | 17 | 22 | 24 | 15 | 19 | 19 | 11 |

[1] Preliminary. *Source: National Agricultural Statistics Service, U.S. Department of Agriculture*

## U.S. Cold Storage Holdings of Frozen Eggs, First of Month In Millions of Pounds[1]

| Year | Jan. | Feb. | Mar. | Apr. | May | June | July | Aug. | Sept. | Oct. | Nov. | Dec. |
|---|---|---|---|---|---|---|---|---|---|---|---|---|
| 1988 | 17.3 | 18.3 | 18.3 | 14.1 | 17.3 | 20.3 | 25.3 | 22.9 | 24.5 | 22.2 | 20.0 | 17.9 |
| 1989 | 19.6 | 19.7 | 19.0 | 14.8 | 15.3 | 16.2 | 15.1 | 16.5 | 15.0 | 14.4 | 14.9 | 13.4 |
| 1990 | 13.6 | 14.2 | 15.2 | 16.8 | 19.7 | 16.8 | 18.1 | 17.1 | 17.1 | 16.6 | 16.8 | 17.2 |
| 1991 | 14.7 | 14.8 | 14.0 | 14.1 | 13.0 | 13.5 | 14.2 | 18.1 | 16.3 | 16.5 | 17.0 | 15.1 |
| 1992 | 16.0 | 20.0 | 19.2 | 19.7 | 18.8 | 18.9 | 21.1 | 19.5 | 20.2 | 20.0 | 21.7 | 18.7 |
| 1993 | 17.2 | 16.7 | 16.9 | 15.1 | 14.3 | 15.5 | 15.1 | 17.6 | 18.1 | 14.4 | 14.0 | 13.5 |
| 1994 | 13.7 | 14.8 | 15.8 | 15.6 | 16.3 | 15.2 | 15.4 | 19.0 | 19.7 | 17.8 | 20.0 | 19.1 |
| 1995 | 19.5 | 19.5 | 18.3 | 18.5 | 17.3 | 18.1 | 22.9 | 20.6 | 18.0 | 16.2 | 14.4 | 12.5 |
| 1996[2] | 13.8 | 15.6 | 16.2 | 12.4 | 11.5 | 11.4 | 11.7 | 13.5 | 15.0 | 14.9 | 12.7 | 10.4 |

[1] Converted on basis 39.5 pounds frozen eggs equal 1 case [2] Preliminary. *Source: National Agricultural Statistics Service, U.S. Department of Agriculture*

# Electric Power

U.S. net generation of electricity in July 1996 was 289 billion kilowatthours, up 7 percent from June 1996 but 1 percent less than was reported for July 1995. For July 1996, the energy sources were 54.8 percent coal, 2.6 percent petroleum, 11.8 percent gas, 9.5 percent hydroelectric and 21.1 percent nuclear. Other sources including geothermal, wood, wind, waste, and solar were 0.2 percent. For the January-July 1996 period, total net generation of electricity was 1.8 trillion kilowatthours. For the first seven months of 1996, electricity generation from nonrenewable energy sources was 1.58 trillion kilowatthours. Of the total, 991 billion kilowatthours were from coal, 43 billion kilowatthours were from petroleum, 150 billion from gas, and 399 billion kilowatthours were generated by nuclear power. For all of 1995, nonrenewable energy sources generated 2.69 trillion kilowatthours of electricity.

For January-July 1996, net generation of electricity by renewable energy sources was 216 billion kilowatthours. Of the total, 213 billion kilowatthours were generated by conventional hydroelectric, 2.6 billion by geothermal sources, 1.1 billion kilowatthours by biomass, 6.2 million kilowatthours by wind, and 2.5 million kilowatthours by photovoltaic sources. For all of 1995, net generation of electricity by renewable energy sources was 303 billion kilowatthours.

U.S. electric utility retail sales of electricity to residential customers in July 1996 were 106 billion kilowatthours, up 16 percent from the previous month. Sales are traditionally highest in the summer months of July and August as well as in January. The months of lowest usage are April and May. For January-July 1996, retail sales of electricity to residential customers were 635 million kilowatthours, up 8 percent from the comparable period in 1995 and 7 percent more than the like period of 1994. For all of 1995, retail sales to residential customers were 1.04 trillion kilowatthours. U.S. electric utility retail sales to commercial customers in July 1996 were 83 billion kilowatthours, up 5 percent from June. For January-July 1996, retail sales to commercial customers were 510 billion kilowatthours, up 5 percent from the comparable period of 1995 and 7 percent above the like period of 1994.

Retail sales of electricity to industrial customers in July 1996 were 87 billion kilowatthours, down less than 1 percent from June. For January-July 1996, sales were 587 billion kilowatthours, about unchanged from the comparable period of 1995 and 3 percent more than the like period of 1994. Sales to other customers, such as for highway lighting and railroads, were 8.6 billion kilowatthours in July 1996. For January-July 1996, they were 57.5 billion kilowatthours. Retail sales to all customers in July 1996 were 284 billion kilowatthours. For January-July 1996 they were 1.79 trillion kilowatthours and for all of 1995 they were 3 trillion kilowatthours.

## World Electricity Production (Monthly Average) In Millions of Kilowatt Hours

| Year | Australia | Canada | China | France | Germany | India | Italy | Japan | Poland | Rep. of Korea | Russia[3] | South Africa | Sweden | Ukraine[3] | United Kingdom | United States |
|---|---|---|---|---|---|---|---|---|---|---|---|---|---|---|---|---|
| 1986 | 10,518 | 39,049 | 37,458 | 28,586 | 43,474 | 15,626 | 15,749 | 55,981 | 11,691 | 4,167 | 133,244 | 12,210 | 11,502 | ------ | 24,846 | 216,610 |
| 1987 | 11,027 | 41,361 | 41,442 | 29,383 | 34,873 | 16,824 | 16,748 | 58,248 | 12,153 | 6,166 | 138,744 | 12,550 | 10,802 | ------ | 25,161 | 226,561 |
| 1988 | 11,592 | 42,164 | 49,460 | 30,456 | 35,228 | 18,427 | 16,931 | 62,811 | 12,028 | 7,122 | 142,090 | 13,062 | 12,451 | ------ | 25,761 | 239,875 |
| 1989 | 12,316 | 41,628 | 49,549 | 33,908 | 36,716 | 20,428 | 17,570 | 66,563 | 12,124 | 7,873 | 143,500 | 13,527 | 11,992 | ------ | 25,153 | 246,659 |
| 1990 | 12,923 | 40,169 | 51,500 | 35,011 | 37,433 | 22,025 | 18,074 | 71,439 | 11,361 | 8,972 | 139,455 | 13,782 | 12,204 | ------ | 26,581 | 250,979 |
| 1991 | 13,071 | 42,326 | 55,918 | 37,846 | 44,949 | 23,893 | 18,503 | 74,007 | 11,225 | 9,885 | 136,156 | 14,026 | 12,282 | ------ | 26,900 | 254,818 |
| 1992 | 13,313 | 41,803 | 61,562 | 38,522 | 44,761 | 25,081 | 18,854 | 74,611 | 11,070 | 10,914 | 84,038 | 14,008 | 12,187 | 21,044 | 27,240 | 256,209 |
| 1993 | 13,646 | 42,591 | 67,723 | 39,635 | 37,722 | 26,961 | 18,566 | 75,559 | 11,156 | 12,036 | 79,716 | 14,572 | 11,883 | 19,159 | 26,834 | 262,158 |
| 1994 | 13,929 | 44,502 | 75,312 | ------ | 37,786 | 29,250 | 19,315 | 80,361 | 11,236 | 13,754 | 75,740 | 15,204 | 11,449 | 17,425 | 27,637 | 272,354 |
| 1995[1] | 13,835 | 44,868 | 81,979 | ------ | 38,207 | 31,121 | 20,079 | 64,683 | 11,583 | 15,388 | 72,291 | 15,655 | 11,799 | ------ | 27,635 | 249,585 |
| 1996[2] | 13,699 | 44,837 | 86,306 | ------ | 47,724 | ------ | ------ | 71,468 | 12,163 | 16,952 | 75,600 | 16,080 | 13,965 | ------ | 30,356 | 251,358 |

[1] Preliminary. [2] Estimate. [3] Formerly part of the U.S.S.R.; data not reported separately until 1992. *Source: United Nations*

## Installed Capacity, Capability & Peak Load of the U.S. Electric Utility Industry In Millions of Kilowatt Hours

| | Installed Generating Capacity at Dec. 31 | | | | | | | | | | | | | | | |
|---|---|---|---|---|---|---|---|---|---|---|---|---|---|---|---|---|
| | | Type of Prime Mover | | | | Type of Ownership | | | | | | | | | | |
| Year | Total Electric Utility Industry | Hydro | Gas Turbine & Steam | Nuclear Power | Internal Com-bustion | Investor Owned | Cooper-ative | Sub-total Gov't. | Munic-ipal Utilities | Federal | Power Districts, State Projects | Capa-bility at Winter Peak Load | Non-Co incident Winter Peak Load | Capacity Margin Non-Co incident Peak Load (%) | Total Electric Utility Industry Gen-eration | Annual Peak Load Factor (%) |
| 1986 | 707.7 | 85.2 | 524.1 | 92.4 | 5.9 | 544.2 | 26.4 | 137.1 | 38.6 | 63.9 | 34.6 | 646.7 | 422.9 | 24.8 | 2,487.3 | 60.7 |
| 1987 | 718.1 | 85.9 | 524.3 | 101.6 | 6.2 | 552.8 | 26.4 | 138.9 | 39.4 | 64.7 | 34.9 | 663.0 | 448.3 | 23.4 | 2,572.1 | 60.8 |
| 1988 | 723.9 | 86.9 | 526.6 | 103.4 | 7.0 | 557.8 | 26.4 | 139.7 | 40.4 | 64.8 | 34.5 | 676.9 | 466.5 | 20.0 | 2,704.3 | 59.5 |
| 1989 | 730.9 | 87.5 | 529.1 | 106.7 | 7.5 | 562.1 | 26.4 | 142.4 | 40.7 | 67.2 | 34.5 | 685.2 | 496.4 | 22.3 | 2,784.3 | 62.2 |
| 1990 | 735.1 | 87.2 | 531.1 | 108.0 | 8.7 | 568.8 | 26.3 | 139.9 | 40.1 | 65.4 | 34.4 | 696.8 | 484.0 | 20.4 | 2,808.2 | 60.4 |
| 1991 | 740.0 | 88.7 | 534.1 | 108.4 | 8.8 | 573.0 | 26.5 | 140.5 | 40.4 | 65.6 | 34.5 | 703.2 | 485.4 | 20.2 | 2,825.0 | 60.9 |
| 1992 | 741.7 | 89.7 | 534.5 | 107.9 | 9.6 | 572.9 | 26.0 | 142.7 | 41.6 | 66.1 | 35.0 | 707.8 | 493.0 | 21.1 | 2,797.2 | 61.1 |
| 1993 | 744.7 | 90.2 | 536.9 | 107.8 | 9.8 | 575.2 | 26.1 | 143.4 | 41.8 | 66.1 | 35.5 | 712.0 | 521.7 | 17.1 | 2,882.5 | 61.0 |
| 1994 | 746.0 | 90.3 | 537.9 | 107.9 | 9.9 | 574.8 | 26.4 | 144.7 | 42.0 | 66.3 | 36.4 | 715.1 | 518.3 | 16.7 | 2,910.7 | 61.2 |
| 1995[1] | 750.9 | 91.1 | 542.0 | 107.9 | 9.9 | 579.2 | 29.6 | 144.8 | 42.2 | 69.9 | 36.7 | 727.7 | 544.7 | 13.2 | 2,994.5 | 59.8 |

[1] Preliminary. *Source: Edison Electric Institute (EEI)*

## Available Electricity & Energy Sales in the United States

In Billions of Kilowatt Hours

| | Net Generation | | | | | | | | | Sales to Ultimate Customers | | | | | | | |
|---|---|---|---|---|---|---|---|---|---|---|---|---|---|---|---|---|---|
| | Electric Utility Industry | | | | | | | | | | | | | | | | |
| Year | Total[2] | Hydro | Natural Gas | Coal | Fuel Oil | Nuclear | Other Sources[3] | Total | Total Million $ | Total | Residential | Inter-Departmental | Commercial | Industrial | Street & Highway Lighting | Other Public Auth. | Railways & Railroads |
| 1982 | 2,241 | 309.2 | 305.3 | 1,192 | 146.4 | 282.8 | 5.2 | 2,302 | 121,584 | 2,100 | 732 | 5.4 | 517.0 | 770 | 14.2 | 55.7 | 4.3 |
| 1983 | 2,310 | 332.1 | 274.1 | 1,259 | 144.5 | 293.7 | 6.5 | 2,368 | 129,589 | 2,160 | 750 | 5.4 | 545.6 | 783 | 13.9 | 57.3 | 4.3 |
| 1984 | 2,416 | 321.2 | 297.4 | 1,342 | 119.8 | 327.6 | 8.6 | 2,488 | 143,093 | 2,281 | 782 | 5.8 | 578.1 | 835 | 14.2 | 59.9 | 4.5 |
| 1985 | 2,470 | 281.1 | 291.9 | 1,402 | 100.2 | 383.7 | 10.7 | 2,568 | 149,162 | 2,306 | 792 | 5.3 | 605.9 | 820 | 14.6 | 62.2 | 4.7 |
| 1986 | 2,487 | 290.8 | 248.5 | 1,386 | 136.6 | 414.0 | 11.5 | 2,599 | 152,467 | 2,355 | 820 | 5.2 | 629.0 | 819 | 15.0 | 61.9 | 4.7 |
| 1987 | 2,572 | 249.7 | 272.6 | 1,464 | 118.5 | 455.3 | 12.3 | 2,719 | 155,700 | 2,435 | 846 | 4.5 | 658.4 | 843 | 14.4 | 63.0 | 4.9 |
| 1988 | 2,704 | 222.9 | 252.8 | 1,541 | 148.9 | 527.0 | 12.0 | 2,879 | 162,388 | 2,554 | 886 | 4.2 | 697.8 | 881 | 14.6 | 64.6 | 5.1 |
| 1989 | 2,784 | 265.1 | 266.6 | 1,554 | 158.3 | 529.4 | 11.3 | 2,985 | 169,627 | 2,621 | 898 | 4.3 | 715.9 | 912 | 14.6 | 69.3 | 5.3 |
| 1990 | 2,808 | 279.9 | 264.1 | 1,560 | 117.0 | 576.9 | 10.7 | 3,041 | 176,468 | 2,684 | 915 | 4.2 | 738.9 | 931 | 15.2 | 72.8 | 5.3 |
| 1991 | 1,825 | 275.5 | 264.2 | 1,551 | 111.5 | 612.6 | 10.1 | 3,100 | 185,118 | 2,764 | 948 | 2.6 | 753.3 | 934 | 15.6 | 76.1 | 5.3 |
| 1992 | 2,797 | 239.6 | 263.9 | 1,576 | 88.9 | 618.8 | 10.2 | 3,107 | 187,283 | 2,735 | 929 | 2.6 | 755.7 | 949 | 15.8 | 77.2 | 5.2 |
| 1993 | 2,883 | 265.1 | 258.9 | 1,639 | 99.5 | 610.3 | 9.6 | 3,210 | 197,857 | 2,850 | 994 | 2.7 | 803.1 | 956 | 18.1 | 69.7 | 5.4 |
| 1994 | 2,911 | 243.7 | 291.1 | 1,635 | 91.0 | 640.4 | 8.9 | 3,283 | 202,515 | 2,930 | 1,008 | 3.0 | 833.5 | 990 | 18.5 | 70.6 | 5.8 |
| 1995[1] | 2,995 | 293.7 | 307.3 | 1,653 | 60.8 | 673.4 | 6.4 | 3,395 | 207,559 | 3,007 | 1,042 | 2.1 | 863.5 | 1,006 | 17.9 | 69.9 | 5.5 |

[1] Preliminary. [2] Includes internal combustion. [3] Includes electricity produced from geothermal, wood, waste, wind, solar, etc.
*Source: Edison Electric Insititute (EEI)*

## Electric Power Production by Electric Utilities in the U.S.

In Millions of Kilowatt Hours

| Year | Jan. | Feb. | Mar. | Apr. | May | June | July | Aug. | Sept. | Oct. | Nov. | Dec. | Total |
|---|---|---|---|---|---|---|---|---|---|---|---|---|---|
| 1982 | 209,403 | 180,299 | 187,687 | 172,580 | 177,147 | 186,128 | 210,584 | 205,656 | 180,662 | 172,966 | 173,377 | 184,722 | 2,241,211 |
| 1983 | 195,579 | 172,479 | 182,488 | 170,372 | 174,392 | 191,048 | 220,165 | 229,957 | 195,604 | 182,931 | 183,949 | 212,319 | 2,310,285 |
| 1984 | 216,632 | 189,564 | 200,107 | 181,084 | 192,217 | 209,648 | 221,245 | 229,296 | 195,198 | 190,936 | 190,380 | 199,996 | 2,416,304 |
| 1985 | 227,856 | 198,242 | 194,970 | 184,877 | 196,790 | 205,363 | 226,722 | 226,050 | 202,499 | 194,789 | 192,427 | 219,255 | 2,469,841 |
| 1986 | 217,470 | 192,336 | 196,834 | 186,074 | 197,315 | 215,015 | 242,672 | 225,166 | 206,692 | 197,754 | 196,432 | 213,551 | 2,487,310 |
| 1987 | 222,749 | 194,034 | 201,849 | 189,496 | 206,074 | 225,589 | 247,915 | 247,645 | 213,008 | 203,009 | 200,258 | 220,500 | 2,572,127 |
| 1988 | 237,897 | 216,937 | 214,013 | 196,000 | 208,371 | 232,747 | 257,461 | 267,693 | 220,179 | 210,608 | 209,593 | 232,752 | 2,704,250 |
| 1989 | 232,747 | 219,826 | 226,742 | 208,042 | 220,124 | 235,689 | 257,050 | 258,687 | 227,150 | 219,910 | 219,300 | 259,038 | 2,784,304 |
| 1990 | 237,289 | 212,880 | 226,034 | 211,070 | 222,908 | 249,175 | 266,375 | 268,527 | 237,017 | 224,694 | 213,748 | 237,434 | 2,808,151 |
| 1991 | 248,455 | 210,821 | 221,400 | 209,004 | 234,373 | 248,427 | 271,976 | 268,115 | 233,885 | 223,430 | 221,377 | 233,760 | 2,825,023 |
| 1992 | 243,970 | 217,761 | 224,665 | 210,837 | 220,355 | 236,842 | 266,148 | 255,203 | 234,760 | 221,289 | 221,263 | 244,126 | 2,797,219 |
| 1993 | 245,782 | 224,617 | 234,801 | 211,374 | 222,396 | 249,633 | 282,292 | 279,132 | 236,603 | 223,629 | 225,855 | 246,412 | 2,882,525 |
| 1994 | 261,697 | 225,011 | 231,544 | 214,817 | 227,703 | 263,859 | 278,149 | 274,645 | 237,663 | 227,972 | 224,745 | 242,906 | 2,910,712 |
| 1995 | 253,077 | 228,127 | 233,675 | 217,381 | 236,381 | 256,083 | 292,827 | 304,709 | 245,574 | 234,409 | 234,117 | 258,170 | 2,994,529 |
| 1996[1] | 268,656 | 245,311 | 247,471 | 226,248 | 251,669 | 268,792 | 288,935 | 290,157 | 250,686 | 240,797 | 241,078 | | 2,819,800 |

[1] Preliminary. *Source: Energy Information Administration, U.S. Department of Energy*

## Use of Fuels for Electric Generation in the United States

| | Consumption of Fuel | | | | | | | | | |
|---|---|---|---|---|---|---|---|---|---|---|
| Year | Coal (Thousand Short Tons) | Fuel Oil (Thousand Barrels)[2] | Gas (Million Cubic Feet) | Total Fuel in Coal Equivalent[3] (Thousand Short Tons) | Net Generation by Fuels[4] (Million Kw. Hr.) | Pounds of Coal Per Kw. Hr. (Pounds) | Cost of Fossil-Fuel at Elec. Util. ¢ Mil. BTU | Average Cost of Fuel Per Kw. Hr. (¢) | Heat Rate BTU Per Kw. Hr. | Cost Per Million BTU Consumed (¢) |
| 1982 | 593,666 | 249,771 | 3,225,518 | 858,869 | 1,644,062 | .996 | 224.9 | 2.46 | 10,517 | 234.0 |
| 1983 | 625,211 | 245,497 | 2,910,767 | 867,621 | 1,678,021 | .993 | 220.6 | 2.40 | 10,547 | 227.1 |
| 1984 | 664,399 | 204,479 | 3,111,342 | 909,156 | 1,758,882 | .990 | 219.1 | 2.41 | 10,385 | 232.0 |
| 1985 | 693,841 | 173,414 | 3,044,083 | 926,793 | 1,794,276 | .990 | 209.4 | 2.27 | 10,429 | 217.7 |
| 1986 | 685,056 | 230,482 | 2,602,370 | 907,720 | 1,770,925 | .989 | 175.0 | 1.92 | 10,423 | 184.5 |
| 1987 | 717,894 | 199,378 | 2,844,051 | 944,420 | 1,854,895 | .981 | 170.6 | 1.84 | 10,354 | 177.7 |
| 1988 | 758,372 | 248,096 | 2,635,613 | 984,969 | 1,942,353 | .984 | 164.3 | 1.76 | 10,328 | 170.7 |
| 1989 | 766,888 | 267,451 | 2,787,012 | 1,004,964 | 1,978,577 | .987 | 167.5 | 1.79 | 10,312 | 174.0 |
| 1990 | 773,549 | 196,054 | 2,787,332 | 988,300 | 1,940,712 | .997 | 168.9 | 1.80 | 10,366 | 174.1 |
| 1991 | 772,268 | 184,886 | 2,789,014 | 987,469 | 1,926,801 | .996 | 160.3 | 1.75 | 10,322 | 169.6 |
| 1992 | 779,860 | 147,335 | 2,765,608 | 983,484 | 1,928,683 | .990 | 159.0 | 1.72 | 10,340 | 166.6 |
| 1993 | 813,508 | 162,454 | 2,682,440 | 1,017,086 | 1,997,605 | .993 | 159.5 | 1.72 | 10,351 | 166.6 |
| 1994 | 817,270 | 151,004 | 2,987,146 | 1,033,575 | 2,017,646 | .999 | 152.6 | 1.59 | 10,425 | 152.6 |
| 1995[1] | 829,007 | 102,150 | 3,196,507 | 1,039,174 | 2,021,064 | 1.003 | 145.3 | 1.48 | 10,173 | 145.2 |

[1] Preliminary. [2] 42-gallon barrels. [3] Coal equivalents are calculated on the basis of Btu instead of generation data. [4] Excludes wood & waste fuels.
*Source: Edison Electric Institute (EEI)*

# Fertilizer

The three primary fertilizer chemicals in the U.S. are nitrogen, phosphorus, and potassium. These chemicals provide the basic nutrients to plants. The basic nitrogen fertilizer is ammonia, which is comprised of natural gas and nitrogen. Ammonia can be applied in liquid form below the surface of the soil or converted into solid nitrogenous fertilizers. Phosphoric acid is the source of most phosphatic acid fertilizer and is made from phosphate rock and sulfuric acid. Diammonium phosphate is the only major fertilizer containing the two basic nutrients, nitrogen and phosphatic fertilizer. Potassium chloride, or potash, is the major potassium fertilizer.

Phosphates are essential for all plant life cycles and are indispensable for all living organisms. Phosphorus is necessary for nutrition. Phosphate rock is the only significant global resource of phosphorus.

According to the U.S. Geological Survey, ten companies in the U.S. operated 22 phosphate rock mines in 1995. The U.S. is the world's leading producer and consumer of phosphate rock which is used to manufacture phosphate fertilizers. In 1995, over 90 percent of the phosphate rock mined was used to produce chemical fertilizers. Production increased for the third consecutive year. Florida and North Carolina produced about 85 percent of the marketable phosphate rock mined in the U.S.

Phosphate rock is also produced in the western states of Idaho and Utah where the mineral is upgraded to phosphate fertilizers as well as elemental phosphorus. In July 1996, U.S. production of phosphate rock was 3.4 million tonnes, down 7 percent from June. For all of 1995, U.S. production of phosphate rock was 43.4 million tonnes with exports of 2.9 million tonnes. At the end of July 1996, U.S. stocks of phosphate rock were 6.5 million tonnes, down 3 percent from June. At the end of December 1995, stocks of phosphate rock were 5.6 million tonnes. Estimated apparent domestic consumption in 1996 was 39.5 million tonnes compared with 42.6 million tonnes in 1995.

Potash is used primarily as an agricultural fertilizer or plant nutrient. Potash is the source of soluble potassium which along with fixed nitrogen and soluble phosphorus make up the three primary plant nutrients. Potassium, in water-soluble form, activates plant enzymes, aids in photosynthesis in the leaves, aids in nitrogen uptake and protein synthesis, and increases the plant's disease resistance. The term "potash" was originally applied to potassium carbonate-potassium hydroxide crystals that were recovered in iron pots from the washings of wood ashes. Potash denotes a variety of mined and manufactured salts, all containing the element potassium in water soluble form.

U.S. production of potash in 1995 was 1.48 million tonnes, up from 1.4 million tonnes in 1994. Sales of all types and grades of potash in 1995 fell to 1.4 million tonnes from 1.47 million tonnes in 1994. Exports of potash in 1995 were 409,000 tonnes, down from 464,000 tonnes in 1994. Producer stocks at the end of 1995 were 312,000 tonnes. World production in 1995 was 24.7 million tonnes.

### *Futures Market*

Diammonium phosphate (DAP) and Anhydrous ammonia ($NH_3$) futures are traded on the Chicago Board of Trade (CBOT).

**World Production of Ammonia** In Thousands of Metric Tons of Contained Nitrogen

| Year | Bulgaria | Canada | China | France | Germany | India | Indonesia | Italy | Japan | Mexico | Netherlands | Poland | Romania | Russia[3] | United Kingdom | United States | Total |
|---|---|---|---|---|---|---|---|---|---|---|---|---|---|---|---|---|---|
| 1988 | 1,342 | 3,289 | 16,500 | 1,832 | 2,980 | 6,205 | 2,367 | 1,561 | 1,524 | 2,067 | 2,695 | 2,338 | 2,795 | 20,200 | 1,105 | 12,544 | 99,265 |
| 1989 | 1,326 | 3,339 | 17,000 | 1,476 | 2,932 | 6,661 | 2,526 | 1,446 | 1,539 | 2,100 | 2,901 | 2,360 | 2,736 | 19,400 | 1,037 | 12,280 | 99,331 |
| 1990 | 1,309 | 3,054 | 17,500 | 1,586 | 2,690 | 7,010 | 2,789 | 1,197 | 1,531 | 2,164 | 3,188 | 1,962 | 1,785 | 18,200 | 1,148 | 12,680 | 97,160 |
| 1991 | 1,093 | 3,016 | 18,000 | 1,604 | 2,123 | 7,132 | 2,706 | 1,147 | 1,553 | 2,221 | 3,033 | 1,531 | 1,128 | 17,100 | 1,011 | 12,803 | 93,800 |
| 1992 | 905 | 3,104 | 18,000 | 1,848 | 2,113 | 7,452 | 2,688 | 1,100 | 1,602 | 2,203 | 2,588 | 1,490 | 1,421 | 8,786 | 869 | 13,400 | 93,600 |
| 1993 | 885 | 3,410 | 19,000 | 1,871 | 2,100 | 7,176 | 2,888 | 729 | 1,447 | 1,758 | 2,472 | 1,420 | 1,328 | 8,138 | 873 | 12,600 | 91,900 |
| 1994[1] | 800 | 3,470 | 19,000 | 1,480 | 2,170 | 7,334 | 2,800 | 504 | 1,450 | 2,030 | 2,500 | 1,500 | ----- | 7,500 | 1,006 | 13,400 | 90,800 |
| 1995[2] | 800 | 3,500 | 19,500 | 1,500 | 2,100 | 7,713 | 2,850 | 600 | 1,400 | 2,100 | 2,500 | 1,500 | 1 | 7,500 | 1,000 | 13,300 | 91,600 |

[1] Preliminary. [2] Estimate. [3] Formerly part of the U.S.S.R.; data not reported separately until 1992. *Source: U.S. Geological Survey*

**U.S. Salient Statistics of Nitrogen[3] (Ammonia)** In Thousands of Metric Tons

| Year | Net Import Reliance as a % of Apparent Consumption | Production[3] (Fixed): Fertilizer | Production[3] (Fixed): Non-fertilizer | Production[3] (Fixed): Total | Imports[4] (Fixed) | Exports | Nitrogen[5] Compounds: Produced | Nitrogen[5] Compounds: Consumption | Stocks, Dec. 31: Ammonia | Stocks, Dec. 31: Fixed Nitrogen Compounds | Ammonia Consumption (Apparent) | Average Price ($ Per Tonne): Urea F.O.B. Gulf[6] Coast | Average Price: Urea F.O.B. Corn Belt | Average Price: Ammonium Nitrate: F.O.B. Corn Belt | Average Price: Ammonia F.O.B. Gulf Coast |
|---|---|---|---|---|---|---|---|---|---|---|---|---|---|---|---|
| 1988 | 14 | 11,400 | 1,144 | 12,544 | 2,751 | 582 | 9,279 | 9,333 | 925 | 705 | 14,742 | 139-145 | 150-155 | 128-135 | 109 |
| 1989 | 17 | 11,131 | 1,148 | 12,280 | 2,861 | 346 | 9,634 | 9,687 | 849 | 787 | 14,871 | 139-145 | 110-120 | 105-115 | 104 |
| 1990 | 15 | 11,573 | 1,107 | 12,680 | 2,673 | 482 | 9,851 | 9,902 | 797 | 1,451 | 14,923 | 155-156 | 155-165 | 120-125 | 106 |
| 1991 | 14 | 11,559 | 1,244 | 12,803 | 2,742 | 580 | 9,770 | 9,815 | 936 | 1,607 | 14,826 | 142-143 | 146-160 | 108-130 | 117 |
| 1992 | 14 | 12,000 | 1,349 | 13,400 | 2,690 | 354 | 10,404 | 10,448 | 1,059 | 1,789 | 15,600 | 142-146 | 149-160 | 138-149 | 106 |
| 1993 | 17 | 11,300 | 1,320 | 12,600 | 2,657 | 378 | 10,000 | 10,100 | 852 | 1,600 | 15,100 | 139-141 | 141-165 | 138-149 | 121 |
| 1994[1] | 19 | 11,600 | 1,750 | 13,400 | 3,450 | 215 | 10,000 | 11,700 | 956 | 1,650 | 16,500 | 219-226 | 204-215 | 165-176 | 211 |
| 1995[2] | 15 | 11,600 | 1,730 | 13,300 | 2,630 | 319 | 10,500 | 10,900 | 963 | 2,230 | 15,600 | 217-222 | 220-235 | 162-170 | 191 |

[1] Preliminary. [2] Estimate. [3] Anhydrous ammonia, synthetic. [4] For consumption. [5] Major downstream nitrogen compounds. [6] Granular.
NA = Not available. *Source: U.S. Geological Survey*

## World Production of Phosphate Rock, Basic Slag & Guano In Thousands of Metric Tons (Gross Weight)

| Year | Algeria | Brazil | China | Egypt | Israel | Jordan | Morocco | Nauru Island | Russia[3] | Senegal | Syria | Togo | Tunisia | United States | World Total |
|---|---|---|---|---|---|---|---|---|---|---|---|---|---|---|---|
| 1986 | 1,203 | 4,509 | 6,700 | 1,271 | 3,673 | 6,249 | 21,178 | 1,494 | 33,900 | 1,850 | 1,606 | 2,314 | 5,951 | 38,710 | 138,869 |
| 1987 | 1,073 | 4,777 | 15,000 | 1,175 | 3,798 | 6,800 | 21,300 | 1,376 | 34,100 | 1,874 | 1,986 | 2,644 | 6,390 | 40,954 | 151,962 |
| 1988 | 1,332 | 4,672 | 17,000 | 1,154 | 3,479 | 6,611 | 25,015 | 1,541 | 37,000 | 2,326 | 2,186 | 3,464 | 6,103 | 45,389 | 166,436 |
| 1989 | 1,124 | 3,655 | 20,000 | 1,355 | 3,922 | 6,900 | 18,067 | 1,181 | 37,500 | 2,273 | 2,256 | 3,355 | 6,610 | 49,817 | 167,342 |
| 1990 | 1,128 | 2,968 | 21,550 | 1,151 | 3,516 | 6,082 | 21,396 | 926 | 36,800 | 2,147 | 1,633 | 2,314 | 6,258 | 46,343 | 162,783 |
| 1991 | 1,090 | 3,280 | 22,000 | 1,652 | 3,370 | 4,433 | 17,900 | 530 | 28,400 | 1,741 | 1,359 | 2,965 | 6,352 | 48,096 | 150,731 |
| 1992 | 1,136 | 2,850 | 21,400 | 2,000 | 3,595 | 4,296 | 19,145 | 747 | 11,500 | 2,284 | 1,266 | 2,083 | 6,400 | 46,965 | 139,000 |
| 1993 | 718 | 3,420 | 21,200 | 1,585 | 3,680 | 4,129 | 18,193 | 634 | 9,400 | 1,667 | 931 | 1,500 | 5,500 | 35,494 | 119,000 |
| 1994[1] | 738 | 3,530 | 24,000 | 1,500 | 3,961 | 4,217 | 19,764 | 613 | 8,000 | 1,670 | 1,203 | 2,250 | 5,699 | 41,100 | 128,000 |
| 1995[2] | 757 | 3,530 | 21,000 | 1,500 | 4,063 | 4,984 | 20,200 | 496 | 8,800 | 1,600 | 1,551 | 2,000 | 7,241 | 43,500 | 131,000 |

[1] Preliminary. [2] Estimate. [3] Formerly part of the U.S.S.R.; data not reported separately until 1992. *Source: U.S. Geological Survey*

## U.S. Salient Statistics of Phosphate Rock In Thousands of Metric Tons

| Year | Mine Production | Marketable Production | Value Million $ | Imports for Consumption | Exports | Apparent Consumption | Stocks, Dec. 31 (Producer) | Price - $ Avg. Per Metric Ton (F.O.B. Mine) | Avg. Price of Florida & North Carolina - $ Tonne - F.O.B. Mine (-60% to +74%) - Domestic | Export | Average |
|---|---|---|---|---|---|---|---|---|---|---|---|
| 1986 | 135,683 | 40,320 | 897 | 528 | 7,848 | 34,456 | 13,277 | 22.25 | 21.64 | 25.02 | 22.31 |
| 1987 | 148,426 | 40,954 | 793 | 464 | 8,454 | 35,683 | 10,884 | 19.37 | 18.93 | 22.87 | 19.77 |
| 1988 | 162,299 | 45,389 | 888 | 676 | 8,092 | 41,025 | 9,323 | 19.56 | 18.29 | 25.24 | 19.56 |
| 1989 | 170,268 | 49,817 | 1,084 | 705 | 7,842 | 42,143 | 11,027 | 21.76 | 20.65 | 28.67 | 21.76 |
| 1990 | 151,277 | 46,343 | 1,075 | 451 | 6,238 | 43,967 | 8,912 | 23.20 | 22.44 | 30.43 | 23.55 |
| 1991 | 154,485 | 48,096 | 1,109 | 552 | 5,082 | 40,177 | 10,168 | 23.06 | 22.67 | 31.69 | 23.69 |
| 1992 | 154,936 | 46,965 | 1,058 | 1,530 | 3,723 | 42,920 | 12,612 | 22.53 | 22.47 | 31.69 | 23.32 |
| 1993 | 106,790 | 35,494 | 759 | 534 | 3,198 | 38,287 | 9,215 | 21.38 | 21.26 | 28.11 | 21.89 |
| 1994[1] | 157,000 | 41,100 | 869 | 620 | 2,800 | 42,900 | 5,980 | 21.14 | 21.79 | 25.60 | 22.08 |
| 1995[2] | 165,000 | 43,500 | 947 | 1,080 | 2,760 | 42,000 | 5,710 | 21.75 | 21.63 | 28.35 | 22.12 |

[1] Preliminary. [2] Estimate. *Source: U.S. Geological Survey*

## World Production of Marketable Potash In Thousands of Metric Tons ($K_2O$ Equivalent)

| Year | Belarus[3] | Brazil | Canada | Chile | China | France | Germany | Israel | Italy | Jordan | Russia[3] | Spain | United Kingdom | United States | World Total |
|---|---|---|---|---|---|---|---|---|---|---|---|---|---|---|---|
| 1986 | ------ | 18 | 6,753 | 20 | 40 | 1,617 | 5,646 | 1,255 | 158 | 660 | 10,228 | 795 | 396 | 1,202 | 28,788 |
| 1987 | ------ | 62 | 7,668 | 23 | 40 | 1,539 | 5,709 | 1,253 | 178 | 734 | 10,888 | 741 | 429 | 1,262 | 30,526 |
| 1988 | ------ | 54 | 8,154 | 25 | 22 | 1,502 | 5,800 | 1,244 | 95 | 785 | 11,301 | 855 | 460 | 1,521 | 31,820 |
| 1989 | ------ | 97 | 7,333 | 45 | 42 | 1,195 | 5,388 | 1,273 | 112 | 792 | 10,200 | 741 | 462 | 1,595 | 29,276 |
| 1990 | ------ | 66 | 6,989 | 45 | 29 | 1,292 | 4,960 | 1,311 | 68 | 841 | 9,000 | 686 | 488 | 1,713 | 27,493 |
| 1991 | ------ | 101 | 7,406 | 55 | 32 | 1,129 | 3,855 | 1,320 | 31 | 818 | 8,560 | 585 | 495 | 1,749 | 26,136 |
| 1992 | 3,311 | 85 | 7,270 | 55 | 21 | 1,141 | 3,460 | 1,300 | 86 | 794 | 3,470 | 594 | 529 | 1,705 | 23,900 |
| 1993 | 1,947 | 173 | 6,841 | 55 | 25 | 890 | 2,860 | 1,310 | 20 | 822 | 2,630 | 661 | 555 | 1,506 | 20,400 |
| 1994[1] | 3,020 | 240 | 8,040 | 50 | 74 | 870 | 3,290 | 1,260 | ------ | 930 | 2,500 | 684 | 580 | 1,400 | 23,100 |
| 1995[2] | 3,210 | 223 | 9,010 | 50 | 80 | 802 | 3,280 | 1,330 | ------ | 1,070 | 2,800 | 650 | 582 | 1,480 | 24,700 |

[1] Preliminary. [2] Estimate. [3] Formerly part of the U.S.S.R.; data not reported separately until 1992. *Source: U.S. Geological Survey*

## U.S. Salient Statistics of Potash In Thousands of Metric Tons ($K_2O$ Equivalent)

| Year | Net Import as % of Consumption | Production | Sales by Producers | Value Million $ | Imports for Consumption | Exports | Apparent Consumption | Producer Stocks, Dec. 31 | $ Per Ton: Avg. Value Per Ton of Product - $ | $ Per Ton: Avg. Value of K2O Equiv. | Avg. Price[3] $ Per Tonne |
|---|---|---|---|---|---|---|---|---|---|---|---|
| 1986 | 76 | 1,202 | 1,147 | 144.9 | 4,212 | 547 | 4,843 | 378 | 63.24 | 126.28 | 82.00 |
| 1987 | 71 | 1,262 | 1,485 | 197.7 | 4,073 | 470 | 5,088 | 155 | 67.98 | 131.73 | 93.00 |
| 1988 | 73 | 1,521 | 1,427 | 240.3 | 4,217 | 380 | 5,264 | 248 | 85.75 | 168.37 | 132.00 |
| 1989 | 66 | 1,595 | 1,536 | 271.5 | 3,410 | 446 | 4,500 | 307 | 90.28 | 176.74 | 137.00 |
| 1990 | 68 | 1,713 | 1,716 | 303.3 | 4,164 | 470 | 5,410 | 303 | 89.46 | 176.80 | 130.00 |
| 1991 | 67 | 1,749 | 1,709 | 304.5 | 4,158 | 624 | 5,243 | 343 | 91.52 | 178.20 | 131.00 |
| 1992 | 67 | 1,705 | 1,766 | 334.4 | 4,248 | 663 | 5,351 | 283 | 96.45 | 189.36 | 134.00 |
| 1993 | 73 | 1,506 | 1,484 | 286.0 | 4,363 | 415 | 5,432 | 305 | 94.36 | 192.72 | 130.74 |
| 1994[1] | 75 | 1,400 | 1,470 | 284.0 | 4,800 | 464 | 5,810 | 234 | 95.94 | 193.32 | 125.34 |
| 1995[2] | 76 | 1,480 | 1,400 | 284.0 | 4,820 | 409 | 5,810 | 312 | 98.61 | 202.43 | 137.87 |

[1] Preliminary. [2] Estimate. [3] Unit of $K_2O$, standard 60% muriate F.O.B. mine. *Source: U.S. Geological Survey*

# Fish

Domestic fish supplies come primarily from landings by the wild catch industry and imports. Aquaculture or domestically raised fish have become an increasingly important industry in the U.S. as well as foreign countries. Data from the Commerce Department's National Marine Fisheries Service indicates that the appetite for seafood is increasing with per capita seafood consumption at 15 pounds. Imports account for over 50 percent U.S. seafood consumption.

The USDA reported that U.S. catfish production in 1996 was projected to reach over 460 million pounds, a record that is slightly above the previous record set in 1993. Over the January-August 1996 period, live catfish deliveries to processing plants totaled 317 million pounds, some 4 percent higher than in the comparable period of 1995. This marks the second consecutive year of higher deliveries. For 1997, the initial outlook is for production to continue to grow due to high farm prices during 1996, increased pond acreage, and larger fish inventories.

In the July 1, 1996 inventory, growers in the four major producing states (Mississippi, Alabama, Arkansas, and Louisiana) indicated that they held larger inventories of fish in almost all size classes. The exception was brood fish where the numbers held on farms fell by 21 percent. Large food-size fish were down 19 percent from the previous year. The growers reported that as of July 1, 1996, the number of small and medium food-size fish inventories were up 36 percent and 8 percent respectively. These are fish that will be marketed in the second half of 1996.

Because of recent favorable prices catfish growers have been expanding their pond acreage. Growers indicated that in the second half of 1996, pond acreage would be 4 percent higher than in the first half of the year. Pond acreage in production in the four major producing states in the second half of 1996 was 162,100 acres. Growers reported that 9,600 acres of ponds were being renovated or are under construction. Whether pond acreage continues to increase is dependent on catfish prices and feed prices in 1997.

During January-June 1996, the U.S. imported 67 million pounds of Atlantic salmon, up 31 percent from the comparable period in 1995. For all of 1996, salmon imports are projected by the USDA to reach 130-140 million pounds. A major change in this market has been that Chile has passed Canada as the major supplier of Atlantic salmon. Canada's exports to the U.S. rose by 7 percent in the first half of 1996 but shipments from Chile increased by 54 percent to 34 million pounds. Canada exported 27 million pounds of Atlantic salmon to the U.S.

U.S. imports of shrimp fell in the first half of 1996. That marked the third year in a row that the quantity of imported shrimp has fallen. Frozen shrimp imports account for over 90 percent of all shrimp imports. The three largest suppliers are Thailand, Mexico and Ecuador.

## U.S. Fishery Products -- Supply  In Millions of Pounds[2]

| | | | | | Domestic Catch | | | | | Imports | | | | |
|---|---|---|---|---|---|---|---|---|---|---|---|---|---|---|
| Year | Grand Total | For Human Food Finfish | For Human Food Shellfish[3] | For Industrial Use[4] | Total | % of Grand Total | For Human Food Finfish | For Human Food Shellfish[3] | For Industrial Use[4] | Total | % of Grand Total | For Human Food Finfish | For Human Food Shellfish[3] | For Industrial Use[4] |
| 1984 | 12,552 | 6,303 | 2,195 | 4,054 | 6,438 | 51.3 | 2,348 | 972 | 3,118 | 6,114 | 48.7 | 3,955 | 1,223 | 936 |
| 1985 | 15,150 | 6,991 | 2,346 | 5,813 | 6,258 | 41.3 | 2,273 | 1,021 | 2,964 | 8,892 | 58.7 | 4,718 | 1,325 | 2,849 |
| 1986 | 14,368 | 7,087 | 2,533 | 4,748 | 6,031 | 42.0 | 2,240 | 1,153 | 2,638 | 8,337 | 58.0 | 4,847 | 1,380 | 2,110 |
| 1987 | 15,744 | 7,919 | 2,642 | 5,183 | 6,896 | 43.8 | 2,769 | 1,177 | 2,950 | 8,848 | 56.2 | 5,150 | 1,465 | 2,233 |
| 1988 | 14,628 | 7,786 | 2,719 | 4,123 | 7,192 | 49.2 | 3,306 | 1,282 | 2,604 | 7,436 | 50.8 | 4,480 | 1,437 | 1,519 |
| 1989 | 15,485 | 9,735 | 2,533 | 3,217 | 8,463 | 54.7 | 4,897 | 1,307 | 2,259 | 7,022 | 45.3 | 4,838 | 1,226 | 958 |
| 1990 | 16,349 | 10,120 | 2,542 | 3,687 | 9,404 | 57.5 | 5,747 | 1,294 | 2,363 | 6,945 | 42.5 | 4,373 | 1,248 | 1,324 |
| 1991 | 16,364 | 10,186 | 2,834 | 3,344 | 9,484 | 58.0 | 5,564 | 1,467 | 2,453 | 6,879 | 42.0 | 4,622 | 1,367 | 890 |
| 1992 | 16,106 | 10,297 | 2,945 | 2,864 | 9,637 | 59.8 | 6,182 | 1,436 | 2,019 | 6,469 | 40.2 | 4,115 | 1,509 | 845 |
| 1993 | 20,334 | 10,796 | 3,025 | 6,513 | 10,467 | 51.5 | 6,770 | 1,444 | 2,253 | 9,867 | 48.5 | 4,026 | 1,581 | 4,260 |
| 1994[1] | 19,309 | 10,719 | 2,995 | 5,595 | 10,461 | 54.2 | 6,612 | 1,324 | 2,525 | 8,848 | 45.8 | 4,107 | 1,671 | 3,070 |

[1] Preliminary. [2] Live weight, except percent. [3] For univalue and bivalues mollusks (conchs, clams, oysters, scallops, etc.) the weight of meats, excluding the shell is reported. [4] Fish meal and sea herring. *Source: Fisheries Statistics Division, U.S. Department of Commerce*

## U.S. Fisheries -- Landings of Principal Species  In Millions of Pounds

| | Fish | | | | | | | | | Shellfish | | | | | |
|---|---|---|---|---|---|---|---|---|---|---|---|---|---|---|---|
| Year | Cod, Atlantic | Flounder | Halibut | Herring, Sea | Menhaden | Pollock | Salmon, Pacific | Tuna | Whiting | Clams (Meats) | Crabs | Lobsters (American) | Oysters (Meats) | Scallops (Meats) | Shrimp |
| 1986 | 61 | 169 | 78 | 210 | 2,391 | 185 | 659 | 88 | 40 | 145 | 356 | 46 | 41 | 22 | 400 |
| 1987 | 59 | 200 | 76 | 207 | 2,712 | 598 | 562 | 100 | 35 | 134 | 386 | 46 | 40 | 41 | 363 |
| 1988 | 76 | 229 | 82 | 222 | 2,086 | 1,290 | 606 | 111 | 36 | 132 | 456 | 49 | 32 | 43 | 331 |
| 1989 | 78 | 202 | 75 | 209 | 1,989 | 2,385 | 786 | 89 | 39 | 138 | 458 | 53 | 30 | 41 | 352 |
| 1990 | 96 | 255 | 70 | 221 | 1,962 | 3,129 | 733 | 62 | 44 | 139 | 499 | 61 | 29 | 42 | 346 |
| 1991 | 93 | 405 | 66 | 230 | 1,977 | 2,873 | 783 | 36 | 37 | 134 | 650 | 63 | 32 | 40 | 320 |
| 1992 | 62 | 646 | 67 | 282 | 1,644 | 2,952 | 716 | 57 | 36 | 142 | 624 | 56 | 36 | 34 | 338 |
| 1993[1] | 51 | 599 | 63 | 216 | 1,983 | 3,258 | 888 | 55 | 36 | 148 | 604 | 57 | 34 | 19 | 293 |
| 1994[1] | NA | 427 | NA | 214 | 2,324 | 3,133 | 901 | 72 | NA | 131 | 447 | 75 | 38 | 25 | 283 |

[1] Preliminary. NA = Not available. *Source: Fisheries Statistics Division, U.S. Department of Commerce*

## U.S. Fisheries: Quantity & Value of Domestic Catch & Consumption & World Fish Oil Production

| Year | Fresh & Frozen (Disposition, Millions Pounds) | Canned | Cured | For Meal, Oil, Etc. | Total | For Human Food | For Industrial Products | Ex-vessel Value[3] Million $ | Average Price ¢ Lb. | Fish Per Capita Consumption Lbs. | World[2] Fish Oil Production 1,000 Tonnes |
|---|---|---|---|---|---|---|---|---|---|---|---|
| 1988 | 3,813 | 1,017 | 86 | 2,276 | 7,192 | 4,588 | 2,604 | 3,520 | 48.9 | 15.1 | 1,613 |
| 1989 | 5,585 | 798 | 128 | 1,952 | 8,463 | 6,204 | 2,259 | 3,238 | 38.3 | 15.6 | 1,393 |
| 1990 | 6,501 | 751 | 126 | 2,026 | 9,404 | 7,041 | 2,363 | 3,522 | 37.4 | 15.0 | 1,386 |
| 1991 | 6,541 | 674 | 119 | 2,150 | 9,484 | 7,031 | 2,453 | 3,308 | 34.9 | 14.8 | 1,105 |
| 1992 | 7,288 | 543 | 110 | 1,696 | 9,637 | 7,618 | 2,019 | 3,678 | 38.2 | 14.7 | 1,187 |
| 1993 | 7,744 | 649 | 115 | 1,959 | 10,467 | 8,214 | 2,253 | 3,471 | 33.2 | 14.9 | 1,224 |
| 1994[1] | 7,475 | 622 | 95 | 2,269 | 10,461 | 7,936 | 2,525 | 3,846 | 36.8 | | |

[1] Preliminary. [2] Crop year on a marketing year basis. [3] At the Dock Prices. *Source: Fisheries Statistics Division, U.S. Department of Commerce*

## Imports of Seafood Products into the U.S. In Thousands of Pounds

| Year | Fresh: Atlantic Salmon | Fresh: Pacific Salmon | Fresh: Shrimp | Frozen: Trout | Frozen: Atlantic Salmon | Frozen: Pacific Salmon | Frozen: Shrimp | Oysters[2] | Mussels[3] | Clams[4] | Canned Salmon | Prepared Shrimp[5] |
|---|---|---|---|---|---|---|---|---|---|---|---|---|
| 1991 | 39,709 | 55,657 | 12,206 | 3,867 | 3,687 | 8,751 | 499,859 | 17,914 | 6,595 | 6,975 | 2,939 | 39,737 |
| 1992 | 48,843 | 40,075 | 8,347 | 6,197 | 5,302 | 10,199 | 558,580 | 16,800 | 7,657 | 6,192 | 2,671 | 36,782 |
| 1993 | 62,860 | 33,920 | 11,649 | 4,741 | 7,714 | 11,659 | 556,213 | 17,293 | 9,658 | 5,818 | 2,053 | 44,765 |
| 1994 | 68,254 | 31,952 | NA | 3,878 | 7,851 | 11,210 | 580,010 | 15,415 | 11,032 | 8,265 | 3,190 | 47,912 |
| 1995 | 95,739 | 33,371 | NA | 4,076 | 9,982 | 8,849 | 539,630 | 14,866 | 15,483 | 5,930 | 3,582 | 57,577 |
| 1996[1] | 116,606 | 43,962 | NA | 4,552 | 10,752 | 8,514 | 507,823 | 14,222 | 21,241 | 6,596 | 4,182 | 74,648 |

[1] Preliminary. [2] Oysters fresh or prepared. [3] Mussels fresh or prepared. [4] Clams, fresh or prepared. [5] Shrimp, canned, breaded or prepare.
NA = Not available. *Source: Bureau of Census, U.S. Department of Commerce*

## Exports of Seafood Products into the U.S. In Thousands of Pounds

| Year | Fresh: Atlantic Salmon | Fresh: Pacific Salmon | Fresh: Shrimp | Frozen: Trout | Frozen: Atlantic Salmon | Frozen: Pacific Salmon | Frozen: Shrimp | Oysters[2] | Mussels[3] | Clams[4] | Canned Salmon | Prepared Shrimp[5] |
|---|---|---|---|---|---|---|---|---|---|---|---|---|
| 1991 | 473 | 14,879 | 2,927 | 1,040 | 123 | 196,668 | 14,980 | 929 | 1,665 | 4,405 | 66,025 | 9,937 |
| 1992 | 1,396 | 20,655 | 3,558 | 1,201 | 406 | 240,072 | 18,082 | 1,105 | 2,317 | 4,999 | 85,369 | 11,134 |
| 1993 | 4,018 | 24,275 | 2,776 | 955 | 373 | 257,751 | 16,524 | 1,454 | 2,291 | 4,217 | 84,520 | 11,539 |
| 1994 | 1,184 | 22,483 | NA | 1,958 | 384 | 260,469 | 13,622 | 2,634 | 1,935 | 3,785 | 90,393 | 15,778 |
| 1995 | 6,823 | 26,142 | NA | 1,545 | 231 | 266,706 | 14,795 | 2,531 | 1,896 | 3,968 | 95,611 | 14,837 |
| 1996[1] | 7,280 | 42,999 | NA | 1,867 | 322 | 233,346 | 11,180 | 2,097 | 1,603 | 5,126 | 94,842 | 17,665 |

[1] Preliminary. [2] Oysters fresh or prepared. [3] Mussels fresh or prepared. [4] Clams, fresh or prepared. [5] Shrimp, canned, breaded or prepare.
NA = Not available. *Source: Bureau of Census, U.S. Department of Commerce*

## World Production of Fish Meal In Thousands of Metric Tons

| Year | Chile | Spain | Denmark | European Union | FSU-12 | Iceland | Japan | Mexico | Norway | Peru | South Africa | Thailand | United States | World Total |
|---|---|---|---|---|---|---|---|---|---|---|---|---|---|---|
| 1988-9 | 1,305.2 | 128.0 | 340.6 | 579.5 | 754.1 | 181.4 | 977.4 | 86.4 | 196.3 | 1,405.9 | 151.7 | 260.8 | 338.8 | 7,002.9 |
| 1989-90 | 1,124.6 | 129.6 | 256.4 | 502.8 | 705.0 | 140.9 | 1,000.8 | 85.0 | 166.8 | 1,180.4 | 103.8 | 265.5 | 299.5 | 6,352.0 |
| 1990-1 | 1,144.2 | 123.9 | 302.6 | 556.2 | 643.9 | 87.6 | 841.8 | 80.1 | 220.8 | 1,308.5 | 87.9 | 292.8 | 310.4 | 6,303.6 |
| 1991-2 | 1,322.1 | 122.1 | 351.7 | 602.5 | 465.1 | 158.9 | 509.6 | 49.8 | 239.9 | 1,095.6 | 150.3 | 313.4 | 312.2 | 5,948.5 |
| 1992-3 | 1,091.2 | 101.6 | 300.1 | 531.2 | 355.0 | 197.7 | 395.0 | 34.6 | 250.8 | 1,767.3 | 128.3 | 349.3 | 352.5 | 6,202.4 |
| 1993-4[1] | 1,526.1 | 91.0 | 352.7 | 569.5 | 295.0 | 190.5 | 335.0 | 41.5 | 216.8 | 2,254.4 | 75.4 | 372.8 | 447.8 | 7,076.2 |
| 1994-5[2] | 1,549.2 | 83.0 | 363.4 | 571.2 | 280.0 | 173.8 | 211.0 | 45.0 | 225.0 | 2,052.9 | 56.2 | 383.5 | 366.2 | 6,663.1 |
| 1995-6[3] | 1,420.0 | 84.0 | 360.0 | 567.8 | 270.0 | 195.0 | 185.0 | 42.9 | 230.0 | 1,700.0 | 65.0 | 380.0 | 400.0 | 6,179.0 |

[1] Preliminary. [2] Estimate. [3] Forecast. *Source: The Oil World*

## World Production of Fish Oil In Thousands of Metric Tons

| Year | Canada | Chile | China | Denmark | Germany | Iceland | Japan | Norway | Peru | South Africa | Former U.S.S.R. | United States | World Total | Fish Oil CIF[4] |
|---|---|---|---|---|---|---|---|---|---|---|---|---|---|---|
| 1988-9 | 13.4 | 236.9 | 13.9 | 96.3 | 7.4 | 70.6 | 482.1 | 77.2 | 319.4 | 30.9 | 114.2 | 102.8 | 1,678.9 | 235 |
| 1989-90 | 9.5 | 204.9 | 11.6 | 73.2 | 7.9 | 66.2 | 445.7 | 49.2 | 209.2 | 12.7 | 124.9 | 127.3 | 1,438.2 | 238 |
| 1990-1 | 10.7 | 201.0 | 12.4 | 107.2 | 9.7 | 39.4 | 331.7 | 97.6 | 215.1 | 12.1 | 132.0 | 127.8 | 1,383.0 | 307 |
| 1991-2 | 11.0 | 155.9 | 8.7 | 114.5 | 9.6 | 63.0 | 186.1 | 92.9 | 102.1 | 16.1 | 104.2 | 84.4 | 1,042.1 | 361 |
| 1992-3 | 11.8 | 165.3 | 9.4 | 90.3 | 9.7 | 86.0 | 102.0 | 112.3 | 250.9 | 17.0 | 71.6 | 119.0 | 1,140.6 | 375 |
| 1993-4[1] | 9.9 | 280.0 | 11.0 | 107.0 | 9.1 | 96.5 | 80.0 | 122.7 | 426.5 | 8.5 | 52.7 | 141.2 | 1,442.7 | 332 |
| 1994-5[2] | 10.1 | 270.0 | 12.0 | 102.0 | 9.0 | 86.0 | 29.0 | 94.1 | 340.0 | 3.8 | 48.5 | 109.1 | 1,215.8 | 405 |
| 1995-6[3] | 10.3 | 245.0 | 12.4 | 105.0 | 9.2 | 90.0 | 17.0 | 100.0 | 270.0 | 8.0 | 43.0 | 120.0 | 1,129.5 | 492 |

[1] Preliminary. [2] Estimate. [3] Forecast. [4] Any origin, N.W. Europe, $ per tonne. *Source: The Oil World*

## Monthly Production of Catfish--Round Weight Processed--in the U.S. In Thousands of Pounds (Live Weight)

| Year | Jan. | Feb. | Mar. | Apr. | May | June | July | Aug. | Sept. | Oct. | Nov. | Dec. | Total |
|---|---|---|---|---|---|---|---|---|---|---|---|---|---|
| 1987 | 20,988 | 22,163 | 27,583 | 26,781 | 21,623 | 19,581 | 21,638 | 24,403 | 26,577 | 27,920 | 20,684 | 20,555 | 280,496 |
| 1988 | 26,018 | 27,786 | 28,179 | 20,805 | 20,351 | 22,839 | 23,687 | 26,941 | 24,611 | 26,221 | 25,037 | 22,634 | 295,109 |
| 1989 | 26,948 | 28,559 | 29,458 | 27,310 | 28,892 | 27,598 | 27,827 | 28,371 | 30,366 | 31,670 | 29,096 | 25,805 | 341,900 |
| 1990 | 33,066 | 31,884 | 33,120 | 30,980 | 31,542 | 28,967 | 29,540 | 31,108 | 27,566 | 29,211 | 27,913 | 25,538 | 360,435 |
| 1991 | 32,206 | 33,036 | 35,951 | 31,205 | 31,322 | 31,588 | 32,720 | 32,912 | 33,244 | 35,400 | 31,114 | 30,172 | 390,870 |
| 1992 | 36,200 | 39,228 | 45,048 | 41,177 | 39,111 | 36,813 | 36,128 | 37,958 | 37,857 | 39,212 | 35,073 | 33,562 | 457,367 |
| 1993 | 40,327 | 40,277 | 43,521 | 39,920 | 37,030 | 35,496 | 37,086 | 37,706 | 37,072 | 39,472 | 36,557 | 34,549 | 459,013 |
| 1994 | 36,714 | 35,035 | 40,446 | 34,494 | 34,163 | 34,595 | 35,901 | 39,813 | 38,716 | 39,072 | 36,054 | 34,266 | 439,269 |
| 1995 | 38,807 | 38,515 | 42,200 | 36,588 | 37,030 | 36,047 | 35,800 | 38,827 | 37,634 | 39,456 | 34,119 | 31,863 | 446,886 |
| 1996[1] | 38,475 | 38,004 | 46,376 | 38,557 | 39,583 | 36,810 | 39,025 | 40,463 | 38,807 | 42,070 | 37,210 | 36,874 | 472,254 |

[1] Preliminary. *Source: Economic Research Service, U.S. Department of Agriculture*

## U.S. Average Price Paid to Producers for Farm-Raised Catfish In Cents Per Pound (Live Weight)

| Year | Jan. | Feb. | Mar. | Apr. | May | June | July | Aug. | Sept. | Oct. | Nov. | Dec. | Average |
|---|---|---|---|---|---|---|---|---|---|---|---|---|---|
| 1987 | 60.0 | 57.0 | 59.0 | 65.0 | 69.0 | 64.0 | 61.0 | 60.0 | 60.0 | 61.0 | 62.0 | 64.0 | 61.8 |
| 1988 | 68.0 | 72.0 | 75.0 | 75.0 | 75.0 | 78.0 | 80.0 | 80.0 | 79.0 | 79.0 | 78.0 | 78.0 | 76.4 |
| 1989 | 78.0 | 78.0 | 77.0 | 76.0 | 76.0 | 75.0 | 71.0 | 68.0 | 65.0 | 64.0 | 64.0 | 68.0 | 71.7 |
| 1990 | 72.0 | 74.0 | 78.0 | 78.0 | 78.0 | 78.0 | 76.0 | 76.0 | 76.0 | 76.0 | 75.0 | 72.0 | 75.8 |
| 1991 | 69.0 | 69.0 | 69.0 | 69.0 | 66.0 | 65.0 | 63.0 | 60.0 | 59.0 | 58.0 | 57.0 | 53.0 | 63.1 |
| 1992 | 53.0 | 56.0 | 60.0 | 63.0 | 63.0 | 61.0 | 59.0 | 58.0 | 59.0 | 61.0 | 62.0 | 63.0 | 59.8 |
| 1993 | 63.0 | 67.0 | 70.0 | 71.0 | 72.0 | 72.0 | 72.0 | 73.0 | 73.0 | 73.0 | 73.0 | 73.0 | 71.0 |
| 1994 | 74.0 | 77.0 | 79.0 | 80.0 | 80.0 | 80.0 | 80.0 | 80.0 | 80.0 | 77.0 | 77.0 | 77.0 | 78.4 |
| 1995 | 78.0 | 79.0 | 79.0 | 79.0 | 79.0 | 79.0 | 79.0 | 79.0 | 78.0 | 78.0 | 78.0 | 78.0 | 78.6 |
| 1996[1] | 77.0 | 78.0 | 78.0 | 78.0 | 79.0 | 79.0 | 79.0 | 78.0 | 77.0 | 76.0 | 75.0 | 73.0 | 77.3 |

[1] Preliminary. *Source: Economic Research Service, U.S. Department of Agriculture*

## U.S. Sales and Prices of Fresh Catfish

| Year | Jan. | Feb. | Mar. | Apr. | May | June | July | Aug. | Sept. | Oct. | Nov. | Dec. | Total/Avg. |
|---|---|---|---|---|---|---|---|---|---|---|---|---|---|
| | | | | | | In Thousands of Pounds | | | | | | | |
| SALES--Whole | | | | | | | | | | | | | |
| 1993 | 4,363 | 4,385 | 4,073 | 3,730 | 3,399 | 3,278 | 3,281 | 3,424 | 3,457 | 3,305 | 3,224 | 3,277 | 43,196 |
| 1994 | 3,664 | 3,677 | 3,752 | 3,192 | 3,176 | 2,892 | 3,036 | 3,173 | 3,179 | 3,197 | 2,888 | 2,862 | 38,688 |
| 1995 | 3,221 | 3,373 | 3,856 | 3,086 | 2,997 | 2,903 | 2,951 | 3,184 | 3,108 | 3,166 | 2,962 | 2,847 | 37,654 |
| 1996[1] | 3,673 | 3,593 | 4,168 | 3,508 | 3,230 | 2,868 | 3,001 | 3,107 | 3,215 | 3,324 | 2,763 | 2,925 | 39,375 |
| Fillets[2] | | | | | | | | | | | | | |
| 1993 | 3,743 | 3,732 | 3,893 | 3,535 | 3,362 | 3,200 | 3,194 | 3,290 | 3,311 | 3,291 | 2,996 | 3,050 | 40,597 |
| 1994 | 3,101 | 3,204 | 3,550 | 3,061 | 3,103 | 3,015 | 3,046 | 3,383 | 3,183 | 3,212 | 2,784 | 2,665 | 37,307 |
| 1995 | 3,054 | 3,281 | 3,646 | 3,369 | 3,350 | 3,246 | 3,115 | 3,348 | 3,162 | 3,295 | 2,897 | 2,845 | 38,608 |
| 1996[1] | 3,439 | 3,866 | 4,366 | 3,883 | 3,824 | 3,374 | 3,556 | 3,615 | 3,645 | 3,758 | 3,254 | 3,222 | 43,802 |
| Other[3] | | | | | | | | | | | | | |
| 1993 | 965 | 915 | 1,068 | 824 | 761 | 734 | 751 | 707 | 824 | 842 | 771 | 803 | 9,965 |
| 1994 | 967 | 926 | 1,019 | 912 | 1,079 | 907 | 914 | 959 | 965 | 965 | 821 | 790 | 11,224 |
| 1995 | 998 | 1,115 | 1,437 | 1,328 | 1,234 | 1,172 | 934 | 1,035 | 1,067 | 1,166 | 1,049 | 938 | 13,473 |
| 1996[1] | 1,097 | 1,263 | 1,438 | 1,154 | 1,124 | 937 | 1,045 | 1,128 | 1,081 | 1,228 | 1,063 | 982 | 13,540 |
| | | | | | | In Dollars Per Pound | | | | | | | |
| PRICE--Whole | | | | | | | | | | | | | |
| 1993 | 1.35 | 1.41 | 1.51 | 1.52 | 1.54 | 1.54 | 1.56 | 1.54 | 1.52 | 1.55 | 1.52 | 1.53 | 1.51 |
| 1994 | 1.54 | 1.62 | 1.71 | 1.73 | 1.73 | 1.74 | 1.76 | 1.76 | 1.72 | 1.72 | 1.70 | 1.66 | 1.70 |
| 1995 | 1.69 | 1.69 | 1.68 | 1.69 | 1.69 | 1.71 | 1.70 | 1.69 | 1.68 | 1.67 | 1.63 | 1.65 | 1.68 |
| 1996[1] | 1.63 | 1.64 | 1.68 | 1.68 | 1.73 | 1.77 | 1.73 | 1.71 | 1.67 | 1.65 | 1.64 | 1.60 | 1.68 |
| Fillets[2] | | | | | | | | | | | | | |
| 1993 | 2.48 | 2.56 | 2.62 | 2.64 | 2.65 | 2.65 | 2.65 | 2.63 | 2.65 | 2.67 | 2.67 | 2.66 | 2.63 |
| 1994 | 2.69 | 2.73 | 2.86 | 2.91 | 2.91 | 2.92 | 2.93 | 2.94 | 2.93 | 2.93 | 2.91 | 2.91 | 2.88 |
| 1995 | 2.89 | 2.90 | 2.92 | 2.93 | 2.90 | 2.90 | 2.91 | 2.90 | 2.91 | 2.92 | 2.90 | 2.89 | 2.91 |
| 1996[1] | 2.88 | 2.85 | 2.86 | 2.87 | 2.88 | 2.92 | 2.91 | 2.88 | 2.85 | 2.83 | 2.84 | 2.81 | 2.87 |
| Other[3] | | | | | | | | | | | | | |
| 1993 | 1.70 | 1.80 | 1.93 | 1.94 | 1.92 | 1.90 | 1.89 | 1.91 | 1.94 | 1.90 | 1.92 | 2.00 | 1.90 |
| 1994 | 1.92 | 1.82 | 1.90 | 1.93 | 2.02 | 2.02 | 1.95 | 1.95 | 1.92 | 1.89 | 1.91 | 1.87 | 1.93 |
| 1995 | 1.82 | 1.80 | 1.93 | 1.99 | 1.99 | 1.97 | 1.81 | 1.86 | 1.84 | 1.84 | 1.87 | 1.81 | 1.88 |
| 1996[1] | 1.77 | 1.75 | 1.77 | 1.84 | 1.87 | 1.90 | 1.86 | 1.81 | 1.77 | 1.74 | 1.75 | 1.73 | 1.80 |

[1] Preliminary. [2] Includes regular, shank and strip fillets; excludes breaded products. [3] Includes steaks, nuggets and all other products not reported.
*Source: Economic Research Service, U.S. Department of Agriculture*

# Flaxseed and Linseed Oil

Flaxseed is a minor U.S. oilseed with annual production averaging less than 3 million bushels, but imports augment the total supply. Linseed oil is derived from flaxseed.

U.S. acreage planted to flaxseed had been sliding lower for several years, but the momentum appears to have quickened since the early 1990's. Planted acreage for the 1996/97 crop of a record low 112,000 acres compares with 165,000 in 1995/96, and acreage of about 300,000 early in the 1990's. Production in 1996/97 (June/May) of 2.0 million bushels compares with 2.2 million in 1995/96. Annual production in the early 1990's averaged 5 million bushels. Since the mid-1970's, U.S. flaxseed production has dropped about 80 percent. The U.S crop is produced mostly in the Northern Plains states, notably North Dakota. Imports of flaxseed, mostly from Canada, the world's largest producer with about a third of total production, were forecast at 7 million bushels in 1996/97, and when coupled with a carrying of 1.2 million bushels puts the year's total supply at 10.2 million bushels vs. 10.6 million in 1995/96. Imports in the 1990's have averaged 6 million bushels, twice the 1980's yearly rate. The U.S. has been a net importer of flaxseed since 1978, prior to which the U.S. was a net exporter. Disappearance in 1996/97 was forecast at 9 million bushels vs. 9.4 million in 1995/96. Most of the crop is crushed, 8.6 million bushels in 1996/97 vs. 9 million in 1995/96.

U.S. domestic demand for linseed oil in 1996/97 of 152 million pounds compares with 155 million in 1995/96. Exports were put at 20 million pounds vs. 23 million. Linseed oil is used as a drying agent in paint, but its use has fallen in line with the acceptance of water based latex paints. U.S. demand for linseed oil for domestic and export apparently peaked years ago. Annual disappearance so far in the 1990's averaged about 175 million pounds, at least 25 million under the like 1980 period. Carryover stocks have averaged near 50 million pounds in recent years. Linseed meal production in 1996/97 of 159,000 short tons compares with 167,000 in 1995/96 with disappearance forecast at 160,000 tons and 171,000, respectively. About a third of the production was exported in both years.

The average price received by U.S. farmers for flaxseed in 1996/97 was expected to average $4.90-6.40 per bushel vs. the 1995/96 average of $5.25. Flaxseed's price volatility appears to have toned down in recent years relative to the 1980's. Linseed oil prices in 1996/97 were forecast between $0.335-.375 per pound vs. $0.365 in 1995/96, basis Minneapolis. Linseed meal prices, basis 34 percent protein, Minneapolis, in 1996/97 were forecast between $140-180 per ton vs. $133.60 in 1995/96 and $91.96 in 1994/95.

***Futures Markets***

Flaxseed futures are traded on the Winnipeg Commodity Exchange (WCE). Prices are quoted in Canadian dollars per metric ton.

**World Production of Flaxseed** In Thousands of Metric Tons

| Crop Year | Argentina | Australia | Bangladesh | Canada | China | Czechoslovakia | Egypt | France | Hungary | India | Poland | Romania | Turkey | United States | Uruguay | Former USSR | World Total |
|---|---|---|---|---|---|---|---|---|---|---|---|---|---|---|---|---|---|
| 1985-6 | 460 | 12 | 8 | 902 | 535 | 15 | 22 | 34 | 7 | 380 | 18 | 36 | 5 | 211 | 6 | 201 | 2,350 |
| 1986-7 | 622 | 9 | 8 | 1,026 | 485 | 15 | 19 | 24 | 6 | 317 | 15 | 32 | 4 | 293 | 3 | 233 | 2,658 |
| 1987-8 | 535 | 8 | 43 | 701 | 400 | 10 | 29 | 21 | 20 | 393 | 11 | 38 | 4 | 189 | 5 | 228 | 2,755 |
| 1988-9 | 446 | 3 | 43 | 328 | 490 | 12 | 28 | 32 | 11 | 361 | 12 | 38 | 3 | 41 | 5 | 220 | 2,215 |
| 1989-90 | 526 | 2 | 47 | 498 | 400 | 16 | 21 | 31 | 11 | 326 | 12 | 49 | 3 | 31 | 4 | 227 | 2,352 |
| 1990-1 | 458 | 4 | 48 | 889 | 535 | 16 | 28 | 34 | 10 | 339 | 11 | 53 | 2 | 97 | 6 | 197 | 2,923 |
| 1991-2 | 341 | 5 | 55 | 635 | 410 | 14 | 24 | 26 | 13 | 292 | 5 | 23 | 1 | 158 | 8 | 140 | 2,458 |
| 1992-3 | 177 | 5 | 49 | 334 | 430 | 14 | 21 | 29 | 10 | 268 | 2 | 18 | 1 | 84 | 4 | 130 | 1,969 |
| 1993-4[1] | 112 | 8 | 49 | 627 | 410 | 12 | 22 | 27 | 11 | 330 | 2 | 28 | 1 | 88 | 2 | 120 | 2,177 |
| 1994-5[2] | 140 | 6 | 50 | 960 | 415 | 12 | 23 | 44 | 11 | 345 | 4 | 27 | 1 | 74 | 3 | 110 | 2,448 |
| 1995-6[3] | 129 | 15 | 50 | 1,097 | 400 | 12 | 24 | 39 | 12 | 340 | 2 | 26 | 1 | 56 | 3 | 120 | 2,555 |

[1] Preliminary. [2] Estimate. [3] Forecast. *Source: Oil World*

**U.S. Supply and Distribution of Flaxseed** In Thousands of Bushels

| Crop Year Beginning June | Planted | Harvested | Yield Per Acre Bushels | Supply: Beginning Stocks | Production | Imports | Total Supply | Distribution: Seed | Crush | Exports | Residual | Total Distribution |
|---|---|---|---|---|---|---|---|---|---|---|---|---|
| | ---- 1,000 Acres ---- | | | | | | | | | | | |
| 1986-7 | 720 | 683 | 16.9 | 1,629 | 11,538 | 2,224 | 15,391 | 362 | 10,000 | 1,448 | 280 | 12,090 |
| 1987-8 | 470 | 463 | 16.1 | 3,301 | 7,444 | 2,925 | 13,671 | 223 | 10,800 | 156 | 167 | 11,346 |
| 1988-9 | 275 | 226 | 7.1 | 2,325 | 1,615 | 6,730 | 10,670 | 158 | 8,500 | 764 | -59 | 9,363 |
| 1989-90 | 195 | 163 | 7.5 | 1,307 | 1,215 | 7,260 | 9,782 | 211 | 8,250 | 1,054 | 23 | 9,538 |
| 1990-1 | 260 | 253 | 15.1 | 244 | 3,812 | 6,715 | 10,771 | 288 | 8,800 | 549 | 163 | 9,800 |
| 1991-2 | 356 | 342 | 18.1 | 971 | 6,200 | 4,371 | 11,542 | 139 | 9,050 | 541 | 256 | 9,986 |
| 1992-3 | 171 | 165 | 19.9 | 1,556 | 3,288 | 6,035 | 10,879 | 167 | 8,600 | 230 | 337 | 9,334 |
| 1993-4 | 206 | 191 | 18.2 | 1,545 | 3,480 | 5,118 | 10,143 | 144 | 8,650 | 126 | 69 | 8,989 |
| 1994-5[1] | 178 | 171 | 17.1 | 1,155 | 2,922 | 6,005 | 10,082 | 134 | 8,550 | 72 | 156 | 8,912 |
| 1995-6[2] | 165 | 147 | 15.0 | 1,170 | 2,211 | 7,300 | 10,681 | 91 | 9,000 | 150 | 210 | 9,451 |
| 1996-7[3] | 112 | 106 | NA | 1,230 | 1,960 | 6,971 | 10,161 | 101 | 8,600 | 125 | 185 | 9,011 |

[1] Preliminary. [2] Estimate. [3] Forecast. NA = not avaliable. *Source: Economic Research Service, U.S. Department of Agriculture*

# FLAXSEED AND LINSEED OIL

## U.S. Production of Flaxseed, by States    In Thousands of Bushels

| Crop Year | Minne-sota | North Dakota | South Dakota | Other States | Total | Crop Year | Minne-sota | North Dakota | South Dakota | Other States | Total |
|---|---|---|---|---|---|---|---|---|---|---|---|
| 1987 | 224 | 6,518 | 702 | ------ | 7,444 | 1992 | 220 | 2,730 | 322 | 16 | 3,288 |
| 1988 | 110 | 1,295 | 210 | ------ | 1,615 | 1993 | 170 | 2,886 | 323 | 101 | 3,480 |
| 1989 | 95 | 980 | 140 | ------ | 1,215 | 1994 | 126 | 2,450 | 304 | 42 | 2,922 |
| 1990 | 238 | 3,118 | 456 | ------ | 3,812 | 1995 | 171 | 1,725 | 260 | 55 | 2,211 |
| 1991 | 640 | 4,860 | 578 | 122 | 6,200 | 1996[1] | 60 | 1,386 | 126 | 30 | 1,602 |

[1] Preliminary.   *Source: National Agricultural Statistics Service, U.S. Department of Agriculture*

## Average Price Received by Farmers for Flaxseed in the U.S.    In Dollars Per Bushel

| Year | July | Aug. | Sept. | Oct. | Nov. | Dec. | Jan. | Feb. | Mar. | Apr. | May | June | Average |
|---|---|---|---|---|---|---|---|---|---|---|---|---|---|
| 1987-8 | 3.47 | 3.33 | 3.15 | 3.07 | 3.03 | 3.20 | 3.45 | 3.80 | 3.95 | 4.11 | 4.19 | 5.28 | 3.39 |
| 1988-9 | 6.29 | 7.19 | 7.67 | 7.85 | 8.09 | 8.34 | 8.34 | 8.70 | 8.09 | 7.78 | 7.54 | 6.79 | 7.72 |
| 1989-90 | 5.90 | 6.49 | 7.07 | 7.09 | 7.15 | 7.14 | 7.24 | 7.69 | 8.03 | 8.60 | 8.23 | 8.31 | 7.41 |
| 1990-1 | 7.56 | 5.86 | 5.36 | 5.15 | 5.16 | 5.15 | 5.12 | 4.82 | 4.90 | 4.66 | 4.33 | 3.98 | 5.17 |
| 1991-2 | 3.92 | 3.69 | 3.55 | 3.39 | 3.31 | 3.46 | 3.39 | 3.43 | 3.51 | 3.53 | 3.61 | 3.66 | 3.54 |
| 1992-3 | 3.70 | 3.68 | 4.12 | 4.09 | 4.08 | 4.24 | 4.11 | 4.46 | 4.52 | 4.40 | 4.42 | 4.45 | 4.19 |
| 1993-4 | 4.29 | 3.79 | 4.24 | 4.09 | 4.05 | 4.18 | 4.38 | 4.61 | 4.64 | 4.60 | 4.43 | 4.25 | 4.30 |
| 1994-5 | 4.28 | 4.52 | 4.54 | 4.49 | 4.51 | 4.71 | 4.76 | 4.94 | 5.13 | 5.10 | 4.91 | 5.03 | 4.74 |
| 1995-6[1] | 5.11 | 5.21 | 5.11 | 5.11 | 5.17 | 5.03 | 5.26 | 5.18 | 5.28 | 5.31 | 6.03 | 5.88 | 5.30 |
| 1996-7[1] | 6.19 | 6.15 | 5.89 | 6.49 | 6.50 | 6.79 | 6.50 | | | | | | 6.36 |

[1] Preliminary.   *Source: National Agricultural Statistics Service, U.S. Department of Agriculture*

## United States Linseed Oil Consumption in Inedible Products    In Millions of Pounds

| Crop Year | July | Aug. | Sept. | Oct. | Nov. | Dec. | Jan. | Feb. | Mar. | Apr. | May | June | Total |
|---|---|---|---|---|---|---|---|---|---|---|---|---|---|
| 1991-2 | ----------- | 29.0 | ----------- | ----------- | 23.2 | ----------- | 15.5 | 15.5 | 13.0 | 15.0 | 15.3 | 11.4 | 137.9 |
| 1992-3 | 16.3 | 14.8 | 11.5 | 11.2 | 6.9 | 8.0 | 8.3 | 8.5 | 11.8 | 10.5 | 12.6 | 13.0 | 133.4 |
| 1993-4 | 14.9 | 8.1 | 11.2 | 9.0 | 7.2 | 10.7 | 10.2 | 7.5 | 9.9 | 8.5 | 11.5 | 11.7 | 120.4 |
| 1994-5 | 10.7 | 10.8 | 12.3 | 12.2 | 9.0 | 10.0 | 12.6 | 8.2 | 11.4 | 8.1 | 10.0 | 9.7 | 124.9 |
| 1995-6 | 8.8 | 10.0 | 9.4 | 10.6 | 7.4 | 6.9 | 8.8 | 8.5 | 7.2 | 8.1 | 10.1 | 9.5 | 105.3 |
| 1996-7[1] | 9.0 | 10.8 | 7.8 | 6.0 | 6.7 | 6.1 | | | | | | | 46.4 |

[1] Preliminary.   *Source: Bureau of Census, U.S. Department of Commerce*

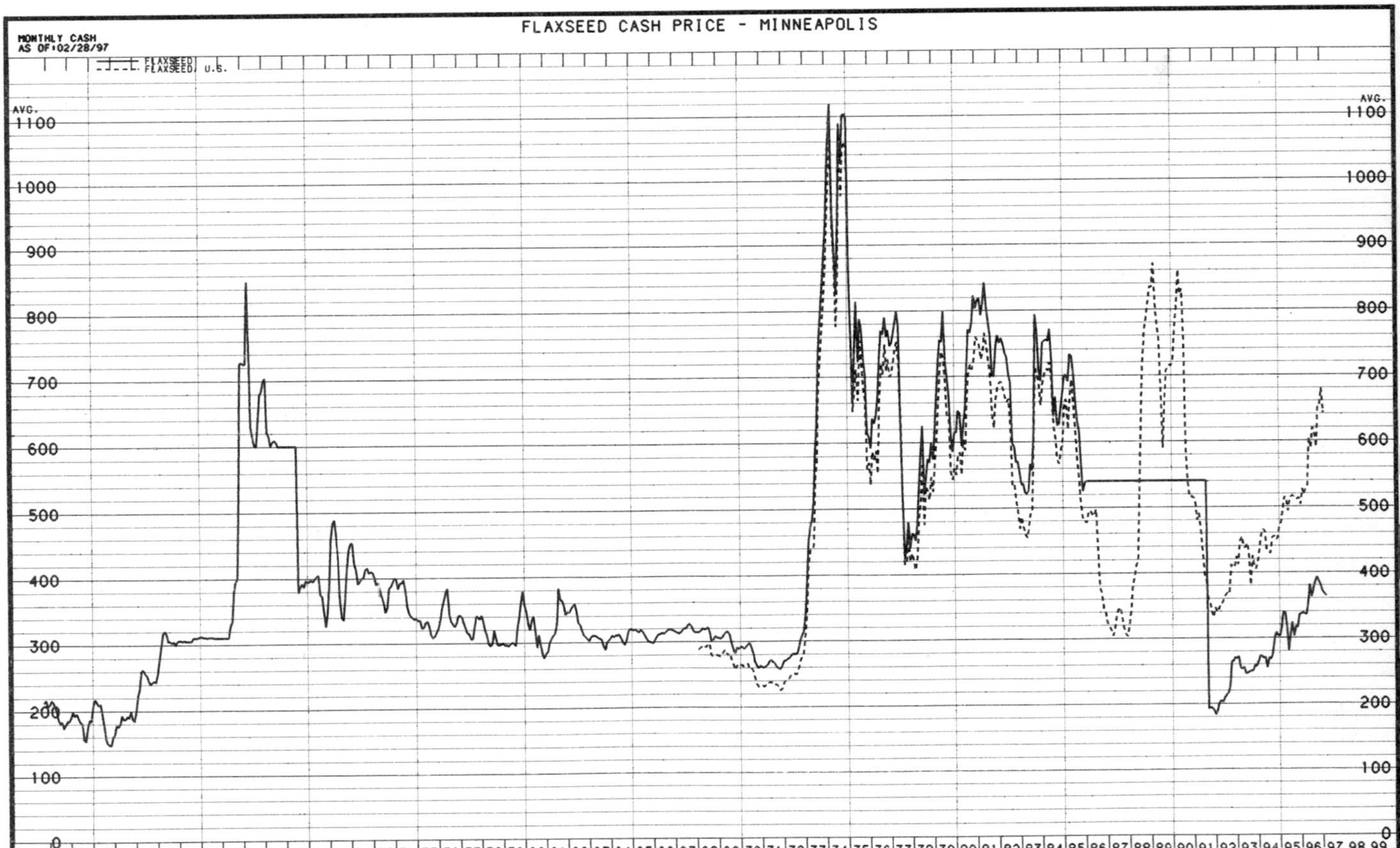

## Supply and Distribution of Linseed Oil in the U.S. In Millions of Pounds

| Crop Year Beginning June | Supply: Stocks June 1 | Supply: Production | Supply: Total | Disappearance: Exports | Disappearance: Domestic | Disappearance: Total Disappearance | Average Price at Minneapolis Cents/Lb. |
|---|---|---|---|---|---|---|---|
| 1986-7 | 39 | 201 | 240 | 6 | 183 | 189 | 26.4 |
| 1987-8 | 51 | 217 | 268 | 8 | 219 | 227 | 24.7 |
| 1988-9 | 41 | 170 | 211 | 12 | 151 | 163 | 39.5 |
| 1989-90 | 48 | 165 | 213 | 12 | 164 | 176 | 40.2 |
| 1990-1 | 37 | 176 | 213 | 6 | 167 | 173 | 38.0 |
| 1991-2 | 40 | 182 | 222 | 12 | 170 | 182 | 32.0 |
| 1992-3 | 40 | 172 | 212 | 8 | 150 | 158 | 31.5 |
| 1993-4 | 54 | 174 | 228 | 7 | 162 | 165 | 31.8 |
| 1994-5 | 63 | 171 | 237 | 24 | 168 | 192 | 33.7 |
| 1995-6[1] | 45 | 180 | 228 | 23 | 155 | 178 | 36.5 |
| 1996-7[2] | 50 | 172 | 222 | 20 | 156 | 172 | 33.5-37.5 |

[1] Preliminary. [2] Forecast. *Source: Economic Research Service, U.S. Department of Agriculture*

## World Production and Price of Linseed Oil In Thousands of Metric Tons

| Year | Argentina | Bangladesh | Belgium | China | Egypt | Ethiopia | Germany | India | Japan | United Kingdom | United States | Former U.S.S.R. | World Total | Price Rotterdam Ex-Tank $ Tonne |
|---|---|---|---|---|---|---|---|---|---|---|---|---|---|---|
| 1986-7 | 198.5 | 9.2 | 6.2 | 125.2 | 12.3 | 12.7 | 135.3 | 90.8 | 31.6 | 17.1 | 97.3 | 11.8 | 837.0 | 319 |
| 1987-8 | 175.5 | 103.0 | 8.3 | 111.3 | 11.1 | 10.5 | 81.1 | 105.7 | 33.6 | 13.5 | 82.4 | 12.6 | 734.9 | 441 |
| 1988-9 | 137.7 | 10.8 | 9.6 | 127.5 | 11.8 | 8.2 | 41.6 | 103.4 | 33.2 | 12.2 | 76.0 | 10.5 | 658.3 | 716 |
| 1989-90 | 158.8 | 11.6 | 12.9 | 104.1 | 11.7 | 6.6 | 44.9 | 92.9 | 31.4 | 11.4 | 76.1 | 11.5 | 646.6 | 756 |
| 1990-1 | 141.5 | 12.0 | 12.2 | 126.9 | 12.3 | 12.1 | 57.5 | 94.2 | 34.7 | 16.8 | 84.0 | 10.1 | 685.8 | 502 |
| 1991-2 | 114.0 | 13.5 | 14.7 | 111.0 | 11.3 | 11.7 | 56.1 | 83.8 | 31.9 | 27.0 | 87.9 | 9.1 | 638.4 | 377 |
| 1992-3 | 62.3 | 12.6 | 25.5 | 114.0 | 8.1 | 10.5 | 56.8 | 78.0 | 28.4 | 27.2 | 80.0 | 9.6 | 571.5 | 450 |
| 1993-4 | 32.2 | 12.7 | 28.8 | 112.5 | 8.6 | 10.1 | 77.2 | 90.7 | 30.7 | 35.2 | 78.7 | 9.9 | 606.9 | 476 |
| 1994-5[1] | 41.1 | 13.0 | 31.3 | 113.1 | 9.8 | 10.1 | 104.0 | 96.7 | 29.2 | 41.4 | 82.1 | 10.2 | 683.4 | 657 |
| 1995-6[2] | 42.9 | 13.0 | 32.0 | 108.0 | 9.2 | 9.8 | 104.0 | 97.3 | 26.9 | 39.2 | 84.7 | 11.7 | 684.9 | 592 |

[1] Preliminary. [2] Forecast. *Source: The Oil World*

## Factory Shipments of Paints, Varnish and Lacquer in the U.S. In Millions of Dollars

| Year | Jan. | Feb. | Mar. | Apr. | May | June | July | Aug. | Sept. | Oct. | Nov. | Dec. | Total |
|---|---|---|---|---|---|---|---|---|---|---|---|---|---|
| 1986 | 698.6 | 681.1 | 760.0 | 903.9 | 913.8 | 891.0 | 862.7 | 856.3 | 841.5 | 863.4 | 660.1 | 614.3 | 9,547 |
| 1987 | 696.7 | 754.6 | 849.5 | 903.2 | 916.0 | 933.0 | 906.6 | 890.8 | 879.6 | 895.4 | 751.7 | 681.3 | 10,168 |
| 1988 | 751.5 | 822.3 | 958.0 | 970.1 | 1,034.0 | 1,067.0 | 937.5 | 1,000.0 | 932.6 | 908.1 | 819.7 | 751.5 | 10,783 |
| 1989 | 820.5 | 841.3 | 952.6 | 985.7 | 1,072.7 | 1,091.5 | 965.9 | 1,114.4 | 1,019.7 | 995.9 | 914.3 | 755.5 | 11,239 |
| 1990 | 853.2 | 881.1 | 1,020.4 | 1,035.1 | 1,076.3 | 1,077.2 | 1,032.7 | 1,084.3 | 963.1 | 1,046.8 | 854.9 | 730.9 | 11,762 |
| 1991 | | 2,498.4 | | | 3,158.7 | | | 3,123.0 | | | 2,611.2 | | 11,707 |
| 1992 | | 2,852.3 | | | 3,464.1 | | | 3,308.7 | | | 2,816.4 | | 12,441 |
| 1993 | | 2,894.1 | | | 3,600.5 | | | 3,448.9 | | | 2,993.7 | | 12,937 |
| 1994 | | 3,039.8 | | | 3,783.0 | | | 3,736.2 | | | 3,240.8 | | 13,800 |
| 1995[1] | | 3,331.9 | | | 3,839.6 | | | 3,816.2 | | | 3,424.3 | | 14,412 |
| 1996[1] | | 3,756.3 | | | 4,589.4 | | | 4,365.2 | | | 3,750.2 | | 16,461 |

[1] Preliminary. *Source: Bureau of Census, U.S. Department of Agriculture*

## U.S. Stocks of Linseed Oil (Crude & Refined) at Factories & Warehouses In Millions of Pounds

| Year | July 1 | Aug. 1 | Sept. 1 | Oct. 1 | Nov. 1 | Dec. 1 | Jan. 1 | Feb. 1 | Mar. 1 | Apr. 1 | May 1 | June 1 |
|---|---|---|---|---|---|---|---|---|---|---|---|---|
| 1986-7 | 46.0 | 45.3 | 40.4 | 40.0 | 50.3 | 68.0 | 60.0 | 68.0 | 60.0 | 64.6 | 55.0 | 51.1 |
| 1987-8 | 52.2 | 45.9 | 40.2 | 52.1 | 54.3 | 50.4 | 50.8 | 56.0 | 39.0 | 35.5 | 35.6 | 40.8 |
| 1988-9 | 35.6 | 36.0 | 44.8 | 24.4 | 33.5 | 36.6 | 46.8 | 54.6 | 47.6 | 49.1 | 54.6 | 47.5 |
| 1989-90 | 48.4 | 43.8 | 23.2 | 21.5 | 23.9 | 30.3 | 29.9 | 39.5 | 36.7 | 39.1 | 38.3 | 36.8 |
| 1990-1 | 28.2 | 21.9 | 17.2 | 41.8 | 41.4 | 47.5 | | 61.7 | | | 75.4 | |
| 1991-2 | | 60.6 | | | 64.2 | | 73.1 | 51.2 | 62.3 | 45.6 | 45.7 | 41.4 |
| 1992-3 | 34.6 | 35.5 | 29.7 | 41.3 | 49.1 | 47.7 | 39.9 | 44.2 | 45.1 | 49.1 | 42.8 | 43.1 |
| 1993-4 | 45.2 | 39.0 | 42.1 | 47.0 | 27.9 | 19.3 | 22.5 | 38.0 | 42.0 | 49.4 | 52.0 | 62.6 |
| 1994-5 | 60.3 | 56.5 | 49.4 | 60.6 | 48.1 | 39.3 | 38.6 | 38.9 | 31.0 | 35.7 | 37.9 | 44.8 |
| 1995-6[1] | 39.5 | 44.6 | 37.4 | 46.0 | 48.0 | 44.5 | 45.3 | 58.9 | 64.0 | 62.0 | 60.6 | 47.2 |
| 1996-7[1] | 51.3 | 50.9 | 59.0 | 46.1 | 38.8 | 41.8 | 48.5 | | | | | |

[1] Preliminary. *Source: Bureau of Census, U.S. Department of Commerce*

# FLAXSEED AND LINSEED OIL

**Wholesale Price of Raw Linseed Oil at Minneapolis in Tank Cars** In Cents Per Pound

| Year | July | Aug. | Sept. | Oct. | Nov. | Dec. | Jan. | Feb. | Mar. | Apr. | May | June | Average |
|---|---|---|---|---|---|---|---|---|---|---|---|---|---|
| 1985-6 | 34.60 | 33.30 | 33.00 | 30.00 | 30.00 | 27.60 | 30.00 | 30.00 | 30.00 | 30.00 | 30.00 | 29.40 | 30.70 |
| 1986-7 | 29.00 | 29.00 | 29.00 | 25.00 | 25.00 | 25.00 | 25.00 | 25.00 | 25.00 | 25.00 | 25.00 | 25.00 | 26.00 |
| 1987-8 | 25.00 | 25.00 | 25.00 | 22.75 | 24.25 | 25.00 | 25.00 | 25.00 | 25.00 | 24.75 | 24.75 | 28.20 | 24.98 |
| 1988-9 | 35.00 | 37.00 | 41.50 | 42.00 | 42.00 | 41.50 | 41.00 | 41.00 | 41.40 | 42.00 | 42.00 | 39.75 | 40.51 |
| 1989-90 | 39.00 | 39.00 | 39.50 | 40.00 | 40.00 | 40.00 | 40.00 | 40.00 | 41.60 | 42.00 | 42.00 | 43.00 | 40.51 |
| 1990-1 | 44.00 | 40.40 | 39.75 | 36.80 | 36.00 | 36.00 | 36.00 | 36.00 | 36.00 | 36.00 | 36.50 | 36.00 | 37.45 |
| 1991-2 | 36.00 | 36.00 | 36.00 | 30.00 | 30.00 | 30.00 | 30.00 | 30.00 | 30.00 | 30.00 | 30.00 | 30.00 | 31.50 |
| 1992-3 | 30.00 | 30.00 | 32.00 | 32.00 | 32.00 | 32.00 | 32.00 | 32.00 | 32.00 | 32.00 | 32.00 | 28.50 | 31.38 |
| 1993-4 | 32.00 | 32.00 | 32.00 | 32.00 | 32.00 | 32.00 | 32.00 | 32.00 | 32.00 | 32.00 | 32.00 | 32.00 | 32.00 |
| 1994-5 | 30.31 | 32.00 | 32.00 | 33.50 | 35.00 | 35.00 | 35.00 | 35.00 | 35.00 | 35.00 | 35.00 | 35.00 | 33.98 |
| 1995-6[1] | 35.00 | 35.50 | 37.00 | 37.00 | 37.00 | 37.00 | 37.00 | 37.00 | 37.00 | 37.00 | 37.00 | 37.00 | 36.71 |
| 1996-7[1] | 37.00 | 37.20 | 37.50 | | | | | | | | | | 37.23 |

[1] Preliminary. *Source: Economic Research Service, U.S. Department of Agriculture*

**Average Open Interest of Flaxseed Futures in Winnipeg** In Contracts

| Year | Jan. | Feb. | Mar. | Apr. | May | June | July | Aug. | Sept. | Oct. | Nov. | Dec. |
|---|---|---|---|---|---|---|---|---|---|---|---|---|
| 1987 | 4,356 | 4,284 | 4,034 | 5,665 | 6,938 | 6,932 | 6,348 | 6,953 | 7,901 | 5,880 | 5,705 | 5,210 |
| 1988 | 5,838 | 6,341 | 5,583 | 6,189 | 6,089 | 7,219 | 5,964 | 7,018 | 7,791 | 8,777 | 10,662 | 7,621 |
| 1989 | 7,864 | 7,875 | 5,422 | 6,038 | 6,479 | 8,297 | 8,609 | 9,234 | 8,191 | 5,120 | 4,613 | 3,349 |
| 1990 | 3,812 | 5,165 | 5,701 | 5,790 | 4,839 | 4,985 | 4,950 | 4,908 | 4,651 | 4,477 | 5,079 | 4,502 |
| 1991 | 4,033 | 4,140 | 4,175 | 4,861 | 4,137 | 4,642 | 5,317 | 6,106 | 6,173 | 5,733 | 5,669 | 5,333 |
| 1992 | 5,620 | 6,772 | 7,864 | 7,984 | 7,786 | 7,321 | 6,299 | 6,553 | 5,623 | 4,860 | 6,734 | 5,979 |
| 1993 | 7,810 | 8,052 | 6,203 | 5,672 | 5,505 | 5,321 | 4,246 | 5,777 | 5,923 | 3,568 | 3,763 | 3,922 |
| 1994 | 6,118 | 6,201 | 5,946 | 5,519 | 4,683 | 3,945 | 4,301 | 4,654 | 4,997 | 3,077 | 4,888 | 5,251 |
| 1995 | 6,242 | 8,731 | 7,505 | 7,121 | 8,107 | 7,212 | 6,436 | 5,557 | 6,230 | 5,245 | 5,937 | 4,414 |
| 1996 | 6,059 | 6,056 | 4,402 | 5,192 | 6,970 | 4,435 | 3,102 | 2,989 | 3,257 | 3,438 | 4,326 | 5,119 |

*Source: Winnipeg Commodity Exchange (WCE)*

# Fruits

According to the USDA, U.S. fruit grower prices were higher than a year ago during the first seven months of 1996, due mostly to smaller apple and pear crops during the fall of 1995. Adding to the price strength was strong domestic and export demand. There was also smaller production of grapefruit, Florida Valencia oranges, Florida temple oranges, and tangelos during 1995/96. There were also smaller peach crops, cherries as well as blueberries, and along with the small pear harvest, prices should remain well supported. Prices for grapes have been strong and are expected to remain that way through early 1997 as the crop was about the same as the year before but demand has remained good. The California crop was reported to be of good quality. All-apple grower prices during 1996/97 will likely average the same as last year's strong level, a result of a relatively unchanged 1996 apple crop and continued tight supplies of processing apples. Strawberry prices could be lower as the crop was expected to be larger.

The USDA forecasts U.S. apple production in 1996 at 10.7 billion pounds, about the same as in 1995. A combination of cold weather and excessive moisture delayed blooms thus reducing the crop's potential. Smaller crops in the central and eastern states would be offset by larger crops in Washington and California. The western states were looking at a production increase of about 15 percent while the central states were down 29 percent and the eastern states down 15 percent. Because of the larger crop in Washington, fresh-market apple prices were expected to decline. Tight supplies of processing apples as well as apple juice stocks should keep all apple prices up.

California grape production was expected to increase 3 percent in 1996 with wine varieties up 1 percent, table varieties unchanged, and raisin varieties 6 percent higher. USDA forecast the 1996 pear crop to be 17 percent smaller than in 1995. Production of Bartlett pears on the Pacific Coast was forecast to be down 18 percent with much smaller crops in Washington and Oregon offsetting a 9 percent gain in California's Bartlett output.

U.S. peach production in 1996 was forecast to be down 13 percent as there were smaller crops in Georgia and South Carolina. California peach production was expected to increase 19 percent in 1996. Total freestone peach production, mainly for fresh use, is forecast down 31 percent. California clingstones, used mostly for canning, were expected to be 16 percent higher.

The 1996 sweet cherry crop was 19 percent less than the year before with smaller crops in Washington, Oregon, Michigan, Pennsylvania, and New York. The 1996 commercial strawberry crop was expected to be up 16 percent. There were larger crops in California and New Jersey, offsetting smaller crops in Florida, Washington, Oregon, and Michigan. In 1995, U.S. fresh strawberry consumption was 3.76 pounds per person.

## U.S. Commercial Production for Selected Fruits In Thousands of Short Tons

| Year | Apples | Cherries[2] | Cranberries | Grapes | Grapefruit | Lemons | Nectarines | Oranges | Peaches | Pears | Pineapples | Prunes & Plums | Strawberries | Tangelos | Tangerines | Total All Fruits |
|---|---|---|---|---|---|---|---|---|---|---|---|---|---|---|---|---|
| 1991 | 4,853 | 244 | 211 | 5,556 | 2,256 | 719 | 215 | 7,848 | 1,348 | 903 | 555 | 831 | 683 | 119 | 166 | 27,110 |
| 1992 | 5,284 | 373 | 208 | 6,052 | 2,224 | 766 | 236 | 8,909 | 1,336 | 923 | 550 | 829 | 668 | 117 | 260 | 29,482 |
| 1993 | 5,342 | 339 | 196 | 6,023 | 2,791 | 942 | 205 | 10,992 | 1,330 | 948 | 370 | 588 | 724 | 137 | 247 | 31,750 |
| 1994 | 5,750 | 359 | 234 | 5,874 | 2,661 | 984 | 242 | 10,329 | 1,257 | 1,046 | 365 | 879 | 825 | 150 | 318 | 31,872 |
| 1995[1] | 5,293 | 363 | 210 | 5,922 | 2,912 | 897 | 176 | 11,432 | 1,151 | 948 | 345 | 744 | 803 | 142 | 287 | 32,177 |
| 1996[1] | 5,217 | 290 | 231 | 5,545 | | | 243 | | 1,035 | 779 | 347 | 936 | 814 | | | |

[1] Preliminary. [2] Sweet and tart. *Source: Economic Research Service, U.S. Department of Agriculture*

## U.S. Utilized Production of Selected Fruits In Thousands of Short Tons

| Year | Utilized Production: Citrus[1] | Utilized Production: Noncitrus[2] | Utilized Production: Total | Value of Production: Citrus[1] | Value of Production: Noncitrus[2] | Value of Production: Total |
|---|---|---|---|---|---|---|
| | In Thousands of Short Tons | | | In Thousands of Dollars | | |
| 1990 | 10,860 | 15,640 | 26,500 | 2,242,862 | 5,525,279 | 7,768,141 |
| 1991 | 11,285 | 15,740 | 27,025 | 2,414,933 | 6,021,210 | 8,436,143 |
| 1992 | 12,452 | 17,124 | 29,576 | 2,401,351 | 6,036,615 | 8,437,966 |
| 1993 | 15,274 | 16,563 | 31,837 | 2,151,173 | 6,135,411 | 8,286,584 |
| 1994 | 14,561 | 17,342 | 31,903 | 2,268,330 | 6,274,599 | 8,542,929 |
| 1995[3] | 15,799 | 16,382 | 32,178 | 2,362,068 | 6,701,404 | 9,063,472 |

[1] Year harvest was completed. [2] Includes bushberries (beginning 1992), cranberries and strawberries. [3] Preliminary. *Source: Economic Research Service, U.S. Department of Agriculture*

## U.S. Annual-Average Retail Prices for Selected Fruits In Dollars Per Pound

| Year | Red Delicious Apples | Bananas | Anjou Pears | Thompson Seedless Grapes | Lemons | Grapefruit | Oranges: Navel | Oranges: Valencias |
|---|---|---|---|---|---|---|---|---|
| 1991 | .885 | .481 | .827 | 1.400 | 1.227 | .618 | .784 | .925 |
| 1992 | .890 | .458 | .837 | 1.288 | 1.007 | .607 | .574 | .559 |
| 1993 | .834 | .439 | .846 | 1.465 | 1.084 | .529 | .557 | .654 |
| 1994 | .803 | .462 | .802 | 1.642 | 1.090 | .513 | .545 | .587 |
| 1995 | .835 | .490 | .774 | 1.551 | 1.136 | .548 | .625 | .648 |
| 1996[1] | .916 | .463 | | 2.072 | 1.011 | .463 | .561 | |

[1] Estimate. *Source: Economic Research Service, U.S. Department of Agriculture*

# FRUITS

## U.S. Utilization of Fruit Production, and Value In Thousands of Short Tons (Fresh Equivalent)

| Year | Utilized Production | Fresh | Processed: Canned | Dried | Juice | Frozen | Wine | Other | Value of Utilized Production $1,000 |
|---|---|---|---|---|---|---|---|---|---|
| 1987 | 16,012 | 5,943 | 2,369 | 2,367 | 1,893 | 475 | 2,647 | 317 | 4,420,956 |
| 1988 | 15,911 | 5,909 | 2,374 | 2,546 | 1,415 | 459 | 2,983 | 224 | 5,102,962 |
| 1989 | 16,345 | 6,104 | 2,266 | 2,857 | 1,580 | 479 | 2,869 | 190 | 5,279,382 |
| 1990 | 15,640 | 6,093 | 2,244 | 2,440 | 1,448 | 506 | 2,717 | 192 | 5,525,279 |
| 1991 | 15,740 | 6,215 | 2,119 | 2,417 | 1,583 | 501 | 2,739 | 167 | 6,021,210 |
| 1992 | 17,124 | 6,522 | 2,386 | 2,369 | 1,743 | 584 | 3,256 | 264 | 6,036,615 |
| 1993 | 16,563 | 6,400 | 2,042 | 2,339 | 1,743 | 627 | 3,029 | 181 | 6,135,411 |
| 1994 | 17,342 | 6,711 | 2,093 | 2,816 | 1,881 | 669 | 2,711 | 227 | 6,274,599 |
| 1995[1] | 16,382 | 6,248 | 1,800 | 2,393 | 1,906 | 635 | 2,992 | 199 | 6,701,404 |

[1] Preliminary. *Source: Economic Research Service, U.S. Department of Agriculture*

## U.S. Average Price Indexes for Fruits

| Year | Index of all Fruit and Nut Prices Received by Growers (1990-92 = 100) | Producer Price Index (1982 = 100): Fresh Fruit | Dried Fruit | Canned Fruits and Juices | Frozen Fruits and Juices | Consumer Price Index (1982-84 = 100): Fresh Fruit | Processed Fruit |
|---|---|---|---|---|---|---|---|
| 1987 | 93 | 112.0 | 95.0 | 115.4 | 113.3 | 132.0 | 110.6 |
| 1988 | 96 | 112.8 | 98.9 | 120.3 | 130.0 | 143.0 | 121.9 |
| 1989 | 99 | 110.4 | 103.1 | 122.6 | 124.5 | 152.4 | 125.9 |
| 1990 | 97 | 116.1 | 107.0 | 126.9 | 138.9 | 170.9 | 136.6 |
| 1991 | 112 | 129.4 | 111.5 | 128.6 | 115.1 | 193.9 | 131.8 |
| 1992 | 99 | 83.2 | 114.3 | 134.6 | 125.7 | 184.2 | 137.7 |
| 1993 | 91 | 84.3 | 117.6 | 126.1 | 110.9 | 188.8 | 132.3 |
| 1994 | 89 | 82.2 | 120.9 | 126.0 | 111.9 | 201.2 | 133.1 |
| 1995 | 97 | 85.6 | 121.0 | 129.4 | 115.8 | 219.0 | 137.2 |
| 1996[1] | 110 | | | | | 228.7 | 143.6 |

[1] Estimate. *Source: Economic Research Service, U.S. Department of Agriculture*

## U.S. Fresh Fruit: Per Capita Consumption[1] In Pounds

| Year | Citrus Fruit: Oranges | Tangerines & Tangelos | Lemons | Grapefruit | Total | Noncitrus Fruit: Apples | Apricots | Avocados | Bananas | Cherries | Cranberries |
|---|---|---|---|---|---|---|---|---|---|---|---|
| 1987 | 12.81 | 1.78 | 2.48 | 6.35 | 23.93 | 20.83 | .08 | 2.35 | 25.02 | .72 | .13 |
| 1988 | 13.90 | 1.77 | 2.47 | 6.69 | 25.39 | 19.84 | .15 | 1.58 | 24.29 | .53 | .11 |
| 1989 | 12.17 | 1.71 | 2.39 | 6.60 | 23.56 | 21.22 | .10 | 1.54 | 24.71 | .62 | .20 |
| 1990 | 12.38 | 1.31 | 2.60 | 4.43 | 21.37 | 19.60 | .16 | 1.07 | 24.36 | .39 | .24 |
| 1991 | 8.46 | 1.38 | 2.60 | 5.87 | 19.07 | 18.18 | .13 | 1.41 | 25.11 | .40 | .26 |
| 1992 | 12.91 | 1.94 | 2.54 | 5.95 | 24.36 | 19.24 | .15 | 1.43 | 27.25 | .53 | .24 |
| 1993 | 14.24 | 1.87 | 2.65 | 6.23 | 25.95 | 19.16 | .13 | 2.17 | 26.79 | .43 | .19 |
| 1994 | 13.06 | 2.11 | 2.68 | 6.10 | 24.93 | 19.57 | .15 | 1.34 | 28.06 | .53 | .30 |
| 1995[2] | 12.25 | 2.01 | 2.87 | 6.04 | 24.37 | 18.93 | .10 | 1.38 | 27.41 | .24 | .30 |

[1] All data on calendar-year basis except for citrus fruits; apples, August; grapes and pears, July; grapefruit, September; lemons, August of prior year; all other citrus, November. [2] Preliminary. *Source: Economic Research Service, U.S. Department of Agriculture*

## U.S. Fresh Fruit: Per Capita Consumption[1] In Pounds

| Year | Noncitrus - Continued: Grapes | Kiwifruit | Mangos | Nectarines & Peaches | Pears | Pineapples | Papaya | Plums & Prunes | Strawberries | Total Noncitrus | Total Fruit |
|---|---|---|---|---|---|---|---|---|---|---|---|
| 1987 | 7.05 | .25 | .56 | 6.05 | 3.51 | 1.70 | .19 | 1.91 | 3.12 | 73.47 | 97.40 |
| 1988 | 7.70 | .25 | .38 | 6.75 | 3.22 | 1.81 | .16 | 1.72 | 3.33 | 71.82 | 97.21 |
| 1989 | 7.94 | .33 | .51 | 5.86 | 3.20 | 2.04 | .14 | 1.41 | 3.25 | 73.07 | 96.63 |
| 1990 | 7.92 | .49 | .54 | 5.54 | 3.22 | 2.05 | .18 | 1.55 | 3.24 | 70.55 | 91.92 |
| 1991 | 7.26 | .44 | .85 | 6.43 | 3.15 | 1.92 | .17 | 1.42 | 3.58 | 70.73 | 89.80 |
| 1992 | 7.19 | .33 | .68 | 6.02 | 3.14 | 2.00 | .24 | 1.78 | 3.61 | 73.84 | 98.20 |
| 1993 | 7.04 | .53 | .90 | 5.95 | 3.38 | 2.05 | .28 | 1.28 | 3.64 | 73.92 | 99.87 |
| 1994 | 7.33 | .50 | .98 | 5.49 | 3.48 | 2.04 | .30 | 1.62 | 4.09 | 75.78 | 100.71 |
| 1995[2] | 7.64 | .51 | 1.13 | 5.44 | 3.40 | 1.93 | .37 | .94 | 3.76 | 73.49 | 97.86 |

[1] All data on calendar-year basis except for citrus fruits; apples, August; grapes and pears, July; grapefruit, September; lemons, August of prior year; all other citrus, November. [2] Preliminary. *Source: Economic Research Service, U.S. Department of Agriculture*

# Gas

Natural gas prices rose in the fourth quarter of 1996 as cold-than-normal temperatures were experienced in the midwestern states. Prices were very volatile as is often the case in late fall and early winter. The U.S. Energy Information Agency noted that the higher prices appeared to be a response to a number of events. First and maybe foremost were the very low temperatures as a strong arctic airmass moved down the central part of the U.S. in December. There continued to be reports of historically low stocks of distillate oil and propane. There were short-term supply cutbacks of 3.5 billion cubic feet a day because of a tropical storm in the Gulf of Mexico and a pipeline service shutdown of 250 million cubic feet per day along a portion of the Tennessee transmission system. These events, along with high crude oil prices, have contributed to high and volatile natural gas prices.

Entering 1997, it appeared there were more fundamental factors likely to support high prices. One factor is that storage levels are at very low levels, particularly in producing regions. Additionally, demand for natural gas is likely to be higher as still low relative prices are encouraging use. There has been little or no growth in U.S. dry gas production over the first nine months of 1996 with most drilling activity adding natural gas to future reserves rather than for immediate delivery.

In October, U.S. total dry gas production was 1.51 trillion cubic feet, up 5 percent from September. In October 1995, total dry gas production was 1.55 trillion cubic feet. Over the January-October 1996 period total gas production was 15.59 trillion cubic feet, down less than 1 percent from the comparable period in 1995 and almost 1 percent more than the like period of 1994. For all of 1995, total gas production was 18.8 trillion cubic feet.

Gas withdrawals in October 1996 were 1.92 trillion cubic feet. This was 5 percent more than in the previous month. For the first 10 months of 1996, total withdrawals of gas were 19.8 trillion cubic feet, down less than 1 percent from the comparable period of 1995 but 2 percent more than the same period in 1994. In October 1996, repressuring took 280 million cubic feet of gas, up 6 percent from the previous month. Marketed production (wet) of natural gas in October 1996 was 1.59 trillion cubic feet, up 5 percent from the previous month. For January-October 1996, marketed production was 16.3 trillion cubic feet, about the same as in 1995 and 1994.

Total consumption of gas in October 1996 was 1.53 trillion cubic feet, up 12 percent from September. For the first 10 months of 1996, U.S. consumption was 17.8 trillion cubic feet, up 2 percent from 1995 and 5 percent above 1994.

### *Futures Markets*

Natural gas futures and options are traded on the New York Mercantile Exchange (NYMEX) and the Kansas City Board of Trade (KCBT). Futures are traded on the International Petroleum Exchange (IPE).

**World Natural Gas Production (Average Monthly Marketed Production[3])** In Terajoule[4]

| Year | Australia | Canada | China | France | Germany | Indonesia | India | Italy | Mexico | Netherlands | Romania | Russia[5] | United Kingdom | United States | Venezuela |
|---|---|---|---|---|---|---|---|---|---|---|---|---|---|---|---|
| 1987 | 49,077 | 271,207 | 45,063 | 17,172 | 48,527 | 89,971 | 24,374 | 46,133 | 82,603 | 195,827 | 106,431 | 2,107,896 | 140,085 | 1,506,613 | 66,607 |
| 1988 | 50,286 | 313,592 | 46,331 | 10,104 | 45,312 | 120,227 | 28,441 | 47,009 | 79,163 | 173,213 | 102,977 | 2,184,357 | 134,778 | 1,550,343 | 68,799 |
| 1989 | 51,406 | 331,923 | 48,816 | 6,774 | 44,734 | 128,193 | 33,715 | 49,618 | 75,131 | 210,184 | 92,312 | 2,245,667 | 143,708 | 1,569,198 | 69,877 |
| 1990 | 66,445 | 342,826 | 49,380 | 6,450 | 44,162 | 195,448 | 36,795 | 54,389 | 79,594 | 211,717 | 79,931 | 2,311,092 | 158,628 | 1,614,310 | 79,683 |
| 1991 | 62,194 | 362,029 | 49,955 | 7,739 | 52,460 | 158,214 | 43,284 | 53,037 | 79,009 | 239,349 | 68,977 | 2,286,626 | 176,344 | 1,609,083 | 83,097 |
| 1992 | 67,696 | 397,229 | 50,052 | 7,470 | 51,911 | 165,761 | 43,297 | 57,117 | 95,688 | 240,043 | 67,900 | 1,743,167 | 176,661 | 1,614,941 | 79,784 |
| 1993 | 72,848 | 437,922 | 52,297 | 7,846 | 47,904 | 171,828 | 44,475 | 60,792 | 93,646 | 244,205 | 68,891 | 1,708,083 | 196,792 | 1,667,401 | 85,907 |
| 1994 | 78,202 | 438,335 | 55,230 | 7,866 | 50,535 | 193,583 | 47,219 | 64,142 | 97,285 | 207,317 | 65,057 | 1,525,232 | 203,875 | 1,700,081 | 91,256 |
| 1995[1] | 92,400 | 607,608 | 55,872 | NA | 55,451 | 276,733 | 53,422 | 65,810 | 143,223 | 209,229 | 62,467 | 1,936,092 | 213,987 | 1,715,397 | NA |
| 1996[2] | NA | NA | 62,540 | NA | 60,387 | 293,592 | 59,397 | NA | 162,655 | NA | 60,784 | 1,971,331 | NA | 1,713,986 | NA |

[1] Preliminary. [2] Estimate. [3] Compares all gas collected & utilized as fuel or as a chemical industry raw material, including gas used in oilfields as a fuel by producers. [4] Terajoule = 10 to the 12th power Joule = approximately 10 to the 9th power BTU. [5] Formerly part of the U.S.S.R., data not reported separately until 1992. NA = not avaliable. *Source: United Nations*

**Marketed Production of Natural Gas by Important States in the U.S.** In Million of Cubic Feet

| Year | Alaska | California | Colorado | Kansas | Louisiana | Michigan | Mississippi | New Mexico | Oklahoma | Texas | Wyoming | Total |
|---|---|---|---|---|---|---|---|---|---|---|---|---|
| 1986 | 304,481 | 462,218 | 163,684 | 465,695 | 4,895,394 | 127,287 | 140,833 | 702,614 | 1,917,493 | 6,151,775 | 403,266 | 16,790,910 |
| 1987 | 359,837 | 424,621 | 164,557 | 457,050 | 5,122,509 | 146,996 | 139,727 | 823,773 | 2,004,797 | 6,126,315 | 497,980 | 17,348,537 |
| 1988 | 378,638 | 399,663 | 191,544 | 592,845 | 5,180,267 | 146,145 | 124,053 | 791,819 | 2,167,050 | 6,286,029 | 509,058 | 17,918,465 |
| 1989 | 393,729 | 362,860 | 216,737 | 601,196 | 5,078,125 | 155,988 | 102,645 | 854,615 | 2,237,037 | 6,241,425 | 665,699 | 18,095,147 |
| 1990 | 402,907 | 362,748 | 242,997 | 573,603 | 5,241,989 | 172,151 | 94,616 | 965,104 | 2,258,471 | 6,343,146 | 735,728 | 18,593,792 |
| 1991 | 437,822 | 378,384 | 285,961 | 628,459 | 5,034,361 | 195,749 | 108,031 | 1,038,284 | 2,153,852 | 6,280,654 | 776,528 | 18,532,439 |
| 1992 | 443,597 | 365,632 | 323,041 | 658,007 | 4,914,300 | 194,815 | 91,697 | 1,268,363 | 2,017,356 | 6,145,862 | 842,576 | 18,711,808 |
| 1993 | 430,350 | 315,851 | 400,985 | 686,347 | 4,991,138 | 204,635 | 80,695 | 1,409,429 | 2,049,942 | 6,249,624 | 634,957 | 18,981,915 |
| 1994 | 555,402 | 309,427 | 453,207 | 712,730 | 5,169,705 | 222,657 | 63,448 | 1,557,689 | 1,934,864 | 6,353,844 | 696,018 | 19,709,525 |
| 1995[1] | 469,550 | 279,555 | 523,084 | 721,436 | 5,108,366 | 238,203 | 95,533 | 1,625,837 | 1,811,734 | 6,330,048 | 673,775 | 19,506,474 |

[1] Preliminary. *Source: Energy Information Administration, U.S. Department of Energy*

## World Natural Gas Plant Liquids Production    Thousand Barrels Per Day

| Year | | Algeria | Canada | Mexico | Saudi Arabia | Former USSR | United States | Persian Gulf[2] | OAPEC[3] | OPEC[4] | World |
|---|---|---|---|---|---|---|---|---|---|---|---|
| 1988 | Average | 120 | 381 | 370 | 499 | 450 | 1,625 | 808 | 979 | 1,077 | 4,481 |
| 1989 | Average | 130 | 410 | 384 | 503 | 425 | 1,546 | 851 | 1,041 | 1,188 | 4,502 |
| 1990 | Average | 130 | 426 | 428 | 620 | 425 | 1,559 | 930 | 1,107 | 1,281 | 4,632 |
| 1991 | Average | 140 | 431 | 457 | 680 | 420 | 1,659 | 931 | 1,113 | 1,299 | 4,827 |
| 1992 | Average | 140 | 460 | 454 | 713 | 390 | 1,697 | 1,003 | 1,185 | 1,364 | 4,973 |
| 1993 | Average | 145 | 506 | 459 | 704 | 380 | 1,736 | 1,040 | 1,238 | 1,435 | 5,169 |
| 1994 | Average | 140 | 539 | 461 | 698 | 340 | 1,727 | 1,081 | 1,272 | 1,475 | 5,297 |
| 1995[1] | Average | 145 | 574 | 447 | 701 | 410 | 1,762 | 1,086 | 1,282 | 1,456 | 5,512 |
| 1996[1] | Average | 145 | 596 | 428 | 696 | 410 | 1,822 | 1,081 | 1,277 | 1,451 | 5,554 |

[1] Preliminary. [2] Bahrain, Iran, Iraq, Kuwait, Qatar, Saudi Arabia and the United Arab Emirates. [3] Organization of Arab Petroleum Exporting Countries. [4] Organization of Petroleum Exporting Countries. *Source: Energy Information Administration, U.S. Department of Energy*

## United States Recoverable Reserves and Deliveries of Natural Gas    In Billions of Cubic Feet

| Year | Gross Withdrawals Natural Gas | Recoverable Reserves of Natural Gas Dec. 31[2] | Deliveries: Residential | Deliveries: Commercial | Deliveries: Electric Utility Plants[3] | Deliveries: Industrial | Deliveries: Total Deliveries | Consumption: Lease & Plant Fuel | Consumption: Used as Pipline Fuel | Heating Value BTU per Cubic Foot |
|---|---|---|---|---|---|---|---|---|---|---|
| 1987 | 20,140 | 187,211 | 4,315 | 2,430 | 2,844 | 5,953 | 15,542 | 1,149 | 519 | 1,031 |
| 1988 | 20,999 | 168,024 | 4,630 | 2,670 | 2,636 | 6,383 | 16,320 | 1,096 | 614 | 1,029 |
| 1989 | 21,074 | 167,116 | 4,781 | 2,718 | 2,787 | 6,816 | 17,102 | 1,070 | 629 | 1,031 |
| 1990 | 21,523 | 169,346 | 4,391 | 2,623 | 2,786 | 7,018 | 16,819 | 1,236 | 660 | 1,031 |
| 1991 | 21,750 | 167,062 | 4,556 | 2,729 | 2,789 | 7,231 | 17,305 | 1,129 | 601 | 1,030 |
| 1992 | 22,132 | 165,015 | 4,690 | 2,803 | 2,766 | 7,527 | 17,786 | 1,171 | 588 | 1,030 |
| 1993 | 22,726 | 162,415 | 4,956 | 2,863 | 2,682 | 7,981 | 18,483 | 1,172 | 624 | 1,027 |
| 1994 | 23,581 | 163,837 | 4,848 | 2,897 | 2,987 | 8,167 | 18,899 | 1,124 | 685 | 1,028 |
| 1995[1] | 23,744 | 165,146 | 4,850 | 3,034 | 3,197 | 8,580 | 19,660 | 1,220 | 700 | 1,027 |

[1] Preliminary. [2] Estimated proved recoverable reserves of dry natural gas. [3] Figures include gas other than natural (impossible to segregate); therefore, shown separately from other consumption. *Source: Energy Information Administration, U.S. Department of Energy*

## Gas Utility Sales in the United States by Types & Class of Service    In Trillions of BTU's

| Year | Total Utility Sales | Number of Customers (Millions) | Class by Service: Residential | Class by Service: Commercial | Class by Service: Industrial | Class by Service: Electric Generation | Class by Service: Other | Revenue -- Million $ From Sales to Customers: Total | Revenue: Residential | Revenue: Commercial | Revenue: Industrial | Revenue: Electric Generation | Revenue: Other |
|---|---|---|---|---|---|---|---|---|---|---|---|---|---|
| 1987 | 10,543 | 51.6 | 4,385 | 2,156 | 2,339 | 1,509 | 155 | 45,492 | 23,622 | 10,271 | 7,279 | 3,789 | 530 |
| 1988 | 10,705 | 52.4 | 4,695 | 2,306 | 2,208 | 1,336 | 160 | 46,162 | 24,828 | 10,681 | 6,713 | 3,400 | 538 |
| 1989 | 10,551 | 53.4 | 4,798 | 2,322 | 1,963 | 1,280 | 188 | 47,493 | 26,172 | 11,074 | 9,217 | 449 | 582 |
| 1990 | 9,842 | 54.3 | 4,468 | 2,192 | 1,890 | 1,120 | 171 | 45,153 | 25,000 | 10,604 | 6,034 | 2,962 | 553 |
| 1991 | 9,601 | 55.2 | 4,546 | 2,198 | 1,743 | 888 | 226 | 44,647 | 25,729 | 10,669 | 5,326 | 2,250 | 674 |
| 1992 | 9,907 | 56.1 | 4,694 | 2,209 | 1,959 | 813 | 231 | 46,178 | 26,702 | 10,865 | 5,837 | 2,077 | 698 |
| 1993 | 10,151 | 57.0 | 5,054 | 2,397 | 2,009 | 524 | 168 | 50,137 | 29,787 | 12,076 | 6,162 | 1,480 | 632 |
| 1994[1] | 9,248 | 58.0 | 4,845 | 2,253 | 1,690 | 420 | 159 | 49,852 | 30,552 | 12,276 | 5,529 | 1,170 | 597 |
| 1995[2] | 9,094 | 58.7 | 4,736 | 2,204 | 1,603 | 328 | 224 | 46,381 | 28,741 | 11,410 | 4,816 | 836 | 579 |

[1] Preliminary. [2] Estimate. NA = Not available. *Source: American Gas Association*

## Salient Statistics of Gas in the United States

| Year | Supply: Marketed Production | Supply: Extraction Loss | Supply: Dry Production | Supply: Storage Withdrawals | Supply: Imports (Consumed) | Supply: Total Supply | Disposition: Consumption | Disposition: Exports | Disposition: Added to Storage | Disposition: Total Disposition | Wellhead Price | Average Price Delivered to Consumers: Imports | Exports | Residential | Commercial | Industrial | Electric Utilities |
|---|---|---|---|---|---|---|---|---|---|---|---|---|---|---|---|---|---|
| | In Billions of Cubic Feet | | | | | | | | | | $ Per Thousand Cubic Feet | | | | | | |
| 1987 | 17,349 | 812 | 16,621 | 1,905 | 993 | 19,176 | 17,211 | 54 | 1,911 | 19,176 | 1.67 | 2.17 | 3.07 | 5.54 | 4.77 | 2.94 | 2.32 |
| 1988 | 17,918 | 816 | 17,103 | 2,270 | 1,294 | 20,315 | 18,030 | 74 | 2,211 | 20,315 | 1.69 | 1.84 | 2.74 | 5.47 | 4.63 | 2.95 | 2.33 |
| 1989 | 18,095 | 785 | 17,311 | 2,854 | 1,382 | 21,435 | 18,801 | 107 | 2,528 | 21,435 | 1.69 | 1.82 | 2.51 | 5.64 | 4.74 | 2.96 | 2.43 |
| 1990 | 18,594 | 784 | 17,810 | 1,986 | 1,532 | 21,302 | 18,716 | 86 | 2,499 | 21,300 | 1.71 | 1.94 | 3.10 | 5.80 | 4.83 | 2.93 | 2.38 |
| 1991 | 18,532 | 835 | 17,698 | 2,752 | 1,773 | 21,836 | 19,035 | 129 | 2,672 | 21,836 | 1.64 | 1.82 | 2.59 | 5.82 | 4.81 | 2.69 | 2.18 |
| 1992 | 18,712 | 872 | 17,840 | 2,772 | 2,138 | 22,360 | 19,544 | 216 | 2,599 | 22,360 | 1.74 | 1.85 | 2.25 | 5.89 | 4.88 | 2.84 | 2.36 |
| 1993 | 18,982 | 886 | 18,095 | 2,799 | 2,350 | 23,254 | 20,279 | 140 | 2,835 | 23,254 | 2.04 | 2.03 | 2.59 | 6.16 | 5.22 | 3.07 | 2.61 |
| 1994[1] | 19,710 | 889 | 18,821 | 2,562 | 2,624 | 23,782 | 20,755 | 162 | 2,865 | 23,782 | 1.88 | 1.87 | 2.50 | 6.41 | 5.44 | 3.05 | 2.28 |
| 1995[2] | 19,506 | 908 | 18,599 | 2,886 | 2,841 | 24,260 | 21,648 | 154 | 2,458 | 24,260 | 1.59 | 1.49 | 2.39 | 6.06 | 5.05 | 2.71 | 2.02 |

[1] Preliminary. [2] Estimate. *Source: Energy Information Administration, U.S. Department of Energy*

## Average Open Interest of Natural Gas Futures in New York In Contracts

| Year | Jan. | Feb. | Mar. | Apr. | May | June | July | Aug. | Sept. | Oct. | Nov. | Dec. |
|---|---|---|---|---|---|---|---|---|---|---|---|---|
| 1990 | | | | 1,320 | 2,699 | 4,268 | 6,130 | 8,760 | 11,077 | 12,998 | 13,813 | 10,814 |
| 1991 | 10,523 | 13,825 | 13,125 | 13,225 | 16,782 | 18,502 | 19,235 | 21,460 | 23,853 | 24,003 | 21,692 | 19,065 |
| 1992 | 24,718 | 28,661 | 29,851 | 33,626 | 41,456 | 49,642 | 49,829 | 57,346 | 68,306 | 77,034 | 80,349 | 74,569 |
| 1993 | 69,499 | 77,053 | 91,132 | 116,366 | 136,074 | 132,667 | 124,038 | 126,443 | 129,940 | 130,619 | 124,627 | 129,963 |
| 1994 | 127,254 | 128,336 | 118,480 | 119,908 | 120,894 | 120,956 | 111,044 | 135,652 | 156,238 | 145,766 | 139,471 | 139,054 |
| 1995 | 148,448 | 151,882 | 157,097 | 150,101 | 148,797 | 144,402 | 143,942 | 140,297 | 135,226 | 133,969 | 140,301 | 166,227 |
| 1996 | 155,024 | 150,521 | 149,809 | 159,132 | 147,616 | 156,959 | 151,913 | 135,191 | 138,657 | 144,944 | 147,854 | 151,498 |

*Source: New York Mercantile Exchange (NYMEX)*

## Volume of Trading of Natural Gas Futures in New York In Contracts

| Year | Jan. | Feb. | Mar. | Apr. | May | June | July | Aug. | Sept. | Oct. | Nov. | Dec. | Total |
|---|---|---|---|---|---|---|---|---|---|---|---|---|---|
| 1990 | | | | 4,112 | 6,400 | 10,521 | 14,313 | 17,298 | 15,222 | 25,312 | 15,886 | 22,307 | 131,371 |
| 1991 | 29,162 | 14,851 | 22,769 | 20,292 | 28,686 | 51,232 | 36,988 | 33,130 | 42,265 | 46,619 | 49,048 | 50,208 | 425,250 |
| 1992 | 89,041 | 45,362 | 77,897 | 98,932 | 137,536 | 116,395 | 156,020 | 192,207 | 268,708 | 300,024 | 213,524 | 227,602 | 1,923,248 |
| 1993 | 194,256 | 274,380 | 318,789 | 443,035 | 471,458 | 365,889 | 335,612 | 353,330 | 459,649 | 417,074 | 449,717 | 613,934 | 4,697,123 |
| 1994 | 667,623 | 470,935 | 373,462 | 344,688 | 411,111 | 465,849 | 438,756 | 724,205 | 578,729 | 594,180 | 621,868 | 721,800 | 6,413,206 |
| 1995 | 733,021 | 557,830 | 676,081 | 524,458 | 621,331 | 622,494 | 641,827 | 745,576 | 548,312 | 664,372 | 762,951 | 988,465 | 8,086,718 |
| 1996 | 887,172 | 655,697 | 694,580 | 619,963 | 590,697 | 681,333 | 828,995 | 628,785 | 679,117 | 924,391 | 802,780 | 820,357 | 8,813,867 |

*Source: New York Mercantile Exchange (NYMEX)*

# Gasoline

U.S. gasoline consumption increased sharply in 1995 due in part to a strong U.S. economy, mild weather in the first quarter of 1995 and decreased fuel efficiency. This in part was due to the switch to reformulated gasoline (RFG). The Environmental Protection Agency's RFG program started on January 1, 1995, causing U.S. refiners to draw down their stocks at the end of 1994 to make room for the new grades which currently account for about 25 percent of U.S. gasoline consumption. Winter weather in early 1995 was for the most part very mild and that encouraged more use of motor vehicles. In late 1995 and early 1996, winter conditions were much different on the East Coast and the Midwest, but despite this gasoline use was good. The peak driving season in the U.S. is between April and September and weather conditions were very favorable. Additionally, the economy performed well adding to the demand for gasoline.

The Energy Information Administration reported that in August 1996, total production of finished motor gasoline was averaging 7.73 million barrels per day, down about 1 percent from the previous month and 1 percent higher than in August 1995. For the January-August 1996 period, motor gasoline production averaged 7.6 million barrels per day, marginally above the comparable period in 1995 and 5 percent more than in the same period of 1994. For all of 1995, daily gasoline production averaged 7.6 million barrels.

U.S. imports of gasoline in August 1996 were averaging 310,000 barrels per day, down 18 percent from the average in July. For the first eight months of 1996, U.S. gasoline imports averaged 377,000 barrels per day. That represented a sharp 37 percent increase from the same period in 1995 when imports averaged 275,000 barrels per day. During the first eight months of 1994, imports averaged 396,000 barrels per day.

The U.S. also exports about 100,000 barrels of gasoline per day to Mexico and Puerto Rico. In August 1996, exports averaged 107,000 barrels per day, down 13 percent from July 1996. Over the first eight months of 1996, exports averaged 106,000 barrels per day. This was 9 percent higher than in the comparable period of 1995 and 34 percent above the same period of 1994. In January 1996, exports averaged 163,000 barrels per day, the highest monthly average since December 1994 when they averaged 231,000 barrels. U.S. exports of gasoline have been increasing. In 1990, they averaged 55,000 barrels per day while in 1984 they were just 6,000 barrels per day.

Total gasoline supplied in August 1996 averaged 8.1 million barrels per day, down 1 percent from the previous month. For the January-August 1996 period, product supplied averaged 7.8 million barrels per day, up almost 1 per cent from the comparable period in 1995 and 3 per cent more than in the like period of 1994.

At the end of August 1996, total stocks of gasoline were 193 million barrels, down from 202 million barrels at the end of July. At the end of December 1995, total gasoline stocks were 202 million barrels. Stocks of finished gasoline (excluding blended components) at the end of August 1996 were 153 million barrels.

***Futures Market***

Unleaded gasoline futures and options are traded on the New York Mercantile Exchange (NYMEX).

**Average Spot Prices of Unleaded Gasoline** In Cents Per Gallon

| Year | Jan. | Feb. | Mar. | Apr. | May | June | July | Aug. | Sept. | Oct. | Nov. | Dec. | Average |
|---|---|---|---|---|---|---|---|---|---|---|---|---|---|
| 1987 | 49.23 | 47.64 | 51.13 | 50.54 | 54.18 | 55.75 | 55.78 | 52.43 | 51.71 | 54.03 | 51.68 | 45.58 | 51.64 |
| 1988 | 45.14 | 45.79 | 45.25 | 50.89 | 52.20 | 51.70 | 55.12 | 48.18 | 46.40 | 51.15 | 52.39 | 47.22 | 49.29 |
| 1989 | 50.24 | 48.47 | 54.91 | 69.98 | 67.97 | 63.75 | 56.34 | 52.81 | 59.29 | 55.76 | 50.80 | 53.94 | 57.02 |
| 1990 | 64.20 | 59.59 | 56.15 | 61.86 | 64.24 | 64.55 | 65.25 | 89.61 | 99.85 | 95.68 | 88.10 | 68.07 | 73.10 |
| 1991 | 68.88 | 65.82 | 74.25 | 72.07 | 70.28 | 63.59 | 65.23 | 69.90 | 62.17 | 64.41 | 65.10 | 55.55 | 66.44 |
| 1992 | 53.04 | 55.14 | 54.10 | 59.75 | 63.48 | 64.51 | 59.94 | 62.06 | 61.63 | 60.81 | 58.22 | 53.24 | 58.83 |
| 1993 | 52.96 | 52.54 | 54.33 | 59.35 | 59.37 | 54.78 | 51.80 | 53.13 | 48.61 | 50.22 | 44.30 | 37.68 | 51.59 |
| 1994 | 42.40 | 43.75 | 44.04 | 48.98 | 50.62 | 52.84 | 54.52 | 55.61 | 46.53 | 51.14 | 52.32 | 46.87 | 49.14 |
| 1995 | 50.99 | 51.43 | 50.74 | 61.01 | 64.76 | 59.47 | 51.45 | 53.45 | 56.10 | 48.89 | 51.15 | 53.44 | 54.41 |
| 1996 | 50.70 | 53.26 | 58.56 | 69.17 | 65.10 | 58.03 | 61.65 | 61.17 | 62.43 | 65.52 | 69.23 | 68.58 | 61.95 |

*Source: New York Mercantile Exchange (NYMEX)*

**Average Open Interest of Unleaded Regular Gasoline Futures in New York** In Contracts

| Year | Jan. | Feb. | Mar. | Apr. | May | June | July | Aug. | Sept. | Oct. | Nov. | Dec. |
|---|---|---|---|---|---|---|---|---|---|---|---|---|
| 1987 | 28,026 | 32,240 | 41,440 | 40,630 | 37,152 | 32,453 | 28,977 | 27,463 | 27,522 | 29,271 | 31,998 | 38,327 |
| 1988 | 39,887 | 43,055 | 44,006 | 46,094 | 46,517 | 50,754 | 57,897 | 51,064 | 49,636 | 49,649 | 49,877 | 50,893 |
| 1989 | 55,838 | 57,011 | 59,012 | 69,547 | 68,478 | 61,519 | 56,913 | 52,158 | 51,910 | 55,312 | 65,392 | 71,464 |
| 1990 | 77,580 | 80,425 | 75,368 | 71,132 | 62,121 | 72,105 | 68,826 | 59,528 | 60,558 | 61,253 | 56,332 | 56,569 |
| 1991 | 54,807 | 75,337 | 81,393 | 74,801 | 71,900 | 73,633 | 74,503 | 87,073 | 90,680 | 100,606 | 111,745 | 125,578 |
| 1992 | 124,896 | 117,155 | 108,388 | 89,775 | 79,680 | 80,394 | 81,110 | 76,741 | 71,264 | 68,059 | 71,110 | 77,508 |
| 1993 | 80,610 | 93,630 | 100,657 | 96,607 | 88,311 | 94,926 | 104,260 | 103,371 | 100,921 | 107,339 | 126,649 | 150,359 |
| 1994 | 135,366 | 120,204 | 118,977 | 122,092 | 96,525 | 89,854 | 86,401 | 76,213 | 67,881 | 70,258 | 71,245 | 63,679 |
| 1995 | 61,015 | 67,631 | 65,201 | 76,323 | 76,269 | 69,676 | 64,379 | 58,426 | 62,089 | 58,782 | 57,902 | 70,098 |
| 1996 | 64,561 | 64,990 | 70,100 | 71,895 | 66,172 | 52,882 | 55,394 | 55,618 | 57,119 | 59,993 | 58,416 | 62,760 |

*Source: New York Mercantile Exchange (NYMEX)*

## Volume of Trading of Unleaded Regular Gasoline Futures in New York In Contracts

| Year | Jan. | Feb. | Mar. | Apr. | May | June | July | Aug. | Sept. | Oct. | Nov. | Dec. | Total |
|---|---|---|---|---|---|---|---|---|---|---|---|---|---|
| 1987 | 135,208 | 139,885 | 211,590 | 214,982 | 178,735 | 175,585 | 182,661 | 154,685 | 155,352 | 166,365 | 152,176 | 190,014 | 2,057,238 |
| 1988 | 196,616 | 191,231 | 245,019 | 217,139 | 257,507 | 330,009 | 401,196 | 254,010 | 294,512 | 355,982 | 308,438 | 240,366 | 3,292,025 |
| 1989 | 354,167 | 258,669 | 373,936 | 510,964 | 407,445 | 443,205 | 356,939 | 310,546 | 412,753 | 375,489 | 328,277 | 352,168 | 4,484,558 |
| 1990 | 540,633 | 349,439 | 461,438 | 481,665 | 527,637 | 472,377 | 456,342 | 549,702 | 373,102 | 386,472 | 314,051 | 248,137 | 5,160,995 |
| 1991 | 366,772 | 351,188 | 525,432 | 541,073 | 482,943 | 446,350 | 396,429 | 562,085 | 386,421 | 477,111 | 537,834 | 529,940 | 5,603,578 |
| 1992 | 565,922 | 558,476 | 604,678 | 668,490 | 580,088 | 620,114 | 600,897 | 545,520 | 469,844 | 563,856 | 435,847 | 461,025 | 6,674,757 |
| 1993 | 531,780 | 558,770 | 584,899 | 539,785 | 571,860 | 611,951 | 594,740 | 721,852 | 642,959 | 629,733 | 674,814 | 729,717 | 7,392,860 |
| 1994 | 634,027 | 526,505 | 615,594 | 677,891 | 636,990 | 673,034 | 601,980 | 748,415 | 569,384 | 684,670 | 582,359 | 519,987 | 7,470,836 |
| 1995 | 592,329 | 506,640 | 736,704 | 663,743 | 780,568 | 680,792 | 565,655 | 556,589 | 573,551 | 473,014 | 480,507 | 461,695 | 7,071,787 |
| 1996 | 543,818 | 449,537 | 570,341 | 676,193 | 623,347 | 467,953 | 533,793 | 463,830 | 469,036 | 527,553 | 487,624 | 499,314 | 6,312,339 |

*Source: New York Mercantile Exchange (NYMEX)*

## United States Production of Finished Motor Gasoline Thousand Barrels Per Day

| Year | Jan. | Feb. | Mar. | Apr. | May | June | July | Aug. | Sept. | Oct. | Nov. | Dec. | Average |
|---|---|---|---|---|---|---|---|---|---|---|---|---|---|
| 1985 | 5,926 | 5,914 | 6,072 | 6,344 | 6,564 | 6,780 | 6,788 | 6,814 | 6,299 | 6,356 | 6,480 | 6,651 | 6,419 |
| 1986 | 6,522 | 6,302 | 6,061 | 6,498 | 7,095 | 7,101 | 6,956 | 7,092 | 6,891 | 6,616 | 6,895 | 6,970 | 6,752 |
| 1987 | 6,714 | 6,365 | 6,569 | 6,850 | 6,991 | 7,089 | 7,043 | 6,933 | 6,921 | 6,668 | 6,907 | 7,015 | 6,841 |
| 1988 | 6,730 | 6,736 | 6,715 | 6,907 | 6,851 | 6,983 | 7,159 | 7,209 | 6,948 | 6,858 | 7,060 | 7,303 | 6,956 |
| 1989 | 6,937 | 6,650 | 6,612 | 6,811 | 6,894 | 7,275 | 7,360 | 7,155 | 7,069 | 6,845 | 7,046 | 6,884 | 6,963 |
| 1990 | 6,879 | 6,989 | 6,613 | 6,775 | 6,610 | 7,101 | 7,238 | 7,326 | 7,274 | 6,880 | 6,940 | 6,887 | 6,959 |
| 1991 | 6,629 | 6,573 | 6,643 | 6,742 | 7,063 | 7,351 | 7,274 | 7,247 | 7,030 | 6,749 | 7,018 | 7,354 | 6,975 |
| 1992 | 7,013 | 6,726 | 6,683 | 6,954 | 7,092 | 7,198 | 7,195 | 6,817 | 7,071 | 7,198 | 7,323 | 7,411 | 7,058 |
| 1993 | 7,228 | 7,144 | 6,904 | 7,126 | 7,446 | 7,442 | 7,337 | 7,335 | 7,573 | 7,394 | 7,652 | 7,725 | 7,360 |
| 1994 | 7,097 | 6,790 | 6,760 | 7,195 | 7,348 | 7,455 | 7,380 | 7,432 | 7,385 | 7,151 | 7,849 | 7,867 | 7,312 |
| 1995 | 7,303 | 7,243 | 7,168 | 7,529 | 7,678 | 7,843 | 7,747 | 7,642 | 7,785 | 7,544 | 7,739 | 7,821 | 7,588 |
| 1996[1] | 7,333 | 7,303 | 7,242 | 7,475 | 7,724 | 7,820 | 7,811 | 7,696 | 7,585 | 7,496 | 7,835 | 7,754 | 7,590 |

[1] Preliminary. *Source: Energy Information Adminstration, U.S. Department of Energy*

# GASOLINE

### United States Disposition of Finished Motor Gasoline, Total Product Supplied     Thousand Barrels Per Day

| Year | Jan. | Feb. | Mar. | Apr. | May | June | July | Aug. | Sept. | Oct. | Nov. | Dec. | Average |
|---|---|---|---|---|---|---|---|---|---|---|---|---|---|
| 1987 | 6,535 | 6,796 | 6,964 | 7,314 | 7,460 | 7,539 | 7,581 | 7,338 | 7,205 | 7,305 | 7,151 | 7,251 | 7,206 |
| 1988 | 6,693 | 7,039 | 7,323 | 7,430 | 7,303 | 7,817 | 7,482 | 7,556 | 7,404 | 7,271 | 7,379 | 7,344 | 7,336 |
| 1989 | 6,745 | 7,119 | 7,421 | 7,157 | 7,381 | 7,780 | 7,296 | 7,717 | 7,240 | 7,302 | 7,353 | 7,410 | 7,328 |
| 1990 | 6,643 | 7,179 | 7,338 | 7,121 | 7,358 | 7,519 | 7,496 | 7,796 | 6,914 | 7,226 | 7,241 | 6,978 | 7,235 |
| 1991 | 6,645 | 6,838 | 7,017 | 7,137 | 7,437 | 7,456 | 7,561 | 7,528 | 7,083 | 7,281 | 7,008 | 7,224 | 7,188 |
| 1992 | 6,869 | 6,963 | 7,137 | 7,238 | 7,328 | 7,460 | 7,639 | 7,380 | 7,344 | 7,338 | 7,102 | 7,396 | 7,268 |
| 1993 | 6,639 | 7,112 | 7,389 | 7,435 | 7,585 | 7,700 | 7,785 | 7,864 | 7,607 | 7,382 | 7,533 | 7,661 | 7,476 |
| 1994 | 6,980 | 7,275 | 7,395 | 7,564 | 7,644 | 7,922 | 7,884 | 7,975 | 7,615 | 7,548 | 7,464 | 7,924 | 7,601 |
| 1995 | 7,163 | 7,481 | 7,788 | 7,651 | 7,894 | 8,220 | 7,888 | 8,187 | 7,786 | 7,781 | 7,866 | 7,742 | 7,789 |
| 1996[1] | 7,254 | 7,552 | 7,729 | 7,869 | 7,998 | 8,089 | 8,135 | 8,216 | 7,641 | 8,038 | 7,875 | 7,802 | 7,850 |

[1] Preliminary. *Source: Energy Information Adminstration, U.S. Department of Energy*

### Stocks of Finished Gasoline[2] on Hand in the United States     In Millions of Barrrels

| Year | Jan. | Feb. | Mar. | Apr. | May | June | July | Aug. | Sept. | Oct. | Nov. | Dec. |
|---|---|---|---|---|---|---|---|---|---|---|---|---|
| 1987 | 213.0 | 209.0 | 207.2 | 202.9 | 197.7 | 194.5 | 190.8 | 190.0 | 193.4 | 184.1 | 190.2 | 191.1 |
| 1988 | 203.1 | 205.1 | 196.4 | 192.1 | 190.8 | 176.7 | 181.2 | 185.4 | 184.6 | 182.3 | 185.8 | 192.0 |
| 1989 | 207.8 | 205.7 | 191.1 | 190.6 | 185.8 | 180.1 | 192.1 | 183.8 | 187.5 | 184.8 | 187.1 | 179.1 |
| 1990 | 197.6 | 203.3 | 187.9 | 186.3 | 180.3 | 177.7 | 182.0 | 175.4 | 190.5 | 181.9 | 178.7 | 182.4 |
| 1991 | 189.1 | 182.7 | 174.4 | 171.9 | 173.7 | 178.5 | 173.5 | 172.8 | 179.1 | 168.3 | 173.3 | 183.3 |
| 1992 | 192.8 | 191.4 | 182.9 | 185.0 | 187.4 | 189.5 | 182.0 | 168.2 | 170.0 | 168.7 | 178.2 | 179.1 |
| 1993 | 197.8 | 201.9 | 189.0 | 184.0 | 186.8 | 184.2 | 176.8 | 166.7 | 171.2 | 175.6 | 182.6 | 187.1 |
| 1994 | 194.1 | 186.2 | 175.6 | 176.4 | 179.0 | 176.9 | 172.9 | 167.6 | 169.2 | 161.7 | 176.6 | 175.9 |
| 1995 | 182.7 | 180.0 | 167.8 | 167.1 | 167.1 | 163.5 | 166.0 | 154.6 | 158.9 | 155.6 | 155.6 | 161.3 |
| 1996[1] | 169.3 | 168.8 | 159.4 | 160.3 | 163.1 | 165.0 | 162.8 | 154.9 | 161.4 | 149.2 | 151.3 | 157.5 |

[1] Preliminary. [2] Includes oxygenated and other finished. *Source: Energy Information Administration, U.S. Department of Energy*

### Refiner Sales Prices of Finished Motor Gasoline to End Users (Excluding Taxes)[1]     In Cents Per Gallon

| Year | Jan. | Feb. | Mar. | Apr. | May | June | July | Aug. | Sept. | Oct. | Nov. | Dec. | Average |
|---|---|---|---|---|---|---|---|---|---|---|---|---|---|
| 1987 | 59.7 | 62.1 | 62.7 | 64.9 | 66.3 | 67.7 | 69.6 | 71.6 | 70.5 | 69.7 | 69.4 | 67.4 | 66.9 |
| 1988 | 64.9 | 63.3 | 62.5 | 66.0 | 68.4 | 68.1 | 69.9 | 71.8 | 70.0 | 68.0 | 67.6 | 66.1 | 67.3 |
| 1989 | 65.6 | 66.1 | 68.4 | 81.7 | 85.5 | 84.5 | 82.0 | 76.6 | 74.9 | 74.7 | 72.7 | 72.1 | 75.6 |
| 1990 | 78.8 | 76.5 | 75.1 | 77.9 | 80.2 | 81.5 | 80.8 | 92.4 | 101.2 | 108.7 | 107.2 | 98.4 | 88.3 |
| 1991 | 88.8 | 79.5 | 74.0 | 77.0 | 82.0 | 81.9 | 78.9 | 81.1 | 80.2 | 77.9 | 79.1 | 76.0 | 79.7 |
| 1992 | 71.2 | 70.2 | 71.0 | 74.6 | 80.3 | 84.0 | 83.5 | 82.3 | 82.3 | 81.3 | 81.4 | 78.5 | 78.4 |
| 1993 | 76.9 | 76.1 | 75.7 | 77.8 | 80.1 | 79.8 | 77.6 | 76.2 | 74.9 | 75.3 | 72.5 | 68.0 | 75.9 |
| 1994 | 66.8 | 67.6 | 67.3 | 69.5 | 71.1 | 74.1 | 77.0 | 81.5 | 79.6 | 76.9 | 77.5 | 75.1 | 73.8 |
| 1995 | 74.5 | 73.3 | 73.1 | 77.3 | 83.4 | 83.9 | 80.0 | 76.9 | 75.8 | 73.6 | 71.8 | 73.0 | 76.5 |
| 1996[2] | 74.6 | 74.8 | 79.8 | 88.1 | 92.7 | 90.3 | 87.5 | 84.9 | 84.4 | 84.4 | 86.7 | | 84.4 |

[1] Excludes aviation. [2] Preliminary. *Source: Energy Information Administration, U.S. Department of Energy*

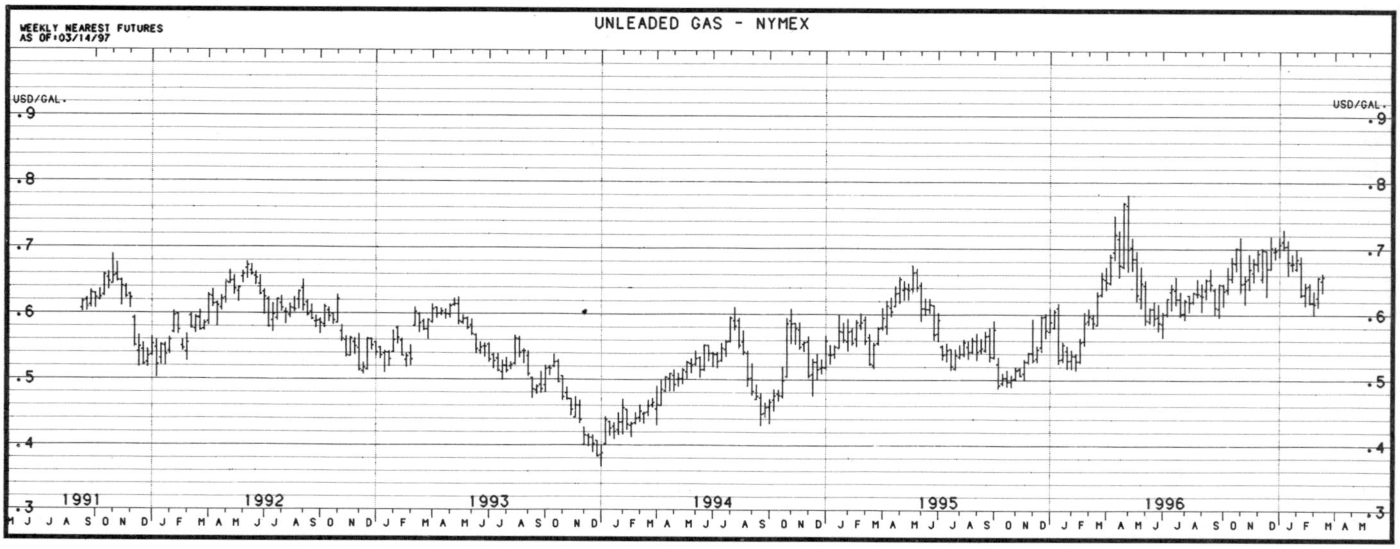

## U.S. Average Retail Selling Prices of Motor Gasoline (Including Taxes) In Cents Per Gallon

| Year | Jan. | Feb. | Mar. | Apr. | May | June | July | Aug. | Sept. | Oct. | Nov. | Dec. | Average |
|---|---|---|---|---|---|---|---|---|---|---|---|---|---|
| | | | | | | | Unleaded Premium | | | | | | |
| 1984 | 136.9 | 136.1 | 136.2 | 137.5 | 138.0 | 137.7 | 137.0 | 135.5 | 136.0 | 136.5 | 136.4 | 135.4 | 136.6 |
| 1985 | 130.4 | 129.0 | 131.0 | 134.0 | 136.0 | 137.1 | 136.7 | 135.9 | 134.9 | 134.2 | 133.9 | 134.4 | 134.0 |
| 1986 | 133.6 | 128.2 | 116.0 | 106.1 | 107.5 | 110.0 | 104.5 | 99.9 | 101.0 | 98.7 | 98.0 | 98.4 | 108.5 |
| 1987 | 100.7 | 104.7 | 105.2 | 107.3 | 107.9 | 109.8 | 111.5 | 113.9 | 113.6 | 112.8 | 112.5 | 111.9 | 109.3 |
| 1988 | 109.5 | 108.2 | 107.4 | 108.8 | 110.5 | 111.1 | 112.3 | 113.8 | 113.0 | 111.9 | 111.6 | 110.1 | 110.7 |
| 1989 | 109.1 | 110.0 | 111.5 | 122.1 | 127.8 | 127.8 | 126.4 | 123.3 | 121.3 | 120.9 | 118.7 | 117.0 | 119.7 |
| 1990 | 123.0 | 122.7 | 121.8 | 123.3 | 124.8 | 127.1 | 127.2 | 136.9 | 146.7 | 155.4 | 155.9 | 153.7 | 134.9 |
| 1991 | 143.1 | 132.1 | 126.4 | 128.1 | 133.1 | 133.8 | 131.3 | 131.8 | 132.4 | 130.7 | 131.8 | 130.9 | 132.1 |
| 1992 | 126.7 | 124.8 | 125.0 | 126.8 | 131.7 | 135.9 | 136.3 | 134.8 | 134.6 | 134.5 | 135.1 | 133.0 | 131.6 |
| 1993 | 131.3 | 130.1 | 129.4 | 130.4 | 131.9 | 132.1 | 130.5 | 129.4 | 128.2 | 132.3 | 130.5 | 126.8 | 130.2 |
| 1994 | 124.0 | 124.5 | 124.3 | 126.0 | 127.4 | 130.0 | 132.7 | 136.7 | 136.4 | 134.5 | 135.4 | 133.7 | 130.5 |
| 1995 | 132.4 | 131.6 | 130.6 | 132.5 | 138.3 | 141.1 | 138.4 | 135.2 | 133.2 | 131.5 | 129.2 | 129.0 | 133.6 |
| 1996[1] | 131.7 | 131.1 | 134.8 | 143.1 | 150.7 | 148.1 | 145.3 | 142.1 | 141.7 | 140.8 | 142.8 | 143.8 | 141.3 |
| | | | | | | | Unleaded Regular | | | | | | |
| 1984 | 121.6 | 120.9 | 121.0 | 122.7 | 123.6 | 122.9 | 121.2 | 119.6 | 120.3 | 120.9 | 120.7 | 119.3 | 121.2 |
| 1985 | 114.8 | 113.1 | 115.9 | 120.5 | 123.1 | 124.1 | 124.2 | 122.9 | 121.6 | 120.4 | 120.7 | 120.8 | 120.2 |
| 1986 | 119.4 | 112.0 | 98.1 | 88.8 | 92.3 | 95.5 | 89.0 | 84.3 | 86.0 | 83.1 | 82.1 | 82.3 | 92.7 |
| 1987 | 86.2 | 90.5 | 91.2 | 93.4 | 94.1 | 95.8 | 97.1 | 99.5 | 99.0 | 97.6 | 97.6 | 96.1 | 94.8 |
| 1988 | 93.3 | 91.3 | 90.4 | 93.0 | 95.5 | 95.5 | 96.7 | 98.7 | 97.4 | 95.7 | 94.9 | 93.0 | 94.6 |
| 1989 | 91.8 | 92.6 | 94.0 | 106.5 | 111.9 | 111.4 | 109.2 | 105.7 | 102.9 | 102.7 | 99.9 | 98.0 | 102.1 |
| 1990 | 104.2 | 103.7 | 102.3 | 104.4 | 106.1 | 108.8 | 108.4 | 119.0 | 129.4 | 137.8 | 137.7 | 135.4 | 116.4 |
| 1991 | 124.7 | 114.3 | 108.2 | 110.4 | 115.6 | 116.0 | 112.7 | 114.0 | 114.3 | 112.2 | 113.4 | 112.3 | 114.0 |
| 1992 | 107.3 | 105.4 | 105.8 | 107.9 | 113.6 | 117.9 | 117.5 | 115.8 | 115.8 | 115.4 | 115.9 | 113.6 | 112.7 |
| 1993 | 111.7 | 110.8 | 109.8 | 111.2 | 112.9 | 113.0 | 110.9 | 109.7 | 108.5 | 112.7 | 111.3 | 107.0 | 110.8 |
| 1994 | 104.3 | 105.1 | 104.5 | 106.4 | 108.0 | 110.6 | 113.6 | 118.2 | 117.7 | 115.2 | 116.3 | 114.3 | 111.2 |
| 1995 | 112.9 | 112.0 | 111.5 | 114.0 | 120.0 | 122.6 | 119.5 | 116.4 | 114.8 | 112.7 | 110.1 | 110.1 | 114.7 |
| 1996[1] | 112.9 | 112.4 | 116.2 | 125.1 | 132.3 | 129.9 | 127.2 | 124.0 | 123.4 | 122.7 | 125.0 | 126.0 | 123.1 |
| | | | | | | | All-Types[2] | | | | | | |
| 1984 | 120.0 | 119.3 | 119.4 | 121.1 | 122.1 | 121.4 | 119.7 | 118.4 | 118.9 | 119.5 | 119.3 | 117.9 | 119.8 |
| 1985 | 114.5 | 112.8 | 115.5 | 119.9 | 122.3 | 123.3 | 123.3 | 122.2 | 120.9 | 119.8 | 120.1 | 120.3 | 119.6 |
| 1986 | 119.0 | 111.9 | 98.3 | 89.5 | 92.7 | 95.8 | 89.5 | 84.8 | 86.4 | 83.7 | 82.7 | 83.0 | 93.1 |
| 1987 | 86.8 | 91.1 | 91.8 | 94.0 | 94.8 | 96.6 | 98.0 | 100.4 | 100.0 | 98.8 | 98.7 | 97.5 | 95.7 |
| 1988 | 94.7 | 92.8 | 92.0 | 94.6 | 97.0 | 97.1 | 98.4 | 100.4 | 99.2 | 97.6 | 97.2 | 95.3 | 96.3 |
| 1989 | 94.4 | 95.5 | 97.4 | 109.8 | 115.2 | 115.0 | 113.2 | 109.6 | 107.3 | 107.1 | 104.6 | 103.0 | 106.0 |
| 1990 | 109.0 | 108.6 | 107.6 | 109.6 | 111.4 | 114.0 | 113.9 | 124.6 | 134.7 | 143.1 | 143.2 | 141.0 | 121.7 |
| 1991 | 130.4 | 119.8 | 113.8 | 115.9 | 120.9 | 121.4 | 118.5 | 119.6 | 119.9 | 118.0 | 119.3 | 118.2 | 119.6 |
| 1992 | 113.5 | 111.7 | 112.2 | 114.3 | 119.7 | 123.9 | 123.8 | 122.1 | 122.2 | 121.9 | 122.3 | 120.1 | 119.0 |
| 1993 | 118.2 | 117.2 | 116.3 | 117.5 | 119.3 | 119.4 | 117.4 | 116.3 | 115.1 | 119.3 | 117.8 | 113.6 | 117.3 |
| 1994 | 110.9 | 111.4 | 110.9 | 112.8 | 114.3 | 116.7 | 119.9 | 124.3 | 123.7 | 121.2 | 122.2 | 120.3 | 117.4 |
| 1995 | 119.0 | 118.1 | 117.3 | 119.7 | 125.6 | 128.1 | 125.2 | 122.2 | 120.6 | 118.5 | 116.1 | 116.0 | 120.5 |
| 1996[1] | 118.6 | 118.1 | 121.9 | 130.5 | 137.8 | 135.4 | 132.8 | 129.8 | 129.3 | 128.7 | 130.8 | 131.8 | 128.8 |

[1] Preliminary. [2] Also includes types of motor oil not shown separately. *Source: Energy Information Administration, U.S. Department of Energy*

## U.S. Refiner Sales Prices of Finished Aviation Gasoline to End Users[2] In Cents Per Gallon

| Year | Jan. | Feb. | Mar. | Apr. | May | June | July | Aug. | Sept. | Oct. | Nov. | Dec. | Average |
|---|---|---|---|---|---|---|---|---|---|---|---|---|---|
| 1984 | 123.9 | 123.7 | 123.8 | 124.4 | 123.9 | 124.6 | 124.3 | 123.2 | 123.7 | 123.3 | 119.3 | 121.9 | 123.4 |
| 1985 | 121.7 | 121.1 | 121.4 | 121.2 | 121.9 | 121.7 | 120.2 | 118.9 | 119.5 | 118.9 | 118.3 | 117.0 | 120.1 |
| 1986 | 116.2 | 117.2 | 111.5 | 104.3 | 102.2 | 101.0 | 98.2 | 94.9 | 93.2 | 91.2 | 87.2 | 88.8 | 101.1 |
| 1987 | 87.9 | 89.7 | 90.3 | 89.8 | 90.6 | 91.3 | 91.5 | 92.4 | 91.9 | 91.4 | 91.0 | 90.0 | 90.7 |
| 1988 | 88.4 | 88.2 | 87.7 | 87.6 | 89.2 | 87.2 | 89.7 | 92.2 | 90.8 | 88.7 | 89.2 | 89.2 | 89.1 |
| 1989 | 89.2 | 89.7 | 90.6 | 99.1 | 107.0 | 107.1 | 105.5 | 101.9 | 100.7 | 100.4 | 98.6 | 97.3 | 99.5 |
| 1990 | 102.0 | 102.4 | 100.9 | 101.4 | 103.6 | 104.2 | 103.9 | 112.8 | 125.6 | 134.4 | 131.7 | 122.5 | 112.0 |
| 1991 | 112.1 | 106.4 | 101.3 | 101.2 | 105.3 | 105.2 | 103.6 | 105.8 | 105.7 | 104.6 | 104.3 | 102.0 | 104.7 |
| 1992 | 98.5 | 98.5 | 98.0 | 99.1 | 102.4 | 106.4 | 106.8 | 105.7 | 104.9 | 104.3 | 103.4 | 101.3 | 102.7 |
| 1993 | 100.3 | 99.9 | 99.4 | 100.7 | 102.2 | 102.5 | 99.7 | 98.8 | 98.2 | 98.0 | 95.7 | 91.2 | 99.0 |
| 1994 | 88.6 | 88.4 | 89.0 | 91.3 | 92.3 | 95.6 | 95.9 | 101.7 | 101.1 | 100.0 | 100.0 | 99.2 | 95.6 |
| 1995 | 99.6 | 99.8 | 99.0 | 101.3 | 105.8 | 106.4 | 101.8 | 99.2 | 101.3 | 96.8 | 95.4 | 96.0 | 100.5 |
| 1996[1] | 97.6 | 100.6 | 105.0 | 111.2 | 114.4 | 113.5 | 113.7 | 114.4 | 114.3 | 115.0 | 115.1 | | 110.4 |

[1] Preliminary. [2] Excluding taxes. *Source: Energy Information Administration, U.S. Department of Energy*

# Gold

Gold traded within a $370-400 per ounce range during 1994 and 1995, but in early 1996 the tight trading range finally gave way as prices penetrated $400. By February prices were nearing $420, basis COMEX futures, the highest level for gold since 1990. However, through the rest of 1996 prices drifted lower in lethargic trading and by yearend prices were trading near $370, the low of the 3-year trading range. Significantly, the ranks of gold bulls appeared to thin during 1996 as there was little overt publicity suggesting that $500 an ounce gold was just around the corner. What was evident was a lack of interest by both bulls and bears.

The psychology towards gold as a safe haven asset has changed, but it would be premature to suggest the change is permanent. Gold's long standing appeal as the one true hedge has diminished due to the myriad of global financial and derivative markets which offer "truer" hedges against economic and/or political uncertainties. Still, gold has a historical edge on contemporary alternatives and it's probably safe to say the metal will always have a speculative following. Gold's world production costs apparently average in the low $200 an ounce range, suggesting that much of the metal's market price above costs and profit margins is a speculative based premium, but one that's eroding.

Traders buying enthusiasm throughout the world in 1996, notably in the U.S., focused on the equity and interest rate markets. On the backburner were inflationary fears, without which it's difficult for gold to sustain higher prices. The bull move in equities siphoned risk capital away from gold, but even when the gold market showed signs of rallying the move was quickly nipped on rumors of increased central bank and/or IMF gold sales.

World gold production (mined) in 1996 of 2250 tons compares with 2272 in 1995 and 2280 in 1994. South Africa, the world's largest producer, mined 520 tons in 1995, the lowest output in years and down from 600 tons in 1994. The U.S., the second largest producer since 1991, mined 313,000 kg in 1995 and 147,000 kg in the first half of 1996. Nevada accounts for nearly two-thirds of U.S. mine production, 222,000 kg in 1995, with California a distant second at 20,500 kg. Net official world gold sales in 1996 were estimated at 250 tons vs. 198 in 1995, and only 85 tons in 1994. Gold scrap yielded about 650 tons in 1996 and 602 in 1995. Total world gold supplies for 1996 of 3150 tons compares with 3072 tons in 1995. World demand in 1996 is estimated at 3170 tons vs. 3470 in 1995, the decline largely reflecting investment demand of only 80 tons vs. 312 tons in 1995. Jewelry use is placed at 2620 tons vs. 2700, respectively.

Identified world gold resources are estimated at 75,000 tons with South Africa having one-half of the resources and the U.S. 12 percent. Of the estimated 120,000 tons of gold mined from historical times through 1995, about 15 percent is believed to have been lost or unaccounted for. Of the remaining 100,000 tons, central banks hold 35,000 tons with the balance privately held in the form of coins, jewelry, and bullion. The European Union gold reserves are estimated at 14,300 tons, half of which are in Germany and France. An uncertainty hanging over the gold market is European central bank sales to meet debt levels required for the introduction of a single European currency in 1999.

The U.S. is a net gold exporter, most of which is refined bullion shipped to Europe and Hong Kong. Exports in 1995 of 347,000 kg compare with imports of 126,000 kg. Through the first half of 1996, exports totaled about 274,000 kg and imports 65,200 kg, with Canada a major supplier. U.S. consumption of gold for industry and arts in the mid-1990's totals only about two-thirds of the late 1980's annual average of more than 110,000 kg.

### *Futures Markets*

Gold futures are traded on the Bolsa de Mercadorias & Futuros (BM&F), The Hong Kong Futures Exchange Ltd. (HKFE), the Tokyo Commodity Exchange (TOCOM), the Singapore International Monetary Exchange Ltd. (SIMEX), the Chicago Board of Trade (CBOT), the Mid America Commodity Exchange, (MidAm), and the New York Mercantile Exchange, COMEX division (COMEX). Gold options are traded on the the Vancouver Stock Exchange (VSE), the European Options Exchange (EOE-Optiebeurs), the MidAm, and the COMEX. Futures and options on Krugerrands are traded on the South Africa Futures Exchange (SAFEX).

**World Mine Production of Gold** In Kilograms (1 Kilogram = 32.1507 Troy Ounces)

| Year | Australia | Brazil | Canada | Chile | China | Colombia | Ghana | Indonesia | Mexico | Papua N.Guinea | Philippines | Russia[3] | South Africa | United States | Uzbekistan[3] | World Total |
|---|---|---|---|---|---|---|---|---|---|---|---|---|---|---|---|---|
| 1984 | 40,309 | 61,585 | 83,444 | 16,829 | 59,097 | 22,726 | 8,927 | 2,447 | 8,429 | 25,971 | 25,727 | 269,000 | 679,952 | 64,839 | ------ | 1,459,671 |
| 1985 | 58,521 | 72,160 | 87,561 | 17,240 | 61,000 | 35,532 | 9,322 | 2,619 | 8,264 | 36,908 | 33,063 | 270,000 | 670,754 | 75,495 | ------ | 1,531,858 |
| 1986 | 75,079 | 67,500 | 102,899 | 17,947 | 66,000 | 39,995 | 8,931 | 3,304 | 7,795 | 35,075 | 40,322 | 275,000 | 638,047 | 116,297 | ------ | 1,606,570 |
| 1987 | 110,696 | 83,700 | 115,818 | 17,035 | 72,000 | 26,546 | 10,201 | 3,643 | 7,988 | 33,250 | 32,599 | 260,000 | 607,000 | 153,870 | ------ | 1,660,535 |
| 1988 | 156,950 | 112,159 | 134,813 | 20,614 | 78,000 | 29,014 | 11,601 | 4,738 | 9,098 | 38,129 | 30,482 | 277,600 | 621,000 | 200,914 | ------ | 1,873,803 |
| 1989 | 203,563 | 52,527 | 159,527 | 22,559 | 90,000 | 29,506 | 13,358 | 6,155 | 10,000 | 27,538 | 30,040 | 304,000 | 607,460 | 265,731 | ------ | 2,013,913 |
| 1990 | 244,137 | 101,913 | 169,412 | 27,503 | 100,000 | 29,352 | 16,840 | 11,158 | 9,682 | 31,938 | 24,591 | 302,000 | 605,100 | 294,189 | ------ | 2,180,000 |
| 1991 | 234,218 | 89,578 | 176,552 | 28,879 | 120,000 | 34,844 | 26,311 | 16,879 | 10,142 | 60,780 | 25,916 | 260,000 | 601,110 | 294,062 | ------ | 2,190,000 |
| 1992 | 243,400 | 85,862 | 161,402 | 33,774 | 125,000 | 32,118 | 31,032 | 37,983 | 9,891 | 71,190 | 25,609 | 146,000 | 614,071 | 330,212 | 70,000 | 2,290,000 |
| 1993 | 247,196 | 74,219 | 152,929 | 33,638 | 130,000 | 27,472 | 39,235 | 42,097 | 11,100 | 60,587 | 21,155 | 149,500 | 619,201 | 331,013 | 70,000 | 2,310,000 |
| 1994[1] | 256,188 | 70,535 | 146,428 | 38,786 | 132,000 | 20,762 | 44,505 | 42,600 | 13,888 | 60,287 | 27,059 | 146,600 | 580,201 | 327,000 | 70,000 | 2,287,756 |
| 1995[2] | 253,504 | 72,000 | 150,273 | 39,180 | 140,000 | 21,160 | 52,200 | 62,800 | 20,292 | 52,635 | 27,144 | 132,170 | 523,820 | 320,000 | 75,000 | 2,381,315 |
| 1996[2] | 294,986 | 76,328 | 159,996 | 54,151 | 151,630 | 25,505 | 50,792 | 77,697 | 19,315 | 61,149 | 33,343 | NA | 561,729 | 349,541 | NA | 2,431,329 |

[1] Preliminary. [2] Estimate. [3] Formerly part of the U.S.S.R.; data not reported separately until 1992. NA = not avaliable. *Source: U.S. Geological Survey*

## Salient U.S. Gold Statistics    In Kilograms (1 Kilogram = 32.1507 Troy Ounces)

| | | | Refinery Production | | | | Stocks, Dec. 31 | | | | Consumption | | | |
|---|---|---|---|---|---|---|---|---|---|---|---|---|---|---|
| Year | Mine Production | Value Million $ | Domestic & Foreign Ores | Secondary (Old Scrap) | Exports (Excluding Coinage) | Imports for Consumption | Treasury Department[3] | Futures Exch. | Industry | Official World Reserves[4] | Dental | Industrial[5] | Jewelry & Arts | Total |
| 1986 | 155,365 | 1,819.0 | 75,618 | 47,266 | 155,365 | 489,863 | 8,149,938 | 87,370 | 28,771 | 35,743 | 7,921 | 36,858 | 65,827 | 110,795 |
| 1987 | 153,870 | 2,216.0 | 112,368 | 63,843 | 119,630 | 119,539 | 8,160,251 | 81,647 | 23,390 | 35,655 | 6,944 | 35,245 | 71,024 | 113,319 |
| 1988 | 200,914 | 2,831.3 | 137,829 | 61,391 | 328,237 | 92,457 | 8,145,696 | 44,634 | 38,360 | 35,829 | 7,576 | 37,226 | 67,027 | 111,836 |
| 1989 | 265,731 | 3,268.6 | 183,685 | 51,943 | 211,091 | 152,504 | 8,147,169 | 69,727 | 30,462 | 35,603 | 7,927 | 37,621 | 69,524 | 115,078 |
| 1990 | 294,189 | 3,640.8 | 225,183 | 43,980 | 296,397 | 97,519 | 8,146,432 | 50,881 | 37,065 | 35,572 | 8,700 | 30,996 | 78,514 | 118,216 |
| 1991 | 294,062 | 3,434.7 | 224,675 | 48,088 | 284,127 | 178,749 | 8,145,696 | 49,893 | 39,411 | 35,501 | 8,485 | 21,793 | 84,096 | 114,375 |
| 1992 | 330,212 | 3,662.4 | 283,951 | 53,396 | 368,851 | 174,341 | 8,145,000 | 46,453 | 36,713 | 35,199 | 6,543 | 20,360 | 83,508 | 110,410 |
| 1993 | 331,013 | 3,840.9 | 243,135 | 65,964 | 792,680 | 169,305 | 8,143,000 | 78,514 | 34,400 | 34,700 | 6,173 | 19,663 | 65,600 | 91,400 |
| 1994[1] | 327,000 | 4,050.0 | 240,584 | 74,332 | 471,000 | 114,000 | 8,142,000 | 49,100 | 32,700 | 34,500 | 5,430 | 17,013 | 53,700 | 76,100 |
| 1995[2] | 320,000 | 3,960.0 | NA | NA | 347,000 | 126,000 | 8,140,000 | 45,400 | NA | NA | NA | NA | NA | NA |

[1] Preliminary. [2] Estimate. [3] Includes gold in Exchange Stabilization Fund. [4] Held by market economy country central banks and governments and international monetary organizations. [5] Including space and defense. *Source: U.S. Geological Survey*

## Monthly Average Gold Price (Handy & Harman at New York)    Dollars Per Troy Ounce

| Year | Jan. | Feb. | Mar. | Apr. | May | June | July | Aug. | Sept. | Oct. | Nov. | Dec. | Average |
|---|---|---|---|---|---|---|---|---|---|---|---|---|---|
| 1984 | 370.90 | 386.00 | 394.40 | 381.70 | 377.30 | 377.70 | 346.40 | 347.70 | 340.90 | 340.10 | 340.90 | 319.00 | 360.23 |
| 1985 | 302.80 | 298.80 | 303.90 | 324.90 | 316.10 | 316.50 | 317.80 | 330.20 | 322.60 | 326.20 | 325.50 | 322.40 | 317.31 |
| 1986 | 345.50 | 339.30 | 345.40 | 304.60 | 340.50 | 342.80 | 348.90 | 376.90 | 419.00 | 423.60 | 398.80 | 391.20 | 367.70 |
| 1987 | 408.30 | 401.30 | 408.90 | 438.70 | 460.10 | 449.60 | 450.80 | 460.90 | 460.20 | 465.50 | 466.50 | 486.00 | 446.40 |
| 1988 | 476.60 | 441.90 | 443.60 | 451.80 | 450.80 | 451.30 | 437.60 | 431.30 | 412.80 | 406.80 | 420.10 | 418.50 | 436.93 |
| 1989 | 404.01 | 387.78 | 390.14 | 384.40 | 371.32 | 367.60 | 394.71 | 364.92 | 361.89 | 366.88 | 392.32 | 408.12 | 382.92 |
| 1990 | 410.10 | 416.80 | 393.10 | 374.30 | 369.20 | 352.30 | 362.50 | 395.00 | 389.50 | 380.70 | 381.70 | 378.20 | 383.61 |
| 1991 | 383.60 | 363.80 | 363.40 | 358.40 | 356.80 | 366.70 | 367.50 | 356.20 | 348.80 | 358.70 | 359.50 | 361.10 | 362.18 |
| 1992 | 354.50 | 353.90 | 344.30 | 338.50 | 337.20 | 340.80 | 353.00 | 343.00 | 345.40 | 344.40 | 335.10 | 334.70 | 343.74 |
| 1993 | 329.00 | 329.40 | 330.10 | 341.90 | 366.70 | 371.90 | 392.40 | 378.50 | 354.90 | 364.20 | 373.50 | 383.70 | 359.67 |
| 1994 | 387.02 | 382.01 | 384.13 | 378.20 | 381.21 | 385.64 | 385.44 | 380.43 | 391.80 | 389.77 | 349.43 | 379.60 | 384.14 |
| 1995 | 378.55 | 376.51 | 382.12 | 391.11 | 385.46 | 387.56 | 386.40 | 383.63 | 382.22 | 383.14 | 385.53 | 387.42 | 384.22 |
| 1996[1] | 399.59 | 404.73 | 396.21 | 392.96 | 391.98 | 385.58 | 383.69 | 387.43 | 382.97 | 381.07 | 378.46 | 369.02 | 387.81 |

[1] Preliminary. *Sources: U.S. Geological Survey; American Metal Market*

# GOLD

**Gold Average Open Interest at New York (COMEX)** In Thousands of Contracts

| Year | Jan. | Feb. | Mar. | Apr. | May | June | July | Aug. | Sept. | Oct. | Nov. | Dec. |
|---|---|---|---|---|---|---|---|---|---|---|---|---|
| 1987 | 137,650 | 134,151 | 146,896 | 172,605 | 169,606 | 147,703 | 147,005 | 149,345 | 147,346 | 139,482 | 137,383 | 154,110 |
| 1988 | 147,067 | 152,789 | 158,224 | 154,788 | 153,465 | 145,951 | 147,822 | 140,311 | 153,556 | 160,591 | 153,497 | 144,839 |
| 1989 | 162,226 | 166,455 | 167,419 | 160,215 | 180,709 | 164,196 | 154,517 | 150,414 | 151,836 | 146,262 | 154,927 | 151,788 |
| 1990 | 147,884 | 132,400 | 126,890 | 118,750 | 117,707 | 113,958 | 105,496 | 120,579 | 116,331 | 113,873 | 111,638 | 110,343 |
| 1991 | 104,666 | 98,000 | 98,429 | 101,266 | 100,341 | 88,961 | 94,467 | 99,790 | 105,053 | 96,302 | 109,030 | 109,004 |
| 1992 | 106,110 | 103,319 | 109,796 | 106,485 | 109,947 | 98,127 | 111,039 | 102,239 | 102,376 | 102,232 | 109,965 | 100,328 |
| 1993 | 112,420 | 109,093 | 115,505 | 142,208 | 172,491 | 170,829 | 200,168 | 180,509 | 166,201 | 152,531 | 152,853 | 154,730 |
| 1994 | 156,045 | 139,354 | 146,269 | 144,386 | 147,738 | 146,255 | 148,915 | 155,641 | 167,981 | 166,041 | 166,536 | 178,998 |
| 1995 | 184,549 | 170,972 | 168,651 | 191,667 | 173,805 | 174,075 | 175,727 | 176,135 | 185,128 | 185,854 | 170,674 | 141,751 |
| 1996 | 210,695 | 226,160 | 203,968 | 201,826 | 203,056 | 192,423 | 185,374 | 159,435 | 185,907 | 192,606 | 187,145 | 185,994 |

*Source: New York Mercantile Exchange, COMEX Division*

**Total Volume of Trading of Gold Futures at New York (COMEX)** In Thousands of Contracts

| Year | Jan. | Feb. | Mar. | Apr. | May | June | July | Aug. | Sept. | Oct. | Nov. | Dec. | Total |
|---|---|---|---|---|---|---|---|---|---|---|---|---|---|
| 1987 | 936.4 | 706.9 | 794.9 | 1,135.2 | 1,021.2 | 793.4 | 796.9 | 760.3 | 747.9 | 951.3 | 847.1 | 748.2 | 10,240 |
| 1988 | 815.0 | 778.7 | 965.0 | 637.7 | 866.2 | 946.3 | 884.2 | 587.5 | 790.9 | 694.5 | 895.5 | 634.9 | 9,496 |
| 1989 | 900.4 | 800.0 | 993.8 | 682.4 | 932.0 | 936.6 | 756.1 | 591.1 | 630.0 | 681.2 | 1,228.4 | 876.4 | 9,989 |
| 1990 | 1,327.1 | 885.1 | 975.6 | 472.4 | 745.2 | 541.0 | 747.4 | 1,191.5 | 729.4 | 879.9 | 705.3 | 530.1 | 9,730 |
| 1991 | 957.3 | 497.8 | 617.7 | 446.1 | 584.4 | 520.0 | 551.4 | 457.2 | 429.1 | 551.0 | 677.3 | 510.6 | 6,771 |
| 1992 | 729.8 | 388.4 | 607.3 | 425.4 | 485.4 | 427.2 | 734.6 | 500.2 | 465.3 | 414.1 | 504.1 | 320.1 | 6,002 |
| 1993 | 506.0 | 446.2 | 661.4 | 640.4 | 1,140.7 | 809.6 | 1,171.7 | 808.8 | 728.9 | 565.2 | 892.3 | 533.2 | 8,916 |
| 1994 | 981.8 | 584.0 | 889.5 | 589.2 | 922.6 | 740.2 | 723.8 | 626.0 | 645.6 | 651.2 | 687.8 | 461.5 | 8,503 |
| 1995 | 881.9 | 420.0 | 1,087.5 | 613.0 | 777.0 | 588.1 | 669.9 | 500.5 | 495.5 | 387.7 | 982.5 | 378.1 | 7,782 |
| 1996 | 1,384.7 | 987.5 | 943.6 | 647.1 | 858.5 | 582.1 | 424.8 | 541.9 | 541.9 | 528.5 | 795.2 | 458.8 | 8,695 |

*Source: New York Mercantile Exchange, COMEX Division*

## Commodity Exchange, Inc. (COMEX) Depository Warehouse Stocks of Gold In Thousands of Troy Ounces

| Year | Jan. 1 | Feb. 1 | Mar. 1 | Apr. 1 | May 1 | June 1 | July 1 | Aug. 1 | Sept. 1 | Oct. 1 | Nov. 1 | Dec. 1 |
|---|---|---|---|---|---|---|---|---|---|---|---|---|
| 1984 | 2,481 | 2,472 | 2,408 | 2,452 | 2,412 | 2,426 | 2,376 | 2,395 | 2,387 | 2,391 | 2,349 | 2,366 |
| 1985 | 2,308 | 2,308 | 2,273 | 2,109 | 2,136 | 2,142 | 2,133 | 2,107 | 2,119 | 2,083 | 2,099 | 2,105 |
| 1986 | 2,109 | 2,352 | 2,580 | 2,593 | 2,567 | 1,986 | 1,992 | 1,621 | 1,664 | 1,726 | 1,787 | 2,193 |
| 1987 | 2,890 | 2,798 | 2,817 | 2,903 | 2,628 | 2,665 | 2,614 | 2,624 | 2,670 | 2,636 | 2,644 | 2,645 |
| 1988 | 2,624 | 2,605 | 2,586 | 1,596 | 1,566 | 1,675 | 1,834 | 2,099 | 2,189 | 1,949 | 1,629 | 1,267 |
| 1989 | 1,434 | 1,408 | 1,454 | 1,532 | 1,606 | 1,634 | 1,602 | 1,602 | 1,433 | 1,483 | 1,731 | 2,263 |
| 1990 | 2,241 | 2,225 | 2,245 | 2,220 | 2,048 | 1,809 | 1,582 | 1,530 | 1,539 | 1,564 | 1,585 | 1,347 |
| 1991 | 1,636 | 1,686 | 1,540 | 1,298 | 1,458 | 1,711 | 1,772 | 1,875 | 1,220 | 1,342 | 1,302 | 1,479 |
| 1992 | 1,605 | 1,362 | 1,435 | 1,411 | 1,591 | 1,618 | 1,605 | 1,733 | 1,688 | 1,947 | 1,766 | 1,524 |
| 1993 | 1,507 | 1,340 | 1,365 | 1,426 | 1,383 | 2,231 | 2,247 | 2,448 | 2,437 | 2,425 | 2,349 | 2,552 |
| 1994 | 2,524 | 2,955 | 2,958 | 2,862 | 2,802 | 2,434 | 2,665 | 2,574 | 2,030 | 1,904 | 1,843 | 1,867 |
| 1995 | 1,577 | 1,498 | 1,386 | 1,360 | 1,391 | 1,488 | 1,505 | 1,608 | 1,448 | 1,745 | 1,395 | 1,315 |
| 1996 | 1,460 | 1,869 | 1,412 | 1,429 | 1,335 | 1,711 | 1,263 | 1,273 | 1,402 | 1,283 | 1,060 | 1,104 |

*Source: New York Mercantile Exchange, COMEX division*

## Central Gold Bank Reserves In Millions of Troy Ounces

| | Industrial Countries | | | | | | | | | | | | | | | |
|---|---|---|---|---|---|---|---|---|---|---|---|---|---|---|---|---|
| Year | Belgium | Canada | France | Germany | Italy | Japan | Netherlands | Switzerland | United Kingdom | United States | Industrial Total | Developing Oil | Developing Non-Oil | IMF[2] | Bank for Int'l Settlements | World Total |
| 1985 | 34.2 | 20.1 | 81.9 | 95.2 | 66.7 | 24.2 | 43.9 | 83.3 | 19.0 | 262.7 | 896.5 | 43.8 | 94.7 | 103.4 | 6.7 | 1,145.2 |
| 1986 | 34.2 | 19.7 | 81.9 | 95.2 | 66.7 | 24.2 | 43.9 | 83.3 | 19.0 | 262.0 | 895.6 | 43.7 | 100.3 | 103.4 | 6.4 | 1,149.5 |
| 1987 | 33.6 | 18.5 | 81.9 | 95.2 | 66.7 | 24.2 | 43.9 | 83.3 | 19.0 | 262.4 | 894.3 | 43.6 | 99.1 | 103.4 | 6.1 | 1,146.5 |
| 1988 | 33.7 | 17.1 | 81.9 | 95.2 | 66.7 | 24.2 | 43.9 | 83.3 | 19.0 | 261.9 | 895.1 | 42.0 | 99.1 | 103.4 | 6.4 | 1,146.1 |
| 1989 | 30.2 | 16.1 | 81.9 | 95.2 | 66.7 | 24.2 | 43.9 | 83.3 | 19.0 | 261.9 | 891.5 | 42.1 | 103.3 | 103.4 | 6.1 | 1,146.4 |
| 1990 | 30.2 | 14.8 | 81.9 | 95.2 | 66.7 | 24.2 | 43.9 | 83.3 | 18.9 | 261.9 | 889.4 | 41.5 | 101.3 | 103.4 | 6.6 | 1,142.2 |
| 1991 | 30.2 | 13.0 | 81.9 | 95.2 | 66.7 | 24.2 | 43.9 | 83.3 | 18.9 | 261.9 | 887.3 | 42.0 | 101.6 | 103.4 | 6.6 | 1,141.0 |
| 1992 | 25.0 | 9.9 | 81.9 | 95.2 | 66.7 | 24.2 | 43.9 | 83.3 | 18.6 | 261.8 | 877.4 | 42.0 | 101.7 | 103.4 | 6.8 | 1,131.3 |
| 1993 | 25.0 | 6.1 | 81.9 | 95.2 | 66.7 | 24.2 | 35.1 | 83.3 | 18.5 | 261.8 | 860.4 | 42.0 | 100.1 | 103.4 | 8.6 | 1,114.6 |
| 1994[1] | 25.0 | 4.0 | 81.9 | 95.2 | 66.7 | 24.2 | 34.8 | 83.3 | 18.4 | 261.8 | 867.3 | 42.0 | 99.7 | 103.4 | 7.3 | 1,109.6 |

[1] Thru October only. [2] International Monetary Fund. *Source: American Metal Market*

## U.S. Mine Production of Recoverable Gold In Kilograms

| Year | Arizona | California | Idaho | Montana | Nevada | Alaska | Colorado | South Dakota | New Mexico | Utah | Other States | Total |
|---|---|---|---|---|---|---|---|---|---|---|---|---|
| 1987 | 1,791 | 18,277 | 3,041 | 7,143 | 83,342 | 3,812 | 5,561 | W | W | W | 30,903 | 153,870 |
| 1988 | 4,549 | 22,442 | 3,218 | 9,175 | 114,322 | 4,210 | 5,126 | 13,981 | W | W | 23,891 | 200,914 |
| 1989 | 2,768 | 29,804 | 3,057 | 12,434 | 153,995 | 5,756 | 3,448 | 16,123 | 1,076 | W | 37,270 | 265,731 |
| 1990 | 5,000 | 29,607 | W | 13,012 | 179,078 | 3,232 | 2,357 | 17,870 | 888 | W | 43,145 | 294,189 |
| 1991 | 6,195 | 30,404 | 3,348 | 13,715 | 178,488 | 3,200 | 3,181 | 16,371 | W | W | 39,161 | 295,957 |
| 1992 | 6,656 | 33,335 | 4,037 | 13,994 | 203,393 | 5,003 | 3,763 | 18,681 | W | W | 41,350 | 329,124 |
| 1993 | 2,710 | 35,800 | 4,324 | 14,300 | 211,000 | 2,780 | W | 19,200 | 995 | W | 37,300 | 331,000 |
| 1994 | 2,540 | 28,880 | 3,610 | 13,300 | 203,000 | 5,740 | 4,420 | W | W | W | 50,100 | 306,000 |
| 1995[1] | 2,780 | 26,200 | 8,850 | 13,600 | 222,000 | W | W | W | W | W | 51,500 | 320,000 |
| 1996[2] | 1,590 | 18,700 | W | 7,820 | 158,000 | W | W | W | W | W | 45,600 | 231,000 |

[1] Preliminary. [2] January thru September. W = Withheld proprietary data, included in "Other States." *Source: U.S. Geological Survey*

## U.S. Consumption of Gold, by End-Use In Kilograms

| | Jewelry and the Arts | | | | | Industrial | | | | |
|---|---|---|---|---|---|---|---|---|---|---|
| Year | Gold-filled & Other | Electro-plating | Karat Gold | Total | Dental | Gold-filled & Other | Electro-plating | Karat Gold | Total | Grand Total |
| 1987 | 9,256 | 3,133 | 58,635 | 71,024 | 6,944 | 21,010 | 12,343 | 1,892 | 35,245 | 113,319 |
| 1988 | 7,598 | 1,469 | 57,959 | 67,027 | 7,576 | 21,034 | 15,088 | 1,104 | 37,226 | 111,836 |
| 1989 | 7,364 | 1,283 | 60,877 | 69,524 | 7,927 | 15,723 | 20,684 | 1,215 | 37,621 | 115,078 |
| 1990 | 8,132 | 429 | 69,952 | 78,514 | 8,700 | 12,725 | 17,251 | 1,020 | 30,996 | 118,216 |
| 1991 | 3,848 | 373 | 79,875 | 84,096 | 8,485 | 8,102 | 12,624 | 1,068 | 21,793 | 114,375 |
| 1992 | 3,546 | 581 | 79,381 | 83,508 | 6,543 | 8,802 | 10,476 | 1,082 | 20,360 | 110,410 |
| 1993 | 3,532 | 373 | 61,700 | 65,600 | 6,173 | 9,474 | 9,094 | 1,095 | 19,663 | 91,400 |
| 1994[1] | 3,652 | 369 | 49,700 | 53,700 | 5,430 | 7,447 | 9,471 | 97 | 17,013 | 76,100 |

[1] Preliminary. *Source: U.S. Geological Survey*

# GOLD

GOLD IN BRITISH POUNDS
WEEKLY CASH
AS OF:03/14/97
RATIO
290
280
270
260
250
240
230
220
210
200
190
180
1994
1995
1996
1997
M A M J J A S O N D J F M A M J J A S O N D J F M A M J J A S O N D J F M A M J J

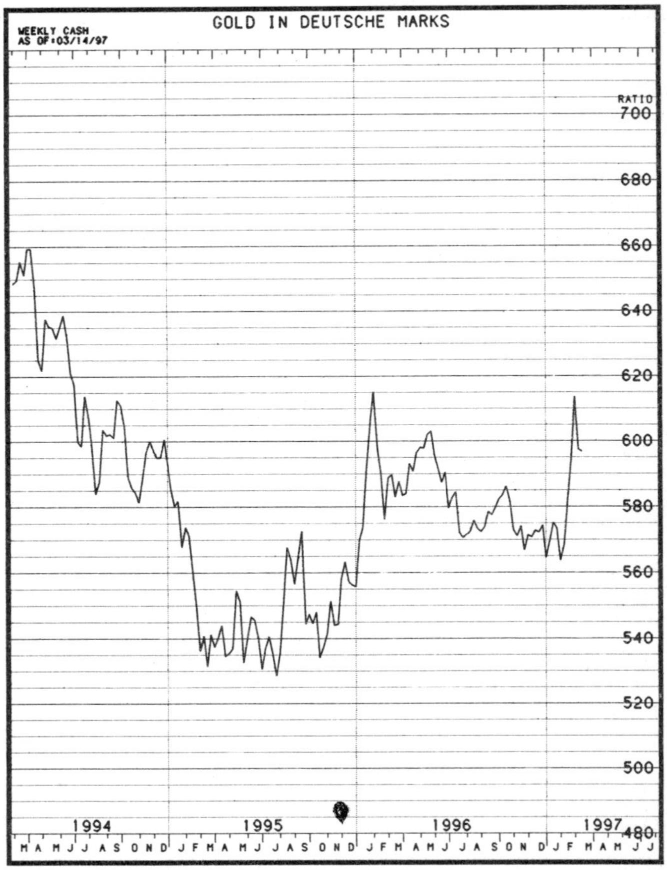
GOLD IN DEUTSCHE MARKS
WEEKLY CASH
AS OF:03/14/97
RATIO
700
680
660
640
620
600
580
560
540
520
500
480
1994
1995
1996
1997
M A M J J A S O N D J F M A M J J A S O N D J F M A M J J A S O N D J F M A M J J

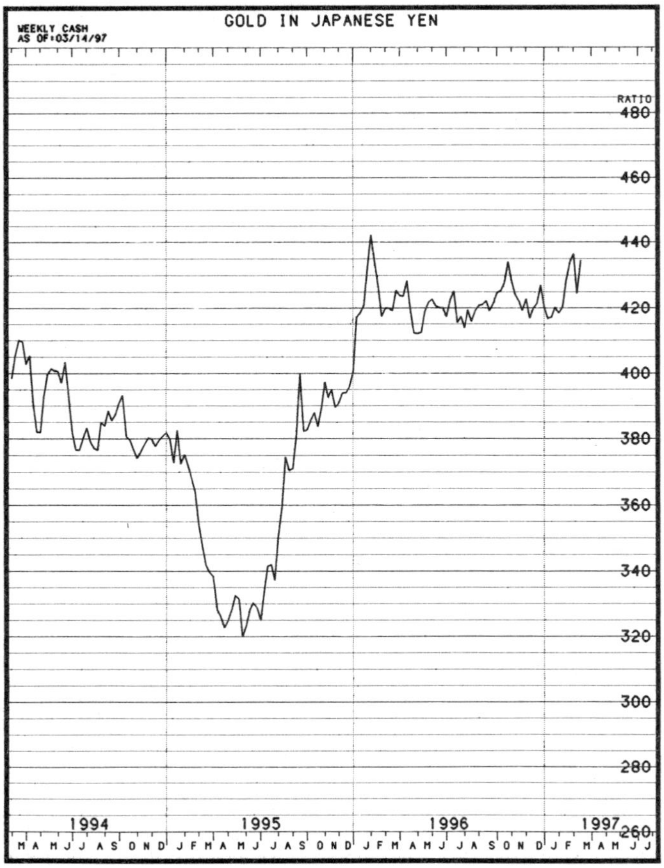
GOLD IN JAPANESE YEN
WEEKLY CASH
AS OF:03/14/97
RATIO
480
460
440
420
400
380
360
340
320
300
280
260
1994
1995
1996
1997
M A M J J A S O N D J F M A M J J A S O N D J F M A M J J A S O N D J F M A M J J

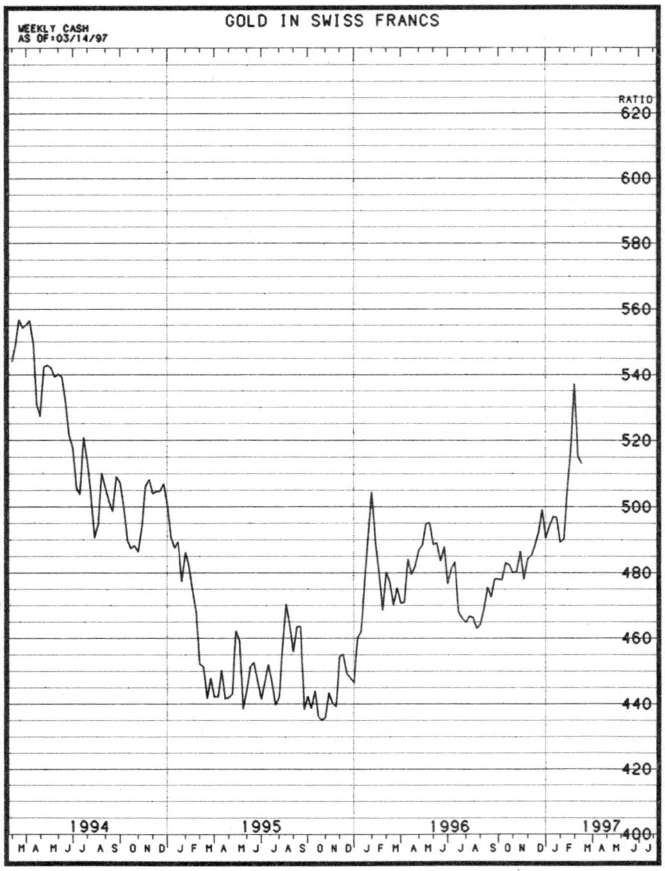
GOLD IN SWISS FRANCS
WEEKLY CASH
AS OF:03/14/97
RATIO
620
600
580
560
540
520
500
480
460
440
420
400
1994
1995
1996
1997
M A M J J A S O N D J F M A M J J A S O N D J F M A M J J A S O N D J F M A M J J

# Grain Sorghum

The U.S. is the world's largest producer of grain sorghum (milo) with India a distant second. World production in 1996/97 of 64.8 million metric tons compares with 54.5 million in 1995/96. The U.S. produced nearly a third of the world crop at 20.2 million tons; but in 1995/96 U.S. production of 11.7 million tons was the lowest of the 1990's and only 21 percent of world output. However, unlike most of the world's sorghum producing nations who consume their production domestically, the U.S. generally consumes two-thirds and exports the balance.

India's 1996/97 crop of 11 million tons compares with 9.7 million in 1995/96. Significantly, India sorghum acreage of 12.6 million hectares in 1996/97 accounts for nearly a third of the world's acreage of 41.7 million, but India's average yield appears to be the world's lowest; 0.87 mt/hectare vs. a world average in 1996/97 of 1.55 and a U.S. average of 4.14 mt/hectare. In contrast, China's 1996/97 average yield was one of the highest at 4.75 mt/hectare on acreage of only 1.2 million hectares yielding a crop of 4.75 million tons vs. 3.9 million in 1995/96.

World sorghum trade is small; 6.5 million tons in 1996/97 vs. 6.1 million in 1995/96 and an early 1990's average of 9 million tons. The U.S. is by far the largest exporter, mostly to Mexico and Japan, the two largest importers. Argentina is the second largest 1996/97 exporter with 500,000 tons vs. the U.S. total of 5.7 million. The world carryover totaled 9.4 million tons at the end of 1992/93, falling to 2.6 million by the end of 1995/96, but was expected to rebound to 3.7 million at the end of 1996/97, almost half of which will be in the U.S.

The U.S. sorghum crop year begins September 1. Kansas and Texas are the largest producing states with Nebraska a distant third. Production rebounded sharply in 1996/97 to 797 million bushels from 460 million in 1995/96. The Kansas crop nearly doubled to 350 million bushels from 174 million. The overall increase, however, largely reflected an increase in harvested acreage; to 12 million acres from 8.3 million and an average yield of 66.4 bushels per acre vs. 55.6 bushels, respectively.

Total U.S. supplies in 1996/97 of 815 million bushels compares with 532 million in 1995/96. No sorghum is imported into the U.S. Disappearance in 1996/97 of 754 million bushels compares with 514 million in 1995/96, of which 525 million bushels will be used in 1996/97 as a feed and 225 million exported vs. 310 million and 200 million, respectively. The projected 1996/97 carryover of 61 million bushels compares with a carryin of 18 million.

Sorghum prices received by farmers during 1996/97 were forecast to have a range of $2.55-$2.95 per bushel vs. a 1990's high of $3.19 in 1995/96 when prices were buoyed by low production. A year earlier, 1994/95, the average farm price was only $2.13. In late calendar 1996, #2 sorghum's cash price of $4.75 per cwt. compared with $6.40 a year earlier, basis Gulf port.

## World Sorghum Supply and Demand — In Thousands of Metric Tons

| Crop Year | Exports: Argentina | Exports: Non-U.S. | Exports: U.S. | Exports: Total | Imports: Japan | Imports: Mexico | Imports: Unaccounted | Imports: Total | Total Production | Utilization: China | Utilization: Japan | Utilization: Mexico | Utilization: U.S. | Utilization: Total | Ending Stocks: Non-U.S. | Ending Stocks: U.S. | Ending Stocks: Total |
|---|---|---|---|---|---|---|---|---|---|---|---|---|---|---|---|---|---|
| 1992-3 | 1,023 | 2,244 | 6,634 | 8,878 | 3,221 | 4,021 | 134 | 8,878 | 65,387 | 4,585 | 3,210 | 7,409 | 12,091 | 61,809 | 4,952 | 4,446 | 9,398 |
| 1993-4 | 426 | 1,750 | 5,318 | 7,068 | 2,852 | 3,089 | 548 | 7,068 | 56,680 | 6,205 | 3,000 | 6,307 | 11,687 | 61,997 | 2,873 | 1,208 | 4,081 |
| 1994-5[1] | 192 | 756 | 5,653 | 6,409 | 2,407 | 2,544 | 45 | 6,409 | 58,143 | 6,355 | 2,650 | 5,644 | 10,223 | 58,111 | 2,294 | 1,819 | 4,113 |
| 1995-6[2] | 811 | 1,592 | 4,757 | 6,349 | 2,325 | 1,765 | 419 | 6,349 | 54,532 | 4,924 | 2,225 | 5,900 | 8,021 | 56,051 | 2,127 | 467 | 2,594 |
| 1996-7[3] | 500 | 725 | 5,750 | 6,475 | 3,000 | 2,100 | 327 | 6,475 | 65,492 | 5,650 | 2,900 | 7,300 | 13,437 | 64,243 | 2,102 | 1,711 | 3,813 |

[1] Preliminary. [2] Estimate. [3] Forecast. *Source: Foreign Agricultural Service, U.S. Department of Agriculture*

## Salient Statistics of Grain Sorghum in the United States

| Year | Acreage Planted[4] for All Purposes (1,000 Acres) | For Grain: Acreage Harvested (1,000 Acres) | For Grain: Production 1,000 Bushels | For Grain: Yield Per Harvested Acre Bushels | For Grain: Price in Cents Per Bushel | For Grain: Value of Production Million $ | For Silage: Acreage Harvested 1,000 Acres | For Silage: Production 1,000 Tons | For Silage: Yield Per Harvested Acre Tons | Sorghum Grain Stocks Dec. 1: On Farms (1,000 Bushels) | Dec. 1: Off Farms | June 1: On Farms | June 1: Off Farms |
|---|---|---|---|---|---|---|---|---|---|---|---|---|---|
| 1991-2 | 11,064 | 9,870 | 584,860 | 59.3 | 225 | 1,331.3 | 483 | 4,846 | 10.0 | 140,000 | 372,340 | 34,140 | 76,247 |
| 1992-3 | 13,177 | 12,050 | 875,022 | 72.6 | 189 | 1,666.9 | 453 | 5,468 | 12.1 | 110,200 | 340,262 | 58,465 | 206,348 |
| 1993-4 | 9,882 | 8,916 | 534,172 | 59.9 | 231 | 1,234.5 | 351 | 3,914 | 11.2 | 105,950 | 340,198 | 32,075 | 96,035 |
| 1994-51 | 9,827 | 8,917 | 649,206 | 72.8 | 213 | 1,323.8 | 329 | 3,932 | 12.0 | 126,650 | 295,809 | 44,570 | 114,212 |
| 1995-6[2] | 9,454 | 8,278 | 460,373 | 55.6 | 319 | 1,395.4 | 368 | 3,652 | 9.9 | 79,090 | 222,186 | 13,955 | 56,420 |
| 1996-7[3] | 13,188 | 11,901 | 802,974 | 67.5 | 220-250 | 2,053.3 | 371 | 4,356 | 11.7 | 144,590 | 315,685 | | |

[1] Preliminary. [2] Estimate. [3] Forecast. NA = Not available. *Source: Economic Research Service, U.S. Department of Agriculture*

## Production of All Sorghum for Grain in the United States, by States — In Thousands of Bushels

| Year | Alabama | Arkansas | Colorado | Illinois | Kansas | Louisiana | Mississippi | Missouri | Nebraska | New Mexico | North Carolina | Oklahoma | South Dakota | Texas |
|---|---|---|---|---|---|---|---|---|---|---|---|---|---|---|
| 1991 | 1,265 | 15,390 | 10,800 | 13,840 | 176,400 | 10,120 | 4,760 | 37,440 | 90,450 | 10,200 | 1,250 | 13,800 | 13,020 | 176,900 |
| 1992 | 1,250 | 31,160 | 6,660 | 26,780 | 244,000 | 15,232 | 10,500 | 62,080 | 143,820 | 12,300 | 1,000 | 17,490 | 14,060 | 279,000 |
| 1993 | 817 | 12,470 | 7,140 | 17,430 | 176,400 | 7,200 | 4,225 | 39,420 | 73,750 | 7,425 | 675 | 14,500 | 10,500 | 156,750 |
| 1994 | 900 | 18,375 | 7,140 | 17,820 | 231,000 | 8,364 | 5,250 | 49,500 | 117,600 | 7,410 | 1,100 | 14,000 | 11,375 | 153,400 |
| 1995 | 320 | 13,135 | 4,620 | 11,730 | 173,600 | 5,880 | 2,665 | 35,770 | 56,840 | 3,380 | 650 | 12,800 | 4,800 | 129,600 |
| 1996[1] | 550 | 16,280 | 13,260 | 18,480 | 354,200 | 11,628 | 5,040 | 52,780 | 97,850 | 7,425 | 570 | 28,910 | 7,975 | 182,400 |

[1] Preliminary. *Source: National Agricultural Statistics Service, U.S Department of Agriculture*

# GRAIN SORGHUM

## U.S. Grain Sorghum Quarterly Supply and Disappearance In Millions of Bushels

| Crop Year Beginning Sept. 1 | Supply: Beginning Stocks | Supply: Production | Supply: Imports | Supply: Total Supply | Disappearance: Domestic Use: Food, Alcohol & Industrial | Domestic Use: Seed | Domestic Use: Feed & Residual | Domestic Use: Total | Export | Disappearance Total | Ending Stocks: Gov't. Owned[3] | Ending Stocks: Privately Owned[4] | Ending Stocks: Total Stocks |
|---|---|---|---|---|---|---|---|---|---|---|---|---|---|
| 1993-4 | 175.0 | 534.2 | 0 | 709.2 | 6.3 | 1.2 | 452.6 | 460.1 | 201.6 | 661.6 | 1.0 | 46.9 | 47.6 |
| Sept.-Nov. | 175.0 | 534.2 | 0 | 709.2 | 1.7 | 0 | 222.1 | 223.8 | 39.2 | 263.0 | 1.9 | 444.2 | 446.1 |
| Dec.-Feb. | 446.1 | ------ | 0 | 446.2 | 1.5 | 0 | 108.0 | 109.5 | 60.4 | 169.9 | 2.0 | 274.2 | 276.2 |
| Mar.-May | 276.2 | ------ | 0 | 276.2 | 1.7 | .8 | 81.9 | 84.4 | 63.7 | 148.1 | 2.0 | 126.1 | 128.1 |
| June-Aug. | 128.1 | ------ | 0 | 128.1 | 1.4 | .4 | 40.5 | 42.3 | 38.2 | 80.5 | 1.0 | 46.9 | 47.6 |
| 1994-5[1] | 47.6 | 655.0 | 0 | 702.6 | 5.8 | 1.2 | 401.7 | 408.7 | 222.7 | 631.4 | 1.0 | 70.2 | 71.2 |
| Sept.-Nov. | 47.6 | 655.0 | 0 | 702.6 | 1.7 | 0 | 214.4 | 216.1 | 64.1 | 280.1 | 3.0 | 419.5 | 422.5 |
| Dec.-Feb. | 422.5 | ------ | 0 | 422.5 | 1.4 | 0 | 79.2 | 80.6 | 60.9 | 141.5 | 2.0 | 278.9 | 280.9 |
| Mar.-May | 280.9 | ------ | 0 | 280.9 | 1.5 | .4 | 65.9 | 67.8 | 54.4 | 122.2 | 1.0 | 157.8 | 158.8 |
| June-Aug. | 158.8 | ------ | 0 | 158.8 | 1.2 | .8 | 42.2 | 44.2 | 43.3 | 87.6 | 1.0 | 70.2 | 71.2 |
| 1995-6[1] | 72.0 | 460.0 | 0 | 532.0 | 5.8 | 1.2 | 312.0 | 322.0 | 198.0 | 514.0 | 1.0 | 40.0 | 18.0 |
| Sept.-Nov. | 72.0 | 460.0 | 0 | 532.0 | | | 176.0 | | 54.0 | 231.0 | | | 301.0 |
| Dec.-Feb. | 301.0 | ------ | 0 | 301.0 | | | 71.0 | | 67.0 | 139.0 | | | 163.0 |
| Mar.-May | 163.0 | ------ | 0 | 163.0 | | | 55.0 | | 36.0 | 92.0 | | | 70.0 |
| June-Aug. | 70.0 | ------ | 0 | 70.0 | | | 10.0 | | 41.0 | 52.0 | | | 18.0 |
| 1996-7[2] | 18.0 | 803.0 | 0 | 821.0 | | | 525.0 | | 225.0 | 754.0 | | | 67.0 |

[1] Preliminary. [2] Forecast. [3] Uncommitted inventory. [4] Includes quantity under loan & farmer-owned reserve. *Source: Economic Research Service, U.S. Department of Agriculture*

## Average Price of Sorghum Grain, No. 2, Yellow at Kansas City In Dollars Per Hundred Pounds (Cwt.)

| Year | Sept. | Oct. | Nov. | Dec. | Jan. | Feb. | Mar. | Apr. | May | June | July | Aug. | Average |
|---|---|---|---|---|---|---|---|---|---|---|---|---|---|
| 1988-9 | 4.27 | 4.17 | 4.00 | 4.23 | 4.24 | 4.26 | 4.32 | 4.17 | 4.29 | 4.15 | 3.96 | 3.92 | 4.17 |
| 1989-90 | 4.73 | 3.91 | 4.00 | 3.98 | 3.91 | 3.84 | 4.01 | 4.32 | 4.47 | 4.54 | 4.48 | 4.27 | 4.21 |
| 1990-1 | 3.89 | 3.79 | 3.85 | 3.97 | 4.12 | 4.21 | 4.35 | 4.34 | 4.13 | 4.02 | 4.05 | 4.22 | 4.08 |
| 1991-2 | 4.24 | 4.30 | 4.27 | 4.35 | 4.44 | 4.62 | 4.78 | 4.41 | 4.54 | 4.51 | 4.05 | 3.77 | 4.36 |
| 1992-3 | 3.76 | 3.60 | 3.61 | 3.70 | 3.70 | 3.66 | 3.70 | 3.72 | 3.82 | 3.58 | 3.99 | 4.01 | 3.74 |
| 1993-4 | 3.89 | 4.03 | 4.60 | 4.91 | 4.93 | 4.81 | 4.64 | 4.33 | 4.38 | 4.43 | 3.79 | 3.73 | 4.37 |
| 1994-5 | 3.72 | 3.55 | 3.60 | 3.81 | 3.92 | 3.90 | 4.01 | 4.08 | 4.27 | 4.50 | 4.93 | 4.85 | 4.10 |
| 1995-6[1] | 5.08 | 5.45 | 5.68 | 6.19 | 6.39 | 6.58 | 6.81 | 7.79 | 8.17 | 7.79 | 7.24 | 6.74 | 6.66 |
| 1996-7[1] | 5.29 | 4.64 | | | | | | | | | | | 4.97 |

[1] Preliminary. *Source: Economic Research Service, U.S. Department of Agriculture*

## U.S. Exports of Grain Sorghum, by Country of Destination In Metric Tons

| Year Beginning October | Canada | Ecuador | Ethiopia | Israel | Japan | Jordon | Mexico | South Africa | Spain | Sudan | Turkey | World Total |
|---|---|---|---|---|---|---|---|---|---|---|---|---|
| 1990-1 | 1,325 | 33,060 | 0 | 165,906 | 1,853,079 | 20,500 | 3,015,944 | 0 | 181,501 | 91,400 | 114,636 | 5,778,792 |
| 1991-2 | 1,613 | 36,000 | 42,150 | 104,952 | 1,738,075 | 120,001 | 4,956,607 | 19,031 | 174,758 | 122,183 | 99,394 | 7,454,616 |
| 1992-3 | 1,795 | 9,501 | 0 | 217,110 | 1,933,012 | 0 | 3,970,069 | 56,186 | 188,893 | 4,287 | 132,182 | 6,651,528 |
| 1993-4 | 1,699 | 0 | 86,697 | 66,264 | 1,681,976 | 0 | 3,118,139 | 0 | 169,454 | 48,042 | 0 | 5,245,524 |
| 1994-5[1] | 0 | 0 | 0 | 214,073 | 1,987,738 | 0 | 2,543,696 | 0 | 398,339 | 0 | 0 | 5,652,585 |
| 1995-6[2] | 0 | 0 | 0 | 356,868 | 1,616,384 | 0 | 1,633,541 | 0 | 431,578 | 0 | 0 | 4,757,055 |

[1] Preliminary. [2] Estimate. *Source: Economic Research Service, U.S. Department of Agriculture*

## Grain Sorghum Price Support Program and Market Prices

| Year | Price Support Operations: Put Under Price Support: Quantity (Million Cwt.) | Put Under Price Support: % of Production | Aquired by CCC (Million Cwt.) | Owned by CCC at Year End (Million Cwt.) | Basic Loan Rate ($ Per Bushel) | Target Price ($ Per Bushel) | Findley Loan Rate ($ Per Bushel) | Effective Base[3] Mil. Acres | Participation Rate[4] % of Base | No. 2 Yellow ($ Per Cwt.): Kansas City | Texas High Plains | Los Angeles | Gulf Ports |
|---|---|---|---|---|---|---|---|---|---|---|---|---|---|
| 1987-8 | 201.3 | 49.2 | 119.7 | 259.6 | 2.17 | 2.88 | 1.82 | 17.4 | 84 | 3.40 | 3.81 | 5.18 | 3.96 |
| 1988-9 | 22.7 | 7.0 | 17.0 | 190.9 | 2.10 | 2.78 | 1.74 | 16.8 | 82 | 4.17 | 4.66 | 6.08 | 4.81 |
| 1989-90 | 11.7 | 3.4 | 10.1 | 91.3 | 1.96 | 2.70 | 1.57 | 16.2 | 71 | 4.21 | 4.38 | 5.53 | 4.76 |
| 1990-1 | 12.1 | 3.8 | 5.0 | 36.4 | 1.86 | 2.61 | 1.49 | 15.4 | 70 | 4.08 | 4.48 | 5.52 | 4.65 |
| 1991-2 | 9.5 | 2.9 | 5.4 | 4.5 | 1.80 | 2.61 | 1.54 | 13.5 | 77 | 4.36 | 4.78 | 5.69 | 4.86 |
| 1992-3 | 27.2 | 5.5 | 0 | 2.2 | 1.91 | 2.61 | 1.63 | 13.6 | 79 | 3.74 | 4.06 | 5.11 | 4.27 |
| 1993-4 | 8.2 | 2.6 | 0 | 1.1 | 1.89 | 2.61 | 1.63 | 13.5 | 82 | 4.37 | 4.95 | | 4.90 |
| 1994-5[1] | 25.2 | 6.9 | 0 | | 1.89 | 2.61 | 1.80 | 13.5 | 81 | 4.10 | 4.75 | | 4.73 |
| 1995-6[2] | 1.5 | .6 | 0 | | ----- | 2.61 | 1.80 | 13.4 | 77 | 5.27 | 5.95 | | 5.94 |

[1] Preliminary. [2] Estimate. [3] National effective crop acreage base as determined by ASCS. [4] Percentage of effective base acres enrolled in acreage reduction programs. *Source: Economic Research Service, U.S. Department of Agriculture*

# Hay

U.S. total hay production in 1996/97 (marketing year, May 1 to April 30) of 152 million tons was down 2 percent from 1995, but a little higher than initially expected. Acreage was a shade higher at 60.1 million acres vs. 59.8 million in 1995, but average yield dipped to 2.51 tons per acre from 2.59. California is generally the largest producing state although bested at times by Texas and South Dakota. Alfalfa and alfalfa mixtures account for more than half of total hay production: 81 million tons in 1996 vs. 85 million in 1995. Alfalfa yields are higher than other hays, especially in California, which set a new record of 7.4 tons per acre in 1996.

Roughage consuming animal units (RCAU) in 1996/97 were expected to be down 2 percent from the 78 million in 1995/96. Hay supplies for 1996/97 of 173 million tons were also down 2 percent from 1995/96. The supply of hay per RCAU was expected to total 2.25 tons, about the same as the 2.24 tons in 1995/96. The key to hay prices rests largely on the number of dairy cows and producer intentions to plant acreage to hay for forage. Much depends on the dairy cow inventory in California and Wisconsin. Alfalfa farm prices in 1995/96 averaged $88.20 per ton, about $4/ton below 1994/95. In the first third of the 1996/97 season prices averaged $97.00 per ton vs. $90/ton a year earlier.

## Salient Statistics of All Hay in the United States

| Year Crop Beginning May | Acres Harvested 1,000 Acres | Yield Per Acre Tons | Production | Carryover May 1 | Disappearance | Supply | Disappearance | Animal Units Fed[3] Millions | Farm Price $ Per Ton | Farm Production Value Million $ | Retail Price Paid by Farmers for Seed, April 15: Alfalfa (Certified) | Timothy | Red Clover | Sudan-Grass |
|---|---|---|---|---|---|---|---|---|---|---|---|---|---|---|
| | | | Millions of Tons | | | Per Animal Unit In Tons | | | | | Dollars Per Cwt. | | | |
| 1990-1 | 61,407 | 2.39 | 146.8 | 27.0 | 146.2 | 2.30 | 1.94 | 73.5 | 80.6 | 10,462 | 253.00 | 82.10 | 145.00 | 47.70 |
| 1991-2 | 62,475 | 2.45 | 153.3 | 27.0 | 150.9 | 2.36 | 1.98 | 74.7 | 71.2 | 10,006 | 266.00 | 66.40 | 134.00 | 48.10 |
| 1992-3 | 58,903 | 2.49 | 146.9 | 28.2 | 154.1 | 2.32 | 2.04 | 75.3 | 74.3 | 10,436 | 252.00 | 66.30 | 122.00 | 47.10 |
| 1993-4 | 59,679 | 2.46 | 146.8 | 21.0 | 145.7 | 2.21 | 1.91 | 76.4 | 84.7 | 10,957 | 269.00 | 80.60 | 148.00 | 45.20 |
| 1994-5[1] | 58,735 | 2.55 | 150.1 | 22.1 | 151.4 | 2.20 | 1.93 | 78.3 | 86.7 | 11,114 | 266.00 | 76.00 | 148.00 | 47.90 |
| 1995-6[2] | 59,629 | 2.59 | 154.2 | 20.8 | | 2.22 | | 86.7 | 82.2 | 11,042 | 274.00 | 71.00 | 134.00 | 51.80 |
| 1996-7[2] | 61,029 | 2.45 | 149.5 | | | | | | 93.0 | 11,970 | | | | |

[1] Preliminary. [2] Estimate. [3] Roughage-consuming animal units fed annually. *Source: Economic Research Service, U.S. Department of Agriculture*

## Production of All Hay in the United States by Important States In Thousands of Tons

| Year | California | Idaho | Illinois | Iowa | Michigan | Minnesota | Missouri | Nebraska | New York | North Dakota | Ohio | Oklahoma | Pennslyvania | South Dakota | Texas | Wisconsin |
|---|---|---|---|---|---|---|---|---|---|---|---|---|---|---|---|---|
| 1991 | 8,610 | 4,294 | 3,162 | 6,285 | 5,255 | 8,090 | 7,110 | 7,473 | 4,102 | 4,780 | 3,150 | 4,360 | 4,026 | 8,045 | 9,700 | 9,060 |
| 1992 | 7,755 | 3,655 | 3,316 | 6,615 | 4,280 | 6,550 | 6,780 | 7,793 | 3,590 | 3,515 | 4,240 | 4,750 | 4,740 | 6,780 | 9,800 | 6,090 |
| 1993 | 7,590 | 4,844 | 4,106 | 4,803 | 5,370 | 5,970 | 7,335 | 7,323 | 3,605 | 5,043 | 3,475 | 4,248 | 4,352 | 8,190 | 7,506 | 6,260 |
| 1994 | 8,210 | 4,438 | 3,175 | 5,775 | 4,865 | 7,530 | 6,770 | 7,415 | 3,961 | 4,510 | 4,384 | 4,198 | 4,528 | 7,330 | 8,455 | 6,550 |
| 1995 | 8,341 | 5,080 | 3,598 | 5,665 | 5,025 | 6,943 | 6,818 | 6,975 | 3,448 | 5,095 | 4,035 | 4,174 | 4,409 | 9,050 | 8,136 | 6,820 |
| 1996[1] | 8,008 | 4,760 | 3,040 | 5,320 | 4,190 | 5,998 | 6,920 | 7,445 | 3,468 | 4,825 | 3,400 | 5,045 | 4,585 | 8,200 | 7,815 | 6,050 |

[1] Preliminary. *Source: Agricultural Statistics Board, U.S. Department of Agriculture*

## U.S. Types of Hay Production & Farm Stocks In Thousands of Short Tons

| Year | Production: Alfalfa & Mixtures | All Others | All Hay | Corn for Silage[1] | Sorghum Silage[1] | Farm Stocks: May 1 | Dec. 1 |
|---|---|---|---|---|---|---|---|
| 1991 | 83,319 | 68,754 | 152,073 | 80,543 | 4,846 | 26,974 | 111,123 |
| 1992 | 79,140 | 67,763 | 146,903 | 87,663 | 5,468 | 28,216 | 105,290 |
| 1993 | 80,305 | 66,494 | 146,799 | 81,829 | 3,914 | 21,010 | 100,953 |
| 1994 | 81,336 | 68,724 | 150,060 | 88,588 | 3,932 | 22,096 | 105,296 |
| 1995 | 84,515 | 69,651 | 154,166 | 77,867 | 3,652 | 20,775 | 109,438 |
| 1996[2] | 79,377 | 70,080 | 149,457 | 83,094 | 4,356 | 20,739 | 105,208 |

[1] Not included in all tame hay. [2] Preliminary. *Source: Agricultural Statistics Board, U.S. Department of Agriculture*

## Mid-Month Price Received by Farmers of All Hay (Baled) In Dollars Per Ton

| Year | May | June | July | Aug. | Sept. | Oct. | Nov. | Dec. | Jan. | Feb. | Mar. | Apr. | Average[2] |
|---|---|---|---|---|---|---|---|---|---|---|---|---|---|
| 1990-1 | 96.00 | 85.00 | 81.60 | 81.00 | 83.20 | 84.00 | 81.40 | 78.70 | 77.90 | 77.80 | 80.50 | 85.50 | 80.60 |
| 1991-2 | 81.10 | 75.20 | 71.80 | 70.80 | 69.80 | 68.50 | 68.20 | 68.90 | 68.70 | 71.10 | 69.90 | 70.90 | 71.20 |
| 1992-3 | 79.50 | 75.80 | 69.70 | 71.90 | 70.10 | 70.30 | 71.00 | 73.50 | 76.10 | 78.00 | 80.50 | 83.60 | 74.30 |
| 1993-4 | 86.60 | 79.60 | 76.90 | 77.50 | 78.80 | 82.30 | 84.20 | 83.50 | 85.70 | 86.90 | 90.80 | 98.20 | 84.70 |
| 1994-5 | 100.00 | 88.70 | 82.50 | 83.10 | 82.40 | 86.80 | 86.60 | 85.50 | 84.80 | 85.00 | 86.70 | 90.30 | 86.00 |
| 1995-6[1] | 90.40 | 83.90 | 80.60 | 81.10 | 80.30 | 83.00 | 81.00 | 80.30 | 81.70 | 81.20 | 83.40 | 90.30 | 83.10 |
| 1996-7[1] | 97.10 | 92.30 | 89.60 | 92.90 | 90.10 | 93.00 | 95.10 | 96.00 | 99.70 | | | | 93.98 |

[1] Preliminary. [2] Marketing year average. *Source: Economic Research Service, U.S. Department of Agriculture*

# Heating Oil

Heating oil use in the U.S. is concentrated in the Northeast section of the country. It is use primarily for residential heating. There is strong competition between private heating oil distributors and regulated natural gas distributors, who are largely regulated utilities. The trend has been for consumers to initially choose natural gas or switch to gas from heating oil when their furnaces need to be replaced. Natural gas pipelines have become more available to more residential customers allowing the switch from heating oil to gas. Natural gas has been promoted as clean and the environmentally safer fuel. Heating oil distributors claim that natural gas by its very nature is not the safer of the two fuels. As private firms, heating oil distributors stress their reliability and responsiveness to their customers. In recent years, the heating oil distributors have hedged the price of their product utilizing the futures market thereby guaranteeing their customers a set price for the heating season. Overall, the trend appears to be in favor of natural gas. One advantage is that natural gas moves through underground pipelines while heating oil requires a storage tank.

Heating oil prices, as represented on the New York Mercantile Exchange, moved higher through all of 1996. Beginning in August what had been a slow but steady eight month advance accelerated into a roaring bull market, although after October gains were narrower and more difficult to sustain. However prices were still registering new highs in early January, 1997.

The overall fundamental situation in heating oil is that the distillate market in the Atlantic Basin remains tight. It is tight in some of the important markets on the U.S. East Coast, the area of highest heating oil use. Among the factors affecting the market are extremely low distillate inventories, the lowest in many years. Stocks in the Northeast remain very tight. Additionally, U.S. refinery activity is running at close to capacity so additional production will be difficult to achieve. On top of that, the demand for distillates is still increasing. The stocks situation in Europe is even tighter than in the U.S. and European distillate has been trading at a premium to the U.S. That would argue for product moving from the U.S. to Europe instead of from Europe to the U.S. All of this would seem to imply that heating oil prices could increase further. The unknown variable is the weather, and if the first quarter of 1997 is colder than normal, heating oil prices have significant upside potential.

U.S. distillate fuel oil production in August 1996 averaged 3.27 million barrels per day, up 4 percent from the previous month. In August 1995, production averaged 3.15 million barrels per day. For the January-August 1996 period, distillate production averaged 3.2 million barrels per day. This was some 4 per cent more than in the comparable period of 1995 and almost 1 per cent above the like period of 1994. For all of 1995, distillate fuel oil production averaged 3.16 million barrels per day.

U.S. imports of distillate in August 1996 were 170,000 barrels per day, down almost 12 per cent from the previous month. Over the first eight months of 1996, daily imports of distillate fuel oil averaged 223,000 barrels per day. In the comparable period of 1995, imports averaged 190,000 barrels per day while in 1994 the average was 217,000 barrels per day. For all of 1995, imports averaged 193,000 barrels

U.S. exports of distillate fuel oil in August 1996 averaged 145,000 barrels per day, up 8 per cent from July. Over the first eight months of 1996, exports averaged 164,000 barrels per day. This was the same as in the comparable period of 1995, but was 31 per cent less than in the like period of 1994.

Total distillate fuel oil supplied in August 1996 averaged 3.1 million barrels per day. Over the January-August 1996 period, distillate supplied averaged 3.3 million barrels per day. This was up 5 per cent from the comparable period of 1995 and 5 per cent above 1994.

The most interesting development in the market has been the decline in stocks. Though stocks increased during the third quarter of 1996, they remained at low levels. At the end of August 1996, distillate fuel oil stocks were 110 million barrels, up close to 4 percent from July. A year earlier, stocks were 131 million barrels while in August 1994 they were 139 million barrels.

### *Futures Markets*

Heating oil futures and options are traded on the New York Mercantile Exchange (NYMEX). In London, gasoil futures and options are listed on the International Petroleum Exchange (IPE).

**Average Spot Prices of Heating Oil #2** In Cents Per Gallon

| Year | Jan. | Feb. | Mar. | Apr. | May | June | July | Aug. | Sept. | Oct. | Nov. | Dec. | Average |
|---|---|---|---|---|---|---|---|---|---|---|---|---|---|
| 1986 | 66.81 | 53.31 | 59.69 | 43.70 | 46.90 | 37.84 | 33.33 | 40.93 | 40.31 | 39.47 | 42.17 | 44.52 | 45.49 |
| 1987 | 52.34 | 47.36 | 49.18 | 48.58 | 51.75 | 52.30 | 54.62 | 52.46 | 52.33 | 56.14 | 55.84 | 53.75 | 52.22 |
| 1988 | 51.73 | 48.10 | 47.43 | 51.46 | 50.82 | 44.76 | 42.79 | 43.41 | 40.71 | 40.52 | 44.84 | 50.91 | 46.46 |
| 1989 | 54.35 | 51.47 | 56.86 | 53.98 | 50.76 | 48.51 | 49.35 | 49.75 | 55.78 | 58.80 | 59.20 | 80.91 | 55.81 |
| 1990 | 73.26 | 57.48 | 57.93 | 58.51 | 53.99 | 48.22 | 53.14 | 75.23 | 88.82 | 93.95 | 87.51 | 79.73 | 68.98 |
| 1991 | 74.96 | 70.80 | 61.92 | 56.36 | 55.04 | 53.67 | 57.74 | 60.48 | 61.54 | 66.58 | 64.33 | 53.35 | 61.31 |
| 1992 | 51.72 | 53.39 | 52.49 | 56.22 | 57.38 | 61.26 | 60.24 | 58.29 | 61.90 | 62.72 | 56.52 | 54.98 | 57.25 |
| 1993 | 53.14 | 56.02 | 58.13 | 55.49 | 54.53 | 52.62 | 49.74 | 50.70 | 51.96 | 54.00 | 50.30 | 43.47 | 52.51 |
| 1994 | 49.93 | 55.81 | 49.18 | 48.01 | 47.98 | 49.37 | 49.93 | 49.51 | 47.90 | 48.23 | 49.62 | 48.41 | 49.49 |
| 1995 | 47.98 | 47.64 | 45.95 | 49.40 | 50.31 | 47.75 | 46.65 | 49.14 | 50.21 | 48.89 | 51.89 | 57.76 | 49.46 |
| 1996 | 55.64 | 61.24 | 65.19 | 67.90 | 57.59 | 51.56 | 55.58 | 60.42 | 67.61 | 72.34 | 70.13 | 72.13 | 63.11 |

*Source: New York Mercantile Exchange (NYMEX)*

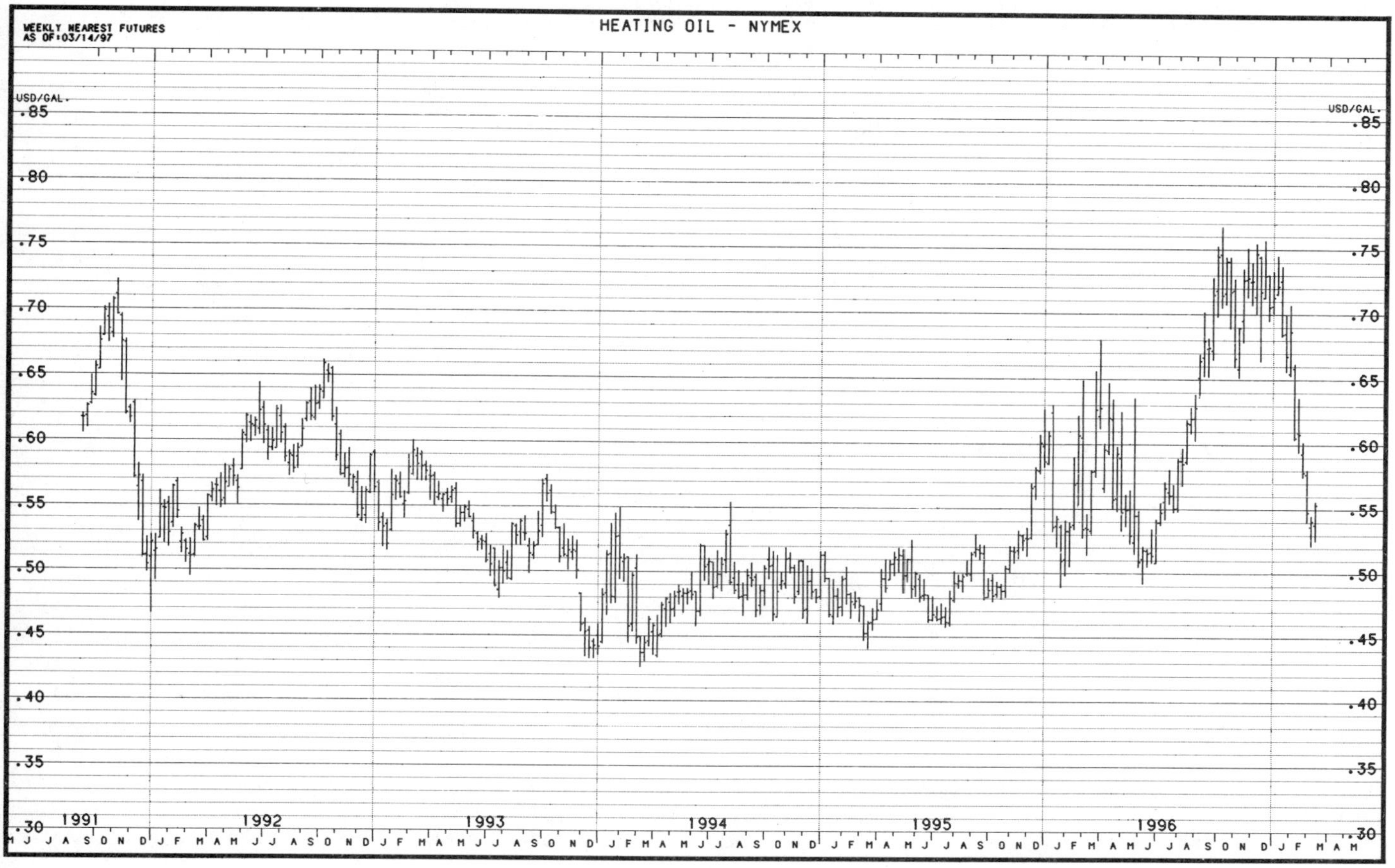


## Average Open Interest of #2 Heating Oil Futures in New York In Contracts

| Year | Jan. | Feb. | Mar. | Apr. | May | June | July | Aug. | Sept. | Oct. | Nov. | Dec. |
|---|---|---|---|---|---|---|---|---|---|---|---|---|
| 1985 | 23,197 | 16,243 | 16,881 | 17,196 | 16,970 | 20,150 | 21,419 | 25,061 | 29,626 | 31,726 | 35,062 | 33,275 |
| 1986 | 28,866 | 29,476 | 32,783 | 33,841 | 37,897 | 50,299 | 63,935 | 65,337 | 70,994 | 79,030 | 75,477 | 70,723 |
| 1987 | 66,228 | 60,479 | 47,798 | 45,494 | 40,865 | 44,530 | 52,480 | 54,696 | 65,781 | 70,167 | 74,093 | 74,945 |
| 1988 | 59,605 | 51,640 | 49,705 | 44,674 | 49,155 | 58,960 | 77,018 | 77,777 | 87,942 | 93,762 | 85,350 | 80,093 |
| 1989 | 75,038 | 63,791 | 60,455 | 57,533 | 49,174 | 49,527 | 59,799 | 69,578 | 88,642 | 97,064 | 99,293 | 105,240 |
| 1990 | 83,020 | 68,065 | 67,389 | 76,954 | 85,349 | 112,506 | 116,108 | 103,280 | 97,589 | 93,631 | 92,399 | 81,864 |
| 1991 | 74,216 | 81,742 | 81,103 | 82,419 | 89,482 | 102,887 | 115,896 | 125,463 | 135,804 | 144,026 | 128,330 | 117,182 |
| 1992 | 108,337 | 96,543 | 91,508 | 90,816 | 87,459 | 101,185 | 98,623 | 109,787 | 119,595 | 129,951 | 140,952 | 135,380 |
| 1993 | 130,536 | 125,603 | 130,438 | 107,363 | 102,708 | 113,898 | 131,816 | 142,054 | 166,253 | 172,940 | 175,781 | 199,299 |
| 1994 | 196,390 | 185,607 | 186,539 | 164,417 | 140,658 | 129,005 | 124,764 | 149,571 | 172,071 | 165,475 | 152,570 | 148,298 |
| 1995 | 128,664 | 112,508 | 118,700 | 121,974 | 115,501 | 122,163 | 136,722 | 140,214 | 149,934 | 152,244 | 139,232 | 138,596 |
| 1996 | 114,324 | 95,745 | 90,080 | 94,161 | 98,038 | 97,699 | 109,524 | 119,366 | 138,513 | 141,217 | 127,512 | 108,558 |

*Source: New York Mercantile Exchange (NYMEX)*

## Volume of Trading of #2 Heating Oil Futures In New York In Contracts

| Year | Jan. | Feb. | Mar. | Apr. | May | June | July | Aug. | Sept. | Oct. | Nov. | Dec. | Total |
|---|---|---|---|---|---|---|---|---|---|---|---|---|---|
| 1985 | 286,264 | 149,403 | 162,503 | 137,064 | 122,699 | 133,339 | 148,117 | 157,552 | 202,785 | 246,558 | 219,126 | 242,323 | 2,207,733 |
| 1986 | 274,057 | 221,156 | 214,501 | 207,748 | 223,943 | 247,552 | 309,662 | 282,636 | 285,246 | 387,054 | 271,497 | 349,992 | 3,275,044 |
| 1987 | 399,813 | 328,327 | 348,204 | 282,109 | 238,048 | 273,708 | 329,078 | 343,355 | 347,152 | 437,157 | 422,982 | 543,462 | 4,293,395 |
| 1988 | 506,182 | 377,379 | 403,181 | 267,233 | 286,365 | 380,550 | 431,231 | 363,276 | 441,939 | 578,648 | 475,675 | 423,356 | 4,935,015 |
| 1989 | 534,041 | 422,660 | 430,447 | 372,640 | 334,973 | 445,822 | 372,388 | 402,420 | 475,402 | 554,733 | 574,693 | 820,748 | 5,740,967 |
| 1990 | 754,945 | 415,420 | 462,479 | 451,708 | 516,989 | 463,263 | 518,993 | 723,152 | 505,810 | 612,310 | 521,969 | 429,833 | 6,376,871 |
| 1991 | 603,683 | 523,870 | 392,484 | 387,232 | 399,919 | 425,082 | 507,755 | 595,913 | 538,240 | 689,143 | 781,291 | 835,559 | 6,680,165 |
| 1992 | 815,199 | 574,007 | 550,113 | 592,056 | 586,707 | 601,067 | 645,020 | 663,743 | 625,675 | 709,532 | 808,201 | 807,142 | 8,005,462 |
| 1993 | 829,340 | 660,546 | 747,299 | 537,543 | 481,957 | 543,356 | 632,168 | 721,852 | 833,800 | 761,764 | 886,565 | 988,871 | 8,625,061 |
| 1994 | 1,085,683 | 875,714 | 766,788 | 631,664 | 629,295 | 723,677 | 612,316 | 783,181 | 706,822 | 721,375 | 652,257 | 798,063 | 8,986,835 |
| 1995 | 779,827 | 608,691 | 715,968 | 622,810 | 729,753 | 618,812 | 612,683 | 563,605 | 714,239 | 650,809 | 659,518 | 990,068 | 8,266,783 |
| 1996 | 977,235 | 768,075 | 666,168 | 586,471 | 530,858 | 402,004 | 530,230 | 624,402 | 766,517 | 1,014,23 | 724,975 | 750,704 | 8,341,877 |

*Source: New York Mercantile Exchange (NYMEX)*

# HEATING OIL

## Stocks of Distillate Fuel in the U.S., First of the Month In Millions of Barrels

| | | | | | | | | | | | | | Residual Fuel ---- Oil Stocks ---- | |
|---|---|---|---|---|---|---|---|---|---|---|---|---|---|---|
| Year | Jan. | Feb. | Mar. | Apr. | May | June | July | Aug. | Sept. | Oct. | Nov. | Dec. | Jan. 1 | July 1 |
| 1986 | 143.7 | 136.5 | 112.4 | 98.8 | 95.9 | 98.9 | 107.9 | 118.9 | 137.7 | 152.4 | 151.6 | 158.3 | 50.4 | 42.8 |
| 1987 | 155.1 | 141.3 | 123.7 | 109.3 | 100.3 | 101.3 | 104.4 | 114.6 | 124.7 | 126.8 | 121.0 | 128.0 | 47.4 | 41.4 |
| 1988 | 134.5 | 128.1 | 110.3 | 89.8 | 95.0 | 104.9 | 110.4 | 120.0 | 125.7 | 131.5 | 128.2 | 128.8 | 47.4 | 42.2 |
| 1989 | 123.5 | 120.3 | 107.5 | 96.6 | 98.4 | 99.3 | 99.6 | 115.0 | 116.3 | 123.2 | 121.7 | 119.8 | 44.6 | 44.1 |
| 1990 | 105.7 | 118.0 | 112.2 | 99.7 | 99.5 | 102.8 | 109.4 | 125.2 | 136.0 | 136.3 | 132.4 | 132.2 | 43.8 | 46.8 |
| 1991 | 112.1 | 111.7 | 101.6 | 98.2 | 102.9 | 106.9 | 113.7 | 124.7 | 131.4 | 140.1 | 138.3 | 144.5 | 47.6 | 43.7 |
| 1992 | 143.5 | 126.7 | 108.8 | 97.7 | 92.1 | 96.4 | 104.5 | 114.6 | 122.8 | 127.8 | 136.8 | 146.3 | 49.9 | 40.9 |
| 1993 | 140.6 | 130.7 | 110.4 | 97.3 | 99.5 | 102.8 | 110.0 | 120.7 | 128.2 | 131.3 | 145.3 | 149.2 | 42.6 | 45.7 |
| 1994 | 140.9 | 117.5 | 102.9 | 99.4 | 102.6 | 112.4 | 119.5 | 134.2 | 138.6 | 144.7 | 146.0 | 147.3 | 44.2 | 39.4 |
| 1995 | 140.2 | 122.1 | 115.4 | 114.6 | 118.3 | 114.7 | 125.0 | 130.9 | 131.7 | 131.4 | 135.4 | 130.2 | 41.9 | 36.0 |
| 1996[1] | 113.1 | 96.8 | 89.7 | 90.1 | 95.6 | 101.6 | 106.3 | 110.2 | 114.9 | 114.8 | 121.6 | | 37.2 | 34.9 |

[1] Preliminary. *Source: Energy Information Administration, U.S. Department of Energy*

## U.S. Production of Distillate Fuel Oil Thousand Barrels Per Day

| Year | Jan. | Feb. | Mar. | Apr. | May | June | July | Aug. | Sept. | Oct. | Nov. | Dec. | Average |
|---|---|---|---|---|---|---|---|---|---|---|---|---|---|
| 1986 | 2,899 | 2,563 | 2,643 | 2,788 | 2,858 | 2,729 | 2,710 | 2,922 | 2,865 | 2,717 | 2,917 | 2,943 | 2,798 |
| 1987 | 2,759 | 2,556 | 2,421 | 2,553 | 2,563 | 2,689 | 2,700 | 2,706 | 2,748 | 2,780 | 3,035 | 3,242 | 2,731 |
| 1988 | 3,010 | 2,667 | 2,706 | 2,867 | 2,936 | 2,893 | 2,784 | 2,848 | 2,778 | 2,827 | 2,909 | 3,068 | 2,859 |
| 1989 | 2,974 | 2,797 | 2,713 | 2,789 | 2,750 | 2,809 | 2,848 | 2,907 | 2,952 | 2,906 | 3,063 | 3,266 | 2,899 |
| 1990 | 3,130 | 2,753 | 2,657 | 2,803 | 2,874 | 2,996 | 3,008 | 3,131 | 2,968 | 2,928 | 2,915 | 2,917 | 2,925 |
| 1991 | 2,845 | 2,870 | 2,865 | 2,819 | 2,929 | 2,941 | 2,998 | 2,961 | 3,055 | 3,040 | 3,103 | 3,107 | 2,962 |
| 1992 | 2,818 | 2,661 | 2,749 | 2,930 | 2,933 | 2,995 | 3,067 | 2,865 | 2,983 | 3,251 | 3,240 | 3,179 | 2,974 |
| 1993 | 2,914 | 2,815 | 2,919 | 3,047 | 2,994 | 3,093 | 3,186 | 3,100 | 3,205 | 3,432 | 3,474 | 3,382 | 3,132 |
| 1994 | 3,114 | 3,018 | 3,096 | 3,249 | 3,317 | 3,285 | 3,191 | 3,187 | 3,285 | 3,203 | 3,270 | 3,232 | 3,205 |
| 1995 | 3,054 | 2,954 | 3,157 | 3,126 | 3,111 | 3,109 | 3,056 | 3,145 | 3,287 | 3,169 | 3,341 | 3,344 | 3,155 |
| 1996[1] | 3,110 | 3,145 | 3,110 | 3,305 | 3,258 | 3,291 | 3,139 | 3,295 | 3,403 | 3,626 | 3,665 | 3,554 | 3,325 |

[1] Preliminary. *Source: Energy Information Administration, U.S. Department of Energy*

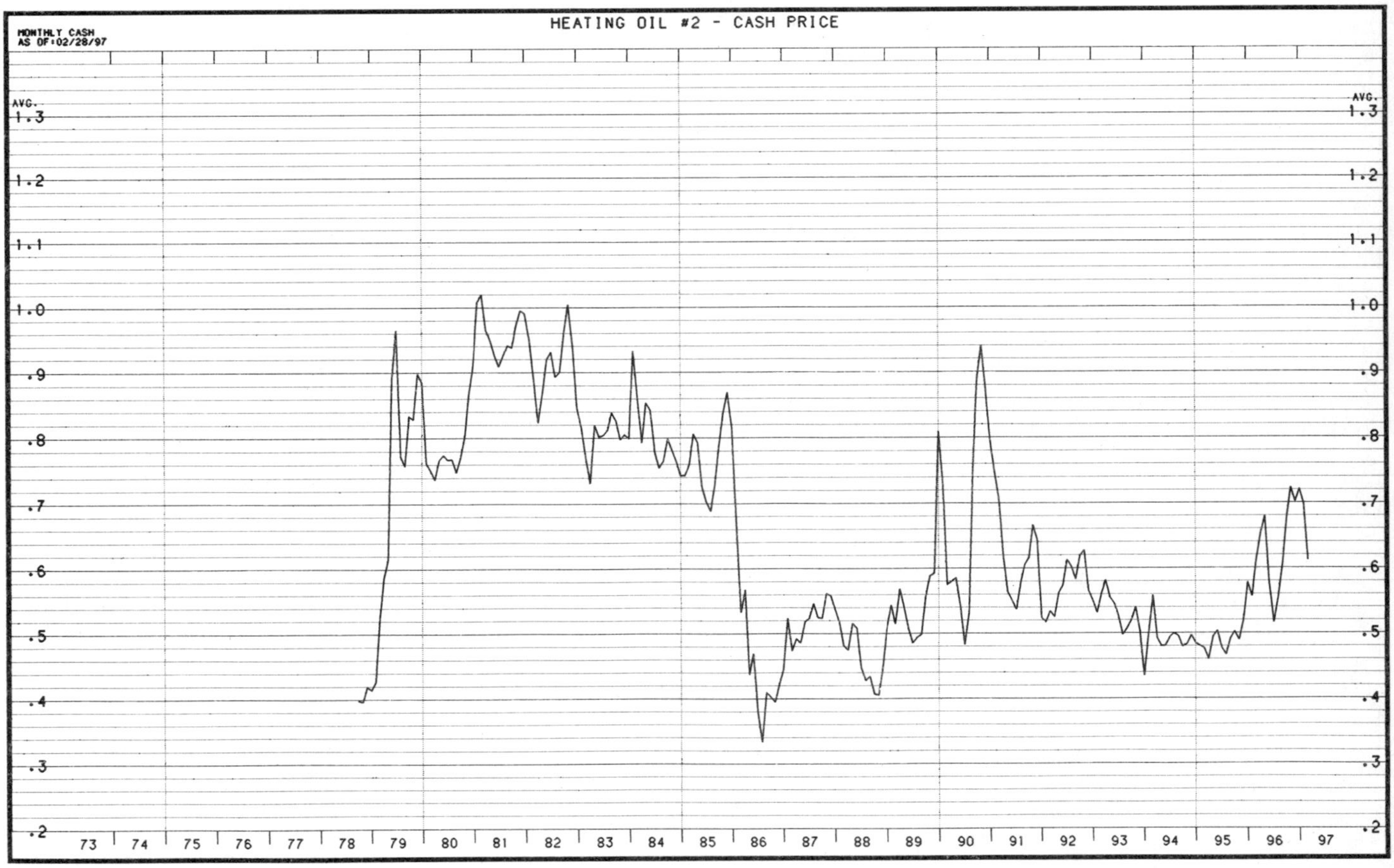

## U.S. Imports of Distillate Fuel Oil Thousand Barrels Per Day

| Year | Jan. | Feb. | Mar. | Apr. | May | June | July | Aug. | Sept. | Oct. | Nov. | Dec. | Average |
|---|---|---|---|---|---|---|---|---|---|---|---|---|---|
| 1986 | 325 | 169 | 217 | 147 | 149 | 169 | 313 | 370 | 262 | 243 | 254 | 339 | 247 |
| 1987 | 222 | 253 | 297 | 192 | 203 | 265 | 381 | 222 | 222 | 237 | 187 | 378 | 255 |
| 1988 | 424 | 383 | 247 | 210 | 253 | 222 | 222 | 279 | 307 | 336 | 327 | 409 | 302 |
| 1989 | 346 | 331 | 439 | 301 | 290 | 233 | 334 | 254 | 249 | 261 | 307 | 324 | 306 |
| 1990 | 505 | 357 | 281 | 308 | 209 | 257 | 236 | 293 | 226 | 190 | 238 | 239 | 278 |
| 1991 | 192 | 139 | 206 | 258 | 186 | 209 | 155 | 168 | 237 | 207 | 249 | 252 | 205 |
| 1992 | 232 | 217 | 238 | 202 | 179 | 157 | 172 | 229 | 237 | 263 | 236 | 229 | 216 |
| 1993 | 182 | 224 | 235 | 209 | 153 | 168 | 130 | 159 | 137 | 242 | 214 | 160 | 184 |
| 1994 | 161 | 276 | 318 | 226 | 202 | 182 | 164 | 211 | 193 | 159 | 166 | 187 | 203 |
| 1995 | 313 | 289 | 188 | 125 | 109 | 176 | 157 | 171 | 142 | 162 | 262 | 235 | 193 |
| 1996[1] | 243 | 271 | 253 | 258 | 215 | 185 | 194 | 195 | 187 | 246 | 192 | 225 | 222 |

[1] Preliminary. *Source: Energy Information Administration, U.S. Department of Energy*

## U.S. Disposition of Distillate Fuel Oil, Total Product Supplied Thousand Barrels Per Day

| Year | Jan. | Feb. | Mar. | Apr. | May | June | July | Aug. | Sept. | Oct. | Nov. | Dec. | Average |
|---|---|---|---|---|---|---|---|---|---|---|---|---|---|
| 1986 | 3,330 | 3,416 | 3,168 | 2,904 | 2,762 | 2,544 | 2,592 | 2,621 | 2,540 | 2,912 | 2,877 | 3,329 | 2,914 |
| 1987 | 3,310 | 3,345 | 3,116 | 2,991 | 2,684 | 2,790 | 2,713 | 2,553 | 2,838 | 3,151 | 2,932 | 3,318 | 2,976 |
| 1988 | 3,558 | 3,557 | 3,539 | 2,864 | 2,765 | 2,854 | 2,640 | 2,873 | 2,821 | 3,218 | 3,183 | 3,560 | 3,122 |
| 1989 | 3,303 | 3,427 | 3,428 | 2,975 | 2,954 | 3,002 | 2,596 | 2,966 | 2,889 | 3,127 | 3,311 | 3,914 | 3,157 |
| 1990 | 3,185 | 3,260 | 3,277 | 3,043 | 2,900 | 2,923 | 2,726 | 3,218 | 2,864 | 2,960 | 3,094 | 2,816 | 3,021 |
| 1991 | 3,367 | 2,976 | 2,984 | 2,839 | 2,765 | 2,775 | 2,648 | 2,770 | 2,865 | 3,047 | 2,921 | 3,087 | 2,921 |
| 1992 | 3,231 | 3,219 | 3,207 | 3,039 | 2,753 | 2,679 | 2,710 | 2,705 | 2,908 | 3,056 | 2,929 | 3,316 | 2,979 |
| 1993 | 3,128 | 3,465 | 3,420 | 2,943 | 2,685 | 2,863 | 2,674 | 2,820 | 2,973 | 2,983 | 3,218 | 3,357 | 3,041 |
| 1994 | 3,698 | 3,581 | 3,307 | 3,116 | 2,912 | 3,062 | 2,663 | 3,063 | 3,133 | 3,066 | 3,180 | 3,203 | 3,162 |
| 1995 | 3,389 | 3,675 | 3,344 | 3,106 | 2,899 | 3,267 | 2,732 | 3,044 | 3,285 | 3,104 | 3,233 | 3,449 | 3,207 |
| 1996[1] | 3,681 | 3,722 | 3,453 | 3,385 | 3,118 | 3,194 | 3,046 | 3,184 | 3,178 | 3,575 | 3,460 | 3,306 | 3,359 |

[1] Preliminary. *Source: Energy Information Administration, U.S. Department of Energy*

## U.S. Production of Residual Fuel Oil Thousand Barrels Per Day

| Year | Jan. | Feb. | Mar. | Apr. | May | June | July | Aug. | Sept. | Oct. | Nov. | Dec. | Average |
|---|---|---|---|---|---|---|---|---|---|---|---|---|---|
| 1986 | 940 | 856 | 813 | 933 | 913 | 818 | 850 | 896 | 854 | 827 | 975 | 987 | 889 |
| 1987 | 920 | 825 | 863 | 831 | 813 | 864 | 901 | 882 | 904 | 887 | 928 | 1,001 | 885 |
| 1988 | 1,002 | 994 | 948 | 960 | 862 | 880 | 906 | 866 | 852 | 852 | 916 | 1,069 | 926 |
| 1989 | 949 | 930 | 937 | 904 | 934 | 953 | 862 | 903 | 856 | 1,001 | 1,075 | 1,140 | 954 |
| 1990 | 1,163 | 1,060 | 976 | 882 | 884 | 926 | 987 | 944 | 909 | 799 | 846 | 1,021 | 950 |
| 1991 | 1,001 | 1,050 | 995 | 916 | 929 | 933 | 871 | 925 | 838 | 814 | 896 | 1,051 | 934 |
| 1992 | 965 | 957 | 990 | 900 | 964 | 894 | 838 | 815 | 810 | 818 | 895 | 862 | 892 |
| 1993 | 820 | 840 | 818 | 896 | 908 | 795 | 762 | 752 | 822 | 841 | 899 | 869 | 835 |
| 1994 | 809 | 852 | 859 | 846 | 860 | 779 | 807 | 838 | 800 | 755 | 835 | 871 | 826 |
| 1995 | 903 | 776 | 778 | 789 | 748 | 746 | 797 | 801 | 811 | 724 | 705 | 874 | 788 |
| 1996[1] | 774 | 776 | 701 | 671 | 732 | 731 | 646 | 732 | 713 | 693 | 712 | 724 | 717 |

[1] Preliminary. *Source: Energy Information Adminstration, U.S. Department of Energy*

## United States Residual Fuel Oil Supply and Disposition

| Year | Supply: Total Production | Supply: Imports | Disposition: Stock Change | Disposition: Exports | Disposition: Product Supplied | Ending Stocks | Average Sales to End Users[3] |
|---|---|---|---|---|---|---|---|
| | Thousand Barrels per Day | | | | | Mil. Barrels | ¢ per Gallon |
| 1986 | 891 | 681 | 12 | 190 | 1,369 | 53 | 34.3 |
| 1987 | 882 | 510 | -7 | 197 | 1,202 | 50 | 42.3 |
| 1988 | 889 | 669 | -8 | 147 | 1,418 | 47 | 33.4 |
| 1989 | 885 | 565 | [2] | 186 | 1,264 | 47 | 38.5 |
| 1990 | 950 | 504 | 13 | 211 | 1,229 | 49 | 44.4 |
| 1991 | 934 | 453 | 4 | 226 | 1,158 | 50 | 34.0 |
| 1992 | 892 | 375 | -20 | 193 | 1,094 | 43 | 33.6 |
| 1993 | 835 | 373 | 4 | 123 | 1,080 | 44 | 33.7 |
| 1994 | 826 | 314 | -6 | 125 | 1,021 | 42 | 35.2 |
| 1995 | 788 | 187 | -13 | 136 | 852 | 37 | 39.1 |
| 1996[1] | 717 | 246 | 21 | 101 | 840 | 44 | 44.2 |

[1] Preliminary. [2] Less than +500 barrels per day and greater than -500 barrels per day. [3] Refiner price excluding taxes.
*Source: Energy Information Administration, U.S. Department of Energy*

# Hides and Leather

The major producers of bovine hides and skins are the U.S., Argentina, Brazil, and Russia. The U.S. is by far the largest producer. World cattle inventories in the major producing countries were expected to increase by less than 1 percent in 1996. Cattle inventories in the U.S., Mexico, and Canada in 1996 were expected to be about the same as in 1995. In the major countries of South America, inventories were expected to increase by close to 2 percent.

The U.S. commercial cattle slaughter in 1995 was estimated at about 35.6 million head. This was about 4 percent above the 1994 level. In terms of trade, 1995 U.S. cattle hide exports were just over 20 million hides, an increase of close to 12 percent from 1994. There were imports of 1.8 million hides, the highest level in many years. Net exports of cattle hides were therefore 18.3 million hides. This represented an increase of almost 13 percent from 1994.

The major markets for U.S. cattle hides are South Korea, Japan, Taiwan, China, Canada, and Mexico. Exports to South Korea were 8.3 million hides or over 40 percent of the total. Exports to Japan were 3.2 million hides or 16 percent of the U.S. total. Taiwan took 15 percent or just over 3 million hides while China's share was almost 7 percent. Canada imported about 950,000 hides while Mexico took just under 900,000.

Much of the leather produced in the U.S. is for the shoe industry. The U.S. Census Bureau reports that U.S. production of men's nonrubber footwear in the second quarter of 1996 was nearly 9 million pairs, down 10 percent from the first quarter of 1996. For the first half of 1996, production of men's nonrubber footwear was 18.9 million pairs, down 9 percent from the comparable period of 1995. U.S. production of women's footwear in the second quarter of 1996 was 13.2 million pair, up almost 3 percent from the first quarter of 1996. For the January-June 1996 period, production of women's footwear was just under 26 million pairs, up 16 percent from the comparable period of 1995. Production of juvenile footwear in the second quarter of 1996 was 2.1 million pairs, down 11 percent from the first quarter of 1996. For the first half of 1996, juvenile footwear production was 4.5 million pairs, down 23 percent from the comparable period of 1995.

Production of athletic shoes in the second quarter of 1996 was 1.5 million pairs. Data for the first quarter was withheld to avoid disclosing figures for individual companies. Production of all other nonrubber footwear in the second quarter of 1996 was 615,000 pairs. Slipper production in the second quarter of 1996 was 9.9 million pairs, down 6 percent from the first quarter of 1996. For the first six months of 1996, slipper production was 20.5 million pairs, down 9 percent from the comparable period of 1995. Total shipments of nonrubber footwear and slippers in the first half of 1996 was 74.1 million pair compared to 75.7 million pairs in the comparable period of 1995.

## World Production of Bovine Hides and Skins In Thousands of Metric Tons

| Year | Agrentina | Australia | Brazil | Canada | Colombia | France | Germany | Italy | Mexico | New Zealand | Russia[3] | South Africa | Turkey | United Kingdom | United States |
|---|---|---|---|---|---|---|---|---|---|---|---|---|---|---|---|
| 1987 | 314 | 144 | 350 | 85 | 86 | 193 | 203 | 91 | 122 | 54 | 1,060 | 59 | 62 | 101 | 1,128 |
| 1988 | 303 | 139 | 390 | 82 | 93 | 185 | 191 | 89 | 176 | 41 | 1,089 | 51 | 63 | 90 | 1,022 |
| 1989 | 304 | 137 | 429 | 84 | 97 | 170 | 228 | 88 | 222 | 35 | 1,090 | 55 | 65 | 91 | 1,086 |
| 1990 | 307 | 149 | 447 | 78 | 105 | 175 | 247 | 92 | 181 | 40 | 503 | 55 | 67 | 92 | 1,057 |
| 1991 | 308 | 153 | 448 | 75 | 104 | 182 | 251 | 95 | 155 | 44 | 502 | 54 | 64 | 93 | 1,061 |
| 1992 | 298 | 162 | 442 | 77 | 88 | 180 | 205 | 98 | 160 | 44 | 466 | 57 | 66 | 88 | 1,073 |
| 1993 | 303 | 154 | 455 | 73 | 79 | 160 | 175 | 95 | 161 | 46 | 460 | 54 | 65 | 77 | 1,078 |
| 1994 | 305 | 152 | 460 | 74 | 77 | 151 | 160 | 93 | 166 | 46 | 350 | 51 | 64 | 81 | 1,106 |
| 1995 | 301 | 145 | 475 | 75 | 84 | 154 | 160 | 91 | 170 | 50 | 310 | 44 | 66 | 83 | 1,153 |
| 1996[1] | 308 | 148 | 496 | 85 | 85 | 153 | 157 | 90 | 160 | 50 | 285 | 44 | 65 | 85 | 1,188 |
| 1997[2] | 291 | 153 | 515 | 94 | 86 | NA | NA | NA | 162 | 52 | 270 | 47 | 65 | NA | 1,200 |

[1] Preliminary. [2] Forecast. [3] Formerly part of the U.S.S.R.; data not reported separately until 1990. NA = not avaliable.
*Source: Foreign Agricultural Service, U.S. Department of Agriculture*

## Salient Statistics of Hides & Leather in the United States

| Year | New Supply of Cattle Hides: Domestic Slaughter: Federally Inspected | Unin-spected[4] | Total Production | Net Exports | Wholesale Prices - ¢ Lb.: Heavy Native Cows[2] | Heavy Native[3] Steers | Production: All U.S. Tanning | Cattle-Hide | Value of Leather Exports $1,000 | Wholesale Leather Indexes: Upper: Men | Women | Footwear: Production[5] | Export |
|---|---|---|---|---|---|---|---|---|---|---|---|---|---|
| | Thousands of Equivalent Hides | | | | | | In 1,000 Equiv. Hides | | | 1982 = 100 | | Mil. Pairs | |
| 1986 | 35,913 | 1,375 | 37,288 | 26,522 | 68.06 | 63.7 | 14,510 | 12,598 | 313,408 | 107.2 | 104.3 | 241,273 | 12,452 |
| 1987 | 34,468 | 1,179 | 35,647 | 24,007 | 83.43 | 79.9 | 14,750 | 12,754 | 395,536 | 111.4 | 107.2 | 225,888 | 14,575 |
| 1988 | 34,048 | 1,031 | 35,079 | 24,527 | 86.50 | 87.3 | 13,300 | 11,475 | 506,483 | 121.3 | 112.5 | 234,852 | 18,394 |
| 1989 | 33,010 | 907 | 33,917 | 22,500 | 83.16 | 89.4 | 12,932 | 11,242 | 624,925 | 127.5 | 116.2 | 221,790 | 14,358 |
| 1990 | 32,391 | 851 | 33,242 | 20,920 | 92.58 | 92.0 | 14,820 | 13,018 | 750,836 | 135.8 | 120.9 | 184,568 | 15,174 |
| 1991 | 31,887 | 803 | 32,690 | 18,636 | 76.92 | 78.9 | 14,800 | 13,021 | 680,348 | 141.0 | 124.0 | 167,386 | 18,109 |
| 1992 | 32,094 | 780 | 32,874 | 17,810 | 81.71 | 75.9 | 15,900 | 14,474 | 705,038 | 145.0 | 126.4 | 168,451 | 21,401 |
| 1993 | 32,593 | 731 | 33,324 | 17,117 | 82.16 | 78.9 | 18,057 | 16,931 | 764,120 | 145.3 | 129.3 | 171,733 | 20,700 |
| 1994 | 33,483 | 713 | 34,196 | 16,259 | 94.99 | 87.3 | 18,842 | 18,117 | 811,951 | 146.5 | 127.5 | 161,711 | 22,505 |
| 1995[1] | 34,879 | 760 | 35,639 | 18,336 | | 87.6 | 18,092 | 17,480 | 869,991 | 151.0 | 131.1 | 159,084 | 20,571 |

[1] Preliminary. [2] Central U.S., heifers. [3] FOB, Chicago. [4] Includes farm slaughter; diseased and condemned animals and hides taken off fallen animals.
[5] Other than rubber. *Sources: Leather Industries of America; U.S. Department of Commerce*

## U.S. Production of All Footwear (Shoes, Sandals, Slippers, Athletic, Etc.) In Millions of Pairs

| Year | Jan. | Feb. | Mar. | Apr. | May | June | July | Aug. | Sept. | Oct. | Nov. | Dec. | Total |
|---|---|---|---|---|---|---|---|---|---|---|---|---|---|
| 1985 | 22.5 | 21.0 | 22.2 | 22.2 | 24.9 | 21.1 | 19.7 | 24.5 | 22.4 | 24.8 | 21.1 | 18.7 | 265.1 |
| 1986 | 22.5 | 21.6 | 21.3 | 21.2 | 20.8 | 18.4 | 18.4 | 20.8 | 19.7 | 21.4 | 18.4 | 16.6 | 240.9 |
| 1987 | 18.2 | 19.2 | 20.7 | 20.0 | 19.7 | 20.7 | 16.1 | 20.6 | 20.9 | 20.6 | 18.2 | 15.2 | 230.0 |
| 1988 | 16.7 | 20.8 | 21.6 | 19.3 | 20.2 | 19.7 | 14.0 | 21.4 | 21.3 | 21.2 | 21.3 | 17.6 | 234.8 |
| 1989 | 18.1 | 18.5 | 19.6 | 16.6 | 18.7 | 17.5 | 13.7 | 19.7 | 17.4 | 19.0 | 17.5 | 14.3 | 221.9 |
| 1990 | 17.8 | 17.2 | 18.5 | 16.7 | 18.9 | 16.7 | 14.3 | 18.8 | 16.5 | 18.2 | 15.4 | 12.6 | 184.6 |
| 1991 | ---------- | 48.1 | ---------- | ---------- | 37.8 | ---------- | ---------- | 41.8 | ---------- | ---------- | 41.2 | ---------- | 169.0 |
| 1992 | ---------- | 41.1 | ---------- | ---------- | 40.8 | ---------- | ---------- | 43.6 | ---------- | ---------- | 39.3 | ---------- | 164.8 |
| 1993 | ---------- | 43.3 | ---------- | ---------- | 44.6 | ---------- | ---------- | 42.8 | ---------- | ---------- | 41.0 | ---------- | 171.7 |
| 1994 | ---------- | 42.5 | ---------- | ---------- | 40.8 | ---------- | ---------- | 40.1 | ---------- | ---------- | 39.5 | ---------- | 163.0 |
| 1995 | ---------- | 37.3 | ---------- | ---------- | 38.3 | ---------- | ---------- | 35.0 | ---------- | ---------- | 36.9 | ---------- | 147.6 |
| 1996[1] | ---------- | 37.8 | ---------- | ---------- | 36.1 | ---------- | ---------- | 33.7 | ---------- | ---------- | 36.2 | ---------- | 143.8 |

[1] Preliminary. *Source: U.S. Department of Commerce*

## Average Factory Price[2] of Footwear in the United States In Dollars Per Pair

| Year | Jan. | Feb. | Mar. | Apr. | May | June | July | Aug. | Sept. | Oct. | Nov. | Dec. | Average |
|---|---|---|---|---|---|---|---|---|---|---|---|---|---|
| 1985 | 15.24 | 14.97 | 14.10 | 14.87 | 14.86 | 15.35 | 14.24 | 14.55 | 14.12 | 13.71 | 13.56 | 15.13 | 14.56 |
| 1986 | 14.60 | 13.86 | 13.82 | 14.22 | 15.00 | 14.98 | 15.53 | 14.38 | 14.64 | 14.38 | 14.40 | 16.50 | 14.69 |
| 1987 | 15.09 | 14.58 | 14.05 | 15.15 | 15.89 | 15.63 | 16.47 | 15.60 | 15.63 | 15.23 | 15.89 | 17.96 | 15.60 |
| 1988 | 16.57 | 14.80 | 13.88 | 15.97 | 13.77 | 14.46 | 17.27 | 14.92 | 15.32 | 15.18 | 14.98 | 16.73 | 15.32 |
| 1989 | 15.94 | 15.35 | 15.00 | 16.90 | 15.77 | 16.45 | 16.36 | 17.17 | 17.38 | 17.20 | 17.73 | 18.68 | 16.98 |
| 1990 | ---------- | 18.04 | ---------- | ---------- | 18.65 | ---------- | ---------- | 19.91 | ---------- | ---------- | 20.72 | ---------- | 19.37 |
| 1991 | ---------- | 22.14 | ---------- | ---------- | 20.40 | ---------- | ---------- | 19.74 | ---------- | ---------- | 18.52 | ---------- | 20.14 |
| 1992 | ---------- | 20.19 | ---------- | ---------- | 22.21 | ---------- | ---------- | 21.15 | ---------- | ---------- | 20.46 | ---------- | 20.96 |
| 1993 | ---------- | 21.62 | ---------- | ---------- | 21.67 | ---------- | ---------- | 21.37 | ---------- | ---------- | 21.79 | ---------- | 21.61 |
| 1994 | ---------- | 25.77 | ---------- | ---------- | 23.60 | ---------- | ---------- | 21.49 | ---------- | ---------- | 22.44 | ---------- | 23.22 |
| 1995 | ---------- | 20.86 | ---------- | ---------- | 23.42 | ---------- | ---------- | 22.72 | ---------- | ---------- | 19.53 | ---------- | 21.54 |
| 1996[1] | ---------- | 21.41 | ---------- | ---------- | 20.63 | ---------- | ---------- | 20.05 | ---------- | ---------- | 18.56 | ---------- | 20.02 |

[1] Preliminary. [2] Average value of factory shipments per pair. *Source: U.S. Department of Commerce*

## U.S. Imports and Exports of All Cattle Hides In Thousands of Hides

| | Imports | | U.S. Exports -- By Country of Destination | | | | | | | | | | | | |
|---|---|---|---|---|---|---|---|---|---|---|---|---|---|---|---|
| Year | Total | From Canada | Total | Canada | France | Germany | Italy | Japan | Rep. of Korea | Mexico | Netherlands | Portugal | Romania | Spain | Taiwan | Thailand |
| 1985 | 1,044 | 883 | 25,428 | 796 | 220 | 125 | 1,169 | 6,835 | 6,453 | 2,309 | 82 | 180 | 1,168 | 340 | 2,831 | 17 |
| 1986 | 761 | 594 | 26,963 | 714 | 275 | 85 | 1,553 | 6,626 | 9,324 | 1,042 | 156 | 247 | 688 | 255 | 3,579 | 20 |
| 1987 | 490 | 338 | 24,235 | 924 | 158 | 56 | 394 | 5,998 | 10,077 | 1,437 | 85 | 82 | 308 | 200 | 3,184 | 37 |
| 1988 | 642 | 481 | 24,687 | 759 | 93 | 97 | 319 | 7,140 | 9,986 | 1,865 | 100 | 44 | 624 | 142 | 2,493 | 35 |
| 1989 | 901 | 1,043 | 23,401 | 614 | 17 | 68 | 343 | 6,268 | 10,322 | 1,284 | 132 | 46 | 1,154 | 64 | 1,886 | 70 |
| 1990 | 661 | 678 | 21,582 | 674 | 28 | 78 | 136 | 6,802 | 9,839 | 1,438 | 99 | 29 | 253 | 175 | 1,476 | 91 |
| 1991 | 1,549 | 1,088 | 20,185 | 561 | 4 | 52 | 138 | 4,662 | 9,300 | 2,702 | 65 | 7 | ----- | 39 | 2,058 | 123 |
| 1992 | 1,536 | 1,457 | 19,347 | 684 | 2 | ----- | 107 | 4,647 | 8,589 | 2,729 | 56 | 100 | 4 | 30 | 1,823 | 160 |
| 1993 | 1,660 | 1,597 | 18,777 | 965 | 8 | 1 | 354 | 4,167 | 7,919 | 2,217 | 9 | 79 | 1 | 60 | 1,950 | 386 |
| 1994 | 1,731 | ----- | 17,990 | 995 | 15 | 2 | 309 | 3,133 | 7,472 | 1,553 | 8 | 168 | 72 | 141 | 2,491 | 332 |
| 1995[1] | 1,759 | ----- | 20,095 | 952 | 6 | 12 | 332 | 3,246 | 8,283 | 899 | 17 | 111 | 63 | 215 | 3,017 | 781 |

[1] Preliminary. *Source: Leather Industries of America*

## Foreign Trade of Bovine Hides and Skins by Selected Countries In Metric Tons

| | Imports | | | | | | | | Exports | | | | | | | |
|---|---|---|---|---|---|---|---|---|---|---|---|---|---|---|---|---|
| Year | Hong Kong | Italy | Japan | Mexico | Rep. of Korea | Spain | Taiwan | United States | Australia | Canada | Germany | Hong Kong | Netherlands | New Zealand | Russia | United States |
| 1990 | 54 | 383 | 236 | 52 | 373 | 96 | 73 | 24 | 134 | 88 | 129 | 53 | 105 | 23 | 16 | 693 |
| 1991 | 67 | 156 | 206 | 70 | 392 | 39 | 100 | 67 | 149 | 90 | 63 | 69 | 70 | 33 | 22 | 637 |
| 1992 | 80 | 131 | 188 | 71 | 385 | 26 | 91 | 65 | 144 | 74 | 38 | 75 | 66 | 31 | 28 | 610 |
| 1993 | 81 | 141 | 188 | 71 | 372 | 35 | 94 | 57 | 142 | 87 | 40 | 76 | 35 | 21 | 150 | 581 |
| 1994 | 95 | 243 | 139 | 60 | 356 | 29 | 112 | 56 | 96 | 79 | 24 | 93 | 37 | 22 | 216 | 602 |
| 1995 | 100 | 255 | 151 | 30 | 342 | 30 | 112 | 55 | 85 | 90 | 20 | 99 | 40 | 22 | 195 | 626 |
| 1996[1] | 108 | 260 | 135 | 40 | 340 | 30 | 121 | 56 | 90 | 96 | 20 | 107 | 40 | 23 | 180 | 645 |
| 1997[2] | 114 | NA | 140 | 43 | 320 | NA | 115 | 55 | 95 | 100 | NA | 113 | NA | 24 | 185 | 651 |

[1] Preliminary. [2] Forecast. NA = not avaliable. *Source: Foreign Agricultural Service, U.S. Department of Agriculture*

# HIDES AND LEATHER

## Utilization of Bovine Hides and Skins by Selected Countries In Metric Tons

| Year | Argentina | Brazil | Colombia | Germany | Italy | Japan | Mexico | Poland | Portugal | Rep. of Korea | Russia | Spain | Taiwan | Turkey | United States |
|---|---|---|---|---|---|---|---|---|---|---|---|---|---|---|---|
| 1990 | 307 | 395 | 100 | 176 | 425 | 261 | 233 | 60 | 67 | 380 | 487 | 129 | 74 | 74 | 388 |
| 1991 | 308 | 396 | 98 | 143 | 435 | 253 | 225 | 70 | 67 | 400 | 480 | 119 | 101 | 78 | 491 |
| 1992 | 298 | 382 | 97 | 129 | 435 | 229 | 231 | 64 | 65 | 400 | 438 | 98 | 91 | 90 | 528 |
| 1993 | 302 | 400 | 94 | 100 | 435 | 226 | 232 | 81 | 62 | 385 | 315 | 98 | 94 | 95 | 554 |
| 1994 | 304 | 392 | 96 | 85 | 550 | 200 | 226 | 75 | 80 | 374 | 139 | 94 | 112 | 85 | 560 |
| 1995 | 300 | 360 | 89 | 120 | 570 | 190 | 200 | 72 | 70 | 355 | 120 | 100 | 112 | 100 | 582 |
| 1996[1] | 307 | 366 | 90 | 117 | 570 | 180 | 200 | 75 | 75 | 350 | 110 | 101 | 121 | 110 | 599 |
| 1997[2] | 290 | 370 | 91 | NA | NA | 185 | 205 | 78 | NA | 345 | 90 | NA | 115 | 110 | 604 |

[1] Preliminary. [2] Forecast. NA = not avaliable. *Source: Foreign Agricultural Service, U.S. Department of Agriculture*

## Wholesale Price of Hides (Packer Native Steer) F.O.B. Chicago In Cents Per Pound

| Year | Jan. | Feb. | Mar. | Apr. | May | June | July | Aug. | Sept. | Oct. | Nov. | Dec. | Average |
|---|---|---|---|---|---|---|---|---|---|---|---|---|---|
| 1983 | 37.10 | 37.70 | 40.40 | 46.00 | 50.80 | 51.80 | 59.20 | 57.30 | 53.30 | 53.80 | 56.70 | 54.80 | 49.91 |
| 1984 | 54.80 | 56.00 | 62.00 | 61.70 | 64.50 | 64.70 | 66.50 | 69.20 | 68.90 | 61.70 | 52.50 | 47.90 | 60.87 |
| 1985 | 46.00 | 41.70 | 45.50 | 54.70 | 57.00 | 53.10 | 54.00 | 55.70 | 57.10 | 57.60 | 63.50 | 60.80 | 53.89 |
| 1986 | 57.70 | 58.40 | 57.70 | 63.10 | 68.60 | 68.70 | 68.30 | 69.90 | 64.50 | 65.90 | 65.20 | 61.80 | 64.15 |
| 1987 | 61.80 | 64.20 | 69.70 | 82.40 | 83.50 | 81.70 | 82.50 | 83.80 | 89.00 | 89.90 | 85.40 | 83.70 | 79.80 |
| 1988 | 82.90 | 86.30 | 97.40 | 100.00 | 99.20 | 87.60 | 84.20 | 93.70 | 87.30 | 80.50 | 77.10 | 76.70 | 87.74 |
| 1989 | 84.00 | 87.40 | 94.60 | 87.50 | 85.20 | 85.00 | 90.30 | 91.70 | 95.90 | 94.70 | 92.90 | 90.90 | 90.01 |
| 1990 | 92.70 | 92.80 | 95.50 | 100.00 | 99.60 | 97.90 | 96.70 | 91.70 | 87.50 | 84.60 | 83.00 | 84.40 | 92.20 |
| 1991 | 81.60 | 76.40 | 75.70 | 86.30 | 88.80 | 86.70 | 84.10 | 77.20 | 74.10 | 75.40 | 75.40 | 71.30 | 79.42 |
| 1992 | 70.60 | 67.80 | 69.90 | 76.00 | 80.00 | 76.80 | 76.50 | 72.80 | 77.60 | 81.20 | 80.10 | 81.00 | 75.86 |
| 1993 | 79.80 | 81.80 | 81.50 | 81.40 | 80.40 | 76.90 | 76.60 | 79.30 | 80.50 | 81.80 | 80.80 | 79.80 | 80.05 |
| 1994 | 75.10 | 75.10 | 79.00 | 84.80 | 87.30 | 88.80 | 90.40 | 89.80 | 93.90 | 93.70 | 93.20 | 91.13 | 86.85 |
| 1995 | 90.10 | 91.42 | 97.99 | 102.32 | 99.64 | 92.45 | 85.74 | 82.46 | 82.45 | 82.16 | 78.02 | 73.02 | 88.15 |
| 1996 | 73.67 | 75.11 | 77.96 | 84.58 | 87.56 | 82.51 | 89.45 | 96.06 | 98.91 | 101.51 | 94.60 | 90.65 | 87.71 |

*Source: The Wall Street Journal*

# Hogs

The January 1, 1996 world hog inventory of 784 million head compares with 762 million a year earlier. China, the world's largest hog producer with more than half the total, had a record high 441 million head in early 1996 vs. 415 million a year earlier. U.S. hog numbers appear to be in a long term slide; The January 1, 1995 inventory of 60 million head compares with 58.2 million a year later and an estimated 57.4 million at the start of 1997, about 8 percent of the world total. U.S. hog slaughter, however, runs about 10-12 percent of world slaughter and pork production somewhat higher, the latter of 7.8 million metric tons in 1996 compares with the world total of 74 million tons.

World pork consumption is rising, paced by China. The 1996 total of nearly 74 million tons compares with less than 70 million in the first half of the 1990's, with China's use put at 37 million tons vs. an average of less than 30 million in the early 1990's. 1996 U.S. consumption of 7.7 million tons compares with about 8 million in the early 1990's. Per capita U.S. pork use totaled slightly more than 30 kilograms in recent years but dropped to 28.8 kg in 1996. A strong advertising campaign in the U.S. stressing pork as a white meat rather than red has helped to maintain per capita use. Per capita consumption in the European Union averages 42 kg.

More than half the inventory share of U.S. hog marketings now come from contract hog operations. In a contractual agreement, the contractor provides the hogs, feed, medication and supplies while the contractee provides the housing, utilities and labor. Southern states, led by North Carolina, have seen a dramatic growth in contractual operations in recent years. Still, most U.S. producers continue to raise hogs in farrow-to-finish operations with Iowa the top producer amongst a list top-heavy with Corn Belt states.

On September 1, 1996, the U.S. total hog inventory of 58.2 million head compared with the year earlier 60.5 million, of which about 51.4 million were marketable hogs vs. 53.6 million in 1995. Stronger hog prices in mid-1996 kept producer returns well above cash costs and averted a larger liquidation of herds.

Commercial 1995 U.S. hog slaughter totaled a record large 96.3 million head with an average dressed weight of 185 pounds and yielding 17.8 billion pounds of pork; for 1996, 93 million head were slaughtered with an average weight of 184 pounds and pork production of 17.2 billion pounds. The 1997 slaughter forecast of 94.9 million head is expected to yield 17.5 billion pounds of pork.

World pork exports in 1996 of 2.3 million tons were marginally higher than in 1995 with another small gain forecast for 1997. The U.S. is the largest exporter, 430,000 tons in 1996, largely to Japan and Canada. U.S. pork imports in 1996 of 280,000 tons compares with 301,000 in 1995. Canada and Denmark are the largest suppliers to the U.S. The U.S. does import live hogs from Canada, often more than 200,000 head per month.

Wholesale barrow and gilt prices during 1996 averaged $53.45 per cwt., basis Iowa/Minnesota, vs. $42.35 in 1995. Prices are forecast to range between $51 to $55 in 1997. 1996 Retail pork prices were expected to average 10 percent above 1995 prices and rise another 2 1/2 percent in 1997.

### *Futures Markets*

Live hog futures and options are traded on the Chicago Mercantile Exchange (CME) and the Mid-American Commodity Exchange (MidAm). Live hog futures are traded on the Budapest Commodity Exchange.

*Beginning in February 1997 Lean Hog futures replace Live Hog contracts on the Chicago Mercantile Exchange (CME). Lean Hog futures settle to the CME Lean Hog Index™ which tracks the value of lean pork at select U.S. packing plants.*

## World Hog Numbers in Specified Countries as of January 1 In Thousands of Head

| Year | Brazil | Canada | China | Denmark | France | Germany | Italy | Japan | Mexico | Philippines | Poland | Russia | Spain | Ukraine | United Kingdom | United States |
|---|---|---|---|---|---|---|---|---|---|---|---|---|---|---|---|---|
| 1991 | 32,550 | 10,468 | 362,408 | 9,282 | 12,013 | 30,818 | 8,837 | 11,355 | 8,593 | 8,007 | 19,739 | 38,500 | 16,001 | 19,427 | 7,380 | 54,416 |
| 1992 | 33,050 | 10,498 | 369,646 | 9,767 | 12,067 | 26,063 | 8,549 | 10,966 | 9,928 | 8,022 | 20,725 | 35,384 | 17,209 | 17,839 | 7,519 | 57,469 |
| 1993 | 31,050 | 10,577 | 384,210 | 10,345 | 13,015 | 26,514 | 8,307 | 10,783 | 11,298 | 7,954 | 21,059 | 31,520 | 18,260 | 16,175 | 7,705 | 58,202 |
| 1994 | 31,200 | 10,851 | 393,000 | 10,870 | 14,291 | 26,075 | 8,348 | 10,622 | 12,083 | 8,227 | 17,422 | 28,557 | 18,234 | 15,298 | 7,869 | 57,904 |
| 1995 | 31,338 | 11,673 | 414,619 | 10,864 | 14,593 | 24,698 | 8,000 | 10,250 | 12,513 | 8,941 | 19,138 | 24,900 | 18,295 | 13,946 | 7,879 | 59,990 |
| 1996[1] | 32,497 | 12,043 | 441,206 | 10,709 | 14,524 | 23,736 | 7,964 | 9,900 | 11,118 | 9,023 | 20,343 | 22,600 | 17,583 | 13,144 | 7,351 | 58,200 |
| 1997[2] | 32,739 | 11,800 | 408,516 | 10,923 | 14,640 | 22,800 | 7,900 | 9,700 | 10,218 | 9,078 | 18,000 | 20,800 | 18,000 | 12,750 | 7,650 | 57,350 |

[1] Preliminary. [2] Forecast. *Source: Foreign Agricultural Service, U.S. Department of Agricultures*

## Salient Statistics of Pigs and Hogs in the U.S.

| | Pig Crop | | | | | | Value of Hogs on Farms, Dec. 1 | | Hog Marketings | Quantity Produced | Value of Production | Hogs Slaughtered in Thousand Heads | | | | |
|---|---|---|---|---|---|---|---|---|---|---|---|---|---|---|---|---|
| | Spring[3] | | | Fall[4] | | | | | | | | Commercial | | | | |
| Year | Sows Farrowed - 1,000s of Head - | Pig Crop - 1,000s of Head - | Pigs Per Liter | Sows Farrowed - 1,000s of Head - | Pig Crop - 1,000s of Head - | Pigs Per Liter | $ Per Head | Total Million $ | Thousand Head | (Live Wt.) Mil. Lbs. | Mil. $ | Federally Inspected | Other | Total | Farm | Total |
| 1990 | 5,732 | 45,223 | 7.89 | 5,709 | 44,877 | 7.86 | 85.4 | 4,648 | 89,240 | 21,287 | 11,346 | 82,901 | 2,235 | 85,136 | 280 | 85,416 |
| 1991 | 5,988 | 47,413 | 7.92 | 6,071 | 47,902 | 7.89 | 68.8 | 3,966 | 92,220 | 22,727 | 11,067 | 85,952 | 2,217 | 88,169 | 266 | 88,435 |
| 1992 | 6,260 | 50,466 | 8.06 | 6,012 | 48,676 | 8.10 | 71.2 | 4,147 | 98,589 | 23,947 | 9,854 | 92,611 | 2,278 | 94,888 | 268 | 95,156 |
| 1993 | 6,028 | 49,006 | 8.13 | 5,954 | 48,044 | 8.07 | 74.9 | 4,338 | 98,351 | 23,693 | 10,628 | 90,933 | 2,135 | 93,069 | 222 | 93,291 |
| 1994 | 6,275 | 51,352 | 8.18 | 6,104 | 50,064 | 8.20 | 53.2 | 3,192 | 100,747 | 24,437 | 9,692 | 93,435 | 2,261 | 95,697 | 195 | 95,892 |
| 1995[1] | 6,056 | 50,224 | 8.29 | 5,791 | 48,292 | 8.34 | 70.7 | 7,256 | 103,309 | 24,121 | 9,750 | 94,203 | 2,125 | 96,326 | 191 | 96,547 |
| 1996[2] | 5,709 | 48,146 | 8.43 | 5,478 | 46,826 | 8.55 | | | | | | 90,534 | 1,905 | 92,439 | | |

[1] Preliminary. [2] Estimate. [3] December-May. [4] June-November. *Source: Economic Research Service, U.S. Department of Agriculture*

# HOGS

## Hogs and Pigs on U.S. Farms on December 1 In Thousands of Head

| Year | Georgia | Illinois | Indiana | Iowa | Kansas | Kentucky | Minne-sota | Missouri | Nebraska | North Carolina | Ohio | Penn-slvanyia | South Dakota | Wis-consin | Total |
|---|---|---|---|---|---|---|---|---|---|---|---|---|---|---|---|
| 1988 | 1,210 | 5,600 | 4,300 | 14,000 | 1,500 | 1,090 | 4,690 | 2,850 | 4,150 | 2,700 | 2,210 | 970 | 1,810 | 1,275 | 55,469 |
| 1989 | 1,200 | 5,700 | 4,350 | 13,500 | 1,450 | 975 | 4,450 | 2,700 | 4,200 | 2,570 | 2,080 | 975 | 1,720 | 1,150 | 53,821 |
| 1990 | 1,100 | 5,700 | 4,400 | 13,800 | 1,500 | 920 | 4,500 | 2,800 | 4,300 | 2,800 | 2,000 | 920 | 1,770 | 1,200 | 54,477 |
| 1991 | 1,130 | 5,900 | 4,600 | 15,000 | 1,430 | 950 | 4,900 | 2,700 | 4,500 | 3,650 | 1,925 | 920 | 1,950 | 1,180 | 57,684 |
| 1992 | 1,100 | 5,900 | 4,600 | 16,400 | 1,440 | 870 | 4,700 | 2,850 | 4,650 | 4,500 | 1,800 | 950 | 1,830 | 1,210 | 59,815 |
| 1993 | 1,000 | 5,450 | 4,300 | 15,000 | 1,350 | 850 | 4,750 | 3,000 | 4,300 | 5,400 | 1,630 | 1,060 | 1,750 | 1,170 | 57,904 |
| 1994 | 1,020 | 5,350 | 4,500 | 14,500 | 1,310 | 780 | 4,850 | 3,500 | 4,350 | 7,000 | 1,800 | 1,090 | 1,740 | 1,040 | 59,990 |
| 1995 | 900 | 4,800 | 4,000 | 13,400 | 1,230 | 800 | 4,950 | 1,100 | 4,050 | 8,200 | 1,800 | 1,000 | 1,450 | 900 | 58,264 |
| 1996[1] | 800 | 4,400 | 3,750 | 12,200 | 1,450 | 625 | 4,850 | 3,500 | 3,600 | 9,300 | 1,500 | 950 | 1,200 | 800 | 56,171 |

[1] Preliminary. *Source: National Agricultural Statistics Service, U.S. Department of Agriculture*

## Quarterly 10 -- U.S. State Hogs & Pigs Report In Thousands of Head

| Year[2] | Inventory[3] | Breeding[3] | Market[3] | Farrowings | Pig Crop | Year[2] | Inventory[3] | Breeding[3] | Market[3] | Farrowings | Pig Crop |
|---|---|---|---|---|---|---|---|---|---|---|---|
| 1991 | 42,900 | 5,257 | 37,643 | 9,516 | 75,330 | 1994 | 57,904 | 7,130 | 50,739 | 12,376 | 101,400 |
| I | 42,900 | 5,257 | 37,643 | 2,129 | 16,700 | I | 57,904 | 7,130 | 50,739 | 2,885 | 23,368 |
| II | 41,990 | 5,450 | 36,540 | 2,577 | 20,555 | II | 57,350 | 7,210 | 50,140 | 3,390 | 27,984 |
| III | 44,520 | 5,700 | 38,820 | 2,413 | 19,260 | III | 60,715 | 7,565 | 53,150 | 3,107 | 25,547 |
| IV | 46,950 | 5,685 | 41,265 | 2,433 | 18,551 | IV | 62,320 | 7,415 | 54,905 | 2,997 | 24,517 |
| 1992 | 45,735 | 5,610 | 40,125 | 10,202 | 82,497 | 1995[1] | 59,990 | 7,060 | 52,930 | 11,847 | 98,516 |
| I | 45,735 | 5,610 | 40,125 | 2,296 | 18,532 | I | 59,990 | 7,060 | 52,930 | 2,886 | 23,851 |
| II | 44,800 | 5,555 | 39,245 | 2,663 | 21,570 | II | 58,465 | 6,998 | 51,467 | 3,170 | 26,373 |
| III | 47,255 | 5,845 | 41,410 | 2,501 | 20,395 | III | 59,560 | 7,180 | 52,380 | 2,976 | 24,813 |
| IV | 49,175 | 5,840 | 43,335 | 2,398 | 19,351 | IV | 60,540 | 6,898 | 53,642 | 2,815 | 23,479 |
| 1993 | 58,202 | 7,109 | 51,093 | 11,982 | 97,050 | 1996[1] | 28,264 | 6,839 | 51,425 | 11,270 | 94,972 |
| I | 58,202 | 7,109 | 51,093 | 3,665 | 29,739 | I | 28,264 | 6,839 | 51,425 | 2,745 | 23,054 |
| II | 47,145 | 5,735 | 41,410 | 2,363 | 19,267 | II | 56,340 | 6,765 | 49,575 | 2,964 | 25,092 |
| III | 58,395 | 7,320 | 51,075 | 2,972 | 24,041 | III | 57,200 | 6,870 | 50,330 | 2,760 | 23,667 |
| IV | 59,030 | 7,130 | 51,900 | 2,982 | 24,003 | IV | 58,200 | 6,770 | 51,430 | 2,801 | 23,159 |

[1] Preliminary. [2] Quarters are December preceding year-February (I), March-May (II), June-August (III) and September-November (IV). [3] Beginning of period. *Source: National Agricultural Statistics Service, U.S.Department of Agriculture*

## Hog-Corn Price Ratio[1] in the U.S.

| Year | Jan. | Feb. | Mar. | Apr. | May | June | July | Aug. | Sept. | Oct. | Nov. | Dec. | Average |
|---|---|---|---|---|---|---|---|---|---|---|---|---|---|
| 1986 | 31.9 | 33.9 | 32.2 | 33.4 | 32.8 | 35.0 | 37.3 | 39.9 | 40.2 | 37.9 | 35.9 | 33.7 | 34.6 |
| 1987 | 24.3 | 25.0 | 22.7 | 22.3 | 23.9 | 19.5 | 16.2 | 16.9 | 36.4 | 31.5 | 25.2 | 23.4 | 21.4 |
| 1988 | 15.7 | 15.6 | 15.1 | 14.4 | 16.1 | 17.9 | 18.6 | 20.1 | 15.7 | 15.0 | 14.4 | 15.7 | 16.7 |
| 1989 | 20.5 | 20.8 | 21.6 | 21.4 | 23.4 | 22.9 | 23.2 | 23.3 | 19.0 | 21.0 | 20.1 | 21.2 | 22.1 |
| 1990 | 22.0 | 22.5 | 21.5 | 21.0 | 22.7 | 23.7 | 23.9 | 22.0 | 22.3 | 23.3 | 25.9 | 21.5 | 22.4 |
| 1991 | 22.0 | 22.5 | 21.5 | 21.0 | 22.7 | 23.7 | 23.9 | 22.0 | 19.9 | 18.9 | 16.6 | 16.6 | 20.9 |
| 1992 | 15.3 | 16.3 | 15.7 | 16.5 | 18.1 | 18.9 | 19.1 | 20.5 | 19.5 | 20.5 | 20.8 | 21.2 | 18.5 |
| 1993 | 20.3 | 22.0 | 22.1 | 21.0 | 21.9 | 23.0 | 20.6 | 21.0 | 21.6 | 20.6 | 17.3 | 15.2 | 20.6 |
| 1994 | 16.1 | 17.2 | 16.2 | 16.1 | 16.4 | 16.3 | 18.6 | 19.4 | 16.2 | 15.4 | 14.1 | 14.5 | 16.4 |
| 1995 | 16.8 | 17.5 | 16.4 | 15.1 | 15.4 | 16.8 | 17.6 | 18.5 | 18.0 | 16.4 | 13.9 | 14.2 | 16.4 |
| 1996[2] | 13.7 | 13.8 | 13.8 | 12.9 | 13.7 | 13.3 | 13.3 | 13.9 | 15.4 | 19.2 | 20.5 | 21.1 | 15.4 |

[1] Bushels of corn equal in value to 100 pounds of hog, live weight [2] Preliminary. *Source: Economic Research Service, U.S. Department of Agriculture*

## Cold Storage Holdings of Frozen Pork[1] in the U.S., on First of Month In Millions of Pounds

| Year | Jan. | Feb. | Mar. | Apr. | May | June | July | Aug. | Sept. | Oct. | Nov. | Dec. |
|---|---|---|---|---|---|---|---|---|---|---|---|---|
| 1986 | 229.4 | 235.4 | 239.1 | 253.5 | 282.0 | 275.6 | 247.7 | 214.9 | 184.7 | 185.9 | 215.8 | 206.2 |
| 1987 | 197.1 | 217.7 | 228.5 | 221.8 | 217.8 | 218.8 | 189.2 | 181.1 | 175.1 | 186.2 | 212.2 | 251.7 |
| 1988 | 285.4 | 291.5 | 308.2 | 345.8 | 397.3 | 388.6 | 362.8 | 337.2 | 287.0 | 288.0 | 320.8 | 361.3 |
| 1989 | 357.9 | 377.6 | 393.5 | 392.8 | 432.6 | 428.1 | 380.1 | 342.6 | 277.9 | 278.0 | 275.8 | 279.2 |
| 1990 | 255.8 | 272.5 | 303.9 | 294.6 | 320.3 | 320.3 | 292.6 | 256.4 | 224.7 | 225.8 | 231.9 | 221.5 |
| 1991 | 233.6 | 247.0 | 281.2 | 289.0 | 340.0 | 333.3 | 312.3 | 277.9 | 282.4 | 280.5 | 299.7 | 308.0 |
| 1992 | 311.1 | 341.2 | 364.0 | 372.2 | 362.6 | 344.9 | 319.0 | 307.0 | 266.7 | 297.3 | 306.8 | 316.7 |
| 1993 | 314.5 | 329.5 | 344.4 | 330.4 | 378.5 | 371.6 | 351.3 | 342.5 | 308.9 | 311.2 | 324.8 | 313.0 |
| 1994 | 299.2 | 348.8 | 356.9 | 393.1 | 429.7 | 437.6 | 410.8 | 393.7 | 364.0 | 352.7 | 385.4 | 383.2 |
| 1995 | 365.3 | 389.6 | 395.1 | 416.8 | 422.3 | 434.9 | 431.1 | 408.3 | 354.0 | 332.6 | 321.6 | 347.1 |
| 1996[2] | 334.8 | 382.2 | 385.5 | 352.9 | 385.5 | 381.3 | 351.8 | 322.7 | 322.9 | 340.3 | 333.3 | 316.4 |

[1] Excludes lard. [2] Preliminary. *Source: Economic Research Service, U.S. Department of Agriculture*

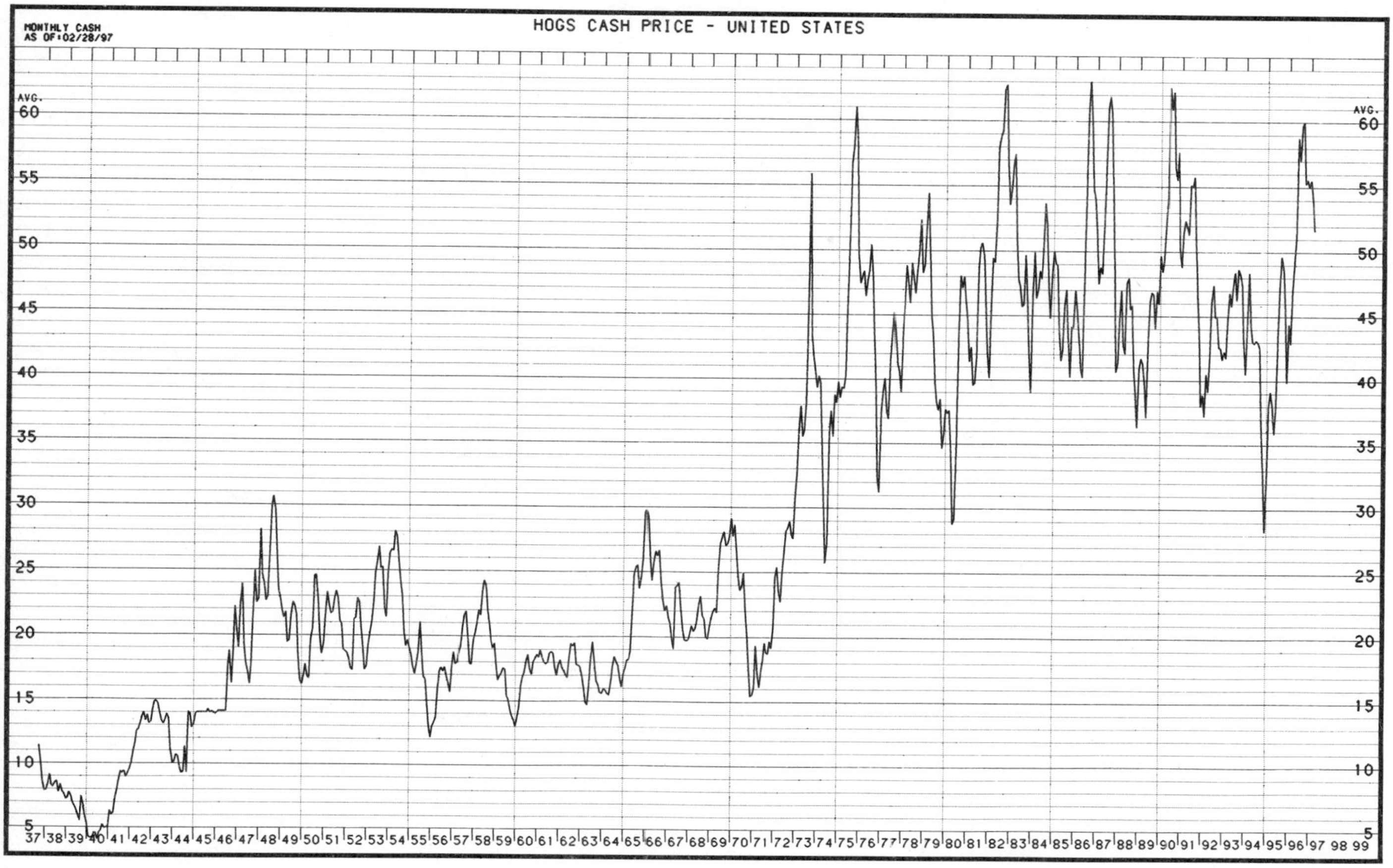


**Average Wholesale Price of Hogs, Average (All Weights) at Sioux City** In Dollars Per Hundred Pounds (Hwt.)

| Year | Jan. | Feb. | Mar. | Apr. | May | June | July | Aug. | Sept. | Oct. | Nov. | Dec. | Average |
|---|---|---|---|---|---|---|---|---|---|---|---|---|---|
| 1987 | 47.56 | 49.08 | 48.67 | 52.10 | 55.79 | 61.37 | 62.69 | 50.56 | 55.19 | 49.28 | 40.74 | 41.56 | 51.22 |
| 1988 | 44.59 | 47.45 | 43.19 | 42.28 | 47.75 | 48.26 | 45.60 | 45.98 | 41.28 | 38.92 | 36.52 | 40.58 | 43.53 |
| 1989 | 41.64 | 41.11 | 39.88 | 37.22 | 42.40 | 46.24 | 47.26 | 47.04 | 44.58 | 47.49 | 47.21 | 49.65 | 44.31 |
| 1990 | 48.41 | 49.48 | 52.56 | 54.63 | 62.80 | 61.34 | 62.54 | 56.37 | 55.64 | 58.02 | 50.17 | 48.96 | 55.08 |
| 1991 | 51.32 | 52.31 | 51.92 | 51.42 | 54.83 | 54.79 | 55.74 | 51.11 | 46.76 | 43.51 | 38.29 | 38.93 | 49.24 |
| 1992 | 37.15 | 40.45 | 39.09 | 42.01 | 45.90 | 47.59 | 44.98 | 44.88 | 42.50 | 42.57 | 41.98 | 42.12 | 42.60 |
| 1993 | 41.66 | 44.57 | 46.76 | 45.46 | 47.10 | 48.52 | 46.38 | 48.67 | 48.40 | 47.27 | 42.76 | 40.38 | 45.66 |
| 1994 | 43.99 | 48.12 | 44.30 | 42.72 | 42.27 | 42.76 | 42.62 | 42.37 | 35.49 | 32.56 | 28.25 | 31.59 | 39.75 |
| 1995 | 37.82 | 39.09 | 37.94 | 35.88 | 37.35 | 43.03 | 47.18 | 49.46 | 48.67 | 45.42 | 40.02 | 43.80 | 42.14 |
| 1996[1] | 42.39 | 46.93 | 49.06 | 50.88 | 58.29 | 56.45 | 59.47 | 60.49 | 54.60 | 55.41 | 54.42 | 55.00 | 53.62 |

[1] Preliminary. *Source: Economic Research Service, U.S. Department of Agriculture*

**Average Price Received by Farmers for Hogs in the U.S.** In Cents Per Pound

| Year | Jan. | Feb. | Mar. | Apr. | May | June | July | Aug. | Sept. | Oct. | Nov. | Dec. | Average |
|---|---|---|---|---|---|---|---|---|---|---|---|---|---|
| 1987 | 47.20 | 48.20 | 47.40 | 50.80 | 54.40 | 59.20 | 59.60 | 58.60 | 54.30 | 48.90 | 40.60 | 40.30 | 50.79 |
| 1988 | 43.00 | 45.80 | 42.20 | 41.90 | 46.30 | 47.10 | 44.10 | 44.70 | 40.70 | 38.70 | 36.20 | 39.70 | 42.53 |
| 1989 | 40.90 | 40.40 | 39.30 | 36.90 | 41.60 | 45.10 | 45.90 | 45.60 | 43.40 | 46.60 | 45.00 | 48.20 | 43.24 |
| 1990 | 47.30 | 48.20 | 51.30 | 53.80 | 61.20 | 60.30 | 60.80 | 55.90 | 54.30 | 56.80 | 50.20 | 47.80 | 53.99 |
| 1991 | 50.00 | 52.20 | 51.50 | 50.90 | 54.10 | 54.70 | 54.20 | 51.20 | 46.40 | 43.60 | 38.00 | 38.60 | 48.78 |
| 1992 | 36.80 | 40.20 | 39.10 | 41.00 | 45.10 | 46.70 | 44.60 | 44.10 | 42.10 | 42.00 | 41.10 | 41.70 | 42.04 |
| 1993 | 41.20 | 44.00 | 46.50 | 45.40 | 46.90 | 48.10 | 45.70 | 47.30 | 47.80 | 46.90 | 42.50 | 40.40 | 45.23 |
| 1994 | 43.50 | 47.90 | 44.40 | 42.70 | 42.70 | 42.70 | 42.20 | 41.80 | 35.40 | 31.80 | 28.00 | 30.80 | 39.49 |
| 1995 | 36.90 | 39.10 | 37.80 | 35.70 | 37.20 | 42.30 | 46.30 | 48.60 | 48.40 | 45.70 | 39.90 | 43.50 | 41.78 |
| 1996[1] | 42.30 | 46.40 | 48.60 | 49.70 | 56.70 | 56.20 | 58.70 | 59.70 | 54.70 | 55.60 | 54.40 | 55.60 | 53.22 |

[1] Preliminary. *Source: Economic Research Service, U.S. Department of Agriculture*

# HOGS

## U.S. Federally Inspected Hog Slaughter   In Thousands of Head

| Week Ended | 1994 | 1995 | 1996 |
|---|---|---|---|
| January[1] | | | |
| 6 | 1,777 | 1,822 | 1,618 |
| 13 | 1,857 | 1,994 | 1,891 |
| 20 | 1,601 | 1,628 | 1,765 |
| 27 | 1,732 | 1,791 | 1,896 |
| February | | | |
| 3 | 1,731 | 1,752 | 1,686 |
| 10 | 1,643 | 1,781 | 1,779 |
| 17 | 1,698 | 1,810 | 1,794 |
| 24 | 1,714 | 1,887 | 1,808 |
| March | | | |
| 2 | 1,756 | 1,908 | 1,824 |
| 9 | 1,826 | 1,888 | 1,758 |
| 16 | 1,769 | 1,808 | 1,845 |
| 23 | 1,751 | 1,876 | 1,780 |
| 30 | 1,799 | 1,837 | 1,776 |
| April | | | |
| 6 | 1,729 | 1,788 | 1,796 |
| 13 | 1,817 | 1,819 | 1,777 |
| 20 | 1,810 | 1,824 | 1,840 |
| 27 | 1,802 | 1,859 | 1,777 |
| May | | | |
| 4 | 1,796 | 1,867 | 1,792 |
| 11 | 1,767 | 1,876 | 1,692 |
| 18 | 1,749 | 1,774 | 1,691 |
| 25 | 1,729 | 1,769 | 1,611 |
| June | | | |
| 1 | 1,489 | 1,603 | 1,439 |
| 8 | 1,731 | 1,762 | 1,568 |
| 15 | 1,675 | 1,722 | 1,629 |
| 22 | 1,634 | 1,702 | 1,582 |
| 29 | 1,644 | 1,735 | 1,573 |

| Week Ended | 1994 | 1995 | 1996 |
|---|---|---|---|
| July | | | |
| 6 | 1,444 | 1,466 | 1,333 |
| 13 | 1,752 | 1,687 | 1,616 |
| 20 | 1,652 | 1,702 | 1,663 |
| 27 | 1,713 | 1,683 | 1,598 |
| August | | | |
| 3 | 1,680 | 1,733 | 1,629 |
| 10 | 1,773 | 1,704 | 1,636 |
| 17 | 1,757 | 1,780 | 1,718 |
| 24 | 1,780 | 1,817 | 1,746 |
| 31 | 1,819 | 1,795 | 1,757 |
| Sept. | | | |
| 7 | 1,638 | 1,650 | 1,525 |
| 14 | 1,973 | 1,896 | 1,935 |
| 21 | 2,000 | 1,888 | 1,827 |
| 28 | 1,976 | 1,888 | |
| October | | | |
| 5 | 1,969 | 1,889 | |
| 12 | 1,984 | 1,834 | |
| 19 | 2,037 | 1,909 | |
| 26 | 2,027 | 1,993 | |
| November | | | |
| 2 | 2,053 | 2,002 | |
| 9 | 1,985 | 1,981 | |
| 16 | 2,059 | 2,011 | |
| 23 | 1,697 | 1,724 | |
| 30 | 2,086 | 1,994 | |
| December | | | |
| 7 | 2,087 | 1,914 | |
| 14 | 2,002 | 1,891 | |
| 21 | 1,796 | 1,840 | |
| 28 | 1,660 | 1,672 | |

[1] Corresponding dates to 1996: 1994, January 15; 1995, January 7.   *Source: Economic Research Service, U.S. Department of Agriculture*

## Federally Inspected Hog Slaughter in the United States   In Thousands of Head

| Year | Jan. | Feb. | Mar. | Apr. | May | June | July | Aug. | Sept. | Oct. | Nov. | Dec. | Total |
|---|---|---|---|---|---|---|---|---|---|---|---|---|---|
| 1988 | 6,803 | 6,518 | 7,505 | 6,929 | 6,713 | 6,715 | 6,199 | 7,101 | 7,534 | 7,887 | 7,908 | 7,703 | 85,516 |
| 1989 | 7,116 | 6,619 | 7,569 | 7,199 | 7,277 | 6,881 | 6,131 | 7,392 | 7,493 | 7,823 | 7,815 | 7,012 | 86,328 |
| 1990 | 7,407 | 6,643 | 7,279 | 6,785 | 6,799 | 6,152 | 5,938 | 7,110 | 6,716 | 7,546 | 7,334 | 7,140 | 82,901 |
| 1991 | 7,461 | 6,469 | 7,044 | 7,320 | 6,948 | 6,296 | 6,557 | 7,098 | 7,177 | 8,292 | 7,744 | 7,708 | 85,951 |
| 1992 | 8,144 | 7,153 | 7,934 | 7,610 | 6,897 | 7,166 | 7,461 | 7,494 | 8,217 | 8,599 | 7,796 | 8,142 | 92,613 |
| 1993 | 7,649 | 6,921 | 7,958 | 7,840 | 6,988 | 7,338 | 7,010 | 7,473 | 7,763 | 7,857 | 7,952 | 8,184 | 90,993 |
| 1994 | 7,285 | 6,783 | 8,148 | 7,609 | 7,383 | 7,452 | 6,941 | 7,997 | 8,192 | 8,585 | 8,516 | 8,547 | 93,435 |
| 1995 | 7,882 | 7,157 | 8,628 | 7,379 | 8,012 | 7,731 | 6,918 | 8,083 | 7,752 | 8,358 | 8,424 | 7,881 | 94,203 |
| 1996[1] | 8,129 | 7,506 | 7,548 | 7,886 | 7,485 | 6,395 | 7,187 | 7,509 | 7,541 | 8,423 | 7,469 | 7,455 | 90,534 |

[1] Preliminary.   *Source: National Agricultural Statistics Service, U.S. Department of Agriculture*

## Average Live Weight of all Hogs Slaughtered Under Federal Inspection   In Pounds Per Head

| Year | Jan. | Feb. | Mar. | Apr. | May | June | July | Aug. | Sept. | Oct. | Nov. | Dec. | Average |
|---|---|---|---|---|---|---|---|---|---|---|---|---|---|
| 1987 | 251 | 248 | 246 | 247 | 247 | 248 | 246 | 244 | 246 | 249 | 252 | 250 | 248 |
| 1988 | 248 | 247 | 247 | 249 | 250 | 250 | 249 | 247 | 248 | 251 | 253 | 251 | 249 |
| 1989 | 249 | 247 | 247 | 251 | 251 | 251 | 247 | 247 | 246 | 248 | 251 | 250 | 249 |
| 1990 | 249 | 248 | 248 | 250 | 251 | 252 | 249 | 249 | 248 | 250 | 253 | 252 | 250 |
| 1991 | 251 | 250 | 250 | 252 | 254 | 253 | 251 | 250 | 251 | 253 | 256 | 255 | 252 |
| 1992 | 255 | 253 | 252 | 253 | 254 | 254 | 251 | 250 | 252 | 252 | 255 | 255 | 253 |
| 1993 | 254 | 253 | 253 | 254 | 254 | 256 | 254 | 252 | 252 | 254 | 257 | 258 | 254 |
| 1994 | 254 | 254 | 254 | 256 | 255 | 256 | 252 | 252 | 255 | 259 | 261 | 260 | 256 |
| 1995 | 258 | 256 | 257 | 258 | 258 | 258 | 256 | 253 | 252 | 255 | 259 | 258 | 257 |
| 1996[1] | 257 | 254 | 255 | 255 | 255 | 256 | 252 | 251 | 251 | 256 | 259 | 258 | 255 |

[1] Preliminary.   *Source: Economic Research Service, U.S. Department of Agriculture*

## Average Open Interest of Lean Hogs Futures[1] in Chicago In Contracts

| Year | Jan. | Feb. | Mar. | Apr. | May | June | July | Aug. | Sept. | Oct. | Nov. | Dec. |
|---|---|---|---|---|---|---|---|---|---|---|---|---|
| 1986 | 22,480 | 21,273 | 19,769 | 17,522 | 23,209 | 25,855 | 30,480 | 31,697 | 34,611 | 28,256 | 30,491 | 27,062 |
| 1987 | 26,275 | 28,125 | 30,794 | 30,195 | 32,431 | 32,889 | 30,752 | 31,553 | 34,197 | 28,562 | 25,138 | 24,440 |
| 1988 | 26,681 | 30,532 | 31,329 | 28,156 | 31,801 | 31,221 | 27,466 | 26,476 | 31,507 | 30,092 | 34,251 | 31,458 |
| 1989 | 31,923 | 30,853 | 29,014 | 30,414 | 29,646 | 27,353 | 25,375 | 25,345 | 28,308 | 33,936 | 35,913 | 29,693 |
| 1990 | 30,335 | 31,018 | 37,789 | 39,257 | 47,291 | 43,631 | 32,942 | 29,964 | 26,982 | 25,691 | 27,648 | 25,757 |
| 1991 | 22,742 | 24,798 | 24,449 | 22,400 | 25,871 | 21,275 | 18,154 | 16,771 | 17,281 | 18,462 | 21,572 | 19,167 |
| 1992 | 23,854 | 31,545 | 32,441 | 32,430 | 30,947 | 26,362 | 24,935 | 24,535 | 27,535 | 32,555 | 32,738 | 30,468 |
| 1993 | 27,210 | 25,620 | 28,264 | 24,139 | 22,581 | 19,840 | 19,026 | 20,761 | 20,544 | 20,051 | 21,167 | 24,096 |
| 1994 | 31,899 | 32,123 | 31,012 | 31,713 | 30,889 | 27,327 | 26,414 | 25,335 | 28,957 | 32,077 | 36,304 | 33,516 |
| 1995 | 36,705 | 30,958 | 30,736 | 28,035 | 28,294 | 28,729 | 29,959 | 31,599 | 34,183 | 31,312 | 31,519 | 35,127 |
| 1996 | 35,253 | 34,823 | 38,730 | 42,900 | 41,916 | 36,620 | 35,616 | 32,541 | 32,591 | 34,329 | 33,148 | 32,163 |

[1] Data prior to November 1995 are for Live Hogs, November 1995 thru December 1996 are Live Hogs and Lean Hogs, January 1997 to date are Lean Hogs.
*Source: Chicago Mercantile Exchange (CME)*

## Volume of Trading of Lean Hogs Futures[1] in Chicago In Thousands of Contracts

| Year | Jan. | Feb. | Mar. | Apr. | May | June | July | Aug. | Sept. | Oct. | Nov. | Dec. | Total |
|---|---|---|---|---|---|---|---|---|---|---|---|---|---|
| 1986 | 156.3 | 108.5 | 113.7 | 153.6 | 157.4 | 160.8 | 224.3 | 168.8 | 196.5 | 183.4 | 171.0 | 142.5 | 1,936.7 |
| 1987 | 159.2 | 138.5 | 172.7 | 190.3 | 189.7 | 212.1 | 219.5 | 169.8 | 174.0 | 175.5 | 121.1 | 118.0 | 2,040.5 |
| 1988 | 172.9 | 143.0 | 172.4 | 137.6 | 169.6 | 267.0 | 171.4 | 140.3 | 160.7 | 150.3 | 166.8 | 156.7 | 2,008.8 |
| 1989 | 188.2 | 135.0 | 152.8 | 130.7 | 175.2 | 147.5 | 141.9 | 131.8 | 149.6 | 181.5 | 205.9 | 151.6 | 1,891.9 |
| 1990 | 181.0 | 119.9 | 189.7 | 188.8 | 278.3 | 277.0 | 212.5 | 170.4 | 147.0 | 160.3 | 186.1 | 130.4 | 2,241.3 |
| 1991 | 177.9 | 150.3 | 148.0 | 157.0 | 155.7 | 120.8 | 131.1 | 120.9 | 102.9 | 118.4 | 104.5 | 94.8 | 1,695.8 |
| 1992 | 135.2 | 137.0 | 140.4 | 138.2 | 116.7 | 131.2 | 148.8 | 102.2 | 116.6 | 149.5 | 117.0 | 123.3 | 1,556.1 |
| 1993 | 131.5 | 101.9 | 160.0 | 131.0 | 120.2 | 121.1 | 112.5 | 91.5 | 109.4 | 102.7 | 116.1 | 103.0 | 1,401.8 |
| 1994 | 144.7 | 97.6 | 146.9 | 93.1 | 127.4 | 144.4 | 116.2 | 122.1 | 110.7 | 129.0 | 150.7 | 172.1 | 1,554.0 |
| 1995 | 155.8 | 115.8 | 181.9 | 116.8 | 145.4 | 155.3 | 139.0 | 144.6 | 135.3 | 132.1 | 142.5 | 136.2 | 1,700.7 |
| 1996 | 177.3 | 138.0 | 150.1 | 216.5 | 208.7 | 177.4 | 185.9 | 157.5 | 158.1 | 203.8 | 170.6 | 152.1 | 2,095.9 |

[1] Data prior to November 1995 are for Live Hogs, November 1995 thru December 1996 are Live Hogs and Lean Hogs, January 1997 to date are Lean Hogs.
*Source: Chicago Mercantile Exchange (CME)*

# Honey

1996 honey production in the world's six major producing countries was 338,400 metric tons, down 26 percent from 1995's 459,096 tons. Production in other countries is small, totaling under 50,000 tons. China is the world's largest producer followed by the U.S. and Argentina. Adverse weather hampered production and distribution in 1996, and in some countries the number of beekeepers has fallen. Also, aggressive Africanized bees have virtually wiped out honey production in some countries.

China's annual honey production held steady from 1992-1995 at 177,000 tons, but poor weather in 1996 reduced the yield per colony to 14.4 kg vs. 28.3 kg in 1995. Also, beekeeper numbers are put at 100,000, down 10,000 since 1990. China's quality control is a lingering problem, especially for domestic consumption which fell 36 percent in 1996 to 49,000 tons. In China, honey is considered a healthy food, but demand for honey used for pharmaceutical purposes has fallen. China is the world's largest honey exporter and more stringent quality control standards are set for exports. Still, China's export fell 37 percent in 1996 to 55,000 tons vs. 87,000 in 1995 and 102,285 tons in 1994.

Argentina's 1996 honey production of 49,200 tons compares with 65,500 in 1995; Mexico's production of 60,000 tons compares with 50,359. U.S. production in 1996, initially forecast at 87,000 tons nearly matched China's total, but was down from 98,000 in 1995. 1996 U.S. imports of 60,000 tons compare with 40,186 in 1995. The U.S. is one of the world's largest markets for industrial honey (used in cereals, bakery and health food products), which accounts for about 45 percent of total domestic use, estimated at 150,000 tons in 1996 vs. 159,317 in 1995. The U.S. had the world's second highest yield per colony in 1996 at 40 kg, topped only by Canada's 54.4 kg. U.S. bee colonies in 1996 of 2.2 million compare with 2.7 million in 1995.

The U.S. Honey Price Support Program was eliminated in the 1996 Farm Act.

### World Production of Honey    In Metric Tons

| Year | Agrentina | Australia | Brazil | Canada | China | Germany[2] | Japan | Mexico | Russia[3] | United States | Total[4] |
|---|---|---|---|---|---|---|---|---|---|---|---|
| 1983 | 30,000 | 24,963 | 22,000 | 38,771 | 138,000 | 19,000 | 6,869 | 68,000 | 210,000 | 93,000 | 650,603 |
| 1984 | 35,000 | 27,997 | 25,000 | 43,298 | 140,000 | 16,000 | 6,798 | 60,000 | 193,000 | 75,000 | 622,093 |
| 1985 | 45,000 | 26,871 | 28,000 | 36,120 | 150,000 | 11,000 | 7,225 | 56,000 | 204,000 | 68,000 | 632,216 |
| 1986 | 36,000 | 25,077 | 27,000 | 34,041 | 160,000 | 16,000 | 5,553 | 54,000 | 210,000 | 90,900 | 658,571 |
| 1987 | 44,000 | 28,000 | 30,500 | 39,776 | 204,000 | 16,000 | 6,023 | 47,850 | 219,245 | 102,875 | 738,269 |
| 1988 | 46,000 | 27,622 | 30,000 | 37,105 | 156,000 | 18,000 | 4,870 | 46,140 | 243,000 | 97,114 | 705,851 |
| 1989 | 40,000 | 26,198 | 32,000 | 27,815 | 189,000 | 29,000 | 5,343 | 48,530 | 225,000 | 80,266 | 703,152 |
| 1990 | 47,000 | 27,561 | 30,000 | 32,115 | 193,000 | 23,000 | 4,854 | 51,000 | 236,219 | 89,717 | 732,466 |
| 1991 | 54,000 | 20,604 | 32,300 | 31,606 | 206,000 | 25,000 | 4,202 | 58,770 | 240,000 | 99,414 | 714,790 |
| 1992 | 61,000 | 18,948 | 18,841 | 30,339 | 178,000 | 24,677 | 3,800 | 48,852 | 47,000 | 100,055 | 531,512 |
| 1993 | 59,000 | 22,556 | 19,000 | 30,760 | 176,000 | 26,357 | 3,500 | 48,000 | 49,600 | 104,620 | 539,393 |
| 1994 | 64,000 | 22,600 | 19,000 | 32,920 | 177,000 | 22,233 | 3,500 | 41,500 | 43,899 | 98,500 | 525,152 |
| 1995[1] | 65,500 | | | 30,352 | 178,000 | 36,885 | | 50,359 | 43,900 | 98,000 | 502,996 |
| 1996[1] | 49,200 | | | 27,200 | 90,000 | 25,000 | | 60,000 | | 87,000 | 338,400 |

[1] Preliminary. [2] Data prior to 1989 are for West Germany. [3] Formerly part of the U.S.S.R.; data not reported separately until 1992. [4] Only for countries listed. *Source: Foreign Agricultural Service, U.S. Department of Agriculture*

### Salient Statistics of Honey in the United States    In Millions of Pounds

| Year | Number of Colonies (1,000) | Yield Per Colony Pounds | Stocks Jan. 1 | Total U.S. Production | Imports for Consumption | Domestic Disappearance | Exports | Total Supply | Program Activity: Placed Under Loan | Program Activity: CCC Take Over | Program Activity: Net Gov't. Expenditure[3] Mil. $ | Domestic Avg. Price All Honey ¢ Lb. | National Avg. Price Support ¢ Lb. | Per Capita Consumption Lbs. |
|---|---|---|---|---|---|---|---|---|---|---|---|---|---|---|
| 1982 | 4,250 | 54.1 | 73.8 | 230.0 | 92.0 | 250.8 | 8.5 | 395.8 | 88.4 | 74.5 | 27.4 | 56.8 | 60.4 | .9 |
| 1983 | 4,275 | 48.0 | 136.5 | 205.0 | 109.8 | 269.0 | 7.5 | 451.3 | 113.6 | 106.4 | 48.0 | 54.4 | 62.2 | 1.0 |
| 1984 | 4,300 | 38.4 | 174.8 | 165.1 | 128.7 | 251.7 | 7.5 | 468.6 | 107.5 | 105.8 | 90.2 | 49.5 | 65.8 | .9 |
| 1985 | 4,325 | 34.7 | 209.4 | 150.1 | 138.2 | 256.9 | 6.5 | 497.7 | 102.0 | 98.0 | 80.8 | 45.5 | 65.3 | .9 |
| 1986 | 3,205 | 62.5 | 234.3 | 200.4 | 120.0 | 282.9 | 9.2 | 554.7 | 180.4 | 41.0 | 89.4 | 51.3 | 64.0 | 1.0 |
| 1987 | 3,190 | 71.1 | 262.6 | 226.8 | 58.3 | 320.9 | 12.4 | 547.7 | 218.0 | 52.7 | 72.6 | 50.3 | 61.0 | 1.1 |
| 1988 | 3,219 | 66.3 | 214.4 | 214.1 | 55.9 | 278.0 | 14.0 | 484.4 | 209.5 | 32.0 | 100.1 | 50.0 | 59.1 | .9 |
| 1989 | 3,443 | 51.4 | 192.4 | 177.0 | 77.3 | 292.0 | 10.0 | 446.7 | 161.7 | 2.8 | 41.7 | 49.8 | 56.4 | 1.0 |
| 1990 | 3,210 | 61.6 | 144.7 | 197.8 | 77.0 | 303.4 | 12.4 | 419.5 | 183.5 | 1.1 | 46.7 | 53.7 | 53.8 | 1.0 |
| 1991 | 3,181 | 68.9 | 103.7 | 219.2 | 92.2 | 303.4 | 9.6 | 415.1 | 112.9 | 3.2 | 18.6 | 55.6 | 53.8 | 1.0 |
| 1992 | 3,030 | 72.8 | 109.3 | 220.6 | 114.6 | 330.5 | 10.4 | 444.5 | 122.7 | 4.1 | 16.6 | 55.0 | 53.8 | 1.0 |
| 1993 | 2,876 | 80.2 | 103.5 | 230.6 | 133.6 | 342.0 | 8.5 | 467.8 | 136.8 | 16.4 | 22.1 | 53.9 | 53.8 | 1.0 |
| 1994 | 2,770 | 78.4 | 117.3 | 217.2 | 123.2 | 355.2 | 8.3 | 457.7 | 73.4 | 0 | -.2 | 52.8 | 50.0 | 1.0 |
| 1995[1] | 2,648 | 79.5 | 94.1 | 210.5 | 88.6 | 351.2 | 9.3 | 402.7 | 64.4 | 0 | -9.3 | 68.5 | 50.0 | 1.0 |
| 1996[2] | 2,566 | 77.2 | 42.2 | 198.1 | 132.3 | 330.7 | 9.5 | 366.3 | | | | 89.4 | | |

[1] Preliminary. [2] Forecast. [3] Fiscal year. *Source: Economic Research Service, U.S. Department of Agriculture*

# Interest Rates, U.S.

1996 U.S. interest rate market action was decidedly different than in 1995 when rates moved steadily lower with the long bond falling about 175 basis points and T-bills more than 50 points. At yearend 1996, the 30 year T-bond yield of 6.60 percent compared with 6.09 percent a year earlier; 3 month T-bills were at 5.20 percent vs 4.89 percent; fed funds were 5.31 percent vs 5.74 percent, the prime rate at 8.25 percent vs 8.50 percent, and the discount rate of 5 percent compared with 5.25 percent.

The U.S. economy emitted mixed signals during 1996 as to its strength. New job creation was strong, but unemployment on average held about 5 1/2 percent; inflationary pressures were well contained even though U.S. consumers were in a buying mood, although the yearend holiday spree, while generally good, lacked zip. On balance, the 1996 economic results were pretty good. Even the nation's chronic trade deficit showed signs of narrowing late in the year.

In February the Fed eased monetary policy apparently in the wake of confirmation that fourth quarter 1995 data put the annualized real growth rate at 0.3 percent. However, the Fed may have miscalculated as within a few weeks of the easing the Fed chairman told Congress that the outlook for the U.S. economy was far from bleak. Indeed, there were signs of stronger than expected economic growth. U.S. rates rose across the yield curve, paced by the longer maturities as earlier ideas of a possible recession and the need for a Fed easing quickly reversed to perceptions of a strengthening inflation prone economy and the need for a Fed tightening. In early March the long bond was yielding 6.40 percent, three months later the yield was 7.40 percent. The market's fears subsided during the second half of 1996 on the realization that economic growth was slowing; annualized real growth in the third quarter of 2.2 percent compared with 4.7 percent in the second quarter. Final sales during the third quarter fell to an annualized rate of only 0.3 percent, the lowest in months and down from a 4.2 percent rate in the second quarter. Clearly there was little reason for the Fed to tighten during the closing months of 1996 and they didn't.

Although growth began to slow in mid-1996, it had been five years since the start of the expansionary phase making it the third longest since World War II. By late 1996 the uncertainty focused on how much longer the cycle could run. Initial forecasts for 1997 GDP growth ranged from a low of -1.3 percent to a high of 3.1 percent. The 2 percent average apparently sits well with the Fed as they consider a growth rate of 2-2.5 percent noninflationary. However, late 1996 economic data seemed to support a slowdown in personal consumption, government spending, and inventory accumulation, with 1997 unemployment holding near 5.5 percent. If the slowdown is realized it would suggest minimal inflationary pressure, giving leeway to the Fed to ease monetary policy and extend the 1991-1996 expansion to the longest on record. The U.S. consumer holds the key to both real growth and inflation during 1997, with the latter forecast under 3 percent, about the same as in 1996.

### *Futures Markets*

A futures (and option) contract exists for almost every maturity on the yield curve, as well as for municipal and commercial credit risks. Major U.S. contracts include T-bills and Eurodollars on Chicago's International Monetary Market (IMM), and T-bonds and 10-Year T-notes on the Chicago Board of Trade (CBOT). Futures are also traded in Chicago on two and five year T-notes, municipal bonds, 30 day fed funds and one month LIBOR. Smaller size contracts on interest rate instruments are listed at the MidAmerica Commodity Exchange (MidAm).

**U.S. Producer Commodity Price Index (Wholesale, All Commodities)** 1982 = 100

| Year | Jan. | Feb. | Mar. | Apr. | May | June | July | Aug. | Sept. | Oct. | Nov. | Dec. | Average |
|---|---|---|---|---|---|---|---|---|---|---|---|---|---|
| 1988 | 104.6 | 104.8 | 104.9 | 105.8 | 106.5 | 107.2 | 107.9 | 108.0 | 108.1 | 108.2 | 108.3 | 109.0 | 106.9 |
| 1989 | 110.5 | 110.8 | 111.5 | 112.3 | 113.2 | 112.9 | 112.8 | 112.0 | 112.3 | 112.7 | 112.7 | 113.0 | 112.2 |
| 1990 | 114.9 | 114.4 | 114.2 | 114.1 | 114.6 | 114.3 | 114.5 | 116.5 | 118.3 | 120.8 | 120.1 | 118.7 | 116.3 |
| 1991 | 119.0 | 117.2 | 116.2 | 116.0 | 116.5 | 116.4 | 116.1 | 116.2 | 116.1 | 116.4 | 116.4 | 115.9 | 116.5 |
| 1992 | 115.6 | 116.0 | 116.1 | 116.3 | 117.2 | 118.0 | 117.9 | 117.7 | 118.0 | 118.1 | 117.8 | 117.6 | 117.2 |
| 1993 | 118.0 | 118.4 | 118.7 | 119.3 | 119.7 | 119.5 | 119.2 | 118.7 | 118.7 | 119.1 | 119.0 | 118.6 | 118.9 |
| 1994 | 119.1 | 119.3 | 119.7 | 119.7 | 119.9 | 120.5 | 120.7 | 121.2 | 120.9 | 120.9 | 121.5 | 121.9 | 120.4 |
| 1995 | 122.9 | 123.5 | 123.9 | 124.6 | 124.9 | 125.3 | 125.3 | 125.1 | 125.2 | 125.3 | 125.4 | 125.7 | 124.8 |
| 1996[1] | 126.3 | 126.2 | 126.4 | 127.4 | 128.1 | 128.0 | 128.0 | 128.1 | 128.0 | 127.9 | 128.1 | | 127.5 |

[1] Preliminary. *Source: Bureau of Labor Statistics, U.S. Department of Commerce*

**U.S. Consumer Price Index[2] (Retail Price Index for All Items: Urban Consumers)** 1982-1984 = 100

| Year | Jan. | Feb. | Mar. | Apr. | May | June | July | Aug. | Sept. | Oct. | Nov. | Dec. | Average |
|---|---|---|---|---|---|---|---|---|---|---|---|---|---|
| 1988 | 115.7 | 116.0 | 116.5 | 117.1 | 117.5 | 118.0 | 118.5 | 119.0 | 119.8 | 120.2 | 120.3 | 120.5 | 118.3 |
| 1989 | 121.1 | 121.6 | 122.3 | 123.1 | 123.8 | 124.1 | 124.4 | 124.6 | 125.0 | 125.6 | 125.9 | 126.1 | 124.0 |
| 1990 | 127.4 | 128.0 | 128.7 | 128.9 | 129.2 | 129.9 | 130.4 | 131.6 | 132.7 | 133.5 | 133.8 | 133.8 | 130.7 |
| 1991 | 134.6 | 134.8 | 135.0 | 135.2 | 135.6 | 136.0 | 136.2 | 136.6 | 137.2 | 137.4 | 137.8 | 137.9 | 136.2 |
| 1992 | 138.1 | 138.6 | 139.3 | 139.5 | 139.7 | 140.2 | 140.5 | 140.9 | 141.3 | 141.8 | 142.0 | 141.9 | 140.3 |
| 1993 | 142.6 | 143.1 | 143.6 | 144.0 | 144.2 | 144.4 | 144.4 | 144.8 | 145.1 | 145.7 | 145.8 | 145.8 | 144.5 |
| 1994 | 146.2 | 146.7 | 147.2 | 147.4 | 147.5 | 148.0 | 148.4 | 149.0 | 149.4 | 149.5 | 149.7 | 149.7 | 148.2 |
| 1995 | 150.3 | 150.9 | 151.4 | 151.9 | 152.2 | 152.5 | 152.5 | 152.9 | 153.2 | 153.7 | 153.6 | 153.5 | 152.4 |
| 1996[1] | 154.4 | 154.9 | 155.7 | 156.3 | 156.6 | 156.7 | 157.0 | 157.3 | 157.8 | 158.3 | 158.6 | 158.6 | 156.9 |

[1] Preliminary. [2] Not seasonally adjusted. *Source: Bureau of Labor Statistics, U.S. Department of Commerce*

# INTEREST RATES

**Average Open Interest of 13 Week[1] Treasury Bill Futures in Chicago** In Thousands of Contracts

| Year | Jan. | Feb. | Mar. | Apr. | May | June | July | Aug. | Sept. | Oct. | Nov. | Dec. |
|---|---|---|---|---|---|---|---|---|---|---|---|---|
| 1985 | 47,022 | 47,171 | 40,954 | 40,069 | 39,624 | 33,712 | 35,817 | 37,911 | 35,473 | 36,887 | 40,830 | 35,963 |
| 1986 | 37,365 | 43,008 | 48,572 | 51,145 | 43,394 | 36,479 | 40,676 | 40,819 | 37,532 | 36,107 | 37,940 | 36,271 |
| 1987 | 40,710 | 48,375 | 39,691 | 35,671 | 32,202 | 23,431 | 24,077 | 25,454 | 20,539 | 26,014 | 24,222 | 20,989 |
| 1988 | 19,571 | 22,956 | 21,460 | 26,134 | 28,166 | 19,081 | 21,812 | 21,626 | 21,374 | 21,930 | 24,711 | 26,923 |
| 1989 | 29,023 | 26,612 | 25,672 | 20,433 | 21,864 | 19,934 | 20,950 | 22,687 | 25,216 | 29,118 | 34,224 | 33,469 |
| 1990 | 39,168 | 38,358 | 27,668 | 31,274 | 25,128 | 21,171 | 26,524 | 37,903 | 35,723 | 46,974 | 53,284 | 50,146 |
| 1991 | 55,371 | 53,484 | 38,259 | 43,538 | 53,941 | 51,178 | 55,514 | 55,999 | 47,509 | 50,865 | 57,680 | 51,750 |
| 1992 | 51,312 | 45,902 | 35,539 | 44,757 | 47,734 | 41,091 | 38,399 | 35,638 | 29,781 | 32,556 | 35,379 | 29,566 |
| 1993 | 32,544 | 35,756 | 32,556 | 39,115 | 40,724 | 34,614 | 30,895 | 34,177 | 28,983 | 30,121 | 33,800 | 30,996 |
| 1994 | 36,456 | 41,150 | 43,243 | 51,485 | 41,164 | 34,580 | 32,572 | 29,559 | 24,522 | 32,325 | 30,077 | 22,322 |
| 1995 | 21,065 | 26,289 | 33,420 | 35,873 | 34,608 | 25,930 | 20,534 | 19,195 | 18,929 | 16,781 | 16,384 | 11,279 |
| 1996 | 14,769 | 16,906 | 14,161 | 14,460 | 15,709 | 10,285 | 8,973 | 9,770 | 6,536 | 6,906 | 7,516 | 7,002 |

[1] 90-day U.S. Treasury Bill. *Source: International Monetary Market (IOM), division of the Chicago Mercantile Exchange (CME)*

**Volume of Trading of 13 Week[1] Treasury Bill Futures in Chicago** In Thousands of Contracts

| Year | Jan. | Feb. | Mar. | Apr. | May | June | July | Aug. | Sept. | Oct. | Nov. | Dec. | Total |
|---|---|---|---|---|---|---|---|---|---|---|---|---|---|
| 1985 | 231.3 | 245.4 | 314.5 | 217.9 | 206.2 | 205.6 | 180.6 | 165.8 | 206.8 | 159.9 | 142.1 | 138.1 | 2,413.0 |
| 1986 | 175.0 | 215.4 | 149.5 | 212.8 | 169.7 | 152.9 | 117.8 | 135.7 | 160.8 | 114.2 | 106.3 | 105.1 | 1,815.2 |
| 1987 | 137.9 | 218.8 | 151.8 | 197.6 | 207.8 | 125.5 | 97.5 | 125.4 | 110.1 | 262.2 | 161.0 | 131.6 | 1,927.0 |
| 1988 | 103.2 | 111.6 | 129.2 | 125.6 | 163.4 | 105.3 | 84.3 | 117.9 | 97.9 | 101.6 | 129.1 | 104.5 | 1,373.6 |
| 1989 | 109.6 | 146.5 | 143.2 | 119.2 | 126.3 | 101.4 | 89.3 | 126.9 | 135.9 | 149.1 | 130.1 | 124.9 | 1,502.4 |
| 1990 | 169.3 | 153.6 | 118.5 | 120.3 | 102.4 | 96.7 | 138.1 | 206.6 | 168.9 | 178.5 | 223.7 | 193.1 | 1,869.6 |
| 1991 | 252.9 | 197.9 | 166.8 | 164.0 | 188.2 | 173.3 | 141.7 | 223.2 | 111.0 | 110.8 | 140.8 | 141.6 | 1,912.2 |
| 1992 | 143.8 | 137.9 | 145.0 | 115.9 | 106.5 | 106.1 | 85.8 | 76.2 | 103.0 | 127.0 | 106.5 | 83.4 | 1,337.1 |
| 1993 | 86.1 | 100.4 | 97.0 | 65.6 | 103.2 | 106.0 | 71.7 | 75.7 | 89.3 | 69.1 | 87.4 | 66.0 | 1,071.3 |
| 1994 | 59.8 | 137.0 | 115.9 | 104.4 | 99.4 | 89.4 | 53.7 | 60.9 | 77.6 | 57.4 | 81.2 | 83.8 | 1,020.5 |
| 1995 | 72.2 | 80.0 | 90.3 | 37.4 | 58.7 | 49.9 | 28.1 | 41.5 | 44.4 | 36.9 | 46.6 | 34.2 | 620.2 |
| 1996 | 32.0 | 36.0 | 36.5 | 17.9 | 16.6 | 25.2 | 12.0 | 19.4 | 19.8 | 10.8 | 10.4 | 14.3 | 250.9 |

[1] 90-day U.S. Treasury Bill. *Source: International Monetary Market (IOM), division of the Chicago Mercantile Exchange (CME)*

## Average Open Interest of 30-Year U.S. Treasury Bond Futures in Chicago In Thousands of Contracts

| Year | Jan. | Feb. | Mar. | Apr. | May | June | July | Aug. | Sept. | Oct. | Nov. | Dec. |
|---|---|---|---|---|---|---|---|---|---|---|---|---|
| 1985 | 196,826 | 223,282 | 224,553 | 215,742 | 224,351 | 209,985 | 209,823 | 229,284 | 229,382 | 279,083 | 315,082 | 307,137 |
| 1986 | 320,040 | 317,197 | 266,005 | 253,991 | 237,236 | 212,415 | 203,921 | 207,524 | 196,672 | 223,588 | 241,717 | 239,695 |
| 1987 | 256,822 | 286,198 | 237,005 | 285,491 | 297,998 | 250,315 | 272,633 | 303,192 | 336,976 | 383,640 | 337,855 | 293,160 |
| 1988 | 296,133 | 328,081 | 307,004 | 317,891 | 366,723 | 406,493 | 441,064 | 489,339 | 475,841 | 478,585 | 472,628 | 411,888 |
| 1989 | 395,874 | 366,704 | 303,891 | 308,850 | 330,016 | 312,318 | 325,851 | 321,493 | 283,133 | 301,719 | 355,555 | 314,252 |
| 1990 | 315,671 | 324,954 | 294,968 | 280,745 | 303,544 | 278,889 | 285,934 | 317,197 | 297,075 | 286,291 | 288,581 | 254,775 |
| 1991 | 257,229 | 279,378 | 250,028 | 283,473 | 279,443 | 254,983 | 273,774 | 325,303 | 310,110 | 304,198 | 317,445 | 301,604 |
| 1992 | 343,156 | 353,782 | 318,737 | 313,742 | 346,542 | 347,293 | 370,850 | 427,723 | 385,645 | 364,250 | 362,231 | 321,706 |
| 1993 | 336,327 | 375,435 | 361,675 | 362,404 | 370,485 | 349,285 | 361,393 | 396,411 | 388,188 | 360,859 | 359,739 | 337,575 |
| 1994 | 380,057 | 422,902 | 454,539 | 500,790 | 497,296 | 421,286 | 441,884 | 451,462 | 447,924 | 436,684 | 449,642 | 397,554 |
| 1995 | 384,356 | 389,908 | 369,989 | 367,964 | 399,500 | 421,234 | 438,267 | 381,237 | 361,394 | 395,346 | 447,409 | 426,384 |
| 1996 | 382,001 | 403,403 | 395,338 | 381,926 | 413,944 | 443,644 | 464,145 | 471,203 | 420,622 | 409,950 | 463,731 | 479,086 |

*Source: Chicago Board of Trade (CBT)*

## Volume of Trading of 30-Year U.S. Treasury Bond Futures in Chicago In Thousands of Contracts

| Year | Jan. | Feb. | Mar. | Apr. | May | June | July | Aug. | Sept. | Oct. | Nov. | Dec. | Total |
|---|---|---|---|---|---|---|---|---|---|---|---|---|---|
| 1985 | 2,974.0 | 3,250.0 | 2,906.0 | 2,272.0 | 3,339.0 | 3,755.0 | 3,308.0 | 3,409.0 | 3,149.0 | 3,558.0 | 4,118.0 | 3,965.0 | 40,448.0 |
| 1986 | 4,640.0 | 5,220.0 | 4,445.0 | 5,115.0 | 4,783.0 | 4,486.0 | 4,114.0 | 4,175.0 | 4,638.0 | 3,853.0 | 3,595.0 | 3,534.0 | 52,599.0 |
| 1987 | 4,188.0 | 4,308.0 | 4,128.0 | 7,110.0 | 6,120.0 | 5,518.0 | 4,839.0 | 6,185.0 | 7,769.0 | 7,388.0 | 4,861.0 | 4,428.0 | 66,841.0 |
| 1988 | 5,550.0 | 5,765.0 | 6,088.0 | 4,984.0 | 5,570.0 | 7,495.0 | 5,133.0 | 6,346.0 | 5,641.0 | 6,136.0 | 6,431.0 | 5,171.0 | 70,307.0 |
| 1989 | 5,806.0 | 6,300.0 | 5,605.0 | 4,858.0 | 6,673.0 | 7,995.0 | 5,231.0 | 7,640.0 | 4,792.0 | 6,329.0 | 5,828.0 | 3,244.0 | 70,303.0 |
| 1990 | 7,215.0 | 7,438.0 | 7,175.0 | 5,653.0 | 6,189.0 | 5,279.0 | 4,895.0 | 8,855.0 | 4,939.0 | 6,659.0 | 6,570.0 | 4,691.0 | 75,559.0 |
| 1991 | 5,804.0 | 5,717.0 | 5,658.0 | 5,957.0 | 6,186.0 | 5,582.0 | 4,293.0 | 6,592.0 | 4,765.0 | 6,450.0 | 6,239.0 | 4,643.0 | 67,886.0 |
| 1992 | 7,523.4 | 6,270.1 | 6,793.4 | 4,810.1 | 5,417.7 | 4,828.8 | 6,081.0 | 6,085.5 | 5,953.3 | 6,870.7 | 5,287.8 | 4,083.0 | 70,004.8 |
| 1993 | 5,577.4 | 6,482.7 | 7,902.9 | 6,156.1 | 6,799.8 | 5,817.2 | 6,218.4 | 6,914.5 | 7,443.9 | 6,537.4 | 8,193.5 | 5,384.5 | 79,428.5 |
| 1994 | 7,287.8 | 8,430.2 | 10,836.7 | 9,557.4 | 9,999.0 | 9,804.0 | 6,987.0 | 7,910.0 | 7,913.0 | 7,004.0 | 8,533.0 | 5,699.0 | 99,960.0 |
| 1995 | 7,058.0 | 7,714.0 | 9,623.8 | 5,835.4 | 8,721.5 | 8,446.7 | 5,790.2 | 7,083.7 | 7,317.1 | 6,927.2 | 6,626.3 | 5,232.1 | 86,375.9 |
| 1996 | 7,528.6 | 8,781.4 | 7,199.3 | 6,010.6 | 7,932.3 | 6,520.6 | 6,422.1 | 6,625.8 | 6,926.1 | 6,772.4 | 7,297.7 | 6,708.4 | 84,725.1 |

*Source: Chicago Board of Trade (CBT)*

# INTEREST RATES

## Average Open Interest of 3-Month Eurodollar Futures in Chicago  In Thousands of Contracts

| Year | Jan. | Feb. | Mar. | Apr. | May | June | July | Aug. | Sept. | Oct. | Nov. | Dec. |
|---|---|---|---|---|---|---|---|---|---|---|---|---|
| 1985 | 93.6 | 105.2 | 107.7 | 105.7 | 123.0 | 120.2 | 118.9 | 129.1 | 125.4 | 127.8 | 154.9 | 144.4 |
| 1986 | 135.7 | 151.9 | 148.1 | 157.3 | 171.3 | 165.0 | 163.3 | 186.9 | 213.5 | 220.0 | 228.2 | 219.9 |
| 1987 | 232.3 | 267.8 | 229.5 | 263.1 | 291.8 | 269.5 | 279.3 | 316.9 | 361.4 | 379.2 | 354.9 | 323.5 |
| 1988 | 317.4 | 358.5 | 340.9 | 376.0 | 422.7 | 421.9 | 440.6 | 510.2 | 509.2 | 477.9 | 519.8 | 567.0 |
| 1989 | 574.8 | 672.3 | 731.3 | 749.7 | 756.9 | 720.4 | 690.2 | 714.0 | 637.9 | 591.5 | 663.6 | 661.9 |
| 1990 | 638.5 | 662.9 | 653.2 | 616.9 | 662.8 | 676.3 | 690.6 | 740.0 | 697.8 | 678.2 | 728.4 | 664.1 |
| 1991 | 630.9 | 722.7 | 741.1 | 767.6 | 857.4 | 835.2 | 797.9 | 883.1 | 916.7 | 949.5 | 1,054.7 | 1,067.2 |
| 1992 | 1,129.8 | 1,213.7 | 1,244.6 | 1,269.1 | 1,377.2 | 1,382.7 | 1,434.1 | 1,549.9 | 1,537.0 | 1,537.6 | 1,547.0 | 1,418.7 |
| 1993 | 1,429.4 | 1,586.7 | 1,643.3 | 1,653.4 | 1,782.8 | 1,739.1 | 1,777.7 | 1,918.4 | 1,940.7 | 2,026.5 | 2,149.0 | 2,150.2 |
| 1994 | 2,300.5 | 2,529.5 | 2,568.1 | 2,627.3 | 2,734.3 | 2,565.2 | 2,599.1 | 2,703.8 | 2,699.6 | 2,561.2 | 2,660.3 | 2,606.3 |
| 1995 | 2,443.6 | 2,535.4 | 2,463.9 | 2,447.4 | 2,503.3 | 2,390.8 | 2,279.5 | 2,374.6 | 2,347.2 | 2,290.3 | 2,405.5 | 2,480.5 |
| 1996 | 2,519.4 | 2,638.6 | 2,511.4 | 2,483.5 | 2,571.8 | 2,590.1 | 2,504.4 | 2,485.5 | 2,392.4 | 2,349.7 | 2,378.2 | 2,225.7 |

*Source: International Monetary Market (IOM), division of the Chicago Mercantile Exchange (CME)*

## Volume of Trading of 3-Month Eurodollar Futures in Chicago  In Thousands of Contracts

| Year | Jan. | Feb. | Mar. | Apr. | May | June | July | Aug. | Sept. | Oct. | Nov. | Dec. | Total |
|---|---|---|---|---|---|---|---|---|---|---|---|---|---|
| 1985 | 524.7 | 723.6 | 877.2 | 764.7 | 753.7 | 891.5 | 798.0 | 697.5 | 769.1 | 694.3 | 695.4 | 710.7 | 8,901.0 |
| 1986 | 888.5 | 825.1 | 627.9 | 933.7 | 982.6 | 1,018.1 | 755.3 | 847.2 | 1,288.7 | 1,046.7 | 836.3 | 774.8 | 10,824.9 |
| 1987 | 1,072.0 | 1,472.0 | 1,197.0 | 2,562.0 | 1,825.0 | 1,760.0 | 1,292.0 | 1,514.0 | 2,495.0 | 2,849.0 | 1,202.0 | 1,177.0 | 20,416.0 |
| 1988 | 1,466.0 | 1,681.0 | 1,635.0 | 1,575.0 | 1,830.0 | 2,288.0 | 1,604.0 | 1,893.0 | 1,957.0 | 1,586.0 | 2,236.0 | 1,952.0 | 21,705.0 |
| 1989 | 2,257.0 | 3,107.0 | 3,848.0 | 4,471.0 | 3,941.0 | 4,116.0 | 3,193.0 | 3,980.0 | 2,977.0 | 3,971.0 | 2,914.0 | 2,043.0 | 40,818.0 |
| 1990 | 3,244.0 | 2,459.0 | 2,727.0 | 2,566.0 | 3,132.0 | 2,473.0 | 2,947.0 | 3,857.0 | 2,730.0 | 2,898.0 | 2,982.0 | 2,680.0 | 34,696.0 |
| 1991 | 2,859.0 | 2,635.0 | 3,445.0 | 3,208.0 | 2,458.0 | 2,972.0 | 2,629.0 | 4,035.0 | 3,000.0 | 3,505.0 | 3,301.0 | 3,196.0 | 37,243.0 |
| 1992 | 5,365.7 | 4,418.5 | 5,582.8 | 4,942.2 | 4,819.0 | 4,602.6 | 5,357.8 | 4,016.3 | 4,705.2 | 6,691.6 | 5,461.3 | 4,568.1 | 60,531.1 |
| 1993 | 5,556.8 | 5,003.8 | 6,013.8 | 4,059.4 | 5,977.8 | 5,672.9 | 5,656.7 | 4,494.2 | 6,340.6 | 4,888.4 | 6,269.8 | 4,477.3 | 64,411.4 |
| 1994 | 6,074.8 | 8,745.3 | 9,468.9 | 9,639.2 | 11,494.0 | 9,348.0 | 7,810.0 | 7,128.0 | 7,641.0 | 7,992.0 | 9,715.0 | 9,766.0 | 104,823.0 |
| 1995 | 10,341.1 | 10,429.3 | 9,549.0 | 6,069.2 | 9,897.1 | 10,104.7 | 6,669.9 | 7,013.5 | 7,171.1 | 6,477.9 | 6,055.2 | 5,952.1 | 95,730.0 |
| 1996 | 7,485.7 | 9,267.2 | 9,526.3 | 6,872.4 | 7,413.7 | 7,415.0 | 8,323.2 | 6,967.5 | 8,232.5 | 7,014.5 | 5,056.9 | 5,308.1 | 88,883.1 |

*Source: International Monetary Market (IOM), division of the Chicago Mercantile Exchange (CME)*

## Average Open Interest of 10-Year U.S. Treasury Note Futures in Chicago  In Contracts

| Year | Jan. | Feb. | Mar. | Apr. | May | June | July | Aug. | Sept. | Oct. | Nov. | Dec. |
|---|---|---|---|---|---|---|---|---|---|---|---|---|
| 1985 | 38,462 | 44,251 | 49,909 | 42,744 | 48,416 | 52,963 | 55,676 | 62,118 | 59,587 | 66,796 | 70,300 | 69,603 |
| 1986 | 76,661 | 78,528 | 75,024 | 63,804 | 70,568 | 72,565 | 67,048 | 62,122 | 60,839 | 56,955 | 64,397 | 58,763 |
| 1987 | 58,926 | 56,177 | 55,093 | 64,924 | 68,797 | 71,033 | 72,033 | 78,281 | 88,939 | 82,672 | 75,139 | 77,631 |
| 1988 | 76,066 | 75,884 | 73,083 | 75,836 | 78,038 | 84,349 | 84,612 | 101,470 | 96,821 | 91,811 | 89,307 | 74,602 |
| 1989 | 76,964 | 84,605 | 78,966 | 86,661 | 88,511 | 76,364 | 77,211 | 76,538 | 71,138 | 82,844 | 82,149 | 72,238 |
| 1990 | 73,155 | 82,211 | 76,939 | 76,030 | 82,174 | 78,498 | 71,413 | 75,644 | 72,900 | 67,309 | 73,744 | 76,697 |
| 1991 | 72,621 | 79,355 | 79,413 | 71,451 | 84,203 | 81,884 | 85,527 | 94,379 | 96,836 | 93,187 | 95,450 | 87,063 |
| 1992 | 119,739 | 114,521 | 106,497 | 102,862 | 112,666 | 126,228 | 143,924 | 158,831 | 179,045 | 191,725 | 199,990 | 195,705 |
| 1993 | 190,018 | 206,852 | 198,653 | 209,221 | 229,378 | 217,521 | 233,458 | 238,189 | 237,243 | 237,877 | 273,336 | 262,831 |
| 1994 | 264,848 | 258,643 | 300,080 | 328,821 | 294,091 | 254,612 | 232,373 | 253,233 | 273,564 | 277,313 | 301,000 | 271,992 |
| 1995 | 282,978 | 285,187 | 265,747 | 263,816 | 273,945 | 289,052 | 306,046 | 323,078 | 277,011 | 278,832 | 270,527 | 249,073 |
| 1996 | 260,374 | 297,850 | 285,501 | 319,234 | 331,032 | 293,416 | 302,330 | 326,391 | 291,208 | 284,581 | 313,298 | 303,702 |

*Source: Chicago Board of Trade (CBT)*

## Volume of Trading of 10-Year U.S. Treasury Note Futures in Chicago  In Thousands of Contracts

| Year | Jan. | Feb. | Mar. | Apr. | May | June | July | Aug. | Sept. | Oct. | Nov. | Dec. | Total |
|---|---|---|---|---|---|---|---|---|---|---|---|---|---|
| 1985 | 171.8 | 216.0 | 215.9 | 175.8 | 274.9 | 266.9 | 219.4 | 282.9 | 212.7 | 234.3 | 297.5 | 292.5 | 2,860.0 |
| 1986 | 269.7 | 401.4 | 383.1 | 381.7 | 434.8 | 470.3 | 309.7 | 363.1 | 459.5 | 319.9 | 328.1 | 305.2 | 4,426.0 |
| 1987 | 304.9 | 358.3 | 347.6 | 643.8 | 541.3 | 405.1 | 269.6 | 446.0 | 512.9 | 662.0 | 369.4 | 392.8 | 5,253.7 |
| 1988 | 335.3 | 462.8 | 420.6 | 298.8 | 467.8 | 469.6 | 327.4 | 566.0 | 455.4 | 383.2 | 537.4 | 476.7 | 5,201.0 |
| 1989 | 450.5 | 547.9 | 468.3 | 431.6 | 625.6 | 637.3 | 453.0 | 629.6 | 465.8 | 555.8 | 516.7 | 327.4 | 6,109.5 |
| 1990 | 491.3 | 650.5 | 480.9 | 381.1 | 638.7 | 427.4 | 415.0 | 703.0 | 399.3 | 449.6 | 574.3 | 442.6 | 6,053.7 |
| 1991 | 507.7 | 519.6 | 508.3 | 466.5 | 566.9 | 456.6 | 318.9 | 705.9 | 467.2 | 573.2 | 661.3 | 591.4 | 6,342.0 |
| 1992 | 929.6 | 866.4 | 824.9 | 531.2 | 758.9 | 683.3 | 859.4 | 1,047.7 | 1,138.5 | 1,300.2 | 1,225.8 | 1,052.1 | 11,218.0 |
| 1993 | 1,134.6 | 1,286.3 | 1,763.1 | 1,089.5 | 1,341.4 | 1,390.6 | 1,147.0 | 1,390.7 | 1,523.7 | 1,279.5 | 1,926.6 | 1,328.2 | 16,601.2 |
| 1994 | 1,484.3 | 1,935.7 | 2,572.4 | 2,213.5 | 2,399.4 | 2,250.2 | 1,621.8 | 2,028.7 | 1,932.9 | 1,635.1 | 2,253.6 | 1,750.2 | 24,078.0 |
| 1995 | 1,752.6 | 1,978.8 | 2,458.7 | 1,368.2 | 2,236.5 | 2,495.8 | 1,588.9 | 2,028.7 | 1,859.0 | 1,459.7 | 1,730.8 | 1,487.6 | 22,445.4 |
| 1996 | 1,649.1 | 2,313.1 | 2,075.8 | 1,632.1 | 2,211.3 | 1,715.6 | 1,556.3 | 1,865.7 | 1,810.4 | 1,494.7 | 1,904.5 | 1,711.2 | 21,939.7 |

*Source: Chicago Board of Trade (CBT)*

## Average Open Interest of 5-Year Treasury Note Futures in Chicago In Contracts

| Year | Jan. | Feb. | Mar. | Apr. | May | June | July | Aug. | Sept. | Oct. | Nov. | Dec. |
|---|---|---|---|---|---|---|---|---|---|---|---|---|
| 1988 | | | | | 2,545 | 5,292 | 10,584 | 11,424 | 12,677 | 18,403 | 24,569 | 34,267 |
| 1989 | 34,728 | 40,203 | 45,320 | 46,371 | 48,195 | 42,496 | 44,985 | 34,675 | 37,474 | 42,669 | 57,901 | 73,798 |
| 1990 | 81,705 | 74,568 | 74,999 | 60,841 | 59,417 | 56,485 | 54,004 | 64,100 | 75,955 | 78,370 | 82,981 | 93,549 |
| 1991 | 80,059 | 82,666 | 83,109 | 74,612 | 75,799 | 65,543 | 72,197 | 86,981 | 85,794 | 91,096 | 102,890 | 99,291 |
| 1992 | 116,322 | 121,667 | 125,155 | 130,826 | 135,111 | 144,386 | 143,928 | 143,203 | 127,418 | 122,113 | 129,548 | 127,690 |
| 1993 | 139,207 | 150,443 | 152,711 | 158,607 | 169,234 | 152,262 | 152,403 | 160,258 | 159,754 | 154,501 | 181,492 | 206,914 |
| 1994 | 200,812 | 213,037 | 200,626 | 185,083 | 192,659 | 186,026 | 189,828 | 182,027 | 181,518 | 181,578 | 176,322 | 205,150 |
| 1995 | 206,539 | 210,192 | 199,357 | 200,087 | 213,531 | 189,332 | 176,329 | 173,897 | 163,419 | 162,121 | 177,915 | 171,023 |
| 1996 | 163,026 | 184,523 | 200,253 | 191,690 | 179,951 | 177,370 | 174,484 | 179,599 | 154,764 | 138,246 | 155,820 | 154,764 |

*Source: Chicago Board of Trade (CBT)*

## Volume of Trading of 5-Year Treasury Note Futures in Chicago In Thousands of Contracts

| Year | Jan. | Feb. | Mar. | Apr. | May | June | July | Aug. | Sept. | Oct. | Nov. | Dec. | Total |
|---|---|---|---|---|---|---|---|---|---|---|---|---|---|
| 1988 | | | | | 20.6 | 56.5 | 45.6 | 66.4 | 73.8 | 54.8 | 97.1 | 91.8 | 243.7 |
| 1989 | 91.1 | 156.8 | 128.1 | 89.2 | 167.3 | 162.0 | 142.3 | 205.2 | 121.2 | 148.3 | 253.4 | 116.9 | 518.6 |
| 1990 | 184.5 | 277.5 | 164.9 | 107.6 | 266.6 | 140.8 | 131.6 | 320.4 | 189.0 | 197.9 | 305.7 | 40.8 | 544.4 |
| 1991 | 220.5 | 318.5 | 252.3 | 181.4 | 307.6 | 232.4 | 179.7 | 385.4 | 243.9 | 291.5 | 419.9 | 353.1 | 1,064.5 |
| 1992 | 498.6 | 543.8 | 560.0 | 322.2 | 590.1 | 551.5 | 484.2 | 565.7 | 582.1 | 539.0 | 640.8 | 563.2 | 1,743.0 |
| 1993 | 539.5 | 673.1 | 886.0 | 447.6 | 755.9 | 753.8 | 506.4 | 711.3 | 753.8 | 472.6 | 908.0 | 715.8 | 2,096.4 |
| 1994 | 695.9 | 1,235.1 | 1,295.4 | 917.1 | 1,202.0 | 1,154.9 | 834.8 | 944.9 | 1,107.3 | 840.6 | 1,156.7 | 1,078.0 | 12,463.0 |
| 1995 | 988.5 | 1,296.2 | 1,386.9 | 783.4 | 1,291.1 | 1,402.9 | 828.6 | 1,100.5 | 1,008.7 | 769.6 | 996.0 | 784.7 | 12,637.1 |
| 1996 | 837.3 | 1,312.0 | 1,084.6 | 815.7 | 1,135.5 | 878.3 | 881.7 | 1,061.8 | 979.0 | 689.5 | 831.1 | 957.1 | 11,463.4 |

*Source: Chicago Board of Trade (CBT)*

## U.S. Federal Funds Rate In Percent

| Year | Jan. | Feb. | Mar. | Apr. | May | June | July | Aug. | Sept. | Oct. | Nov. | Dec. | Annual |
|---|---|---|---|---|---|---|---|---|---|---|---|---|---|
| 1985 | 8.35 | 8.50 | 8.58 | 8.27 | 7.97 | 7.53 | 7.88 | 7.90 | 7.92 | 7.99 | 8.05 | 8.27 | 8.10 |
| 1986 | 8.14 | 7.86 | 7.48 | 6.99 | 6.85 | 6.92 | 6.56 | 6.17 | 5.89 | 5.85 | 6.04 | 6.91 | 6.81 |
| 1987 | 6.43 | 6.10 | 6.13 | 6.37 | 6.85 | 6.73 | 6.58 | 6.73 | 7.22 | 7.29 | 6.69 | 6.77 | 6.66 |
| 1988 | 6.83 | 6.58 | 6.58 | 6.87 | 7.09 | 7.51 | 7.76 | 8.01 | 8.19 | 8.30 | 8.35 | 8.76 | 7.57 |
| 1989 | 9.12 | 9.36 | 9.85 | 9.84 | 9.81 | 9.53 | 9.24 | 8.99 | 9.02 | 8.84 | 8.55 | 8.45 | 9.22 |
| 1990 | 8.23 | 8.24 | 8.28 | 8.26 | 8.18 | 8.29 | 8.15 | 8.13 | 8.20 | 8.11 | 7.81 | 7.31 | 8.10 |
| 1991 | 6.91 | 6.25 | 6.12 | 5.91 | 5.78 | 5.90 | 5.82 | 5.66 | 5.45 | 5.21 | 4.81 | 4.43 | 5.69 |
| 1992 | 4.03 | 4.06 | 3.98 | 3.73 | 3.82 | 3.76 | 3.25 | 3.30 | 3.22 | 3.10 | 3.09 | 2.92 | 3.52 |
| 1993 | 3.02 | 3.03 | 3.07 | 2.96 | 3.00 | 3.04 | 3.06 | 3.03 | 3.09 | 2.99 | 3.02 | 2.96 | 3.02 |
| 1994 | 3.05 | 3.25 | 3.34 | 3.56 | 4.01 | 4.25 | 4.26 | 4.47 | 4.73 | 4.76 | 5.29 | 5.45 | 4.20 |
| 1995 | 5.53 | 5.92 | 5.98 | 6.05 | 6.01 | 6.00 | 5.85 | 5.74 | 5.80 | 5.76 | 5.80 | 5.60 | 5.84 |
| 1996 | 5.56 | 5.22 | 5.31 | 5.22 | 5.56 | 5.27 | 5.40 | 5.22 | 5.30 | 5.24 | 5.31 | 5.29 | 5.33 |

*Source: Bureau of Economic Analysis, U.S. Department of Commerce*

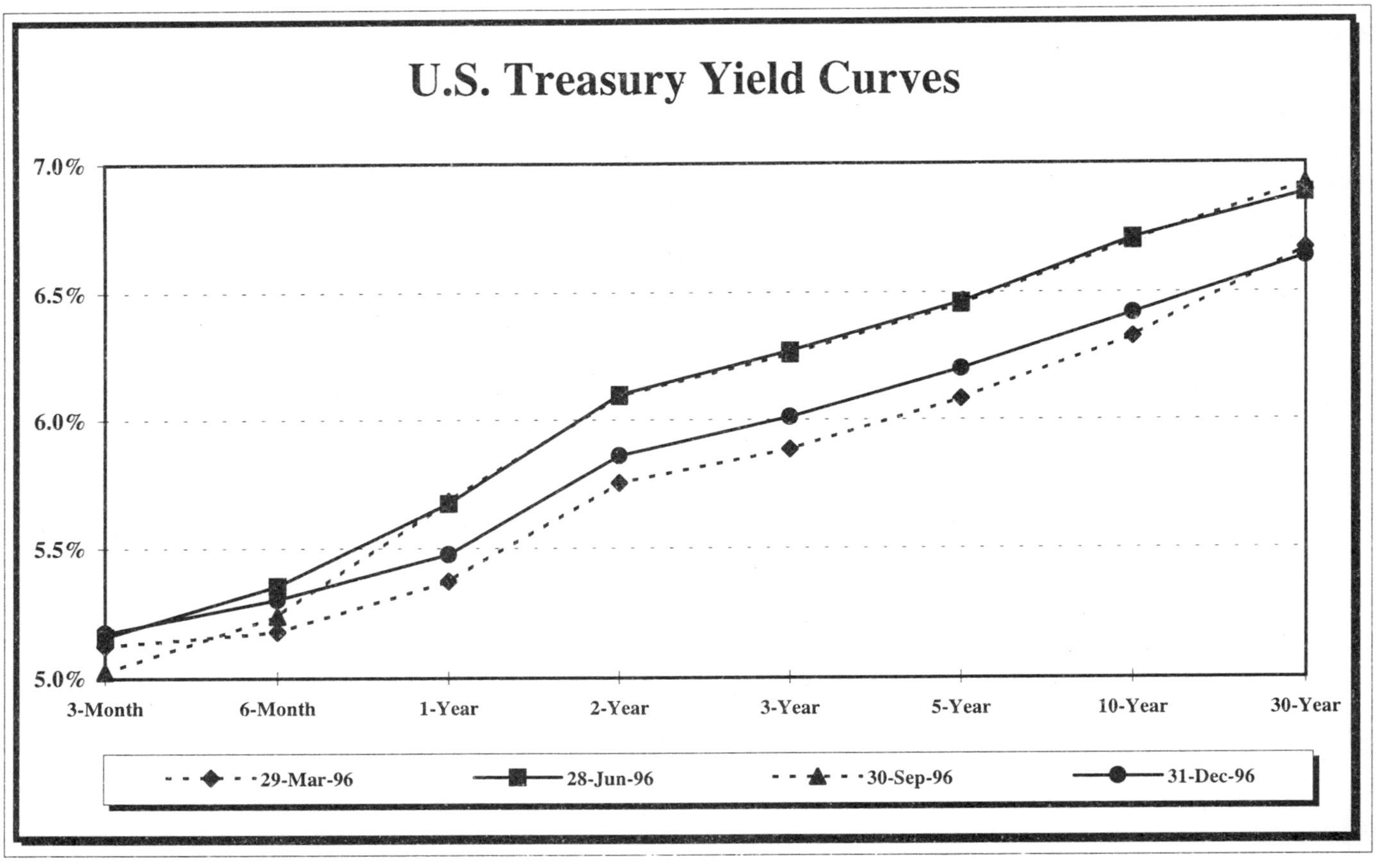


## U.S. Industrial Production Index[1] (Seasonally Adjusted) 1992 = 100

| Year | Jan. | Feb. | Mar. | Apr. | May | June | July | Aug. | Sept. | Oct. | Nov. | Dec. | Average |
|---|---|---|---|---|---|---|---|---|---|---|---|---|---|
| 1985 | 86.9 | 87.6 | 87.8 | 88.0 | 88.2 | 88.0 | 87.6 | 88.1 | 88.6 | 87.9 | 88.4 | 89.0 | 88.0 |
| 1986 | 89.6 | 88.9 | 88.0 | 88.7 | 88.5 | 88.2 | 88.5 | 88.7 | 88.7 | 89.5 | 89.9 | 90.7 | 89.0 |
| 1987 | 90.2 | 91.2 | 91.5 | 91.9 | 92.3 | 93.1 | 93.7 | 93.8 | 93.7 | 94.9 | 95.2 | 95.8 | 93.1 |
| 1988 | 95.8 | 96.1 | 96.2 | 96.7 | 96.8 | 96.8 | 97.4 | 98.0 | 97.6 | 97.9 | 98.6 | 99.1 | 97.3 |
| 1989 | 99.7 | 98.9 | 99.8 | 100.1 | 99.5 | 99.3 | 98.3 | 98.7 | 98.5 | 98.1 | 98.5 | 98.9 | 99.0 |
| 1990 | 98.5 | 99.0 | 99.4 | 98.9 | 99.3 | 99.3 | 99.2 | 99.4 | 99.5 | 99.0 | 97.7 | 97.1 | 98.9 |
| 1991 | 96.7 | 95.9 | 95.0 | 95.3 | 96.0 | 97.2 | 97.2 | 97.4 | 98.3 | 98.2 | 98.1 | 97.4 | 96.9 |
| 1992 | 97.5 | 98.1 | 98.9 | 99.6 | 100.0 | 99.7 | 100.4 | 100.1 | 100.5 | 101.3 | 101.9 | 101.9 | 100.0 |
| 1993 | 102.3 | 102.8 | 102.8 | 103.2 | 102.6 | 102.8 | 103.1 | 102.8 | 103.9 | 104.1 | 104.6 | 105.4 | 103.4 |
| 1994 | 105.7 | 106.2 | 107.0 | 107.4 | 108.1 | 108.6 | 109.1 | 109.2 | 109.3 | 109.9 | 110.6 | 111.6 | 108.6 |
| 1995 | 111.9 | 111.6 | 111.7 | 111.4 | 111.5 | 111.7 | 111.7 | 112.6 | 113.0 | 112.5 | 112.7 | 112.8 | 112.1 |
| 1996[2] | 112.4 | 113.8 | 113.2 | 114.3 | 114.8 | 115.5 | 115.5 | 115.8 | 116.0 | 116.0 | 116.9 | 117.7 | 115.2 |

[1] Total Index of the Federal Reserve Index of Quantity Output. [2] Preliminary. *Source: Bureau of Economic Analysis, U.S. Department of Commerce*

## U.S. Gross National Product, National Income, and Personal Income In Billions of Current Dollars[1]

| | Gross Domestic Product | | | | | National Income | | | | | Personal Income | | | | |
|---|---|---|---|---|---|---|---|---|---|---|---|---|---|---|---|
| Year | I | II | III | IV | Annual Average | I | II | III | IV | Annual Average | I | II | III | IV | Annual Average |
| 1986 | 4,181 | 4,195 | 4,253 | 4,297 | 4,232 | 3,363 | 3,395 | 3,419 | 3,473 | 3,413 | 3,457 | 3,510 | 3,540 | 3,598 | 3,526 |
| 1987 | 4,412 | 4,498 | 4,578 | 4,691 | 4,545 | 3,572 | 3,646 | 3,722 | 3,829 | 3,692 | 3,716 | 3,760 | 3,814 | 3,919 | 3,802 |
| 1988 | 4,764 | 4,863 | 4,952 | 5,054 | 4,908 | 3,889 | 3,966 | 4,028 | 4,128 | 4,003 | 3,968 | 4,038 | 4,103 | 4,195 | 4,076 |
| 1989 | 5,144 | 5,218 | 5,280 | 5,351 | 5,248 | 4,203 | 4,231 | 4,245 | 4,301 | 4,245 | 4,304 | 4,352 | 4,391 | 4,474 | 4,380 |
| 1990 | 5,433 | 5,506 | 5,577 | 5,583 | 5,525 | 4,396 | 4,461 | 4,475 | 4,507 | 4,460 | 4,581 | 4,655 | 4,719 | 4,765 | 4,680 |
| 1991 | 5,615 | 5,674 | 5,726 | 5,764 | 5,917 | 4,493 | 4,529 | 4,555 | 4,599 | 4,720 | 4,753 | 4,807 | 4,846 | 4,907 | 4,969 |
| 1992 | 6,122 | 6,201 | 6,272 | 6,383 | 6,244 | 4,889 | 4,941 | 4,912 | 5,062 | 4,951 | 5,152 | 5,225 | 5,265 | 5,415 | 5,264 |
| 1993 | 6,443 | 6,503 | 6,571 | 6,684 | 6,550 | 5,095 | 5,160 | 5,213 | 5,310 | 5,194 | 5,349 | 5,458 | 5,501 | 5,609 | 5,479 |
| 1994 | 6,773 | 6,885 | 6,988 | 7,080 | 6,936 | 5,301 | 5,494 | 5,551 | 5,635 | 5,502 | 5,562 | 5,743 | 5,802 | 5,894 | 5,753 |
| 1995[2] | 7,150 | 7,205 | 7,310 | 7,351 | 7,254 | 5,710 | 5,755 | 5,861 | 5,927 | 5,814 | 6,005 | 6,074 | 6,147 | 6,235 | 6,115 |
| 1996[2] | 7,427 | 7,545 | 7,616 | | 7,529 | 6,015 | 6,119 | 6,203 | | 6,112 | 6,309 | 6,412 | 6,501 | | 6,407 |

[1] Seasonally adjusted at annual rates. [2] Preliminary *Source: Bureau of Economic Analysis, U.S. Department of Commerce*

## U.S. Money Supply M1 in Constant Dollars[2] In Billions of Dollars

| Year | Jan. | Feb. | Mar. | Apr. | May | June | July | Aug. | Sept. | Oct. | Nov. | Dec. | Average |
|---|---|---|---|---|---|---|---|---|---|---|---|---|---|
| 1986 | 800.7 | 806.2 | 819.2 | 829.4 | 841.1 | 849.4 | 859.8 | 870.1 | 876.0 | 884.1 | 896.9 | 917.7 | 854.2 |
| 1987 | 919.2 | 916.3 | 917.2 | 926.7 | 927.9 | 919.7 | 917.3 | 916.6 | 915.1 | 922.0 | 915.6 | 910.1 | 918.6 |
| 1988 | 916.9 | 916.6 | 917.6 | 921.4 | 921.7 | 925.5 | 925.8 | 923.3 | 918.8 | 916.2 | 914.6 | 913.6 | 919.3 |
| 1989 | 907.3 | 902.4 | 896.8 | 887.5 | 878.0 | 874.5 | 878.1 | 878.0 | 877.6 | 879.2 | 878.0 | 882.1 | 885.0 |
| 1990 | 877.5 | 877.0 | 876.4 | 877.9 | 873.2 | 875.2 | 872.5 | 872.6 | 872.9 | 865.5 | 865.9 | 868.4 | 872.9 |
| 1991 | 865.1 | 869.3 | 876.2 | 876.6 | 880.4 | 889.2 | 889.7 | 893.0 | 893.4 | 898.5 | 906.3 | 912.7 | 887.5 |
| 1992 | 922.9 | 936.7 | 944.4 | 949.5 | 955.6 | 955.2 | 960.6 | 975.1 | 982.5 | 994.1 | 1,005.0 | 1,011.8 | 966.1 |
| 1993 | 1,015.8 | 1,015.0 | 1,017.9 | 1,023.7 | 1,042.4 | 1,049.6 | 1,057.4 | 1,064.6 | 1,072.6 | 1,077.2 | 1,084.6 | 1,089.6 | 1,050.9 |
| 1994 | 1,090.8 | 1,092.7 | 1,093.3 | 1,094.0 | 1,093.9 | 1,093.1 | 1,094.0 | 1,089.2 | 1,087.3 | 1,084.0 | 1,083.0 | 1,082.4 | 1,089.8 |
| 1995[1] | 1,078.6 | 1,075.4 | 1,073.9 | 1,072.8 | 1,066.3 | 1,064.0 | 1,063.7 | 1,059.9 | 1,056.3 | 1,046.4 | 1,043.1 | 1,037.8 | 1,061.5 |
| 1996[1] | 1,030.4 | 1,027.0 | 1,032.4 | 1,026.0 | 1,018.5 | 1,017.3 | 1,007.6 | 998.9 | 989.8 | 972.9 | 970.9 | 970.4 | 1,005.2 |

[1] Preliminary. [2] M1--This measure is currency, travelers checks, plus demand deposits at commercial banks and interest-earning checkable deposits at all depository institutions. *Source: Bureau of Economic Analysis, U.S. Department of Commerce*

## U.S. Money Supply M2 in Constant Dollars[2] In Billions of Dollars

| Year | Jan. | Feb. | Mar. | Apr. | May | June | July | Aug. | Sept. | Oct. | Nov. | Dec. | Average |
|---|---|---|---|---|---|---|---|---|---|---|---|---|---|
| 1986 | 3,233.9 | 3,248.6 | 3,282.7 | 3,318.1 | 3,343.5 | 3,356.5 | 3,378.1 | 3,396.9 | 3,409.0 | 3,428.7 | 3,439.6 | 3,464.2 | 3,358.3 |
| 1987 | 3,462.5 | 3,453.3 | 3,451.1 | 3,455.4 | 3,454.2 | 3,443.2 | 3,440.6 | 3,436.8 | 3,434.9 | 3,439.9 | 3,435.7 | 3,440.5 | 3,445.7 |
| 1988 | 3,459.6 | 3,482.8 | 3,493.9 | 3,500.4 | 3,504.6 | 3,502.9 | 3,498.5 | 3,491.0 | 3,478.4 | 3,476.5 | 3,483.5 | 3,480.6 | 3,487.7 |
| 1989 | 3,465.1 | 3,454.7 | 3,447.2 | 3,432.0 | 3,423.8 | 3,434.7 | 3,453.6 | 3,474.7 | 3,484.3 | 3,491.2 | 3,502.5 | 3,514.2 | 3,464.8 |
| 1990 | 3,504.2 | 3,502.7 | 3,497.7 | 3,498.1 | 3,484.8 | 3,483.5 | 3,481.7 | 3,477.4 | 3,470.0 | 3,451.0 | 3,447.5 | 3,451.6 | 3,479.2 |
| 1991 | 3,449.3 | 3,458.8 | 3,476.0 | 3,475.7 | 3,474.5 | 3,481.1 | 3,474.2 | 3,462.7 | 3,450.5 | 3,447.6 | 3,443.2 | 3,442.1 | 3,461.3 |
| 1992 | 3,439.9 | 3,450.3 | 3,442.5 | 3,431.2 | 3,422.9 | 3,408.9 | 3,396.8 | 3,412.0 | 3,402.8 | 3,402.9 | 3,401.4 | 3,396.4 | 3,417.3 |
| 1993 | 3,384.1 | 3,367.1 | 3,358.7 | 3,351.4 | 3,371.6 | 3,374.4 | 3,371.3 | 3,368.4 | 3,370.9 | 3,362.3 | 3,368.7 | 3,373.4 | 3,368.5 |
| 1994 | 3,371.0 | 3,364.3 | 3,359.2 | 3,362.3 | 3,356.6 | 3,338.8 | 3,333.2 | 3,318.6 | 3,311.5 | 3,305.8 | 3,305.9 | 3,306.6 | 3,336.2 |
| 1995[1] | 3,298.1 | 3,292.5 | 3,289.5 | 3,288.0 | 3,297.2 | 3,318.0 | 3,331.1 | 3,342.8 | 3,354.7 | 3,354.5 | 3,363.2 | 3,374.3 | 3,325.3 |
| 1996[1] | 3,380.4 | 3,389.2 | 3,410.9 | 3,404.9 | 3,396.0 | 3,410.5 | 3,409.0 | 3,419.0 | 3,422.6 | 3,420.6 | 3,435.9 | 3,456.0 | 3,412.9 |

[1] Preliminary. [2] M2--This measure adds to M1 overnight repurchase agreements (RPs) issued by commercial banks and certain overnight Eurodollars (those issued by Caribbean branches of member banks) held by U.S. nonbank residents, general purpose and broker/dealer money market mutual shares (MMMF), and savings and small-denomination time deposits. *Source: Bureau of Economic Analysis, U.S. Department of Commerce*

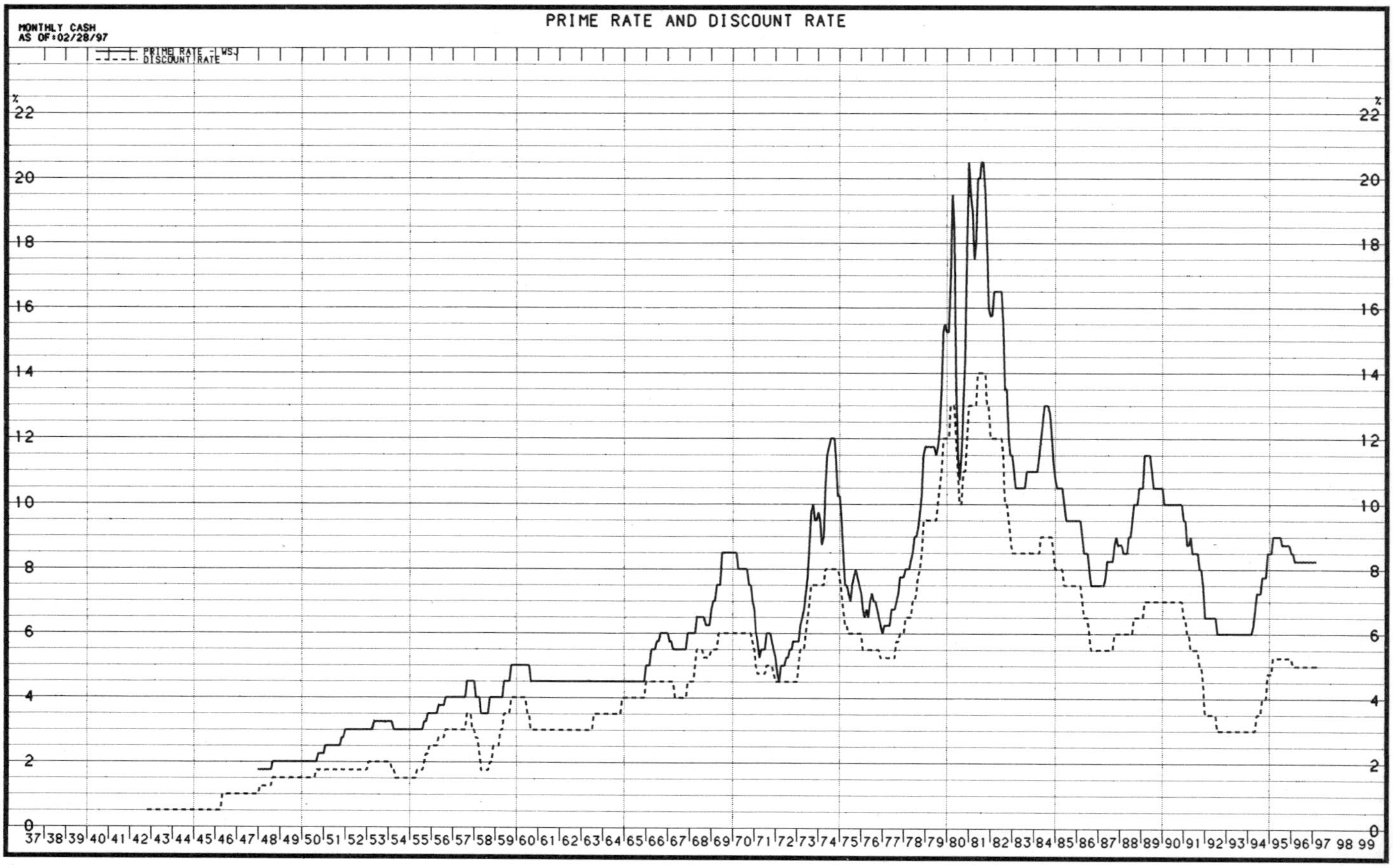
PRIME RATE AND DISCOUNT RATE
MONTHLY CASH
AS OF:02/28/97
PRIME RATE - WSJ
DISCOUNT RATE
%
22
20
18
16
14
12
10
8
6
4
2
0
37 38 39 40 41 42 43 44 45 46 47 48 49 50 51 52 53 54 55 56 57 58 59 60 61 62 63 64 65 66 67 68 69 70 71 72 73 74 75 76 77 78 79 80 81 82 83 84 85 86 87 88 89 90 91 92 93 94 95 96 97 98 99

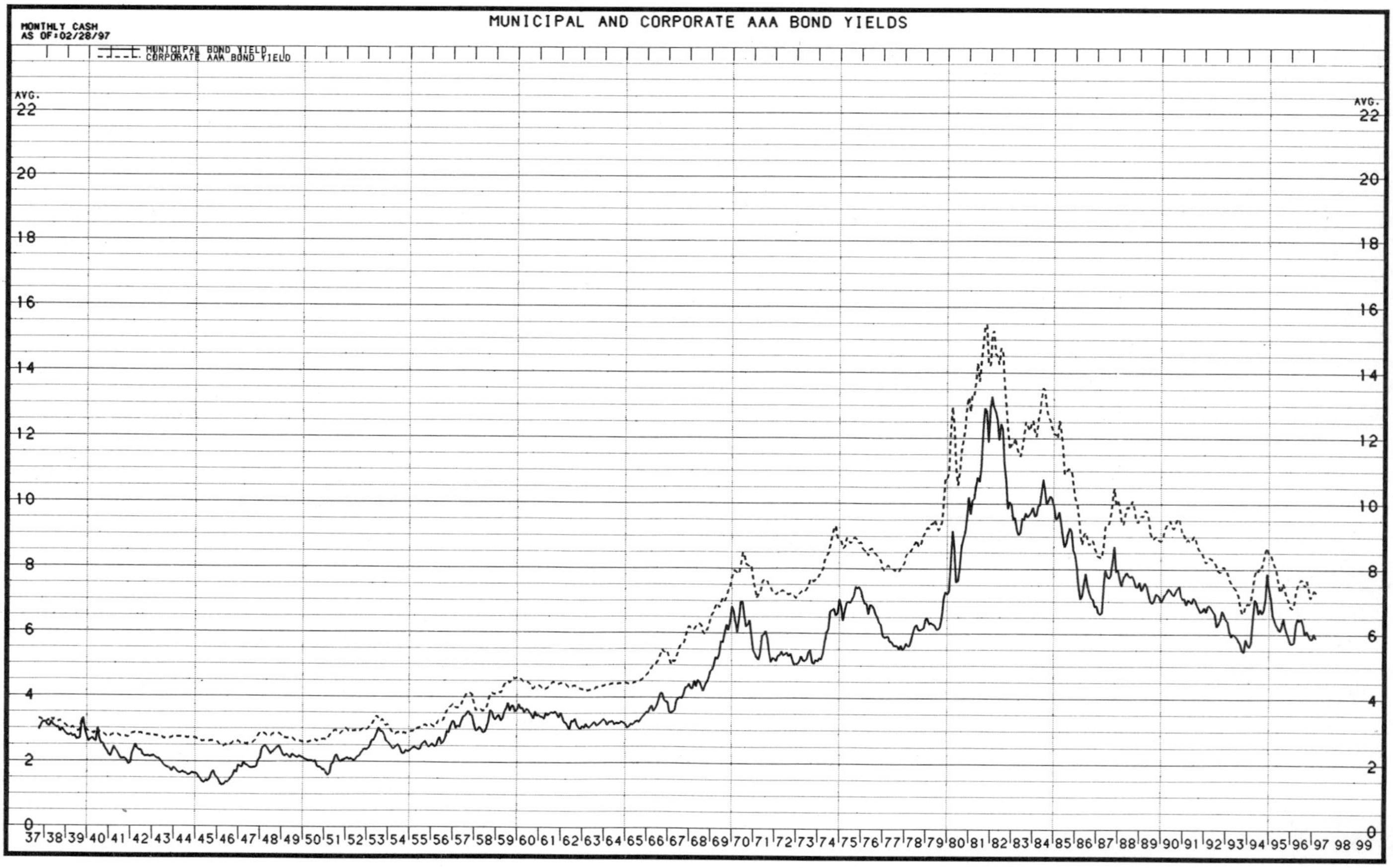
MUNICIPAL AND CORPORATE AAA BOND YIELDS
MONTHLY CASH
AS OF:02/28/97
MUNICIPAL BOND YIELD
CORPORATE AAA BOND YIELD
AVG.
22
20
18
16
14
12
10
8
6
4
2
0
37 38 39 40 41 42 43 44 45 46 47 48 49 50 51 52 53 54 55 56 57 58 59 60 61 62 63 64 65 66 67 68 69 70 71 72 73 74 75 76 77 78 79 80 81 82 83 84 85 86 87 88 89 90 91 92 93 94 95 96 97 98 99

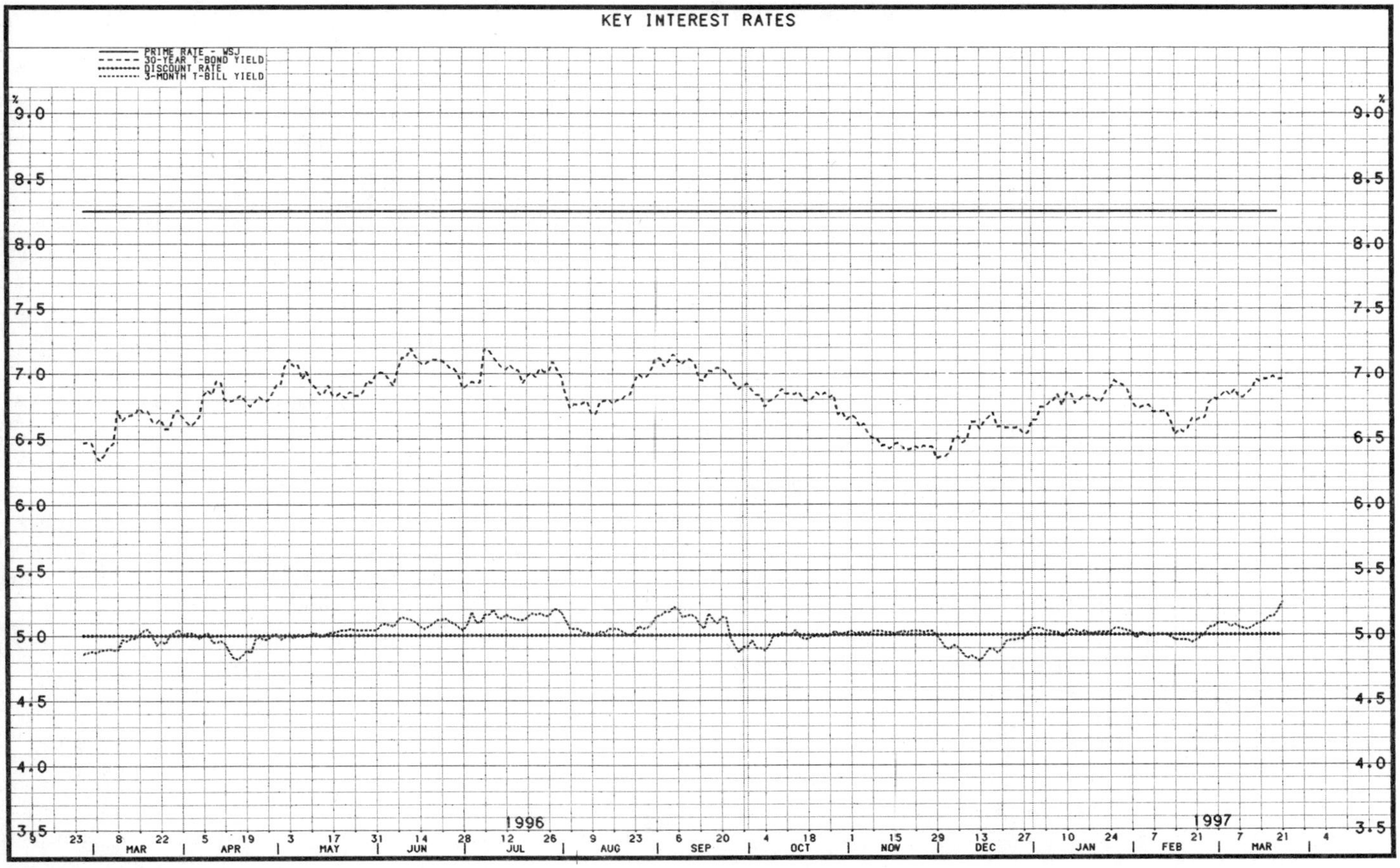
KEY INTEREST RATES
PRIME RATE - WSJ
30-YEAR T-BOND YIELD
DISCOUNT RATE
3-MONTH T-BILL YIELD
1996
1997

CBT 2-YR T-NOTE - CBOT
WEEKLY NEAREST FUTURES
AS OF:03/14/97
NOMINAL VALUE
1991
1992
1993
1994
1995
1996

# Interest Rates, Worldwide

Another year of slow economic growth inhibited many of the world's leading economies in 1996, enabling the major central banks to maintain easier monetary polices. Inflationary pressures were generally minimal in response to high unemployment which held both labor costs and consumer demand in check. Although economic improvement was expected to take hold in a number of countries during 1997, it was not likely to be strong enough to trigger any inflationary fears, suggesting that at least during the first half of the year monetary policy will be in a holding pattern and short-term rates are likely to pivot around late 1996 levels. The second half of 1997, however, may see some tightening of short term rates with only a couple of notable exceptions. In the U.S. short term rates are likely to show little change while in Italy they may even drop as inflationary fears diminish. Long-term rates, however, are apt to trend slightly higher in anticipation of strengthening domestic demand. Inflation fears appear minimal: indeed, the powerful bull market in bonds during the past few years reflects disinflationary pressures. Since the late 1970's, in virtually every western country, consumer price inflation has dropped from a double-digit pace to below 3 percent. Still, bondholders opt for a premium in yields as insurance against a surprise inflation surge, but the latter is not likely to happen in 1997.

A common thread was evident among the key central banks during 1996: monetary policy was eased or held steady. For example: the Bank of Canada lowered the cost of overnight money a cumulative total of 225 basis points resulting in a year-end major bank prime rate of 4.75 percent, the lowest level since 1956; France, in late October, lowered the money market intervention rate to 3.20 percent, down 5 basis points; Sweden, in November, lowered its repo-rate 25 basis points to 4.35 percent, bringing the cumulative decline since late 1995 to 456 basis points. Moreover, confidence that the EMU will occur was a factor prompting a convergence in European bond yields; in France a 5 basis point discount over German bonds was in place in late 1996 vs. a premium of 64 basis points a year earlier; and the premium that Australian 10-year bonds had over comparable U.S. bonds narrowed to 98 basis points from 258 points at year-end 1995. Clearly there was a need for monetary stimulus. Unemployment in the European Union averaged 11 percent in 1996 with Spain at 22 percent, Belgium at 14 percent, and Germany at 11 percent. In Eastern Europe, unemployment was even higher and the economic malaise filtered through much of the world; Canada's unemployment neared 10 percent, but in the U.S. the official level never rose above 5.8 percent in 1996.

In Europe, the U.K. stands out as having the healthiest economy and may be the only country to experience above trend growth in 1997. Unemployment is falling in contrast to the Continent where it's at a record high, suggesting that only the U.K. may have to tighten monetary policy in 1997. Contributing to the U.K.'s resurgence is its divorce in 1992 from the fixed exchange rate arrangement which benefitted the U.K.'s currency at the expense of continental Europe, and highlighted the problems that could emerge after the EMU is implemented, assuming it is. In late 1996, there was considerable uncertainty about which countries will meet the Maastricht criteria. Germany's Bundesbank and the European Monetary Institute (EMI), the embryonic European Central Bank, may take a hard line in 1997 towards a strict adherence to the criteria; the treaty itself apparently has loopholes that could check full implementation, but the odds favor the EMU's realization.

1997 inflation and interest rate forecasts for Europe generally focus on a slight rise for both in the second half of the year: the yield on 10-year U.K. bonds was estimated around 7 1/2 percent in the first half, followed by a move towards 8 percent; in Germany, France, and the Netherlands, 10-year bond yields were forecast around 6 percent, moving 25 to 50 basis points higher by year-end; Switzerland could prove to have one of the Continent's lowest yields with 10-year bonds trading in a range for the year of 4 to 4 1/2 percent.

Japan's long standing economic problems carried into 1996, but signs of improvement were thought to be taking hold late in the year. The Bank of Japan's monetary policy into 1997 is expected to be geared toward establishing a stronger base from which a solid recovery could develop. Ironically, a little dose of inflation is thought to be beneficial to Japan's economy and the central bank may opt to get inflation up to about 1 1/2 percent by late 1997 vs. near zero in 1996. Japan's 10-year bond yield forecasts for 1997 focus on less than 3 percent in the first half of 1997 and toward 3 1/2 percent by year-end.

### *Futures Markets*

A number of actively traded interest rate futures markets exist worldwide. The London International Financial Futures Exchange (LIFFE) trades contracts on 3-month Sterling prices and British government bonds, called long gilts. LIFFE also offers futures on Euromarks, Euroswiss, Italian government bonds, the FT-SE 100 index and German government bonds, called bunds. The latter is also traded in Frankfurt. Canadian Bankers Acceptances are traded on the Montreal Exchange. Notional bond and PIBOR futures are traded on the Paris MATIF. Euroyen futures and Japanese yen government bonds are traded in Tokyo. Libor and eurodollars are traded on Chicago's Mercantile Exchange, with the latter also on the Mid-America Exchange. A Eurotop 100 is traded on New York's Commodity Exchange.

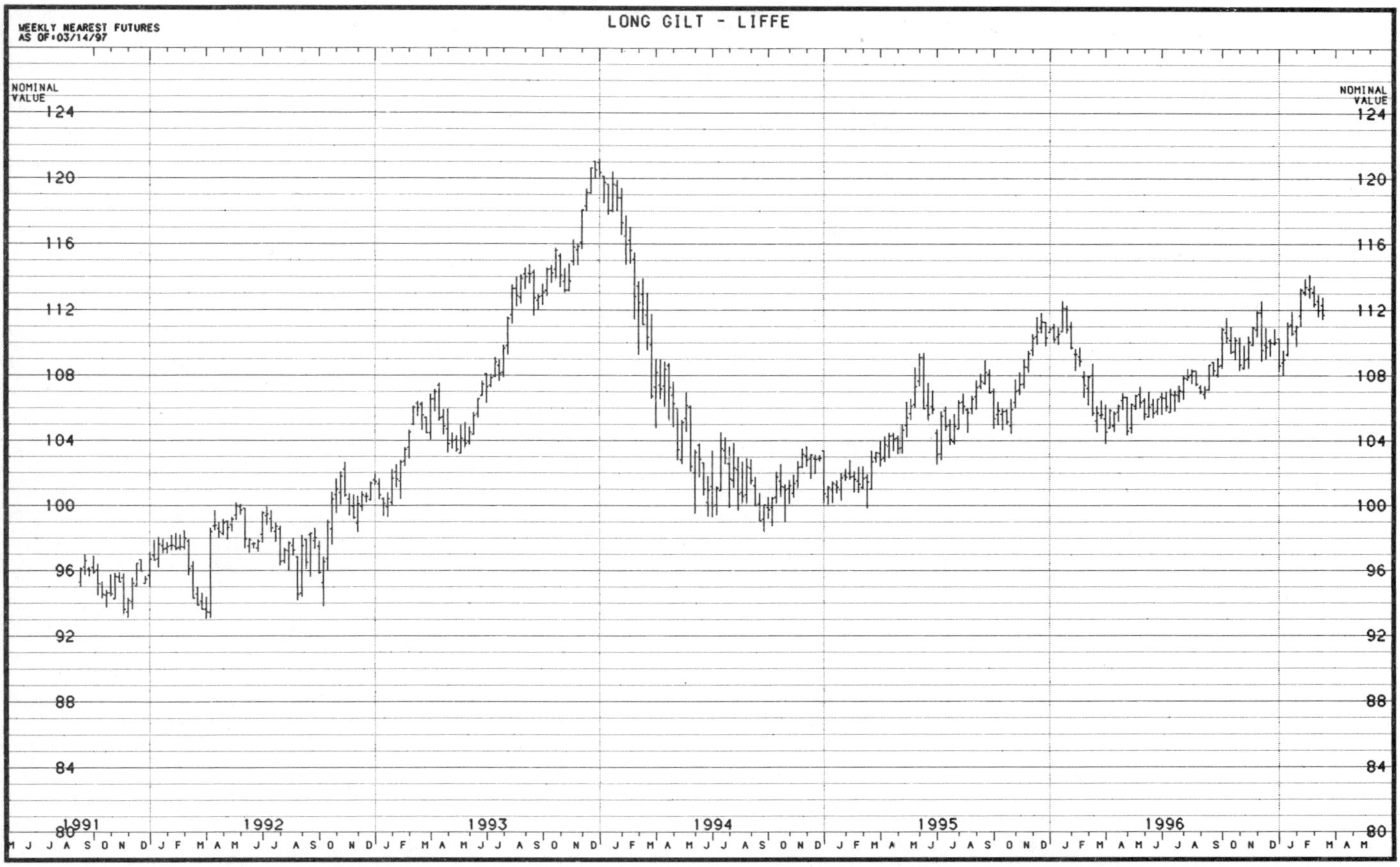
WEEKLY NEAREST FUTURES
AS OF:03/14/97
LONG GILT - LIFFE
NOMINAL VALUE
124
120
116
112
108
104
100
96
92
88
84
80
1991
1992
1993
1994
1995
1996
M J J A S O N D J F M A M J J A S O N D J F M A M J J A S O N D J F M A M J J A S O N D J F M A M J J A S O N D J F M A M J J A S O N D J F M A M

WEEKLY NEAREST FUTURES
AS OF:03/14/97
STERLING, 3-MONTH - LIFFE
POINTS OF 100%
97
96
95
94
93
92
91
90
89
88
87
86
1991
1992
1993
1994
1995
1996
M J J A S O N D J F M A M J J A S O N D J F M A M J J A S O N D J F M A M J J A S O N D J F M A M J J A S O N D J F M A M J J A S O N D J F M A M

10-YR YEN BOND - TSE
WEEKLY NEAREST FUTURES
AS OF:03/14/97
NOMINAL VALUE
136
132
128
124
120
116
112
108
104
100
96
92
1991
1992
1993
1994
1995
1996

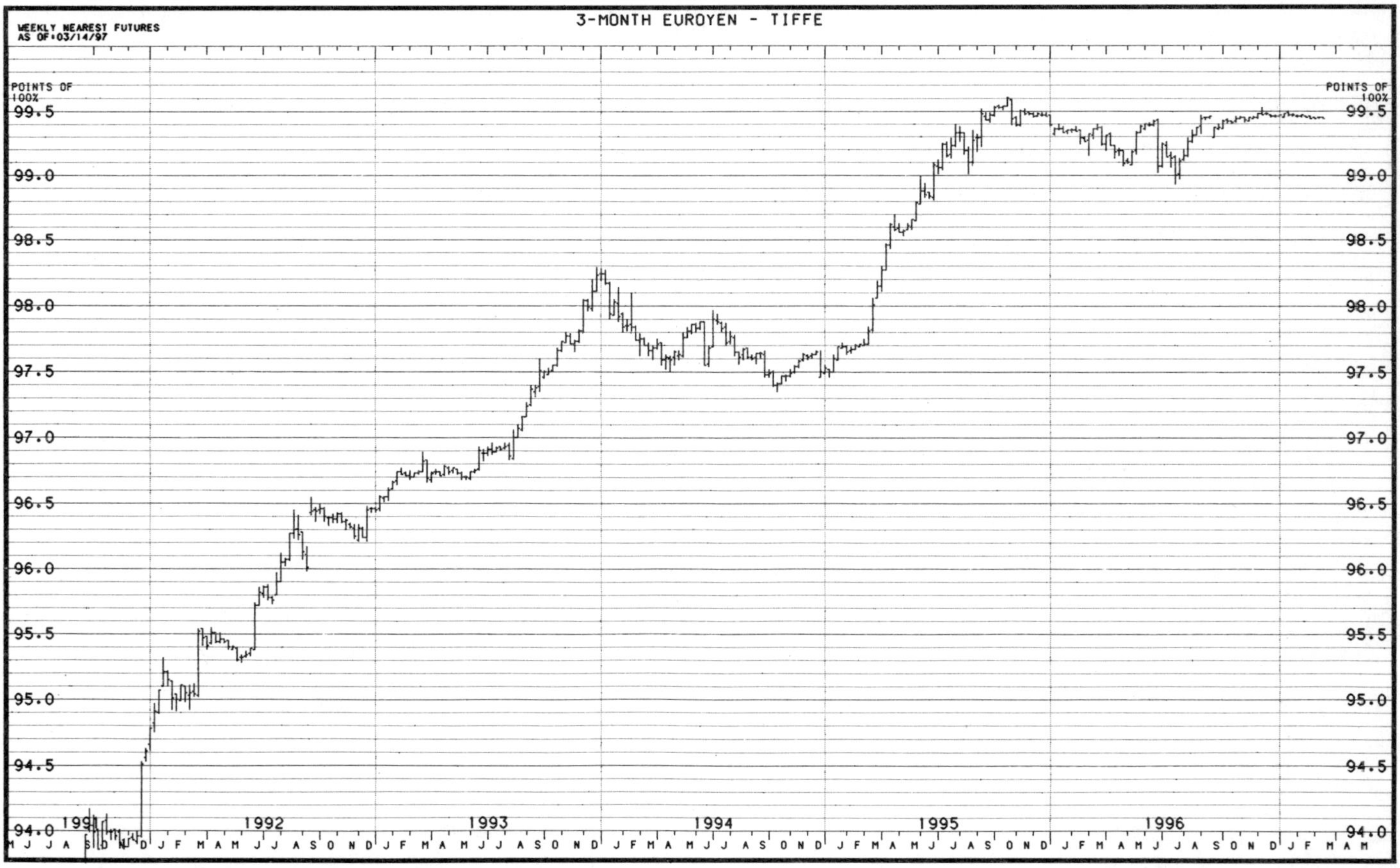
3-MONTH EUROYEN - TIFFE
WEEKLY NEAREST FUTURES
AS OF:03/14/97
POINTS OF 100%
99.5
99.0
98.5
98.0
97.5
97.0
96.5
96.0
95.5
95.0
94.5
94.0
1992
1993
1994
1995
1996

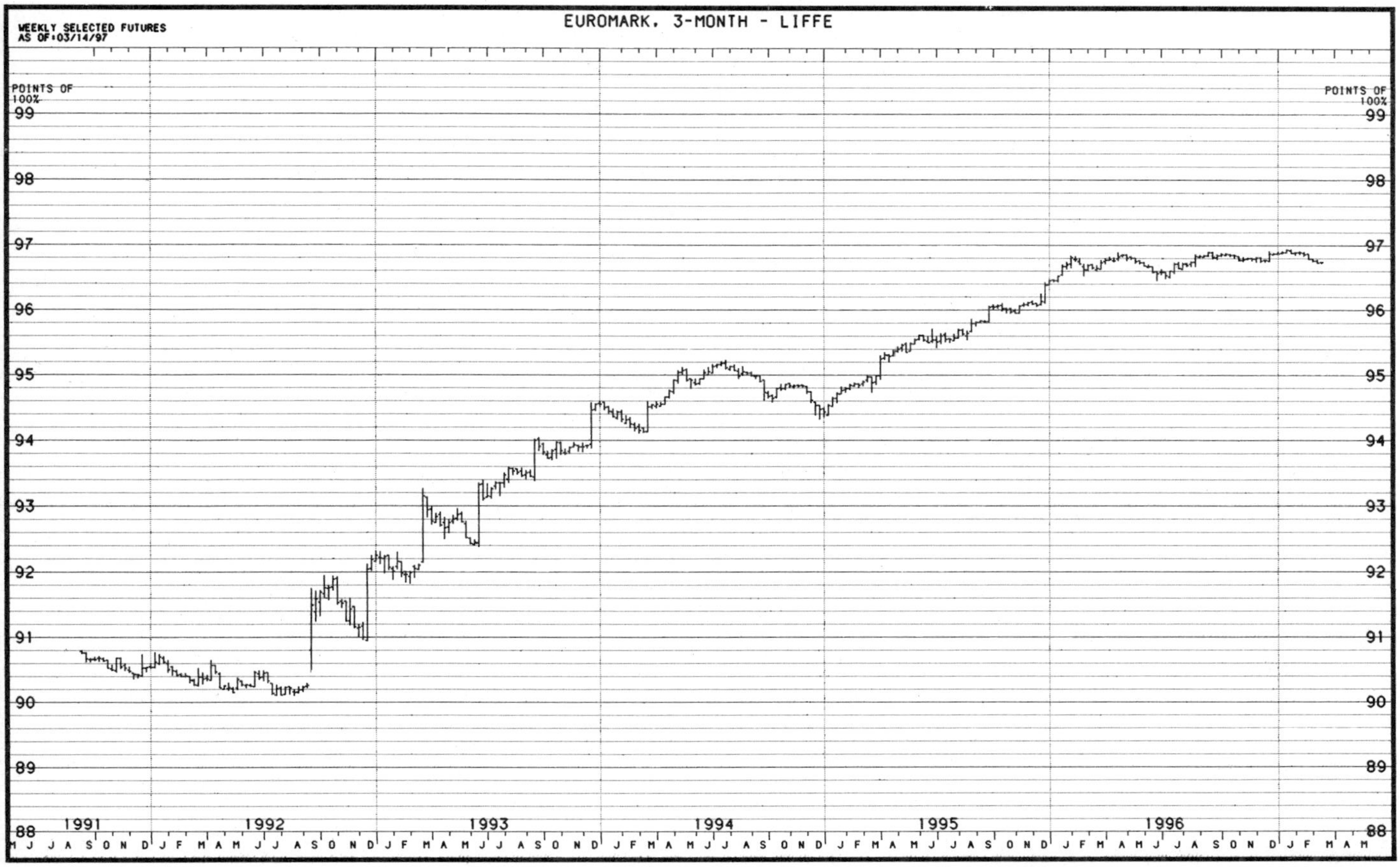
WEEKLY SELECTED FUTURES
AS OF:03/14/97
EUROMARK, 3-MONTH - LIFFE
POINTS OF 100%
99
98
97
96
95
94
93
92
91
90
89
88
1991
1992
1993
1994
1995
1996
M J J A S O N D J F M A M J J A S O N D J F M A M J J A S O N D J F M A M J J A S O N D J F M A M J J A S O N D J F M A M J J A S O N D J F M A M

WEEKLY NEAREST FUTURES
AS OF:03/14/97
GERMAN BOND, BUND - LIFFE
NOMINAL VALUE
106
104
102
100
98
96
94
92
90
88
86
84
1991
1992
1993
1994
1995
1996
M J J A S O N D J F M A M J J A S O N D J F M A M J J A S O N D J F M A M J J A S O N D J F M A M J J A S O N D J F M A M J J A S O N D J F M A M

# INTEREST RATES, WORLDWIDE

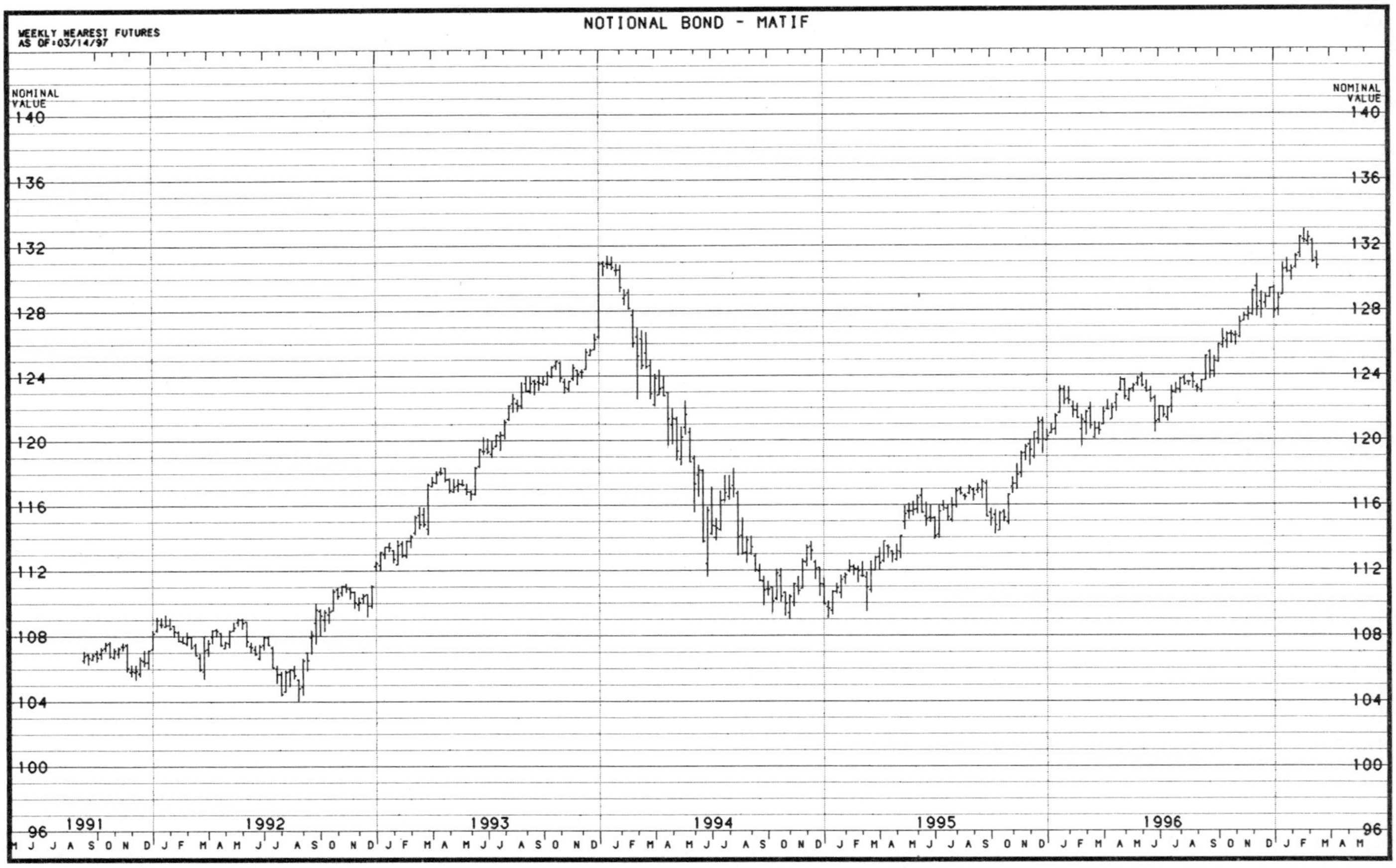

## Japan--Economic Statistics  Percentage Change from Previous Period

| Year | Real GDP | Nominal GDP | Real Private Consumption | Real Public Consumption | Grossed Fixed Investment | Real Total Domestic Demand | Real Exports of Goods & Services | Real Imports of Goods & Services | Consumer Prices[1] | Unemployment Rate |
|---|---|---|---|---|---|---|---|---|---|---|
| 1988 | 6.2 | 6.9 | 5.3 | 2.3 | 11.5 | 7.4 | 5.9 | 20.9 | .7 | 2.5 |
| 1989 | 4.8 | 7.0 | 4.8 | 2.0 | 8.2 | 5.6 | 9.1 | 18.6 | 2.3 | 2.3 |
| 1990 | 5.1 | 7.5 | 4.4 | 1.5 | 8.5 | 5.2 | 6.9 | 7.9 | 3.1 | 2.1 |
| 1991 | 4.0 | 6.7 | 2.5 | 2.0 | 3.3 | 2.9 | 5.4 | -4.7 | 3.3 | 2.1 |
| 1992 | 1.1 | 2.8 | 2.1 | 2.0 | -1.5 | .4 | 4.9 | -1.1 | 1.7 | 2.2 |
| 1993 | .1 | .8 | 1.2 | 2.4 | -2.0 | .1 | 1.3 | 1.7 | 1.2 | 2.5 |
| 1994 | .5 | .8 | 1.8 | 2.2 | -1.0 | .8 | 4.5 | 9.0 | .7 | 2.9 |
| 1995 | .9 | .4 | 1.7 | 2.0 | .9 | 1.7 | 5.0 | 13.5 | -.1 | 3.2 |
| 1996[2] | 3.6 | 3.5 | 2.7 | 2.1 | 9.6 | 4.7 | 1.7 | 11.4 | NA | 3.3 |
| 1997[2] | 1.6 | 2.1 | 1.9 | 1.7 | 1.1 | 1.6 | 8.3 | 8.3 | NA | 3.2 |

[1] National accounts implicit private consumption deflator. [2] Forecast. *Source: Organization for Economic Co-operation and Development (OECD)*

## United Kingdom--Economic Statistics  Percentage Change from Previous Period

| Year | Real GDP | Nominal GDP | Real Private Consumption | Real Public Consumption | Grossed Fixed Investment | Real Total Domestic Demand | Real Exports of Goods & Services | Real Imports of Goods & Services | Consumer Prices[1] | Unemployment Rate |
|---|---|---|---|---|---|---|---|---|---|---|
| 1988 | 5.0 | 11.3 | 7.5 | .7 | 13.9 | 7.9 | .5 | 12.6 | 4.9 | 7.8 |
| 1989 | 2.2 | 9.4 | 3.2 | 1.4 | 6.0 | 2.9 | 4.7 | 7.4 | 7.8 | 6.0 |
| 1990 | .4 | 6.8 | .6 | 2.5 | -3.5 | -.6 | 5.0 | .5 | 9.5 | 5.8 |
| 1991 | -2.0 | 4.5 | -2.2 | 2.6 | -9.5 | -3.1 | -.7 | -5.2 | 5.9 | 8.2 |
| 1992 | -.5 | 4.0 | -.1 | -.1 | -1.5 | .2 | 4.1 | 6.6 | 3.7 | 9.9 |
| 1993 | 2.3 | 5.3 | 2.5 | -.1 | .6 | 2.0 | 3.5 | 3.0 | 1.6 | 10.2 |
| 1994 | 3.8 | 5.8 | 2.6 | 1.7 | 2.9 | 2.9 | 9.2 | 5.4 | 2.5 | 9.2 |
| 1995 | 2.4 | 4.9 | 2.0 | 1.0 | -.1 | 1.5 | 7.2 | 3.9 | 3.4 | 8.2 |
| 1996[2] | 2.4 | 4.8 | 2.9 | .8 | 3.4 | 2.6 | 6.5 | 7.3 | NA | 7.9 |
| 1997[2] | 3.3 | 5.5 | 3.7 | .8 | 6.3 | 3.5 | 6.0 | 6.8 | NA | 7.4 |

[1] National accounts implicit private consumption deflator. [2] Forecast. *Source: Organization for Economic Co-operation and Development (OECD)*

## France--Economic Statistics  Percentage Change from Previous Period

| Year | Real GDP | Nominal GDP | Real Private Consumption | Real Public Consumption | Grossed Fixed Investment | Real Total Domestic Demand | Real Exports of Goods & Services | Real Imports of Goods & Services | Consumer Prices[1] | Unemployment Rate |
|---|---|---|---|---|---|---|---|---|---|---|
| 1988 | 4.5 | 7.5 | 3.3 | 3.4 | 9.6 | 4.7 | 8.1 | 8.6 | 2.7 | 10.0 |
| 1989 | 4.3 | 7.4 | 3.1 | .5 | 7.9 | 3.9 | 10.2 | 8.1 | 3.6 | 9.4 |
| 1990 | 2.5 | 5.7 | 2.7 | 2.1 | 2.8 | 2.8 | 5.4 | 6.1 | 3.4 | 8.9 |
| 1991 | .8 | 4.1 | 1.4 | 2.8 | 0 | .6 | 4.1 | 3.0 | 3.2 | 9.4 |
| 1992 | 1.2 | 3.3 | 1.4 | 3.4 | -2.8 | .2 | 4.9 | 1.2 | 2.4 | 10.3 |
| 1993 | -1.3 | 1.1 | .2 | 3.4 | -6.7 | -2.2 | -.4 | -3.5 | 2.1 | 11.7 |
| 1994 | 2.8 | 4.4 | 1.4 | 1.1 | 1.3 | 3.0 | 6.0 | 6.7 | 1.7 | 12.3 |
| 1995 | 2.2 | 3.9 | 1.8 | .9 | 2.7 | 2.1 | 6.0 | 5.4 | 1.7 | 11.7 |
| 1996[2] | 1.3 | 3.0 | 2.4 | 1.6 | .6 | .9 | 2.4 | 1.1 | NA | 12.4 |
| 1997[2] | 2.5 | 3.8 | 1.7 | 1.1 | 2.5 | 2.3 | 5.8 | 5.3 | NA | 12.5 |

[1] National accounts implicit private consumption deflator. [2] Forecast. *Source: Organization for Economic Co-operation and Development (OECD)*

## Germany[2]--Economic Statistics  Percentage Change from Previous Period

| Year | Real GDP | Nominal GDP | Real Private Consumption | Real Public Consumption | Grossed Fixed Investment | Real Total Domestic Demand | Real Exports of Goods & Services | Real Imports of Goods & Services | Consumer Prices[1] | Unemployment Rate |
|---|---|---|---|---|---|---|---|---|---|---|
| 1988 | 3.7 | 5.3 | 2.7 | 2.1 | 4.4 | 3.6 | 5.5 | 5.1 | 1.3 | 7.6 |
| 1989 | 3.6 | 6.1 | 2.8 | -1.6 | 6.3 | 2.9 | 10.2 | 8.3 | 2.8 | 6.9 |
| 1990 | 5.7 | 9.1 | 5.4 | 2.2 | 8.5 | 5.2 | 11.0 | 10.3 | 2.7 | 6.2 |
| 1991 | 5.0 | 9.1 | 5.6 | .5 | 6.0 | 4.8 | 12.3 | 12.8 | 3.6 | 6.7 |
| 1992 | 2.2 | 7.8 | 2.8 | 4.3 | 3.5 | 2.8 | -.3 | 2.0 | 5.1 | 7.7 |
| 1993 | -1.1 | 2.7 | .3 | 5.0 | -5.6 | -1.3 | -4.9 | -5.7 | 4.5 | 8.9 |
| 1994 | 2.9 | 5.1 | 1.0 | 1.3 | 4.2 | 2.8 | 8.0 | 7.6 | 2.7 | 9.6 |
| 1995 | 1.9 | 4.1 | 1.8 | 2.0 | 1.5 | 2.1 | 5.9 | 6.4 | 1.8 | 9.4 |
| 1996[3] | 1.1 | 2.5 | 1.7 | 2.7 | -2.2 | .8 | 3.7 | 2.4 | NA | 10.3 |
| 1997[3] | 2.2 | 3.4 | 2.0 | .7 | 1.4 | 1.7 | 5.9 | 4.0 | NA | 10.4 |

[1] National accounts implicit private consumption deflator. [2] Data are for Western Germany only, except for foreign trade statistics. [3] Forecast.
*Source: Organization for Economic Co-operation and Development (OECD)*

# Iron and Steel

Iron and steel scrap are the vital raw materials for the production of new steel and cast iron products. Since scrap is readily available for manufacturing operations and from the recovery of products that have reached the end of their useful lives, the steel industry and the foundry industry in the U.S. have been structured to efficiently recycle scrap and as a result are highly dependent on it.

Iron (or blast furnace) and steel slags are silicate byproducts of iron and steel making, and contain most of the nonferrous components of the original ores, fluxes, reductants, and metallic feeds to the iron and steel furnaces. Slag has been used for construction purposes since ancient times. Since the Industrial Revolution in Europe, slag production has increased substantially. Slag production began to outpace consumption resulting in the development of slag heaps. Research in the mid 19th century showed that slag had various uses, particularly if mixed with concrete. Consumption did not really increase significantly until the 20th century when a new use for slag was discovered. It was found it could be mixed with asphalt in road paving. This use, along with slag consumption in concrete, has allowed the consumption of slag to keep pace with production. The use of slag is considered one of the recycling industry's greatest successes.

For 1995, U.S. usage of iron and steel slag was 21 million tonnes, an increase of 4 percent from 1994. Use of steel slag was 7.2 million tonnes, down 8 percent from 1994, while blast furnace slag was 13.8 million tonnes, up 12 percent. Of the steel slag used in 1995, road bases used 39 percent, fill took 19 percent, asphaltic concrete aggregate took 15 percent, railroad ballast 2 percent, and other uses 25 percent.

U.S. production of iron ore in the first seven months of 1996 totaled 34.5 million tonnes with virtually all production in the Lake Superior district. This represented a decline of 3 percent from the same period in 1995. For all of 1995, iron ore production was 62.5 million tonnes. U.S. production of iron ore in July 1996 was 5.8 million tonnes compared to 5.7 million tonnes in July 1995. Stocks of iron ore at the end of July 1996 were 7.9 million tonnes, up about 12 percent from July 1995.

U.S. imports of iron ore and agglomerates in the first half of 1996 were 7.6 million tonnes, an increase of almost 4 percent from the first half of 1995. The major suppliers were Canada, Brazil, and Venezuela.

U.S. raw steel production in July 1996 was 7.8 million tonnes, an increase of over 3 percent from July 1995. Raw steel capability utilization was 86.6 percent, down from 86.8 percent a year earlier. For January-July 1996, U.S. raw steel production was 55.8 million tonnes, up 2 percent from the same period of 1995. For all of 1995, U.S. raw steel production was 93.6 percent.

U.S. exports of iron and steel scrap in June 1996 were 797,000 tonnes. For the first half of 1996, exports totaled 4.5 million tonnes. The major destinations were South Korea, Canada, Mexico, and Turkey. U.S. imports for consumption of iron and steel scrap in June 1996 were 167,000 tonnes and for the first half of 1996 they were 1.24 million tonnes. Most scrap is imported from Canada.

## World Production of Raw Steel (Ingots & Castings) In Thousands of Metric Tons

| Year | Belgium | Brazil | Canada | China | Czech Republic[4] | France | Germany | Italy | Japan | Rep. of Korea | Russia[3] | Spain | Ukraine[3] | United Kindom | United States | World Total |
|---|---|---|---|---|---|---|---|---|---|---|---|---|---|---|---|---|
| 1986 | 9,771 | 21,234 | 14,101 | 52,070 | 15,112 | 17,624 | 45,101 | 22,883 | 98,277 | 14,554 | 160,553 | 11,976 | ------ | 14,811 | 74,033 | 712,704 |
| 1987 | 9,787 | 22,231 | 14,737 | 56,280 | 15,356 | 17,693 | 44,491 | 22,859 | 98,513 | 16,782 | 161,887 | 11,691 | ------ | 17,425 | 80,877 | 734,319 |
| 1988 | 11,222 | 24,657 | 14,866 | 59,430 | 15,319 | 19,122 | 49,154 | 23,760 | 105,681 | 19,117 | 163,037 | 11,685 | ------ | 19,013 | 90,650 | 780,318 |
| 1989 | 10,952 | 25,055 | 15,458 | 61,200 | 15,465 | 19,335 | 48,902 | 25,213 | 107,908 | 21,873 | 160,096 | 12,684 | ------ | 18,813 | 88,852 | 786,712 |
| 1990 | 11,419 | 20,567 | 12,281 | 66,100 | 14,877 | 19,032 | 43,981 | 25,439 | 110,339 | 23,125 | 154,414 | 12,705 | ------ | 17,908 | 89,726 | 771,169 |
| 1991 | 11,335 | 22,616 | 12,987 | 70,600 | 12,133 | 18,434 | 42,169 | 25,046 | 109,649 | 26,001 | 77,093 | 12,933 | 45,002 | 16,474 | 79,738 | 737,000 |
| 1992 | 10,377 | 23,900 | 13,924 | 80,900 | 10,846 | 17,961 | 39,711 | 24,904 | 98,132 | 28,054 | 67,029 | 12,295 | 41,759 | 16,212 | 84,322 | 724,000 |
| 1993 | 10,173 | 25,170 | 14,300 | 89,600 | 6,732 | 17,179 | 37,625 | 25,701 | 99,623 | 33,000 | 58,346 | 12,646 | 32,357 | 16,625 | 88,793 | 730,000 |
| 1994[1] | 11,319 | 25,700 | 13,897 | 92,600 | 7,075 | 18,028 | 40,847 | 26,114 | 98,295 | 33,745 | 48,812 | 13,574 | 24,111 | 17,286 | 91,200 | 730,000 |
| 1995[2] | 11,606 | 25,100 | 14,415 | 93,000 | 6,746 | 18,100 | 42,100 | 27,800 | 101,640 | 36,772 | 51,300 | 13,800 | 22,300 | 17,600 | 95,172 | 752,000 |

[1] Preliminary. [2] Estimate. [3] Formerly part of the U.S.S.R.; data not reported separately until 1992. [4] Formerly part of Czechoslovakia; data not reported separately until 1993. *Source: U.S. Geological Survey*

## Average Wholesale Prices of Iron and Steel in the U.S.

| Year | No. 1 Heavy Melting Steel Scrap | | Pittsburgh Prices | | | | | | | | |
|---|---|---|---|---|---|---|---|---|---|---|---|
| | Pittsburgh | Chicago | Hot Rolled Sheet[2] | Sheet Bars: Hot Rolled | Sheet Bars: Cold Finished | Hot Rolled Strip | Carbon Steel Plates | Cold Rolled Strip | Galvanized Sheets | Rail Road Steel Scrap[3] | Used Steel Cans[4] |
| | $ Per Gross Ton | | Cents Per Pound | | | | | | | $ Per Gross Ton | |
| 1986 | 74.87 | 73.49 | 21.15 | 24.10 | 32.00 | 23.30 | 18.27 | 37.24 | 27.89 | 94.07 | NA |
| 1987 | 90.58 | 87.22 | 21.92 | 17.12 | 21.23 | 22.50 | 19.29 | 37.24 | 29.97 | 117.65 | NA |
| 1988 | 113.78 | 113.47 | 21.50 | 17.25 | 21.23 | 22.10 | 21.64 | 37.24 | 31.05 | 150.25 | NA |
| 1989 | 106.80 | 108.33 | 22.21 | 19.60 | 25.21 | 22.10 | 23.50 | 37.24 | 32.48 | 145.23 | 60.18 |
| 1990 | 106.61 | 108.62 | 22.25 | 20.43 | 25.37 | 22.10 | 23.75 | 37.24 | 33.55 | 131.59 | 77.16 |
| 1991 | 95.18 | 95.19 | 22.88 | 20.60 | 25.75 | 23.15 | 24.50 | 38.86 | 35.35 | 129.69 | 89.00 |
| 1992 | 88.72 | 88.52 | 19.13 | 17.48 | 24.03 | 23.50 | 24.50 | 39.40 | 30.88 | 117.40 | 88.73 |
| 1993 | 116.30 | 115.26 | 17.25 | 18.44 | 23.83 | 23.50 | 25.12 | 39.40 | 30.90 | 142.18 | 91.79 |
| 1994 | 136.76 | 131.91 | 17.25 | NA | 25.70 | 23.50 | 27.61 | 39.40 | 32.24 | 169.00 | 102.33 |
| 1995[1] | 142.34 | 143.17 | 17.25 | NA | 25.70 | 23.50 | 29.98 | 39.40 | 34.47 | NA | 126.32 |

[1] Preliminary. [2] 10 gauge. [3] Specialties scrap. [4] Consumer buying prices. NA = Not available. *Source: American Metal Market*

## Salient Statistics of Steel in the United States  In Thousands of Net Tons

| Year | Pig Iron Production | Producer Price Index for Steel Mill Products (1982=100) | Raw Steel Production: By Type of Furnace: Basic Oxygen | Open Hearth | Electric[2] | Stainless | Carbon | Alloy | Total | Net Shipments Steel Mill Products | Total Steel Products: Exports | Imports |
|---|---|---|---|---|---|---|---|---|---|---|---|---|
| 1987 | 48,410 | 102.3 | 52,496 | 2,666 | 33,989 | 2,028 | 77,976 | 9,147 | 89,151 | 76,654 | 1,647 | 22,005 |
| 1988 | 55,745 | 110.7 | 57,960 | 5,118 | 36,846 | 2,199 | 86,823 | 10,902 | 99,924 | 83,840 | 2,469 | 22,989 |
| 1989 | 55,873 | 114.5 | 58,348 | 4,442 | 35,154 | 1,926 | 86,230 | 9,786 | 97,943 | 84,100 | 5,098 | 19,699 |
| 1990 | 54,750 | 112.1 | 58,471 | 3,496 | 36,939 | 2,037 | 86,590 | 10,279 | 98,606 | 84,981 | 5,001 | 19,401 |
| 1991 | 48,637 | 109.5 | 52,714 | 1,408 | 33,774 | 1,878 | 77,879 | 8,139 | 87,896 | 78,846 | 7,112 | 17,743 |
| 1992 | 52,224 | 106.4 | 57,642 | NA | 35,308 | 1,993 | 82,458 | 8,498 | 92,949 | 82,241 | 5,016 | 19,033 |
| 1993 | 53,082 | 108.2 | 59,353 | NA | 38,524 | 1,956 | 86,865 | 9,056 | 97,877 | 89,022 | 4,727 | 21,796 |
| 1994 | 54,426 | 113.4 | 61,028 | NA | 39,551 | 2,022 | 89,535 | 9,022 | 100,579 | 95,084 | 4,852 | 32,705 |
| 1995[1] | 56,097 | 117.3 | 62,523 | NA | 42,407 | 2,265 | 92,656 | 10,009 | 104,930 | 97,494 | 7,080 | 24,409 |
| 1996[1] | 54,428 | 116.5 | 60,433 | NA | 43,923 | 1,943 | 93,026 | 5,562 | 100,531 | 100,531 | 5,031 | 29,164 |

[1] Preliminary. [2] Includes crucible sheets. NA = Not available. *Sources: American Iron & Steel Institute; U.S. Geological Survey*

## U.S. Production of Steel Ingots, Rate of Capability Utilization[1]  In Percents

| Year | Jan. | Feb. | Mar. | Apr. | May | June | July | Aug. | Sept. | Oct. | Nov. | Dec. | Average |
|---|---|---|---|---|---|---|---|---|---|---|---|---|---|
| 1987 | 65.5 | 69.5 | 77.3 | 80.3 | 80.2 | 79.7 | 77.3 | 79.1 | 83.9 | 84.4 | 85.2 | 82.8 | 79.5 |
| 1988 | 88.1 | 89.7 | 92.2 | 91.4 | 93.1 | 87.4 | 88.0 | 86.6 | 90.1 | 87.7 | 85.8 | 83.8 | 89.2 |
| 1989 | 88.2 | 89.8 | 90.9 | 92.2 | 88.1 | 86.2 | 80.8 | 79.2 | 80.0 | 83.0 | 77.4 | 73.3 | 84.5 |
| 1990 | 83.1 | 85.1 | 85.7 | 85.2 | 85.7 | 84.5 | 82.0 | 85.5 | 84.6 | 85.1 | 83.8 | 75.0 | 84.0 |
| 1991 | 74.6 | 73.1 | 71.7 | 72.5 | 70.0 | 71.7 | 74.8 | 75.2 | 78.5 | 78.0 | 78.0 | 74.4 | 74.2 |
| 1992 | 80.5 | 82.4 | 83.5 | 85.3 | 83.5 | 82.1 | 78.9 | 78.7 | 78.3 | 80.9 | 80.4 | 77.7 | 82.2 |
| 1993 | 84.8 | 89.0 | 87.0 | 87.4 | 88.3 | 87.5 | 86.9 | 86.2 | 87.7 | 90.2 | 86.3 | 85.9 | 89.1 |
| 1994 | 87.7 | 92.2 | 91.3 | 91.4 | 91.2 | 88.7 | 87.1 | 87.7 | 90.0 | 92.0 | 92.6 | 94.3 | 93.0 |
| 1995 | 93.8 | 95.6 | 96.0 | 92.9 | 91.6 | 90.1 | 86.8 | 88.3 | 93.6 | 90.3 | 92.1 | 90.2 | 91.7 |
| 1996[2] | 92.2 | 92.6 | 93.8 | 90.5 | 89.7 | 91.3 | 86.6 | 87.1 | 87.7 | 88.0 | 87.0 | | 89.7 |

[1] Based on tonnage capability to produce raw steel for a full order book. [2] Preliminary. *Sources: American Iron and Steel Institute; U.S. Geological Survey*

## United States Production of Steel Ingots  In Thousands of Short Tons

| Year | Jan. | Feb. | Mar. | Apr. | May | June | July | Aug. | Sept. | Oct. | Nov. | Dec. | Total |
|---|---|---|---|---|---|---|---|---|---|---|---|---|---|
| 1987 | 6,248 | 5,992 | 7,375 | 7,402 | 7,641 | 7,349 | 7,324 | 7,494 | 7,694 | 8,073 | 7,882 | 7,916 | 89,151 |
| 1988 | 8,380 | 7,984 | 8,763 | 8,398 | 8,832 | 8,031 | 8,313 | 8,181 | 8,237 | 8,332 | 7,883 | 7,954 | 99,924 |
| 1989 | 8,729 | 8,022 | 8,997 | 8,738 | 8,633 | 8,171 | 7,955 | 7,790 | 7,617 | 8,175 | 7,386 | 7,222 | 97,943 |
| 1990 | 8,241 | 7,624 | 8,505 | 8,209 | 8,529 | 8,142 | 8,101 | 8,452 | 8,094 | 8,424 | 8,021 | 7,422 | 98,906 |
| 1991 | 7,577 | 6,608 | 7,283 | 7,089 | 7,076 | 7,017 | 7,338 | 7,386 | 7,457 | 7,711 | 7,461 | 7,348 | 87,896 |
| 1992 | 7,754 | 7,432 | 8,043 | 7,875 | 7,968 | 7,584 | 7,542 | 7,526 | 7,249 | 7,742 | 7,449 | 7,438 | 92,949 |
| 1993 | 7,942 | 7,528 | 8,148 | 7,926 | 8,278 | 7,937 | 8,066 | 8,001 | 7,878 | 8,409 | 7,786 | 8,008 | 97,877 |
| 1994 | 8,003 | 7,598 | 8,323 | 8,180 | 8,437 | 7,941 | 7,996 | 8,053 | 7,993 | 8,477 | 8,256 | 8,684 | 100,579 |
| 1995 | 8,918 | 8,211 | 9,131 | 8,548 | 8,696 | 8,286 | 8,308 | 8,455 | 8,668 | 8,685 | 8,574 | 8,678 | 103,142 |
| 1996[1] | 8,981 | 8,438 | 9,136 | 8,588 | 8,798 | 8,661 | 8,585 | 8,627 | 8,407 | 8,702 | 8,276 | 8,689 | 103,888 |

[1] Preliminary. *Source: American Iron and Steel Institute*

## Shipments of Steel Products[1] by Market Classifications in the United States  In Thousands of Net Tons

| Year | Appliances Utensils & Cutlery | Auto-motive | Con-tainers, Packaging & Shipping Materials | Cons-truction Including Maint. | Con-tactors Products | Electrical Equip-ment | Export | Machinery, Industrial Equipment & Tools | Oil and Gas | Rail Trans-portation | Steel for Converting & Pro-cessing[2] | Steel Service Center & Dis-tributors | All Other[3] | Total Ship-ments |
|---|---|---|---|---|---|---|---|---|---|---|---|---|---|---|
| 1987 | 1,633 | 11,343 | 4,372 | 7,681 | 3,337 | 2,373 | 515 | 2,277 | 1,489 | 758 | 7,195 | 19,840 | 13,841 | 76,654 |
| 1988 | 1,638 | 12,555 | 4,421 | 8,607 | 3,495 | 2,459 | 1,233 | 2,798 | 1,477 | 1,146 | 8,792 | 21,037 | 14,182 | 83,840 |
| 1989 | 1,721 | 11,763 | 4,459 | 8,318 | 3,182 | 2,449 | 3,183 | 2,409 | 1,203 | 1,229 | 8,235 | 20,769 | 15,180 | 84,100 |
| 1990 | 1,540 | 11,100 | 4,474 | 9,245 | 2,870 | 2,453 | 2,487 | 2,388 | 1,892 | 1,080 | 9,441 | 21,111 | 14,900 | 84,981 |
| 1991 | 1,388 | 10,015 | 4,278 | 9,161 | 2,306 | 2,102 | 4,476 | 1,982 | 1,425 | 999 | 8,265 | 19,464 | 12,985 | 78,846 |
| 1992 | 1,503 | 11,092 | 3,974 | 9,536 | 2,694 | 2,136 | 2,650 | 1,951 | 1,454 | 1,052 | 9,226 | 21,328 | 13,645 | 82,241 |
| 1993 | 1,592 | 12,719 | 4,355 | 10,516 | 2,913 | 2,213 | 2,110 | 2,191 | 1,526 | 1,223 | 9,451 | 23,714 | 14,499 | 89,022 |
| 1994 | 1,736 | 14,753 | 4,495 | 10,935 | 3,348 | 2,299 | 1,710 | 2,427 | 1,703 | 1,248 | 10,502 | 24,153 | 15,775 | 95,084 |
| 1995 | 1,538 | 13,512 | 3,877 | 11,761 | 3,337 | 2,320 | 3,767 | 2,024 | 2,736 | 1,136 | 8,444 | 20,573 | 21,832 | 96,859 |
| 1996[4] | 1,648 | 14,400 | 3,998 | 12,981 | 3,348 | 2,329 | 2,211 | 2,329 | 2,987 | 1,134 | 8,070 | 22,156 | 26,286 | 100,531 |

[1] All grades including carbon, alloy and stainless steel. [2] Net total after deducting shipments to reporting companies for conversion or resale. [3] Includes agricultural; bolts, nuts, rivets and screws; forgings (other than automotive); shipbuilding and marine equipment; aircraft; mining, quarrying and lumbering; other domestic and commercial equipment machinery; ordinance and other direct military; seven shipments of non-reporting companies. [4] Preliminary.
*Source: American Iron and Steel Institute*

# IRON AND STEEL

## Net Shipments of Steel Products in the United States[1] In Thousands of Net Tons

| Year | Cold Finished Bars | Rails & Acces-sories | Wire Drawn | Tin Mill Products | Plates (Cut & Coils) | Sheet & Strip Galv. (Hot Dipped) | Hot Rolled Bars | Pipe & Tubing | Structural Shapes & Steel Piling | Rein-forcing Bars | Hot Rolled Sheets | Cold Rolled Sheets | Carbon | Alloy | Stain-less |
|---|---|---|---|---|---|---|---|---|---|---|---|---|---|---|---|
| 1987 | 1,361 | 62 | 800 | 3,988 | 4,048 | 7,660 | 6,048 | 3,569 | 4,839 | 4,918 | 13,048 | 13,859 | 68,116 | 7,120 | 1,418 |
| 1988 | 1,499 | 118 | 1,073 | 4,069 | 7,328 | 8,115 | 6,460 | 4,443 | 4,860 | 5,091 | 12,969 | 13,871 | 77,702 | 4,552 | 1,586 |
| 1989 | 1,472 | 562 | 1,002 | 4,126 | 7,384 | 8,543 | 6,301 | 4,011 | 4,987 | 5,015 | 13,281 | 13,854 | 78,485 | 4,143 | 1,472 |
| 1990 | 1,486 | 519 | 918 | 4,031 | 7,945 | 7,878 | 6,655 | 4,652 | 5,670 | 5,305 | 13,388 | 13,199 | 78,818 | 4,647 | 1,516 |
| 1991 | 1,341 | 486 | 865 | 4,041 | 6,942 | 6,910 | 5,431 | 4,488 | 5,245 | 4,859 | 13,161 | 11,532 | 73,480 | 3,917 | 1,449 |
| 1992 | 1,458 | 562 | 900 | 3,927 | 7,102 | 8,199 | 5,806 | 4,198 | 5,081 | 4,781 | 13,361 | 12,692 | 76,625 | 4,101 | 1,514 |
| 1993 | 1,580 | 679 | 802 | 4,123 | 7,538 | 9,712 | 6,339 | 4,445 | 4,973 | 5,033 | 14,873 | 12,758 | 83,106 | 4,381 | 1,534 |
| 1994 | 1,786 | 631 | 788 | 4,137 | 8,556 | 10,943 | 7,088 | 4,965 | 5,506 | 4,929 | 15,654 | 13,016 | 88,505 | 4,859 | 1,720 |
| 1995 | 1,758 | 609 | 703 | 3,942 | 9,044 | 11,345 | 7,004 | 5,436 | 6,611 | 4,714 | 16,402 | 12,677 | 90,485 | 5,115 | 1,894 |
| 1996[2] | 1,678 | 668 | 652 | 4,108 | 8,660 | 11,914 | 7,025 | 5,895 | 6,141 | 5,710 | 16,056 | 14,120 | 93,026 | 5,562 | 1,943 |

[1] All grades, including carbon, alloy and stainless steel. [2] Preliminary. *Source: American Iron and Steel Institute*

## World Production of Pig Iron (Excludes Ferro-Alloys) In Thousands of Metric Tons

| Year | Australia | Belgium | Brazil | Canada | China | Czech Repub.[3] | France | Ger-many | India | Italy | Japan | Poland | Russia[4] | Ukraine[4] | United Kindom | United States | World Total |
|---|---|---|---|---|---|---|---|---|---|---|---|---|---|---|---|---|---|
| 1987 | 5,569 | 8,244 | 21,509 | 10,446 | 55,030 | 9,788 | 13,449 | 31,272 | 11,083 | 11,335 | 73,418 | 10,476 | 115,038 | ------ | 12,017 | 44,034 | 522,720 |
| 1988 | 5,730 | 9,147 | 23,649 | 10,245 | 57,040 | 9,706 | 14,786 | 34,676 | 11,925 | 11,349 | 79,295 | 10,264 | 116,158 | ------ | 13,056 | 50,861 | 553,395 |
| 1989 | 6,094 | 8,868 | 24,621 | 10,849 | 58,200 | 9,911 | 15,071 | 35,197 | 12,420 | 11,795 | 80,197 | 9,488 | 116,628 | ------ | 12,638 | 50,977 | 561,762 |
| 1990 | 6,125 | 9,416 | 21,360 | 8,080 | 62,380 | 9,667 | 14,415 | 32,058 | 13,395 | 11,883 | 80,229 | 8,658 | 111,763 | ------ | 12,277 | 50,058 | 549,000 |
| 1991 | 5,633 | 9,354 | 22,926 | 8,268 | 67,650 | 8,479 | 13,408 | 30,608 | 14,176 | 10,856 | 79,985 | 6,515 | 90,900 | ------ | 11,883 | 44,510 | 528,000 |
| 1992 | 6,384 | 8,533 | 23,152 | 8,621 | 75,890 | 8,039 | 12,730 | 28,547 | 15,126 | 10,462 | 73,144 | 6,498 | 45,824 | 34,663 | 11,542 | 47,890 | 523,000 |
| 1993 | 6,714 | 8,178 | 23,982 | 8,633 | 87,390 | 4,668 | 12,335 | 26,970 | 15,674 | 11,066 | 73,738 | 6,298 | 40,871 | 26,999 | 11,534 | 48,640 | 529,000 |
| 1994[1] | 7,466 | 9,029 | 25,177 | 8,150 | 97,409 | 5,287 | 13,293 | 29,923 | 17,808 | 11,157 | 73,776 | 7,082 | 36,116 | 19,984 | 11,943 | 49,880 | 541,000 |
| 1995[2] | 7,475 | 9,000 | 25,090 | 8,464 | 101,700 | 5,289 | 13,150 | 30,038 | 18,626 | 11,684 | 74,905 | 7,500 | 39,762 | 17,701 | 12,238 | 51,360 | 554,000 |

[1] Preliminary. [2] Estimate. [3] Formerly part of Czechoslovakia; data not reported separately until 1993. [4] Formerly part of the U.S.S.R.; data not reported separately until 1992. *Source: U.S. Geological Survey*

## U.S Pig Iron Production (Excluding Production of Ferro-Alloys) In Thousands of Short Tons

| Year | Jan. | Feb. | Mar. | Apr. | May | June | July | Aug. | Sept. | Oct. | Nov. | Dec. | Total |
|---|---|---|---|---|---|---|---|---|---|---|---|---|---|
| 1987 | 3,214 | 3,069 | 3,891 | 4,048 | 4,256 | 4,079 | 4,235 | 4,165 | 4,208 | 4,407 | 4,351 | 4,447 | 48,137 |
| 1988 | 4,683 | 4,443 | 4,842 | 4,699 | 4,932 | 4,497 | 4,762 | 4,584 | 4,612 | 4,646 | 4,455 | 4,712 | 55,745 |
| 1989 | 4,964 | 4,654 | 5,112 | 4,990 | 4,917 | 4,707 | 4,604 | 4,172 | 4,403 | 4,692 | 4,322 | 4,202 | 55,873 |
| 1990 | 4,638 | 4,221 | 4,681 | 4,549 | 4,746 | 4,530 | 4,656 | 4,788 | 4,629 | 4,673 | 4,523 | 4,264 | 54,925 |
| 1991 | 4,077 | 3,470 | 4,047 | 3,830 | 3,885 | 3,830 | 4,179 | 4,121 | 4,175 | 4,251 | 4,300 | 4,338 | 48,503 |
| 1992 | 4,390 | 4,175 | 4,524 | 4,400 | 4,444 | 4,232 | 4,347 | 4,299 | 4,065 | 5,329 | 4,268 | 4,306 | 52,224 |
| 1993 | 4,503 | 4,503 | 4,454 | 4,328 | 4,555 | 4,351 | 4,522 | 4,504 | 4,367 | 4,652 | 4,218 | 4,514 | 53,103 |
| 1994 | 3,970 | 3,858 | 3,957 | 4,099 | 4,394 | 4,519 | 4,518 | 4,446 | 4,320 | 4,564 | 4,619 | 4,928 | 54,426 |
| 1995 | 4,820 | 4,453 | 4,916 | 4,568 | 4,674 | 4,499 | 4,576 | 4,688 | 4,727 | 4,687 | 4,738 | 4,762 | 56,115 |
| 1996[1] | 4,811 | 4,476 | 4,813 | 4,430 | 4,556 | 4,578 | 4,524 | 4,498 | 4,404 | 4,443 | 4,307 | 4,523 | 54,428 |

[1] Preliminary. *Source: American Iron and Steel Institute*

## Salient Statistics of Ferrous Scrap & Pig Iron in the U.S. In Thousands of Metric Tons

| | Consumption: Ferrous Scrap & Pig Iron Charged To | | | | | | | | | | | | Stocks--Dec. 31 Ferrous Scrap & Pig Iron at Consumers | | |
|---|---|---|---|---|---|---|---|---|---|---|---|---|---|---|---|
| | Mfg. of Pig Iron & Steel Ingots & Castings | | | Iron Foundries & Misc. Users | | | Mfg. of Steel Castings | All Uses | | | | | | | |
| Year | Scrap | Pig Iron | Total | Scrap | Pig Iron | Total | (Scrap) | Ferrous Scrap | Pig Iron | Grand Total | Imports of Scrap[2] | Exports of Scrap[3] | Scrap | Pig Iron | Total Stocks |
| 1986 | 45,053 | 40,211 | 85,264 | 13,034 | 1,113 | 14,147 | 1,657 | 59,745 | 41,372 | 101,117 | 657 | 10,618 | 3,941 | 171 | 4,112 |
| 1987 | 46,870 | 44,421 | 91,291 | 13,371 | 955 | 14,326 | 1,723 | 61,964 | 45,387 | 107,351 | 765 | 9,405 | 4,394 | 255 | 4,649 |
| 1988 | 51,054 | 52,163 | 103,217 | 16,513 | 1,393 | 17,906 | 2,126 | 69,692 | 53,567 | 123,259 | 942 | 9,161 | 4,131 | 188 | 4,319 |
| 1989 | 52,733 | 50,210 | 102,943 | 13,270 | 892 | 14,162 | 1,894 | 67,897 | 51,122 | 119,019 | 1,016 | 11,149 | 4,293 | 246 | 4,539 |
| 1990 | 54,361 | 49,337 | 103,698 | 13,085 | 835 | 13,920 | 1,850 | 69,296 | 50,193 | 119,489 | 1,324 | 11,580 | 4,292 | 147 | 4,439 |
| 1991 | 48,778 | 44,095 | 92,873 | 11,126 | 656 | 11,782 | 1,609 | 61,513 | 44,765 | 106,278 | 1,073 | 9,502 | 4,072 | 190 | 4,262 |
| 1992 | 50,144 | 47,263 | 97,407 | 11,444 | 619 | 12,063 | 1,640 | 63,228 | 47,894 | 111,122 | 1,316 | 9,262 | 3,752 | 181 | 3,933 |
| 1993 | 53,084 | 48,092 | 101,176 | 12,658 | 676 | 13,334 | 1,900 | 68,000 | 48,777 | 116,777 | 1,390 | 9,805 | 3,725 | 220 | 3,945 |
| 1994 | 53,801 | 50,257 | 104,057 | 14,000 | 1,000 | 15,000 | 2,000 | 70,000 | 51,000 | 121,000 | 1,740 | 8,813 | 4,100 | 400 | 4,500 |
| 1995[1] | 56,000 | 51,000 | 107,000 | 13,000 | 1,100 | 14,100 | 2,000 | 72,000 | 52,000 | 124,000 | 2,090 | 10,400 | 4,200 | 630 | 4,830 |

[1] Preliminary. [2] Includes tinplate and terneplate. [3] Excludes used rails for rerolling and other uses and ships, boats, and other vessels for scrapping.
*Source: U.S. Geological Survey*

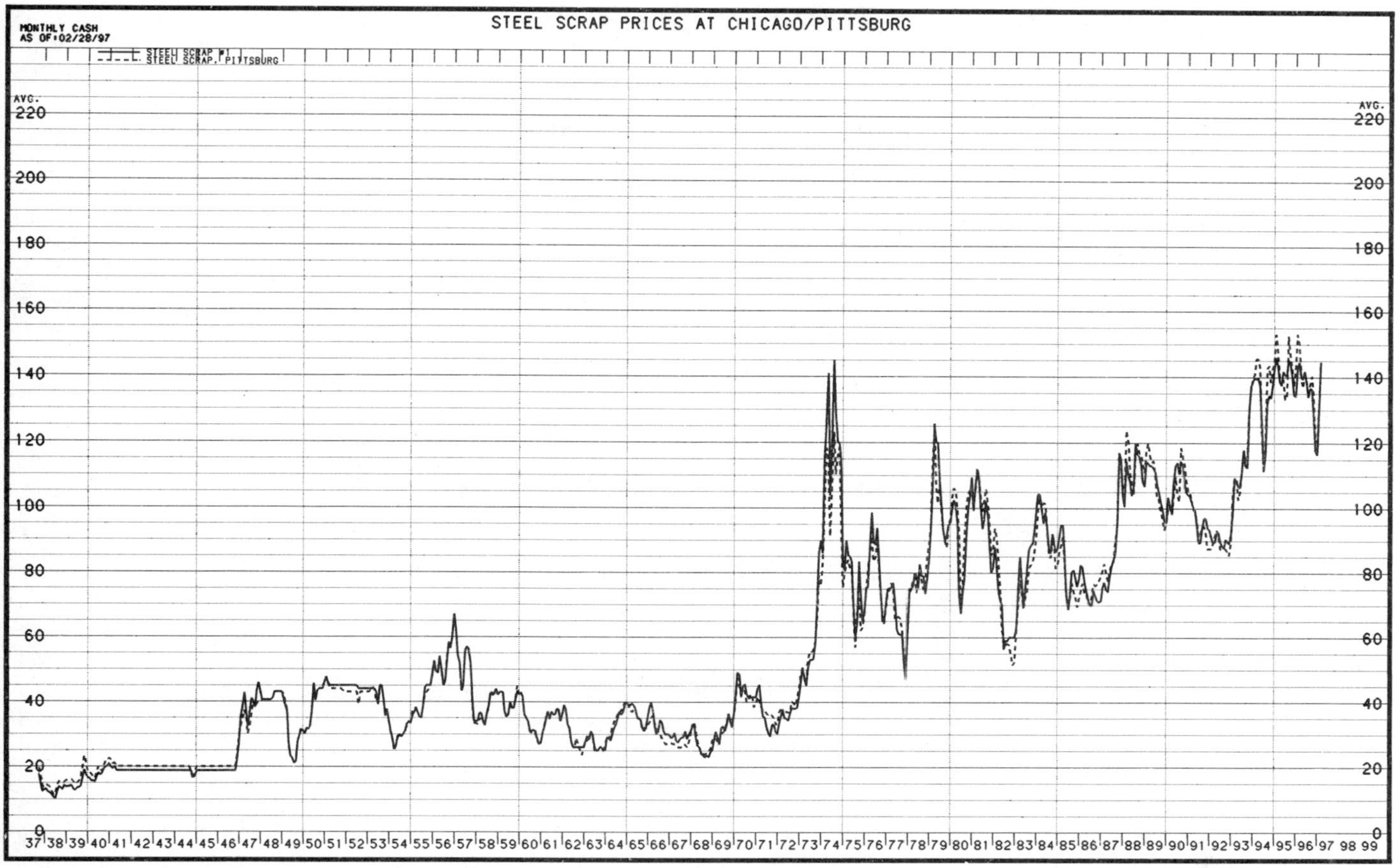


## Consumption of Pig Iron in the U.S. by Type of Furance or Equipment In Thousands of Metric Tons

| Year | Open Hearth | Electric | Cupola | Basic Oxygen Process | Air & Other Furnace | Direct Casting | Total | Year | Open Hearth | Electric | Cupola | Basic Oxygen Process | Air & Other Furnace | Direct Casting | Total |
|---|---|---|---|---|---|---|---|---|---|---|---|---|---|---|---|
| 1984 | 5,187 | 334 | 425 | 41,324 | 83 | 909 | 48,262 | 1990 | 2,072 | 982 | 332 | 47,307 | 19 | 387 | 51,099 |
| 1985 | 4,297 | 456 | 455 | 40,384 | 51 | 998 | 46,641 | 1991 | 997 | 574 | 265 | 42,955 | 13 | 106 | 44,910 |
| 1986 | 2,109 | 284 | 388 | 37,723 | 53 | 816 | 41,373 | 1992 | ------ | 429 | 215 | 47,194 | 7 | 49 | 47,894 |
| 1987 | 1,866 | 1,322 | 336 | 38,468 | 51 | 891 | 42,934 | 1993 | ------ | 519 | 292 | 47,848 | 34 | 84 | 48,777 |
| 1988 | 3,500 | 1,269 | 679 | 47,199 | 40 | 879 | 53,566 | 1994[1] | ------ | 1,700 | 520 | 49,138 | 4 | 39 | 51,401 |
| 1989 | 1,582 | 1,051 | 389 | 49,380 | 30 | 536 | 52,968 | 1995[2] | ------ | 1,700 | 500 | 50,000 | NA | 72 | 52,272 |

[1] Preliminary. [2] Estimate. NA = not avaliable. *Source: U.S. Geological Survey*

## Wholesale Price of No. 1 Heavy Melting Steel Scrap at Chicago In Dollars Per Gross Ton

| Year | Jan. | Feb. | Mar. | Apr. | May | June | July | Aug. | Sept. | Oct. | Nov. | Dec. | Average |
|---|---|---|---|---|---|---|---|---|---|---|---|---|---|
| 1984 | 88.29 | 89.00 | 87.09 | 85.14 | 85.00 | 84.71 | 79.00 | 78.00 | 81.00 | 81.09 | 83.00 | 76.00 | 83.12 |
| 1985 | 78.86 | 82.16 | 84.76 | 79.59 | 68.00 | 62.00 | 64.24 | 73.00 | 72.00 | 71.87 | 69.00 | 69.19 | 72.89 |
| 1986 | 74.23 | 76.89 | 74.05 | 74.00 | 74.00 | 71.00 | 71.00 | 76.71 | 73.14 | 70.87 | 73.00 | 73.00 | 73.49 |
| 1987 | 78.00 | 78.00 | 73.00 | 72.00 | 74.15 | 77.00 | 78.73 | 84.00 | 96.52 | 116.00 | 115.47 | 103.73 | 87.22 |
| 1988 | 100.80 | 119.43 | 119.02 | 117.24 | 111.38 | 108.55 | 120.00 | 119.78 | 115.00 | 115.00 | 109.16 | 106.33 | 113.47 |
| 1989 | 114.10 | 118.32 | 113.00 | 113.00 | 113.00 | 113.00 | 108.00 | 108.00 | 108.00 | 101.09 | 96.00 | 94.50 | 108.33 |
| 1990 | 104.00 | 102.29 | 98.00 | 109.43 | 114.55 | 111.67 | 108.50 | 116.00 | 113.76 | 112.50 | 107.73 | 105.00 | 108.62 |
| 1991 | 104.76 | 100.74 | 98.00 | 97.80 | 93.18 | 87.50 | 87.74 | 94.14 | 98.50 | 97.50 | 91.97 | 90.50 | 95.19 |
| 1992 | 90.50 | 90.50 | 90.50 | 90.50 | 89.70 | 87.68 | 87.50 | 87.55 | 88.50 | 85.50 | 85.50 | 88.36 | 88.52 |
| 1993 | 98.34 | 109.50 | 109.50 | 106.50 | 106.50 | 111.27 | 118.50 | 114.18 | 113.50 | 125.88 | 131.50 | 138.00 | 115.26 |
| 1994 | 138.00 | 138.00 | 138.00 | 138.00 | 123.64 | 110.50 | 117.20 | 133.63 | 134.50 | 132.50 | 137.50 | 141.50 | 131.91 |
| 1995 | 152.05 | 147.50 | 140.20 | 141.50 | 144.50 | 141.64 | 141.50 | 149.76 | 144.90 | 141.50 | 136.50 | 136.50 | 143.17 |
| 1996 | 143.41 | 144.50 | 139.50 | 139.50 | 142.50 | 139.50 | 134.50 | 136.95 | 140.35 | 130.89 | 120.76 | 120.50 | 136.07 |

*Source: American Metal Market*

# IRON AND STEEL

## World Production of Iron Ore[3], by Specific Countries — In Thousands of Metric Tons (Gross Weight)

| Year | Australia | Brazil | Canada | Chile | China | France | India | Maur-itania | Mexico | North Korea | Russia[4] | South Africa | Sweden | Ukraine[4] | United States | Vene-zula | World Total |
|---|---|---|---|---|---|---|---|---|---|---|---|---|---|---|---|---|---|
| 1986 | 94,015 | 129,405 | 36,167 | 6,981 | 90,000 | 12,437 | 47,800 | 9,170 | 7,298 | 8,500 | 249,959 | 24,483 | 20,475 | ------ | 39,486 | 16,753 | 863,650 |
| 1987 | 101,748 | 134,497 | 37,702 | 6,637 | 113,000 | 11,267 | 51,018 | 9,002 | 7,523 | 8,500 | 250,874 | 22,008 | 19,636 | ------ | 47,648 | 17,782 | 902,737 |
| 1988 | 99,450 | 146,008 | 39,934 | 7,710 | 154,380 | 9,872 | 49,961 | 10,004 | 8,431 | 9,000 | 249,754 | 25,248 | 20,440 | ------ | 57,515 | 18,932 | 967,218 |
| 1989 | 105,810 | 157,900 | 40,509 | 9,030 | 171,850 | 9,368 | 53,418 | 12,110 | 15,000 | 9,500 | 241,348 | 29,958 | 21,763 | ------ | 59,032 | 18,053 | 1,013,383 |
| 1990 | 110,508 | 152,300 | 34,855 | 7,903 | 168,300 | 8,729 | 53,700 | 11,590 | 15,000 | 10,000 | 236,000 | 30,291 | 19,877 | ------ | 56,408 | 20,119 | 983,000 |
| 1991 | 117,134 | 151,500 | 39,307 | 8,692 | 176,070 | 7,472 | 56,880 | 10,246 | 9,994 | 10,000 | 199,000 | 29,075 | 19,328 | ------ | 56,761 | 21,296 | 955,618 |
| 1992 | 112,101 | 146,447 | 33,167 | 7,643 | 197,600 | 5,707 | 54,870 | 8,202 | 10,964 | 10,500 | 82,100 | 28,226 | 19,277 | 75,700 | 55,593 | 18,070 | 924,887 |
| 1993 | 120,534 | 150,000 | 31,830 | 7,010 | 234,660 | 3,520 | 57,375 | 9,360 | 11,435 | 10,500 | 76,100 | 29,385 | 18,728 | 65,000 | 55,661 | 16,841 | 953,098 |
| 1994[1] | 128,493 | 167,900 | 37,703 | 8,341 | 240,200 | 2,550 | 58,388 | 11,400 | 8,538 | 11,000 | 73,300 | 30,489 | 19,663 | 42,200 | 58,382 | 18,318 | 969,435 |
| 1995[2] | 142,836 | 186,000 | 38,560 | 8,174 | 249,350 | 2,000 | 59,000 | 11,500 | 8,523 | 11,000 | 78,300 | 31,946 | 21,700 | 45,000 | 62,489 | 19,484 | 1,034,847 |

[1] Preliminary. [2] Estimate. [3] Iron ore, iron ore concentrates and iron ore agglomerates. [4] Formerly part of the U.S.S.R.; data not reported separately until 1992. *Source: U.S. Geological Survey*

## Salient Statistics of Iron Ore[3] in the U.S. — In Thousands of Metric Tons

| Year | Net Import Reliance % of Apparent Consumption | Production: Total | Production: Lake Superior | Production: Other Regions | Ship-ments | Value Million $ (at Mine) | Average Value $ at Mine Per Ton | Stocks--Dec. 31: Mines | Stocks--Dec. 31: Con-suming Plants | Stocks--Dec. 31: Lake Erie Docks | Imports | Exports | Con-sumption | Value Million $ Imports |
|---|---|---|---|---|---|---|---|---|---|---|---|---|---|---|
| 1986 | 33 | 39,486 | 38,203 | 1,283 | 41,991 | 1,472.5 | 35.07 | 3,307 | 17,439 | 2,019 | 17,011 | 4,553 | 62,097 | 460.6 |
| 1987 | 22 | 47,648 | 46,756 | 892 | 47,983 | 1,503.1 | 31.33 | 2,402 | 16,565 | 2,056 | 16,849 | 5,093 | 67,768 | 408.8 |
| 1988 | 18 | 57,515 | 56,038 | 1,477 | 57,113 | 1,716.7 | 30.06 | 2,957 | 18,005 | 2,537 | 20,183 | 5,285 | 83,694 | 484.5 |
| 1989 | 22 | 59,032 | 56,981 | 2,052 | 58,299 | 1,939.9 | 33.27 | 4,575 | 15,730 | 2,171 | 19,596 | 5,365 | 80,447 | 522.3 |
| 1990 | 21 | 56,408 | 54,628 | 1,780 | 57,010 | 1,570.0 | 27.52 | 4,795 | 15,911 | 2,273 | 18,054 | 3,199 | 76,855 | 559.5 |
| 1991 | 14 | 56,761 | 55,636 | 1,124 | 56,775 | 1,900.0 | 33.40 | 4,850 | 17,612 | 2,981 | 13,335 | 4,045 | 66,366 | 436.8 |
| 1992 | 10 | 55,593 | 55,018 | 575 | 55,569 | 1,730.0 | 31.10 | 3,780 | 16,093 | 2,981 | 12,504 | 5,055 | 75,067 | 395.8 |
| 1993 | 12 | 55,661 | 54,814 | 848 | 56,251 | 1,570.0 | 27.90 | 2,500 | 16,548 | 2,288 | 14,097 | 5,061 | 76,800 | 419.0 |
| 1994[1] | 16 | 58,215 | 57,848 | 367 | 57,917 | 1,600.0 | 27.70 | 2,790 | 16,300 | 2,230 | 17,513 | 4,975 | 80,200 | 499.0 |
| 1995[2] | 15 | 62,450 | 62,026 | 427 | 60,898 | 1,900.0 | 31.00 | 4,340 | 17,100 | 2,140 | 17,500 | 5,270 | 83,100 | 485.0 |

[1] Preliminary. [2] Estimate. [3] Usable iron ore exclusive of ore containing 5% or more manganese and includes byproduct ore. *Source: U.S. Geological Survey*

## U.S. Imports (for Consumption) of Iron Ore[2] from Principal Countries — In Thousands of Metric Tons

| Year | Australia | Brazil | Canada | Chile | Maur-itania | Peru | Sweden | Vene-zuela | Total |
|---|---|---|---|---|---|---|---|---|---|
| 1987 | 194 | 3,698 | 7,981 | 636 | 412 | 84 | 139 | 2,622 | 16,849 |
| 1988 | 1,076 | 4,935 | 9,157 | 139 | 522 | 181 | 88 | 3,568 | 20,183 |
| 1989 | 394 | 5,169 | 8,538 | 61 | 594 | 186 | 57 | 4,232 | 19,596 |
| 1990 | 14 | 4,276 | 9,344 | 138 | 666 | 59 | 54 | 3,503 | 18,054 |
| 1991 | NA | 2,481 | 7,299 | 103 | 459 | 157 | 51 | 2,763 | 13,335 |
| 1992 | 163 | 2,442 | 6,834 | 107 | 280 | 70 | 64 | 2,540 | 12,504 |
| 1993 | 254 | 2,872 | 7,442 | 68 | 206 | 1 | 60 | 3,170 | 14,097 |
| 1994 | 675 | 3,610 | 10,073 | 134 | 124 | 2 | 45 | 2,778 | 17,466 |
| 1995[1] | 570 | 4,271 | 9,048 | 57 | 317 | 54 | 47 | 2,501 | 17,555 |
| 1996[1] | 444 | 4,593 | 7,309 | 164 | 275 | 43 | 48 | 1,743 | 14,856 |

[1] Preliminary. [2] Including agglomerates. *Source: U.S. Geological Survey*

## Total[1] Iron Ore Stocks at End of Month in the U.S. — In Thousands of Metric Tons

| Year | Jan. | Feb. | Mar. | Apr. | May | June | July | Aug. | Sept. | Oct. | Nov. | Dec. |
|---|---|---|---|---|---|---|---|---|---|---|---|---|
| 1986 | 26,829 | 25,770 | 24,743 | 23,618 | 24,652 | 24,677 | 24,546 | 23,047 | 23,331 | 23,251 | 22,336 | 21,783 |
| 1987 | 21,472 | 21,406 | 20,580 | 19,571 | 18,875 | 19,008 | 19,235 | 19,085 | 19,343 | 19,994 | 20,264 | 20,613 |
| 1988 | 20,997 | 20,925 | 20,041 | 20,119 | 19,789 | 19,341 | 19,835 | 20,801 | 22,210 | 22,140 | 22,485 | 22,755 |
| 1989 | 23,189 | 23,252 | 22,685 | 21,145 | 21,670 | 21,544 | 22,286 | 22,275 | 22,588 | 21,429 | 21,448 | 22,476 |
| 1990 | 22,088 | 21,986 | 20,958 | 20,609 | 20,501 | 21,019 | 21,863 | 22,110 | 22,268 | 22,027 | 22,042 | 22,978 |
| 1991 | 22,572 | 22,218 | 21,316 | 20,757 | 21,756 | 23,174 | 23,319 | 24,329 | 25,148 | 25,117 | 25,358 | 25,445 |
| 1992 | 24,527 | 23,162 | 20,922 | 20,550 | 21,501 | 22,492 | 23,046 | 21,721 | 22,735 | 23,190 | 23,433 | 22,856 |
| 1993 | 21,296 | 20,806 | 19,235 | 18,996 | 19,180 | 22,036 | 22,905 | 21,575 | 22,629 | 21,355 | 21,615 | 21,341 |
| 1994[2] | 19,013 | 17,816 | 15,953 | 14,883 | 15,251 | 16,592 | 17,864 | 18,931 | 20,554 | 20,760 | 21,552 | 21,339 |
| 1995[2] | 20,316 | 19,330 | 18,200 | 18,340 | 19,369 | 20,905 | 22,336 | 23,668 | | | | |

[1] All stocks at mines, furnance yards and at U.S. docks. [2] Preliminary. *Source: U.S. Geological Survey*

# Lard

Production of lard is directly related to commercial pork production. As such, the largest producers of hogs are also the largest producers of lard. China is by far the world's largest producer of lard with over a third of the world total. The U.S. is the next largest producer followed closely by the former Soviet Union and Germany. While production in the U.S. and China has been increasing about in line with population growth, there have been steep declines in lard production in both Germany and the former Soviet Union.

The USDA indicated that U.S. beginning stocks of lard on October 1, 1996 were 31.3 billion pounds or 14.2 million tonnes. This represents an increase of almost 29 percent from stocks at the beginning of the 1995/96 season. The reason for the increase in stocks was a decline in lard disappearance in the 1995/96 season.

U.S. production of lard over the 1996/97 (October-September) season was forecast by the USDA at one billion pounds or 453 thousand tonnes. This represents a decline of 1 percent from the 1995/96 marketing year. This would be the lowest level of production since the 1990/91 season. Over the last five years, U.S. lard production has averaged 1.02 billion pounds per year. Imports of lard are minimal and for 1995/96 they are estimated at 2 million pounds. Taking into account beginning stocks, production, and imports, the total supply of lard in 1996/97 is forecast by the USDA to be 1.03 billion pounds, down less than 1 percent from the previous year.

The USDA forecasts domestic disappearance of lard at 905 million pounds, unchanged from the previous season. Over the last five years, domestic use has averaged 902 million pounds. Exports of lard were forecast to be 100 million pounds, the same as in 1995/96. With supply of 1.033 billion pounds, and disappearance of 1.005 billion pounds, season-ending stocks were forecast at 28.3 million pounds.

**World Production of Lard** In Thousands of Metric Tons

| Year Beginning Oct. 1 | Brazil | Canada | China | Czecho-slovak | France | Germany | Italy | Japan | Poland | Romania | Spain | Taiwan | United States | Former U.S.S.R. | World Total |
|---|---|---|---|---|---|---|---|---|---|---|---|---|---|---|---|
| 1987-8 | 162.9 | 79.9 | 1,381.0 | 120.6 | 132.5 | 572.6 | 182.3 | 92.1 | 136.1 | 156.7 | 155.2 | 55.1 | 415.5 | 838.7 | 5,395.0 |
| 1988-9 | 147.5 | 79.0 | 1,438.3 | 124.6 | 126.5 | 518.7 | 181.0 | 91.0 | 137.7 | 130.4 | 154.8 | 54.9 | 426.2 | 852.1 | 5,382.8 |
| 1989-90 | 151.0 | 75.6 | 1,519.5 | 123.9 | 129.2 | 534.4 | 178.5 | 91.0 | 136.8 | 130.1 | 156.1 | 59.1 | 412.3 | 844.4 | 5,441.8 |
| 1990-1 | 158.6 | 75.6 | 1,605.6 | 112.4 | 137.3 | 476.3 | 187.6 | 87.0 | 288.3 | 129.0 | 169.7 | 65.5 | 415.0 | 762.8 | 5,586.2 |
| 1991-2 | 165.7 | 76.9 | 1,698.4 | 111.0 | 135.5 | 411.3 | 188.0 | 85.0 | 303.3 | 117.7 | 170.6 | 66.5 | 447.7 | 653.6 | 5,497.5 |
| 1992-3 | 175.5 | 77.0 | 1,767.6 | 96.8 | 142.9 | 418.2 | 192.1 | 85.8 | 292.9 | 113.7 | 185.8 | 68.2 | 445.0 | 573.8 | 5,523.6 |
| 1993-4[1] | 186.2 | 76.0 | 1,984.8 | 88.0 | 151.3 | 409.5 | 189.5 | 82.4 | 251.6 | 114.3 | 192.8 | 71.1 | 451.0 | 509.6 | 5,654.5 |
| 1994-5[2] | 199.3 | 78.3 | 2,145.6 | 87.8 | 153.3 | 405.1 | 192.0 | 83.8 | 276.8 | 113.5 | 189.9 | 73.8 | 471.2 | 426.3 | 5,791.4 |
| 1995-6[3] | 210.4 | 80.0 | 2,269.9 | 89.9 | 153.7 | 391.2 | 196.0 | 80.0 | 295.1 | 114.4 | 187.3 | 74.8 | 464.0 | 381.0 | 5,889.4 |

[1] Preliminary. [2] Estimate. [3] Forecast. *Source: The Oil World*

**Supply and Distribution of Lard in the United States** In Millions of Pounds

| | Supply | | | Disappearance | | | | | | |
|---|---|---|---|---|---|---|---|---|---|---|
| Year | Production | Stocks Oct. 1 | Total Supply | Domestic | Baking or Frying Fats | Margarine[2] | Exports | Total Disappearance | Direct Use | Per Capita (Lbs.) |
| 1988-9 | 940.0 | 39.0 | 965.0 | 811.0 | 265.0 | 35.0 | 127.0 | 928.0 | 433.0 | 3.2 |
| 1989-90 | 909.0 | 42.0 | 972.0 | 845.0 | 295.0 | 32.0 | 85.0 | 940.0 | 442.0 | 3.3 |
| 1990-1 | 933.6 | 22.9 | 959.9 | 825.4 | 264.0 | 35.0 | 110.0 | 935.8 | 439.2 | 3.3 |
| 1991-2 | 1,016.3 | 24.1 | 1,042.9 | 884.8 | 274.0 | 43.0 | 131.0 | 1,015.7 | 423.7 | 3.3 |
| 1992-3 | 1,011.2 | 27.2 | 1,041.5 | 886.1 | 310.0 | 37.0 | 129.2 | 1,015.3 | 438.6 | 3.5 |
| 1993-4 | 1,014.7 | 26.2 | 1,043.6 | 890.4 | 296.0 | 31.0 | 118.8 | 1,009.2 | 573.0 | 3.4 |
| 1994-5 | 1,052.4 | 34.4 | 1,089.0 | 924.4 | 287.0 | 42.0 | 140.4 | 1,064.7 | 584.4 | 3.4 |
| 1995-6[1] | 1,012.6 | 24.3 | 1,038.8 | 921.8 | 325.0 | 41.0 | 94.3 | 1,016.1 | 623.0 | 3.5 |
| 1996-7[3] | 1,000.0 | 22.7 | 1,024.7 | 896.0 | NA | NA | 100.0 | 996.0 | NA | NA |

[1] Preliminary. [2] Includes edible tallow. [3] Forecast. NA = not avaliable. *Source: Economic Research Service, U.S. Department of Agriculture*

**Consumption (Edible & Inedible) of Lard in the United States** In Millions of Pounds

| Year | Jan. | Feb. | Mar. | Apr. | May | June | July | Aug. | Sept. | Oct. | Nov. | Dec. | Total |
|---|---|---|---|---|---|---|---|---|---|---|---|---|---|
| 1988 | 25.6 | 27.7 | 31.1 | 29.3 | 28.5 | 27.4 | 25.9 | 28.0 | 37.9 | 34.6 | 36.3 | 35.3 | 367.6 |
| 1989 | 28.9 | 27.5 | 34.0 | 31.1 | 33.5 | 32.2 | 28.9 | 33.5 | 34.1 | 39.0 | 42.5 | 32.7 | 397.9 |
| 1990 | 27.0 | 27.3 | 30.9 | 26.3 | 32.1 | 29.2 | 22.8 | 32.0 | 31.3 | 34.6 | 33.8 | 30.6 | 357.9 |
| 1991 | ---------- | 97.3 | ---------- | ---------- | 94.7 | ---------- | ---------- | 95.2 | ---------- | ---------- | 105.9 | ---------- | 393.1 |
| 1992 | 33.9 | 31.6 | 39.9 | 40.0 | 38.7 | 39.6 | 42.9 | 41.1 | 47.6 | 46.4 | 41.0 | 37.2 | 479.9 |
| 1993 | 40.1 | 34.4 | 45.9 | 36.8 | 38.2 | 38.8 | 32.6 | 38.4 | 41.8 | 44.0 | 43.0 | 40.3 | 474.3 |
| 1994 | 33.5 | 33.9 | 36.2 | 34.6 | 35.9 | 34.4 | 32.4 | 37.5 | 43.4 | 43.8 | 44.7 | 41.7 | 452.0 |
| 1995 | 37.5 | 34.7 | 41.2 | 36.2 | 42.2 | 44.4 | 34.9 | 35.9 | 35.9 | 40.1 | 38.9 | 36.8 | 458.7 |
| 1996[1] | 30.5 | 35.4 | 36.7 | 46.9 | 36.8 | 31.4 | 32.6 | 33.9 | 30.9 | 34.5 | 34.7 | 33.6 | 417.9 |

[1] Preliminary. *Source: Bureau of Census, U.S. Department of Commerce*

# LARD

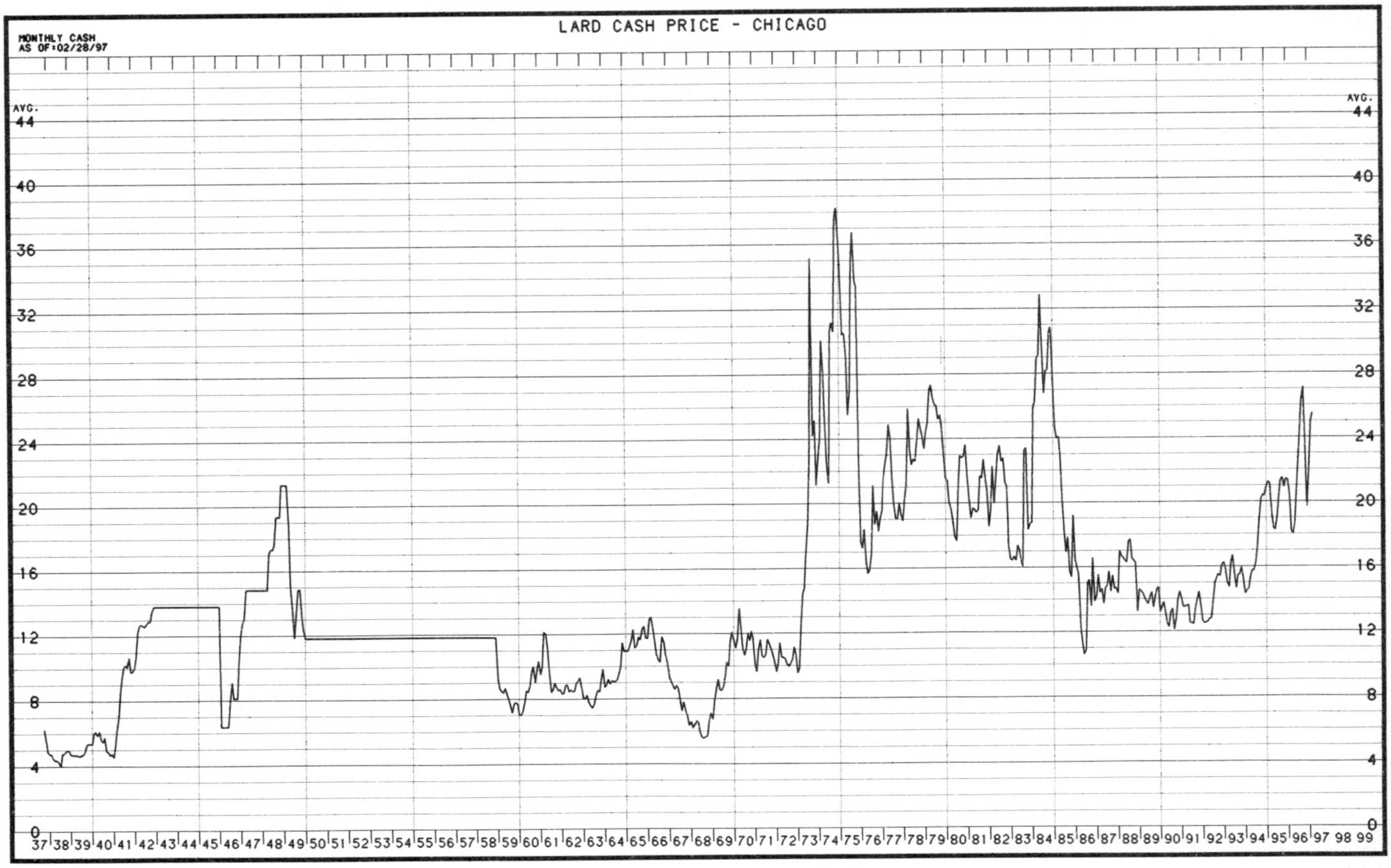


## Average Wholesale Price of Lard--Loose, Tank Cars, Chicago In Cents Per Pound

| Year | Jan. | Feb. | Mar. | Apr. | May | June | July | Aug. | Sept. | Oct. | Nov. | Dec. | Average |
|---|---|---|---|---|---|---|---|---|---|---|---|---|---|
| 1987 | 15.50 | 14.40 | 14.60 | 13.70 | 14.70 | 14.90 | 15.70 | 14.50 | 15.50 | 14.70 | 14.70 | 14.40 | 14.78 |
| 1988 | 17.00 | 16.70 | 16.60 | 16.40 | 16.30 | 17.60 | 17.70 | 16.50 | 16.40 | 16.30 | 13.20 | 14.60 | 16.28 |
| 1989 | 14.50 | 14.40 | 14.10 | 13.80 | 13.70 | 14.10 | 14.40 | 13.50 | 14.20 | 14.60 | 14.80 | 13.20 | 14.11 |
| 1990 | 13.50 | 13.80 | 13.20 | 12.50 | 12.30 | 13.20 | 13.40 | 12.10 | 12.70 | 14.00 | 14.50 | 14.10 | 13.28 |
| 1991 | 13.50 | 13.50 | 13.50 | 13.70 | 12.50 | 12.50 | 12.40 | 13.40 | 14.00 | 14.40 | 13.60 | 12.20 | 13.27 |
| 1992 | 12.50 | 12.50 | 12.60 | 12.60 | 13.90 | 15.00 | 15.00 | 15.30 | 15.50 | 15.40 | 16.10 | 16.30 | 14.39 |
| 1993 | 15.80 | 15.00 | 14.70 | 16.20 | 16.70 | 15.50 | 14.60 | 15.40 | 15.50 | 15.90 | 15.30 | 14.30 | 15.41 |
| 1994 | 14.50 | 14.60 | 15.40 | 15.70 | 15.80 | 16.30 | 17.20 | 18.90 | 20.10 | 20.40 | 20.40 | 20.90 | 17.52 |
| 1995 | 21.21 | 21.13 | 19.25 | 18.34 | 18.25 | 19.02 | 20.25 | 21.30 | 21.48 | 20.90 | 21.38 | 21.35 | 20.32 |
| 1996 | 20.52 | 18.17 | 18.01 | 18.67 | 20.47 | 22.61 | 24.55 | 26.30 | 27.09 | 23.11 | 19.70 | 22.17 | 21.78 |

*Source: The Wall Street Journal*

## United States Cold Storage Holdings of all Lard[1], on First of Month In Millions of Pounds

| Year | Jan. | Feb. | Mar. | Apr. | May | June | July | Aug. | Sept. | Oct. | Nov. | Dec. |
|---|---|---|---|---|---|---|---|---|---|---|---|---|
| 1987 | 21.9 | 31.5 | 30.9 | 27.2 | 28.9 | 29.9 | 27.4 | 27.8 | 28.9 | 28.8 | 38.2 | 36.2 |
| 1988 | 33.0 | 37.2 | 33.8 | 37.1 | 31.2 | 31.9 | 37.8 | 41.1 | 30.1 | 39.0 | 41.7 | 36.7 |
| 1989 | 37.4 | 38.2 | 37.1 | 27.3 | 34.2 | 37.6 | 41.3 | 32.4 | 28.9 | 41.6 | 29.0 | 36.6 |
| 1990 | 32.0 | 33.7 | 37.6 | 28.5 | 31.6 | 27.4 | 25.2 | 25.9 | 22.8 | 22.9 | 22.2 | 30.3 |
| 1991 | ---------- | 24.4 | ---------- | ---------- | 28.3 | ---------- | ---------- | 24.0 | ---------- | ---------- | 24.1 | ---------- |
| 1992 | 37.4 | 27.2 | 28.9 | 28.3 | 26.7 | 23.2 | 24.8 | 29.2 | 26.9 | 27.2 | 22.2 | 24.8 |
| 1993 | 22.7 | 25.9 | 27.2 | 24.0 | 22.8 | 25.8 | 31.1 | 27.4 | 23.6 | 26.2 | 24.6 | 30.1 |
| 1994 | 37.7 | 38.0 | 31.8 | 28.8 | 25.1 | 27.4 | 27.0 | 25.5 | 29.7 | 34.4 | 34.0 | 35.8 |
| 1995 | 40.6 | 50.3 | 46.4 | 43.0 | 36.8 | 27.1 | 25.8 | 22.1 | 30.2 | 24.3 | 19.9 | 21.6 |
| 1996[2] | 38.4 | 38.6 | 25.8 | 28.8 | 21.5 | 23.2 | 23.7 | 30.5 | 20.7 | 22.7 | 20.1 | 18.8 |

[1] Stocks in factories and warehouses (except that in hands of retailers). [2] Preliminary. *Source: Bureau of Census, U.S. Department of Commerce*

# Lead

Lead finds widespread use in batteries, fuel tanks, ammunition, building construction, electrical equipment, cans and containers, and as solder for pipes and plumbing. Lead and compounds that contain lead are very toxic. As a result, there has been a concerted effort to reduce the use of lead, especially in areas where humans are exposed to it. Substitutes for lead include plastic, aluminum, tin, and iron. There has been research into the use of bismuth as a non-toxic substitute for lead in a variety of uses from ceramic glazes to solder. Currently there is a great deal of research occurring in developing a new type of battery using lithium-polymer materials. Lead finds the most use in batteries. Batteries without lead would be much lighter and could find use in electric automobiles. Lithium is the lightest metal on the atomic chart and lead is one of the heaviest.

A major development in the lead market was the announcement on April 15, 1996, by Asarco, Incorporated, that it had reached an agreement with the City of Omaha, Nebraska to cease all operations at its Omaha refinery as of February 1, 1998. The property will be turned into a park. The company ceased lead refining at Omaha on June 1, 1996, but is still processing other materials such as bismuth. The U.S. Geological Survey has noted that as a result of the cessation of lead refining, U.S. primary lead production was down just over 20 percent.

The National Defense Stockpile cash disposal of lead in June 1996 was 5,600 tonnes. Cash disposal of lead in the October 1995 through June 1996 period totaled 29,999 tonnes.

U.S. mine production of lead in June 1996 was 35,600 tonnes, down 5 percent from production in May. For the first six months of 1996, mine production of lead was 217,000 tonnes, up 12 percent from the comparable period in 1995. For all of 1995, lead production was 384,000 tonnes. Primary refinery production of lead in June 1996 was 21,700 tonnes, down 21 percent from May. This was due in part to the closing of the refinery in Omaha for lead production. For January-June 1996, refinery lead production was 174,000 tonnes, down 7 percent from the same period in 1995. For all of 1995, refinery production was 374,000 tonnes.

Secondary refinery lead production in June 1996 was 80,700 tonnes, down 5 percent from May. For the January-June 1996 period, secondary refinery production was 485,000 tonnes, up 4 percent from the same period in 1995. For all of 1995, production was 945,000 tonnes.

Lead stocks at primary refineries as of June 1996 were 15,000 tonnes, the same as in May. Stocks at secondary smelters and consumer stocks in June 1996 were 47,600 tonnes, down from 48,200 tonnes at the end of May 1996.

U.S. imports of lead ore in May 1996 were 1,170 tonnes, all of which came from Canada. For January-May 1996, imports of ore were 2,880 tonnes, up 17 percent from the comparable period of 1995.

U.S. consumption of lead in June 1996 was 106,000 tonnes, down 6 percent from May. For January-June 1996, consumption was 653,000 tonnes, down 5 percent from the comparable period in 1995. For all of 1995, U.S. lead consumption was 838,000 tonnes.

## World Smelter (Primary & Secondary) Production of Lead In Thousands of Metric Tons

| Year | Australia[3] | Belgium[4] | Bulgaria | Canada[3] | China[2] | France | Germany | Italy | Japan | Kazakhstan[5] | Mexico[3] | Peru[3] | Spain | United Kingdom[3] | United States | World Total |
|---|---|---|---|---|---|---|---|---|---|---|---|---|---|---|---|---|
| 1988 | 185.0 | 105.2 | 101.0 | 268.1 | 241.4 | 255.7 | 384.7 | 177.7 | 340.0 | 727.0 | 250.0 | 53.6 | 110.8 | 373.8 | 1,090.5 | 5,518 |
| 1989 | 205.0 | 109.4 | 101.5 | 242.8 | 260.0 | 427.6 | 363.9 | 186.2 | 332.4 | 745.0 | 235.0 | 78.4 | 114.5 | 350.5 | 1,287.8 | 6,077 |
| 1990 | 229.0 | 105.8 | 66.6 | 183.6 | 296.0 | 432.7 | 411.0 | 166.8 | 327.4 | 700.0 | 232.2 | 74.3 | 110.0 | 329.4 | 1,330.0 | 5,950 |
| 1991 | 239.4 | 110.7 | 56.2 | 212.4 | 330.0 | 438.0 | 362.5 | 208.2 | 332.4 | 630.0 | 161.8 | 79.5 | 169.0 | 311.0 | 1,230.3 | 5,770 |
| 1992 | 231.8 | 116.3 | 53.1 | 252.9 | 365.0 | 444.6 | 354.3 | 186.3 | 330.2 | 210.0 | 177.0 | 89.0 | 120.0 | 346.8 | 1,220.0 | 5,420 |
| 1993 | 243.0 | 126.9 | 54.0 | 217.0 | 412.0 | 438.0 | 334.2 | 182.8 | 309.5 | 150.0 | 188.0 | 92.2 | 125.0 | 364.0 | 1,230.0 | 5,370 |
| 1994[1] | 232.5 | 123.5 | 62.3 | 251.6 | 467.9 | 444.0 | 331.7 | 205.9 | 292.3 | 95.0 | 180.0 | 93.1 | 140.0 | 352.5 | 1,260.0 | 5,380 |
| 1995[2] | 235.4 | 125.0 | 63.0 | 277.4 | 420.0 | 425.0 | 335.0 | 205.0 | 286.5 | 70.0 | 174.0 | 94.6 | 140.0 | 350.0 | 1,350.0 | 5,400 |

[1] Preliminary. [2] Estimate. [3] Refined & bullion. [4] Includes scrap. [5] Formerly part of the U.S.S.R.; data not reported separately until 1992.
NA - not avaliable. *Source: U.S. Bureau of Mines*

## Consumption of Lead in the United States by Products In Metric Tons

| Year | Ammunition | Bearing Metals | Pipes, Traps & Bends[2] | Cable Covering | Calking Lead | Casting Metals | Other Metal Products[3] | Total Other Oxides[4] | Sheet Lead | Solder | --- Storage Battery --- Grids, Post, etc. | Oxides | Brass and Bronze | Total Consumption |
|---|---|---|---|---|---|---|---|---|---|---|---|---|---|---|
| 1988 | 52,708 | 6,034 | 11,193 | 16,170 | 1,618 | 15,872 | 7,614 | 62,524 | 17,458 | 19,064 | 514,694 | 454,964 | 9,994 | 1,245,170 |
| 1989 | 57,310 | 2,586 | 9,818 | 22,605 | 1,831 | 16,175 | 6,850 | 57,984 | 20,987 | 17,009 | 552,308 | 459,847 | 9,610 | 1,283,234 |
| 1990 | 58,210 | 5,212 | 9,281 | 18,253 | 1,688 | 14,843 | 3,812 | 56,484 | 21,013 | 16,490 | 571,187 | 448,450 | 9,943 | 1,275,226 |
| 1991 | 58,458 | 3,669 | 8,975 | 17,472 | 1,074 | 14,141 | 3,254 | 59,617 | 22,334 | 14,750 | 591,884 | 415,233 | 8,997 | 1,246,337 |
| 1992 | 64,845 | 4,785 | 11,652 | 15,992 | 1,045 | 17,111 | 3,024 | 63,225 | 21,006 | 13,518 | 629,147 | 373,185 | 9,175 | 1,236,571 |
| 1993 | 65,100 | 4,830 | 5,740 | 17,165 | 961 | 18,500 | 5,360 | 63,600 | 21,200 | 14,400 | 677,000 | 374,000 | 5,750 | 1,290,000 |
| 1994 | 62,400 | 5,560 | 3,370 | 16,000 | 764 | 18,900 | 5,330 | 62,700 | 21,500 | 12,200 | 797,000 | 425,000 | 6,320 | 1,450,000 |
| 1995[1] | 70,900 | 6,490 | 2,210 | 5,640 | NA | 18,100 | 5,220 | 61,700 | 27,900 | 16,200 | 823,000 | 533,000 | 5,260 | 1,600,000 |

[1] Preliminary. [2] Including building. [3] Including terne metal, type metal, and lead consumed in foil, collapsible tubes, annealing, plating, galvanizing and fishing weights. [4] Includes paints, glass and ceramic products, and other pigments and chemicals. NA = not avaliable. W = Withheld proprietary data.
*Source: U.S. Geological Survey*

# LEAD

## Salient Statistics of Lead in the United States In Thousands of Metric Tons

| Year | Net Import Reliance as a % of Apparent Consumption | Production of Refined Lead from: Domestic Ores[3] | Foreign Ores[3] | Total Primary | Total Value of Refined Million $ | Secondary Lead Recovered: As Soft Lead | In Antimonial Lead | In Other Alloys | Total | Total Value of Secondary Million $ | Stocks, Dec. 31: Primary | Consumer[4] | Average Price ¢ Per Pound: New York | London[5] |
|---|---|---|---|---|---|---|---|---|---|---|---|---|---|---|
| 1979 | 5 | 530.0 | 45.6 | 575.6 | 668.0 | 352.2 | 378.8 | 70.3 | 801.4 | 930.0 | 89.3 | 153.2 | 52.64 | 54.52 |
| 1980 | E | 508.2 | 39.4 | 547.6 | 512.6 | 315.2 | 306.7 | 53.7 | 675.6 | 632.4 | 126.0 | 126.2 | 42.46 | 41.21 |
| 1981 | 1 | 440.2 | 55.1 | 495.3 | 398.9 | 282.2 | 304.4 | 54.6 | 641.1 | 516.3 | 140.2 | 123.2 | 36.53 | 33.30 |
| 1982 | 11 | 459.9 | 52.3 | 512.2 | 288.4 | 240.5 | 284.4 | 46.4 | 615.7 | 321.7 | 125.5 | 97.2 | 25.54 | 24.66 |
| 1983 | 20 | 463.9 | 55.2 | 519.2 | 248.1 | 189.6 | 271.6 | 42.3 | 503.5 | 240.7 | 53.4 | 100.8 | 21.68 | 19.27 |
| 1984 | 20 | 324.0 | 65.4 | 389.4 | 219.3 | 263.4 | 327.8 | 42.1 | 633.4 | 266.3 | 45.1 | 97.1 | 25.55 | 20.12 |
| 1985 | 12 | 422.7 | 71.4 | 494.0 | 207.7 | 273.7 | 299.3 | 42.7 | 615.7 | 258.9 | 84.5 | 93.1 | 19.07 | 17.84 |
| 1986 | 20 | 348.2 | 22.1 | 370.3 | 180.0 | 289.5 | 291.9 | 43.3 | 624.8 | 303.7 | 20.4 | 83.8 | 22.05 | 18.43 |
| 1987 | 17 | 336.5 | 37.1 | 373.6 | 296.0 | 345.1 | 323.3 | 41.7 | 710.1 | 562.6 | 21.6 | 88.6 | 35.94 | 26.99 |
| 1988 | 13 | 371.3 | 20.7 | 392.1 | 321.0 | 367.1 | 331.3 | 38.0 | 736.4 | 603.0 | 15.4 | 89.9 | 37.14 | 29.73 |
| 1989 | 8 | 379.0 | 17.4 | 396.5 | 343.9 | 438.0 | 418.6 | 34.7 | 891.3 | 773.3 | 15.6 | 82.4 | 39.35 | 30.63 |
| 1990 | 3 | 385.6 | 18.0 | 403.7 | 409.5 | 461.4 | 425.4 | 35.6 | 922.2 | 935.6 | 25.5 | 86.3 | 46.02 | 37.05 |
| 1991 | E | 323.9 | 21.9 | 345.7 | 255.2 | 421.9 | 426.9 | 35.8 | 884.6 | 652.9 | 9.1 | 71.7 | 33.48 | 25.30 |
| 1992 | 4 | 284.0 | 20.8 | 304.8 | 235.9 | 452.9 | 424.5 | 23.1 | 916.3 | 709.1 | 20.5 | 82.3 | 35.10 | 24.50 |
| 1993 | 7 | 310.7 | 24.9 | 335.6 | 234.4 | 444.0 | 417.0 | 17.0 | 893.0 | 625.0 | 14.3 | 80.5 | 31.74 | 18.42 |
| 1994[1] | 8 | 328.0 | 23.4 | 351.4 | 288.0 | 527.0 | 371.0 | 16.1 | 931.0 | 763.0 | 9.3 | 68.8 | 37.17 | 24.83 |
| 1995[2] | 8 | 374.0 | W | 374.0 | 348.0 | 588.0 | 348.0 | 19.2 | 972.0 | 906.0 | 14.2 | 76.0 | 42.28 | 28.60 |

[1] Preliminary. [2] Estimate. [3] And base bullion. [4] Also at secondary smelters. [5] LME data in dollars per metric ton beginning July 1993.
W = Withheld Proprietary data. E = Net exporter. *Source: U.S. Geological Survey*

## U.S. Mine Production of Recoverable Lead In Metric Tons

| Year | Total | Missouri | Missouri's % of Total | Year | Total | Missouri | Missouri's % of Total |
|---|---|---|---|---|---|---|---|
| 1982 | 512,500 | 474,500 | 93% | 1989 | 410,915 | 366,931 | 89% |
| 1983 | 449,295 | 409,280 | 91% | 1990 | 483,704 | 380,781 | 79% |
| 1984 | 322,677 | 278,329 | 86% | 1991 | 465,931 | 351,995 | 76% |
| 1985 | 413,955 | 371,008 | 90% | 1992 | 397,923 | 300,589 | 76% |
| 1986 | 339,793 | 319,900 | 94% | 1993 | 353,607 | 276,569 | 78% |
| 1987 | 311,381 | W | NA | 1994[1] | 363,443 | 290,738 | 80% |
| 1988 | 384,983 | 353,194 | 92% | 1995[2] | 383,900 | 290,000 | 76% |

1 Preliminary. 2 Estimate. W = Withheld. NA = Not available. *Source: U.S. Geological Survey*

## U.S. Foreign Trade of Lead In Thousands of Metric Tons

| Year | Exports: Ore Concentrate | Unwrought Lead[3] | Wrought Lead[4] | Scrap | Ash & Residues[5] | Imports for Consumption: Ores, Flue Dust or Fume & Mattes | Base Bullion | Pigs & Bars | Reclaimed Scrap, Etc. | Value Million $ | General Imports From: Ore, Flue Dust & Matte: Australia | Canada | Peru | Pigs & Bars: Australia | Canada | Mexico | Peru |
|---|---|---|---|---|---|---|---|---|---|---|---|---|---|---|---|---|---|
| 1979 | 32.9 | 7.4 | 3.3 | 119.7 | ----- | 44.4 | 1.7 | 182.6 | 4.0 | 248.3 | 1.9 | 12.8 | 12.4 | 17.3 | ----- | 73.6 | 17.9 |
| 1980 | 27.6 | 156.5 | 8.0 | 119.7 | ----- | 29.6 | 0.3 | 81.3 | 2.9 | 116.5 | 3.0 | 8.5 | 18.0 | 11.3 | 34.9 | 28.6 | 3.3 |
| 1981 | 33.0 | 16.8 | 6.5 | 59.4 | ----- | 27.2 | 0.4 | 100.1 | 2.7 | 110.5 | 2.2 | 23.5 | 14.1 | 10.9 | 50.8 | 33.7 | 2.9 |
| 1982 | 29.1 | 51.0 | 4.6 | 51.8 | ----- | 18.9 | ----- | 94.9 | 4.8 | 69.9 | 7.7 | 4.8 | 14.5 | 7.3 | 49.8 | 23.5 | 8.3 |
| 1983 | 20.1 | 17.7 | 2.8 | 50.9 | ----- | 19.8 | 0.1 | 134.4 | 4.2 | 89.9 | 10.0 | 6.1 | 22.7 | 10.9 | 72.7 | 34.9 | 10.1 |
| 1984 | 11.9 | 5.0 | 2.5 | 45.1 | 9.1 | 29.9 | ----- | 161.5 | 5.0 | 104.2 | 17.0 | 14.1 | 22.7 | 10.9 | 94.9 | 39.5 | 9.2 |
| 1985 | 10.0 | 25.4 | 2.0 | 59.9 | 10.0 | 2.6 | 0.8 | 131.4 | 3.2 | 56.5 | 12.3 | 5.2 | 15.2 | 3.6 | 90.1 | 33.8 | 5.2 |
| 1986 | 4.4 | 11.2 | 1.4 | 59.0 | 7.2 | 4.6 | 0.1 | 140.2 | 3.3 | 62.1 | 11.5 | 62.9 | 8.4 | ----- | 105.3 | 29.5 | 1.1 |
| 1987 | 8.8 | 4.4 | 5.8 | 52.8 | 3.5 | 0.9 | 10.8 | 185.7 | 6.6 | 133.8 | 1.7 | 201.2 | 19.1 | 0.1 | 92.6 | 42.6 | 0.4 |
| 1988 | 20.9 | 7.5 | 6.0 | 81.9 | 15.5 | 20.6 | 4.0 | 148.6 | 7.3 | 124.8 | 1.4 | 221.8 | 11.4 | 6.7 | 104.8 | 30.9 | ----- |
| 1989 | 57.0 | 28.5 | 5.4 | 59.9 | 10.0 | 5.1 | 5.8 | 115.7 | 0.7 | 95.7 | 1.9 | 189.9 | 12.9 | ----- | 90.5 | 19.2 | 2.3 |
| 1990 | 56.6 | 57.2 | 6.8 | 75.0 | 13.0 | 10.7 | 2.7 | 90.6 | 0.3 | 91.2 | 1.2 | 124.3 | 7.1 | 6.9 | 70.7 | 25.0 | 1.0 |
| 1991 | 88.0 | 94.4 | 7.6 | 72.0 | 11.0 | 12.4 | 0.4 | 116.5 | 0.1 | 82.6 | 1.0 | 226.7 | 3.9 | 8.0 | 83.6 | 11.9 | 0.5 |
| 1992 | 72.3 | 64.3 | 5.3 | 63.2 | 2.1 | 5.3 | 0.2 | 190.7 | 0.2 | 120.6 | ----- | 239.9 | 21.2 | ----- | 124.7 | 56.1 | 9.8 |
| 1993 | 41.8 | 51.4 | 7.1 | 54.1 | 1.7 | 0.5 | ----- | 195.6 | 0.1 | 99.4 | ----- | 55.7 | 13.6 | 1.0 | 130.8 | 40.3 | 18.3 |
| 1994[1] | 38.7 | 48.2 | 5.3 | 88.1 | 20.6 | 0.5 | 0.6 | 230.8 | 0.1 | 146.6 | ----- | 0.3 | 11.7 | 0.5 | 159.0 | 31.9 | 25.6 |
| 1995[2] | 65.5 | 57.2 | 3.2 | 105.0 | 8.0 | 2.6 | ----- | 264.0 | 0.1 | NA | 1.5 | 106.0 | 12.8 | NA | 182.0 | 54.3 | 22.1 |

[1] Preliminary. [2] Estimate. [3] And lead alloys. [4] Blocks, pigs, etc. [5] Formerly drosses and flue dust. *Source: U.S. Geological Survey*

## Average Price of Pig Lead, U.S. Primary Producers (Common Corroding)[1] In Cents Per Pound

| Year | Jan. | Feb. | Mar. | Apr. | May | June | July | Aug. | Sept. | Oct. | Nov. | Dec. | Average |
|---|---|---|---|---|---|---|---|---|---|---|---|---|---|
| 1985 | 20.45 | 19.76 | 19.24 | 20.48 | 20.50 | 20.00 | 19.88 | 19.32 | 19.44 | 18.97 | 19.06 | 19.05 | 19.68 |
| 1986 | 18.70 | 18.41 | 18.55 | 18.93 | 19.58 | 22.41 | 22.63 | 22.52 | 23.43 | 25.53 | 27.23 | 28.37 | 22.19 |
| 1987 | 27.75 | 26.03 | 26.00 | 27.01 | 35.10 | 36.77 | 41.82 | 42.00 | 42.00 | 42.00 | 42.00 | 42.00 | 35.87 |
| 1988 | 38.00 | 34.83 | 34.00 | 34.00 | 34.67 | 36.59 | 37.00 | 37.04 | 38.81 | 39.58 | 40.75 | 42.04 | 37.28 |
| 1989 | 40.22 | 37.00 | 35.00 | 35.03 | 36.14 | 38.82 | 39.97 | 41.30 | 43.00 | 43.00 | 40.55 | 38.55 | 39.05 |
| 1990 | 39.73 | 41.74 | 54.45 | 48.10 | 45.00 | 45.14 | 50.62 | 51.00 | 49.08 | 44.52 | 41.33 | 37.03 | 45.65 |
| 1991 | 34.18 | 33.00 | 33.00 | 33.00 | 32.00 | 31.80 | 33.00 | 33.00 | 33.70 | 35.00 | 35.00 | 35.00 | 33.47 |
| 1992 | 35.00 | 35.00 | 35.00 | 35.00 | 35.00 | 35.00 | 36.91 | 40.00 | 40.00 | 36.64 | 32.63 | 32.00 | 35.68 |
| 1993 | 32.00 | 32.00 | 32.00 | 32.00 | 32.00 | 32.00 | 32.00 | 32.00 | 32.00 | 32.00 | 32.00 | 33.00 | 32.08 |
| 1994 | 34.00 | 34.00 | 34.00 | 34.00 | 34.00 | 35.73 | 37.70 | 38.00 | 40.00 | 42.00 | 43.70 | 44.00 | 37.59 |
| 1995 | 44.00 | 44.00 | 42.00 | 42.00 | 42.00 | 42.00 | 42.00 | 43.65 | 44.00 | 44.00 | 46.10 | 48.00 | 43.65 |
| 1996 | 48.00 | 49.50 | 50.96 | 52.00 | 52.00 | 52.00 | 50.29 | 49.18 | 50.00 | 50.00 | 50.00 | 50.00 | 50.33 |

[1] New York Delivery. *Source: American Metal Market*

## Refiners Production[1] of Lead in the United States In Metric Tons

| Year | Jan. | Feb. | Mar. | Apr. | May | June | July | Aug. | Sept. | Oct. | Nov. | Dec. | Total |
|---|---|---|---|---|---|---|---|---|---|---|---|---|---|
| 1985 | 39,100 | 45,632 | 51,075 | 47,809 | 48,444 | 46,176 | 29,484 | 42,276 | 40,733 | 35,653 | 27,307 | 40,370 | 494,003 |
| 1986 | 43,001 | 37,740 | 44,816 | 36,469 | 36,469 | 24,041 | 15,332 | 28,395 | 24,948 | 25,946 | 25,855 | 27,307 | 370,288 |
| 1987 | 35,199 | 30,482 | 32,659 | 30,119 | 31,026 | 26,762 | 26,127 | 28,032 | 30,300 | 34,111 | 35,834 | 33,113 | 373,610 |
| 1988 | 31,117 | 32,115 | 35,472 | 31,117 | 32,841 | 31,571 | 28,849 | 22,952 | 29,121 | 44,997 | 36,288 | 35,653 | 392,087 |
| 1989 | 37,195 | 32,659 | 35,381 | 30,845 | 32,841 | 32,206 | 32,387 | 34,474 | 35,653 | 31,480 | 32,024 | 29,303 | 396,455 |
| 1990 | 34,927 | 34,383 | 33,476 | 35,018 | 33,022 | 30,210 | 30,845 | 34,474 | 33,929 | 38,375 | 33,476 | 31,571 | 403,657 |
| 1991 | 30,763 | 30,863 | 33,771 | 30,248 | 27,031 | 22,371 | 27,973 | 28,204 | 29,411 | 29,846 | 26,428 | 28,813 | 345,714 |
| 1992 | 29,121 | 27,691 | 33,366 | 27,456 | 26,742 | 22,441 | 24,993 | 21,587 | 19,365 | 22,945 | 23,674 | 25,414 | 304,791 |
| 1993 | 29,627 | 26,693 | 30,197 | 27,578 | 29,814 | 28,253 | 16,734 | 22,817 | 32,725 | 31,220 | 27,953 | 31,312 | 335,014 |
| 1994 | 29,908 | 30,685 | 31,420 | 29,059 | 31,588 | 31,707 | 30,661 | 27,335 | 31,185 | 32,874 | 29,301 | 30,447 | 366,170 |
| 1995 | 32,100 | 29,100 | 32,600 | 32,300 | 32,600 | 28,300 | 31,000 | 29,300 | 30,600 | 34,200 | 30,100 | 31,500 | 374,000 |
| 1996[2] | 34,700 | 30,400 | 30,900 | 28,600 | 27,500 | 21,700 | 25,500 | 24,700 | 25,400 | 25,300 | 26,100 | | 300,800 |

[1] Represents refined lead produced from domestic ores by primary smelters plus small amounts of secondary material passing through these smelters. Includes GSA metal purchased for remelt. [2] Preliminary. *Source: U.S. Geological Survey*

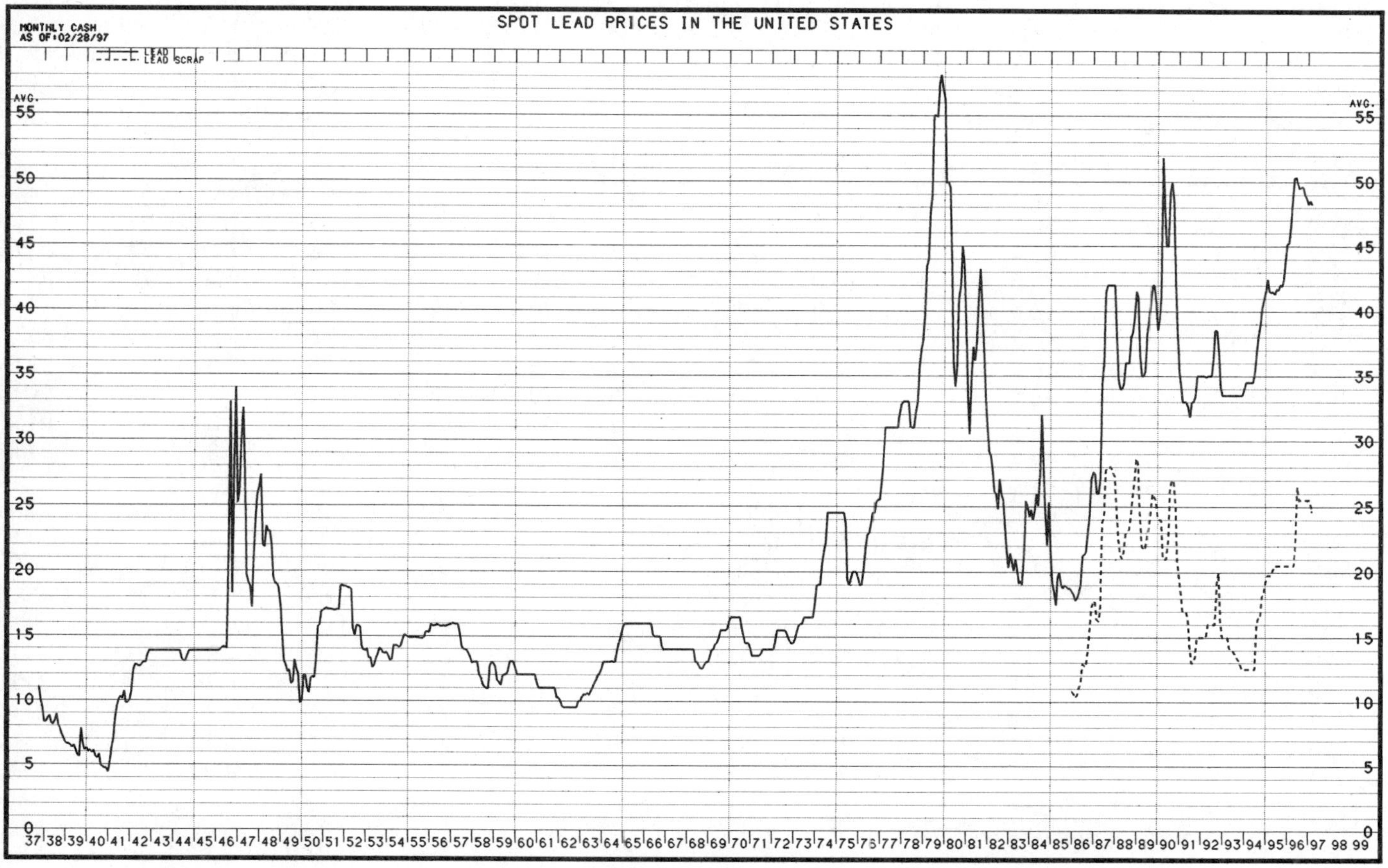

# LEAD

## U.S. Mine Production of Recoverable Lead    In Thousands of Metric Tons

| Year | Jan. | Feb. | Mar. | Apr. | May | June | July | Aug. | Sept. | Oct. | Nov. | Dec. | Total |
|---|---|---|---|---|---|---|---|---|---|---|---|---|---|
| 1988 | 27.9 | 28.2 | 36.0 | 32.7 | 30.3 | 32.5 | 30.4 | 36.3 | 33.1 | 34.4 | 31.1 | 31.8 | 385.0 |
| 1989 | 33.3 | 31.0 | 34.4 | 33.2 | 33.8 | 36.1 | 33.2 | 38.6 | 34.3 | 35.1 | 32.9 | 30.1 | 410.9 |
| 1990 | 42.4 | 39.0 | 39.9 | 37.4 | 40.8 | 38.8 | 42.3 | 47.2 | 37.9 | 43.0 | 38.5 | 36.6 | 483.7 |
| 1991 | 41.5 | 41.1 | 41.6 | 37.8 | 43.5 | 36.4 | 47.5 | 41.1 | 36.1 | 38.9 | 28.0 | 26.1 | 465.9 |
| 1992 | 36.0 | 34.0 | 34.0 | 31.2 | 31.5 | 32.4 | 33.8 | 32.5 | 32.5 | 33.3 | 30.8 | 31.7 | 392.7 |
| 1993 | 33.3 | 30.5 | 34.2 | 30.6 | 28.5 | 29.5 | 25.8 | 27.5 | 28.4 | 27.3 | 29.5 | 28.5 | 355.2 |
| 1994 | 27.6 | 28.8 | 33.0 | 31.3 | 32.4 | 29.1 | 29.4 | 30.4 | 31.2 | 28.0 | 31.7 | 29.9 | 363.4 |
| 1995 | 29.6 | 30.3 | 35.2 | 28.9 | 32.7 | 34.8 | 32.5 | 33.5 | 29.9 | 34.1 | 31.6 | 32.1 | 385.0 |
| 1996[1] | 36.9 | 36.4 | 35.6 | 35.9 | 37.5 | 33.8 | 35.6 | 34.1 | 26.9 | 35.2 | 33.0 | | 380.9 |

[1] Preliminary. *Source: U.S. Geological Survey*

## Total Stocks of Lead[1] in the United States at Refiners, at End of Month    In Metric Tons

| Year | Jan. | Feb. | Mar. | Apr. | May | June | July | Aug. | Sept. | Oct. | Nov. | Dec. |
|---|---|---|---|---|---|---|---|---|---|---|---|---|
| 1988 | 22,408 | 27,670 | 27,397 | 28,849 | 24,041 | 15,060 | 14,697 | 5,988 | 4,627 | 10,524 | 11,884 | 15,422 |
| 1989 | 26,037 | 32,931 | 39,191 | 37,558 | 29,665 | 28,940 | 31,389 | 27,942 | 27,488 | 18,779 | 14,606 | 15,604 |
| 1990 | 14,697 | 18,325 | 16,420 | 21,138 | 19,323 | 19,596 | 20,775 | 19,958 | 20,593 | 23,769 | 22,771 | 25,492 |
| 1991 | 24,177 | 24,333 | 26,990 | 21,261 | 17,474 | 16,195 | 15,362 | 9,072 | 6,608 | 4,091 | 4,491 | 9,089 |
| 1992 | 9,774 | 15,785 | 21,682 | 25,220 | 28,940 | 26,490 | 26,634 | 22,347 | 17,736 | 14,971 | 14,796 | 20,543 |
| 1993 | 28,069 | 33,338 | 34,058 | 34,306 | 35,775 | 32,162 | 22,753 | 14,797 | 15,086 | 14,408 | 13,456 | 14,289 |
| 1994 | 11,964 | 12,633 | 12,048 | 11,445 | 11,598 | 10,251 | 12,368 | 9,256 | 8,897 | 10,659 | 9,060 | 9,271 |
| 1995 | 8,200 | 9,750 | 11,500 | 14,500 | 16,700 | 16,200 | 21,300 | 14,000 | 12,800 | 9,820 | 9,830 | 14,200 |
| 1996[2] | 15,000 | 15,000 | 15,000 | 15,000 | 15,000 | 19,600 | 19,900 | 14,200 | 12,200 | 7,060 | 7,830 | |

[1] Primary refineries. [2] Preliminary. *Source: U.S. Geological Survey*

## Total[1] Lead Consumption in the United States    In Thousands of Metric Tons

| Year | Jan. | Feb. | Mar. | Apr. | May | June | July | Aug. | Sept. | Oct. | Nov. | Dec. | Total |
|---|---|---|---|---|---|---|---|---|---|---|---|---|---|
| 1988 | 99.8 | 101.4 | 116.0 | 99.3 | 104.0 | 103.6 | 92.1 | 102.5 | 103.0 | 110.6 | 103.4 | 95.1 | 1,231 |
| 1989 | 104.7 | 98.3 | 101.2 | 99.2 | 101.3 | 101.6 | 95.2 | 102.7 | 105.9 | 114.0 | 106.2 | 97.3 | 1,283 |
| 1990 | 104.1 | 106.7 | 111.9 | 101.1 | 106.2 | 103.2 | 97.7 | 112.4 | 104.6 | 109.0 | 104.3 | 97.3 | 1,275 |
| 1991 | 101.3 | 105.3 | 101.2 | 101.3 | 98.4 | 92.4 | 90.8 | 101.9 | 102.7 | 106.9 | 102.4 | 92.7 | 1,246 |
| 1992 | 102.5 | 99.3 | 108.3 | 98.5 | 96.0 | 103.5 | 94.8 | 104.8 | 106.6 | 105.4 | 98.2 | 92.9 | 1,215 |
| 1993 | 108.9 | 107.5 | 112.3 | 104.6 | 109.2 | 113.8 | 106.8 | 112.6 | 117.1 | 113.2 | 109.3 | 102.2 | 1,357 |
| 1994 | 107.0 | 115.2 | 112.8 | 111.6 | 113.5 | 115.2 | 114.3 | 115.5 | 115.9 | 121.2 | 118.7 | 113.0 | 1,384 |
| 1995 | 119.0 | 119.0 | 119.0 | 109.0 | 110.0 | 113.0 | 115.0 | 105.0 | 115.0 | 116.0 | 118.0 | 116.0 | 1,370 |
| 1996[2] | 107.0 | 100.0 | 106.0 | 111.0 | 113.0 | 106.0 | 104.0 | 146.0 | 140.0 | 147.0 | 163.0 | | 1,343 |

[1] Represents total consumption of primary and secondary lead as metal, in chemicals, or in alloys. [2] Preliminary. *Source: U.S. Bureau of Mines*

## U.S. Lead Recovered from Scrap    In Thousands of Metric Tons (Lead Content)

| Year | Jan. | Feb. | Mar. | Apr. | May | June | July | Aug. | Sept. | Oct. | Nov. | Dec. | Total |
|---|---|---|---|---|---|---|---|---|---|---|---|---|---|
| 1988 | 52.2 | 57.5 | 60.1 | 55.9 | 52.2 | 59.4 | 55.3 | 56.3 | 60.7 | 61.8 | 61.6 | 59.7 | 737.0 |
| 1989 | 62.1 | 58.6 | 67.5 | 64.1 | 65.3 | 66.3 | 61.6 | 65.9 | 64.4 | 73.5 | 67.1 | 66.9 | 808.6 |
| 1990 | 68.7 | 69.6 | 73.0 | 69.4 | 66.9 | 67.9 | 67.0 | 71.8 | 71.0 | 77.5 | 72.3 | 77.3 | 923.0 |
| 1991 | 79.0 | 74.4 | 71.0 | 72.0 | 72.0 | 70.7 | 69.8 | 70.0 | 72.3 | 74.6 | 70.7 | 75.9 | 883.7 |
| 1992 | 76.1 | 71.5 | 66.5 | 71.0 | 73.3 | 72.3 | 71.1 | 77.7 | 77.5 | 79.6 | 76.9 | 74.3 | 888.5 |
| 1993 | 71.1 | 76.8 | 71.7 | 80.2 | 78.9 | 72.5 | 70.3 | 76.6 | 76.3 | 77.0 | 77.9 | 79.3 | 903.6 |
| 1994 | 74.0 | 76.0 | 84.2 | 81.7 | 81.1 | 79.0 | 78.9 | 79.8 | 78.4 | 76.4 | 81.0 | 80.4 | 949.0 |
| 1995 | 82.5 | 80.8 | 84.4 | 72.8 | 73.7 | 72.5 | 79.9 | 71.5 | 82.3 | 80.0 | 82.3 | 82.1 | 945.0 |
| 1996[1] | 75.7 | 76.2 | 84.2 | 83.7 | 84.7 | 80.7 | 81.2 | 89.0 | 92.1 | 98.8 | 97.3 | | 943.6 |

[1] Preliminary. *Source: U.S. Geological Survey*

## Domestic Shipments[1] of Lead in the United States by Refiners    In Thousands of Short Tons

| Year | Jan. | Feb. | Mar. | Apr. | May | June | July | Aug. | Sept. | Oct. | Nov. | Dec. | Total |
|---|---|---|---|---|---|---|---|---|---|---|---|---|---|
| 1988 | 33.5 | 29.5 | 39.2 | 33.0 | 41.4 | 44.7 | 32.0 | 34.7 | 33.7 | 43.0 | 38.5 | 35.5 | 438.7 |
| 1989 | 29.3 | 28.5 | 32.2 | 35.7 | 45.1 | 36.4 | 32.8 | 41.5 | 40.0 | 44.2 | 40.2 | 31.1 | 437.1 |
| 1990 | 39.3 | 33.9 | 39.1 | 33.5 | 38.4 | 32.9 | 32.6 | 38.9 | 36.6 | 38.9 | 37.9 | 31.7 | 433.7 |
| 1991 | 35.4 | 33.8 | 34.3 | 39.8 | 33.9 | 26.0 | 31.8 | 37.9 | 35.1 | 35.7 | 28.7 | 26.7 | 399.2 |
| 1992 | 31.3 | 23.9 | 30.4 | 26.3 | 25.6 | 27.2 | 27.3 | 28.7 | 26.3 | 28.5 | 26.3 | 21.7 | 323.5 |
| 1993 | 24.6 | 23.6 | 32.5 | 30.0 | 31.3 | 35.1 | 28.9 | 34.0 | 35.5 | 35.5 | 31.7 | 33.5 | 376.2 |
| 1994 | 35.9 | 32.8 | 352.4 | 32.7 | 34.7 | 36.7 | 31.6 | 33.4 | 34.8 | 34.3 | 34.0 | 33.3 | 409.3 |
| 1995[2] | 36.5 | 30.3 | 35.1 | 31.1 | 33.7 | 31.9 | 28.6 | 40.3 | 34.9 | 40.9 | 33.2 | 29.8 | 406.4 |

[1] Includes GSA metal. *Source: American Metal Market*

# Lumber & Plywood

Lumber prices displayed extreme volatility during 1996. In the first half of 1996 prices became more volatile in the second quarter as a result of the signing of the Canadian trade pact. To implement the pact, the Canadian government put restrictions on how much lumber could be exported, and allocated export quotas to mills. These policies added to the overall uncertainty and volatility in the marketplace. Any time the supply of a commodity is artificially restricted, be it petroleum, coffee, or lumber, price movement is bound to increase until the market adjusts to the new market reality. In the second quarter of 1996 lumber demand was still strong after a strong housing market in the first four months of 1996. A decline in interest rates had made housing more affordable leading to improved demand for lumber. The signing of the trade pact, along with a slowing in housing starts in May 1996, added to the uncertainty about future price direction. Under the Canadian export quota, exports to the U.S. would be restricted to 14.7 billion board feet of lumber per year and only 28 per cent of the yearly total can be exported each quarter. At the time of the agreement, further details were lacking and that lack of details contributed to the price volatility.

Late in the second quarter of 1996, lumber futures moved down toward $300 per thousand board feet. From that level, they staged a strong rally that carried about $100, or over 30 per cent higher by the fourth quarter of 1996. The initial reason for the rally was a decline in inventories at the retail level as the peak building season was reaching an end. This, along with reduced lumber exports from Canada due to the export quota, allowed lumber prices to stage a very strong rally.

Going into September 1996, lumber prices were moving still higher as short-term supplies were tight. On the housing front the data gave mixed indications. Existing home sales for the month of July were lower, which was bearish, but new home sales as of late August were strong. There were indications that the economy was slowing but interest rates were holding steady. In September 1996, lumber prices began to move lower for the first time in several weeks. There were a couple of hurricanes that brushed the Southeastern part of the U.S. but the damage was not as bad as expected and a weather premium that had been built into the price structure was eliminated.

As of September 3, 1996, the Canadian export quota had used 69.7 per cent of the quarterly quota and 47.9 per cent of the annual quota. It was reported that a plan was reached in September to allocate the quota. The plan allocated 59 per cent of the quota to British Columbia, 23 per cent to Quebec, 10.3 per cent to Ontario, and 7.7 per cent to Alberta. The allocation should reduce the uncertainty in the lumber market. New data on the housing market released in September 1996 pointed to a slowdown. Lumber prices moved lower but in October began to rally again on concerns about the Canadian export quota.

In late 1996, lumber prices continued their volatile pattern of strong rallies followed by sharp pullbacks. Retailers continued to hold smaller inventories and there were concerns about the Canadian quotas. The housing data reported in December 1996, for September and October, was weaker than expectations. Going into 1997, the lumber market was being influenced by two fundamental forces each pulling in the opposite direction. The U.S. housing market was slowing by virtually every measurement. Housing starts and building permits were down as were sales expectations of builders. While all of this pointed to lower lumber prices, the Canadian export quota issue remained a potentially bullish factor. Because the supply of lumber that could be obtained from Canada was not known with certainty, there continued to be the potential for a strong rally.

Random Lengths reported that wholesalers in the U.S. were having difficulty buying lumber from Canada since the quota on exports was started. They blamed the quota for periodic disruptions of shipments and higher lumber prices. Because of the uncertainty of receiving supplies without a problem, more buyers were turning to U.S. producers. Other buyers were looking at Canadian mills that were not covered by the quota such as the Maritime provinces. Another problem that had developed was that lower grades of lumber were becoming harder to buy as Canadian mills were reserving their quotas for higher-value products.

In other developments, the USDA reported that U.S. exports in January-March 1996 of softwood logs were 2.5 million cubic meters, down 11 per cent from the same period of 1995. Hardwood log exports in the first quarter of 1996 were 315,872 cubic meters, down 13 per cent from the first quarter of 1995. The major market for softwood logs is Japan.

### *Futures Markets*

Lumber futures and options are traded on the Chicago Mercantile Exchange (CME). The CME also began trading an Oriented Strand Board contract late in 1996.

**U.S. Housing Starts: Seasonally Adjusted Annual Rate** In Thousands

| Year | Jan. | Feb. | Mar. | Apr. | May | June | July | Aug. | Sept. | Oct. | Nov. | Dec. | Average |
|---|---|---|---|---|---|---|---|---|---|---|---|---|---|
| 1988 | 1,391 | 1,511 | 1,528 | 1,576 | 1,392 | 1,463 | 1,478 | 1,459 | 1,463 | 1,532 | 1,567 | 1,577 | 1,495 |
| 1989 | 1,678 | 1,465 | 1,409 | 1,343 | 1,308 | 1,414 | 1,424 | 1,325 | 1,263 | 1,423 | 1,347 | 1,273 | 1,389 |
| 1990 | 1,568 | 1,488 | 1,307 | 1,216 | 1,206 | 1,189 | 1,153 | 1,131 | 1,107 | 1,026 | 1,130 | 971 | 1,208 |
| 1991 | 844 | 1,008 | 918 | 978 | 983 | 1,036 | 1,053 | 1,053 | 1,022 | 1,085 | 1,085 | 1,118 | 1,015 |
| 1992 | 1,180 | 1,285 | 1,318 | 1,095 | 1,197 | 1,141 | 1,106 | 1,229 | 1,218 | 1,226 | 1,226 | 1,286 | 1,209 |
| 1993 | 1,170 | 1,194 | 1,092 | 1,232 | 1,241 | 1,238 | 1,245 | 1,319 | 1,359 | 1,409 | 1,406 | 1,612 | 1,293 |
| 1994 | 1,266 | 1,318 | 1,499 | 1,463 | 1,489 | 1,370 | 1,440 | 1,463 | 1,511 | 1,451 | 1,536 | 1,527 | 1,444 |
| 1995 | 1,370 | 1,322 | 1,241 | 1,278 | 1,300 | 1,301 | 1,450 | 1,401 | 1,401 | 1,351 | 1,458 | 1,425 | 1,358 |
| 1996[1] | 1,453 | 1,505 | 1,435 | 1,505 | 1,461 | 1,474 | 1,460 | 1,529 | 1,440 | 1,386 | 1,514 | 1,329 | 1,458 |

[1] Preliminary. Total privately owned. *Source: American Forest & Paper Association*

# LUMBER

## World Production of Industrial Roundwood by Selected Countries In Thousands of Cubic Meters

| Year | Austria | Canada | Czech[3] Republic | Finland | France | Germany | Japan | Norway | Poland | Russia[4] | Spain | Sweden | Switzer-land | Turkey | United Kingdom | United States |
|---|---|---|---|---|---|---|---|---|---|---|---|---|---|---|---|---|
| 1989 | 13,575 | 170,625 | 16,856 | 42,670 | 34,276 | 41,806 | 31,202 | 10,590 | 18,980 | 305,300 | 15,691 | 51,430 | 3,729 | 5,728 | 6,207 | 416,900 |
| 1990 | 14,160 | 173,897 | 16,398 | 40,196 | 34,913 | 40,934 | 29,300 | 10,900 | 15,549 | 305,300 | 13,790 | 49,071 | 5,383 | 5,960 | 6,125 | 430,200 |
| 1991 | 12,535 | 159,039 | 13,770 | 31,616 | 33,754 | 29,823 | 27,938 | 10,345 | 14,334 | 275,300 | 12,988 | 47,600 | 3,751 | 5,502 | 6,122 | 388,310 |
| 1992 | 9,255 | 165,436 | 8,820 | 35,279 | 52,854 | 29,159 | 26,934 | 9,200 | 15,720 | 164,000 | 12,614 | 49,720 | 3,638 | 8,458 | 5,740 | 403,100 |
| 1993[1] | 9,107 | 173,133 | 9,706 | 37,758 | 29,566 | 29,357 | 25,570 | 9,253 | 15,940 | 136,030 | 11,477 | 50,200 | 3,501 | 9,408 | 7,185 | 401,520 |
| 1994[2] | 11,101 | NA | 11,400 | 43,502 | 33,050 | 33,217 | NA | 8,274 | 16,621 | 94,700 | NA | 52,700 | NA | 9,211 | 7,915 | 399,725 |

[1] Preliminary. [2] Estimate. [3] Formerly part of Czechoslovakia; data not reported separately until 1992. [4] Formerly part of the U.S.S.R.; data not reported separately until 1992. NA = Not available. *Source: Food and Agricultural Organization of the United Nations*

## United States Lumber Production and Consumption In Millions of Board Feet

| Year | Production | | | | | | Domestic Consumption | | | | | | | |
|---|---|---|---|---|---|---|---|---|---|---|---|---|---|---|
| | Softwood | | | | | | Softwood | | | | | | | |
| | California Redwood | Inland Region | Southern Pine | West Coast | Total | Total Hardwood | Inland Region | Southern Pine | West Coast | Softwood Imports | Total | U.S. Hardwood | Hardwood Imports | Total Lumber |
| 1985 | 1,730 | 9,276 | 10,730 | 8,062 | 31,321 | 8,866 | 8,977 | 10,480 | 7,250 | 14,608 | 44,240 | 8,864 | 364 | 53,468 |
| 1986 | 2,021 | 10,482 | 11,678 | 9,412 | 35,273 | 10,877 | 10,273 | 11,383 | 8,377 | 14,238 | 47,492 | 10,469 | 347 | 58,308 |
| 1987 | 2,181 | 11,407 | 12,473 | 10,354 | 38,235 | 11,695 | 11,008 | 12,240 | 9,117 | 14,680 | 50,558 | 11,235 | 511 | 62,304 |
| 1988 | 2,214 | 11,395 | 12,676 | 10,029 | 38,130 | 12,170 | 11,180 | 12,108 | 8,096 | 13,806 | 48,513 | 10,636 | 390 | 59,539 |
| 1989 | 2,053 | 11,348 | 12,544 | 9,811 | 37,545 | 12,415 | 11,134 | 12,125 | 7,950 | 13,638 | 47,966 | 11,970 | 375 | 60,311 |
| 1990 | 1,972 | 10,452 | 12,911 | 8,751 | 35,791 | 12,660 | 10,390 | 12,388 | 7,184 | 12,148 | 45,003 | 11,070 | 255 | 56,328 |
| 1991 | 1,657 | 9,510 | 12,507 | 7,908 | 33,161 | 11,633 | 9,302 | 12,147 | 6,454 | 11,742 | 42,225 | 10,278 | 226 | 52,730 |
| 1992 | 1,571 | 9,263 | 14,106 | 7,948 | 34,526 | 11,639 | 9,107 | 13,893 | 6,709 | 13,381 | 45,737 | 10,853 | 276 | 56,866 |
| 1993 | 1,354 | 8,312 | 14,392 | 7,319 | 32,947 | 11,914 | 8,129 | 14,020 | 6,043 | 15,260 | 45,810 | 10,556 | 335 | 56,702 |
| 1994 | 1,474 | 8,097 | 15,010 | 7,902 | 34,107 | 12,311 | 7,855 | 14,618 | 6,834 | 16,380 | 48,104 | 11,128 | 394 | 59,626 |
| 1995 | 1,305 | 7,015 | 14,708 | 7,452 | 32,233 | 12,434 | 6,956 | 14,384 | 6,530 | 17,396 | 47,749 | 11,372 | 379 | 59,501 |
| 1996[1] I | 319 | 1,720 | 3,616 | 1,872 | 7,959 | NA | 1,671 | 3,511 | 1,620 | 4,496 | 11,925 | NA | NA | NA |
| II | 349 | 1,794 | 3,998 | 2,076 | 8,689 | NA | 1,801 | 3,998 | 1,886 | 4,558 | 12,958 | NA | NA | NA |
| III | 362 | 1,841 | 3,976 | 2,234 | 8,896 | NA | 1,904 | 3,981 | 1,999 | 4,892 | 13,513 | NA | NA | NA |

[1] Preliminary. NA = not avaliable. *Source: American Forest & Paper Association*

## Stocks (Gross) of Softwood Lumber in the United States, Beginning of Month In Millions of Board Feet

| Year | Jan. | Feb. | Mar. | Apr. | May | June | July | Aug. | Sept. | Oct. | Nov. | Dec. |
|---|---|---|---|---|---|---|---|---|---|---|---|---|
| 1985 | 4,594 | 4,533 | 4,637 | 4,733 | 4,508 | 4,415 | 4,633 | 4,680 | 4,687 | 4,699 | 4,850 | 4,870 |
| 1986 | 4,765 | 4,842 | 4,959 | 4,846 | 4,886 | 4,748 | 4,605 | 4,615 | 4,722 | 4,840 | 4,929 | 5,038 |
| 1987 | 5,040 | 5,039 | 5,112 | 5,203 | 5,181 | 5,097 | 4,927 | 4,928 | 4,755 | 4,855 | 4,787 | 4,823 |
| 1988 | 4,771 | 4,867 | 4,950 | 4,994 | 4,939 | 4,894 | 4,685 | 4,677 | 4,765 | 4,823 | 4,951 | 4,979 |
| 1989 | 4,999 | 4,896 | 4,818 | 4,837 | 4,810 | 4,740 | 4,746 | 4,748 | 4,797 | 4,762 | 4,908 | 4,934 |
| 1990 | 4,898 | 5,022 | 5,022 | 5,020 | 4,961 | 5,043 | 4,831 | 4,783 | 4,752 | 4,810 | 4,834 | 4,809 |
| 1991 | 4,734 | 4,925 | 4,949 | 4,946 | 4,849 | 4,600 | 4,699 | 4,684 | 4,793 | 4,786 | 4,741 | 4,710 |
| 1992 | 4,616 | 4,603 | 4,567 | 4,608 | 4,730 | 4,731 | 4,678 | 4,606 | 4,418 | 4,419 | 4,365 | 4,263 |
| 1993 | 4,669 | 4,217 | 4,166 | 4,239 | 4,490 | 4,618 | 4,599 | 4,526 | 4,418 | 4,445 | 4,282 | 4,298 |
| 1994 | 4,207 | 4,512 | 4,656 | 4,816 | 4,883 | 4,649 | 4,738 | 4,432 | 4,349 | 4,539 | 4,235 | 4,294 |
| 1995 | 4,403 | 4,336 | 4,344 | 4,653 | 4,352 | 4,663 | 4,508 | 4,323 | 4,342 | 4,359 | 4,361 | 4,335 |
| 1996[1] | 4,293 | 4,435 | 4,459 | 4,357 | 4,251 | 4,153 | 4,156 | 4,038 | 3,918 | 3,965 | 3,939 | 3,906 |

[1] Preliminary. *Source: American Forest & Paper Association*

## Lumber Production in the United States (Softwood)[2] In Millions of Board Feet

| Year | Jan. | Feb. | Mar. | Apr. | May | June | July | Aug. | Sept. | Oct. | Nov. | Dec. | Total |
|---|---|---|---|---|---|---|---|---|---|---|---|---|---|
| 1985 | 2,727 | 2,718 | 3,085 | 3,296 | 3,256 | 3,101 | 3,034 | 3,299 | 3,196 | 3,387 | 2,851 | 2,649 | 36,599 |
| 1986 | 3,092 | 3,046 | 3,347 | 3,362 | 3,405 | 3,355 | 2,961 | 3,441 | 3,397 | 3,820 | 3,496 | 3,623 | 40,345 |
| 1987 | 3,293 | 3,307 | 3,742 | 3,616 | 3,518 | 3,905 | 3,662 | 3,737 | 3,617 | 3,942 | 3,458 | 3,829 | 43,626 |
| 1988 | 3,814 | 4,042 | 4,389 | 4,247 | 4,245 | 4,137 | 3,671 | 4,056 | 4,180 | 4,040 | 3,715 | 3,641 | 48,177 |
| 1989 | 3,849 | 3,311 | 3,758 | 3,773 | 4,025 | 4,273 | 3,683 | 4,023 | 3,787 | 4,172 | 3,811 | 3,615 | 46,080 |
| 1990 | 4,160 | 3,862 | 4,300 | 4,121 | 4,084 | 3,944 | 3,976 | 4,060 | 3,602 | 4,015 | 3,412 | 2,914 | 46,450 |
| 1991 | 3,534 | 3,410 | 3,661 | 3,958 | 3,837 | 3,762 | 3,664 | 3,808 | 3,682 | 3,933 | 3,473 | 3,254 | 43,976 |
| 1992 | 3,836 | 3,628 | 4,121 | 3,862 | 3,632 | 3,911 | 3,882 | 3,746 | 3,736 | 4,048 | 3,617 | 3,425 | 45,444 |
| 1993 | 3,545 | 3,596 | 3,954 | 3,809 | 3,555 | 3,787 | 3,685 | 3,930 | 3,824 | 4,103 | 3,883 | 3,576 | 45,247 |
| 1994 | 3,839 | 3,662 | 4,097 | 3,735 | 3,972 | 4,113 | 3,785 | 4,124 | 4,135 | 4,145 | 3,636 | 3,851 | 47,094 |
| 1995 | 4,084 | 3,577 | 3,931 | 3,675 | 3,805 | 3,897 | 3,641 | 3,866 | 3,757 | 4,105 | 3,549 | 3,297 | 45,184 |
| 1996[1] | 2,600 | 2,606 | 2,757 | 2,903 | 2,833 | 2,819 | 2,942 | 3,077 | 2,858 | 3,179 | 2,720 | | 31,294 |

[1] Preliminary. [2] Data prior to 1996 are for Softwood and Hardwood. *Source: American Forest & Paper Association*

## United States Lumber Shipments (Softwood)[2] In Millions of Board Feet

| Year | Jan. | Feb. | Mar. | Apr. | May | June | July | Aug. | Sept. | Oct. | Nov. | Dec. | Total |
|---|---|---|---|---|---|---|---|---|---|---|---|---|---|
| 1987 | 3,350 | 3,302 | 3,735 | 3,686 | 3,656 | 4,039 | 3,671 | 3,812 | 3,540 | 4,034 | 3,470 | 3,865 | 50,311 |
| 1988 | 3,790 | 4,092 | 4,320 | 4,257 | 4,261 | 4,309 | 3,688 | 3,929 | 4,038 | 3,871 | 3,656 | 3,649 | 49,839 |
| 1989 | 3,914 | 3,417 | 3,877 | 3,846 | 4,163 | 4,420 | 3,760 | 3,977 | 3,823 | 4,081 | 3,854 | 3,626 | 50,476 |
| 1990 | 4,035 | 3,870 | 4,317 | 4,173 | 3,952 | 4,176 | 3,912 | 3,987 | 3,453 | 3,890 | 3,357 | 2,873 | 47,773 |
| 1991 | 3,240 | 3,301 | 3,617 | 4,037 | 4,028 | 3,764 | 3,412 | 3,926 | 3,676 | 4,012 | 3,477 | 3,370 | 44,559 |
| 1992 | 3,912 | 3,693 | 4,078 | 3,682 | 3,565 | 3,936 | 3,884 | 3,878 | 3,692 | 4,147 | 3,745 | 3,491 | 45,703 |
| 1993 | 3,575 | 3,649 | 3,852 | 3,563 | 3,402 | 3,759 | 3,721 | 3,997 | 3,724 | 4,211 | 3,798 | 3,617 | 44,868 |
| 1994 | 3,576 | 3,663 | 3,912 | 3,761 | 4,192 | 4,091 | 4,039 | 4,163 | 3,914 | 4,321 | 3,603 | 3,696 | 46,931 |
| 1995 | 3,971 | 3,584 | 3,855 | 3,831 | 3,765 | 4,026 | 3,826 | 3,870 | 3,760 | 4,055 | 3,478 | 3,367 | 45,388 |
| 1996[1] | 2,460 | 2,581 | 2,863 | 3,002 | 2,934 | 2,813 | 3,058 | 3,196 | 2,813 | 3,206 | 2,752 | | 31,678 |

[1] Preliminary. [2] Data prior to 1996 are for Softwood and Hardwood. *Source: American Forest & Paper Association*

## United States Trade of Lumber by Type In Millions of Board Feet

| | Imports[2] | | | | | | | | Exports[2] | | | | | | |
|---|---|---|---|---|---|---|---|---|---|---|---|---|---|---|---|
| | Softwood | | | | | | | | Softwood | | | | | | |
| Year | Cedar | Douglas Fir | Hemlock | Pine | Spurce | Total | Total Hardwood | Total Lumber | Douglas Fir | Hemlock | Ponderosa/White Pine | Southern Pine | Total | Total Hardwood | Total Lumber |
| 1987 | 792.2 | 631.4 | 553.6 | 499.6 | 10,964.4 | 14,680.4 | 511.0 | 15,219.3 | 660.8 | 663.9 | 269.1 | 247.5 | 2,423.3 | 775.1 | 3,216.9 |
| 1988 | 786.8 | 721.4 | 539.7 | 332.3 | 10,284.5 | 13,806.0 | 390.1 | 14,225.3 | 888.6 | 714.9 | 233.4 | 492.3 | 3,263.9 | 1,232.0 | 4,528.0 |
| 1989 | 786.0 | 603.4 | 469.5 | 335.8 | 7,387.4 | 13,638.4 | 375.1 | 14,022.5 | 1,018.2 | 670.9 | 197.0 | 442.3 | 3,319.1 | 856.0 | 4,213.1 |
| 1990 | 652.8 | 375.4 | 362.4 | 87.6 | 3,535.7 | 12,148.2 | 255.4 | 12,429.4 | 818.5 | 549.4 | 215.2 | 374.7 | 2,970.4 | 877.7 | 3,900.0 |
| 1991 | 700.6 | 354.1 | 287.8 | 55.7 | 2,248.3 | 11,741.5 | 226.2 | 11,998.2 | 798.1 | 497.7 | 222.9 | 396.0 | 2,863.2 | 934.3 | 3,858.9 |
| 1992 | 666.4 | 355.3 | 300.0 | 91.4 | 2,410.5 | 13,380.5 | 276.4 | 13,681.9 | 735.0 | 396.7 | 308.7 | 440.5 | 2,650.7 | 977.2 | 3,687.1 |
| 1993 | 615.3 | 327.6 | 354.9 | 84.6 | 3,104.1 | 15,259.9 | 335.0 | 15,625.4 | 664.9 | 340.4 | 273.3 | 339.6 | 2,376.4 | 1,008.9 | 3,468.9 |
| 1994 | 702.6 | 336.2 | 399.2 | 97.2 | 2,948.5 | 16,380.3 | 394.4 | 16,787.1 | 591.9 | 283.2 | 157.2 | 356.7 | 2,186.6 | 1,040.9 | 3,333.4 |
| 1995 | 768.0 | 395.4 | 258.1 | 97.1 | 2,827.7 | 17,395.3 | 379.7 | 17,786.9 | 637.9 | 227.0 | 106.7 | 334.6 | 1,987.5 | 1,100.5 | 3,189.5 |
| 1996[1] I | 182.0 | 55.3 | 65.7 | 29.3 | 595.1 | 4,495.9 | 98.4 | 4,597.1 | 164.4 | 52.0 | 25.0 | 81.4 | 471.7 | 279.3 | 779.4 |
| II | 181.2 | 67.4 | 60.1 | 31.2 | 544.0 | 4,558.2 | 98.5 | 4,666.0 | 174.7 | 47.5 | 23.4 | 78.0 | 487.4 | 294.5 | 813.6 |
| III | 211.4 | 79.0 | 69.9 | 43.2 | 509.9 | 4,892.4 | 97.7 | 4,999.8 | 165.8 | 43.9 | 21.8 | 71.4 | 465.4 | 271.1 | 756.8 |

[1] Preliminary. [2] Includes sawed timber, board planks and scantings, flooring, box shook and railroad ties. *Source: American Forest & Paper Association*

# LUMBER

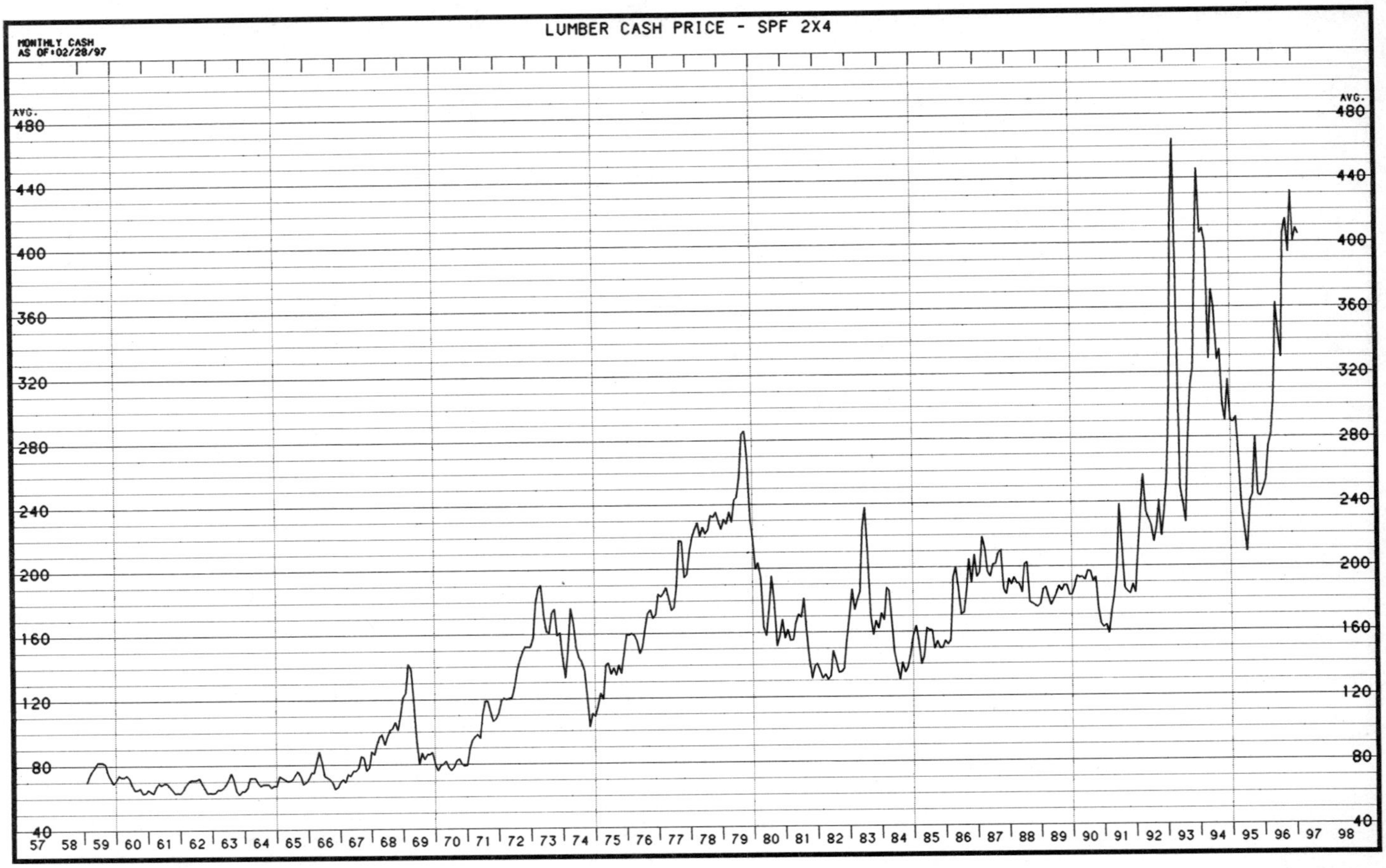


## Average Open Interest of Random Lumber Futures at Chicago[1] In Contracts

| Year | Jan. | Feb. | Mar. | Apr. | May | June | July | Aug. | Sept. | Oct. | Nov. | Dec. |
|---|---|---|---|---|---|---|---|---|---|---|---|---|
| 1985 | 9,953 | 9,704 | 8,102 | 9,115 | 9,115 | 10,038 | 8,823 | 8,672 | 7,672 | 7,247 | 6,819 | 6,567 |
| 1986 | 5,486 | 6,121 | 8,866 | 9,287 | 8,171 | 6,112 | 5,441 | 5,197 | 5,701 | 5,262 | 5,275 | 5,732 |
| 1987 | 6,077 | 7,330 | 6,406 | 6,950 | 6,019 | 6,770 | 6,563 | 7,439 | 6,961 | 7,247 | 6,579 | 6,572 |
| 1988 | 6,212 | 6,701 | 5,791 | 6,395 | 5,548 | 5,644 | 5,586 | 6,272 | 5,527 | 5,697 | 5,368 | 5,919 |
| 1989 | 7,982 | 7,484 | 7,436 | 8,244 | 7,363 | 7,921 | 8,248 | 8,055 | 7,065 | 7,192 | 6,600 | 6,167 |
| 1990 | 6,078 | 6,061 | 4,991 | 4,957 | 4,538 | 4,359 | 3,570 | 3,028 | 2,881 | 3,105 | 2,632 | 2,001 |
| 1991 | 1,922 | 2,003 | 2,023 | 2,354 | 2,076 | 2,601 | 2,571 | 2,181 | 2,276 | 2,480 | 2,206 | 1,606 |
| 1992 | 1,969 | 2,651 | 2,743 | 2,467 | 1,900 | 1,774 | 1,338 | 1,369 | 1,507 | 1,441 | 1,745 | 2,155 |
| 1993 | 2,194 | 2,432 | 2,163 | 2,055 | 2,302 | 2,658 | 2,254 | 2,141 | 2,011 | 2,080 | 2,140 | 2,721 |
| 1994 | 2,571 | 2,814 | 2,638 | 2,563 | 1,936 | 1,838 | 1,705 | 1,854 | 2,102 | 2,169 | 1,702 | 1,967 |
| 1995 | 1,757 | 1,923 | 2,142 | 2,509 | 2,742 | 3,252 | 2,896 | 2,918 | 2,809 | 3,039 | 2,626 | 2,940 |
| 1996 | 3,378 | 4,040 | 3,752 | 4,395 | 5,666 | 4,972 | 3,280 | 5,243 | 4,743 | 4,797 | 4,341 | 3,691 |

[1] Data July 1995 thru March 1996, Lumber and Random Lumber. *Source: Chicago Mercantile Exchange (CME)*

## Volume of Trading of Random Lumber Futures at Chicago[1] In Contracts

| Year | Jan. | Feb. | Mar. | Apr. | May | June | July | Aug. | Sept. | Oct. | Nov. | Dec. | Total |
|---|---|---|---|---|---|---|---|---|---|---|---|---|---|
| 1985 | 71,719 | 55,737 | 56,718 | 65,762 | 62,766 | 57,422 | 43,525 | 39,151 | 36,517 | 34,703 | 29,556 | 27,972 | 581,548 |
| 1986 | 29,570 | 34,647 | 61,718 | 64,176 | 44,778 | 49,929 | 35,203 | 42,212 | 44,961 | 35,847 | 28,912 | 30,577 | 502,530 |
| 1987 | 40,351 | 49,167 | 40,504 | 39,211 | 27,954 | 33,505 | 31,345 | 38,876 | 34,039 | 39,437 | 32,052 | 30,648 | 437,089 |
| 1988 | 35,451 | 32,410 | 32,886 | 30,386 | 28,100 | 37,508 | 27,550 | 33,454 | 29,743 | 24,632 | 26,131 | 23,238 | 371,489 |
| 1989 | 29,963 | 25,857 | 23,947 | 31,427 | 26,789 | 26,712 | 20,258 | 19,514 | 18,790 | 18,965 | 17,286 | 14,395 | 273,903 |
| 1990 | 27,416 | 21,914 | 20,948 | 18,362 | 19,053 | 16,084 | 16,465 | 13,446 | 8,914 | 11,839 | 15,794 | 11,749 | 201,984 |
| 1991 | 10,535 | 13,460 | 10,326 | 11,309 | 15,135 | 19,029 | 19,350 | 14,912 | 12,214 | 14,054 | 10,295 | 9,902 | 160,521 |
| 1992 | 17,073 | 16,778 | 17,557 | 13,713 | 14,059 | 13,807 | 12,177 | 13,043 | 12,127 | 11,261 | 11,514 | 17,425 | 170,534 |
| 1993 | 14,915 | 15,080 | 14,808 | 14,661 | 14,241 | 15,308 | 13,287 | 13,358 | 12,400 | 13,248 | 18,150 | 18,728 | 178,184 |
| 1994 | 16,837 | 15,204 | 17,323 | 17,380 | 14,996 | 14,348 | 11,542 | 13,327 | 14,856 | 13,032 | 10,997 | 13,121 | 172,963 |
| 1995 | 12,150 | 12,909 | 15,088 | 12,139 | 14,536 | 20,126 | 13,766 | 16,919 | 15,718 | 18,981 | 15,551 | 14,803 | 182,686 |
| 1996 | 22,954 | 19,960 | 20,956 | 27,094 | 28,271 | 26,100 | 19,302 | 27,792 | 31,982 | 32,042 | 25,236 | 22,525 | 304,214 |

[1] Data July 1995 thru March 1996, Lumber and Random Lumber. *Source: Chicago Mercantile Exchange (CME)*

## Production of Plywood by Selected Countries In Thousands of Cubic Meters

| Year | Austria | Canada | Czech Republic[2] | Finland | France | Germany | Italy | Japan | Poland | Romania | Russia[3] | Slovenia[4] | Spain | Sweden | Turkey | United States |
|---|---|---|---|---|---|---|---|---|---|---|---|---|---|---|---|---|
| 1989 | 111 | 2,165 | 245 | 657 | 498 | 439 | 445 | 6,707 | 154 | 181 | 2,298 | 138 | 150 | 68 | 65 | 19,700 |
| 1990 | 120 | 2,228 | 234 | 643 | 518 | 436 | 445 | 6,738 | 126 | 123 | 1,744 | 79 | 141 | 68 | 65 | 18,771 |
| 1991 | 140 | 1,927 | 157 | 477 | 470 | 424 | 450 | 6,588 | 111 | 51 | 1,548 | 71 | 140 | 67 | 65 | 16,508 |
| 1992 | 150 | 1,838 | 87 | 462 | 484 | 429 | 427 | 5,954 | 132 | 100 | 1,268 | 65 | 120 | 55 | 74 | 17,109 |
| 1993 | 150 | 1,824 | 75 | 621 | 460 | 416 | 415 | 5,263 | 133 | 100 | 1,042 | 63 | 200 | 73 | 77 | 17,093 |
| 1994[1] | 150 | 1,834 | 80 | 700 | 485 | 416 | 427 | NA | 143 | NA | 870 | 64 | 210 | 85 | 77 | 17,500 |

[1] Preliminary. [2] Formerly part of Czechoslovakia; data not reported separately until 1992. [3] Formerly part of the U.S.S.R.; data not reported separately until 1992. [4] Formerly part of Yugoslavia; data not reported separately until 1992. NA = Not available.
*Source: Food and Agricultural Organization of the United Nations*

## Imports of Plywood by Selected Countries In Thousands of Cubic Meters

| Year | Austria | Belgium | Belarus[2] | Canada | Denmark | France | Germany | Italy | Japan | Netherlands | Norway | Sweden | Switzerland | United Kingdom | United States |
|---|---|---|---|---|---|---|---|---|---|---|---|---|---|---|---|
| 1989 | 58 | 325 | 28 | 135 | 173 | 376 | 574 | 188 | 3,098 | 582 | 62 | 143 | 149 | 1,643 | 1,790 |
| 1990 | 61 | 361 | 22 | 231 | 206 | 442 | 706 | 212 | 2,941 | 655 | 68 | 158 | 137 | 1,454 | 1,493 |
| 1991 | 76 | 385 | 14 | 262 | 161 | 414 | 664 | 204 | 3,046 | 619 | 51 | 131 | 121 | 1,271 | 1,338 |
| 1992 | 79 | 300 | 157 | 242 | 198 | 423 | 879 | 216 | 3,003 | 583 | 58 | 106 | 110 | 1,397 | 1,649 |
| 1993 | 77 | 436 | 127 | 288 | 152 | 341 | 865 | 241 | 4,105 | 612 | 57 | 98 | 118 | 1,157 | 1,630 |
| 1994[1] | 104 | NA | NA | 288 | 171 | 304 | 967 | 257 | NA | 560 | 71 | 126 | 144 | 1,202 | 1,547 |

[1] Preliminary. [2] Formerly part of the U.S.S.R.; data not reported separately until 1992. NA = Not available.
*Source: Food and Agricultural Organization of the United Nations*

## Exports of Plywood by Selected Countries In Thousands of Cubic Meters

| Year | Austria | Baltic States[2] | Belgium | Canada | Czech Republic[3] | Finland | France | Germany | Italy | Netherlands | Poland | Russia[2] | Spain | United Kingdom | United States |
|---|---|---|---|---|---|---|---|---|---|---|---|---|---|---|---|
| 1989 | 105 | 419 | 145 | 310 | 55 | 512 | 210 | 83 | 160 | 51 | 30 | ------- | 44 | 26 | 931 |
| 1990 | 128 | 361 | 133 | 391 | 72 | 515 | 210 | 83 | 94 | 50 | 44 | ------- | 41 | 40 | 1,563 |
| 1991 | 130 | 240 | 169 | 288 | 35 | 347 | 222 | 81 | 95 | 63 | 49 | ------- | 39 | 45 | 1,374 |
| 1992 | 119 | 25 | 132 | 412 | 12 | 348 | 228 | 122 | 90 | 72 | 56 | 226 | 32 | 25 | 1,618 |
| 1993 | 129 | 90 | 87 | 416 | 69 | 542 | 252 | 110 | 104 | 99 | 43 | 464 | 60 | 13 | 1,562 |
| 1994[1] | 158 | 133 | NA | 416 | 55 | 627 | 250 | 131 | 108 | 102 | NA | 650 | 67 | 23 | 1,346 |

[1] Preliminary. [2] Formerly part of the U.S.S.R.; data not reported separately until 1992. [3] Formerly part of Czechoslovakia; data not reported separately until 1992. NA = Not available. *Source: Food and Agricultural Organization of the United Nations*

## Selected World Prices of Plywood

| Year | Jan. | Feb. | Mar. | Apr. | May | June | July | Aug. | Sept. | Oct. | Nov. | Dec. | Average |
|---|---|---|---|---|---|---|---|---|---|---|---|---|---|
| Philippines, Lauan, Wholesale Price, Spot Tokyo In U.S. Cents Per Sheet[1] | | | | | | | | | | | | | |
| 1992 | 403.7 | 396.0 | 380.6 | 370.7 | 338.5 | 347.6 | 350.2 | 348.4 | 358.5 | 414.4 | 419.8 | 446.8 | 381.3 |
| 1993 | 512.0 | 611.8 | 700.4 | 708.0 | 712.0 | 715.0 | 696.2 | 703.8 | 664.8 | 617.3 | 644.3 | 630.7 | 659.7 |
| 1994 | 610.4 | 625.0 | 639.4 | 654.9 | 655.7 | 606.8 | 631.9 | 600.4 | 545.6 | 564.3 | 578.3 | 543.5 | 604.7 |
| 1995 | 557.5 | 622.5 | 712.1 | 715.4 | 629.7 | 629.8 | 595.3 | 563.1 | 597.9 | 602.6 | 581.0 | 573.0 | 615.0 |
| 1996 | 596.8 | 607.6 | 615.7 | 627.1 | 633.1 | | | | | | | | 616.1 |
| Canada, Export Unit Value, F.O.B. In Canadian Dollar Per Cubic Meter | | | | | | | | | | | | | |
| 1992 | 426.14 | 409.62 | 373.22 | 396.94 | 387.59 | 395.95 | 354.61 | 373.58 | 385.20 | 395.29 | 410.59 | 353.95 | 388.56 |
| 1993 | 392.59 | 396.65 | 393.73 | 424.19 | 515.51 | 448.76 | 408.39 | 435.72 | 505.58 | 517.58 | 494.52 | 476.08 | 450.78 |
| 1994 | 442.04 | 574.74 | 553.92 | 553.81 | 542.95 | 458.48 | 472.29 | 510.01 | 526.42 | 454.20 | 462.90 | 499.71 | 504.29 |
| 1995 | 473.77 | 480.78 | | | | | | | | | | | 477.28 |
| Finland, Export Unit Value, F.O.B. In Markka Per Cubic Meter | | | | | | | | | | | | | |
| 1992 | 4,548 | 4,501 | 4,523 | 4,425 | 4,488 | 4,474 | 4,532 | 4,399 | 4,807 | 4,465 | 4,662 | 3,999 | 4,485 |
| 1993 | 4,135 | 3,939 | 4,088 | 3,752 | 3,876 | 3,906 | 3,962 | 3,817 | 3,914 | 4,046 | 3,890 | 3,719 | 3,920 |
| 1994 | 3,758 | 3,518 | 3,829 | 3,822 | 3,800 | 4,029 | 3,963 | 3,916 | 4,041 | 3,680 | 3,631 | 3,569 | 3,796 |
| 1995 | 3,681 | 3,809 | 3,751 | 3,897 | 3,752 | 3,769 | 3,771 | 3,543 | 3,430 | | | | 3,711 |
| United Kingdom, Import Unit Value, C.I.F. In Pound Sterling Per Cubic Meter | | | | | | | | | | | | | |
| 1992 | 143.52 | 182.04 | 215.30 | 230.92 | 204.20 | 156.32 | 229.29 | 202.98 | 215.69 | 255.57 | 252.41 | 266.59 | 212.90 |
| 1993 | 227.26 | 255.36 | 269.62 | 204.76 | 270.40 | 249.27 | 265.25 | 273.33 | 291.90 | 261.68 | 328.13 | 304.04 | 266.75 |
| 1994 | 256.36 | 252.50 | 263.47 | 299.61 | 291.19 | 209.08 | 275.85 | 272.06 | 294.44 | 276.46 | 213.94 | 247.54 | 262.71 |
| 1995 | 232.68 | 239.77 | 257.68 | 264.72 | 229.18 | 268.11 | 256.09 | 241.61 | 263.31 | 285.36 | 275.38 | 282.68 | 258.05 |

[1] Sheet measurement = 1.2cm X 90.0cm X 1.8cm. *Source: Food and Agricultural Organization of the United Nations*

# Magnesium

Magnesium alloy finds widespread use in aircraft and automobile parts, photo optical instruments, engines, luggage, pipelines, water heaters, and dry-cell batteries. Because magnesium has a density only two-thirds that of aluminum, it finds applications where weight is a consideration. Among the magnesium compounds, magnesium sulfate is consumed in explosives, fertilizers, and paper production. Magnesium oxide is used in water treatment, household cleaners, and pharmaceuticals. Demand for magnesium is expected to rise further as U.S. automobile manufacturers introduce new magnesium compounds in the 1997 and 1998 models.

The U.S. Geological Survey noted that the largest magnesite production facilities in the world are in China, North Korea, and Russia. Together, these three countries account for 58 percent of the world magnesite production capacity. As part of broader negotiations with North Korea, the U.S. Department of Treasury issued regulations that would allow the importation of North Korean magnesite or magnesia into the U.S. for the first time since the Korean War.

Japan and the U.S. account for 60 percent of the world's magnesium compounds production capacity from seawater or brine. Fused magnesia is produced in a number of countries including the U.S. Norway is the largest producer of olivine, used for foundry and refractory applications.

World production of magnesite in 1995 was 9.2 million tonnes, up from 8.6 million in 1994. The major producers were Turkey, North Korea, Slovakia, and China.

U.S. imports of caustic-calcined magnesia in 1995 were 139,000 tonnes. Major suppliers were China, Canada, and Greece. Imports of dead-burned and fused magnesia in 1995 were 393,000 tonnes with the major supplier being China. Other magnesia imports were 126,000 tonnes supplied primarily by Mexico. U.S. crude magnesite imports in 1995 were 13,600 tonnes with the major suppliers being the Netherlands and Greece.

U.S. imports of magnesium in the January-May 1996 period were 16,700 tonnes. Metal imports were 7,160 tonnes, scrap imports were 1,760 tonnes, alloys were 7,510 tonnes, and sheet, tubing, and others were 297 tonnes. U.S. exports of magnesium in January-May 1996 were 16,700 tonnes. Metal exports were 6,990 tonnes, waste and scrap were 3,310 tonnes, alloys (gross weight) were 2,390 tonnes, and sheet, tubing, and others were 3,970 tonnes.

## World Production of Magnesium (Primary and Secondary) In Metric Tons

| | Primary Production | | | | | | | | | | | Secondary Procuction | | | |
|---|---|---|---|---|---|---|---|---|---|---|---|---|---|---|---|
| Year | Brazil | Canada | China | France | Italy | Japan | Kazakhstan[3] | Norway | Russia[4] | United States | World Total[2] | Japan | United Kingdom | United States | Former USSR |
| 1984[3] | 1,323 | 8,800 | 7,700 | 14,299 | 8,257 | 7,830 | ----- | 54,343 | 94,000 | 159,207 | 360,459 | 17,258 | 1,102 | 48,357 | 9,000 |
| 1985 | 2,615 | 7,200 | 3,000 | 13,639 | 7,863 | 8,456 | ----- | 54,704 | 87,000 | 135,728 | 325,183 | 20,894 | 900 | 41,298 | 8,000 |
| 1986 | 4,356 | 5,100 | 3,000 | 13,361 | 12,417 | 8,116 | ----- | 56,522 | 89,000 | 125,639 | 322,408 | 13,400 | 1,000 | 41,807 | 8,000 |
| 1987 | 5,488 | 8,800 | 3,000 | 13,601 | 7,626 | 8,180 | ----- | 56,907 | 90,000 | 124,396 | 323,930 | 10,124 | 1,000 | 45,165 | 8,000 |
| 1988 | 5,865 | 7,600 | 3,200 | 13,776 | 5,436 | 9,012 | ----- | 50,317 | 91,000 | 141,983 | 334,348 | 15,099 | 1,000 | 50,207 | 8,000 |
| 1989 | 6,200 | 7,000 | 3,500 | 14,600 | 5,768 | 8,381 | ----- | 49,827 | 91,000 | 152,066 | 344,447 | 20,270 | 1,000 | 51,200 | 8,000 |
| 1990 | 8,700 | 25,300 | 5,900 | 14,000 | 5,725 | 12,843 | ----- | 48,222 | 88,000 | 139,333 | 354,000 | 23,308 | 900 | 54,808 | 7,500 |
| 1991 | 7,800 | 35,512 | 8,600 | 14,050 | 3,919 | 11,559 | ----- | 44,322 | 80,000 | 131,288 | 342,000 | 17,158 | 800 | 50,543 | 7,000 |
| 1992 | 7,300 | 25,800 | 10,600 | 13,660 | 1,211 | 7,119 | 3,000 | 30,404 | 40,000 | 136,947 | 295,000 | 12,978 | 800 | 57,045 | 6,500 |
| 1993 | 9,700 | 23,000 | 11,800 | 10,982 | ----- | 7,471 | 2,000 | 27,300 | 30,000 | 132,144 | 269,000 | 13,215 | 1,000 | 58,890 | 6,000 |
| 1994[1] | 9,700 | 28,900 | 24,000 | 12,280 | ----- | 3,412 | ----- | 27,635 | 35,400 | 128,000 | 284,000 | 19,009 | 1,000 | 62,100 | 5,000 |
| 1995[2] | 9,700 | 48,100 | 40,000 | 12,000 | ----- | 4,688 | ----- | 35,000 | 37,500 | 142,000 | 339,000 | 16,760 | 1,000 | 65,000 | 6,000 |

[1] Preliminary. [2] Estimate. [3] Data prior to 1985 reported in short tons. [4] Formerly part of the U.S.S.R.; data not reported separately until 1992.
*Source: U.S. Geological Survey*

## Salient Statistics of Magnesium in the United States In Metric Tons

| | Production | | | | | | | | Domestic Consumption of Primary Magnesium | | | | | |
|---|---|---|---|---|---|---|---|---|---|---|---|---|---|---|
| | | Secondary | | | | | | | Structural Products | | | | | |
| Year | Primary (Ingot) | New Scrap | Old Scrap | Total | Exports[3] | Imports for Consumption | Stocks Dec. 31[4] | $ Price per Pound[5] | Castings | Wrought | Total | Aluminum Alloys | Other Uses[6] | Total |
| 1983 | 115,431 | 21,591 | 24,738 | 46,329 | 46,690 | 6,350 | 28,000 | 1.38 | 3,341 | 11,435 | 14,776 | 46,026 | 21,174 | 81,976 |
| 1984[7] | 159,207 | 21,594 | 26,763 | 48,357 | 48,337 | 9,381 | 35,000 | 1.43-1.48 | 4,193 | 10,246 | 14,439 | 48,673 | 26,775 | 89,887 |
| 1985 | 135,728 | 19,579 | 25,944 | 41,298 | 36,680 | 8,411 | 39,000 | 1.48-1.53 | 4,536 | 10,840 | 15,376 | 31,059 | 31,317 | 83,752 |
| 1986 | 125,639 | 18,813 | 22,994 | 41,807 | 39,909 | 8,355 | 39,000 | 1.53 | 5,767 | 7,737 | 13,504 | 39,290 | 26,167 | 78,961 |
| 1987 | 134,396 | 21,712 | 23,452 | 45,164 | 44,182 | 10,851 | 28,000 | 1.53 | 6,285 | 8,300 | 14,585 | 52,172 | 27,863 | 94,620 |
| 1988 | 141,983 | 22,567 | 27,640 | 50,207 | 49,802 | 14,407 | 25,000 | 1.58-1.63 | 7,069 | 10,138 | 17,207 | 53,671 | 29,915 | 100,793 |
| 1989 | 152,066 | 23,229 | 27,971 | 51,200 | 56,631 | 12,289 | 26,000 | 1.63 | 7,455 | 9,653 | 17,108 | 53,821 | 34,297 | 88,118 |
| 1990 | 139,333 | 23,424 | 31,384 | 54,808 | 51,834 | 26,755 | 26,000 | 1.43-1.63 | 9,078 | 10,944 | 20,022 | 45,060 | 31,026 | 76,086 |
| 1991 | 131,288 | 23,059 | 27,484 | 50,543 | 55,160 | 31,863 | 27,000 | 1.43 | 8,857 | 8,802 | 17,659 | 45,809 | 28,404 | 74,213 |
| 1992 | 136,947 | 26,191 | 30,854 | 57,045 | 51,951 | 11,844 | 13,000 | 1.46-1.53 | 10,223 | 8,843 | 19,066 | 41,003 | 33,758 | 74,761 |
| 1993 | 132,144 | 28,313 | 30,577 | 58,890 | 38,815 | 37,248 | 26,000 | 1.43-1.46 | 12,543 | 9,870 | 22,413 | 46,498 | 32,202 | 78,700 |
| 1994[1] | 128,000 | 32,500 | 29,600 | 62,100 | 45,200 | 29,100 | 20,030 | 1.63 | 15,676 | 7,690 | 23,366 | 61,100 | 27,900 | 89,000 |
| 1995[2] | 142,000 | 35,400 | 29,800 | 65,100 | 38,300 | 34,800 | 21,193 | 1.93-2.25 | 15,231 | 8,520 | 23,751 | 60,200 | 25,100 | 85,300 |

[1] Preliminary. [2] Estimate. [3] Metal & alloys in crude form & scrap. [4] Estimate of Industry Stocks, metal. [5] Magnesium (99.8%), F.O.B. Valasco, Texas. [6] Distributive or sacrificial purposes. [7] Data prior to 1985 reported in short tons. *Source: U.S. Geological Survey*

# Manganese

Manganese finds its primary use in the steel industry where it is employed as an alloy. Virtually all steel contains some manganese, which increases hardness. Manganese is essential to iron and steel production due to its sulfur-fixing, deoxidizing, and alloying properties. No practical approach currently exists for replacing it with other materials or for obtaining the bulk of U.S. requirements from domestic sources. Manganese ore, when converted to a metallic alloy with iron, forms the compound ferromanganese. Nonmetallurgical uses for manganese include plant fertilizer and animal feed. Manganese is the key component of some widely used aluminum alloys and is used in oxide form in dry cell batteries. The use of manganese in batteries has been denoted by the expansion of domestic production of electrolytic manganese dioxide, as well as record imports of manganese dioxide.

World production of manganese ore has been declining for several years. In 1985 it reached 27,948 tonnes but by 1994 it had fallen under 21,000 tonnes. The major producer is China with about a quarter of the world total. Other major producers are South Africa, the Ukraine, Brazil, and Australia.

The U.S. Geological Survey reported that U.S. consumption of manganese ore containing 35 percent or more manganese in July 1996, exclusive of that at iron and steel plants, was 17,900 tonnes, down sharply from the June 1996 total. Over the first seven months of 1996, reported consumption of manganese ore was 231,000 tonnes. Corresponding industry stocks of manganese ore at the end of July 1996 were estimated at 310,000 tonnes, an increase of about 3 percent from the previous month.

U.S. imports for consumption in June 1996 of manganese ore and dioxide were 26,300 tonnes. For the January-June 1996 period, imports were 104,000 tonnes which compares with 78,400 tonnes in the same period of 1995. Imports of manganese ferroalloy and metal in June 1996 were 45,000 tonnes. Imports for the first six months of 1996 were 284,000 tonnes. For the same six month period of 1995 they were 221,000 tonnes. U.S. imports of silicomanganese in June 1996 had a gross weight of 20,100 tonnes, with total manganese content of 13,200 tonnes. The major suppliers were India, Romania, Mexico, Venezuela, and France.

## World Production of Manganese Ore    In Thousands of Metric Tons (Gross Weight)

| Year | Australia[2] 37-53[4] | Brazil 30-50 | Bulgaria 29 | China 30 | Gabon 50-53 | Georgia[5] 29-30 | Ghana 30-50 | Hungary[3] 30-33 | India 10-54 | Iran 25-35 | Mexico 27-50 | Morocco 50-53 | South Africa 30-48 + | Ukraine[5] 29-30 | World Total |
|---|---|---|---|---|---|---|---|---|---|---|---|---|---|---|---|
| 1985 | 2,208 | 2,781 | 42 | 2,900 | 2,579 | ----- | 351 | 69 | 1,367 | 61 | 437 | 48 | 3,969 | 10,900 | 27,948 |
| 1986 | 1,818 | 2,973 | 41 | 3,000 | 2,767 | ----- | 335 | 69 | 1,337 | 37 | 506 | 44 | 4,100 | 10,300 | 27,523 |
| 1987 | 2,043 | 2,279 | 42 | 2,900 | 2,649 | ----- | 303 | 86 | 1,435 | 69 | 425 | 47 | 3,631 | 10,313 | 26,404 |
| 1988[6] | 1,985 | 1,991 | 34 | 3,212 | 2,254 | ----- | 260 | 81 | 1,333 | 75 | 444 | 30 | 4,023 | 9,108 | 25,013 |
| 1989 | 2,124 | 1,904 | 32 | 3,200 | 2,592 | ----- | 297 | 84 | 1,334 | 81 | 394 | 32 | 4,884 | 9,141 | 26,260 |
| 1990 | 1,920 | 2,300 | 39 | 4,080 | 2,423 | ----- | 247 | 60 | 1,385 | 54 | 451 | 49 | 4,402 | 8,500 | 26,108 |
| 1991 | 1,412 | 2,000 | 34 | 5,150 | 1,620 | ----- | 320 | 30 | 1,401 | 48 | 254 | 59 | 3,146 | 7,240 | 22,900 |
| 1992 | 1,251 | 1,993 | 29 | 5,300 | 1,556 | 1,200 | 276 | 18 | 1,810 | 40 | 407 | 44 | 2,464 | 5,819 | 22,500 |
| 1993 | 2,092 | 1,837 | ----- | 5,860 | 1,290 | 1,000 | 295 | 59 | 1,655 | 55 | 363 | 43 | 2,507 | 3,800 | 21,200 |
| 1994 | 1,920 | 2,320 | ----- | 3,570 | 1,440 | 700 | 270 | 55 | 1,630 | 40 | 307 | 31 | 2,851 | 2,980 | 18,500 |
| 1995[1] | 2,176 | 2,320 | ----- | 5,000 | 1,940 | 500 | 176 | ----- | 1,650 | ----- | 472 | ----- | 3,199 | 3,200 | 21,300 |

[1] Preliminary. [2] Metallurgical Ore. [3] Concentrate. [4] Range of percentage of manganese. [5] Formerly part of the U.S.S.R.; data not reported separately until 1992. [6] Data reported in short tons prior to 1988. *Source: U.S. Geological Survey*

## Salient Statistics of Manganese in the United States    In Thousands of Metric Tons (Gross Weight)

| | | Manganese Ore (35% or More Manganese) | | | | Ferromanganese | | | | Silicomanganese | |
|---|---|---|---|---|---|---|---|---|---|---|---|
| Year | Net Import Reliance as a % of Apparent Consumption | Imports for Consumption | Exports | Consumption | Stocks, Dec. 31[3] | Imports for Consumption | Exports | Consumption | Avg. Price Mn. Metallurgical Ore $ Lg. Ton Unit[4] | Exports | Imports |
| 1985 | 61 | 387 | 56 | 545 | 589 | 367 | 7 | 466 | 1.43 | 3.1 | 165.5 |
| 1986 | 84 | 463 | 42 | 500 | 455 | 396 | 4 | 376 | 1.34 | 2.0 | 198.6 |
| 1987 | 52 | 341 | 63 | 533 | 456 | 368 | 3 | 409 | 1.27 | .7 | 191.4 |
| 1988[5] | 80 | 464 | 62 | 503 | 415 | 482 | 3 | 425 | 1.75 | 8.3 | 256.0 |
| 1989 | 94 | 580 | 52 | 559 | 470 | 432 | 8 | 399 | 2.76 | 6.5 | 281.5 |
| 1990 | 48 | 307 | 70 | 497 | 379 | 380 | 7 | 413 | 3.78 | 1.8 | 224.5 |
| 1991 | 36 | 234 | 66 | 473 | 275 | 320 | 15 | 346 | 3.72 | 2.9 | 258.3 |
| 1992 | 53 | 247 | 13 | 438 | 276 | 304 | 13 | 339 | 3.25 | 9.2 | 257.2 |
| 1993 | 56 | 232 | 16 | 389 | 302 | 347 | 18 | 341 | 2.60 | 9.4 | 316.0 |
| 1994[1] | 70 | 331 | 15 | 449 | 269 | 336 | 11 | 347 | 2.40 | 6.8 | 273.0 |
| 1995[2] | 78 | 394 | 15 | 486 | 309 | 310 | 11 | 348 | 2.40 | 7.8 | 305.0 |

[1] Preliminary. [2] Estimate. [3] Including bonded warehouses; excludes Government stocks; also excludes small tonnages of dealers' stocks. [4] 46-48% Mn, C.I.F., U.S. Ports. [5] Data reported in short tons prior to 1988. *Source: U.S. Geological Survey*

# MANGANESE

## U.S. Consumption of Manganese by End Uses    In Thousands of Metric Tons

| Year | Appliances & Equipment | Batteries | Cans & Containers | Chem-icals | Con-struction | Mach-inery | Oil & Gas Industry | Trans-portation | Other | Total |
|---|---|---|---|---|---|---|---|---|---|---|
| 1979 | 59 | 17 | 61 | 59 | 291 | 217 | 70 | 296 | 180 | 1,250 |
| 1980 | 49 | 17 | 49 | 50 | 243 | 167 | 79 | 214 | 161 | 1,029 |
| 1981[3] | 46 | 15 | 42 | 45 | 229 | 155 | 81 | 194 | 125 | 932 |
| 1982 | 27 | 19 | 28 | 26 | 138 | 83 | 36 | 104 | 147 | 610 |
| 1983 | 30 | 23 | 25 | 20 | 137 | 82 | 25 | 117 | 147 | 606 |
| 1984 | 33 | 31 | 34 | 31 | 154 | 88 | 33 | 126 | 39 | 569 |
| 1985 | 29 | 35 | 32 | 20 | 149 | 71 | 31 | 112 | 154 | 633 |
| 1986 | 24 | 39 | 28 | 21 | 134 | 59 | 23 | 86 | 248 | 662 |
| 1987 | 28 | 39 | 32 | 40 | 150 | 70 | 27 | 95 | 153 | 634 |
| 1988 | 17 | 44 | 28 | 42 | 221 | 100 | 19 | 93 | 119 | 682 |
| 1989 | 11 | 41 | 21 | 39 | 138 | 75 | 9 | 49 | 340 | 723 |
| 1990 | 9 | 42 | 22 | 36 | 138 | 74 | 14 | 45 | 250 | 630 |
| 1991[1] | 8 | 52 | 20 | 33 | 122 | 45 | 10 | 47 | 260 | 598 |
| 1992[2] | 8 | 50 | 20 | 34 | 101 | 63 | 10 | 60 | 250 | 596 |

[1] Preliminary. [2] Estimate. [3] Data reported in short tons prior to 1981. *Source: U.S. Geological Survey*

## Manganese Ore (20% or More Mn) Imported[3] into the U.S.    In Metric Tons (Mn Content)

| Year | Australia | Brazil | Gabon | Mexico | Morocco | South Africa | Total | Customs Value Thous. $ |
|---|---|---|---|---|---|---|---|---|
| 1980 | 106,043 | 33,648 | 79,858 | 18,568 | 5,260 | 86,373 | 329,750 | 46,413 |
| 1981 | 34,259 | 38,909 | 90,629 | 25,813 | 13,594 | 97,536 | 300,740 | 42,643 |
| 1982 | 18,842 | 2,962 | 23,156 | 1,492 | 4,996 | 57,873 | 111,054 | 16,160 |
| 1983 | 15,118 | 39,112 | 85,509 | 25,598 | 20 | 12,703 | 178,060 | 19,867 |
| 1984 | 21,005 | 44,259 | 66,135 | 16,298 | 39 | 17,286 | 165,023 | 16,024 |
| 1985 | 43,104 | 59,816 | 64,093 | 21,761 | 65 | ----- | 188,840 | 22,561 |
| 1986 | 35,539 | 38,728 | 119,068 | 14,771 | 186 | 13,988 | 225,608 | 23,122 |
| 1987 | 48,747 | 29,673 | 88,413 | 3,712 | 30 | ----- | 170,576 | 15,079 |
| 1988[4] | 39,324 | 27,004 | 146,654 | 35,490 | 94 | ----- | 248,566 | 29,074 |
| 1989 | 60,436 | 93,283 | 109,637 | 9,828 | 20 | 21,618 | 298,485 | 43,794 |
| 1990 | 35,873 | 22,776 | 74,766 | 3,012 | 20 | 10,977 | 164,180 | 40,054 |
| 1991[5] | 16,485 | 2,583 | 79,997 | 4,673 | 44 | ----- | 117,255 | 40,332 |
| 1992 | 25,519 | 15,541 | 75,354 | 3,930 | 56 | ----- | 120,400 | 29,967 |
| 1993 | 30,171 | 5,573 | 66,659 | 7,317 | 43 | 6,006 | 115,770 | 24,927 |
| 1994[1] | 23,200 | 4,530 | 112,000 | 13,700 | 56 | 7,780 | 161,000 | 29,800 |
| 1995[2] | 31,600 | 7,080 | 104,000 | 23,600 | 37 | 13,100 | 187,000 | 33,300 |

[1] Preliminary. [2] Estimate. [3] Imports for consumption. [4] Manganese content of 35% or more prior to 1989. [5] Data reported in short tons prior to 1991.
*Source: U.S. Geological Survey*

## Average Price of Ferromanganese[1] (High Carbon[2] - F.O.B. Plant)    In Dollars Per Gross Ton -- Carloads

| Year | Jan. | Feb. | Mar. | Apr. | May | June | July | Aug. | Sept. | Oct. | Nov. | Dec. | Average |
|---|---|---|---|---|---|---|---|---|---|---|---|---|---|
| 1978 | 399.50 | 399.50 | 399.50 | 399.50 | 422.17 | 425.00 | 425.00 | 425.00 | 425.00 | 425.00 | 425.00 | 425.00 | 416.26 |
| 1979 | 440.00 | 440.00 | 440.00 | 465.00 | 490.00 | 490.00 | 490.00 | 490.00 | 490.00 | 493.00 | 510.00 | 510.00 | 479.04 |
| 1980 | 510.00 | 510.00 | 510.00 | 510.00 | 510.00 | 510.00 | 510.00 | 510.00 | 510.00 | 510.00 | 510.00 | 510.00 | 510.00 |
| 1981 | 510.00 | 510.00 | 510.00 | 510.00 | 510.00 | 510.00 | 510.00 | 510.00 | 510.00 | 510.00 | 510.00 | 510.00 | 510.00 |
| 1982 | 510.00 | 510.00 | 510.00 | 510.00 | 510.00 | 510.00 | 510.00 | 510.00 | 510.00 | 510.00 | 510.00 | 510.00 | 510.00 |
| 1983 | 510.00 | 510.00 | 510.00 | 510.00 | 510.00 | 510.00 | 510.00 | 510.00 | 510.00 | 510.00 | 510.00 | 510.00 | 510.00 |
| 1984 | 510.00 | 510.00 | 510.00 | 510.00 | 510.00 | 510.00 | 510.00 | 510.00 | 510.00 | NQ | NQ | NQ | 510.00 |
| 1985 | NQ | NQ | NQ | NQ | NQ | NQ | NQ | NQ | NQ | NQ | NQ | NQ | NQ |
| 1986 | NQ | NQ | NQ | NQ | NQ | NQ | NQ | NQ | NQ | NQ | NQ | NQ | NQ |
| 1987 | NQ | NQ | NQ | NQ | 326.25 | 331.88 | 339.50 | 345.00 | 355.00 | 358.00 | 363.00 | 373.00 | 348.95 |
| 1988 | 382.50 | 382.50 | 414.50 | 422.50 | 435.63 | 440.00 | 457.50 | 475.00 | 530.00 | 550.00 | 550.00 | 550.00 | 465.84 |
| 1989 | 550.00 | 550.50 | 573.75 | 597.50 | 640.00 | 640.00 | 640.00 | 634.00 | 610.00 | 610.00 | 610.00 | 610.00 | 605.48 |
| 1990 | 610.00 | 610.00 | 610.00 | 610.00 | 610.00 | 610.00 | 610.00 | 610.00 | 610.00 | 610.00 | 610.00 | 610.00 | 610.00 |
| 1991 | 610.00 | 610.00 | 610.00 | 610.00 | 610.00 | 610.00 | 610.00 | 610.00 | 610.00 | 610.00 | 610.00 | 610.00 | 610.00 |
| 1992 | 610.00 | 610.00 | 610.00 | 610.00 | 610.00 | 610.00 | 610.00 | 610.00 | 610.00 | 610.00 | 610.00 | 610.00 | 610.00 |
| 1993 | 610.00 | 610.00 | 610.00 | 610.00 | 610.00 | 610.00 | 610.00 | 610.00 | 610.00 | 610.00 | 610.00 | 610.00 | 610.00 |
| 1994 | 610.00 | 610.00 | 610.00 | 610.00 | 610.00 | 527.50 | 500.00 | 500.00 | 500.00 | 500.00 | 500.00 | 500.00 | 548.13 |
| 1995 | 500.00 | 500.00 | 500.00 | 500.00 | 500.00 | 500.00 | 500.00 | 518.75 | 525.00 | 525.00 | 542.50 | 560.00 | 514.27 |

[1] Domestic standard. [2] Prior to May 1987, prices are for 78% Mn-F.O.B. plant. NQ = No quote. *Source: American Metal Market*

# Meats

U.S. commercial red meat production–the combined total of beef, veal, lamb, and pork output–dipped in 1996 to 43.3 billion pounds vs. the 1995 record high 43.6 billion pounds. Forecasts for 1997 put total production at a record large 43.9 billion pounds. Red meat accounts for about 60 percent of total U.S. meat production and poultry the balance. Beef accounted for 25.6 billion pounds of the 1996 total vs. 25.1 billion in 1995. Pork took most of the balance with 17.1 billion pounds and 17.8 billion, respectively. Worldwide, China is the largest red meat producer with a record large 43 million metric tons in 1996, about one-third of the world total with the U.S. second at 19.8 million tons. For 1997, world production is forecast at 128.5 million tons with China at 43.1 million. Annual production in the former USSR continues to slide, from 9.5 million tons in 1993 to 7 million in 1996 and down to 6.5 million in 1997.

U.S. per capita beef usage (carcass weight) in both 1996 and 1995 of 97.0 pounds compares with 96.4 pounds in 1994. During the 1980's per capita use averaged about 105 pounds. Pork use has slipped, which is surprising considering the aggressive advertising campaign by the pork industry associating pork as a white meat: per capita use in 1996 of 62.9 pounds compares with 67.6 pounds in 1995 and 68.4 in 1994. On a retail weight basis, per capita beef use runs about 30 pounds lower and pork about 14 pounds. For both meats consumer preferences continue to favor foods containing less fat; the impact favoring poultry at red meat's expense.

Choice steers (basis Nebraska) averaged $63-64/cwt. in 1996 vs. $66.26 in 1995; forecasts for 1997 range from $62-68.00. Midwest barrow prices of $53.45/cwt. compare with $42.35/cwt. in 1995 and estimates for 1997 have a $51-55.00 range.

U.S. red meat imports in 1996 of 1.2 million metric tons (carcass weight) compare with 1.3 million in 1995 and forecasts of 1.2 million in 1997; beef imports account for about 75 percent of the totals. U.S. exports, again mostly beef, totaled 1.3 million tons in 1996 vs. 1.2 million in 1995 and a 1997 estimate of 1.5 million. Japan is the world's largest red meat importer with almost 1.8 million tons in 1996. The world's largest exporter (mostly beef) is Australia with about 1.1 million tons annually during the 1990's. The U.S. imports live cattle from Canada and Mexico while beef and veal are mostly imported from Australia and New Zealand. U.S. pork imports have been stagnant in recent years, but exports have doubled of late–to 430,000 tons in 1996 from less than 200,000 in the early 1990's.

## World Total Meat Production[4] In Thousands of Metric Tons

| Year | Agrentina | Australia | Brazil | Canada | China[5] | Denmark | France | Germany | Italy | Japan | Mexico | New Zealand | Poland | Russia[6] | Ukraine[6] | United Kingdom | United States |
|---|---|---|---|---|---|---|---|---|---|---|---|---|---|---|---|---|---|
| 1988 | 2,697 | 2,377 | 3,600 | 2,161 | 21,870 | 1,386 | 3,532 | 4,477 | 2,378 | 2,147 | 2,791 | 1,811 | 2,635 | ------ | 15,893 | 2,314 | 18,146 |
| 1989 | 2,696 | 2,452 | 4,750 | 2,164 | 23,262 | 1,372 | 3,670 | 6,006 | 2,515 | 2,142 | 3,125 | 1,168 | 2,621 | ------ | 16,501 | 2,326 | 17,963 |
| 1990 | 2,738 | 2,683 | 4,650 | 2,022 | 25,132 | 1,100 | 3,816 | 6,111 | 2,583 | 2,104 | 2,658 | 1,014 | 2,736 | 8,204 | 3,608 | 2,331 | 17,597 |
| 1991 | 2,735 | 2,704 | 5,513 | 2,022 | 27,238 | 1,485 | 3,963 | 5,552 | 2,608 | 2,057 | 2,535 | 1,053 | 2,768 | 7,526 | 3,339 | 2,389 | 17,956 |
| 1992 | 2,602 | 2,810 | 5,620 | 2,107 | 29,406 | 1,600 | 3,997 | 4,994 | 2,648 | 2,024 | 2,626 | 1,036 | 2,708 | 6,748 | 2,874 | 2,297 | 18,589 |
| 1993 | 2,630 | 2,780 | 5,795 | 2,052 | 32,254 | 1,727 | 3,901 | 4,796 | 2,642 | 2,026 | 2,718 | 1,095 | 2,022 | 6,260 | 2,419 | 2,236 | 18,488 |
| 1994 | 2,682 | 2,763 | 5,775 | 2,137 | 36,957 | 1,729 | 3,872 | 4,518 | 2,618 | 1,992 | 2,852 | 1,085 | 1,799 | 5,670 | 2,371 | 2,323 | 19,361 |
| 1995 | 2,630 | 2,612 | 6,050 | 2,215 | 43,500 | 1,707 | 3,959 | 4,464 | 2,596 | 1,951 | 2,948 | 1,100 | 1,937 | 4,950 | 2,213 | 2,346 | 19,778 |
| 1996[1] | 2,606 | 2,692 | 6,480 | 2,270 | 43,000 | 1,716 | 3,950 | 4,501 | 2,433 | 1,845 | 2,827 | 1,120 | 1,932 | 4,600 | 1,812 | 2,084 | 19,739 |
| 1997[2] | 2,555 | 2,813 | 6,730 | 2,395 | 43,100 | 1,744 | 4,002 | 4,423 | 2,540 | 1,800 | 2,829 | 1,050 | 1,819 | 4,260 | 1,745 | 2,131 | 20,104 |

[1] Preliminary. [2] Estimate. [3] Forecast. [4] Includes beef, veal, pork, sheep and goat meat. [5] Predominately pork production. [6] Formerly part of the U.S.S.R.; data not reported separately until 1990. *Source: Foreign Agricultural Service, U.S. Department of Agriculture*

## Production and Consumption of Red Meats in the United States (Carcass Weight)

| | Beef | | | Veal | | | Lamb & Mutton | | | Pork (Excluding Lard) | | | All Meats | | |
|---|---|---|---|---|---|---|---|---|---|---|---|---|---|---|---|
| | Commercial Production | Consumption | | Commercial Production | Consumption | | Commercial Production | Consumption | | Commercial Production | Consumption | | Commercial Production | Consumption | |
| Year | -- Million Pounds -- | Total | Per Capita Lb.[4] | - Million Pounds - | Total | Per Capita Lb.[4] | - Million Pounds - | Total | Per Capita Lb.[4] | -- Million Pounds -- | Total | Per Capita Lb.[4] | -- Million Pounds -- | Total | Per Capita Lb.[4] |
| 1986 | 24,213 | 25,257 | 108.0 | 524 | 509 | 2.3 | 331 | 378 | 1.6 | 13,998 | 15,135 | 62.9 | 39,051 | 42,051 | 174.7 |
| 1987 | 23,405 | 25,252 | 104.0 | 430 | 417 | 1.9 | 309 | 362 | 1.5 | 14,311 | 15,352 | 63.2 | 38,442 | 41,422 | 170.6 |
| 1988 | 23,424 | 24,330 | 103.1 | 396 | 387 | 1.7 | 329 | 387 | 1.6 | 15,623 | 16,549 | 67.5 | 39,763 | 42,599 | 173.9 |
| 1989 | 22,974 | 24,030 | 98.4 | 355 | 344 | 1.4 | 341 | 386 | 1.6 | 15,759 | 16,571 | 67.0 | 39,418 | 41,644 | 168.4 |
| 1990 | 22,634 | 24,114 | 96.2 | 327 | 316 | 1.3 | 358 | 397 | 1.6 | 15,300 | 16,030 | 64.1 | 38,608 | 40,782 | 163.2 |
| 1991 | 22,800 | 24,261 | 95.4 | 306 | 296 | 1.2 | 358 | 397 | 1.6 | 15,948 | 16,399 | 64.9 | 39,402 | 41,214 | 163.1 |
| 1992 | 22,968 | 24,261 | 95.0 | 310 | 299 | 1.2 | 343 | 388 | 1.5 | 17,185 | 17,475 | 68.4 | 40,795 | 42,437 | 166.1 |
| 1993 | 22,942 | 24,006 | 93.0 | 267 | 286 | 1.1 | 329 | 381 | 1.5 | 17,030 | 17,419 | 67.5 | 40,568 | 42,092 | 163.1 |
| 1994 | 24,278 | 25,124 | 96.4 | 283 | 290 | 1.2 | 304 | 345 | 1.3 | 17,658 | 17,829 | 68.4 | 42,523 | 43,588 | 167.3 |
| 1995[1] | 25,115 | 25,534 | 97.0 | 308 | 319 | 1.2 | 283 | 348 | 1.3 | 17,811 | 17,785 | 67.6 | 43,517 | 43,986 | 167.1 |
| 1996[2] | 25,585 | 25,949 | 97.7 | 363 | 375 | 1.4 | 263 | 330 | 1.2 | 17,157 | 16,876 | 63.5 | 43,368 | 43,530 | 163.8 |
| 1997[3] | 26,100 | 26,032 | 97.2 | 307 | 318 | 1.2 | 254 | 314 | 1.2 | 17,500 | 17,099 | 63.8 | 44,161 | 43,763 | 163.4 |

[1] Preliminary. [2] Estimate. [3] Forecast. [4] Carcass Weight. *Source: Economic Research Service, U.S. Department of Agriculture*

## Total Red Meat Imports (Carcass Weight Equivalent) of Principal Countries — In Thousands of Metric Tons

| Year | Belgium & Lux. | Canada | Czecho-slovakia | France | Ger-many | Greece | Hong Kong | Italy | Japan | Rep. of Korea | Nether-lands | Russia[3] | Singa-pore | Spain | Switzer-land | United Kingdom | United States |
|---|---|---|---|---|---|---|---|---|---|---|---|---|---|---|---|---|---|
| 1983 | 107 | 121 | 25 | 676 | 728 | 216 | 82 | 832 | 599 | 78 | 108 | 779 | 24 | 26 | 27 | 1,072 | 1,212 |
| 1984 | 79 | 130 | 15 | 711 | 796 | 194 | 238 | 823 | 636 | 39 | 105 | 691 | 22 | 36 | 21 | 1,015 | 1,280 |
| 1985 | 79 | 132 | 15 | 760 | 843 | 208 | 296 | 948 | 647 | 19 | 116 | 587 | 0 | 36 | 15 | 955 | 1,476 |
| 1986 | 77 | 130 | 15 | 841 | 837 | 221 | 300 | 961 | 712 | 14 | 104 | 537 | 38 | 92 | 16 | 1,007 | 1,506 |
| 1987 | 78 | 157 | 15 | 829 | 880 | 246 | 281 | 952 | 869 | 16 | 109 | 495 | 42 | 90 | 20 | 1,036 | 1,602 |
| 1988 | 76 | 170 | 15 | 869 | 940 | 232 | 313 | 906 | 994 | 45 | 132 | 353 | 40 | 93 | 18 | 1,081 | 1,630 |
| 1989 | 81 | 175 | 25 | 908 | 952 | 239 | 292 | 974 | 1,150 | 111 | 119 | 355 | 47 | 127 | 14 | 1,033 | 1,421 |
| 1990 | 110 | 198 | 15 | 967 | 1,033 | 209 | 311 | 1,025 | 1,153 | 120 | 143 | 545 | 43 | 971 | 17 | 76 | 1,503 |
| 1991 | 71 | 232 | 0 | 1,035 | 1,240 | 179 | 306 | 1,106 | 1,206 | 201 | 181 | 740 | 41 | 140 | 13 | 896 | 1,463 |
| 1992 | 100 | 237 | 108 | 1,027 | 1,338 | 248 | 265 | 1,231 | 1,388 | 187 | 208 | 292 | 54 | 147 | 14 | 885 | 1,424 |
| 1993 | 126 | 292 | 44 | 1,010 | 1,319 | 236 | 280 | 1,139 | 1,480 | 134 | 207 | 227 | 56 | 150 | 16 | 889 | 1,449 |
| 1994 | 29 | 313 | 25 | 1,044 | 1,447 | 232 | 298 | 1,103 | 1,628 | 191 | 238 | 865 | 50 | 28 | 19 | 785 | 1,434 |
| 1995 | 2 | 283 | 28 | 40 | 149 | 14 | 223 | 37 | 1,840 | 247 | 25 | 1,084 | 52 | 28 | 10 | 285 | 1,284 |
| 1996[1] | 1 | 285 | 25 | 63 | 137 | 14 | 247 | 33 | 1,854 | 263 | 25 | 1,164 | 48 | 32 | 11 | 295 | 1,247 |
| 1997[2] | 1 | 250 | 24 | 51 | 148 | 14 | 269 | 40 | 1,917 | 315 | 25 | 1,225 | 48 | 26 | 11 | 285 | 1,217 |

[1] Preliminary. [2] Forecast. [3] Formerly part of the U.S.S.R.; data not reported separately until 1992. *Source: Foreign Agricultural Service, U.S. Department of Agriculture*

## Total Red Meat Exports (Carcass Weight Equivalent) of Principal Countries — In Thousands of Metric Tons

| Year | Agren-tina | Aust-ralia | Brazil | Canada | China | Den-mark | France | India | Ireland | Nether-lands | New Zealand | Poland | Romania | Ukraine[3] | United Kingdom | United States | Uruguay |
|---|---|---|---|---|---|---|---|---|---|---|---|---|---|---|---|---|---|
| 1982 | 546 | 1,184 | 361 | 247 | 230 | 909 | 401 | 62 | 311 | 879 | 846 | 52 | 160 | 32 | 194 | 213 | 182 |
| 1983 | 438 | 947 | 404 | 242 | 264 | 945 | 387 | 83 | 341 | 957 | 938 | 93 | 185 | 25 | 296 | 225 | 236 |
| 1984 | 266 | 747 | 483 | 280 | 273 | 952 | 489 | 88 | 301 | 1,066 | 815 | 68 | 177 | 27 | 344 | 227 | 142 |
| 1985 | 272 | 860 | 540 | 313 | 278 | 958 | 503 | 65 | 370 | 1,158 | 876 | 13 | 265 | 30 | 284 | 210 | 131 |
| 1986 | 261 | 1,031 | 355 | 376 | 222 | 1,007 | 649 | 64 | 473 | 1,216 | 863 | 122 | 280 | 353 | 306 | 279 | 198 |
| 1987 | 294 | 1,122 | 304 | 394 | 238 | 986 | 604 | 79 | 496 | 1,265 | 922 | 128 | 310 | 1,157 | 313 | 327 | 104 |
| 1988 | 464 | 1,102 | 567 | 405 | 227 | 1,005 | 630 | 69 | 431 | 1,309 | 901 | 131 | 305 | 747 | 270 | 402 | 142 |
| 1989 | 369 | 1,069 | 304 | 407 | 261 | 990 | 586 | 70 | 478 | 1,357 | 908 | 140 | 320 | 704 | 301 | 606 | 177 |
| 1990 | 461 | 1,312 | 243 | 424 | 395 | 995 | 644 | 133 | 469 | 1,395 | 794 | 107 | 25 | 545 | 188 | 565 | 192 |
| 1991 | 402 | 1,391 | 290 | 375 | 494 | 1,097 | 757 | 151 | 529 | 1,438 | 845 | 31 | 31 | 740 | 299 | 669 | 117 |
| 1992 | 288 | 1,496 | 390 | 453 | 195 | 1,173 | 864 | 91 | 643 | 1,485 | 884 | 34 | 40 | 291 | 348 | 787 | 125 |
| 1993 | 283 | 1,469 | 425 | 494 | 315 | 1,272 | 917 | 120 | 672 | 1,470 | 858 | 27 | 64 | 256 | 421 | 779 | 105 |
| 1994 | 378 | 1,473 | 383 | 518 | 295 | 1,394 | 1,054 | 110 | 613 | 1,499 | 896 | 41 | 60 | 167 | 513 | 976 | 152 |
| 1995 | 463 | 1,329 | 315 | 520 | 310 | 1,313 | 999 | 129 | 372 | 1,425 | 923 | 39 | 47 | 167 | 430 | 1,211 | 150 |
| 1996[1] | 451 | 1,382 | 380 | 600 | 356 | 410 | 141 | 147 | 203 | 90 | 905 | 83 | 46 | 170 | 33 | 1,327 | 170 |

Preliminary. [2] Estimate. [3] Formerly part of the U.S.S.R.; data not reported separately until 1992. *Source: Foreign Agricultural Service, U.S. Department of Agriculture*

## U.S. Exports and Imports of Meats into the United States (Carcass Weight Equivalent)[3]

| | Exports | | | | Imports | | | |
|---|---|---|---|---|---|---|---|---|
| Year | Beef and Veal | Lamb and Mutton | Pork[4] | All Meat | Beef and Veal | Lamb and Mutton | Pork[4] | All Meat |
| | In Millions of Pounds | | | | | | | |
| 1981 | 221 | 2 | 307 | 531 | 1,761 | 31 | 541 | 2,333 |
| 1982 | 254 | 2 | 214 | 470 | 1,958 | 21 | 612 | 2,591 |
| 1983 | 276 | 1 | 219 | 497 | 1,974 | 18 | 707 | 2,717 |
| 1984 | 335 | 2 | 164 | 500 | 1,847 | 20 | 954 | 2,821 |
| 1985 | 332 | 1 | 128 | 461 | 2,091 | 36 | 1,128 | 3,255 |
| 1986 | 526 | 1 | 86 | 613 | 2,156 | 41 | 1,122 | 3,319 |
| 1987 | 611 | 1 | 109 | 722 | 2,293 | 44 | 1,195 | 3,533 |
| 1988 | 690 | 1 | 195 | 887 | 2,406 | 51 | 1,137 | 3,594 |
| 1989 | 1,023 | 5 | 262 | 1,290 | 2,178 | 46 | 896 | 3,120 |
| 1990 | 1,006 | 6 | 238 | 1,250 | 2,356 | 41 | 898 | 3,295 |
| 1991 | 1,188 | 10 | 283 | 1,481 | 1,406 | 41 | 775 | 3,223 |
| 1992 | 1,324 | 8 | 407 | 1,739 | 2,440 | 50 | 645 | 3,135 |
| 1993 | 1,275 | 8 | 435 | 1,718 | 2,401 | 53 | 740 | 3,194 |
| 1994 | 1,611 | 9 | 532 | 2,152 | 2,368 | 49 | 744 | 3,162 |
| 1995[1] | 1,821 | 7 | 771 | 2,599 | 2,103 | 64 | 664 | 2,831 |
| 1996[2] | 1,878 | 8 | 952 | 2,838 | 2,072 | 72 | 619 | 2,764 |

[1] Preliminary. [2] Estimate. [3] Includes meat content of minor meats and of mixed products. *Source: Economic Research Service, U.S. Department of Agriculture*

## United States Meat Imports by Type of Product In Metric Tons

| Year | Beaf and Veal: Fresh, Chilled & Frozen | Beaf and Veal: Canned, including Sausage | Beaf and Veal: Other Prepared or Preserved | Lamb Mutton and Goat, Except Canned | Pork: Fresh and Frozen | Pork: Canned[2] | Pork: Other Prepared or Preserved | Pork: Sausage, all Types | Mixed Sausage | Other Meats[3] | Variety Meats, Fresh or Frozen | Total |
|---|---|---|---|---|---|---|---|---|---|---|---|---|
| 1984 | 516,960 | 57,863 | 19,864 | 8,693 | 207,703 | 142,423 | 3,372 | 2,243 | 2,121 | 5,088 | 5,707 | 972,037 |
| 1985 | 594,476 | 64,277 | 19,314 | 15,565 | 254,538 | 160,802 | 6,312 | 2,192 | 2,672 | 5,305 | 5,622 | 1,130,075 |
| 1986 | 637,718 | 45,779 | 20,778 | 16,596 | 263,488 | 151,730 | 8,221 | 2,640 | 2,849 | 4,621 | 6,475 | 1,160,895 |
| 1987 | 671,152 | 56,653 | 17,450 | 17,204 | 302,392 | 145,464 | 9,387 | 2,688 | 4,222 | 4,126 | 9,590 | 1,240,328 |
| 1988 | 703,415 | 66,919 | 10,367 | 19,239 | 282,728 | 139,847 | 10,214 | 2,906 | 2,732 | 3,977 | 8,905 | 1,251,249 |
| 1989 | 638,999 | 68,710 | 1,434 | 20,917 | 225,304 | 107,267 | 8,651 | 2,656 | 2,620 | 3,509 | 11,102 | 1,091,169 |
| 1990 | 694,163 | 67,054 | 1,520 | 19,056 | 232,253 | 98,479 | 10,055 | 3,421 | 1,874 | 1,239 | 11,423 | 1,140,537 |
| 1991 | 709,997 | 71,570 | 1,870 | 19,100 | 215,933 | 72,666 | 11,760 | 2,144 | 1,533 | 3,904 | 18,266 | 1,128,744 |
| 1992 | 728,922 | 72,631 | 2,112 | 23,853 | 185,672 | 54,114 | 13,104 | 2,453 | 1,674 | 1,607 | 20,059 | 1,106,201 |
| 1993 | 720,079 | 71,351 | 2,995 | 24,468 | 207,652 | 70,577 | 14,295 | 2,695 | 1,368 | 2,274 | 25,298 | 1,143,052 |
| 1994 | 714,448 | 72,235 | 2,675 | 23,277 | 209,026 | 79,307 | 13,713 | 2,237 | 1,900 | 2,119 | 27,407 | 1,148,270 |
| 1995[1] | 641,919 | 62,938 | 2,602 | 29,844 | 194,386 | 77,475 | 12,105 | 2,553 | 1,935 | 2,449 | 36,446 | 1,018,319 |
| 1996[1] | 587,844 | 59,124 | 3,141 | 30,253 | 167,022 | 65,072 | 10,771 | 2,172 | 1,596 | 3,612 | 38,576 | 922,951 |

[1] Preliminary. [2] Includes canned hams, shoulders and bacon. [3] Mostly mixed lucheon meats. *Scurce: Foreign Agricultural Service, U.S. Department of Agriculture*

## United States Meat Exports by Type of Product In Metric Tons

| Year | Beef and Veal: Fresh, Chilled & Frozen | Beef and Veal: Prepared and Preserved | Lamb and Mutton, Fresh or Frozen | Pork: Fresh, Chilled & Frozen | Pork: Hams & Shoulders, Cured | Pork: Bacon | Pork: Other Pork Prepared or Preserved: Not Canned | Pork: Other Pork Prepared or Preserved: Canned | Sausage, Bologna & Frankfurters | Variety Meats, Fresh, Chilled & Frozen | Other Meats[2] | Total |
|---|---|---|---|---|---|---|---|---|---|---|---|---|
| 1984 | 99,208 | 12,322 | 878 | 46,098 | 1,474 | 621 | 3,837 | 513 | 2,603 | 213,180 | 35,457 | 416,191 |
| 1985 | 99,923 | 9,605 | 460 | 34,394 | 1,175 | 450 | 4,066 | 638 | 2,908 | 239,451 | 38,395 | 431,465 |
| 1986 | 173,884 | 10,519 | 558 | 20,969 | 650 | 474 | 4,796 | 349 | 3,214 | 241,051 | 46,760 | 503,224 |
| 1987 | 200,180 | 10,789 | 668 | 29,145 | 1,227 | 617 | 3,597 | 376 | 4,582 | 222,342 | 61,812 | 535,335 |
| 1988 | 214,530 | 14,083 | 619 | 54,598 | 2,138 | 1,045 | 4,924 | 268 | 8,439 | 302,087 | 75,084 | 677,815 |
| 1989 | 373,110 | 8,810 | 2,076 | 79,318 | 6,101 | 3,788 | 2,204 | 1,395 | 11,968 | 245,235 | 78,550 | 812,555 |
| 1990 | 339,925 | 7,783 | 2,490 | 66,756 | 5,567 | 4,518 | 4,310 | 1,036 | 14,208 | 226,623 | 70,558 | 731,566 |
| 1991 | 395,697 | 10,248 | 3,790 | 76,193 | 4,702 | 5,443 | 6,133 | 1,278 | 24,025 | 280,721 | 61,440 | 869,670 |
| 1992 | 436,455 | 12,064 | 3,278 | 116,496 | 8,181 | 7,396 | 5,812 | 2,352 | 22,796 | 303,295 | 57,154 | 975,279 |
| 1993 | 411,003 | 14,464 | 3,608 | 129,240 | 5,208 | 7,092 | 4,579 | 2,349 | 34,198 | 338,689 | 45,905 | 996,335 |
| 1994 | 517,481 | 13,539 | 3,763 | 149,311 | 8,479 | 12,062 | 4,455 | 2,973 | 46,926 | 371,816 | 70,642 | 1,201,447 |
| 1995[1] | 581,731 | 13,653 | 2,509 | 228,164 | 12,074 | 13,830 | 6,263 | 3,564 | 56,829 | 449,599 | 93,455 | 1,461,671 |
| 1996[1] | 542,521 | 13,419 | 2,194 | 245,369 | 8,419 | 15,004 | 6,648 | 5,046 | 83,301 | 431,356 | 246,655 | 1,599,932 |

[1] Preliminary. [2] Includes sausage ingredients, cured (excluding canned); meat and meat products canned; and baby food, canned.
*Source: Foreign Agricultural Service, U.S. Department of Agriculture*

## Average Wholesale Prices of Meats In Cents Per Pound

| Year | Composite Retail Price of Beef, Choice, Grade 3 | Composite Retail Price of Pork[3] | Wholesale Value[4]: Beef | Wholesale Value[4]: Pork | Net Farm Value of Pork[5] | Cow Beef Canner & Cutter, Central US | Boxed Beef Cut-out, Choice 1-3, Central US, 550-700 lbs. | Pork Carcass Cut-out, U.S., No. 2 | Lamb Carcass, Choice-Prime, East Coast, 55-65 lbs. | Pork[6] Loins, Central US, 14-18 lbs. | Skinned Ham, Central US, 20-26 lbs.[7] | Pork Bellies, Central US, 12-14 lbs. |
|---|---|---|---|---|---|---|---|---|---|---|---|---|
| 1983 | 234.10 | 169.80 | 160.10 | 108.90 | 76.50 | 78.48 | 101.96 | 59.91 | 125.86 | 97.30 | 73.99 | 61.69 |
| 1984 | 235.50 | 162.00 | 162.50 | 110.10 | 77.40 | 74.70 | 103.80 | 61.35 | 130.99 | 96.36 | 75.41 | 60.31 |
| 1985 | 228.60 | 162.00 | 148.80 | 101.10 | 71.50 | 74.13 | 97.95 | 50.38 | 140.23 | 91.51 | 67.27 | 59.51 |
| 1986 | 226.80 | 178.40 | 146.50 | 110.90 | 80.60 | 71.31 | 94.61 | 69.05 | 140.32 | 104.78 | 77.96 | 65.82 |
| 1987 | 238.40 | 188.40 | 160.00 | 113.00 | 82.70 | 85.26 | 103.85 | 69.40 | 150.41 | 106.23 | 79.29 | 63.11 |
| 1988 | 250.30 | 183.40 | 169.40 | 101.00 | 69.40 | 87.77 | 110.35 | 59.57 | 137.81 | 97.49 | 69.05 | 41.25 |
| 1989 | 265.70 | 182.90 | 176.80 | 99.20 | 70.40 | 94.43 | 114.78 | 60.62 | 131.35 | 101.11 | 69.25 | 34.14 |
| 1990 | 281.00 | 212.60 | 189.60 | 118.30 | 87.20 | 102.41 | 123.21 | 74.00 | 121.47 | 117.52 | 84.87 | 53.80 |
| 1991 | 288.30 | 211.90 | 182.50 | 108.90 | 78.40 | 99.42 | 118.31 | 67.02 | 117.33 | 108.39 | 75.68 | 47.79 |
| 1992 | 284.60 | 198.00 | 179.60 | 98.90 | 67.80 | 93.85 | 116.73 | 58.37 | 131.66 | 101.41 | 67.42 | 30.39 |
| 1993 | 293.40 | 197.60 | 182.50 | 102.90 | 72.50 | 95.43 | 118.74 | 62.19 | 143.97 | 107.47 | 67.85 | 41.62 |
| 1994 | 282.90 | 198.10 | 166.80 | 98.90 | 62.90 | 84.39 | 108.47 | 57.29 | 147.62 | 101.50 | 58.12 | 40.00 |
| 1995[1] | 284.49 | 195.10 | 163.90 | | | 68.22 | 106.18 | 60.54 | 165.36 | 108.72 | 56.82 | 43.68 |

[1] Preliminary. [2] Estimate. [3] Sold as retail cuts (ham, bacon, loin, etc.). [4] Quantity equivalent to 1 pound of retail cuts. [5] Portion of gross farm value minus farm by-product allowance. [6] Prior to 1983, 8-14 pounds. [7] Prior to 1995, 17-20 pounds.
*Source: Economic Research Service, U.S. Department of Agriculture*

## Average Wholesale Price of Boxed Beef Cut-Out[1], Choice, at Central Markets In Cents Per Pound

| Year | Jan. | Feb. | Mar. | Apr. | May | June | July | Aug. | Sept. | Oct. | Nov. | Dec. | Average |
|---|---|---|---|---|---|---|---|---|---|---|---|---|---|
| 1986 | 96.70 | 91.22 | 89.02 | 88.17 | 90.56 | 90.37 | 96.05 | 98.40 | 98.48 | 98.00 | 101.41 | 96.95 | 94.61 |
| 1987 | 96.71 | 98.56 | 98.40 | 106.45 | 114.03 | 113.18 | 104.55 | 101.52 | 104.33 | 103.97 | 102.62 | 101.82 | 103.85 |
| 1988 | 102.55 | 105.94 | 108.50 | 110.79 | 116.73 | 111.96 | 107.09 | 110.37 | 112.72 | 112.74 | 112.37 | 112.45 | 110.35 |
| 1989 | 113.62 | 114.30 | 117.09 | 118.58 | 118.53 | 114.53 | 113.17 | 112.83 | 110.08 | 110.04 | 115.06 | 119.52 | 114.78 |
| 1990 | 121.75 | 120.97 | 122.10 | 123.62 | 124.56 | 121.53 | 118.54 | 121.52 | 121.18 | 124.96 | 128.32 | 129.48 | 123.21 |
| 1991 | 125.04 | 123.24 | 125.45 | 125.96 | 123.76 | 120.61 | 115.82 | 111.54 | 110.61 | 113.04 | 113.43 | 111.18 | 118.31 |
| 1992 | 114.38 | 119.65 | 119.14 | 118.66 | 119.18 | 117.53 | 112.79 | 114.36 | 114.40 | 115.51 | 115.26 | 119.95 | 116.73 |
| 1993 | 122.69 | 122.13 | 124.80 | 126.12 | 127.19 | 120.52 | 114.48 | 116.73 | 114.65 | 111.52 | 113.26 | 110.83 | 118.74 |
| 1994 | 112.11 | 112.23 | 115.03 | 114.98 | 108.85 | 102.92 | 104.19 | 108.38 | 105.49 | 103.63 | 106.66 | 107.22 | 108.47 |
| 1995 | 112.17 | 111.12 | 107.87 | 103.03 | 104.21 | 107.65 | 103.03 | 102.55 | 105.82 | 107.77 | 108.88 | 106.08 | 106.68 |
| 1996[2] | 101.71 | 98.86 | 96.36 | 96.01 | 96.90 | 100.70 | 101.53 | 104.43 | 105.93 | 109.10 | 117.53 | 108.03 | 103.09 |

[1] Choice 1-3, 550-700 pounds. [2] Preliminary. *Source: Economic Research Service, U.S. Department of Agriculture*

## Production (Commercial) of All Red Meats in the U.S. In Millions of Pounds (Carcass Weight)

| Year | Jan. | Feb. | Mar. | Apr. | May | June | July | Aug. | Sept. | Oct. | Nov. | Dec. | Total |
|---|---|---|---|---|---|---|---|---|---|---|---|---|---|
| 1986 | 3,483 | 2,942 | 3,133 | 3,476 | 3,388 | 3,157 | 3,281 | 3,179 | 3,260 | 3,505 | 2,986 | 3,261 | 39,051 |
| 1987 | 3,410 | 2,875 | 3,198 | 3,161 | 2,976 | 3,103 | 3,158 | 3,135 | 3,330 | 3,521 | 3,197 | 3,378 | 38,442 |
| 1988 | 3,246 | 3,071 | 3,355 | 3,158 | 3,206 | 3,319 | 3,170 | 3,507 | 3,462 | 3,512 | 3,399 | 3,358 | 39,763 |
| 1989 | 3,265 | 3,004 | 3,325 | 3,131 | 3,397 | 3,343 | 3,048 | 3,483 | 3,317 | 3,523 | 3,411 | 3,171 | 39,418 |
| 1990 | 3,354 | 2,972 | 3,259 | 3,049 | 3,320 | 3,175 | 3,100 | 3,431 | 3,096 | 3,499 | 3,273 | 3,080 | 38,608 |
| 1991 | 3,430 | 2,954 | 3,081 | 3,285 | 3,291 | 3,059 | 3,253 | 3,425 | 3,308 | 3,708 | 3,324 | 3,284 | 39,402 |
| 1992 | 3,623 | 3,090 | 3,376 | 3,259 | 3,237 | 3,423 | 3,441 | 3,406 | 3,560 | 3,656 | 3,289 | 3,434 | 40,794 |
| 1993 | 3,304 | 3,012 | 3,396 | 3,299 | 3,212 | 3,481 | 3,342 | 3,504 | 3,516 | 3,499 | 3,449 | 3,554 | 40,568 |
| 1994 | 3,366 | 3,126 | 3,591 | 3,382 | 3,431 | 3,615 | 3,361 | 3,756 | 3,720 | 3,795 | 3,666 | 3,714 | 42,523 |
| 1995 | 3,560 | 3,210 | 3,751 | 3,304 | 3,758 | 3,798 | 3,424 | 3,860 | 3,697 | 3,795 | 3,748 | 3,553 | 43,458 |
| 1996[1] | 3,823 | 3,519 | 3,512 | 3,690 | 3,767 | 3,439 | 3,585 | 3,707 | 3,396 | 3,827 | 3,435 | 3,432 | 43,132 |

[1] Preliminary. *Source: Economic Research Service, U.S. Department of Agriculture*

## Cold Storage Holdings of All[1] Meat in the United States, at End of Month In Millions of Pounds

| Year | Jan. | Feb. | Mar. | Apr. | May | June | July | Aug. | Sept. | Oct. | Nov. | Dec. |
|---|---|---|---|---|---|---|---|---|---|---|---|---|
| 1986 | 616.8 | 615.3 | 622.5 | 658.2 | 667.2 | 638.8 | 618.6 | 572.0 | 541.1 | 572.4 | 564.3 | 566.2 |
| 1987 | 597.6 | 599.0 | 598.2 | 590.8 | 560.2 | 498.7 | 515.6 | 495.9 | 523.0 | 575.6 | 613.8 | 622.9 |
| 1988 | 664.6 | 689.5 | 716.6 | 759.4 | 721.2 | 670.7 | 670.7 | 633.9 | 644.3 | 644.0 | 701.5 | 716.4 |
| 1989 | 745.0 | 758.7 | 474.5 | 747.5 | 763.7 | 683.5 | 652.0 | 576.3 | 557.0 | 538.2 | 554.2 | 536.0 |
| 1990 | 564.7 | 609.6 | 637.5 | 653.0 | 632.8 | 591.6 | 565.9 | 507.4 | 507.5 | 536.7 | 536.7 | 536.4 |
| 1991 | 566.2 | 588.6 | 606.2 | 597.7 | 640.1 | 614.1 | 589.7 | 593.2 | 592.8 | 594.7 | 650.2 | 644.9 |
| 1992 | 707.9 | 690.5 | 725.4 | 706.8 | 692.2 | 665.3 | 646.0 | 595.6 | 613.4 | 637.8 | 626.6 | 615.1 |
| 1993 | 649.4 | 654.6 | 652.9 | 692.0 | 671.0 | 660.8 | 664.2 | 650.7 | 671.7 | 702.4 | 720.3 | 726.7 |
| 1994 | 807.7 | 800.5 | 842.5 | 858.0 | 837.5 | 822.6 | 816.2 | 771.9 | 788.5 | 822.7 | 827.5 | 802.0 |
| 1995 | 838.7 | 833.8 | 834.0 | 852.7 | 831.2 | 820.8 | 803.6 | 733.4 | 711.3 | 732.3 | 757.0 | 749.7 |
| 19962 | 779.5 | 781.6 | 729.3 | 748.6 | 716.2 | 687.9 | 642.7 | 654.6 | 678.4 | 652.0 | 627.1 | 621.3 |

[1] Includes beef and veal, mutton and lamb, pork and products, rendered pork fat, and miscellaneous meats. Excludes lard. [2] Preliminary.
*Source: Economic Research Service, U.S. Department of Agriculture*

## Cold Storage Holdings of Frozen Beef in the United States In Millions of Pounds

| Year | Jan. 1 | Feb. 1 | Mar. 1 | Apr. 1 | May 1 | June 1 | July 1 | Aug. 1 | Sept. 1 | Oct. 1 | Nov. 1 | Dec. 1 |
|---|---|---|---|---|---|---|---|---|---|---|---|---|
| 1986 | 317.4 | 318.4 | 302.3 | 297.1 | 301.2 | 318.5 | 321.6 | 337.0 | 319.4 | 291.6 | 292.3 | 297.5 |
| 1987 | 310.6 | 320.6 | 306.0 | 311.1 | 312.3 | 280.1 | 252.7 | 278.7 | 269.3 | 286.5 | 307.6 | 304.3 |
| 1988 | 288.7 | 316.7 | 325.4 | 313.2 | 305.0 | 275.1 | 248.4 | 269.6 | 294.9 | 307.6 | 296.5 | 300.4 |
| 1989 | 317.5 | 315.1 | 313.4 | 298.9 | 275.4 | 244.1 | 241.8 | 249.2 | 242.4 | 231.8 | 220.7 | 237.6 |
| 1990 | 251.7 | 259.8 | 267.6 | 304.3 | 293.3 | 270.4 | 256.5 | 265.4 | 240.5 | 243.0 | 267.4 | 277.2 |
| 1991 | 300.4 | 298.9 | 271.3 | 276.9 | 265.6 | 234.7 | 247.1 | 273.2 | 259.4 | 276.7 | 298.2 | 306.3 |
| 1992 | 315.9 | 329.1 | 298.9 | 313.7 | 302.1 | 303.5 | 299.4 | 294.1 | 288.9 | 275.2 | 291.2 | 275.9 |
| 1993 | 272.8 | 286.4 | 279.9 | 293.9 | 276.7 | 262.1 | 271.7 | 285.3 | 307.5 | 326.8 | 344.4 | 376.3 |
| 1994 | 401.0 | 430.2 | 414.4 | 423.2 | 399.5 | 367.9 | 379.4 | 388.9 | 377.2 | 406.8 | 410.6 | 419.5 |
| 1995 | 411.2 | 420.3 | 407.7 | 385.4 | 392.2 | 359.1 | 352.3 | 359.3 | 344.9 | 347.7 | 381.6 | 381.4 |
| 1996[1] | 389.6 | 367.9 | 362.6 | 347.3 | 335.6 | 307.4 | 306.7 | 291.1 | 305.1 | 312.2 | 295.5 | 288.1 |

[1] Preliminary. *Source: Economic Research Service, U.S. Department of Agriculture*

# Mercury

U.S. consumption of mercury has been in a downward trend since the early 1970's. Moreover, strict environmental policy and new technology is expected to further reduce the future use of mercury. Many nonessential uses are likely to be banned or voluntarily eliminated. U.S. production of primary mercury will rely on the mining of other minerals while secondary production becomes an even more important component of domestic supply, especially if the ban (imposed in 1994) on sales of mercury from the National Defense Stockpile continues. The trend for the past several years has been to substitute other materials for mercury rather than develop large-scale recycling programs.

In the U.S., the last producing primary mercury mine (in Nevada) closed in 1990. Since then the only prime virgin mercury produced in the U.S. has been recovered as a by-product of gold mining operations in California, Nevada, and Utah; the recovery is required to prevent contamination of the environment.

World production of mercury is limited to a few countries. However, mine output increased 57 percent in 1995 from a year earlier to 2,820 metric tons from 1,800 tons, respectively; the highest total since 1990 when 4,100 tons were produced. Most of the increase was generated by renewed production in Spain, once the world's largest producer of primary mercury. Spain's production jumped to 1,497 tons in 1995 from 393 tons in 1994 as a major mine reopened following plant repairs directed to environmental concerns. Prior to Spain's resurgence, much of the world's mercury during the 1990's was produced by China and Algeria, whose combined 1995 output of 842 tons compares with 884 tons in 1994. (One ton=29+ flasks of 76 pounds each.) World reserves and reserve base (mostly in Spain) are estimated at 130,000 and 240,000 tons, respectively. Where mined, mercury occurs with gold ores and must be recovered to avoid contamination, but the process is costly and recovery restrictions are lax in some countries.

Mercury is a recoverable metal. U.S. secondary production increased during the first half of the 1990's from only 108 tons in 1990 to 466 tons in 1994 and 534 tons in 1995. The larger secondary production since 1993 reflected new EPA restrictions banning landfill disposal and/or transport of mercury-containing wastes. Stockpiled mercury is another source of supply. Industry stocks at U.S. sites in late 1995 were estimated at 352 tons vs. 469 tons a year earlier. The U.S. government has a mercury stockpile; tight restrictions are in place as to how much can be sold, if any, each year.

U.S. industrial consumption of refined mercury totaled 436 metric tons in 1995, down from 483 tons in 1994. In the mid-1980's, battery production alone consumed almost 30,000 tons; in 1995 the total was near zero. Domestic battery manufacturers now produce alkaline and zinc-carbon batteries without any added mercury. Chlorine and caustic soda manufacture is now the largest domestic use for mercury, 154 tons in 1995 vs. 135 tons in 1994. Substitutes for mercury include lithium and composite ceramic materials.

U.S. foreign trade in mercury is small, but the flow reversed in 1995 from 1994. Imports, mostly from Canada and Russia, totaled 377 tons in 1995 vs. 129 tons in 1994, whereas exports fell to 179 tons from 316 tons, respectively. India and Hong Kong received one half of 1995 U.S. exports.

Mercury is usually sold in 34.5 kilogram flasks. The U.S. average price in 1995 was $247.39/flask (N.Y.) vs. $194.45 in 1994. Prices during the 1980's averaged near $300/fl. U.S. prices have been slowly climbing since a low of $122/flask was set in 1991 and the upward trend is expected to persist. European prices, however, are generally lower than in the U.S. and considered more reflective of true market values.

## World Mine Production of Mercury    In Metric Tons (1 tonne = 29.008216 flasks)

| Year | Algeria | China | Finland | Kyrgyz stan[3] | Mexico | Spain | Tajik-istan[3] | Turkey | Ukraine[3] | United States | World Total |
|---|---|---|---|---|---|---|---|---|---|---|---|
| 1987 | 705 | 700 | 144 | ------ | 124 | 1,395 | ------ | 211 | 2,300 | 100 | 5,810 |
| 1988 | 662 | 940 | 130 | ------ | 345 | 1,716 | ------ | 97 | 850 | 378 | 5,357 |
| 1989 | 587 | 1,200 | 159 | ------ | 651 | 1,224 | ------ | 197 | 850 | 414 | 5,464 |
| 1990 | 637 | 1,000 | 141 | ------ | 735 | 425 | ------ | 60 | 800 | 562 | 4,100 |
| 1991 | 431 | 760 | 74 | ------ | 340 | 100 | ------ | 25 | 750 | 58 | 2,540 |
| 1992 | 476 | 580 | 85 | 300 | 21 | 36 | 100 | 5 | 100 | 64 | 1,920 |
| 1993 | 459 | 520 | 98 | 250 | 12 | 643 | 80 | ------ | 80 | 70 | 2,270 |
| 1994[1] | 414 | 470 | 83 | 200 | 10 | 393 | 55 | ------ | 50 | W | 1,800 |
| 1995[2] | 292 | 550 | 90 | 170 | 15 | 1,497 | 50 | ------ | 40 | W | 2,820 |

[1] Preliminary. [2] Estimate. [3] Formerly part of the U.S.S.R.; data not reported separately until 1992. NA = Not available. *Source: U.S. Geological Survey*

## Salient Statistics of Mercury in the U.S.    In Metric Tons

| Year | Producing Mines | Secondary Production: Industrial | Secondary Production: Govern-ment[3] | Secondary Production: N.D.S.[4] Shipments | Consumer & Dealer Stocks, Dec. 31 | Industrial Demand | Exports | Imports |
|---|---|---|---|---|---|---|---|---|
| 1989 | 10 | 137 | 180 | 170 | 217 | 121 | 221 | 131 |
| 1990 | 9 | 108 | 193 | 52 | 197 | 720 | 311 | 15 |
| 1991 | 8 | 165 | 215 | 103 | 313 | 554 | 786 | 56 |
| 1992 | 9 | 176 | 103 | 267 | 436 | 621 | 977 | 92 |
| 1993 | 9 | 350 | ----- | 543 | 384 | 558 | 389 | 40 |
| 1994[1] | 7 | 466 | ----- | 86 | 469 | 483 | 316 | 129 |
| 1995[2] | 8 | 534 | ----- | 17 | 352 | 436 | 179 | 377 |

[1] Preliminary. [2] Estimate. [3] Secondary mercury shipped from the Department of Energy. [4] National Defense Stockpile. NA = Not available.
*Source: U.S. Geological Survey*

# MERCURY

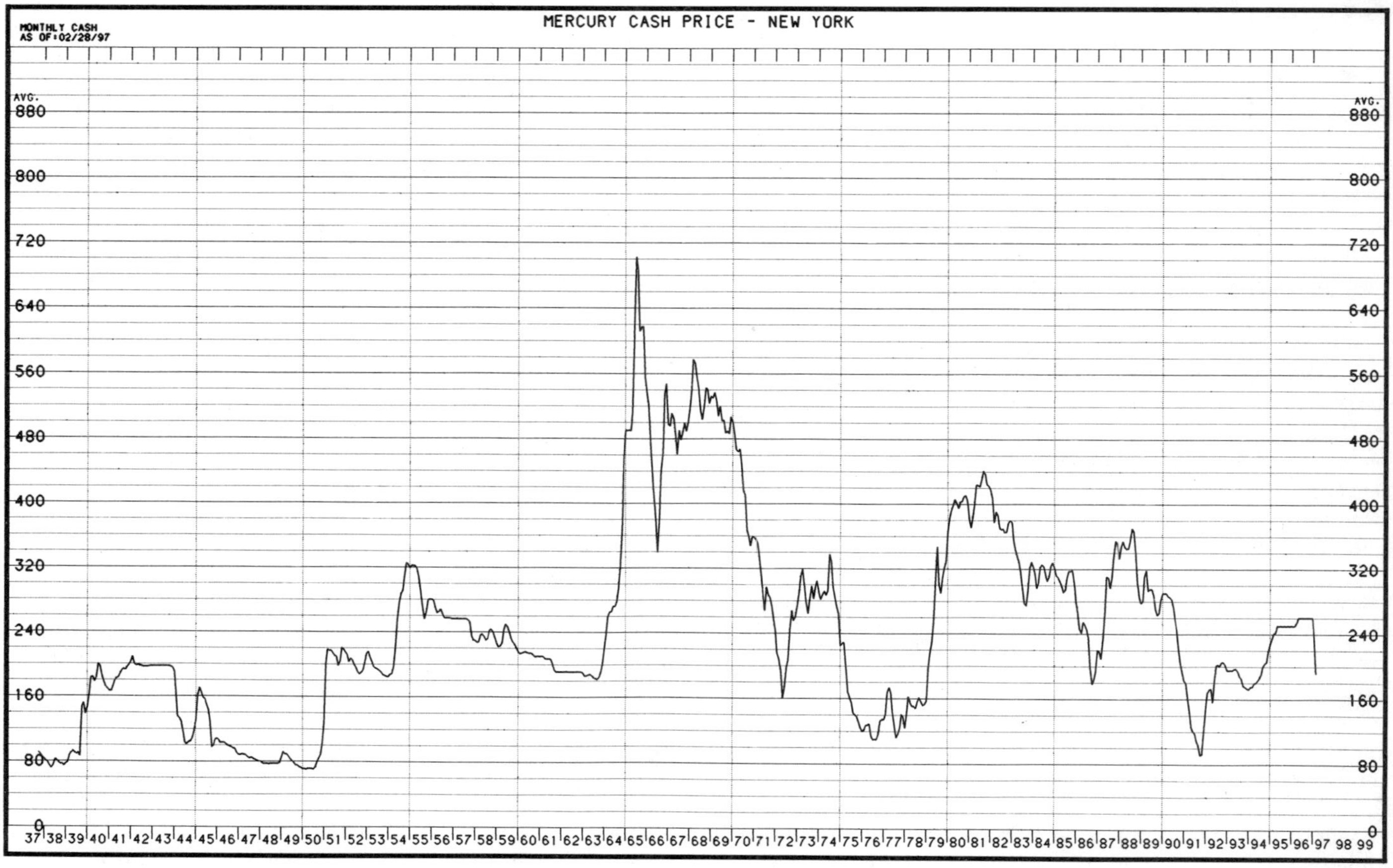


**Average Price of Mercury in New York** In Dollars Per Flask of 76 Pounds (34.5 Kilograms)

| Year | Jan. | Feb. | Mar. | Apr. | May | June | July | Aug. | Sept. | Oct. | Nov. | Dec. | Average |
|---|---|---|---|---|---|---|---|---|---|---|---|---|---|
| 1986 | 285.68 | 261.97 | 252.44 | 272.05 | 277.50 | 276.07 | 260.00 | 218.10 | 181.91 | 193.80 | 215.19 | 219.43 | 242.85 |
| 1987 | 216.70 | 211.03 | 223.73 | 260.00 | 297.63 | 297.73 | 286.82 | 306.55 | 337.86 | 345.91 | 348.95 | 342.27 | 289.60 |
| 1988 | 354.00 | 357.00 | 350.00 | 337.14 | 326.90 | 352.28 | 367.13 | 360.43 | 349.29 | 322.74 | 299.34 | 293.45 | 339.14 |
| 1989 | 292.50 | 318.42 | 330.00 | 327.50 | 315.68 | 308.86 | 293.03 | 273.80 | 265.13 | 267.61 | 282.50 | 292.50 | 297.29 |
| 1990 | 292.50 | 292.50 | 287.84 | 285.00 | 285.00 | 285.00 | 281.45 | 262.50 | 259.34 | 235.54 | 198.75 | 182.50 | 262.33 |
| 1991 | 181.55 | 169.08 | 150.36 | 140.68 | 129.77 | 119.75 | 110.36 | 102.50 | 98.00 | 94.02 | 127.50 | 150.12 | 131.14 |
| 1992 | 162.86 | 177.24 | 180.00 | 180.00 | 190.63 | 202.50 | 202.50 | 203.45 | 207.50 | 207.50 | 207.50 | 207.50 | 194.10 |
| 1993 | 207.50 | 207.50 | 207.50 | 207.50 | 207.50 | 201.30 | 191.00 | 191.00 | 185.00 | 185.00 | 181.00 | 175.00 | 195.57 |
| 1994 | 175.00 | 175.00 | 179.78 | 180.00 | 180.95 | 186.64 | 196.50 | 200.00 | 203.10 | 205.00 | 217.50 | 230.71 | 194.18 |
| 1995 | 235.00 | 240.00 | 241.30 | 250.00 | 250.00 | 250.00 | 250.00 | 250.00 | 250.00 | 250.00 | 250.00 | 250.00 | 247.19 |
| 1996 | 250.00 | 250.00 | 261.67 | 268.33 | 265.00 | 265.00 | 265.00 | 265.00 | 265.00 | 265.00 | 262.63 | 235.48 | 259.84 |

*Source: American Metal Market*

**Mercury Consumed in the United States** In Metric Tons

| Year | Batteries | Chlorine & Caustic Soda | Catalysts, Misc. | Dental Equip. | Electrical Lighting | General Lab Use | Measuring Control Instrument | Paints | Wiring Devices & Switches | Other Uses | Grand Total |
|---|---|---|---|---|---|---|---|---|---|---|---|
| 1985 | 952 | 235 | 61 | 50 | 40 | 14 | 79 | 169 | 95 | 20 | 1,718 |
| 1986 | 750 | 259 | 90 | 52 | 41 | 20 | 63 | 179 | 103 | 31 | 1,588 |
| 1987 | 533 | 311 | 59 | 56 | 45 | 20 | 59 | 198 | 131 | 34 | 1,446 |
| 1988 | 448 | 354 | 86 | 53 | 31 | 26 | 77 | 197 | 176 | 55 | 1,503 |
| 1989 | 250 | 379 | 40 | 39 | 31 | 18 | 87 | 192 | 141 | 32 | 1,212 |
| 1990 | 106 | 247 | 29 | 44 | 33 | 32 | 108 | 14 | 70 | 38 | 720 |
| 1991 | 18 | 184 | 26 | 41 | 39 | 30 | 90 | 6 | 71 | 49 | 554 |
| 1992 | 13 | 209 | 20 | 42 | 55 | 28 | 80 | ----- | 82 | 92 | 621 |
| 1993 | 10 | 180 | 18 | 35 | 38 | 26 | 65 | ----- | 83 | 103 | 558 |
| 1994[1] | 6 | 135 | 25 | 24 | 27 | 24 | 53 | ----- | 79 | 110 | 483 |
| 1995[2] | ----- | 154 | ----- | 32 | 30 | ----- | 43 | ----- | 84 | 93 | 436 |

[1] Preliminary. [2] Estimate. [3] Data reported in flasks prior to 1985. NA = Not available. *Source: U.S. Geological Survey*

# Milk

Wholesale milk prices soared higher in 1996, reaching a record high $15.37 for 100 pounds of raw milk, up from $12.73 in January and a 1995 average of $11.83. Retail prices also moved higher, but showed considerably more variance largely due to differences in transportation and marketing costs. Contributing to the price gains were higher feed costs and lower quality feed from which producers realized less milk per cow. Supplies of high quality alfalfa feed, for example, were very tight. However, a fresh factor may have impacted on milk's price structure in 1996, perhaps buoying demand at a time when new supply was checked. At midyear the nation witnessed a temporary milk shortage which was reflected quickly by higher prices. For the first time ever the $14 billion milk industry began aggressively advertising milk as a beverage in an effort to reverse the tide of fluid milk's 30-year consumption decline and defend itself from competing iced teas and bottled water. The strategy may yet work with children, but adults are questionable; it's believed that more than half of U.S. adults over 35 have eliminated milk from their diet.

22 states account for 87 percent of U.S. milk output. California and Wisconsin are the leading milk producing states. 1996 dairy cow numbers totaled about 8.0 million head while the total number of milk cows averaged 9.45 million.

Seasonally, milk production is highest during the April-June quarter during which a nationwide 39.7 billion pounds were produced in 1996 vs. 40.5 billion a year earlier. The year's total production was expected to dip about 1 percent from the 156 billion pounds produced in 1995. In 1997, the industry's response to the high 1996 prices are expected to restore milk output, but only back to the 1995 level which may lower the wholesale price by 50 cents to $1. However, feed conditions are expected to trouble dairy farmers into mid-1997 as low forage quality feed supplies are likely to hinder producer efforts to expand milk production.

Milk prices in much of 1997 are projected to be dominated by strong demand and the lingering forage/grain problems, although the magnitude may be less than in 1996. In either case, wholesale prices are expected to average above $14 per cwt. for only the second time. The potential for price weakness is much greater in 1998, depending upon what happens to 1996-97 feed and milk prices.

The U.S. is the world's largest fluid milk producer, the 71 million metric tons produced in both 1995 and 1996 account for about 18 percent of world production of 383 and 384 million tons, respectively. Russia is second with 1996 output of 37.8 million tons, down from 39.4 million in 1995; in 1991, Russia produced 52 million tons. Other major producers include India, Germany, and France, each in excess of 25 million tons during 1996. The U.S., however, is not the world's largest consumer of fluid milk, that honor goes to India with 28.5 million tons in 1996 vs. the U.S. total of 26.7 million tons. On a per capita basis, the U.S. total of 100 kilograms is well under most European nations. Pricewise, U.S. fluid milk prices are lower than abroad, but dried milk prices tend to be higher due largely to a government support program. The average U.S. producer price for milk eligible for fluid use in 1995 of $12.78/cwt. compares with $13.03 in 1994. Generally, fluid milk prices average near $20.00/cwt. in Europe and are even higher in Japan.

### *Futures Markets*

Nonfat dry milk and raw milk futures and options are traded on the Coffee, Sugar, & Cocoa Exchange Inc. (CSCE). Fluid milk futures and options are traded on the Chicago Mercantile Exchange (CME).

**World Fluid Milk Production (Cow's Milk)** In Thousands of Metric Tons

| Year | Australia | Brazil | Canada | France | Germany | India | Italy | Japan | Mexico | Netherlands | New Zealand | Poland | Russia[3] | Ukraine[3] | United Kingdom | United States |
|---|---|---|---|---|---|---|---|---|---|---|---|---|---|---|---|---|
| 1989 | 6,465 | 13,400 | 7,980 | 26,150 | 32,400 | 24,000 | 10,828 | 8,059 | 8,970 | 11,321 | 7,406 | 16,371 | 55,742 | 24,237 | 14,647 | 65,424 |
| 1990 | 6,435 | 14,500 | 7,975 | 26,400 | 31,200 | 27,500 | 11,491 | 8,190 | 9,330 | 11,285 | 7,746 | 15,801 | 55,715 | 24,360 | 14,952 | 67,005 |
| 1991 | 6,578 | 14,200 | 7,790 | 25,700 | 28,916 | 28,200 | 11,400 | 8,260 | 10,200 | 11,047 | 8,122 | 14,504 | 51,971 | 22,409 | 14,503 | 66,994 |
| 1992 | 6,918 | 15,000 | 7,633 | 25,315 | 28,106 | 29,400 | 11,300 | 8,581 | 10,700 | 10,901 | 8,603 | 13,060 | 46,776 | 19,114 | 14,428 | 68,440 |
| 1993 | 7,530 | 15,300 | 7,500 | 25,049 | 28,080 | 30,600 | 10,400 | 8,627 | 10,720 | 10,953 | 8,735 | 12,650 | 46,300 | 18,377 | 14,645 | 68,303 |
| 1994 | 8,300 | 16,700 | 7,750 | 25,322 | 27,866 | 31,000 | 10,365 | 8,388 | 11,010 | 10,964 | 9,719 | 11,822 | 42,800 | 18,138 | 14,920 | 69,701 |
| 1995[1] | 8,430 | 17,400 | 7,920 | 25,491 | 28,800 | 32,000 | 10,400 | 8,382 | 11,120 | 11,294 | 9,684 | 11,410 | 39,400 | 17,050 | 14,700 | 70,599 |
| 1996[2] | 8,735 | 18,200 | 7,750 | 25,600 | 28,500 | 33,000 | 10,200 | 8,290 | 11,450 | 11,080 | 10,000 | 11,100 | 37,800 | 16,500 | 14,600 | 72,577 |

[1] Preliminary. [2] Estimate. [3] Formerly part of the U.S.S.R.; data not reported separately until 1989. *Source: Foreign Agricultural Service, U.S. Department of Agriculture*

**U.S. Milk-Feed Price Ratio[1]** In Pounds

| Year | Jan. | Feb. | Mar. | Apr. | May | June | July | Aug. | Sept. | Oct. | Nov. | Dec. | Average |
|---|---|---|---|---|---|---|---|---|---|---|---|---|---|
| 1989 | 2.51 | 2.45 | 2.30 | 2.26 | 2.25 | 2.38 | 2.52 | 2.83 | 2.97 | 3.22 | 3.34 | 3.39 | 2.70 |
| 1990 | 3.25 | 3.02 | 2.84 | 2.59 | 2.54 | 2.72 | 2.79 | 2.92 | 2.93 | 2.82 | 2.83 | 2.59 | 2.82 |
| 1991 | 2.57 | 2.52 | 2.42 | 2.34 | 2.41 | 2.54 | 2.73 | 2.82 | 2.94 | 3.14 | 3.25 | 3.19 | 2.74 |
| 1992 | 3.04 | 2.86 | 2.77 | 2.79 | 2.68 | 2.81 | 3.06 | 3.20 | 3.22 | 3.23 | 3.23 | 3.13 | 3.00 |
| 1993 | 2.96 | 2.87 | 2.77 | 2.79 | 2.81 | 2.91 | 2.78 | 2.70 | 2.80 | 2.79 | 2.77 | 2.65 | 2.80 |
| 1994 | 2.62 | 2.51 | 2.51 | 2.50 | 2.36 | 2.44 | 2.61 | 2.74 | 2.81 | 2.92 | 2.96 | 2.81 | 2.65 |
| 1995 | 2.73 | 2.75 | 2.73 | 2.60 | 2.53 | 2.46 | 2.39 | 2.50 | 2.55 | 2.60 | 2.69 | 2.55 | 2.59 |
| 1996[2] | 2.57 | 2.44 | 2.30 | 2.16 | 2.07 | 2.14 | 2.20 | 2.27 | 2.61 | 2.89 | 2.78 | 2.61 | 2.42 |

[1] Pounds of 16% protein mixed dairy feed equal in value to one pound of whole milk. [2] Preliminary. *Source: Economic Research Service, U.S. Department of Agriculture*

## Salient Statistics of Milk in the United States    In Millions of Pounds

| Year | Number of Milk Cows on Farms[3] (Thousands) | Supply: Production: Per Cow[4] (Pounds) | Supply: Production: Total[4] | Supply: Beginning Stocks[5] | Supply: Imports | Supply: Total Supply | Utilization: Exports[5] | Utilization: Domestic: Fed to Calves | Utilization: Domestic: Humans | Utilization: Total Use | Average Farm Price Received Per Cwt.: All Milk, Wholesale | Average Farm Price Received Per Cwt.: Milk Eligible for Fluid Market | Average Farm Price Received Per Cwt.: Milk, Manufacturing Grade | Per Capita Consumption[6] (Fluid Milk in Lbs.) |
|---|---|---|---|---|---|---|---|---|---|---|---|---|---|---|
| 1989 | 10,046 | 14,323 | 143,893 | 8,378 | 2,498 | 154,769 | 3,995 | 1,496 | 139,463 | 145,733 | 13.56 | 13.67 | 12.49 | 236 |
| 1990 | 9,993 | 14,782 | 147,721 | 9,036 | 2,690 | 159,447 | 1,886 | 1,484 | 142,067 | 146,088 | 13.68 | 13.80 | 12.28 | 234 |
| 1991 | 9,826 | 15,031 | 147,697 | 13,359 | 2,625 | 163,681 | 2,845 | 1,480 | 142,897 | 147,841 | 12.24 | 12.33 | 11.12 | 233 |
| 1992 | 9,688 | 15,570 | 150,847 | 15,840 | 2,520 | 169,246 | 7,569 | 1,436 | 144,519 | 155,032 | 13.09 | 13.16 | 11.87 | 231 |
| 1993 | 9,589 | 15,704 | 150,582 | 14,214 | 2,806 | 167,602 | 7,894 | 1,408 | 148,178 | 158,032 | 12.80 | 12.86 | 11.76 | 227 |
| 1994[1] | 9,500 | 16,175 | 153,664 | 9,569 | 2,880 | 166,072 | 5,555 | 1,353 | 152,791 | 160,312 | 12.97 | 13.03 | 11.83 | 226 |
| 1995[2] | 9,458 | 14,633 | 155,425 | 5,760 | 2,936 | 164,121 | | | | | 12.76 | 12.80 | 11.77 | |

[1] Preliminary. [2] Estimate. [3] Average number on farms during year including dry cows, excluding heifers not yet fresh. [4] Excludes milk sucked by calves. [5] Government and commercial. [6] Product pounds of commercial sales and on farm consumption. *Source: Economic Research Service, U.S. Department of Agriculture*

## Utilization of Milk in the United States    In Millions of Pounds (Milk Equivalent)

| Year | Butter from Whey Cream | Creamery Butter[2] | Cheese[3] | Cottage Cheese (Creamed) | Canned Milk[4] | Bulk Condensed Whole Milk: Unsweetened | Bulk Condensed Whole Milk: Sweetened | Dry Whole Milk Products | Ice Cream[5] | Other Frozen Dairy Products | Other Manufactured Products[6] | Used on Farms: Farm-Churned Butter | Used on Farms: Total |
|---|---|---|---|---|---|---|---|---|---|---|---|---|---|
| 1989 | 3,961 | 28,486 | 43,548 | 704 | 1,144 | 428 | 215 | 1,286 | 2,069 | 12,531 | 357 | 563 | 2,059 |
| 1990 | 4,348 | 29,391 | 47,368 | 672 | 1,332 | 351 | 243 | 1,292 | 2,014 | 12,307 | 332 | 512 | 1,996 |
| 1991 | 4,296 | 30,039 | 46,769 | 644 | 1,194 | 364 | 236 | 785 | 2,092 | 12,726 | 356 | 494 | 1,974 |
| 1992 | 4,150 | 30,478 | 49,458 | 592 | 1,872 | 417 | 301 | 1,227 | 2,367 | 11,825 | 188 | 455 | 1,892 |
| 1993 | 4,500 | 29,493 | 49,871 | 557 | 1,178 | 374 | 324 | 1,130 | 1,995 | 12,063 | 199 | 428 | 1,836 |
| 1994[1] | 4,592 | 29,127 | 51,115 | 524 | 1,184 | 205 | 277 | 1,227 | 1,997 | 12,543 | 216 | 404 | 1,758 |

[1] Preliminary. [2] Excludes whey butter. [3] American and other. [4] Includes evaporated and sweetened condensed. [5] Milk equivalent of butter and condensed milk used in ice cream. [6] Whole milk equivalent of dry cream, malted milk powder, part-skim milk, dry or concentrated ice cream mix, dehydrated butterfat and other miscellaneous products using milkfat. *Source: National Agricultural Statistics Service, U.S. Department of Agriculture*

## Milk Production[1] in the United States    In Millions of Pounds

| Year | Jan. | Feb. | Mar. | Apr. | May | June | July | Aug. | Sept. | Oct. | Nov. | Dec. | Total |
|---|---|---|---|---|---|---|---|---|---|---|---|---|---|
| 1990 | 12,283 | 11,491 | 12,988 | 12,749 | 13,256 | 12,635 | 12,562 | 12,312 | 11,737 | 12,098 | 11,831 | 12,372 | 148,314 |
| 1991 | 12,587 | 11,732 | 13,106 | 12,888 | 13,268 | 12,477 | 12,348 | 12,202 | 11,705 | 12,102 | 11,763 | 12,347 | 148,477 |
| 1992 | 12,671 | 12,132 | 13,155 | 12,838 | 13,346 | 12,893 | 12,844 | 12,577 | 12,094 | 12,476 | 12,064 | 12,626 | 150,847 |
| 1993 | 10,728 | 9,908 | 11,060 | 10,927 | 11,410 | 12,957 | 12,894 | 12,492 | 11,978 | 12,272 | 11,872 | 12,427 | 150,582 |
| 1994 | 12,721 | 11,662 | 13,209 | 13,118 | 13,719 | 13,079 | 13,020 | 12,837 | 12,360 | 12,732 | 12,330 | 12,871 | 153,664 |
| 1995 | 13,147 | 12,142 | 13,640 | 13,343 | 13,875 | 13,302 | 13,152 | 12,793 | 12,381 | 12,716 | 12,297 | 12,844 | 155,425 |
| 1996[2] | 13,082 | 12,449 | 13,555 | 13,269 | 13,604 | 12,833 | 12,852 | 12,608 | 12,273 | 12,715 | 12,318 | 12,921 | 154,479 |

[1] Excludes milk sucked by calves. [2] Preliminary. *Source: Economic Research Service, U.S. Department of Agriculture*

## Average Price Received by U.S. Farmers for All Milk (Sold to Plants)    In Dollars Per Hundred Pounds (Cwt.)

| Year | Jan. | Feb. | Mar. | Apr. | May | June | July | Aug. | Sept. | Oct. | Nov. | Dec. | Average |
|---|---|---|---|---|---|---|---|---|---|---|---|---|---|
| 1990 | 15.50 | 14.50 | 13.90 | 13.40 | 13.50 | 13.80 | 14.00 | 14.20 | 13.90 | 13.10 | 12.70 | 11.70 | 13.68 |
| 1991 | 11.70 | 11.60 | 11.40 | 11.30 | 11.30 | 11.40 | 11.80 | 12.40 | 12.80 | 13.50 | 13.90 | 13.80 | 12.24 |
| 1992 | 13.40 | 12.90 | 12.50 | 12.60 | 12.80 | 13.20 | 13.40 | 13.50 | 13.50 | 13.40 | 13.10 | 12.80 | 13.09 |
| 1993 | 12.50 | 12.20 | 12.20 | 12.60 | 12.90 | 13.00 | 12.80 | 12.40 | 12.80 | 13.10 | 13.60 | 13.50 | 12.80 |
| 1994 | 13.60 | 13.40 | 13.50 | 13.40 | 12.80 | 12.60 | 12.20 | 12.40 | 12.80 | 13.00 | 13.10 | 12.80 | 12.97 |
| 1995 | 12.60 | 12.60 | 12.70 | 12.30 | 12.30 | 12.10 | 12.00 | 12.40 | 12.80 | 13.40 | 14.00 | 13.90 | 12.76 |
| 1996[1] | 14.00 | 13.80 | 13.70 | 13.90 | 14.30 | 14.60 | 15.30 | 15.70 | 16.30 | 16.10 | 15.00 | 14.10 | 14.73 |

[1] Preliminary. *Source: Economic Research Service, U.S. Department of Agriculture*

## Farm Price of Milk Eligible for Fluid Market    In Dollars Per Hundred Pounds (Cwt.)

| Year | Jan. | Feb. | Mar. | Apr. | May | June | July | Aug. | Sept. | Oct. | Nov. | Dec. | Average |
|---|---|---|---|---|---|---|---|---|---|---|---|---|---|
| 1990 | 15.60 | 14.70 | 14.00 | 13.40 | 13.60 | 13.90 | 14.10 | 14.30 | 14.00 | 13.30 | 12.90 | 11.80 | 13.80 |
| 1991 | 11.80 | 11.70 | 11.50 | 11.40 | 11.40 | 11.50 | 11.90 | 12.40 | 12.90 | 13.60 | 13.90 | 13.90 | 12.33 |
| 1992 | 13.50 | 13.00 | 12.50 | 12.60 | 12.90 | 13.30 | 13.40 | 13.50 | 13.60 | 13.50 | 13.20 | 12.90 | 13.16 |
| 1993 | 12.60 | 12.30 | 12.20 | 12.70 | 13.00 | 13.10 | 12.80 | 12.50 | 12.80 | 13.10 | 13.60 | 13.60 | 12.86 |
| 1994 | 13.60 | 13.50 | 13.50 | 13.50 | 12.90 | 12.70 | 12.20 | 12.50 | 12.80 | 13.10 | 13.10 | 12.90 | 13.03 |
| 1995 | 12.70 | 12.60 | 12.60 | 12.30 | 12.30 | 12.20 | 12.10 | 12.50 | 12.80 | 13.40 | 14.00 | 14.00 | 12.79 |
| 1996[1] | 14.00 | 13.90 | 13.70 | 13.90 | 14.30 | 14.70 | 15.40 | 15.70 | 16.40 | 16.20 | 15.10 | 14.20 | 14.79 |

[1] Preliminary. *Source: Economic Research Service, U.S. Department of Agriculture*

# Molasses

Molasses is produced during the refinement of cane and beet sugar. U.S. supplies of molasses, including production and imports, total about three million tonnes per year. Of this total, about a third comes from mainland sugar mills. a quarter from beet sugar refiners, smaller amounts from Hawaiian cane and cane refiner's blackstrap, and the remainder from imports. Beet molasses is used primarily as a livestock feed and as a yeast by the pharmaceutical industry.

According to the USDA, molasses production from sugar cane from mainland mills in 1995 was 886,826 tonnes, up almost 8 percent from 1994. This was the highest level of molasses production in a number of years. Cane refiners blackstrap molasses production in 1995 was 114,000 tonnes, the same as in 1994. Shipments of molasses from cane sugar in Hawaii to the U.S. mainland were 146,000 tonnes, down 3 percent from 1994. Production of molasses from sugar beets in 1995 was 1.04 million tonnes, down 5 percent. Estimated domestic supplies of molasses in 1995 were 2.19 million tonnes, less than 1 percent more than in 1994.

The U.S. is also an importer of inedible molasses. For 1995, U.S. imports were 1.05 million tonnes, down 33 percent from 1994. The major suppliers were Guatemala, Mexico, Colombia, the Dominican Republic, and Poland. U.S. mainland exports of molasses in 1995 were 274,868 tonnes, down 1 percent from 1994. Total available supplies of molasses in 1995 were estimated at 2.96 million tonnes, down 14 percent from 1994.

In terms of utilization, distilled use of molasses in 1995 was estimated at 206,000 tonnes, up 7 percent from 1994. Industrial use of molasses (includes lysine, yeast, citric acid, edible molasses, and pharmaceuticals) was 545,000 tonnes, down 10 percent. Desugarization molasses was 750,000 tonnes, up 22 percent from 1994. Molasses used in mixed feeds was 1.5 million tonnes, down 29 percent from 1994. Total utilization of molasses in 1995 was 3 million tonnes in 1995, down 14 percent.

## World Production of Sugarcane and Sugarbeets by Selected Countries In Thousands of Metric Tons

| | Sugarcane | | | | | | | | Sugerbeets | | | | | | | |
|---|---|---|---|---|---|---|---|---|---|---|---|---|---|---|---|---|
| Crop Year | Australia | Brazil | China | Cuba | India | Indonesia | Pakistan | Thailand | China | France | Germany | Poland | Russia[3] | Turkey | Ukraine[3] | United States |
| 1985-6 | 24,414 | 87,000 | 51,549 | 68,300 | 79,307 | 21,000 | 12,060 | 24,000 | 8,919 | 23,764 | 28,060 | 14,664 | ----- | 9,830 | 82,392 | 20,438 |
| 1986-7 | 25,413 | 95,000 | 50,219 | 66,900 | 102,229 | 23,870 | 14,485 | 24,441 | 8,306 | 21,387 | 27,285 | 14,217 | 29,201 | 10,660 | 42,920 | 22,827 |
| 1987-8 | 28,013 | 88,000 | 47,363 | 68,400 | 108,753 | 21,270 | 20,300 | 27,189 | 8,140 | 24,115 | 26,732 | 13,989 | 34,156 | 12,400 | 49,743 | 25,466 |
| 1988-9 | 28,073 | 88,000 | 49,064 | 73,500 | 98,825 | 26,800 | 21,708 | 36,667 | 12,810 | 25,380 | 23,215 | 14,069 | 32,825 | 11,530 | 48,205 | 22,507 |
| 1989-90 | 27,562 | 73,000 | 48,795 | 70,000 | 124,348 | 26,850 | 20,500 | 33,560 | 9,243 | 23,915 | 26,901 | 14,374 | 37,378 | 10,930 | 51,917 | 22,798 |
| 1990-1 | 25,140 | 75,000 | 57,620 | 67,500 | 135,494 | 28,074 | 22,604 | 40,563 | 14,525 | 25,520 | 30,366 | 16,721 | 31,091 | 13,986 | 44,265 | 24,959 |
| 1991-2 | 21,306 | 87,000 | 67,898 | 62,000 | 148,814 | 28,100 | 24,796 | 47,505 | 16,289 | 24,403 | 25,926 | 11,412 | 24,280 | 15,474 | 36,168 | 25,485 |
| 1992-3 | 29,400 | 90,000 | 73,011 | 47,150 | 123,985 | 32,000 | 27,276 | 34,711 | 15,069 | 26,491 | 27,177 | 11,052 | 25,548 | 15,563 | 28,783 | 26,438 |
| 1993-4 | 31,951 | 91,000 | 63,549 | 46,000 | 116,638 | 33,000 | 34,182 | 37,569 | 11,938 | 25,514 | 28,606 | 15,621 | 25,468 | 15,463 | 33,717 | 23,813 |
| 1994-5 | 34,860 | 110,000 | 60,300 | 39,000 | 159,593 | 30,545 | 34,193 | 50,459 | 12,406 | 23,943 | 24,211 | 11,630 | 13,945 | 12,757 | 28,138 | 29,024 |
| 1995-6[1] | 37,537 | 120,000 | 65,417 | 45,500 | 182,600 | 30,000 | 27,570 | 57,693 | 13,984 | 25,121 | 26,049 | 13,340 | 19,110 | 10,989 | 29,400 | 25,425 |
| 1996-7[2] | 40,600 | 125,000 | 66,700 | 45,500 | 163,500 | 32,500 | 30,100 | 59,000 | 13,500 | 24,000 | 27,000 | 15,000 | 16,500 | 14,300 | 25,500 | 24,277 |

[1] Preliminary. [2] Estimate. [3] Formerly part of the U.S.S.R.; data not reported separately until 1986. *Source: Economic Reseach Service, U.S. Department of Agriculture*

## U.S. Annual Average Prices of Molasses, by Types (F.O.B. Tank Car or Truck) In Dollars Per Short Ton[2]

| | Blackstrap | | | | | | | Beet Molasses | |
|---|---|---|---|---|---|---|---|---|---|
| Year | New Orleans | South Florida | Baltimore | Upper Mississippi[3] | Savannah[4] | California Ports[5] | Houston[6] | Montana/ Wyoming & Nebraska | Red River Valley[7] |
| 1982 | 48.00 | 56.55 | 64.15 | 70.85 | 81.90 | 60.50 | 69.40 | 63.70 | 44.50 |
| 1983 | 56.50 | 63.10 | 73.05 | 76.90 | 91.90 | 70.40 | 79.45 | 65.95 | 60.55 |
| 1984 | 61.50 | 71.00 | 77.65 | 81.00 | 94.45 | 71.95 | 82.50 | 79.15 | 70.65 |
| 1985 | 50.28 | 59.79 | 64.66 | 72.83 | 85.00 | 61.89 | NA | 67.50 | 57.33 |
| 1986 | 69.61 | 78.10 | 83.05 | 92.03 | NA | 73.26 | 80.33 | 73.75 | 68.44 |
| 1987 | 53.23 | 61.96 | 72.83 | 80.05 | NA | 67.17 | 60.31 | 54.69 | 62.22 |
| 1988 | 64.89 | 74.54 | 82.93 | 90.07 | NA | 74.61 | 72.95 | 69.94 | 55.71 |
| 1989 | 55.63 | 65.31 | 75.15 | 81.12 | NA | 70.36 | 79.94 | 74.50 | 55.00 |
| 1990 | 61.70 | 68.37 | 80.59 | 88.48 | 76.13 | 75.40 | 64.26 | 75.00 | 58.33 |
| 1991 | 67.02 | 74.58 | 89.15 | 94.78 | 82.52 | 80.00 | 69.52 | 71.92 | 66.16 |
| 1992 | 61.27 | 68.36 | 80.41 | 92.95 | 76.70 | 78.43 | 63.75 | 67.81 | 57.50 |
| 1993 | 55.48 | 62.36 | 76.03 | 89.26 | 70.00 | 74.24 | 57.12 | 72.63 | 64.44 |
| 1994 | 65.53 | 72.23 | 85.94 | 91.97 | 79.23 | 83.31 | 69.86 | NA | NA |
| 1995 | 72.00 | 79.92 | 86.30 | 99.11 | 87.48 | 90.30 | 76.37 | NA | NA |
| 1996[1] | 74.95 | 86.56 | 93.88 | 107.50 | 95.75 | 98.05 | 83.09 | NA | NA |

[1] Preliminary. [2] To convert dollars per short ton to cents per gallon divide by 171. [3] Prior to 1989, prices are for Minneapolis. [4] Prior to 1989, prices are for Omaha. [5] Los Angeles and Stockton. [6] Prior to 1990, prices are for Colorado. [7] North Dakota and Minnesota. NA = Not available.
*Source: Agricultural Marketing Service, U.S. Department of Agriculture*

# MOLASSES

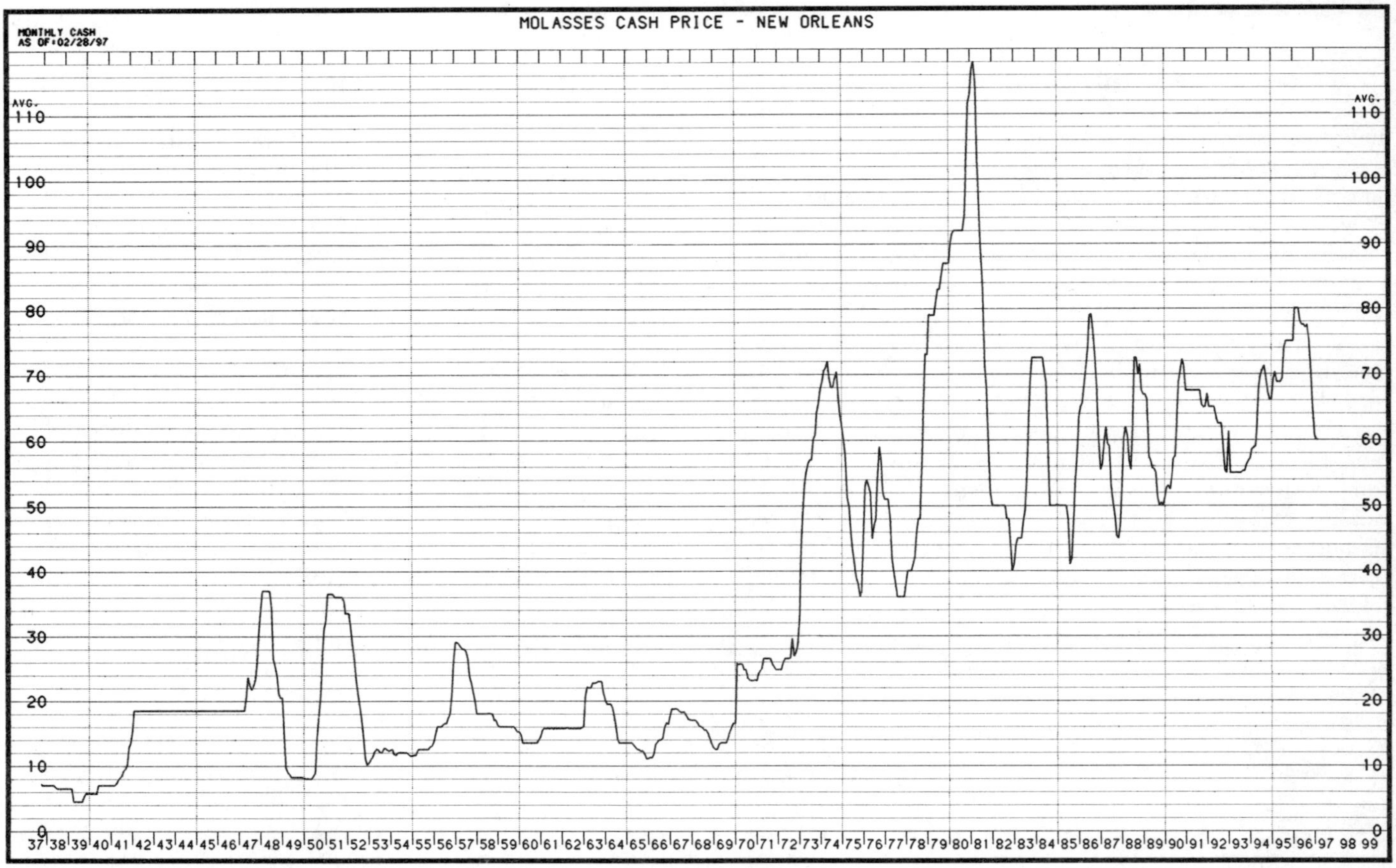


## Salient Statistics of Molasses[3] in the United States In Metric Tons

| Year | Production: Hawaii | Production: Mainland Mills[4] | Production: Mainland Refiners Blackstrap | Production: Mainland Beet | Production: Puerto Rico | In Shipments From Hawaii | Inedible Imports From: Total Imports | Brazil | Dominican Republic | Mexico | Mainland Exports[5] | Total U.S. Supply | Production of Edible Molasses (1,000 Gallons) |
|---|---|---|---|---|---|---|---|---|---|---|---|---|---|
| 1987 | 260,930 | 726,854 | 110,784 | 1,137,014 | 35,385 | 152,087 | 962,151 | 95,004 | 123,619 | 183,525 | 366,957 | 2,721,954 | 1,630 |
| 1988 | 252,516 | 775,936 | 101,257 | 1,006,353 | 40,694 | 178,476 | 969,870 | 142,897 | 102,792 | 93,605 | 299,217 | 2,749,692 | 1,925 |
| 1989 | 218,009 | 808,355 | 122,786 | 974,179 | 34,864 | 169,270 | 926,870 | 107,109 | 147,235 | 75,634 | 293,535 | 2,707,925 | 1,990 |
| 1990 | 228,968 | 741,749 | 105,124 | 948,820 | 24,959 | 214,045 | 1,078,924 | 70,986 | 145,543 | 88,401 | 212,263 | 2,876,399 | 1,405 |
| 1991 | 188,252 | 807,652 | 126,000 | 1,165,962 | 27,882 | 184,337 | 1,258,637 | 10,342 | 137,271 | 235,244 | 242,635 | 3,299,953 | 1,825 |
| 1992 | 182,849 | 782,566 | 123,000 | 950,312 | 25,097 | 183,657 | 1,115,863 | ----- | 127,500 | 117,722 | 282,098 | 2,873,300 | 1,460 |
| 1993 | 187,915 | 831,661 | 113,000 | 692,465 | 22,802 | 190,371 | 1,040,858 | ----- | 163,180 | 47,596 | 255,907 | 2,612,448 | 1,480 |
| 1994[1] | 180,884 | 824,453 | 114,000 | 1,200,000 | 18,531 | 151,172 | 1,556,640 | ----- | 121,320 | 197,753 | 277,098 | 3,459,167 | 1,500 |
| 1995[2] | 146,000 | 886,826 | 114,000 | 1,040,000 | 16,156 | 146,000 | 1,048,726 | ----- | 132,983 | 172,177 | 274,868 | 2,960,684 | |

[1] Preliminary. [2] Estimate. [3] Feed and industrial molasses. [4] Includes high-test molasses from frozen cane. [5] Excluding exports from Hawaii and Puerto Rico. NA = Not available. *Source: Agricultural Marketing Service, U.S. Department of Agriculture*

## Wholesale Price of Blackstrap Molasses (Cane) at New Orleans In Dollars Per Short Ton

| Year | Jan. | Feb. | Mar. | Apr. | May | June | July | Aug. | Sept. | Oct. | Nov. | Dec. | Average |
|---|---|---|---|---|---|---|---|---|---|---|---|---|---|
| 1987 | 56.25 | 59.40 | 62.00 | 59.40 | 59.10 | 53.00 | 50.60 | 48.60 | 45.30 | 45.00 | 47.00 | 53.10 | 53.23 |
| 1988 | 60.30 | 62.00 | 60.60 | 56.90 | 55.50 | 62.50 | 72.50 | 72.50 | 70.00 | 71.50 | 67.50 | 66.90 | 64.89 |
| 1989 | 66.90 | 66.25 | 57.50 | 56.90 | 55.75 | 55.60 | 55.00 | 51.25 | 50.00 | 50.50 | 50.00 | 51.25 | 55.58 |
| 1990 | 52.75 | 53.13 | 52.50 | 54.25 | 57.19 | 57.50 | 62.75 | 68.75 | 70.63 | 72.25 | 71.25 | 67.50 | 61.70 |
| 1991 | 67.50 | 67.50 | 67.50 | 67.50 | 67.50 | 67.50 | 67.50 | 67.50 | 65.25 | 65.00 | 65.00 | 65.00 | 66.69 |
| 1992 | 65.00 | 65.00 | 65.00 | 65.00 | 63.75 | 62.50 | 62.50 | 62.50 | 58.75 | 55.31 | 55.00 | 55.00 | 61.28 |
| 1993 | 55.00 | 55.00 | 55.00 | 55.00 | 55.00 | 55.00 | 55.00 | 55.25 | 55.31 | 56.25 | 56.75 | 57.19 | 55.48 |
| 1994 | 57.75 | 57.50 | 59.38 | 62.50 | 68.00 | 70.00 | 70.63 | 71.25 | 69.38 | 67.50 | 66.25 | 66.25 | 65.53 |
| 1995 | 69.00 | 70.31 | 68.75 | 68.75 | 68.75 | 69.38 | 74.25 | 75.00 | 75.00 | 75.00 | 75.00 | 75.00 | 72.02 |
| 1996[1] | 80.00 | 80.00 | 80.00 | 78.00 | 77.50 | 77.50 | 77.50 | 77.50 | 75.00 | 70.00 | 65.60 | 60.75 | 74.95 |

[1] Preliminary. *Source: Agricultural Marketing Service, U.S. Department of Agriculture*

# Molybdenum

Molybdenum is a silver-gray metal which is strong at high temperatures, hard, and resistant to corrosion. It is a refractory metallic element used principally as an alloying agent in steels, cast irons, and superalloys to enhance strength, toughness, and wear resistance. Primarily added in the form of molybdic oxide or ferromolybdenum, it is frequently used in combination with chromium, manganese, nickel, tungsten, or other alloy metals to achieve desired metallurgical properties. Molybdenum's versatility ensures a significant role in contemporary technology and industry. Molybdenum finds significant usage as a refractory metal in numerous chemical applications, including catalysts, lubricants, and pigments. The variety of uses for molybdenum materials has resulted in a demand that is expected to increase at a greater rate than most other ferrous metals.

U.S. production of molybdenum concentrate in June 1996 was 4,960 tonnes (contained molybdenum), the same as in May. For the January-June 1996 period, U.S. molybdenum production was 28,700 tonnes. For all of 1995 production was 58,000 tonnes.

U.S. reported consumption of molybdenum materials in June 1996 was 14.2 million kilograms. About half the consumption is of molybdic oxides with 7.6 million kilograms. Most of the use of molybdic oxides is in production of steel, especially stainless, heat-resisting, and full alloy. Superalloys and chemical catalysts also consume much of the molybdic oxides. Consumption of ferromolybdenum in June 1996 was 2.8 million kilograms, about half of which is used to make full alloy steel. Cast iron and carbon steel also use ferromolybdenum. Consumption of ammonium and sodium molybate was 798,000 kilograms, with molybdenum scrap consumption at 369,000 kilograms. Molybdenum scrap is used primarily in superalloys.

U.S. consumer stocks of molybdenum materials on June 30, 1996 were 15.5 million kilograms. Stocks of molybdic oxides were 4.8 million kilograms, ammonium and sodium molybdate 97,000 kilograms, molybdenum scrap 626,000 kilograms, and other materials 2.6 million kilograms.

U.S. exports of molybdenum ore and concentrate in May 1996 were 42.9 million kilograms, up from 39.5 million in April 1996. For January-May 1996, exports totaled 201 million kilograms. Major destinations included Belgium, the United Kingdom, Chile, Mexico and the Netherlands.

## World Mine Production of Molybdenum In Metric Tons (Contained Molybdenum)

| Year | Bulgaria | Canada[3] | Chile | China | Iran | Kazakhstan[4] | Mexico | Mongolia | Peru | Russia[4] | United States | Uzbekisten[4] | World Total |
|---|---|---|---|---|---|---|---|---|---|---|---|---|---|
| 1985 | 175 | 7,195 | 16,850 | 1,829 | 457 | ------ | 3,446 | 914 | 3,488 | 10,349 | 45,058 | ------ | 90,174 |
| 1986 | 190 | 11,251 | 16,581 | 2,000 | 900 | ------ | 3,350 | 1,100 | 3,484 | 11,400 | 42,627 | ------ | 93,218 |
| 1987 | 200 | 14,771 | 16,941 | 12,000 | 500 | ------ | 4,400 | 1,400 | 3,353 | 11,500 | 34,063 | ------ | 89,871 |
| 1988 | 200 | 13,535 | 15,515 | 14,400 | 700 | ------ | 4,456 | 1,400 | 2,444 | 17,000 | 43,051 | ------ | 112,860 |
| 1989 | 190 | 14,073 | 16,550 | 15,700 | 785 | ------ | 4,189 | 1,580 | 3,177 | 17,000 | 63,105 | ------ | 136,494 |
| 1990 | 150 | 11,994 | 13,830 | 15,700 | 542 | ------ | 2,000 | 1,578 | 2,510 | 17,000 | 61,611 | ------ | 127,028 |
| 1991 | 120 | 11,329 | 14,434 | 13,200 | 395 | ------ | 1,716 | 1,716 | 3,031 | 16,000 | 53,364 | ------ | 115,000 |
| 1992 | 120 | 9,405 | 14,840 | 19,200 | 1,320 | 700 | 1,458 | 1,610 | 3,220 | 5,000 | 49,725 | 700 | 108,000 |
| 1993 | 120 | 9,700 | 14,899 | 18,300 | 1,000 | 600 | 1,705 | 2,050 | 2,980 | 4,800 | 36,803 | 700 | 94,000 |
| 1994[1] | 100 | 10,250 | 16,028 | 17,500 | 1,000 | 500 | 2,610 | 2,100 | 2,765 | 4,500 | 46,800 | 700 | 105,000 |
| 1995[2] | 400 | 9,536 | 17,889 | 17,500 | 1,200 | 700 | 3,810 | 1,830 | 3,630 | 7,300 | 60,900 | 500 | 126,000 |

[1] Preliminary. [2] Estimate. [3] Shipments. [4] Formerly part of the U.S.S.R.; data not reported separately until 1992. *Source: U.S. Geological Survey*

## U.S. Salient Statistics of Molybdenum In Metric Tons (Contained Molybdenum)

| | Concentrate | | | | | | | Primary Products[4] | | | | | | | | |
|---|---|---|---|---|---|---|---|---|---|---|---|---|---|---|---|---|
| | | Shipments | | | | | | Net Production | | | | Shipments | | | | |
| Year | Production | Total (Includes Exports) | Value Mil. $ | For Exports | Consumption | Imports for Consumption | Stocks, Dec. 31[3] | Grand Total | Molybdic Oxide[5] | Molybdenum Metal Powder | Price Avg. Value $ Kl.[6] | To Domestic Destinations | Oxide for Exports (Gross Weight) | Consumption | Producer Stocks, Dec. 31 |
| 1985 | 45,058 | 46,524 | 347.8 | 16,062 | W | 47 | 3,874 | 25,728 | 20,262 | 1,552 | 3.33 | 30,699 | 15,074 | 13,903 | 8,734 |
| 1986 | 39,058 | 39,487 | 240.5 | 7,592 | 22,054 | 508 | 3,953 | 7,462 | 2,555 | 1,769 | 2.92 | 24,046 | 8,863 | 13,258 | 8,603 |
| 1987 | 34,073 | 31,692 | 179.3 | 18,377 | 16,983 | 573 | 6,841 | 11,257 | 7,076 | 4,181 | 7.28 | 18,447 | 5,567 | 14,800 | 10,055 |
| 1988 | 43,051 | 45,240 | 266.9 | 23,500 | 35,690 | 514 | 4,777 | 29,782 | 25,404 | 4,378 | 7.61 | 20,535 | W | 17,422 | 7,116 |
| 1989 | 63,105 | 61,733 | 421.4 | 51,232 | 41,877 | 238 | 6,969 | 16,545 | 16,545 | W | 8.05 | 18,277 | 1,391 | 17,204 | 6,675 |
| 1990 | 61,611 | 61,580 | 346.3 | 41,380 | 35,455 | 478 | 7,672 | 15,727 | 15,727 | W | 7.39 | 17,983 | 787 | 18,060 | 5,919 |
| 1991 | 53,364 | 53,607 | 249.9 | 22,424 | 32,998 | 161 | 5,291 | 20,782 | 18,739 | 2,043 | 5.27 | 19,105 | 1,571 | 16,901 | 9,422 |
| 1992 | 49,725 | 45,098 | 189.9 | 33,439 | 15,243 | 831 | 11,905 | 13,880 | 11,916 | 1,964 | 4.85 | 17,305 | 557 | 17,200 | 7,480 |
| 1993 | 36,803 | 39,209 | 165.1 | 28,280 | 13,794 | 3,398 | 11,200 | 11,989 | 10,697 | 1,292 | 5.13 | 15,981 | 1,042 | 17,700 | 6,150 |
| 1994[1] | 46,800 | 46,000 | 284.0 | 14,568 | 17,200 | 2,280 | 5,510 | 16,000 | 14,900 | 1,070 | 4.60 | 21,400 | 2,240 | 19,100 | 3,940 |
| 1995[2] | 60,900 | 61,700 | 651.0 | 18,600 | 13,700 | 5,570 | 5,390 | 22,000 | 20,900 | 1,070 | 17.47 | 24,000 | 2,840 | 20,200 | 4,820 |

[1] Preliminary. [2] Estimate. [3] At mines and at plants making molybdenum products. [4] Comprises ferromolybdenum, molybdic oxide, and molybdenum salts and metal. [5] Includes molybdic oxide briquets, molybdic acid, molybdenum trioxide, and all others. [6] U.S. producer price per kilogram of molybdenum contained in technical-grade molybdic oxide. W = Withheld proprietary data. *Source: U.S. Geological Survey*

# Nickel

Most commercial nickel is used in stainless steel and other corrosion-resistant alloys. Approximately one-fifth of the nickel produced in the U.S. is used in plating to give hard, tarnish-resistant, polishable surfaces. Plating techniques, like electroless coating or single-slurry coating, are employed for such applications as helicopter rotors, turbine blades, extrusion dies, and rolled steel strip. Nickel finds use in coins to replace silver and has been utilized in ceramics, rechargeable batteries, and electronic circuitry. Nickel-base alloys are consumed in wire, bars, sheets, and tubular forms fabricated into finished products.

U.S. consumption of nickel (exclusive of scrap) over the first six months of 1996 was 51,300 tonnes vs. 52,500 tonnes for the same period of 1995. By form of nickel material, cathodes, pellets, briquets, and powder comprised 41,000 tonnes. Ferronickel comprised 8,710 tonnes while oxide-sinter, salts, and other forms comprised 1,660 tonnes. Total 1995 consumption was 105,000 tonnes.

In the January-June 1996 period nickel scrap consumption was 26,800 tonnes, ferrous scrap consumption was 22,100 tonnes, and nonferrous scrap consumption was 4,740 tonnes. For all of 1995, total scrap consumption was 58,100 tonnes with 48,900 tonnes of ferrous scrap and 9,200 tonnes of nonferrous scrap. At the end of June 1996, ferrous scrap stocks were 3,370 tonnes, nonferrous scrap stocks were 100 tonnes, and total scrap stocks 3,470 tonnes.

Consumer stocks of nickel at the end of June 1996 were 3,980 tonnes. At the end of June 1996, stocks of nickel cathodes, pellets, briquets, and powder were 3,560 tonnes. Stocks of ferronickel were 330 tonnes. Stocks of oxide-sinter, salts, and other forms were 98 tonnes. Nickel stocks at the end of 1995 were 6,030 tonnes.

U.S. imports for consumption of nickel over the January-May 1996 period were 69,400 tonnes (nickel content). Imports of cathodes, pellets, and briquets were 52,400 tonnes, powder and flakes 4,360 tonnes, and ferronickel 7,550 tonnes. The major supplier of nickel materials in 1996 was Canada with 39 percent, Norway 15 percent, Russia 15 percent, and Australia 10 percent. For all of 1995, imports of nickel materials were 157,000 tonnes.

The U.S. exports smaller amounts of nickel materials. For January-May 1996, exports were 17,200 tonnes. Exports of stainless steel scrap were 8,410 tonnes while waste and scrap exports were 4,220 tonnes. Exports of nickel chemicals were 1,630 tonnes and ferronickel exports 1,010 tonnes. Major export destinations were Canada, South Korea, Spain, and Japan.

### *Futures Markets*

Nickel futures are traded on the London Metals Exchange.

## World Mine Production of Nickel    In Metric Tons (Contained Nickel)

| Year | Australia[3] | Botswana | Brazil | Canada | China | Dominican Republic | Finland[3] | Greece | Indonesia | New Caledonia | Philippines | Russia[4] | South Africa | United States | Zimbabwe | World Total |
|---|---|---|---|---|---|---|---|---|---|---|---|---|---|---|---|---|
| 1986 | 76,740 | 25,583 | 21,103 | 163,642 | 25,000 | 21,878 | 11,886 | 14,424 | 53,680 | 61,780 | 12,791 | 259,000 | 31,026 | 1,066 | 3,720 | 852,151 |
| 1987 | 74,554 | 25,900 | 22,092 | 189,086 | 25,000 | 32,521 | 10,557 | 9,202 | 57,764 | 56,850 | 7,819 | 270,000 | 34,300 | ------ | 6,300 | 890,539 |
| 1988 | 62,358 | 26,000 | 18,677 | 216,589 | 32,700 | 29,345 | 11,699 | 13,131 | 57,982 | 71,200 | 10,349 | 280,000 | 30,000 | ------ | 12,600 | 952,215 |
| 1989 | 67,041 | 23,700 | 18,826 | 200,899 | 34,250 | 31,264 | 10,480 | 16,097 | 62,987 | 96,200 | 15,380 | 280,000 | 28,900 | ------ | 12,721 | 984,078 |
| 1990 | 67,000 | 23,200 | 24,100 | 196,225 | 33,000 | 28,700 | 11,524 | 18,500 | 68,308 | 85,100 | 15,818 | 280,000 | 29,000 | 330 | 12,654 | 974,000 |
| 1991 | 69,000 | 23,500 | 26,400 | 192,259 | 31,000 | 29,062 | 9,900 | 19,300 | 71,681 | 114,492 | 13,658 | 245,000 | 27,700 | 5,523 | 12,371 | 991,000 |
| 1992 | 64,000 | 23,500 | 29,400 | 192,086 | 37,000 | 25,000 | 9,171 | 17,000 | 77,600 | 113,100 | 13,000 | 280,000 | 28,400 | 6,671 | 12,200 | 981,000 |
| 1993 | 64,717 | 23,000 | 32,200 | 188,378 | 30,700 | 23,863 | 8,290 | 12,940 | 65,800 | 97,100 | 7,660 | 243,000 | 30,000 | 2,464 | 12,769 | 905,000 |
| 1994[1] | 71,900 | 23,000 | 32,000 | 150,000 | 33,000 | 30,500 | 7,250 | 19,000 | 81,100 | 96,000 | 9,800 | 240,000 | 31,000 | 2,540 | 13,500 | 895,000 |
| 1995[2] | 101,334 | 16,692 | 15,604 | 180,986 | 31,026 | 31,208 | 3,538 | 16,692 | 83,735 | ------ | 17,237 | ------ | 29,756 | 2,540 | 10,705 | 827,911 |

[1] Preliminary. [2] Estimate. [3] Content of nickel and sulfate and concentrates. *Source: U.S. Geological Survey*

## Salient Statistics of Nickel in the United States    In Metric Tons (Contained Nickel)

| | | Production | | Nickel Consumed[1], By Uses | | | | | | | | | Stocks, Dec. 31 | | Primary & Secondary Nickel | | |
|---|---|---|---|---|---|---|---|---|---|---|---|---|---|---|---|---|---|
| Year | Net Import Reliance as a % of Apparent Consumption | Plant[4] | Secondary[5] | Alloy Steels | Cast Irons | Copper Base Alloys | Electroplating Anodes | Nickel Alloys | Stainless & Heat Resisting Steels | Super Alloys | Chemicals | Apparent Consumption | At Consumers' Plants | At Producer Plants | Exports | Imports | Avg. Price LME[6] $ Lb. |
| 1986 | 73 | 1,498 | 41,039 | 7,458 | 2,370 | 9,609 | 19,050 | 18,086 | 54,580 | 11,563 | 1,692 | 164,483 | 19,256 | 9,344 | 19,586 | 117,114 | 1.76 |
| 1987 | 79 | ------- | 32,331 | 8,139 | 1,591 | 10,169 | 20,548 | 17,377 | 71,797 | 16,605 | 1,765 | 183,397 | 13,474 | 6,191 | 20,951 | 134,511 | 2.19 |
| 1988 | 74 | ------- | 49,371 | 7,330 | 2,359 | 6,890 | 19,520 | 19,046 | 80,107 | 13,537 | 1,816 | 159,156 | 15,081 | 6,967 | 27,916 | 127,680 | 6.25 |
| 1989 | 71 | 347 | 52,131 | 6,094 | 2,318 | 9,928 | 21,604 | 18,757 | 68,866 | 10,956 | 1,164 | 157,103 | 16,562 | 6,326 | 31,460 | 137,017 | 6.04 |
| 1990 | 64 | 3,701 | 57,367 | 7,007 | 2,646 | 7,594 | 15,550 | 16,315 | 96,120 | 15,713 | 1,500 | 170,042 | 13,971 | 8,065 | 37,057 | 145,600 | 4.02 |
| 1991 | 61 | 7,065 | 53,521 | 5,536 | 1,185 | 6,938 | 15,474 | 16,882 | 84,292 | 13,787 | 1,363 | 156,663 | 15,940 | 11,794 | 36,902 | 138,210 | 3.70 |
| 1992 | 59 | 8,962 | 55,871 | 4,988 | 1,202 | 6,313 | 16,538 | 15,946 | 83,460 | 10,872 | 51 | 159,373 | 17,480 | 10,140 | 33,867 | 128,510 | 3.18 |
| 1993 | 63 | 4,878 | 54,702 | 4,940 | 805 | 6,078 | 16,611 | 17,004 | 87,300 | 10,783 | 1,170 | 158,000 | 14,430 | 15,700 | 33,199 | 132,710 | 2.40 |
| 1994[2] | 66 | ------- | ------- | 5,930 | 499 | 7,940 | 15,500 | 20,500 | 88,700 | 11,700 | 2,670 | 164,000 | 10,200 | 10,200 | 41,940 | 133,060 | 2.88 |
| 1995[3] | | | | 8,100 | W | W | 13,700 | 19,300 | 40,300 | 13,200 | W | | | | | | |

[1] Exclusive of scrap. [2] Preliminary. [3] Estimate. [4] Smelter & refinery. [5] From purchased scrap (ferrous & nonferrous). [6] London Metal Exchange
W = Withheld proprietary data. *Source: U.S. Geological Survey*

# Oats

Within the U.S. feed grain complex oats production is the smallest, totaling about 2 percent that of corn. The 1996/97 record low crop (June to May) of 155 million bushels compares with the previous low of 162 million in 1995/96. The planted oats acreage in 1996/97 of 2.7 million (vs. 3 million in 1995/96) extended the downtrend that took hold early in the 1980's when planted acreage averaged near 15 million acres. Average yield, however, rose in 1996/97 to 57.8 bushels per acre from 54.7 in 1995/96. South Dakota was the largest producing state in 1996 with 21.6 million bushels followed by North Dakota and Wisconsin. Despite the small 1996/97 crop, imports, mostly from Canada, are forecast at only 85 million bushels vs. 81 million in 1995/96 and underscoring the well entrenched contraction in U.S. oats demand.

1996/97 oat carryin stocks, as of June 1, 1996, of 66 million bushels, a record low, compare with 101 million a year earlier. The total supply for 1996/97 of 307 million bushels compares with 343 million in 1995/96. Disappearance was estimated at 238 million vs. 277 million, respectively. Feed use was forecast at only 115 million bushels vs. 152 million in 1995/96, and feed/seed/industrial use placed at 120 million vs. 123 million in 1995/96. U.S. oat exports are insignificant. Carryover stocks on May 31, 1997 are placed at 69 million bushels.

Despite the dwindling statistical data crop prices declined into late calendar 1996, from a high of $2.96 per bushel in April to less than $1.50 by yearend, basis nearby futures. The average farm price for 1996/97 was forecast at $1.65-2.05/bushel vs. $1.68 in 1995/96, the highest average farm price of the 1990's.

World oats production has also been declining: in 1985/86 about 50 million metric tons were produced, by 1995/96 the total was less than 29 million as less acreage was allocated to oats. In 1996/97 world acreage of 18.2 million hectare compares with 18.3 million in 1995/96 and almost 20 million in 1994/95. Average yield, however, increased in 1996/97 to 1.73 tons per hectare vs. 1.57 in 1995/96, bolstering 1996/97 production to 31.6 million tons of which the U.S. produced about 7 percent. Russia remains the world's largest producer, but their 1996/97 crop of 9.5 million tons is about one-third below their mid 1980's production. Among the few major producers only Canada has shown any real growth in production, the record high 4.5 million tons in 1996/97 compares with 2.7 million in 1995/96 and a 1980's average of about 3 million tons. Most of the world's oats production is consumed domestically and world trade is small. In 1996/97, exports were put at 1.9 million tons with Canada accounting for 1.4 million; importing nations are more numerous, but the U.S. is the consistent leader with 1.5 million tons forecast for 1996/97.

### *Futures Markets*

Oat futures and options are traded on the Chicago Board of Trade (CBOT) and the Winnipeg Commodity Exchange (WCE). Oat futures are traded on the Mid America Commodity Exchange (MidAm).

**World Production of Oats** In Thousands of Metric Tons

| Crop Year | Agrentina | Australia | Canada | China | Denmark | France | Germany | Italy | Poland | Spain | Sweden | Turkey | United Kingdom | United States | Former U.S.S.R. | World Total |
|---|---|---|---|---|---|---|---|---|---|---|---|---|---|---|---|---|
| 1981-2 | 339 | 1,617 | 3,188 | 1,700 | 176 | 1,774 | 3,200 | 422 | 2,731 | 445 | 1,816 | 325 | 620 | 7,391 | 15,000 | 45,343 |
| 1982-3 | 637 | 848 | 3,637 | 1,660 | 178 | 1,802 | 3,777 | 359 | 2,608 | 443 | 1,663 | 330 | 575 | 8,602 | 15,500 | 47,866 |
| 1983-4 | 593 | 2,296 | 2,773 | 1,650 | 86 | 1,374 | 2,489 | 307 | 2,377 | 464 | 1,268 | 310 | 465 | 6,923 | 17,000 | 45,115 |
| 1984-5 | 610 | 1,367 | 2,670 | 780 | 150 | 1,892 | 2,973 | 433 | 2,604 | 780 | 1,904 | 300 | 516 | 6,875 | 19,200 | 48,391 |
| 1985-6 | 400 | 1,339 | 2,997 | 664 | 152 | 1,803 | 3,278 | 363 | 2,682 | 719 | 1,668 | 314 | 615 | 7,559 | 20,500 | 50,062 |
| 1986-7 | 400 | 1,584 | 3,251 | 599 | 111 | 1,007 | 2,687 | 397 | 2,486 | 433 | 1,486 | 300 | 505 | 5,608 | 21,929 | 47,471 |
| 1987-8 | 650 | 1,738 | 2,995 | 642 | 94 | 1,045 | 2,406 | 361 | 2,428 | 502 | 1,440 | 310 | 450 | 5,424 | 18,495 | 43,270 |
| 1988-9 | 451 | 1,867 | 2,993 | 670 | 202 | 984 | 2,941 | 383 | 2,222 | 537 | 1,330 | 300 | 545 | 3,158 | 15,287 | 37,506 |
| 1989-90 | 620 | 1,640 | 3,546 | 622 | 125 | 970 | 2,010 | 296 | 2,186 | 494 | 1,455 | 270 | 530 | 5,423 | 14,972 | 39,554 |
| 1990-1 | 434 | 1,530 | 2,692 | 685 | 121 | 830 | 2,104 | 298 | 2,119 | 512 | 1,584 | 270 | 550 | 5,189 | 15,081 | 39,042 |
| 1991-2 | 400 | 1,690 | 1,794 | 650 | 125 | 740 | 1,867 | 359 | 1,873 | 410 | 1,426 | 280 | 545 | 3,534 | 12,342 | 32,785 |
| 1992-3 | 450 | 1,937 | 2,823 | 640 | 93 | 700 | 1,314 | 333 | 1,229 | 320 | 807 | 280 | 525 | 4,298 | 13,974 | 33,587 |
| 1993-4 | 440 | 1,652 | 3,550 | 640 | 150 | 710 | 1,730 | 370 | 1,500 | 400 | 1,295 | 280 | 500 | 2,994 | 14,422 | 35,162 |
| 1994-5[1] | 350 | 920 | 3,640 | 600 | ----- | 680 | 1,660 | 360 | 1,240 | ----- | 990 | 300 | 600 | 3,320 | 13,850 | 33,160 |
| 1995-6[2] | 350 | 1,940 | 2,860 | 640 | ----- | 620 | 1,420 | 310 | 1,500 | ----- | 950 | 280 | 600 | 2,350 | 10,690 | 28,970 |
| 1996-7[3] | 320 | 1,600 | 4,380 | 650 | ----- | 600 | 1,600 | 300 | 1,500 | ----- | 1,130 | 250 | ----- | 2,250 | 11,230 | 31,440 |

[1] Preliminary. [2] Estimate. [3] Forecast. *Source: Foreign Agricultural Service, U.S. Department of Agriculture*

**United States Official Oats Crop Production Reports** In Thousands of Bushels

| Year | July 1 | Aug. 1 | Sept. 1 | Oct. 1 | Dec. | Final | Year | July 1 | Aug. 1 | Sept. 1 | Oct. 1 | Dec. | Final |
|---|---|---|---|---|---|---|---|---|---|---|---|---|---|
| 1985 | 498,953 | 519,028 | 537,443 | ------ | 518,626 | 520,800 | 1991 | 280,016 | 259,666 | 259,666 | 242,526 | ------ | 243,851 |
| 1986 | ------ | 443,183 | 413,025 | ------ | 383,553 | 386,356 | 1992 | 256,381 | 276,381 | ------ | ------ | ------ | 294,229 |
| 1987 | ------ | 392,843 | ------ | ------ | ------ | 373,713 | 1993 | 262,860 | 249,830 | 249,830 | 208,138 | ------ | 206,770 |
| 1988 | ------ | 206,330 | 206,330 | 210,766 | ------ | 217,375 | 1994 | 248,151 | 247,753 | 247,753 | 229,717 | ------ | 229,008 |
| 1989 | 387,593 | 380,690 | 380,690 | 370,693 | ------ | 373,587 | 1995 | 181,508 | 186,167 | 186,167 | ------ | ------ | 162,027 |
| 1990 | 374,457 | 365,337 | 365,337 | 358,288 | ------ | 357,654 | 1996 | 154,968 | 157,663 | ------ | ------ | ------ | 155,225 |

*Source: National Agricultural Statistics Service, U.S. Department of Agriculture*

# OATS

## Oat Stocks in the United States In Thousands of Bushels

| Year | On Farms Mar. 1 | On Farms June 1 | On Farms Sept. 1 | On Farms Dec. 1 | Off Farms Mar. 1 | Off Farms June 1 | Off Farms Sept. 1 | Off Farms Dec. 1 | Total Stocks Mar. 1 | Total Stocks June 1 | Total Stocks Sept. 1 | Total Stocks Dec. 1 |
|---|---|---|---|---|---|---|---|---|---|---|---|---|
| 1990 | 140,000 | 82,850 | 234,700 | 194,700 | 74,749 | 74,062 | 117,009 | 99,398 | 214,749 | 156,912 | 351,709 | 294,098 |
| 1991 | 138,600 | 92,400 | 173,600 | 148,100 | 90,659 | 78,831 | 110,487 | 96,508 | 229,259 | 171,231 | 284,087 | 244,608 |
| 1992 | 98,150 | 61,000 | 199,900 | 161,200 | 76,735 | 66,721 | 94,717 | 81,292 | 174,885 | 127,721 | 294,617 | 242,492 |
| 1993 | 110,250 | 66,130 | 161,000 | 124,200 | 64,875 | 47,063 | 58,004 | 69,517 | 175,125 | 113,193 | 219,004 | 193,717 |
| 1994 | 85,050 | 53,940 | 144,300 | 113,400 | 61,502 | 51,583 | 75,551 | 78,664 | 146,552 | 105,523 | 219,851 | 192,064 |
| 1995 | 78,400 | 46,750 | 107,200 | 87,200 | 70,575 | 53,848 | 72,967 | 65,804 | 148,975 | 100,598 | 180,167 | 153,004 |
| 1996[1] | 57,350 | 32,600 | 93,400 | 80,650 | 55,268 | 33,708 | 39,503 | 47,872 | 112,618 | 66,308 | 132,903 | 128,522 |

[1] Preliminary. *Source: National Agriucultural Statistics Service, U.S. Department of Agriculture*

## Oats Supply and Utilization in the United States

| Crop Year Beginning June 1 | Acreage Planted (1,000 Acres) | Acreage Harvested (1,000 Acres) | Yield Per Acre (Bushels) | Production (In Millions of Bushels) | Imports | Total Supply | Feed & Residual | Food, Alcohol & Industrial | Seed | Exports | Total Use | Ending Stocks | Farm Price (Dollars Per Bushel) | Findley Loan Rate | Target Price |
|---|---|---|---|---|---|---|---|---|---|---|---|---|---|---|---|
| 1981-2 | 13,632 | 9,407 | 54.2 | 509.5 | 1.5 | 688.0 | 458.0 | 41.2 | 34.2 | 2.7 | 536.1 | 151.9 | 1.88 | 1.24 | 0 |
| 1982-3 | 13,951 | 10,258 | 57.8 | 592.6 | 3.5 | 748.0 | 442.4 | 41.7 | 43.3 | .8 | 528.2 | 219.8 | 1.49 | 1.31 | 1.50 |
| 1983-4 | 20,289 | 9,062 | 52.6 | 476.5 | 29.9 | 726.2 | 474.0 | 40.9 | 29.5 | .9 | 545.3 | 180.9 | 1.62 | 1.36 | 1.60 |
| 1984-5 | 12,414 | 8,163 | 58.0 | 473.7 | 33.6 | 688.2 | 435.6 | 41.0 | 31.2 | .5 | 508.3 | 179.9 | 1.67 | 1.31 | 1.60 |
| 1985-6 | 13,235 | 8,147 | 63.6 | 518.5 | 27.2 | 725.6 | 464.2 | 44.0 | 32.5 | 1.2 | 541.9 | 183.7 | 1.23 | 1.31 | 1.60 |
| 1986-7 | 14,671 | 6,840 | 56.3 | 385.0 | 32.4 | 601.0 | 384.4 | 45.0 | 38.0 | .9 | 468.3 | 132.7 | 1.21 | .99 | 1.60 |
| 1987-8 | 17,907 | 6,888 | 54.3 | 373.7 | 45.7 | 552.1 | 358.2 | 49.8 | 31.6 | .5 | 440.1 | 112.0 | 1.56 | .94 | 1.60 |
| 1988-9 | 13,910 | 5,533 | 39.3 | 217.6 | 62.9 | 392.5 | 193.8 | 72.7 | 27.1 | .6 | 294.2 | 98.3 | 2.61 | .90 | 1.55 |
| 1989-90 | 12,085 | 6,882 | 54.3 | 373.6 | 66.4 | 538.3 | 265.6 | 91.6 | 23.4 | .8 | 381.4 | 156.9 | 1.49 | .85 | 1.50 |
| 1990-1 | 10,423 | 5,945 | 60.1 | 357.5 | 63.4 | 578.0 | 286.1 | 100.9 | 19.1 | .6 | 406.7 | 171.2 | 1.14 | .81 | 1.45 |
| 1991-2 | 8,654 | 4,806 | 50.6 | 243.5 | 74.8 | 489.4 | 235.2 | 107.2 | 17.8 | 1.9 | 362.1 | 127.7 | 1.21 | .83 | 1.45 |
| 1992-3 | 7,961 | 4,492 | 65.4 | 294.8 | 55.0 | 476.9 | 233.0 | 107.2 | 17.8 | 5.7 | 363.7 | 113.2 | 1.32 | .88 | 1.45 |
| 1993-4 | 7,937 | 3,803 | 54.4 | 206.8 | 106.8 | 426.8 | 193.3 | 110.0 | 15.0 | 3.0 | 321.3 | 105.5 | 1.36 | .88 | 1.45 |
| 1994-5 | 6,639 | 4,010 | 57.1 | 229.0 | 93.2 | 427.7 | 201.1 | 111.0 | 14.0 | 1.0 | 327.1 | 100.6 | 1.22 | .97 | 1.45 |
| 1995-6[1] | 6,336 | 2,959 | 54.7 | 163.2 | 105.0 | 368.8 | 155.0 | 110.2 | 14.8 | 1.0 | 281.0 | 87.8 | 1.30-1.70 | .97 | 1.45 |
| 1996-7[2] | 4,600 | 2,700 | 58.0 | 155.0 | 105.0 | 306.0 | 115.0 | 110.2 | 14.8 | 2.0 | 237.0 | 69.0 | 1.30-1.70 | .97 | 1.45 |

[1] Preliminary. [2] Forecast. *Source: Economic Research Service, U.S. Department of Agriculture*

## Production of Oats in the United States by States In Thousands of Bushels

| Year | California | Illinois | Indiana | Iowa | Michigan | Minnesota | Missouri | Nebraska | New York | North Dakota | Ohio | Oregon | Pennsylvania | South Dakota | Texas | Wisconsin |
|---|---|---|---|---|---|---|---|---|---|---|---|---|---|---|---|---|
| 1981 | 3,600 | 13,530 | 5,525 | 59,520 | 21,080 | 90,090 | 4,590 | 15,800 | 17,920 | 44,160 | 17,010 | 4,550 | 20,010 | 70,520 | 18,860 | 52,606 |
| 1982 | 3,350 | 11,800 | 6,720 | 54,150 | 28,350 | 97,920 | 3,276 | 26,680 | 18,200 | 55,650 | 23,460 | 6,375 | 19,765 | 123,540 | 10,730 | 49,290 |
| 1983 | 2,925 | 12,600 | 4,560 | 38,250 | 15,600 | 76,950 | 2,538 | 13,640 | 11,400 | 63,630 | 15,360 | 6,000 | 16,200 | 79,200 | 24,000 | 45,050 |
| 1984 | 3,450 | 11,385 | 4,960 | 47,360 | 21,700 | 78,000 | 1,584 | 15,680 | 10,620 | 49,980 | 13,860 | 6,600 | 15,960 | 86,800 | 8,750 | 53,320 |
| 1985 | 3,015 | 12,480 | 7,590 | 57,760 | 26,130 | 77,000 | 5,775 | 25,620 | 17,710 | 44,520 | 26,350 | 9,200 | 21,000 | 79,520 | 15,000 | 51,480 |
| 1986 | 3,150 | 14,400 | 6,390 | 39,060 | 17,010 | 43,350 | 5,000 | 21,240 | 12,920 | 38,500 | 12,160 | 7,600 | 16,120 | 46,200 | 8,400 | 52,700 |
| 1987 | 2,800 | 13,110 | 6,365 | 35,750 | 17,100 | 45,600 | 3,420 | 17,640 | 12,000 | 36,400 | 17,500 | 5,200 | 14,820 | 52,900 | 9,900 | 43,200 |
| 1988 | 2,730 | 9,180 | 3,000 | 25,000 | 6,000 | 24,750 | 1,520 | 12,160 | 7,540 | 7,200 | 9,000 | 6,500 | 13,000 | 20,000 | 9,000 | 46,860 |
| 1989 | 3,375 | 16,000 | 6,840 | 54,000 | 20,100 | 46,750 | 3,600 | 8,640 | 9,145 | 20,150 | 15,750 | 6,860 | 13,770 | 44,000 | 6,600 | 46,860 |
| 1990 | 3,375 | 11,560 | 4,830 | 40,800 | 13,050 | 48,180 | 2,226 | 13,440 | 8,235 | 16,100 | 2,280 | 4,590 | 15,840 | 53,200 | 9,225 | 47,570 |
| 1991 | 3,375 | 6,600 | 2,565 | 21,250 | 5,400 | 22,800 | 1,632 | 11,880 | 5,000 | 10,200 | 1,292 | 4,725 | 8,400 | 38,500 | 7,200 | 26,500 |
| 1992 | 2,800 | 7,930 | 2,800 | 25,125 | 8,400 | 35,000 | 2,430 | 15,400 | 7,700 | 37,400 | 12,070 | 4,230 | 13,735 | 42,900 | 5,720 | 34,410 |
| 1993 | 2,400 | 4,590 | 2,240 | 9,000 | 7,150 | 23,750 | 686 | 6,880 | 6,510 | 37,100 | 9,000 | 3,000 | 10,000 | 26,520 | 7,420 | 24,150 |
| 1994 | 2,400 | 5,490 | 1,855 | 26,660 | 6,270 | 24,750 | 1,768 | 7,500 | 7,040 | 33,550 | 6,720 | 4,500 | 8,480 | 31,360 | 5,200 | 25,380 |
| 1995 | 2,550 | 5,360 | 2,040 | 14,625 | 5,130 | 18,000 | 1,363 | 4,500 | 5,310 | 21,600 | 6,900 | 3,395 | 9,440 | 11,500 | 5,040 | 18,700 |
| 1996[1] | 2,250 | 4,620 | 1,600 | 12,920 | 3,600 | 15,120 | 1,537 | 7,455 | 4,275 | 19,000 | 5,130 | 3,395 | 7,560 | 21,600 | 3,400 | 17,400 |

[1] Preliminary. *Source: National Agricultural Statistics Service, U.S. Department of Agriculture*

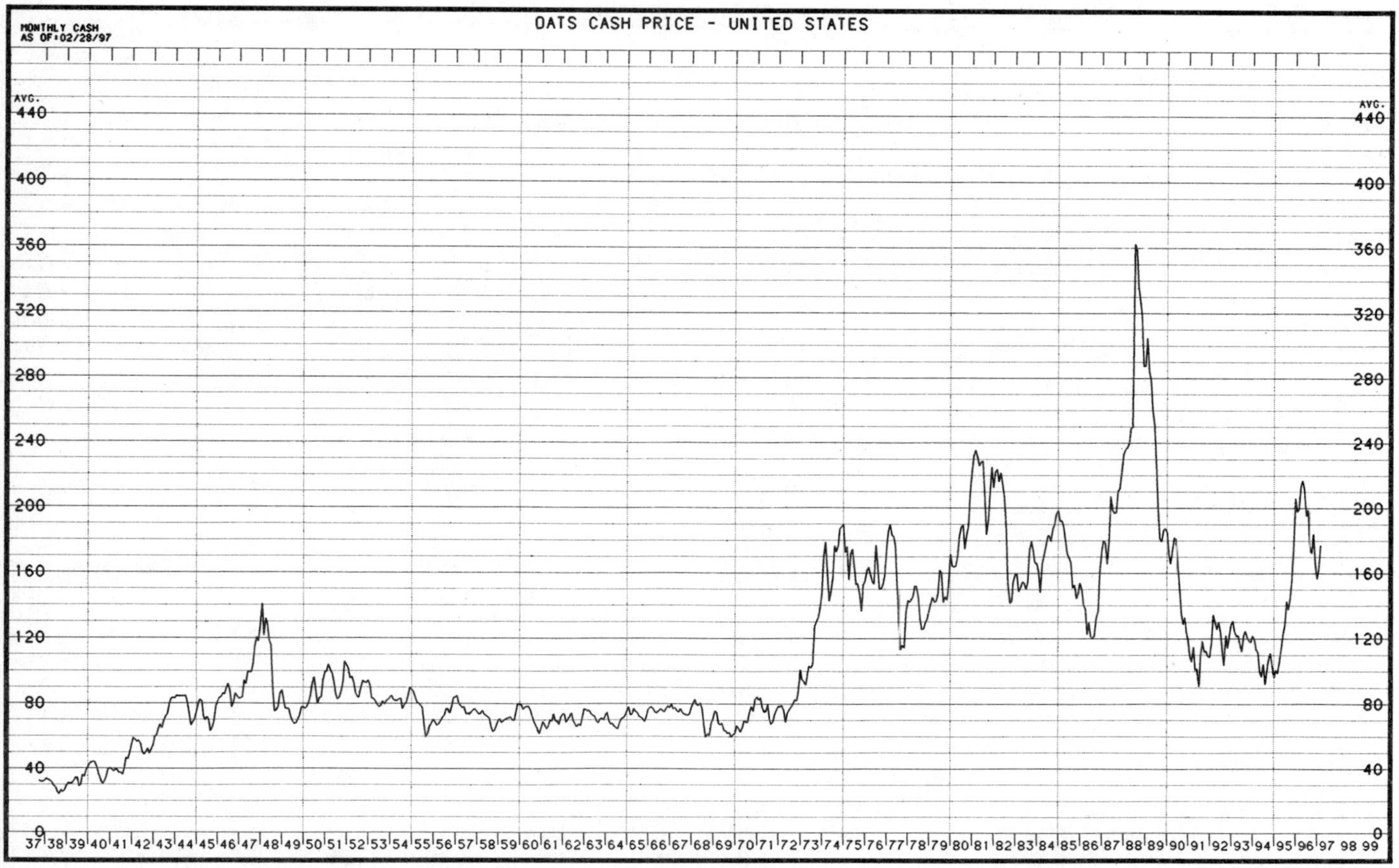


## Volume of Trading in Oat Futures in Chicago — In Millions of Bushels

| Year | Jan | Feb | Mar | Apr | May | June | July | Aug | Sept | Oct | Nov | Dec | Total |
|---|---|---|---|---|---|---|---|---|---|---|---|---|---|
| 1987 | 94.0 | 138.3 | 120.6 | 106.2 | 121.3 | 117.0 | 103.7 | 153.6 | 109.4 | 135.4 | 139.4 | 116.6 | 1,455.5 |
| 1988 | 92.1 | 121.2 | 146.6 | 162.1 | 162.6 | 267.1 | 160.3 | 121.1 | 107.6 | 108.1 | 183.0 | 141.1 | 1,772.9 |
| 1989 | 168.5 | 136.6 | 150.7 | 188.7 | 138.7 | 195.2 | 148.7 | 174.9 | 104.2 | 86.7 | 191.9 | 64.5 | 1,749.3 |
| 1990 | 123.3 | 158.7 | 169.4 | 225.7 | 270.0 | 231.8 | 160.2 | 248.0 | 126.0 | 139.0 | 236.9 | 77.8 | 2,166.8 |
| 1991 | 100.2 | 151.4 | 151.6 | 213.6 | 102.9 | 224.7 | 185.5 | 205.3 | 89.3 | 101.5 | 172.8 | 76.0 | 1,774.8 |
| 1992 | 155.1 | 420.1 | 211.3 | 235.3 | 210.1 | 272.7 | 111.0 | 200.8 | 125.5 | 82.9 | 176.1 | 97.0 | 2,297.9 |
| 1993 | 102.4 | 132.5 | 130.3 | 315.7 | 167.1 | 215.6 | 166.5 | 160.4 | 134.4 | 203.9 | 361.6 | 186.3 | 2,276.7 |
| 1994 | 239.9 | 285.3 | 199.0 | 269.1 | 171.5 | 348.8 | 103.8 | 196.7 | 144.2 | 124.5 | 284.7 | 98.4 | 2,465.9 |
| 1995 | 67.6 | 185.1 | 147.5 | 227.7 | 170.6 | 535.4 | 149.3 | 228.4 | 158.4 | 193.2 | 261.6 | 235.0 | 2,559.7 |
| 1996 | 307.3 | 260.4 | 173.0 | 387.0 | 235.8 | 172.5 | 194.8 | 166.6 | 154.0 | 187.9 | 189.3 | 80.8 | 2,509.3 |

*Source: Chicago Board of Trade (CBT)*

## Average Open Interest of Oat Futures in Chicago — In Thousands of Bushels

| Year | Jan. | Feb. | Mar. | Apr. | May | June | July | Aug. | Sept. | Oct. | Nov. | Dec. |
|---|---|---|---|---|---|---|---|---|---|---|---|---|
| 1987 | 31,648 | 36,004 | 33,508 | 30,655 | 26,271 | 24,536 | 28,090 | 36,166 | 35,212 | 35,173 | 28,988 | 29,724 |
| 1988 | 35,008 | 42,084 | 39,209 | 43,132 | 43,594 | 48,130 | 40,230 | 35,936 | 34,095 | 35,978 | 45,844 | 46,842 |
| 1989 | 50,341 | 51,226 | 50,761 | 50,283 | 47,606 | 48,831 | 48,967 | 47,272 | 48,824 | 55,834 | 59,311 | 56,240 |
| 1990 | 56,134 | 59,043 | 56,777 | 61,213 | 62,563 | 54,455 | 53,714 | 60,559 | 64,824 | 74,022 | 75,574 | 58,791 |
| 1991 | 59,450 | 64,161 | 69,476 | 78,100 | 71,117 | 65,457 | 55,584 | 54,469 | 51,842 | 57,798 | 56,284 | 46,776 |
| 1992 | 47,776 | 77,496 | 76,797 | 75,261 | 76,646 | 73,863 | 63,793 | 55,501 | 49,345 | 45,889 | 43,906 | 36,433 |
| 1993 | 36,990 | 38,696 | 38,274 | 57,897 | 66,783 | 60,098 | 54,472 | 56,906 | 55,855 | 70,578 | 100,285 | 102,734 |
| 1994 | 105,964 | 100,687 | 100,971 | 99,412 | 91,561 | 72,873 | 58,550 | 69,616 | 73,715 | 81,330 | 76,768 | 66,882 |
| 1995 | 65,665 | 66,155 | 65,001 | 77,131 | 80,272 | 68,054 | 55,096 | 56,741 | 55,059 | 59,848 | 62,710 | 65,016 |
| 1996 | 66,264 | 70,476 | 71,154 | 72,485 | 69,487 | 58,487 | 56,680 | 59,013 | 57,286 | 59,589 | 55,749 | 42,748 |

*Source: Chicago Board of Trade (CBT)*

# OATS

## Average Cash Price of No. 2 Heavy White Oats at Minneapolis In Dollars Per Bushel

| Year | June | July | Aug. | Sept. | Oct. | Nov. | Dec. | Jan. | Feb. | Mar. | Apr. | May | Average | No. 2 -- Heavy, White -- Portland | Toledo |
|---|---|---|---|---|---|---|---|---|---|---|---|---|---|---|---|
| 1986-7 | 1.18 | 1.05 | 1.12 | 1.29 | 1.39 | 1.72 | 1.66 | 1.64 | 1.56 | 1.46 | 1.59 | 1.83 | 1.46 | 1.53 | 1.20 |
| 1987-8 | 1.64 | 1.61 | 1.77 | 1.85 | 1.97 | 2.05 | 2.02 | 2.10 | 2.06 | 1.93 | 1.94 | 2.12 | 1.92 | 1.76 | 1.68 |
| 1988-9 | 3.26 | 3.25 | 3.09 | 3.07 | 2.99 | 2.71 | 2.74 | 2.87 | 2.59 | 2.49 | 2.30 | 2.22 | 2.80 | 2.24 | 2.26 |
| 1989-90 | 1.97 | 1.72 | 1.59 | 1.58 | 1.61 | 1.68 | 1.70 | 1.56 | 1.48 | 1.57 | 1.63 | 1.68 | 1.65 | 1.63 | 1.40 |
| 1990-1 | 1.52 | 1.37 | 1.25 | 1.23 | 1.29 | 1.30 | 1.24 | 1.22 | 1.18 | 1.27 | 1.32 | 1.36 | 1.30 | 1.58 | 1.17 |
| 1991-2 | 1.25 | 1.33 | 1.38 | 1.35 | 1.41 | 1.42 | 1.49 | 1.50 | 1.68 | 1.66 | 1.57 | 1.59 | 1.47 | 1.60 | 1.37 |
| 1992-3 | 1.55 | 1.49 | 1.45 | 1.58 | 1.52 | 1.59 | 1.63 | 1.66 | 1.63 | 1.63 | 1.66 | 1.57 | 1.58 | 1.73 | 1.51 |
| 1993-4 | 1.54 | 1.63 | 1.63 | 1.66 | 1.56 | 1.51 | 1.56 | 1.57 | 1.52 | 1.55 | 1.46 | 1.37 | 1.55 | NA | 1.40 |
| 1994-5 | 1.47 | 1.36 | 1.44 | 1.44 | 1.44 | 1.41 | NQ | 1.46 | 1.42 | 1.54 | 1.62 | 1.76 | 1.36 | NA | 1.37 |
| 1995-6 | 1.73 | 1.92 | 1.96 | 2.04 | 2.11 | 2.63 | 2.50 | 2.40 | 2.31 | 2.47 | 2.56 | 2.68 | 2.28 | NA | NA |
| 1996-7[1] | 2.11 | 2.48 | 2.36 | 2.08 | 2.06 | 1.87 | 1.86 | 2.40 | 2.31 | 2.47 | 2.56 | 2.68 | 2.12 | NA | NA |

[1] Preliminary. NQ = No Quote. NA = Not avaliable. *Source: Economic Research Service, U.S. Department of Agriculture*

## Average Price Received by U.S. Farmers for Oats In Dollars Per Bushel

| Year | Jan. | Feb. | Mar. | Apr. | May | June | July | Aug. | Sept. | Oct. | Nov. | Dec. | Marketing Year Average |
|---|---|---|---|---|---|---|---|---|---|---|---|---|---|
| 1986 | 1.10 | .90 | .86 | .99 | 1.10 | 1.32 | 1.44 | 1.46 | 1.47 | 1.45 | 1.50 | 1.57 | 1.21 |
| 1987 | 1.52 | 1.29 | 1.40 | 1.49 | 1.60 | 1.62 | 1.76 | 1.79 | 1.84 | 1.78 | 1.82 | 1.84 | 1.56 |
| 1988 | 2.63 | 2.86 | 2.54 | 2.57 | 2.56 | 2.41 | 2.47 | 2.52 | 2.46 | 2.41 | 2.24 | 2.13 | 2.61 |
| 1989 | 2.52 | 2.46 | 2.41 | 2.24 | 2.13 | 1.82 | 1.53 | 1.47 | 1.38 | 1.47 | 1.48 | 1.53 | 1.49 |
| 1990 | 1.47 | 1.43 | 1.39 | 1.44 | 1.45 | 1.33 | 1.15 | 1.06 | 1.09 | 1.14 | 1.16 | 1.17 | 1.14 |
| 1991 | 1.13 | 1.13 | 1.16 | 1.16 | 1.16 | 1.08 | 1.08 | 1.09 | 1.12 | 1.21 | 1.25 | 1.25 | 1.21 |
| 1992 | 1.31 | 1.44 | 1.44 | 1.46 | 1.43 | 1.38 | 1.32 | 1.23 | 1.28 | 1.31 | 1.35 | 1.36 | 1.32 |
| 1993 | 1.42 | 1.42 | 1.43 | 1.45 | 1.51 | 1.43 | 1.36 | 1.32 | 1.31 | 1.33 | 1.39 | 1.42 | 1.36 |
| 1994 | 1.42 | 1.42 | 1.39 | 1.32 | 1.49 | 1.31 | 1.20 | 1.16 | 1.18 | 1.21 | 1.18 | 1.18 | 1.22 |
| 1995 | 1.22 | 1.22 | 1.33 | 1.36 | 1.41 | 1.38 | 1.52 | 1.48 | 1.43 | 1.50 | 1.72 | 1.91 | 1.46 |
| 1996[1] | 1.93 | 1.96 | 2.04 | 2.14 | 2.46 | 2.16 | 2.12 | 2.01 | 1.83 | 1.82 | 1.83 | 1.72 | 2.00 |

[1] Preliminary. *Source: National Agricultural Statistics Service, U.S. Department of Agriculture*

# Olive Oil

Despite its steep price premium to other cooking oils, olive oil remains the oil of choice for many due to its taste and health benefits. Perhaps due to its higher price, olive oil consumption has shown virtually no growth in recent years. The olive harvest begins in the northern Mediterranean region in mid-November and moves south, ending in March. The main producers are Italy, Spain, and Greece, with Tunisia, Turkey, and Morocco accounting for smaller amounts. Between 1990-91 and 1994-95, average olive oil production by Spain was 578,000 tonnes, Italy 418,000 tonnes, Greece 293,000 tonnes and Tunisia 181,000 tonnes. As a tree crop, olive oil production is cyclical with large crops typically followed by smaller ones.

The USDA forecasts that world olive oil production will fall substantially in 1995-96 (Aug.-Sept.). Production is estimated at 1.47 million tonnes, down 12.5 percent from the previous season's output of 1.68 million tonnes. *Oil World* estimates that production by the fifteen nations of the European Union will fall to a five year low in 1995/96, down 130,000 tonnes from the 1994-95 season and 170,000 tonnes below the recent five year average. A serious drought took a toll on Spanish production insuring that Spain's olive oil output will be the lowest in 20 years. This in turn could force Spain to increase imports of olive oil from Italy, Greece, and North Africa to 150,000-200,000 tonnes to cover domestic and export requirements. Olive oil stocks were estimated at 200,000 tonnes at the start of the new season, a four year low. Somewhat offsetting the smaller Spanish crop will be larger crops in Italy and Greece.

Much of the world's olive oil is consumed where it is grown. It is expected the steep production decline and very tight stocks could increase prices substantially. This could cause a switch by consumers to other cooking oils such as soybean oil or corn oil. The U.S., a major importer of olive oil, forecast 1995 usage at 289 million pounds, a four percent increase from 1994. On a net basis. U.S. imports of olive oil were forecast at 287 million pounds versus 276 million in 1994.

**World Production of Olive Oil (Pressed Oil)** In Thousands of Metric Tons

| Crop Year | Algeria | Argentina | Greece | Israel | Italy | Jordan | Lebanon | Libya | Morocco | Portugal | Spain | Syria | Tunisia | Turkey | World Total |
|---|---|---|---|---|---|---|---|---|---|---|---|---|---|---|---|
| 1984-5 | 15.0 | 9.7 | 266.0 | 4.0 | 371.8 | 7.1 | 7.0 | 12.0 | 28.5 | 48.0 | 724.2 | 66.6 | 99.8 | 91.0 | 1,769.8 |
| 1985-6 | 18.0 | 9.5 | 386.4 | 2.0 | 656.0 | 9.1 | 5.0 | 9.0 | 43.4 | 36.0 | 432.2 | 52.0 | 114.7 | 81.0 | 1,870.3 |
| 1986-7 | 15.0 | 7.5 | 257.0 | 3.0 | 383.1 | 15.4 | 6.0 | 7.4 | 38.0 | 44.0 | 529.8 | 81.0 | 127.5 | 138.0 | 1,670.2 |
| 1987-8 | 10.0 | 9.5 | 322.0 | 3.0 | 742.5 | 3.1 | 5.0 | 6.5 | 41.5 | 38.0 | 792.0 | 36.0 | 101.5 | 63.0 | 2,198.0 |
| 1988-9 | 10.0 | 11.0 | 319.2 | 4.0 | 390.0 | 13.0 | 8.0 | 6.0 | 31.5 | 24.6 | 431.4 | 100.0 | 61.0 | 102.0 | 1,552.0 |
| 1989-90 | 16.0 | 10.5 | 316.3 | 2.5 | 624.2 | 7.5 | 5.5 | 8.0 | 70.0 | 44.3 | 594.9 | 33.0 | 137.0 | 39.0 | 1,938.6 |
| 1990-1 | 6.0 | 11.0 | 187.0 | 7.5 | 176.4 | 9.0 | 6.5 | 7.0 | 40.0 | 22.0 | 690.6 | 92.0 | 189.0 | 92.0 | 1,579.1 |
| 1991-2 | 37.0 | 9.5 | 423.5 | 2.5 | 727.9 | 5.5 | 5.0 | 10.0 | 55.5 | 72.7 | 640.5 | 47.0 | 264.0 | 70.0 | 2,393.5 |
| 1992-3 | 26.5 | 10.5 | 339.0 | 7.5 | 469.8 | 15.5 | 8.0 | 6.0 | 43.0 | 26.9 | 673.9 | 95.0 | 133.0 | 65.0 | 1,974.0 |
| 1993-4[1] | 21.0 | 8.5 | 275.0 | 1.5 | 451.5 | 9.5 | 2.0 | 8.0 | 45.5 | 36.1 | 593.2 | 71.0 | 251.0 | 55.0 | 1,875.2 |
| 1994-5[2] | 14.0 | 10.0 | 389.8 | 4.5 | 464.4 | 16.5 | 5.0 | 6.5 | 49.5 | 36.0 | 520.0 | 101.5 | 148.0 | 184.0 | 2,004.9 |
| 1995-6[3] | 18.0 | 11.5 | 330.0 | 4.0 | 420.0 | 14.5 | 5.0 | 4.0 | 34.0 | 35.0 | 325.0 | 75.0 | 85.0 | 60.0 | 1,467.7 |

[1] Preliminary. [2] Estimate. [3] Forecast. *Source: The Oil World*

**Average Unit Value of U.S. Olive Oil Imports** In Dollars Per Metric Ton

| Year | Jan. | Feb. | Mar. | Apr. | May | June | July | Aug. | Sept. | Oct. | Nov. | Dec. | Average |
|---|---|---|---|---|---|---|---|---|---|---|---|---|---|
| 1987 | 1,690 | 1,763 | 1,652 | 1,726 | 1,635 | 1,577 | 1,588 | 1,608 | 1,563 | 1,646 | 1,609 | 1,696 | 1,646 |
| 1988 | 1,682 | 1,694 | 1,736 | 1,699 | 1,701 | 1,669 | 1,465 | 1,562 | 1,691 | 1,582 | 1,493 | 1,606 | 1,632 |
| 1989 | 1,642 | 1,642 | 1,890 | 1,930 | 2,005 | 1,981 | 1,919 | 1,919 | 1,862 | 1,917 | 1,910 | 2,017 | 1,886 |
| 1990 | 1,892 | 1,940 | 1,931 | 2,034 | 2,047 | 2,047 | 2,044 | 2,169 | 2,142 | 2,029 | 2,245 | 2,170 | 2,058 |
| 1991 | 2,195 | 2,213 | 2,355 | 2,188 | 2,283 | 2,274 | 2,281 | 2,282 | 2,401 | 2,250 | 2,417 | 2,523 | 2,305 |
| 1992 | 2,448 | 2,365 | 2,317 | 2,271 | 2,270 | 2,267 | 2,299 | 2,302 | 2,206 | 2,204 | 2,189 | 2,295 | 2,286 |
| 1993 | 2,132 | 2,071 | 1,853 | 1,823 | 1,779 | 1,820 | 1,805 | 1,815 | 1,836 | 1,788 | 1,885 | 1,852 | 1,872 |
| 1994 | 1,838 | 1,752 | 1,891 | 1,850 | 1,872 | 1,889 | 1,943 | 2,001 | 2,032 | 2,141 | 2,215 | 2,126 | 1,963 |
| 1995[1] | 2,245 | 2,316 | 2,470 | 2,629 | 2,795 | 2,857 | 3,032 | 3,112 | 3,110 | 3,253 | 3,256 | 3,322 | 2,866 |
| 1996[1] | 3,704 | 4,056 | 4,267 | 4,411 | 4,361 | 4,233 | 4,300 | 4,149 | 4,131 | 4,129 | | | 4,174 |

[1] Preliminary. *Source: Foreign Agricultural Service, U.S. Department of Agriculture*

**World Olive Oil Supply and Distribution** In Thousands of Metric Tons

| Crop Year | Production | Exports | Imports | Consumption | Ending Stocks | Crop Year | Production | Exports | Imports | Consumption | Ending Stocks |
|---|---|---|---|---|---|---|---|---|---|---|---|
| 1984-5 | 1,600 | 484 | 503 | 1,729 | 799 | 1990-1 | 1,579 | 316 | 333 | 1,879 | 419 |
| 1985-6 | 1,626 | 367 | 500 | 1,718 | 839 | 1991-2 | 2,394 | 346 | 349 | 1,916 | 899 |
| 1986-7 | 1,670 | 746 | 730 | 1,849 | 764 | 1992-3 | 1,974 | 379 | 373 | 2,054 | 813 |
| 1987-8 | 2,095 | 509 | 519 | 1,929 | 1,936 | 1993-4[1] | 1,875 | 407 | 414 | 2,030 | 665 |
| 1988-9 | 1,552 | 558 | 575 | 1,870 | 634 | 1994-5[2] | 2,005 | 478 | 477 | 1,951 | 718 |
| 1989-90 | 1,939 | 579 | 573 | 1,861 | 706 | 1995-6[3] | 1,468 | 346 | 348 | 1,796 | 391 |

[1] Preliminary. [2] Estimate. [3] Forecast. *Source: The Oil World*

# Onions

## Salient Statistics of Onions in the United States

| Crop Year | Harvested Acres | Yield Per Acre | Production 1,000 Cwt. | Price Per Cwt. | Farm Value $1,000 | Jan. 1 Stocks Frozen | Annual Pack Frozen | Imports Canned | Exports (Fresh) | Imports (Fresh) | Per Capita[3] Utilization --Lbs., Farm Weight-- All | Fresh |
|---|---|---|---|---|---|---|---|---|---|---|---|---|
| | | | | | | Millions of Pounds | | | | | | |
| 1987 | 123,720 | 364 | 45,113 | 12.50 | 505,163 | 35.7 | 185.2 | 13.0 | 282.0 | 387.9 | 14.9 | 13.4 |
| 1988 | 128,950 | 362 | 46,733 | 9.75 | 413,996 | 29.6 | 198.9 | 14.1 | 322.9 | 425.1 | 16.2 | 14.5 |
| 1989 | 132,660 | 361 | 47,902 | 11.40 | 496,971 | 33.4 | 208.8 | 3.3 | 256.8 | 364.0 | 16.4 | 14.8 |
| 1990 | 138,340 | 382 | 52,781 | 10.50 | 488,786 | 39.6 | 243.1 | 3.7 | 378.3 | 381.8 | 17.1 | 15.1 |
| 1991 | 133,970 | 378 | 50,702 | 12.50 | 582,556 | 34.4 | 226.5 | 3.4 | 345.0 | 496.1 | 17.3 | 15.7 |
| 1992 | 141,730 | 386 | 54,731 | 13.00 | 629,019 | 32.1 | 202.3 | 3.4 | 359.9 | 421.4 | 17.6 | 16.2 |
| 1993 | 152,580 | 380 | 57,956 | 16.80 | 831,986 | 34.2 | 213.7 | 4.7 | 437.9 | 510.2 | 18.5 | 16.5 |
| 1994 | 160,350 | 396 | 63,531 | 10.90 | 626,778 | 36.1 | 241.3 | 4.2 | 802.1 | 544.7 | 17.5 | 16.5 |
| 1995[1] | 164,000 | 391 | 64,182 | 11.10 | 633,692 | 51.2 | 246.8 | 4.0 | 662.1 | 483.7 | 19.0 | 17.7 |
| 1996[2] | 160,610 | 383 | 61,568 | 9.58 | 589,938 | 48.8 | | | 590.0 | 500.0 | 18.7 | 17.4 |

[1] Preliminary. [2] Forecast. [3] Includes fresh and processing. *Source: Economic Research Service, U.S. Department of Agriculture*

## Production of Onions in the United States In Thousands of Hundred Pounds (Cwt.)

| Year | Spring: Arizona | California | Texas | Total (All) | Summer: California | Colorado | Idaho | Michigan | Minnesota | New Mexico | New York | Oregon (Malheur) | Texas | Total (All) | Grand Total |
|---|---|---|---|---|---|---|---|---|---|---|---|---|---|---|---|
| 1987 | 585 | 3,198 | 2,750 | 6,533 | 10,730 | 4,688 | 4,620 | 1,900 | 195 | 2,106 | 3,132 | 7,032 | 799 | 39,334 | 45,867 |
| 1988 | 450 | 3,315 | 3,220 | 6,985 | 10,512 | 5,535 | 4,028 | 2,000 | 126 | 2,752 | 2,925 | 6,649 | 861 | 39,748 | 46,733 |
| 1989 | 440 | 3,080 | 3,225 | 7,380 | 10,125 | 5,520 | 3,996 | 2,212 | 161 | 3,000 | 2,912 | 6,710 | 1,040 | 40,516 | 47,902 |
| 1990 | 473 | 3,570 | 2,520 | 7,655 | 12,675 | 5,130 | 4,180 | 2,442 | 208 | 2,870 | 5,120 | 6,865 | 1,377 | 45,853 | 53,508 |
| 1991 | 441 | 3,160 | 3,264 | 7,093 | 11,250 | 4,953 | 4,543 | 2,044 | 294 | 2,960 | 3,510 | 7,588 | 960 | 42,017 | 49,110 |
| 1992 | 450 | 3,600 | 2,793 | 8,229 | 10,313 | 5,460 | 5,063 | 2,448 | 285 | 3,200 | 4,392 | 6,649 | 740 | 46,502 | 54,213 |
| 1993 | 631 | 3,300 | 2,768 | 8,193 | 13,035 | 5,735 | 4,698 | 2,201 | 22 | 4,074 | 3,720 | 5,940 | 936 | 49,763 | 57,956 |
| 1994 | 688 | 2,948 | 4,704 | 10,297 | 12,710 | 6,125 | 5,547 | 2,178 | 312 | 3,318 | 3,844 | 7,378 | 837 | 53,324 | 63,531 |
| 1995 | 672 | 3,300 | 3,763 | 10,110 | 12,658 | 6,141 | 5,481 | 1,856 | 125 | 4,095 | 4,032 | 7,134 | 870 | 54,072 | 64,182 |
| 1996[1] | 760 | 2,736 | 4,030 | 9,290 | 13,330 | 5,525 | 5,590 | 1,798 | 114 | 3,266 | 2,736 | 7,080 | 924 | 52,278 | 61,568 |

[1] Preliminary. *Source: Agricultural Statistics Board, U.S. Department of Agriculture*

## Cold Storage Stocks of Fresh Onions in the United States In Thousands of Pounds

| Year | Jan. 1 | Feb. 1 | Mar. 1 | Apr. 1 | May 1 | June 1 | July 1 | Aug. 1 | Sept. 1 | Oct. 1 | Nov. 1 | Dec. 1 |
|---|---|---|---|---|---|---|---|---|---|---|---|---|
| 1987 | 6,773 | 5,330 | 2,710 | 1,883 | 1,560 | 2,403 | 1,181 | 137 | 1,276 | 2,500 | 3,823 | 6,641 |
| 1988 | 4,406 | 1,982 | 192 | 35 | 575 | 2,551 | 1,587 | 268 | 3,508 | 7,453 | 10,499 | 9,018 |
| 1989 | 7,608 | 4,914 | 2,348 | 70 | 462 | 670 | 184 | 140 | 2,133 | 13,283 | 16,492 | 16,000 |
| 1990 | 11,858 | 12,787 | 7,282 | 5,226 | 2,633 | 3,346 | 2,394 | 984 | 2,296 | 13,927 | 23,224 | 21,731 |
| 1991 | 17,030 | 14,387 | 5,918 | 2,885 | 995 | 1,957 | 2,225 | 1,695 | 2,164 | 26,746 | 35,362 | 29,414 |
| 1992 | 9,894 | 7,717 | 5,799 | 595 | 357 | 2,072 | 1,882 | 951 | 6,476 | 22,115 | 28,573 | 16,839 |
| 1993 | 12,032 | 5,196 | 3,536 | 1,642 | 733 | 600 | 747 | 1,270 | 16,948 | 11,735 | 19,967 | 16,875 |
| 1994 | 6,353 | 2,668 | 1,678 | 1,390 | 838 | 2,973 | 2,106 | 2,060 | 1,631 | 3,858 | 6,300 | 4,058 |
| 1995 | 2,520 | 908 | 562 | 149 | 237 | 1,861 | 747 | 385 | 485 | 2,227 | 4,149 | 3,519 |
| 1996[1] | 2,352 | 1,115 | 1,986 | 744 | 579 | 1,358 | 1,535 | 1,276 | 1,682 | 5,273 | 18,895 | 16,084 |

[1] Preliminary. *Source: National Agricultural Statistics Service, U.S. Department of Agriculture*

## F.O.B. Price Received by Growers for Onions in the U.S. In Dollars Per Hundred Pounds (Cwt.)

| Year | Jan. | Feb. | Mar. | Apr. | May | June | July | Aug. | Sept. | Oct. | Nov. | Dec. | Season Average |
|---|---|---|---|---|---|---|---|---|---|---|---|---|---|
| 1987 | 16.50 | 18.30 | 20.60 | 26.30 | 22.30 | 16.80 | 14.90 | 10.60 | 9.71 | 8.77 | 9.38 | 10.60 | 12.50 |
| 1988 | 15.70 | 15.70 | 15.00 | 16.80 | 8.90 | 8.52 | 10.40 | 8.97 | 12.50 | 12.10 | 12.20 | 12.00 | 9.75 |
| 1989 | 11.50 | 10.90 | 9.70 | 10.90 | 9.47 | 12.90 | 16.90 | 16.00 | 11.20 | 10.10 | 9.62 | 9.70 | 11.40 |
| 1990 | 10.90 | 15.70 | 18.40 | 19.40 | 13.40 | 10.50 | 9.49 | 10.80 | 9.01 | 8.29 | 9.54 | 10.90 | 10.50 |
| 1991 | 13.80 | 10.20 | 11.90 | 18.40 | 21.50 | 14.10 | 17.70 | 12.90 | 11.20 | 10.00 | 10.60 | 10.40 | 12.50 |
| 1992 | 10.70 | 12.80 | 20.80 | 23.60 | 12.40 | 10.00 | 12.20 | 13.80 | 12.40 | 11.60 | 12.00 | 14.80 | 13.00 |
| 1993 | 16.60 | 14.00 | 17.30 | 31.00 | 23.60 | 10.40 | 12.70 | 14.80 | 13.30 | 12.10 | 18.70 | 24.50 | 16.70 |
| 1994 | 29.80 | 32.10 | 17.90 | 10.70 | 8.64 | 8.54 | 12.80 | 9.44 | 9.14 | 10.40 | 12.00 | 12.10 | 10.90 |
| 1995[1] | 12.10 | 13.20 | 18.60 | 22.30 | 17.40 | 12.60 | 12.30 | 10.60 | 11.00 | 11.10 | 10.90 | 9.80 | 11.10 |
| 1996[1] | 11.20 | 9.50 | 8.06 | 9.54 | 9.81 | 11.30 | 11.40 | 12.40 | 13.10 | 12.20 | | | |

[1] Preliminary. *Source: Economic Research Service, U.S. Department of Agriculture*

# Oranges and Orange Juice

Frozen concentrated orange juice (FCOJ) prices in 1996 showed signs of strength as well as weakness. Early in the year prices moved higher, approaching $1.40 per pound on the seasonal concerns about cold weather in Florida and the potential for a crop-damaging freeze. With the coldest part of the season past and no problem from the weather, orange juice prices began to slip lower as it appeared the 1996/97 crop had the potential to be record large. Despite an active hurricane season the Florida crop was largely untouched. Adding to the declining price trend were imports which exceeded the previous season by a wide margin. This brought more juice to an already large inventory which pressured new crop prices under $1.00 per pound in the fall.

Early in the fourth quarter of 1995 the supply situation looked very bearish. The Florida Citrus Processors reported that imports of FCOJ into the U.S. were running close to 80 percent above the level of 1994/95. Most U.S. imports originate in Brazil and attractive prices were causing juice to flow into the U.S. with the possibility that imports for the 1995/96 season could reached 50 million gallons. Movement of juice was also slowing down in late 1995/96 though total movement was still outpacing 1994/95 by about 2 percent. It appeared that for the 1995/96 season, movement of FCOJ would be near 270 million gallons.

The 1995/96 season pack of FCOJ was just over 202 million gallons, down 7 percent from the 1994/95 pack of 216.5 million gallons.

Since the freezes of the late 1980's, most producers in Florida have moved their groves to the south. The Florida Agricultural Statistics Service released its bi-annual Commercial Citrus Inventory report in September. It showed that Florida's total commercial citrus trees increased to a record high in January 1996 of 107 million, up 3.5 percent from January 1994. Orange trees in January 1996 were 84.2 million, up 3 percent from 81.6 million two years earlier. The number of bearing trees is 78.5 million. Florida's orange crop acreage in January 1996 increased to 656,598 acres, up from 653,370 acres in January 1994.

With more trees reaching their most productive years, the 1996/97 season, which begins in December, had the potential to be record large. The USDA reported that the 1996/97 Florida crop would be 220 million boxes, up over 8 percent from 1995/96 and a new record. The previous record was in 1979/80 at 206.7 million boxes. Early midseason and navel oranges were forecast at 130 million boxes while the Valencia crop was put at 90 million boxes. Florida yield for the 1996/97 season was forecast at 1.53 gallons per box at 42.0 degrees Brix. The 1995/96 yield was 1.52 gallons per box. The California orange crop was estimated at 63 million boxes, down 5 percent from 1995/96. All U.S. orange production was estimated at 285.95 million boxes, up just over 5 percent.

### *Futures Market*

Frozen concentrated orange juice futures and options are traded on the Citrus Associates of the New York Cotton Exchange (NYCE).

# ORANGES AND ORANGE JUICE

## World Production of Oranges In Thousands of Metric Tons

| Season | Agren-tina | Aust-ralia | Brazil | Cuba | Cyprus | Egypt | Greece | Israel | Italy | Mexico | Morocco | South Africa | Spain | Turkey | United States | Grand Total |
|---|---|---|---|---|---|---|---|---|---|---|---|---|---|---|---|---|
| 1987-8 | 650 | 394 | 10,400 | 508 | 138 | 1,387 | 462 | 627 | 1,343 | 1,942 | 891 | 681 | 2,442 | 700 | 7,903 | 30,990 |
| 1988-9 | 620 | 544 | 14,150 | 474 | 170 | 1,199 | 770 | 546 | 2,170 | 2,000 | 994 | 629 | 2,216 | 740 | 8,272 | 35,835 |
| 1989-90 | 750 | 458 | 12,036 | 604 | 223 | 1,397 | 932 | 877 | 2,067 | 1,900 | 775 | 697 | 2,400 | 740 | 7,083 | 33,361 |
| 1990-1 | 600 | 485 | 12,362 | 600 | 169 | 1,574 | 819 | 567 | 1,760 | 2,300 | 1,103 | 648 | 2,590 | 735 | 7,222 | 33,938 |
| 1991-2 | 640 | 595 | 14,974 | 428 | 168 | 1,694 | 820 | 513 | 1,842 | 2,100 | 780 | 680 | 2,651 | 830 | 8,175 | 38,193 |
| 1992-3 | 660 | 578 | 14,484 | 379 | 160 | 1,771 | 1,042 | 377 | 2,111 | 2,913 | 874 | 712 | 2,926 | 820 | 10,074 | 41,582 |
| 1993-4 | 746 | 651 | 13,710 | 350 | 160 | 1,324 | 854 | 365 | 2,100 | 3,174 | 916 | 739 | 2,509 | 840 | 9,462 | 39,595 |
| 1994-5[1] | 712 | 416 | 16,520 | 350 | 166 | 1,513 | 930 | 405 | 1,800 | 3,570 | 657 | 770 | 2,697 | 920 | 10,474 | 43,650 |
| 1995-6[2] | 580 | 543 | 16,360 | 380 | 170 | 1,555 | 870 | 472 | 2,200 | 3,000 | 1,013 | 930 | 2,434 | 840 | 10,723 | 43,910 |
| 1996-7[3] | NA | NA | NA | 350 | 165 | 1,608 | 850 | 472 | 1,515 | 2,800 | 780 | NA | 2,153 | 1,000 | 11,333 | 43,000 |

[1] Preliminary. [2] Estimate. [3] Forecast. NA = Not available. *Source: Foreign Agricultural Service, U.S. Department of Agriculture*

## U.S. Salient Statistics of Oranges & Orange Juice

| | Production[4] | | | Farm Price | Farm Value | Florida Crop Processed | | | | Frozen Concentrated Orange Juice-Florida | | | | Brazilian U.S. Imports of Frozen Concentrated OJ | | |
|---|---|---|---|---|---|---|---|---|---|---|---|---|---|---|---|---|
| | California | Florida | Total U.S. | $ Per | Value | Frozen Concen-trates | Chilled Products | Total Pro-cessed | Yield Per Box Gallons[5] | Carry-in | Pack | Total Supply | Total Season Movement | Pack | Exports Total | Exports To U.S. |
| Season | Million Boxes | | | Box | Million $ | Million Boxes | | | | In Million Gallons (42° Brix) | | | | | | |
| 1985-6 | 53.9 | 119.2 | 175.7 | 6.18 | 1,090.4 | 96.1 | 17.3 | 114.7 | 1.4 | 48.3 | 215.1 | 263.4 | 226.4 | 285.9 | 190.7 | 112.2 |
| 1986-7 | 57.9 | 119.7 | 181.2 | 7.29 | 1,322.5 | 96.2 | 19.7 | 116.8 | 1.5 | 37.0 | 227.9 | 264.9 | 225.1 | 210.4 | 277.8 | 139.8 |
| 1987-8 | 59.0 | 138.0 | 200.3 | 8.52 | 1,773.7 | 110.2 | 23.3 | 134.4 | 1.6 | 39.8 | 240.9 | 280.7 | 238.5 | 244.8 | 254.5 | 120.5 |
| 1988-9 | 58.9 | 146.6 | 207.2 | 8.90 | 1,848.5 | 107.4 | 29.5 | 146.6 | 1.5 | 42.1 | 239.1 | 281.2 | 235.0 | 245.8 | 243.8 | 123.1 |
| 1989-90 | 71.4 | 110.2 | 184.5 | 7.96 | 1,465.1 | 70.1 | 33.5 | 110.2 | 1.2 | 46.3 | 184.7 | 231.0 | 191.1 | 362.0 | 330.7 | 132.4 |
| 1990-1 | 25.6 | 151.6 | 179.0 | 8.70 | 1,584.7 | 100.4 | 38.2 | 151.6 | 1.5 | 40.0 | 221.2 | 261.2 | 229.2 | 294.8 | 284.5 | 87.7 |
| 1991-2 | 67.4 | 139.8 | 209.6 | 7.43 | 1,545.2 | 90.6 | 37.0 | 139.8 | 1.6 | 31.8 | 211.7 | 243.5 | 212.6 | 274.1 | 279.3 | 107.8 |
| 1992-3 | 66.8 | 186.6 | 255.8 | 5.77 | 1,489.9 | 128.3 | 47.2 | 186.6 | 1.6 | 31.0 | 292.0 | 322.9 | 269.4 | 394.8 | 418.2 | 103.1 |
| 1993-4[1] | 63.6 | 174.4 | 240.5 | 6.37 | 1,541.3 | 111.7 | 51.0 | 174.4 | 1.6 | 53.5 | 312.2 | 303.2 | 244.5 | 388.2 | 387.5 | 102.0 |
| 1994-5[2] | 61.0 | 205.4 | 268.5 | 5.76 | 1,563.5 | 140.8 | 53.4 | 205.5 | 1.5 | 58.6 | 216.5 | 320.1 | 269.0 | 356.9 | 370.7 | |
| 1995-6[3] | 66.0 | 202.0 | 270.3 | | | 129.3 | 62.1 | 203.2 | | | | | | | | |

[1] Preliminary. [2] Estimate. [3] Forecast. [4] Fruit ripened on trees, but destroyed prior to picking in not included. [5] 42° Brix equivalent.
*Sources: Economic Research Service, U.S. Department of Agriculture; Florida Department of Citrus*

## U.S. Cold Storage Stocks of Orange Juice Concentrate[2] In Millions of Pounds

| Year | Jan. 1 | Feb. 1 | Mar. 1 | Apr. 1 | May 1 | June 1 | July 1 | Aug. 1 | Sept. 1 | Oct. 1 | Nov. 1 | Dec. 1 |
|---|---|---|---|---|---|---|---|---|---|---|---|---|
| 1987 | 621.2 | 874.8 | 1,012.7 | 933.8 | 999.0 | 1,109.1 | 1,105.1 | 942.1 | 792.6 | 840.0 | 652.8 | 569.0 |
| 1988 | 662.4 | 903.8 | 1,072.9 | 1,004.1 | 1,019.0 | 1,122.1 | 1,171.8 | 998.5 | 827.0 | 693.3 | 638.7 | 589.5 |
| 1989 | 721.6 | 980.9 | 1,155.9 | 1,087.0 | 1,144.8 | 1,296.1 | 1,324.8 | 1,167.5 | 932.6 | 808.4 | 725.7 | 669.7 |
| 1990 | 749.6 | 926.6 | 1,046.5 | 1,119.2 | 980.9 | 1,148.2 | 1,074.8 | 1,008.1 | 901.4 | 797.1 | 802.0 | 871.3 |
| 1991 | 1,031.6 | 1,195.8 | 1,199.5 | 1,236.9 | 1,363.2 | 1,304.7 | 1,110.6 | 1,007.5 | 876.9 | 765.2 | 617.3 | 655.4 |
| 1992 | 828.4 | 1,130.7 | 1,150.0 | 1,102.9 | 1,269.3 | 1,294.8 | 1,143.8 | 978.0 | 874.9 | 741.9 | 665.5 | 638.0 |
| 1993 | 892.9 | 1,135.9 | 1,282.8 | 1,297.5 | 1,440.9 | 1,462.3 | 1,351.8 | 1,147.0 | 1,029.6 | 875.7 | 813.3 | 890.9 |
| 1994 | 955.5 | 1,248.9 | 1,429.0 | 1,273.8 | 1,499.6 | 1,615.2 | 1,521.8 | 1,449.1 | 1,257.5 | 1,119.6 | 1,026.1 | 1,055.9 |
| 1995 | 1,353.1 | 1,704.0 | 1,685.1 | 1,773.3 | 1,864.6 | 1,833.8 | 1,631.6 | 1,424.1 | 1,233.7 | 1,038.3 | 830.3 | 897.7 |
| 1996[1] | 1,050.6 | 1,295.4 | 1,353.0 | 1,322.3 | 1,443.9 | 1,597.6 | 1,535.0 | 1,427.5 | 1,238.6 | 965.6 | 728.2 | 691.0 |

[1] Preliminary. *Source: Agricultural Statistics Board, U.S. Department of Agriculture*

## Average Open Interest of Frozen Concentrated Orange Juice Futures in New York In Contracts

| Year | Jan. | Feb. | Mar. | Apr. | May | June | July | Aug. | Sept. | Oct. | Nov. | Dec. |
|---|---|---|---|---|---|---|---|---|---|---|---|---|
| 1987 | 11,222 | 10,283 | 10,031 | 9,206 | 8,658 | 8,104 | 6,994 | 6,665 | 7,229 | 8,810 | 9,000 | 10,212 |
| 1988 | 11,683 | 14,089 | 16,708 | 14,576 | 11,861 | 11,427 | 11,235 | 11,192 | 9,708 | 6,564 | 9,170 | 8,697 |
| 1989 | 7,169 | 6,959 | 7,009 | 7,821 | 8,374 | 9,767 | 8,340 | 7,531 | 6,857 | 7,218 | 7,029 | 9,887 |
| 1990 | 9,667 | 11,067 | 11,877 | 11,952 | 10,528 | 10,229 | 9,413 | 7,485 | 6,867 | 5,939 | 5,802 | 6,983 |
| 1991 | 6,773 | 6,457 | 5,739 | 6,255 | 5,762 | 6,338 | 5,653 | 6,556 | 9,854 | 11,924 | 9,877 | 9,101 |
| 1992 | 9,095 | 10,033 | 9,872 | 11,309 | 10,791 | 9,776 | 10,109 | 12,132 | 11,910 | 14,224 | 16,669 | 17,455 |
| 1993 | 17,733 | 18,199 | 19,030 | 20,210 | 18,525 | 19,267 | 20,000 | 18,899 | 18,287 | 18,825 | 18,422 | 20,367 |
| 1994 | 17,544 | 18,137 | 19,073 | 21,607 | 21,450 | 23,530 | 24,829 | 21,874 | 22,739 | 23,385 | 26,859 | 26,413 |
| 1995 | 27,439 | 25,885 | 26,407 | 30,172 | 27,057 | 26,844 | 23,537 | 17,881 | 20,918 | 22,460 | 26,303 | 24,202 |
| 1996 | 22,943 | 21,670 | 25,232 | 23,788 | 21,724 | 20,934 | 20,159 | 19,834 | 18,029 | 18,000 | 22,513 | 26,405 |

*Source: Citrus Association of the New York Cotton Exchange (NYCE)*

## Volume of Trading of Frozen Concentrated Orange Juice Futures in New York In Contracts

| Year | Jan. | Feb. | Mar. | Apr. | May | June | July | Aug. | Sept. | Oct. | Nov. | Dec. | Total |
|---|---|---|---|---|---|---|---|---|---|---|---|---|---|
| 1987 | 28,566 | 24,342 | 27,999 | 19,569 | 10,651 | 15,470 | 8,805 | 10,710 | 12,330 | 20,321 | 20,724 | 26,758 | 266,641 |
| 1988 | 40,976 | 42,153 | 37,295 | 28,937 | 22,931 | 36,877 | 23,752 | 27,118 | 26,228 | 26,922 | 19,399 | 25,451 | 358,039 |
| 1989 | 26,156 | 26,419 | 28,501 | 26,855 | 30,272 | 32,051 | 23,403 | 19,698 | 17,119 | 18,069 | 15,893 | 39,668 | 304,104 |
| 1990 | 53,133 | 32,035 | 31,676 | 28,025 | 23,656 | 45,028 | 21,302 | 24,029 | 13,131 | 21,793 | 16,473 | 30,739 | 342,574 |
| 1991 | 35,037 | 28,221 | 17,298 | 17,116 | 17,991 | 20,956 | 14,905 | 20,187 | 26,412 | 42,016 | 23,228 | 24,171 | 287,076 |
| 1992 | 30,508 | 28,177 | 21,371 | 31,725 | 21,253 | 22,473 | 21,877 | 27,208 | 26,912 | 29,604 | 33,133 | 44,979 | 339,230 |
| 1993 | 43,634 | 46,067 | 58,298 | 52,554 | 53,566 | 60,330 | 49,415 | 52,381 | 56,838 | 63,808 | 44,167 | 58,073 | 640,131 |
| 1994 | 46,166 | 51,123 | 43,075 | 55,955 | 48,236 | 60,110 | 37,069 | 55,711 | 52,209 | 73,155 | 54,978 | 76,037 | 653,824 |
| 1995 | 50,875 | 66,370 | 51,292 | 78,288 | 32,607 | 80,165 | 41,357 | 67,528 | 38,781 | 64,904 | 45,688 | 71,077 | 688,932 |
| 1996 | 59,666 | 82,057 | 46,272 | 65,752 | 62,247 | 44,827 | 40,884 | 58,346 | 44,239 | 40,680 | 39,291 | 70,676 | 654,937 |

*Source: Citrus Association of the New York Cotton Exchange (NYCE)*

## U.S Retail and Nonretail Sales of Orange Juice In Millions of SSE Gallons

| Crop Year | Retail Sales | % Change[2] | Nonretail Sales | % Change[2] | Apparent Consumption | % Change[2] | Per Capita Consumption | % Change[2] |
|---|---|---|---|---|---|---|---|---|
| 1984-5 | 817 | -4.6% | 376 | 72.5% | 1,193 | 11.1% | 5.0 | 11.1% |
| 1985-6 | 884 | 8.2% | 321 | -14.6% | 1,205 | 1.0% | 5.0 | 0 |
| 1986-7 | 701 | -20.7% | 385 | 19.9% | 1,243 | 3.2% | 5.1 | 2.0% |
| 1987-8 | 667 | -4.9% | 432 | 12.2% | 1,229 | -1.1% | 5.0 | -2.0% |
| 1988-9 | 690 | 3.4% | 401 | -7.2% | 1,238 | .7% | 5.0 | 0 |
| 1989-90 | 628 | -9.0% | 317 | -20.9% | 1,079 | -12.8% | 4.3 | -14.0% |
| 1990-1 | 701 | 11.6% | 296 | -6.6% | 1,146 | 6.2% | 4.5 | 4.7% |
| 1991-2 | 689 | -1.7% | 268 | -9.5% | 1,112 | -3.0% | 4.3 | -4.4% |
| 1992-3 | 748 | 8.6% | 371 | 38.4% | 1,328 | 19.4% | 5.1 | 18.6% |
| 1993-4 | 740 | -1.1% | | | 1,368 | 3.0% | 5.2 | 2.0% |
| 1994-5 | 740 | 0 | | | 1,355 | -1.0% | 5.1 | -1.9% |
| 1995-6[1] | 718 | -2.9% | | | 1,363 | .6% | 4.9 | -3.9% |
| 1996-7[1] | 700 | -2.5% | | | 1,320 | -3.1% | NA | NA |

[1] Estimate. [2] Percentage change from previous period. *Source: Florida Department of Citrus*

## Producer Price Index of Frozen Orange Concentrate 1982 = 100

| Year | Jan. | Feb. | Mar. | Apr. | May | June | July | Aug. | Sept. | Oct. | Nov. | Dec. | Average |
|---|---|---|---|---|---|---|---|---|---|---|---|---|---|
| 1987 | 106.9 | 106.9 | 107.4 | 109.5 | 109.7 | 110.0 | 110.1 | 111.0 | 110.6 | 110.6 | 117.2 | 129.9 | 111.7 |
| 1988 | 132.1 | 140.1 | 142.4 | 140.5 | 142.0 | 141.1 | 141.6 | 142.0 | 141.7 | 140.7 | 140.8 | 139.1 | 140.3 |
| 1989 | 136.4 | 127.7 | 126.5 | 126.5 | 131.7 | 139.2 | 140.6 | 140.3 | 134.0 | 131.6 | 123.1 | 121.7 | 131.6 |
| 1990 | 137.6 | 162.4 | 162.8 | 159.9 | 159.7 | 160.0 | 160.4 | 160.8 | 150.9 | 147.2 | 120.9 | 117.8 | 150.0 |
| 1991 | 114.4 | 114.4 | 111.7 | 111.7 | 111.0 | 111.0 | 111.0 | 107.2 | 107.4 | 116.0 | 127.3 | 131.5 | 114.6 |
| 1992 | 135.1 | 134.7 | 134.7 | 134.3 | 126.2 | 118.5 | 115.5 | 114.5 | 112.5 | 106.5 | 104.2 | 98.8 | 119.6 |
| 1993 | 91.6 | 88.8 | 88.2 | 89.0 | 89.3 | 97.5 | 104.5 | 104.5 | 104.7 | 104.7 | 107.9 | 107.9 | 98.2 |
| 1994 | 107.9 | 104.8 | 104.2 | 104.2 | 102.7 | 101.2 | 100.2 | 100.1 | 99.9 | 99.8 | 100.7 | 100.5 | 102.2 |
| 1995 | 107.4 | 105.4 | 107.6 | 107.6 | 109.1 | 109.1 | 109.1 | 105.3 | 101.0 | 101.6 | 106.1 | 107.3 | 106.4 |
| 1996[1] | 109.4 | 112.5 | 117.2 | 119.5 | 119.5 | 119.5 | 115.3 | 113.6 | 114.9 | 114.8 | 112.8 | | 115.4 |

[1] Preliminary. *Source: Bureau of Labor Statistics, U.S. Department of Commerce*

## Average Price of Oranges (Equivalent On-Tree) Received by Growers In Dollar Per Box

| Year | Jan. | Feb. | Mar. | Apr. | May | June | July | Aug. | Sept. | Oct. | Nov. | Dec. | Average |
|---|---|---|---|---|---|---|---|---|---|---|---|---|---|
| 1987 | 4.64 | 4.80 | 4.96 | 5.40 | 5.99 | 6.40 | 6.02 | 5.41 | 7.43 | 10.43 | 9.10 | 6.35 | 6.41 |
| 1988 | 6.43 | 6.59 | 6.87 | 7.76 | 8.79 | 8.78 | 6.47 | 5.44 | 5.56 | 3.39 | 6.15 | 6.76 | 6.58 |
| 1989 | 6.51 | 6.45 | 6.26 | 7.28 | 8.39 | 8.51 | 7.27 | 6.52 | 6.54 | 6.29 | 7.34 | 6.34 | 6.98 |
| 1990 | 5.92 | 5.82 | 6.00 | 6.47 | 6.97 | 6.61 | 5.74 | 4.38 | 4.48 | 5.04 | 5.78 | 5.76 | 5.75 |
| 1991 | 5.64 | 6.28 | 6.94 | 7.09 | 7.95 | 19.43 | 17.40 | 18.45 | 21.39 | 9.87 | 6.27 | 5.79 | 11.04 |
| 1992 | 5.90 | 6.02 | 5.81 | 6.14 | 6.16 | 4.26 | 1.85 | 1.02 | 1.05 | 2.43 | 4.10 | 3.67 | 4.03 |
| 1993 | 3.37 | 3.21 | 3.41 | 4.00 | 4.03 | 4.09 | 5.02 | 7.25 | 11.85 | 11.44 | 5.95 | 3.81 | 5.62 |
| 1994 | 3.76 | 3.90 | 4.66 | 4.83 | 5.04 | 4.94 | 4.08 | 4.24 | 3.44 | 2.50 | 2.74 | 3.01 | 3.93 |
| 1995 | 3.21 | 3.51 | 4.11 | 4.70 | 4.96 | 5.11 | 6.04 | 4.25 | 7.26 | 7.90 | 3.57 | 3.55 | 4.85 |
| 1996[1] | 3.97 | 4.39 | 4.49 | 5.70 | 6.61 | 6.32 | 5.74 | 8.15 | 11.05 | 8.62 | 4.07 | 3.54 | 6.05 |

[1] Preliminary. *Source: Economic Research Service, U.S. Department of Agriculture*

# Palm Oil

Palm oil is the leading vegetable oil in foreign trade and has shown the world's fastest year to year supply/demand growth rate of the major edible oils over the last decade. Palm oil is a tropical oil which competes directly with soybean and sunflower oil. Almost all the world's production comes from Malaysia and Indonesia.

1996/97 palm oil production (October/September) of a record 16.2 million metric tons compares with 15.6 million in 1995/96. Much of the production is exported to meet world consumption estimated at a record 16.2 million tons in 1996/97, vs. 15.2 million in 1995/96, and an early 1990's usage average of 11.5 million tons. Palm oil exports go mostly to Europe, the world's largest importer of vegetable oils. World palm oil stocks were an estimated 1.60 million tons in September 1996, unchanged from a year earlier.

Malaysia's 1995/96 production of 8.4 million tons compares with 8.2 million in 1995/96, but nearly twice the production of the mid-1980's. Malaysia's 1996/97 exports of 7.1 million tons compare with 6.7 million in 1995/96. Malaysia's ending carryover has grown to 917,000 tons, the same as a year earlier but up sharply from 650,000 tons or less in each of the two prior crop years. Indonesia's 1996/97 crop of 4.8 million tons compares with 4.5 million in 1995/96. Palm kernel production is also concentrated: the world's 1996/97 total of 5 million tons compares with 4.7 million the year before, with Malaysia producing more than half of the total.

U.S. palm oil imports during the first ten months of 1995/96 totaled 96,000 tons vs. 79,000 during the like 1994/95 period, with a value of $49.8 million vs. $42.8 million, respectively. The U.S. does not reexport any palm oil.

World palm oil prices have traversed a wide range over the last decade, from a high of $651 in 1994/95, to a low of $271 in 1989/90. The 10 year average is $395 per metric ton. The 1995/96 average was $523, basis Malaysia FOB. Helping to support prices is the strong growth in consumption from Europe and at times from China and India. However, the hefty growth in production and the availability of competing oils on the world market can quickly depress palm oil prices as seen in 1995/96.

### *Futures Markets*

Crude Palm Oil and Crude Palm Kernal Oil are traded on the Kuala Lumpur Commodity Exchange (KLCE).

## World Palm Oil Statistics — In Thousands of Metric Tons

| | Production | | | | | | | | | Imports | | | | Exports | | | |
|---|---|---|---|---|---|---|---|---|---|---|---|---|---|---|---|---|---|
| Crop Year | Colombia | Ecuador | Indonesia | Ivory Coast | Malaysia | Nigeria | Papua/ N.Guinea | Thailand | World Total | China | Pakistan | Singapore | World Total | Indonesia | Malaysia | Singapore | World Total |
| 1990-1 | 251 | 127 | 2,574 | 277 | 6,036 | 631 | 184 | 234 | 11,269 | 1,291 | 818 | 848 | 8,539 | 1,626 | 5,717 | 644 | 8,611 |
| 1991-2 | 281 | 139 | 2,803 | 278 | 6,224 | 633 | 192 | 254 | 11,834 | 877 | 1,002 | 696 | 8,389 | 1,268 | 5,783 | 572 | 8,305 |
| 1992-3 | 303 | 156 | 3,453 | 310 | 7,122 | 640 | 217 | 289 | 13,499 | 1,162 | 1,102 | 745 | 9,350 | 1,733 | 6,212 | 501 | 9,351 |
| 1993-4 | 346 | 176 | 3,630 | 299 | 7,103 | 640 | 226 | 311 | 13,773 | 1,687 | 1,080 | 469 | 10,366 | 1,965 | 6,737 | 346 | 10,359 |
| 1994-5[1] | 390 | 175 | 4,039 | 285 | 7,771 | 655 | 223 | 345 | 14,951 | 1,786 | 1,215 | 562 | 10,720 | 1,904 | 6,728 | 402 | 10,655 |
| 1995-6[2] | 391 | 185 | 4,435 | 295 | 8,264 | 660 | 228 | 366 | 15,913 | 1,178 | 1,170 | 456 | 10,543 | 2,080 | 6,901 | 308 | 10,645 |
| 1996-7[3] | 384 | 206 | 4,880 | 315 | 8,349 | NA | 238 | 378 | 16,527 | 1,780 | 1,215 | 500 | 11,630 | 2,650 | 7,280 | 320 | 11,669 |

[1] Preliminary. [2] Estimate. [3] Forecast. *Source: The Oil World*

## Palm Oil--U.S. Supply and Distribution — In Thousands of Metric Tons

| | | | | Consumption | | | | | Prices | | |
|---|---|---|---|---|---|---|---|---|---|---|---|
| Year Beginning Oct. | Stocks Oct. 1 | Imports | Total Supply | Edible Products | Inedible Products | Total End Products | Total Disappearance | Exports | U.S. Import Value[4] | Malaysia, F.O.B., RBD | Palm Kernel Oil, Malaysia, C.I.F. Rotterdam |
| | | | | In Millions of Pounds | | | | | U.S. $ Per Metric Ton | | |
| 1991-2 | 23.7 | 100.1 | 123.8 | 98.6 | 101.5 | 200.1 | 100.4 | 3.3 | 347 | 365 | 586 |
| 1992-3 | 20.1 | 120.6 | 140.7 | 83.5 | 113.5 | 197.0 | 122.5 | 3.3 | 377 | 379 | 439 |
| 1993-4 | 14.9 | 167.0 | 181.9 | 86.2 | 118.2 | 204.4 | 162.0 | 3.6 | 370 | 451 | 566 |
| 1994-5[1] | 16.4 | 98.7 | 115.1 | 38.1 | 113.6 | 151.7 | 101.8 | 5.9 | 538 | 647 | 680 |
| 1995-6[2] | 7.4 | 107.0 | 114.4 | 6.7 | 103.9 | 110.6 | 91.0 | 6.4 | 511 | 545 | 729 |
| 1996-7[3] | 8.0 | 120.0 | 128.0 | | 96.7 | | 115.0 | | 408 | 558 | 734 |

[1] Preliminary. [2] Estimate. [3] Forecast. [4] Market value in the foreign country, excluding import duties, ocean freight and marine insurance.
*Sources: The Oil World; Economic Research Service, U.S. Department of Agriculture*

## Average Wholesale Palm Oil Prices, CIF, Bulk, U.S. Ports — In Cents Per Pound

| Year | Jan. | Feb. | Mar. | Apr. | May | June | July | Aug. | Sept. | Oct. | Nov. | Dec. | Average |
|---|---|---|---|---|---|---|---|---|---|---|---|---|---|
| 1990 | 15.14 | 13.94 | 14.53 | 14.68 | 13.91 | 14.98 | 14.16 | 15.04 | 14.63 | 15.21 | 16.24 | 15.73 | 14.85 |
| 1991 | 19.49 | 19.50 | 19.25 | 19.18 | 19.05 | 19.40 | 20.32 | 19.14 | 18.86 | 20.63 | 21.63 | 18.99 | 19.62 |
| 1992 | 21.91 | 21.05 | 21.92 | 22.05 | 21.51 | 21.77 | 21.19 | 21.00 | 21.50 | 21.86 | 22.18 | 22.24 | 21.68 |
| 1993 | 23.18 | 23.09 | 22.99 | 22.26 | 21.95 | 21.01 | 20.31 | 19.84 | 19.43 | 18.83 | 19.74 | 21.90 | 21.21 |
| 1994 | 21.91 | 21.67 | 21.72 | 23.08 | 26.27 | 28.94 | 27.44 | 30.18 | 32.15 | 31.93 | 34.95 | 36.83 | 28.09 |
| 1995 | 34.26 | 33.82 | 36.18 | 35.56 | 32.80 | 33.06 | 33.68 | 32.59 | 30.86 | 31.45 | 31.96 | 30.00 | 33.02 |
| 1996[1] | 27.08 | 26.52 | 26.33 | 27.52 | 28.57 | 25.43 | 24.78 | 24.46 | 27.24 | | | | 26.44 |

[1] Preliminary. *Source: Economic Research Service, U.S. Department of Agriculture*

# Paper

The American Forest and Paper Association reported that U.S. seasonally-adjusted paper and paperboard production was 7.71 million short tons in September 1996, down from the record high 7.77 million tons in August 1996. Paper and paperboard production in the first nine months of 1996 was 1.8 percent less than in the comparable period of 1995. In the third quarter of 1996, paper and paperboard production was 3.8 percent more than in the third quarter of 1995. Part of the improvement was due to better demand. Through August 1996, U.S. exports of paper, paperboard, and converted products were up 4.9 percent compared to the same period of 1995. In the same period of 1996, imports were down 9.8 percent from a year ago according to the Bureau of the Census.

Canada is the world's largest producer of newsprint, followed by the U.S., Japan, and Sweden. For 1995, average monthly production of newsprint in Canada was 768,000 tonnes, down 1 percent from the prior year. Average monthly production in the U.S. was 527,000 tonnes, about the same as in 1994. Newsprint production in Japan averaged 260,000 tonnes per month, up almost 5 percent from the previous year. Other important producers of newsprint include Germany, Finland, and China.

The American Forest and Paper Association has estimated annual newsprint capacity. 1995 U.S. production capacity was estimated at 6.57 million tonnes. For 1996 and 1997 it was 6.58 million tonnes. For Canada, 1995 production capacity was 9.69 million tonnes. In 1996 it was 9.64 million tonnes while for 1997 Canadian newsprint capacity was forecast to be 9.6 million tonnes.

In late 1996 in Japan, the New Oji Paper Company merged with Honshu Paper Company to become that country's biggest paper manufacturer. It will also be the world's third largest paper manufacturer.

## Production of Paper and Paperboard by Selected Countries    In Thousands of Metric Tons

| Year | Austria | Canada | Czech Republic[2] | Finland | France | Germany | Italy | Japan | Netherlands | Norway | Russia[3] | Spain | Sweden | Switzerland | United Kingdom | United States |
|---|---|---|---|---|---|---|---|---|---|---|---|---|---|---|---|---|
| 1990 | 2,932 | 16,466 | 1,300 | 8,967 | 7,049 | 12,759 | 5,587 | 28,088 | 2,770 | 1,820 | 10,718 | 3,446 | 8,419 | 1,295 | 4,824 | 71,965 |
| 1991 | 3,090 | 16,559 | 1,087 | 8,776 | 7,190 | 12,904 | 5,795 | 29,056 | 2,862 | 1,784 | 9,590 | 3,579 | 8,349 | 1,259 | 4,951 | 72,724 |
| 1992 | 3,252 | 16,585 | 688 | 9,147 | 7,690 | 13,214 | 6,040 | 28,324 | 2,835 | 1,684 | 5,765 | 3,449 | 8,378 | 1,305 | 5,151 | 75,161 |
| 1993 | 3,300 | 17,528 | 643 | 9,990 | 7,975 | 13,034 | 6,019 | 27,764 | 2,855 | 1,968 | 4,459 | 3,348 | 8,781 | 1,332 | 5,406 | 77,167 |
| 1994[1] | 3,603 | 18,342 | 735 | 10,909 | 8,481 | 14,457 | 6,705 | ----- | 3,011 | ----- | 3,407 | 3,503 | 9,283 | ----- | 5,829 | 80,911 |

[1] Preliminary. [2] Formerly part of Czechoslovakia; data not reported separately until 1992. [3] Formerly part of the U.S.S.R.; data not reported separately until 1992. *Source: Food and Agricultural Organization of the United Nations*

## Production of Newsprint by Selected Countries (Monthly Average)    In Thousands of Metric Tons

| Year | Australia | Brazil | Canada | China | Finland | France | Germany | India | Japan | Rep. of Korea | Norway | Russia[3] | Sweden | United Kingdom | United States |
|---|---|---|---|---|---|---|---|---|---|---|---|---|---|---|---|
| 1991 | 33.2 | 21.3 | 748.1 | 36.5 | 108.8 | 34.8 | 104.7 | 24.3 | 292.9 | 47.4 | 79.6 | 128.6 | 192.3 | 56.0 | 517.2 |
| 1992 | 33.6 | 18.9 | 729.0 | 40.8 | 104.8 | 55.8 | 94.2 | 24.7 | 271.1 | 50.2 | 77.9 | 78.6 | 147.5 | 58.3 | 535.3 |
| 1993 | 33.1 | 22.2 | 761.0 | 48.3 | 118.7 | 66.7 | 105.8 | 23.5 | 243.1 | 61.9 | 83.9 | 70.4 | 193.8 | 61.7 | 534.3 |
| 1994 | 33.5 | 22.1 | 776.8 | 52.6 | 119.4 | 70.3 | 156.3 | 22.3 | 247.7 | 72.3 | ----- | 86.5 | 201.3 | ----- | 528.3 |
| 1995[1] | 37.4 | 23.5 | 770.8 | 64.0 | 117.8 | 56.4 | 146.0 | 24.9 | 258.2 | 79.7 | ----- | ----- | 196.1 | ----- | 529.3 |
| 1996[2] | 37.7 | 23.2 | 744.1 | 68.6 | 110.0 | ----- | 142.1 | 28.7 | 259.0 | 97.8 | ----- | ----- | 190.0 | ----- | 519.2 |

[1] Preliminary. [2] Estimate. [3] Formerly part of the U.S.S.R.; data not reported separately until 1992. *Source: Statistical Division, United Nations*

## Salient Stastistics of Newsprint in the the United States and Canada    In Thousands of Metric Tons

| | United States | | | | | | | | | | | | | | Canada | | |
|---|---|---|---|---|---|---|---|---|---|---|---|---|---|---|---|---|---|
| | | | Imports by Countries of Origin | | | | | | | | | Stocks, Dec. 31 | | | | | |
| Year | Production | Exports | Canada | Finland | Italy | Norway | South Africa | Sweden | United Kingdom | Total | Consumption | At Mills | At Publishers | Production | Exports | Stocks at Mills |
| 1991 | 6,206 | 570 | 5,623 | 22 | 0 | 29 | 0 | 46 | 0 | 6,795 | 11,268 | 98 | 932 | 8,855 | 9,165 | 565 |
| 1992 | 6,424 | 753 | 5,690 | 14 | 0 | 25 | 0 | 38 | 0 | 6,658 | 11,505 | 59 | 938 | 8,753 | 7,924 | 351 |
| 1993 | 6,412 | 768 | 5,805 | 14 | 0 | 37 | 0 | 54 | 6 | 7,061 | 11,535 | 81 | 956 | 9,130 | 8,003 | 362 |
| 1994 | 6,984 | 672 | 5,906 | 12 | 0 | 28 | 1 | 30 | 1 | 7,150 | 11,695 | 66 | 879 | 9,321 | 8,326 | 246 |
| 1995[1] | 7,002 | 829 | 7,722 | | | | | | | | | 84 | 1,133 | 9,252 | 8,062 | 252 |
| 1996[1] | 6,945 | 591 | 6,881 | | | | | | | | | 104 | | | | |

[1] Preliminary. Not seasonally adjusted. *Source: Newsprint Division, American Forest & Paper Association*

## Index Price of Paperboard    1982 = 100

| Year | Jan. | Feb. | Mar. | Apr. | May | June | July | Aug. | Sept. | Oct. | Nov. | Dec. | Average |
|---|---|---|---|---|---|---|---|---|---|---|---|---|---|
| 1990 | 139.2 | 138.9 | 138.9 | 137.6 | 136.0 | 135.5 | 135.0 | 133.4 | 133.1 | 134.3 | 134.2 | 132.8 | 135.7 |
| 1991 | 132.6 | 132.0 | 129.6 | 128.4 | 127.0 | 127.2 | 127.1 | 127.8 | 131.8 | 132.7 | 132.8 | 132.9 | 130.2 |
| 1992 | 133.4 | 133.6 | 133.4 | 134.3 | 134.3 | 134.3 | 134.2 | 134.6 | 135.9 | 135.7 | 133.9 | 133.6 | 134.3 |
| 1993 | 133.0 | 131.6 | 131.3 | 130.6 | 129.9 | 128.9 | 128.6 | 128.0 | 128.0 | 129.7 | 130.2 | 130.5 | 130.0 |
| 1994 | 130.2 | 130.1 | 131.1 | 133.4 | 133.1 | 133.5 | 137.8 | 143.5 | 146.9 | 153.6 | 156.0 | 156.7 | 140.5 |
| 1995 | 165.3 | 171.2 | 172.3 | 183.8 | 188.2 | 188.4 | 189.9 | 190.6 | 190.3 | 188.8 | 185.7 | 182.2 | 183.1 |
| 1996[1] | 175.7 | 172.6 | 166.6 | 161.8 | 154.0 | 150.6 | 148.0 | 148.6 | 148.5 | 147.0 | 148.4 | | 156.5 |

[1] Preliminary. *Source: Bureau of Labor Statistics, U.S. Department of Commerce*

# PAPER

## Index Price of Wood Pulp, Bleached Suphate Softwood 1982 = 100

| Year | Jan. | Feb. | Mar. | Apr. | May | June | July | Aug. | Sept. | Oct. | Nov. | Dec. | Average |
|---|---|---|---|---|---|---|---|---|---|---|---|---|---|
| 1990 | 183.2 | 183.0 | 180.9 | 179.3 | 177.1 | 174.9 | 174.5 | 173.5 | 173.5 | 170.2 | 170.9 | 170.4 | 176.0 |
| 1991 | 152.2 | 150.0 | 143.6 | 142.1 | 136.8 | 132.4 | 126.2 | 124.2 | 123.2 | 120.0 | 120.7 | 114.8 | 132.2 |
| 1992 | 121.6 | 123.7 | 125.2 | 131.8 | 132.1 | 131.4 | 134.2 | 136.1 | 135.1 | 133.7 | 132.0 | 132.8 | 130.8 |
| 1993 | 121.6 | 118.1 | 112.7 | 112.3 | 112.7 | 112.7 | 110.7 | 108.9 | 108.6 | 107.1 | 105.5 | 104.0 | 111.2 |
| 1994 | 106.7 | 106.9 | 109.6 | 113.5 | 113.4 | 118.0 | 119.4 | 124.3 | 130.3 | 137.1 | 141.4 | 142.2 | 121.9 |
| 1995 | 150.9 | 153.0 | 187.5 | 193.0 | 202.4 | 215.2 | 217.8 | 223.3 | 218.8 | 223.3 | 217.0 | 212.7 | 201.2 |
| 1996[1] | 195.0 | 175.4 | 155.5 | 123.5 | 111.1 | 120.1 | 126.9 | 130.9 | 129.6 | 131.0 | 130.0 | | 139.0 |

[1] Preliminary. *Source: Bureau of Labor Statistics, U.S. Department of Commerce*

## Index Price of Shipping Sack Paper[2] 1982 = 100

| Year | Jan. | Feb. | Mar. | Apr. | May | June | July | Aug. | Sept. | Oct. | Nov. | Dec. | Average |
|---|---|---|---|---|---|---|---|---|---|---|---|---|---|
| 1990 | 144.4 | 144.4 | 144.4 | 144.4 | 144.4 | 144.4 | 144.4 | 144.4 | NA | NA | NA | NA | 144.4 |
| 1991 | 148.9 | 148.9 | 148.9 | 148.9 | 148.9 | 148.9 | 148.9 | 148.9 | 148.9 | 148.9 | 148.9 | 148.9 | 148.9 |
| 1992 | 148.9 | 148.9 | 154.0 | 154.0 | 154.0 | 148.9 | 148.9 | 148.9 | 155.7 | 155.7 | 155.7 | 155.7 | 152.4 |
| 1993 | 155.7 | 155.7 | 155.7 | 155.7 | 151.8 | 151.8 | 151.8 | 151.8 | 151.8 | 151.8 | 152.5 | 152.5 | 153.2 |
| 1994 | 151.3 | 150.9 | 154.3 | 154.5 | 159.3 | 163.9 | 169.9 | 170.3 | 176.6 | 178.2 | 184.9 | 185.5 | 166.6 |
| 1995 | 190.4 | 204.5 | 209.5 | 212.0 | 221.5 | 224.2 | 224.2 | 224.2 | 224.0 | 223.4 | 212.8 | 207.3 | 214.8 |
| 1996[1] | 205.2 | 202.2 | 201.5 | 194.7 | 194.3 | 193.1 | 189.9 | 185.5 | 182.7 | 183.8 | 186.0 | | 192.6 |

[1] Preliminary. [2] Unbleached kraft. NA = Not avaliable. *Source: Bureau of Labor Statistics, U.S. Department of Commerce*

## Producer Price Index of Standard Newsprint 1982 = 100

| Year | Jan. | Feb. | Mar. | Apr. | May | June | July | Aug. | Sept. | Oct. | Nov. | Dec. | Average |
|---|---|---|---|---|---|---|---|---|---|---|---|---|---|
| 1990 | 116.8 | 115.4 | 115.6 | 115.5 | 116.6 | 121.6 | 122.2 | 122.2 | 121.8 | 122.5 | 122.3 | 122.7 | 119.6 |
| 1991 | 126.8 | 127.2 | 127.1 | 121.7 | 121.4 | 120.1 | 119.5 | 118.8 | 118.1 | 117.3 | 116.4 | 115.8 | 120.9 |
| 1992 | 115.3 | 114.8 | 112.3 | 108.8 | 108.3 | 106.6 | 106.6 | 106.7 | 109.5 | 109.2 | 110.6 | 109.6 | 109.9 |
| 1993 | 110.4 | 111.2 | 114.1 | 113.9 | 113.0 | 113.1 | 112.7 | 112.6 | 111.3 | 111.2 | 111.0 | 111.0 | 112.1 |
| 1994 | 109.9 | 109.5 | 110.7 | 110.6 | 112.2 | 113.8 | 116.9 | 116.9 | 121.7 | 123.8 | 126.8 | 127.3 | 116.7 |
| 1995 | 135.8 | 134.6 | 140.1 | 147.4 | 152.3 | 164.8 | 166.1 | 166.1 | 174.5 | 186.2 | 186.2 | 186.2 | 161.7 |
| 1996[1] | 186.2 | 186.2 | 185.2 | 182.7 | 173.5 | 164.4 | 157.4 | 149.7 | 143.0 | 131.4 | 124.0 | | 162.2 |

[1] Preliminary. *Source: Bureau of Labor Statistics, U.S. Department of Commerce*

## Index Price of Coated Printing Paper, No. 3 1982 = 100

| Year | Jan. | Feb. | Mar. | Apr. | May | June | July | Aug. | Sept. | Oct. | Nov. | Dec. | Average |
|---|---|---|---|---|---|---|---|---|---|---|---|---|---|
| 1990 | 130.3 | 130.2 | 130.2 | 130.3 | 130.3 | 130.3 | 130.2 | 130.2 | 130.2 | 130.2 | 130.2 | 130.2 | 130.2 |
| 1991 | 129.3 | 129.4 | 129.4 | 129.1 | 128.7 | 128.1 | 128.1 | 128.1 | 128.1 | 128.7 | 128.7 | 127.8 | 128.6 |
| 1992 | 126.8 | 123.6 | 123.7 | 123.7 | 122.3 | 121.7 | 122.1 | 121.7 | 121.7 | 124.2 | 123.4 | 123.3 | 123.2 |
| 1993 | 123.4 | 123.3 | 123.3 | 123.4 | 123.4 | 123.3 | 123.0 | 123.0 | 123.2 | 122.9 | 122.9 | 122.9 | 123.2 |
| 1994 | 122.0 | 122.1 | 121.8 | 122.2 | 121.6 | 121.6 | 121.6 | 125.2 | 130.7 | 131.7 | 132.9 | 136.3 | 125.8 |
| 1995 | 139.5 | 145.8 | 150.2 | 153.1 | 147.7 | 152.0 | 159.3 | 159.3 | 160.4 | 160.3 | 160.3 | 160.3 | 154.0 |
| 1996[1] | 160.2 | 159.7 | 159.4 | 159.2 | 155.6 | 153.5 | 153.0 | 153.0 | 151.8 | 151.8 | 151.9 | | 155.4 |

[1] Preliminary. *Source: Bureau of Labor Statistics, U.S. Department of Commerce*

## International Paper Prices--Export Unit Value

| Year | Jan. | Feb. | Mar. | Apr. | May | June | July | Aug. | Sept. | Oct. | Nov. | Dec. | Average |
|---|---|---|---|---|---|---|---|---|---|---|---|---|---|
| NEWSPRINT - Canada | | | In Canadian Dollars Per Metric Ton | | | | | | | | | | |
| 1993 | 687 | 676 | 668 | 690 | 692 | 690 | 676 | 674 | 664 | 666 | 658 | 642 | 674 |
| 1994 | 634 | 618 | 638 | 657 | 656 | 642 | 663 | 672 | 658 | 657 | 749 | 755 | 667 |
| 1995 | 781 | 787 | | | | | | | | | | | 784 |
| NEWSPRINT - Finland | | | In Markka Per Metric Ton | | | | | | | | | | |
| 1993 | 2,362 | 2,414 | 2,415 | 2,461 | 2,324 | 2,336 | 2,265 | 2,371 | 2,386 | 2,437 | 2,376 | 2,371 | 2,377 |
| 1994 | 2,339 | 2,273 | 2,320 | 2,366 | 2,349 | 2,364 | 2,318 | 2,360 | 2,295 | 2,262 | 2,236 | 2,275 | 2,313 |
| 1995 | 2,563 | 2,589 | 2,577 | 2,614 | 2,598 | 2,667 | 3,037 | 3,122 | 3,172 | | | | 2,771 |
| PRINTING AND WRITING - Canada | | | | In Canadian Dollars Per Metric Ton | | | | | | | | | |
| 1993 | 885 | 861 | 860 | 891 | 902 | 920 | 923 | 921 | 924 | 919 | 927 | 931 | 905 |
| 1994 | 910 | 920 | 925 | 923 | 915 | 922 | 955 | 978 | 987 | 1,024 | 1,078 | 1,127 | 972 |
| 1995 | 1,225 | 1,240 | | | | | | | | | | | 1,233 |
| PRINTING AND WRITING - Finland | | | | In Markka Per Metric Ton | | | | | | | | | |
| 1993 | 3,510 | 3,580 | 3,652 | 3,652 | 3,668 | 3,536 | 3,522 | 3,587 | 3,568 | 3,576 | 3,517 | 3,500 | 3,572 |
| 1994 | 3,471 | 3,290 | 3,370 | 3,375 | 3,484 | 3,507 | 3,524 | 3,490 | 3,498 | 3,472 | 3,501 | 3,666 | 3,471 |
| 1995 | 3,816 | 3,897 | 3,905 | 4,066 | 4,165 | 4,284 | 4,473 | 4,416 | 4,439 | | | | 4,162 |

*Source: Food and Agricultural Organization of the United Nations*

# Peanuts and Peanut Oil

World raw peanut (groundnut) production of a record 26.4 million metric tons in 1996/97 compares with 26 million in 1995/96, and to the previous record of 26.3 million in 1994/95. On a shelled basis the totals would be about 25 percent lower. Peanuts vie for the position as the world's fourth largest oilseed crop, generally just eking out sunflowerseed. However, among the major oilseeds for which world acreage has generally increased, the area devoted to peanuts in the 1990's has held steady at about 19.5 million hectares.

China (9.8 million tons in 1996/97) and India (8.20 million) produce more than half the world's crop with the U.S. a distant third with about 8 percent. Foreign trade in peanuts is small as most crops are consumed locally. World imports during 1996/97 of 1.5 million tons were marginally higher than in 1995/96; exports of 1.5 million tons compares with 1.6 million, respectively. The world's peanut crush is among the smallest of the major oilseeds; 14.5 million tons in 1996/97, about a tenth of the soybean crush and the gap has been growing. More of the world's peanut crop is allocated to meal production than oil, production of which totaled 5.9 million tons in 1996/97 vs. 5.7 million in 1995/96 and about equal to consumption in both years. Peanut oil production in 1996/97 of 4.1 million tons compares with 4 million in 1995/96. Foreign trade in meal and oil is small.

The 1995/96 (October/September) average world peanut oil price of $986 per metric ton, basis Rotterdam, compares with $856 in 1994/95 and a 1984/85-1994/95 average of $951 per ton, during which time the yearly average saw a high of $1539 and a low of $713. Rotterdam meal prices in 1995/96 averaged $201 per metric ton vs. $161 in 1994/95 and the ten year average of $176; oil prices of $928 per ton compare with $1005 and $973, respectively. In the U.S., the average price for peanut meal during 1996/97 was forecast between $220-245 per ton vs. $190.90 in 1995/96, and an average of only $128.90 per ton in 1994/95; peanut oil prices were forecast at $0.38-.42 cents a pound in 1996/97 vs. $0.403 in 1995/96 and $0.443 in 1994/95.

U.S. peanut production tends to be erratic: a record large 4.9 billion pounds were produced in 1991/92 while the low since the mid-1970's was 2.3 billion in 1980/81. The 1996/97 crop of 3.4 billion pounds compares with 3.5 billion in 1995/96. U.S. peanut production is largely concentrated in the Southeast. Peanuts are also grown in the southern plains states where irrigation may be needed and production costs run higher. The average yield for the 1996 crop was put at 2,421 pounds per acre vs. 2,282 a year earlier. The acreage harvested of 1.4 million acres compares with 1.5 million, respectively. Georgia is the largest producing state with at least a third of total production (1.4 million pounds in 1996) followed by North Carolina and Alabama. Total supplies in 1996/97 of 4.3 billion pounds compare with 4.8 billion in 1995/96, and include an August 1, 1996 carryin of 758 million pounds vs. stocks of 1.2 billion a year earlier. The carryin for the 1997/98 crop was forecast at 675 million pounds. Peanut imports are generally small, 100 million pounds in 1996/97. Imports, however, have seen wide swings at times, from 401 million pounds in 1980 to 2 million in the early 1990's.

Total U.S. peanut disappearance in 1996/97 of 3.6 billion pounds compares with 4.1 billion in 1995/96. The decline largely reflects a smaller crush of 675 million pounds vs. 999 million, and exports of 675 million vs. 824 million.

As a direct food, 2 billion pounds were forecast for 1996/97, about unchanged from 1995/96. Peanut use as a direct foodstuff has slipped during the past decade. Per capita U.S. peanut use has fallen from a high of 7 pounds (kernel basis) in 1989 to 5.7 pounds in 1995/96, the lowest in 14 years. Initial usage was similarly off to a slow start in 1996/97. Contributing to the decline is reduced demand for peanut butter, a drop in snack peanut consumption, and no growth in peanut based candies. Exports of peanut oil in 1996/97 of 60 million pounds compares with 108 million in 1995/96; exports of meal of 10,000 shorts tons compares with 32,000 in 1995/96.

The average peanut price received by farmers in 1996/97 was forecast at 27.5-29.5 cents per pound vs. 29.3 cents in 1995/96.

***Futures Markets***

Peanut futures are traded on the Beijing Commodity Exchange (BCE).

**World Production of Peanuts (in the Shell)** In Thousands of Metric Tons

| Crop Year | Agren-tina | Brazil | Burma | China | India | Indo-nesia | Mali | Nigeria | Senegal | South Africa | Sudan | Taiwan | Thailand | United States | Zaire | World Total |
|---|---|---|---|---|---|---|---|---|---|---|---|---|---|---|---|---|
| 1984-5 | 270 | 337 | 667 | 4,815 | 6,436 | 755 | 45 | 500 | 196 | 560 | 390 | 89 | 172 | 1,998 | 375 | 19,683 |
| 1985-6 | 439 | 216 | 560 | 6,664 | 5,120 | 780 | 90 | 400 | 111 | 587 | 275 | 77 | 172 | 1,870 | 375 | 19,900 |
| 1986-7 | 518 | 195 | 544 | 5,882 | 5,875 | 750 | 90 | 400 | 235 | 817 | 350 | 83 | 169 | 1,677 | 380 | 20,383 |
| 1987-8 | 450 | 170 | 519 | 6,170 | 5,854 | 786 | 100 | 475 | 204 | 932 | 435 | 100 | 162 | 1,640 | 380 | 20,863 |
| 1988-9 | 243 | 156 | 438 | 5,693 | 9,000 | 843 | 115 | 350 | 163 | 350 | 450 | 74 | 164 | 1,806 | 380 | 23,279 |
| 1989-90 | 336 | 137 | 459 | 5,365 | 8,088 | 875 | 90 | 350 | 113 | 350 | 400 | 58 | 161 | 1,810 | 380 | 22,059 |
| 1990-1 | 574 | 157 | 440 | 6,368 | 7,514 | 860 | 100 | 250 | 703 | 112 | 325 | 73 | 162 | 1,634 | 380 | 22,206 |
| 1991-2 | 400 | 160 | 440 | 6,300 | 7,065 | 890 | 95 | 220 | 724 | 114 | 400 | 83 | 160 | 2,235 | 380 | 22,138 |
| 1992-3 | 225 | 150 | 425 | 5,953 | 8,850 | 890 | 95 | 250 | 580 | 172 | 390 | 65 | 162 | 1,943 | 380 | 23,050 |
| 1993-4 | 210 | 150 | 390 | 8,420 | 7,760 | 870 | ----- | 250 | 620 | 190 | 390 | ----- | 170 | 1,540 | 380 | 23,990 |
| 1994-5 | 280 | 150 | 450 | 9,680 | 8,260 | 1,090 | ----- | 250 | 720 | 110 | 390 | ----- | 170 | 1,930 | 380 | 26,480 |
| 1995-6[1] | 350 | 150 | 500 | 10,200 | 7,400 | 1,040 | ----- | 250 | 810 | 200 | 400 | ----- | 170 | 1,570 | 380 | 26,080 |
| 1996-7[2] | 360 | 150 | 500 | 9,500 | 8,200 | 1,000 | ----- | 250 | 850 | 200 | 400 | ----- | 170 | 1,650 | 380 | 26,280 |

[1] Preliminary. [2] Estimate. *Source: Foreign Agricultural Service, U.S. Department of Agriculture*

## Salient Statistics of Peanuts in the United States

| Crop Year | Acreage Planted (1,000 Acres) | Acreage Harvested for Nuts (1,000 Acres) | Average Yield Per Acre In Lbs. | Production 1,000 Lbs. | Season Farm Price ¢ Lb. | Farm Value Million Dollars | Thousand Pounds (Year Beg. August): Exports Unshelled | Exports Shelled | Imports Unshelled | Imports Shelled |
|---|---|---|---|---|---|---|---|---|---|---|
| 1983-4 | 1,411.0 | 1,373.5 | 2,399 | 3,295,530 | 24.7 | 814.6 | 39,509 | 529,949 | 298 | 1,715 |
| 1984-5 | 1,558.6 | 1,528.0 | 2,883 | 4,405,745 | 27.9 | 1,230.8 | 72,907 | 592,333 | 79 | 2,167 |
| 1985-6 | 1,490.4 | 1,467.4 | 2,810 | 4,122,787 | 24.3 | 1,003.4 | 83,747 | 721,690 | 1,493 | 1,942 |
| 1986-7 | 1,564.7 | 1,535.2 | 2,408 | 3,700,745 | 29.2 | 1,073.3 | 75,687 | 441,954 | 328 | 1,598 |
| 1987-8 | 1,567.4 | 1,547.4 | 2,337 | 3,619,440 | 28.0 | 1,021.9 | 76,345 | 407,557 | 880 | 1,949 |
| 1988-9 | 1,657.4 | 1,628.4 | 2,445 | 3,980,917 | 27.9 | 1,115.2 | 105,746 | 437,867 | 650 | 2,094 |
| 1989-90 | 1,665.2 | 1,644.7 | 2,426 | 3,989,995 | 28.0 | 1,116.5 | 126,682 | 577,807 | 55 | 1,477 |
| 1990-1 | 1,840.0 | 1,809.5 | 1,991 | 3,602,770 | 34.7 | 1,257.2 | 250,851 | 401,149 | 6,429 | 20,571 |
| 1991-2 | 2,039.2 | 2,015.7 | 2,444 | 4,926,570 | 28.3 | 1,392.0 | ------- 997,000 ------- | | ------- 5,000 ------- | |
| 1992-3 | 1,686.6 | 1,669.1 | 2,567 | 4,284,416 | 30.0 | 1,285.4 | ------- 951,000 ------- | | ------- 2,000 ------- | |
| 1993-4 | 1,733.5 | 1,689.8 | 2,008 | 3,392,415 | 30.4 | 1,030.9 | ------- 555,000 ------- | | ------- 2,000 ------- | |
| 1994-5 | 1,641.0 | 1,618.5 | 2,624 | 4,247,455 | 28.9 | 1,229.0 | ------- 878,000 ------- | | ----- 74,000 ------- | |
| 1995-6[1] | 1,537.5 | 1,517.0 | 2,282 | 3,461,475 | 29.3 | 1,013.3 | ------- 825,000 ------- | | --- 104,000 ------- | |
| 1996-7[2] | 1,428.0 | 1,391.5 | 2,619 | 2,644,660 | 27.5-29.5 | 973.2 | ------- 675,000 ------- | | --- 125,000 ------- | |

[1] Preliminary. [2] Estimate. *Source: Economic Research Service, U.S. Department of Agriculture*

## Peanut Supply and Disposition (Farmer's Stock Basis) & Support Program in the United States

| Crop Year Beginning Aug. 1 | Supply: Production | Supply: Imports | Supply: Stocks Aug. 1 | Supply: Total | Disposition: Exports | Disposition: Crushed for Oil | Disposition: Seed, Loss & Residual | Disposition: Food | Disposition: Total Disappearance | Government Support Program: Support Price (¢ per Lb.) | Additional (¢ per Lb.) | Amount Put Under Support: Quantity Mil. Lbs. | Amount Put Under Support: % of Prod. |
|---|---|---|---|---|---|---|---|---|---|---|---|---|---|
| | Million Pounds | | | | | | | | | | | | |
| 1983-4 | 3,296 | 2 | 864 | 4,162 | 744 | 387 | 564 | 1,856 | 3,551 | 27.50 | 9.3 | 367 | 11.1 |
| 1984-5 | 4,406 | 2 | 611 | 5,019 | 860 | 625 | 199 | 1,911 | 3,595 | 27.50 | 9.3 | 1,370 | 30.9 |
| 1985-6 | 4,123 | 2 | 1,424 | 5,549 | 1,043 | 812 | 826 | 2,023 | 4,704 | 27.95 | 7.4 | 1,359 | 33.0 |
| 1986-7 | 3,697 | 2 | 845 | 4,544 | 663 | 514 | 291 | 2,073 | 3,541 | 30.37 | 7.5 | 290 | 7.8 |
| 1987-8 | 3,616 | 2 | 1,003 | 4,621 | 618 | 560 | 539 | 2,071 | 3,788 | 30.41 | 7.5 | 700 | 19.3 |
| 1988-9 | 3,981 | 2 | 833 | 4,816 | 688 | 814 | 217 | 2,254 | 3,974 | 30.76 | 7.5 | 540 | 13.6 |
| 1989-90 | 3,990 | 2 | 843 | 4,835 | 989 | 624 | 211 | 2,312 | 4,136 | 30.79 | 7.5 | 401 | 10.0 |
| 1990-1 | 3,603 | 27 | 701 | 4,331 | 652 | 689 | 288 | 2,020 | 3,649 | 31.57 | 7.5 | 576 | 16.0 |
| 1991-2 | 4,927 | 5 | 683 | 5,615 | 997 | 1,103 | 254 | 2,207 | 4,561 | 32.14 | 7.5 | 1,070 | 21.7 |
| 1992-3 | 4,284 | 2 | 1,055 | 5,341 | 951 | 891 | 227 | 2,122 | 3,991 | 33.75 | 6.6 | 436 | 10.2 |
| 1993-4 | 3,392 | 2 | 1,350 | 4,744 | 553 | 670 | 372 | 2,088 | 3,683 | 33.75 | 6.6 | 324 | 9.6 |
| 1994-5 | 4,247 | 74 | 1,061 | 5,382 | 878 | 982 | 315 | 2,009 | 4,184 | 33.92 | 6.6 | | |
| 1995-6[1] | 3,461 | 153 | 1,198 | 4,812 | 824 | 999 | 238 | 1,993 | 4,054 | 33.92 | 6.6 | | |
| 1996-7[2] | 3,645 | 125 | 758 | 4,528 | 700 | 742 | 271 | 2,015 | 3,728 | 30.50 | 6.6 | | |

[1] Preliminary. [2] Estimate. *Source: Economic Research Service, U.S. Department of Agriculture*

## U.S. Production of Peanuts (Harvested for Nuts) by States In Thousands of Pounds

| Crop Year | Alabama | Florida | Georgia | New Mexico | North Carolina | Oklahoma | South Carolina | Texas | Virgina | Total |
|---|---|---|---|---|---|---|---|---|---|---|
| 1983 | 454,500 | 166,800 | 1,567,980 | 25,630 | 318,255 | 176,540 | 25,000 | 362,275 | 198,550 | 3,295,530 |
| 1984 | 648,550 | 246,400 | 2,160,000 | 32,190 | 449,500 | 189,000 | 39,150 | 371,295 | 269,660 | 4,405,745 |
| 1985 | 590,000 | 216,000 | 1,921,320 | 31,992 | 451,990 | 170,980 | 34,200 | 422,625 | 283,680 | 4,122,787 |
| 1986 | 494,940 | 233,160 | 1,632,575 | 28,700 | 440,440 | 184,500 | 25,530 | 385,000 | 275,900 | 3,700,745 |
| 1987 | 465,300 | 215,800 | 1,575,000 | 29,760 | 392,200 | 222,750 | 31,200 | 441,000 | 243,000 | 3,616,010 |
| 1988 | 561,680 | 228,600 | 1,801,550 | 30,552 | 419,985 | 225,040 | 32,110 | 417,500 | 263,900 | 3,980,917 |
| 1989 | 537,750 | 214,890 | 1,849,500 | 43,680 | 370,120 | 210,700 | 32,500 | 484,700 | 246,155 | 3,989,995 |
| 1990 | 386,560 | 233,120 | 1,347,500 | 50,000 | 475,600 | 235,320 | 30,105 | 534,650 | 309,915 | 3,602,770 |
| 1991 | 638,485 | 279,660 | 2,228,550 | 51,075 | 461,700 | 243,800 | 33,600 | 682,500 | 307,200 | 4,926,570 |
| 1992 | 591,180 | 202,510 | 1,820,465 | 58,236 | 406,980 | 236,180 | 32,500 | 680,150 | 256,215 | 4,284,416 |
| 1993 | 473,220 | 194,880 | 1,383,545 | 56,680 | 299,585 | 233,580 | 24,500 | 550,175 | 176,250 | 3,392,415 |
| 1994 | 446,220 | 207,480 | 1,862,630 | 51,660 | 485,465 | 261,000 | 36,250 | 605,570 | 291,180 | 4,247,455 |
| 1995 | 483,360 | 193,590 | 1,414,880 | 43,000 | 347,040 | 201,880 | 30,800 | 540,000 | 206,925 | 3,461,475 |
| 1996[1] | 456,950 | 219,960 | 1,439,100 | 36,300 | 363,750 | 194,400 | 30,000 | 679,200 | 225,000 | 3,644,660 |

[1] Preliminary. *Source: Agricultural Statistics Board, U.S. Department of Agriculture*

## Supply and Reported Uses of Shelled Peanuts and Products in the U.S. In Thousands of Pounds

| Crop Year Beginning Aug. 1 | Shelled Peanuts -- Stocks Aug.1 --- | | Shelled Peanuts ------ Production ----- | | Reported Used (Shelled Peanuts--Raw Basis | | | | | | | | |
|---|---|---|---|---|---|---|---|---|---|---|---|---|---|
| | | | | | Edible Grades Used in | | | | | | | | Cake & Meal |
| | Edible | Oil Stock[2] | Edible | Oil Stock[2] | Candy[3] | Snacks[4] | Sandwich Spread | Butter[5] | Other Products | Total | Shelled Peanuts Crushed[6] | Crude Oil Production | Production |
| 1983-4 | 537,855 | 19,208 | 1,776,069 | 342,477 | 298,065 | 301,971 | 24,279 | 671,430 | 15,469 | 1,311,214 | 291,084 | 119,008 | 159,340 |
| 1984-5 | 402,449 | 33,063 | 2,414,852 | 422,026 | 290,318 | 309,050 | 26,240 | 697,137 | 19,201 | 1,341,945 | 470,264 | 187,283 | 264,658 |
| 1985-6 | 860,508 | 30,407 | 2,238,427 | 496,928 | 313,836 | 358,542 | 24,623 | 701,289 | 23,515 | 1,421,805 | 610,897 | 256,545 | 336,232 |
| 1986-7 | 559,256 | 4,734 | 2,123,054 | 299,651 | 321,191 | 384,286 | 33,858 | 679,373 | 41,065 | 1,459,773 | 386,388 | 152,423 | 214,526 |
| 1987-8 | 683,622 | 21,300 | 2,015,144 | 301,379 | 325,583 | 373,773 | 45,808 | 701,436 | 37,791 | 1,484,391 | 421,214 | 168,263 | 247,851 |
| 1988-9 | 565,779 | 22,647 | 2,095,351 | 406,626 | 326,907 | 381,481 | 28,373 | 831,928 | 35,978 | 1,604,667 | 612,200 | 250,498 | 348,662 |
| 1989-90 | 513,679 | 44,397 | 2,319,780 | 374,859 | 330,158 | 392,811 | ----- | 897,318 ----- | 36,682 | 1,656,969 | 469,351 | 193,000 | 261,465 |
| 1990-1 | 455,586 | 15,194 | 1,836,052 | 330,102 | 305,324 | 355,258 | ----- | 742,384 ----- | 37,888 | 1,440,854 | 517,712 | 213,112 | 299,820 |
| 1991-2 | 386,155 | 65,950 | 2,538,398 | 616,170 | 327,617 | 346,255 | ----- | 886,367 ----- | 34,173 | 1,594,412 | 828,986 | 356,276 | 459,457 |
| 1992-3 | 871,207 | 57,829 | 2,376,782 | 533,641 | 328,324 | 352,775 | ----- | 797,910 ----- | 24,981 | 1,503,990 | 669,942 | 285,904 | 377,301 |
| 1993-4 | 679,639 | 42,054 | 1,748,734 | 425,710 | 362,418 | 348,867 | ----- | 727,006 ----- | 36,301 | 1,474,592 | 503,674 | 212,216 | 292,093 |
| 1994-5 | 732,272 | 57,188 | 1,741,824 | 511,635 | 349,630 | 301,548 | ----- | 709,823 ----- | 36,854 | 1,397,855 | 738,221 | 314,189 | 415,394 |
| 1995-6[1] | 752,814 | 58,188 | 1,253,119 | 491,712 | 350,666 | 246,862 | ----- | 727,980 ----- | 32,020 | 1,387,528 | 751,281 | 320,909 | 420,919 |

[1] Preliminary. [2] Includes straight run oil stock peanuts. [3] Includes peanut butter made by manufacturers for own use in candy. [4] Formerly titled "Salted Peanuts." [5] Includes peanut butter made by manufacturers for own use in cookies and sandwiches, but excludes peanut butter used in candy. [6] All crushings regardless of grade. *Source: National Agricultural Statistics Service, U.S. Department of Agriculture*

## Shelled Peanuts (Raw Basis) Used in Primary Products by Type In Thousands of Pounds

| Crop Year Beginning Aug. 1 | Virginia | | | | Runner | | | | Spanish | | | |
|---|---|---|---|---|---|---|---|---|---|---|---|---|
| | Candy[2] | Snack Peanuts | Peanut Butter[3] | Total | Candy[2] | Snack Peanuts | Peanut Butter[3] | Total | Candy[2] | Snack Peanuts | Peanut Butter[3] | Total |
| 1983-4 | 15,402 | 101,980 | 44,091 | 163,268 | 237,075 | 164,389 | 600,226 | 1,032,248 | 45,588 | 35,602 | 33,263 | 115,698 |
| 1984-5 | 31,276 | 96,181 | 46,735 | 176,237 | 209,765 | 175,404 | 620,057 | 1,050,877 | 49,276 | 37,466 | 26,896 | 114,831 |
| 1985-6 | 32,900 | 113,577 | 54,794 | 206,557 | 240,198 | 207,503 | 648,566 | 1,091,850 | 40,739 | 37,463 | 43,159 | 123,400 |
| 1986-7 | 27,591 | 171,679 | 61,405 | 280,765 | 261,630 | 169,715 | 633,307 | 1,053,159 | 31,970 | 42,892 | 48,706 | 125,849 |
| 1987-8 | 40,251 | 120,084 | 42,841 | 216,987 | 249,673 | 220,511 | 613,231 | 1,152,848 | 35,659 | 33,178 | 43,224 | 114,556 |
| 1988-9 | 37,145 | 112,101 | 75,436 | 241,130 | 259,680 | 237,008 | 644,555 | 1,256,252 | 30,082 | 32,372 | 43,668 | 107,285 |
| 1989-90 | 28,701 | 130,000 | 90,622 | 263,014 | 278,062 | 234,661 | 773,985 | 1,306,810 | 23,395 | 28,150 | 32,711 | 87,145 |
| 1990-1 | 26,043 | 142,113 | 101,069 | 286,242 | 259,995 | 189,254 | 580,691 | 1,049,423 | 19,286 | 23,841 | 60,624 | 105,189 |
| 1991-2 | 51,312 | 142,514 | 89,045 | 297,570 | 244,815 | 180,609 | 759,747 | 1,203,233 | 31,490 | 23,132 | 37,575 | 93,609 |
| 1992-3 | 49,223 | 124,875 | 92,355 | 275,895 | 259,498 | 203,732 | 674,962 | 1,152,775 | 19,603 | 24,168 | 30,593 | 75,320 |
| 1993-4 | 44,889 | 99,381 | 63,270 | 222,641 | 298,325 | 227,286 | 365,047 | 1,179,396 | 19,204 | 22,200 | 28,689 | 72,555 |
| 1994-5 | 26,857 | 97,389 | 51,354 | 190,916 | 302,697 | 185,377 | 644,711 | 1,152,110 | 20,076 | 18,782 | 13,758 | 54,829 |
| 1995-6[1] | 25,176 | 92,973 | 71,310 | 203,115 | 304,285 | 169,012 | 635,604 | 1,124,848 | 21,205 | 14,877 | 21,066 | 59,565 |

[1] Preliminary. [2] Includes peanut butter made by manufacturers for own use in candy. [3] Includes peanut butter made by manufacturers for own use in cookies and sandwiches, but excludes peanut butter used in candy. *Source: National Agricultural Statistics Service, U.S. Department of Agriculture*

## Production, Consumption, Stocks and Foreign Trade of Peanut Oil in the U.S. In Millions of Pounds

| Crop Year Beginning Aug. 1 | Production | | Consumption | | Stocks Dec. 31 | | Imports for Consumption | Exports |
|---|---|---|---|---|---|---|---|---|
| | Crude | Refined | In Refining | In End Products | Crude | Refined | | |
| 1983-4 | 119.0 | 139.6 | 183.9 | 132.9 | 17.9 | 4.0 | .6 | 7 |
| 1984-5 | 187.3 | 119.9 | 148.4 | NA | 9.6 | 4.8 | 2.2 | 29 |
| 1985-6 | 256.5 | 139.7 | 124.6 | NA | 64.9 | 4.0 | .5 | 93 |
| 1986-7 | 152.4 | 160.0 | 145.7 | 153.2 | 17.0 | 3.6 | 2.4 | 6 |
| 1987-8 | 168.3 | 199.6 | 169.0 | 179.3 | 10.9 | 3.8 | 33.1 | 7 |
| 1988-9 | 250.5 | 185.5 | 207.5 | NA | 18.6 | 4.4 | 1.9 | 11 |
| 1989-90 | 193.0 | 212.5 | 192.4 | NA | 17.6 | 4.1 | 5.0 | 19 |
| 1990-1 | 213.1 | 131.7 | 229.1 | 169.0 | 19.3 | 5.8 | 10.0 | 25 |
| 1991-2 | 261.5 | 125.6 | 132.3 | 141.0 | 27.5 | 3.1 | 1.0 | 151 |
| 1992-3 | 285.9 | 181.1 | 188.4 | 182.1 | 46.2 | 5.3 | 0 | 59 |
| 1993-4 | 212.2 | 155.2 | 163.7 | 149.1 | 6.5 | 3.9 | 11.0 | 61 |
| 1994-5 | 319.9 | 120.0 | 126.1 | 118.9 | 5.0 | 2.8 | 5.0 | 22 |
| 1995-6[1] | 329.0 | 125.7 | 129.9 | 126.0 | 19.9 | 2.8 | 3.2 | 48 |

[1] Preliminary. NA = Not available. Source: Bureau of Census, U.S. Department of Commerce

# PEANUTS AND PEANUT OIL

## Average Price Received by Producers in U.S. for Peanuts in the Shell  In Cents Per Pound

| Crop Year | Aug. | Sept. | Oct. | Nov. | Dec. | Jan. | Feb. | Mar. | Apr. | May. | June | July | Average[1] |
|---|---|---|---|---|---|---|---|---|---|---|---|---|---|
| 1981-2 | 25.7 | 28.9 | 26.7 | 25.1 | 25.8 | 24.9 | NQ | NQ | NQ | NQ | NQ | NQ | 26.2 |
| 1982-3 | 27.1 | 25.1 | 24.9 | 25.3 | 26.1 | 22.9 | NQ | NQ | NQ | NQ | NQ | NQ | 25.2 |
| 1983-4 | NQ | 25.2 | 24.3 | 24.5 | 26.0 | 27.8 | NQ | NQ | NQ | NQ | NQ | NQ | 25.6 |
| 1984-5 | NQ | 29.9 | 27.1 | 25.6 | 26.3 | NQ | NQ | NQ | NQ | NQ | NQ | NQ | 27.2 |
| 1985-6 | 24.7 | 24.4 | 24.3 | 24.6 | 23.3 | 20.6 | NQ | NQ | NQ | NQ | NQ | NQ | 23.7 |
| 1986-7 | 29.6 | 27.0 | 28.8 | 29.8 | 32.5 | 24.5 | NQ | NQ | NQ | NQ | NQ | NQ | 28.7 |
| 1987-8 | 29.7 | 29.2 | 27.9 | 27.4 | 27.6 | 28.5 | NQ | NQ | NQ | NQ | NQ | NQ | 28.4 |
| 1988-9 | 20.0 | 29.9 | 28.0 | 26.4 | 25.8 | 27.8 | NQ | NQ | NQ | NQ | NQ | NQ | 26.3 |
| 1989-90 | 28.4 | 28.2 | 27.7 | 26.9 | 28.2 | 24.6 | NQ | NQ | NQ | NQ | NQ | NQ | 27.3 |
| 1990-1 | 26.5 | 32.2 | 34.0 | 40.1 | 43.6 | 44.8 | NQ | NQ | NQ | NQ | NQ | NQ | 34.7 |
| 1991-2 | 30.4 | 29.3 | 28.1 | 24.4 | 25.1 | NQ | NQ | NQ | NQ | NQ | NQ | NQ | 28.3 |
| 1992-3 | NQ | 31.3 | 29.9 | 28.2 | 25.7 | 29.5 | NQ | NQ | NQ | NQ | NQ | NQ | 30.0 |
| 1993-4 | NQ | 32.0 | 30.0 | 29.5 | 29.7 | 36.1 | NQ | NQ | NQ | NQ | NQ | NQ | 30.4 |
| 1994-5 | NQ | 30.6 | 28.6 | 25.9 | 25.8 | 25.7 | NQ | NQ | NQ | NQ | NQ | NQ | 27.9 |
| 1995-6[2] | 30.6 | 29.7 | 28.6 | 29.5 | 28.3 | 29.8 | NQ | NQ | NQ | NQ | NQ | NQ | 29.4 |
| 1996-7[2] | NQ | 27.7 | 25.8 | 25.0 | 25.6 | 24.3 | | | | | | | 25.7 |

[1] Weighted average by sale. [2] Preliminary. NQ = No quote. *Source: National Agricultural Statistics Service, U.S. Department of Agriculture*

## Crude Peanut Oil Produced in the United States  In Millions of Pounds

| Year | Jan. | Feb. | Mar. | Apr. | May | June | July | Aug. | Sept. | Oct. | Nov. | Dec. | Total |
|---|---|---|---|---|---|---|---|---|---|---|---|---|---|
| 1981 | 6.1 | 6.0 | 10.5 | 17.3 | 19.1 | 19.5 | 13.6 | 9.8 | 5.3 | 9.7 | 12.0 | 12.7 | 141.6 |
| 1982 | 11.3 | 11.1 | 19.4 | 26.3 | 22.3 | 19.0 | 15.0 | 11.8 | NA | NA | NA | NA | 136.2 |
| 1983 | NA | NA | NA | NA | NA | NA | NA | NA | NA | NA | NA | NA | NA |
| 1984 | 12.1 | 13.3 | 10.8 | 12.5 | 10.1 | 8.9 | 5.1 | 5.3 | 4.3 | 9.9 | 8.6 | 7.3 | 108.2 |
| 1985 | 9.8 | 13.9 | 15.8 | 15.5 | 14.5 | 12.4 | 10.4 | 10.0 | 10.1 | 9.2 | 10.2 | 14.9 | 146.7 |
| 1986 | 19.2 | 21.1 | 19.9 | 20.8 | 24.0 | 26.4 | 14.2 | 9.6 | NA | 4.1 | 11.9 | 10.7 | 181.9 |
| 1987 | 9.8 | 13.6 | 20.5 | 11.6 | 17.8 | 15.8 | 14.5 | 9.7 | 4.2 | 7.5 | 13.7 | 13.1 | 151.8 |
| 1988 | 13.8 | 14.9 | 10.1 | 8.3 | 19.5 | 12.5 | 17.0 | 11.4 | 2.8 | 9.7 | 17.0 | 18.4 | 155.4 |
| 1989 | 10.5 | 20.8 | 27.8 | 24.3 | 19.0 | 33.4 | 26.6 | 22.4 | NA | 7.4 | 11.6 | 9.8 | 213.6 |
| 1990 | 11.1 | 15.8 | 14.2 | 22.2 | 24.9 | 24.1 | 14.0 | 8.5 | 2.1 | 14.4 | 12.5 | 15.9 | 179.7 |
| 1991 | ------------ | 70.8 | ------------ | ------------ | 71.1 | ------------ | ------------ | 59.5 | ------------ | ------------ | 60.1 | ------------ | 261.5 |
| 1992 | 28.0 | 26.8 | 42.5 | 40.9 | 39.8 | 40.6 | 37.3 | 31.3 | 35.1 | 24.2 | 19.2 | 15.6 | 381.3 |
| 1993 | 16.9 | 17.0 | 24.1 | 28.8 | 23.3 | 29.0 | 25.6 | 22.5 | 3.6 | 8.6 | 16.4 | 14.6 | 230.4 |
| 1994 | 18.1 | 18.3 | 21.2 | 18.7 | 25.6 | 15.4 | 21.7 | 16.8 | 17.2 | 11.9 | 18.4 | 24.2 | 227.5 |
| 1995 | 27.9 | 28.6 | 42.7 | 36.9 | 39.2 | 29.2 | 26.9 | 26.3 | 17.4 | 13.2 | 19.5 | 24.3 | 332.0 |
| 1996[1] | 29.2 | 31.9 | 36.8 | 36.8 | 36.7 | 33.3 | 31.4 | 31.5 | 27.1 | 21.1 | 20.6 | 21.8 | 358.2 |

[1] Preliminary. NA = Not available. *Source: Bureau of Census, U.S. Department of Commerce*

## Average Price of Domestic Crude Peanut Oil (in Tanks) F.O.B. Southeast Mills  In Cents Per Pounds

| Year | Oct. | Nov. | Dec. | Jan. | Feb. | Mar. | Apr. | May | June | July | Aug. | Sept. | Average |
|---|---|---|---|---|---|---|---|---|---|---|---|---|---|
| 1981-2 | 34.50 | 34.50 | 30.90 | 27.30 | 31.40 | 23.30 | 29.10 | 29.90 | 26.20 | 24.70 | 22.70 | 22.50 | 28.08 |
| 1982-3 | 22.90 | 25.20 | 26.10 | 25.60 | 25.70 | 24.10 | 25.10 | 26.40 | 26.40 | 26.70 | 30.70 | 50.50 | 27.95 |
| 1983-4 | 50.70 | 48.80 | 48.10 | 47.30 | 46.50 | 48.40 | 52.60 | 58.20 | 59.10 | 57.70 | 54.80 | 39.20 | 50.95 |
| 1984-5 | 36.70 | 41.20 | 41.40 | 39.20 | 38.80 | 40.30 | 49.60 | 46.20 | 40.70 | 39.70 | 37.60 | 33.90 | 40.44 |
| 1985-6 | 38.30 | 42.20 | 36.10 | 29.50 | 22.60 | 21.50 | 24.40 | 27.60 | 28.00 | 27.50 | 30.50 | 28.30 | 29.71 |
| 1986-7 | 27.80 | 29.80 | 26.50 | 25.10 | 25.00 | 23.75 | 24.00 | 26.15 | 25.68 | 25.27 | 24.61 | 26.74 | 25.87 |
| 1987-8 | 33.48 | 31.50 | 32.10 | 35.73 | 32.40 | 29.61 | 29.50 | 30.02 | 34.00 | 39.80 | 37.86 | 36.00 | 33.50 |
| 1988-9 | 42.50 | 36.75 | 34.25 | 26.50 | 25.09 | 29.98 | 32.39 | 36.25 | 39.80 | NA | 35.75 | 34.40 | 33.97 |
| 1989-90 | 39.06 | 41.50 | 41.60 | 43.25 | 46.00 | 43.40 | 41.25 | 45.25 | 46.90 | 46.88 | 49.05 | 51.13 | 44.64 |
| 1990-1 | 48.13 | 44.20 | 43.00 | 41.00 | 42.83 | 47.60 | 46.75 | 43.33 | 42.25 | 41.50 | 35.33 | 30.66 | 42.22 |
| 1991-2 | 34.33 | 27.67 | 23.50 | 23.50 | 23.63 | 23.17 | 25.00 | 27.88 | 25.60 | 26.19 | 23.88 | 22.00 | 25.53 |
| 1992-3 | 23.63 | 25.58 | 30.30 | 30.88 | 27.17 | 26.00 | 27.50 | 30.00 | 30.20 | 33.00 | 39.50 | 35.93 | 29.97 |
| 1993-4 | 40.20 | 43.33 | 43.17 | 46.10 | 46.12 | 44.50 | 43.40 | 44.25 | 43.75 | 44.00 | 45.00 | 43.10 | 43.91 |
| 1994-5 | 46.00 | 50.88 | 53.80 | 50.25 | 41.83 | 41.00 | 41.25 | 40.25 | 39.00 | 39.13 | 41.50 | 41.30 | 43.85 |
| 1995-6[1] | 42.50 | 41.63 | 39.20 | 37.25 | 36.00 | 36.60 | 39.25 | 42.80 | 43.00 | 43.00 | 42.60 | 40.80 | 40.39 |
| 1996-7[1] | 41.50 | 39.20 | 40.75 | 43.50 | | | | | | | | | 41.24 |

[1] Preliminary. *Source: Agricultural Marketing Service, U.S. Department of Agriculture*

# Pepper

Pepper prices rose in 1995 only to decline in the first few months of 1996. By September 1996, pepper prices had again risen. Indonesian Lampong black pepper was quoted at $1.265 per pound, basis spot New York, 6 percent above prices in August. For all of 1995, black pepper prices averaged $1.165 per pound, 23 percent more than in 1994. Indonesian Muntok white pepper was quoted at $1.815 per pound in September 1996, basis spot New York, 7 percent above the price in August. For all of 1995, white pepper averaged $1.823 per pound while in 1994 it was $1.519.

Much of the statistical supply and demand data on pepper is laggard. Much of the production data is complicated by the tendency of countries to hold stocks. Pepper is a commodity that can be stored for long periods of time.

One characteristic of the pepper market has been the tendency for world production to not keep pace with world consumption. Low pepper prices between 1990 and 1994 caused some pepper producers to switch to other crops. Recent increases in pepper prices should put more land into production resulting in larger crops over the next few years.

The International Pepper Community reported that world production in 1994 was 182,876 tonnes, up 7 percent from 1993 but still well below the 1991 total of 233,355 tonnes. For 1994, the world's largest producer continued to be India with a crop estimated at 50,000 tonnes, down 9 percent from 1993; next came Indonesia with 1994 production of 42,500 tonnes, an increase of 81 percent from the small 1993 crop. In 1991 and 1992, Indonesia was the world's largest pepper producer with crops of over 60,000 tonnes. Brazilian pepper production declined 8 percent in 1994 to 23,000 tonnes and well below the 1991 crop of 50,000 tonnes. Malaysian production in 1994 was put at 16,000 tonnes, down 9 percent from 1993.

Vietnam is a country that has expanded production significantly. In 1994 production was 20,000 tonnes, up 8 percent from the previous year. In 1992, production was only 7,830 tonnes. 1994 Chinese production was 12,409 tonnes, up 19 percent from 1993. Production by Thailand in 1994 was 10,104 tonnes, up 12 percent from 1993. Other important producers are Sri Lanka, Madagascar, and Mexico.

For 1994, world exports of pepper were 144,687 tonnes, down 2 percent from 1993. The largest exporter in 1994 was Indonesia with shipments of 35,418 tonnes. Just over half of the exports are of white pepper. The major destinations for Indonesian white pepper were Singapore, the U.S., the Netherlands, Japan, and Germany. For black pepper the major destinations were the U.S. with most of the shipments, followed by Poland, Singapore, and Hungary. India was the next largest exporter with 34,000 tonnes. All of the exports were black pepper. The major market was the U.S. with over half of the total. The next largest market was Russia followed by Italy and Egypt. Malaysia exported 22,480 tonnes of pepper in 1994. The major markets for Malaysian black pepper were Singapore, Japan, Germany, and South Korea. The other major pepper exporters are Brazil and Vietnam.

## World Exports of Pepper (Black & White) and U.S. Prices

| | Exports (In Metric Tons) | | | | | | | | | New York Spot Prices (¢ Per Pound) | | | | |
|---|---|---|---|---|---|---|---|---|---|---|---|---|---|---|
| | | | | | | | | | | Indonesian | | | Indian | |
| Year | Brazil | India | Indonesia | Madagascar | Malaysia | Mexico | Sri Lanka | Thailand | Vietnam | Lampong Black | Muntok White | Brazilian Black | Malabar Black | Tellicherry[2] |
| 1986 | 22,069 | 49,808 | 29,566 | 972 | 15,380 | 1,794 | 1,286 | 1,816 | 3,133 | 215.0 | 275.3 | 212.5 | 214.6 | 235.1 |
| 1987 | 26,260 | 32,971 | 29,995 | 1,851 | 14,185 | 2,125 | 2,014 | 1,477 | 4,275 | 237.1 | 267.7 | 235.9 | 236.0 | 262.8 |
| 1988 | 24,393 | 47,258 | 41,568 | 2,497 | 19,190 | 2,602 | 2,714 | 910 | 2,612 | 173.9 | 243.4 | 170.3 | 170.3 | 220.6 |
| 1989 | 27,717 | 25,120 | 42,138 | 1,417 | 26,260 | 2,388 | 1,576 | 2,077 | 7,551 | 138.2 | 146.2 | 136.2 | 135.9 | 174.8 |
| 1990 | 28,014 | 34,429 | 47,675 | 1,222 | 27,706 | 2,663 | 2,609 | 4,042 | 1,288 | 99.1 | 90.3 | 97.1 | 97.1 | 139.1 |
| 1991 | 47,553 | 18,735 | 49,667 | 1,844 | 25,458 | 1,861 | 2,058 | 3,838 | 16,252 | 71.1 | 70.1 | 67.1 | 67.1 | 117.8 |
| 1992 | 26,277 | 22,684 | 62,136 | 1,948 | 22,919 | 3,636 | 2,143 | 6,156 | 22,347 | 56.1 | 70.8 | 54.7 | 54.7 | 86.1 |
| 1993 | 26,254 | 47,677 | 27,684 | 2,001 | 16,737 | 2,430 | 5,032 | 4,541 | 18,200 | 62.5 | 114.6 | 62.3 | 62.3 | 84.0 |
| 1994[1] | 22,231 | 36,315 | 36,036 | 2,066 | 23,301 | 2,615 | 1,850 | 1,124 | 17,500 | 95.3 | 151.9 | 95.0 | 95.0 | 110.7 |
| 1995[1] | | | | | | | | | | 116.8 | 182.3 | 116.8 | 116.8 | 150.9 |

[1] Preliminary. [2] Extra bold. *Sources: Foreign Agricultural Service, U.S. Department of Agriculture; Food and Agricultural Organization of the United Nations*

## United States Imports of Unground Pepper from Specified Countries In Metric Tons

| | Black Pepper | | | | | | | | | | White Pepper | | | | | | |
|---|---|---|---|---|---|---|---|---|---|---|---|---|---|---|---|---|---|
| Year | Brazil | China | India | Indonesia | Malaysia | Mexico | Singapore | Spain | Sri Lanka | Total | Brazil | China | Germany | Indonesia | Malaysia | Singapore | Total |
| 1986 | 9,416 | 243 | 20,976 | 5,980 | 634 | 7 | 120 | 1 | 255 | 38,063 | 134 | 171 | 7 | 2,846 | 65 | 140 | 3,578 |
| 1987 | 11,981 | 107 | 9,341 | 6,958 | 1,667 | 23 | 379 | ----- | 388 | 31,372 | 65 | 6 | 1 | 4,238 | 22 | 110 | 4,533 |
| 1988 | 6,033 | 14 | 7,481 | 11,131 | 1,400 | 119 | 104 | ----- | 344 | 26,939 | 20 | 2 | 25 | 4,169 | 12 | 26 | 4,326 |
| 1989 | 11,038 | 109 | 1,272 | 11,016 | 6,732 | 20 | 324 | ----- | 375 | 31,819 | 37 | 38 | 1 | 5,272 | 63 | 90 | 5,549 |
| 1990 | 8,778 | 70 | 6,679 | 8,444 | 6,768 | 20 | 457 | 20 | 644 | 32,980 | 17 | 15 | 1 | 5,506 | 24 | 86 | 5,721 |
| 1991 | 15,069 | 4 | 2,308 | 11,330 | 8,154 | 20 | 391 | ----- | 396 | 38,860 | 2 | 7 | 1 | 4,938 | 37 | 96 | 5,174 |
| 1992 | 6,601 | 1 | 9,892 | 20,768 | 2,073 | 160 | 52 | 1 | 310 | 40,590 | 51 | 2 | ----- | 5,089 | 29 | 261 | 5,544 |
| 1993 | 4,580 | 6 | 21,985 | 7,666 | 209 | ----- | ----- | ----- | 539 | 35,969 | 322 | 114 | 3 | 4,304 | 137 | 363 | 5,481 |
| 1994[1] | 8,215 | 1 | 21,097 | 11,877 | 829 | ----- | 90 | 1 | 386 | 43,011 | 312 | 756 | 58 | 3,974 | 228 | 302 | 6,102 |
| 1995[1] | 3,165 | ----- | 10,836 | 19,630 | 258 | 20 | 30 | 1 | 327 | 34,465 | 414 | 280 | 0 | 4,037 | 164 | 211 | 5,266 |

[1] Preliminary. *Source: Foreign Agricultural Service, U.S. Department of Agriculture*

# PEPPER

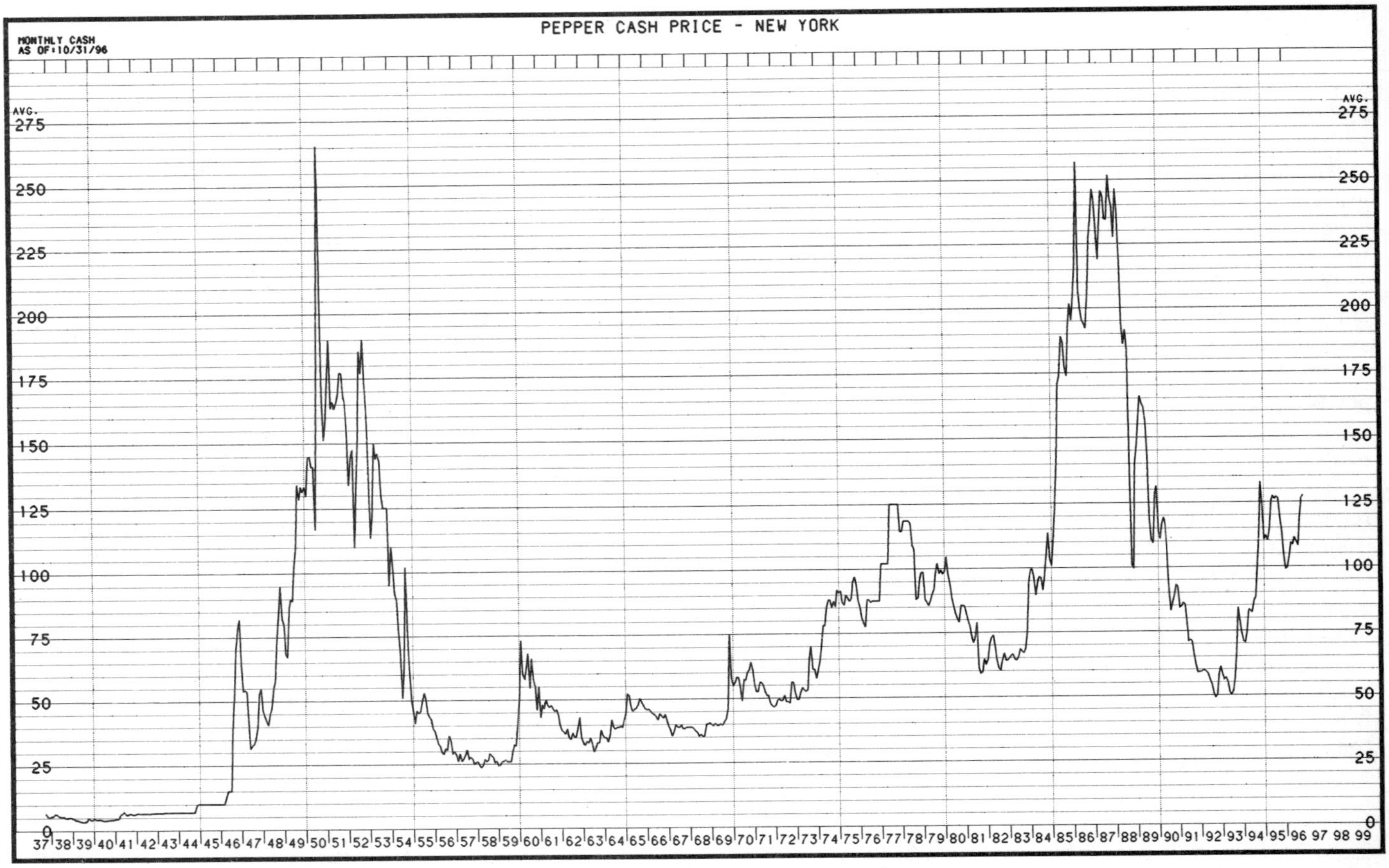


## Average Black Pepper Prices in New York (Brazilian) In Cents Per Pound

| Year | Jan. | Feb. | Mar. | Apr. | May | June | July | Aug. | Sept. | Oct. | Nov. | Dec. | Average |
|---|---|---|---|---|---|---|---|---|---|---|---|---|---|
| 1987 | 241.4 | 231.0 | 218.8 | 232.5 | 245.2 | 241.8 | 232.6 | 232.5 | 251.5 | 241.4 | 238.5 | 233.8 | 236.8 |
| 1988 | 233.3 | 228.8 | 210.5 | 190.3 | 184.3 | 190.5 | 182.8 | 141.5 | 100.2 | 99.5 | 138.3 | 143.0 | 170.3 |
| 1989 | 156.8 | 161.8 | 159.0 | 160.0 | 154.5 | 141.8 | 115.5 | 108.0 | 108.2 | 124.7 | 131.3 | 112.4 | 136.2 |
| 1990 | 107.0 | 110.8 | 115.4 | 115.0 | 106.0 | 91.0 | 82.3 | 85.8 | 88.5 | 92.3 | 89.6 | 81.8 | 97.1 |
| 1991 | 79.0 | 78.5 | 78.6 | 74.5 | 66.8 | 70.0 | 68.8 | 61.6 | 59.5 | 56.8 | 55.8 | 55.0 | 67.1 |
| 1992 | 55.6 | 54.5 | 56.0 | 55.3 | 54.0 | 54.0 | 50.8 | 49.0 | 50.0 | 57.8 | 61.0 | 58.0 | 54.7 |
| 1993 | 56.0 | 56.5 | 54.3 | 51.2 | 50.0 | 51.5 | 55.8 | 64.8 | 84.0 | 79.0 | 74.2 | 70.8 | 62.3 |
| 1994 | 69.3 | 74.3 | 82.0 | 82.8 | 82.0 | 86.5 | 87.8 | 97.8 | 112.2 | 131.5 | 123.5 | 110.4 | 95.0 |
| 1995 | 111.0 | 110.0 | 114.2 | 124.8 | 127.3 | 126.0 | 127.0 | 126.3 | 118.2 | 113.5 | 104.8 | 99.0 | 116.8 |
| 1996 | 99.3 | 103.3 | 109.2 | 108.3 | 111.2 | 109.5 | 108.0 | 119.8 | 126.5 | 127.5 | 127.6 | | 113.7 |

*Source: Foreign Agricultural Service, U.S. Department of Agriculture*

## Average White Pepper Prices in New York (Indonesian)[1] In Cents Per Pound

| Year | Jan. | Feb. | Mar. | Apr. | May | June | July | Aug. | Sept. | Oct. | Nov. | Dec. | Average |
|---|---|---|---|---|---|---|---|---|---|---|---|---|---|
| 1987 | 288.2 | 280.3 | 263.3 | 244.5 | 257.8 | 251.3 | 246.8 | 257.0 | 285.0 | 280.0 | 283.8 | 273.8 | 267.7 |
| 1988 | 273.3 | 275.0 | 277.5 | 285.0 | 291.3 | 296.3 | 262.0 | 235.0 | 204.0 | 172.5 | 177.8 | 171.2 | 243.4 |
| 1989 | 176.3 | 178.8 | 179.8 | 169.2 | 156.3 | 147.6 | 141.5 | 135.0 | 125.6 | 121.2 | 116.0 | 107.6 | 146.2 |
| 1990 | 102.3 | 100.5 | 99.2 | 95.5 | 93.8 | 82.8 | 80.0 | 88.2 | 91.5 | 88.0 | 83.2 | 78.0 | 90.3 |
| 1991 | 77.0 | 72.5 | 71.4 | 70.0 | 67.4 | 66.0 | 66.3 | 63.2 | 67.0 | 70.8 | 78.6 | 71.5 | 70.1 |
| 1992 | 70.0 | 70.0 | 70.0 | 70.0 | 68.0 | 65.0 | 64.2 | 65.0 | 72.7 | 79.2 | 78.5 | 77.4 | 70.8 |
| 1993 | 79.0 | 89.0 | 85.3 | 84.0 | 81.3 | 87.3 | 97.0 | 121.5 | 181.3 | 172.6 | 154.7 | 142.4 | 114.6 |
| 1994 | 144.5 | 139.5 | 141.3 | 140.8 | 137.0 | 143.3 | 143.4 | 156.3 | 159.2 | 167.5 | 176.5 | 173.0 | 151.9 |
| 1995 | 179.5 | 175.8 | 168.0 | 181.3 | 195.0 | 184.2 | 187.5 | 190.8 | 191.0 | 182.0 | 178.5 | 174.2 | 182.3 |
| 1996 | 174.5 | 177.5 | 181.6 | 179.5 | 172.6 | 164.8 | 154.0 | 169.6 | 181.5 | 193.5 | 191.8 | | 174.7 |

[1] Muntok white. *Source: Foreign Agricultural Service, U.S. Department of Agriculture*

# Petroleum

The U.S. Energy Information Administration reported that for September 1996, U.S. field production of crude oil was 6.49 million barrels per day. This represented a 2 percent increase from August. For the January-September 1996 period, field production of crude oil averaged 6.47 million barrels per day. For the same period of 1995, production averaged 6.58 million barrels while for the comparable period of 1994 the average was 6.65 million barrels. For all of 1995, crude oil production averaged 6.56 million barrels. U.S. crude oil production has been on a steady decline for a number of years as reserves have been depleted. In 1990, average daily production of crude oil was 7.36 million barrels. In 1980, the daily average was 8.60 million barrels while in 1973, it was 9.2 million. The current level of U.S. production is some 30 percent less than in 1973.

Natural gas plant liquids production averaged 1.84 million barrels per day in September 1996. This was some 2 percent less than in August. For the first nine months of 1996, production averaged 1.8 million barrels a day, an increase of 2 percent from the comparable period of 1995, and 6 percent more than in the like period of 1994. For all of 1995, natural gas plant liquids production averaged 1.76 million barrels per day. Production of natural gas plant liquids has been slowly increasing in recent years.

Total petroleum production (crude oil, natural gas plant liquids, and other liquids) averaged 8.61 million barrels per day in September 1996, virtually the same as in August. This was 1 percent less than in 1995, and about the same as in the comparable period of 1994.

Of the average daily crude oil production of 6.49 million barrels in September 1996, 1.39 million barrels per day came from Alaska. This represented 21 percent of U.S. production. For the January-September 1996 period, Alaskan petroleum production averaged 1.39 million barrels per day. In the same period of 1995, Alaskan production averaged 1.49 million barrels while in the like period of 1994 it averaged 1.55 million barrels. For all of 1995, Alaskan crude oil production averaged 1.48 million barrels per day or 23 percent of U.S. production. In 1990, Alaskan daily crude oil production was 1.77 million barrels or 24 percent of the U.S. output. In 1980, Alaskan production averaged 1.62 million barrels or 19 percent of the U.S. total. In 1973 production was only 198,000 barrels per day or 2 percent of U.S. crude oil output.

Total U.S. petroleum products supplied in September 1996 were 17.98 million barrels per day, down 3 percent from the August total. Over the first nine months of 1996, petroleum products supplied averaged 18.14 million barrels daily, up 3 percent from the comparable period of 1995 and almost 3 percent more than the like period of 1994. For all of 1995, the daily supply of petroleum products was 17.73 million barrels.

U.S. ending stocks of crude oil and petroleum products (crude oil, natural gas plant liquids, and other liquids) at the end of September 1996 were 1.54 billion barrels. This was down 1 percent from August 1996. At the end of December 1995, U.S. stocks were 1.56 billion barrels.

Since U.S. energy requirements cannot be met out of current production, crude oil and petroleum products must be imported. As U.S. crude oil reserves have declined and energy requirements have increased, imports have risen. In September 1996, U.S. imports of crude oil averaged 7.38 million barrels per day, an increase of 1 percent from the same period of 1995 and almost 5 percent more than in the like period of 1994. For all of 1995, U.S. crude oil imports averaged 7.23 million barrels per day. In 1990, imports averaged 5.89 million barrels daily while in 1980 the average was 5.26 million. In 1973, imports averaged 3.24 million barrels. Total petroleum imports (crude oil and products) in September 1996 averaged 9.04 million barrels per day.

### *Futures Markets*

Futures and options contracts on light sweet crude oil, heating oil and unleaded gasoline are traded on the New York Mercantile Exchange (NYMEX). Propane and natural gas futures also are traded there. London's International Petroleum Exchange (IPE) trades Brent crude oil futures and options on those futures. The IPE also trades heating oil futures and options (termed gas oil) and unleaded gasoline futures. High-sulfur fuel oil futures are traded on the SIMEX in Singapore.

**World Production of Crude Petroleum, by Specified Countries** In Thousands of Barrels Per Day

| Year | Algeria | Canada | China | Libya | Indonesia | Iran | Iraq | Kuwait | Mexico | Nigeria | Russia[3] | Saudi Arabia | United Kingdom | United States | Venezuela | Total World |
|---|---|---|---|---|---|---|---|---|---|---|---|---|---|---|---|---|
| 1984 | 1,014 | 1,438 | 2,296 | 1,087 | 1,412 | 2,174 | 1,209 | 1,157 | 2,780 | 1,388 | 11,861 | 4,663 | 2,480 | 8,879 | 1,798 | 54,488 |
| 1985 | 1,037 | 1,471 | 2,505 | 1,059 | 1,325 | 2,250 | 1,433 | 1,023 | 2,745 | 1,495 | 11,585 | 3,388 | 2,530 | 8,971 | 1,677 | 53,981 |
| 1986 | 945 | 1,474 | 2,620 | 1,034 | 1,390 | 2,035 | 1,690 | 1,419 | 2,435 | 1,467 | 11,895 | 4,870 | 2,539 | 8,680 | 1,787 | 56,227 |
| 1987 | 1,048 | 1,535 | 2,690 | 972 | 1,343 | 2,298 | 2,079 | 1,585 | 2,548 | 1,341 | 12,050 | 4,265 | 2,406 | 8,349 | 1,752 | 56,666 |
| 1988 | 1,040 | 1,616 | 2,730 | 1,175 | 1,342 | 2,240 | 2,685 | 1,492 | 2,512 | 1,450 | 12,053 | 5,086 | 2,232 | 8,140 | 1,903 | 58,737 |
| 1989 | 1,095 | 1,560 | 2,757 | 1,150 | 1,409 | 2,810 | 2,897 | 1,783 | 2,520 | 1,716 | 11,715 | 5,064 | 1,802 | 7,613 | 1,907 | 59,863 |
| 1990 | 1,175 | 1,553 | 2,774 | 1,375 | 1,462 | 3,088 | 2,040 | 1,175 | 2,553 | 1,810 | 10,975 | 6,410 | 1,820 | 7,355 | 2,137 | 60,566 |
| 1991 | 1,230 | 1,548 | 2,835 | 1,483 | 1,592 | 3,312 | 305 | 190 | 2,680 | 1,892 | 9,992 | 8,115 | 1,797 | 7,417 | 2,375 | 60,207 |
| 1992 | 1,214 | 1,605 | 2,845 | 1,433 | 1,504 | 3,429 | 425 | 1,058 | 2,669 | 1,943 | 7,632 | 8,332 | 1,825 | 7,171 | 2,371 | 60,216 |
| 1993 | 1,162 | 1,679 | 2,890 | 1,361 | 1,511 | 3,540 | 512 | 1,852 | 2,673 | 1,960 | 6,730 | 8,198 | 1,915 | 6,847 | 2,450 | 60,246 |
| 1994 | 1,180 | 1,793 | 2,939 | 1,378 | 1,514 | 3,635 | 553 | 2,034 | 2,689 | 2,037 | 6,135 | 8,147 | 2,375 | 6,662 | 2,588 | 61,358 |
| 1995[1] | 1,197 | 1,817 | 3,015 | 1,390 | 1,523 | 3,643 | 555 | 2,057 | 2,618 | 2,028 | 5,768 | 8,231 | 2,489 | 6,560 | 2,750 | 62,230 |
| 1996[2] | 1,240 | 1,820 | 3,131 | 1,400 | 1,545 | 3,690 | 555 | 2,060 | 2,851 | 2,185 | 5,866 | 8,205 | 2,550 | 6,479 | 3,036 | 63,821 |

Includes lease condensate. [1] Preliminary. [2] Estimate. [3] Formerly part of the U.S.S.R.; data not reported separately until 1992.

*Source: Energy Information Administration, U.S. Department of Energy*

## Refiner Sales Prices of Petroleum Products for Resale (Excluding Taxes) In Cents Per Gallon

| Year | Jan. | Feb. | Mar. | Apr. | May | June | July | Aug. | Sept. | Oct. | Nov. | Dec. | Average |
|---|---|---|---|---|---|---|---|---|---|---|---|---|---|
| Residual Fuel Oil (Sulfur 1% or less) | | | | | | | | | | | | | |
| 1990 | 56.0 | 44.4 | 39.7 | 36.1 | 34.5 | 31.1 | 33.2 | 49.1 | 56.4 | 64.1 | 63.3 | 57.6 | 47.2 |
| 1991 | 52.1 | 36.5 | 36.0 | 33.6 | 36.6 | 32.1 | 32.6 | 33.4 | 33.7 | 34.1 | 36.6 | 34.8 | 36.4 |
| 1992 | 30.3 | 32.7 | 30.8 | 31.6 | 33.1 | 35.9 | 38.0 | 37.7 | 37.9 | 41.4 | 39.2 | 35.9 | 35.1 |
| 1993 | 36.8 | 35.5 | 39.1 | 38.4 | 34.8 | 33.7 | 32.7 | 31.6 | 31.9 | 32.1 | 30.7 | 27.5 | 33.7 |
| 1994 | 33.8 | 39.3 | 30.0 | 29.4 | 31.7 | 35.8 | 37.8 | 37.1 | 32.6 | 32.6 | 35.7 | 36.9 | 34.5 |
| 1995 | 38.4 | 37.1 | 38.3 | 36.8 | 40.4 | 39.9 | 36.8 | 35.2 | 36.4 | 35.2 | 36.6 | 44.5 | 38.1 |
| 1996[1] | 49.9 | 42.8 | 47.1 | 48.3 | 45.0 | 40.4 | 41.4 | 42.0 | 42.8 | 47.9 | 49.1 | | 45.2 |
| No. 2 Fuel Oil | | | | | | | | | | | | | |
| 1990 | 73.8 | 57.8 | 57.9 | 57.4 | 54.5 | 49.4 | 51.9 | 72.1 | 85.3 | 95.0 | 90.6 | 80.9 | 69.7 |
| 1991 | 76.6 | 67.9 | 59.6 | 57.2 | 56.0 | 54.0 | 56.7 | 60.6 | 62.1 | 66.3 | 66.6 | 55.9 | 62.2 |
| 1992 | 51.9 | 54.0 | 53.7 | 56.5 | 58.8 | 61.7 | 61.3 | 60.1 | 62.7 | 64.6 | 58.8 | 55.7 | 57.9 |
| 1993 | 54.4 | 56.9 | 59.0 | 57.5 | 56.9 | 55.0 | 51.0 | 51.0 | 54.8 | 58.1 | 53.1 | 45.1 | 54.4 |
| 1994 | 50.7 | 54.2 | 49.7 | 48.9 | 49.0 | 49.8 | 50.9 | 51.4 | 50.1 | 50.8 | 51.0 | 49.5 | 50.6 |
| 1995 | 49.4 | 49.1 | 48.1 | 50.4 | 52.4 | 49.3 | 48.1 | 51.0 | 52.0 | 50.5 | 53.4 | 57.3 | 51.1 |
| 1996[1] | 56.8 | 58.9 | 62.8 | 67.5 | 61.1 | 53.7 | 57.1 | 62.1 | 68.7 | 72.7 | 71.4 | | 63.0 |
| No. 2 Diesel Fuel | | | | | | | | | | | | | |
| 1990 | 69.3 | 57.1 | 57.6 | 57.6 | 55.4 | 50.5 | 52.0 | 73.7 | 87.2 | 99.4 | 93.6 | 79.8 | 69.4 |
| 1991 | 75.5 | 67.4 | 57.7 | 57.4 | 57.2 | 54.5 | 57.1 | 61.9 | 62.9 | 65.6 | 66.5 | 55.6 | 61.5 |
| 1992 | 51.4 | 54.1 | 54.0 | 57.0 | 60.1 | 62.7 | 61.8 | 60.4 | 63.3 | 65.5 | 60.4 | 56.4 | 59.1 |
| 1993 | 54.9 | 57.4 | 60.0 | 59.8 | 59.6 | 57.2 | 53.2 | 53.2 | 58.9 | 65.8 | 58.9 | 46.8 | 57.0 |
| 1994 | 49.1 | 52.8 | 52.9 | 52.3 | 51.7 | 52.2 | 53.7 | 54.1 | 54.2 | 55.2 | 55.1 | 50.8 | 52.9 |
| 1995 | 50.1 | 50.6 | 51.2 | 54.8 | 55.9 | 52.6 | 51.4 | 54.2 | 55.7 | 54.6 | 56.3 | 57.6 | 53.8 |
| 1996[1] | 56.2 | 57.9 | 61.9 | 70.1 | 67.0 | 59.1 | 60.0 | 64.9 | 71.7 | 75.4 | 73.3 | | 65.2 |
| Kerosine-Type Jet Fuel | | | | | | | | | | | | | |
| 1990 | 76.6 | 66.7 | 61.6 | 59.5 | 57.1 | 54.6 | 55.5 | 71.4 | 92.9 | 114.7 | 107.0 | 90.1 | 77.3 |
| 1991 | 82.0 | 74.0 | 62.4 | 58.9 | 60.8 | 58.8 | 59.4 | 63.3 | 65.9 | 67.1 | 68.2 | 60.1 | 65.0 |
| 1992 | 53.9 | 55.2 | 54.6 | 56.9 | 60.8 | 63.3 | 64.8 | 63.9 | 64.3 | 66.0 | 61.5 | 58.9 | 60.5 |
| 1993 | 57.7 | 60.4 | 60.3 | 59.8 | 60.1 | 58.5 | 55.1 | 55.1 | 56.6 | 60.5 | 58.7 | 51.0 | 57.7 |
| 1994 | 52.6 | 56.0 | 52.4 | 50.8 | 50.6 | 51.5 | 53.8 | 54.4 | 54.0 | 54.4 | 56.3 | 53.1 | 53.4 |
| 1995 | 52.3 | 52.1 | 50.1 | 52.6 | 54.7 | 53.1 | 51.3 | 53.1 | 55.2 | 54.1 | 56.3 | 58.6 | 53.9 |
| 1996[1] | 60.3 | 57.2 | 59.6 | 65.3 | 62.2 | 57.5 | 59.6 | 64.5 | 71.6 | 73.6 | 72.2 | | 64.0 |
| Propane (Consumer Grade) | | | | | | | | | | | | | |
| 1990 | 54.4 | 34.1 | 27.1 | 25.2 | 24.0 | 24.9 | 27.3 | 36.3 | 43.5 | 53.5 | 50.5 | 44.6 | 38.6 |
| 1991 | 42.2 | 31.6 | 31.3 | 31.8 | 31.9 | 29.3 | 27.6 | 29.6 | 34.9 | 40.2 | 43.0 | 37.7 | 34.9 |
| 1992 | 30.9 | 30.2 | 29.5 | 29.0 | 29.4 | 31.6 | 31.5 | 32.9 | 35.4 | 36.6 | 36.2 | 36.3 | 32.8 |
| 1993 | 40.2 | 36.7 | 38.2 | 36.2 | 34.0 | 33.8 | 33.3 | 33.3 | 34.1 | 34.7 | 33.6 | 30.9 | 35.1 |
| 1994 | 32.3 | 34.0 | 31.8 | 30.5 | 30.4 | 29.9 | 29.8 | 31.0 | 31.7 | 33.5 | 35.0 | 35.8 | 32.5 |
| 1995 | 35.6 | 34.5 | 34.3 | 33.0 | 33.2 | 32.6 | 32.1 | 33.2 | 33.8 | 34.4 | 34.7 | 37.9 | 34.4 |
| 1996[1] | 41.6 | 44.1 | 41.1 | 37.8 | 36.2 | 36.2 | 36.9 | 38.9 | 45.3 | 51.1 | 58.2 | | 42.5 |

[1] Preliminary. *Source: Energy Information Administration, U.S. Department of Energy*

## United States Crude Oil Supply & Disposition

| Yearly Average | Supply: Field Production: Total Domestic | Supply: Field Production: Alaskan | Supply: Imports: Total | Supply: Imports: SPR[2] | Supply: Imports: Other | Supply: Unaccounted for Crude Oil | Stock Withdrawal[3]: SPR[2] | Stock Withdrawal[3]: Other | Disposition: Refinery Inputs | Disposition: Exports | Ending Stocks: Total | Ending Stocks: SPR[2] | Ending Stocks: Other Primary |
|---|---|---|---|---|---|---|---|---|---|---|---|---|---|
| | Thousands of Barrels Per Day | | | | | | | | | | Million of Barrels | | |
| 1987 | 8,349 | 1,962 | 4,674 | 73 | 4,601 | 145 | 80 | 49 | 12,854 | 151 | 890 | 541 | 349 |
| 1988 | 8,140 | 2,017 | 5,107 | 51 | 5,055 | 196 | 52 | -51 | 13,246 | 155 | 890 | 560 | 330 |
| 1989 | 7,613 | 1,874 | 5,843 | 56 | 5,787 | 200 | 56 | 30 | 13,401 | 142 | 921 | 580 | 341 |
| 1990 | 7,355 | 1,773 | 5,894 | 27 | 5,867 | 258 | 16 | -51 | 13,409 | 109 | 908 | 586 | 323 |
| 1991 | 7,417 | 1,798 | 5,782 | 0 | 5,782 | 195 | -47 | 5 | 13,301 | 116 | 893 | 569 | 325 |
| 1992 | 7,171 | 1,714 | 6,083 | 10 | 6,073 | 258 | 17 | -18 | 13,411 | 89 | 893 | 575 | 318 |
| 1993 | 6,847 | 1,582 | 6,787 | 15 | 6,772 | 168 | 34 | 47 | 13,613 | 98 | 922 | 587 | 335 |
| 1994 | 6,662 | 1,559 | 7,063 | 12 | 7,051 | 266 | 13 | 5 | 13,866 | 99 | 929 | 592 | 337 |
| 1995 | 6,560 | 1,484 | 7,230 | 0 | 7,230 | 193 | 0 | -93 | 13,973 | 95 | 895 | 592 | 303 |
| 1996[1] | 6,471 | 1,396 | 7,482 | 0 | 7,482 | 227 | -71 | -47 | 14,181 | 110 | 850 | 566 | 285 |

[1] Preliminary. [2] Strategic Petroleum Reserve. [3] A negative number indicates a decrease in stocks and a positive number indicates an increase. Note: Crude oil includes lease condensate. Stocks of Alaskan crude oil in transit were included beginning in January 1981. *Source: Energy Information Administration, U.S. Department of Energy*

## Crude Petroleum Refinery Operations Ration[1] In Percent of Capacity

| Year | Jan. | Feb. | Mar. | Apr. | May | June | July | Aug. | Sept. | Oct. | Nov. | Dec. | Average |
|---|---|---|---|---|---|---|---|---|---|---|---|---|---|
| 1986 | 81.0 | 78.0 | 76.0 | 82.0 | 86.0 | 86.0 | 84.0 | 87.0 | 86.0 | 83.0 | 84.0 | 84.0 | 83.1 |
| 1987 | 82.0 | 80.0 | 79.0 | 81.0 | 82.0 | 85.0 | 87.0 | 87.0 | 86.0 | 83.0 | 82.0 | 84.0 | 83.2 |
| 1988 | 83.0 | 81.0 | 83.0 | 84.0 | 86.0 | 86.0 | 86.0 | 87.0 | 84.0 | 83.0 | 84.0 | 85.0 | 84.3 |
| 1989 | 86.0 | 83.0 | 84.0 | 84.0 | 86.0 | 90.0 | 89.0 | 89.0 | 88.0 | 86.0 | 86.0 | 84.0 | 86.3 |
| 1990 | 88.0 | 88.0 | 84.0 | 85.0 | 87.0 | 89.0 | 93.0 | 91.0 | 91.0 | 84.0 | 84.0 | 83.0 | 87.3 |
| 1991 | 83.0 | 84.0 | 83.0 | 85.0 | 87.0 | 90.0 | 89.0 | 89.0 | 88.0 | 83.0 | 84.0 | 87.0 | 86.0 |
| 1992 | 83.0 | 81.0 | 85.0 | 86.0 | 89.0 | 92.0 | 92.0 | 89.0 | 91.0 | 89.0 | 90.0 | 88.0 | 87.9 |
| 1993 | 87.0 | 87.0 | 89.0 | 91.0 | 93.0 | 95.0 | 95.0 | 93.0 | 93.0 | 92.0 | 92.0 | 91.0 | 91.5 |
| 1994 | 89.8 | 88.7 | 87.6 | 92.4 | 95.4 | 95.8 | 95.5 | 96.4 | 94.4 | 89.8 | 92.7 | 92.6 | 92.6 |
| 1995 | 89.6 | 87.9 | 86.7 | 90.5 | 94.0 | 95.6 | 94.0 | 94.0 | 95.6 | 90.5 | 92.1 | 93.3 | 92.0 |
| 1996[2] | 90.6 | 89.1 | 90.6 | 93.7 | 94.4 | 95.4 | 93.9 | 95.0 | 95.5 | 94.6 | 94.7 | | 93.4 |

[1] Based on the ration of the daily average crude runs to stills to the rated capacity of refineries per day. [2] Preliminary.
*Source: Energy Information Administration, U.S. Department of Energy*

## United States Crude Oil Refinery Inputs In Thousands of Barrels Per Day

| Year | Jan. | Feb. | Mar. | Apr. | May | June | July | Aug. | Sept. | Oct. | Nov. | Dec. | Average |
|---|---|---|---|---|---|---|---|---|---|---|---|---|---|
| 1986 | 12,374 | 11,918 | 11,652 | 12,512 | 13,279 | 13,261 | 12,917 | 13,287 | 13,097 | 12,636 | 12,831 | 12,777 | 12,716 |
| 1987 | 12,570 | 12,290 | 12,081 | 12,512 | 12,653 | 13,202 | 13,430 | 13,380 | 13,168 | 12,733 | 12,981 | 13,212 | 12,854 |
| 1988 | 12,920 | 12,644 | 13,016 | 13,135 | 13,425 | 13,487 | 13,617 | 13,752 | 13,261 | 13,126 | 13,156 | 13,381 | 13,246 |
| 1989 | 13,330 | 12,765 | 12,963 | 12,956 | 13,405 | 13,905 | 13,848 | 13,861 | 13,791 | 13,360 | 13,420 | 13,165 | 13,401 |
| 1990 | 13,491 | 13,487 | 12,876 | 13,051 | 13,386 | 13,689 | 14,212 | 14,142 | 14,104 | 12,825 | 12,953 | 12,708 | 13,409 |
| 1991 | 12,735 | 13,046 | 12,839 | 13,042 | 13,539 | 13,918 | 13,703 | 13,800 | 13,694 | 12,896 | 12,929 | 13,465 | 13,301 |
| 1992 | 12,923 | 12,486 | 13,083 | 13,260 | 13,679 | 14,059 | 13,953 | 13,426 | 13,714 | 13,584 | 13,547 | 13,194 | 13,411 |
| 1993 | 12,938 | 12,865 | 13,200 | 13,538 | 13,829 | 14,129 | 14,136 | 13,844 | 13,841 | 13,729 | 13,686 | 13,571 | 13,613 |
| 1994 | 13,286 | 13,130 | 12,985 | 13,809 | 14,272 | 14,351 | 14,344 | 14,491 | 14,234 | 13,529 | 13,968 | 13,951 | 13,866 |
| 1995 | 13,604 | 13,365 | 13,480 | 13,817 | 14,303 | 14,553 | 14,403 | 14,276 | 14,402 | 13,598 | 13,833 | 14,011 | 13,973 |
| 1996[1] | 13,708 | 13,529 | 13,755 | 14,263 | 14,401 | 14,535 | 14,319 | 14,423 | 14,483 | 14,276 | 14,276 | 14,194 | 14,181 |

[1] Preliminary. *Source: Energy Information Administration, U.S. Department of Energy*

## Production of Major Refined Petroleum Products in the Continental U.S. In Millions of Barrels

| | | | Fuel Oil | | | | | Natural | | Liquefied Gases | | |
|---|---|---|---|---|---|---|---|---|---|---|---|---|
| Year | Asphalt | Aviation Gasoline | Distillate | Residual | Gasoline | Jet Fuel | Kerosene | Gas Plant Liquids | Lubricants | Total | at L.P.G.[2] | at L.P.G.[3] |
| 1986 | 149.7 | 11.7 | 1,021.2 | 324.3 | 2,476 | 472.0 | 32.6 | 587.1 | 58.2 | 618.5 | 466.2 | 152.3 |
| 1987 | 158.4 | 9.1 | 996.6 | 323.2 | 2,506 | 490.1 | 28.7 | 605.6 | 60.9 | 638.2 | 474.5 | 163.7 |
| 1988 | 162.1 | 9.3 | 1,046.3 | 338.7 | 2,555 | 501.3 | 28.8 | 614.2 | 62.3 | 665.2 | 482.6 | 182.6 |
| 1989 | 154.9 | 9.2 | 1,152.2 | 500.1 | 2,684 | 543.6 | 30.8 | 586.1 | 58.1 | 653.5 | 451.3 | 202.2 |
| 1990 | 164.0 | 8.5 | 1,067.5 | 346.6 | 2,650 | 555.6 | 15.5 | 598.3 | 59.7 | 638.4 | 456.2 | 182.2 |
| 1991 | 156.8 | 8.0 | 1,081.0 | 341.1 | 2,554 | 525.0 | 14.0 | 639.2 | 57.0 | 683.1 | 487.5 | 195.6 |
| 1992 | 153.0 | 7.9 | 1,088.4 | 326.1 | 2,591 | 512.0 | 14.8 | 668.0 | 57.5 | 721.9 | 499.7 | 222.2 |
| 1993 | 165.6 | 7.9 | 1,139.7 | 303.9 | 2,644 | 518.8 | 17.5 | 631.2 | 58.4 | 849.4 | 633.5 | 215.9 |
| 1994 | 164.8 | 7.9 | 1,169.7 | 301.4 | 2,621 | 528.4 | 21.1 | 630.2 | 62.1 | 734.2 | 511.1 | 223.2 |
| 1995[1] | 170.4 | 7.8 | 1,151.7 | 287.6 | 2,722 | 516.8 | 19.2 | 643.2 | 63.7 | 759.9 | 521.1 | 238.8 |

[1] Preliminary. *Source: Energy Information Administration, U.S. Department of Energy*

## Stocks of Petroleum & Products in the United States on January 1 In Millions of Barrels

| | | | Refined Products | | | | | | | | | | Motor Gasoline | |
|---|---|---|---|---|---|---|---|---|---|---|---|---|---|---|
| | | | | | | Fuel Oil | | | | | | | | |
| Year | Crude Petroleum | Strategic Reserve | Total | Asphalt | Aviation Gasoline | Distillate | Residual | Finished Gasoline | Jet Fuel | Kerosene | Liquefied Gases[2] | Lubricants | Total | Finished[3] |
| 1986 | 814.2 | 493.3 | 556.6 | 21.2 | 2.1 | 143.7 | 50.4 | 192.4 | 40.5 | 7.5 | 73.5 | 11.8 | 223 | 190 |
| 1987 | 842.8 | 511.6 | 609.4 | 17.7 | 2.2 | 155.1 | 47.4 | 196.4 | 49.7 | 8.4 | 102.7 | 14.2 | 233 | 194 |
| 1988 | 889.6 | 540.6 | 579.5 | 18.8 | 2.3 | 134.5 | 47.4 | 191.1 | 49.9 | 8.4 | 97.1 | 13.3 | 226 | 189 |
| 1989 | 889.9 | 559.5 | 561.6 | 20.8 | 2.1 | 123.5 | 44.6 | 192.0 | 43.8 | 7.3 | 97.3 | 13.3 | 228 | 190 |
| 1990 | 921.1 | 579.9 | 508.3 | 20.6 | 2.1 | 105.7 | 43.8 | 179.1 | 40.9 | 5.1 | 80.2 | 13.8 | 213 | 177 |
| 1991 | 908.4 | 585.7 | 566.8 | 18.7 | 1.7 | 132.2 | 48.6 | 182.4 | 52.1 | 5.6 | 97.9 | 12.4 | 220 | 181 |
| 1992 | 893.1 | 568.5 | 576.7 | 22.3 | 1.6 | 143.5 | 49.9 | 183.3 | 48.8 | 5.8 | 92.3 | 12.3 | 219 | 182 |
| 1993 | 892.9 | 574.7 | 549.1 | 17.7 | 1.6 | 140.6 | 42.6 | 179.1 | 43.1 | 5.7 | 88.7 | 13.3 | 216 | 178 |
| 1994 | 922.5 | 587.1 | 465.8 | 19.1 | 1.8 | 140.9 | 44.2 | 185.7 | 40.4 | 4.1 | 106.6 | 11.8 | 226 | 187 |
| 1995 | 928.9 | 591.7 | 468.0 | 18.6 | 2.3 | 145.2 | 41.9 | 175.9 | 46.8 | 8.0 | 108.0 | 11.5 | 215 | 176 |
| 1996[1] | 892.5 | 591.6 | 401.2 | 26.3 | 2.2 | 106.3 | 34.8 | 162.8 | 38.4 | 4.0 | 99.2 | 11.7 | 206 | 163 |

1 Preliminary. [2] Includes ethane and ethylene at plants and refineries. [3] Includes oxygenated. *Source: Energy Information Administration, U.S. Department of Energy*

## Stocks of Crude Petroleum in the United States at the Beginning of the Month — In Millions of Barrels

| Year | Jan. | Feb. | Mar. | Apr. | May | June | July | Aug. | Sept. | Oct. | Nov. | Dec. |
|---|---|---|---|---|---|---|---|---|---|---|---|---|
| 1986 | 814.2 | 826.1 | 827.1 | 837.8 | 836.6 | 828.5 | 828.4 | 845.2 | 837.7 | 844.2 | 851.4 | 848.6 |
| 1987 | 842.8 | 847.9 | 848.6 | 852.4 | 850.9 | 849.8 | 854.8 | 853.8 | 864.4 | 871.1 | 891.5 | 902.2 |
| 1988 | 889.6 | 888.3 | 892.2 | 898.9 | 904.6 | 907.6 | 908.9 | 900.8 | 885.7 | 883.2 | 895.6 | 895.7 |
| 1989 | 889.9 | 894.8 | 896.6 | 892.5 | 907.4 | 915.7 | 903.0 | 907.6 | 916.3 | 912.0 | 914.3 | 930.5 |
| 1990 | 921.1 | 932.9 | 924.0 | 955.9 | 953.1 | 968.7 | 970.9 | 966.2 | 959.2 | 932.7 | 935.7 | 924.7 |
| 1991 | 908.4 | 905.3 | 912.8 | 905.3 | 907.2 | 924.3 | 915.3 | 910.6 | 913.8 | 909.1 | 910.7 | 912.0 |
| 1992 | 893.1 | 909.7 | 914.8 | 907.1 | 916.5 | 912.0 | 894.6 | 902.2 | 898.3 | 893.5 | 906.2 | 899.4 |
| 1993 | 892.9 | 902.0 | 908.1 | 914.7 | 930.4 | 935.0 | 935.1 | 935.2 | 919.6 | 906.4 | 916.5 | 924.1 |
| 1994 | 922.5 | 925.3 | 922.6 | 932.6 | 930.6 | 922.7 | 919.6 | 924.2 | 920.2 | 927.0 | 934.9 | 938.0 |
| 1995 | 922.2 | 920.8 | 931.0 | 929.4 | 924.1 | 919.6 | 907.3 | 899.5 | 897.5 | 902.8 | 910.6 | 894.9 |
| 1996[1] | 894.9 | 893.1 | 888.7 | 889.5 | 890.6 | 898.8 | 892.5 | 892.8 | 878.0 | 883.6 | 870.5 | |

[1] Preliminary. *Source: Energy Information Administration, U.S. Department of Agriculture*

## Production of Crude Petroleum in the United States — In Thousands of Barrels Per Day

| Year | Jan. | Feb. | Mar. | Apr. | May | June | July | Aug. | Sept. | Oct. | Nov. | Dec. | Average |
|---|---|---|---|---|---|---|---|---|---|---|---|---|---|
| 1986 | 9,137 | 9,173 | 9,013 | 8,864 | 8,838 | 8,623 | 8,660 | 8,374 | 8,328 | 8,419 | 8,412 | 8,352 | 8,680 |
| 1987 | 8,480 | 8,389 | 8,464 | 8,498 | 8,336 | 8,279 | 8,251 | 8,210 | 8,205 | 8,364 | 8,397 | 8,318 | 8,349 |
| 1988 | 8,250 | 8,374 | 8,374 | 8,288 | 8,229 | 8,170 | 8,040 | 8,079 | 7,895 | 8,023 | 8,023 | 7,942 | 8,140 |
| 1989 | 7,937 | 7,788 | 7,575 | 7,772 | 7,816 | 7,624 | 7,444 | 7,544 | 7,548 | 7,453 | 7,536 | 7,337 | 7,613 |
| 1990 | 7,546 | 7,497 | 7,433 | 7,407 | 7,328 | 7,106 | 7,173 | 7,287 | 7,224 | 7,542 | 7,387 | 7,338 | 7,355 |
| 1991 | 7,500 | 7,637 | 7,546 | 7,509 | 7,409 | 7,320 | 7,347 | 7,316 | 7,368 | 7,437 | 7,328 | 7,299 | 7,417 |
| 1992 | 7,361 | 7,389 | 7,348 | 7,293 | 7,169 | 7,167 | 7,131 | 6,922 | 7,030 | 7,126 | 7,024 | 7,103 | 7,171 |
| 1993 | 6,961 | 6,943 | 6,974 | 6,881 | 6,847 | 6,795 | 6,688 | 6,758 | 6,712 | 6,839 | 6,912 | 6,858 | 6,847 |
| 1994 | 6,817 | 6,770 | 6,746 | 6,612 | 6,688 | 6,611 | 6,501 | 6,544 | 6,609 | 6,658 | 6,628 | 6,760 | 6,662 |
| 1995[1] | 6,682 | 6,794 | 6,600 | 6,604 | 6,629 | 6,579 | 6,449 | 6,447 | 6,416 | 6,421 | 6,585 | 6,530 | 6,560 |
| 1996[2] | 6,495 | 6,550 | 6,516 | 6,479 | 6,443 | 6,502 | 6,383 | 6,389 | 6,503 | 6,490 | 6,465 | 6,448 | 6,471 |

[1] Preliminary. [2] Estimate. *Source: Energy Information Administration, U.S. Department of Energy*

## U.S. Foreign Trade of Petroleum and Products — In Thousands of Barrels Per Day

| | Exports | | Imports | | | | | | Exports | | Imports | | | | |
|---|---|---|---|---|---|---|---|---|---|---|---|---|---|---|---|
| Year | Total[2] | Petroleum Products | Crude | Petroleum Products | Distillate Fuel Oil | Residual Fuel Oil | Net Imports[3] | Year | Total[2] | Petroleum Products | Crude | Petroleum Products | Distillate Fuel Oil | Residual Fuel Oil | Net Imports[3] |
| 1977 | 243 | 193 | 6,615 | 2,193 | 250 | 1,359 | 8,565 | 1987 | 764 | 613 | 4,674 | 2,004 | 255 | 565 | 5,914 |
| 1978 | 362 | 204 | 6,356 | 2,008 | 173 | 1,355 | 8,002 | 1988 | 815 | 661 | 5,107 | 2,295 | 302 | 644 | 6,587 |
| 1979 | 471 | 236 | 6,519 | 1,937 | 193 | 1,151 | 7,985 | 1989 | 859 | 717 | 5,843 | 2,217 | 306 | 629 | 7,202 |
| 1980 | 544 | 258 | 5,263 | 1,646 | 142 | 939 | 6,365 | 1990 | 857 | 748 | 5,894 | 2,123 | 278 | 504 | 7,161 |
| 1981 | 595 | 367 | 4,396 | 1,599 | 173 | 800 | 5,401 | 1991 | 1,001 | 885 | 5,782 | 1,844 | 205 | 453 | 6,626 |
| 1982 | 815 | 579 | 3,488 | 1,325 | 93 | 776 | 4,298 | 1992 | 950 | 861 | 6,083 | 1,805 | 216 | 375 | 6,938 |
| 1983 | 739 | 575 | 3,329 | 1,722 | 174 | 699 | 4,312 | 1993 | 1,003 | 904 | 6,787 | 1,833 | 184 | 373 | 7,618 |
| 1984 | 722 | 541 | 3,426 | 2,011 | 272 | 681 | 4,715 | 1994 | 942 | 843 | 7,063 | 1,933 | 203 | 314 | 8,054 |
| 1985 | 781 | 577 | 3,201 | 1,866 | 200 | 510 | 4,286 | 1995 | 949 | 855 | 7,230 | 1,605 | 193 | 187 | 7,886 |
| 1986 | 785 | 631 | 4,178 | 2,045 | 247 | 669 | 5,439 | 1996[1] | 981 | 871 | 7,482 | 1,917 | 224 | 247 | 8,419 |

[1] Preliminary. [2] Includes crude oil. [3] Equals imports minus exports. *Source: Energy Information Administration, U.S. Department of Energy*

## Domestic First Purchase Price of Crude Petroleum at Wells[1] — In Dollars Per Barrel

| Year | Jan. | Feb. | Mar. | Apr. | May | June | July | Aug. | Sept. | Oct. | Nov. | Dec. | Average |
|---|---|---|---|---|---|---|---|---|---|---|---|---|---|
| 1986 | 23.12 | 17.65 | 12.62 | 10.68 | 10.75 | 10.68 | 9.25 | 9.77 | 11.09 | 11.00 | 11.05 | 11.73 | 12.51 |
| 1987 | 13.79 | 14.51 | 14.54 | 14.95 | 15.29 | 15.95 | 16.88 | 17.06 | 16.25 | 15.95 | 15.46 | 14.27 | 15.40 |
| 1988 | 13.64 | 13.43 | 12.96 | 13.92 | 14.12 | 13.59 | 12.38 | 12.22 | 11.63 | 10.62 | 10.31 | 11.99 | 12.58 |
| 1989 | 13.80 | 14.24 | 15.65 | 17.04 | 16.76 | 16.42 | 16.32 | 15.01 | 15.58 | 16.25 | 16.30 | 17.01 | 15.86 |
| 1990 | 18.49 | 18.16 | 16.57 | 14.52 | 13.82 | 12.79 | 14.03 | 21.87 | 28.46 | 30.86 | 27.53 | 22.63 | 20.03 |
| 1991 | 19.60 | 16.28 | 15.13 | 16.16 | 16.44 | 15.58 | 16.36 | 16.60 | 16.71 | 17.72 | 17.12 | 14.68 | 16.54 |
| 1992 | 13.99 | 14.04 | 14.12 | 15.36 | 16.38 | 17.96 | 17.80 | 17.07 | 17.20 | 17.16 | 16.00 | 14.94 | 15.99 |
| 1993 | 14.70 | 15.53 | 15.94 | 16.15 | 16.03 | 15.06 | 13.83 | 13.75 | 13.39 | 13.72 | 12.45 | 10.38 | 14.25 |
| 1994 | 10.49 | 10.71 | 10.94 | 12.31 | 14.02 | 14.93 | 15.34 | 14.50 | 13.62 | 13.84 | 14.14 | 13.43 | 13.19 |
| 1995 | 14.00 | 14.69 | 14.68 | 15.84 | 15.85 | 15.02 | 14.01 | 14.13 | 14.49 | 13.68 | 14.03 | 15.02 | 14.62 |
| 1996[2] | 15.42 | 15.55 | 17.63 | 19.58 | 17.96 | 16.94 | 17.63 | 18.29 | 19.92 | 21.09 | 20.21 | | 18.20 |

[1] Buyers posted prices. [2] Preliminary. *Source: Energy Information Adiministration, U.S. Department of Energy*

## Volume of Trading of Crude Oil Futures in New York In Thousands of Contracts

| Year | Jan. | Feb. | Mar. | Apr. | May | June | July | Aug. | Sept. | Oct. | Nov. | Dec. | Total |
|---|---|---|---|---|---|---|---|---|---|---|---|---|---|
| 1986 | 520.1 | 490.9 | 560.0 | 691.4 | 677.0 | 612.7 | 860.5 | 701.6 | 666.7 | 986.4 | 604.4 | 941.8 | 8,313.5 |
| 1987 | 873.2 | 968.4 | 1,199.0 | 1,059.0 | 937.3 | 1,196.0 | 1,412.0 | 1,505.0 | 1,126.0 | 1,205.0 | 1,287.0 | 1,813.0 | 14,582.0 |
| 1988 | 1,626.0 | 1,336.0 | 1,809.0 | 1,352.0 | 1,205.0 | 1,507.0 | 1,754.0 | 1,219.0 | 1,956.0 | 2,040.0 | 1,609.0 | 1,450.0 | 18,859.0 |
| 1989 | 1,919.0 | 1,524.0 | 2,053.0 | 2,070.0 | 1,911.0 | 2,082.0 | 1,663.0 | 1,343.0 | 1,541.0 | 1,521.0 | 1,425.0 | 1,483.0 | 20,535.0 |
| 1990 | 2,164.0 | 1,790.0 | 1,794.0 | 1,813.0 | 1,945.0 | 1,839.0 | 2,046.0 | 2,716.0 | 2,073.0 | 2,437.0 | 1,769.0 | 1,302.0 | 23,687.0 |
| 1991 | 1,997.0 | 1,478.0 | 1,605.0 | 1,885.0 | 1,741.0 | 1,411.0 | 1,675.0 | 1,598.0 | 1,543.0 | 2,064.0 | 2,051.0 | 1,960.0 | 21,008.0 |
| 1992 | 2,097.0 | 1,630.0 | 1,620.0 | 1,889.0 | 1,885.0 | 2,006.0 | 1,796.0 | 1,531.0 | 1,541.0 | 1,797.0 | 1,542.0 | 1,778.0 | 21,110.0 |
| 1993 | 2,139.0 | 1,886.0 | 1,895.0 | 1,459.0 | 1,641.0 | 2,018.0 | 2,616.0 | 2,200.0 | 2,679.0 | 1,945.0 | 2,378.0 | 2,122.0 | 24,869.0 |
| 1994 | 2,296.0 | 1,933.0 | 2,228.0 | 2,382.0 | 2,602.0 | 2,576.0 | 2,186.0 | 2,544.0 | 1,897.0 | 2,195.0 | 2,195.9 | 1,778.2 | 16,812.0 |
| 1995 | 2,133.5 | 1,657.3 | 2,289.8 | 2,220.1 | 2,408.9 | 2,172.4 | 1,749.3 | 1,793.8 | 1,968.0 | 1,834.6 | 1,739.1 | 1,647.2 | 23,614.0 |
| 1996 | 2,260.1 | 1,928.3 | 2,399.3 | 2,489.9 | 2,161.3 | 1,601.7 | 1,732.1 | 1,657.0 | 1,912.6 | 2,098.0 | 1,643.1 | 1,604.3 | 23,487.8 |

*Source: New York Mercantile Exchange (NYMEX)*

## Average Open Interest of Crude Oil Futures in New York In Contracts

| Year | Jan. | Feb. | Mar. | Apr. | May | June | July | Aug. | Sept. | Oct. | Nov. | Dec. |
|---|---|---|---|---|---|---|---|---|---|---|---|---|
| 1986 | 69,614 | 66,811 | 73,167 | 88,203 | 100,012 | 103,300 | 122,760 | 113,286 | 104,874 | 117,423 | 113,077 | 113,631 |
| 1987 | 127,129 | 144,569 | 160,668 | 155,686 | 143,305 | 147,501 | 177,760 | 195,468 | 197,623 | 183,276 | 165,489 | 199,806 |
| 1988 | 202,830 | 200,813 | 210,878 | 192,074 | 177,155 | 180,019 | 177,978 | 177,879 | 220,973 | 221,628 | 196,454 | 196,109 |
| 1989 | 204,066 | 210,299 | 224,322 | 248,032 | 231,390 | 222,748 | 221,389 | 209,702 | 230,990 | 235,716 | 242,677 | 257,974 |
| 1990 | 273,193 | 300,069 | 287,013 | 287,538 | 278,600 | 285,384 | 275,771 | 262,746 | 266,313 | 269,167 | 242,500 | 232,405 |
| 1991 | 249,759 | 272,396 | 285,417 | 303,942 | 286,159 | 277,587 | 278,704 | 267,186 | 264,223 | 298,434 | 292,889 | 284,453 |
| 1992 | 310,763 | 331,050 | 316,544 | 340,315 | 335,545 | 364,155 | 331,972 | 316,066 | 314,446 | 301,381 | 308,467 | 330,134 |
| 1993 | 352,316 | 369,180 | 385,768 | 381,954 | 384,309 | 396,832 | 423,041 | 428,418 | 404,172 | 397,121 | 404,046 | 427,756 |
| 1994 | 427,705 | 438,929 | 424,462 | 410,974 | 427,071 | 414,257 | 409,251 | 396,657 | 395,194 | 413,206 | 388,932 | 391,151 |
| 1995 | 373,798 | 379,329 | 353,805 | 364,929 | 350,826 | 346,051 | 357,718 | 343,636 | 342,360 | 334,170 | 329,786 | 348,954 |
| 1996 | 389,935 | 400,236 | 427,306 | 460,841 | 424,994 | 376,164 | 367,405 | 364,458 | 395,358 | 410,387 | 385,415 | 368,331 |

*Source: New York Mercantile Exchange (NYMEX)*

# Plastics

Plastics are one of the most used materials on a volume basis for industrial and commercial purposes in the United States. The plastics industry in the U.S. is now in its second century but the most important developments in the industry have occurred since 1910. The period of 1930-1940 saw the initial commercial development of today's major thermoplastics: polyvinyl chloride, low density polyethylene, polystyrene, and polymethyl methacrylate. The Second World War in 1939 brought plastics into great demand mostly as substitutes for material that was in short supply, such as natural rubber. In the U.S., the production of synthetic rubbers led to the development of more plastic materials. The demand for plastics has increased steadily and plastics are now accepted as basic materials along with more traditional materials.

Plastics find wide use in a variety of products ranging from packaging materials to replacement material for wood, metals, glass, and paper. The environmental impact of the disposal of plastic materials has led to the development of a recycling industry. One area where plastic is making an important contribution is in the automobile industry. Part of this is due to the need by automakers to keep the prices of cars down while at the same time making vehicles lighter to improve gasoline efficiency. Plastic material is finding use in bumpers, gas tanks, hoods, fenders, and other body panels.

The major markets for plastic resins are packaging, building and construction, consumer and institutional products (including disposable food serviceware, toys and sporting goods, healthcare and medical products), transportation, furniture and furnishings, and electrical/electronic. For 1995, total plastic resin sales were 71.2 billion pounds, dry weight basis. Packaging took 19.3 billion pounds, building and construction 14.3 billion pounds, with consumer and institutional 9.1 billion pounds. By end use category; the packaging industry, 27.2 percent, building and construction 20.1 percent, consumer and institutional 12.7 percent, transportation 5.5 percent, furniture and furnishings 4.5 percent, electrical/electronic 4.2 percent, adhesives, inks and coatings 2.5 percent, industrial/machinery 1.1 percent, and other 11.3 percent. Exports made up the remaining 10.9 percent.

All plastic resin use grew less than 1 percent in 1995. The largest decline in use was in electrical/electronic which fell about 11 percent. Exports grew 12.4 percent while transportation increased 3.2 percent and furniture and furnishings rose 2.6 percent. Total U.S. production of plastic resins in 1995 was 78.7 billion pounds, up close to 4 percent from 1994.

The major types of plastic resins are thermosets and thermoplastics. According to the Society of the Plastics Industry, 1995 thermoset use was 7.49 billion pounds. The building and construction industry took 4.8 billion pounds or 63.7 percent of the thermosets. The next largest user was transportation with 710 million pounds or 9.5 percent. Exports were 309 million pounds or 4.1 percent. Thermoplastic use in 1995 was 63.7 billion pounds. Packaging took 19.3 billion pounds or 30.3 percent with building and construction 9.6 billion pounds or 15 percent of the total. Exports of thermoplastics in 1995 were 7.4 billion pounds or 11.7 percent of thermoplastic use.

## Plastics Production by Resin in the United States — In Millions of Pounds

| | Thermosets | | | | Thermoplastics | | | | | | | | | | |
|---|---|---|---|---|---|---|---|---|---|---|---|---|---|---|---|
| Year | Polyester Unsaturated | Phenolic | Epoxy | Total Thermosets | Thermoplastic Polyester | Polyvinyl Chloride | Polystyrene | Polypropylene | Nylon | Low Density Polyethylene[1] | High Density Polyethylene | Total Thermoplastics | Total Selected Plastics | Other Plastics | Total Plastics |
| 1986 | 1,271 | 2,735 | 398 | 5,848 | 1,175 | 7,256 | 4,470 | 5,812 | 465 | 8,903 | 7,182 | 36,447 | 42,295 | 8,554 | 50,849 |
| 1987 | 1,367 | 2,869 | 433 | 6,263 | 1,394 | 7,971 | 4,780 | 6,647 | 507 | 9,599 | 7,995 | 40,194 | 46,457 | 9,294 | 55,751 |
| 1988 | 1,404 | 3,066 | 486 | 6,588 | 1,652 | 8,350 | 5,187 | 7,274 | 566 | 10,397 | 8,400 | 43,251 | 49,839 | 9,923 | 59,762 |
| 1989 | 1,319 | 2,879 | 510 | 6,407 | 1,630 | 8,478 | 5,104 | 7,238 | 569 | 9,695 | 8,102 | 42,189 | 48,596 | 9,933 | 58,529 |
| 1990 | 1,221 | 2,946 | 499 | 6,364 | 1,879 | 9,096 | 5,021 | 8,310 | 558 | 11,148 | 8,337 | 45,646 | 52,010 | 9,950 | 61,960 |
| 1991 | 1,075 | 2,658 | 497 | 5,909 | 2,115 | 9,164 | 4,954 | 8,330 | 576 | 11,582 | 9,213 | 47,146 | 53,055 | 9,731 | 62,786 |
| 1992 | 1,175 | 2,923 | 457 | 6,335 | 2,413 | 9,989 | 5,096 | 8,421 | 668 | 11,917 | 9,808 | 49,751 | 56,086 | 10,285 | 66,371 |
| 1993 | 1,264 | 3,078 | 512 | 6,868 | 2,549 | 10,257 | 5,382 | 8,628 | 768 | 12,067 | 9,941 | 51,159 | 58,027 | 10,777 | 68,854 |
| 1994 | 1,468 | 3,229 | 601 | 7,513 | 3,196 | 11,712 | 5,848 | 9,539 | 943 | 12,600 | 11,117 | 56,794 | 64,307 | 11,664 | 75,971 |
| 1995 | 1,577 | 3,204 | 632 | 7,519 | 3,785 | 12,295 | 5,656 | 10,890 | 1,020 | 12,886 | 11,211 | 59,331 | 66,850 | 11,834 | 78,684 |

[1] Includes LDPE and LLDPE. *Source: The Society of the Plastics Industry, Inc.*

## Total Resin Sales and Captive Use by Important Markets — In Millions of Pounds (Dry Weight Basis)

| Year | Adhesive, Inks & Coatings | Building & Construction | Consumer & Industrial | Electrical & Electronics | Exports | Furniture & Furnishings | Industrial & Machinery | Packaging | Transportation | Other | Total |
|---|---|---|---|---|---|---|---|---|---|---|---|
| 1989 | 1,211 | 11,096 | 6,217 | 3,145 | [1] | 2,285 | 475 | 14,711 | 2,547 | 10,911 | 52,598 |
| 1990 | 1,373 | 11,803 | 5,861 | 3,165 | [1] | 2,190 | 636 | 16,568 | 2,504 | 11,811 | 55,910 |
| 1991 | 1,391 | 10,650 | 5,689 | 2,896 | 7,418 | 2,255 | 587 | 16,723 | 2,328 | 6,616 | 56,553 |
| 1992 | 1,723 | 11,876 | 6,093 | 2,766 | 6,950 | 2,559 | 617 | 18,284 | 2,817 | 6,877 | 60,562 |
| 1993 | 1,572 | 12,885 | 6,015 | 2,981 | 6,632 | 2,759 | 768 | 19,569 | 3,221 | 7,234 | 63,636 |
| 1994 | 1,789 | 14,715 | 9,266 | 3,325 | 6,889 | 3,118 | 836 | 19,551 | 3,795 | 7,515 | 70,799 |
| 1995 | 1,795 | 14,321 | 9,054 | 2,966 | 7,742 | 3,198 | 818 | 19,334 | 3,916 | 8,050 | 71,194 |

[1] Included in other. *Source: The Society of the Plastics Industry, Inc.*

## Average Producer Price Index of Plastic Materials in the United States 1982 = 100

| Year | Jan. | Feb. | Mar. | Apr. | May | June | July | Aug. | Sept. | Oct. | Nov. | Dec. | Average |
|---|---|---|---|---|---|---|---|---|---|---|---|---|---|
| | | | | | Plastic Resins and Materials (066) | | | | | | | | |
| 1988 | 121.5 | 123.5 | 124.4 | 127.6 | 130.1 | 131.2 | 134.8 | 136.9 | 138.9 | 139.8 | 140.2 | 140.1 | 132.4 |
| 1989 | 140.3 | 141.1 | 140.6 | 140.7 | 139.8 | 138.0 | 135.3 | 127.7 | 126.1 | 124.7 | 123.7 | 123.3 | 133.4 |
| 1990 | 122.2 | 121.6 | 122.2 | 123.0 | 123.5 | 123.0 | 122.1 | 122.3 | 123.6 | 125.1 | 128.6 | 131.2 | 124.0 |
| 1991 | 131.1 | 128.7 | 125.4 | 122.9 | 120.6 | 117.0 | 115.0 | 114.9 | 114.9 | 116.4 | 116.7 | 116.0 | 120.0 |
| 1992 | 115.4 | 115.6 | 114.2 | 114.2 | 114.7 | 115.2 | 115.9 | 117.7 | 117.5 | 118.2 | 118.1 | 118.1 | 116.2 |
| 1993 | 118.3 | 118.0 | 117.6 | 117.1 | 116.3 | 116.9 | 116.9 | 117.6 | 117.4 | 116.9 | 116.2 | 116.2 | 117.1 |
| 1994 | 115.0 | 114.7 | 114.5 | 116.5 | 117.7 | 119.1 | 119.6 | 121.5 | 126.3 | 131.9 | 134.1 | 138.1 | 122.4 |
| 1995 | 142.5 | 144.1 | 145.9 | 148.5 | 149.0 | 148.9 | 147.0 | 144.8 | 142.7 | 139.2 | 135.8 | 132.2 | 143.4 |
| 1996[1] | 129.9 | 128.4 | 128.4 | 127.7 | 130.6 | 132.1 | 133.2 | 134.7 | 137.1 | 138.4 | 138.3 | | 132.6 |
| | | | | | Thermoplastic Resins (0662) | | | | | | | | |
| 1988 | 124.4 | 126.7 | 127.8 | 131.1 | 133.7 | 134.9 | 139.0 | 141.2 | 143.5 | 144.3 | 144.4 | 144.2 | 136.3 |
| 1989 | 114.5 | 145.2 | 144.4 | 143.9 | 143.2 | 141.1 | 137.7 | 128.5 | 126.7 | 125.1 | 124.0 | 124.0 | 133.2 |
| 1990 | 122.9 | 121.9 | 122.5 | 123.5 | 124.1 | 123.4 | 122.4 | 122.5 | 124.1 | 125.8 | 130.5 | 134.0 | 124.8 |
| 1991 | 132.1 | 129.4 | 125.5 | 122.9 | 120.2 | 116.2 | 113.8 | 113.7 | 114.6 | 115.5 | 116.0 | 115.3 | 119.6 |
| 1992 | 114.7 | 114.7 | 113.0 | 112.9 | 113.4 | 114.1 | 114.8 | 117.1 | 116.8 | 117.6 | 117.6 | 117.5 | 115.4 |
| 1993 | 117.5 | 117.1 | 116.3 | 115.8 | 114.8 | 115.4 | 115.5 | 116.4 | 116.4 | 116.4 | 115.5 | 114.6 | 116.0 |
| 1994 | 113.0 | 112.7 | 112.5 | 115.0 | 116.2 | 117.9 | 118.4 | 120.1 | 125.4 | 131.6 | 133.9 | 138.4 | 121.3 |
| 1995 | 143.1 | 145.0 | 147.1 | 150.3 | 151.0 | 151.2 | 148.7 | 146.2 | 143.7 | 139.6 | 135.5 | 131.1 | 144.4 |
| 1996[1] | 128.4 | 126.7 | 126.8 | 125.9 | 129.4 | 131.1 | 132.5 | 134.1 | 136.9 | 138.4 | 138.3 | | 131.7 |
| | | | | | PE Resin, Low, Film & Sheeting (0662-0301) | | | | | | | | |
| 1988 | 145.9 | 150.3 | 153.8 | 157.9 | 171.4 | 172.0 | 178.3 | 192.3 | 201.3 | 203.5 | 202.7 | 201.6 | 177.6 |
| 1989 | 202.0 | 206.6 | 206.0 | 204.0 | 200.8 | 195.3 | 191.9 | 151.5 | 150.3 | 150.9 | 152.3 | 153.0 | 180.4 |
| 1990 | 151.9 | 145.3 | 146.1 | 145.9 | 152.5 | 151.7 | 144.9 | 141.9 | 152.3 | 145.6 | 149.8 | 157.4 | 148.8 |
| 1991 | 158.1 | 150.7 | 142.6 | 135.8 | 130.1 | 121.9 | 117.8 | 114.8 | 113.9 | 123.2 | 131.3 | 124.6 | 130.4 |
| 1992 | 126.5 | 130.9 | 126.7 | 121.3 | 123.5 | 122.4 | 132.9 | 138.9 | 145.2 | 149.3 | 148.6 | 150.6 | 134.7 |
| 1993 | NA | 151.4 | 145.6 | 141.8 | 135.5 | 137.1 | 132.2 | 136.6 | 129.2 | 128.4 | 127.6 | 127.4 | 135.7 |
| 1994 | 121.6 | 119.4 | 119.3 | 120.8 | 127.6 | 134.5 | 136.3 | 140.8 | 146.6 | 155.4 | 172.8 | 182.2 | 139.8 |
| 1995 | 188.5 | 196.0 | 202.0 | 210.6 | 215.4 | 211.1 | 205.7 | 194.4 | 185.0 | 173.4 | 167.5 | 157.4 | 192.3 |
| 1996[1] | 146.4 | 139.9 | 137.6 | 139.5 | 147.6 | 158.8 | 166.0 | 156.5 | 184.0 | 211.5 | 195.0 | | 162.1 |
| | | | | | Styrene Plastics Materials (0662-06) | | | | | | | | |
| 1988 | 122.2 | 125.2 | 127.0 | 128.9 | 129.0 | 131.7 | 133.6 | 134.1 | 134.1 | 135.4 | 134.7 | 134.8 | 130.9 |
| 1989 | 135.3 | 136.3 | 134.4 | 135.8 | 135.1 | 133.1 | 124.6 | 119.5 | 119.0 | 116.8 | 114.2 | 114.4 | 126.5 |
| 1990 | 113.1 | 114.7 | 117.2 | 116.8 | 116.8 | 115.2 | 113.7 | 113.7 | 116.8 | 123.4 | 127.8 | 124.2 | 117.8 |
| 1991 | 123.3 | 122.7 | 115.4 | 115.5 | 112.4 | 121.9 | 109.2 | 107.7 | 108.3 | 113.0 | 113.0 | 111.5 | 114.5 |
| 1992 | 109.5 | 109.6 | 109.1 | 109.1 | 110.3 | 109.4 | 110.4 | 112.6 | 111.2 | 112.5 | 111.7 | 111.5 | 110.6 |
| 1993 | 110.7 | 110.5 | 110.0 | 110.4 | 111.0 | 111.3 | 111.2 | 111.1 | 110.6 | 109.1 | 106.5 | 106.4 | 109.9 |
| 1994 | 105.8 | 104.1 | 104.1 | 108.1 | 108.3 | 109.2 | 110.4 | 110.6 | 116.0 | 123.3 | 125.3 | 126.2 | 112.6 |
| 1995 | 129.0 | 127.0 | 132.5 | 134.7 | 135.9 | 137.5 | 135.1 | 133.2 | 132.1 | 130.1 | 127.9 | 126.1 | 131.8 |
| 1996[1] | 125.7 | 123.5 | 125.0 | 118.3 | 120.1 | 122.7 | 123.4 | 122.9 | 123.4 | 123.3 | 122.8 | | 122.8 |
| | | | | | Thermosetting Resins (0663) | | | | | | | | |
| 1988 | 110.2 | 110.4 | 110.7 | 113.5 | 115.4 | 115.7 | 116.8 | 118.4 | 119.2 | 120.0 | 122.4 | 122.7 | 116.3 |
| 1989 | 122.4 | 124.0 | 124.9 | 127.9 | 126.6 | 126.5 | 126.8 | 127.5 | 126.9 | 126.6 | 125.9 | 123.8 | 125.8 |
| 1990 | 122.8 | 124.0 | 124.1 | 124.4 | 124.3 | 124.7 | 124.7 | 124.8 | 125.0 | 125.6 | 124.0 | 126.6 | 124.6 |
| 1991 | 130.1 | 129.1 | 128.9 | 127.1 | 126.3 | 125.2 | 124.9 | 124.9 | 123.9 | 124.5 | 123.8 | 123.1 | 126.0 |
| 1992 | 123.1 | 124.1 | 123.9 | 124.3 | 124.4 | 124.4 | 124.7 | 125.0 | 125.0 | 125.3 | 125.1 | 125.2 | 124.5 |
| 1993 | 126.1 | 126.5 | 127.4 | 127.5 | 127.8 | 128.0 | 127.7 | 127.7 | 127.9 | 127.8 | 127.8 | 128.3 | 127.5 |
| 1994 | 128.2 | 128.1 | 128.1 | 127.8 | 128.7 | 129.1 | 129.7 | 132.1 | 134.9 | 137.7 | 140.1 | 141.5 | 132.2 |
| 1995 | 144.3 | 145.1 | 145.4 | 145.2 | 144.7 | 143.5 | 144.0 | 143.5 | 142.9 | 142.3 | 142.4 | 142.1 | 143.8 |
| 1996[1] | 141.8 | 141.9 | 141.2 | 141.3 | 141.4 | 141.2 | 140.6 | 141.8 | 141.7 | 142.2 | 142.1 | | 141.6 |
| | | | | | Phenolic & Tar Acid Resins (0663-02) | | | | | | | | |
| 1988 | 126.8 | 126.2 | 126.4 | 128.8 | 135.4 | 136.2 | 141.6 | 143.6 | 147.1 | 150.9 | 154.8 | 157.1 | 139.6 |
| 1989 | 156.7 | 158.9 | 162.6 | 166.8 | 164.2 | 164.4 | 166.2 | 159.5 | 158.6 | 158.0 | 156.9 | 152.3 | 160.4 |
| 1990 | 148.2 | 149.4 | 149.1 | 148.7 | 148.5 | 147.3 | 143.9 | 142.5 | 141.5 | 139.0 | 138.2 | 143.7 | 145.0 |
| 1991 | 146.4 | 147.3 | 142.4 | 140.7 | 138.3 | 132.8 | 131.6 | 131.5 | 128.3 | 129.7 | 126.5 | 125.5 | 135.1 |
| 1992 | 125.4 | 126.4 | 125.1 | 124.7 | 125.6 | 125.6 | 127.7 | 127.6 | 127.9 | 129.7 | 128.8 | 128.5 | 126.9 |
| 1993 | 128.5 | 130.3 | 130.5 | 131.4 | 133.7 | 134.1 | 133.9 | 132.8 | 133.1 | 132.1 | 132.0 | 132.9 | 132.1 |
| 1994 | 133.0 | 130.9 | 129.7 | 131.3 | 134.1 | 135.9 | 139.2 | 143.7 | 147.2 | 154.7 | 161.0 | 161.5 | 141.9 |
| 1995 | 164.6 | 166.4 | 165.1 | 162.5 | 158.6 | 153.5 | 152.0 | 148.5 | 147.7 | 146.2 | 143.2 | 142.6 | 154.2 |
| 1996[1] | 142.7 | 142.6 | 141.9 | 142.2 | 143.1 | 143.4 | 143.2 | 147.8 | 149.5 | 148.7 | 149.8 | | 145.0 |

[1] Preliminary. NA = Not available. *Source: Bureau of Labor Statistics, U.S. Department of Commerce*

# Platinum-Group Metals

Both the platinum and palladium markets spent 1996 trending lower in a continuation of the declines which began in mid-1995. Palladium has recently been the more volatile of the two markets with prices moving from a 10-year low of $75.00 per ounce in June, 1992, to a peak of $183.00/ounce in April, 1995. From that high point the market reversed course and began a down trend which continued through most of 1996, bottoming at $114.40/ounce in November before staging a minor recovery in December.

Platinum mirrored palladium's price movements although in a much more benign fashion. Platinum bottomed at $331.00 per ounce very late in 1991, but traded as low as all $336.00/ounce in early 1993 before beginning a modest advance that peaked at $463.00/ounce in April, 1995. From $463.00/ounce prices declined all through 1996, posting a closing low for the year on the last day of the year at $369.30/ounce. All price quotes are based on nearby futures prices at the New York Mercantile Exchange.

The steady weakness during 1996 came despite a strong U.S. economy and good car demand. However, platinum tends to be viewed as a precious metal and its price, justified or not, tends to mirror gold and silver's price action; palladium in turn follows platinum. In 1996, traders' interest in the precious metals complex dropped, partly due to the buoyancy in the equity markets that siphoned capital away from the precious metals. Moreover, inflation fears were held in check which depressed gold and silver prices, in turn influencing platinum prices even though the latter is generally not seen as an inflation hedge. Adding to the pressure was the absence of any serious political disruptions in South Africa that may have hindered mine production and/or shipments of the metals. Generally the short term variables on platinum's price are more supply sensitive.

Six metals make up the platinum group (PGM), but up to date statistical data is limited to platinum and palladium; for iridium, osmium, rhodium (the most expensive), and ruthenium (the least expensive) the data is spotty at best. Mineable deposits of the PGM's are rare, production occurs as a by-product of some other metal, usually nickel or copper. World production in 1995 of 286,000 kilograms compares with 269,000 in 1994, and 287,000 in 1991. However, a shift has apparently developed in the production breakdown. Until 1991 more palladium was produced than platinum, generally by about 10,000 kg. But in 1994, platinum's output was higher by 36,000 kg.; in 1995 some 145,000 kg. of platinum were produced and 112,000 kg. of palladium. Other 1995 PGM metals production of 28,400 kg. compares with 27,100 kg. in 1994. Identified world PGM resources at yearend 1995 were estimated at 100 million kg., of which 90 percent were in South Africa, 9 percent in Russia, and 1 percent in the U.S. At yearend 1995, accountable PGM stocks in the U.S. Government's National Defense Stockpile totaled 14,100 kg. of platinum, 39,300 kg. of palladium, and 920 kg. of iridium, all unchanged from a year earlier. The next largest stockpile of U.S. supplies were held in approved NYMEX vaults; 2,376 kg. of platinum at yearend 1995 vs. 7,720 kg. a year earlier, and palladium at 1,075 kg. vs. 991 kg., respectively.

South Africa is the largest producer with a record 118,000 kg. of platinum in 1995 vs. 114,000 in 1994; palladium production at a record high 49,000 kg. compares with 47,800 in 1994. In the late 1980s, the USSR's annual production averaged about 125,000 kg.; production has since fallen sharply. Russia is believed to have produced 18,000 kg. of platinum in 1995 and 48,000 kg. of palladium, both higher than in 1994. Canada's combined record production in 1995 of 13,140 kg. compares with 13,000 in 1994. U.S. production is well below demand leaving the U.S. dependent on imports. The Stillwater Mine in Montana accounts for nearly all domestic PGM production. Stillwater smelts the ore locally, but the resulting PGM-bearing matte is shipped to Belgium for refining. Stillwater is said to be planing on a near doubling in ore production, to more than 660,000 tons by mid-1997. Reportedly there are large deposits of PGM in the Montana region, but high extraction costs are a restraining factor. The U.S. produced 1,600 kg. of platinum in 1995, and 5,300 kg. of palladium vs. 2,000 kg. and 6,400 kg., respectively, in 1994.

In the U.S., the automotive industry is the largest consumer. The metal(s) have no competitive substitutes when used as an emission control catalyst, but the percentage of each metal used in the catalysts can be varied. On a world basis, demand for "platinum" in 1995 is forecast at 5 million ounces vs. 4.8 million in 1994, of which about 1.9 million will be used by the automotive industry, 1.8 million for jewelry, 1.0 million for industrial, and 345,000 ounces for investment. Percentagewise, the biggest year to year change was in investment use, down 50,000 ounces.

The U.S. imports half of the world's PGM production. U.S. imports of platinum during 1992-95 totaled about 240,000 kg. of platinum with South Africa supplying about 60 percent. During the same period the U.S. imported about 356,000 kg. of palladium with Russia supplying about 36 percent and South Africa 25 percent. More than half of U.S. PGM exports in 1995 were refined palladium, 26,000 kg., with Japan, Belgium, and Mexico taking about 13,320 kg.

Producers maintain an artificial price for the platinum group metals, leaving dealer and market prices generally much lower. Platinum's producer price averaged about $425.00 per ounce in 1995 vs. $406.00 in 1994; palladium averaged $153.00 in 1995 and $144.00 in 1994. Generally platinum has a premium to gold, but at yearend 1996 the metal was only $3-5.00 over gold vs. a year earlier differential near $25.00/oz.

### *Futures Markets*

Platinum and palladium futures and options are traded on the New York Mercantile Exchange (NYMEX). In Japan, platinum and palladium futures a listed on the Tokyo Commodity Exchange (TOCOM).

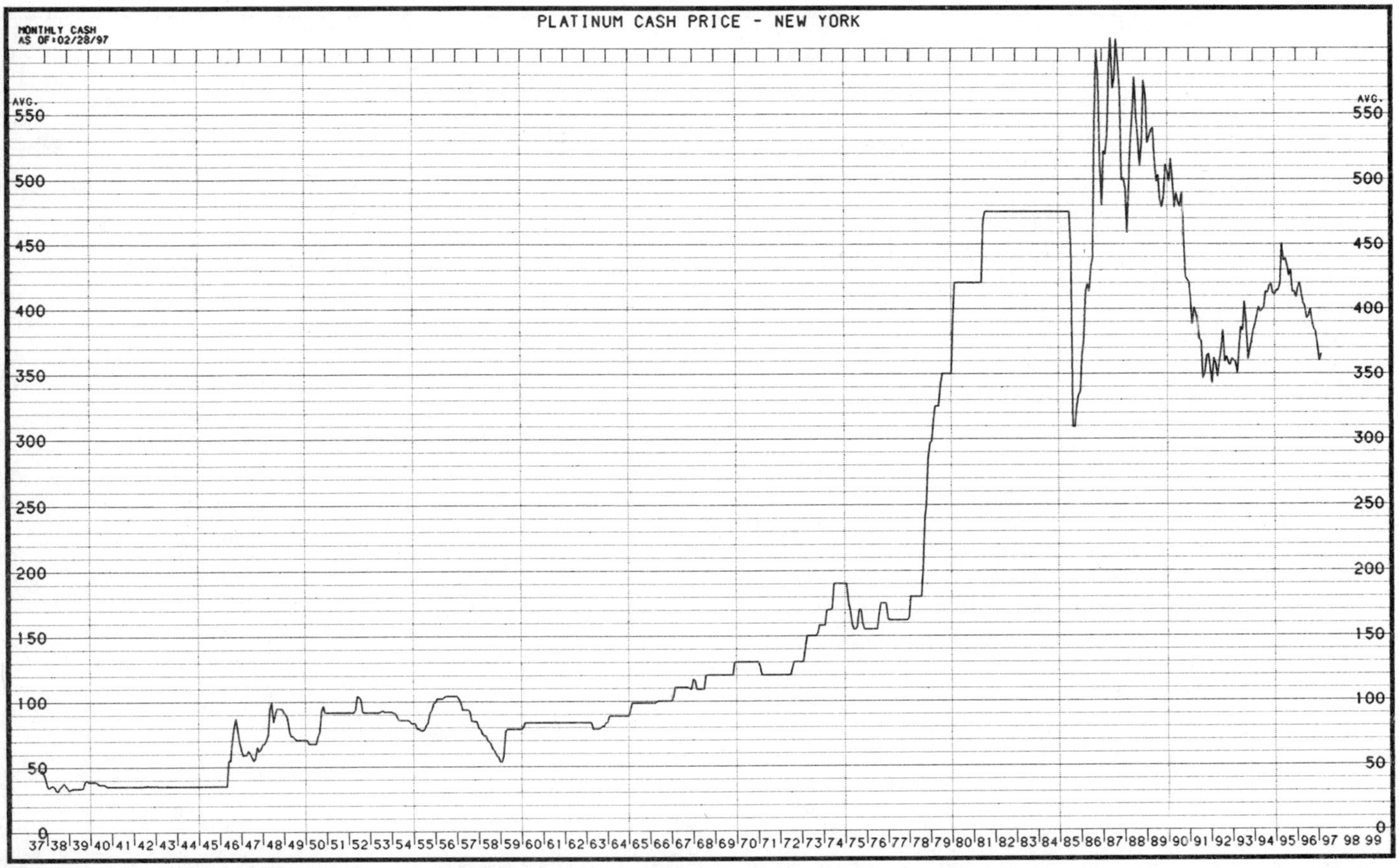


## World Mine Production of Platinum--Group Metals    In Kilograms

| Year | Aust-ralia | Canada Platinum | Canada Palladium | Canada Total | Colom-bia[3] | Japan Platinum | Japan Palladium | Russia[4] Platinum | Russia[4] Palladium | Russia[4] Total | South Africa Platinum | South Africa Palladium | South Africa Total | United States Platinum | United States Palladium | World Total |
|---|---|---|---|---|---|---|---|---|---|---|---|---|---|---|---|---|
| 1986 | 543 | 5,242 | 5,486 | 12,190 | 447 | 663 | 1,453 | 30,000 | 81,000 | 121,300 | 73,100 | 32,300 | 123,200 | W | W | 260,193 |
| 1987 | 620 | 4,354 | 5,910 | 10,930 | 638 | 753 | 1,417 | 31,000 | 83,000 | 124,400 | 78,400 | 33,900 | 128,000 | 780 | 2,330 | 270,281 |
| 1988 | 517 | 5,393 | 5,643 | 12,541 | 815 | 647 | 1,170 | 32,000 | 85,000 | 127,500 | 80,322 | 34,400 | 131,722 | 1,240 | 3,730 | 280,282 |
| 1989 | 500 | 4,467 | 4,676 | 10,389 | 973 | 1,031 | 821 | 32,000 | 85,000 | 127,500 | 82,884 | 35,800 | 133,684 | 1,430 | 4,850 | 281,629 |
| 1990 | 500 | 5,044 | 5,269 | 11,709 | 1,316 | 1,425 | 1,047 | 31,000 | 84,000 | 125,000 | 87,813 | 38,300 | 141,913 | 1,810 | 5,930 | 291,015 |
| 1991 | 500 | 4,683 | 6,439 | 11,120 | 1,603 | 988 | 1,053 | 30,000 | 82,000 | 121,500 | 88,861 | 38,000 | 126,900 | 1,500 | 5,200 | 287,000 |
| 1992 | 500 | 4,800 | 5,800 | 10,600 | 1,956 | 629 | 986 | 28,000 | 70,000 | 98,000 | 94,891 | 41,000 | 135,900 | 1,600 | 5,400 | 280,000 |
| 1993 | 500 | 5,000 | 6,000 | 11,000 | 1,720 | 661 | 1,180 | 20,000 | 50,000 | 70,000 | 109,000 | 48,000 | 157,000 | 2,100 | 6,800 | 276,000 |
| 1994[1] | 500 | 6,000 | 7,000 | 13,000 | 1,080 | 700 | 1,280 | 15,000 | 40,000 | 55,000 | 114,000 | 47,800 | 161,800 | 2,000 | 6,400 | 269,000 |
| 1995[2] | 500 | 6,040 | 7,100 | 13,140 | 1,100 | 580 | 2,000 | 18,000 | 48,000 | 66,000 | 118,000 | 494,000 | 167,400 | 1,600 | 5,300 | 286,000 |

[1] Preliminary. [2] Estimate. [3] Placer platinum. [4] Formerly part of the U.S.S.R.; data not reported separately until 1992 W = Withheld proprietary data.
*Source: U.S. Geological Survey*

## Salient Statistics of Platinum and Allied Metals[3] in the U.S.    In Kilograms

| Year | Net Import Reliance as a % of Apparent Con-sumption | Mine Production Platinum | Mine Production Palladium | Refinery Produc-tion (Secon-dary) | Total Refined | Refiner, Importer & Dealer Stocks as of Dec. 31 Platinum | Stocks Palladium | Stocks Other[4] | Stocks Total | Imports for Consumption Refined | Imports for Consumption Total | Exports Refined | Exports Total | Apparent Con-sumption |
|---|---|---|---|---|---|---|---|---|---|---|---|---|---|---|
| 1986 | 90 | W | W | 46,939 | 47,074 | 20,426 | 16,958 | 2,803 | 40,187 | 115,925 | 139,256 | 11,880 | 23,349 | 109,904 |
| 1987 | 91 | 780 | 2,330 | 50,053 | 50,243 | 19,004 | 17,356 | 2,052 | 38,412 | 98,878 | 118,397 | 13,423 | 22,031 | 95,458 |
| 1988 | 91 | 1,240 | 3,730 | 51,190 | 51,488 | 18,438 | 14,837 | 2,239 | 35,514 | 110,947 | 124,324 | 20,301 | 28,787 | 103,302 |
| 1989 | 90 | 1,430 | 4,850 | 50,186 | 50,525 | 14,791 | 15,182 | 2,570 | 32,543 | 111,107 | 113,278 | 23,082 | 38,301 | 101,209 |
| 1990 | 88 | 1,810 | 5,930 | 71,248 | 71,312 | 13,421 | 14,425 | 2,478 | 30,324 | 120,631 | 125,354 | 20,148 | 55,044 | 117,043 |
| 1991 | 90 | 1,730 | 6,050 | 72,349 | 72,564 | 10,349 | 12,263 | 1,701 | 24,313 | 121,741 | 125,661 | 27,401 | 39,624 | 111,798 |
| 1992 | 87 | 1,840 | 6,470 | 64,309 | 64,309 | 14,187 | 10,641 | 2,118 | 26,946 | 129,419 | 132,006 | 31,060 | 57,830 | 109,469 |
| 1993 | 89 | 1,800 | 6,500 | 65,792 | 65,792 | 10,263 | 8,324 | 176 | 18,763 | 148,790 | 153,165 | 43,798 | 78,486 | 123,273 |
| 1994[1] | 91 | 2,000 | 6,400 | 63,000 | 63,000 | 10,304 | 9,345 | 123 | 19,772 | 167,681 | 170,907 | 46,259 | 88,561 | 127,000 |
| 1995[2] | NA | 1,600 | 5,300 | NA | NA | NA | NA | NA | NA | 214,143 | 220,613 | 41,825 | 50,575 | NA |

[1] Preliminary. [2] Estimate. [3] Includes platinum, palladium, iridium, osmium, rhodium, and ruthenium. [4] Includes iridium, osmium, rhodium, and ruthenium. W = Withheld proprietary data. *Source: U.S. Geological Survey*

# PLATINUM-GROUP METALS

**Average Merchant's Price of Platinum in the U.S.** In Dollars Per Troy Ounce

| Year | Jan | Feb | Mar | Apr | May | Jun | Jul | Aug | Sep | Oct | Nov | Dec | Average |
|---|---|---|---|---|---|---|---|---|---|---|---|---|---|
| 1977 | 167.00 | 167.00 | 167.00 | 167.00 | 167.00 | 167.00 | 167.00 | 167.00 | 167.00 | 167.00 | 167.65 | 174.81 | 167.71 |
| 1978[2] | 186.55 | 206.58 | 217.07 | 220.00 | 220.00 | 227.73 | 237.89 | 241.74 | 250.23 | 253.18 | 284.00 | 300.00 | 237.08 |
| 1979 | 303.41 | 325.00 | 325.00 | 327.38 | 350.00 | 350.00 | 350.00 | 357.83 | 380.00 | 380.00 | 380.00 | 393.33 | 351.83 |
| 1980 | 420.00 | 420.00 | 420.00 | 420.00 | 420.00 | 420.00 | 420.00 | 425.24 | 475.00 | 475.00 | 475.00 | 475.00 | 436.77 |
| 1981 | 475.00 | 475.00 | 475.00 | 475.00 | 475.00 | 475.00 | 475.00 | 475.00 | 475.00 | 475.00 | 475.00 | 475.00 | 475.00 |
| 1982 | 369.26 | 361.95 | 322.46 | 338.95 | 314.43 | 278.26 | 286.90 | 290.41 | 334.98 | 324.58 | 346.65 | 370.95 | 328.32 |
| 1983 | 441.07 | 468.34 | 400.17 | 410.38 | 446.69 | 420.23 | 431.63 | 438.30 | 431.93 | 399.87 | 389.33 | 399.70 | 423.14 |
| 1984 | 375.11 | 391.38 | 398.47 | 395.17 | 388.95 | 386.31 | 345.55 | 336.03 | 327.36 | 324.65 | 328.45 | 309.11 | 358.83 |
| 1985 | 275.76 | 274.37 | 255.36 | 287.23 | 273.24 | 267.94 | 269.52 | 303.91 | 304.59 | 321.73 | 334.53 | 327.75 | 291.33 |
| 1986 | 362.77 | 377.74 | 412.48 | 422.93 | 415.52 | 431.23 | 436.50 | 526.52 | 597.92 | 578.50 | 524.65 | 480.14 | 463.91 |
| 1987 | 520.08 | 518.30 | 533.27 | 587.38 | 607.08 | 569.14 | 573.57 | 610.12 | 590.55 | 568.65 | 500.02 | 479.29 | 554.79 |
| 1988 | 494.14 | 458.64 | 496.49 | 527.73 | 548.91 | 581.32 | 548.51 | 532.80 | 513.16 | 527.35 | 577.74 | 567.36 | 531.18 |
| 1989 | 528.69 | 532.66 | 538.26 | 539.96 | 517.20 | 498.81 | 503.16 | 485.20 | 479.29 | 485.48 | 508.73 | 507.24 | 510.39 |
| 1990 | 949.93 | 517.34 | 500.32 | 478.33 | 485.89 | 486.60 | 476.93 | 492.02 | 463.87 | 423.78 | 424.12 | 446.94 | 474.26 |
| 1991 | 408.92 | 385.53 | 403.12 | 398.16 | 373.06 | 374.25 | 375.38 | 351.68 | 348.01 | 362.52 | 364.01 | 356.65 | 375.11 |
| 1992 | 341.88 | 362.97 | 356.84 | 347.73 | 354.75 | 368.17 | 378.89 | 360.20 | 361.60 | 359.75 | 355.81 | 361.98 | 359.21 |
| 1993 | 359.99 | 361.53 | 349.31 | 365.98 | 385.50 | 384.54 | 401.10 | 394.69 | 365.29 | 369.19 | 376.98 | 383.85 | 374.75 |
| 1994 | 390.30 | 393.95 | 398.29 | 400.38 | 395.41 | 401.42 | 408.25 | 411.91 | 415.93 | 421.11 | 415.73 | 408.83 | 405.13 |
| 1995 | 414.27 | 415.22 | 415.37 | 446.24 | 439.02 | 436.58 | 435.21 | 425.61 | 430.31 | 414.49 | 413.55 | 410.17 | 424.67 |
| 1996[1] | 416.13 | 420.02 | 411.19 | 404.28 | 401.60 | 392.64 | 393.86 | 400.03 | 389.86 | 384.24 | 382.36 | 370.60 | 397.23 |

[1] Preliminary. [2] Prior to 1978 prices are for producer prices. *Source: American Metal Market*

## Platinum–Group Metals Sold to Consuming Industries in the United States In Kilograms

| Year | ----Automotive---- | | ----Chemical----- | | -----Electrical----- | | Dental & -----Medical----- | | Jewelry & ----Decorative---- | | ----Petroleum---- | | ------All Platinum–Group Metals------ | | | |
|---|---|---|---|---|---|---|---|---|---|---|---|---|---|---|---|---|
| | Platinum | Other[3] | Platinum | Other[3] | Platinum | Other[3] | Platinum | Other[3] | Platinum | Other[3] | Platinum | Other[3] | Platinum | Palladium | Other[3] | Total |
| 1985 | 19,251 | 7,785 | 2,651 | 2,718 | 3,603 | 11,169 | 762 | 10,576 | 499 | 397 | 895 | 2,518 | 31,901 | 32,976 | 5,765 | 70,642 |
| 1986 | 19,438 | 7,234 | 2,416 | 2,346 | 3,219 | 11,082 | 645 | 8,363 | 352 | 304 | 951 | 1,896 | 30,509 | 27,677 | 6,511 | 64,698 |
| 1987 | 18,816 | 6,935 | 1,919 | 1,283 | 1,821 | 10,879 | 479 | 10,526 | 177 | 478 | 543 | 1,286 | 25,469 | 30,953 | 3,851 | 60,273 |
| 1988 | 19,346 | 7,186 | 3,184 | 4,499 | 3,494 | 14,429 | 581 | 6,650 | 385 | 407 | 1,027 | 1,560 | 31,125 | 34,241 | 5,632 | 70,998 |
| 1989 | 18,774 | 6,869 | 2,424 | 2,233 | 3,894 | 19,514 | 632 | 8,601 | 418 | 396 | 2,859 | 2,570 | 33,698 | 39,273 | 5,512 | 78,483 |
| 1990 | 20,967 | 5,990 | 2,080 | 2,574 | 3,907 | 19,791 | 687 | 6,287 | 431 | 387 | 3,274 | 1,488 | 36,055 | 35,116 | 6,316 | 77,487 |
| 1991 | 18,643 | 5,338 | 861 | 1,749 | 3,910 | 14,428 | 598 | 4,918 | 626 | 500 | 3,163 | 181 | 31,112 | 25,747 | 5,738 | 62,597 |
| 1992 | 20,290 | 5,789 | 1,716 | 2,297 | 2,922 | 15,738 | 640 | 5,386 | 881 | 1,417 | 1,036 | 790 | 31,095 | 28,935 | 6,816 | 66,846 |
| 1993[1] | 19,444 | 10,123 | 2,364 | 3,121 | 2,125 | 12,699 | 687 | 5,562 | 1,024 | 1,422 | 1,204 | 709 | 29,879 | 26,840 | 8,544 | 65,063 |
| 1994[2] | 21,754 | 11,412 | 3,104 | 1,889 | 2,790 | 7,961 | 902 | 5,092 | 1,345 | 824 | 1,581 | 422 | 34,044 | 21,509 | 7,387 | 62,940 |

[1] Preliminary. [2] Estimate. [3] Includes palladium, iridium, osmium, rhodium, and ruthenium. *Source: U.S. Geological Survey*

## Average Open Interest of Platinum Futures in New York In Contracts

| Year | Jan. | Feb. | Mar. | Apr. | May | June | July | Aug. | Sept. | Oct. | Nov. | Dec. |
|---|---|---|---|---|---|---|---|---|---|---|---|---|
| 1986 | 17,496 | 18,587 | 20,993 | 17,591 | 16,007 | 18,867 | 17,473 | 20,989 | 27,426 | 19,825 | 20,256 | 17,485 |
| 1987 | 16,641 | 16,544 | 18,629 | 20,777 | 19,675 | 17,977 | 17,290 | 22,890 | 24,421 | 22,631 | 20,458 | 19,756 |
| 1988 | 17,133 | 18,080 | 16,737 | 16,718 | 18,643 | 22,735 | 19,668 | 17,671 | 19,936 | 19,097 | 22,022 | 24,384 |
| 1989 | 19,334 | 18,648 | 19,736 | 19,895 | 19,661 | 20,597 | 17,310 | 19,121 | 19,165 | 16,981 | 19,934 | 20,392 |
| 1990 | 19,510 | 17,970 | 15,888 | 15,915 | 16,688 | 15,652 | 15,496 | 17,254 | 18,494 | 17,472 | 16,313 | 16,994 |
| 1991 | 15,497 | 16,043 | 16,083 | 14,334 | 15,779 | 18,273 | 17,503 | 19,214 | 18,611 | 15,933 | 13,579 | 14,533 |
| 1992 | 15,464 | 14,231 | 14,272 | 14,130 | 15,353 | 19,070 | 20,402 | 18,444 | 17,574 | 14,079 | 13,532 | 14,282 |
| 1993 | 11,889 | 14,315 | 12,990 | 15,490 | 19,641 | 17,919 | 20,931 | 18,892 | 16,883 | 15,690 | 16,658 | 19,633 |
| 1994 | 18,779 | 19,655 | 21,673 | 22,834 | 21,880 | 22,835 | 24,804 | 25,049 | 24,245 | 24,159 | 26,287 | 26,661 |
| 1995 | 23,285 | 23,058 | 23,470 | 23,657 | 20,984 | 21,533 | 20,801 | 25,288 | 23,489 | 24,498 | 22,137 | 21,534 |
| 1996 | 23,130 | 21,535 | 23,156 | 25,081 | 26,343 | 27,720 | 25,861 | 25,455 | 28,511 | 28,305 | 27,423 | 29,143 |

*Source: New York Mercantile Exchange (NYMEX)*

## Volume of Trading of Platinum Futures in New York In Thousands of Contracts

| Year | Jan. | Feb. | Mar. | Apr. | May | June | July | Aug. | Sept. | Oct. | Nov. | Dec. | Total |
|---|---|---|---|---|---|---|---|---|---|---|---|---|---|
| 1986 | 101.3 | 114.7 | 139.8 | 100.3 | 77.0 | 122.2 | 75.4 | 189.8 | 289.4 | 164.8 | 136.6 | 113.3 | 1,624.6 |
| 1987 | 117.2 | 85.7 | 134.1 | 149.3 | 110.8 | 116.5 | 87.1 | 133.2 | 122.7 | 127.2 | 88.6 | 89.2 | 1,361.5 |
| 1988 | 82.8 | 77.6 | 119.2 | 74.3 | 123.3 | 182.2 | 111.5 | 105.8 | 125.1 | 114.6 | 164.8 | 179.2 | 1,460.5 |
| 1989 | 113.6 | 96.6 | 148.5 | 107.3 | 111.6 | 126.9 | 69.8 | 86.8 | 85.1 | 56.4 | 99.8 | 88.1 | 1,190.5 |
| 1990 | 85.6 | 80.9 | 81.3 | 55.3 | 65.2 | 70.1 | 52.7 | 73.8 | 77.2 | 68.0 | 50.1 | 56.8 | 817.1 |
| 1991 | 50.8 | 42.3 | 72.7 | 43.0 | 51.1 | 55.7 | 40.6 | 45.7 | 55.8 | 42.9 | 41.9 | 60.3 | 598.6 |
| 1992 | 47.9 | 38.3 | 54.1 | 29.3 | 37.7 | 82.0 | 61.0 | 50.6 | 51.8 | 28.5 | 42.3 | 53.8 | 577.3 |
| 1993 | 29.4 | 55.6 | 61.4 | 50.6 | 65.8 | 72.5 | 59.8 | 56.4 | 58.6 | 37.0 | 44.0 | 60.3 | 651.2 |
| 1994 | 48.3 | 65.3 | 94.4 | 62.6 | 65.1 | 88.3 | 84.2 | 75.4 | 92.4 | 60.9 | 77.3 | 81.6 | 895.8 |
| 1995 | 61.4 | 38.6 | 131.3 | 69.9 | 60.4 | 75.4 | 53.4 | 62.5 | 98.8 | 55.9 | 56.3 | 82.8 | 846.7 |
| 1996 | 80.5 | 70.3 | 86.3 | 54.2 | 47.9 | 88.8 | 53.3 | 53.7 | 90.1 | 47.1 | 42.0 | 88.3 | 802.5 |

*Source: New York Mercantile Exchange (NYMEX)*

## Average Open Interest of Palladium Futures in New York In Contracts

| Year | Jan. | Feb. | Mar. | Apr. | May | June | July | Aug. | Sept. | Oct. | Nov. | Dec. |
|---|---|---|---|---|---|---|---|---|---|---|---|---|
| 1988 | 6,094 | 6,434 | 6,194 | 6,269 | 6,419 | 7,038 | 7,330 | 7,160 | 6,360 | 6,263 | 6,188 | 6,289 |
| 1988 | 6,094 | 6,434 | 6,194 | 6,269 | 6,419 | 7,038 | 7,330 | 7,160 | 6,360 | 6,263 | 6,188 | 6,289 |
| 1988 | 6,094 | 6,434 | 6,194 | 6,269 | 6,419 | 7,038 | 7,330 | 7,160 | 6,360 | 6,263 | 6,188 | 6,289 |
| 1988 | 6,094 | 6,434 | 6,194 | 6,269 | 6,419 | 7,038 | 7,330 | 7,160 | 6,360 | 6,263 | 6,188 | 6,289 |
| 1989 | 6,460 | 6,758 | 6,636 | 9,082 | 9,173 | 9,116 | 8,307 | 7,616 | 7,105 | 6,847 | 7,123 | 6,660 |
| 1990 | 6,296 | 6,350 | 5,276 | 5,359 | 5,476 | 5,361 | 5,493 | 5,717 | 5,165 | 5,100 | 5,316 | 4,565 |
| 1991 | 4,658 | 4,559 | 4,319 | 4,686 | 4,559 | 4,302 | 4,454 | 4,429 | 4,429 | 4,384 | 4,337 | 4,042 |
| 1992 | 3,984 | 4,071 | 4,101 | 4,206 | 4,137 | 3,852 | 3,762 | 3,362 | 3,041 | 2,982 | 2,901 | 3,246 |
| 1993 | 3,718 | 4,213 | 4,365 | 4,897 | 5,312 | 4,513 | 4,655 | 5,080 | 4,360 | 4,495 | 4,472 | 4,484 |
| 1994 | 4,626 | 4,995 | 4,672 | 4,303 | 5,116 | 4,530 | 5,807 | 6,851 | 6,625 | 6,511 | 7,726 | 6,917 |
| 1995 | 7,484 | 7,579 | 7,102 | 7,231 | 6,519 | 6,413 | 6,739 | 6,852 | 5,950 | 6,120 | 6,486 | 6,090 |

*Source: New York Mercantile Exchange (NYMEX)*

## Volume of Trading of Palladium Futures in New York In Contracts

| Year | Jan. | Feb. | Mar. | Apr. | May | June | July | Aug. | Sept. | Oct. | Nov. | Dec. | Total |
|---|---|---|---|---|---|---|---|---|---|---|---|---|---|
| 1986 | 12,115 | 21,296 | 8,680 | 9,796 | 12,348 | 6,456 | 4,460 | 22,764 | 16,266 | 10,565 | 13,611 | 6,726 | 145,083 |
| 1987 | 9,870 | 14,469 | 9,849 | 19,005 | 22,323 | 7,728 | 9,660 | 18,270 | 6,741 | 17,514 | 17,724 | 9,303 | 162,456 |
| 1988 | 12,348 | 16,065 | 8,673 | 11,970 | 15,435 | 15,456 | 15,393 | 11,781 | 6,363 | 7,077 | 14,973 | 11,739 | 147,273 |
| 1989 | 12,852 | 16,296 | 12,978 | 48,699 | 28,266 | 13,062 | 15,477 | 15,351 | 11,235 | 8,862 | 17,745 | 10,836 | 211,659 |
| 1990 | 4,893 | 19,026 | 6,930 | 5,355 | 13,104 | 5,670 | 4,452 | 11,130 | 5,407 | 7,150 | 9,592 | 3,178 | 95,887 |
| 1991 | 5,017 | 10,542 | 5,380 | 7,245 | 10,521 | 4,447 | 5,230 | 10,114 | 2,914 | 5,668 | 8,150 | 2,971 | 78,199 |
| 1992 | 7,217 | 7,323 | 3,429 | 2,833 | 8,011 | 2,881 | 4,965 | 6,752 | 5,066 | 5,359 | 6,461 | 7,912 | 68,209 |
| 1993 | 7,708 | 14,461 | 8,057 | 10,034 | 12,190 | 7,368 | 7,043 | 13,356 | 6,977 | 9,220 | 12,477 | 4,790 | 113,681 |
| 1994 | 8,250 | 14,953 | 6,067 | 6,676 | 15,481 | 6,514 | 9,024 | 21,741 | 15,690 | 9,603 | 21,384 | 8,390 | 143,773 |
| 1995 | 10,684 | 17,092 | 21,001 | 12,775 | 17,413 | 9,615 | 11,816 | 18,948 | 9,754 | 9,320 | 16,662 | 11,633 | 166,713 |
| 1996 | 13,725 | 33,519 | 11,931 | 16,416 | 27,467 | 8,989 | 9,896 | 23,740 | 10,721 | 8,149 | 28,870 | 12,187 | 205,610 |

*Source: New York Mercantile Exchange (NYMEX)*

## Average Dealer[1] Price of Palladium in the United States In Dollars Per Troy Ounce

| Year | Jan. | Feb. | Mar. | Apr. | May | June | July | Aug. | Sept. | Oct. | Nov. | Dec. | Average |
|---|---|---|---|---|---|---|---|---|---|---|---|---|---|
| 1986 | 101.83 | 103.18 | 110.62 | 110.64 | 109.23 | 110.40 | 112.00 | 127.05 | 142.30 | 136.68 | 125.36 | 118.15 | 117.29 |
| 1987 | 124.13 | 121.32 | 122.74 | 136.58 | 146.55 | 140.00 | 141.34 | 143.32 | 137.93 | 132.72 | 113.42 | 121.99 | 131.84 |
| 1988 | 125.26 | 120.40 | 122.67 | 123.62 | 124.06 | 128.77 | 126.25 | 123.84 | 121.04 | 122.59 | 126.80 | 133.30 | 124.89 |
| 1989 | 135.74 | 141.79 | 152.84 | 165.46 | 155.17 | 152.92 | 151.36 | 135.97 | 137.85 | 137.84 | 139.35 | 139.75 | 145.50 |
| 1990 | 135.80 | 136.63 | 131.25 | 128.18 | 120.08 | 117.40 | 116.60 | 116.17 | 106.62 | 96.12 | 94.84 | 90.93 | 115.89 |
| 1991 | 86.61 | 85.11 | 86.44 | 95.25 | 96.61 | 97.39 | 95.57 | 84.55 | 82.49 | 81.87 | 85.96 | 82.72 | 88.38 |
| 1992 | 82.96 | 86.04 | 84.50 | 83.71 | 82.90 | 80.98 | 86.49 | 86.04 | 90.67 | 95.07 | 95.01 | 104.88 | 88.27 |
| 1993 | 110.39 | 112.57 | 106.22 | 113.79 | 119.94 | 125.36 | 139.74 | 137.37 | 121.95 | 130.04 | 123.62 | 125.60 | 122.22 |
| 1994 | 124.40 | 130.92 | 132.43 | 133.22 | 135.76 | 137.03 | 145.28 | 151.83 | 152.99 | 154.90 | 158.10 | 153.80 | 142.56 |
| 1995 | 156.67 | 157.53 | 161.18 | 170.91 | 160.87 | 158.59 | 156.27 | 138.81 | 143.76 | 137.36 | 135.57 | 132.37 | 150.83 |
| 1996[2] | 131.59 | 142.10 | 140.67 | 138.05 | 134.36 | 132.95 | 134.55 | 128.82 | 123.10 | 119.39 | 119.30 | 119.90 | 130.40 |

[1] Based on wholesale quantities, prompt delivery. [2] Preliminary. *Sources: American Metal Market; U.S. Geological Survey*

# Pork Bellies

Pork bellies, or more commonly known as bacon, are obtained from the underside of a hog. A hog has two bellies, generally weighing about 8-18 pounds each, depending on the hog's commercial slaughter weight. Bellies account for about 12 percent of a hog's live weight, but represent a somewhat larger percentage of the total cutout value of the realized pork products. Bellies deliverable against futures generally weigh around 12-14 pounds.

Although pork belly futures trading volume has contracted in recent years, the market is still a viable pricing media for producers and users.

Definitive seasonal trends for pork bellies exist. Bellies are storable and the movement into cold storage builds early in the calendar year and peaks about mid-year. Net withdrawals from storage then carry stocks to a low around October. The cycle then begins anew. Retail bacon demand also follows a well established pattern. Demand is strongest in the summer when consumer preference shifts to lighter foods and then tapers off to a low during the winter months.

Pricewise, a weak seasonality is evident if the swings in futures values serve as a clue. Demand patterns would suggest the highest prices in the summer and the lowest in the winter. The opposite is not unusual. Such contra-seasonal price moves can be partially attributed to supply logistics, notably, the availability of storage stocks deliverable against futures at exchange approved warehouses. When it happens, underlying demand factors for bacon are on the backburner as a market making variable. The fact that no futures contract months are traded between August and the following February adds to the price distortion.

Belly prices (cash and futures) are sensitive to the inventory in cold storage during the year and to the weekly net movement in and out of storage. Storage movements can afford a clue to demand although a better measure is the weekly quantity of bellies being sliced into bacon.

Belly prices strengthened sharply early in 1996, pushing past $0.90 a pound by early May, their highest level since the early 1980's. A precipitous 20 cent drop then followed. The market's earlier price strength laid the seeds for the break as the higher prices encouraged placing more supply into storage and at the same time discouraged retail bacon demand which in some parts of the country had reached $4 a pound. Although personal income in the first half of 1996 was rising, bacon is not a consumer necessity. Moreover, consumer dietary tastes and nutritional standards have changed dramatically in recent years and are not necessarily favorable to bacon consumption. Also, U.S. pork belly exports to Eastern Europe fell in the first half of 1996. On the positive side as a price supporting factor in the second half of 1996 was the apparent strong consumer acceptance of bacon containing foodstuffs at the nation's fast food chains and expectations for improved export demand. Retail bacon prices in mid-1996 were averaging about $2.50 a pound, up about 60 cents from a year earlier and the highest mid-year levels since the early 1980's.

### *Futures Markets*

Pork belly futures and options are traded on the Chicago Mercantile Exchange (CME).

**Average Bureau of Labor Statistics Retail Price of Bacon, Sliced** In Dollars Per Pound

| Year | Jan. | Feb. | Mar. | Apr. | May | June | July | Aug. | Sept. | Oct. | Nov. | Dec. | Average |
|---|---|---|---|---|---|---|---|---|---|---|---|---|---|
| 1987 | 2.12 | 2.09 | 2.10 | 2.08 | 2.11 | 2.13 | 2.23 | 2.28 | 2.28 | 2.19 | 2.07 | 2.02 | 2.14 |
| 1988 | 1.95 | 1.94 | 1.92 | 1.91 | 1.90 | 1.90 | 1.91 | 1.88 | 1.84 | 1.86 | 1.80 | 1.79 | 1.88 |
| 1989 | 1.80 | 1.80 | 1.79 | 1.75 | 1.68 | 1.69 | 1.71 | 1.72 | 1.72 | 1.77 | 1.82 | 1.96 | 1.77 |
| 1990 | 1.97 | 2.01 | 1.99 | 1.98 | 2.04 | 2.15 | 2.21 | 2.24 | 2.18 | 2.21 | 2.24 | 2.28 | 2.13 |
| 1991 | 2.26 | 2.30 | 2.32 | 2.27 | 2.31 | 2.31 | 2.31 | 2.22 | 2.16 | 2.12 | 2.07 | 1.99 | 2.22 |
| 1992 | 1.96 | 1.95 | 1.92 | 1.92 | 1.90 | 1.93 | 1.95 | 1.94 | 1.93 | 1.89 | 1.85 | 1.86 | 1.92 |
| 1993 | 1.87 | 1.84 | 1.80 | 1.89 | 1.91 | 1.95 | 2.00 | 1.95 | 1.98 | 1.99 | 2.01 | 2.02 | 1.93 |
| 1994 | 2.04 | 2.02 | 2.02 | 2.06 | 1.99 | 1.99 | 2.00 | 1.99 | 1.97 | 1.97 | 1.92 | 1.89 | 1.99 |
| 1995 | 1.93 | 1.93 | 1.91 | 1.89 | 1.92 | 1.90 | 1.91 | 1.97 | 2.04 | 2.12 | 2.16 | 2.17 | 1.99 |
| 1996[1] | 2.14 | 2.20 | 2.20 | 2.24 | 2.35 | 2.49 | 2.54 | 2.68 | 2.81 | 2.72 | 2.66 | 2.64 | 2.47 |

[1] Preliminary. *Source: Economic Research Service, U.S. Department of Agriculture*

| Year | Jan. | Feb. | Mar. | Apr. | May | June | July | Aug. | Sept. | Oct. | Nov. | Dec. |
|---|---|---|---|---|---|---|---|---|---|---|---|---|
| 1986 | 51,314 | 47,633 | 51,218 | 62,508 | 68,325 | 65,895 | 61,547 | 40,333 | 20,797 | 12,941 | 17,022 | 24,528 |
| 1987 | 37,771 | 34,900 | 34,717 | 41,821 | 50,482 | 58,245 | 47,367 | 28,649 | 18,938 | 12,620 | 14,850 | 35,487 |
| 1988 | 62,089 | 62,996 | 67,035 | 90,347 | 102,543 | 111,484 | 103,401 | 73,747 | 42,623 | 31,054 | 49,550 | 93,254 |
| 1989 | 113,137 | 116,191 | 121,556 | 127,617 | 143,751 | 142,340 | 126,676 | 94,107 | 49,083 | 32,031 | 39,358 | 67,489 |
| 1990 | 85,026 | 77,255 | 85,789 | 96,945 | 102,899 | 105,482 | 87,983 | 55,859 | 23,352 | 4,785 | 5,506 | 24,044 |
| 1991 | 46,998 | 48,750 | 54,529 | 68,094 | 80,382 | 79,936 | 72,032 | 45,915 | 29,832 | 15,944 | 25,558 | 48,311 |
| 1992 | 71,318 | 76,894 | 75,925 | 85,095 | 96,653 | 92,677 | 78,646 | 54,544 | 26,854 | 21,973 | 26,044 | 49,970 |
| 1993 | 70,576 | 65,280 | 65,919 | 66,064 | 79,430 | 77,903 | 70,251 | 46,630 | 20,811 | 10,964 | 14,345 | 33,563 |
| 1994 | 53,168 | 55,999 | 54,921 | 63,099 | 72,230 | 79,018 | 73,583 | 57,747 | 30,636 | 18,260 | 22,656 | 40,725 |
| 1995 | 61,073 | 62,776 | 64,228 | 78,975 | 78,539 | 77,919 | 67,607 | 47,055 | 17,435 | 6,255 | 13,478 | 37,092 |
| 1996[1] | 47,587 | 46,498 | 46,381 | 47,655 | 57,174 | 63,522 | 56,767 | 28,533 | 18,996 | 12,702 | 16,206 | 30,943 |

[1] Preliminary. *Source: National Agricultural Statistics Service, U.S. Department of Agriculture*

# PORK BELLIES

## Weekly Pork Belly Storage Movement

| 1995 Week Ending | | Stocks[1] in Thousands of Pounds In | Out | On Hand | Net Move-ment | 1996 Week Ending | | Stocks[1] in Thousands of Pounds In | Out | On Hand | Net Move-ment |
|---|---|---|---|---|---|---|---|---|---|---|---|
| Jan. | 7 | 748 | 287 | 44,157 | 461 | Jan. | 6 | 1,119 | 83 | 33,884 | 1,036 |
| | 13 | 294 | 790 | 43,661 | -496 | | 13 | 749 | 439 | 34,194 | 310 |
| | 21 | 939 | 953 | 43,647 | -14 | | 20 | 995 | 827 | 34,362 | 168 |
| | 28 | 289 | 570 | 43,366 | -281 | | 27 | 546 | 1,320 | 33,588 | -774 |
| Feb. | 4 | 627 | 846 | 43,147 | -219 | Feb. | 3 | 844 | 1,842 | 32,590 | -998 |
| | 11 | 579 | 613 | 43,113 | -34 | | 10 | 69 | 692 | 31,967 | -623 |
| | 18 | 1,300 | 1,047 | 43,366 | 253 | | 17 | 61 | 1,390 | 30,638 | -1,329 |
| | 25 | 735 | 732 | 43,369 | 3 | | 24 | 315 | 485 | 30,468 | -170 |
| Mar. | 4 | 1,511 | 933 | 43,947 | 578 | Mar. | 2 | 1,599 | 552 | 31,515 | 1,047 |
| | 11 | 2,698 | 242 | 46,403 | 2,456 | | 9 | 488 | 1,151 | 30,852 | -663 |
| | 18 | 2,329 | 479 | 48,253 | 1,850 | | 16 | 815 | 594 | 31,073 | 221 |
| | 25 | 2,380 | 399 | 50,234 | 1,981 | | 23 | 1,014 | 305 | 31,782 | 709 |
| Apr. | 1 | 2,207 | 132 | 52,309 | 2,075 | | 30 | 499 | 399 | 31,882 | 100 |
| | 8 | 1,137 | 287 | 53,159 | 850 | Apr. | 6 | 1,407 | 682 | 32,607 | 725 |
| | 15 | 779 | 210 | 53,728 | 569 | | 13 | 2,951 | 488 | 35,070 | 2,463 |
| | 22 | 1,331 | 272 | 54,787 | 1,059 | | 20 | 2,093 | 293 | 36,870 | 1,800 |
| | 29 | 660 | 384 | 55,063 | 276 | | 27 | 999 | 735 | 37,134 | 264 |
| May | 6 | 922 | 262 | 55,723 | 660 | May | 4 | 739 | 397 | 37,476 | 342 |
| | 13 | 1,411 | 60 | 57,074 | 1,351 | | 11 | 1,289 | 381 | 38,384 | 908 |
| | 20 | 1,366 | 113 | 58,326 | 1,253 | | 18 | 3,101 | 291 | 41,194 | 2,810 |
| | 27 | 870 | 384 | 58,812 | 486 | | 25 | 1,992 | 286 | 42,900 | 1,706 |
| June | 3 | 247 | 528 | 58,531 | -281 | June | 1 | 2,026 | 1,824 | 43,102 | 202 |
| | 10 | 18 | 623 | 57,926 | -605 | | 8 | 2,058 | 1,630 | 43,530 | 428 |
| | 17 | 199 | 1,219 | 56,906 | -1,020 | | 15 | 564 | 366 | 43,728 | 198 |
| | 24 | 16 | 3,034 | 53,888 | -3,018 | | 22 | 182 | 1,210 | 42,700 | -1,028 |
| July | 1 | 293 | 2,788 | 51,393 | -2,495 | | 29 | 227 | 1,385 | 41,542 | -1,158 |
| | 8 | 235 | 1,192 | 50,436 | -957 | July | 6 | 4 | 1,854 | 39,692 | -1,850 |
| | 15 | 95 | 2,966 | 47,565 | -2,871 | | 13 | 0 | 3,414 | 36,278 | -3,414 |
| | 22 | 54 | 5,607 | 42,012 | -5,553 | | 20 | 12 | 4,364 | 31,926 | -4,352 |
| | 29 | 26 | 5,122 | 36,916 | -5,096 | | 27 | 0 | 3,577 | 28,349 | -3,577 |
| Aug. | 5 | 297 | 4,688 | 32,525 | -4,391 | Aug. | 3 | 162 | 3,721 | 24,790 | -3,559 |
| | 12 | 382 | 4,021 | 28,913 | -3,639 | | 10 | 0 | 3,723 | 21,067 | -3,723 |
| | 19 | 188 | 5,199 | 23,875 | -5,011 | | 17 | 0 | 1,802 | 19,265 | -1,802 |
| | 26 | 0 | 6,061 | 17,814 | -6,061 | | 24 | 235 | 486 | 19,014 | -251 |
| Sept. | 2 | 41 | 4,978 | 12,836 | -4,978 | | 31 | 490 | 1,638 | 17,866 | -1,148 |
| | 9 | 19 | 3,202 | 9,675 | -3,161 | Sept. | 7 | 664 | 1,746 | 16,784 | -1,082 |
| | 16 | 43 | 3,381 | 6,313 | -3,362 | | 14 | 1,268 | 1,526 | 16,526 | -258 |
| | 23 | 304 | 2,249 | 4,107 | -2,206 | | 21 | 906 | 2,857 | 14,575 | -1,951 |
| | 30 | 80 | 1,249 | 3,162 | -945 | | 28 | 122 | 3,069 | 11,628 | -2,947 |
| Oct. | 7 | 86 | 121 | 3,121 | -41 | Oct. | 5 | 43 | 2,549 | 9,122 | -2,506 |
| | 15 | 149 | 214 | 2,993 | -128 | | 12 | 981 | 970 | 9,133 | 11 |
| | 21 | 2,850 | 776 | 2,366 | -627 | | 19 | 1,765 | 893 | 10,005 | 872 |
| | 28 | 3,748 | 203 | 5,013 | 2,647 | | 26 | 1,932 | 946 | 11,091 | 1,086 |
| Nov. | 4 | 3,837 | 39 | 8,804 | 3,791 | Nov. | 2 | 2,165 | 697 | 12,559 | 1,468 |
| | 11 | 4,404 | 40 | 12,525 | 3,721 | | 9 | 3,108 | 278 | 15,389 | 2,830 |
| | 18 | 4,503 | 207 | 17,010 | 4,191 | | 16 | 2,409 | 167 | 17,631 | 2,242 |
| | 25 | 4,028 | 43 | 21,219 | 4,503 | | 23 | 1,134 | 296 | 18,469 | 838 |
| Dec. | 2 | 3,985 | 123 | 25,081 | 3,862 | | 30 | 3,626 | 313 | 21,782 | 3,313 |
| | 9 | 3,024 | 368 | 27,737 | 2,656 | Dec. | 7 | 2,244 | 465 | 23,561 | 1,779 |
| | 16 | 1,492 | 128 | 29,101 | 1,364 | | 14 | 2,154 | 410 | 25,305 | 1,744 |
| | 23 | 1,878 | 41 | 30,938 | 1,837 | | 21 | 1,323 | 138 | 26,490 | 1,185 |
| | 30 | 1,910 | | 32,848 | 1,910 | | 28 | 1,328 | 0 | 27,818 | 1,328 |

[1] 57 Chicago and Outside Combined Chicago Mercantile Exchange approved warehouses. *Source: Chicago Mercantile Exchange (CME)*

## Average Open Interest of Pork Bellies Futures in Chicago In Contracts

| Year | Jan. | Feb. | Mar. | Apr. | May | June | July | Aug. | Sept. | Oct. | Nov. | Dec. |
|---|---|---|---|---|---|---|---|---|---|---|---|---|
| 1985 | 13,804 | 14,545 | 13,138 | 12,356 | 11,526 | 11,315 | 9,770 | 6,878 | 6,710 | 7,507 | 8,481 | 9,018 |
| 1986 | 8,313 | 7,969 | 7,357 | 8,635 | 9,509 | 10,781 | 9,135 | 7,462 | 8,515 | 8,287 | 10,412 | 11,440 |
| 1987 | 11,617 | 10,159 | 10,936 | 13,586 | 14,277 | 12,863 | 11,291 | 8,940 | 8,301 | 9,550 | 9,924 | 11,846 |
| 1988 | 11,250 | 10,942 | 13,421 | 16,229 | 17,887 | 18,428 | 15,782 | 11,874 | 14,678 | 15,860 | 19,292 | 19,723 |
| 1989 | 20,453 | 20,444 | 21,897 | 22,117 | 24,931 | 25,898 | 20,053 | 12,724 | 11,916 | 12,501 | 14,802 | 13,844 |
| 1990 | 12,885 | 12,114 | 13,017 | 15,338 | 14,513 | 13,038 | 11,146 | 6,104 | 6,059 | 7,851 | 11,419 | 12,589 |
| 1991 | 11,777 | 10,187 | 9,776 | 11,509 | 10,436 | 10,111 | 7,356 | 6,176 | 7,532 | 10,813 | 13,173 | 12,844 |
| 1992 | 12,521 | 12,195 | 11,901 | 12,345 | 12,497 | 13,598 | 12,623 | 7,149 | 6,540 | 7,033 | 9,251 | 10,953 |
| 1993 | 10,623 | 9,244 | 8,283 | 8,626 | 10,096 | 11,092 | 9,031 | 5,427 | 4,644 | 7,241 | 8,701 | 9,121 |
| 1994 | 11,053 | 10,426 | 9,375 | 9,894 | 8,092 | 8,248 | 7,836 | 7,841 | 8,398 | 10,072 | 10,141 | 10,216 |
| 1995 | 10,294 | 9,080 | 7,809 | 7,367 | 8,017 | 7,036 | 5,666 | 4,271 | 6,246 | 7,007 | 7,103 | 7,282 |
| 1996 | 7,094 | 8,028 | 10,521 | 10,753 | 10,018 | 8,136 | 6,432 | 6,296 | 6,056 | 6,395 | 6,050 | 6,480 |

*Source: Chicago Mercantile Exchange (CME)*

## Volume of Trading of Pork Bellies Futures in Chicago In Contracts

| Year | Jan. | Feb. | Mar. | Apr. | May | June | July | Aug. | Sept. | Oct. | Nov. | Dec. | Total |
|---|---|---|---|---|---|---|---|---|---|---|---|---|---|
| 1985 | 173,488 | 137,334 | 133,509 | 148,489 | 149,809 | 135,139 | 136,026 | 89,784 | 77,326 | 99,291 | 85,377 | 91,634 | 1,457,386 |
| 1986 | 92,033 | 81,768 | 75,830 | 96,642 | 106,958 | 100,331 | 109,981 | 78,967 | 91,470 | 87,712 | 91,779 | 86,868 | 1,100,339 |
| 1987 | 104,134 | 95,108 | 92,707 | 118,107 | 112,112 | 120,598 | 118,996 | 89,564 | 60,670 | 66,423 | 53,903 | 64,688 | 1,097,010 |
| 1988 | 70,150 | 76,741 | 85,947 | 99,754 | 116,780 | 179,505 | 112,356 | 90,371 | 79,667 | 94,646 | 84,236 | 96,446 | 1,186,599 |
| 1989 | 107,577 | 89,922 | 84,768 | 90,353 | 145,975 | 152,207 | 119,733 | 91,200 | 75,155 | 106,389 | 141,983 | 105,714 | 1,310,976 |
| 1990 | 109,036 | 100,813 | 129,476 | 133,946 | 165,880 | 143,663 | 122,187 | 74,653 | 53,428 | 76,549 | 112,752 | 80,746 | 1,303,129 |
| 1991 | 106,078 | 89,975 | 88,056 | 111,195 | 119,773 | 96,273 | 74,255 | 59,176 | 65,604 | 80,707 | 63,331 | 50,773 | 1,005,196 |
| 1992 | 80,697 | 79,700 | 67,470 | 57,565 | 73,137 | 73,081 | 78,588 | 54,663 | 39,839 | 64,248 | 60,724 | 54,440 | 784,152 |
| 1993 | 77,380 | 62,871 | 63,988 | 62,403 | 62,400 | 70,124 | 65,496 | 42,613 | 37,992 | 47,780 | 60,163 | 49,099 | 698,799 |
| 1994 | 60,316 | 67,250 | 58,183 | 53,839 | 56,575 | 58,424 | 50,450 | 47,626 | 38,375 | 45,525 | 49,280 | 47,803 | 633,646 |
| 1995 | 62,994 | 54,330 | 59,324 | 43,501 | 49,453 | 53,571 | 45,869 | 36,623 | 31,112 | 35,444 | 47,061 | 42,631 | 561,913 |
| 1996 | 48,563 | 56,623 | 61,669 | 61,703 | 61,868 | 55,337 | 55,121 | 45,399 | 39,182 | 48,973 | 42,709 | 35,502 | 612,649 |

*Source: Chicago Mercantile Exchange (CME)*

# PORK BELLIES

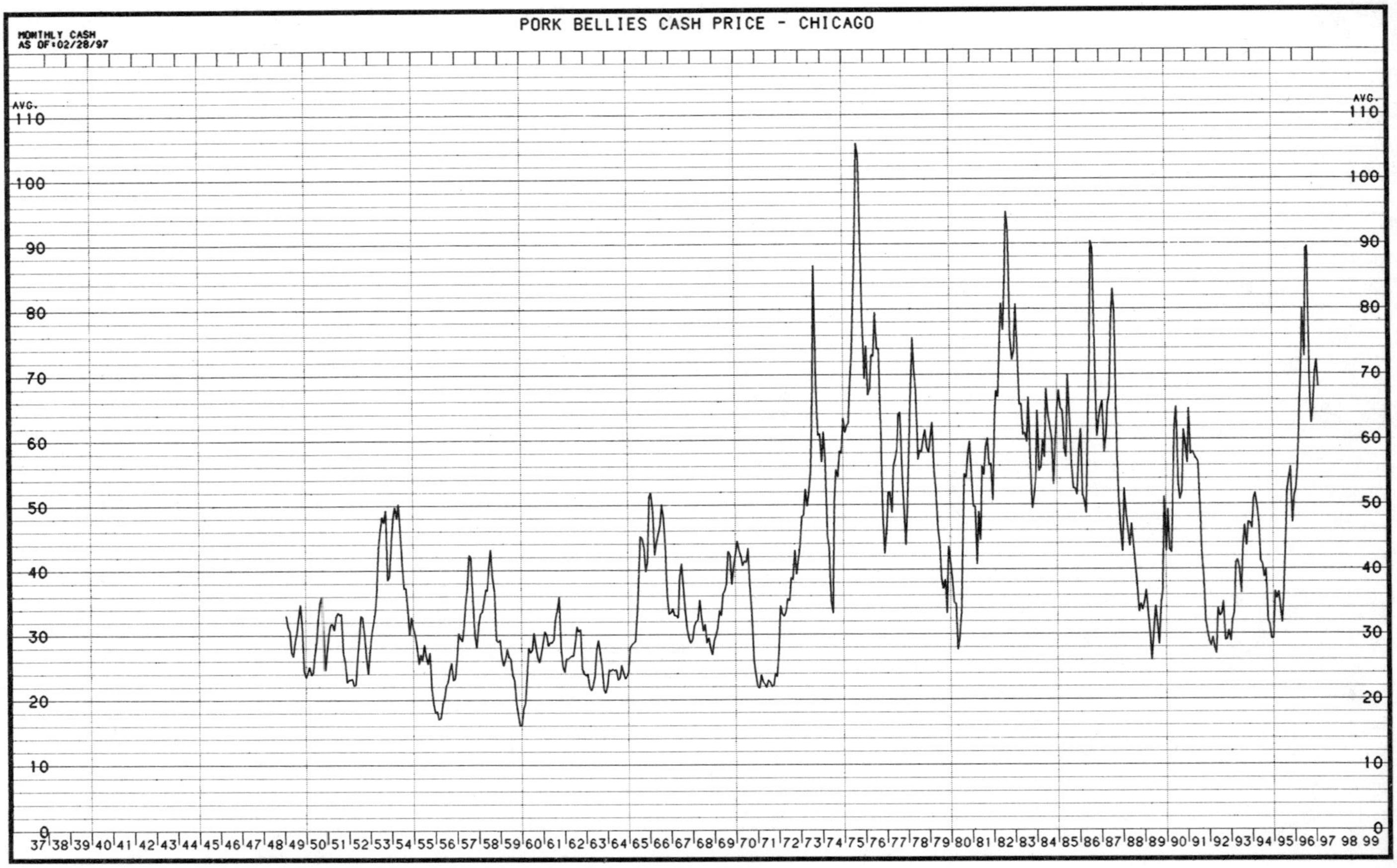


**Average Price of Pork Bellies (12-14 Pounds) Midwest** In Cents Per Pound

| Year | Jan. | Feb. | Mar. | Apr. | May | June | July | Aug. | Sept. | Oct. | Nov. | Dec. | Average |
|---|---|---|---|---|---|---|---|---|---|---|---|---|---|
| 1983 | 80.91 | 73.88 | 65.11 | 64.71 | 60.81 | 60.19 | 59.06 | 65.72 | 55.25 | 49.10 | 50.96 | 54.59 | 61.69 |
| 1984 | 65.03 | 54.68 | 56.04 | 59.53 | 57.38 | 67.12 | 64.75 | 62.17 | 58.00 | 52.80 | 61.88 | 64.31 | 60.31 |
| 1985 | 67.50 | 64.14 | 64.25 | 58.83 | 58.64 | 70.15 | 62.53 | 54.17 | 51.40 | 52.09 | 51.73 | 58.63 | 59.51 |
| 1986 | 61.27 | 51.50 | 50.80 | 49.45 | 61.82 | 71.83 | 90.08 | 89.10 | 75.64 | 60.32 | 63.29 | 64.72 | 65.82 |
| 1987 | 66.32 | 57.81 | 60.02 | 65.79 | 67.21 | 78.44 | 83.62 | 80.46 | 59.74 | 49.39 | 45.87 | 42.60 | 63.11 |
| 1988 | 51.82 | 48.40 | 45.32 | 43.13 | 46.09 | 45.51 | 40.84 | 37.46 | 33.05 | 34.97 | 33.64 | 34.82 | 41.25 |
| 1989 | 36.91 | 31.41 | 30.19 | 25.49 | 29.11 | 32.90 | 31.52 | 28.82 | 34.23 | 36.88 | 49.96 | 42.23 | 34.14 |
| 1990 | 48.65 | 42.53 | 42.60 | 52.60 | 61.48 | 65.15 | 53.18 | 51.08 | 51.31 | 59.83 | 60.57 | 56.58 | 53.80 |
| 1991 | 64.11 | 57.20 | 58.52 | 57.25 | 57.50 | 56.48 | 50.40 | 42.01 | 38.97 | 32.26 | 30.04 | 28.79 | 47.79 |
| 1992 | 28.05 | 29.44 | 28.01 | 26.93 | 34.09 | 32.78 | 32.77 | 35.13 | 29.09 | 29.13 | 30.48 | 28.80 | 30.39 |
| 1993 | 31.97 | 33.22 | 41.28 | 41.19 | 39.86 | 36.24 | 44.51 | 46.68 | 43.82 | 47.25 | 47.21 | 46.21 | 41.62 |
| 1994 | 50.63 | 51.66 | 49.68 | 46.84 | 41.40 | 40.39 | 38.64 | 39.60 | 31.50 | 31.33 | 29.09 | 29.29 | 40.00 |
| 1995 | 36.03 | 35.80 | 36.30 | 33.83 | 31.70 | 37.94 | 43.10 | 52.42 | 54.43 | 56.20 | 47.28 | 51.45 | 43.04 |
| 1996[1] | 52.33 | 56.33 | 64.50 | 69.89 | 79.50 | 72.64 | 89.49 | 88.40 | 68.12 | 63.07 | 65.27 | 70.07 | 69.97 |

[1] Preliminary. *Source: Economic Research Service, U.S. Department of Agriculture*

# Potatoes

U.S. potato production in 1995 of 444 million cwt. was 23 million cwt. under the record 1994 crop reflecting an average yield of 323 cwt. per acre vs. 339 cwt. in 1994. Total consumption also fell due to higher retail prices and shifting consumer tastes. The annualized growth in processed potato demand was braked in 1995 as total use fell to 256 million cwt. from 1994's record high 261 million cwt.; with the decline largely in frozen french fry usage (129 million cwt. vs. 137 million). Despite the nation's ever expanding number of fast food outlets, consumer affinity for deep fried foods has slowed. Tablestock use (fresh potatoes) in 1995 of 124 million cwt. compares with 134 million in 1994.

Potatoes are grown in all fifty states. However, the crop is divided into four seasonal groups based on harvest time. The fall crop accounts for 85-90 percent of total production and is harvested September through November in about two dozen states. The winter crop is the smallest and harvested only in Florida and California from January into March. Spring and summer crop production tends to be fairly close in size. The seasonal disparities reflect major differences in planted acreage and realized yield which is consistently higher in the fall producing states. The marketing season follows the harvest, but the movement of the fall crop can extend into the following July with supplies drawn from storage. The inventoried fall crop can serve as a supply buffer in the event the spring and summer crops are short. Large fall stocks can be a depressant on prices should earlier crops prove large. Generally about 30 percent of farm marketings occur in September/October.

Harvested acreage fell slightly in 1995 to 1.37 million acres from 1.38 million in 1994, of which fall acreage accounted for 1.20 million acres and 1.18 million, respectively. Idaho is the nation's largest producer with a 1995 fall crop of 133 million cwt., down 6 million cwt. from 1994. Washington's crop was second at 81 million cwt. vs. 89 million. Washington's 1995 average yield of 550 cwt./acre was the nation's highest while Idaho's yield averaged 333 cwt./acre. In years past, Maine was the largest fall producing state, but now ranks eighth with 17 million cwt. in 1995. Reasons for Maine's slide include the wide variety of tubers grown, about 80, whereas in Idaho production is focused on one type of potato, the Russet Burbank, making it easier to guarantee marketing consistency and consumer preference.

The value of the 1995 crop was estimated at $3.0 billion, up 15 percent from 1994. The average price received by farmers in 1995 was $6.77 per cwt. vs. $5.58 in 1994. On the retail level, processed potatoes at about $1.00 per pound are usually about three times higher than tablestock prices.

Almost 60 percent of U.S. production is processed, either into frozen products or as a direct consumer food, such as chips. Frozen french fries account for most of all frozen use. Chips and shoestrings generally account for more than 20 percent of total processing use; in 1995 there were 126 chip producing plants in the U.S. vs. 131 in 1994. Per capita use of potatoes, the largest U.S. vegetable crop, totals 135 pounds, about 60 percent of which is processed potatoes.

Foreign trade in U.S. potatoes is small. Japan is the largest importer of U.S. processed potatoes. Canada exports fresh potatoes to the U.S. which are used mostly for seed.

***Futures Markets***

Potato futures and options are traded on the New York Cotton Exchange (NYCE) and the London Commodity Exchange (LCE). Potato futures are traded on the Marche a Terme International de France (MATIF).

## Salient Statistics of Potatoes in the United States

| Crop Year | Acreage: Planted (1,000 Acres) | Acreage: Harvested (1,000 Acres) | Yield Per Harvested Acre (Cwt.) | Total Production (In Thousands of Cwt.) | Farm Disposition — Used Where Grown: Seed & Feed (In Thousands of Cwt.) | Farm Disposition — Used Where Grown: Shrinkage & Loss (In Thousands of Cwt.) | Sold[2] (In Thousands of Cwt.) | Farm Price ($ Cwt.) | Value of: Production[3] (Million $) | Value of: Sales (Million $) | Stocks on Jan. 1 (1,000 Cwt) | Foreign Trade[5] (Fresh): Domestic Exports (Millions of Lbs.) | Foreign Trade[5]: Imports (Millions of Lbs.) | Consumption[5] Per Capita in Pounds: Fresh | Consumption[5] Per Capita in Pounds: Total |
|---|---|---|---|---|---|---|---|---|---|---|---|---|---|---|---|
| 1989 | 1,305 | 1,282 | 289 | 370,444 | 5,722 | 24,974 | 339,748 | 7.36 | 2,717 | 2,501 | 177,750 | 467,836 | 509,347 | 50.0 | 127.1 |
| 1990 | 1,400 | 1,371 | 293 | 402,110 | 5,949 | 28,329 | 367,832 | 6.08 | 2,409 | 2,240 | 173,550 | 327,333 | 482,903 | 45.8 | 127.7 |
| 1991 | 1,408 | 1,374 | 304 | 417,622 | 5,995 | 32,429 | 379,198 | 4.96 | 2,043 | 1,880 | 194,460 | 341,682 | 437,349 | 46.4 | 130.4 |
| 1992 | 1,339 | 1,315 | 323 | 425,367 | 5,925 | 33,807 | 385,637 | 5.52 | 2,336 | 2,129 | 211,005 | 537,939 | 273,515 | 48.9 | 132.4 |
| 1993 | 1,385 | 1,317 | 326 | 428,693 | 5,931 | 30,152 | 392,610 | 6.17 | 2,637 | 2,424 | 215,990 | 539,345 | 541,382 | 49.7 | 136.9 |
| 1994 | 1,413 | 1,383 | 338 | 467,054 | 5,878 | 37,166 | 424,010 | 5.58 | 2,590 | 2,367 | 217,800 | 655,026 | 405,899 | 48.6 | 140.2 |
| 1995[1] | 1,398 | 1,372 | 323 | 443,606 | 5,745 | 29,530 | 408,331 | 6.77 | 2,992 | 2,762 | 237,960 | 583,938 | 405,899 | 50.7 | 137.9 |
| 1996[1] | | 1,426 | 345 | 491,445 | | | | | | | 223,150 | | | 49.2 | 142.3 |

[1] Preliminary. [2] For all purposes, including food, seed processing & livestock feed. [3] Farm weight basis, excluding canned and frozen potatoes.
*Source: Economic Research Service, U.S. Department of Agriculture*

## U.S. Cold Storage Stocks of All Frozen Potatoes (First of Month) In Millions of Pounds

| Year | Jan. | Feb. | Mar. | Apr. | May | June | July | Aug. | Sept. | Oct. | Nov. | Dec. |
|---|---|---|---|---|---|---|---|---|---|---|---|---|
| 1989 | 988.7 | 927.4 | 944.3 | 947.3 | 968.7 | 986.7 | 961.5 | 739.9 | 611.3 | 734.2 | 878.7 | 938.0 |
| 1990 | 917.3 | 932.7 | 995.6 | 1,041.2 | 1,059.0 | 1,061.3 | 977.6 | 769.3 | 688.1 | 852.5 | 995.6 | 999.5 |
| 1991 | 975.8 | 993.3 | 988.9 | 1,041.5 | 1,052.3 | 1,167.2 | 1,216.5 | 935.5 | 880.1 | 985.5 | 1,148.0 | 1,037.2 |
| 1992 | 980.8 | 996.5 | 1,036.3 | 1,082.7 | 1,077.6 | 1,137.3 | 1,131.4 | 966.4 | 948.7 | 949.1 | 1,067.1 | 1,038.7 |
| 1993 | 963.2 | 971.2 | 1,028.2 | 1,046.6 | 912.7 | 979.5 | 989.8 | 932.8 | 902.8 | 1,019.5 | 1,184.7 | 1,130.7 |
| 1994 | 1,006.4 | 1,019.9 | 1,057.1 | 1,054.4 | 1,050.5 | 1,118.9 | 1,099.9 | 979.8 | 1,028.2 | 1,108.7 | 1,189.0 | 1,163.5 |
| 1995 | 1,096.6 | 1,156.0 | 1,179.9 | 1,169.0 | 1,138.0 | 1,125.4 | 1,116.5 | 992.4 | 992.6 | 1,145.3 | 1,225.6 | 1,174.5 |
| 1996[1] | 1,123.7 | 1,147.2 | 1,174.5 | 1,166.4 | 1,108.9 | 1,074.8 | 1,057.5 | 907.1 | 957.8 | 1,124.9 | 1,225.3 | 1,146.3 |

[1] Preliminary. *Source: Agricultural Statistics Board, U.S. Department of Agriculture*

# POTATOES

## Potato Crop Production Estimates, Stocks & Disappearance in the U.S. In Millions of Cwt.

| | Crop Production Estimates | | | | | Total Storage Stocks[2] | | | | | | Fall Crop | | | | |
|---|---|---|---|---|---|---|---|---|---|---|---|---|---|---|---|---|
| | Total Crop | | | Fall Crop | | Following Year | | | | | | 1,000 Cwt. | | | | |
| Year | Oct. 1 | Nov. 1 | Dec. 1 | Oct. 1 | Nov. 1 | Dec. 1 | Jan. 1 | Feb. 1 | Mar. 1 | Apr. 1 | May 1 | Pro-duction | Disap-pearance (Sold) | Dec. 1 Stocks | Average Price $/Cwt. | Value of Sales $1,000 |
| 1983 | 329.8 | 329.8 | 325.7 | 292.7 | 292.7 | 192.5 | 165.3 | 138.9 | 112.7 | 81.7 | 50.4 | 294,679 | 265,598 | 192,150 | 5.46 | 1,449,394 |
| 1984 | 358.8 | 358.8 | 361.6 | 310.0 | 346.1 | 201.4 | 173.4 | 144.8 | 118.4 | 86.4 | 52.5 | 312,662 | 279,270 | 201,410 | 5.03 | 1,402,425 |
| 1985 | ------ | 400.4 | 404.1 | ------ | 307.5 | 235.5 | 202.8 | 171.5 | 138.7 | 104.5 | 65.4 | 343,984 | 295,032 | 235,475 | 3.42 | 1,007,953 |
| 1986 | ------ | 352.3 | 352.3 | ------ | 342.7 | 209.4 | 180.9 | 154.5 | 128.7 | 95.1 | 59.8 | 307,928 | 284,721 | 209,435 | 4.68 | 1,335,419 |
| 1987 | ------ | 361.5 | ------ | ------ | 309.9 | 225.9 | 196.8 | 167.3 | 138.8 | 105.9 | 70.0 | 335,607 | 309,279 | 225,890 | 3.69 | 1,142,731 |
| 1988 | ------ | 352.1 | ------ | ------ | 322.7 | 206.4 | 177.8 | 151.1 | 124.5 | 92.6 | 59.4 | 305,623 | 284,205 | 206,420 | 5.82 | 1,652,864 |
| 1989 | ------ | 367.3 | ------ | ------ | 342.5 | 202.1 | 173.6 | 144.3 | 116.6 | 84.3 | 50.7 | 316,097 | 295,605 | 202,050 | 6.76 | 1,999,104 |
| 1990 | ------ | 393.2 | ------ | ------ | 371.7 | 225.5 | 194.5 | 162.9 | 134.5 | 101.2 | 63.0 | 344,200 | 320,033 | 225,500 | 5.42 | 1,734,476 |
| 1991 | ------ | 417.6 | ------ | ------ | 379.5 | 242.1 | 211.0 | 178.5 | 145.8 | 108.9 | 69.1 | 363,541 | 334,893 | 242,070 | 4.16 | 1,393,749 |
| 1992 | ------ | 425.4 | ------ | ------ | 372.4 | 246.8 | 216.0 | 184.6 | 152.8 | 115.8 | 75.0 | 368,516 | 341,209 | 246,820 | 5.17 | 1,762,984 |
| 1993 | ------ | 428.7 | ------ | ------ | 372.4 | 249.7 | 217.8 | 186.1 | 154.1 | 116.0 | 73.9 | 375,004 | 351,161 | 249,710 | 5.65 | 1,981,017 |
| 1994 | ------ | 467.9 | ------ | ------ | 412.4 | 272.3 | 238.0 | 201.9 | 168.1 | 128.4 | 87.4 | 408,139 | 378,333 | 272,290 | 5.06 | 1,914,311 |
| 1995 | ------ | 444.8 | ------ | ------ | 402.4 | 256.3 | 223.2 | 189.0 | 155.7 | 116.3 | 76.2 | 392,942 | 368,946 | 256,310 | 6.43 | 2,372,983 |
| 1996[1] | ------ | 491.5 | ------ | ------ | 447.9 | 291.3 | 256.5 | 220.5 | | | | 441,083 | | 291,300 | | |

[1] Preliminary. [2] Held by growers and local dealers in the fall producing areas. *Source: Agricultural Statistics Board, U.S. Department of Agriculture*

## United States Potato Production by Seasonal Groups In Thousands of Cwt.

| | | Spring | | | Summer | | | Fall | | | | | | | | |
|---|---|---|---|---|---|---|---|---|---|---|---|---|---|---|---|---|
| Year | Winter | Cali-fornia | Florida | Total | New Mexico | Virgina | Total | Colo-rado | Idaho | Maine | Minne-sota | North Dakota | Oregan | Washing-ton | Wis-consin | Total |
| 1983 | 2,193 | 8,330 | 5,121 | 18,338 | 1,625 | 1,001 | 18,701 | 13,950 | 85,990 | 22,560 | 10,313 | 20,480 | 20,710 | 54,080 | 18,910 | 294,679 |
| 1984 | 2,640 | 11,115 | 6,740 | 23,798 | 2,639 | 1,540 | 23,086 | 17,225 | 86,500 | 21,360 | 13,775 | 20,615 | 23,515 | 56,925 | 21,350 | 313,088 |
| 1985 | 2,691 | 10,588 | 6,643 | 22,986 | 2,860 | 3,300 | 27,794 | 17,920 | 102,515 | 28,215 | 14,145 | 23,630 | 26,888 | 63,630 | 24,130 | 353,638 |
| 1986 | 2,991 | 7,605 | 7,031 | 19,865 | 2,790 | 1,112 | 20,689 | 18,810 | 90,220 | 21,930 | 13,650 | 21,600 | 23,172 | 61,950 | 20,125 | 318,198 |
| 1987 | 2,501 | 7,881 | 5,567 | 18,988 | 3,500 | 1,974 | 22,833 | 19,500 | 99,710 | 23,240 | 16,330 | 24,050 | 25,924 | 66,960 | 22,100 | 344,438 |
| 1988 | 2,616 | 7,546 | 6,753 | 20,110 | 3,060 | 2,048 | 20,154 | 19,040 | 102,610 | 22,000 | 13,860 | 15,525 | 20,735 | 63,250 | 20,000 | 313,558 |
| 1989 | 2,764 | 7,875 | 6,860 | 20,852 | 4,025 | 1,440 | 22,155 | 20,603 | 102,475 | 22,000 | 13,860 | 15,070 | 23,308 | 64,310 | 23,120 | 324,673 |
| 1990 | 2,343 | 8,438 | 8,714 | 24,163 | 3,400 | 1,980 | 23,097 | 22,750 | 119,070 | 20,520 | 14,280 | 16,675 | 23,450 | 67,980 | 23,075 | 352,507 |
| 1991 | 2,609 | 8,284 | 6,600 | 20,636 | 3,450 | 1,485 | 22,647 | 23,800 | 122,175 | 18,170 | 17,160 | 30,030 | 22,170 | 75,435 | 23,275 | 371,730 |
| 1992 | 2,998 | 7,238 | 7,750 | 21,535 | 952 | 1,980 | 21,309 | 22,110 | 127,050 | 24,300 | 16,080 | 27,690 | 21,075 | 69,300 | 25,160 | 379,525 |
| 1993 | 2,552 | 7,508 | 6,068 | 19,654 | 1,290 | 1,760 | 14,922 | 25,270 | 126,192 | 19,890 | 14,780 | 21,090 | 23,103 | 88,500 | 22,588 | 391,565 |
| 1994 | 2,372 | 7,790 | 8,588 | 22,646 | 1,088 | 1,425 | 17,381 | 25,795 | 138,801 | 18,375 | 20,035 | 28,200 | 27,514 | 88,920 | 25,740 | 424,655 |
| 1995 | 2,473 | 6,230 | 7,830 | 20,193 | 1,344 | 2,040 | 17,931 | 23,808 | 132,657 | 17,160 | 20,790 | 25,410 | 24,788 | 80,850 | 26,000 | 403,009 |
| 1996[1] | 3,273 | 7,538 | 7,765 | 22,417 | 1,404 | 1,800 | 19,390 | 28,786 | 139,960 | 21,175 | 24,600 | 28,820 | 31,684 | 94,990 | 31,590 | 452,039 |

[1] Preliminary. *Source: Agricultural Statistics Board, U.S. Department of Agriculture*

## Utilization of Potatoes in the United States In Thousands of Cwt.

| | Sales | | | | | | | | | | | Non-sales | | | |
|---|---|---|---|---|---|---|---|---|---|---|---|---|---|---|---|
| | | For Processing | | | | | | | Other Sales | | | | | | |
| Crop Year | Table Stock | Chips, Shoe-strings | For Dehyd-ration | Frozen French Fries | Other Frozen Products | Canned Potatoes | Other Canned Products[2] | Starch & Flour | Livestock Feed | Seed | Total Sale | Used on Farms Where Grown | Shrink-age & Loss | Total Non-sales | Total |
| 1983 | 107,295 | 43,311 | 26,754 | 74,350 | 19,655 | 2,137 | 1,991 | 3,028 | 3,734 | 20,870 | 303,125 | 4,605 | 24,664 | 30,601 | 333,726 |
| 1984 | 113,187 | 42,339 | 27,845 | 87,350 | 20,322 | 2,589 | 1,834 | 3,401 | 4,662 | 22,752 | 326,281 | 4,407 | 30,057 | 35,758 | 362,039 |
| 1985 | 125,006 | 42,217 | 29,958 | 94,741 | 17,856 | 2,971 | 1,610 | 3,489 | 8,098 | 19,895 | 345,841 | 5,060 | 52,707 | 60,768 | 406,609 |
| 1986 | 109,331 | 45,814 | 28,445 | 96,244 | 15,708 | 2,790 | 1,308 | 2,808 | 3,992 | 20,700 | 327,140 | 5,070 | 28,355 | 34,603 | 361,743 |
| 1987 | 129,097 | 40,593 | 30,823 | 101,377 | 18,305 | 2,958 | 1,597 | 2,184 | 3,808 | 21,023 | 351,765 | 4,521 | 31,901 | 37,555 | 389,320 |
| 1988 | 108,348 | 44,539 | 28,786 | 95,466 | 17,558 | 2,941 | 2,031 | 1,416 | 3,330 | 21,146 | 325,561 | 4,827 | 25,067 | 30,877 | 356,438 |
| 1989 | 113,932 | 43,071 | 32,187 | 100,459 | 19,115 | 3,138 | 1,858 | 898 | 2,800 | 22,290 | 339,748 | 4,735 | 24,974 | 30,696 | 370,444 |
| 1990 | 119,545 | 44,489 | 38,838 | 108,455 | 23,915 | 2,526 | 2,075 | 1,699 | 3,264 | 23,026 | 367,832 | 5,035 | 28,329 | 34,278 | 402,110 |
| 1991 | 126,953 | 45,850 | 40,395 | 111,128 | 23,097 | 2,465 | 1,886 | 1,739 | 3,652 | 22,033 | 379,198 | 4,988 | 32,429 | 38,424 | 417,622 |
| 1992 | 127,215 | 48,455 | 38,078 | 112,496 | 23,016 | 2,710 | 2,557 | 1,610 | 3,928 | 23,529 | 385,637 | 4,746 | 33,807 | 39,730 | 425,367 |
| 1993 | 123,802 | 48,987 | 40,795 | 121,087 | 25,190 | 1,879 | 2,458 | 1,691 | 2,498 | 24,223 | 392,610 | 4,808 | 30,152 | 36,083 | 428,693 |
| 1994 | 133,989 | 49,299 | 41,381 | 136,531 | 26,362 | 2,503 | 3,006 | 2,176 | 4,147 | 24,616 | 424,010 | 4,732 | 37,166 | 43,044 | 467,054 |
| 1995[1] | 123,989 | 47,908 | 44,465 | 129,029 | 26,573 | 3,413 | 2,492 | 1,668 | 3,224 | 25,570 | 408,331 | 4,787 | 29,530 | 35,275 | 443,606 |

[1] Preliminary. [2] Hash, stews and soups. *Source: Agricultural Statistics Board, U.S. Department of Agriculture*

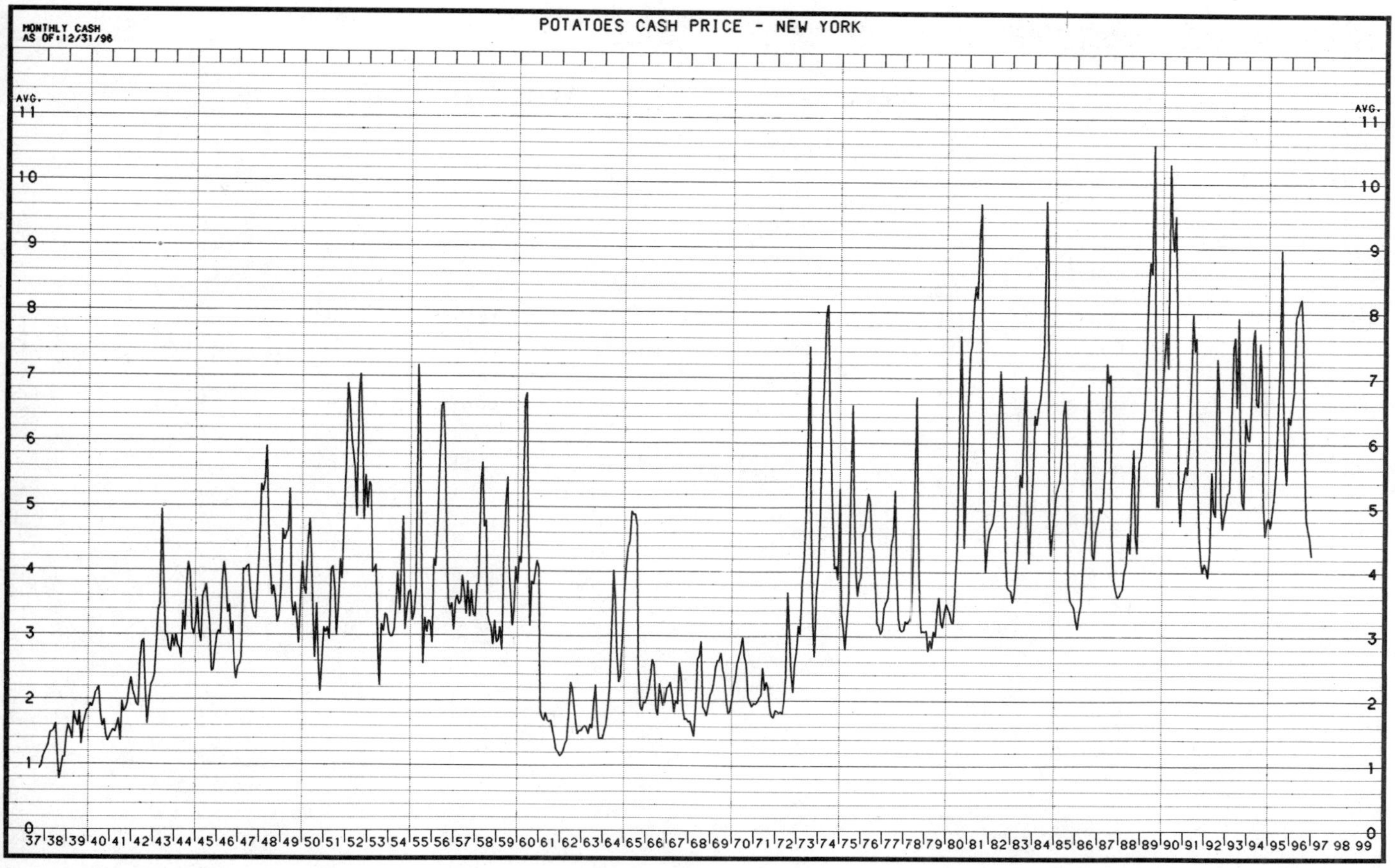


## Potatoes U.S. Total Per Capita Utilization in Pounds (Farm Weight)

| | | | Processing | | | | |
|---|---|---|---|---|---|---|---|
| Year | Total | Fresh | Freezing | Chips & Shoe-string | Dehy-drating | Canning | Total |
| 1987 | 126.0 | 47.9 | 47.9 | 17.6 | 10.8 | 1.8 | 78.1 |
| 1988 | 122.4 | 49.6 | 43.3 | 17.2 | 10.4 | 1.9 | 72.8 |
| 1989 | 127.1 | 50.0 | 46.8 | 17.5 | 10.8 | 2.0 | 77.1 |
| 1990 | 127.7 | 45.8 | 50.2 | 17.0 | 12.8 | 1.9 | 81.9 |
| 1991 | 130.4 | 46.4 | 51.3 | 17.3 | 13.7 | 1.7 | 84.0 |
| 1992 | 132.4 | 48.9 | 51.0 | 17.5 | 13.2 | 1.8 | 83.5 |
| 1993 | 136.9 | 49.7 | 54.5 | 17.6 | 13.4 | 1.7 | 87.2 |
| 1993 | 136.9 | 49.7 | 54.5 | 17.6 | 13.4 | 1.7 | 87.2 |
| 1994 | 140.2 | 48.6 | 59.3 | 17.1 | 13.5 | 1.7 | 91.6 |
| 1995[1] | 137.9 | 50.7 | 55.3 | 16.9 | 13.0 | 2.0 | 87.2 |
| 1996[2] | 142.3 | 49.2 | 59.0 | 17.0 | 15.0 | 2.1 | 93.1 |

[1] Preliminary. [2] Forecast. *Source: Agricultural Statistics Board, U.S. Department of Agriculture*

## U.S. Average Price Received by Farmers for Potatoes In Dollars Per Cwt.

| Year | Jan. | Feb. | Mar. | Apr. | May | June | July | Aug. | Sept. | Oct. | Nov. | Dec. | Season Average |
|---|---|---|---|---|---|---|---|---|---|---|---|---|---|
| 1986 | 3.12 | 3.35 | 3.50 | 3.99 | 4.39 | 4.79 | 6.91 | 5.68 | 4.28 | 4.20 | 4.63 | 4.78 | 5.03 |
| 1987 | 5.01 | 4.93 | 5.05 | 5.66 | 7.23 | 6.94 | 7.06 | 4.52 | 3.89 | 3.74 | 3.62 | 3.63 | 4.38 |
| 1988 | 3.70 | 3.74 | 4.02 | 4.11 | 4.62 | 4.30 | 5.28 | 5.91 | 4.55 | 4.30 | 5.72 | 5.79 | 6.02 |
| 1989 | 6.24 | 6.43 | 7.34 | 8.33 | 8.78 | 8.61 | 10.60 | 7.58 | 5.06 | 5.03 | 6.32 | 6.81 | 7.36 |
| 1990 | 7.36 | 7.71 | 9.17 | 10.30 | 9.32 | 8.96 | 9.50 | 8.09 | 5.36 | 4.73 | 5.24 | 5.46 | 6.08 |
| 1991 | 5.66 | 5.53 | 6.15 | 7.03 | 7.98 | 7.51 | 7.95 | 5.39 | 4.51 | 4.06 | 3.99 | 4.29 | 4.96 |
| 1992 | 4.07 | 4.08 | 4.64 | 5.16 | 4.43 | 4.71 | 7.00 | 6.64 | 4.89 | 4.55 | 4.90 | 5.06 | 5.52 |
| 1993 | 5.15 | 5.29 | 6.06 | 7.19 | 7.18 | 6.45 | 7.61 | 6.05 | 5.12 | 4.96 | 6.40 | 6.12 | 6.17 |
| 1994 | 6.02 | 6.43 | 7.67 | 6.69 | 6.59 | 6.67 | 7.49 | 6.99 | 5.03 | 4.57 | 4.80 | 4.86 | 5.58 |
| 1995 | 4.88 | 4.90 | 5.39 | 5.54 | 5.77 | 6.98 | 8.60 | 6.81 | 5.76 | 5.38 | 6.42 | 6.29 | 6.77 |
| 1996[1] | 6.53 | 6.81 | 7.94 | 8.00 | 8.13 | 8.22 | 7.69 | 5.83 | 4.82 | 4.67 | 4.55 | 4.26 | |

[1] Preliminary. *Source: Agricultural Statistics Board, U.S. Department of Agriculture*

# POTATOES

**United States Potatoes Processed[1], Eight States** In Thousands of Cwt.

| States | Storage Season | to Dec. 1 | to Jan. 1 | to Feb. 1 | to Mar. 1 | to Apr. 1 | to May 1 | Entire Season |
|---|---|---|---|---|---|---|---|---|
| Idaho and Oregon-Malheur Co | 1987-8 | 18,260 | 23,320 | 28,680 | 34,340 | 40,380 | 46,440 | 64,495 |
| | 1988-9 | 18,740 | 24,270 | 29,420 | 34,720 | 41,360 | 48,080 | 64,425 |
| | 1989-90 | 22,200 | 28,140 | 34,240 | 40,270 | 46,330 | 51,810 | 66,010 |
| | 1990-1 | 24,780 | 31,100 | 37,550 | 44,220 | 51,030 | 58,660 | 78,500 |
| | 1991-2 | 22,980 | 28,910 | 35,700 | 42,840 | 50,260 | 57,290 | 78,690 |
| | 1992-3 | 22,180 | 29,080 | 35,710 | 42,800 | 50,090 | 57,090 | 80,570 |
| | 1993-4 | 24,090 | 30,540 | 37,150 | 44,720 | 53,070 | 61,440 | 85,780 |
| | 1994-5 | 26,620 | 34,230 | 42,330 | 49,890 | 57,990 | 66,680 | 90,300 |
| | 1995-6 | 27,310 | 35,040 | 43,260 | 51,530 | 59,060 | 66,690 | 89,250 |
| | 1996-7 | 31,060 | 38,210 | 45,420 | | | | |
| Maine[2] | 1987-8 | 1,770 | 2,440 | 3,145 | 3,745 | 4,410 | 4,865 | 6,745 |
| | 1988-9 | 1,685 | 2,190 | 2,830 | 3,455 | 4,230 | 4,915 | 6,915 |
| | 1989-90 | 2,055 | 2,660 | 3,510 | 4,000 | 4,620 | 5,210 | 6,900 |
| | 1990-1 | 2,105 | 2,690 | 3,420 | 3,900 | 4,460 | 5,120 | 6,750 |
| | 1991-2 | 2,015 | 2,450 | 3,050 | 3,350 | 3,900 | 4,445 | 5,210 |
| | 1992-3 | 1,195 | 1,630 | 2,205 | 2,720 | 3,390 | 4,020 | 5,055 |
| | 1993-4 | 1,350 | 1,720 | 2,210 | 2,505 | 2,890 | 3,275 | 4,555 |
| | 1994-5 | 1,505 | 1,840 | 2,265 | 2,540 | 2,985 | 3,330 | 4,770 |
| | 1995-6 | 1,335 | 1,690 | 2,180 | 2,520 | 3,025 | 3,465 | 5,225 |
| | 1996-7 | 1,400 | 1,725 | 2,225 | | | | |
| Washington and Oregon-Other | 1987-8 | 22,265 | 25,950 | 30,790 | 35,800 | 40,900 | 44,925 | 58,085 |
| | 1988-9 | 19,200 | 23,455 | 27,280 | 31,960 | 37,575 | 41,795 | 51,555 |
| | 1989-90 | 23,635 | 28,015 | 33,170 | 38,610 | 44,510 | 49,595 | 57,695 |
| | 1990-1 | 24,780 | 29,830 | 35,170 | 39,950 | 45,600 | 50,780 | 61,450 |
| | 1991-2 | 26,345 | 30,570 | 35,320 | 41,320 | 47,120 | 52,605 | 65,210 |
| | 1992-3 | 26,840 | 31,550 | 35,950 | 41,670 | 46,530 | 51,630 | 63,510 |
| | 1993-4 | 28,260 | 33,350 | 39,010 | 45,020 | 51,290 | 57,180 | 70,690 |
| | 1994-5 | 28,670 | 33,480 | 39,120 | 46,070 | 52,940 | 59,540 | 76,780 |
| | 1995-6 | 30,000 | 35,170 | 39,460 | 45,280 | 51,730 | 57,360 | 70,250 |
| | 1996-7 | 31,650 | 36,590 | 41,690 | | | | |
| Other States[3] | 1987-8 | 5,750 | 7,370 | 9,200 | 11,250 | 13,305 | 15,270 | 20,155 |
| | 1988-9 | 5,805 | 7,450 | 9,040 | 10,645 | 12,340 | 14,075 | 18,385 |
| | 1989-90 | 6,340 | 8,010 | 9,860 | 11,535 | 13,240 | 15,100 | 20,610 |
| | 1990-1 | 6,585 | 8,605 | 10,405 | 12,425 | 14,635 | 17,010 | 24,005 |
| | 1991-2 | 7,515 | 9,350 | 11,580 | 13,585 | 15,685 | 17,935 | 24,990 |
| | 1992-3 | 7,140 | 9,220 | 11,265 | 13,305 | 15,550 | 17,555 | 25,070 |
| | 1993-4 | 7,605 | 9,515 | 11,605 | 13,720 | 16,080 | 18,705 | 25,690 |
| | 1994-5 | 9,725 | 13,110 | 15,630 | 18,260 | 21,115 | 24,060 | 32,260 |
| | 1995-6 | 12,450 | 15,330 | 18,415 | 21,485 | 24,910 | 28,010 | 33,305 |
| | 1996-7 | 13,660 | 16,570 | 20,140 | | | | |
| Total | 1987-8 | 48,045 | 59,080 | 71,815 | 85,135 | 98,995 | 111,500 | 149,480 |
| | 1988-9 | 45,430 | 57,365 | 68,570 | 80,780 | 95,505 | 108,865 | 144,280 |
| | 1989-90 | 54,230 | 66,825 | 80,780 | 94,415 | 108,700 | 121,715 | 151,215 |
| | 1990-1 | 58,250 | 72,225 | 86,545 | 100,495 | 115,725 | 131,570 | 170,705 |
| | 1991-2 | 58,855 | 71,280 | 85,650 | 101,095 | 116,965 | 132,275 | 174,100 |
| | 1992-3 | 57,355 | 71,480 | 85,130 | 100,495 | 115,560 | 130,295 | 174,205 |
| | 1993-4 | 61,305 | 75,125 | 89,975 | 105,965 | 123,330 | 140,600 | 186,715 |
| | 1994-5 | 66,520 | 82,660 | 99,345 | 116,760 | 135,030 | 153,610 | 204,110 |
| | 1995-6 | 71,095 | 87,230 | 103,315 | 120,815 | 138,725 | 155,525 | 198,030 |
| | 1996-7 | 77,770 | 93,095 | 109,475 | | | | |

[1] Total quantity received and used for processing regardless of the state in which the potatoes were produced. Excluding quantities used for potato chips in Maine, Michigan, Minnesota, North Dakota or Wisconsin. [2] Includes Maine grown potatoes only. [3] Michigan, Minnesota, North Dakota and Wisconsin.

*Source: National Agricultural Statistics Service, U.S. Department of Agriculture*

# Rayon and Other Synthetic Fibers

## Worldwide Cellulosic Fiber Production   In Thousands of Metric Tons

| Year | Austria | Brazil | China | Czech Republic | Finland | Germany | India | Japan | Poland | Romania | Taiwan | United Kingdom | United States | Former U.S.S.R. | Yugo-slavia | Total |
|---|---|---|---|---|---|---|---|---|---|---|---|---|---|---|---|---|
| 1987 | 120.0 | 48.9 | 187.0 | 55.2 | 54.0 | 274.6 | 167.5 | 300.5 | 73.3 | 66.0 | 119.6 | 55.0 | 274.6 | 591.5 | 63.3 | 2,826 |
| 1988 | 132.0 | 51.5 | 184.4 | 58.3 | 60.4 | 277.1 | 174.1 | 290.6 | 74.2 | 75.6 | 125.8 | 64.0 | 278.3 | 601.0 | 68.0 | 2,896 |
| 1989 | 136.0 | 55.0 | 204.0 | 56.9 | 64.8 | 278.4 | 198.7 | 272.9 | 65.6 | 95.9 | 147.6 | 55.0 | 263.3 | 584.0 | 71.1 | 2,943 |
| 1990 | 135.0 | 54.5 | 214.3 | 55.0 | 63.8 | 199.1 | 216.7 | 275.8 | 36.2 | 59.9 | 147.9 | 71.0 | 229.2 | 544.0 | 72.7 | 2,757 |
| 1991 | 120.0 | 53.0 | 242.0 | 33.5 | 47.4 | 118.0 | 215.4 | 266.4 | 25.6 | 38.0 | 149.1 | 63.0 | 220.7 | 401.7 | 49.3 | 2,433 |
| 1992 | 128.3 | 54.2 | 249.0 | 39.3 | 56.0 | 139.9 | 219.9 | 254.4 | 22.1 | 28.5 | 139.3 | 65.0 | 224.5 | 292.3 | 18.2 | 2,327 |
| 1993 | 131.2 | 56.7 | 276.2 | 41.0 | 56.5 | 127.1 | 238.9 | 244.4 | 23.6 | 13.3 | 130.8 | 67.2 | 228.9 | 258.3 | 15.0 | 2,286 |
| 1994 | 134.3 | 62.8 | 336.1 | 41.7 | 58.5 | 136.2 | 239.7 | 218.9 | 18.0 | 11.5 | 149.3 | 67.4 | 226.0 | 176.0 | 19.6 | 2,340 |
| 1995[1] | 139.4 | 65.2 | 435.4 | 35.0 | 57.5 | 136.1 | 262.2 | 212.6 | 22.2 | 11.4 | 139.6 | 67.1 | 240.1 | 172.3 | 17.7 | 2,471 |
| 1996[2] | 145.0 | 71.3 | 545.0 | 51.2 | 62.0 | 152.2 | 303.4 | 290.7 | 40.2 | 44.0 | 153.0 | 69.5 | 320.2 | 588.0 | 51.0 | 3,404 |

[1] Preliminary. [2] Producing capacity. *Source: Fiber Economics Bureau, Inc.*

## Worldwide Noncellulosic Fiber Production (Except Olefin)   In Thousands of Metric Tons

| Year | Brazil | China | France | Germany | India | Italy/ Malta | Japan | Rep. of Korea | Mexico | Romania | Spain | Taiwan | United Kingdom | United States | Former U.S.S.R. | Total |
|---|---|---|---|---|---|---|---|---|---|---|---|---|---|---|---|---|
| 1987 | 248.1 | 846.0 | 161.0 | 759.3 | 266.0 | 564.6 | 1,340.6 | 970.1 | 333.2 | 201.9 | 268.5 | 1,391.3 | 203.0 | 3,094.3 | 591.5 | 13,741 |
| 1988 | 239.7 | 1,074.5 | 159.1 | 926.3 | 321.6 | 568.2 | 1,351.9 | 1,115.0 | 340.3 | 192.3 | 302.3 | 1,430.2 | 193.0 | 3,146.9 | 601.0 | 14,418 |
| 1989 | 245.8 | 1,223.2 | 152.1 | 952.3 | 366.7 | 547.7 | 1,380.9 | 1,189.9 | 352.8 | 159.3 | 252.3 | 1,523.1 | 178.5 | 3,119.4 | 874.0 | 14,747 |
| 1990 | 207.8 | 1,342.8 | 137.2 | 777.0 | 436.6 | 578.3 | 1,425.0 | 1,269.7 | 366.8 | 139.9 | 255.0 | 1,621.5 | 179.8 | 2,886.0 | 893.5 | 14,894 |
| 1991 | 219.1 | 1,488.9 | 107.0 | 797.0 | 439.6 | 564.6 | 1,429.8 | 1,365.2 | 395.3 | 138.8 | 241.1 | 1,841.4 | 179.3 | 2,902.9 | 804.8 | 15,273 |
| 1992 | 218.2 | 1,586.7 | 105.2 | 817.3 | 538.0 | 589.9 | 1,448.8 | 1,451.4 | 426.6 | 110.1 | 257.0 | 2,042.6 | 187.4 | 2,980.6 | 656.8 | 15,911 |
| 1993 | 233.3 | 1,871.9 | 103.7 | 758.8 | 608.9 | 551.6 | 1,365.1 | 1,581.3 | 406.5 | 103.5 | 240.3 | 2,122.8 | 174.3 | 3,016.1 | 669.8 | 16,653 |
| 1994 | 239.1 | 2,299.2 | 124.7 | 807.6 | 681.0 | 599.9 | 1,374.0 | 1,673.5 | 418.4 | 118.5 | 273.6 | 2,295.9 | 161.3 | 3,193.3 | 658.1 | 17,908 |
| 1995[1] | 232.5 | 2,264.0 | 135.6 | 771.3 | 730.5 | 551.3 | 1,403.9 | 1,895.2 | 494.6 | 118.9 | 252.3 | 4,211.0 | 157.1 | 3,313.0 | 636.1 | 18,472 |
| 1996[2] | 292.8 | 3,245.0 | ------ | ------ | 1,083.8 | ------ | 1,853.6 | ------ | 554.0 | 217.3 | ------ | 4,851.0 | ------ | 3,803.3 | 1,359.8 | 24,215 |

[1] Preliminary. [2] Producing capacity. *Source: Fiber Economics Bureau, Inc.*

## World Production of Synthetic Fibers   In Thousands of Metric Tons

| | Noncellulosic Fiber Production (Except Olefin) | | | | | | | Glass Fiber Production | | | | | | | |
|---|---|---|---|---|---|---|---|---|---|---|---|---|---|---|---|
| | By Fibers | | | | World Total | | | | | | | | | | |
| Year | Acrylic & Mod-acrylic | Nylon & Aramid | Polyester | Other Fibers[3] | Yarn & Monofil-aments | Staple & Tow & Fiberfill | Total | Europe | Japan | Other Americas | United States | Total | China | Former U.S.S.R. | Cigarette Tow Pro-duction |
| 1987 | 2,521 | 3,638 | 7,438 | 144 | 6,040 | 7,701 | 13,741 | 407 | 300 | 50 | 725 | 1,517 | 55 | 110 | 400 |
| 1988 | 2,452 | 3,725 | 8,102 | 138 | 6,572 | 7,845 | 14,417 | 465 | 340 | 65 | 730 | 1,655 | 65 | 125 | 412 |
| 1989 | 2,341 | 3,795 | 8,459 | 152 | 6,847 | 7,900 | 14,747 | 470 | 345 | 65 | 735 | 1,680 | 70 | 133 | 443 |
| 1990 | 2,320 | 3,738 | 8,678 | 158 | 7,035 | 7,859 | 14,894 | 445 | 371 | 60 | 675 | 1,631 | 75 | 120 | 464 |
| 1991 | 2,385 | 3,605 | 9,116 | 167 | 7,241 | 8,032 | 15,273 | 441 | 293 | 75 | 650 | 1,561 | 65 | 133 | 480 |
| 1992 | 2,363 | 3,662 | 9,729 | 157 | 7,673 | 8,238 | 15,911 | 442 | 307 | 83 | 700 | 1,652 | 75 | 130 | 475 |
| 1993 | 2,297 | 3,707 | 10,512 | 136 | 8,478 | 8,174 | 16,652 | 508 | 312 | 86 | 794 | 1,865 | 77 | 69 | 482 |
| 1994 | 2,472 | 3,770 | 11,500 | 162 | 9,107 | 8,797 | 17,904 | 545 | 313 | 87 | 959 | 2,076 | 78 | 64 | 536 |
| 1995[1] | 2,420 | 3,911 | 11,958 | 182 | 9,754 | 8,717 | 18,471 | 567 | 310 | 96 | 981 | 2,133 | 85 | 65 | 552 |
| 1996[2] | 3,191 | 5,333 | 15,387 | 304 | 12,724 | 11,491 | 24,215 | 731 | 318 | 108 | 1,027 | 2,396 | 130 | 125 | 362 |

[1] Preliminary. [2] Producing capacity. [3] Alginate, azion, spandex, saran, etc. *Source: Fiber Economics Bureau, Inc.*

## U.S. Artificial (Cellulosic) Distribution   In Millions of Pounds

| | Yarn & Monofilament | | | | | Staple & Tow | | | | | Glass Fiber Ship-ments |
|---|---|---|---|---|---|---|---|---|---|---|---|
| | Producers' Shipments | | | | Domestic Con-sumption | Producers' Shipments | | | | Domestic Con-sumption | |
| Year | Domestic | Exports | Total | Imports | | Domestic | Exports | Total | Imports | | |
| 1987 | 166.8 | 24.9 | 191.7 | 12.8 | 179.6 | 383.6 | 32.4 | 416.0 | 13.8 | 397.4 | 1,513.1 |
| 1988 | 182.6 | 34.1 | 216.7 | 17.6 | 200.2 | 386.0 | 20.5 | 406.5 | 20.4 | 406.4 | 1,587.6 |
| 1989 | 187.3 | 31.7 | 219.0 | 26.3 | 213.6 | 338.2 | 16.2 | 354.4 | 54.0 | 392.2 | 1,530.1 |
| 1990 | 172.7 | 34.0 | 206.7 | 24.2 | 196.9 | 291.7 | 12.5 | 304.2 | 111.6 | 403.3 | 1,519.1 |
| 1991 | 179.9 | 32.3 | 212.2 | 30.8 | 210.7 | 255.5 | 8.1 | 263.6 | 92.0 | 347.5 | 1,488.5 |
| 1992 | 182.9 | 35.1 | 218.0 | 32.1 | 215.0 | 260.7 | 6.9 | 267.6 | 85.6 | 346.3 | 1,629.7 |
| 1993 | 196.5 | 31.5 | 228.0 | 40.4 | 236.9 | 273.6 | 10.3 | 283.9 | 89.5 | 363.1 | 1,780.6 |
| 1994 | 190.3 | 32.9 | 223.2 | 32.9 | 223.2 | 252.3 | 30.7 | 283.0 | 65.7 | 318.0 | 2,016.0 |
| 1995[1] | 169.3 | 41.5 | 210.8 | 34.0 | 203.3 | 259.8 | 28.7 | 288.5 | 40.8 | 300.6 | 2,089.0 |

[1] Preliminary. *Source: Fiber Economics Bureau, Inc.*

# RAYON AND OTHER SYNTHETIC FIBERS

## Man-Made Fiber Production in the United States In Millions of Pounds

| | Artificial (Cellulosic) Fibers - Rayon & Acetate | | | Synthetic (Noncellulosic) Fibers | | | | | | | | | | | |
|---|---|---|---|---|---|---|---|---|---|---|---|---|---|---|---|
| | | | | Yarn & Monofilament | | | | Staple & Tow | | | | | | | |
| Year | Filament Yarn & Monofilament | Staple & Tow | Total Cellulostic | Nylon | Polyester | Olefin | Total Yarn | Nylon | Polyester | Acrylic & Modacrylic | Olefin | Total Staple | Total Noncellulosic | Total Manufactured Fibers | Total Glass Fiber |
| 1987 | 191 | 414 | 605 | 1,697 | 1,179 | 1,134 | 4,010 | 992 | 2,362 | 592 | 360 | 4,306 | 8,316 | 8,921 | 1,598 |
| 1988 | 214 | 400 | 614 | 1,728 | 1,228 | 1,224 | 4,180 | 942 | 2,452 | 588 | 364 | 4,346 | 8,526 | 9,140 | 1,609 |
| 1989 | 217 | 363 | 580 | 1,759 | 1,209 | 1,257 | 4,225 | 981 | 2,385 | 543 | 382 | 4,291 | 8,516 | 9,096 | 1,620 |
| 1990 | 206 | 299 | 505 | 1,671 | 1,107 | 1,417 | 4,194 | 990 | 2,090 | 505 | 406 | 3,991 | 8,185 | 8,690 | 1,488 |
| 1991 | 213 | 273 | 486 | 1,667 | 1,208 | 1,408 | 4,282 | 869 | 2,202 | 454 | 459 | 3,984 | 8,266 | 8,752 | 1,433 |
| 1992 | 220 | 275 | 495 | 1,651 | 1,270 | 1,528 | 4,449 | 904 | 2,308 | 439 | 474 | 4,125 | 8,573 | 9,068 | 1,543 |
| 1993 | 227 | 278 | 505 | 1,700 | 1,284 | 1,659 | 4,643 | 959 | 2,274 | 433 | 483 | 4,149 | 8,791 | 9,296 | 1,751 |
| 1994 | 225 | 273 | 498 | 1,805 | 1,492 | 1,870 | 5,167 | 935 | 2,366 | 442 | 549 | 4,292 | 9,459 | 9,957 | 2,114 |
| 1995[1] | 208 | 290 | 498 | 1,829 | 1,597 | 1,907 | 5,333 | 874 | 2,290 | 432 | 521 | 4,117 | 9,450 | 9,948 | 2,163 |
| 1996[2] | 219 | 245 | 464 | 1,920 | 1,564 | 1,958 | 5,437 | 874 | 2,258 | 474 | 439 | 4,045 | 9,482 | 9,946 | 2,264 |

[1] Preliminary. [2] Estimate. *Source: Fiber Economics Bureau, Inc.*

## U.S. Domestic Distribution of Synthetic (Noncellulosic) Fibers In Millions of Pounds

| | Yarn & Monofilament | | | | | | | | Staple & Tow | | | | | | | | |
|---|---|---|---|---|---|---|---|---|---|---|---|---|---|---|---|---|---|
| | Producers' Shipments | | | | | | | | Producers' Shipments | | | | | | | | |
| | Domestic | | | | | | | | Domestic | | | | | | | | |
| Year | Nylon | Polyester | Olefin | Total | Exports | Total | Imports | Domestic Consumption | Nylon | Polyester | Acrylic & Modacrylic | Olefin | Total | Exports | Total | Imports | Domestic Consumption |
| 1987 | 1,554.3 | 1,113.4 | 1,135.5 | 3,803.2 | 214.7 | 4,017.9 | 123.9 | 3,927.1 | 966.0 | 2,201.0 | 479.3 | 341.1 | 3,987.4 | 325.6 | 4,313.0 | 189.0 | 4,176.4 |
| 1988 | 1,572.4 | 1,157.4 | 1,199.8 | 3,929.6 | 260.5 | 4,190.1 | 116.3 | 4,045.9 | 944.9 | 2,311.8 | 421.1 | 344.2 | 4,022.0 | 344.8 | 4,366.8 | 196.2 | 4,218.2 |
| 1989 | 1,575.3 | 1,110.7 | 1,226.0 | 3,912.0 | 237.9 | 4,149.9 | 182.2 | 4,094.2 | 955.3 | 2,261.3 | 414.8 | 363.4 | 3,994.8 | 253.3 | 4,248.1 | 192.4 | 4,187.2 |
| 1990 | 1,537.5 | 1,046.2 | 1,404.9 | 3,988.6 | 265.1 | 4,253.7 | 154.7 | 4,143.3 | 950.2 | 2,015.4 | 352.2 | 387.9 | 3,705.7 | 278.9 | 3,984.6 | 209.8 | 3,915.5 |
| 1991 | 1,493.9 | 1,114.0 | 1,380.6 | 3,988.5 | 246.9 | 4,235.4 | 174.8 | 4,163.3 | 835.0 | 2,127.9 | 319.2 | 437.5 | 3,719.6 | 277.8 | 3,997.4 | 263.1 | 3,982.7 |
| 1992 | 1,570.1 | 1,229.6 | 1,496.1 | 4,295.8 | 194.8 | 4,490.6 | 209.3 | 4,505.1 | 891.7 | 2,202.1 | 322.3 | 441.0 | 3,857.1 | 267.2 | 4,124.3 | 397.7 | 4,255.0 |
| 1993 | 1,612.7 | 1,228.4 | 1,631.5 | 4,472.6 | 174.6 | 4,647.2 | 295.8 | 4,768.4 | 907.9 | 2,157.8 | 333.0 | 468.2 | 3,866.9 | 297.1 | 4,164.0 | 509.0 | 4,375.9 |
| 1994 | 1,700.0 | 1,402.8 | 1,838.2 | 4,941.0 | 204.9 | 5,145.9 | 377.7 | 5,318.7 | 911.7 | 2,221.3 | 319.6 | 489.0 | 3,941.6 | 390.9 | 4,332.5 | 622.9 | 4,564.5 |
| 1995[1] | 1,741.1 | 1,439.8 | 1,870.3 | 5,051.2 | 259.0 | 5,310.2 | 393.6 | 5,444.8 | 828.5 | 2,100.2 | 266.1 | 458.0 | 3,652.8 | 402.8 | 4,055.6 | 624.8 | 4,277.6 |

[1] Preliminary. *Source: Fiber Economics Bureau, Inc.*

## U.S. Mill Consumption of Fiber & Products & Per Capita Consumption In Millions of Pounds

| | Cellulosic Fibers | | | | Noncellulosic Fibers | | | | | | | | Per Capita[4] Mill Consumption (Pounds) | | | | |
|---|---|---|---|---|---|---|---|---|---|---|---|---|---|---|---|---|---|
| Year | Yarn & Monofilament | Staple & Tow | Net Waste | Total Cellulostic | Noncellulostic | Net Waste | Total Noncellulostic | Total Manufactured Fibers[2] | Cotton | Wool | Other Fibers[3] | Grand Total | Man-made Fibers[2] | Cotton | Wool | Other Fibers[3] | Total All Fibers |
| 1987 | 179.6 | 397.4 | 8.6 | 585.6 | 8,103.5 | 172.6 | 8,276.1 | 8,861.7 | 3,736.5 | 167.6 | 104.8 | 12,870.6 | 41.3 | 23.7 | 1.7 | 2.5 | 69.2 |
| 1988 | 200.2 | 406.4 | 5.8 | 612.4 | 8,264.1 | 140.9 | 8,405.0 | 9,017.4 | 3,470.1 | 156.1 | 83.8 | 12,727.4 | 40.9 | 21.4 | 1.5 | 2.1 | 65.9 |
| 1989 | 213.6 | 392.2 | -5.0 | 600.8 | 8,281.4 | 127.4 | 8,408.8 | 9,009.6 | 3,985.9 | 139.6 | 77.9 | 13,213.0 | 40.6 | 23.4 | 1.1 | 2.0 | 67.1 |
| 1990 | 196.9 | 403.3 | -1.3 | 598.9 | 8,058.8 | 179.3 | 8,238.1 | 8,837.0 | 4,036.5 | 135.4 | 75.7 | 13,084.6 | 39.3 | 23.2 | 1.1 | 2.2 | 65.8 |
| 1991 | 210.7 | 347.5 | -1.7 | 556.5 | 8,135.9 | 168.8 | 8,304.7 | 8,861.2 | 4,347.5 | 159.0 | 78.6 | 13,446.3 | 39.1 | 24.6 | 1.2 | 2.0 | 66.9 |
| 1992 | 215.0 | 346.3 | -3.6 | 557.7 | 8,760.1 | 181.1 | 8,941.2 | 9,498.9 | 4,714.7 | 159.1 | 76.3 | 14,449.0 | 41.5 | 27.6 | 1.2 | 1.9 | 72.2 |
| 1993 | 236.9 | 363.1 | -5.6 | 594.4 | 9,144.3 | 189.8 | 9,334.1 | 9,928.5 | 4,921.9 | 166.6 | 73.8 | 15,090.8 | 43.2 | 29.2 | 1.3 | 1.8 | 75.5 |
| 1994 | 223.2 | 318.0 | -21.4 | 519.8 | 9,883.2 | 102.4 | 9,985.6 | 10,505.4 | 5,191.6 | 168.1 | 73.4 | 15,938.5 | 45.4 | 30.2 | 1.4 | 2.2 | 79.2 |
| 1995[1] | 203.3 | 300.6 | -22.7 | 481.2 | 9,722.7 | 76.3 | 9,799.0 | 10,280.2 | 5,199.9 | 161.5 | 75.0 | 15,716.6 | 44.6 | 30.2 | 1.5 | 2.1 | 78.4 |

[1] Preliminary. [2] Excludes Glass Fiber. [3] Includes silk, linen, jute and sisel & others. [4] Mill consumption plus imports less exports of semimanufactured and unmanufactured products. *Source: Fiber Economics Bureau, Inc.*

## Producer Price Index of Grey Synthetic Broadwovens 1982 = 100

| Year | Jan. | Feb. | Mar. | Apr. | May | June | July | Aug. | Sept. | Oct. | Nov. | Dec. | Average |
|---|---|---|---|---|---|---|---|---|---|---|---|---|---|
| 1987 | 101.9 | 101.9 | 102.2 | 103.4 | 103.9 | 105.3 | 106.4 | 106.9 | 107.9 | 108.6 | 109.0 | 109.2 | 105.6 |
| 1988 | 110.0 | 111.1 | 111.6 | 111.8 | 112.2 | 113.0 | 113.4 | 113.8 | 113.0 | 113.5 | 113.9 | 114.6 | 112.7 |
| 1989 | 114.3 | 112.0 | 112.2 | 112.2 | 112.1 | 113.1 | 114.7 | 115.0 | 115.0 | 115.8 | 115.9 | 115.3 | 114.0 |
| 1990 | 115.6 | 115.7 | 115.6 | 115.7 | 115.5 | 115.6 | 115.7 | 115.2 | 115.3 | 115.6 | 115.8 | 116.1 | 115.7 |
| 1991 | 115.7 | 114.7 | 114.4 | 114.1 | 114.3 | 113.9 | 114.8 | 116.4 | 116.5 | 116.5 | 116.8 | 118.2 | 115.5 |
| 1992 | 119.0 | 119.9 | 120.3 | 120.9 | 121.8 | 122.0 | 122.6 | 122.0 | 121.7 | 120.8 | 119.4 | 119.9 | 120.9 |
| 1993 | 119.6 | 119.1 | 119.1 | 119.2 | 117.1 | 118.4 | 118.0 | 118.0 | 116.9 | 117.3 | 115.2 | 114.5 | 117.7 |
| 1994 | 113.5 | 112.8 | 112.9 | 113.2 | 113.2 | 113.3 | 113.1 | 113.3 | 114.1 | 111.8 | 112.9 | 113.8 | 113.2 |
| 1995 | 114.8 | 116.8 | 116.7 | 116.3 | 116.6 | 117.1 | 115.4 | 114.8 | 116.9 | 116.4 | 114.7 | 116.2 | 116.1 |
| 1996[1] | 114.3 | 114.1 | 116.9 | 117.9 | 116.8 | 115.7 | 116.1 | 117.1 | 116.8 | 117.1 | 116.5 | 117.4 | 116.4 |

[1] Preliminary. *Source: Bureau of Labor Statistics, U.S. Department of Commerce*

# Rice

Rice is the world's second most popular foodstock after wheat, but international trading is small (5 percent) relative to world production. Global rice trade during calendar year 1996 of 18.8 million metric tons (milled basis) compares with the record high 21 million tons in 1995; initial forecasts for 1997 call for at 18.3 million tons. Until recently it was rare to find a country with annual rice imports in excess of 1 million tons, but in 1995 four nations imported at least that much paced by Indonesia with 3.0 million tons. 1996 Indonesian imports fell to 1.3 million tons and China's needs dropped from 2 million tons to 850,000 tons. However, Bangladesh, Brazil, and Iran each imported a million tons. Thailand is the largest exporter: 5.2 million tons in 1996 vs. a record high 5.9 million in 1995 and a forecast of 5.5 million in 1997. India is the second largest exporter followed by Vietnam.

World rice production in 1996/97 of a record 376.1 million metric tons (milled) compares with 375.7 million in 1995/96, the equivalent of 558 million tons and 551 million, respectively, of rough rice. World consumption of a record high 377.4 million tons in 1996/97 compares with 372.3 million in 1995/96.

China is the world's largest producer and consumer of rice with about a third of each; production in 1996/97 of 130 million tons (milled) was marginally higher than in 1995/96. China's recent annual rice acreage has been holding near 31 million hectares. China's consumption in 1996/97 of 132 million tons compares with 130 million in 1995/96., suggesting a need for larger imports in calendar 1997. India, the second largest producer and consumer produced 82 million tons in 1996/97, up 1 million from 1995/96, but India remains a net exporter of rice. Thailand, whose 1996/97 rice production was 4 percent of the world total is the largest exporter. The U.S. ranks fourth. The Western hemisphere is now the primary destination for U.S. rice. U.S. export prices are traditionally higher than competing Asian exporters.

U.S. rough rice production in 1996 of 176.1 million cwt. compares with 173.9 million in 1995 and the record 197.8 million in 1994. U.S. rice acreage peaked in 1981 at 3.8 million acres and has never returned to that level, 2.9 million were planted in 1996/97. The long grain yield for the 1996/97 crop of a record 6,053 lbs./acre compares with 5,621 lbs. in 1995/96. U.S. rice exports (rough and milled) in 1996/97 of 74 million cwt. compare with 82 million in 1995/96 and 100 million in 1994/95. U.S. ending 1996/97 stocks at 27.7 million cwt. (rough) compare with 25 million a year earlier and represent about 15.3 percent of total use. The 1996 U.S. average farm price in 1996/97 was forecast to range between $8.50 and $9.50 per cwt. vs. $9.09 in 1995/96.

### *Futures Market*

Rough rice futures and options are traded on the Chicago Board of Trade (CBOT).

**World Rice Supply and Distribution**[4] In Thousands of Metric Tons

| Year | Production | Exports | | | Imports | | | | | Utilization | | | Ending Stocks | | |
|---|---|---|---|---|---|---|---|---|---|---|---|---|---|---|---|
| | | U.S. | Non-U.S. | Total | Brazil | Iran | Saudi Arabia | Unaccounted | Total | China | India | Total | China | India | Total |
| 1992-3 | 526,888 | 2,644 | 12,271 | 14,915 | 831 | 1,161 | 859 | 1,939 | 14,915 | 127,000 | 75,368 | 357,926 | 29,602 | 10,600 | 54,780 |
| 1993-4 | 526,962 | 2,794 | 13,671 | 16,465 | 1,098 | 645 | 698 | 1,656 | 16,465 | 128,000 | 76,045 | 358,802 | 25,173 | 14,230 | 51,526 |
| 1994-5[1] | 541,248 | 3,073 | 17,951 | 21,024 | 987 | 1,633 | 615 | 871 | 21,024 | 129,000 | 77,106 | 367,364 | 21,256 | 14,083 | 49,518 |
| 1995-6[2] | 550,038 | 2,600 | 16,411 | 19,011 | 800 | 1,400 | 750 | 984 | 19,011 | 130,000 | 78,210 | 369,874 | 21,456 | 12,083 | 50,527 |
| 1996-7[3] | 559,413 | 2,300 | 15,830 | 18,130 | 1,200 | 1,200 | 750 | 1,007 | 18,130 | 132,000 | 79,500 | 376,437 | 22,206 | 11,583 | 51,349 |

[1] Preliminary. [2] Estimate. [3] Forecast. [4] Production is on a rough basis; all other data are reported on a milled basis. *Source: Foreign Agricultural Service, U.S. Department of Agriculture*

**World Exports of Rice (Milled Basis), by Country of Origin** In Thousands of Metric Tons

| Year | Bangladesh | Brazil | Burma | China | Egypt | India | Indonesia | Japan | Kazakhstan | Rep. of Korea | Pakistan | Philippines | Russia | Thailand | Vietnam |
|---|---|---|---|---|---|---|---|---|---|---|---|---|---|---|---|
| 1992-3 | 27,513 | 9,901 | 13,400 | 186,220 | 3,908 | 109,313 | 48,182 | 13,216 | 468 | 7,257 | 4,674 | 9,523 | 755 | 19,917 | 22,195 |
| 1993-4 | 27,064 | 10,515 | 15,086 | 177,700 | 4,198 | 120,462 | 46,638 | 9,793 | 403 | 6,404 | 5,993 | 9,923 | 769 | 19,200 | 24,302 |
| 1994-5[1] | 25,252 | 10,885 | 16,000 | 175,930 | 4,565 | 121,752 | 49,743 | 14,977 | 277 | 6,882 | 5,171 | 10,475 | 462 | 21,400 | 24,632 |
| 1995-6[2] | 26,533 | 10,050 | 17,241 | 185,214 | 3,387 | 119,202 | 50,308 | 13,435 | 277 | 6,386 | 5,905 | 11,174 | 462 | 21,818 | 26,667 |
| 1996-7[3] | 27,753 | 9,118 | 18,000 | 188,571 | 4,032 | 121,512 | 51,538 | 12,930 | ------ | 7,189 | 6,391 | 11,231 | ------ | 21,818 | 25,758 |

[1] Preliminary. [2] Estimate. [3] Forecast. *Source: Foreign Agricultural Service, U.S. Department of Agriculture*

**World Exports of Rice (Milled Basis), by Country of Origin** In Thousands of Metric Tons

| Year | Agrentina | Australia | Burma | China | Egypt | European Union | Guyana | India | Indonesia | Pakistan | Taiwan | Thailand | Uruguay | Vietnam | United States |
|---|---|---|---|---|---|---|---|---|---|---|---|---|---|---|---|
| 1992 | 204 | 500 | 185 | 933 | 209 | 376 | 114 | 563 | 60 | 1,358 | 188 | 4,776 | 327 | 1,914 | 2,107 |
| 1993 | 276 | 540 | 223 | 1,374 | 133 | 153 | 122 | 625 | 469 | 937 | 101 | 4,798 | 451 | 1,765 | 2,644 |
| 1994 | 215 | 570 | 619 | 1,519 | 262 | 185 | 183 | 600 | 225 | 1,399 | 117 | 4,738 | 396 | 2,222 | 2,794 |
| 1995[1] | 342 | 519 | 645 | 32 | 150 | 325 | 203 | 4,201 | 225 | 1,592 | 189 | 5,931 | 470 | 2,308 | 3,073 |
| 1996[2] | 395 | 475 | 265 | 300 | 75 | 175 | 225 | 3,250 | 0 | 1,663 | 150 | 5,251 | 550 | 3,100 | 2,600 |
| 1997[3] | 550 | 800 | 500 | 250 | 75 | 350 | 225 | 2,000 | 0 | 1,650 | 50 | 5,500 | 475 | 2,750 | 2,300 |

[1] Preliminary. [2] Estimate. [3] Forecast. *Source: Foreign Agricultural Service, U.S. Department of Agriculture*

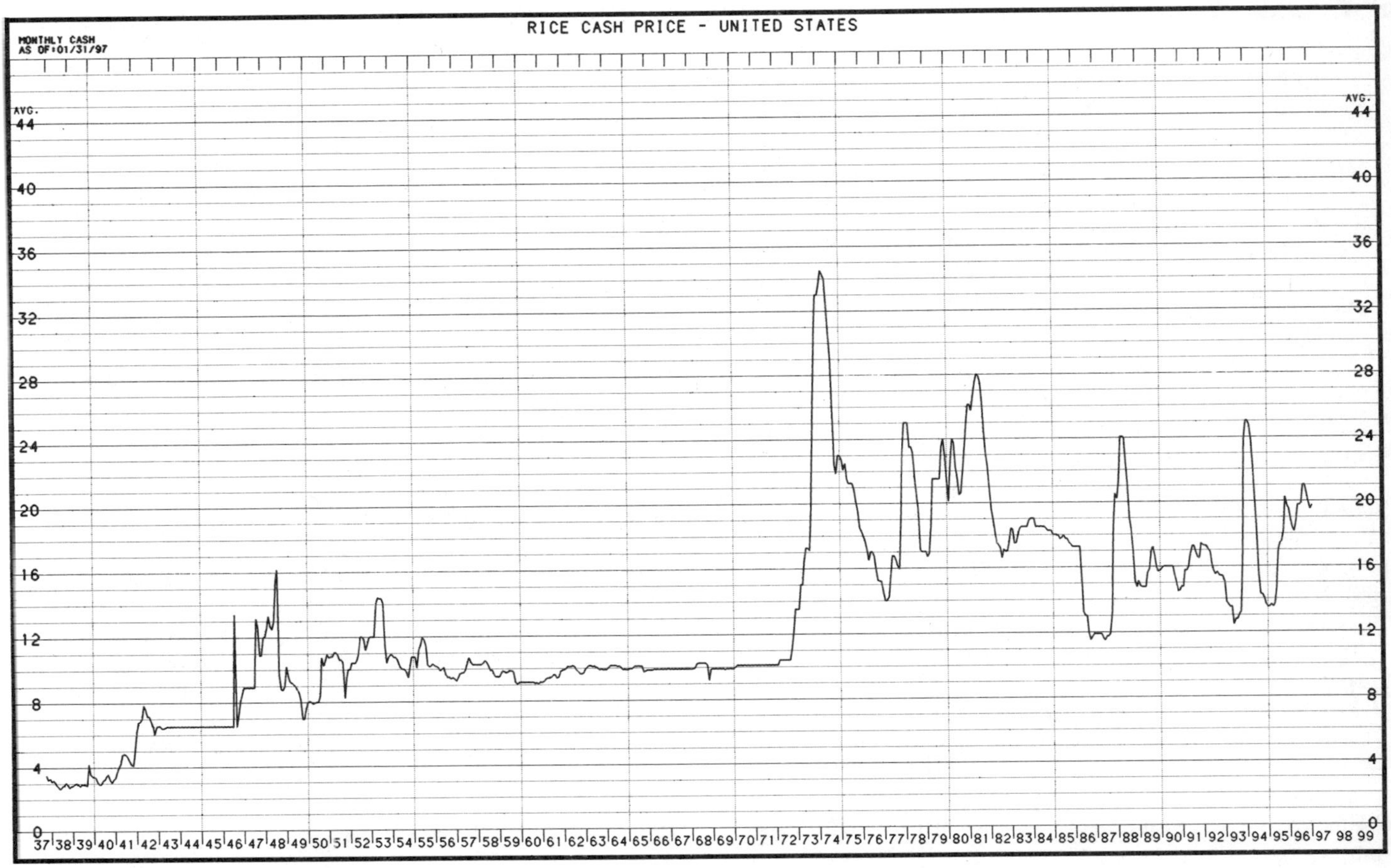


## Average Wholesale Price of Rice No. 2 (Medium)[1] Southwest Louisiana In Dollars Per Cwt. Bagged

| Year | Aug. | Sept. | Oct. | Nov. | Dec. | Jan. | Feb. | Mar. | Apr. | May | June | July | Average |
|---|---|---|---|---|---|---|---|---|---|---|---|---|---|
| 1982-3 | 16.50 | 16.50 | 16.50 | 16.70 | 17.80 | 17.30 | 16.50 | 16.50 | 16.50 | 17.10 | 17.50 | 17.50 | 16.90 |
| 1983-4 | 17.50 | 17.50 | 17.50 | 17.50 | 17.50 | 17.50 | 17.50 | 17.50 | 17.50 | 17.50 | 17.50 | 17.50 | 17.50 |
| 1984-5 | 16.00 | 16.00 | 15.50 | 15.50 | 15.50 | 15.50 | 15.50 | 16.00 | 16.20 | 16.30 | 18.00 | 16.20 | 16.00 |
| 1985-6 | 16.00 | 16.00 | 16.00 | 16.00 | 16.00 | 16.00 | 15.67 | 15.50 | 14.60 | 11.90 | 12.00 | 11.35 | 14.75 |
| 1986-7 | 10.00 | 10.00 | 10.00 | 10.00 | 10.00 | 10.00 | 10.00 | 10.50 | 11.25 | 11.15 | 11.20 | 11.20 | 10.45 |
| 1987-8 | 11.10 | 11.95 | 16.60 | 17.25 | 16.75 | 18.50 | 19.80 | 20.15 | 20.00 | 18.00 | 17.40 | 16.70 | 17.00 |
| 1988-9 | 16.40 | 16.20 | 14.50 | 14.50 | 14.00 | 13.90 | 13.75 | 13.50 | 13.50 | 14.60 | 14.65 | 15.75 | 14.60 |
| 1989-90 | 15.55 | 15.30 | 14.80 | 14.30 | 14.04 | 14.80 | 15.13 | 15.13 | 15.50 | 15.75 | 15.65 | 15.30 | 15.10 |
| 1990-1 | 14.75 | 13.90 | 13.50 | 13.50 | 13.50 | 14.90 | 14.90 | 15.05 | 16.05 | 16.15 | 16.50 | 16.35 | 14.90 |
| 1991-2 | 15.85 | 16.00 | 16.00 | 16.00 | 16.00 | 16.00 | 15.90 | 15.50 | 15.50 | 15.15 | 14.50 | 14.50 | 15.60 |
| 1992-3 | 14.50 | 14.00 | 14.50 | 14.15 | 13.40 | 13.40 | 13.00 | 12.80 | 12.40 | 11.94 | 12.00 | 12.00 | 13.15 |
| 1993-4 | 12.25 | 12.45 | 15.65 | 21.95 | 24.00 | 24.00 | 23.88 | 23.80 | 24.00 | 23.70 | 22.00 | 20.00 | 20.65 |
| 1994-5 | 18.30 | 15.88 | 15.00 | 15.00 | 14.00 | 13.80 | 14.16 | 14.38 | 14.38 | 14.70 | 14.75 | 14.55 | 14.91 |
| 1995-6 | 15.44 | 17.50 | 20.25 | 20.13 | 20.00 | 20.00 | 19.88 | 19.25 | 19.13 | 19.38 | 19.40 | 19.50 | 19.15 |
| 1996-7[2] | 19.50 | 19.50 | 19.25 | 19.25 | | | | | | | | | 19.38 |

[1] U.S. No. 2--broken not to exceed 4%. [2] Preliminary. *Source: Economic Research Service, U.S. Department of Agriculture*

## U.S. Rice (Rough) Production by Type and Variety In Thousands of Hundred of Pounds (Cwt.)

| Year | Long Grain | Medium Grain | Short Grain | Total | Year | Long Grain | Medium Grain | Short Grain | Total |
|---|---|---|---|---|---|---|---|---|---|
| 1987 | 88,995 | 37,651 | 2,957 | 129,603 | 1992 | 128,015 | 50,633 | 1,010 | 179,658 |
| 1988 | 119,364 | 36,891 | 3,642 | 159,897 | 1993 | 103,064 | 51,873 | 1,173 | 156,110 |
| 1989 | 109,161 | 41,441 | 3,885 | 154,487 | 1994 | 133,445 | 63,390 | 944 | 197,779 |
| 1990 | 107,806 | 47,328 | 954 | 156,088 | 1995 | 121,730 | 51,241 | 900 | 173,871 |
| 1991 | 109,137 | 47,567 | 753 | 157,457 | 1996[1] | 113,462 | 56,790 | 1,069 | 171,321 |

[1] Preliminary. *Source: National Agricultural Statistics Service, U.S. Department of Agriculture*

## Salient Statistics of Rice, Rough & Milled (Rough Equivalent) in the United States In Millions of Cwt.

| Crop Year Beginning August | Supply | | | | Disappearance | | | | | | | | Government Support Program | | | | |
|---|---|---|---|---|---|---|---|---|---|---|---|---|---|---|---|---|---|
| | | | | | Domestic | | | | | | | | | Loan Rate ($ Per Cwt.) | | | |
| | | | | | | | | | | | | | | Rough[3] | | | |
| | Stocks August 1 | Production | Imports | Total Supply | Food | Brewers | Seed | Total | Residual | Exports | Total Disappearance | CCC Stocks July 31 | Put Under Price Support | Long | Medium | All Classes | Milled Long |
| 1991-2 | 24.6 | 159.4 | 5.3 | 189.3 | 67.1 | 15.5 | 4.1 | 86.7 | 8.8 | 66.4 | 161.8 | .4 | 108.3 | 6.65 | 6.11 | 6.50 | 10.74 |
| 1992-3 | 27.4 | 179.7 | 6.1 | 213.2 | 69.0 | 15.1 | 3.8 | 87.9 | 8.8 | 77.0 | 173.7 | .1 | 125.8 | 6.66 | 6.13 | 6.50 | 10.74 |
| 1993-4 | 39.4 | 156.1 | 6.9 | 202.5 | 71.2 | 14.3 | 4.3 | 89.8 | 11.7 | 75.2 | 176.7 | 0 | 30.9 | 6.66 | 6.13 | 6.50 | 10.75 |
| 1994-5 | 25.8 | 197.8 | 7.0 | 230.6 | 74.0 | 14.5 | 4.1 | 92.6 | 7.4 | 99.4 | 199.3 | .1 | 131.2 | 6.65 | 6.12 | 6.50 | 10.72 |
| 1995-6[1] | 31.3 | 173.9 | 7.4 | 212.6 | 77.0 | 15.2 | 3.8 | 96.0 | 8.5 | 83.0 | 187.6 | 0 | 100.9 | 6.65 | 6.11 | 6.50 | 10.69 |
| 1996-7[2] | 25.0 | 171.3 | 7.8 | 204.1 | 78.5 | 15.1 | 3.7 | 97.3 | 7.5 | 75.0 | 179.8 | 0 | 67.8 | 6.68 | 6.17 | 6.50 | 10.77 |

[1] Preliminary. [2] Estimate. [3] Loan rate for each class of rice is the sum of the whole kernels' loan rate weighted by its milling yield (average 56%) and the broken kernels' loan rate weighted by its milling yield (average 12%). *Source: Economic Research Service, U.S. Department of Agriculture*

## Acreage, Yield, Production and Prices of Rice in the United States

| Crop Year | Acreage Harvested (1,000 Acres) | | | Yield Per Harvested Acre (In Lbs.) | | Production 1,000 Cwt. | | | Value of Production $1,000 | Wholesale Prices ($ Per Cwt.) | | Milled Rice, Average C.I.F. at Rotterdam ($ Per Metric Ton) | | |
|---|---|---|---|---|---|---|---|---|---|---|---|---|---|---|
| | Southern States | California | United States | California | United States | Southern States | California | United States | | Arkansas[2] | Houston[3] | U.S. No. 2[4] | Thai "A"[5] | Thai "B"[5] |
| 1991-2 | 2,425 | 350 | 2,775 | 8,100 | 5,674 | 129,107 | 30,260 | 159,367 | 1,200,629 | 16.20 | 17.15 | 359 | 396 | 328 |
| 1992-3 | 2,738 | 394 | 3,132 | 8,500 | 5,736 | 146,168 | 33,490 | 179,658 | 1,057,272 | 14.30 | 15.25 | 287 | 385 | 290 |
| 1993-4 | 2,396 | 437 | 2,833 | 8,300 | 5,510 | 119,839 | 36,271 | 156,110 | 1,246,875 | 21.15 | 20.75 | 413 | 413 | 335 |
| 1994-5 | 2,831 | 485 | 3,316 | 8,500 | 5,964 | 156,555 | 41,224 | 197,779 | 1,336,570 | 14.47 | 14.70 | 325 | 412 | 331 |
| 1995-6 | 2,628 | 465 | 3,093 | 7,600 | 5,621 | 138,519 | 35,352 | 173,871 | 1,587,236 | 19.10 | 19.15 | 404 | NA | 407 |
| 1996-7[1] | 2,299 | 500 | 2,799 | 7,490 | 6,121 | 133,862 | 37,459 | 171,321 | 1,611,959 | 19.33 | 20.52 | 422 | NA | 377 |

[1] Preliminary. [2] F.O.B. mills, Arkansas, medium. [3] Houston, Texas (long grain). [4] Milled, 4%, container, FAS. 5 SWR, 100%, bulk. NA = Not available. *Source: Economic Research Service, U.S. Department of Agriculture*

## U.S. Exports of Milled Rice, by Country of Destination In Thousands of Metric Tons

| Year Beginning October | Canada | Germany | Haiti | Iran | Ivory Coast | Jamaica | Mexico | Netherlands | Peru | Russia[2] | Saudi Arabia | Senegal | South Africa | Switzerland | United Kingdom | Total |
|---|---|---|---|---|---|---|---|---|---|---|---|---|---|---|---|---|
| 1990-1 | 127.4 | 49.9 | 124.8 | 0 | 69.4 | 75.5 | 96.5 | 91.6 | 61.5 | 0 | 189.1 | 63.2 | 115.9 | 108.6 | 38.8 | 2,395.1 |
| 1991-2 | 143.7 | 44.9 | 116.9 | 11.6 | 73.4 | 46.3 | 157.0 | 67.7 | 43.6 | 55.6 | 179.6 | 61.7 | 136.6 | 94.2 | 59.8 | 2,279.0 |
| 1992-3 | 146.0 | 67.6 | 152.9 | 184.3 | 107.3 | 39.4 | 241.5 | 120.9 | 61.6 | 74.8 | 223.5 | 91.5 | 122.1 | 71.2 | 72.2 | 2,709.9 |
| 1993-4 | 141.3 | 41.7 | 57.2 | 60.4 | 34.2 | 53.8 | 234.0 | 92.8 | 47.0 | 6.4 | 180.5 | 90.1 | 110.9 | 64.8 | 82.4 | 2,432.5 |
| 1994-5 | 160.0 | 43.1 | 210.2 | 240.6 | 92.0 | 88.5 | 309.6 | 170.3 | 81.8 | 0 | 176.1 | 28.1 | 106.1 | 91.2 | 58.7 | 3,763.1 |
| 1995-6[1] | 172.1 | 42.7 | 149.6 | 24.5 | 61.3 | 63.1 | 359.1 | 113.9 | 97.7 | 0 | 141.5 | 0 | 169.9 | 80.3 | 85.4 | 2,825.9 |

[1] Preliminary. [2] Formerly part of the U.S.S.R.; data not reported separately until 1992. *Source: Economic Research Service, U.S. Department of Agriculture*

## U.S. Rice Exports by Export Program In Thousands of Metric Tons

| Fiscal Year | PL 480 | Section 416 | CCC Credit Programs[2] | CCC African Relief Exports | EEP[3] | Export Programs[4] | Exports Outside Specified Export Programs | Total U.S. Rice Exports | % Export Programs as a Share of Total Exports |
|---|---|---|---|---|---|---|---|---|---|
| 1991 | 411 | 0 | 183 | 0 | 76 | 669 | 1,611 | 2,395 | 28 |
| 1992 | 382 | 0 | 220 | 0 | 358 | 982 | 1,177 | 2,279 | 43 |
| 1993 | 496 | 0 | 235 | 0 | 278 | 1,108 | 1,486 | 2,710 | 41 |
| 1994 | 352 | 0 | 155 | 0 | 46 | 553 | 2,010 | 2,433 | 23 |
| 1995 | 233 | 0 | 321 | 0 | 113 | 667 | 3,096 | 3,763 | 18 |
| 1996[1] | 182 | 0 | 215 | 0 | 0 | 397 | 2,429 | 2,826 | 14 |

[1] Preliminary. [2] May not completely reflect exports made under these programs. [3] Sales not shipments. [4] Adjusted for estimated overlap between CCC export credit and EEP shipments. *Source: Economic Research Service, U.S. Department of Agriculture*

## Average Price Received by Farmers for Rice (Rough) in the U.S. In Dollars Per Hundred Pounds (Cwt.)

| Year | Aug. | Sept. | Oct. | Nov. | Dec. | Jan. | Feb. | Mar. | Apr. | May | June | July | Average[2] |
|---|---|---|---|---|---|---|---|---|---|---|---|---|---|
| 1991-2 | 7.16 | 7.67 | 7.65 | 7.84 | 7.98 | 7.84 | 7.97 | 7.78 | 7.46 | 7.18 | 6.97 | 6.99 | 7.58 |
| 1992-3 | 6.60 | 6.41 | 6.40 | 6.42 | 6.39 | 6.36 | 6.06 | 5.64 | 5.52 | 5.24 | 5.02 | 4.92 | 5.89 |
| 1993-4 | 5.19 | 5.21 | 6.10 | 8.06 | 8.91 | 8.98 | 10.10 | 10.20 | 9.93 | 10.00 | 8.88 | 7.80 | 7.98 |
| 1994-5 | 6.87 | 6.89 | 6.47 | 6.53 | 6.56 | 6.78 | 6.71 | 6.64 | 6.70 | 6.75 | 7.03 | 7.17 | 6.78 |
| 1995-6 | 7.64 | 7.95 | 8.77 | 9.12 | 9.36 | 9.33 | 9.10 | 9.31 | 9.34 | 9.69 | 9.74 | 9.68 | 9.15 |
| 1996-7[1] | 9.92 | 9.95 | 9.54 | 9.53 | 9.63 | 9.65 | | | | | | | 9.70 |

[1] Preliminary. [2] Weighted average by sales. *Source: Economic Research Service, U.S. Department of Agriculture*

# Rubber

According to the International Rubber Study Group (IRSG), world production of natural rubber in June 1996 was 470,000 tonnes, an increase of over 4 percent from May. Of the June total, 75,000 tonnes were produced on rubber estates and 395,000 tonnes by smallholdings. Over the January-June 1996 period, world production of natural rubber was 2.92 million tonnes. Over the comparable period of 1995, production was 2.79 million tonnes, or 4 percent less. For all of 1995, production of natural rubber was 5.87 million tonnes, the highest total in a number of years. Of the total, 19 percent was from rubber estates and 81 percent was produced by smallholdings.

Consumption of natural rubber in June 1996 was 500,000 tonnes, down 2 percent from May. For the first half of 1996, world natural rubber consumption was 3.1 million tonnes, up 3 percent from the comparable period of 1995. For all of 1995, world consumption was 5.91 million tonnes, one of the highest levels in years. For 1995, world consumption exceeded production by 40,000 tonnes. In 1994, production exceeded consumption by 50,000 tonnes. For the first half of 1996, consumption has exceeded production by 130,000 tonnes.

Producer's stocks of natural rubber in June 1996 were 380,000 tonnes, the same as in May and almost 3 percent more than in December 1995. Consumers reported stocks in June 1996 were 214,000 tonnes, down 11 percent from the previous month. At the end of December 1995, consumers reported stocks were 279,000 tonnes. Consumers total stocks of natural rubber in June 1996 were 710,000 tonnes, down 4 percent from the previous month. At the end of 1995, consumers total stocks were 780,000 tonnes. Stocks afloat in June 1996 were 500,000 tonnes. Total stocks of natural rubber in June 1996 were 1.5 million tonnes, down 2 percent from the previous month. In December 1995, world stocks were 1.7 million tonnes.

The major producers of natural rubber are Indonesia, Malaysia, and Thailand. For 1995, Thailand produced 1.8 million tonnes of natural rubber or about 30 percent of the world total. Indonesia produced 1.5 million tonnes or 24 percent of world production. Malaysian production was 1.1 million tonnes or 19 percent of global output. Other large producers of natural rubber in 1995 included India with 500,000 tonnes, China with 360,000 tonnes, and Sri Lanka with 106,000 tonnes. In 1994, Indonesia reported it had 3.2 million hectares of plantation rubber. In 1995, Thailand had 1.9 million hectares of plantation rubber while Malaysia had 1.7 million.

World production of synthetic rubber in June 1996 was 790,000 tonnes, the same as in the previous month. For the first half of 1996, world synthetic rubber production was 4.8 million tonnes. This was about the same level as in the comparable period of 1995. For all of 1995, world production of synthetic rubber was 9.4 million tonnes, the highest level since 1990. The major producers of synthetic rubber are the U.S., Japan, Russia, and France. In 1995, U.S. synthetic rubber production was 2.5 million tonnes. This represented 27 percent of the world total. Russia produced 830,000 tonnes or about 9 percent of world output. Japan's production was 1.5 million tonnes or almost 16 percent of global output. French production of synthetic rubber in 1995 was 618,000 tonnes. Other large producers include China, Germany and Italy.

World consumption of synthetic rubber in June 1996 was 790,000 tonnes, down 2 percent from the previous month. For the January-June 1996 period, world consumption was 4.8 million tonnes. This was some 2 percent above the comparable period of 1995. For all of 1995, global consumption of synthetic rubber was 9.3 million tonnes, the highest total since 1992. For 1995, production of synthetic rubber exceeded consumption by 160,000 tonnes.

Reported stocks of synthetic rubber in June 1996 were 981,000 tonnes, down 1 percent from the previous month. Russian Federation stocks of synthetic rubber in June 1996 were 210,000 tonnes, the same as in May. Synthetic rubber stocks in China in June 1996 were 100,000 tonnes, the same as in May. Synthetic rubber stocks elsewhere in June 1996 were 520,000 tonnes, down 2 percent from the prior month. Stocks afloat in June 1996 were 230,000 tonnes, up close to 10 percent from May. Total world stocks of synthetic rubber in June 1996 were 2.04 million tonnes, the same level as in May 1996. At the end of 1996, stocks were 2.02 million tonnes.

### *Futures Markets*

Rubber futures are traded on the Kobe Rubber Exchange (KRE), the Tokyo Commodity Exchange, (TOCOM), the Kuala Lumpur Commodity Exchange (KLCE), and the Singapore Commodity Exchange Ltd.

**U.S. Imports of Natural Rubber (Includes Latex & Guayule)** In Thousands of Metric Tons

| Year | Jan. | Feb. | Mar. | Apr. | May | June | July | Aug. | Sept. | Oct. | Nov. | Dec. | Total |
|---|---|---|---|---|---|---|---|---|---|---|---|---|---|
| 1986 | 66.7 | 71.5 | 77.9 | 84.5 | 48.4 | 54.9 | 70.1 | 45.2 | 63.9 | 73.5 | 54.0 | 56.7 | 721.0 |
| 1987 | 55.9 | 91.3 | 82.0 | 33.3 | 64.6 | 58.9 | 64.2 | 47.6 | 59.4 | 57.7 | 63.9 | 78.9 | 769.1 |
| 1988 | 83.2 | 69.6 | 87.0 | 68.6 | 67.2 | 64.9 | 49.5 | 83.3 | 59.1 | 69.3 | 77.4 | 74.7 | 791.8 |
| 1989 | 99.3 | 52.2 | 99.1 | 74.6 | 87.5 | 63.8 | 77.9 | 65.6 | 69.1 | 69.5 | 78.9 | 69.1 | 880.9 |
| 1990 | 72.3 | 58.6 | 81.9 | 63.1 | 89.5 | 77.7 | 60.4 | 61.0 | 83.0 | 55.7 | 81.7 | 75.7 | 820.1 |
| 1991 | 59.9 | 54.1 | 69.5 | 90.9 | 59.6 | 56.7 | 53.4 | 52.4 | 65.5 | 74.4 | 71.3 | 68.9 | 776.2 |
| 1992 | 77.5 | 75.2 | 84.7 | 64.7 | 79.0 | 73.8 | 80.5 | 77.2 | 73.9 | 81.3 | 68.1 | 77.5 | 913.4 |
| 1993 | 95.3 | 79.9 | 93.9 | 86.3 | 74.1 | 81.2 | 83.6 | 77.8 | 69.2 | 73.4 | 86.0 | 86.9 | 987.6 |
| 1994 | 87.5 | 74.7 | 102.6 | 78.9 | 88.3 | 77.8 | 66.7 | 85.0 | 78.8 | 89.3 | 70.0 | 76.0 | 975.6 |
| 1995[1] | 81.7 | 86.9 | 102.3 | 90.2 | 94.1 | 93.4 | 78.0 | 81.0 | 81.5 | 89.2 | 79.1 | 68.7 | 1,026.1 |
| 1996[1] | 105.4 | 86.1 | 82.2 | 90.6 | 65.1 | 70.4 | 79.0 | 81.0 | 82.1 | 113.6 | | | 855.5 |

[1] Preliminary. *Source: International Rubber Study Group*

## World Rubber Production[1] In Thousands of Metric Tons

| Year | Natural: China | India | Indonesia | Malaysia | Nigeria | Philippines | Sri Lanka | Thailand | Vietnam | World Total | Synthetic: Canada | Germany | Japan | United Kingdom | United States | Russia[3] | World Total |
|---|---|---|---|---|---|---|---|---|---|---|---|---|---|---|---|---|---|
| 1986 | 209.7 | 219.0 | 1,049.2 | 1,538.6 | 36.8 | 146.0 | 137.8 | 786.0 | 54.0 | 4,490 | 187.1 | 452.5 | 1,150.1 | 249.2 | 2,119.1 | 2,320 | 9,260 |
| 1987 | 237.6 | 227.4 | 1,203.3 | 1,578.7 | 55.3 | 147.2 | 121.8 | 925.6 | 55.0 | 4,840 | 179.8 | 468.4 | 1,191.9 | 257.0 | 2,182.1 | 2,366 | 9,450 |
| 1988 | 239.8 | 254.8 | 1,235.0 | 1,661.6 | 80.5 | 51.6 | 122.4 | 978.9 | 60.0 | 5,020 | 197.0 | 499.6 | 1,298.8 | 312.8 | 2,334.7 | 2,435 | 10,160 |
| 1989 | 242.8 | 288.6 | 1,256.0 | 1,415.6 | 118.4 | 56.7 | 110.7 | 1,178.9 | 85.0 | 5,150 | 188.0 | 507.6 | 1,352.7 | 311.4 | 2,261.4 | 2,358 | 10,150 |
| 1990 | 264.2 | 323.5 | 1,262.0 | 1,291.0 | 152.0 | 61.2 | 113.1 | 1,275.3 | 103.0 | 5,120 | 195.0 | 524.5 | 1,425.8 | 274.3 | 2,114.5 | 2,277 | 9,910 |
| 1991 | 296.4 | 360.2 | 1,284.0 | 1,255.7 | 155.7 | 59.6 | 103.9 | 1,341.2 | 87.0 | 5,170 | 180.0 | 504.4 | 1,377.3 | 251.3 | 2,050.0 | 2,105 | 9,270 |
| 1992 | 309.0 | 383.0 | 1,387.0 | 1,173.2 | 126.0 | 56.9 | 106.1 | 1,531.0 | 114.0 | 5,460 | 206.0 | 544.7 | 1,389.9 | 280.1 | 2,300.0 | 1,495 | 9,240 |
| 1993 | 326.0 | 428.1 | 1,301.3 | 1,074.3 | 105.0 | 57.5 | 104.2 | 1,553.4 | 90.0 | 5,340 | 187.0 | 569.7 | 1,309.8 | 289.8 | 2,180.0 | 1,030 | 8,560 |
| 1994 | 341.0 | 464.0 | 1,360.8 | 1,100.6 | 95.0 | 58.9 | 105.3 | 1,717.9 | 88.0 | 5,670 | 197.0 | 621.6 | 1,349.0 | 290.7 | 2,390.0 | 630 | 8,870 |
| 1995[2] | 360.0 | 499.6 | 1,456.8 | 1,089.3 | 93.0 | 59.8 | 105.7 | 1,784.4 | 95.0 | 5,870 | 175.0 | 487.5 | 1,497.6 | 319.8 | 2,540.0 | 830 | 9,410 |

[1] Including rubber in the form of latex. [2] Preliminary. *Source: International Rubber Study Group*

## World Consumption of Natural and Synthetic Rubber In Thousands of Metric Tons

| Year | Natural: Australia | Brazil | Canada | France | Germany | Japan | United Kingdom | United States | World Total | Synthetic: Canada | France | Germany | Japan | United Kingdom | United States | World Total |
|---|---|---|---|---|---|---|---|---|---|---|---|---|---|---|---|---|
| 1986 | 30.6 | 105.6 | 86.0 | 158.7 | 198.7 | 535.0 | 130.0 | 743.0 | 4,460 | 190.2 | 315.0 | 426.0 | 910.0 | 195.0 | 2,019.6 | 9,280 |
| 1987 | 35.5 | 115.4 | 98.0 | 170.0 | 198.5 | 568.0 | 134.0 | 789.0 | 4,800 | 210.0 | 316.4 | 453.4 | 946.0 | 216.0 | 2,017.3 | 9,650 |
| 1988 | 40.5 | 125.3 | 82.5 | 181.0 | 203.6 | 623.0 | 140.0 | 858.3 | 5,100 | 202.0 | 315.0 | 471.0 | 1,042.0 | 226.5 | 2,016.8 | 9,940 |
| 1989 | 43.5 | 124.3 | 84.9 | 184.0 | 221.1 | 657.0 | 132.5 | 866.9 | 5,190 | 191.1 | 358.0 | 476.0 | 1,103.0 | 240.0 | 2,051.0 | 10,070 |
| 1990 | 34.0 | 121.3 | 84.0 | 179.0 | 208.7 | 677.0 | 136.0 | 807.5 | 5,200 | 185.4 | 351.0 | 511.0 | 1,133.0 | 223.0 | 1,820.8 | 9,710 |
| 1991 | 34.0 | 125.0 | 76.3 | 183.0 | 210.7 | 689.5 | 119.0 | 755.8 | 5,100 | 183.9 | 342.0 | 502.0 | 1,118.5 | 201.0 | 1,768.1 | 9,310 |
| 1992 | 36.5 | 119.4 | 86.5 | 179.0 | 212.8 | 685.4 | 124.5 | 910.2 | 5,390 | 198.0 | 365.4 | 506.0 | 1,080.6 | 231.0 | 1,959.6 | 9,330 |
| 1993 | 45.0 | 125.0 | 91.5 | 168.5 | 174.9 | 631.0 | 119.0 | 966.7 | 5,380 | 200.0 | 314.7 | 488.0 | 1,022.0 | 212.0 | 2,001.0 | 8,650 |
| 1994 | 48.5 | 124.0 | 106.0 | 179.8 | 186.4 | 639.8 | 135.0 | 1,001.7 | 5,620 | 205.0 | 400.1 | 512.2 | 1,026.2 | 217.0 | 2,117.6 | 8,880 |
| 1995[1] | 49.0 | 140.0 | 121.0 | 179.0 | 207.0 | 692.0 | 122.0 | 1,003.9 | 5,910 | 198.1 | 420.0 | 421.0 | 1,085.0 | 233.0 | 2,172.0 | 9,250 |

[1] Preliminary. *Source: International Rubber Study Group*

## World Stocks of Natural & Synthetic Rubber (by Countries) on January 1 In Thousands of Metric Tons

| Year | Total Synthetic | In Producing Countries: Africa | Cambodia | Indonesia | Malaysia | Singapore | Sri Lanka | Thailand | Vietnam | Other Asia | Total Natural | In Consuming Countries (Reported Stocks): Brazil | India | Japan | United States | Total |
|---|---|---|---|---|---|---|---|---|---|---|---|---|---|---|---|---|
| 1986 | 1,750 | 17.8 | 1.0 | 90.0 | 191.8 | 22.0 | 12.2 | 47.1 | 6.0 | 16.0 | 520 | 13.5 | 58.2 | 70.7 | 95.2 | 238 |
| 1987 | 1,710 | 16.2 | 1.0 | 90.0 | 207.3 | 21.6 | 23.6 | 32.5 | 6.0 | 15.1 | 530 | 13.3 | 85.5 | 61.9 | 73.0 | 234 |
| 1988 | 1,520 | 19.1 | 1.0 | 100.0 | 208.5 | 21.6 | 20.0 | 37.8 | 6.0 | 13.8 | 510 | 13.5 | 58.2 | 70.7 | 95.2 | 224 |
| 1989 | 1,800 | 23.2 | 1.0 | 100.0 | 286.5 | 32.2 | 23.2 | 53.0 | 6.0 | 6.7 | 540 | 20.5 | 80.9 | 97.2 | 61.7 | 260 |
| 1990 | 988 | 26.9 | 1.0 | 110.0 | 248.3 | 24.0 | 27.0 | 53.7 | 8.0 | 7.3 | 510 | 16.0 | 78.4 | 105.6 | 92.0 | 292 |
| 1991 | 1,011 | 21.7 | 1.0 | 114.0 | 190.3 | 20.2 | 29.8 | 83.7 | 11.0 | 7.1 | 490 | 12.0 | 92.9 | 91.6 | 94.3 | 291 |
| 1992 | 973 | 24.4 | 1.0 | 68.0 | 196.1 | 25.9 | 17.3 | 89.3 | 9.0 | 6.9 | 460 | 9.0 | 106.0 | 92.7 | 109.4 | 317 |
| 1993 | 965 | 22.6 | 1.0 | 70.0 | 187.2 | 15.3 | 16.0 | 89.0 | 12.0 | 7.1 | 510 | 2.0 | 90.9 | 82.9 | 108.0 | 284 |
| 1994 | 893 | 22.2 | 1.0 | 40.0 | 159.2 | 10.6 | 17.2 | 115.4 | 9.0 | 7.4 | 480 | 5.0 | 96.4 | 85.4 | 71.3 | 258 |
| 1995 | 863 | 20.8 | 1.0 | 40.0 | 187.0 | 10.5 | 16.5 | 96.1 | 8.0 | 8.5 | 400 | 5.0 | 94.1 | 72.9 | 45.2 | 217 |
| 1996[1] | 967 | 18.5 | 1.0 | 40.0 | 175.6 | 1.0 | 17.0 | 95.0 | 9.0 | 8.2 | 370 | 7.0 | 127.4 | 77.1 | 67.1 | 279 |

[1] Preliminary. *Source: International Rubber Study Group*

## Net Exports of Natural Rubber from Producing Areas In Thousands of Metric Tons

| Year | Cambodia | Guatemala | Indonesia | Liberia | Malaysia | Nigeria | Sri Lanka | Thailand | Vietnam | Other Africa[2] | Other Asia[3] | World Total |
|---|---|---|---|---|---|---|---|---|---|---|---|---|
| 1986 | 20.0 | 6.2 | 958.7 | 90.4 | 1,485.2 | 26.0 | 110.0 | 755.2 | 35.0 | 78.0 | 35.2 | 3,630 |
| 1987[4] | 20.0 | 10.4 | 1,092.8 | 91.1 | 1,578.5 | 43.7 | 106.0 | 873.2 | 35.0 | 94.0 | 28.1 | 3,950 |
| 1988 | 21.0 | 9.8 | 1,132.0 | 105.6 | 1,563.6 | 65.8 | 99.3 | 906.4 | 37.9 | 107.0 | 36.8 | 4,070 |
| 1989 | 32.0 | 11.0 | 1,151.8 | 106.0 | 1,364.8 | 101.3 | 86.0 | 1,100.6 | 57.7 | 115.0 | 38.2 | 4,170 |
| 1990 | 28.0 | 13.4 | 1,077.3 | 19.0 | 1,185.6 | 121.0 | 86.7 | 1,150.8 | 75.9 | 118.0 | 37.6 | 3,990 |
| 1991 | 21.0 | 14.3 | 1,220.0 | 32.0 | 1,041.2 | 63.0 | 76.4 | 1,231.9 | 62.9 | 126.0 | 44.0 | 3,950 |
| 1992 | 20.0 | 15.7 | 1,268.1 | 30.0 | 939.1 | 107.0 | 78.6 | 1,412.9 | 80.9 | 135.0 | 44.6 | 4,070 |
| 1993 | 21.0 | 16.9 | 1,214.3 | 45.0 | 769.8 | 87.0 | 69.6 | 1,396.8 | 63.0 | 134.0 | 52.8 | 3,920 |
| 1994 | 32.0 | 22.3 | 1,244.8 | 31.0 | 782.1 | 76.0 | 69.1 | 1,605.0 | 59.0 | 143.0 | 65.0 | 4,220 |
| 1995[1] | 34.0 | 21.0 | 1,323.8 | 13.0 | 777.5 | 71.0 | 68.2 | 1,635.5 | 63.0 | 138.3 | 54.1 | 4,230 |

[1] Preliminary. [2] Includes Cameroon, Cote d'Ivoire, Gabon, Ghana and Zaire. [3] Includes Myanmar, Papua New Guinea and the Philippines. [4] Prior to 1987, data shown for Central American Common Market (C.A.C.M.) *Source: International Rubber Study Group*

# RUBBER

**Average Spot Crude Rubber Prices (Smoked Sheets[1]) in New York** In Cents Per Pound

| Year | Jan. | Feb. | Mar. | Apr. | May | June | July | Aug. | Sept. | Oct. | Nov. | Dec. | Average |
|---|---|---|---|---|---|---|---|---|---|---|---|---|---|
| 1987 | 45.9 | 46.5 | 43.8 | 47.4 | 49.1 | 50.6 | 53.5 | 53.7 | 54.2 | 53.8 | 53.1 | 54.0 | 50.5 |
| 1988 | 54.6 | 53.8 | 54.9 | 55.7 | 58.6 | 67.6 | 66.1 | 63.8 | 60.1 | 55.2 | 53.0 | 54.1 | 58.1 |
| 1989 | 56.0 | 59.3 | 54.1 | 55.2 | 52.1 | 49.5 | 49.2 | 47.2 | 46.1 | 46.1 | 45.6 | 44.8 | 50.4 |
| 1990 | 44.7 | 45.8 | 45.9 | 45.6 | 45.8 | 46.0 | 45.8 | 47.5 | 48.4 | 46.5 | 46.3 | 47.1 | 46.3 |
| 1991 | 47.5 | 48.8 | 49.1 | 46.0 | 45.2 | 45.3 | 44.6 | 44.4 | 44.3 | 44.5 | 44.8 | 44.2 | 45.7 |
| 1992 | 43.1 | 44.0 | 44.5 | 45.9 | 46.4 | 46.6 | 46.8 | 47.1 | 46.9 | 47.8 | 48.0 | 48.0 | 46.3 |
| 1993 | 48.5 | 48.3 | 46.4 | 44.2 | 43.8 | 43.8 | 43.3 | 43.9 | 44.5 | 44.2 | 44.9 | 44.7 | 45.0 |
| 1994 | 44.9 | 46.1 | 49.6 | 50.8 | 51.4 | 55.1 | 62.5 | 66.4 | 67.2 | 73.5 | 71.8 | 77.4 | 59.7 |
| 1995 | 85.7 | 92.6 | 94.2 | 93.4 | 89.5 | 80.6 | 72.1 | 68.5 | 70.7 | 73.6 | 83.2 | 83.4 | 82.3 |
| 1996 | 80.3 | 79.9 | 79.8 | 75.1 | 77.0 | 75.1 | 71.0 | 69.1 | 68.8 | 66.3 | 66.3 | 66.1 | 72.9 |

[1] No. 1 ribbed, plantation rubber. *Source: Wall Street Journal*

**Natural Rubber Prices in London** In British Pounds Per Metric Ton

| Year | Jan. | Feb. | Mar. | Apr. | May | June | July | Aug. | Sept. | Oct. | Nov. | Dec. | Average |
|---|---|---|---|---|---|---|---|---|---|---|---|---|---|
| Buyers' Price RSS 1 (CIF) | | | | | | | | | | | | | |
| 1993 | 644.4 | 683.5 | 635.7 | 584.2 | 576.1 | 585.0 | 588.0 | 597.3 | 593.9 | 599.4 | 605.1 | 610.9 | 608.6 |
| 1994 | 612.6 | 639.5 | 686.0 | 698.9 | 712.6 | 771.7 | 878.5 | 886.8 | 884.7 | 911.8 | 875.8 | 1,004.5 | 797.0 |
| 1995 | 1,141.9 | 1,170.8 | 1,209.6 | 1,189.2 | 1,174.9 | 1,004.9 | 894.9 | 886.0 | 921.4 | 946.7 | 1,082.6 | 1,099.7 | 1,060.2 |
| 1996 | 1,063.1 | 1,066.1 | 1,057.3 | 990.8 | 1,025.1 | 999.6 | 912.0 | 881.2 | 880.5 | 829.8 | 803.3 | 800.3 | 942.4 |
| Buyers' Prices RSS 3 (CIF) | | | | | | | | | | | | | |
| 1993 | 614.4 | 667.5 | 625.3 | 578.0 | 566.3 | 573.2 | 575.6 | 581.5 | 565.3 | 570.5 | 574.8 | 578.1 | 589.2 |
| 1994 | 586.2 | 629.2 | 671.0 | 688.2 | 706.0 | 766.0 | 872.6 | 880.8 | 875.0 | 901.8 | 866.8 | 975.2 | 784.9 |
| 1995 | 1,122.9 | 1,157.0 | 1,188.2 | 1,174.2 | 1,161.0 | 988.2 | 882.7 | 859.2 | 911.3 | 941.4 | 1,074.2 | 1,093.6 | 1,046.2 |
| 1996 | 1,057.3 | 1,058.6 | 1,049.9 | 981.4 | 1,015.5 | 984.6 | 895.2 | 863.0 | 862.0 | 814.7 | 790.7 | 782.1 | 929.6 |
| Sellers' Prices SMR 20 (CIF) | | | | | | | | | | | | | |
| 1993 | 602.5 | 640.6 | 607.1 | 585.6 | 571.8 | 571.5 | 568.1 | 568.8 | 550.0 | 546.9 | 571.2 | 598.0 | 581.8 |
| 1994 | 619.4 | 658.8 | 718.5 | 757.5 | 713.8 | 719.8 | 780.6 | 821.0 | 823.1 | 877.5 | 897.5 | 1,088.1 | 789.6 |
| 1995 | 1,227.5 | 1,228.8 | 1,151.5 | 1,116.9 | 1,053.0 | 926.3 | 796.9 | 839.1 | 871.2 | 887.5 | 1,066.5 | 1,065.0 | 1,019.2 |
| 1996 | 1,059.5 | 1,019.4 | 1,006.3 | 915.0 | 894.0 | 838.1 | 821.0 | 830.6 | 844.4 | 814.5 | 778.8 | 777.5 | 883.3 |

*Source: International Rubber Study Group*

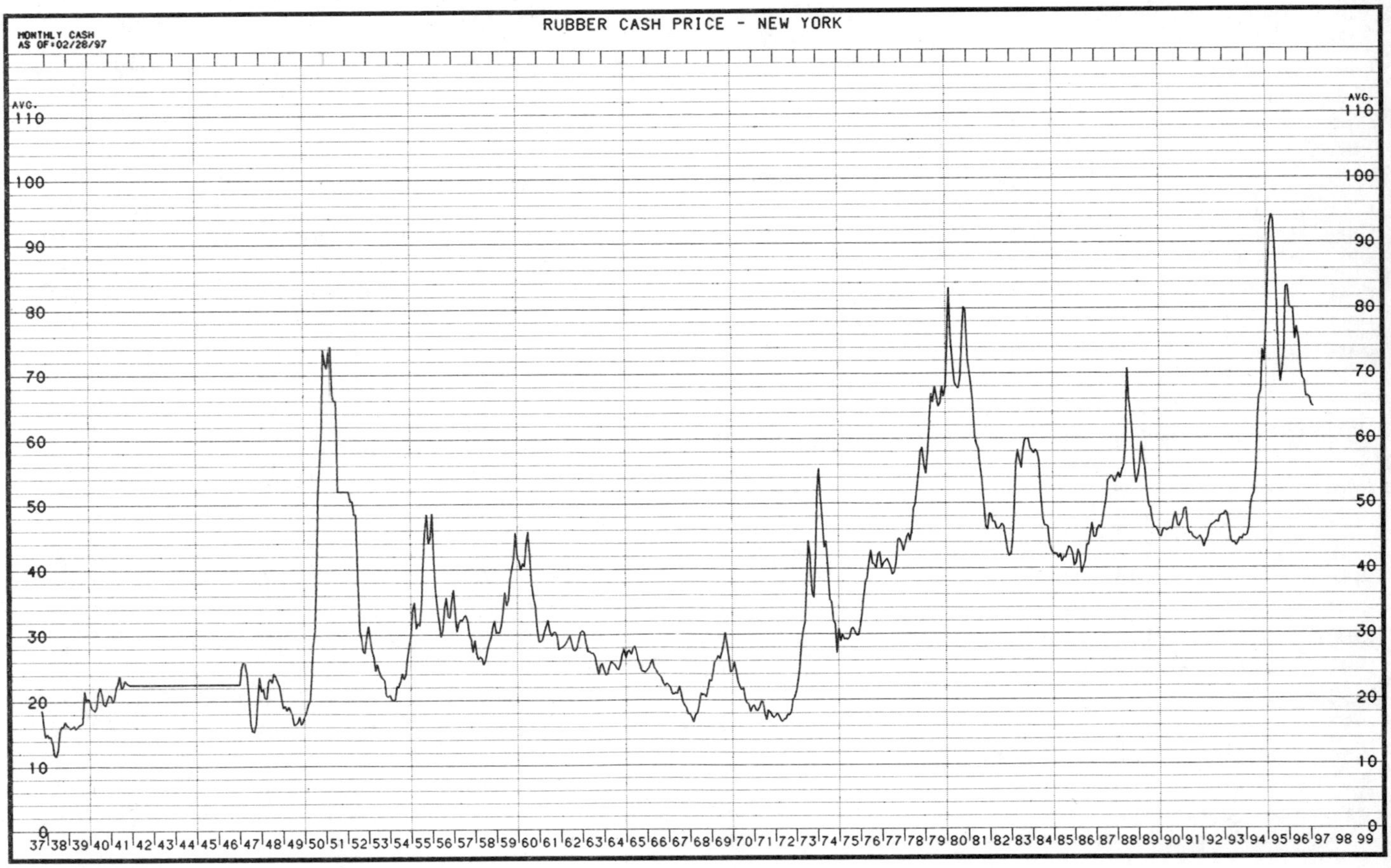

**Consumption of Natural Rubber in the United States** In Thousands of Metric Tons

| Year | Jan. | Feb. | Mar. | Apr. | May | June | July | Aug. | Sept. | Oct. | Nov. | Dec. | Total |
|---|---|---|---|---|---|---|---|---|---|---|---|---|---|
| 1985 | 71.8 | 65.7 | 91.5 | 51.7 | 89.0 | 45.2 | 55.4 | 47.3 | 68.1 | 47.2 | 65.7 | 52.4 | 774.7 |
| 1986 | 59.4 | 71.8 | 71.3 | 81.9 | 45.5 | 54.6 | 69.9 | 49.9 | 57.0 | 80.3 | 50.8 | 51.2 | 743.0 |
| 1987 | 49.9 | 85.4 | 81.3 | 62.3 | 62.6 | 56.3 | 67.4 | 61.4 | 61.9 | 57.4 | 60.6 | 69.4 | 789.0 |
| 1988 | 80.9 | 66.3 | 91.6 | 60.8 | 68.7 | 66.2 | 53.5 | 80.6 | 64.6 | 74.5 | 75.4 | 75.2 | 858.3 |
| 1989 | 89.9 | 51.1 | 96.6 | 68.4 | 87.9 | 65.1 | 82.7 | 70.8 | 72.0 | 62.1 | 84.6 | 50.9 | 866.9 |
| 1990 | 62.6 | 57.3 | 79.0 | 65.2 | 87.4 | 73.9 | 57.4 | 74.1 | 78.8 | 59.8 | 75.6 | 69.8 | 807.5 |
| 1991 | 60.0 | 60.0 | 65.0 | 65.0 | 65.0 | 60.0 | 55.0 | 55.0 | 65.0 | 70.0 | 65.0 | 66.0 | 755.8 |
| 1992 | 83.4 | 63.3 | 85.9 | 66.9 | 80.6 | 78.6 | 82.6 | 79.5 | 70.2 | 84.6 | 64.4 | 70.2 | 910.2 |
| 1993 | 96.3 | 76.0 | 93.4 | 93.4 | 67.9 | 76.8 | 77.3 | 84.9 | 72.0 | 73.6 | 82.9 | 72.2 | 966.7 |
| 1994 | 92.8 | 84.9 | 93.1 | 82.7 | 89.6 | 84.6 | 76.2 | 87.8 | 74.8 | 90.1 | 66.4 | 78.7 | 1,001.7 |
| 1995 | 70.5 | 75.8 | 98.4 | 90.3 | 92.2 | 93.3 | 85.0 | 82.7 | 83.1 | 89.9 | 81.4 | 61.3 | 1,003.9 |
| 1996[1] | 102.5 | 85.8 | 81.2 | 87.9 | 65.6 | 76.7 | 81.9 | 88.0 | 85.0 | | | | 754.6 |

[1] Preliminary. *Source: International Rubber Study Group*

**Stocks of Natural Rubber in the United States, Beginning of the Month** In Thousands of Metric Tons

| Year | Jan. | Feb. | Mar. | Apr. | May | June | July | Aug. | Sept. | Oct. | Nov. | Dec. |
|---|---|---|---|---|---|---|---|---|---|---|---|---|
| 1985 | 96.4 | 94.3 | 97.3 | 91.4 | 101.9 | 95.9 | 95.6 | 97.9 | 93.9 | 84.9 | 81.1 | 85.1 |
| 1986 | 95.2 | 97.0 | 96.9 | 100.4 | 98.6 | 98.6 | 96.7 | 93.8 | 86.4 | 91.6 | 75.3 | 78.2 |
| 1987 | 38.5 | 76.7 | 78.8 | 70.2 | 80.2 | 79.5 | 79.0 | 82.5 | 77.0 | 70.6 | 65.9 | 65.5 |
| 1988 | 72.5 | 74.9 | 75.3 | 70.7 | 74.6 | 72.9 | 71.6 | 68.7 | 71.2 | 63.9 | 57.9 | 58.4 |
| 1989 | 61.7 | 71.1 | 67.5 | 77.4 | 82.2 | 86.7 | 86.2 | 86.2 | 88.1 | 83.3 | 87.7 | 83.9 |
| 1990 | 92.0 | 100.2 | 100.2 | 101.6 | 97.1 | 97.3 | 99.8 | 101.6 | 87.2 | 90.3 | 84.7 | 89.6 |
| 1991 | 94.3 | 94.0 | 88.0 | 93.0 | 119.0 | 113.0 | 110.0 | 108.0 | 106.0 | 106.0 | 110.0 | 117.0 |
| 1992 | 109.4 | 103.6 | 112.7 | 110.4 | 107.5 | 105.9 | 101.1 | 99.0 | 96.7 | 100.3 | 97.0 | 100.7 |
| 1993 | 108.0 | 49.4 | 53.3 | 53.7 | 46.7 | 52.9 | 57.3 | 63.6 | 56.5 | 53.7 | 53.4 | 56.5 |
| 1994 | 71.3 | 65.9 | 55.7 | 65.2 | 61.4 | 60.0 | 53.2 | 43.8 | 41.0 | 45.0 | 44.2 | 47.8 |
| 1995 | 45.2 | 56.4 | 67.5 | 71.4 | 71.2 | 72.6 | 73.0 | 66.0 | 64.4 | 62.8 | 62.1 | 59.8 |
| 1996[1] | 67.1 | 70.0 | 70.3 | 71.2 | 73.9 | 73.4 | 67.1 | 64.2 | 57.2 | 54.0 | | |

[1] Preliminary. *Source: International Rubber Study Group*

**Stocks of Synthetic Rubber in the United States, Beginning of the Month** In Thousands of Metric Tons

| Year | Jan. | Feb. | Mar. | Apr. | May | June | July | Aug. | Sept. | Oct. | Nov. | Dec. |
|---|---|---|---|---|---|---|---|---|---|---|---|---|
| 1985 | 272.1 | 281.2 | 271.8 | 288.6 | 294.0 | 398.0 | 247.8 | 295.8 | 413.5 | 397.3 | 374.9 | 367.0 |
| 1986 | 213.9 | 352.8 | 217.5 | 397.7 | 403.0 | 238.6 | 247.5 | 239.9 | 233.4 | 236.5 | 231.1 | 224.6 |
| 1987 | 235.6 | 247.0 | 249.5 | 242.6 | 239.9 | 242.2 | 241.8 | 251.9 | 240.6 | 222.8 | 213.6 | 213.8 |
| 1988 | 229.0 | 237.8 | 235.1 | 229.6 | 237.5 | 246.2 | 249.6 | 261.0 | 259.9 | 258.6 | 259.0 | 258.2 |
| 1989 | 276.3 | 288.9 | 287.7 | 294.4 | 289.6 | 300.4 | 303.7 | 308.7 | 314.1 | 323.4 | 329.6 | 414.8 |
| 1990 | 404.0 | 393.5 | 392.5 | 385.8 | 406.8 | 397.5 | 395.0 | 414.9 | 420.8 | 419.6 | 405.0 | 393.9 |
| 1991 | 403.7 | 406.0 | 403.0 | 404.0 | 402.0 | 388.0 | 394.0 | 385.0 | 356.0 | 334.0 | 330.0 | 325.0 |
| 1992 | 403.7 | 386.0 | 381.2 | 383.9 | 393.2 | 389.2 | 372.8 | 382.7 | 382.1 | 375.1 | 378.6 | 401.1 |
| 1993 | 406.9 | 345.9 | 345.7 | 346.0 | 340.5 | 351.8 | 342.1 | 341.6 | 333.6 | 326.4 | 319.9 | 321.4 |
| 1994 | 331.1 | 313.3 | 313.3 | 307.9 | 306.0 | 314.2 | 302.5 | 323.2 | 318.5 | 304.6 | 299.4 | 299.5 |
| 1995 | 305.4 | 307.4 | 302.8 | 293.5 | 319.4 | 315.6 | 325.9 | 349.2 | 355.7 | 354.6 | 347.0 | 351.5 |
| 1996[1] | 366.2 | 355.3 | 342.0 | 354.8 | 365.4 | 360.0 | 367.0 | 377.3 | 366.0 | 360.0 | | |

[1] Preliminary. *Source: International Rubber Study Group*

**Production of Synthetic Rubber in the United States** In Thousands of Metric Tons

| Year | Jan. | Feb. | Mar. | Apr. | May | June | July | Aug. | Sept. | Oct. | Nov. | Dec. | Total |
|---|---|---|---|---|---|---|---|---|---|---|---|---|---|
| 1985 | 155.2 | 153.9 | 170.1 | 160.5 | 171.1 | 164.6 | 154.4 | 146.7 | 159.6 | 174.5 | 189.4 | 160.2 | 1,936 |
| 1986 | 183.3 | 173.0 | 190.3 | 193.2 | 191.4 | 183.7 | 166.7 | 178.4 | 173.0 | 179.7 | 158.3 | 147.5 | 2,156 |
| 1987 | 169.9 | 161.6 | 182.1 | 166.0 | 154.2 | 139.5 | 150.4 | 154.2 | 160.3 | 153.6 | 149.2 | 131.8 | 1,838 |
| 1988 | 166.5 | 156.7 | 189.1 | 178.6 | 167.8 | 164.9 | 155.3 | 170.5 | 178.6 | 186.7 | 145.6 | 174.7 | 2,335 |
| 1989 | 206.3 | 177.5 | 193.6 | 174.1 | 179.7 | 175.0 | 186.2 | 164.2 | 176.0 | 191.0 | 182.9 | 194.8 | 2,261 |
| 1990 | 173.5 | 180.1 | 182.5 | 187.8 | 174.6 | 172.0 | 171.9 | 180.9 | 180.4 | 190.3 | 167.4 | 153.1 | 2,115 |
| 1991 | 168.0 | 163.0 | 184.0 | 174.0 | 173.0 | 159.0 | 154.0 | 133.0 | 159.0 | 159.0 | 173.0 | 164.0 | 2,050 |
| 1992 | 180.0 | 190.0 | 200.0 | 210.0 | 200.0 | 190.0 | 190.0 | 200.0 | 210.0 | 200.0 | 195.0 | 175.0 | 2,300 |
| 1993 | 120.0 | 160.0 | 220.0 | 190.0 | 200.0 | 180.0 | 190.0 | 180.0 | 180.0 | 180.0 | 190.0 | 180.0 | 2,180 |
| 1994 | 180.0 | 180.0 | 210.0 | 200.0 | 210.0 | 200.0 | 200.0 | 210.0 | 190.0 | 210.0 | 200.0 | 200.0 | 2,390 |
| 1995 | 220.0 | 200.0 | 210.0 | 210.0 | 240.0 | 220.0 | 210.0 | 230.0 | 210.0 | 200.0 | 200.0 | 190.0 | 2,540 |
| 1996[1] | 210.0 | 190.0 | 230.0 | 220.0 | 200.0 | 220.0 | 210.0 | 210.0 | 220.0 | | | | 1,910 |

[1] Preliminary. *Source: International Rubber Study Group*

# RUBBER

## Consumption of Synthetic Rubber in the United States In Thousands of Metric Tons

| Year | Jan. | Feb. | Mar. | Apr. | May | June | July | Aug. | Sept. | Oct. | Nov. | Dec. | Total |
|---|---|---|---|---|---|---|---|---|---|---|---|---|---|
| 1985 | 177.5 | 175.4 | 180.5 | 166.7 | 167.1 | 171.0 | 147.1 | 173.9 | 151.5 | 184.1 | 166.3 | 147.2 | 2,062 |
| 1986 | 155.8 | 169.5 | 159.6 | 154.8 | 163.6 | 137.9 | 139.8 | 150.6 | 171.6 | 174.3 | 154.0 | 140.3 | 1,802 |
| 1987 | 160.7 | 145.0 | 175.7 | 157.6 | 163.9 | 148.0 | 151.5 | 168.5 | 160.6 | 177.5 | 145.8 | 155.7 | 2,020 |
| 1988 | 162.8 | 166.1 | 182.8 | 160.6 | 163.1 | 157.8 | 161.9 | 163.6 | 172.2 | 185.1 | 167.6 | 174.1 | 2,017 |
| 1989 | 158.5 | 166.8 | 186.8 | 163.1 | 172.1 | 166.3 | 160.9 | 171.1 | 162.5 | 170.6 | 180.5 | 150.5 | 2,051 |
| 1990 | 159.6 | 158.7 | 161.6 | 144.1 | 161.5 | 151.6 | 137.1 | 149.5 | 155.6 | 175.3 | 147.1 | 119.1 | 1,821 |
| 1991 | 145.0 | 140.0 | 160.0 | 150.0 | 160.0 | 135.0 | 140.0 | 140.0 | 160.0 | 140.0 | 150.0 | 149.0 | 1,768 |
| 1992 | 167.8 | 159.5 | 174.7 | 158.9 | 162.6 | 184.2 | 154.5 | 177.7 | 180.2 | 171.5 | 155.1 | 148.2 | 1,960 |
| 1993 | 161.3 | 154.4 | 189.4 | 172.8 | 164.5 | 173.6 | 166.0 | 173.9 | 162.0 | 169.4 | 162.3 | 151.4 | 2,001 |
| 1994 | 177.7 | 160.8 | 191.8 | 173.0 | 173.5 | 187.5 | 164.9 | 187.1 | 176.0 | 178.8 | 175.7 | 170.8 | 2,118 |
| 1995 | 188.6 | 182.2 | 194.3 | 179.1 | 212.7 | 188.7 | 160.0 | 190.7 | 182.4 | 178.1 | 169.7 | 145.5 | 2,172 |
| 1996[1] | 188.0 | 173.7 | 186.9 | 176.8 | 184.9 | 178.5 | 177.0 | 197.3 | 195.0 | | | | 1,658 |

[1] Preliminary. *Source: International Rubber Study Group*

## Exports of Synthetic Rubber in the United States In Thousands of Metric Tons

| Year | Jan. | Feb. | Mar. | Apr. | May | June | July | Aug. | Sept. | Oct. | Nov. | Dec. | Total |
|---|---|---|---|---|---|---|---|---|---|---|---|---|---|
| 1986 | 23.9 | 28.1 | 24.4 | 36.0 | 26.1 | 25.4 | 26.8 | 32.3 | 34.8 | 30.9 | 28.2 | 27.5 | 366.0 |
| 1987 | 32.4 | 33.2 | 36.1 | 37.1 | 39.4 | 36.9 | 34.1 | 33.3 | 38.8 | 33.5 | 37.5 | 37.1 | 470.5 |
| 1988 | 39.7 | 37.4 | 41.8 | 41.7 | 40.4 | 41.1 | 29.8 | 44.0 | 38.6 | 37.2 | 36.3 | 32.1 | 514.0 |
| 1989 | 42.4 | 45.7 | 55.0 | 41.3 | 54.4 | 51.3 | 43.7 | 48.2 | 54.5 | 54.6 | 43.6 | 44.4 | 450.6 |
| 1990 | 45.6 | 39.0 | 50.2 | 42.6 | 42.7 | 41.0 | 37.4 | 43.1 | 42.0 | 50.8 | 50.3 | 39.0 | 523.7 |
| 1991 | 43.8 | 46.1 | 44.0 | 45.2 | 47.9 | 40.4 | 42.8 | 43.2 | 43.1 | 46.3 | 47.3 | 42.2 | 532.3 |
| 1992 | 52.3 | 55.1 | 51.3 | 59.1 | 58.2 | 51.6 | 46.5 | 52.8 | 58.0 | 51.4 | 48.1 | 39.7 | 624.1 |
| 1993 | 47.1 | 34.1 | 57.7 | 47.4 | 52.4 | 46.9 | 46.9 | 43.8 | 48.8 | 46.6 | 49.0 | 41.9 | 562.6 |
| 1994 | 48.8 | 46.4 | 55.4 | 57.0 | 52.4 | 49.6 | 50.2 | 62.8 | 60.7 | 59.9 | 56.9 | 55.0 | 655.1 |
| 1995 | 54.9 | 51.6 | 62.7 | 55.6 | 58.6 | 58.6 | 50.0 | 54.9 | 53.0 | 60.4 | 53.9 | 52.6 | 666.8 |
| 1996[1] | 61.1 | 57.7 | 64.0 | 68.0 | 48.2 | 66.8 | 62.3 | 57.1 | 63.9 | 65.2 | | | 614.3 |

[1] Preliminary. *Source: International Rubber Study Group*

## Production of Tyres (Car and Truck) in the United States In Thousands of Units

| Year | Jan. | Feb. | Mar. | Apr. | May | June | July | Aug. | Sept. | Oct. | Nov. | Dec. | Total |
|---|---|---|---|---|---|---|---|---|---|---|---|---|---|
| 1985 | 18,381 | 17,375 | 18,704 | 17,388 | 16,781 | 15,216 | 12,989 | 16,635 | 16,844 | 17,626 | 15,198 | 13,786 | 196,923 |
| 1986 | 16,306 | 15,966 | 16,968 | 16,037 | 15,003 | 14,647 | 14,203 | 16,112 | 16,540 | 18,180 | 15,144 | 15,183 | 190,289 |
| 1987 | 16,879 | 16,593 | 17,733 | 16,680 | 16,982 | 16,548 | 15,796 | 16,723 | 17,204 | 18,956 | 16,455 | 16,428 | 202,978 |
| 1988 | 17,345 | 18,027 | 19,305 | 17,642 | 17,403 | 17,941 | 15,022 | 18,058 | 18,115 | 19,138 | 17,253 | 16,102 | 211,351 |
| 1989 | 18,944 | 18,102 | 19,670 | 19,224 | 19,090 | 18,312 | 14,835 | 18,288 | 16,963 | 18,400 | 16,323 | 14,721 | 212,870 |
| 1990 | 19,017 | 17,376 | 19,522 | 17,680 | 17,990 | 18,186 | 14,996 | 18,555 | 17,612 | 19,965 | 16,077 | 13,687 | 210,663 |
| 1991 | 17,713 | 17,375 | 16,208 | 17,017 | 19,360 | 16,419 | 14,354 | 17,784 | 17,045 | 19,588 | 16,354 | 15,173 | 202,391 |
| 1992 | 18,772 | 18,762 | 20,356 | 19,065 | 18,874 | 19,380 | 17,273 | 20,306 | 19,975 | 21,602 | 18,384 | 17,501 | 230,250 |
| 1993 | ---------- | 61,809 | ---------- | ---------- | 60,752 | ---------- | ---------- | 57,702 | ---------- | ---------- | 57,184 | ---------- | 237,447 |
| 1994 | ---------- | 63,586 | ---------- | ---------- | 63,331 | ---------- | ---------- | 57,018 | ---------- | ---------- | 59,442 | ---------- | 243,377 |
| 1995[1] | ---------- | 63,800 | ---------- | ---------- | 63,800 | ---------- | ---------- | 63,800 | ---------- | ---------- | 63,754 | ---------- | 255,154 |

[1] Preliminary. [2] Estimate. *Source: International Rubber Study Group*

## Foreign Trade of Tyres (Car and Truck) in the United States In Thousands of Units

| | Imports | | | | | Exports | | | | |
|---|---|---|---|---|---|---|---|---|---|---|
| Year | First Quarter | Second Quarter | Third Quarter | Fourth Quarter | Total | First Quarter | Second Quarter | Third Quarter | Fourth Quarter | Total |
| 1986 | 9,346 | 10,148 | 11,458 | 10,215 | 41,167 | 1,268 | 1,146 | 1,267 | 1,474 | 5,223 |
| 1987 | 11,584 | 12,820 | 11,722 | 11,341 | 47,467 | 2,095 | 2,327 | 2,389 | 3,371 | 10,182 |
| 1988 | 11,383 | 12,059 | 12,383 | 12,783 | 48,608 | 4,203 | 4,120 | 3,712 | 4,034 | 16,069 |
| 1989 | 12,802 | 14,518 | 12,609 | 12,749 | 52,678 | 4,104 | 4,254 | 5,267 | 4,704 | 18,329 |
| 1990 | 13,713 | 13,564 | 11,951 | 11,633 | 50,861 | 5,453 | 5,532 | 6,031 | 6,730 | 23,746 |
| 1991 | 12,011 | 13,008 | 11,320 | 10,158 | 46,497 | 6,407 | 6,388 | 6,623 | 6,342 | 25,760 |
| 1992 | 10,760 | 12,496 | 11,850 | 12,285 | 47,391 | 6,243 | 6,475 | 7,125 | 6,646 | 26,489 |
| 1993 | 11,519 | 13,045 | 12,688 | 13,036 | 50,288 | 7,266 | 6,930 | 7,163 | 7,133 | 28,492 |
| 1994[1] | 13,809 | 15,352 | 14,906 | 14,774 | 58,841 | 7,444 | 8,035 | 7,945 | 8,678 | 32,102 |
| 1995[2] | 14,883 | 14,977 | 13,762 | 12,718 | 56,340 | 8,438 | 8,502 | 8,478 | 9,174 | 34,592 |

[1] Preliminary. [2] Estimate. *Source: International Rubber Study Group*

# Rye

U.S. rye production continues to slide, from an annual average during the 1980's of more than 20 million bushels to about 10 million during the 1990's. The U.S. is a net importer of rye, importing almost half of domestic production. The major producing states are Georgia and South Dakota. In 1995/96 (June/May) production totaled about 9.9 million bushels (260,000 metric tons); for 1996/97 slightly more than 9 million bushels (230,000 tons) were produced. The decrease reflected 347,000 harvested acres and an average yield of 26 bushels per acre, both record lows.

In the U.S., rye is used as an animal feed and as an ingredient in bread and some whiskeys, with about a third of the total supply used as a feedstuff, a third as a foodstuff, and the balance as seed and for whisky. U.S. rye exports are minimal at best. Carryover stocks are also small, averaging during the past five years 1.5 million bushels and in sharp contrast to only a decade ago when carryover averaged near 20 million bushels. Rye's steadily declining U.S. statistics during the 1990's underscore the lack of interest towards the grain by producers and users alike; a trend that has yet to show any sign of bottoming.

On a worldwide basis, however, production shows signs of stabilizing, although not likely to recover back to the mid-1980's average of more than 30 million tons. World production in 1996/97 of 22 million metric tons compares with the previous two crop years at 21.9 million each. The steadiness reflects a moderate increase in world acreage that offset lower average yields. Eastern Europe is the major producing area with Poland the largest producer (about half of world's crop) followed by Russia and Belarus. Germany produces about 18 percent of total production. Percentagewise, U.S. output at about 1 percent is insignificant. Much of the world's production is consumed domestically, except for Canada, whose output is not much larger than the U.S., but mostly exported to the U.S.

World trade in 1996/97 was estimated at 2.6 million metric tons vs. 2.5 million in 1995/96. The Republic of Korea is the world's largest importer, with one million tons in 1996/97, unchanged from 1995/96. Significantly, Korea imported no rye in 1992/93 and 1993/94. China has also increased its import demand, from virtually nothing early in the 1990's to 400,000 tons in both 1996/97 and 1995/96. Japan's annual imports average about 420,000 tons. Eastern Europe supplies most of the world's rye exports, about 2 million tons during the past three crop years.

**World Production of Rye** In Thousands of Metric Tons

| Crop Year | Argentina | Austria | Canada | Czech Republic[5] | Denmark | France | Germany | Hungary | Netherlands | Poland | Russia[4] | Spain | Turkey | Ukraine[4] | United States | World Total |
|---|---|---|---|---|---|---|---|---|---|---|---|---|---|---|---|---|
| 1984-5 | 140 | 380 | 664 | 710 | 608 | 321 | 4,493 | 192 | 25 | 9,540 | ----- | 325 | 360 | 13,400 | 827 | 33,398 |
| 1985-6 | 100 | 339 | 569 | 620 | 565 | 283 | 4,382 | 163 | 19 | 7,600 | ----- | 295 | 360 | 15,700 | 524 | 32,217 |
| 1986-7 | 60 | 284 | 609 | 547 | 546 | 200 | 4,224 | 172 | 19 | 7,074 | ----- | 220 | 350 | 15,248 | 496 | 30,782 |
| 1987-8 | 88 | 309 | 493 | 496 | 513 | 275 | 3,928 | 186 | 25 | 6,816 | ----- | 320 | 350 | 18,055 | 503 | 33,034 |
| 1988-9 | 42 | 356 | 267 | 530 | 366 | 260 | 3,419 | 245 | 28 | 7,232 | ----- | 357 | 360 | 18,517 | 373 | 32,989 |
| 1989-90 | 70 | 381 | 873 | 708 | 487 | 270 | 3,867 | 200 | 33 | 6,216 | ----- | 336 | 320 | 18,288 | 347 | 33,412 |
| 1990-1 | 96 | 396 | 599 | 736 | 545 | 240 | 3,988 | 226 | 36 | 6,044 | ----- | 267 | 240 | 21,193 | 258 | 36,861 |
| 1991-2 | 45 | 350 | 339 | 484 | 395 | 210 | 3,324 | 221 | 34 | 5,899 | ----- | 242 | 240 | 14,061 | 248 | 27,359 |
| 1992-3 | 34 | 278 | 265 | 255 | 308 | 205 | 2,422 | 140 | 34 | 3,981 | 13,890 | 230 | 240 | 1,160 | 304 | 28,656 |
| 1993-4 | 62 | 290 | 320 | 300 | 323 | 190 | 2,984 | 110 | 35 | 5,000 | 9,150 | 300 | 230 | 1,180 | 263 | 26,090 |
| 1994-5[1] | 80 | 320 | 400 | 280 | 380 | 180 | 3,450 | 200 | 35 | 5,300 | 6,000 | 220 | 250 | 940 | 290 | 21,890 |
| 1995-6[2] | ----- | 310 | 310 | 260 | 500 | 200 | 4,520 | 170 | ----- | 6,290 | 4,100 | 170 | 260 | 1,210 | 260 | 21,970 |
| 1996-7[3] | ----- | 160 | 320 | 220 | 370 | 190 | 4,150 | 100 | ----- | 5,600 | 5,900 | 300 | 250 | 1,100 | 230 | 22,570 |

[1] Preliminary. [2] Estimate. [3] Forecast. [4] Formerly part of the U.S.S.R.; data not reported separately until 1992. [5] Formerly part of Czechoslovakia; data not reported separately until 1992. *Source: Foreign Agricultural Service, U.S. Department of Agriculture (FAS-USDA)*

**Production of Rye in the United States** In Thousands of Bushels

| Year | Georgia | Illinois | Indiana | Kansas | Michigan | Minnesota | Nebraska | North Dakota | Ohio | Oklahoma | Pennylvania | South Carolina | South Dakota | Texas | Virginia | Wisconsin |
|---|---|---|---|---|---|---|---|---|---|---|---|---|---|---|---|---|
| 1984 | 1,760 | 308 | 336 | 312 | 588 | 6,650 | 1,392 | 5,400 | 175 | 704 | 578 | 546 | 10,800 | 240 | 378 | 216 |
| 1985 | 2,070 | 256 | 308 | 300 | 651 | 3,300 | 1,242 | 2,640 | 172 | 828 | 470 | 532 | 4,440 | 400 | 312 | 234 |
| 1986 | 1,785 | 210 | 280 | 210 | 713 | 1,600 | 1,035 | 4,250 | 175 | 840 | 630 | 391 | 4,440 | 190 | 364 | 168 |
| 1987 | 1,540 | 144 | 162 | 270 | 640 | 1,200 | 1,150 | 5,115 | 180 | 360 | 525 | 528 | 5,040 | 150 | 435 | 100 |
| 1988 | 1,890 | 140 | 210 | 130 | 650 | 920 | 1,375 | 1,350 | 185 | 720 | 684 | 720 | 2,250 | 150 | 560 | 120 |
| 1989 | 1,610 | 312 | 204 | 80 | 825 | 1,088 | 600 | 1,064 | 155 | 532 | 576 | 644 | 3,240 | 126 | 264 | 360 |
| 1990 | 1,320 | 165 | 124 | 130 | 580 | 868 | 750 | 780 | 175 | 420 | 496 | 594 | 1,870 | 140 | 256 | 465 |
| 1991 | 1,300 | 162 | 100 | 115 | 360 | 648 | 1,000 | 992 | 155 | 665 | 297 | 630 | 1,152 | 228 | 264 | 435 |
| 1992 | 1,560 | 280 | 156 | 130 | 496 | 720 | 1,040 | 1,496 | 175 | 798 | 720 | 675 | 1,666 | 280 | 288 | 330 |
| 1993 | 1,380 | 224 | 150 | 693 | 420 | 667 | 500 | 1,050 | 150 | 660 | 340 | 380 | 1,600 | 363 | 165 | 260 |
| 1994 | 1,890 | 144 | 120 | 325 | 442 | 810 | 546 | 700 | 170 | 945 | 320 | 600 | 1,485 | 435 | 252 | 875 |
| 1995 | 1,155 | 240 | 116 | 400 | 544 | 609 | 480 | 726 | 180 | 810 | 330 | 440 | 1,650 | 380 | 175 | 480 |
| 1996[1] | 1,820 | 186 | 44 | 150 | 351 | 480 | 418 | 528 | 93 | 900 | 216 | 520 | 1,476 | 190 | 330 | 384 |

[1] Preliminary. *Source: Agricultural Statistics Board, U.S. Department of Agriculture (ASB-USDA)*

# RYE

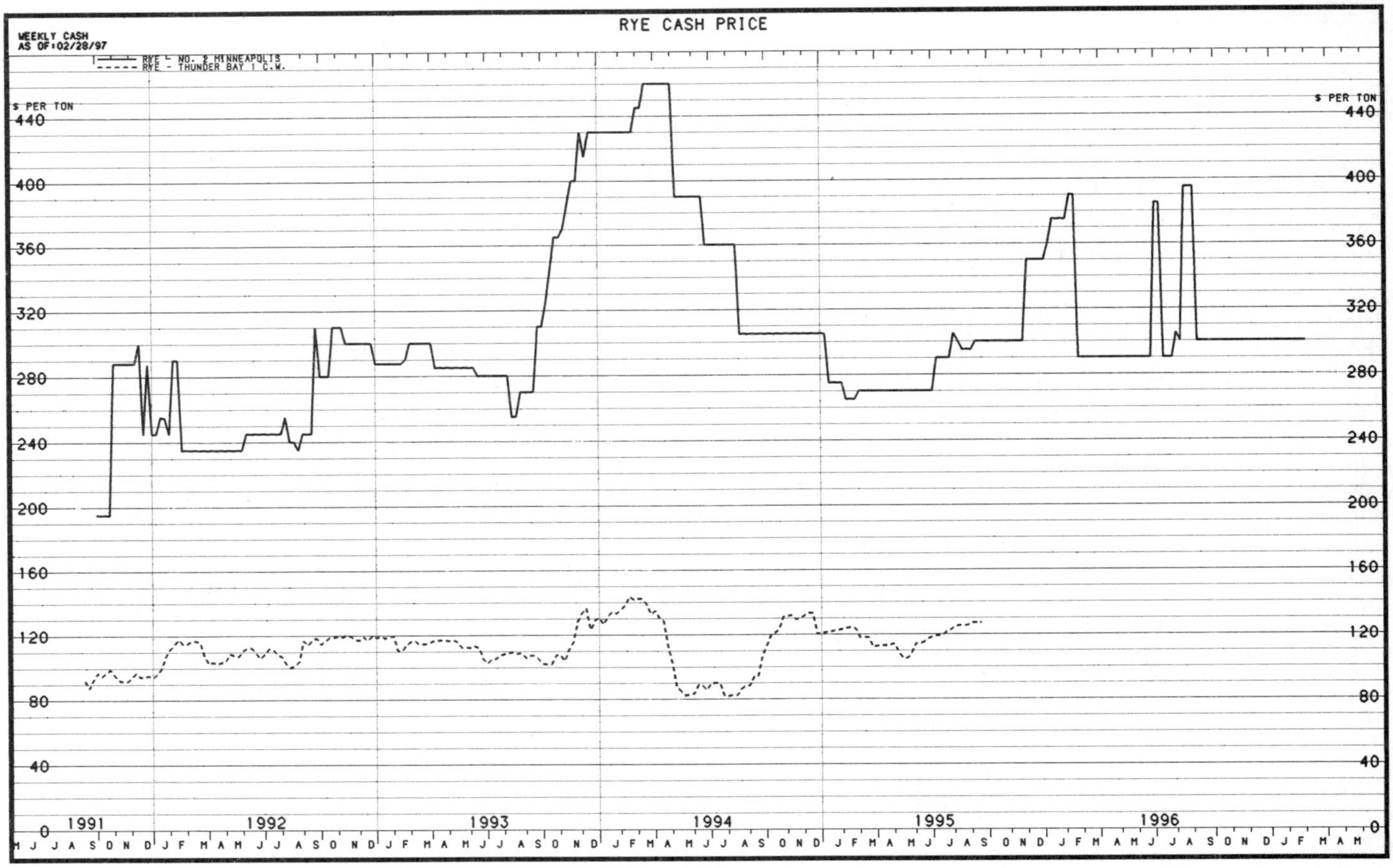


## Salient Statistics of Rye in the United States    In Thousands of Bushels

| Crop Year Beginning June 1 | Supply: Stocks June 1 | Supply: Production | Supply: Imports | Supply: Total Supply | Disappearance, Domestic Use: Food | Industry | Seed | Feed & Residual | Total | Exports | Total Disappearance | Acreage: Planted (1,000 Acres) | Harvested for Grain (1,000 Acres) | Yield Per Harvested Acre (Bushels) |
|---|---|---|---|---|---|---|---|---|---|---|---|---|---|---|
| 1987-8 | 18,583 | 19,526 | 1,204 | 39,313 | 3,500 | 2,000 | 3,800 | 10,601 | 19,901 | 500 | 20,401 | 2,428 | 671 | 29.1 |
| 1988-9 | 18,912 | 14,689 | 200 | 33,801 | 3,500 | 2,000 | 3,200 | 11,401 | 20,101 | 3,400 | 23,501 | 2,374 | 595 | 24.7 |
| 1989-90 | 10,300 | 13,647 | 30 | 23,977 | 3,500 | 2,000 | 3,000 | 9,035 | 17,535 | 800 | 18,335 | 2,014 | 484 | 28.2 |
| 1990-1 | 5,642 | 10,176 | 3,895 | 19,713 | 3,500 | 2,000 | 3,000 | 7,670 | 16,173 | 213 | 16,383 | 1,625 | 375 | 27.1 |
| 1991-2 | 3,327 | 9,761 | 4,542 | 17,630 | 3,500 | 2,000 | 3,000 | 7,528 | 16,028 | 53 | 16,081 | 1,671 | 396 | 24.6 |
| 1992-3 | 1,523 | 11,952 | 3,099 | 16,100 | 3,500 | 2,000 | 3,000 | 5,984 | 14,484 | 14 | 14,498 | 1,582 | 406 | 29.4 |
| 1993-4 | 1,555 | 10,340 | 4,607 | 16,502 | 3,600 | 2,000 | 3,000 | 6,915 | 15,515 | 16 | 15,531 | 1,493 | 381 | 27.1 |
| 1994-5[1] | 971 | 11,341 | 4,386 | 16,698 | 3,600 | 2,000 | 3,000 | 6,612 | 15,212 | 35 | 15,247 | 1,613 | 407 | 27.9 |
| 1995-6[2] | 1,451 | 10,064 | 3,800 | 15,315 | 3,200 | 2,000 | 3,000 | 6,100 | 14,300 | 100 | 14,400 | 1,602 | 385 | 26.1 |
| 1996-7[3] | 898 | 9,016 | 4,000 | 13,914 | 3,200 | 2,000 | 3,000 | 4,700 | 12,900 | 100 | 12,900 | 1,467 | 347 | 26.0 |

[1] Preliminary. [2] Estimate. [3] Forecast. *Source: Economic Research Service, U.S. Department of Agriculture (ERS-USDA)*

## U.S. Rye Crop Production Reports and CCC Operations    In Thousands of Bushels

| Crop Year Beginning June 1 | Official Crop Reports: July 1 | Aug. 1 | Dec. 1 | Final | National Average Support Rate: $ Per Bushel | % of Parity | Placed Under Loan Total | Percentage of Production | Acquired by CCC |
|---|---|---|---|---|---|---|---|---|---|
| 1987-8 | ------ | 19,098 | 19,718 | 19,526 | 1.55 | 38 | 8,600 | 44.1 | 1,600 |
| 1988-9 | ------ | 15,062 | ------ | 14,689 | 1.50 | 37 | 300 | 2.0 | 800 |
| 1989-90 | ------ | 13,610 | ------ | 13,647 | 1.40 | 32 | 600 | 4.4 | 0 |
| 1990-1 | ------ | 10,098 | ------ | 10,176 | 1.33 | 31 | 200 | 2.0 | 0 |
| 1991-2 | ------ | 9,761 | ------ | 9,761 | 1.38 | 32 | 100 | 1.0 | 0 |
| 1992-3 | ------ | 11,952 | ------ | 11,952 | 1.46 | 34 | 200 | 1.7 | 0 |
| 1993-4 | ------ | 10,340 | ------ | 10,340 | 1.46 | 35 | 100 | 1.0 | 0 |
| 1994-5[1] | ------ | 11,138 | ------ | 11,341 | 1.61 | 38 | 100 | .9 | 0 |
| 1995-6[2] | ------ | 9,928 | ------ | 10,064 | 1.61 | ------ | 100 | ------ | 0 |
| 1996-7[3] | ------ | ------ | ------ | 9,016 | 1.61 | ------ | 0 | ------ | 0 |

[1] Preliminary. [2] Estimate. [3] Forecast. *Source: National Agricultural Statistics Service, U.S. Department of Agriculture (NASS-USDA)*

## Average Price of Cash Rye No. 2 at Minneapolis In Cents Per Bushel

| Year | July | Aug. | Sept. | Oct. | Nov. | Dec. | Jan. | Feb. | Mar. | Apr. | May | June | Average |
|---|---|---|---|---|---|---|---|---|---|---|---|---|---|
| 1985-6 | 210 | 215 | 223 | 233 | 248 | 259 | 246 | 228 | 226 | 226 | 219 | 178 | 226 |
| 1986-7 | 156 | 151 | 160 | 168 | 173 | 202 | 195 | 185 | 185 | 173 | 196 | 163 | 176 |
| 1987-8 | 165 | 165 | 175 | 198 | 199 | 189 | 185 | 189 | 175 | 167 | 181 | 278 | 189 |
| 1988-9 | 266 | 264 | 264 | 247 | 269 | 280 | 268 | 268 | 264 | 270 | 257 | 201 | 260 |
| 1989-90 | 206 | 203 | 214 | 235 | 229 | 225 | 245 | 220 | 222 | 241 | 242 | 232 | 226 |
| 1990-1 | 215 | 222 | 220 | 220 | 190 | 245 | 252 | 243 | 242 | 242 | 245 | 245 | 232 |
| 1991-2 | 216 | 238 | 195 | 288 | 288 | 279 | 251 | 263 | 235 | 235 | 235 | 245 | 247 |
| 1992-3 | 245 | 241 | 267 | 295 | 303 | 298 | 288 | 290 | 300 | 289 | 285 | 282 | 282 |
| 1993-4 | 280 | 270 | 280 | 354 | 387 | 427 | 430 | 430 | 452 | 460 | 400 | 383 | 372 |
| 1994-5 | 360 | 336 | 305 | 305 | 305 | 305 | 285 | 267 | 270 | 270 | 270 | 270 | 296 |
| 1995-6 | 287 | 298 | 299 | 300 | 300 | 350 | 368 | 346 | 290 | 290 | 290 | 304 | 310 |
| 1996-7[1] | 325 | 364 | 314 | 300 | 300 | 300 | 300 | 300 | | | | | 313 |

[1] Preliminary. *Source: Agricultural Marketing Service, U.S. Department of Agriculture (AMS-USDA)*

## Average Open Interest[1] of Rye Futures in Winnipeg In 20 Metric Ton Units

| Year | Jan. | Feb. | Mar. | Apr. | May | June | July | Aug. | Sept. | Oct. | Nov. | Dec. |
|---|---|---|---|---|---|---|---|---|---|---|---|---|
| 1984 | 2,224 | 4,566 | 3,980 | 3,883 | 3,731 | 3,023 | 2,888 | 5,430 | 7,098 | 6,320 | 5,894 | 4,158 |
| 1985 | 4,267 | 4,826 | 4,175 | 4,227 | 3,893 | 3,919 | 4,031 | 5,022 | 4,872 | 5,478 | 4,289 | 3,786 |
| 1986 | 4,287 | 4,335 | 3,302 | 4,211 | 3,039 | 2,553 | 2,900 | 3,317 | 3,479 | 2,767 | 2,827 | 2,031 |
| 1987 | 2,128 | 2,406 | 1,892 | 2,813 | 3,778 | 4,427 | 2,866 | 3,167 | 4,209 | 3,228 | 3,211 | 2,494 |
| 1988 | 2,690 | 2,645 | 2,760 | 2,809 | 2,176 | 3,635 | 3,562 | 3,628 | 3,537 | 3,139 | 2,827 | 2,160 |
| 1989 | 2,382 | 2,556 | 1,768 | 1,586 | 1,666 | 1,963 | 1,990 | 3,027 | 3,004 | 2,954 | 3,434 | 2,537 |
| 1990 | 2,828 | 2,840 | 1,943 | 2,335 | 2,500 | 2,408 | 2,673 | 3,062 | 2,669 | 2,379 | 2,116 | 1,625 |
| 1991 | 1,713 | 1,834 | 1,765 | 1,685 | 1,165 | 1,078 | 1,017 | 1,447 | 1,724 | 1,842 | 1,630 | 1,168 |
| 1992 | 1,153 | 1,954 | 2,330 | 2,336 | 1,996 | 1,902 | 1,385 | 1,642 | 1,416 | 1,218 | 965 | 1,058 |
| 1993 | 935 | 1,053 | 785 | 860 | 792 | 760 | 644 | 623 | 558 | 461 | 476 | 476 |
| 1994 | 472 | 474 | 275 | 113 | 51 | 40 | 34 | 37 | 20 | 23 | 17 | 22 |
| 1995[2] | 20 | 20 | 34 | 42 | 31 | 31 | 17 | 15 | 15 | | | |

[1] Data prior to 1986 are for end of month. [2] Trading of contract ceased on September 20, 1995. *Source: Winnipeg Commodity Exchange (WCE)*

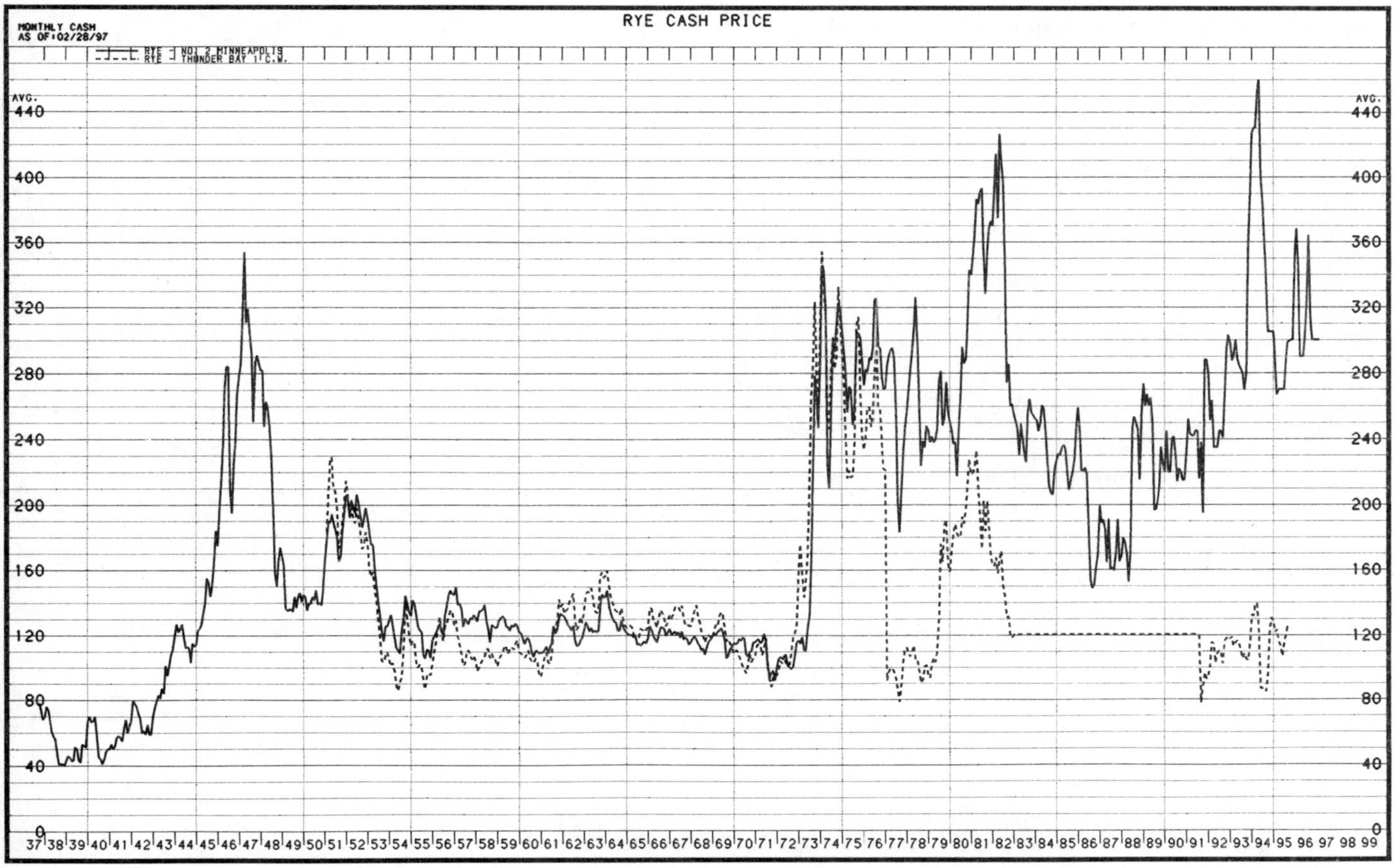

# Salt

World resources of salt are practically unlimited. Domestic resources of rock salt and salt from brine are in the northeast, central western, and southern gulf coast states. Saline lakes and solar evaporation salt facilities are near populated regions in the western United States. Almost every country in the world has salt deposits or solar evaporation operations of various sizes. There are no economic substitutes for salt. Calcium chloride and calcium magnesium acetate, hydrochloric acid, and potassium chloride can be substituted for salt in deicing, certain chemical processes, and food flavoring but at a higher cost.

World production of salt in 1995 was estimated at 185 million tonnes, up 3 percent from 1994. The U.S. is by far the world's largest producer of salt. The next largest producer is China which in 1995 produced 30 million tonnes, up 1 percent from 1994. Germany produced 13 million tonnes of salt, up more than 2 percent from 1994. The next largest producer is Canada with 1995 output of 11.1 million tonnes, down 3 percent from 1994. Other large producers include India, Australia, Mexico, the U.K., and Brazil.

U.S. production of salt in 1995 totaled 43.3 million tonnes, up 9 percent from 1994. Salt sold or used by producers in 1995 was 42.3 million tonnes, up 7 percent from the previous year. The estimated percentage of salt sold or used, by type, was salt in brine, 46 percent; rock salt, 36 percent; vacuum pan, 9 percent; and solar salt, 9 percent.

The chemical industry consumed about 39 percent of total salt sales, with salt brine representing about 88 percent of the type of salt used for feedstock. Chlorine and caustic soda manufacture was the main consuming sector within the chemical industry. Salt for highway deicing accounted for 35 percent of U.S. demand. The remaining markets for salt, in declining order, were distributors, 10 percent; food and agricultural, 6 percent; general industrial, 6 percent; primary water treatment, 1 percent; and other, 3 percent.

## World Production of All Salt In Thousands of Metric Tons

| Year | Australia | Canada | China | France | Germany | India | Italy | Japan | Mexico | Netherlands | Poland | Spain | Ukraine[3] | United Kingdom | United States | World Total |
|---|---|---|---|---|---|---|---|---|---|---|---|---|---|---|---|---|
| 1988 | 7,165 | 10,687 | 22,000 | 7,575 | 17,861 | 9,204 | 4,289 | 1,363 | 6,788 | 3,693 | 6,179 | 3,880 | 14,800 | 6,130 | 34,325 | 185,542 |
| 1989 | 7,069 | 11,021 | 28,000 | 8,267 | 17,129 | 9,603 | 4,186 | 1,367 | 6,703 | 3,756 | 4,670 | 3,090 | 15,000 | 6,720 | 35,251 | 191,660 |
| 1990 | 7,227 | 11,261 | 20,000 | 6,605 | 15,719 | 9,503 | 4,432 | 1,377 | 7,135 | 3,653 | 4,055 | 3,377 | 14,700 | 6,434 | 36,918 | 183,000 |
| 1991 | 7,791 | 11,993 | 24,100 | 6,500 | 14,870 | 9,503 | 3,954 | 1,374 | 7,533 | 3,417 | 3,840 | 4,070 | 14,000 | 6,828 | 36,400 | 191,000 |
| 1992 | 7,693 | 11,171 | 28,100 | 6,116 | 12,708 | 9,503 | 3,821 | 1,405 | 7,395 | 3,628 | 3,887 | 3,610 | 4,400 | 6,101 | 36,100 | 184,000 |
| 1993 | 7,737 | 10,900 | 29,530 | 6,980 | 12,688 | 9,502 | 3,730 | 1,378 | 7,490 | 3,500 | 3,817 | 3,410 | 4,000 | 6,790 | 39,300 | 187,000 |
| 1994[1] | 7,685 | 11,700 | 29,700 | 7,536 | 10,532 | 9,500 | 3,900 | 1,387 | 7,458 | 3,500 | 4,074 | 3,400 | 3,500 | 7,000 | 39,800 | 190,000 |
| 1995[2] | 8,480 | 10,893 | 25,000 | 7,350 | 10,800 | 9,500 | 3,400 | 1,400 | 7,670 | 3,500 | 4,000 | 3,400 | 3,000 | 7,100 | 42,100 | 189,000 |

[1] Preliminary. [2] Estimate. [3] Formerly part of the U.S.S.R.; data not reported separately until 1992. *Source: U.S. Geological Survey*

## Salient Statistics of the Salt Industry in the United States In Thousands of Metric Tons

| | Net Import Reliance as a % of Apparent Consumption | Average Value FOB Mine Vacuum & Open Pan $ Ton | Production | | | | | Sold or Used by Producers | | | | | | Exports | | |
|---|---|---|---|---|---|---|---|---|---|---|---|---|---|---|---|---|
| Year | | | Total | Open & Vacuum Pan | Solar | Rock | Brine | Open & Vacuum Pan | Rock Salt | Brine | Total Salt | Value[3] Million $ | Imports for Consumption | Total | To Canada | Apparent Consumption |
| 1988 | 11 | 97.71 | 35,534 | 3,469 | 3,065 | 11,567 | 17,434 | 3,467 | 11,703 | 17,782 | 35,326 | 699.3 | 4,966 | 802 | 650 | 39,490 |
| 1989 | 10 | 102.22 | 35,632 | 3,606 | 2,849 | 12,682 | 16,496 | 3,599 | 15,364 | 16,509 | 35,250 | 776.8 | 5,519 | 1,422 | 1,240 | 39,347 |
| 1990 | 9 | 110.58 | 36,794 | 3,662 | 2,985 | 12,772 | 17,374 | 3,655 | 13,056 | 17,724 | 36,916 | 826.7 | 5,969 | 2,266 | 2,087 | 40,619 |
| 1991 | 11 | 114.75 | 36,316 | 3,654 | 2,813 | 11,188 | 18,660 | 3,623 | 11,064 | 18,640 | 35,902 | 801.5 | 6,188 | 1,777 | 1,288 | 40,313 |
| 1992 | 11 | 113.20 | 36,016 | 3,811 | 3,221 | 11,411 | 17,574 | 3,763 | 10,910 | 34,784 | 34,784 | 802.6 | 5,394 | 992 | 718 | 39,186 |
| 1993 | 12 | 111.97 | 39,200 | 3,864 | 2,960 | 14,253 | 18,100 | 3,850 | 13,401 | 18,100 | 38,200 | 904.0 | 5,868 | 688 | 499 | 43,400 |
| 1994[1] | 18 | 115.35 | 40,100 | 3,960 | 3,020 | 15,100 | 18,000 | 3,930 | 14,900 | 18,000 | 39,700 | 990.0 | 9,630 | 742 | 573 | 48,600 |
| 1995[2] | 14 | 118.63 | 42,100 | 3,950 | 3,540 | 14,000 | 20,600 | 3,920 | 13,000 | 20,500 | 40,800 | 1,000.0 | 7,090 | 670 | 558 | 47,200 |

[1] Preliminary. [2] Estimate. [3] Values are fob mine or refinery and do not include cost of cooperage or containers. *Source: U.S. Geological Survey*

## Salt Sold or Used by Producers in the U.S. by Classes & Consumers or Uses In Thousands of Metric Tons

| Year | Chemical[2] | Tanning Leather | Textile & Dyeing | Meat Packers | Canning | Baking | Agricultural Distribution | Feed Dealers | Feed Manufacturers | Rubber | Oil | Paper & Pulp | Metal Processing | Water Treatment | Grocery Stores | Water Conditioning Distrib. | Ice Control and/or Stabilization |
|---|---|---|---|---|---|---|---|---|---|---|---|---|---|---|---|---|---|
| 1988 | 18,810 | 112 | 208 | 417 | 252 | 138 | 320 | 905 | 396 | 24 | 743 | 341 | 339 | 420 | 866 | 953 | 10,093 |
| 1989 | 18,105 | 105 | 211 | 394 | 263 | 152 | 530 | 810 | 363 | 31 | 653 | 338 | 363 | 469 | 880 | 880 | 10,397 |
| 1990 | 19,258 | 99 | 206 | 543 | 288 | 155 | 562 | 999 | 495 | 41 | 719 | 257 | 314 | 449 | 811 | 1,019 | 10,253 |
| 1991 | 20,014 | 76 | 232 | 370 | 255 | 142 | 546 | 1,097 | 335 | 138 | 554 | 237 | 293 | 432 | 897 | 889 | 9,360 |
| 1992 | 18,538 | 67 | 271 | 389 | 252 | 161 | 553 | 1,020 | 392 | 34 | 1,208 | 230 | 217 | 435 | 849 | 899 | 7,814 |
| 1993 | 19,273 | 67 | 313 | 418 | 322 | 152 | 808 | 1,120 | 476 | 37 | 1,220 | 110 | 216 | 419 | 823 | 527 | 13,600 |
| 1994 | 18,400 | 82 | 304 | 410 | 342 | 157 | 842 | 1,070 | 478 | 33 | 1,290 | 150 | 239 | 440 | 934 | 505 | 16,400 |
| 1995[1] | 21,100 | 74 | 290 | 410 | 332 | 155 | 726 | 1,090 | 468 | 67 | 2,420 | 152 | 236 | 413 | 847 | 563 | 13,100 |

[1] Preliminary. [2] Chlralkali producers and other chemical. *Source: U.S. Geological Survey*

# Sheep & Lambs

The U.S. sheep herd continues to contract, setting a new low in 1996. The mid-1996 the sheep/lamb inventory of 10.3 million head was 6 percent lower than a year earlier. Of the total, the breeding inventory was down to 6.2 million head vs. 6.5 million in mid-1995.

Commercial lamb production in 1996 of 257 million pounds compares with 287 million in 1995. The U.S. is a net importer of lamb, mostly from New Zealand and Australia with live sheep coming from Canada. Per capita retail consumption of lamb in the U.S. is small, totaling only 1.2 pounds in 1994 and 1995, and 1.0 pounds in 1996.

Slaughter lamb prices rose toward mid-1996, peaking at $88.92/cwt., basis San Angelo, declining to the mid-$70's by fall. For the year, prices averaged about $83.00/cwt.

In contrast to the U.S., world demand for lamb has improved considerably, overwhelming the weak recovery in wool prices that began in early 1995. As a result, the movement of flocks from wool production to meat production is likely to persist. World sheep numbers were expected to increase slightly in 1996 and 1997 after seven years of steady decline. The recovery largely reflecting increases in China and a moderate gain in Australia's flock.

## World Sheep and Goat Numbers in Specified Countries, January 1 In Thousands of Head

| Year | Agrentina | Australia | China | France | Greece | India | Italy | Kazakhstan[3] | New Zealand | Romania | Russia[3] | South Africa | Spain | Turkey | United Kingdom | United States |
|---|---|---|---|---|---|---|---|---|---|---|---|---|---|---|---|---|
| 1987 | 28,998 | 158,800 | 166,220 | 10,580 | 10,000 | 55,482 | 11,451 | 36,408 | 69,204 | 18,762 | 64,100 | 29,753 | 17,600 | 43,500 | 25,976 | 10,334 |
| 1988 | 29,202 | 162,500 | 180,340 | 10,360 | 10,512 | 51,684 | 11,450 | 36,388 | 64,244 | 18,900 | 63,000 | 29,640 | 20,310 | 40,000 | 27,820 | 10,784 |
| 1989 | 29,345 | 171,292 | 201,527 | 11,495 | 10,694 | 155,204 | 11,623 | 36,498 | 64,600 | 16,210 | 62,700 | 30,935 | 23,797 | 45,700 | 29,045 | 10,858 |
| 1990 | 28,571 | 177,841 | 211,642 | 11,208 | 10,150 | 157,706 | 11,695 | 36,223 | 60,569 | 15,442 | 61,300 | 38,349 | 22,730 | 45,300 | 29,521 | 12,132 |
| 1991 | 27,552 | 173,982 | 210,021 | 11,071 | 9,759 | 160,207 | 10,848 | 35,700 | 57,852 | 14,062 | 58,200 | 37,585 | 24,037 | 45,000 | 30,147 | 11,930 |
| 1992 | 25,706 | 161,073 | 206,210 | 11,761 | 9,694 | 161,084 | 11,749 | 34,556 | 55,162 | 13,879 | 55,255 | 36,076 | 24,625 | 44,700 | 28,932 | 11,507 |
| 1993 | 24,500 | 140,542 | 207,329 | 11,451 | 9,659 | 162,155 | 11,724 | 34,420 | 52,568 | 12,079 | 51,368 | 35,770 | 24,615 | 44,600 | 29,493 | 10,906 |
| 1994 | 23,500 | 132,569 | 217,310 | 11,505 | 9,604 | 163,156 | 11,835 | 34,208 | 50,298 | 12,276 | 43,712 | 33,800 | 23,872 | 44,000 | 29,333 | 9,714 |
| 1995 | 21,626 | 123,210 | 240,528 | 11,385 | 9,559 | 164,242 | 12,070 | 25,132 | 50,135 | 12,119 | 34,541 | 33,385 | 29,484 | 43,000 | 29,484 | 8,886 |
| 1996[1] | 17,956 | 126,320 | 254,626 | 11,390 | 9,386 | 165,384 | 12,000 | 19,383 | 47,270 | 11,529 | 28,336 | 35,145 | 28,797 | 42,400 | 28,797 | 8,457 |
| 1997[2] | 17,306 | 128,100 | 264,326 | 11,390 | 9,201 | 166,010 | 12,000 | 14,200 | 47,050 | 11,500 | 23,800 | 37,310 | 22,100 | 41,800 | 28,720 | 8,303 |

[1] Preliminary. [2] Forecast. [3] Formerly part of the U.S.S.R.; data not reported separately until 1986. *Source: Foreign Agricultural Service, U.S. Department of Agriculture*

## Salient Statistics of Sheep & Lamb in the United States In Thousands of Head

| Year | Inventory, Jan. 1: Without New Crop Lambs | Inventory, Jan. 1: With New Crop Lambs | Lamb Crop | Total Supply | Marketings[3]: Sheep | Marketings[3]: Lambs | Slaughter: Farm | Slaughter: Commercial | Slaughter: Total[4] | Net Exports | Total Disappearance | Production (Live Weight) Mil. Lbs. | Farm Value, Jan. 1: All Million $ | Farm Value, Jan. 1: $ Per Hear |
|---|---|---|---|---|---|---|---|---|---|---|---|---|---|---|
| 1987 | 10,572 | 11,417 | 7,190 | 18,607 | 1,195 | 6,194 | 112 | 5,200 | 5,312 | 15 | 12,085 | 733.1 | 799.3 | 75.7 |
| 1988 | 10,945 | 11,799 | 7,205 | 19,004 | 1,610 | 6,350 | 99 | 5,294 | 5,393 | 134 | 12,268 | 730.9 | 985.0 | 90.0 |
| 1989 | 10,853 | 11,674 | 7,721 | 19,395 | 1,129 | 7,201 | 97 | 5,466 | 5,563 | 188 | 12,412 | 811.3 | 894.4 | 82.4 |
| 1990 | 11,358 | 12,132 | 7,685 | 19,817 | 1,628 | 6,823 | 96 | 5,654 | 5,750 | 448 | 12,290 | 780.8 | 901.1 | 79.3 |
| 1991 | 11,174 | 11,930 | 7,651 | 19,581 | 1,719 | 7,187 | 91 | 5,722 | 5,813 | 787 | 11,763 | 796.1 | 732.6 | 65.6 |
| 1992 | 10,797 | 11,507 | 7,225 | 18,732 | 1,923 | 7,007 | 88 | 5,497 | 5,585 | 770 | 11,173 | 746.0 | 660.7 | 61.2 |
| 1993 | 10,201 | 10,906 | 6,379 | 17,285 | 1,952 | 6,752 | 84 | 5,184 | 5,268 | 750 | 10,159 | 688.6 | 714.2 | 70.6 |
| 1994 | 9,079 | 9,714 | 5,897 | 15,611 | 1,527 | 6,358 | 69 | 4,939 | 5,008 | 760 | 8,899 | 625.9 | 681.4 | 69.9 |
| 1995[1] | 8,008 | 8,886 | 5,606 | 14,492 | NA | NA | 72 | 4,559 | 4,631 | 680 | 8,289 | NA | 663.4 | 74.7 |
| 1996[2] | 7,598 | 8,461 | 5,282 | 13,743 | NA | NA | 65 | 4,185 | 4,250 | 264 | 8,299 | NA | 731.4 | 86.5 |

[1] Preliminary. [2] Estimate. [3] Excludes interfarm sales. [4] Includes all commercial and farm. NA = Not avaliable.
*Source: Economic Research Service, U.S. Department of Agriculture*

## Sheep and Lambs on Farms in the United States, January 1 In Thousands of Head

| Year | California | Colorado | Idaho | Iowa | Minnesota | Missouri | Montana | New Mexico | Ohio | South Dakota | Texas | Utah | Wyoming | Total[3] |
|---|---|---|---|---|---|---|---|---|---|---|---|---|---|---|
| 1987 | 980 | 690 | 314 | 375 | 237 | 110 | 523 | 480 | 300 | 605 | 1,930 | 464 | 775 | 10,334 |
| 1988 | 990 | 755 | 324 | 405 | 258 | 103 | 530 | 489 | 270 | 610 | 1,960 | 478 | 865 | 10,945 |
| 1989 | 940 | 825 | 287 | 420 | 290 | 125 | 600 | 516 | 246 | 590 | 1,870 | 503 | 837 | 10,858 |
| 1990 | 1,000 | 840 | 286 | 490 | 285 | 138 | 663 | 495 | 270 | 590 | 2,090 | 509 | 805 | 11,363 |
| 1991 | 1,015 | 710 | 272 | 465 | 300 | 134 | 683 | 462 | 305 | 640 | 2,000 | 508 | 830 | 11,200 |
| 1992 | 995 | 710 | 273 | 345 | 293 | 111 | 658 | 445 | 215 | 602 | 2,140 | 488 | 870 | 10,749 |
| 1993 | 995 | 685 | 250 | 320 | 245 | 97 | 554 | 405 | 190 | 591 | 2,000 | 490 | 885 | 10,500 |
| 1994 | 1,120 | 647 | 266 | 267 | 231 | 91 | 534 | 340 | 198 | 550 | 1,895 | 442 | 813 | 9,742 |
| 1995 | 1,060 | 545 | 270 | 294 | 190 | 83 | 490 | 315 | 162 | 530 | 1,700 | 445 | 790 | 8,886 |
| 1996[1] | 1,000 | 535 | 273 | 345 | 185 | 73 | 465 | 265 | 153 | 500 | 1,650 | 395 | 680 | 8,461 |
| 1997[2] | 960 | 575 | 285 | 285 | 180 | 68 | 432 | 235 | 130 | 450 | 1,400 | 375 | 720 | 7,937 |

[1] Preliminary. [2] Estimate. [3] Includes sheep & lambs on feed for market and stock sheep & lambs. *Source: Economic Research Service, U.S. Department of Agriculture*

## SHEEP AND LAMBS

### Average Wholesale Price of Slaughter Lambs (Choice) at San Angelo, Texas    In Dollars Per 100 Pounds

| Year | Jan. | Feb. | Mar. | Apr. | May | June | July | Aug. | Sept. | Oct. | Nov. | Dec. | Average |
|---|---|---|---|---|---|---|---|---|---|---|---|---|---|
| 1988 | 83.53 | 77.25 | 83.75 | 76.50 | 72.67 | 59.38 | 59.00 | 56.19 | 59.50 | 63.94 | 65.55 | 68.83 | 68.84 |
| 1989 | 68.13 | 68.83 | 70.90 | 78.17 | 73.56 | 72.63 | 67.79 | 67.28 | 63.81 | 59.63 | 56.06 | 60.83 | 67.30 |
| 1990 | 54.80 | 60.38 | 63.69 | 63.13 | 62.25 | 53.56 | 53.25 | 51.20 | 51.75 | 52.50 | 50.42 | 48.08 | 55.42 |
| 1991 | 47.63 | 45.81 | 54.88 | 55.50 | 57.70 | 55.75 | 55.50 | 54.31 | 53.25 | 51.20 | 52.08 | 54.92 | 53.21 |
| 1992 | 58.56 | 57.69 | 66.55 | 74.63 | 68.88 | 64.50 | 58.17 | 52.38 | 53.61 | 52.81 | 56.93 | 67.25 | 61.00 |
| 1993 | 69.88 | 73.38 | 75.50 | 71.25 | 62.50 | 57.75 | 57.00 | 58.97 | 66.08 | 63.75 | 65.69 | 68.44 | 65.85 |
| 1994 | 56.67 | 62.31 | 61.19 | 51.25 | 60.94 | 66.92 | 75.33 | 79.50 | 76.08 | 69.96 | 73.60 | 67.50 | 66.77 |
| 1995 | 65.38 | 75.08 | 73.75 | 68.58 | 77.20 | 81.63 | 83.70 | 87.00 | 80.00 | 75.50 | 72.00 | 70.50 | 75.86 |
| 1996[1] | 74.44 | 85.63 | 84.07 | 83.10 | 86.17 | 97.50 | 92.67 | 83.75 | 84.40 | 82.58 | 80.00 | 88.88 | 85.27 |

[1] Preliminary. *Source: Economic Research Service, U.S. Department of Agriculture*

### Federally Inspected Slaughter of Sheep & Lambs in the United States    In Thousands of Head

| Year | Jan. | Feb. | Mar. | Apr. | May. | June | July | Aug. | Sept. | Oct. | Nov. | Dec. | Total |
|---|---|---|---|---|---|---|---|---|---|---|---|---|---|
| 1988 | 380 | 408 | 535 | 388 | 414 | 413 | 387 | 442 | 452 | 437 | 418 | 447 | 5,121 |
| 1989 | 418 | 415 | 505 | 393 | 435 | 423 | 398 | 476 | 440 | 468 | 467 | 457 | 5,295 |
| 1990 | 479 | 431 | 481 | 466 | 465 | 426 | 430 | 463 | 422 | 490 | 465 | 449 | 5,467 |
| 1991 | 495 | 449 | 546 | 436 | 442 | 388 | 431 | 438 | 456 | 501 | 449 | 471 | 5,502 |
| 1992 | 468 | 422 | 481 | 503 | 374 | 419 | 427 | 400 | 470 | 452 | 413 | 460 | 5,289 |
| 1993 | 380 | 384 | 476 | 461 | 396 | 462 | 394 | 413 | 410 | 391 | 403 | 430 | 5,000 |
| 1994 | 383 | 409 | 515 | 402 | 418 | 377 | 302 | 382 | 384 | 381 | 393 | 411 | 4,756 |
| 1995 | 373 | 363 | 456 | 420 | 355 | 347 | 296 | 355 | 344 | 356 | 364 | 358 | 4,388 |
| 1996[1] | 352 | 353 | 403 | 374 | 313 | 271 | 313 | 315 | 313 | 365 | 324 | 336 | 4,032 |

[1] Preliminary. *Source: Economic Research Service, U.S. Department of Agriculture*

### Cold Storage Holdings of Lamb and Mutton, on First of Month    In Thousands of Pounds

| Year | Jan. | Feb. | Mar. | Apr. | May | June | July | Aug. | Sept. | Oct. | Nov. | Dec. |
|---|---|---|---|---|---|---|---|---|---|---|---|---|
| 1988 | 7,949 | 8,069 | 6,190 | 7,056 | 7,639 | 8,018 | 8,738 | 8,537 | 7,253 | 6,827 | 6,396 | 6,001 |
| 1989 | 6,115 | 7,267 | 6,487 | 6,947 | 6,135 | 6,827 | 8,003 | 7,841 | 7,731 | 7,057 | 7,707 | 7,990 |
| 1990 | 7,625 | 7,844 | 8,468 | 7,905 | 8,390 | 8,052 | 9,685 | 10,107 | 9,144 | 8,929 | 8,458 | 8,099 |
| 1991 | 8,414 | 9,438 | 9,829 | 8,070 | 7,277 | 8,436 | 8,002 | 6,917 | 6,130 | 5,287 | 5,739 | 6,659 |
| 1992 | 6,296 | 7,255 | 6,670 | 8,455 | 8,580 | 9,870 | 10,968 | 11,711 | 9,314 | 8,751 | 8,520 | 8,406 |
| 1993 | 7,864 | 6,343 | 6,620 | 6,661 | 11,064 | 11,181 | 13,152 | 13,495 | 12,241 | 12,615 | 11,843 | 10,161 |
| 1994 | 8,372 | 9,198 | 9,507 | 11,194 | 11,505 | 11,368 | 12,124 | 12,026 | 11,016 | 9,261 | 8,946 | 8,796 |
| 1995 | 10,913 | 11,621 | 10,825 | 12,679 | 14,934 | 13,992 | 12,306 | 10,679 | 10,240 | 7,412 | 7,503 | 7,846 |
| 1996[1] | 7,606 | 9,794 | 13,017 | 12,247 | 13,649 | 12,187 | 13,726 | 13,164 | 14,705 | 11,249 | 10,494 | 9,803 |

[1] Preliminary. *Source: Economic Research Service, U.S. Department of Agriculture*

### Average Price Received by Farmers for Sheep in the U.S.    In Dollars Per Hundred Pounds (Cwt.)

| Year | Jan. | Feb. | Mar. | Apr. | May | June | July | Aug. | Sept. | Oct. | Nov. | Dec. | Average |
|---|---|---|---|---|---|---|---|---|---|---|---|---|---|
| 1988 | 34.70 | 30.10 | 29.70 | 26.00 | 23.90 | 23.20 | 25.00 | 25.30 | 25.00 | 25.30 | 27.80 | 29.10 | 27.09 |
| 1989 | 34.20 | 35.70 | 30.30 | 25.40 | 21.60 | 22.20 | 24.60 | 23.40 | 23.10 | 22.70 | 29.50 | 31.10 | 26.98 |
| 1990 | 32.20 | 30.90 | 30.00 | 23.50 | 19.70 | 19.60 | 24.70 | 24.30 | 18.90 | 19.20 | 20.40 | 22.40 | 23.82 |
| 1991 | 23.50 | 19.90 | 21.50 | 21.30 | 18.30 | 21.00 | 20.30 | 19.20 | 18.90 | 18.20 | 19.80 | 22.60 | 20.38 |
| 1992 | 28.10 | 29.80 | 31.60 | 28.30 | 23.10 | 22.60 | 24.00 | 25.80 | 25.00 | 25.30 | 25.50 | 33.20 | 26.86 |
| 1993 | 33.10 | 35.20 | 36.10 | 27.30 | 29.10 | 28.90 | 29.00 | 28.50 | 25.80 | 24.60 | 25.70 | 30.30 | 29.47 |
| 1994 | 35.10 | 37.00 | 34.30 | 29.60 | 29.30 | 33.60 | 30.10 | 29.40 | 27.90 | 27.30 | 30.50 | 34.70 | 31.57 |
| 1995 | 32.80 | 37.50 | 31.90 | 29.50 | 27.90 | 28.30 | 28.60 | 27.00 | 26.00 | 24.50 | 23.80 | 26.00 | 28.65 |
| 1996[1] | 34.40 | 33.80 | 34.30 | 27.70 | 25.60 | 27.50 | 30.30 | 29.10 | 30.10 | 28.80 | 29.70 | 33.10 | 30.37 |

[1] Preliminary. *Source: Economic Research Service, U.S. Department of Agriculture*

### Average Price Received by Farmers for Lambs in the U.S.    In Dollars Per Hundred Pounds (Cwt.)

| Year | Jan. | Feb. | Mar. | Apr. | May | June | July | Aug. | Sept. | Oct. | Nov. | Dec. | Average |
|---|---|---|---|---|---|---|---|---|---|---|---|---|---|
| 1988 | 80.70 | 80.40 | 80.20 | 74.80 | 72.60 | 60.20 | 60.00 | 59.80 | 64.20 | 66.20 | 66.30 | 68.60 | 69.50 |
| 1989 | 67.40 | 68.40 | 72.50 | 75.20 | 73.10 | 70.60 | 68.60 | 66.60 | 65.90 | 62.00 | 58.70 | 59.00 | 67.33 |
| 1990 | 56.40 | 59.80 | 66.00 | 62.90 | 59.80 | 55.40 | 54.40 | 54.00 | 52.80 | 51.90 | 50.10 | 48.60 | 56.01 |
| 1991 | 48.00 | 45.80 | 51.10 | 54.80 | 57.60 | 55.30 | 57.70 | 53.40 | 51.80 | 51.70 | 50.70 | 52.00 | 52.49 |
| 1992 | 53.50 | 55.20 | 63.40 | 69.30 | 68.80 | 65.60 | 62.20 | 55.90 | 56.70 | 55.40 | 58.20 | 65.20 | 60.78 |
| 1993 | 67.30 | 72.70 | 76.00 | 68.10 | 61.50 | 55.70 | 53.90 | 59.20 | 64.50 | 64.50 | 65.80 | 66.00 | 64.60 |
| 1994 | 60.60 | 59.40 | 58.60 | 54.50 | 54.50 | 63.00 | 72.80 | 75.50 | 71.20 | 68.00 | 70.60 | 69.10 | 64.82 |
| 1995 | 67.50 | 70.40 | 74.80 | 74.60 | 80.40 | 85.70 | 85.70 | 85.60 | 82.70 | 77.60 | 77.10 | 76.50 | 78.22 |
| 1996[1] | 76.10 | 84.30 | 86.40 | 85.60 | 90.70 | 99.90 | 98.30 | 89.00 | 88.20 | 86.90 | 84.50 | 88.30 | 88.18 |

[1] Preliminary. *Source: Economic Research Service, U.S. Department of Agriculture*

# Silk

The world's largest producer of silk by far is China. In 1994, Chinese production of silk was 84,001 tonnes or 73 percent of the world total silk production of 114,509 tonnes. Chinese silk production has been on a steady increase. In 1990, Chinese silk production was 55,003 tonnes. In 1985, Chinese silk production was 38,956 tonnes. The second largest producer of silk is India. In 1994, production was 17,000 tonnes or about 15 percent of the world total. India has also been increasing its silk output. In 1990, Indian silk production was 11,000 tonnes. In 1985, Indian silk production was 7,029 tonnes. The next largest producer of silk is North Korea which in 1994 produced 4,800 tonnes. North Korea has been slowly increasing its production of silk. Of interest is Japan where production is on the decline. In 1994, Japanese production was 2,400 tonnes. In 1990, Japan produced 6,000 tonnes of silk while in 1985, production was 9,591 tonnes.

The major importers of silk are Japan, Hong Kong, Italy, India, and South Korea. The major exporters of silk are China, Brazil, and North Korea.

### Futures Markets

Raw silk is traded in Japan on the Kobe Raw Silk Exchange (KSE). Dry Cocoons are traded on the Manila International Futures Exchange Inc., (MIFE).

## World Production of Silk  In Metric Tons

| Year | Brazil | China | India | Iran | Japan | North Korea | South Korea | Kyrgyzstan[3] | Tajikistan[3] | Thailand | Turkey | Turkmenistan[3] | Uzbekistan[3] | Viet Nam | World Total |
|---|---|---|---|---|---|---|---|---|---|---|---|---|---|---|---|
| 1985 | 1,200 | 38,956 | 7,029 | 280 | 9,591 | 3,500 | 1,436 | ----- | ----- | 1,300 | 80 | ----- | 3,908 | 330 | 68,090 |
| 1986 | 1,200 | 39,098 | 9,300 | 280 | 8,336 | 3,600 | 1,342 | ----- | ----- | 1,400 | 85 | ----- | 3,710 | 350 | 69,178 |
| 1987 | 1,800 | 40,940 | 9,498 | 900 | 7,864 | 3,700 | 1,413 | ----- | ----- | 1,200 | 216 | ----- | 4,200 | 360 | 72,597 |
| 1988 | 1,900 | 42,041 | 10,255 | 900 | 6,862 | 3,800 | 1,355 | ----- | ----- | 1,250 | 251 | ----- | 4,300 | 420 | 73,866 |
| 1989 | 1,697 | 50,244 | 10,500 | 537 | 6,078 | 4,000 | 1,400 | ----- | ----- | 1,250 | 250 | ----- | 3,900 | 400 | 80,745 |
| 1990 | 1,693 | 55,003 | 11,000 | 537 | 6,000 | 4,200 | 971 | ----- | ----- | 1,250 | 290 | ----- | 4,094 | 500 | 85,987 |
| 1991 | 2,077 | 60,002 | 14,000 | 537 | 5,527 | 4,400 | 837 | ----- | ----- | 1,300 | 180 | ----- | 4,100 | 500 | 93,880 |
| 1992 | 2,296 | 70,302 | 15,000 | 537 | 5,085 | 4,500 | 870 | 1,200 | 300 | 1,300 | 105 | 600 | 2,200 | 500 | 105,220 |
| 1993[1] | 2,450 | 76,801 | 16,000 | 537 | 4,000 | 4,600 | 683 | 1,000 | 300 | 1,500 | 135 | 500 | 2,000 | 550 | 111,473 |
| 1994[2] | 2,450 | 84,001 | 17,000 | 550 | 2,400 | 4,800 | 683 | NA | NA | 1,500 | 135 | NA | NA | 588 | 114,509 |

[1] Preliminary. [2] Estimate. [3] Formerly part of the U.S.S.R.; data not reported separately until 1992. NA = Not available.
*Source: Food and Agricultural Organization of the United Nations*

## World Trade of Silk by Selected Countries  In Metric Tons

| | Imports | | | | | | | | Exports | | | | | | |
|---|---|---|---|---|---|---|---|---|---|---|---|---|---|---|---|
| Year | France | Hong Kong | India | Italy | Japan | South Korea | United States | World Total | Brazil | China | Hong Kong | Japan | North Korea | Russia[2] | World Total |
| 1986 | 572 | 3,179 | 2,100 | 7,133 | 8,943 | 3,747 | 475 | 29,835 | 692 | 16,349 | 4,115 | 586 | 1,060 | 2,816 | 27,931 |
| 1987 | 770 | 6,652 | 2,100 | 7,339 | 8,342 | 5,582 | 661 | 35,864 | 648 | 18,368 | 7,778 | 794 | 1,200 | 3,367 | 34,886 |
| 1988 | 771 | 7,489 | 1,411 | 8,094 | 10,259 | 4,851 | 435 | 39,216 | 670 | 20,168 | 8,553 | 442 | 1,200 | 4,432 | 37,276 |
| 1989 | 1,012 | 6,362 | 1,400 | 7,740 | 8,512 | 3,763 | 535 | 35,968 | 534 | 19,314 | 6,748 | 417 | 1,100 | 5,754 | 39,064 |
| 1990 | 796 | 3,928 | 1,647 | 4,775 | 7,111 | 3,204 | 326 | 27,322 | 1,064 | 13,066 | 4,102 | 380 | 1,200 | 1,703 | 27,977 |
| 1991 | 579 | 4,347 | 2,100 | 5,297 | 6,933 | 3,519 | 439 | 29,623 | 2,052 | 15,178 | 4,186 | 405 | 900 | 2,000 | 29,188 |
| 1992 | 693 | 4,400 | 2,843 | 4,337 | 5,137 | 3,627 | 288 | 28,239 | 1,552 | 13,474 | 4,358 | 701 | 800 | 410 | 26,433 |
| 1993 | 1,001 | 5,475 | 4,977 | 5,634 | 5,982 | 4,494 | 375 | 35,832 | 1,495 | 15,652 | 7,204 | 904 | 600 | 166 | 34,984 |
| 1994[1] | 1,047 | 6,165 | 5,439 | 9,228 | 5,772 | 4,128 | 337 | 43,664 | 1,739 | 21,005 | 6,149 | 1,265 | 1,300 | 200 | 41,455 |

[1] Preliminary. [2] Formerly part of the U.S.S.R.; data not reported separately until 1992.
*Source: Food and Agricultural Organization of the United Nations*

## U.S. Raw Silk Deliveries  In Bales of 132-Pounds

| Year | Jan. | Feb. | Mar. | Apr. | May | June | July | Aug. | Sept. | Oct. | Nov. | Dec. | Total |
|---|---|---|---|---|---|---|---|---|---|---|---|---|---|
| 1985 | 462 | 689 | 344 | 480 | 415 | NA | NA | NA | NA | NA | NA | NA | 4,813 |
| 1986 | 410 | 504 | 197 | 244 | 225 | 227 | 555 | NA | NA | NA | NA | NA | 4,272 |
| 1987 | 411 | 680 | 572 | 526 | 245 | 447 | 253 | 327 | 330 | 470 | 239 | 448 | 4,948 |
| 1988 | 292 | 430 | 559 | 317 | 302 | 189 | 203 | 613 | 310 | 126 | 367 | 108 | 3,816 |
| 1989 | 358 | 234 | 471 | 329 | 405 | 564 | 353 | 401 | 288 | 317 | 475 | 442 | 4,637 |
| 1990 | 455 | 352 | 387 | 158 | 342 | 150 | 248 | 53 | 49 | 103 | 152 | 139 | 2,588 |
| 1991 | 124 | 126 | 206 | 187 | 100 | 250 | 445 | 305 | 220 | 345 | 325 | 351 | 2,984 |
| 1992 | 145 | 192 | 425 | 209 | 122 | 459 | 173 | 166 | 146 | 223 | 249 | 132 | 2,641 |
| 1993 | 457 | 173 | 281 | 215 | 315 | 197 | NA | NA | NA | NA | NA | NA | 3,066 |
| 1994 | 363 | 71 | 224 | 233 | 227 | 479 | 315 | 227 | 195 | 193 | 315 | 201 | 3,043 |
| 1995[1] | NA | NA | NA | NA | NA | NA | NA | NA | NA | NA | NA | NA | 2,041 |

[1] Preliminary. NA = Not available. *Source: Fiber Economics Bureau, Inc.*

# Silver

Silver prices had a short lived rally during the first quarter of 1996 that topped out near $6.00/ounce, basis March '97 COMEX futures. Through the rest of 1996 prices drifted lower, bottoming towards yearend in the $4.75-5.00 area. Daily futures trading volume was often lethargic and COMEX open interest contracted towards 80,000 contracts by yearend vs. over 100,000 in mid-year.

Many variables impact on the price of silver at any given time, but it is difficult to determine which are the most important. The fundamental approach focuses on tangible supply/demand data which can help rationalize a price swing in either direction. However, on its own such price action can usually not be sustained. Market intangibles, often defying quantitative analysis, may enter the picture in turn exaggerating the price action when technically structured computer generated buy or sell signals are triggered. Compounding silver's uncertainty is that the metal's price is quoted in different markets, and perhaps at the same time, different prices. The primary price references are the London spot, fixed daily at 12:15 P.M., the COMEX spot settlement, and the Handy & Harmon price which is the cash quotation accepted by most commercial users.

Historically inflation fears, real or perceived, coupled with a belief of a direct price correlation between gold and silver have exerted strong market reactions, especially on silver which has been called the poor man's gold. In recent years the relationship appears to have dissipated.

Contributing to the curtailed trading interest in silver during 1996 were the buoyant equity markets which siphoned risk capital away from silver. Moreover, there was persistent assurance from the government and credit markets that inflation posed no threat. Even the drawdown on COMEX approved silver vault stocks failed to reawaken buying enthusiasm; at yearend 1995 COMEX stocks totaled 159 million ounces, down almost 100 million from a year earlier, toward the end of 1996 stocks had fallen to about 130 million pounces. However, declining COMEX silver inventories do not necessarily mean increased consumption, but more likely a reallocation of inventory placement. U.S. silver exports doubled to almost 1900 tons during the first half of 1996 from the like 1995 period, destined for Europe, but believed to be then transshipped to Asia. The unknown factor behind these shipments was the purpose they were intended for, inventory accumulation, actual use, or both.

World mine production of silver in 1995 of 469 million ounces compares with 444 million in 1994 which was the lowest since 1986. Only 16 percent of 1995's silver came from primary mines, most was obtained as a by-product of copper, lead, zinc, and gold mining. Forecast for the next few years put mine production toward 500 million ounces with production more a function of the price of the host metals associated with silver. Mexico is the world's largest producer with about 75 million ounces in 1995, followed by Peru at 61 million. U.S. production in 1995 of almost 50 million ounces compares with 48 million in 1994. Nevada is the largest producing state. The worldwide recovery of silver from secondary supplies such as scrap and old coinage totaled 141 million ounces in 1995 vs. 136 million in 1994. U.S. secondary production of 30 million ounces in 1995 was the world's largest, followed by Japan with 27 million ounces, and Germany at 15 million.

Silver fabrication demand in 1995 of 764 million ounces compares with 758 million in 1994. Of the total, U.S. demand was 139.7 million ounces (vs. 132.5) and Japan 112.7 million (vs. 108.4). Collectively, European demand was the largest at 220 million ounces vs. 224 million in 1994, with Italy and Germany accounting for 100 million ounces in each year. Fabrication demand includes (1) industrial and decorative, (2) photography, (3) jewelry/silverware and (4) coinage; of the four only Western World coinage use fell in 1995, down 48 percent to 22 million ounces.

### *Futures Markets*

Silver futures are traded on the Tokyo Commodity Exchange (TOCOM), the Chicago Board of Trade (CBOT), the Mid America Commodity Exchange (MidAm), and the New York Mercantile Exchange, COMEX division (COMEX). Options are traded on the European Options Exchange (EOE-Optiebeurs), the CBOT, and the COMEX.

**World Mine Production of Silver, by Selected Countries** In Thousands of Kilograms (Metric Tons)

| Year | Australia | Bolivia | Brazil | Canada[3] | Chile | China | Japan | Kazakhstan[4] | Rep. of Korea | Mexico | Peru | Poland | South Africa | Spain | Sweden | United States | World Total[2] |
|---|---|---|---|---|---|---|---|---|---|---|---|---|---|---|---|---|---|
| 1981 | 743 | 199 | 24 | 1,129 | 361 | 78 | 280 | 1,446 | 95 | 1,646 | 1,460 | 640 | 235 | 166 | 161 | 1,265 | 11,246 |
| 1982 | 907 | 170 | 24 | 1,314 | 382 | 78 | 306 | 1,459 | 101 | 1,840 | 1,305 | 657 | 216 | 118 | 168 | 1,252 | 11,543 |
| 1983 | 1,033 | 187 | 15 | 1,106 | 468 | 78 | 307 | 1,468 | 105 | 1,978 | 1,570 | 678 | 203 | 47 | 207 | 1,351 | 12,058 |
| 1984 | 972 | 142 | 26 | 1,327 | 490 | 78 | 324 | 1,474 | 117 | 2,343 | 1,651 | 744 | 218 | 290 | 239 | 1,387 | 13,064 |
| 1985 | 1,086 | 111 | 32 | 1,197 | 517 | 80 | 339 | 1,490 | 124 | 2,153 | 1,811 | 831 | 208 | 367 | 231 | 1,227 | 13,051 |
| 1986 | 1,023 | 95 | 58 | 1,088 | 500 | 90 | 351 | 1,500 | 157 | 2,303 | 1,926 | 829 | 222 | 327 | 263 | 1,074 | 13,034 |
| 1987 | 1,119 | 142 | 110 | 1,375 | 500 | 100 | 281 | 1,510 | 209 | 2,415 | 2,054 | 831 | 208 | 350 | 254 | 1,241 | 14,019 |
| 1988 | 1,118 | 232 | 124 | 1,443 | 507 | 110 | 252 | 2,500 | 227 | 2,359 | 1,552 | 1,063 | 200 | 353 | 208 | 1,661 | 15,484 |
| 1989 | 1,075 | 267 | 114 | 1,371 | 545 | 125 | 156 | 2,500 | 239 | 2,400 | 1,840 | 1,003 | 180 | 668 | 228 | 2,008 | 16,425 |
| 1990 | 1,173 | 311 | 171 | 1,501 | 655 | 130 | 150 | 2,500 | 238 | 2,425 | 1,930 | 832 | 161 | 500 | 243 | 2,121 | 16,600 |
| 1991 | 1,180 | 376 | 154 | 1,339 | 678 | 150 | 171 | 2,200 | 265 | 2,295 | 1,927 | 899 | 171 | 182 | 239 | 1,860 | 15,600 |
| 1992 | 1,218 | 282 | 162 | 1,220 | 1,029 | 170 | 178 | 900 | 333 | 2,098 | 1,614 | 798 | 183 | 160 | 210 | 1,800 | 14,600 |
| 1993 | 1,092 | 333 | 155 | 896 | 970 | 200 | 137 | 900 | 215 | 2,420 | 1,631 | 767 | 192 | 180 | 255 | 1,640 | 14,200 |
| 1994[1] | 1,045 | 352 | 155 | 740 | 983 | 210 | 133 | 800 | 258 | 2,330 | 1,742 | 1,064 | 196 | 132 | 276 | 1,490 | 14,000 |
| 1995[2] | 920 | 410 | 155 | 1,195 | 1,032 | 250 | 100 | 800 | 258 | 2,400 | 1,908 | 1,000 | 174 | 135 | 268 | 1,640 | 14,600 |

[1] Preliminary. [2] Estimate. [3] Shipments. [4] Formerly part of the U.S.S.R.; data not reported separately until 1992. *Source: U.S. Geological Survey*

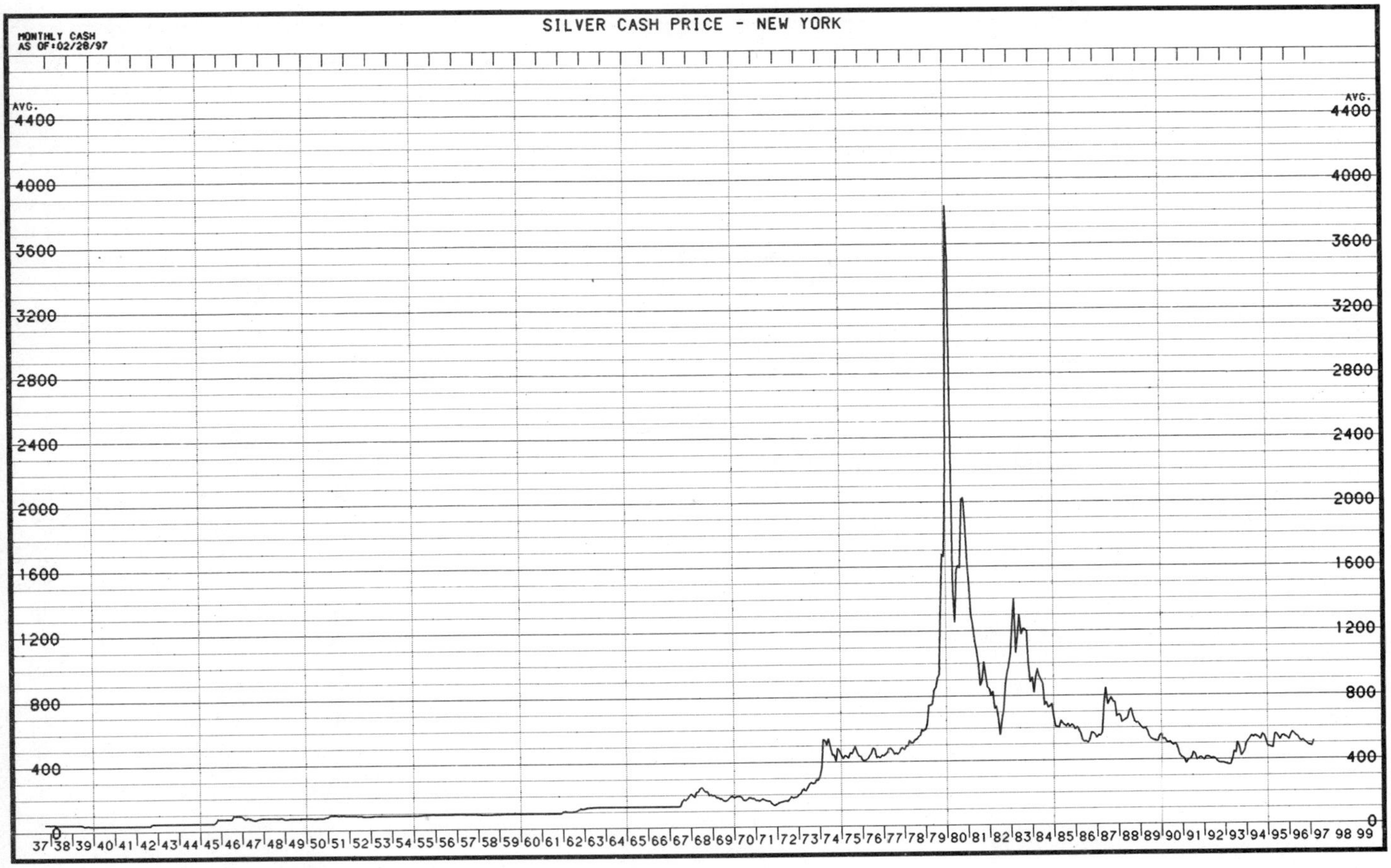


**Average Price of Silver in New York (Handy & Harman)** In Cents Per Troy Ounce (.999 Fine)

| Year | Jan. | Feb. | Mar. | Apr. | May | June | July | Aug. | Sept. | Oct. | Nov. | Dec. | Average |
|---|---|---|---|---|---|---|---|---|---|---|---|---|---|
| 1973 | 201.66 | 223.62 | 230.92 | 220.72 | 240.12 | 262.09 | 270.56 | 263.65 | 267.51 | 288.56 | 285.99 | 313.67 | 255.96 |
| 1974 | 363.70 | 535.90 | 532.55 | 503.60 | 543.18 | 489.61 | 441.55 | 443.14 | 404.88 | 482.98 | 469.39 | 439.13 | 470.80 |
| 1975 | 419.27 | 437.00 | 434.53 | 420.92 | 453.81 | 448.91 | 470.45 | 492.50 | 451.60 | 432.86 | 433.24 | 408.50 | 441.97 |
| 1976 | 406.27 | 408.64 | 418.91 | 435.05 | 448.85 | 481.17 | 477.95 | 423.70 | 429.52 | 422.51 | 437.27 | 434.68 | 435.38 |
| 1977 | 440.90 | 452.74 | 484.16 | 477.71 | 469.20 | 444.30 | 449.81 | 444.43 | 453.86 | 476.32 | 482.84 | 470.60 | 462.30 |
| 1978 | 493.40 | 493.57 | 526.80 | 511.59 | 511.95 | 531.59 | 533.07 | 549.50 | 557.48 | 591.79 | 586.49 | 592.95 | 540.02 |
| 1979 | 625.45 | 741.69 | 745.35 | 749.25 | 836.57 | 853.83 | 913.50 | 933.43 | 1,395.92 | 1,678.07 | 1,655.27 | 2,179.28 | 1,108.97 |
| 1980 | 3,827.21 | 3,508.50 | 2,413.33 | 1,384.09 | 1,253.29 | 1,574.76 | 1,605.97 | 1,589.71 | 2,014.38 | 2,018.14 | 1,864.82 | 1,639.33 | 2,063.29 |
| 1981 | 1,475.15 | 1,306.50 | 1,236.91 | 1,091.73 | 1,084.75 | 1,000.07 | 863.11 | 892.29 | 1,003.55 | 925.12 | 854.68 | 843.16 | 1,048.09 |
| 1982 | 803.05 | 826.79 | 721.30 | 731.07 | 667.35 | 557.79 | 649.67 | 713.61 | 872.52 | 946.75 | 991.83 | 1,058.63 | 795.03 |
| 1983 | 1,239.57 | 1,396.37 | 1,061.87 | 1,169.43 | 1,295.26 | 1,174.93 | 1,208.75 | 1,209.56 | 1,191.50 | 984.13 | 883.73 | 912.07 | 1,143.93 |
| 1984 | 818.24 | 912.65 | 965.11 | 922.05 | 897.20 | 874.38 | 741.57 | 761.30 | 726.34 | 731.68 | 748.89 | 669.42 | 814.07 |
| 1985 | 609.82 | 606.95 | 601.36 | 645.83 | 628.05 | 617.18 | 610.43 | 624.68 | 605.37 | 618.80 | 613.39 | 588.78 | 614.22 |
| 1986 | 605.30 | 587.37 | 563.93 | 522.91 | 511.48 | 515.26 | 504.93 | 521.83 | 568.29 | 566.69 | 559.56 | 536.40 | 547.00 |
| 1987 | 552.88 | 548.76 | 568.16 | 742.79 | 843.90 | 741.09 | 767.84 | 784.74 | 759.05 | 755.80 | 666.18 | 679.02 | 700.85 |
| 1988 | 673.25 | 632.48 | 641.28 | 647.83 | 654.26 | 703.68 | 714.65 | 670.80 | 636.48 | 628.45 | 627.53 | 610.83 | 653.46 |
| 1989 | 597.17 | 589.08 | 592.98 | 579.08 | 544.70 | 528.02 | 523.65 | 517.93 | 513.30 | 513.30 | 546.53 | 554.28 | 550.00 |
| 1990 | 524.30 | 527.84 | 505.82 | 504.58 | 507.39 | 490.60 | 485.90 | 498.15 | 479.03 | 436.59 | 416.90 | 406.84 | 482.00 |
| 1991 | 402.82 | 372.34 | 396.90 | 397.07 | 404.07 | 438.85 | 430.38 | 393.80 | 403.60 | 410.22 | 406.05 | 390.90 | 403.92 |
| 1992 | 412.08 | 413.71 | 410.36 | 403.00 | 406.83 | 405.64 | 394.89 | 379.67 | 376.33 | 373.66 | 376.32 | 370.98 | 393.62 |
| 1993 | 367.93 | 364.39 | 364.80 | 396.36 | 445.02 | 437.50 | 503.74 | 480.61 | 417.19 | 433.45 | 450.25 | 496.83 | 429.84 |
| 1994 | 513.14 | 527.24 | 545.11 | 530.87 | 543.64 | 539.34 | 528.65 | 519.54 | 552.88 | 544.10 | 519.60 | 476.88 | 528.42 |
| 1995 | 476.36 | 469.53 | 464.83 | 552.42 | 555.25 | 535.27 | 517.58 | 539.59 | 540.78 | 534.48 | 529.30 | 514.75 | 519.18 |
| 1996 | 547.03 | 562.75 | 551.38 | 540.14 | 536.02 | 513.58 | 502.95 | 500.98 | 510.50 | 492.76 | 482.76 | 479.23 | 518.34 |

*Source: American Metal Market*

## World Silver Consumption[1] In Millions of Troy Ounces

| | Industrial Uses | | | | | | | | | | Coinage | | | | | | | | |
|---|---|---|---|---|---|---|---|---|---|---|---|---|---|---|---|---|---|---|---|
| Year | Canada | France | Germany | India | Italy | Japan | Mexico | United Kingdom | United States | World Total | Austria | Canada | France | Germany | Mexico | United States | World Total | World Total |
| 1974 | 10.3 | 21.0 | 55.0 | 15.0 | 38.6 | 46.5 | 10.2 | 25.0 | 176.0 | 470.0 | 5.7 | 9.0 | 3.6 | 7.6 | NA | 1.0 | 31.6 | 501.6 |
| 1975 | 10.3 | 21.0 | 38.9 | 13.0 | 28.9 | 46.4 | 8.8 | 28.0 | 157.7 | 407.7 | 9.1 | 10.4 | 1.8 | 5.4 | NA | 2.7 | 33.4 | 441.1 |
| 1976 | 9.3 | 31.8 | 52.9 | 18.0 | 32.1 | 60.7 | 10.2 | 28.0 | 170.6 | 484.7 | 6.9 | 8.4 | 6.2 | 1.8 | NA | 1.3 | 30.0 | 514.7 |
| 1977 | 9.1 | 32.6 | 48.1 | 17.6 | 33.8 | 63.2 | 8.6 | 32.2 | 153.6 | 459.9 | 8.9 | .5 | 7.1 | 4.6 | 4.2 | .1 | 34.5 | 494.4 |
| 1978 | 9.6 | 24.6 | 42.0 | 20.0 | 41.8 | 64.9 | 9.1 | 29.0 | 160.2 | 452.4 | 9.6 | 1.0 | 9.0 | 3.6 | 6.6 | 0 | 39.5 | 491.9 |
| 1979 | 7.3 | 24.1 | 39.8 | 19.0 | 33.3 | 68.8 | 8.6 | 27.6 | 157.3 | 448.2 | 4.0 | .8 | 10.6 | 3.7 | 5.0 | .2 | 31.0 | 479.2 |
| 1980 | 8.7 | 19.8 | 31.9 | 19.0 | 21.8 | 61.5 | 4.9 | 19.5 | 124.7 | 364.3 | 2.3 | .2 | .1 | 0 | 6.1 | .1 | 15.0 | 379.3 |
| 1981 | 8.5 | 18.9 | 29.3 | 19.0 | 21.5 | 59.6 | 5.0 | 18.4 | 116.7 | 355.4 | 3.1 | .3 | .1 | .5 | 0 | .2 | 9.5 | 364.9 |
| 1982 | 9.0 | 17.1 | 32.7 | 16.1 | 20.8 | 63.2 | 5.7 | 18.1 | 118.8 | 361.4 | 4.5 | .3 | 1.4 | .3 | 0 | 1.8 | 12.0 | 373.4 |
| 1983 | 8.9 | 16.5 | 30.3 | 12.9 | 15.0 | 72.1 | 3.5 | 17.7 | 116.3 | 356.5 | 1.8 | .4 | 2.2 | 0 | 0 | 2.1 | 10.2 | 366.7 |
| 1984 | 9.3 | 17.1 | 32.2 | 16.1 | 19.4 | 78.8 | 5.5 | 19.2 | 114.8 | 376.2 | 2.4 | .3 | 3.9 | 0 | 2.5 | 2.0 | 13.7 | 389.9 |
| 1985 | 9.1 | 17.0 | 34.1 | 20.9 | 23.9 | 72.6 | 8.0 | 19.1 | 118.7 | 500.0 | 4.9 | .3 | 2.2 | 0 | 3.5 | .4 | 13.4 | 513.4 |
| 1986 | 9.6 | 17.1 | 36.3 | 22.5 | 33.7 | 78.5 | 7.7 | 19.0 | 118.9 | 542.3 | 1.2 | 1.3 | 2.2 | 0 | 2.0 | 10.3 | 26.8 | 569.1 |
| 1987 | 10.4 | 17.6 | 39.1 | 20.1 | 38.6 | 90.9 | 6.9 | 21.1 | 115.1 | 538.7 | .6 | 1.2 | 2.2 | 3.2 | 2.3 | 12.2 | 30.4 | 569.1 |
| 1988 | 11.0 | 21.3 | 44.0 | 22.4 | 37.9 | 100.4 | 7.1 | 22.8 | 112.0 | 568.6 | .6 | 1.1 | 2.2 | 3.2 | 2.0 | 7.9 | 25.3 | 593.9 |
| 1989 | 12.0 | 22.1 | 46.7 | 25.6 | 43.1 | 100.8 | 7.2 | 24.6 | 120.0 | 599.2 | .4 | 3.3 | 2.2 | 3.2 | 1.7 | 6.8 | 26.3 | 625.5 |
| 1990 | 4.0 | 22.4 | 51.7 | 42.3 | 45.7 | 106.9 | 14.1 | 24.7 | 118.9 | 651.8 | .5 | 1.9 | 2.2 | 2.4 | 1.2 | 9.1 | 31.6 | 683.4 |
| 1991 | 3.8 | 26.9 | 52.2 | 44.9 | 57.4 | 109.3 | 14.3 | 24.7 | 112.3 | 672.3 | .6 | .9 | 2.0 | 5.5 | 1.6 | 10.5 | 28.4 | 700.7 |
| 1992 | 1.6 | 29.7 | 49.3 | 58.1 | 61.1 | 105.4 | 15.6 | 26.3 | 114.5 | 687.7 | .5 | .8 | 2.1 | 5.4 | 8.7 | 8.1 | 32.8 | 720.5 |
| 1993 | 1.6 | 29.0 | 45.6 | 109.9 | 57.4 | 105.5 | 16.4 | 27.6 | 117.4 | 729.4 | .5 | 1.2 | 1.0 | 2.6 | 17.1 | 7.9 | 39.0 | 768.4 |
| 1994 | 1.6 | 29.2 | 45.8 | 91.2 | 52.8 | 108.5 | 16.1 | 31.2 | 124.3 | 715.8 | .5 | 1.5 | 1.0 | 7.0 | 13.0 | 8.2 | 42.3 | 758.1 |
| 1995[2] | 2.0 | 32.3 | 44.1 | 97.5 | 50.8 | 112.7 | 18.5 | 32.3 | 132.2 | 741.6 | .6 | .7 | 1.2 | 2.3 | .6 | 7.5 | 22.9 | 764.4 |

[1] Non-communist areas only. [2] Preliminary. NA = Not available. *Source: The Silver Institute*

## U.S. Mine Production of Recoverable Silver In Metric Tons

| Year | Arizona | Idaho | Montana | Nevada | Total | Year | Arizona | Idaho | Montana | Nevada | Total |
|---|---|---|---|---|---|---|---|---|---|---|---|
| 1984 | 137 | 607 | 182 | 208 | 1,434 | 1990 | 173 | 442 | 220 | 646 | 2,125 |
| 1985 | 152 | 586 | 125 | 154 | 1,227 | 1991 | 148 | 337 | 222 | 578 | 1,848 |
| 1986 | 140 | 349 | 148 | 199 | 1,074 | 1992 | 153 | 255 | 195 | 586 | 1,740 |
| 1987 | 114 | NA | 185 | 379 | 1,241 | 1993 | 157 | 190 | 125 | 713 | 1,610 |
| 1988 | 152 | 340 | 192 | 608 | 1,661 | 1994 | 183 | 158 | 71 | 602 | 1,390 |
| 1989 | 171 | 439 | 194 | 625 | 2,007 | 1995[1] | 220 | 182 | 76 | 766 | 1,640 |

[1] Preliminary. [2] Estimate. NA = Not available. *Source: U.S. Geological Survey*

## U.S. Consumption of Silver, by End Use In Millions of Troy Ounces

| Year | Batteries | Brazing Alloys & Solders | Catalysts | Electrical Contacts - Conductors | Mirrors | Photo-graphic Materials | Silver-plate | Jewelry | Sterling Ware | Total Net Industrial Con-sumption | Coinage | Total Con-sumption |
|---|---|---|---|---|---|---|---|---|---|---|---|---|
| 1981 | 3.8 | 7.7 | 3.8 | 26.4 | .6 | 51.0 | 3.9 | 5.4 | 4.4 | 116.6 | .2 | 116.8 |
| 1982 | 4.2 | 7.4 | 2.4 | 27.7 | 1.0 | 51.8 | 3.3 | 6.3 | 6.6 | 118.9 | 1.8 | 120.7 |
| 1983 | 2.6 | 5.8 | 2.4 | 26.3 | 1.0 | 51.8 | 3.2 | 6.9 | 7.0 | 116.3 | 2.1 | 118.4 |
| 1984 | 2.7 | 5.9 | 2.4 | 25.6 | 1.0 | 55.3 | 3.5 | 5.8 | 3.6 | 114.8 | 2.7 | 117.5 |
| 1985 | 2.5 | 5.6 | 2.4 | 27.5 | 1.0 | 57.9 | 3.7 | 5.8 | 3.5 | 118.7 | .4 | 119.1 |
| 1986 | 3.7 | 6.4 | 2.3 | 27.4 | 1.0 | 55.4 | 3.7 | 4.6 | 3.9 | 118.9 | 10.3 | 129.2 |
| 1987 | 2.4 | 5.6 | 2.4 | 22.7 | 1.0 | 60.2 | 2.5 | 4.2 | 3.8 | 115.1 | 12.2 | 127.3 |
| 1988 | 2.5 | NA | 2.6 | 23.0 | 1.1 | 62.5 | 2.6 | 2.9 | 3.5 | 117.5 | 7.9 | 125.4 |
| 1989 | 2.8 | NA | 2.8 | 23.5 | 1.1 | 65.2 | 2.7 | 2.4 | 3.4 | 126.0 | 6.8 | 132.8 |
| 1990 | 3.0 | NA | 3.0 | 22.8 | 1.2 | 67.0 | 2.8 | 2.0 | 3.5 | 118.2 | 9.1 | 127.3 |
| 1991 | 3.1 | NA | 3.3 | 18.3 | 1.1 | 65.0 | 2.8 | 2.0 | 3.5 | 112.3 | 10.5 | 122.8 |
| 1992 | 3.1 | NA | 3.8 | 18.3 | 1.2 | 63.5 | 2.9 | 3.0 | 3.9 | 114.5 | 8.1 | 122.6 |
| 1993 | 3.3 | NA | 4.0 | 18.8 | 1.3 | 64.0 | 3.0 | 3.3 | 4.0 | 117.4 | 7.9 | 125.3 |
| 1994 | ---------- | ---------- | 46.0 | ---------- | ---------- | ----- 66.3 | ----- | ----- 12.0 | ----- | 124.3 | 8.2 | 132.5 |
| 1995[1] | ---------- | ---------- | 49.4 | ---------- | ---------- | ----- 70.3 | ----- | ----- 12.5 | ----- | 132.2 | 7.5 | 139.7 |

[1] Preliminary. NA = Not available. *Source: The Silver Institute*

## Commodity Exchange, Inc. (COMEX) Warehouse of Stocks of Silver In Thousands of Troy Ounces

| Year | Jan. 1 | Feb. 1 | Mar. 1 | Apr. 1 | May 1 | June 1 | July 1 | Aug. 1 | Sept. 1 | Oct. 1 | Nov. 1 | Dec. 1 |
|---|---|---|---|---|---|---|---|---|---|---|---|---|
| 1985 | 121,516 | 123,320 | 106,614 | 106,777 | 104,238 | 132,431 | 139,285 | 143,439 | 143,970 | 149,178 | 153,743 | 155,343 |
| 1986 | 143,219 | 145,276 | 148,158 | 155,207 | 147,946 | 151,887 | 150,202 | 158,667 | 156,794 | 137,654 | 144,901 | 145,358 |
| 1987 | 150,187 | 159,955 | 157,277 | 157,695 | 156,089 | 152,179 | 152,122 | 160,096 | 156,352 | 154,762 | 155,768 | 156,271 |
| 1988 | 155,429 | 157,592 | 155,755 | 161,276 | 164,348 | 168,198 | 169,743 | 176,309 | 178,773 | 175,282 | 178,457 | 174,359 |
| 1989 | 182,657 | 190,243 | 194,802 | 200,995 | 203,207 | 206,049 | 210,385 | 207,286 | 212,283 | 226,570 | 237,946 | 238,773 |
| 1990 | 240,796 | 243,421 | 252,104 | 253,773 | 255,421 | 251,626 | 253,326 | 255,814 | 260,184 | 258,614 | 257,685 | 265,339 |
| 1991 | 266,206 | 263,832 | 257,851 | 263,563 | 263,686 | 266,087 | 276,961 | 270,804 | 269,661 | 265,874 | 262,835 | 270,734 |
| 1992 | 271,692 | 278,990 | 270,449 | 262,239 | 267,003 | 267,818 | 271,259 | 273,743 | 278,575 | 278,526 | 280,712 | 275,156 |
| 1993 | 272,824 | 273,629 | 271,856 | 265,580 | 270,800 | 273,947 | 277,228 | 278,745 | 276,819 | 275,370 | 277,666 | 263,138 |
| 1994 | 251,685 | 250,730 | 239,374 | 240,187 | 233,950 | 236,459 | 246,291 | 249,417 | 255,198 | 259,634 | 265,710 | 258,618 |
| 1995 | 260,708 | 264,045 | 235,114 | 211,028 | 189,668 | 184,570 | 181,269 | 175,764 | 156,544 | 156,529 | 156,110 | 156,932 |
| 1996 | 159,695 | 143,426 | 151,336 | 139,059 | 141,789 | 150,141 | 168,079 | 155,441 | 151,283 | 141,673 | 129,911 | 148,451 |

*Source: New York Mercantile Exchange, COMEX Division*

## United States Production[1] of Refined Silver from all Sources In Metric Tons

| Year | Jan. | Feb. | Mar. | Apr. | May | June | July | Aug. | Sept. | Oct. | Nov. | Dec. | Total |
|---|---|---|---|---|---|---|---|---|---|---|---|---|---|
| 1984 | 7,094 | 8,414 | 8,446 | 9,827 | 10,423 | 8,921 | 8,879 | 11,226 | 8,971 | 8,386 | 10,200 | 13,920 | 116,400 |
| 1985 | 8,414 | 7,930 | 8,645 | 9,238 | 9,344 | 9,850 | 8,578 | 9,885 | 8,191 | 8,429 | 8,987 | 11,467 | 109,000 |
| 1986 | 7,897 | 7,835 | 7,340 | 8,727 | 7,547 | 7,129 | 3,988 | 6,404 | 6,932 | 7,869 | 8,216 | 10,197 | 90,081 |
| 1987 | 8,170 | 6,098 | 7,047 | 7,946 | 8,473 | 7,839 | 8,777 | 7,731 | 7,703 | 6,692 | 6,955 | 9,024 | 92,455 |
| 1988 | 7,852 | 7,264 | 9,453 | 7,956 | 7,891 | 9,453 | 10,562 | 9,903 | 7,374 | 8,074 | 9,545 | 9,726 | 105,053 |
| 1989 | 10,025 | 9,488 | 9,883 | 9,650 | 12,006 | 8,956 | 7,722 | 9,337 | 7,978 | 7,901 | 10,099 | 8,999 | 112,044 |
| 1990 | 8,938 | 7,839 | 7,106 | 8,725 | 8,571 | 8,819 | 8,230 | 7,747 | 7,619 | 8,019 | 9,732 | 8,106 | 99,451 |
| 1991 | 8,767 | 6,715 | 7,378 | 7,334 | 9,162 | 7,579 | 7,070 | 8,165 | 8,444 | 8,335 | 8,023 | 8,614 | 95,586 |
| 1992[2] | ---------- | 1,031 | ---------- | ---------- | 1,031 | ---------- | ---------- | 933 | ---------- | ---------- | 557 | ---------- | 3,921 |
| 1993 | ---------- | 1,032 | ---------- | ---------- | 1,080 | ---------- | ---------- | 795 | ---------- | ---------- | 712 | ---------- | 4,059 |
| 1994[3] | ---------- | 802 | ---------- | ---------- | 908 | ---------- | ---------- | 808 | ---------- | ---------- | 803 | ---------- | 3,321 |
| 1995[3] | ---------- | NA | ---------- | ---------- | NA | ---------- | ---------- | NA | ---------- | ---------- | NA | ---------- | NA |

[1] Output of commercial bars .999 fine, including U.S. Mint purchases of crude. Production is from both foreign and domestic silver. [2] Prior to 1992, shown in thousands of troy ounces. [3] Preliminary. NA = Not Avaliable. *Source: U.S. Geological Survey*

## U.S. Exports of Refined Silver to Selected Countries In Thousands of Troy Ounces

| Year | Australia | Canada | France | Germany | Hong Kong | Japan | Singapore | South Korea | Switzer-land | United Arab Emirates | United Kingdom | Uruguay | Other Countries | Total |
|---|---|---|---|---|---|---|---|---|---|---|---|---|---|---|
| 1987 | NA | 2,086 | 134 | 261 | NA | 5,426 | NA | NA | NA | NA | 2,568 | NA | 157 | 11,241 |
| 1988 | NA | 1,073 | 157 | 480 | NA | 6,030 | NA | 166 | 70 | NA | 4,894 | NA | 82 | 14,270 |
| 1989 | NA | 2,597 | 61 | 519 | NA | 5,997 | NA | 588 | 88 | NA | 3,722 | NA | 55 | 13,828 |
| 1990 | NA | 2,586 | 64 | 749 | NA | 16,568 | 1,005 | 298 | 74 | NA | 2,060 | 152 | 93 | 23,664 |
| 1991 | NA | 736 | 22 | 350 | 755 | 6,519 | 1,593 | 2,823 | 8 | 3,462 | 8,628 | 259 | 73 | 25,318 |
| 1992 | 593 | 2,177 | 44 | 140 | 497 | 4,554 | 2,126 | NA | 70 | 6,922 | 10,856 | 671 | 47 | 29,274 |
| 1993 | 520 | 4,910 | NA | 34 | 1,002 | 3,414 | 2,500 | 1,492 | 38 | 4,403 | 3,673 | 530 | 44 | 22,673 |
| 1994 | NA | 4,289 | NA | 8 | 456 | 9,275 | 16 | 3,084 | NA | 3,627 | 4,896 | 1,353 | 193 | 27,902 |
| 1995[1] | NA | 1,667 | 431 | NA | NA | 2,737 | 2,209 | 2,929 | 1,170 | 10,285 | 63,882 | 937 | 41 | 86,644 |

[1] Preliminary. NA = Not available, included in "Other Countries," if any. *Source: American Bureau of Metal Statistics*

## U.S. Imports of Silver from Selected Countries In Thousands of Troy Ounces

| | Ores and Concentrates | | | | Refined Bullion | | | | | | |
|---|---|---|---|---|---|---|---|---|---|---|---|
| Year | Canada | Mexico | Other Countries | Total | Canada | Chile | Mexico | Peru | Uruguay | Other Countries | Total |
| 1987 | 650 | 1,561 | 59 | 2,681 | 16,665 | 113 | 40,779 | 243 | NA | 71 | 67,959 |
| 1988 | 288 | 1,511 | 31 | 6,151 | 31,361 | 211 | 37,471 | 11 | NA | 139 | 72,663 |
| 1989 | 56 | 129 | 28 | 225 | 37,203 | 724 | 53,262 | 2,761 | 1,958 | 0 | 98,429 |
| 1990 | 12 | 189 | 2 | 203 | 33,518 | 1,671 | 40,204 | 8,141 | 2,265 | 165 | 86,741 |
| 1991 | 42 | 277 | 29 | 348 | 25,389 | 6,640 | 34,448 | 13,748 | NA | 17 | 81,198 |
| 1992 | 646 | 126 | 11 | 814 | 24,937 | 2,002 | 40,230 | 16,841 | 400 | 2 | 85,572 |
| 1993 | 299 | 836 | 11 | 1,147 | 28,622 | 1,058 | 27,241 | 12,709 | NA | 28 | 70,189 |
| 1994 | 369 | 3,805 | 5 | 4,271 | 28,678 | 1,923 | 22,135 | 12,663 | NA | 32 | 66,141 |
| 1995[1] | 312 | 6,269 | NA | 6,825 | 27,640 | 4,694 | 29,200 | 13,732 | NA | 78 | 84,446 |

[1] Preliminary. NA = Not available, included in "Other Countries," if any. *Source: American Bureau of Metal Statistics*

## Average Open Interest of Silver Futures at New York (COMEX) In Contracts

| Year | Jan. | Feb. | Mar. | Apr. | May | June | July | Aug. | Sept. | Oct. | Nov. | Dec. |
|---|---|---|---|---|---|---|---|---|---|---|---|---|
| 1984 | 62,135 | 64,640 | 68,763 | 72,204 | 65,424 | 62,890 | 61,644 | 63,700 | 63,655 | 66,339 | 78,744 | 78,492 |
| 1985 | 82,285 | 83,773 | 74,987 | 75,583 | 74,587 | 76,985 | 71,610 | 73,325 | 71,100 | 81,987 | 87,775 | 86,249 |
| 1986 | 82,915 | 81,670 | 75,891 | 79,653 | 74,781 | 72,411 | 67,063 | 74,916 | 79,376 | 81,192 | 93,567 | 88,962 |
| 1987 | 93,442 | 94,823 | 94,366 | 114,498 | 98,917 | 91,469 | 82,200 | 87,131 | 79,747 | 84,420 | 78,669 | 71,204 |
| 1988 | 76,788 | 79,031 | 68,994 | 66,187 | 69,137 | 83,428 | 84,517 | 82,793 | 82,369 | 85,261 | 92,026 | 90,081 |
| 1989 | 93,582 | 95,876 | 93,953 | 99,598 | 90,996 | 86,804 | 83,466 | 88,886 | 85,248 | 88,406 | 91,459 | 93,606 |
| 1990 | 94,397 | 93,713 | 96,182 | 96,701 | 95,784 | 103,575 | 99,098 | 99,668 | 92,436 | 91,093 | 84,181 | 80,364 |
| 1991 | 91,685 | 101,352 | 99,564 | 99,791 | 94,921 | 105,646 | 97,554 | 95,536 | 87,079 | 90,791 | 89,765 | 91,390 |
| 1992 | 97,179 | 93,352 | 88,445 | 96,427 | 87,355 | 84,002 | 80,879 | 81,695 | 74,265 | 72,090 | 77,633 | 72,296 |
| 1993 | 80,155 | 86,241 | 87,127 | 100,985 | 105,931 | 102,539 | 107,537 | 109,427 | 93,891 | 93,316 | 101,576 | 110,029 |
| 1994 | 112,584 | 116,652 | 112,745 | 119,314 | 121,296 | 126,255 | 122,138 | 118,081 | 113,261 | 117,224 | 126,666 | 134,099 |
| 1995 | 132,158 | 139,806 | 132,317 | 129,063 | 112,723 | 108,941 | 101,842 | 111,251 | 95,433 | 101,763 | 105,453 | 95,551 |
| 1996 | 99,316 | 107,667 | 92,186 | 101,011 | 99,529 | 110,247 | 105,627 | 103,618 | 93,448 | 95,809 | 93,238 | 83,879 |

*Source: New York Mercantile Exchange, COMEX Division*

## Volume of Trading of Silver Futures at New York (COMEX) In Thousands of Contracts

| Year | Jan. | Feb. | Mar. | Apr. | May | June | July | Aug. | Sept. | Oct. | Nov. | Dec. | Total |
|---|---|---|---|---|---|---|---|---|---|---|---|---|---|
| 1984 | 570,786 | 698,768 | 695,748 | 629,865 | 626,746 | 587,366 | 554,669 | 601,549 | 431,257 | 449,221 | 534,232 | 362,301 | 6,742,508 |
| 1985 | 531,833 | 487,990 | 518,440 | 449,760 | 424,766 | 377,900 | 377,681 | 388,531 | 267,653 | 313,964 | 332,770 | 349,918 | 4,821,206 |
| 1986 | 394,008 | 368,915 | 277,591 | 438,800 | 280,131 | 336,070 | 187,896 | 317,799 | 454,638 | 286,680 | 338,934 | 168,225 | 3,849,687 |
| 1987 | 247,346 | 247,958 | 343,178 | 932,731 | 438,614 | 486,410 | 378,740 | 502,729 | 390,266 | 468,064 | 355,893 | 263,723 | 5,055,652 |
| 1988 | 274,098 | 301,119 | 348,905 | 313,927 | 341,145 | 726,860 | 638,934 | 411,665 | 299,858 | 268,383 | 475,374 | 264,387 | 4,664,655 |
| 1989 | 317,152 | 408,485 | 447,323 | 354,235 | 278,496 | 484,711 | 272,254 | 360,381 | 244,926 | 261,102 | 622,123 | 345,423 | 4,376,611 |
| 1990 | 343,175 | 413,287 | 210,193 | 364,055 | 328,804 | 433,848 | 242,288 | 524,815 | 201,273 | 308,449 | 323,664 | 219,758 | 3,913,609 |
| 1991 | 309,841 | 420,092 | 446,491 | 395,957 | 255,548 | 547,495 | 344,683 | 320,639 | 268,660 | 252,983 | 349,698 | 242,617 | 4,154,704 |
| 1992 | 408,179 | 320,226 | 229,010 | 322,364 | 184,825 | 295,358 | 197,946 | 266,347 | 173,165 | 125,537 | 355,728 | 127,654 | 3,016,339 |
| 1993 | 167,201 | 315,916 | 242,974 | 476,554 | 433,460 | 523,961 | 503,935 | 531,772 | 428,366 | 338,189 | 520,591 | 373,005 | 4,855,924 |
| 1994 | 489,055 | 555,136 | 484,134 | 585,058 | 516,396 | 729,414 | 339,298 | 535,722 | 377,540 | 455,049 | 589,220 | 348,323 | 5,994,345 |
| 1995 | 390,453 | 501,454 | 541,807 | 592,620 | 500,522 | 476,481 | 280,651 | 655,854 | 344,182 | 272,362 | 447,095 | 179,755 | 5,183,236 |
| 1996 | 415,801 | 583,767 | 368,175 | 547,629 | 334,973 | 549,631 | 296,905 | 460,686 | 316,366 | 321,781 | 415,441 | 259,653 | 4,870,808 |

*Source: New York Mercantile Exchange, COMEX Division*

# Soybean Meal

Soybean meal, a high protein feed used in formulating livestock and poultry rations, is obtained from the processing (crush) of soybeans and is the world's top protein meal with about 60 percent of total production. Cottonseed and rapeseed meal account for a combined total of about 20 percent. The U.S. is the largest producer followed by Brazil.

World soybean meal production increased steadily during the first half of the 1990's, from about 70 million metric tons in 1990 to a record large 89 million in 1996/97. Percentagewise, China's production gain has been the most dynamic. Brazil's production during the period also increased sharply. Part of the growth in meal production has been indirectly derived from the strong worldwide demand for vegetable oils, but the primary reason for the growth is that more countries have increasing livestock numbers and an expanding need for high protein feed; a fact that is underscored by the continued strength in the world's soybean meal trade. Significantly, many of the recent gains in foreign trade have come from developing nations in Latin America and Asia, a trend which is very likely to continue in the years ahead.

World meal consumption in 1996/97 of a record large 89 million tons compares with 88.6 million tons in 1995/96. The U.S. is the largest single consumer with about 25 million tons, but the European Union runs a close second with 23 million tons used in 1995/96, and may easily be the primary user by the end of the 1990's. Asia's usage at 20.5 million tons has nearly doubled during the past decade. Contributing to the gain in EU and Asian imports is the strong growth in poultry production in those regions, the primary user of soybean meal. World carryover at the end of the 1996/97 season is forecast at 3.9 million tons vs. a year earlier carryin of 4.1 million, with Argentina and Brazil accounting for a combined total of at least 1.2 million tons.

U.S. soymeal production in 1996/97 of a near record large 33 million short tons compares with 32.5 million in 1995/96 and the record high 33.3 million in 1994/95. Total 1996/97 supplies of 33.4 million tons compare with 32.8 in 1995/96, including a carryin of about 0.2 million tons at the start of each crop year (October 1). Total supplies in the early 1990's averaged near 30 million tons. Domestic usage has climbed steadily since 1990 and is expected to total a record high 26.9 million tons in 1996/97 vs. 26.5 million in 1995/96, the gain largely due to increases in poultry production. It is possible that poultry demand in 1996/97 will control the U.S. crush, instead of the more typical demand for soybean oil. Cattle feeding accounts for little soybean meal use, hogs a little more.

U.S. soybean meal exports totaled 7.9 million short tons in 1979, slipping to 4.9 million by 1984 due to increased competition from South American producers. Exports in 1996/97 were forecast at 6.3 million tons, higher than initially expected and comparing with about 6 million in 1995/96. Abetting the foreign demand in 1996/97 for U.S. meal is a decline in South American meal export availability and the possibility of net imports by China; as recently as 1994/95 China was a net exporter of soybean meal. If the 1996/97 supply/demand forecasts are realized, ending carryover on September 30, 1997 should total about 225,000 tons.

U.S. soybean meal prices were expected to average $210-$225.00 per ton in 1996/97 vs. $236.00 in 1995/96, and a ten-year low of $162.55 in 1994/95, basis 48 percent protein, Decatur, Illinois.

### *Futures Markets*

Soybean meal futures and options are traded on the Chicago Board of Trade. A smaller futures contract is traded on the Mid-America Commodity Exchange.

**World Soybean Meal Supply & Demand** In Thousands of Metric Tons

| Year Beginning Oct. 1 | Production | | | | | Exports | | | Imports | | Consumption | | | Ending Stocks | | |
|---|---|---|---|---|---|---|---|---|---|---|---|---|---|---|---|---|
| | Brazil | China | EC-12 | United States | Total | Brazil | United States | Total | France | Total | EC-12 | United States | Total | Brazil | United States | Total |
| 1986-7 | 11,280 | 3,000 | 10,740 | 25,182 | 67,210 | 8,370 | 6,617 | 25,940 | 3,660 | 26,630 | 19,240 | 18,539 | 67,680 | 520 | 218 | 3,070 |
| 1987-8 | 10,130 | 3,980 | 10,400 | 25,460 | 67,555 | 7,350 | 6,191 | 24,560 | 3,110 | 25,310 | 18,930 | 19,344 | 67,660 | 970 | 140 | 3,720 |
| 1988-9 | 11,360 | 3,570 | 9,100 | 22,630 | 64,230 | 8,680 | 4,940 | 24,980 | 2,910 | 26,310 | 17,810 | 17,680 | 66,050 | 790 | 160 | 3,220 |
| 1989-90 | 12,350 | 3,020 | 10,580 | 25,150 | 70,089 | 9,430 | 4,830 | 26,010 | 3,480 | 25,730 | 19,900 | 20,220 | 68,950 | 1,114 | 290 | 4,070 |
| 1990-1 | 11,160 | 3,280 | 9,950 | 25,700 | 69,500 | 8,200 | 4,960 | 26,890 | 3,430 | 27,200 | 20,190 | 20,810 | 70,130 | 860 | 260 | 3,660 |
| 1991-2 | 11,740 | 2,750 | 10,530 | 27,060 | 73,200 | 8,780 | 6,300 | 28,620 | 3,550 | 28,250 | 21,170 | 20,870 | 73,360 | 520 | 210 | 3,140 |
| 1992-3 | 12,170 | 3,630 | 10,980 | 27,550 | 76,380 | 8,170 | 5,650 | 27,550 | 3,500 | 27,870 | 22,240 | 22,000 | 76,050 | 600 | 190 | 3,800 |
| 1993-4 | 14,500 | 6,160 | 9,850 | 27,680 | 81,200 | 10,310 | 4,860 | 29,950 | 3,800 | 29,260 | 22,680 | 22,940 | 80,600 | 610 | 140 | 3,710 |
| 1994-5 | 15,870 | 6,550 | 11,490 | 30,180 | 87,190 | 10,680 | 6,090 | 31,150 | 3,790 | 31,220 | 24,420 | 24,080 | 86,630 | 690 | 200 | 4,330 |
| 1995-6[1] | 16,820 | 6,040 | 10,750 | 29,500 | 88,960 | 11,670 | 5,450 | 32,560 | 3,340 | 32,260 | 23,620 | 24,110 | 88,800 | 640 | 210 | 4,190 |
| 1996-7[2] | 16,740 | 6,240 | 10,900 | 30,250 | 90,390 | 11,400 | 6,030 | 32,870 | 3,400 | 33,280 | 23,560 | 24,310 | 90,870 | 630 | 180 | 4,110 |

[1] Preliminary. [2] Forecast. *Source: Foreign Agricultural Service, U.S. Department of Agriculture*

# SOYBEAN MEAL

**Stocks (at Oil Mills)[2] of Soybean Cake & Meal in the United States** In Thousands of Short Tons

| Year | Oct. 1 | Nov. 1 | Dec. 1 | Jan. 1 | Feb. 1 | Mar. 1 | Apr. 1 | May 1 | June 1 | July 1 | Aug. 1 | Sept. 1 |
|---|---|---|---|---|---|---|---|---|---|---|---|---|
| 1977-8 | 228.3 | 270.0 | 239.8 | 245.1 | 251.7 | 239.7 | 227.3 | 308.2 | 263.3 | 191.1 | 262.6 | 234.1 |
| 1978-9 | 242.9 | 210.4 | 178.2 | 260.5 | 215.1 | 198.7 | 210.4 | 231.6 | 207.4 | 205.3 | 232.2 | 140.3 |
| 1979-80 | 224.3 | 204.1 | 164.2 | 207.7 | 158.7 | 160.6 | 219.1 | 193.9 | 265.0 | 262.0 | 232.4 | 225.1 |
| 1980-1 | 189.7 | 211.1 | 350.0 | 221.8 | 209.7 | 214.4 | 232.2 | 184.4 | 254.0 | 209.7 | 156.1 | 199.7 |
| 1981-2 | 233.8 | 309.2 | 314.8 | 279.4 | 315.7 | 324.9 | 190.3 | 172.1 | 309.3 | 224.9 | 209.1 | 189.7 |
| 1982-3 | 175.2 | 342.8 | 349.6 | 332.3 | 400.2 | 422.8 | 341.0 | 356.1 | 341.5 | 272.3 | 365.2 | 378.5 |
| 1983-4 | 474.1 | 419.3 | 466.8 | 391.1 | 475.8 | 446.7 | 460.7 | 418.6 | 427.2 | 391.2 | 355.5 | 242.7 |
| 1984-5 | 255.4 | 236.1 | 285.7 | 336.8 | 319.6 | 334.1 | 444.6 | 429.8 | 495.8 | 569.6 | 562.5 | 458.0 |
| 1985-6 | 386.9 | 318.4 | 369.2 | 358.4 | 372.4 | 281.3 | 386.6 | 300.8 | 282.4 | 278.7 | 250.6 | 298.3 |
| 1986-7 | 211.7 | 218.0 | 387.3 | 240.3 | 311.2 | 277.5 | 235.8 | 244.0 | 321.7 | 261.3 | 292.9 | 301.3 |
| 1987-8 | 240.2 | 267.6 | 311.8 | 296.2 | 390.4 | 304.9 | 243.7 | 299.5 | 255.6 | 294.4 | 437.4 | 264.6 |
| 1988-9 | 153.5 | 267.8 | 295.6 | 353.6 | 442.3 | 395.7 | 237.9 | 296.8 | 260.4 | 218.0 | 264.9 | 152.0 |
| 1989-90 | 172.9 | 220.5 | 194.3 | 328.2 | 254.0 | 262.0 | 311.8 | 307.9 | 252.6 | 262.5 | 267.7 | 232.0 |
| 1990-1 | 318.3 | 290.9 | 313.6 | ------------ | 455.8 | ------------ | ------------ | 527.8 | ------------ | ------------ | 425.0 | ------------ |
| 1991-2 | ------------ | 285.0 | ------------ | 281.0 | 258.3 | 291.3 | 315.6 | 310.4 | 310.2 | 274.7 | 260.5 | 209.9 |
| 1992-3 | 230.0 | 307.9 | 411.3 | 360.8 | 440.0 | 420.5 | 336.9 | 268.5 | 328.4 | 257.3 | 386.1 | 353.8 |
| 1993-4 | 204.4 | 375.1 | 282.3 | 290.1 | 230.0 | 283.1 | 277.3 | 333.0 | 325.2 | 254.3 | 267.5 | 144.9 |
| 1994-5 | 149.6 | 240.9 | 231.6 | 241.1 | 197.7 | 227.1 | 173.1 | 382.7 | 337.6 | 222.6 | 252.0 | 203.8 |
| 1995-6[1] | 223.4 | 196.9 | 241.3 | 394.8 | 301.9 | 229.9 | 369.3 | 382.1 | 311.6 | 416.1 | 297.3 | 215.3 |
| 1996-7[1] | 228.8 | 231.1 | 316.8 | 293.2 | | | | | | | | |

[1] Preliminary. [2] Including millfeed and lecithin. *Source: Economic Research Service, U.S. Department of Agriculture*

## Supply and Distribution of Soybean Meal in the United States    In Thousands of Short Tons

| Year Beginning Oct. 1 | Supply: For Stocks Oct. 1 | Supply: Production | Supply: Total Supply | Distribution: Domestic | Distribution: Exports | Distribution: Total | $ Ton Decatur 48% Protein Solvent | $ Tonne: Decatur 44% Solvent | $ Tonne: Brazil FOB 45-46% Protein | $ Tonne: Rotterdam CIF |
|---|---|---|---|---|---|---|---|---|---|---|
| 1989-90 | 173 | 27,719 | 27,928 | 22,291 | 5,319 | 27,610 | 186.48 | 192 | 181 | 204 |
| 1990-1 | 318 | 28,325 | 28,688 | 22,934 | 5,469 | 28,403 | 181.40 | 187 | 178 | 198 |
| 1991-2 | 285 | 29,831 | 30,183 | 23,008 | 6,945 | 29,953 | 189.20 | 194 | 184 | 203 |
| 1992-3 | 230 | 30,364 | 30,687 | 24,251 | 6,232 | 30,483 | 193.75 | 201 | 185 | 207 |
| 1993-4 | 204 | 30,514 | 30,788 | 25,283 | 5,356 | 30,638 | 192.86 | 199 | 182 | 202 |
| 1994-5[1] | 150 | 33,265 | 33,479 | 26,538 | 6,717 | 33,256 | 162.55 | 167 | 172 | 184 |
| 1995-6[2] | 223 | 32,514 | 32,813 | 26,581 | 6,002 | 32,584 | 236.00 | 248 | 256 | 256 |
| 1996-7[3] | 229 | 33,341 | 33,650 | 26,800 | 6,650 | 33,450 | 230-245 | 266 | 281 | 276 |

[1] Preliminary. [2] Estimate. [3] Forecast. *Source: Economic Research Service, U.S. Department of Agriculture*

## U.S. Exports of Soybean Cake & Meal by Country of Destination    In Thousands of Metric Tons

| Year | Algeria | Australia | Canada | Dominican Republic | Egypt | Ireland | Italy | Japan | Mexico | Netherlands | Philippines | Russia[2] | Spain | United Kingdom | Venezuela | Total |
|---|---|---|---|---|---|---|---|---|---|---|---|---|---|---|---|---|
| 1989 | 389.1 | 7.7 | 569.2 | 66.2 | 165.9 | 5.7 | 188.6 | 10.8 | 269.5 | 269.0 | 59.1 | 1,417.9 | 44.2 | 29.6 | 283.8 | 4,712 |
| 1990 | 373.5 | 28.2 | 555.5 | 130.5 | 174.8 | 7.5 | 146.4 | 20.8 | 253.0 | 229.7 | 200.7 | 1,568.4 | 19.6 | 32.0 | 332.2 | 4,826 |
| 1991 | 323.5 | 99.4 | 651.2 | 142.6 | 118.6 | 7.5 | 33.5 | 24.1 | 303.6 | 339.8 | 150.4 | 2,271.0 | 5.5 | 29.6 | 405.9 | 5,536 |
| 1992 | 237.8 | 75.9 | 582.5 | 146.7 | 56.5 | 57.2 | 93.4 | 167.2 | 454.4 | 420.0 | 434.8 | 765.1 | 92.3 | 70.6 | 473.8 | 6,236 |
| 1993 | 266.1 | 90.6 | 646.7 | 200.8 | 120.6 | 84.1 | 91.5 | 208.7 | 187.8 | 580.8 | 295.7 | 697.1 | 203.8 | 32.1 | 425.0 | 5,536 |
| 1994 | 248.3 | 247.0 | 706.3 | 209.2 | 142.0 | 36.8 | 27.1 | 76.9 | 367.5 | 465.6 | 257.9 | 159.5 | 92.6 | 80.9 | 258.9 | 4,825 |
| 1995[1] | 216.7 | 190.2 | 798.7 | 219.2 | 147.3 | 137.9 | 70.2 | 246.7 | 340.0 | 750.7 | 593.4 | 11.1 | 127.7 | 72.3 | 181.4 | 5,894 |

[1] Preliminary. [2] Formerly part of the U.S.S.R.; data not reported separately until 1992. *Source: The Oil World*

## Production of Soybean Cake & Meal[2] in the U.S.    In Thousands of Short Tons

| Crop Year | Production: Oct. | Nov. | Dec. | Jan. | Feb. | Mar. | Apr. | May | June | July | Aug. | Sept. | Total | Yield of Meal from Soybeans in lbs. |
|---|---|---|---|---|---|---|---|---|---|---|---|---|---|---|
| 1989-90 | 2,246.2 | 2,492.5 | 2,519.6 | 2,548.6 | 2,187.2 | 2,432.3 | 2,263.7 | 2,224.2 | 2,183.4 | 2,196.6 | 2,237.1 | 2,187.3 | 27,718 | 47.63 |
| 1990-1 | 2,508.8 | 2,513.2 | 2,431.5 | | 7,082.0 | | | 6,640.8 | | | 7,148.9 | | 28,325 | 47.47 |
| 1991-2 | | 7,920.4 | | 2,665.5 | 2,393.8 | 2,544.4 | 2,411.3 | 2,262.5 | 2,372.4 | 2,434.2 | 2,429.0 | 2,397.3 | 29,831 | 47.51 |
| 1992-3 | 2,698.1 | 2,697.3 | 2,763.4 | 2,781.2 | 2,430.4 | 2,691.3 | 2,519.1 | 2,536.3 | 2,373.0 | 2,324.1 | 2,188.3 | 2,361.8 | 30,364 | 47.54 |
| 1993-4 | 2,707.1 | 2,714.8 | 2,696.7 | 2,632.3 | 2,458.1 | 2,696.3 | 2,510.0 | 2,446.4 | 2,330.7 | 2,398.0 | 2,406.6 | 2,517.1 | 30,514 | 47.62 |
| 1994-5 | 2,812.5 | 2,903.5 | 3,027.8 | 3,007.5 | 2,755.0 | 3,048.5 | 2,829.8 | 2,697.9 | 2,492.1 | 2,565.4 | 2,589.8 | 2,535.8 | 33,269 | 47.33 |
| 1995-6[1] | 2,893.2 | 2,948.9 | 2,972.3 | 2,943.3 | 2,645.3 | 2,757.5 | 2,683.1 | 2,534.6 | 2,566.2 | 2,657.5 | 2,509.9 | 2,395.3 | 32,514 | 47.66 |
| 1996-7[1] | 2,993.0 | 3,151.8 | 3,265.8 | | | | | | | | | | 9,411 | |

[1] Preliminary. [2] At oil mills; including millfeed and lecithin. *Source: Economic Research Service, U.S. Department of Agriculture*

## Average Open Interest of Soybean Futures in Chicago    In Contracts

| Year | Jan. | Feb. | Mar. | Apr. | May | June | July | Aug. | Sept. | Oct. | Nov. | Dec. |
|---|---|---|---|---|---|---|---|---|---|---|---|---|
| 1989 | 71,792 | 71,599 | 67,542 | 58,923 | 58,794 | 64,212 | 59,547 | 60,925 | 59,271 | 60,038 | 63,552 | 57,219 |
| 1990 | 60,010 | 71,773 | 74,762 | 76,897 | 77,307 | 69,658 | 63,824 | 62,033 | 58,915 | 68,888 | 76,899 | 70,901 |
| 1991 | 62,172 | 60,017 | 56,179 | 59,107 | 49,973 | 57,068 | 55,629 | 54,342 | 67,765 | 68,627 | 68,263 | 71,900 |
| 1992 | 67,575 | 56,453 | 55,370 | 59,528 | 57,204 | 60,519 | 66,315 | 66,861 | 66,648 | 72,403 | 73,255 | 72,881 |
| 1993 | 63,178 | 70,384 | 64,550 | 66,121 | 78,386 | 74,191 | 91,435 | 73,770 | 75,267 | 77,065 | 83,802 | 85,039 |
| 1994 | 87,612 | 91,142 | 82,193 | 89,453 | 85,553 | 81,721 | 84,461 | 82,691 | 85,508 | 94,483 | 101,030 | 98,717 |
| 1995 | 97,661 | 101,253 | 101,846 | 99,898 | 90,237 | 86,090 | 83,712 | 74,233 | 79,450 | 85,290 | 103,824 | 110,193 |
| 1996 | 95,903 | 90,010 | 87,468 | 101,204 | 91,453 | 88,641 | 77,961 | 80,727 | 93,373 | 88,969 | 90,007 | 84,399 |

*Source: Chicago Board of Trade (CBT)*

## Volume of Trading of Soybean Meal Futures in Chicago    In Thousands of Contracts

| Year | Jan. | Feb. | Mar. | Apr. | May | June | July | Aug. | Sept. | Oct. | Nov. | Dec. | Total |
|---|---|---|---|---|---|---|---|---|---|---|---|---|---|
| 1989 | 408.1 | 320.7 | 382.4 | 388.8 | 406.7 | 403.8 | 410.7 | 393.1 | 382.8 | 364.8 | 330.1 | 294.8 | 4,487 |
| 1990 | 308.6 | 276.4 | 400.2 | 428.4 | 421.0 | 398.3 | 460.2 | 435.3 | 401.6 | 476.3 | 448.7 | 448.5 | 4,904 |
| 1991 | 323.4 | 281.8 | 310.3 | 429.3 | 296.8 | 412.5 | 484.3 | 463.6 | 394.7 | 410.8 | 351.6 | 339.6 | 4,498 |
| 1992 | 368.7 | 290.5 | 312.6 | 312.2 | 388.1 | 381.0 | 426.0 | 333.6 | 327.6 | 320.2 | 327.9 | 357.1 | 4,146 |
| 1993 | 295.5 | 288.1 | 346.6 | 307.9 | 356.7 | 518.2 | 575.5 | 460.5 | 402.4 | 315.6 | 469.3 | 380.6 | 4,718 |
| 1994 | 405.6 | 339.8 | 330.7 | 380.7 | 467.2 | 456.3 | 384.5 | 354.4 | 366.3 | 317.4 | 370.4 | 420.5 | 4,594 |
| 1995 | 283.6 | 307.5 | 404.4 | 410.9 | 532.7 | 479.6 | 610.8 | 491.8 | 481.9 | 449.0 | 523.4 | 625.6 | 5,601 |
| 1996 | 496.4 | 442.9 | 435.8 | 656.0 | 439.2 | 442.4 | 507.2 | 490.3 | 425.9 | 581.1 | 491.9 | 452.1 | 5,861 |

*Source: Chicago Board of Trade (CBT)*

# SOYBEAN MEAL

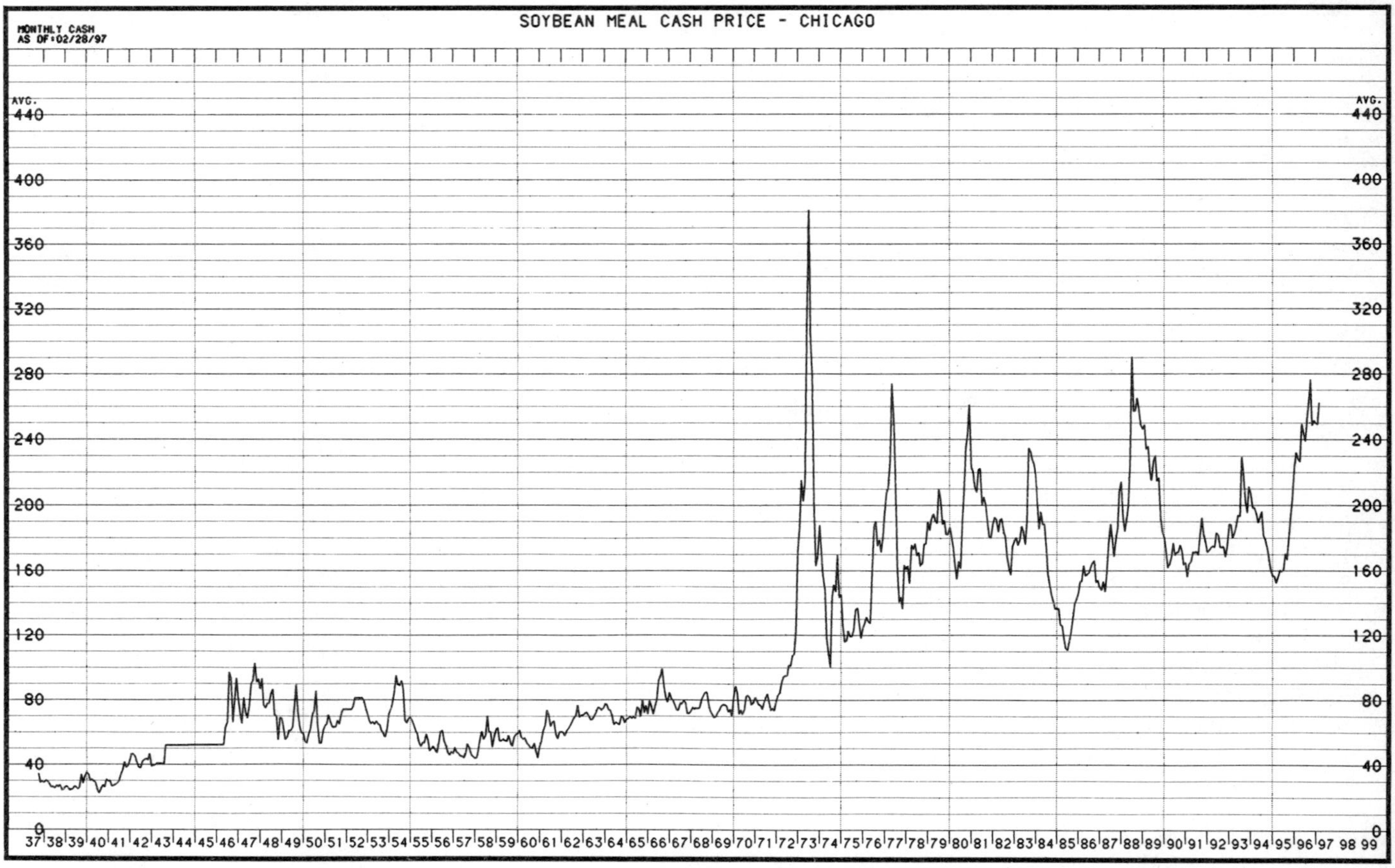


**Average Price of Soybean Meal (48% Solvent) at Decatur** In Dollars Per Short Ton--Bulk

| Year | Oct. | Nov. | Dec. | Jan. | Feb. | Mar. | Apr. | May | June | July | Aug. | Sept. | Average |
|---|---|---|---|---|---|---|---|---|---|---|---|---|---|
| 1985-6 | 146.40 | 152.25 | 153.60 | 162.00 | 162.50 | 174.90 | 167.90 | 168.90 | 170.40 | 174.40 | 178.75 | 182.40 | 166.20 |
| 1986-7 | 165.40 | 167.40 | 164.30 | 158.00 | 169.25 | 161.20 | 173.40 | 190.00 | 200.70 | 196.50 | 186.40 | 195.20 | 177.31 |
| 1987-8 | 201.60 | 224.75 | 231.70 | 211.75 | 199.60 | 207.60 | 218.25 | 238.60 | 305.40 | 275.10 | 273.80 | 284.00 | 239.35 |
| 1988-9 | 280.10 | 268.90 | 266.90 | 270.10 | 252.10 | 254.00 | 238.00 | 232.30 | 246.25 | 251.00 | 234.30 | 234.90 | 252.40 |
| 1989-90 | 208.10 | 194.90 | 191.60 | 183.80 | 172.90 | 176.40 | 178.00 | 189.40 | 182.00 | 183.92 | 186.75 | 190.00 | 186.48 |
| 1990-1 | 185.40 | 174.25 | 175.90 | 167.00 | 174.50 | 177.60 | 182.50 | 182.10 | 183.25 | 181.00 | 188.75 | 204.25 | 181.38 |
| 1991-2 | 196.30 | 190.25 | 183.10 | 184.00 | 185.40 | 185.90 | 187.20 | 195.25 | 203.90 | 186.25 | 186.00 | 187.00 | 189.21 |
| 1992-3 | 180.60 | 181.90 | 187.60 | 188.75 | 179.90 | 183.60 | 187.40 | 193.25 | 193.10 | 229.90 | 219.10 | 199.90 | 193.75 |
| 1993-4 | 194.50 | 209.40 | 206.00 | 198.30 | 198.40 | 195.40 | 188.90 | 193.75 | 195.50 | 181.10 | 178.60 | 174.50 | 192.86 |
| 1994-5 | 168.50 | 161.00 | 156.90 | 156.40 | 151.30 | 156.90 | 161.90 | 159.10 | 160.40 | 170.45 | 166.70 | 180.99 | 162.55 |
| 1995-6 | 193.90 | 204.10 | 223.60 | 232.00 | 228.30 | 226.57 | 249.30 | 244.30 | 238.80 | 252.50 | 261.20 | 276.40 | 235.90 |
| 1996-7 | 248.50 | 251.50 | 250.60 | 249.20 | | | | | | | | | 249.95 |

*Source: Economic Research Service, U.S. Department of Agriculture*

# Soybean Oil

World soybean oil production in 1996/97 of a record high 20.3 million metric tons compares with the previous year's high of 20.1 million. The U.S., the world's largest bean oil producer, generally accounts for about a third of total production and produces nearly double that of Brazil, the world's second largest producer. Of the important edible vegetable oils soyoil is the world's largest with a 29 percent market share in 1996/97, followed by palm oil with 23 percent, and rapeseed oil with 15 percent. World usage of soyoil in 1996/97 was forecast at a record 20.2 million tons, marginally higher than in 1995/96. The U.S. is the largest consumer with Brazil a distant second. World carryover stocks at the end of 1996/97 were estimated at 2.3 million tons, a shade under 1995/96. Nearly half of the carryover is in the U.S. with Brazil holding about 15 percent.

Global soybean oil exports in 1996/97 of 5.7 million tons compare with 5.3 million in 1995/96, and the record high 6.1 million in 1994/95. Argentina is the largest exporter and Brazil second, each with at least 1.5 million tons. U.S. exports in 1996/97 of 800,000 tons compare with 470,000 in 1995/96 with the increase largely due to increased shipments to China. Importing nations are scattered with China now the largest single importer, 1.5 million tons in 1996/97, unchanged from 1995/96.

U.S. soybean oil production in 1996/97 of a near record high 15.4 billion pounds compares with 15.3 billion in 1995/96, and the high of 15.6 billion in 1994/95. During the first half of the 1990's production averaged about 14 billion pounds. The oil content of U.S. soybeans correlates directly with temperatures and sunshine during the pod-filling stages, which proved favorable during the 1996 growing season. Carryin stocks on October 1, 1996 totaled about 2 billion pounds, nearly twice the year earlier total, but not a record high. The U.S. supply in 1996/97 of a record high 17.5 billion pounds compares with 16.5 billion in 1995/96. Disappearance in 1996/97 of 15.4 billion pounds compares with 14.5 billion in 1995/96, but lags the record high 15.6 billion pounds in 1994/95. Bean oil stocks will build during 1996/97, but not as much as initially expected. The earlier projected ending carryover of a near record high 2.2 billion pounds may prove about 100 million pounds too high.

Domestic soybean oil use in 1996/97 may reach a record high 13.7 billion pounds vs. 13.5 billion in 1995/96 as domestic prices should prove competitive to other fats and oils.

Crude soybean oil prices (basis Decatur) in 1996/97 were expected to range from 22.50-24.50¢ per pound vs. a 24.80¢ per pound average in 1995/96. The record high 30.60¢ per pound was realized during 1983/84.

### *Futures Markets*

Soybean oil futures and options are traded on the Chicago Board of Trade (CBT).

## World Supply & Demand of Soybean Oil — In Thousands of Metric Tons

| Year Beginning Oct. 1 | Production | | | | Exports | | | Imports | | Consumption | | | | | Stocks[3] | |
|---|---|---|---|---|---|---|---|---|---|---|---|---|---|---|---|---|
| | Brazil | EC-12 | United States | Total | Brazil | United States | Total | India | Total | Brazil | EC-12 | India | United States | Total | United States | Total |
| 1987-8 | 2,440 | 2,280 | 5,890 | 15,240 | 610 | 850 | 3,800 | 420 | 3,770 | 1,930 | 1,560 | 620 | 4,960 | 15,110 | 950 | 2,090 |
| 1988-9 | 2,740 | 2,010 | 5,320 | 14,630 | 700 | 750 | 3,710 | 30 | 3,490 | 2,140 | 1,590 | 410 | 4,800 | 14,870 | 780 | 1,660 |
| 1989-90 | 2,980 | 2,350 | 5,900 | 16,000 | 870 | 610 | 3,940 | 30 | 3,970 | 2,000 | 1,610 | 340 | 5,480 | 15,950 | 590 | 1,740 |
| 1990-1 | 2,679 | 2,243 | 6,082 | 15,909 | 686 | 356 | 3,635 | 20 | 3,587 | 2,136 | 1,661 | 370 | 5,515 | 15,886 | 810 | 1,988 |
| 1991-2 | 2,815 | 2,337 | 6,507 | 16,851 | 658 | 748 | 3,558 | 100 | 3,487 | 2,167 | 1,703 | 442 | 5,554 | 16,366 | 1,016 | 2,470 |
| 1992-3 | 2,910 | 2,540 | 6,250 | 17,200 | 690 | 640 | 4,210 | 40 | 3,900 | 2,280 | 2,000 | 560 | 5,920 | 17,220 | 710 | 2,050 |
| 1993-4 | 3,470 | 2,240 | 6,330 | 18,250 | 1,350 | 690 | 4,850 | 40 | 4,730 | 2,320 | 1,850 | 710 | 5,870 | 18,410 | 500 | 1,770 |
| 1994-5 | 3,800 | 2,580 | 7,080 | 19,710 | 1,550 | 1,220 | 6,080 | 60 | 6,100 | 2,470 | 1,920 | 560 | 5,860 | 19,440 | 520 | 2,050 |
| 1995-6[1] | 4,020 | 2,420 | 6,910 | 20,180 | 1,600 | 450 | 5,420 | 60 | 5,230 | 2,530 | 1,960 | 760 | 6,110 | 19,770 | 910 | 2,280 |
| 1996-7[2] | 4,000 | 2,450 | 6,960 | 20,390 | 1,500 | 840 | 5,720 | 110 | 5,700 | 2,600 | 1,960 | 740 | 6,190 | 20,380 | 890 | 2,270 |

[1] Preliminary. [2] Forecast. [3] End of season. *Source: Foreign Agricultural Service, U.S. Department of Agriculture*

## Supply & Distribution of Soybean Oil in the U.S. — In Millions of Pounds

| Year Beginning Oct. 1 | Production | Imports | Stocks Oct. 1 | Exports | Domestic Disappearance: Total Domestic | Food: Shortening | Food: Margarine | Food: Cooking & Salad Oils | Food: Other Edible | Food: Total Food | Non-Food: Paint & Varnish | Non-Food: Resins & Plastics | Non-Food: Total Non-Food | Total Disappearance |
|---|---|---|---|---|---|---|---|---|---|---|---|---|---|---|
| 1987-8 | 12,974 | 194 | 1,725 | 1,873 | 10,930 | 3,627 | 1,629 | 5,043 | 130 | 10,429 | 54 | 106 | 285 | 12,803 |
| 1988-9 | 11,737 | 137 | 2,092 | 1,661 | 10,591 | 3,419 | 1,537 | 4,497 | 137 | 9,636 | 35 | 124 | 282 | 12,252 |
| 1989-90 | 13,004 | 22 | 1,715 | 1,353 | 12,083 | 3,934 | 1,754 | 4,726 | 124 | 10,537 | 38 | 112 | 272 | 13,436 |
| 1990-1 | 13,408 | 17 | 1,305 | 780 | 12,164 | 4,090 | 1,811 | 4,693 | 130 | 10,722 | 49 | 106 | 295 | 12,944 |
| 1991-2 | 14,345 | 1 | 1,786 | 1,648 | 12,245 | 4,091 | 1,911 | 4,961 | 148 | 11,112 | 46 | 98 | 301 | 13,893 |
| 1992-3 | 13,778 | 10 | 2,239 | 1,419 | 14,473 | 4,465 | 1,970 | 4,717 | 254 | 11,505 | 38 | 95 | 296 | 14,473 |
| 1993-4 | 13,951 | 68 | 1,555 | 1,529 | 14,471 | 4,773 | 1,840 | 4,999 | 221 | 11,832 | 46 | 115 | 304 | 14,471 |
| 1994-5 | 15,613 | 17 | 1,103 | 2,680 | 15,597 | 4,714 | 1,693 | 5,546 | 222 | 12,175 | 49 | 124 | 287 | 15,597 |
| 1995-6[1] | 15,234 | 95 | 1,137 | 992 | 14,451 | 4,701 | 1,697 | 5,320 | 159 | 11,878 | 48 | 119 | 297 | 14,451 |
| 1996-7[2] | 15,350 | 100 | 2,015 | 1,850 | 15,500 | | | | | | 42 | 109 | 292 | 15,500 |

[1] Preliminary. [2] Forecast. *Source: Economic Research Service, U.S. Department of Agriculture*

# SOYBEAN OIL

## Crude and Refined Stocks of Soybean Oil in the U.S., at End of Month    In Millions of Pounds

| Crop Year Beginning Oct. | | Oct. | Nov. | Dec. | Jan. | Feb. | Mar. | Apr. | May | June | July | Aug. | Sept. |
|---|---|---|---|---|---|---|---|---|---|---|---|---|---|
| 1991-2 | Crude | ---------- | ---------- | 1,955.9 | 1,915.8 | 2,156.8 | 2,175.8 | 2,211.3 | 2,213.9 | 2,216.8 | 2,205.0 | 2,126.8 | 2,026.2 |
| | Refined | ---------- | ---------- | 259.8 | 243.7 | 245.7 | 224.3 | 211.2 | 219.6 | 209.7 | 215.9 | 236.0 | 213.2 |
| 1992-3 | Crude | 1,856.1 | 1,885.0 | 2,041.5 | 2,177.8 | 2,110.4 | 2,029.0 | 2,068.9 | 2,006.4 | 1,967.0 | 1,848.8 | 1,518.6 | 1,352.9 |
| | Refined | 220.2 | 220.2 | 238.6 | 232.3 | 226.4 | 217.1 | 229.0 | 234.3 | 207.0 | 211.8 | 201.2 | 201.9 |
| 1993-4 | Crude | 1,239.6 | 1,209.9 | 1,189.3 | 1,184.2 | 1,184.0 | 1,192.3 | 1,329.8 | 1,346.2 | 1,330.0 | 1,352.6 | 1,124.0 | 904.7 |
| | Refined | 213.1 | 189.7 | 217.5 | 230.4 | 216.9 | 209.8 | 223.5 | 220.6 | 223.8 | 218.2 | 215.4 | 198.4 |
| 1994-5 | Crude | 850.8 | 811.4 | 826.6 | 880.6 | 876.7 | 838.3 | 860.5 | 893.9 | 885.9 | 906.3 | 895.3 | 905.7 |
| | Refined | 204.7 | 215.5 | 231.7 | 236.2 | 252.1 | 221.3 | 229.1 | 236.5 | 225.8 | 235.7 | 204.7 | 231.0 |
| 1995-6[1] | Crude | 990.4 | 908.9 | 1,154.3 | 1,237.4 | 1,264.2 | 1,366.6 | 1,490.1 | 1,531.7 | 1,672.4 | 1,951.4 | 1,874.3 | 1,799.3 |
| | Refined | 205.5 | 223.1 | 254.6 | 275.2 | 257.2 | 287.0 | 257.3 | 227.2 | 216.1 | 205.1 | 217.1 | 216.1 |
| 1996-7[1] | Crude | 1,796.5 | 1,711.6 | 1,805.1 | 1,929.7 | | | | | | | | |
| | Refined | 196.4 | 186.8 | 222.0 | 242.7 | | | | | | | | |

[1] Preliminary.   *Source: Bureau of Census, U.S. Department of Commerce*

## U.S. Exports of Soybean Oil[1], by Country of Destination    In Metric Tons

| Year Beginning Oct. 1 | Bolivia | Canada | Ecuador | Ethiopia | Haiti | India | Israel | Mexico | Morocco | Pakistan | Panama | Peru | Philip-pines | Turkey | Vene-zuela | Grand Total |
|---|---|---|---|---|---|---|---|---|---|---|---|---|---|---|---|---|
| 1986-7 | 2,293 | 6,940 | 18,814 | 561 | 6,940 | 47,098 | 560 | 21,883 | 59,547 | 146,663 | 2,975 | 1,292 | 5,926 | 0 | 18,652 | 538,466 |
| 1987-8 | 2,123 | 7,344 | 19,050 | 17,605 | 3,411 | 151,600 | 416 | 11,537 | 35,821 | 396,737 | 3,736 | 1,144 | 6,734 | 17,098 | 4,866 | 850,015 |
| 1988-9 | 998 | 5,364 | 30,930 | 8,960 | 2,846 | 28,127 | 454 | 17,730 | 80,023 | 453,067 | 6,695 | 5,778 | 3,657 | 0 | 29,055 | 753,576 |
| 1989-90 | 1,037 | 5,443 | 26,314 | 22,858 | 1,688 | 16,391 | 442 | 4,435 | 77,985 | 309,502 | 3,174 | 5,206 | 1,868 | 0 | 8,198 | 613,902 |
| 1990-1 | 1,549 | 3,790 | 20,832 | 14,948 | 4,946 | 13,544 | 321 | 11,087 | 73,255 | 66,209 | 8,123 | 6,566 | 3,006 | 16,460 | 0 | 353,959 |
| 1991-2 | 1,829 | 11,153 | 528 | 19,619 | 4,737 | 67,577 | 356 | 23,383 | 127,602 | 250 | 11,143 | 32,696 | 1,996 | 81,976 | 13 | 747,465 |
| 1992-3 | 280 | 28,585 | 17 | 8,272 | 6,753 | 49,452 | 480 | 44,194 | 57,995 | 0 | 641 | 36,340 | 634 | 58,436 | 0 | 643,796 |
| 1993-4 | 0 | 4,401 | 0 | 24,509 | 1,747 | 46,846 | 200 | 18,499 | 31,563 | 72,204 | 248 | 24,081 | 100 | 34,920 | 26 | 693,697 |
| 1994-5[2] | 0 | 24,886 | 12,698 | 8,391 | 49,793 | 28,949 | 0 | 58,623 | 29,053 | 25,500 | 13,342 | 8,692 | 0 | 5,750 | 0 | 1,215,804 |
| 1995-6[3] | 0 | 43,910 | 1,155 | 4,546 | 15,040 | 20,841 | 0 | 46,645 | 0 | 0 | 9,512 | 35,999 | 0 | 0 | 0 | 449,869 |

[1] Crude & refined oil combined as such.   [2] Preliminary.   *Source: Economic Research Service, U.S. Department of Agriculture*

## U.S. Production of Crude Soybean Oil[2]    In Millions of Pounds

| Year | Oct. | Nov. | Dec. | Jan. | Feb. | Mar. | Apr. | May | June | July | Aug. | Sept. | Total |
|---|---|---|---|---|---|---|---|---|---|---|---|---|---|
| 1986-7 | 1,163 | 1,172 | 1,152 | 1,186 | 1,110 | 1,149 | 1,047 | 1,038 | 981 | 1,014 | 891 | 881 | 12,783 |
| 1987-8 | 1,120 | 1,207 | 1,208 | 1,170 | 1,092 | 1,187 | 1,133 | 1,087 | 996 | 994 | 879 | 901 | 12,974 |
| 1988-9 | 1,047 | 1,109 | 1,110 | 1,106 | 952 | 1,041 | 1,010 | 977 | 856 | 836 | 855 | 843 | 11,737 |
| 1989-90 | 1,057 | 1,146 | 1,161 | 1,187 | 1,022 | 1,142 | 1,067 | 1,050 | 1,036 | 1,038 | 1,059 | 1,038 | 13,004 |
| 1990-1 | 1,188 | 1,168 | 1,138 | ---------- | 3,331 | ---------- | ---------- | 3,171 | ---------- | ---------- | 3,412 | ---------- | 13,408 |
| 1991-2 | ---------- | 3,772 | ---------- | 1,270 | 1,147 | 1,228 | 1,167 | 1,096 | 1,152 | 1,177 | 1,179 | 1,158 | 14,345 |
| 1992-3 | 1,238 | 1,200 | 1,239 | 1,247 | 1,102 | 1,216 | 1,148 | 1,152 | 1,083 | 1,070 | 1,006 | 1,078 | 13,778 |
| 1993-4 | 1,241 | 1,228 | 1,218 | 1,192 | 1,122 | 1,231 | 1,155 | 1,123 | 1,070 | 1,099 | 1,104 | 1,168 | 13,951 |
| 1994-5 | 1,328 | 1,342 | 1,403 | 1,400 | 1,289 | 1,419 | 1,333 | 1,275 | 1,183 | 1,205 | 1,228 | 1,208 | 15,613 |
| 1995-6[1] | 1,354 | 1,360 | 1,382 | 1,360 | 1,236 | 1,292 | 1,259 | 1,197 | 1,221 | 1,263 | 1,171 | 1,139 | 15,234 |
| 1996-7[1] | 1,401 | 1,430 | 1,474 | | | | | | | | | | 4,304 |

[1] Preliminary.   [2] Not seasonally adjusted.   *Source: Economic Research Service, U.S. Department of Agriculture*

## U.S. Production of Refined Soybean Oil    In Millions of Pounds

| Year | Oct. | Nov. | Dec. | Jan. | Feb. | Mar. | Apr. | May | June | July | Aug. | Sept. | Total |
|---|---|---|---|---|---|---|---|---|---|---|---|---|---|
| 1986-7 | 911.3 | 848.1 | 850.0 | 790.2 | 763.6 | 900.7 | 871.2 | 826.9 | 871.3 | 921.8 | 898.6 | 946.5 | 10,400 |
| 1987-8 | 975.5 | 925.8 | 902.5 | 880.3 | 843.4 | 925.6 | 843.5 | 894.1 | 890.1 | 947.4 | 903.6 | 838.7 | 10,771 |
| 1988-9 | 867.1 | 826.9 | 800.8 | 776.7 | 709.6 | 830.1 | 800.6 | 867.4 | 801.4 | 791.4 | 866.6 | 866.6 | 9,805 |
| 1989-90 | 936.8 | 912.0 | 873.9 | 887.8 | 800.6 | 800.6 | 812.7 | 952.8 | 915.1 | 903.7 | 931.1 | 935.7 | 10,745 |
| 1990-1 | 1,028.0 | 980.6 | 934.7 | ---------- | 2,717.1 | ---------- | ---------- | 2,865.5 | ---------- | ---------- | 2,952.8 | ---------- | 11,479 |
| 1991-2 | ---------- | 2,918.1 | ---------- | 933.8 | 876.7 | 1,041.3 | 973.1 | 993.3 | 977.9 | 979.2 | 997.6 | 1,040.7 | 11,732 |
| 1992-3 | 1,095.6 | 999.4 | 951.0 | 960.1 | 935.4 | 1,054.9 | 1,039.7 | 950.6 | 1,042.8 | 978.2 | 1,066.7 | 1,109.7 | 12,184 |
| 1993-4 | 1,094.3 | 1,053.5 | 1,030.8 | 960.1 | 945.5 | 1,056.6 | 1,018.5 | 1,012.0 | 1,017.3 | 968.0 | 1,107.2 | 1,044.6 | 12,308 |
| 1994-5 | 1,123.0 | 1,079.2 | 1,060.6 | 1,002.5 | 968.2 | 1,063.6 | 1,010.4 | 1,077.0 | 993.5 | 940.9 | 1,076.8 | 1,039.8 | 12,435 |
| 1995-6[1] | 1,119.2 | 1,088.8 | 1,018.5 | 979.9 | 934.3 | 1,042.6 | 997.3 | 1,009.3 | 962.8 | 971.9 | 1,115.8 | 1,058.7 | 12,299 |
| 1996-7[1] | 1,111.7 | 1,064.1 | 1,025.7 | 975.0 | | | | | | | | | 3,177 |

[1] Preliminary.   *Source: Bureau of Census, U.S. Department of Commerce*

## Soybean Oil Consumption in End Products in the U.S. In Millions of Pounds

| Year | Jan. | Feb. | Mar. | Apr. | May | June | July | Aug. | Sept. | Oct. | Nov. | Dec. | Total |
|---|---|---|---|---|---|---|---|---|---|---|---|---|---|
| 1985 | 989.0 | 804.0 | 867.1 | 885.9 | 940.8 | 810.5 | 825.9 | 856.1 | 863.7 | 922.4 | 864.2 | 851.6 | 10,481 |
| 1986 | 836.7 | 794.0 | 889.7 | 849.1 | 850.3 | 856.8 | 835.1 | 843.1 | 890.3 | 927.6 | 840.6 | 891.2 | 10,305 |
| 1987 | 800.9 | 799.4 | 862.0 | 869.6 | 824.4 | 918.9 | 932.7 | 902.9 | 949.6 | 961.4 | 876.0 | 891.5 | 10,589 |
| 1988 | 913.9 | 820.5 | 930.0 | 839.9 | 870.5 | 937.9 | 936.5 | 907.3 | 829.1 | 862.2 | 829.1 | 846.6 | 10,524 |
| 1989 | 780.8 | 729.5 | 834.7 | 800.8 | 851.9 | 854.2 | 774.7 | 876.9 | 876.2 | 923.2 | 889.7 | 887.0 | 10,080 |
| 1990 | 901.3 | 815.7 | 952.0 | 893.6 | 950.9 | 927.8 | 866.0 | 905.4 | 895.7 | 984.1 | 912.9 | 878.0 | 10,883 |
| 1991 | | 2,690.3 | | | 2,831.8 | | | 2,837.7 | | | 2,907.8 | | 11,268 |
| 1992 | 880.4 | 867.0 | 1,010.1 | 947.9 | 956.7 | 962.1 | 935.5 | 932.4 | 1,019.8 | 1,061.7 | 951.8 | 946.1 | 11,472 |
| 1993 | 934.5 | 942.2 | 1,092.6 | 1,044.6 | 981.2 | 1,036.0 | 1,019.3 | 1,097.3 | 1,103.3 | 1,123.6 | 1,092.1 | 1,029.2 | 12,496 |
| 1994 | 924.5 | 939.1 | 1,084.7 | 1,040.6 | 1,001.4 | 1,023.8 | 974.9 | 1,119.2 | 1,075.4 | 1,123.3 | 1,103.4 | 1,063.8 | 12,474 |
| 1995 | 991.1 | 950.0 | 1,093.8 | 1,006.2 | 1,077.3 | 1,020.8 | 948.7 | 1,046.1 | 1,042.3 | 1,092.0 | 1,067.7 | 1,002.6 | 12,339 |
| 1996[1] | 964.9 | 927.4 | 1,026.4 | 999.8 | 1,020.6 | 946.2 | 959.9 | 1,123.3 | 1,042.8 | 1,137.1 | 1,080.9 | 1,093.1 | 12,322 |

[1] Preliminary. *Source: Bureau of Censue, U.S. Department of Commerce*

## U.S. Exports of Soybean Oil (Crude & Refined) In Millions of Pounds

| Year | Jan. | Feb. | Mar. | Apr. | May | June | July | Aug. | Sept. | Oct. | Nov. | Dec. | Total |
|---|---|---|---|---|---|---|---|---|---|---|---|---|---|
| 1985 | 66.7 | 198.3 | 184.9 | 66.9 | 52.4 | 138.8 | 174.4 | 70.1 | 102.8 | 125.4 | 38.1 | 74.3 | 1,293 |
| 1986 | 80.6 | 100.7 | 92.8 | 124.0 | 50.7 | 115.1 | 44.6 | 187.7 | 223.4 | 118.2 | 27.4 | 22.8 | 1,188 |
| 1987 | 67.9 | 74.0 | 52.1 | 28.2 | 47.4 | 85.0 | 175.6 | 261.0 | 224.8 | 100.1 | 139.0 | 134.0 | 1,389 |
| 1988 | 25.7 | 281.0 | 279.4 | 87.7 | 138.6 | 269.0 | 157.2 | 78.1 | 183.2 | 200.1 | 110.6 | 119.9 | 1,931 |
| 1989 | 104.5 | 65.8 | 112.4 | 105.5 | 161.4 | 72.1 | 159.3 | 181.1 | 265.6 | 116.2 | 82.5 | 113.4 | 1,540 |
| 1990 | 95.4 | 136.2 | 164.4 | 33.0 | 112.0 | 161.9 | 122.6 | 82.8 | 132.9 | 85.4 | 43.9 | 12.1 | 1,183 |
| 1991 | | 71.8 | | | 132.3 | | | 434.8 | | | 336.1 | | 975 |
| 1992 | 140.0 | 171.9 | 134.6 | 155.4 | 69.1 | 129.1 | 163.7 | 205.2 | 142.5 | 169.5 | 113.2 | 91.6 | 1,686 |
| 1993 | 146.8 | 188.0 | 143.3 | 61.1 | 154.8 | 75.4 | 59.9 | 116.0 | 99.7 | 190.4 | 88.6 | 200.2 | 1,524 |
| 1994 | 120.4 | 144.6 | 94.4 | 46.1 | 111.6 | 36.1 | 57.7 | 184.6 | 254.0 | 154.8 | 303.2 | 305.9 | 1,813 |
| 1995 | 217.4 | 367.6 | 564.2 | 236.2 | 90.8 | 160.4 | 91.0 | 109.4 | 79.4 | 69.3 | 205.4 | 95.9 | 2,287 |
| 1996[1] | 189.1 | 97.0 | 68.0 | 75.3 | 63.9 | 16.1 | 27.1 | 28.0 | 56.7 | 121.0 | 303.8 | | 1,046 |

[1] Preliminary. *Source: Economic Research Service, U.S. Department of Agriculture*

# SOYBEAN OIL

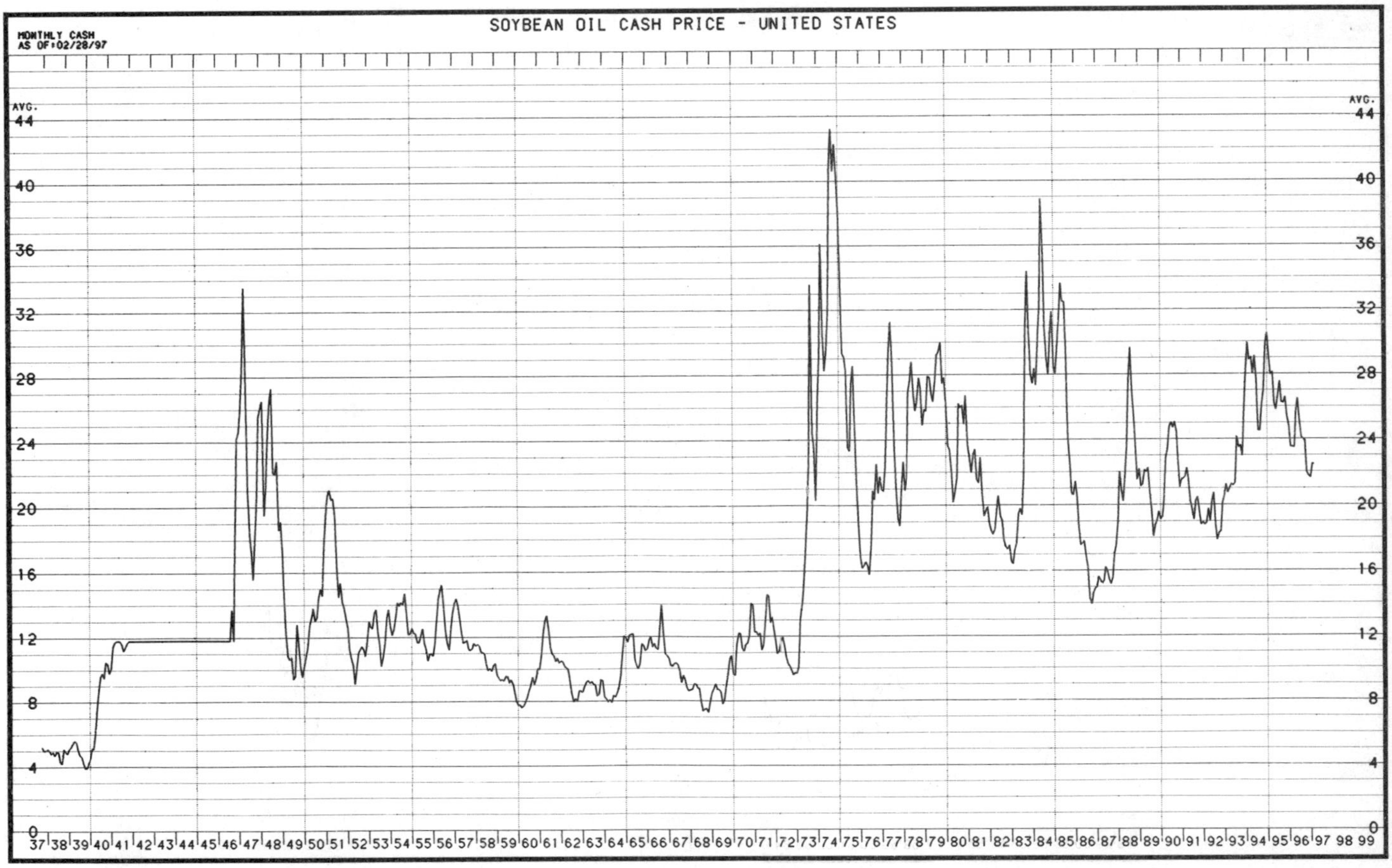


## U.S. Stocks of Soybean Oil (Crude & Refined) at Factory & Warehouse In Millions of Pounds

| Year | Oct. 1 | Nov. 1 | Dec. 1 | Jan. 1 | Feb. 1 | Mar. 1 | Apr. 1 | May 1 | June 1 | July 1 | Aug. 1 | Sept. 1 |
|---|---|---|---|---|---|---|---|---|---|---|---|---|
| 1985-6 | 632 | 636 | 810 | 969 | 1,167 | 1,181 | 1,247 | 1,219 | 1,360 | 1,225 | 1,321 | 1,152 |
| 1986-7 | 947 | 964 | 1,269 | 1,507 | 1,837 | 2,017 | 2,352 | 2,344 | 2,416 | 2,339 | 2,184 | 1,979 |
| 1987-8 | 1,725 | 1,661 | 1,834 | 2,050 | 2,391 | 2,239 | 2,343 | 2,385 | 2,570 | 2,361 | 2,203 | 2,212 |
| 1988-9 | 2,092 | 2,046 | 2,303 | 2,540 | 2,703 | 2,902 | 2,893 | 2,759 | 2,743 | 2,683 | 2,427 | 2,070 |
| 1989-90 | 1,715 | 1,515 | 1,532 | 1,605 | 1,718 | 1,703 | 1,695 | 1,716 | 1,551 | 1,422 | 1,433 | 1,380 |
| 1990-1 | 1,305 | 1,216 | 1,320 | | 1,464 | | | 1,875 | | | 1,853 | |
| 1991-2 | | 1,786 | | 2,217 | 2,159 | 2,402 | 2,400 | 2,423 | 2,433 | 2,427 | 2,421 | 2,363 |
| 1992-3 | 2,239 | 2,076 | 2,111 | 2,280 | 2,410 | 2,337 | 2,246 | 2,298 | 2,241 | 2,174 | 2,061 | 1,720 |
| 1993-4 | 1,555 | 1,453 | 1,400 | 1,407 | 1,415 | 1,401 | 1,402 | 1,553 | 1,567 | 1,554 | 1,571 | 1,339 |
| 1994-5 | 1,103 | 1,056 | 1,027 | 1,055 | 1,117 | 1,129 | 1,060 | 1,090 | 1,130 | 1,112 | 1,142 | 1,100 |
| 1995-6[1] | 1,137 | 1,196 | 1,132 | 1,409 | 1,513 | 1,521 | 1,654 | 1,747 | 1,759 | 1,888 | 2,156 | 2,091 |
| 1996-7[1] | 2,015 | 1,993 | 1,898 | | | | | | | | | |

[1] Preliminary. *Source: Economic Research Service, U.S. Department of Agriculture*

## Average Prices of Crude Domestic Soybean Oil (in Tank Cars) F.O.B. Decatur In Cents Per Pound

| Year | Oct. | Nov. | Dec. | Jan. | Feb. | Mar. | Apr. | May | June | July | Aug. | Sept. | Average |
|---|---|---|---|---|---|---|---|---|---|---|---|---|---|
| 1985-6 | 20.71 | 20.62 | 21.39 | 20.63 | 18.64 | 17.56 | 17.65 | 17.79 | 16.80 | 16.22 | 14.28 | 13.94 | 18.02 |
| 1986-7 | 14.63 | 14.88 | 14.94 | 15.60 | 15.40 | 15.21 | 15.31 | 16.22 | 15.96 | 15.41 | 15.16 | 15.58 | 15.36 |
| 1987-8 | 17.03 | 17.55 | 19.00 | 21.98 | 20.94 | 20.22 | 21.67 | 23.56 | 27.68 | 29.65 | 27.16 | 25.55 | 22.67 |
| 1988-9 | 23.42 | 21.55 | 22.16 | 21.13 | 21.21 | 22.11 | 21.97 | 22.23 | 20.75 | 19.66 | 18.08 | 18.77 | 21.09 |
| 1989-90 | 19.02 | 19.57 | 19.11 | 19.28 | 20.27 | 22.80 | 23.35 | 24.72 | 25.03 | 24.69 | 25.05 | 24.45 | 22.28 |
| 1990-1 | 22.59 | 21.05 | 21.55 | 21.56 | 21.66 | 22.21 | 21.50 | 20.23 | 19.65 | 19.05 | 20.23 | 20.46 | 21.00 |
| 1991-2 | 19.57 | 18.78 | 18.99 | 18.77 | 18.88 | 19.74 | 19.00 | 20.15 | 20.71 | 18.82 | 17.87 | 18.28 | 19.10 |
| 1992-3 | 18.36 | 20.10 | 20.52 | 21.23 | 20.72 | 21.00 | 21.24 | 21.15 | 21.30 | 24.13 | 23.47 | 23.61 | 21.40 |
| 1993-4 | 22.98 | 25.37 | 28.09 | 29.91 | 28.84 | 29.03 | 27.94 | 29.10 | 27.60 | 24.53 | 24.51 | 26.11 | 27.00 |
| 1994-5 | 27.06 | 29.84 | 30.61 | 29.01 | 28.15 | 28.33 | 27.16 | 26.00 | 26.78 | 27.60 | 26.56 | 26.26 | 27.71 |
| 1995-6[1] | 26.56 | 25.41 | 24.76 | 23.69 | 23.65 | 23.60 | 25.82 | 26.50 | 24.95 | 24.10 | 23.99 | 23.92 | 24.70 |
| 1996-7[1] | 21.95 | 21.80 | 21.60 | 22.45 | | | | | | | | | 21.95 |

[1] Preliminary. *Source: Economic Research Service, U.S. Department of Agriculture*

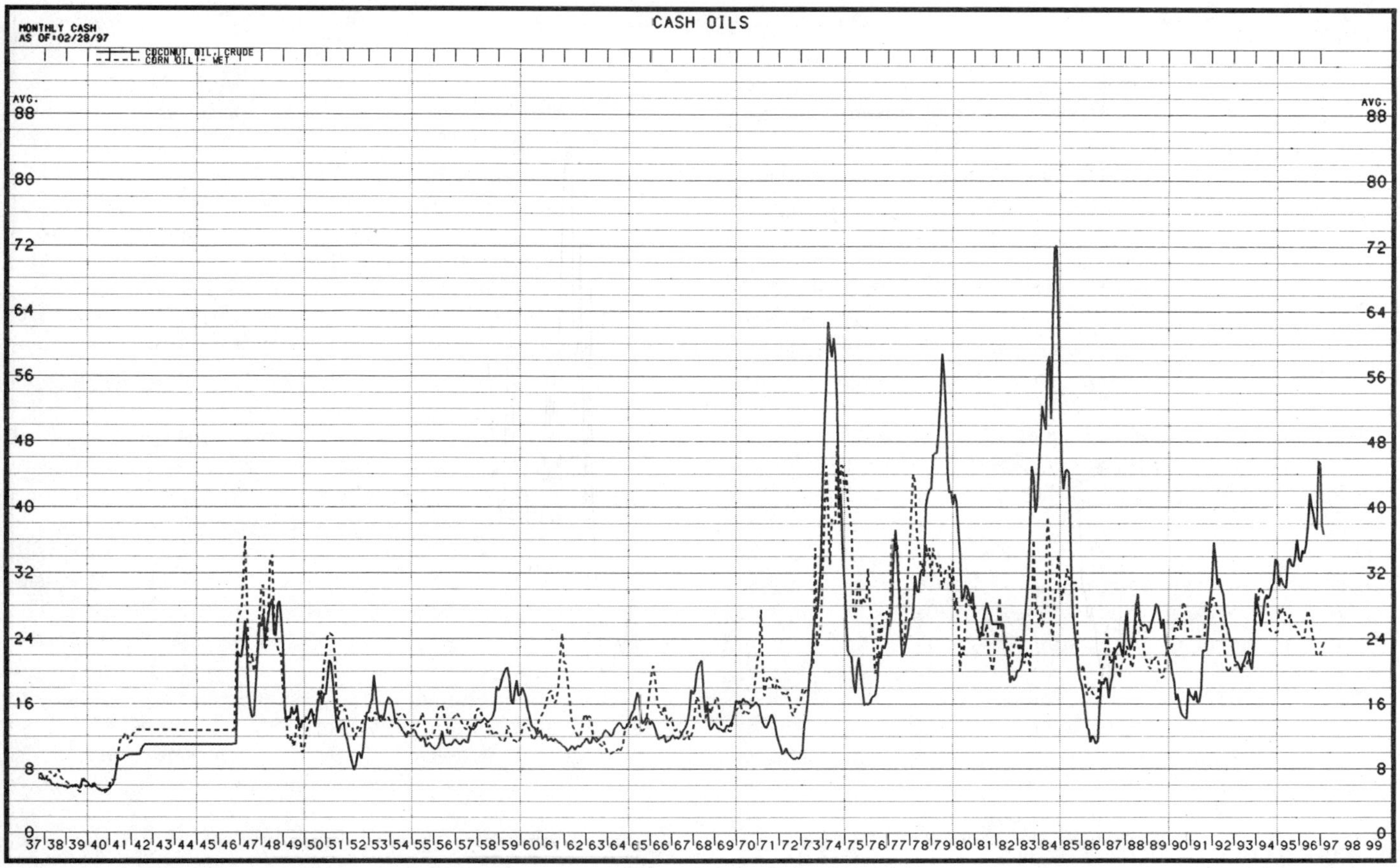


## Average Open Interest of Soybean Oil Futures in Chicago In Contracts

| Year | Jan. | Feb. | Mar. | Apr. | May | June | July | Aug. | Sept. | Oct. | Nov. | Dec. |
|---|---|---|---|---|---|---|---|---|---|---|---|---|
| 1985 | 37,482 | 42,458 | 47,038 | 56,246 | 58,675 | 60,357 | 55,448 | 53,111 | 53,351 | 47,026 | 42,732 | 46,469 |
| 1986 | 48,384 | 52,875 | 55,877 | 56,114 | 53,063 | 60,035 | 63,034 | 60,095 | 54,905 | 57,256 | 69,227 | 67,871 |
| 1987 | 71,509 | 81,610 | 73,916 | 75,154 | 82,843 | 86,672 | 83,041 | 68,373 | 65,973 | 68,860 | 73,194 | 79,985 |
| 1988 | 85,953 | 88,260 | 86,472 | 85,712 | 87,253 | 94,791 | 95,931 | 87,566 | 86,994 | 82,541 | 82,477 | 75,688 |
| 1989 | 77,741 | 81,676 | 78,235 | 77,249 | 73,623 | 76,572 | 70,644 | 68,652 | 63,751 | 63,911 | 69,248 | 68,166 |
| 1990 | 73,368 | 80,842 | 87,615 | 92,845 | 103,116 | 103,747 | 88,763 | 81,310 | 73,841 | 78,548 | 86,786 | 75,995 |
| 1991 | 72,987 | 71,607 | 76,800 | 70,361 | 70,954 | 73,870 | 73,864 | 70,058 | 66,128 | 61,227 | 69,657 | 63,901 |
| 1992 | 68,619 | 73,919 | 75,508 | 68,749 | 65,084 | 71,507 | 64,450 | 72,569 | 70,228 | 65,243 | 76,168 | 76,908 |
| 1993 | 73,683 | 68,887 | 66,803 | 68,598 | 65,814 | 73,892 | 83,730 | 72,746 | 64,927 | 62,348 | 80,136 | 94,990 |
| 1994 | 97,198 | 99,640 | 100,334 | 98,659 | 97,595 | 83,165 | 93,994 | 88,196 | 81,735 | 86,901 | 108,327 | 114,928 |
| 1995 | 101,171 | 103,856 | 97,715 | 87,300 | 76,175 | 75,171 | 81,650 | 77,064 | 70,410 | 71,652 | 85,241 | 84,138 |
| 1996 | 87,214 | 85,611 | 87,859 | 95,954 | 95,422 | 86,366 | 81,440 | 80,090 | 83,211 | 98,514 | 97,496 | 86,119 |

*Source: Chicago Board of Trade (CBT)*

## Volume of Trading of Soybean Oil Futures in Chicago In Thousands of Contracts

| Year | Jan. | Feb. | Mar. | Apr. | May | June | July | Aug. | Sept. | Oct. | Nov. | Dec. | Total |
|---|---|---|---|---|---|---|---|---|---|---|---|---|---|
| 1985 | 264.2 | 256.0 | 311.6 | 405.0 | 416.4 | 308.7 | 341.1 | 281.5 | 233.0 | 270.0 | 281.5 | 278.4 | 3,647 |
| 1986 | 263.1 | 235.9 | 254.0 | 311.7 | 273.8 | 262.0 | 296.0 | 237.9 | 202.7 | 324.8 | 261.4 | 259.6 | 3,183 |
| 1987 | 347.3 | 304.8 | 267.7 | 303.4 | 374.2 | 363.9 | 356.3 | 267.6 | 301.1 | 349.8 | 315.1 | 361.2 | 3,912 |
| 1988 | 437.0 | 390.7 | 346.8 | 442.7 | 399.2 | 580.2 | 461.4 | 403.6 | 390.0 | 303.1 | 377.3 | 364.2 | 4,896 |
| 1989 | 317.8 | 347.7 | 368.1 | 384.7 | 426.4 | 386.3 | 414.5 | 348.8 | 320.8 | 341.0 | 344.2 | 298.6 | 4,301 |
| 1990 | 294.1 | 397.1 | 413.9 | 447.7 | 488.8 | 441.5 | 462.3 | 405.6 | 319.2 | 344.1 | 370.2 | 266.3 | 4,651 |
| 1991 | 330.2 | 259.4 | 355.0 | 342.1 | 364.6 | 322.9 | 433.8 | 399.8 | 303.2 | 340.6 | 297.9 | 369.3 | 4,119 |
| 1992 | 344.2 | 293.1 | 400.0 | 255.8 | 381.8 | 352.3 | 413.1 | 298.0 | 425.9 | 346.8 | 365.8 | 405.5 | 4,283 |
| 1993 | 341.4 | 281.1 | 378.4 | 291.5 | 261.6 | 434.7 | 513.3 | 444.6 | 449.3 | 302.1 | 465.2 | 448.6 | 4,612 |
| 1994 | 442.0 | 401.6 | 366.0 | 391.2 | 442.4 | 378.2 | 397.5 | 357.9 | 415.4 | 476.9 | 516.7 | 477.4 | 5,063 |
| 1995 | 424.4 | 363.7 | 464.4 | 355.9 | 457.7 | 418.2 | 377.4 | 330.5 | 303.9 | 317.2 | 431.7 | 366.4 | 4,611.3 |
| 1996 | 354.6 | 355.2 | 375.2 | 443.4 | 376.7 | 423.1 | 512.6 | 449.0 | 425.9 | 414.0 | 396.2 | 454.3 | 4,980.3 |

*Source: Chicago Board of Trade (CBT)*

# Soybeans

The 1996/97 U.S. soybean crop of a near record high 2.4 billion bushels was 10 percent higher than the 2.2 billion produced in 1995/96, and about 100 million bushels below the 1994/95 record of 2.5 billion. The U.S. produces nearly half of the world's soybeans while Brazil, the second largest producer, contributes about 20 percent. World production in 1996/97 of 132.7 million metric tons proved larger than expected by at least 2 million tons, up from 124.3 million in 1995/96. The large crop, especially in the U.S., depressed prices in late 1996 with new crop beans falling more than a $1.00/bushel during October and $0.40 in November, basis May 1997 Chicago futures. World soybean production in the late 1980's averaged under 100 million tons; in the first half of the 1990's the average reached 120 million tons with a record high crop of 137.8 million tons in 1994/95.

Soybean production is expanding in a number of countries but the U.S. ranking is well entrenched as is Brazil's runner up slot. A key question is China, who during the past few years has vied with Argentina to be the third largest producer, each of whom produced about 13.5 million tons in 1996/97. In 1995/96 China also produced 13.5 million tons, while Argentina produced 12.6 million. The odds would seem to favor stronger growth in China in line with their expanding poultry flocks and the derived need for high protein soybean meal. However, as China's economy becomes more market sensitive growers may switch to higher priced crops as happened in 1995 and 1996, when soybean acreage was switched into corn and cotton production. Unless the reduced acreage trend is braked, China's 1990's bean production may have peaked in 1994/95 at 16 million tons.

Brazil's soybean crop is sown about the same time the U.S. is finishing their harvest. Brazilian production was forecast at 26 million tons in 1996/97 vs. 23.2 million in 1995/96. Argentina's 1996/97 crop was a record high. Unlike Brazil, Argentine soybean farmers have significantly lower production costs and a better transportation structure. Brazilian soybean acreage is generally about twice that of Argentina, 12.2 million hectares vs. 6 million respectively last year, but yield per acre is lower, 2.13 tons/hectare vs. 2.25 tons in Argentina. Brazil's crop year encompasses February to January, in Argentina it's April to March.

World soybean trade in 1996/97 of a record large 32.4 million tons compares with 31.7 million in 1995/96. The U.S. generally accounts for about two-thirds of world exports; a record large 23.1 million tons in 1996/97 vs. 23 million in 1995/96. Brazil's exports account for about 10 percent of total exports. Importing nations are numerous, the biggest are generally Japan, Germany, and the Netherlands. The ending 1996/97 world bean carryover of 17.8 million tons compares with the year earlier carryin of 17.2 million; generally the U.S., Brazil, and Argentina account for about 80 percent of total world stocks.

U.S. farmers planted 64.3 million acres to soybeans in 1996 vs. 62.6 million in 1995/96, with an estimated 98.6 percent of the acreage harvested. An average yield of 37.9 bushels per acre was realized vs. 35.3 bushels in 1995/96, and the record high 41.4 bushels in 1994/95.

U.S. soybean carryover stocks on August 31, 1996 of 183 million bushels brought total 1996/97 supplies to 2.6 billion bushels vs. 2.5 billion in 1995/96. Total disappearance in 1996/97 was put at of 2.4 billion bushels, of which at least 1.4 billion will be crushed, 0.9 billion exported, and about 120 million allocated to seed and residual. Carryover as of August 31, 1997 is forecast at 210 million bushels, but not a burdensome supply. Projected carryover as a percentage of use in 1996/97 was forecast at 8.8 percent vs. 7.8 percent in 1995/96, and a hefty 14 percent in 1994/95 when that season's ending carryover reached 335 million bushels. The 1996/97 season could yet prove to have a more intense demand than expected, much will depend on the crush (and export demand) during December-February which tends to be the seasonal high; on the other hand, competition from the large corn crop could check the crush demand for beans. Still, when a more positive soybean usage outlook shows signs of materializing it's apt to show in early calendar year prices. Demand bull years in soybeans generally show counterseasonal strength in January and February, however, if total usage holds neutral then prices, manifested chiefly in futures, tend to witness what is referred to as the "February break." If the latter develops it's not unusual for prices to penetrate the harvest lows of the previous October-December quarter.

The USDA's average price received by farmers in 1996/97 was initially forecast at $6.50 to $7.40 per bushel, then revised to $6.15 to $6.85 per bushel vs. $6.77 in 1995/96. The downward adjustment partially reflected the sharp, if not exaggerated, break in futures during October. The highest farm price during the past decade was $7.42 in 1988/89, and the low was $4.78 in 1986/87.

***Futures Markets***

Soybean futures are traded on the Bolsa de Mercadorias & Futuros (BM&F), the Kansai Agricultural Commodities Exchange (KANEX), the Tokyo Grain Exchange (TGE), the Manila International Futures Exchange Inc. (MIFE), the Chicago Board of Trade (CBOT), and the Mid America Commodity Exchange (MidAm). Options are traded on the TGE, the CBOT, and the MidAm.

## World Production of Soybeans In Thousands of Metric Tons

| Crop Year[4] | Argentina | Bolivia | Brazil | Canada | China | India | Indonesia | Japan | Rep. of Korea | Mexico | Romania | Paraguay | Thailand | United States | former USSR | World Total |
|---|---|---|---|---|---|---|---|---|---|---|---|---|---|---|---|---|
| 1987-8 | 9,700 | 158 | 18,020 | 1,267 | 12,470 | 980 | 950 | 287 | 203 | 750 | 350 | 1,100 | 338 | 52,746 | 712 | 103,810 |
| 1988-9 | 6,500 | 294 | 23,600 | 1,100 | 11,650 | 1,400 | 1,285 | 277 | 239 | 300 | 340 | 1,620 | 517 | 42,153 | 880 | 95,650 |
| 1989-90 | 10,750 | 173 | 20,340 | 1,219 | 10,227 | 1,806 | 1,315 | 272 | 252 | 984 | 304 | 1,575 | 672 | 52,354 | 956 | 107,367 |
| 1990-1 | 11,500 | 352 | 15,750 | 1,262 | 11,000 | 2,602 | 1,400 | 220 | 233 | 575 | 141 | 1,300 | 530 | 52,416 | 880 | 104,155 |
| 1991-2 | 11,315 | 384 | 19,456 | 1,460 | 9,713 | 2,492 | 1,555 | 197 | 183 | 725 | 179 | 1,315 | 436 | 54,065 | 830 | 108,050 |
| 1992-3 | 11,240 | 278 | 22,710 | 1,455 | 10,304 | 3,106 | 1,870 | 188 | 176 | 573 | 126 | 1,794 | 435 | 59,546 | 620 | 117,508 |
| 1993-4 | 12,200 | 491 | 24,963 | 1,851 | 14,600 | 3,700 | 1,709 | 101 | 170 | 497 | 95 | 1,890 | 480 | 50,919 | 660 | 117,058 |
| 1994-5[1] | 12,200 | 510 | 25,934 | 2,251 | 15,100 | 3,100 | 1,565 | 99 | 154 | 569 | 94 | 2,100 | 528 | 67,900 | 520 | 135,506 |
| 1995-6[2] | 12,640 | 700 | 23,400 | 2,279 | 13,500 | 4,450 | 1,600 | 119 | 159 | 135 | 107 | 2,300 | 452 | 59,240 | 600 | 124,390 |
| 1996-7[3] | 13,500 | | 26,500 | | 12,500 | | | | | | | 2,500 | | 64,840 | | 132,810 |

[1] Preliminary. [2] Estimate. [3] Forecast. [4] Split year includes Northern Hemisphere crops harvested in the late months of the first year shown combined with Southern Hemisphere crops harvested in the early months of the following year. *Source: Foreign Agricultural Service, U.S. Department of Agriculture*

## Supply and Distribution of Soybeans in the United States In Millions of Bushels

| Crop Year Beginning Sept. 1 | Supply: Stocks, Sept. 1: Farms | Supply: Stocks, Sept. 1: Mills, Elevators[3] | Supply: Stocks, Sept. 1: Total | Supply: Production | Supply: Total Supply | Distribution: Crushings | Distribution: Exports | Distribution: Seed, Feed & Residual | Distribution: Total Distribution |
|---|---|---|---|---|---|---|---|---|---|
| 1987-8 | 108.0 | 328.5 | 436 | 1,938 | 2,375 | 1,174 | 804 | 95 | 2,073 |
| 1988-9 | 105.1 | 197.4 | 302 | 1,549 | 1,855 | 1,058 | 527 | 87 | 1,673 |
| 1989-90 | 87.3 | 94.7 | 182 | 1,924 | 2,109 | 1,146 | 622 | 101 | 1,870 |
| 1990-1 | 86.0 | 153.1 | 239 | 1,926 | 2,169 | 1,187 | 557 | 95 | 1,840 |
| 1991-2 | 118.4 | 210.6 | 329 | 1,987 | 2,319 | 1,254 | 684 | 103 | 2,041 |
| 1992-3 | 105.0 | 173.4 | 278 | 2,190 | 2,471 | 1,279 | 770 | 130 | 2,179 |
| 1993-4 | 125.0 | 167.3 | 292 | 1,871 | 2,170 | 1,276 | 589 | 96 | 1,961 |
| 1994-5 | 59.1 | 150.0 | 209 | 2,517 | 2,731 | 1,405 | 838 | 153 | 2,396 |
| 1995-6[1] | 105.1 | 229.7 | 335 | 2,177 | 2,518 | 1,389 | 851 | 112 | 2,333 |
| 1996-7[2] | 59.5 | 123.9 | 183 | 2,382 | 2,570 | 1,410 | 905 | 116 | 2,431 |

[1] Preliminary. [2] Estimate. [3] Also warehouses. *Source: Economic Research Service, U.S. Department of Agriculture*

## U.S. Soybean Price Support Program & Official Crop Production Reports In Millions of Bushels

| Crop Year Beginning Sept. | Quantity Put Under Support | % of Production | Stocks Sept. 1 | National Average Support: % of Parity | National Average Support: $ Per Bu. | Crop Production Reports In Thousands of Bushels: Aug. 1 | Sept. 1 | Oct. 1 | Nov. 1 | Dec. 1 | Final |
|---|---|---|---|---|---|---|---|---|---|---|---|
| 1987-8 | 274.7 | 14.2 | 436.4 | 39 | 4.77 | 2,000,349 | 1,956,859 | 1,968,069 | 1,959,949 | 1,904,712 | 1,938,087 |
| 1988-9 | 120.1 | 7.8 | 302.5 | 40 | 4.77 | 1,473,986 | 1,472,376 | 1,501,381 | 1,511,876 | ---------- | 1,548,841 |
| 1989-90 | 208.9 | 10.9 | 182.0 | 37 | 4.53 | 1,905,300 | 1,889,265 | 1,926,385 | 1,936,545 | ---------- | 1,926,806 |
| 1990-1 | 241.4 | 12.5 | 239.1 | 36 | 4.50 | 1,836,017 | 1,834,602 | 1,823,462 | 1,903,832 | ---------- | 1,925,947 |
| 1991-2 | 158.8 | 8.0 | 329.0 | 40 | 5.02 | 1,868,825 | 1,816,825 | 1,933,570 | 1,961,840 | ---------- | 1,986,539 |
| 1992-3 | 182.1 | 8.3 | 278.4 | 41 | 5.02 | 2,079,487 | NA | NA | NA | ---------- | 2,190,354 |
| 1993-4 | 87.1 | 4.8 | 292.3 | 40 | 5.02 | 1,902,023 | 1,909,188 | 1,890,808 | 1,833,788 | ---------- | 1,870,958 |
| 1994-5 | 375.0 | 14.9 | 209.1 | 40 | 4.92 | 2,282,367 | 2,316,077 | 2,458,087 | 2,522,527 | ---------- | 2,516,694 |
| 1995-6 | 181.8 | 2.9 | 335.0 | | 4.92 | 2,245,901 | 2,284,551 | 2,190,661 | 2,182,991 | ---------- | 2,176,814 |
| 1996-7[1] | 190.7 | | | | | 2,299,675 | 2,269,505 | 2,346,220 | 2,402,610 | ---------- | 2,382,364 |

[1] Preliminary. NA = Not available. *Source: National Agricultural Statistics Service, U.S. Department of Agriculture*

## Soybean Stocks in the United States In Thousands of Bushels

| Year | On Farms: Mar. 1 | On Farms: Jun. 1 | On Farms: Sept. 1 | On Farms: Dec. 1 | Off Farms[1]: Mar. 1 | Off Farms[1]: Jun. 1 | Off Farms[1]: Sept. 1 | Off Farms[1]: Dec. 1 | Total Stocks: Mar. 1 | Total Stocks: Jun. 1 | Total Stocks: Sept. 1 | Total Stocks: Dec. 1 |
|---|---|---|---|---|---|---|---|---|---|---|---|---|
| 1987 | 589,000 | 282,100 | 107,950 | 865,300 | 749,958 | 554,654 | 328,497 | 889,981 | 1,338,958 | 836,754 | 436,447 | 1,755,281 |
| 1988 | 553,100 | 304,900 | 105,050 | 650,000 | 594,620 | 351,382 | 197,426 | 716,812 | 1,147,720 | 656,282 | 302,476 | 1,366,812 |
| 1989 | 415,000 | 229,200 | 87,320 | 793,400 | 475,246 | 235,311 | 94,709 | 816,583 | 890,246 | 464,511 | 182,029 | 1,609,983 |
| 1990 | 535,800 | 255,300 | 86,000 | 754,000 | 519,705 | 340,614 | 153,139 | 929,963 | 1,055,505 | 595,914 | 239,139 | 1,683,963 |
| 1991 | 555,500 | 336,500 | 118,400 | 810,000 | 634,619 | 387,022 | 210,642 | 968,957 | 1,190,119 | 723,522 | 329,042 | 1,778,957 |
| 1992 | 505,000 | 279,000 | 105,000 | 876,100 | 672,343 | 416,671 | 173,437 | 959,885 | 1,177,343 | 695,671 | 278,437 | 1,835,985 |
| 1993 | 576,900 | 319,800 | 124,970 | 697,400 | 638,667 | 363,613 | 167,314 | 876,220 | 1,215,567 | 683,413 | 292,284 | 1,573,620 |
| 1994 | 425,700 | 195,000 | 59,080 | 985,800 | 595,917 | 360,260 | 150,037 | 1,116,156 | 1,021,617 | 555,260 | 209,117 | 2,101,956 |
| 1995 | 635,300 | 348,800 | 105,130 | 861,500 | 734,898 | 443,072 | 229,684 | 971,929 | 1,370,198 | 791,872 | 334,814 | 1,833,429 |
| 1996 | 512,000 | 234,100 | 59,523 | 935,100 | 678,356 | 388,944 | 123,655 | 887,563 | 1,190,356 | 623,044 | 183,178 | 1,822,663 |

[1] Includes stocks at mills, elevators, warehouses, terminals and processors. NA = Not available. *Source: National Agricultural Statistics Service, U.S. Department of Agriculture*

# SOYBEANS

## U.S. Commercial Stocks of Soybeans on the First of the Month In Millions of Bushels

| Year | Jan. | Feb. | Mar. | Apr. | May | June | July | Aug. | Sept. | Oct. | Nov. | Dec. |
|---|---|---|---|---|---|---|---|---|---|---|---|---|
| 1984 | 77.2 | 74.4 | 65.2 | 58.6 | 49.2 | 41.1 | 35.4 | 20.8 | 7.9 | 6.7 | 23.3 | 41.7 |
| 1985 | 41.1 | 44.0 | 38.2 | 33.3 | 22.8 | 14.7 | 12.7 | 11.3 | 6.9 | 9.6 | 47.6 | 60.9 |
| 1986 | 61.7 | 63.9 | 57.3 | 53.6 | 40.2 | 30.5 | 24.9 | 24.5 | 24.8 | 30.1 | 52.5 | 61.5 |
| 1987 | 62.0 | 61.4 | 56.9 | 52.5 | 49.4 | 46.3 | 38.4 | 26.0 | 16.6 | 21.3 | 56.5 | 57.1 |
| 1988 | 63.0 | 66.9 | 63.6 | 61.2 | 54.6 | 51.7 | 53.2 | 54.5 | 46.0 | 41.6 | 74.7 | 80.9 |
| 1989 | 81.3 | 75.6 | 63.8 | 53.4 | 35.8 | 31.2 | 21.1 | 18.6 | 14.1 | 11.4 | 62.1 | 71.3 |
| 1990 | 65.8 | 62.1 | 57.8 | 53.2 | 56.2 | 54.4 | 48.1 | 41.4 | 26.1 | 24.1 | 89.7 | 90.7 |
| 1991 | 90.2 | 78.1 | 70.5 | 56.2 | 43.5 | 35.5 | 33.3 | 25.5 | 25.3 | 29.7 | 80.6 | 84.0 |
| 1992 | 76.0 | 75.9 | 67.1 | 67.8 | 58.5 | 57.2 | 51.7 | 32.1 | 18.6 | 59.0 | 75.1 | 79.9 |
| 1993 | 71.5 | 63.5 | 54.5 | 48.5 | 44.0 | 32.1 | 26.6 | 24.4 | 15.8 | 9.6 | 52.3 | 60.2 |
| 1994 | 62.6 | 65.3 | 54.4 | 46.3 | 40.7 | 34.7 | 29.9 | 24.3 | 19.8 | 11.5 | 68.1 | 83.4 |
| 1995 | 80.7 | 72.5 | 67.8 | 63.5 | 51.8 | 50.8 | 44.3 | 35.7 | 33.6 | 23.0 | 60.8 | 61.7 |
| 1996 | 57.2 | 57.2 | 59.2 | 54.7 | 56.2 | 44.9 | 36.9 | 32.7 | 12.0 | 5.3 | 55.2 | 50.6 |

*Source: Livestock Division, U.S. Department of Agriculture*

## Salient Statistics of Soybeans in the United States

| Crop Year | Acreage Planted | Acreage Harvested | Yield Per Acre (Bu.) | Farm Price ($ Bu.) | Farm Value (Million Dollars) | Pounds Per Bushel Crushed: Yield of Oil | Pounds Per Bushel Crushed: Yield of Meal | U.S. Exports of Soybeans Crop Year (Oct.-Sept.) in Thousands of Metric Tons: Grand Total | Bel.-Luxem. | Canada | Germany | Japan | Netherlands | Spain | Taiwan | former USSR |
|---|---|---|---|---|---|---|---|---|---|---|---|---|---|---|---|---|
| | --- 1,000 Acres --- | | | | | | | | | | | | | | | |
| 1979-80 | 71,411 | 70,343 | 32.1 | 6.28 | 14,204 | 10.74 | 48.01 | 23,818 | 584 | 392 | 1,318 | 3,868 | 6,035 | 2,203 | 780 | 813 |
| 1980-1 | 60,930 | 67,813 | 26.5 | 7.57 | 13,601 | 11.09 | 47.93 | 19,712 | 670 | 345 | 1,791 | 3,816 | 3,839 | 1,383 | 1,063 | NA |
| 1981-2 | 67,543 | 66,163 | 30.1 | 6.07 | 12,005 | 10.72 | 47.86 | 25,285 | 1,404 | 310 | 2,135 | 4,196 | 5,349 | 3,855 | 1,059 | 683 |
| 1982-3 | 70,884 | 69,442 | 31.5 | 5.71 | 12,463 | 10.76 | 47.88 | 24,634 | 1,259 | 324 | 1,813 | 4,580 | 4,648 | 2,313 | 1,300 | 199 |
| 1983-4 | 63,779 | 62,525 | 26.2 | 7.83 | 12,775 | 11.26 | 47.36 | 20,215 | 882 | 248 | 967 | 4,394 | 2,988 | 1,800 | 1,382 | 408 |
| 1984-5 | 67,755 | 66,113 | 28.1 | 5.84 | 10,748 | 11.05 | 47.15 | 16,279 | 658 | 140 | 718 | 3,828 | 2,857 | 1,084 | 1,389 | 0 |
| 1985-6 | 63,145 | 61,599 | 34.1 | 5.05 | 10,571 | 11.01 | 47.27 | 20,158 | 784 | 114 | 934 | 4,293 | 3,056 | 1,519 | 1,506 | 1,519 |
| 1986-7 | 60,405 | 58,312 | 33.3 | 4.78 | 9,263 | 10.86 | 47.08 | 20,600 | 888 | 206 | 1,393 | 4,024 | 3,540 | 1,775 | 1,968 | 71 |
| 1987-8 | 58,180 | 57,172 | 33.9 | 5.88 | 11,391 | 11.04 | 47.76 | 21,870 | 825 | 154 | 1,416 | 3,914 | 4,267 | 1,593 | 1,857 | 831 |
| 1988-9 | 58,840 | 57,373 | 27.0 | 7.42 | 11,488 | 11.16 | 47.43 | 14,356 | 474 | 113 | 601 | 3,251 | 2,531 | 1,152 | 1,439 | 240 |
| 1989-90 | 60,820 | 59,538 | 32.3 | 5.69 | 10,916 | 11.17 | 47.63 | 16,933 | 666 | 276 | 818 | 3,480 | 2,721 | 1,565 | 2,016 | 342 |
| 1990-1 | 57,795 | 56,512 | 34.1 | 5.74 | 11,042 | 11.23 | 47.47 | 15,161 | 413 | 156 | 760 | 3,584 | 2,085 | 1,027 | 1,087 | 354 |
| 1991-2 | 59,180 | 58,011 | 34.2 | 5.58 | 11,092 | 11.42 | 47.51 | 19,277 | 797 | 76 | 814 | 3,891 | 3,167 | 1,459 | 2,034 | 543 |
| 1992-3 | 59,180 | 58,233 | 37.6 | 5.56 | 12,168 | 10.84 | 47.54 | 20,400 | 814 | 249 | 893 | 3,984 | 3,362 | 1,424 | 2,369 | 46 |
| 1993-4 | 60,135 | 57,347 | 32.6 | 6.40 | 11,950 | 10.87 | 47.62 | 16,364 | 602 | 26 | 807 | 3,527 | 2,661 | 921 | 1,700 | 0 |
| 1994-5 | 61,670 | 60,859 | 41.4 | 5.48 | 13,756 | 11.08 | 47.33 | 23,584 | 778 | 0 | 1,228 | 4,061 | 4,130 | 1,714 | 2,586 | 0 |
| 1995-6[1] | 62,575 | 61,624 | 35.3 | 6.77 | 14,617 | 11.18 | 47.69 | 22,372 | 621 | 0 | 1,286 | 3,730 | 3,706 | 1,218 | 2,631 | 0 |
| 1996-7[2] | 64,205 | 63,409 | 37.6 | 7.14 | 16,277 | 10.89 | 47.37 | | | | | | | | | |

[1] Preliminary. [2] Forecast. NA = Not available. *Source: Economic Research Service, U.S. Department of Agriculture*

## Production of Soybeans for Beans in the U.S., by Selected States In Millions of Bushels

| Year | Arkansas | Illinois | Indiana | Iowa | Kentucky | Louisiana | Michigan | Minnesota | Mississippi | Missouri | Nebraska | North Carolina | Ohio | South Carolina | Tennessee |
|---|---|---|---|---|---|---|---|---|---|---|---|---|---|---|---|
| 1979 | 144.2 | 379.1 | 159.1 | 306.4 | 54.0 | 93.8 | 30.3 | 162.6 | 118.9 | 183.6 | 54.7 | 45.8 | 144.8 | 39.8 | 70.7 |
| 1980 | 65.3 | 309.9 | 157.7 | 318.4 | 36.0 | 67.0 | 30.4 | 149.9 | 61.6 | 135.5 | 53.1 | 34.7 | 135.4 | 20.8 | 45.9 |
| 1981 | 99.0 | 351.5 | 151.8 | 326.0 | 47.9 | 64.2 | 29.1 | 139.2 | 75.6 | 155.6 | 78.7 | 46.3 | 99.8 | 31.0 | 61.1 |
| 1982 | 105.6 | 354.2 | 173.3 | 306.6 | 51.3 | 75.4 | 35.3 | 169.1 | 92.3 | 171.0 | 78.8 | 52.5 | 133.2 | 39.6 | 61.0 |
| 1983 | 70.3 | 267.0 | 122.5 | 278.6 | 24.5 | 68.1 | 33.8 | 151.8 | 58.9 | 103.0 | 59.0 | 33.0 | 105.0 | 23.6 | 31.5 |
| 1984 | 101.4 | 284.1 | 150.1 | 264.6 | 42.3 | 66.8 | 32.1 | 172.9 | 76.8 | 108.7 | 66.3 | 46.5 | 137.6 | 29.8 | 48.1 |
| 1985 | 98.1 | 382.5 | 185.1 | 309.7 | 41.8 | 44.1 | 34.6 | 160.0 | 70.7 | 180.4 | 85.0 | 39.1 | 160.6 | 24.6 | 45.3 |
| 1986 | 66.0 | 360.0 | 157.3 | 350.7 | 35.8 | 35.0 | 28.8 | 162.8 | 41.7 | 170.6 | 93.1 | 36.7 | 146.6 | 13.7 | 35.5 |
| 1987 | 71.5 | 330.6 | 174.0 | 343.7 | 24.0 | 38.8 | 38.2 | 181.4 | 47.8 | 154.6 | 83.4 | 32.8 | 147.3 | 15.7 | 28.8 |
| 1988 | 83.2 | 234.9 | 115.5 | 251.1 | 24.1 | 56.6 | 35.1 | 124.8 | 49.5 | 112.1 | 70.8 | 35.4 | 99.9 | 18.6 | 32.0 |
| 1989 | 75.2 | 354.0 | 166.1 | 322.9 | 36.9 | 38.5 | 38.9 | 185.0 | 40.0 | 121.8 | 81.9 | 41.9 | 125.4 | 20.2 | 29.8 |
| 1990 | 90.5 | 354.9 | 171.4 | 327.9 | 39.0 | 42.0 | 43.3 | 179.4 | 39.9 | 124.5 | 81.4 | 32.4 | 135.7 | 13.9 | 33.8 |
| 1991 | 89.6 | 341.3 | 171.6 | 349.5 | 36.7 | 30.7 | 52.8 | 195.3 | 46.8 | 135.1 | 82.4 | 38.6 | 135.7 | 13.7 | 31.5 |
| 1992 | 104.3 | 405.5 | 194.4 | 359.5 | 42.2 | 35.1 | 47.5 | 172.8 | 59.5 | 161.5 | 103.3 | 36.5 | 147.2 | 14.7 | 33.3 |
| 1993 | 92.3 | 387.0 | 223.1 | 257.3 | 38.0 | 31.2 | 54.7 | 115.0 | 42.9 | 118.8 | 90.0 | 30.0 | 156.2 | 7.8 | 32.2 |
| 1994 | 115.6 | 429.1 | 215.3 | 442.9 | 42.4 | 31.9 | 57.0 | 224.0 | 57.0 | 173.3 | 134.4 | 41.9 | 173.6 | 15.7 | 38.3 |
| 1995 | 88.4 | 378.3 | 196.7 | 407.4 | 41.4 | 26.0 | 59.6 | 234.9 | 37.8 | 132.8 | 101.0 | 26.8 | 153.1 | 12.7 | 34.6 |
| 1996[1] | 112.0 | 398.9 | 203.7 | 415.8 | 44.8 | 35.6 | 46.7 | 224.2 | 54.3 | 149.9 | 135.5 | 34.8 | 157.2 | 13.5 | 40.3 |

[1] Preliminary. *Source: Agricultural Statistics Board, U.S. Department of Agriculture*

**Soybean Stocks at U.S. Mills on First of Month** In Millions of Bushels

| Crop Year | Sept. | Oct. | Nov. | Dec. | Jan. | Feb. | Mar. | Apr. | May | June | July | Aug. |
|---|---|---|---|---|---|---|---|---|---|---|---|---|
| 1979-80 | 37.5 | 39.2 | 166.5 | 184.5 | 163.3 | 145.4 | 130.7 | 118.6 | 95.8 | 79.7 | 75.7 | 73.9 |
| 1980-1 | 56.9 | 80.4 | 166.0 | 172.0 | 138.7 | 125.9 | 105.4 | 97.2 | 84.4 | 67.8 | 49.2 | 43.9 |
| 1981-2 | 33.4 | 31.5 | 105.8 | 135.2 | 114.5 | 99.8 | 84.6 | 79.2 | 72.2 | 60.8 | 51.2 | 43.6 |
| 1982-3 | 30.0 | 29.0 | 114.2 | 145.5 | 125.1 | 116.2 | 98.5 | 96.2 | 84.6 | 69.8 | 62.0 | 55.4 |
| 1983-4 | 58.6 | 63.9 | 124.5 | 142.3 | 124.0 | 125.3 | 114.8 | 105.3 | 94.2 | 101.7 | 83.4 | 57.7 |
| 1984-5 | 35.3 | 19.7 | 53.9 | 116.4 | 98.4 | 85.9 | 65.8 | 69.7 | 65.2 | 53.4 | 47.6 | 36.0 |
| 1985-6 | 26.7 | 25.7 | 92.8 | 113.4 | 119.9 | 124.6 | 97.5 | 84.9 | 67.6 | 53.2 | 40.7 | 40.2 |
| 1986-7 | 28.5 | 38.3 | 108.1 | 127.4 | 117.2 | 113.1 | 105.4 | 90.2 | 85.2 | 72.9 | 63.6 | 49.8 |
| 1987-8 | 31.2 | 65.7 | 158.5 | 155.5 | 145.0 | 141.8 | 139.3 | 133.8 | 113.9 | 95.4 | 90.1 | 66.2 |
| 1988-9 | 59.7 | 61.4 | 136.6 | 147.4 | 138.6 | 131.9 | 112.0 | 99.2 | 72.8 | 52.5 | 46.1 | 31.0 |
| 1989-90 | 23.8 | 24.5 | 96.3 | 108.5 | 89.7 | 93.6 | 91.4 | 83.5 | 73.0 | 67.5 | 58.8 | 46.9 |
| 1990-1 | 45.2 | 34.5 | 130.1 | 130.7 | ----------- | 106.5 | ----------- | ------------- | 78.5 | ----------- | ----------- | 61.2 |
| 1991-2 | ------ | ----------- | 67.0 | ----------- | 126.9 | 121.4 | 109.6 | 94.7 | 79.8 | 73.5 | 65.7 | 56.2 |
| 1992-3 | 43.8 | 46.3 | 132.3 | 137.4 | 119.1 | 111.2 | 97.2 | 90.1 | 83.6 | 67.7 | 67.1 | 55.3 |
| 1993-4 | 42.0 | 28.0 | 108.6 | 114.9 | 120.9 | 126.1 | 118.5 | 119.7 | 98.7 | 97.8 | 90.0 | 63.5 |
| 1994-5 | 47.9 | 46.8 | 114.1 | 124.3 | 108.0 | 114.7 | 114.3 | 112.6 | 94.1 | 81.2 | 69.1 | 55.1 |
| 1995-6[1] | 52.8 | 54.2 | 125.6 | 129.1 | 120.0 | 123.3 | 121.9 | 110.6 | 104.2 | 92.5 | 70.4 | 57.5 |
| 1996-7[1] | 40.5 | 23.3 | 101.1 | 117.7 | | | | | | | | |

[1] Preliminary. *Source: Economic Research Service, U.S. Department of Agriculture*

**Soybean Exports from the United States** In Millions of Bushels

| Year | Sept. | Oct. | Nov. | Dec. | Jan. | Feb. | Mar. | Apr. | May | June | July | Aug. | Total |
|---|---|---|---|---|---|---|---|---|---|---|---|---|---|
| 1980-1 | 41.4 | 60.3 | 75.0 | 74.5 | 71.7 | 55.5 | 103.2 | 60.0 | 69.6 | 41.8 | 29.6 | 41.8 | 724.3 |
| 1981-2 | 50.9 | 100.8 | 103.7 | 73.6 | 84.3 | 89.4 | 79.0 | 85.7 | 90.6 | 59.8 | 53.8 | 57.5 | 929.1 |
| 1982-3 | 58.0 | 94.4 | 93.6 | 90.1 | 86.3 | 87.2 | 84.4 | 73.3 | 58.5 | 67.7 | 51.6 | 60.2 | 905.2 |
| 1983-4 | 53.9 | 67.6 | 69.2 | 74.5 | 80.4 | 79.7 | 78.8 | 68.5 | 56.8 | 41.1 | 39.2 | 30.7 | 686.6 |
| 1984-5 | 19.0 | 40.9 | 93.5 | 84.8 | 70.3 | 72.6 | 59.8 | 60.4 | 33.1 | 18.2 | 19.2 | 26.3 | 598.2 |
| 1985-6 | 31.5 | 55.3 | 79.6 | 94.1 | 84.7 | 92.1 | 89.9 | 80.4 | 57.2 | 28.7 | 26.6 | 20.4 | 740.7 |
| 1986-7 | 30.2 | 89.7 | 96.6 | 89.0 | 71.7 | 73.8 | 67.8 | 53.9 | 37.6 | 37.9 | 54.3 | 54.5 | 756.9 |
| 1987-8 | 59.4 | 101.1 | 100.4 | 81.1 | 80.8 | 97.0 | 78.5 | 66.7 | 39.7 | 29.3 | 30.4 | 37.2 | 801.7 |
| 1988-9 | 26.7 | 50.2 | 61.3 | 69.3 | 66.3 | 56.1 | 66.8 | 40.8 | 23.2 | 31.2 | 16.4 | 18.3 | 526.5 |
| 1989-90 | 17.9 | 74.0 | 76.6 | 65.7 | 76.3 | 74.9 | 87.3 | 43.6 | 22.8 | 35.2 | 20.8 | 28.3 | 623.4 |
| 1990-1 | 27.9 | 29.8 | 62.8 | 55.8 | ----------- | 190.1 | ----------- | ----------- | 117.7 | ----------- | 73.9 | ----------- | 557.9 |
| 1991-2 | 26.8 | ----------- | 235.6 | ----------- | 73.8 | 90.6 | 63.3 | 56.6 | 28.3 | 27.3 | 42.6 | 39.2 | 683.9 |
| 1992-3 | 50.1 | 98.0 | 84.2 | 73.6 | 89.1 | 104.7 | 79.7 | 48.7 | 34.6 | 39.4 | 42.7 | 24.6 | 769.5 |
| 1993-4 | 30.1 | 73.6 | 72.4 | 73.9 | 71.0 | 67.8 | 53.6 | 34.8 | 27.5 | 26.7 | 17.1 | 40.7 | 589.1 |
| 1994-5 | 42.3 | 99.9 | 78.5 | 104.2 | 89.3 | 91.4 | 83.1 | 80.7 | 45.2 | 35.5 | 41.2 | 46.7 | 838.1 |
| 1995-6[1] | 70.7 | 77.4 | 65.5 | 89.6 | 106.2 | 82.9 | 93.5 | 52.9 | 42.1 | 51.8 | 46.0 | 52.6 | 851.2 |
| 1996-7[1] | 41.6 | 95.7 | 152.4 | | | | | | | | | | 289.7 |

[1] Preliminary. *Source: Economic Research Service, U.S. Department of Agriculture*

**Volume of Trading in Soybean Futures in Chicago** In Millions of Bushels

| Year | Jan. | Feb. | Mar. | Apr. | May | June | July | Aug. | Sept. | Oct. | Nov. | Dec. | Total |
|---|---|---|---|---|---|---|---|---|---|---|---|---|---|
| 1982 | 3,120 | 3,497 | 4,478 | 4,484 | 3,517 | 4,245 | 4,017 | 3,822 | 3,197 | 4,014 | 4,282 | 3,198 | 45,828 |
| 1983 | 3,942 | 3,820 | 4,247 | 4,375 | 4,259 | 4,409 | 6,224 | 8,799 | 7,852 | 8,071 | 6,793 | 5,609 | 68,402 |
| 1984 | 5,550 | 5,247 | 6,008 | 4,945 | 7,300 | 6,323 | 5,314 | 4,045 | 2,505 | 3,687 | 3,427 | 2,463 | 56,813 |
| 1985 | 3,315 | 2,749 | 2,657 | 2,821 | 2,766 | 3,309 | 3,779 | 2,581 | 2,525 | 3,364 | 3,881 | 3,213 | 36,961 |
| 1986 | 3,692 | 2,484 | 2,435 | 2,976 | 2,546 | 2,199 | 2,925 | 2,049 | 1,812 | 3,266 | 2,473 | 1,811 | 30,668 |
| 1987 | 2,174 | 1,816 | 1,794 | 3,118 | 3,969 | 4,356 | 3,785 | 1,935 | 2,305 | 4,109 | 3,674 | 3,859 | 36,894 |
| 1988 | 4,436 | 4,252 | 4,284 | 4,822 | 6,339 | 7,975 | 5,574 | 5,214 | 4,516 | 5,235 | 5,001 | 4,777 | 62,485 |
| 1989 | 5,222 | 4,265 | 4,760 | 4,720 | 4,587 | 4,466 | 3,977 | 3,172 | 2,854 | 4,011 | 3,247 | 2,893 | 48,174 |
| 1990 | 3,278 | 2,673 | 4,133 | 4,422 | 5,630 | 5,209 | 5,188 | 4,528 | 3,214 | 5,660 | 4,299 | 3,275 | 67,887 |
| 1991 | 3,725 | 3,104 | 3,577 | 4,040 | 3,422 | 3,881 | 4,962 | 4,716 | 3,312 | 4,381 | 2,856 | 3,095 | 44,871 |
| 1992 | 4,022 | 3,692 | 3,440 | 2,794 | 4,369 | 5,273 | 4,666 | 3,154 | 2,861 | 4,337 | 3,066 | 3,327 | 45,001 |
| 1993 | 3,417 | 3,123 | 3,379 | 3,806 | 3,890 | 6,435 | 8,216 | 5,900 | 4,625 | 4,811 | 5,940 | 4,707 | 58,247 |
| 1994 | 5,673 | 4,493 | 4,610 | 4,597 | 5,792 | 5,985 | 4,462 | 3,442 | 3,113 | 4,285 | 4,129 | 3,166 | 53,745 |
| 1995 | 3,070 | 2,859 | 3,998 | 3,491 | 4,746 | 5,254 | 5,983 | 4,085 | 4,001 | 5,639 | 4,202 | 5,726 | 53,058 |
| 1996 | 6,512 | 5,614 | 5,046 | 8,415 | 5,746 | 4,947 | 6,479 | 4,948 | 5,250 | 5,013 | 8,477 | 4,700 | 71,154 |

*Source: Chicago Board of Trade (CBT)*

# SOYBEANS

**Average Open Interest of Soybean Futures in Chicago** In Millions of Bushels

| Year | Jan. | Feb. | Mar. | Apr. | May | June | July | Aug. | Sept. | Oct. | Nov. | Dec. |
|---|---|---|---|---|---|---|---|---|---|---|---|---|
| 1981 | 760,433 | 618,363 | 556,355 | 586,500 | 516,510 | 517,640 | 497,162 | 452,323 | 440,217 | 472,908 | 485,995 | 482,498 |
| 1982 | 404,223 | 406,528 | 393,035 | 460,729 | 418,686 | 391,052 | 374,053 | 380,213 | 355,169 | 397,810 | 425,089 | 438,322 |
| 1983 | 442,828 | 456,830 | 416,479 | 505,813 | 462,581 | 420,022 | 455,472 | 670,320 | 714,951 | 748,973 | 655,300 | 631,981 |
| 1984 | 558,727 | 544,108 | 564,202 | 535,411 | 546,508 | 495,022 | 360,313 | 286,738 | 270,991 | 326,171 | 353,568 | 356,011 |
| 1985 | 348,140 | 364,738 | 327,450 | 317,610 | 306,381 | 329,845 | 314,415 | 324,314 | 315,912 | 353,915 | 375,558 | 367,207 |
| 1986 | 377,175 | 375,378 | 374,277 | 382,321 | 342,736 | 333,767 | 303,102 | 290,679 | 298,112 | 366,628 | 410,962 | 405,791 |
| 1987 | 373,975 | 374,970 | 384,749 | 448,282 | 472,715 | 460,889 | 396,495 | 364,262 | 373,807 | 524,582 | 537,224 | 589,553 |
| 1988 | 592,560 | 617,929 | 609,312 | 692,576 | 763,473 | 849,772 | 644,812 | 574,151 | 598,951 | 607,404 | 558,608 | 603,549 |
| 1989 | 598,499 | 572,342 | 579,959 | 513,682 | 484,011 | 472,263 | 417,035 | 379,628 | 404,830 | 503,966 | 482,161 | 493,360 |
| 1990 | 478,591 | 496,834 | 556,976 | 615,027 | 655,864 | 590,047 | 483,946 | 458,531 | 489,646 | 599,204 | 625,678 | 617,759 |
| 1991 | 546,555 | 552,104 | 551,590 | 534,973 | 511,847 | 516,809 | 457,245 | 430,659 | 490,248 | 571,031 | 562,037 | 563,908 |
| 1992 | 574,356 | 591,586 | 663,193 | 605,856 | 606,990 | 689,478 | 581,040 | 534,148 | 520,573 | 628,670 | 594,385 | 571,307 |
| 1993 | 608,628 | 633,411 | 633,405 | 690,776 | 689,104 | 713,606 | 998,406 | 917,111 | 818,236 | 798,207 | 805,850 | 843,468 |
| 1994 | 888,241 | 836,087 | 780,293 | 737,844 | 728,991 | 751,017 | 660,050 | 605,630 | 634,736 | 735,989 | 685,934 | 681,753 |
| 1995 | 691,726 | 693,969 | 689,213 | 693,120 | 667,663 | 715,597 | 718,354 | 677,921 | 722,043 | 836,000 | 873,873 | 970,104 |
| 1996 | 993,655 | 995,749 | 964,634 | 1,036,420 | 959,947 | 897,742 | 904,086 | 911,618 | 981,804 | 894,358 | 779,683 | 764,829 |

*Source: Chicago Board of Trade (CBT)*

## Spread Between Value of Products and Soybean Price in the U.S. In Cents Per Bushel

| Year | Sept. | Oct. | Nov. | Dec. | Jan. | Feb. | Mar. | Apr. | May | June | July | Aug. | Average |
|---|---|---|---|---|---|---|---|---|---|---|---|---|---|
| 1981-2 | 35 | 15 | 4 | 22 | 19 | 26 | 25 | 22 | 24 | 16 | 21 | 24 | 21 |
| 1982-3 | 33 | 47 | 30 | 31 | 21 | 22 | 15 | 18 | 30 | 27 | 25 | 39 | 28 |
| 1983-4 | 42 | 40 | 23 | 40 | 28 | 7 | 8 | 14 | 26 | 24 | 41 | 31 | 27 |
| 1984-5 | 46 | 49 | 37 | 23 | 19 | 18 | 36 | 35 | 25 | 33 | 28 | 29 | 37 |
| 1985-6 | 40 | 49 | 43 | 43 | 40 | 27 | 32 | 29 | 25 | 18 | 28 | 48 | 35 |
| 1986-7 | 90 | 60 | 44 | 50 | 44 | 77 | 51 | 63 | 72 | 83 | 85 | 77 | 66 |
| 1987-8 | 108 | 134 | 166 | 167 | 131 | 83 | 89 | 89 | 133 | 125 | 135 | 107 | 122 |
| 1988-9 | 111 | 131 | 109 | 95 | 90 | 73 | 70 | 72 | 61 | 93 | 107 | 155 | 97 |
| 1989-90 | 171 | 141 | 113 | 87 | 78 | 58 | 70 | 85 | 109 | 103 | 97 | 99 | 101 |
| 1990-1 | 99 | 77 | 58 | 64 | 63 | 73 | 79 | 75 | 72 | 74 | 91 | 99 | 77 |
| 1991-2 | 118 | 120 | 94 | 82 | 74 | 74 | 75 | 78 | 87 | 104 | 80 | 83 | 89 |
| 1992-3 | 98 | 93 | 87 | 93 | 94 | 77 | 77 | 79 | 82 | 84 | 120 | 97 | 90 |
| 1993-4 | 95 | 108 | 105 | 92 | 93 | 99 | 88 | 85 | 89 | 88 | 94 | 118 | 96 |
| 1994-5 | 146 | 167 | 143 | 137 | 130 | 109 | 114 | 109 | 86 | 102 | 87 | 90 | 118 |
| 1995-6 | 88 | 107 | 82 | 88 | 82 | 77 | 79 | 94 | 73 | 76 | 77 | 71 | 82 |
| 1996-7 | 107 | 117 | 126 | 114 | | | | | | | | | 116 |

*Source: Economic Research Service, U.S. Department of Agriculture*

## Soybean Crushed (Factory Consumption) in the U.S. In Millions of Bushels--One Bushel=60 Pounds

| Year | Sept. | Oct. | Nov. | Dec. | Jan. | Feb. | Mar. | Apr. | May | June | July | Aug. | Total |
|---|---|---|---|---|---|---|---|---|---|---|---|---|---|
| 1981-2 | 75.4 | 104.5 | 97.6 | 102.5 | 94.9 | 86.7 | 85.1 | 81.0 | 86.6 | 77.1 | 70.6 | 67.8 | 1,030 |
| 1982-3 | 76.0 | 100.2 | 108.1 | 111.9 | 110.0 | 93.0 | 94.6 | 81.8 | 83.7 | 81.5 | 81.6 | 85.7 | 1,108 |
| 1983-4 | 86.6 | 96.4 | 86.6 | 89.4 | 93.8 | 79.2 | 86.0 | 74.6 | 79.4 | 70.6 | 69.0 | 71.1 | 983 |
| 1984-5 | 65.5 | 89.2 | 98.9 | 101.1 | 94.5 | 80.8 | 85.6 | 83.2 | 89.3 | 82.7 | 82.0 | 77.5 | 1,030 |
| 1985-6 | 76.5 | 94.3 | 96.7 | 100.8 | 99.6 | 81.4 | 91.6 | 84.4 | 86.3 | 79.6 | 83.1 | 78.4 | 1,053 |
| 1986-7 | 79.4 | 107.0 | 109.4 | 107.6 | 110.3 | 102.3 | 106.0 | 95.9 | 95.3 | 90.6 | 92.6 | 82.4 | 1,179 |
| 1987-8 | 79.7 | 102.5 | 111.2 | 110.8 | 106.7 | 99.8 | 107.6 | 102.6 | 98.0 | 89.2 | 88.0 | 78.3 | 1,174 |
| 1988-9 | 79.9 | 94.4 | 101.0 | 100.7 | 99.8 | 85.8 | 93.5 | 89.6 | 87.0 | 76.0 | 74.0 | 75.9 | 1,058 |
| 1989-90 | 74.1 | 94.8 | 104.1 | 105.4 | 107.2 | 91.8 | 102.1 | 95.1 | 93.4 | 92.0 | 92.2 | 94.2 | 1,146 |
| 1990-1 | 92.1 | 106.1 | 106.0 | 102.7 | ----------- | 297.9 | ----------- | ----------- | 280.1 | ----------- | 202.5 | ----------- | 1,187 |
| 1991-2 | 98.9 | ----------- | 333.3 | ----------- | 112.0 | 100.8 | 107.2 | 101.6 | 95.2 | 100.0 | 102.3 | 102.3 | 1,254 |
| 1992-3 | 101.2 | 113.9 | 113.1 | 116.2 | 116.8 | 102.2 | 113.0 | 105.9 | 106.5 | 99.9 | 98.0 | 92.2 | 1,279 |
| 1993-4 | 98.4 | 113.7 | 114.4 | 114.1 | 110.7 | 103.3 | 113.3 | 105.6 | 103.0 | 97.2 | 101.0 | 101.0 | 1,276 |
| 1994-5 | 105.9 | 119.3 | 122.5 | 128.5 | 127.3 | 116.5 | 128.1 | 119.4 | 114.2 | 105.6 | 108.4 | 109.5 | 1,405 |
| 1995-6[1] | 107.4 | 120.6 | 123.4 | 125.1 | 122.7 | 111.2 | 115.5 | 112.1 | 106.3 | 107.5 | 111.9 | 105.6 | 1,369 |
| 1996-7[1] | 100.5 | 127.0 | 133.1 | 138.2 | | | | | | | | | 499 |

[1] Preliminary. *Source: Economic Research Service, U.S. Department of Agriculture*

## Average Price Received by Farmers for Soybeans in the U.S. In Cents Per Bushel

| Year | Sept. | Oct. | Nov. | Dec. | Jan. | Feb. | Mar. | Apr. | May | June | July | Aug. | Average |
|---|---|---|---|---|---|---|---|---|---|---|---|---|---|
| 1981-2 | 621 | 606 | 603 | 600 | 613 | 604 | 604 | 617 | 627 | 612 | 599 | 559 | 604 |
| 1982-3 | 522 | 506 | 534 | 546 | 556 | 566 | 582 | 609 | 606 | 590 | 627 | 757 | 565 |
| 1983-4 | 828 | 796 | 780 | 774 | 785 | 728 | 768 | 783 | 812 | 799 | 695 | 650 | 783 |
| 1984-5 | 609 | 607 | 601 | 582 | 591 | 577 | 588 | 588 | 570 | 562 | 542 | 510 | 584 |
| 1985-6 | 499 | 485 | 492 | 501 | 516 | 518 | 523 | 523 | 525 | 519 | 511 | 499 | 505 |
| 1986-7 | 485 | 455 | 464 | 467 | 470 | 469 | 473 | 490 | 520 | 536 | 525 | 502 | 478 |
| 1987-8 | 502 | 504 | 536 | 563 | 573 | 596 | 605 | 639 | 698 | 818 | 850 | 833 | 588 |
| 1988-9 | 793 | 753 | 743 | 753 | 769 | 741 | 751 | 729 | 720 | 705 | 683 | 607 | 742 |
| 1989-90 | 570 | 554 | 566 | 564 | 565 | 556 | 565 | 582 | 597 | 588 | 597 | 600 | 570 |
| 1990-1 | 599 | 587 | 578 | 572 | 572 | 565 | 577 | 577 | 559 | 555 | 536 | 566 | 575 |
| 1991-2 | 564 | 549 | 548 | 545 | 554 | 559 | 567 | 566 | 587 | 594 | 559 | 540 | 560 |
| 1992-3 | 535 | 526 | 536 | 546 | 558 | 556 | 565 | 573 | 581 | 564 | 657 | 655 | 571 |
| 1993-4 | 621 | 601 | 632 | 664 | 672 | 671 | 673 | 657 | 677 | 672 | 592 | 558 | 640 |
| 1994-5 | 547 | 530 | 536 | 541 | 547 | 540 | 551 | 555 | 556 | 568 | 590 | 583 | 548 |
| 1995-6[1] | 598 | 615 | 640 | 676 | 677 | 701 | 700 | 743 | 769 | 741 | 762 | 782 | 677 |
| 1996-7[1] | 779 | 695 | 690 | 691 | 716 | | | | | | | | 714 |

[1] Preliminary. *Source: Economic Research Service, U.S. Department of Agriculture*

# SOYBEANS

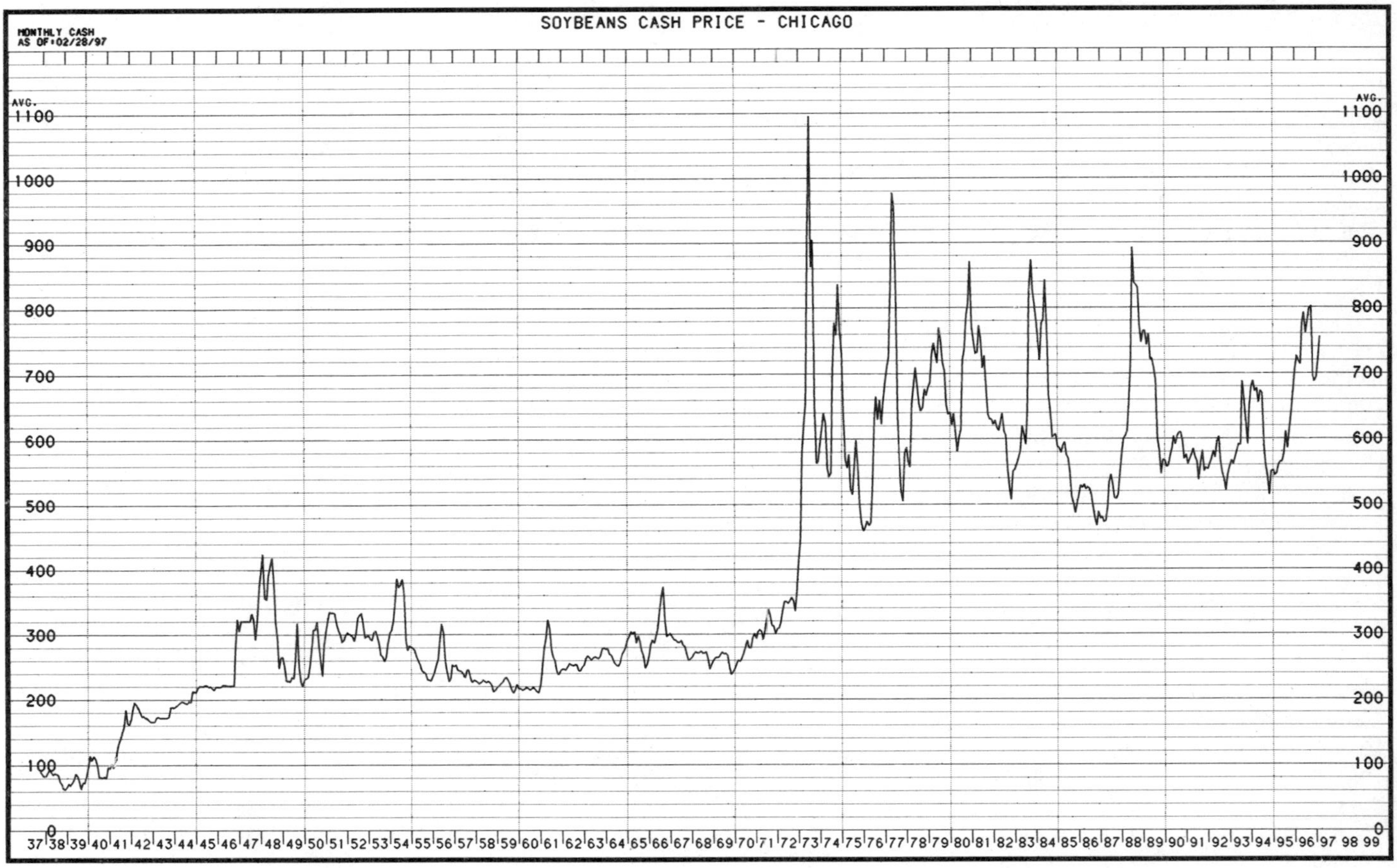


**Average Cash Price of No. 1 Yellow Soybeans at Illinois Processor** In Cents Per Bushel

| Year | Sept. | Oct. | Nov. | Dec. | Jan. | Feb. | Mar. | Apr. | May | June | July | Aug. | Average |
|---|---|---|---|---|---|---|---|---|---|---|---|---|---|
| 1977-8 | 642 | 507 | 584 | 594 | 573 | 565 | 658 | 681 | 701 | 676 | 662 | 647 | 624 |
| 1978-9 | 704 | 672 | 668 | 681 | 689 | 728 | 745 | 727 | 721 | 768 | 764 | 728 | 716 |
| 1979-80 | 813 | 656 | 652 | 653 | 636 | 642 | 607 | 580 | 604 | 610 | 722 | 745 | 660 |
| 1980-1 | 644 | 827 | 891 | 773 | 757 | 734 | 737 | 772 | 758 | 713 | 736 | 694 | 753 |
| 1981-2 | 540 | 630 | 628 | 623 | 630 | 624 | 616 | 642 | 656 | 631 | 620 | 573 | 618 |
| 1982-3 | 540 | 526 | 570 | 573 | 581 | 586 | 598 | 635 | 627 | 606 | 659 | 846 | 612 |
| 1983-4 | 893 | 846 | 820 | 777 | 767 | 737 | 797 | 798 | 861 | 791 | 685 | 663 | 786 |
| 1984-5 | 621 | 627 | 625 | 607 | 604 | 597 | 608 | 613 | 595 | 588 | 565 | 528 | 598 |
| 1985-6 | 519 | 505 | 519 | 532 | 545 | 538 | 547 | 540 | 544 | 543 | 533 | 500 | 530 |
| 1986-7 | 496 | 489 | 508 | 469 | 498 | 489 | 492 | 512 | 552 | 563 | 547 | 528 | 512 |
| 1987-8 | 527 | 532 | 564 | 594 | 617 | 621 | 630 | 671 | 731 | 913 | 859 | 852 | 676 |
| 1988-9 | 852 | 792 | 767 | 783 | 783 | 760 | 778 | 739 | 740 | 725 | 708 | 606 | 753 |
| 1989-90 | 600 | 564 | 570 | 582 | 572 | 585 | 600 | 600 | 620 | 609 | 619 | 626 | 596 |
| 1990-1 | 628 | 614 | 587 | 591 | 576 | 585 | 592 | 601 | 589 | 583 | 554 | 578 | 590 |
| 1991-2 | 598 | 568 | 571 | 568 | 577 | 581 | 593 | 585 | 609 | 619 | 580 | 564 | 584 |
| 1992-3 | 554 | 535 | 560 | 572 | 582 | 575 | 587 | 597 | 607 | 606 | 689 | 679 | 595 |
| 1993-4 | 643 | 606 | 664 | 694 | 701 | 686 | 692 | 670 | 689 | 685 | 603 | 576 | 659 |
| 1994-5 | 557 | 531 | 566 | 567 | 558 | 560 | 574 | 578 | 580 | 577 | 623 | 602 | 573 |
| 1995-6[1] | 632 | 656 | 686 | 717 | 737 | 730 | 726 | 791 | 808 | 778 | 795 | 816 | 739 |
| 1996-7[1] | 820 | 711 | 704 | 708 | | | | | | | | | 736 |

[1] Preliminary. *Source: Economic Research Service, U.S. Department of Agriculture*

# Stock Index Futures, U.S.

The year 1995 was described as phenomenal for the U.S. equity markets, but 1996 proved spectacular. In back to back years, the major indices rose 68 percent to new highs on record trading volume, and the corrections that developed proved short lived. Little appeared capable of braking the rush into equities during 1996, not even a warning call by the Chairman of the Federal Reserve on December 5, designed to cool the market's "irrational exuberance." To the novice and professional market participants, the equity markets were viewed as the only game in town. The bullish momentum fed upon itself, especially in the second half of 1996. The bellwether Dow Jones 30 Industrials Stock Average closed the year at 6448.27, up 26 percent; the S & P 500 Index finished at 740.74, up 23 percent; and the Nasdaq Composite closed at 1291, also up 23 percent from yearend 1995. 1996 trading volume on the New York Stock Exchange of 105 billion shares compared with 87 billion in 1995; Nasdaq volume of 138 billion shares compared with 100 billion, respectively.

Slow growth, low interest rates, and no signs of inflation all combined to fuel the fires of the bull market. Consumer confidence ended 1996 at a seven year high, as newly created wealth from equity investments brightened spirits of investors.

Capital from 401k and IRA pension funds, both corporate and individual, poured into mutual funds. In the first five months of 1996, traditionally the mutual fund industry's five biggest months for equity fund inflows, $123 billion was invested, nearly twice as much as in all of 1995. By the fourth quarter of 1996 mutual fund assets were estimated at $3.4 trillion, up more than $1 trillion in less than two years, of which stock fund assets were placed at $1.65 trillion vs. $866 billion at yearend 1994.

The ownership breakdown was also an eye opener; almost 37 million American households owned mutual funds in 1996, a jump of nearly 7 million in less than two years; of which nearly 9 million had funds in tax-advantage retirement programs by the end of 1996. Moreover, about 45 percent of the households that owned mutual funds had annual incomes of less than $50,000, suggesting that the massive flow of capital into equities during 1996 was not skewed by higher income households.

The economic news in 1996 was generally positive, with no major changes forecast for 1997. Real growth slowed to about 2.5 percent in the second half of 1996 from over 4 percent in the first half, but job creation held well and in parts of the country the available labor supply proved tight, bolstering labor costs at times, but cost push price increases were difficult to pass along. In 1996, both producer and consumer inflationary pressures were well contained giving the Fed little reason to seriously tighten monetary policy. However, there were some disturbing economic signs; consumer credit debt, not including mortgages and home equity loans, reached a record high and delinquency problems were rising. Still, the "bad news is good news" scenario had strong roots in late 1996. Moreover, the flow of pension funds into equities is not likely to abate, imparting firm underlying support to the markets into 1997.

***Futures Markets***

S & P 500 futures and options and the S & P Midcap Index of 400 stocks are traded on the Chicago Mercantile Exchange (CME). Options on the S & P Midcap Index are traded on the American Stock Exchange (AMEX). A New York Stock Exchange Composite index is traded on the New York Futures Exchange (NYFE). Other U.S. stock indices listed for futures and/or options trading include: the Value Line Arithmetic Index and mini Value line Index, and the Major Market Index and Russell 2000 Index.

## Dow Jones Industrial Average (30 Stocks)

| Year | Jan. | Feb. | Mar. | Apr. | May | June | July | Aug. | Sept. | Oct. | Nov. | Dec. | Average |
|---|---|---|---|---|---|---|---|---|---|---|---|---|---|
| 1989 | 2,234.7 | 2,304.3 | 2,283.1 | 2,348.9 | 2,439.6 | 2,494.9 | 2,554.0 | 2,691.1 | 2,693.4 | 2,692.0 | 2,642.5 | 2,728.5 | 2,508.9 |
| 1990 | 2,679.2 | 2,614.2 | 2,700.1 | 2,708.3 | 2,793.8 | 2,894.8 | 2,934.2 | 2,681.9 | 2,550.7 | 2,460.5 | 2,518.6 | 2,610.9 | 2,678.9 |
| 1991 | 2,587.6 | 2,863.0 | 2,920.1 | 2,925.5 | 2,928.4 | 2,968.1 | 2,978.2 | 3,006.1 | 3,010.4 | 3,019.7 | 2,986.1 | 2,958.6 | 2,929.3 |
| 1992 | 3,227.1 | 3,257.3 | 3,247.4 | 3,294.1 | 3,376.8 | 3,337.8 | 3,329.4 | 3,307.4 | 3,293.9 | 3,198.7 | 3,238.5 | 3,303.2 | 3,284.3 |
| 1993 | 3,277.7 | 3,367.3 | 3,440.7 | 3,423.6 | 3,478.2 | 3,513.8 | 3,529.4 | 3,597.0 | 3,592.3 | 3,625.8 | 3,674.7 | 3,744.1 | 3,522.1 |
| 1994 | 3,868.4 | 3,905.6 | 3,817.0 | 3,661.5 | 3,708.0 | 3,737.6 | 3,718.3 | 3,797.5 | 3,880.6 | 3,868.1 | 3,792.5 | 3,770.3 | 3,793.8 |
| 1995 | 3,872.5 | 3,953.7 | 4,062.8 | 4,230.7 | 4,391.6 | 4,510.8 | 4,684.8 | 4,639.3 | 4,746.8 | 4,760.5 | 4,935.8 | 5,136.1 | 4,493.8 |
| 1996 | 5,179.4 | 5,518.7 | 5,612.2 | 5,579.9 | 5,616.7 | 5,671.5 | 5,496.3 | 5,685.5 | 5,804.0 | 5,995.1 | 6,318.4 | 6,435.9 | 5,742.8 |

*Source: The Wall Street Journal*

## Dow Jones Transportation (20 Stocks)

| Year | Jan. | Feb. | Mar. | Apr. | May | June | July | Aug. | Sept. | Oct. | Nov. | Dec. | Average |
|---|---|---|---|---|---|---|---|---|---|---|---|---|---|
| 1989 | 1,009.3 | 1,073.2 | 1,046.3 | 1,098.0 | 1,139.8 | 1,158.9 | 1,223.1 | 1,407.1 | 1,462.7 | 1,342.0 | 1,188.1 | 1,183.0 | 1,194.3 |
| 1990 | 1,139.8 | 1,083.4 | 1,160.3 | 1,164.8 | 1,163.1 | 1,181.9 | 1,150.0 | 951.1 | 881.3 | 850.8 | 848.1 | 908.4 | 1,040.3 |
| 1991 | 962.4 | 1,110.3 | 1,113.2 | 1,139.1 | 1,167.6 | 1,205.1 | 1,204.6 | 1,204.7 | 1,182.4 | 1,283.1 | 1,237.1 | 1,233.3 | 1,170.2 |
| 1992 | 1,378.7 | 1,412.2 | 969.9 | 1,356.9 | 1,380.4 | 1,333.3 | 1,303.1 | 1,254.6 | 1,275.2 | 1,286.2 | 1,375.9 | 1,430.1 | 1,349.6 |
| 1993 | 1,488.1 | 1,533.2 | 1,541.6 | 1,619.7 | 1,583.4 | 1,533.9 | 1,553.7 | 1,631.6 | 1,623.9 | 1,660.5 | 1,732.6 | 1,763.2 | 1,605.5 |
| 1994 | 1,812.1 | 1,810.4 | 1,719.9 | 1,614.7 | 1,602.2 | 1,619.2 | 1,596.2 | 1,602.8 | 1,553.7 | 1,485.8 | 1,473.7 | 1,415.3 | 1,608.8 |
| 1995 | 1,515.8 | 1,547.2 | 1,584.6 | 1,648.9 | 1,646.2 | 1,699.3 | 1,852.1 | 1,883.9 | 1,961.4 | 1,922.9 | 2,008.3 | 2,029.5 | 1,775.0 |
| 1996 | 1,932.7 | 2,030.0 | 2,136.0 | 2,180.0 | 2,229.1 | 2,213.4 | 2,053.1 | 2,060.4 | 2,050.8 | 2,100.1 | 2,224.3 | 2,273.9 | 2,123.7 |

*Source: The Wall Street Journal*

# STOCK INDEX FUTURES

## Dow Jones Public Utilities (15 Stocks)

| Year | Jan. | Feb. | Mar. | Apr. | May | June | July | Aug. | Sept. | Oct. | Nov. | Dec. | Average |
|---|---|---|---|---|---|---|---|---|---|---|---|---|---|
| 1988 | 182.2 | 185.0 | 177.7 | 171.4 | 169.3 | 180.0 | 178.7 | 178.6 | 179.9 | 185.0 | 184.1 | 185.2 | 179.8 |
| 1989 | 188.9 | 186.6 | 182.8 | 188.0 | 196.3 | 206.7 | 215.5 | 218.1 | 216.0 | 216.6 | 221.0 | 232.1 | 205.7 |
| 1990 | 223.2 | 221.2 | 217.0 | 210.7 | 212.4 | 211.2 | 205.0 | 210.1 | 199.8 | 207.2 | 210.3 | 210.6 | 210.8 |
| 1991 | 205.3 | 213.7 | 213.2 | 214.5 | 211.2 | 204.6 | 199.6 | 204.4 | 208.0 | 213.5 | 216.7 | 219.3 | 210.3 |
| 1992 | 215.7 | 206.8 | 204.4 | 206.1 | 213.2 | 212.5 | 219.1 | 220.2 | 220.0 | 217.2 | 217.7 | 220.2 | 214.4 |
| 1993 | 222.0 | 234.2 | 240.0 | 242.1 | 237.8 | 241.5 | 246.5 | 252.0 | 253.0 | 243.1 | 227.1 | 227.1 | 238.9 |
| 1994 | 222.3 | 215.6 | 207.0 | 196.5 | 185.5 | 182.9 | 181.8 | 188.9 | 179.6 | 179.9 | 177.7 | 181.0 | 191.6 |
| 1995 | 186.9 | 194.0 | 187.9 | 192.7 | 197.6 | 204.5 | 202.5 | 202.8 | 207.2 | 216.4 | 215.3 | 221.4 | 202.4 |
| 1996 | 228.4 | 228.6 | 216.3 | 209.5 | 211.2 | 210.0 | 212.8 | 214.8 | 217.2 | 222.3 | 234.0 | 232.1 | 219.8 |

*Source: The Wall Street Journal*

## Standard & Poor's 500 Composite Price Index

| Year | Jan. | Feb. | Mar. | Apr. | May | June | July | Aug. | Sept. | Oct. | Nov. | Dec. | Average |
|---|---|---|---|---|---|---|---|---|---|---|---|---|---|
| 1988 | 250.5 | 258.1 | 265.7 | 262.6 | 256.1 | 270.7 | 269.1 | 263.7 | 268.0 | 277.4 | 271.0 | 276.5 | 265.8 |
| 1989 | 285.4 | 294.0 | 292.7 | 302.3 | 313.9 | 323.7 | 331.9 | 246.6 | 247.3 | 247.4 | 340.2 | 348.6 | 322.8 |
| 1990 | 340.0 | 330.5 | 338.5 | 338.2 | 350.3 | 360.4 | 360.0 | 330.8 | 315.4 | 307.1 | 315.3 | 328.8 | 334.6 |
| 1991 | 325.5 | 362.3 | 372.3 | 379.7 | 378.0 | 378.3 | 380.2 | 389.4 | 387.2 | 386.9 | 385.9 | 388.5 | 376.2 |
| 1992 | 416.1 | 412.6 | 407.4 | 407.4 | 414.8 | 408.3 | 415.1 | 417.9 | 418.5 | 412.5 | 422.8 | 435.6 | 415.8 |
| 1993 | 435.2 | 441.7 | 450.2 | 443.1 | 445.3 | 448.1 | 447.3 | 454.1 | 459.2 | 463.9 | 462.9 | 466.0 | 451.4 |
| 1994 | 473.0 | 471.6 | 463.8 | 447.2 | 451.0 | 454.8 | 451.4 | 464.2 | 467.0 | 463.8 | 461.0 | 455.2 | 460.3 |
| 1995 | 465.3 | 481.9 | 493.2 | 507.9 | 523.8 | 539.4 | 557.4 | 559.1 | 578.8 | 582.9 | 595.5 | 614.6 | 541.6 |
| 1996 | 614.4 | 649.5 | 647.1 | 547.2 | 661.2 | 668.5 | 644.1 | 662.7 | 674.9 | 701.5 | 735.7 | 743.3 | 662.5 |

*Source: The Wall Street Journal*

WEEKLY NEAREST FUTURES
AS OF:03/14/97
MAJOR MARKET INDEX (MMI) - IOM
INDEX VALUE
720
680
640
600
560
520
480
440
400
360
320
280
1991
1992
1993
1994
1995
1996

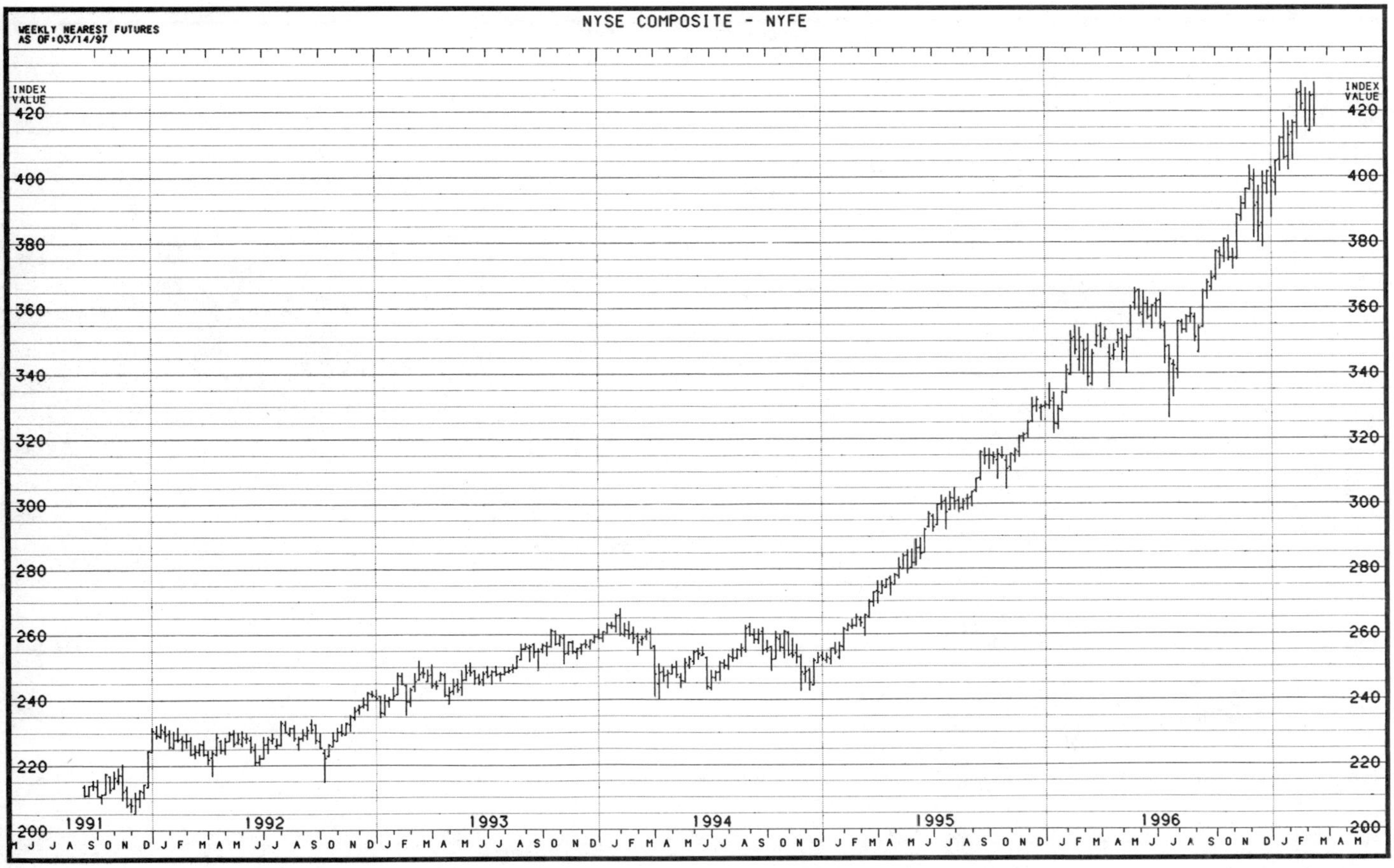
WEEKLY NEAREST FUTURES
AS OF:03/14/97
NYSE COMPOSITE - NYFE
INDEX VALUE
420
400
380
360
340
320
300
280
260
240
220
200
1991
1992
1993
1994
1995
1996

WEEKLY NEAREST FUTURES
AS OF:03/14/97
S&P 500 - IOM
INDEX VALUE
850
800
750
700
650
600
550
500
450
400
350
300
1991
1992
1993
1994
1995
1996
M J J A S O N D J F M A M J J A S O N D J F M A M J J A S O N D J F M A M J J A S O N D J F M A M J J A S O N D J F M A M J J A S O N D J F M A M

WEEKLY NEAREST FUTURES
AS OF:03/14/97
VALUE-LINE 'A' - KCBT
INDEX VALUE
720
680
640
600
560
520
480
440
400
360
320
280
1991
1992
1993
1994
1995
1996
M J J A S O N D J F M A M J J A S O N D J F M A M J J A S O N D J F M A M J J A S O N D J F M A M J J A S O N D J F M A M J J A S O N D J F M A M

## Composite of Leading Indicators 1987 = 100

| Year | Jan. | Feb. | Mar. | Apr. | May | June | July | Aug. | Sept. | Oct. | Nov. | Dec. | Average |
|---|---|---|---|---|---|---|---|---|---|---|---|---|---|
| 1988 | 99.8 | 100.2 | 100.5 | 100.3 | 100.4 | 100.8 | 100.3 | 100.3 | 100.2 | 100.3 | 100.2 | 100.3 | 100.3 |
| 1989 | 100.3 | 100.0 | 99.6 | 99.9 | 99.4 | 99.3 | 99.3 | 99.5 | 99.6 | 99.4 | 99.6 | 99.7 | 99.6 |
| 1990 | 100.0 | 99.6 | 99.9 | 99.7 | 99.7 | 99.7 | 99.6 | 99.1 | 98.8 | 98.2 | 97.9 | 98.0 | 99.2 |
| 1991 | 97.8 | 98.1 | 98.5 | 98.8 | 99.1 | 99.3 | 99.8 | 99.5 | 99.5 | 99.5 | 99.4 | 99.1 | 99.0 |
| 1992 | 99.4 | 99.7 | 99.9 | 99.9 | 100.0 | 99.9 | 99.9 | 99.9 | 99.9 | 100.1 | 100.4 | 101.0 | 100.0 |
| 1993 | 100.7 | 100.7 | 100.1 | 100.4 | 100.2 | 100.3 | 100.1 | 100.3 | 100.4 | 100.5 | 100.8 | 101.2 | 100.5 |
| 1994 | 101.2 | 101.0 | 101.5 | 101.4 | 101.4 | 101.4 | 101.2 | 101.5 | 101.4 | 101.5 | 101.6 | 101.6 | 101.4 |
| 1995 | 101.5 | 101.1 | 100.7 | 100.6 | 100.4 | 100.5 | 100.7 | 101.0 | 101.1 | 100.9 | 100.9 | 101.2 | 100.9 |
| 1996[1] | 100.5 | 101.4 | 101.6 | 101.8 | 102.1 | 102.3 | 102.3 | 102.4 | 102.5 | 102.5 | 102.7 | 102.8 | 102.1 |

[1] Preliminary. *Source: Bureau of Economic Analysis, U.S. Department of Commerce*

## Civilian Unemployment Rate

| Year | Jan. | Feb. | Mar. | Apr. | May | June | July | Aug. | Sept. | Oct. | Nov. | Dec. | Average |
|---|---|---|---|---|---|---|---|---|---|---|---|---|---|
| 1988 | 5.7 | 5.7 | 5.7 | 5.4 | 5.6 | 5.4 | 5.4 | 5.6 | 5.4 | 5.4 | 5.3 | 5.3 | 5.5 |
| 1989 | 5.4 | 5.2 | 5.0 | 5.2 | 5.2 | 5.3 | 5.2 | 5.2 | 5.3 | 5.3 | 5.4 | 5.4 | 5.3 |
| 1990 | 5.4 | 5.3 | 5.2 | 5.4 | 5.4 | 5.2 | 5.5 | 5.7 | 5.9 | 5.9 | 6.2 | 6.3 | 5.6 |
| 1991 | 6.4 | 6.6 | 6.8 | 6.7 | 6.9 | 6.9 | 6.8 | 6.9 | 6.9 | 7.0 | 7.0 | 7.3 | 6.9 |
| 1992 | 7.3 | 7.4 | 7.4 | 7.4 | 7.6 | 7.8 | 7.7 | 7.6 | 7.6 | 7.3 | 7.4 | 7.4 | 7.5 |
| 1993 | 7.3 | 7.1 | 7.0 | 7.1 | 7.1 | 7.0 | 6.9 | 6.8 | 6.7 | 6.8 | 6.6 | 6.5 | 6.9 |
| 1994 | 6.7 | 6.6 | 6.5 | 6.4 | 6.0 | 6.1 | 6.1 | 6.1 | 5.9 | 5.8 | 5.6 | 5.4 | 6.1 |
| 1995 | 5.6 | 5.5 | 5.4 | 5.7 | 5.6 | 5.6 | 5.7 | 5.7 | 5.7 | 5.5 | 5.6 | 5.6 | 5.6 |
| 1996[1] | 5.7 | 5.5 | 5.5 | 5.5 | 5.5 | 5.3 | 5.4 | 5.2 | 5.2 | 5.2 | 5.3 | 5.3 | 5.4 |

[1] Preliminary. *Source: Bureau of Economic Analysis, U.S. Department of Commerce*

## Capacity Utilization Rates (Total Industry) Percent

| Year | Jan. | Feb. | Mar. | Apr. | May | June | July | Aug. | Sept. | Oct. | Nov. | Dec. | Average |
|---|---|---|---|---|---|---|---|---|---|---|---|---|---|
| 1988 | 83.1 | 83.3 | 83.2 | 83.6 | 83.6 | 83.5 | 84.0 | 84.3 | 84.0 | 84.1 | 84.6 | 85.0 | 83.9 |
| 1989 | 85.3 | 84.5 | 85.1 | 85.2 | 84.6 | 84.3 | 83.3 | 83.5 | 83.2 | 82.7 | 82.9 | 83.2 | 84.0 |
| 1990 | 82.6 | 82.9 | 83.2 | 82.6 | 82.8 | 82.7 | 82.5 | 82.5 | 82.5 | 81.9 | 80.7 | 80.1 | 82.3 |
| 1991 | 79.6 | 78.9 | 78.1 | 78.2 | 78.7 | 79.5 | 79.5 | 79.5 | 80.1 | 79.9 | 79.7 | 79.1 | 79.2 |
| 1992 | 79.0 | 79.4 | 79.9 | 80.4 | 80.6 | 80.2 | 80.6 | 80.2 | 80.5 | 81.0 | 81.3 | 81.2 | 80.4 |
| 1993 | 81.4 | 81.7 | 81.6 | 81.7 | 81.2 | 81.2 | 81.3 | 81.0 | 81.7 | 81.8 | 82.1 | 82.5 | 81.6 |
| 1994 | 82.6 | 82.8 | 83.2 | 83.3 | 83.7 | 83.9 | 84.1 | 83.9 | 83.8 | 84.1 | 84.4 | 84.9 | 83.9 |
| 1995 | 84.9 | 84.5 | 84.3 | 83.9 | 83.7 | 83.6 | 83.4 | 83.8 | 83.9 | 83.3 | 83.2 | 83.0 | 83.8 |
| 1996[1] | 82.4 | 83.2 | 82.6 | 83.1 | 83.2 | 83.5 | 83.2 | 83.2 | 83.1 | 82.8 | 83.2 | 83.5 | 83.1 |

[1] Preliminary. *Source: Bureau of Economic Analysis, U.S. Department of Commerce*

## Manufacturers New Orders, Durable Goods In Billions of Constant Dollars

| Year | Jan. | Feb. | Mar. | Apr. | May | June | July | Aug. | Sept. | Oct. | Nov. | Dec. | Average |
|---|---|---|---|---|---|---|---|---|---|---|---|---|---|
| 1988 | 127.24 | 128.46 | 126.88 | 126.99 | 128.31 | 131.29 | 130.35 | 131.23 | 130.77 | 132.10 | 130.13 | 142.65 | 130.53 |
| 1989 | 137.70 | 133.27 | 132.31 | 133.42 | 126.53 | 129.50 | 127.01 | 125.49 | 128.47 | 123.84 | 131.25 | 134.44 | 130.27 |
| 1990 | 124.02 | 127.57 | 135.14 | 127.83 | 131.90 | 129.10 | 131.58 | 127.67 | 128.36 | 130.67 | 117.87 | 123.12 | 127.90 |
| 1991 | 119.26 | 120.00 | 112.54 | 117.55 | 120.64 | 116.85 | 132.82 | 125.62 | 122.36 | 123.66 | 124.96 | 116.97 | 121.10 |
| 1992 | 122.15 | 122.14 | 124.63 | 127.60 | 125.65 | 128.77 | 125.51 | 123.79 | 125.86 | 128.69 | 125.49 | 135.19 | 126.29 |
| 1993 | 129.56 | 133.47 | 128.50 | 130.20 | 126.93 | 131.29 | 128.27 | 128.99 | 130.31 | 133.01 | 135.60 | 136.82 | 131.08 |
| 1994 | 142.23 | 138.88 | 140.91 | 141.21 | 142.61 | 146.15 | 142.60 | 145.92 | 146.93 | 145.72 | 149.89 | 152.88 | 144.66 |
| 1995 | 153.42 | 151.82 | 151.72 | 146.32 | 149.74 | 148.21 | 147.45 | 152.12 | 156.78 | 154.37 | 154.09 | 158.89 | 152.08 |
| 1996[1] | 158.86 | 155.10 | 157.67 | 156.01 | 162.59 | 162.30 | 164.66 | 158.93 | 166.24 | 167.39 | 164.55 | 161.97 | 161.36 |

[1] Preliminary. *Source: Bureau of Economic Analysis, U.S. Department of Commerce*

## Change in Manufacturing and Trade Inventories In Billions of Dollars

| Year | Jan. | Feb. | Mar. | Apr. | May | June | July | Aug. | Sept. | Oct. | Nov. | Dec. | Average |
|---|---|---|---|---|---|---|---|---|---|---|---|---|---|
| 1988 | 35.0 | 66.5 | 50.2 | 48.3 | 49.8 | 92.5 | 41.4 | 89.2 | 62.8 | 4.1 | 44.1 | 104.8 | 57.4 |
| 1989 | 84.5 | 71.6 | 54.7 | 77.5 | 82.9 | 76.1 | 54.3 | 22.3 | -11.5 | 37.0 | 47.6 | -17.7 | 48.3 |
| 1990 | 19.9 | 7.6 | 22.2 | 39.8 | 64.5 | -15.2 | 64.0 | 55.9 | 41.3 | 24.2 | 25.3 | -50.3 | 24.9 |
| 1991 | 60.8 | -24.8 | -99.2 | -25.7 | -50.0 | -32.7 | -10.5 | -1.1 | 37.2 | 16.2 | 8.8 | 47.3 | -6.1 |
| 1992 | -60.6 | -0.3 | 13.8 | 28.3 | -22.3 | 53.6 | 28.4 | 21.4 | -8.4 | 4.6 | 11.8 | 23.9 | 7.9 |
| 1993 | 34.9 | 31.8 | 66.7 | 43.7 | 12.9 | 25.6 | 7.3 | 39.0 | 34.8 | 27.2 | 63.2 | 1.6 | 32.4 |
| 1994 | 15.3 | 45.1 | -8.1 | 42.1 | 114.2 | 56.3 | 60.8 | 98.6 | 60.3 | 71.8 | 65.3 | 64.5 | 57.2 |
| 1995 | 127.4 | 78.5 | 100.6 | 97.6 | 54.4 | 48.1 | 42.9 | 50.6 | 51.4 | 61.8 | 24.1 | -39.7 | 58.1 |
| 1996[1] | 66.2 | 7.9 | -24.0 | 53.0 | -17.4 | 28.1 | 37.0 | 36.4 | 11.9 | 58.0 | 8.3 | | 24.1 |

[1] Preliminary. *Source: Bureau of Economic Analysis, U.S. Department of Commerce*

## Comparison of International Stock Price Indexes 1967 = 100

| Year | Jan. | Feb. | Mar. | Apr. | May | June | July | Aug. | Sept. | Oct. | Nov. | Dec. | Average |
|---|---|---|---|---|---|---|---|---|---|---|---|---|---|
| United States | | | | | | | | | | | | | |
| 1991 | 354.1 | 394.1 | 405.0 | 413.0 | 411.2 | 411.5 | 413.6 | 423.6 | 421.2 | 420.8 | 419.8 | 422.6 | 409.2 |
| 1992 | 452.6 | 448.8 | 443.1 | 443.2 | 451.2 | 444.1 | 451.5 | 454.6 | 455.2 | 448.7 | 460.0 | 473.9 | 452.2 |
| 1993 | 473.4 | 480.5 | 489.7 | 482.0 | 484.3 | 487.4 | 486.6 | 494.0 | 499.6 | 504.6 | 503.5 | 506.9 | 491.0 |
| 1994 | 514.5 | 513.0 | 504.5 | 486.5 | 490.5 | 494.8 | 491.0 | 505.0 | 508.0 | 504.5 | 501.5 | 495.2 | 500.8 |
| 1995 | 506.1 | 524.2 | 536.4 | 552.5 | 569.8 | 586.7 | 606.3 | 608.2 | 629.6 | 634.1 | 647.8 | 668.5 | 589.2 |
| 1996[1] | 668.4 | 706.6 | 703.9 | 704.0 | 719.3 | 727.2 | 700.6 | 720.9 | 734.1 | 763.0 | 800.3 | 808.5 | 729.7 |
| Canada | | | | | | | | | | | | | |
| 1991 | 369.8 | 391.2 | 395.0 | 392.0 | 400.7 | 391.6 | 400.0 | 397.5 | 382.8 | 397.3 | 390.3 | 396.9 | 392.1 |
| 1992 | 406.3 | 404.7 | 385.6 | 379.2 | 382.8 | 382.8 | 389.1 | 384.5 | 372.6 | 377.0 | 370.8 | 378.6 | 384.5 |
| 1993 | 373.5 | 390.0 | 407.1 | 428.2 | 437.4 | 448.2 | 448.3 | 467.5 | 450.9 | 480.9 | 472.3 | 488.3 | 441.1 |
| 1994 | 514.7 | 499.9 | 489.2 | 482.2 | 488.9 | 454.8 | 472.2 | 491.5 | 492.0 | 484.9 | 462.5 | 474.9 | 484.0 |
| 1995 | 454.0 | 466.1 | 487.4 | 483.6 | 502.7 | 511.5 | 521.5 | 510.4 | 511.9 | 503.9 | 526.7 | 532.6 | 501.0 |
| 1996[1] | 561.4 | 557.5 | 561.4 | 580.7 | 592.3 | 569.1 | 557.5 | 580.7 | 600.1 | 627.2 | 668.3 | 668.6 | 593.7 |
| France | | | | | | | | | | | | | |
| 1991 | 669.0 | 744.8 | 768.8 | 753.0 | 788.0 | 739.7 | 742.7 | 713.1 | 735.1 | 737.5 | 749.7 | 786.3 | 744.0 |
| 1992 | 793.7 | 839.5 | 822.1 | 859.7 | 860.6 | 804.4 | 742.7 | 713.1 | 735.1 | 737.5 | 749.7 | 786.3 | 787.0 |
| 1993 | 750.1 | 839.6 | 859.7 | 820.7 | 799.4 | 834.6 | 882.8 | 938.1 | 895.0 | 923.5 | 893.1 | 960.0 | 866.4 |
| 1994 | 988.0 | 947.3 | 881.2 | 916.7 | 859.2 | 800.8 | 878.2 | 875.7 | 795.4 | 806.6 | 836.3 | 796.2 | 865.1 |
| 1995 | 761.0 | 752.0 | 828.9 | 812.0 | 824.5 | 786.7 | 812.7 | 797.1 | 756.9 | 767.8 | 773.8 | 870.4 | 788.8 |
| 1996[1] | 938.0 | 929.6 | 954.9 | 980.3 | 980.3 | 988.7 | 929.6 | 912.7 | 988.7 | 997.2 | 1,033.7 | 1,051.8 | 973.8 |
| Germany[2] | | | | | | | | | | | | | |
| 1991 | 280.6 | 300.9 | 314.8 | 324.0 | 327.9 | 339.3 | 329.3 | 326.5 | 330.4 | 315.8 | 313.3 | 301.2 | 317.0 |
| 1992 | 315.1 | 326.9 | 331.8 | 334.7 | 337.5 | 336.1 | 316.2 | 292.0 | 285.2 | 266.4 | 269.6 | 269.2 | 306.7 |
| 1993 | 277.8 | 292.0 | 297.0 | 293.4 | 286.3 | 293.4 | 311.6 | 325.4 | 322.9 | 337.9 | 345.7 | 363.1 | 312.2 |
| 1994 | 374.2 | 372.7 | 380.2 | 396.9 | 399.8 | 373.1 | 372.0 | 389.4 | 379.8 | 361.7 | 362.4 | 359.2 | 376.8 |
| 1995 | 361.7 | 366.0 | 343.6 | 338.9 | 349.6 | 354.6 | 364.1 | 373.8 | 376.4 | 360.9 | 366.4 | 519.0 | 361.2 |
| 1996[1] | 557.8 | 553.0 | 553.0 | 553.0 | 557.8 | 572.4 | 553.0 | 562.7 | 582.1 | 582.1 | 596.2 | 616.0 | 569.9 |
| Italy | | | | | | | | | | | | | |
| 1991 | 532.5 | 577.3 | 615.8 | 628.2 | 618.6 | 640.0 | 602.8 | 591.0 | 578.0 | 555.2 | 539.4 | 523.5 | 583.5 |
| 1992 | 564.2 | 568.3 | 537.3 | 531.1 | 514.6 | 501.5 | 445.7 | 424.3 | 387.1 | 422.3 | 475.3 | 453.3 | 485.4 |
| 1993 | 497.4 | 528.4 | 534.6 | 544.2 | 575.2 | 560.0 | 580.0 | 634.4 | 633.1 | 617.2 | 575.2 | 622.7 | 575.2 |
| 1994 | 646.8 | 703.3 | 699.9 | 815.6 | 823.9 | 757.1 | 738.5 | 721.2 | 710.2 | 668.9 | 668.9 | 651.7 | 717.2 |
| 1995 | 691.6 | 697.8 | 643.4 | 644.1 | 682.7 | 656.5 | 667.5 | 690.2 | 675.1 | 624.8 | 604.8 | 604.8 | 656.9 |
| 1996[1] | 633.8 | 647.5 | 626.9 | 654.4 | 702.6 | 702.6 | 668.2 | 640.6 | 633.8 | 655.5 | 675.1 | 688.8 | 660.8 |
| Japan | | | | | | | | | | | | | |
| 1991 | 1,544.0 | 1,698.2 | 1,787.2 | 1,805.0 | 1,777.3 | 1,714.0 | 1,640.9 | 1,595.4 | 1,615.2 | 1,696.2 | 1,633.0 | 1,536.1 | 1,670.2 |
| 1992 | 1,476.8 | 1,427.4 | 1,334.4 | 1,178.3 | 1,243.5 | 1,176.3 | 1,132.8 | 1,095.2 | 1,243.5 | 1,178.3 | 1,152.6 | 1,198.0 | 1,236.4 |
| 1993 | 1,158.5 | 1,172.3 | 1,235.6 | 1,411.5 | 1,468.9 | 1,462.9 | 1,468.9 | 1,510.4 | 1,506.4 | 1,490.6 | 1,381.9 | 1,308.7 | 1,381.4 |
| 1994 | 1,376.0 | 1,445.1 | 1,466.9 | 1,457.0 | 1,488.6 | 1,526.2 | 1,498.5 | 1,494.6 | 1,441.2 | 1,433.3 | 1,383.9 | 1,383.9 | 1,449.6 |
| 1995 | 1,344.3 | 1,277.1 | 1,190.1 | 1,182.2 | 1,180.2 | 1,109.1 | 1,176.3 | 1,257.3 | 1,302.8 | 1,298.9 | 1,304.8 | 1,395.7 | 1,251.6 |
| 1996[1] | 1,443.2 | 1,443.2 | 1,423.4 | 1,522.3 | 1,522.3 | 1,542.0 | 1,482.7 | 1,443.2 | 1,423.4 | 1,441.8 | 1,435.9 | 1,372.3 | 1,458.0 |
| United Kingdom | | | | | | | | | | | | | |
| 1991 | 971.3 | 1,049.6 | 1,139.4 | 1,168.7 | 1,159.3 | 1,158.2 | 1,169.7 | 1,201.0 | 1,223.0 | 1,208.4 | 1,179.1 | 1,132.1 | 1,146.7 |
| 1992 | 1,179.1 | 1,196.9 | 1,179.1 | 1,208.4 | 1,285.6 | 1,234.5 | 1,148.8 | 1,095.6 | 1,133.2 | 1,188.5 | 1,241.8 | 1,283.6 | 1,197.9 |
| 1993 | 1,303.4 | 1,326.4 | 1,352.5 | 1,325.3 | 1,326.4 | 1,341.0 | 1,325.3 | 1,405.7 | 1,414.1 | 1,440.2 | 1,430.8 | 1,509.1 | 1,375.0 |
| 1994 | 1,584.3 | 1,584.3 | 1,520.6 | 1,488.3 | 1,472.6 | 1,409.9 | 1,430.8 | 1,503.9 | 1,463.2 | 1,427.7 | 1,441.3 | 1,413.1 | 1,478.3 |
| 1995 | 1,420.4 | 1,420.4 | 1,421.4 | 1,472.6 | 1,514.4 | 1,539.4 | 1,573.9 | 1,608.4 | 1,627.2 | 1,612.5 | 1,615.7 | 1,636.6 | 1,538.6 |
| 1996[1] | 1,671.0 | 1,691.9 | 1,702.3 | 1,765.0 | 1,754.6 | 1,744.1 | 1,702.3 | 1,744.1 | 1,775.5 | 1,788.0 | 1,754.2 | 1,748.7 | 1,736.8 |

[1] Preliminary. [2] Federal Republic of Germany. Not seasonally adjusted. *Source: Economic and Statistics Administration, U.S. Department of Census*

## Corporate Profits After Tax--Quarterly In Billions of Dollars

| Year | I | II | III | IV | Average | Year | I | II | III | IV | Average |
|---|---|---|---|---|---|---|---|---|---|---|---|
| 1987 | 144.4 | 167.3 | 173.8 | 180.6 | 166.5 | 1992 | 267.2 | 275.2 | 240.4 | 270.6 | 263.4 |
| 1988 | 201.0 | 217.1 | 220.3 | 231.0 | 217.4 | 1993 | 285.6 | 295.0 | 298.6 | 322.8 | 300.5 |
| 1989 | 219.3 | 206.7 | 196.9 | 204.4 | 206.8 | 1994 | 304.1 | 333.3 | 347.4 | 358.8 | 335.9 |
| 1990 | 221.7 | 232.2 | 233.9 | 237.1 | 231.2 | 1995[1] | 377.2 | 375.3 | 382.8 | 385.5 | 380.2 |
| 1991 | 240.7 | 236.4 | 238.6 | 247.6 | 240.8 | 1996[1] | 408.8 | 408.1 | 402.2 | | 406.4 |

[1] Preliminary. *Source: Bureau of Economic Analysis, U.S. Department of Commerce*

## Productivity: Index of Output Per Hour, All Persons, Nonfarm Business--Quarterly 1992 = 100

| Year | I | II | III | IV | Average | Year | I | II | III | IV | Average |
|---|---|---|---|---|---|---|---|---|---|---|---|
| 1987 | 94.1 | 94.7 | 94.5 | 95.2 | 94.6 | 1992 | 99.3 | 99.9 | 99.7 | 101.1 | 100.0 |
| 1988 | 94.9 | 95.0 | 95.4 | 95.9 | 95.3 | 1993 | 100.1 | 99.7 | 100.1 | 100.8 | 100.2 |
| 1989 | 95.5 | 95.7 | 96.0 | 96.1 | 95.8 | 1994 | 100.2 | 100.5 | 101.0 | 101.2 | 100.7 |
| 1990 | 96.4 | 96.7 | 96.4 | 95.5 | 96.3 | 1995 | 100.5 | 100.9 | 101.3 | 101.1 | 101.0 |
| 1991 | 96.1 | 96.8 | 97.4 | 97.6 | 97.0 | 1996[1] | 101.5 | 101.7 | 101.6 | | 101.6 |

[1] Preliminary. *Source: Bureau of Economic Analysis, U.S. Department of Commerce*

## Consumer Confidence, The Conference Board 1985 = 100

| Year | Jan. | Feb. | Mar. | Apr. | May | June | July | Aug. | Sept. | Oct. | Nov. | Dec. | Average |
|---|---|---|---|---|---|---|---|---|---|---|---|---|---|
| 1988 | 109.9 | 114.9 | 112.7 | 115.7 | 120.2 | 115.7 | 113.5 | 119.7 | 110.7 | 116.9 | 112.9 | 119.4 | 115.2 |
| 1989 | 115.8 | 120.7 | 117.4 | 116.6 | 116.7 | 117.2 | 120.4 | 115.4 | 116.3 | 117.0 | 115.1 | 113.0 | 116.8 |
| 1990 | 106.5 | 106.7 | 110.6 | 107.3 | 107.3 | 102.4 | 101.7 | 84.7 | 85.6 | 62.6 | 61.7 | 61.3 | 91.5 |
| 1991 | 55.1 | 59.4 | 81.1 | 79.4 | 76.4 | 78.0 | 77.7 | 76.1 | 72.9 | 60.1 | 52.7 | 52.5 | 68.5 |
| 1992 | 50.2 | 47.3 | 56.5 | 65.1 | 71.9 | 72.6 | 61.2 | 59.0 | 57.3 | 54.6 | 65.6 | 78.1 | 61.6 |
| 1993 | 76.7 | 68.5 | 63.2 | 67.6 | 61.9 | 58.6 | 59.2 | 59.3 | 63.8 | 60.5 | 71.9 | 79.8 | 65.9 |
| 1994 | 82.6 | 79.9 | 86.7 | 92.1 | 88.9 | 92.5 | 91.3 | 90.4 | 89.5 | 89.1 | 100.4 | 103.4 | 90.6 |
| 1995 | 101.4 | 99.4 | 100.2 | 104.6 | 102.0 | 94.6 | 101.4 | 102.4 | 97.3 | 96.3 | 101.6 | 99.2 | 100.0 |
| 1996[1] | 88.4 | 98.0 | 98.4 | 104.8 | 103.5 | 100.1 | 107.0 | 112.0 | 111.8 | 107.3 | 109.5 | 114.2 | 104.6 |

[1] Preliminary. *Source: The Conference Board*

## Average Open Interest of NYSE Composite Stock Index Futures in New York In Contracts

| Year | Jan. | Feb. | Mar. | Apr. | May | June | July | Aug. | Sept. | Oct. | Nov. | Dec. |
|---|---|---|---|---|---|---|---|---|---|---|---|---|
| 1988 | 5,530 | 5,760 | 6,013 | 6,785 | 8,372 | 7,400 | 7,003 | 7,668 | 6,689 | 6,816 | 7,600 | 6,419 |
| 1989 | 6,460 | 7,211 | 7,860 | 7,605 | 8,001 | 6,771 | 6,386 | 6,247 | 6,449 | 7,045 | 6,491 | 6,084 |
| 1990 | 6,350 | 6,098 | 5,443 | 4,925 | 5,129 | 5,160 | 4,732 | 6,079 | 6,003 | 5,272 | 4,983 | 4,554 |
| 1991 | 4,736 | 5,720 | 5,264 | 5,488 | 6,190 | 6,010 | 5,056 | 5,997 | 5,869 | 5,512 | 6,438 | 6,195 |
| 1992 | 5,216 | 5,290 | 5,469 | 4,575 | 4,867 | 5,858 | 6,491 | 7,049 | 6,647 | 6,034 | 6,430 | 5,890 |
| 1993 | 5,033 | 5,083 | 4,113 | 3,613 | 4,222 | 4,340 | 3,714 | 4,178 | 3,997 | 4,315 | 4,721 | 4,539 |
| 1994 | 4,653 | 4,471 | 4,823 | 3,720 | 3,839 | 3,969 | 3,903 | 3,982 | 4,142 | 4,494 | 4,244 | 4,617 |
| 1995 | 3,695 | 4,159 | 4,113 | 3,476 | 3,396 | 3,254 | 3,205 | 3,029 | 2,966 | 2,683 | 3,125 | 3,403 |
| 1996 | 3,644 | 4,139 | 3,245 | 2,822 | 2,839 | 2,547 | 2,492 | 2,526 | 2,759 | 2,798 | 2,649 | 3,050 |

*Source: New York Futures Exchange (NYFE)*

## Average Open Interest of KC Value Line Stock Index Futures in Kansas City In Contracts

| Year | Jan. | Feb. | Mar. | Apr. | May | June | July | Aug. | Sept. | Oct. | Nov. | Dec. |
|---|---|---|---|---|---|---|---|---|---|---|---|---|
| 1988 | 1,538 | 1,655 | 2,814 | 3,059 | 3,266 | 2,269 | 1,570 | 1,389 | 1,332 | 1,229 | 1,564 | 1,580 |
| 1989 | 1,394 | 1,189 | 1,288 | 1,262 | 1,421 | 1,513 | 1,615 | 1,710 | 1,522 | 1,250 | 1,200 | 1,182 |
| 1990 | 1,245 | 1,355 | 1,463 | 1,514 | 1,544 | 1,404 | 1,311 | 1,297 | 1,250 | 1,210 | 1,325 | 1,381 |
| 1991 | 1,534 | 2,211 | 2,107 | 2,326 | 2,384 | 2,138 | 1,860 | 1,884 | 1,764 | 1,509 | 1,857 | 2,100 |
| 1992 | 2,127 | 2,208 | 1,657 | 1,169 | 1,117 | 1,049 | 833 | 867 | 1,029 | 962 | 1,101 | 1,632 |
| 1993 | 1,999 | 1,822 | 1,356 | 934 | 1,188 | 1,118 | 1,100 | 1,181 | 1,039 | 1,057 | 1,302 | 1,461 |
| 1994 | 1,921 | 1,649 | 1,289 | 768 | 839 | 823 | 812 | 850 | 898 | 915 | 1,011 | 1,478 |
| 1995 | 1,600 | 1,365 | 1,077 | 802 | 759 | 648 | 580 | 565 | 568 | 489 | 627 | 1,025 |
| 1996 | 1,163 | 783 | 571 | 530 | 418 | 435 | 347 | 411 | 403 | 318 | 370 | 503 |

*Source: Kansas City Board of Trade (KCBT)*

## Average Open Interest of Maxi Major Market Stock Index Futures in Chicago In Contracts

| Year | Jan. | Feb. | Mar. | Apr. | May | June | July | Aug. | Sept. | Oct. | Nov. | Dec. |
|---|---|---|---|---|---|---|---|---|---|---|---|---|
| 1988 | 2,442 | 2,849 | 3,901 | 6,309 | 8,000 | 4,890 | 3,072 | 2,957 | 3,591 | 5,878 | 4,956 | 7,206 |
| 1989 | 7,060 | 6,421 | 5,554 | 6,335 | 6,280 | 4,130 | 6,213 | 5,235 | 4,043 | 7,169 | 4,835 | 5,552 |
| 1990 | 5,274 | 4,273 | 5,261 | 5,847 | 7,686 | 8,773 | 8,398 | 6,480 | 7,837 | 8,106 | 7,873 | 9,891 |
| 1991 | 9,705 | 9,856 | 7,894 | 7,739 | 7,715 | 7,130 | 5,519 | 5,501 | 5,042 | 4,296 | 3,877 | 5,118 |
| 1992 | 5,326 | 5,568 | 4,627 | 4,776 | 5,495 | 5,518 | 4,505 | 4,336 | 4,681 | 4,409 | 4,236 | 5,771 |
| 1993 | 5,880 | 5,122 | 3,730 | 3,137 | 3,116 | 2,913 | 2,033 | 1,903 | 1,849 | 2,040 | 2,867 | 3,699 |
| 1994 | 3,467 | 3,722 | 4,048 | 4,280 | 4,516 | 5,015 | 4,517 | 3,690 | 2,937 | 3,842 | 3,511 | 1,899 |
| 1995 | 2,009 | 3,457 | 2,397 | 1,263 | 1,297 | 1,048 | 1,015 | 746 | 705 | 334 | 313 | 344 |
| 1996 | 333 | 302 | 208 | 165 | 116 | 86 | 81 | 99 | 92 | 46 | 6 | 21 |

*Source: Index and Option Market (IOM), division of the Chicago Mercantile Exchange (CME)*

# STOCK INDEX FUTURES

## Average Open Interest of S & P 500 Index Futures in Chicago    In Contracts

| Year | Jan. | Feb. | Mar. | Apr. | May | June | July | Aug. | Sept. | Oct. | Nov. | Dec. |
|---|---|---|---|---|---|---|---|---|---|---|---|---|
| 1987 | 107,367 | 116,765 | 119,444 | 110,154 | 127,090 | 131,406 | 115,722 | 127,385 | 128,930 | 139,741 | 141,059 | 130,387 |
| 1988 | 115,006 | 120,909 | 114,792 | 114,269 | 129,134 | 116,524 | 104,644 | 118,008 | 120,657 | 121,970 | 137,715 | 131,134 |
| 1989 | 129,453 | 136,285 | 137,068 | 136,664 | 140,627 | 128,578 | 116,935 | 129,989 | 129,949 | 126,039 | 126,444 | 117,875 |
| 1990 | 112,196 | 124,279 | 124,460 | 118,350 | 127,718 | 118,865 | 113,050 | 132,568 | 159,607 | 151,990 | 157,440 | 160,260 |
| 1991 | 148,112 | 168,803 | 158,994 | 148,106 | 157,103 | 154,848 | 142,665 | 152,067 | 151,609 | 144,279 | 153,898 | 145,324 |
| 1992 | 147,434 | 143,013 | 141,942 | 136,991 | 141,757 | 149,962 | 153,035 | 163,613 | 168,263 | 170,065 | 178,342 | 179,942 |
| 1993 | 164,614 | 173,691 | 178,939 | 174,277 | 182,896 | 190,053 | 182,189 | 191,311 | 208,390 | 195,109 | 201,374 | 196,175 |
| 1994 | 188,225 | 195,824 | 210,065 | 200,818 | 219,109 | 299,567 | 217,028 | 227,871 | 237,934 | 230,594 | 243,581 | 251,370 |
| 1995 | 213,502 | 221,314 | 222,792 | 210,052 | 221,648 | 226,682 | 210,012 | 211,304 | 208,906 | 201,397 | 220,890 | 223,764 |
| 1996 | 203,200 | 214,029 | 209,844 | 184,310 | 199,535 | 203,957 | 184,624 | 191,133 | 206,972 | 187,363 | 208,051 | 224,191 |

*Source: International Monetary Market (IMM); division of the Chicago Mercantile Exchange (CME)*

## Average Open Interest of S & P 400 Midcap Index Futures in Chicago    In Contracts

| Year | Jan. | Feb. | Mar. | Apr. | May | June | July | Aug. | Sept. | Oct. | Nov. | Dec. |
|---|---|---|---|---|---|---|---|---|---|---|---|---|
| 1992 | | 2,776 | 3,060 | 3,017 | 3,712 | 4,476 | 4,073 | 4,350 | 4,762 | 4,355 | 5,778 | 6,883 |
| 1993 | 7,197 | 9,048 | 9,095 | 8,759 | 8,640 | 9,336 | 8,731 | 10,183 | 10,728 | 12,955 | 13,343 | 13,261 |
| 1994 | 13,183 | 11,999 | 12,748 | 10,801 | 10,829 | 11,902 | 11,970 | 12,369 | 15,002 | 13,702 | 13,896 | 14,494 |
| 1995 | 13,787 | 13,355 | 11,130 | 9,275 | 9,329 | 9,929 | 11,198 | 11,708 | 13,107 | 11,702 | 12,341 | 12,863 |
| 1996 | 11,088 | 10,474 | 11,375 | 8,700 | 9,254 | 10,403 | 9,763 | 10,867 | 11,168 | 9,641 | 10,596 | 11,107 |

*Source: International Monetary Market (IMM); division of the Chicago Mercantile Exchange (CME)*

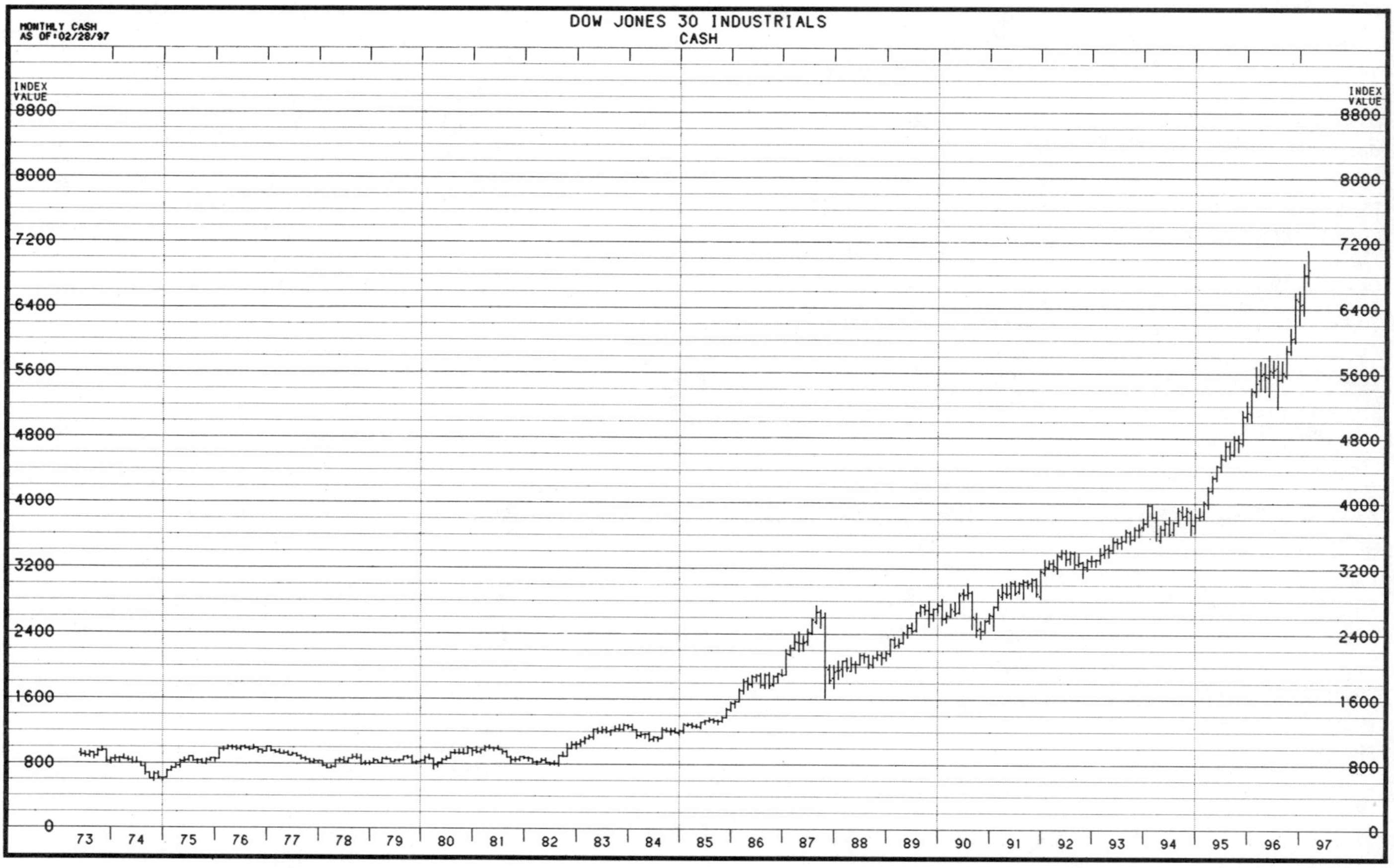

# Stock Index Futures, Worldwide

With the notable exception of Japan's Nikkei 225 index, the world's equity markets moved higher in 1996 with some finishing the year with dynamic gains vs. yearend 1995. The prices surges were accompanied by record high trading volumes on nearly every exchange.

In the U.S., the bellwether Dow Jones 30 Industrials Stock Average advanced 26 percent; the S & P 500 was up 20 percent; the Nasdaq Index, which is heavily weighted with high-tech corporations, surged 23 percent; and the Dow Jones World Index advanced almost 11 percent.

Hong Kong's Hang Seng Average gained 33 percent; Germany's Dax was up 28 percent; the United Kingdom's FTSE-100 gained 12 percent; Toronto's 35 Stock Index was up 26 percent; and Mexico's IPC was up 21 percent. Among the more dynamic percentage moves was Venezuela's 228 percent gain.

Japan's Nikkei, however, closed the year at 19,361 vs. 19,868 a year earlier, down 2.8 percent for 1996 and continuing the slide which took root in 1990-92 and has since halved the Nikkei's value. Ironically, the gains in European stock indices came despite generally lackluster economies and easier, but not necessarily effective, monetary policies aimed to jump-start economic growth. However, high unemployment in Europe braked consumer demand which in turn held down inflationary fears. Moreover, with the U.S. markets booming it was hard for other world stock markets not to join in, regardless of the economic malaise in their own countries. Meanwhile, stock markets are taking root in a number of countries that only a few years ago perceived such symbols of capitalism as decadent; worldwide almost ninety countries now have equity markets.

In the U.S., stocks reacted positively to a basically robust low-inflation economy. Cyclically, the economy's expansionary phase was the third longest since World War II and the favorable outlook for 1997, if realized, would move the phase to a record length. Although the Federal Reserve did snug monetary policy a bit in early 1996, it failed to slow the flow of capital into equities at the expense of low yielding bank deposits. Moreover, the sizeable infusion of capital into pension programs was largely allocated to equities, the demand for which at times seemed insatiable. The markets seemed to have no place to go but up.

In Europe, Germany's DAX Index was a star performer, setting a string of new highs during 1996 and peaking at 2910 in early December. The reasons for the strength included positive earnings expectations for most of Germany's industrial sector, falling interest rates, and corporate restructuring. A weaker D-Mark against the U.S. Dollar enhanced the outlook for Germany's chemical and automotive industries.

In France, the CAC-40 Index was slower than most European markets to respond to the mix of lower interest rates and corporate restructuring, but the bulls took notice in mid-summer and by yearend the index was up 24 percent and close to its all time high of 2361 set in 1994.

The U.K.'s Financial Times-Stock Index gained in 1996, but it was a struggle at times. British stocks were held in check by political worries, a strong B-Pound, and being out of the European Monetary Union (EMU). The U.K. was the only European country that tightened monetary policy in 1996; only 25 basis points, but enough to dampen bullish enthusiasm. The U.K.'s strong economy in 1996 was expected to carry into 1997, which could trigger another 25 basis point rise in the first quarter.

The Scandinavian markets sizzled in 1996, reflecting low inflation and solid corporate earnings, but comparable gains in 1997 were forecast as unlikely if interest rates go up. Indeed, the 1997 outlook for most European equity markets, while positive, is not ecstatic.

Canada's TSE Index took off in 1996, bolstered by declining interest rates. The Bank of Canada cut rates 19 times between mid-1995 and late 1996 in an effort to prime Canada's economy. Moreover, the Quebec separation turmoil that took hold in late 1995 was relegated to the back-burner during 1996.

Mexico's IPC Index, while higher at yearend, did not witness the volatility of 1995. In Peso's the index gained 21 percent, 17 percent in dollar terms. Conglomerates made a strong recovery in 1996, but most Mexican equity prices still lagged behind their 1994 prevaluation highs in dollar terms.

The markets in Asia, China, Hong Kong, and Taiwan did well while Japan's Nikkei 225 index faltered. Japanese investors seemed torn between two beliefs. One being that Japan's 5 year economic slump was nearing an end and the other that it was not. The uncertainty seems likely to persist into at least the first half of 1997. In Hong Kong, however, a perception took hold in 1996 that China's takeover in mid-1997 will prove smooth, which if realized, may propel the Hang Seng Index to new highs, possibly to the 15,000 level from the yearend 1996 close of 13,451. But China's intentions towards Taiwan remain an enigma. In spite of the uncertainty the island's stock index rose 34 percent in 1996, partially in response to lower interest rates.

### *Futures Markets*

A number of stock index futures and options markets are traded in the world's major financial centers. The Chicago Mercantile Exchange (CME) offers the S & P 500, the S & P Midcap 400, the Major Market Index and the Russell 2000 index. A Nikkei 225 stock average is traded in Chicago, Tokyo, Osaka and Singapore. In New York, the NYSE Composite index is offered. The Kansas City Board of Trade (KC) lists the Value Line index. The Canadian 25 stock index is traded on the Toronto Futures Exchange (TFE). The Sydney Futures Exchange (SFE) trades the Australian All-Ordinaries Share Price index. In Europe, the FT-SE 100 index is traded on the London International Financial Futures Exchange (LIFFE); in Paris, the CAC-40 stock index is traded on the MATIF.

WEEKLY CASH
AS OF:03/14/97
FT-SE 100
CASH
INDEX VALUE
4400
4200
4000
3800
3600
3400
3200
3000
2800
2600
2400
2200
1991
1992
1993
1994
1995
1996
M J J A S O N D J F M A M J J A S O N D J F M A M J J A S O N D J F M A M J J A S O N D J F M A M J J A S O N D J F M A M J J A S O N D J F M A M

WEEKLY CASH
AS OF:03/14/97
TORONTO 35 INDEX
CASH
INDEX VALUE
360
340
320
300
280
260
240
220
200
180
160
140
1991
1992
1993
1994
1995
1996
M J J A S O N D J F M A M J J A S O N D J F M A M J J A S O N D J F M A M J J A S O N D J F M A M J J A S O N D J F M A M J J A S O N D J F M A M

WEEKLY CASH
AS OF:03/14/97
CAC 40
CASH
INDEX VALUE
2700
2600
2500
2400
2300
2200
2100
2000
1900
1800
1700
1600
1994
1995
1996
1997
M A M J J A S O N D J F M A M J J A S O N D J F M A M J J A S O N D J F M A M J J

WEEKLY CASH
AS OF:03/14/97
GERMAN STOCK INDEX (DAX)
CASH
INDEX VALUE
3800
3600
3400
3200
3000
2800
2600
2400
2200
2000
1800
1600
1994
1995
1996
1997
M A M J J A S O N D J F M A M J J A S O N D J F M A M J J A S O N D J F M A M J J

WEEKLY CASH
AS OF:03/14/97
TOPIX INDEX
CASH
INDEX VALUE
2000
1900
1800
1700
1600
1500
1400
1300
1200
1100
1000
900
1994
1995
1996
1997
M A M J J A S O N D J F M A M J J A S O N D J F M A M J J A S O N D J F M A M J J

WEEKLY CASH
AS OF:03/14/97
TORONTO 300
CASH
INDEX VALUE
6500
6250
6000
5750
5500
5250
5000
4750
4500
4250
4000
3750
1994
1995
1996
1997
M A M J J A S O N D J F M A M J J A S O N D J F M A M J J A S O N D J F M A M J J

WEEKLY CASH
AS OF:03/14/97
HANG SENG INDEX
CASH
INDEX VALUE
14000
13000
12000
11000
10000
9000
8000
7000
6000
5000
4000
3000
1991
1992
1993
1994
1995
1996

WEEKLY CASH
AS OF:03/14/97
NIKKEI 225 INDEX
CASH
INDEX VALUE
320
300
280
260
240
220
200
180
160
140
120
100
1991
1992
1993
1994
1995
1996

# Sugar

Raw sugar is produced from either sugar cane or sugar beets. The sugar is sucrose in both plants. While there are many types of sugar, sucrose is the most common. Generally it takes about 1.07 tonnes of raw sugar to produce a tonnes of refined sugar. Sugar cane is a grass that grows best in warm, moist, typically tropical climates. A large number of countries produce sugar cane including Brazil, Cuba, Mexico, Thailand, Australia, South Africa, and India. The sugar cane plant through the process of photosynthesis converts sunlight, water, and carbon dioxide into sugar. The plant stores a huge amount of sugar.

The cane is harvested and sent to a sugar mill where it is pressed. The juice is removed and boiled under a vacuum until it becomes a brown syrup with the sugar becoming a crystalline solid. The remaining liquid is molasses.

The crystalized sugar is put into a drum and dried through centrifugal force. The resulting raw sugar is then sent to a refinery where it is washed. It is then subjected to spinning or centrifuging becoming almost pure sucrose. This sugar is further crystalized to become virtually pure white refined sugar. Beet sugar is produced primarily in Europe, China and the U.S. Sugar beets grow best in cooler climates and store sucrose in their roots. At a beet sugar refinery, the beets are sliced and then soaked in hot water which removes the sugar. There is no raw sugar stage.

World sugar production is 1996/97 (September-August) is estimated at 125 million tonnes (raw value). This is up about 2 percent from 1995/96 global output of 121 million tonnes. The reasons for the increase were somewhat larger crops in Western Europe, Brazil, and Thailand. Western Europe is the largest producer of white sugar. While world production of sugar in the last two years has been very large, consumption has also been increasing with global use in 1996/97 forecast at 120 million tonnes. The previous season consumption was 117 million tonnes. Most of the increase in sucrose sugar consumption is taking place in non-industrialized nations. Countries such as China and India continue to increase their use of sugar as populations rise and sugar is used in more products like soft drinks and foods. In the industrialized countries of Western Europe and North America, sucrose sugar consumption has leveled off or declined. High fructose corn syrup (HFCS), which is made from corn as well as other non-sucrose sweeteners, has made substantial inroads in the sugar market. In part this has been due to the fact that HFCS is priced at a discount to refined sugar, encouraging the substitution of corn sweeteners for sucrose sugar wherever feasible.

With world sugar production exceeding consumption in 1996/97, world sugar stocks were forecast to continue increasing, possibly exceeding 50 million tonnes. While this would represent a record level of sugar stocks, it did not necessarily imply that prices would decline. For example, India was expected to have about 8 million tonnes of sugar in storage at the end of 1996/97. Of that total, exports were expected to be about a million tonnes. This implies that while world stocks are huge, not all of that sugar was available to countries looking to import.

The European Union (EU) produced 17 million tonnes, about the same as in 1995/96. It was another dry summer, though by early fall there were rains and warm temperatures allowing the crop to recover some. The major surprise was in Turkey where the crop of nearly 2 million tonnes was up close to 40 percent from the year before as beet plantings increased. It was a poor season in parts of Eastern Europe where raw sugar production fell about 5 percent to just over 9 million tonnes. Late planting, poor weather, and shortages of equipment led to forecasts of reduced output in Russia and the Ukraine. Russia's crop of 1.9 million tonnes was off almost 10 percent from 1995/96. Similar problems beset the Ukraine where the crop barely reached 3 million tonnes, down over 20 percent from the year before. Poland, on the other hand, planted a lot more acreage to beets and the crop of 2.2 million tonnes was up over 25 percent from 1995/96.

After reaching record levels in 1995/96, Asian sugar production was expected to fall back in 1996/97. India has produced three very large crops in a row. The 1996/97 crop is 17 million tonnes, down 7 percent from the previous season. The large crops have resulted in a huge buildup in stocks and pressure from the domestic industry on the government to increase the export quota. One problem for India has been a limited physical ability to export sugar.

The USDA estimated U.S. sugar production in 1996/97 at 7.1 million short tons, down 3 percent from the 1995/96 crop of 7.4 million tons. Beet sugar production was 4 million tons, up marginally from 3.9 million tons the year before. Cane sugar, grown in Florida, Texas, Louisiana, and Hawaii was 3.2 million tons, down 8 percent. Imports of sugar under the tariff rate quota were 2.7 million tons. U.S. sugar ending stocks were 1.5 million tons.

### *Futures Markets*

Sugar futures are traded on the Bolsa de Mercadorias & Futuros (BM&F), the Marche a Terme International de France (MATIF), Kansai Agricultural Commodities Exchange (KANEX), the Tokyo Grain Exchange (TGE), the Manila International Futures Exchange Inc. (MIFE), the London Commodity Exchange (LCE), and the New York Coffee, Sugar, and Cocoa Exchange Inc. (CSCE). Options are traded on the KANEX, the TGE, the LCE, and the CSCE.

# SUGAR

## World Sugar Production, Supply & Stocks/Consumption Ratio — In Thousands of Metric Tons (Raw Value)

| Marketing Year | Beginning Stocks | Production | Imports | Total Supply | Exports | Domestic Consumption | Ending Stocks | Stocks/ Consumption Percentage |
|---|---|---|---|---|---|---|---|---|
| 1987-8 | 23,117 | 103,786 | 27,076 | 153,979 | 27,076 | 106,554 | 20,349 | 19.1 |
| 1988-9 | 20,349 | 105,562 | 28,671 | 154,582 | 28,671 | 106,516 | 19,395 | 18.2 |
| 1989-90 | 19,395 | 108,772 | 33,179 | 161,346 | 33,179 | 108,709 | 19,458 | 17.9 |
| 1990-1 | 19,458 | 113,458 | 32,538 | 165,391 | 32,538 | 111,926 | 20,927 | 18.8 |
| 1991-2 | 20,967 | 116,512 | 30,802 | 168,281 | 30,802 | 113,929 | 23,550 | 20.7 |
| 1992-3 | 23,550 | 112,089 | 29,022 | 164,661 | 29,022 | 114,102 | 21,537 | 18.9 |
| 1993-4 | 21,537 | 109,787 | 29,753 | 161,077 | 29,753 | 112,801 | 18,523 | 16.4 |
| 1994-5 | 18,574 | 115,842 | 30,532 | 164,948 | 30,532 | 113,622 | 20,794 | 18.3 |
| 1995-6[1] | 20,794 | 122,509 | 35,084 | 178,387 | 35,084 | 118,608 | 24,695 | 20.8 |
| 1996-7[2] | 24,694 | 124,989 | 35,475 | 185,158 | 35,475 | 122,930 | 26,753 | 21.8 |

[1] Preliminary. [2] Forecast. *Source: Foreign Agricultural Service, U.S. Department of Agriculture*

## World Production of Sugar (Centrifugal Sugar-Raw Value) — In Thousands of Metric Tons

| Year | Australia | Brazil | China | Cuba | France | Germany | India | Indonesia | Mexico | Philippines | Poland | South Africa | Thailand | United States | Ukraine[3] | World Total |
|---|---|---|---|---|---|---|---|---|---|---|---|---|---|---|---|---|
| 1985-6 | 3,404 | 8,100 | 5,535 | 7,200 | 4,297 | 3,430 | 7,983 | 1,728 | 3,928 | 1,561 | 1,811 | 2,287 | 2,586 | 5,473 | 8,260 | 98,798 |
| 1986-7 | 3,457 | 8,650 | 5,774 | 7,220 | 3,707 | 3,469 | 9,474 | 2,024 | 3,970 | 1,350 | 1,891 | 2,289 | 2,639 | 6,246 | 8,700 | 103,951 |
| 1987-8 | 3,528 | 8,457 | 4,706 | 7,400 | 3,966 | 2,968 | 10,000 | 2,127 | 3,806 | 1,400 | 1,823 | 2,165 | 2,704 | 6,483 | 9,560 | 103,786 |
| 1988-9 | 3,680 | 8,582 | 5,312 | 8,100 | 4,372 | 3,003 | 10,150 | 1,889 | 3,678 | 1,600 | 1,825 | 2,240 | 4,055 | 6,089 | 8,900 | 105,562 |
| 1989-90 | 3,797 | 7,793 | 5,618 | 8,000 | 4,204 | 4,087 | 12,575 | 2,080 | 3,100 | 1,750 | 1,865 | 2,289 | 3,502 | 6,070 | 5,627 | 108,772 |
| 1990-1 | 3,637 | 7,900 | 6,765 | 7,620 | 4,736 | 4,675 | 13,707 | 2,120 | 3,900 | 1,718 | 2,214 | 2,152 | 3,954 | 6,330 | 5,369 | 113,484 |
| 1991-2 | 3,192 | 9,200 | 8,492 | 7,030 | 4,413 | 4,250 | 15,249 | 2,250 | 3,500 | 2,010 | 1,640 | 2,429 | 5,062 | 6,627 | 4,178 | 116,512 |
| 1992-3 | 4,367 | 9,800 | 8,300 | 4,280 | 4,723 | 4,401 | 12,456 | 2,300 | 4,330 | 2,060 | 1,567 | 1,600 | 3,750 | 7,111 | 3,965 | 112,088 |
| 1993-4 | 4,412 | 9,930 | 6,505 | 4,000 | 4,725 | 4,736 | 11,660 | 2,480 | 3,780 | 1,809 | 2,170 | 1,243 | 3,975 | 6,945 | 4,188 | 109,787 |
| 1994-5 | 5,196 | 12,500 | 5,900 | 3,300 | 4,363 | 3,991 | 16,410 | 2,450 | 4,556 | 1,647 | 1,492 | 1,770 | 5,448 | 7,191 | 3,600 | 115,842 |
| 1995-6[1] | 5,136 | 13,700 | 6,750 | 4,450 | 4,601 | 4,150 | 18,270 | 2,100 | 4,660 | 1,787 | 1,714 | 1,769 | 6,300 | 6,686 | 3,800 | 122,509 |
| 1996-7[2] | 5,600 | 14,500 | 7,000 | 4,600 | 4,400 | 4,550 | 17,000 | 2,450 | 4,600 | 1,850 | 2,200 | 2,500 | 6,500 | 6,468 | 3,000 | 124,989 |

[1] Preliminary. [2] Forecast. [3] Formerly part of the U.S.S.R.; data not reported separately until 1989. *Source: Foreign Agricultural Service, U.S. Department of Agriculture*

## World Stocks of Centrifugal Sugar at Beginning of Marketing Year — In Thousands of Metric Tons (Raw Value)

| Year | Australia | Brazil | China | Cuba | France | Germany | India | Iran | Italy | Japan | Mexico | Netherlands | Philippines | Switzerland | United Kingdom | United States | World Total |
|---|---|---|---|---|---|---|---|---|---|---|---|---|---|---|---|---|---|
| 1987-8 | 310 | 845 | 1,679 | 360 | 1,034 | 707 | 2,960 | 296 | 439 | 192 | 1,485 | 233 | 209 | 237 | 398 | 1,358 | 23,117 |
| 1988-9 | 236 | 771 | 2,575 | 460 | 710 | 432 | 2,700 | 246 | 479 | 180 | 577 | 223 | 160 | 205 | 338 | 1,194 | 20,349 |
| 1989-90 | 256 | 1,382 | 2,674 | 340 | 642 | 409 | 1,315 | 246 | 332 | 242 | 605 | 114 | 275 | 200 | 343 | 1,128 | 19,395 |
| 1990-1 | 256 | 1,164 | 1,350 | 475 | 434 | 330 | 2,376 | 220 | 425 | 192 | 750 | 58 | 308 | 197 | 300 | 1,111 | 19,458 |
| 1991-2 | 220 | 757 | 1,350 | 500 | 689 | 428 | 3,563 | 275 | 475 | 85 | 1,505 | 125 | 242 | 172 | 228 | 1,371 | 21,016 |
| 1992-3 | 194 | 950 | 2,002 | 500 | 589 | 340 | 5,245 | 300 | 333 | 110 | 910 | 137 | 515 | 149 | 281 | 1,340 | 23,602 |
| 1993-4 | 156 | 880 | 905 | 130 | 701 | 358 | 3,501 | 400 | 375 | 144 | 1,040 | 147 | 679 | 144 | 416 | 1,546 | 21,063 |
| 1994-5 | 125 | 455 | 573 | 170 | 784 | 511 | 2,731 | 400 | 170 | 140 | 575 | 85 | 412 | 139 | 450 | 1,213 | 18,574 |
| 1995-6[1] | 152 | 710 | 1,559 | 400 | 437 | 271 | 5,430 | 270 | 140 | 137 | 601 | 23 | 100 | 124 | 453 | 1,126 | 20,794 |
| 1996-7[2] | 124 | 510 | 1,659 | 400 | 684 | 331 | 7,710 | 300 | 190 | 237 | 431 | 43 | 506 | 124 | 457 | 1,356 | 24,694 |

[1] Preliminary. [2] Forecast. *Source: Foreign Agricultural Service, U.S. Department of Agriculture*

## Average Refined Beet Sugar[1] (Wholesale)--Midwest Market — In Cents Per Pound

| Year | Jan. | Feb. | Mar. | Apr. | May | June | July | Aug. | Sept. | Oct. | Nov. | Dec. | Average |
|---|---|---|---|---|---|---|---|---|---|---|---|---|---|
| 1985 | 23.50 | 23.42 | 23.00 | 23.12 | 23.55 | 23.12 | 23.25 | 23.50 | 23.44 | 23.13 | 22.50 | 22.62 | 23.18 |
| 1986 | 23.45 | 23.31 | 23.25 | 23.50 | 23.30 | 23.00 | 23.38 | 24.20 | 24.19 | 23.50 | 23.00 | 23.00 | 23.38 |
| 1987 | 23.30 | 23.50 | 23.50 | 23.50 | 24.15 | 24.44 | 24.50 | 24.50 | 24.00 | 22.85 | 22.50 | 22.50 | 23.60 |
| 1988 | 23.25 | 22.75 | 22.75 | 23.45 | 24.19 | 25.25 | 27.10 | 27.75 | 27.50 | 27.25 | 26.75 | 27.80 | 25.44 |
| 1989 | 28.75 | 29.00 | 29.50 | 29.50 | 29.50 | 29.50 | 29.38 | 29.25 | 29.06 | 28.20 | 29.50 | 31.38 | 29.06 |
| 1990 | 30.50 | 30.50 | 30.50 | 30.50 | 30.50 | 30.50 | 30.50 | 30.50 | 30.50 | 29.13 | 28.60 | 27.38 | 29.97 |
| 1991 | 26.88 | 26.50 | 26.50 | 26.13 | 26.00 | 25.75 | 25.50 | 25.50 | 25.00 | 24.94 | 24.60 | 24.50 | 25.65 |
| 1992 | 25.40 | 26.50 | 26.50 | 26.50 | 26.40 | 26.00 | 25.00 | 25.00 | 25.00 | 24.90 | 24.13 | 23.90 | 25.44 |
| 1993 | 23.25 | 23.00 | 23.00 | 23.50 | 23.50 | 23.50 | 25.50 | 27.75 | 27.50 | 27.50 | 27.25 | 26.50 | 25.15 |
| 1994 | 25.75 | 25.50 | 25.50 | 24.50 | 24.75 | 25.25 | 25.00 | 25.00 | 24.70 | 25.00 | 25.38 | 26.50 | 25.15 |
| 1995 | 25.50 | 25.50 | 25.50 | 25.50 | 25.13 | 25.10 | 24.75 | 24.75 | 25.50 | 25.75 | 28.13 | 28.85 | 25.83 |
| 1996[2] | 28.69 | 29.00 | 29.50 | 29.50 | 29.70 | 29.50 | 29.50 | 29.00 | 29.00 | 29.00 | 29.00 | | 29.22 |

[1] These are f.o.b. basis prices in bulk, not delivered prices. [2] Preliminary. *Source: Economic Research Service, U.S. Department of Agriculture*

## World Raw Sugar Price[1] In Cents Per Pound

| Year | Jan. | Feb. | Mar. | Apr. | May | June | July | Aug. | Sept. | Oct. | Nov. | Dec. | Average |
|---|---|---|---|---|---|---|---|---|---|---|---|---|---|
| 1985 | 3.59 | 3.66 | 3.78 | 3.37 | 2.77 | 2.74 | 3.15 | 4.35 | 5.14 | 5.01 | 5.53 | 5.37 | 4.04 |
| 1986 | 4.87 | 5.55 | 7.07 | 8.36 | 7.64 | 6.36 | 5.58 | 5.50 | 4.67 | 5.42 | 5.93 | 5.66 | 6.05 |
| 1987 | 6.47 | 7.32 | 7.51 | 6.64 | 6.71 | 6.40 | 6.03 | 5.57 | 5.79 | 6.60 | 7.28 | 8.25 | 6.71 |
| 1988 | 9.64 | 8.40 | 8.48 | 8.49 | 8.85 | 10.52 | 14.04 | 11.09 | 10.18 | 10.29 | 10.82 | 11.28 | 10.17 |
| 1989 | 6.69 | 10.49 | 11.54 | 12.14 | 11.93 | 12.63 | 14.01 | 13.96 | 14.13 | 14.42 | 15.02 | 13.52 | 12.79 |
| 1990 | 14.38 | 14.63 | 15.39 | 15.24 | 14.62 | 12.99 | 11.92 | 10.92 | 11.00 | 9.77 | 10.00 | 9.72 | 12.55 |
| 1991 | 8.88 | 8.57 | 9.22 | 8.55 | 7.88 | 9.37 | 10.26 | 9.45 | 9.39 | 9.10 | 8.79 | 9.03 | 9.04 |
| 1992 | 8.43 | 8.06 | 8.22 | 9.53 | 9.62 | 10.52 | 10.30 | 9.78 | 9.28 | 8.66 | 8.54 | 8.15 | 9.09 |
| 1993 | 8.27 | 8.61 | 10.75 | 11.30 | 11.87 | 10.35 | 9.60 | 9.30 | 9.52 | 10.27 | 10.10 | 10.47 | 10.03 |
| 1994 | 10.29 | 10.80 | 11.71 | 11.10 | 11.79 | 12.04 | 11.73 | 12.05 | 12.62 | 12.75 | 13.88 | 14.76 | 12.13 |
| 1995 | 14.87 | 14.43 | 14.58 | 13.63 | 13.49 | 13.99 | 13.46 | 13.75 | 12.72 | 11.94 | 11.96 | 12.40 | 13.44 |
| 1996[2] | 12.57 | 12.97 | 13.07 | 12.43 | 11.94 | 12.54 | 12.83 | 12.33 | 11.87 | 11.65 | 11.29 | | 12.64 |

[1] Contract No. 11 fob stowed Caribbean port, including Brazil, bulk spot price. [2] Preliminary. *Source: Economic Research Service, U.S. Department of Agriculture*

## Raw Sugar N.Y. Spot Price (C.I.F., Duty/Free Paid, Contract #12 & #14) In Cents Per Pound

| Year | Jan. | Feb. | Mar. | Apr. | May | June | July | Aug. | Sept. | Oct. | Nov. | Dec. | Average |
|---|---|---|---|---|---|---|---|---|---|---|---|---|---|
| 1985 | 20.72 | 20.38 | 20.91 | 20.97 | 21.09 | 21.27 | 21.23 | 20.59 | 19.51 | 18.68 | 18.89 | 19.89 | 20.34 |
| 1986 | 20.67 | 21.01 | 20.95 | 20.85 | 20.88 | 20.99 | 20.97 | 20.87 | 20.87 | 21.08 | 21.17 | 21.12 | 20.95 |
| 1987 | 21.50 | 21.76 | 21.76 | 21.81 | 22.01 | 22.06 | 22.07 | 21.88 | 21.88 | 21.69 | 21.75 | 21.76 | 21.83 |
| 1988 | 21.83 | 22.11 | 22.16 | 22.16 | 22.13 | 22.54 | 23.43 | 21.90 | 21.77 | 21.74 | 21.70 | 21.99 | 22.12 |
| 1989 | 21.88 | 22.07 | 22.12 | 22.30 | 22.45 | 22.99 | 23.56 | 23.57 | 23.50 | 23.14 | 23.24 | 22.84 | 22.81 |
| 1990 | 23.11 | 22.93 | 23.58 | 23.81 | 23.58 | 23.33 | 23.42 | 23.27 | 23.23 | 23.29 | 23.15 | 22.47 | 23.26 |
| 1991 | 21.86 | 21.42 | 21.46 | 21.23 | 21.29 | 21.42 | 21.25 | 21.83 | 22.06 | 21.76 | 21.75 | 21.50 | 21.57 |
| 1992 | 21.38 | 21.56 | 21.36 | 21.38 | 21.04 | 20.92 | 21.10 | 21.34 | 21.55 | 21.61 | 21.39 | 21.11 | 21.31 |
| 1993 | 20.76 | 21.16 | 21.56 | 21.76 | 21.36 | 21.42 | 21.89 | 21.85 | 21.97 | 21.80 | 21.87 | 22.00 | 21.62 |
| 1994 | 22.00 | 21.95 | 21.95 | 22.08 | 22.18 | 22.44 | 22.72 | 21.84 | 21.78 | 21.58 | 21.57 | 22.35 | 22.04 |
| 1995 | 22.65 | 22.69 | 22.46 | 22.76 | 23.10 | 23.09 | 24.47 | 23.18 | 23.21 | 22.67 | 22.60 | 22.63 | 22.96 |
| 1996[1] | 22.39 | 22.68 | 22.57 | 22.71 | 22.62 | 22.48 | 21.80 | 22.51 | 22.38 | 22.37 | 22.12 | | 22.42 |

[1] Preliminary. *Source: Economic Research Service, U.S. Department of Agriculture*

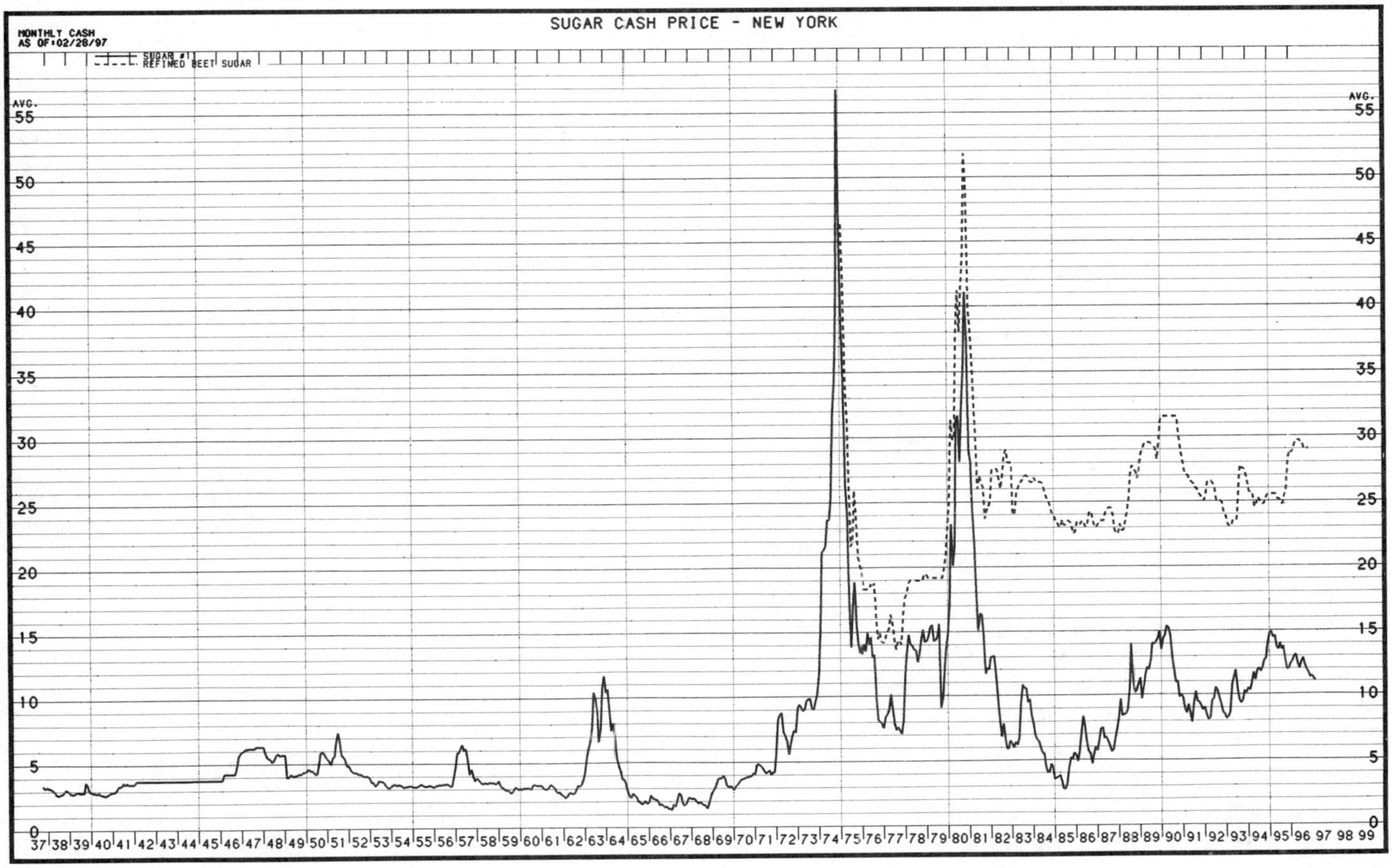

# SUGAR

## Centrifugal Sugar (Raw Value) Imported into Selected Countries  In Thousands of Metric Tons

| Year | Algeria | Canada | China | France | Germany | Iran | Israel | Rep. of Korea | Malaysia | Morocco | Nigeria | Russia[4] | Peru | United Kingdom | United States | World Total |
|---|---|---|---|---|---|---|---|---|---|---|---|---|---|---|---|---|
| 1988-9 | 650 | 711 | 2,462 | 382 | 630 | 650 | ----- | 1,109 | 797 | 283 | 400 | 5,300 | 126 | 1,429 | 1,753 | 28,671 |
| 1989-90 | 840 | 824 | 1,132 | 357 | 482 | 774 | 260 | 1,110 | 841 | 276 | 396 | 4,550 | 130 | 1,350 | 2,351 | 33,179 |
| 1990-1 | 990 | 1,109 | 1,055 | 343 | 209 | 875 | 280 | 1,233 | 900 | 350 | 480 | 3,580 | 237 | 1,143 | 2,619 | 32,558 |
| 1991-2 | 980 | 961 | 1,230 | 398 | 173 | 825 | 290 | 1,258 | 921 | 380 | 560 | 3,850 | 267 | 1,442 | 2,071 | 30,822 |
| 1992-3 | 980 | 1,095 | 506 | 487 | 154 | 780 | 300 | 1,233 | 900 | 408 | 430 | 3,500 | 305 | 1,352 | 1,827 | 29,605 |
| 1993-4 | 990 | 1,219 | 874 | 156 | 142 | 950 | 300 | 1,258 | 958 | 417 | 510 | 3,150 | 342 | 1,363 | 1,604 | 29,753 |
| 1994-5[1] | 990 | 1,020 | 3,500 | 361 | 181 | 800 | 300 | 1,345 | 1,030 | 455 | 460 | 2,700 | 368 | 1,261 | 1,664 | 30,532 |
| 1995-6[2] | 1,000 | 1,085 | 2,500 | 523 | 125 | 940 | 300 | 1,340 | 1,100 | 407 | 447 | 3,200 | 299 | 1,361 | 2,539 | 35,084 |
| 1996-7[3] | 1,000 | 1,130 | 2,600 | 553 | 150 | 1,100 | 320 | 1,350 | 1,190 | 480 | 500 | 3,300 | 270 | 1,260 | 2,741 | 35,475 |

[1] Preliminary. [2] Estimate. [3] Forecast. [4] Formerly part of the U.S.S.R.; data not reported separately until 1989-90. *Source: Foreign Agricultural Service, U.S. Department of Agriculture*

## Centrifugal Sugar (Raw Value) Exported from Selected Countries  In Thousands of Metric Tons

| Year | Australia | Brazil | Czech Republic[4] | Cuba | Dominican Republic | France | Germany | Mauritius | Mexico | Netherlands | Philippines | South Africa | Swaziland | Thailand | United Kingdom | World Total |
|---|---|---|---|---|---|---|---|---|---|---|---|---|---|---|---|---|
| 1988-9 | 2,860 | 1,371 | 140 | 7,420 | 550 | 2,804 | 1,264 | 690 | 410 | 446 | 210 | 900 | 428 | 3,004 | 366 | 28,671 |
| 1989-90 | 2,927 | 1,500 | 91 | 7,065 | 393 | 2,748 | 1,539 | 589 | 17 | 548 | 271 | 927 | 449 | 2,611 | 385 | 33,179 |
| 1990-1 | 2,819 | 1,300 | 133 | 6,800 | 328 | 2,751 | 1,857 | 621 | 285 | 538 | 286 | 757 | 469 | 2,741 | 255 | 32,558 |
| 1991-2 | 2,345 | 1,607 | 100 | 6,100 | 344 | 2,682 | 1,557 | 590 | 50 | 379 | 178 | 969 | 474 | 3,657 | 368 | 30,822 |
| 1992-3 | 3,476 | 2,425 | 95 | 3,800 | 327 | 2,822 | 1,607 | 621 | 0 | 523 | 253 | 123 | 409 | 2,332 | 300 | 29,605 |
| 1993-4 | 3,663 | 2,861 | 33 | 3,300 | 346 | 2,636 | 1,785 | 590 | 0 | 626 | 261 | 27 | 395 | 2,718 | 410 | 29,753 |
| 1994-5[1] | 4,321 | 4,300 | 33 | 2,600 | 295 | 3,004 | 1,417 | 508 | 235 | 291 | 150 | 369 | 296 | 3,809 | 263 | 30,532 |
| 1995-6[2] | 4,306 | 5,800 | 55 | 3,750 | 325 | 2,735 | 1,180 | 560 | 700 | 237 | 229 | 403 | 307 | 4,500 | 327 | 35,084 |
| 1996-7[3] | 4,580 | 5,750 | 50 | 3,700 | 310 | 2,730 | 1,430 | 600 | 300 | 255 | 300 | 1,100 | 290 | 4,500 | 388 | 35,475 |

[1] Preliminary. [2] Estimate. [3] Forecast. [4] Formerly part of Czechoslovakia.; data not reported separately until 1989-90. *Source: Foreign Agricultural Service, U.S. Department of Agriculture*

## United States Sugar (Cane & Beet) Supply and Utilization  In Thousands of Short Tons (Raw Value)

| | Supply: Production | | | Supply: Offshore Receipts | | | Supply | | Utilization | | | | Utilization: Domestic Disappearance | | |
|---|---|---|---|---|---|---|---|---|---|---|---|---|---|---|---|
| Year | Cane | Beet | Total | Foreign | Territories | Total | Beginning Stocks | Total Supply | Total Use | Exports | Net Changes in Invisible Stocks | Refining Loss Adjustment | In Polyhydric Alcohol[4] | Total | Per Capita |
| 1988-9 | 3,316 | 3,396 | 6,712 | 2,025 | 12 | 2,037 | 1,326 | 10,155 | 8,911 | 460 | 7 | 53 | 6 | 7,689 | 62.4 |
| 1989-90 | 3,157 | 3,466 | 6,623 | 2,568 | 0 | 2,568 | 1,244 | 10,503 | 9,279 | 561 | 53 | 7 | 10 | 7,933 | 63.7 |
| 1990-1 | 3,124 | 3,854 | 6,978 | 2,825 | 0 | 2,825 | 1,224 | 11,027 | 9,503 | 627 | -86 | 61 | 8 | 9,503 | 64.6 |
| 1991-2 | 3,641 | 3,845 | 7,486 | 2,194 | 0 | 2,194 | 1,524 | 11,024 | 9,547 | 554 | -13 | 0 | 11 | 9,547 | 64.4 |
| 1992-3 | 3,446 | 4,392 | 7,838 | 2,039 | 0 | 2,039 | 1,477 | 11,354 | 9,650 | 405 | 48 | 0 | 15 | 8,916 | 64.6 |
| 1993-4 | 3,565 | 4,090 | 7,655 | 1,772 | 0 | 1,772 | 1,704 | 11,131 | 9,794 | 454 | 7 | 0 | 15 | 9,794 | 66.1 |
| 1994-5[1] | 3,434 | 4,494 | 7,927 | 1,853 | 0 | 1,853 | 1,337 | 11,117 | 9,876 | 502 | 37 | 0 | 10 | 9,876 | 65.5 |
| 1995-6[2] | 3,454 | 3,916 | 7,370 | 2,860 | 0 | 2,860 | 1,241 | 11,491 | 10,100 | 400 | | 0 | 10 | 10,100 | 67.5 |
| 1996-7[3] | 3,130 | 4,000 | 7,130 | 3,021 | 0 | 3,021 | 1,391 | 11,462 | 10,025 | 200 | | 0 | 10 | 10,025 | 67.7 |

[1] Preliminary. [2] Estimate. [3] Forecast. [4] Includes feed use. *Source: Economic Research Service, U.S. Department of Agriculture*

## Sugar Cane for Sugar & Seed and Production of Cane Sugar and Molasses in the United States

| | | | Production (1,000 Tons) | | | | | Farm Value (1,000 Dollars) | | Sugar Production: Raw Value | | Sugar Production | Molasses Made (1,000 Gallons) | |
|---|---|---|---|---|---|---|---|---|---|---|---|---|---|---|
| Year | Acreage Harvested 1,000 Acres | Yield of Cane Per Havested Acre Net Tons | for Sugar | for Seed | Total | Sugar Yield Per Acre Short Tons | Farm Price $ Per Ton | of Cane Used for Sugar | of Cane Used for Sugar & Seed | Total 1,000 Tons | Per Ton of Cane Lbs. | Refined Basis 1,000 Tons | Edible | Total[3] |
| 1988 | 845 | 35.4 | 28,479 | 1,425 | 29,904 | 4.14 | 29.4 | 836,810 | 877,817 | 3,489 | 239 | 3,176 | 1,925 | 197,608 |
| 1989 | 852 | 34.5 | 28,069 | 1,357 | 29,426 | 3.83 | 29.2 | 819,057 | 857,678 | 3,244 | 226 | 2,967 | 1,990 | 197,732 |
| 1990 | 794 | 35.4 | 26,475 | 1,661 | 28,136 | 4.20 | 30.8 | 815,630 | 863,497 | 3,226 | 238 | 2,945 | 1,405 | 186,487 |
| 1991 | 897 | 33.7 | 28,960 | 1,292 | 30,252 | 3.95 | 29.0 | 840,194 | 876,479 | 3,497 | 237 | 3,206 | 1,825 | 193,117 |
| 1992 | 925 | 32.8 | 28,873 | 1,490 | 30,363 | 3.79 | 28.1 | 811,350 | 852,235 | 3,437 | 234 | 3,193 | 1,460 | 184,974 |
| 1993 | 924 | 32.8 | 29,652 | 1,449 | 31,101 | 3.82 | 28.5 | 846,132 | 886,285 | 3,532 | 235 | 3,351 | 1,480 | 198,167 |
| 1994[1] | 937 | 33.0 | 29,405 | 1,524 | 30,929 | 3.96 | 29.2 | 857,438 | 900,827 | 3,595 | | 3,308 | NA | 193,628 |
| 1995[1] | 932 | 33.0 | 29,155 | 1,641 | 30,796 | 3.90 | 29.4 | 857,157 | 906,956 | 3,489 | | | NA | 195,429 |
| 1996[2] | 888 | 32.9 | 27,511 | 1,713 | 29,224 | | | | | | | | | |

[1] Preliminary. [2] Estimate. [3] Excludes edible molasses. *Source: Economic Research Service, U.S. Department of Agriculture*

## U.S. Sugar Beets, Beet Sugar, Pulp & Molasses Produced from Sugar Beets & Raw Sugar Spot Prices

| Year of Harvest | Acreage: Planted (1,000 Acres) | Acreage: Harvested (1,000 Acres) | Yield Per Harvested Acre Tons | Production 1,000 Tons | Sugar Yield Per Acre Sh. Tons | Price[3] Dollars | Farm Value $1,000 | Sugar Production: Equivalent Raw Value[4] (1,000 Short Tons) | Sugar Production: Refined Basis (1,000 Short Tons) | Raw Sugar Prices: World[5] Refined #5 (Cents Per Pound) | Raw Sugar Prices: Cof., Sugar Exch. #11 World (Cents Per Pound) | Raw Sugar Prices: Cof., Sugar Exch. N.Y. Duty Paid (Cents Per Pound) | Wholesale List Price HFCS (42%) Midwest |
|---|---|---|---|---|---|---|---|---|---|---|---|---|---|
| 1987 | 1,267 | 1,252 | 22.4 | 28,072 | 3.19 | 38.20 | 1,073,584 | 3,998 | 3,736 | 8.75 | 6.71 | 21.83 | 16.50 |
| 1988 | 1,327 | 1,301 | 19.1 | 24,810 | 2.70 | 41.20 | 1,022,284 | 3,507 | 3,278 | 12.01 | 10.17 | 22.12 | 16.47 |
| 1989 | 1,324 | 1,295 | 19.4 | 25,131 | 2.66 | 42.10 | 1,058,298 | 3,442 | 3,217 | 17.15 | 12.79 | 22.81 | 19.24 |
| 1990 | 1,400 | 1,377 | 20.0 | 27,513 | 2.79 | 43.00 | 1,182,221 | 3,842 | 3,591 | 17.32 | 12.55 | 23.26 | 19.69 |
| 1991 | 1,427 | 1,412 | 20.3 | 28,203 | 2.68 | 38.50 | 1,085,728 | 3,729 | 3,485 | 13.41 | 9.04 | 21.57 | 20.93 |
| 1992 | 1,437 | 1,412 | 20.6 | 29,143 | 3.10 | 41.40 | 1,206,480 | 4,386 | 4,099 | 12.39 | 9.09 | 21.31 | 20.70 |
| 1993 | 1,438 | 1,409 | 18.6 | 26,249 | 2.87 | 38.50 | 1,023,687 | 4,047 | 3,792 | 12.79 | 10.03 | 21.62 | 18.83 |
| 1994 | 1,476 | 1,443 | 22.1 | 31,853 | 3.17 | 38.80 | 1,234,470 | 4,578 | 4,090 | 15.66 | 12.13 | 22.04 | 20.17 |
| 1995[1] | 1,445 | 1,417 | 19.8 | 28,026 | 2.78 | 38.10 | 1,070,663 | 3,944 | | 17.99 | 13.44 | 22.96 | 17.04 |
| 1996[2] | 1,424 | 1,324 | 20.2 | 26,761 | 2.92 | | | 3,900 | | | | | |

[1] Preliminary. [2] Estimate. [3] Includes support payments, but excludes Government sugar beet payments. [4] Refined sugar multiplies by the factor of 1.07. [5] F.O.B. Europe. *Source: Economic Research Service, U.S. Department of Agriculture*

## Sugar Deliveries and Stocks in the United States In Thousands of Short Tons (Raw Value)

| Year | Quota Allocation | Actual Imports | Deliveries by Primary Distributors: Cane Sugar Refineries | Deliveries: Beet Sugar Factories | Deliveries: Importers of Direct Consumption Sugar | Deliveries: Mainland Cane Sugar Mills[3] | Deliveries: Total Deliveries | Total Domestic Consumption | Stocks (January 1): Cane Sugar Refineries[4] | Stocks: Beet Sugar Factories | Stocks: Commodity Credit Corp. | Stocks: Refiners' Raw | Stocks: Mainland Cane Mills | Stocks: Total |
|---|---|---|---|---|---|---|---|---|---|---|---|---|---|---|
| 1987 | 1,003.4 | 997.1 | 4,454 | 3,656 | 18 | 4 | 8,131 | 8,897 | 211 | 1,304 | 177 | 516 | 830 | 3,038 |
| 1988 | 1,056.7 | 1,024.8 | 4,290 | 3,832 | 20 | 5 | 8,147 | 8,557 | 184 | 1,546 | 0 | 401 | 996 | 3,128 |
| 1989 | 3,093.1 | 2,995.8 | 4,764 | 3,449 | 76 | 6 | 8,295 | 8,952 | 187 | 1,372 | 0 | 487 | 1,008 | 3,053 |
| 1990 | 2,314.9 | 2,242.8 | 4,998 | 3,570 | 39 | 8 | 8,615 | 9,309 | 155 | 1,412 | 0 | 381 | 899 | 2,947 |
| 1991 | 1,526.7 | 1,477.0 | 4,786 | 3,713 | 30 | 11 | 8,540 | 9,470 | 168 | 1,327 | 0 | 371 | 812 | 2,729 |
| 1992 | 2,500.0 | 2,275.4 | 4,808 | 3,966 | 52 | 7 | 8,936 | 8,772 | 194 | 1,336 | 0 | 619 | 890 | 3,039 |
| 1993 | [5] | [5] | 4,781 | 4,087 | 52 | 10 | 9,064 | 9,577 | 183 | 1,640 | 0 | 507 | 895 | 3,225 |
| 1994 | [5] | [5] | 4,929 | 4,170 | 78 | NA | 9,321 | 9,813 | 218 | 1,696 | 0 | 438 | 1,160 | 3,512 |
| 1995[1] | 2,413.2 | 2,308.0 | 4,808 | 4,486 | 44 | NA | 9,451 | 9,971 | 185 | 1,594 | 6 | 448 | 906 | 3,139 |
| 1996[2] | 2,559.6 | | | | | | | | 192 | 1,383 | | 334 | 996 | 2,904 |

[1] Preliminary. [2] Estimate. [3] Sugar for direct consumption only. [4] Refined. [5] Combined with 1992. *Source: Economic Research Service, U.S. Department of Agriculture*

## Sugar, Refined--Delivered to End User in the U.S. In Thousands of Short Tons

| Year | Bakery & Cereal Products | Beverages | Confectionery[2] | Hotels, Restaurant & Institutions | Ice Cream & Dairy Products | Canned, Bottled & Frozen Foods | All Other Food Uses | Retail Grocers[3] | Wholesale Grocers[4] | Non-food Uses | Non-Industrial Uses | Industrial Uses | Total Deliveries |
|---|---|---|---|---|---|---|---|---|---|---|---|---|---|
| 1987 | 1,513 | 212 | 1,146 | 91 | 449 | 393 | 534 | 996 | 2,040 | 149 | 3,199 | 4,400 | 7,599 |
| 1988 | 1,541 | 237 | 1,107 | 89 | 394 | 354 | 529 | 940 | 2,200 | 121 | 3,316 | 4,283 | 7,614 |
| 1989 | 1,532 | 215 | 1,187 | 106 | 426 | 342 | 637 | 1,026 | 2,051 | 126 | 3,259 | 4,465 | 7,730 |
| 1990 | 1,608 | 228 | 1,279 | 108 | 462 | 332 | 642 | 1,077 | 2,130 | 109 | 3,391 | 4,660 | 8,051 |
| 1991 | 1,632 | 204 | 1,277 | 100 | 439 | 331 | 623 | 1,182 | 2,079 | 88 | 3,469 | 4,594 | 8,063 |
| 1992 | 1,719 | 164 | 1,246 | 101 | 429 | 315 | 649 | 1,230 | 2,104 | 69 | 3,668 | 4,591 | 8,259 |
| 1993 | 1,785 | 158 | 1,292 | 108 | 424 | 336 | 725 | 1,235 | 2,075 | 85 | 3,589 | 4,805 | 8,394 |
| 1994 | 1,952 | 156 | 1,313 | 93 | 453 | 322 | 704 | 1,269 | 2,039 | 77 | 3,598 | 4,977 | 8,575 |
| 1995[1] | 1,905 | 169 | 1,372 | 103 | 452 | 279 | 860 | 1,236 | 2,173 | 64 | 3,691 | 5,101 | 8,792 |

[1] Preliminary. [2] And related products. [3] Chain stores, supermarkets. [4] Jobbers, sugar dealers. *Source: Economic Research Service, U.S. Department of Agriculture*

## U.S. Deliveries[1] of All Sugar by Primary Distributors by Quarters In Thousands of Short Tons (Raw Value)

| Year | First Quarter | Second Quarter | Third Quarter | Fourth Quarter | Total | Year | First Quarter | Second Quarter | Third Quarter | Fourth Quarter | Total |
|---|---|---|---|---|---|---|---|---|---|---|---|
| 1985 | 1,909 | 1,972 | 2,150 | 2,044 | 8,035 | 1991 | 1,878 | 1,955 | 2,173 | 2,057 | 8,063 |
| 1986 | 1,819 | 1,907 | 2,069 | 1,991 | 7,786 | 1992 | 1,985 | 2,178 | 2,390 | 2,273 | 8,826 |
| 1987 | 1,908 | 2,001 | 2,146 | 2,112 | 8,167 | 1993 | 2,039 | 2,172 | 2,432 | 2,277 | 8,920 |
| 1988 | 1,951 | 1,983 | 2,147 | 2,107 | 8,183 | 1994 | 2,121 | 2,265 | 2,533 | 2,222 | 9,141 |
| 1989 | 1,923 | 2,051 | 2,181 | 2,185 | 8,340 | 1995 | 2,093 | 2,308 | 2,536 | 2,379 | 9,316 |
| 1990 | 1,837 | 1,911 | 2,154 | 2,149 | 8,051 | 1996[2] | 2,191 | 2,355 | 2,501 | | 7,047 |

[1] Includes for domestic consumption and for export. [2] Preliminary. *Source: Economic Research Service, U.S. Department of Agriculture*

# SUGAR

## Average Open Interest of World Sugar (#11) Futures in New York In Contracts

| Year | Jan. | Feb. | Mar. | Apr. | May | June | July | Aug. | Sept. | Oct. | Nov. | Dec. |
|---|---|---|---|---|---|---|---|---|---|---|---|---|
| 1986 | 92,744 | 92,403 | 106,334 | 113,717 | 100,925 | 93,288 | 85,582 | 87,092 | 90,033 | 82,403 | 86,598 | 90,652 |
| 1987 | 98,697 | 103,115 | 95,910 | 93,886 | 96,153 | 98,463 | 97,889 | 98,401 | 100,395 | 99,286 | 103,205 | 126,916 |
| 1988 | 147,508 | 147,629 | 132,539 | 133,524 | 137,472 | 167,829 | 159,071 | 137,351 | 135,121 | 115,138 | 119,873 | 144,931 |
| 1989 | 123,554 | 126,504 | 146,798 | 157,254 | 146,878 | 162,097 | 186,211 | 179,077 | 168,840 | 152,276 | 171,354 | 164,757 |
| 1990 | 164,235 | 160,509 | 163,155 | 168,962 | 170,351 | 161,320 | 133,208 | 121,665 | 112,065 | 109,986 | 110,047 | 108,939 |
| 1991 | 124,637 | 129,361 | 114,432 | 115,704 | 110,142 | 105,607 | 106,406 | 107,852 | 102,546 | 91,649 | 90,976 | 93,827 |
| 1992 | 96,255 | 105,166 | 93,774 | 109,137 | 95,101 | 106,310 | 96,038 | 87,089 | 77,740 | 69,023 | 74,292 | 93,039 |
| 1993 | 91,426 | 105,147 | 123,023 | 115,400 | 112,085 | 101,843 | 94,296 | 94,932 | 91,312 | 92,832 | 96,246 | 99,592 |
| 1994 | 108,936 | 123,148 | 137,582 | 115,060 | 117,030 | 126,843 | 106,749 | 118,057 | 141,361 | 140,011 | 171,843 | 191,801 |
| 1995 | 186,893 | 167,451 | 149,027 | 152,600 | 127,978 | 121,877 | 114,027 | 119,787 | 114,069 | 119,561 | 140,008 | 157,779 |
| 1996 | 156,047 | 159,563 | 150,093 | 142,773 | 137,897 | 148,447 | 144,527 | 153,845 | 153,202 | 144,830 | 150,866 | 150,573 |

*Source: Coffee, Sugar & Cocoa Exchange, Inc. (CSCE)*

## Volume of Trading of World Sugar (#11) Futures in New York In Contracts

| Year | Jan. | Feb. | Mar. | Apr. | May | June | July | Aug. | Sept. | Oct. | Nov. | Dec. | Total |
|---|---|---|---|---|---|---|---|---|---|---|---|---|---|
| 1986 | 308,044 | 268,053 | 382,053 | 519,027 | 343,746 | 289,900 | 281,124 | 235,555 | 328,830 | 258,744 | 173,612 | 195,126 | 3,583,814 |
| 1987 | 387,630 | 381,393 | 323,047 | 381,972 | 278,857 | 313,001 | 248,133 | 235,263 | 367,074 | 331,052 | 268,226 | 337,851 | 3,853,499 |
| 1988 | 603,565 | 605,773 | 348,510 | 391,971 | 474,693 | 705,498 | 807,381 | 422,101 | 450,116 | 276,010 | 332,463 | 381,040 | 5,819,121 |
| 1989 | 499,199 | 520,018 | 575,486 | 600,852 | 557,386 | 660,521 | 624,969 | 517,295 | 526,834 | 328,469 | 456,485 | 375,927 | 6,243,361 |
| 1990 | 519,886 | 523,591 | 588,021 | 505,492 | 598,320 | 532,937 | 384,116 | 441,608 | 448,195 | 372,925 | 303,065 | 206,645 | 5,424,801 |
| 1991 | 313,915 | 510,163 | 388,672 | 477,954 | 286,120 | 534,639 | 309,836 | 352,351 | 366,007 | 240,812 | 253,201 | 234,876 | 4,268,546 |
| 1992 | 376,704 | 395,793 | 255,501 | 583,535 | 246,360 | 454,854 | 264,528 | 275,677 | 334,962 | 163,263 | 168,470 | 147,844 | 3,667,481 |
| 1993 | 330,474 | 481,506 | 507,370 | 518,292 | 415,283 | 390,261 | 255,581 | 307,181 | 368,194 | 222,082 | 272,579 | 217,142 | 4,285,945 |
| 1994 | 289,593 | 486,222 | 360,787 | 472,388 | 407,343 | 443,002 | 252,012 | 349,079 | 471,899 | 316,330 | 484,943 | 387,620 | 4,719,218 |
| 1995 | 591,861 | 489,274 | 472,519 | 478,757 | 352,000 | 485,131 | 298,756 | 402,358 | 360,086 | 246,584 | 278,906 | 254,850 | 4,711,082 |
| 1996 | 550,780 | 544,514 | 341,940 | 526,255 | 384,302 | 496,745 | 279,707 | 290,732 | 562,082 | 264,290 | 203,921 | 306,584 | 4,751,852 |

*Source: Coffee, Sugar & Cocoa Exchange, Inc. (CSCE)*

# Sulfur

Elemental sulfur is used in the synthesis of sulfur compounds. It finds use in construction where it is added to concrete to aide in corrosion resistance, and it is added to asphalt for highway construction.

According to the U.S. Geological Survey, U.S. production of sulfur in July 1996 was 860,000 tonnes. Production of sulfur from petroleum, including coking operations, was 433,000 tonnes during the month while production from natural gas, including Frasch producers, was 427,000 tonnes. For the January-July 1996 period, production of sulfur from petroleum operations was 3.03 million tonnes, a decline of 4 percent from the same period of 1995. Sulfur production from natural gas operations in the first seven months of 1996 was 2.96 million tonnes, an increase of 6 percent. Total sulfur production, including that of Frasch producers, was 6 million tonnes, a decline of 13 percent from the same period of 1995. For all of 1995, sulfur production was 10.4 million tonnes with 7 percent from Frasch producers, 48 percent from petroleum operations, and 44 percent from natural gas operations.

U.S. imports of sulfur in June 1996 were 122,000 tonnes. For January-June 1996, U.S. imports were 827,000 tonnes, down 23 percent from the same period in 1995. In the first half of 1996, 571,000 tonnes of sulfur were supplied by Canada and 202,000 tonnes by Mexico. For all of 1995, U.S. imports of sulfur were 2.2 million tonnes with 76 percent supplied by Canada and 23 percent by Mexico.

U.S. consumption of sulfur in June 1996 was 761,000 tonnes. Of the total, domestic sources provided 639,000 tonnes and imports 122,000 tonnes. For the first six months of 1996, U.S. sulfur consumption was 5.52 million tonnes with 4.7 million tonnes from domestic sources and 827,000 tonnes from imports. For all of 1995, U.S. sulfur consumption was 12 million tonnes with 9.8 million tonnes from domestic sources and 2.2 million tonnes from imports.

### World Production of Sulfur (All Forms) In Thousands of Metric Tons

| Year | Canada | China | Finland | France | Germany | Iraq | Italy | Japan | Mexico | Poland | Romania | Russia[3] | Saudi Arabia | Spain | Ukraine[3] | United States | World Total |
|---|---|---|---|---|---|---|---|---|---|---|---|---|---|---|---|---|---|
| 1988 | 6,908 | 4,750 | 600 | 1,181 | 2,153 | 1,185 | 618 | 2,432 | 2,378 | 5,200 | 750 | 10,765 | 1,378 | 1,177 | ------ | 10,746 | 59,160 |
| 1989 | 6,600 | 5,170 | 527 | 1,036 | 1,701 | 1,330 | 640 | 2,559 | 2,372 | 5,137 | 725 | 9,900 | 1,423 | 1,211 | ------ | 11,592 | 58,924 |
| 1990 | 6,790 | 5,370 | 636 | 1,049 | 1,550 | 1,180 | 587 | 2,630 | 2,413 | 4,902 | 660 | 9,025 | 1,435 | 1,147 | ------ | 11,560 | 57,800 |
| 1991 | 7,130 | 5,910 | 636 | 1,200 | 1,282 | 300 | 480 | 2,626 | 2,094 | 4,104 | 600 | 8,100 | 2,000 | 905 | ------ | 10,820 | 54,600 |
| 1992 | 7,487 | 5,900 | 607 | 1,150 | 1,164 | 350 | 470 | 2,745 | 2,300 | 3,087 | 585 | 3,500 | 2,370 | 860 | 1,200 | 10,663 | 50,700 |
| 1993 | 8,430 | 6,360 | 607 | 1,260 | 1,171 | 450 | 475 | 2,922 | 1,640 | 2,119 | 580 | 3,600 | 2,400 | 687 | 1,000 | 10,959 | 51,300 |
| 1994[1] | 8,850 | 6,900 | ----- | 1,180 | 1,240 | 475 | 500 | 2,820 | 2,890 | 2,435 | ----- | 3,510 | 2,300 | 702 | 1,000 | 11,500 | 54,100 |
| 1995[2] | 9,010 | 6,530 | ----- | 1,100 | 1,230 | 475 | ----- | 2,860 | 2,880 | 2,440 | ----- | 4,000 | 2,200 | 702 | ------ | 11,800 | 54,300 |

[1] Preliminary. [2] Estimate. [3] Formerly part of the U.S.S.R.; data not reported separately until 1992. *Source: U.S. Geological Survey (USGS)*

### Salient Statistics of Sulfur in the United States In Thousands of Metric Tons (Sulfur Content)

| | Production of | | | | | | | | | | Apparent | Sales Value of Shipments F.O.B. Mine/Plant | | |
|---|---|---|---|---|---|---|---|---|---|---|---|---|---|---|
| | Elemental Sulfur | | | | | | | | | | | | | |
| | Native - Sulfur[3] - | Recovered | | | By-product | Other Sulf. Acid | Production | Imports | Exports | Producer | Con-sumption | Frasch | Recovered | Average |
| Year | Frasch | Petroleum & Coke | Natural Gas | Total | Sulfuric Acid[4] | Com-pounds | (All Forms) | Sulfuric Acid[4] | Sulfuric Acid[4] | Stocks, Dec. 31[5] | (All Forms) | $ Per Tonne | | |
| 1988 | 3,174 | 3,941 | 2,503 | 6,444 | 1,125 | 3 | 10,746 | 1,996 | 147 | 1,112 | 12,712 | 99.24 | 77.03 | 85.95 |
| 1989 | 3,888 | 3,971 | 2,539 | 6,510 | 1,190 | 4 | 11,592 | 2,260 | 146 | 1,301 | 12,685 | 100.18 | 78.70 | 86.62 |
| 1990 | 3,726 | 4,199 | 2,337 | 6,536 | 1,294 | 4 | 11,560 | 2,571 | 162 | 1,423 | 13,056 | 91.17 | 73.89 | 80.14 |
| 1991 | 2,869 | 4,243 | 2,402 | 6,645 | 1,302 | 4 | 10,820 | 3,020 | 149 | 1,194 | 12,932 | 87.05 | 64.17 | 71.45 |
| 1992 | 2,320 | 4,524 | 2,524 | 7,048 | 1,292 | 3 | 10,663 | 2,725 | 139 | 809 | 12,747 | 58.15 | 44.47 | 48.14 |
| 1993 | 1,904 | 4,820 | 2,905 | 7,725 | 1,430 | 3 | 11,100 | 2,440 | 145 | 1,382 | 12,600 | 51.60 | 25.06 | 31.86 |
| 1994[1] | 2,960 | 4,930 | 2,240 | 7,160 | 1,390 | | 11,500 | 2,130 | 140 | 1,160 | 13,100 | W | W | 28.60 |
| 1995[2] | 3,150 | 5,040 | 2,210 | 7,250 | 1,400 | | 11,800 | 1,920 | 170 | 583 | 14,300 | W | W | 43.74 |

[1] Preliminary. [2] Estimate. [3] Or sulfur ore. [4] Basis 100% $H_2SO_4$, sulfur equivalent. [5] Frasch & recovered. W = Withheld. *Source: U.S. Geological Survey*

### Sulfur Consumption & Foreign Trade of the United States In Thousands of Metric Tons (Sulfur Content)

| | Consumption | | | Sulfuric Acid Sold or Used, by End Use[2] | | | | | | Foreign Trade | | | | | |
|---|---|---|---|---|---|---|---|---|---|---|---|---|---|---|---|
| | | | | | | | | | | Exports | | | Imports | | |
| Year | Native Sulfur (Frasch) | Re-covered Sulfur | Total Elemental Form | Total Sulfuric Acid | Pulpmills & Paper Products | Inorganic Chem-icals[3] | Synthetic Rubber & Plastic | Pho-sphatic Fertilizers | Petro-leum Refining[4] | Frasch | Re-covered | Value Thous. $ | Frasch | Re-covered | Value Thous. $ |
| 1988 | 4,956 | 6,628 | 11,584 | 12,334 | 280 | 435 | 339 | 8,404 | 786 | 464 | 759 | 131,863 | 1,079 | 917 | 185,864 |
| 1989 | 4,536 | 6,955 | 11,491 | 12,563 | 320 | 423 | 383 | 8,642 | 683 | 330 | 694 | 107,126 | 1,086 | 1,174 | 209,465 |
| 1990 | 4,457 | 7,301 | 11,758 | 12,600 | 290 | 653 | 273 | 8,664 | 400 | 348 | 624 | 109,327 | 1,129 | 1,442 | 206,450 |
| 1991 | 3,931 | 7,694 | 11,625 | 12,842 | 279 | 901 | 272 | 8,311 | 383 | 448 | 748 | 119,713 | 1,259 | 1,760 | 241,749 |
| 1992 | 3,083 | 8,368 | 11,451 | 12,340 | 296 | 617 | 278 | 8,300 | 385 | 362 | 604 | 69,662 | 845 | 1,877 | 129,894 |
| 1993 | 1,331 | 9,046 | 10,377 | 11,886 | 304 | 549 | 259 | 7,906 | 388 | 246 | 656 | 39,726 | 100 | 2,070 | 49,800 |
| 1994 | W | 11,100 | 11,100 | 11,300 | 295 | 448 | 256 | 8,040 | 236 | ---- | 899 | 48,400 | ---- | 1,650 | 62,000 |
| 1995[1] | W | 12,300 | 12,300 | 10,300 | 306 | 283 | 244 | 8,200 | 236 | ---- | 906 | 66,200 | ---- | 2,510 | 143,000 |

[1] Preliminary. [2] Sulfur equivalent. [3] Including inorganic pigments, paints & allied products, and other inorganic chemicals & products. [4] Including other petroleum and coal products. NA = Not available. W = Withheld. *Source: U.S. Geological Survey (USGS)*

# Sunflowerseed, Meal, and Oil

World sunflowerseed production is a fifth of soybean's total, but the protein meal that is derived from the oilseed totals about 10 percent that of soybeans. However, unlike soybeans for which most of the crop is crushed for meal, sunflowerseed yields nearly equal amounts of meal and oil.

The U.S. produces only about 6 percent of global production, but has a larger role in the world export market. World production in 1996/97 of 23.7 million metric tons was slightly higher than expected, but trailed the 1995/96 record of 25.8 million tons. Argentina is the largest producer with a 1996/97 crop of 5.6 million tonnes, down slightly from the record 1995/96 crop of 5.9 million tons. Initial estimates for Argentina's 1997/98 crop are 4.5 million tons, the decline reflecting lower acreage. Russia, once the largest producer, forecast 3.4 million tons in 1996/97 vs. 4.2 million in 1995/96; production in the EU in 1996/97 of 3.8 million tons compares with 3.2 million, respectively.

The acreage planted to sunflowerseed production in the U.S. shows an irregular pattern, as does average yield. A record 5.6 million acres were planted in 1979, falling to an average of 2 million by 1986, rising to 3.5 million in 1994 and 1995, then dropping to 2.8 million in 1996. The Dakotas, notably North Dakota, are the largest producing states, accounting for about two-thirds of total production.

U.S. sunflowerseed meal production in 1996/97 (October/September) of 426,000 metric tons compares with 435,000 in 1995/96 and 660,000 tons in 1994/95. Meal carryin supplies are small, 5,000 tons for 1996/97, unchanged from a year earlier. Disappearance in 1996/97 of 431,000 tons compares with 436,000 in 1995/96, of which about 9 percent will be exported. Sunflowerseed oil production in 1996/97 of 346,000 tons compares with 351,000 in 1995/96 and 528,000 in 1994/95. However, unlike meal, most of U.S. sunflowerseed oil production is exported; 280,000 tons in 1996/97, about unchanged from 1995/96 and well under the record large 444,000 in 1994/95. Domestic oil use has recently hovered around 70,000 tons. Carryin oil stocks for 1996/97 of 43,000 tons compares with 37,000 a year earlier. U.S. sunflowerseed oil exports are dependent on a number of variables including the fact that some countries, like Mexico, have a preference for sunflowerseed oil. The U.S. also exports sunflowerseed, much of it going to the European Union. Seed exports of 188,000 tons in 1996/97 compare with 209,000 in 1995/96.

The 1996/97 sunflowerseed oil price was forecast at $530-575.00 per metric ton vs. $559.00 in 1995/96, basis average crude Minneapolis. The sunflowerseed meal price was forecast to range from $130-152.00 per metric ton vs. $136.00 in 1995/96, basis 28 percent protein.

The foreign oil price for 1995/96 averaged $312.00 per metric ton, basis Rotterdam vs. with $309 the year before; for protein meal the average of $151 compares with $103, respectively.

## World Production of Sunflowerseed In Thousands of Metric Tons

| Crop Year | Argentina | Australia | Bulgaria | Myanmar (Burma) | China | France | Hungary | India | Romania | South Africa | Spain | Turkey | United States | Former U.S.S.R. | Yugoslavia | World Total |
|---|---|---|---|---|---|---|---|---|---|---|---|---|---|---|---|---|
| 1992-3 | 3,100 | 70 | 595 | 87 | 1,473 | 2,110 | 765 | 1,185 | 774 | 250 | 1,343 | 950 | 1,181 | 5,734 | 440 | 21,642 |
| 1993-4 | 4,010 | 127 | 442 | 96 | 1,340 | 1,643 | 702 | 1,400 | 696 | 362 | 1,309 | 815 | 1,167 | 5,230 | 460 | 21,390 |
| 1994-5 | 5,900 | 128 | 596 | 115 | 1,367 | 2,053 | 664 | 1,204 | 764 | 352 | 979 | 740 | 2,194 | 4,612 | 380 | 24,020 |
| 1995-6[1] | 5,552 | 87 | 655 | 105 | 1,269 | 1,993 | 785 | 1,270 | 946 | 546 | 575 | 830 | 1,819 | 7,390 | 365 | 25,975 |
| 1996-7[2] | 5,000 | 152 | 475 | | 1,320 | 2,000 | 882 | 1,300 | 1,170 | 755 | 1,174 | 730 | 1,491 | 5,570 | 460 | 24,450 |

[1] Preliminary. [2] Forecast. *Source: The Oil World*

## Sunflowerseed Statistics in the United States In Thousands of Metric Tons

| Crop Year Beginning September | Harvested Acres 1,000 | Harvested Yield Per Cwt. | Farm Price $ Per Metric Ton | Value of Production Mil. $ | Supply: Stocks, Sept. 1 | Supply: Production | Supply: Imports | Supply: Total | Disappearance: Crush | Disappearance: Exports | Disappearance: Non-Oil Use & Seed | Disappearance: Total |
|---|---|---|---|---|---|---|---|---|---|---|---|---|
| 1992-3 | 2,043 | 12.55 | 215 | 254.3 | 262 | 1,163 | 47 | 1,472 | 923 | 118 | 363 | 1,404 |
| 1993-4 | 2,486 | 10.35 | 284 | 332.0 | 69 | 1,167 | 25 | 1,261 | 661 | 99 | 429 | 1,189 |
| 1994-5 | 3,430 | 14.10 | 236 | 512.8 | 71 | 2,194 | 42 | 2,306 | 1,313 | 287 | 604 | 2,203 |
| 1995-6[1] | 3,368 | 11.90 | 254 | 457.6 | 103 | 1,819 | 21 | 1,943 | 915 | 224 | 598 | 1,737 |
| 1996-7[2] | 2,499 | 14.35 | 249-267 | 405.4 | 205 | 1,627 | 23 | 1,855 | 821 | 163 | 651 | 1,635 |

[1] Preliminary. [2] Forecast. *Source: Economic Research Service, U.S. Department of Agriculture*

## Sunflowerseed Product Statistics in the United States In Thousands of Metric Tons

| Crop Year Beginning October | Sunflower Oil — Supply: Stocks, Oct. 1 | Supply: Production | Supply: Total[3] | Disappearance: Exports | Disappearance: Domestic | Disappearance: Total | Price $ Per Metric Ton[4] | Sunflower Meal — Supply: Stocks, Oct. 1 | Supply: Production | Supply: Total[3] | Disappearance: Exports | Disappearance: Domestic | Disappearance: Total | Price $ Per Metric Ton 28% Protein |
|---|---|---|---|---|---|---|---|---|---|---|---|---|---|---|
| 1992-3 | 45 | 331 | 376 | 266 | 85 | 351 | 558 | 6 | 440 | 451 | 48 | 401 | 449 | 98 |
| 1993-4 | 25 | 263 | 292 | 204 | 59 | 262 | 683 | 2 | 327 | 331 | 37 | 291 | 328 | 104 |
| 1994-5 | 29 | 528 | 558 | 444 | 78 | 521 | 622 | 5 | 653 | 660 | 89 | 566 | 655 | 72 |
| 1995-6[1] | 37 | 370 | 406 | 285 | 56 | 341 | 560 | 5 | 458 | 464 | 25 | 434 | 459 | 136 |
| 1996-7[2] | 67 | 328 | 396 | 285 | 66 | 351 | 512-545 | 5 | 408 | 417 | 36 | 376 | 412 | 119-135 |

[1] Preliminary. [2] Forecast. [3] Includes imports. [4] Crude at Minneapolis. *Source: Economic Research Service, U.S. Department of Agriculture*

# Tall Oil

Tall oil is the major by-product of the kraft or sulfate processing of pinewood. After the lumber is pulped, the resulting liquor concentrate is skimmed. These skimmings are then acidified to produce crude tall oil.

Crude tall oil contains 40-50 percent fatty acids; and 5-10 percent sterols, alcohols, and other neutral components. When distilled, these resins and fatty acids are consumed in alkyd and synthetic resins, lubricants, adhesives, soaps and detergents, linoleum, flotation agents, and water proofing agents.

The U.S. Department of Commerce, Bureau of Census, reported that U.S. tall oil production in the October-December 1995 quarter was 317.6 million pounds, down 1 percent from the comparable quarter of 1994. For the 1994-95 marketing year (October-September), U.S. crude tall oil production was 1.26 billion pounds. Over the previous five years, crude tall oil production averaged 1.35 billion pounds.

U.S. tall oil consumption in inedible products in calendar year 1995 was 1.14 billion pounds or 95 million pounds per month. Consumption in 1995 was down 17 percent from 1994. Over the last five years, U.S. consumption averaged 1.04 billion pounds. The inedible products tall oil is used in are resin and plastics, soap, paint, varnish, lubricants, and fatty acids. The majority of the use is in fatty acid production.

Stocks of tall oil on December 1, 1995 were 106.3 million pounds, down 12 percent from the stocks on November 1, 1995. Stocks of crude tall oil on December 1, 1995 were 100.3 million pounds, down 11 percent from the previous month. Refined tall oil stocks were 6 million pounds.

## U.S. Tall Oil Consumption in Inedible Products In Millions of Pounds

| Year | Jan. | Feb. | Mar. | Apr. | May | June | July | Aug. | Sept. | Oct. | Nov. | Dec. | Total |
|---|---|---|---|---|---|---|---|---|---|---|---|---|---|
| 1990 | 100.4 | 105.9 | 91.2 | 86.5 | 86.5 | 84.6 | 78.5 | 82.4 | 69.1 | 69.7 | 78.4 | 78.2 | 1,017 |
| 1991 | ------- | 249.1 | ------- | ------- | 237.3 | ------- | ------- | 223.1 | ------- | ------- | 230.5 | ------- | 940 |
| 1992 | 77.8 | 7.5 | 73.2 | 67.6 | 77.8 | 74.8 | 71.5 | 78.4 | 77.1 | 78.9 | 63.8 | 69.2 | 884 |
| 1993 | 68.6 | 64.8 | 73.1 | 68.1 | 76.3 | 68.8 | 79.0 | 78.1 | 78.0 | 75.4 | 78.4 | 83.2 | 892 |
| 1994 | 117.4 | 98.8 | 124.0 | 118.4 | 115.0 | 118.8 | 106.8 | 114.9 | 119.8 | 113.7 | 101.9 | 113.0 | 1,363 |
| 1995 | 99.8 | 93.6 | 96.9 | 95.8 | 87.3 | 96.5 | 93.1 | 102.3 | 89.4 | 91.6 | 100.5 | 88.9 | 1,136 |
| 1996[1] | 93.1 | 103.4 | 89.2 | 104.1 | 100.5 | 96.6 | 85.4 | 100.7 | 94.9 | 111.5 | 101.4 | 98.8 | 1,180 |

[1] Preliminary. *Source: Bureau of Census, U.S. Department of Commerce*

## Tall Oil Production in the United States In Millions of Pounds

| Crop Year | | Oct. | Nov. | Dec. | Jan. | Feb. | Mar. | Apr. | May | June | July | Aug. | Sept. | Total |
|---|---|---|---|---|---|---|---|---|---|---|---|---|---|---|
| 1990-1 | Crude | 120.8 | 119.1 | 126.5 | ------- | 389.5 | ------- | ------- | 362.4 | ------- | ------- | 375.0 | ------- | 1,469.6 |
| | Refined | 5.6 | 6.2 | 4.2 | ------- | 15.7 | ------- | ------- | 15.3 | ------- | ------- | 17.6 | ------- | 64.6 |
| 1991-2 | Crude | ------- | 342.7 | ------- | 131.4 | 121.5 | 131.2 | 133.2 | 121.9 | 129.8 | 130.6 | 129.9 | 119.7 | 1,372.2 |
| | Refined | ------- | 15.7 | ------- | 5.4 | 5.6 | 6.2 | W | W | W | W | W | W | W |
| 1992-3 | Crude | 120.2 | 114.7 | 122.7 | 119.4 | 128.4 | 142.1 | 131.8 | 120.0 | 126.6 | 117.0 | 104.3 | 117.3 | 1,347.2 |
| 1993-4 | Crude | 107.5 | 120.7 | 124.6 | 127.0 | 115.4 | 148.1 | 131.0 | 119.1 | 109.1 | 108.7 | 110.8 | 117.4 | 1,322.0 |
| 1994-5 | Crude | 111.1 | 114.5 | 115.1 | 108.3 | 108.1 | 123.0 | 111.1 | 116.5 | 118.2 | 116.4 | 119.2 | 102.9 | 1,261.6 |
| 1995-6[1] | Crude | 109.8 | 105.2 | 105.2 | 115.5 | 123.3 | 126.9 | 108.9 | 120.3 | 120.3 | 120.5 | 124.9 | 112.9 | 1,281.0 |
| 1996-7[1] | Crude | 119.2 | 113.9 | 114.5 | 124.1 | | | | | | | | | 471.7 |

[1] Preliminary. W = Withheld proprietary data. *Source: Bureau of Census, U.S. Department of Commerce*

## Tall Oil Stocks in the United States In Millions of Pounds

| Crop Year | | Oct. 1 | Nov. 1 | Dec. 1 | Jan. 1 | Feb. 1 | Mar. 1 | Apr. 1 | May 1 | June 1 | July 1 | Aug. 1 | Sept. 1 |
|---|---|---|---|---|---|---|---|---|---|---|---|---|---|
| 1990-1 | Crude | 101.5 | 83.1 | 76.6 | ------- | 144.5 | ------- | ------- | 119.8 | ------- | ------- | 140.4 | ------- |
| | Refined | 15.3 | 34.0 | 35.8 | ------- | 29.7 | ------- | ------- | 30.2 | ------- | ------- | 33.9 | ------- |
| 1991-2 | Crude | ------- | 139.1 | ------- | 188.9 | 153.9 | 163.1 | 163.2 | 156.9 | 158.4 | 161.0 | 190.7 | 186.1 |
| | Refined | ------- | 36.0 | ------- | 35.0 | 35.0 | 35.7 | 36.2 | 13.5 | 16.1 | 15.2 | 15.9 | 28.4 |
| 1992-3 | Crude | 173.3 | 167.5 | 143.7 | 137.8 | 162.5 | 170.8 | 184.7 | 187.3 | 165.3 | 179.2 | 173.1 | 149.9 |
| | Refined | 17.4 | 18.1 | 13.8 | 14.1 | 14.0 | 12.6 | 13.7 | 9.4 | 7.7 | 7.3 | 7.5 | 7.2 |
| 1993-4 | Crude | 132.8 | 124.0 | 113.0 | 103.7 | 109.5 | 109.7 | 118.2 | 124.4 | 112.6 | 105.3 | 101.1 | 97.5 |
| | Refined | 7.0 | 7.5 | 8.5 | 10.7 | 13.7 | 13.5 | 13.5 | 12.0 | 10.2 | 9.7 | 11.6 | 10.9 |
| 1994-5 | Crude | 86.3 | 82.7 | 94.1 | 104.1 | 107.6 | 117.2 | 123.4 | 132.1 | 118.1 | 132.3 | 134.7 | 135.0 |
| | Refined | 12.0 | 14.4 | 16.3 | 13.5 | 15.4 | 14.1 | 11.7 | 10.8 | 10.2 | 10.0 | 9.9 | 8.9 |
| 1995-6[1] | Crude | 120.9 | 117.5 | 112.9 | 100.7 | 105.7 | 120.3 | 146.0 | 131.8 | 127.0 | 130.5 | 138.7 | 147.3 |
| | Refined | 10.1 | 11.6 | 7.9 | 6.0 | 7.9 | 9.7 | 8.5 | 10.4 | 8.5 | 6.0 | 6.1 | 7.2 |
| 1996-7[1] | Crude | 172.3 | 192.1 | 167.4 | 182.4 | 173.0 | | | | | | | |
| | Refined | 8.3 | 7.0 | 7.5 | 8.9 | 6.4 | | | | | | | |

[1] Preliminary. *Source: Bureau of Census, U.S. Department of Commerce*

# Tallow and Greases

According to the USDA, U.S. edible tallow stocks on August 1, 1996 were 40 million pounds. This was down from 43 million pounds at the end of July and 48 million pounds a year ago. At the beginning of the marketing year on October 1, 1995, edible tallow stocks were 52 million pounds.

For August 1996, U.S. production of edible tallow was estimated at 115 million pounds, down 10 percent from production in July of 128 million pounds. For the October 1995 to August 1996 period, tallow production totaled 1.4 billion pounds or about 127 million pounds per month. Minor amounts of tallow were imported, usually about 10 million pounds per year. For the period October 1995 to August 1996, the U.S. supply of edible tallow was estimated at 1.5 billion pounds.

In terms of use, tallow and grease are used in a wide variety of cooking situations including baking. Per capita domestic use of edible tallow has been estimated at just under 5 pounds. Use of edible tallow in food products has been on the increase and that may in part be due to the increase in consumption of fried foods like french fries. The USDA estimates that in July 1996, domestic use of tallow was 113 million pounds, down from 115 million pounds in June. For the October 1995 to July 1996 period, U.S. consumption of edible tallow was estimated at 1.1 billion pounds. For all of 1994/95 tallow consumption was 1.3 billion pounds.

The USDA reported that for July 1996, U.S. exports of tallow were 18 million pounds which compared with 16 million pounds in June 1996. For the period of October 1995 to July 1996, U.S. tallow exports were 201 million pounds. For all of 1994/95 exports were 277 million pounds. Total disappearance of tallow between October 1995 and August 1996 was estimated at 1.4 billion pounds.

For the October 1996 to September 1997 marketing year, the USDA forecasts the supply of edible tallow at 1.6 billion pounds. This would be some 3 percent above the forecast for the 1995/96 season. Imports were projected to be 10 million pounds. The total supply of tallow for 1996/97 was put at 1.7 billion pounds, up about 2 percent from 1995/96. Domestic use of edible tallow for the 1996/97 marketing year was forecast to be 1.4 billion pounds, up less than 1 percent from 1995/96. Exports were estimated at 260 million pounds, up close to 11 percent from 1995/96.

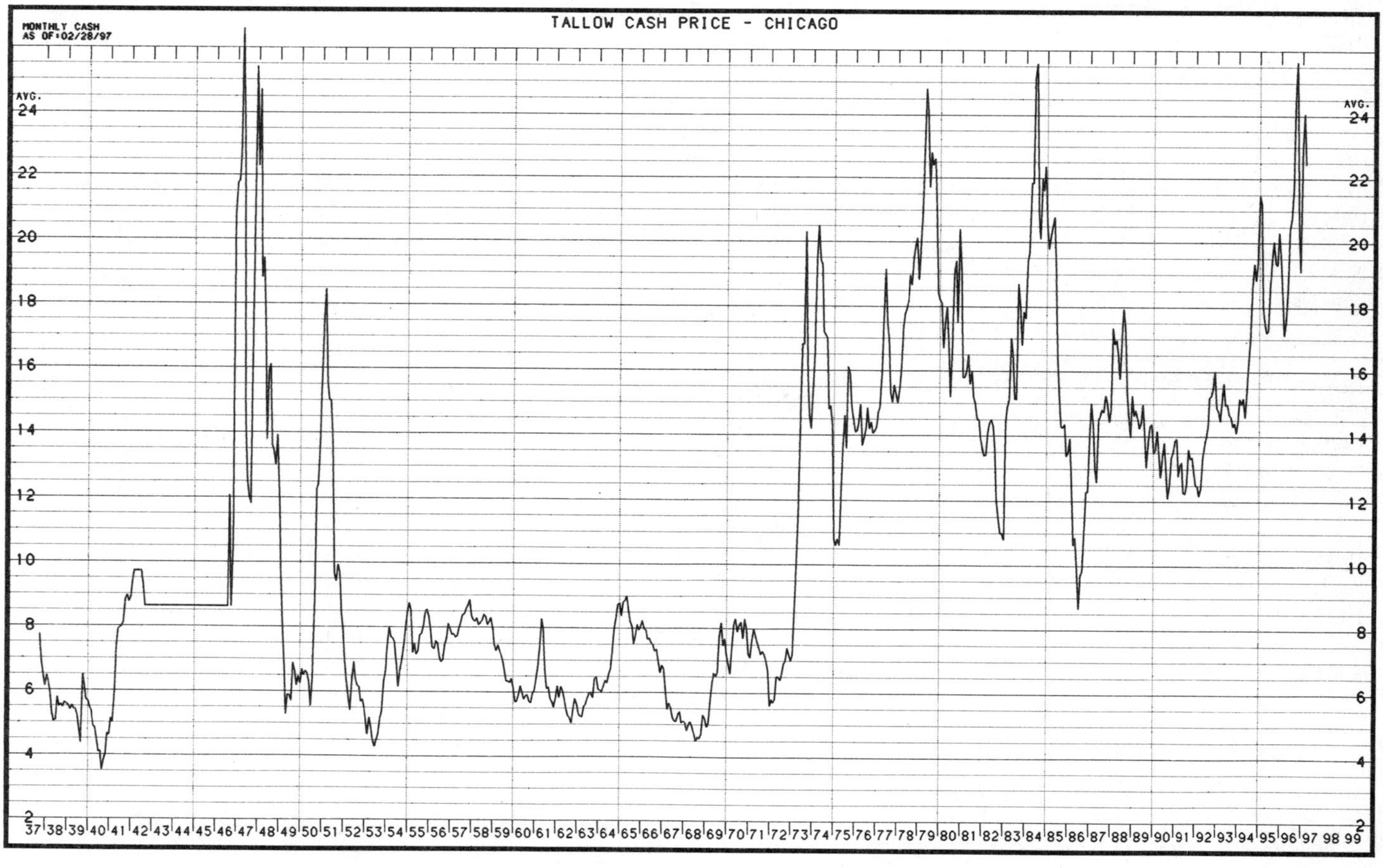

# TALLOW AND GREASES

## World Production of Tallow and Greases (Edible and Inedible) In Thousands of Metric Tons

| Year | Agren-tina | Aust-ralia | Brazil | Canada | Den-mark | France | Ger-many | Italy | Japan | Rep. of Korea | Mexico | Nether-lands | New Zealand | Russia[4] | United Kingdom | United States | World Total |
|---|---|---|---|---|---|---|---|---|---|---|---|---|---|---|---|---|---|
| 1986 | 305 | 328 | 200 | 217 | 69 | 175 | 256 | 115 | 215 | 25 | 58 | 119 | 126 | 375 | 220 | 3,375 | 6,580 |
| 1987 | 289 | 350 | 170 | 205 | 70 | 182 | 282 | 110 | 219 | 46 | 43 | 127 | 132 | 380 | 233 | 3,190 | 6,420 |
| 1988 | 279 | 456 | 190 | 200 | 65 | 186 | 278 | 100 | 218 | 53 | 54 | 125 | 146 | 370 | 200 | 3,382 | 6,726 |
| 1989 | 278 | 489 | 272 | 203 | 83 | 179 | 280 | 90 | 168 | 60 | 65 | 125 | 133 | 400 | 207 | 3,212 | 6,614 |
| 1990 | 285 | 530 | 340 | 193 | 122 | 185 | 270 | 96 | 164 | 85 | 55 | 150 | 132 | 108 | 230 | 3,180 | 6,538 |
| 1991 | 268 | 472 | 336 | 212 | 129 | 275 | 197 | 99 | 153 | 121 | 58 | 150 | 134 | 106 | 225 | 3,309 | 6,677 |
| 1992 | 260 | 526 | 345 | 209 | 118 | 240 | 178 | 98 | 165 | 115 | 59 | 163 | 145 | 115 | 212 | 3,487 | 7,511 |
| 1993 | 250 | 446 | 350 | 213 | 104 | 206 | 167 | 96 | 150 | 120 | 62 | 159 | 135 | 90 | 215 | 3,851 | 7,716 |
| 1994[1] | 248 | 423 | 361 | 217 | 99 | 220 | 166 | 96 | 157 | 118 | 65 | 158 | 147 | 55 | 230 | 3,756 | 7,738 |
| 1995[2] | 250 | 441 | 377 | 245 | 100 | 220 | 172 | 83 | 148 | 130 | 65 | 150 | 151 | 50 | 150 | 3,681 | 7,664 |
| 1996[3] | 244 | 463 | 391 | 270 | 102 | 220 | 166 | 88 | 144 | 130 | 65 | 148 | 150 | 48 | 156 | 3,773 | 7,817 |

[1] Preliminary. [2] Estimate. [3] Forecast. [4] Formerly part of the U.S.S.R.; data not reported separately until 1990.
*Source: Foreign Agricultural Service, U.S. Department of Agriculture*

## Salient Statistics of Tallow and Greases (Inedible) in the United States In Millions of Pounds

| | Supply | | | | Consumption | | | Wholesale Prices, ¢ Per Lb. | |
|---|---|---|---|---|---|---|---|---|---|
| Year | Production | Stocks Jan. 1 | Total | Exports | Soap | Feed | Total | Edible, (Loose) Chicago | Inedible, Chicago No. 1 |
| 1987 | 5,602 | 316 | 5,918 | 2,491 | 571 | 1,727 | 3,082 | 15.6 | 14.9 |
| 1988 | 6,158 | 407 | 6,565 | 2,807 | 461 | 1,864 | 3,147 | 17.9 | 16.6 |
| 1989 | 5,848 | 399 | 6,247 | 2,679 | 368 | 1,919 | 3,194 | 15.8 | 14.4 |
| 1990 | 5,217 | 374 | 6,097 | 2,267 | 402 | 2,000 | 3,061 | 14.6 | 13.7 |
| 1991 | 5,759 | 357 | 6,116 | 1,936 | 392 | 1,748 | 2,949 | 14.3 | 13.3 |
| 1992 | 5,768 | 349 | 6,117 | 2,276 | 334 | 1,954 | 3,050 | 15.5 | 14.4 |
| 1993 | 6,621 | 309 | 6,930 | 2,117 | 300 | 1,995 | 3,018 | 16.2 | 14.9 |
| 1994 | 6,364 | 320 | 6,684 | 3,039 | 301 | 2,183 | 3,246 | 18.4 | 17.4 |
| 1995[1] | 6,481 | 350 | 6,831 | 2,486 | 264 | 2,071 | 2,334 | 21.4 | 19.2 |
| 1996[2] | 6,242 | 266 | 6,508 | 1,807 | 245 | 2,389 | 2,634 | 22.0 | 20.3 |

[1] Preliminary. [2] Estimate. *Sources: Economic Research Service, U.S. Department of Agriculture; Bureau of Census, U.S. Department of Commerce*

## Edible Tallow: Supply and Disappearance in the U.S. In Millions of Pounds, Rendered Basis

| | Supply | | | Disappearance | | | | | |
|---|---|---|---|---|---|---|---|---|---|
| Year | Stocks Jan. 1 | Production | Total | Domestic | Exports | Total | Direct Use | Baking or Frying Fats | Per Capita (Lbs.) |
| 1986 | 41 | 1,523 | 1,564 | 1,469 | 62 | 1,531 | 428 | 973 | 6.1 |
| 1987 | 33 | 1,258 | 1,291 | 1,186 | 65 | 1,251 | 220 | 890 | 4.9 |
| 1988 | 40 | 1,296 | 1,336 | 1,149 | 139 | 1,288 | 197 | 840 | 4.7 |
| 1989 | 48 | 1,167 | 1,215 | 975 | 202 | 1,177 | 223 | 752 | 3.9 |
| 1990 | 34 | 1,202 | 1,247 | 955 | 251 | 1,206 | 342 | 637 | 3.8 |
| 1991 | 41 | 1,515 | 1,944 | 1,197 | 333 | 1,530 | 604 | 460 | 3.9 |
| 1992 | 33 | 1,414 | 1,456 | 1,109 | 306 | 1,415 | 537 | 427 | 4.7 |
| 1993 | 41 | 1,499 | 1,556 | 1,204 | 316 | 1,519 | 700 | 404 | 4.4 |
| 1994 | 33 | 1,510 | 1,559 | 1,228 | 295 | 1,523 | 731 | 405 | 4.7 |
| 1995[1] | 36 | 1,541 | 1,595 | 1,273 | 279 | 1,552 | 715 | 374 | 4.8 |
| 1996[2] | 43 | 1,448 | 1,491 | 1,342 | 260 | 1,602 | 457 | 320 | 6.4 |

[1] Preliminary. [2] Forecast. *Sources: Economic Research Service, U.S. Department of Agriculture; Bureau of Census, U.S. Department of Commerce*

## Average Wholesale Price of Tallow, Inedible, No. 1 Packers (Prime), Delivered, Chicago In Cents Per Lb.

| Year | Jan. | Feb. | Mar. | Apr. | May | June | July | Aug. | Sept. | Oct. | Nov. | Dec. | Average |
|---|---|---|---|---|---|---|---|---|---|---|---|---|---|
| 1986 | 12.00 | 11.80 | 9.40 | 8.90 | 8.70 | 7.60 | 7.80 | 7.80 | 8.10 | 8.40 | 8.50 | 9.50 | 9.04 |
| 1987 | 15.84 | 15.15 | 13.03 | 12.98 | 15.42 | 14.73 | 15.17 | 14.50 | 15.53 | 15.23 | 15.17 | 15.56 | 14.86 |
| 1988 | 18.00 | 17.08 | 17.25 | 16.17 | 15.93 | 17.18 | 18.81 | 17.44 | 16.00 | 15.02 | 14.18 | 16.33 | 16.62 |
| 1989 | 14.90 | 16.00 | 14.86 | 14.60 | 14.70 | 15.10 | 14.48 | 13.52 | 14.13 | 15.25 | 15.50 | 15.50 | 14.88 |
| 1990 | 14.87 | 14.50 | 14.47 | 13.77 | 13.66 | NA | 13.50 | 10.12 | 12.00 | 13.42 | 14.09 | 14.75 | 13.56 |
| 1991 | 13.88 | 14.28 | 14.43 | 14.80 | 13.02 | 12.36 | 12.96 | 14.00 | 13.50 | 13.68 | 13.08 | 12.50 | 13.54 |
| 1992 | 12.25 | 12.63 | 12.68 | 13.25 | 13.75 | 13.98 | 14.75 | 15.42 | 15.25 | 15.94 | 16.75 | 16.13 | 14.40 |
| 1993 | 15.36 | 14.70 | 15.24 | 16.15 | 15.41 | 14.51 | 14.36 | 14.53 | 14.66 | 14.62 | 14.69 | 14.63 | 14.91 |
| 1994 | 15.00 | 15.00 | 15.22 | 15.19 | 15.25 | 15.63 | 16.67 | 18.64 | 19.50 | 19.78 | 20.38 | 22.48 | 17.40 |
| 1995 | 21.75 | 18.86 | 18.00 | 17.75 | 17.50 | 17.89 | 19.61 | 19.81 | 19.53 | 19.46 | 19.75 | 20.08 | 19.17 |
| 1996[1] | 19.45 | 17.00 | 17.03 | 17.54 | 19.37 | 19.50 | 20.98 | 22.40 | 27.00 | 20.68 | 19.10 | 22.95 | 20.25 |

[1] Preliminary. *Source: Economic Research Service, U.S. Department of Agriculture*

# Tea

World production of tea in 1994 was estimated at 2.6 million tonnes, down 1 percent from the previous year. Over the last five years, world output of tea averaged 2.6 million tonnes. India is by far the world's largest producer of tea. In 1994, India's production was estimated at 743,800 tonnes or 28 percent of the world total. For 1995, India's production was estimated at 715,000 tonnes, down 4 percent from the prior year. Tea acreage in India was slightly higher but yields were lower particularly for whole leaf tea. While India has been attempting to produce more tea, production has declined. The Indian tea industry has been concentrating on producing higher quality teas. There have been concerns over the use of pesticides and there has been an effort to produce tea using organic methods of weed and pest control.

China is the second largest producer of tea. In 1994, production was estimated at 588,000 tonnes. For 1995, the USDA estimated Chinese production at 590,000 tonnes. Harvested acreage was estimated at 860,000 hectares, up 1 percent from the previous year. The Chinese government continues to encourage tea farmers to produce high quality teas. The primary tea grown in China is green tea which is used for local consumption. Its consumption has been increasing. Black (manufactured) tea is produced primarily for the export market.

Sri Lanka is another major producer of tea. For 1995, production was estimated by USDA at 240,000 tonnes, down slightly from 1994. Harvested acreage was lower. Sri Lanka produces orthodox tea. Kenya's 1995 tea crop was estimated at 230,000 tonnes, up close to 12 percent from 1994. Harvested acreage increased by almost 9 percent. While Kenya has been gradually increasing its tea production, the industry continues to be troubled by a weak infrastructure.

The U.S. is a major importer of tea. For 1994, U.S. tea imports were estimated at 96,476 tonnes, up over 15 percent from the previous year. By far, the type of tea imported most is black tea which in 1994 totaled 90,873 tonnes or 94 percent of the U.S. import total. Green tea imports were 4,517 tonnes, with 689 tonnes of oolong tea and 397 tonnes of mixed tea. The major supplier of tea to the U.S. is Argentina with exports of 25,120 tonnes in 1994. Argentine exports have been on a steady increase. The next largest supplier has been China with 24,549 tonnes in 1994. After these two major suppliers, the next largest source for U.S. tea is Indonesia with 15,011 tonnes. Other important suppliers include Sri Lanka, Kenya, Brazil, India, and Malawi.

U.S. sales of tea by retail stores in 1993 were 57,697 tonnes. Of that total, 34,534 tonnes was in the form of tea bags or some 60 percent. Another 23 percent, or 13,283 tonnes, was in the form of instant mixes. Instant tea sales were 5,239 tonnes or 9 percent of the total. Herbal teas were 2,581 tonnes or 4 percent, with 730 tonnes of loose tea sold. In 1994, U.S. per capita consumption of tea was 7.1 gallons. That compared to 23.4 gallons of coffee and 18.9 gallons of milk.

## World Tea Production, in Major Producing Countries In Thousands of Metric Tons

| Year | Agrentina | Bangladesh | China | India | Indonesia | Iran | Japan | Kenya | Malawi | Mozambique | Sri Lanka | Taiwan | Tanzania | Turkey | Former USSR[2] | Grand Total |
|---|---|---|---|---|---|---|---|---|---|---|---|---|---|---|---|---|
| 1985 | 35.0 | 43.3 | 432.0 | 656.2 | 132.3 | 41.5 | 95.5 | 147.1 | 40.0 | 7.0 | 215.3 | 23.2 | 16.5 | 137.1 | 152.1 | 2,292 |
| 1986 | 40.0 | 37.6 | 461.0 | 620.8 | 129.5 | 48.5 | 93.6 | 143.3 | 39.0 | 5.0 | 212.7 | 23.9 | 15.1 | 148.3 | 146.6 | 2,285 |
| 1987 | 43.0 | 40.6 | 508.0 | 665.3 | 126.1 | 45.6 | 96.3 | 155.8 | 31.9 | 3.0 | 214.6 | 25.6 | 14.5 | 140.7 | 120.0 | 2,356 |
| 1988 | 44.0 | 43.6 | 545.0 | 700.0 | 133.8 | 55.6 | 89.8 | 164.0 | 40.2 | 1.5 | 228.2 | 23.6 | 14.6 | 166.4 | 118.0 | 2,490 |
| 1989 | 48.0 | 39.1 | 535.0 | 688.1 | 141.4 | 46.0 | 90.5 | 180.6 | 39.5 | 1.8 | 208.0 | 22.1 | 17.0 | 141.6 | 119.2 | 2,444 |
| 1990 | 50.0 | 45.9 | 540.0 | 720.3 | 145.2 | 44.0 | 89.9 | 197.0 | 39.1 | 2.0 | 234.1 | 22.3 | 18.4 | 126.7 | 123.2 | 2,528 |
| 1991 | 40.0 | 45.2 | 542.0 | 741.7 | 133.4 | 45.0 | 87.9 | 203.6 | 40.5 | 2.0 | 241.6 | 21.4 | 19.3 | 135.3 | 110.0 | 2,541 |
| 1992 | 43.0 | 46.0 | 580.0 | 704.0 | 163.0 | 55.0 | 92.0 | 188.0 | 28.0 | 1.0 | 179.0 | 20.7 | 18.0 | 144.0 | 57.0 | 2,439 |
| 1993 | 55.0 | 49.0 | 600.0 | 757.0 | 169.0 | 57.0 | 92.0 | 211.0 | 39.0 | 1.0 | 232.0 | 21.0 | 21.0 | 117.0 | 81.0 | 2,645 |
| 1994 | 56.0 | 51.0 | 600.0 | 720.0 | 174.0 | 75.0 | 86.0 | 209.0 | 42.0 | 1.0 | 240.0 | | 22.0 | 125.0 | 78.0 | 2,623 |
| 1995[1] | 40.0 | | 590.0 | 715.0 | 140.0 | | | 230.0 | | | 240.0 | | | | | |

[1] Preliminary. [2] Mostly Georgia and Azerbaijan. *Sources: Foreign Agricultural Service, U.S.D.A.; Food and Agriculture Organization of the United Nations*

## World Tea Exports from Producing Countries In Metric Tons

| Year | Argentina | Bangladesh | Brazil | China | India | Indonesia | Japan | Kenya | Malawi | Mozambique | P. New Guinea | Sri Lanka | Taiwan | Vietnam | Zimbabwe | Grand Total |
|---|---|---|---|---|---|---|---|---|---|---|---|---|---|---|---|---|
| 1984 | 42,102 | 23,100 | 9,301 | 145,346 | 217,400 | 85,664 | 2,787 | 91,198 | 37,208 | 7,550 | 7,530 | 204,226 | 11,862 | 11,000 | 9,835 | 942,733 |
| 1985 | 30,657 | 30,306 | 8,807 | 136,864 | 214,021 | 90,121 | 1,805 | 126,086 | 37,777 | 3,190 | 7,025 | 197,580 | 9,127 | 12,000 | 10,036 | 957,083 |
| 1986 | 36,279 | 27,675 | 10,851 | 172,028 | 203,149 | 78,957 | 1,261 | 116,456 | 40,189 | 1,820 | 5,213 | 207,567 | 9,011 | 12,500 | 11,819 | 997,534 |
| 1987 | 33,647 | 21,606 | 8,073 | 174,274 | 201,891 | 90,422 | 1,107 | 134,779 | 33,404 | 2,100 | 5,491 | 200,774 | 7,375 | 13,000 | 10,105 | 978,368 |
| 1988 | 34,258 | 26,187 | 9,686 | 198,289 | 200,956 | 92,687 | 1,260 | 138,201 | 36,961 | 830 | 5,834 | 219,710 | 7,631 | 14,800 | 14,190 | 1,039,313 |
| 1989 | 43,335 | 23,426 | 9,400 | 204,584 | 211,622 | 114,709 | 671 | 163,188 | 39,891 | 800 | 5,439 | 203,763 | 6,745 | 15,016 | 12,768 | 1,121,251 |
| 1990 | 45,966 | 26,970 | 7,976 | 195,471 | 209,085 | 110,964 | 322 | 169,586 | 43,039 | 700 | 5,375 | 215,251 | 5,853 | 24,698 | 11,507 | 1,141,026 |
| 1991 | 36,029 | 26,860 | 7,347 | 190,188 | 215,144 | 110,207 | 289 | 175,625 | 41,185 | 1,339 | 3,747 | 212,017 | 5,317 | 7,953 | 11,304 | 1,206,282 |
| 1992 | 36,530 | 24,990 | 8,211 | 180,834 | 166,359 | 121,243 | 290 | 172,053 | 37,056 | 600 | 5,638 | 181,259 | 5,296 | 12,967 | 6,088 | 1,130,355 |
| 1993[1] | 44,258 | 29,620 | 8,335 | 206,659 | 153,159 | 123,925 | 328 | 199,379 | 35,264 | 100 | 6,441 | 134,742 | | 16,200 | 8,065 | 1,190,662 |
| 1994[2] | 43,355 | 27,415 | 8,377 | 184,050 | 151,047 | 84,916 | 345 | 174,926 | 38,670 | 100 | 3,400 | 115,097 | | 17,300 | 8,579 | 1,030,915 |

[1] Preliminary. [2] Estimate. *Source: Food and Agriculture Organization of the United Nations*

# TEA

## United States Imports of Tea In Metric Tons

| Year | Agren-tina | Brazil | China | Ger-many | India | Indo-nesia | Kenya | Malawi | Nether-lands | Papua New Guinea | Sri Lanka | Total | ------ Passed for U.S. Entry by Type ------ Black Teas | Green Teas | Oolong Teas | Mixed Teas | Total |
|---|---|---|---|---|---|---|---|---|---|---|---|---|---|---|---|---|---|
| 1981 | 10,345 | 2,806 | 7,962 | 205 | 4,159 | 13,913 | 6,762 | 2,147 | 5,936 | 200 | 12,216 | 83,819 | 80,857 | 3,754 | 541 | 755 | 85,907 |
| 1982 | 10,011 | 3,537 | 7,143 | 289 | 4,724 | 14,676 | 5,498 | 2,356 | 7,668 | 56 | 12,991 | 86,299 | 78,273 | 3,290 | 541 | 768 | 82,872 |
| 1983 | 15,114 | 3,926 | 6,399 | 646 | 2,894 | 14,352 | 4,536 | 1,288 | 4,657 | 25 | 8,106 | 77,318 | 71,709 | 2,371 | 517 | 551 | 75,148 |
| 1984 | 18,142 | 3,611 | 9,622 | 1,161 | 3,758 | 15,501 | 3,932 | 915 | 4,792 | 76 | 9,383 | 88,256 | 82,486 | 5,385 | 646 | 634 | 89,151 |
| 1985 | 15,234 | 4,281 | 10,877 | 3,046 | 2,943 | 12,844 | 4,152 | 935 | 4,213 | 62 | 9,796 | 79,206 | 69,210 | 6,570 | 811 | 618 | 77,209 |
| 1986 | 16,367 | 5,554 | 16,925 | 2,535 | 3,884 | 16,270 | 4,330 | 1,205 | 4,053 | 14 | 7,756 | 90,549 | 81,036 | 5,543 | 722 | 471 | 87,772 |
| 1987 | 15,897 | 5,418 | 16,728 | 3,422 | 3,042 | 10,395 | 4,145 | 1,991 | 3,258 | 75 | 4,799 | 77,391 | 70,881 | 6,590 | 770 | 496 | 78,737 |
| 1988 | 13,815 | 4,147 | 22,950 | 5,198 | 3,625 | 14,380 | 6,198 | 1,645 | 3,843 | 321 | 5,919 | 90,144 | 79,430 | 4,547 | 689 | 572 | 85,238 |
| 1989 | 17,219 | 4,735 | 19,641 | 5,731 | 2,914 | 12,293 | 6,005 | 1,871 | 2,508 | 571 | 5,693 | 89,582 | 78,898 | 5,870 | 804 | 634 | 86,206 |
| 1990 | 17,100 | 3,882 | 19,579 | 4,931 | 2,565 | 10,650 | 3,996 | 1,585 | 2,633 | 822 | 3,762 | 76,997 | 70,885 | 5,183 | 845 | 534 | 77,447 |
| 1991 | 19,457 | 3,453 | 21,859 | 4,834 | 2,648 | 13,477 | 4,056 | 1,958 | 1,839 | 1,153 | 3,702 | 84,330 | 76,762 | 5,056 | 704 | 412 | 82,934 |
| 1992 | 22,879 | 3,679 | 24,026 | 4,408 | 2,893 | 16,350 | 4,357 | 2,650 | 811 | 831 | 3,907 | 91,365 | 83,510 | 5,551 | 788 | 526 | 90,375 |
| 1993 | 21,268 | 2,684 | 24,035 | 3,961 | 2,912 | 13,247 | 3,938 | 3,146 | 937 | 1,126 | 3,750 | 84,893 | 75,470 | 4,628 | 751 | 484 | 81,333 |
| 1994 | 25,121 | 3,843 | 24,549 | 4,481 | 3,705 | 15,011 | 3,406 | 3,865 | 640 | 1,087 | 4,842 | 96,184 | 89,518 | 4,166 | 667 | 455 | 94,807 |
| 1995[1] | 25,191 | 2,798 | 20,634 | 5,126 | 3,227 | 9,379 | 2,700 | 2,562 | 793 | 734 | 5,240 | 83,308 | 80,699 | 5,712 | 852 | 292 | 87,556 |

[1] Preliminary. *Source: Foreign Agricultural Service, U.S. Department of Agriculture*

## U.S. Per Capita Consumption of Specific Beverages and Tea Sales by U.S. Retail Stores

| | Per Capita Consumption | | | | | | | | | | Sales by Retail Stores[4] | | | | | |
|---|---|---|---|---|---|---|---|---|---|---|---|---|---|---|---|---|
| Year | Soft Drinks | Coffee[2] | Beer | Milk | Tea[2] | Bottled Water | Juices | Powder Drinks | Wine[3] | Distilled Spirits | Tea Bags | Loose Tea | Instant Tea | Instant Mixes | Herbal | Total |
| | In Gallons | | | | | | | | | | In Metric Tons | | | | | |
| 1982 | 35.6 | 26.6 | 24.4 | 19.7 | 7.5 | 3.3 | 6.8 | 6.0 | 2.2 | 1.9 | 40,638 | 3,023 | 14,905 | 11,742 | 1,875 | 72,183 |
| 1983 | NA | NA | NA | NA | NA | NA | NA | NA | NA | NA | 41,876 | 2,685 | 14,878 | 13,136 | 2,096 | 74,671 |
| 1984 | 38.8 | 26.4 | 23.9 | 19.7 | 7.2 | 4.0 | 6.6 | 6.4 | 2.3 | 1.9 | 40,685 | 2,329 | 13,287 | 12,192 | 2,109 | 70,602 |
| 1985 | 40.8 | 26.8 | 23.8 | 19.8 | 7.3 | 5.2 | 7.9 | 6.3 | 2.4 | 1.8 | 40,951 | 2,081 | 12,688 | 11,412 | 2,151 | 69,283 |
| 1986 | 42.1 | 25.8 | 24.1 | 19.9 | 7.3 | 5.7 | 7.3 | 6.0 | 2.4 | 1.7 | 40,410 | 1,816 | 12,065 | 10,573 | 2,350 | 67,214 |
| 1987 | NA | NA | NA | NA | NA | NA | NA | NA | NA | NA | 32,596 | 1,124 | 7,226 | 10,437 | 2,141 | 53,524 |
| 1988 | 46.0 | 25.4 | 23.7 | 19.3 | 7.4 | 7.2 | 7.1 | 5.2 | 2.2 | 1.6 | 31,924 | 939 | 6,521 | 10,589 | 2,191 | 52,164 |
| 1989 | 46.7 | 26.4 | 23.6 | 19.6 | 7.2 | 8.1 | 8.0 | 5.4 | 2.1 | 1.5 | 35,359 | 1,045 | 7,606 | 11,322 | 2,380 | 58,060 |
| 1990 | 47.7 | 26.4 | 24.1 | 19.4 | 7.0 | 8.0 | 7.1 | 5.7 | 2.0 | 1.5 | 34,806 | 972 | 6,858 | 11,659 | 2,458 | 57,153 |
| 1991 | 47.8 | 26.5 | 23.3 | 19.4 | 6.7 | 8.0 | 7.6 | 5.9 | 1.9 | 1.4 | 35,068 | 871 | 6,561 | 12,599 | 2,380 | 58,060 |
| 1992 | 48.0 | 26.1 | 23.0 | 19.1 | 6.8 | 8.2 | 7.1 | 5.8 | 2.0 | 1.3 | 35,025 | 749 | 5,761 | 12,846 | 2,477 | 57,607 |
| 1993 | 49.0 | 25.4 | 22.9 | 18.9 | 6.9 | 8.8 | 7.0 | 5.5 | 1.7 | 1.3 | 34,534 | 730 | 5,239 | 13,283 | 2,581 | 57,697 |
| 1994 | 50.6 | 22.6 | 23.4 | 18.9 | 8.9 | 10.3 | 7.1 | 5.6 | 1.7 | 1.3 | 34,879 | 644 | 4,681 | 13,926 | 2,692 | 58,491 |
| 1995[1] | 51.8 | 22.1 | 21.6 | 18.8 | 9.0 | 11.3 | 6.8 | 5.6 | 1.8 | 1.3 | 33,369 | 588 | 4,221 | 14,069 | 2,776 | 57,928 |
| 1996[1] | 52.8 | 21.9 | 20.4 | 18.7 | 9.2 | 12.3 | 6.8 | 5.6 | 1.8 | 1.3 | | | | | | |

[1] Preliminary. [2] Based on 3-year moving average. [3] Includes wine coolers beginning 1985. [4] Excludes sales by hotels, restaurants and institutional users. NA = Not available. *Source: Foreign Agricultural Service, U.S. Department of Agriculture*

## London Auction Tea Prices In U.S. Cents Per Pound

| Year | Jan. | Feb. | Mar. | Apr. | May | June | July | Aug. | Sept. | Oct. | Nov. | Dec. | Average |
|---|---|---|---|---|---|---|---|---|---|---|---|---|---|
| 1981 | 98.6 | 101.2 | 100.5 | 97.9 | 94.7 | 90.4 | 84.6 | 80.0 | 81.7 | 87.4 | 91.3 | 91.6 | 91.7 |
| 1982 | 92.0 | 94.2 | 88.5 | 84.7 | 84.8 | 83.3 | 79.9 | 80.8 | 86.7 | 91.4 | 89.8 | 96.1 | 87.7 |
| 1983 | 98.5 | 93.1 | 89.8 | 92.1 | 91.0 | 85.2 | 86.6 | 90.6 | 99.0 | 117.4 | 158.8 | 163.8 | 105.5 |
| 1984 | 194.2 | 169.0 | 166.7 | 160.4 | 161.3 | 144.8 | 130.3 | 133.2 | 154.1 | 164.2 | 155.2 | 147.9 | 156.8 |
| 1985 | 143.1 | 127.3 | 110.4 | 98.6 | 75.2 | 74.6 | 71.5 | 72.2 | 73.3 | 78.7 | 80.2 | 75.3 | 90.0 |
| 1986 | 82.1 | 85.7 | 91.5 | 91.3 | 85.9 | 79.7 | 79.8 | 86.5 | 91.6 | 94.1 | 93.6 | 88.6 | 87.5 |
| 1987 | 89.7 | 83.6 | 83.2 | 67.9 | 65.4 | 60.8 | 69.5 | 72.3 | 72.7 | 84.1 | 87.4 | 94.0 | 77.6 |
| 1988 | 96.1 | 88.0 | 87.2 | 83.6 | 77.3 | 75.3 | 66.4 | 67.2 | 74.7 | 82.5 | 87.4 | 89.4 | 81.3 |
| 1989 | 87.5 | 82.4 | 80.6 | 77.3 | 76.7 | 80.4 | 88.1 | 83.2 | 97.7 | 118.4 | 106.7 | 115.5 | 91.2 |
| 1990 | 114.7 | 95.9 | 87.3 | 88.5 | 84.8 | 82.6 | 86.3 | 79.2 | 84.1 | 100.0 | 103.8 | 99.6 | 92.2 |
| 1991 | 107.2 | 90.2 | 83.6 | 84.3 | 78.7 | 73.8 | 70.4 | 73.5 | 79.6 | 84.4 | 89.4 | 89.7 | 83.7 |
| 1992 | 78.7 | 73.8 | 76.1 | 89.6 | 98.2 | 95.7 | 93.7 | 100.6 | 99.2 | 91.4 | 93.7 | 105.4 | 91.3 |
| 1993 | 108.6 | 92.5 | 86.9 | 80.6 | 78.3 | 75.9 | 74.7 | 75.8 | 82.4 | 90.9 | 84.3 | 84.4 | 84.6 |
| 1994 | 74.7 | 78.9 | 84.7 | 84.3 | 83.4 | 90.2 | 82.4 | 83.3 | 91.2 | 86.5 | 81.4 | 78.1 | 83.3 |
| 1995 | 74.0 | 76.8 | 77.9 | 76.3 | 74.6 | 66.0 | 65.7 | 68.3 | 74.2 | 80.2 | 78.9 | 81.6 | 74.5 |
| 1996[1] | 79.3 | 80.2 | 76.5 | 78.3 | | | | | | | | | 78.6 |

[1] Preliminary. *Source: Foreign Agricultural Service, U.S. Department of Agriculture*

# Tin

Tin is manufactured into a coating for steel containers used to preserve food and beverages. It is also used in solder alloys, electroplating, ceramics, and in plastic. Tin is mined in approximately 28 countries but the top five account for about three-fourths of world output. China is the largest producer with about a quarter of world output followed by Indonesia, Brazil, Bolivia, and Peru. Other major producers include Portugal, Malaysia, Australia, and Thailand. World tin reserves were estimated at about seven million tonnes and were considered adequate to meet the world's tin requirements in the near future. The bulk of the world's reserves are located in Asia and South America. The only tin mine in the U.S. is located in Alaska and it is currently not in production.

The U.S. is believed to be the world's largest producer of secondary tin. Tin metal recovered from new tinplate scrap and from used tin cans was the only type of secondary tin available in the marketplace as free tin. Other secondary tin was available in scrap materials as an alloying ingredient. Secondary tin from recycled fabricated parts was a major source of material, particularly for the solder, brass, and bronze industries.

In a market development, the American Metal Market reported that Bethlehem Steel Corp. had received a U.S. patent for the development of a more environmentally friendly process for the high-speed tinplating of steel and a plating bath composition that is free of ferrocyanides. Ferrocyanide is a chemical that is commonly added to halogen tinplating baths in large quantities to counter the effect of dissolved iron during the tinplating process. The iron ferrocyanides that result become a major ingredient in the sludge that accumulates in the plating cells, storage tanks, and other plating system components. The new process uses more environmentally friendly antioxidants instead of ferrocyanides. These new antioxidants are reported to substantially reduce the environmental requirements typical in operating a tin-plating line and the associated costs of sludge disposal. Work is now being done to commercialize the process.

U.S. production (scrap) of tin from brass and bronze in July 1996 was 900 tonnes, the same as in June. For January-July 1996, production was 6,300 tonnes. For all of 1995 it was 10,800 tonnes. Statistics on production of tin scrap as tin metal were withheld to avoid disclosing company proprietary data. U.S. tinplate production in July 1996 in all forms was 141,000 tonnes (gross weight) with a tin content of 857 tonnes. There are 6.1 kilograms of tin per metric ton. Tinplate waste (waste, strips, cobbles, and other forms) production in July 1996 was 15,700 tonnes. For all of 1995, tinplate waste production was 205,000 tonnes. Tinplate production (in all forms) in 1995 was 1.66 million tonnes.

U.S. tin metal (unwrought tin) imports for consumption in June 1996 were 2,270 tonnes, down 1 percent from May. For January-June 1996, imports were 14,700 tonnes. The major suppliers were Brazil with 30 percent, Bolivia 24 percent, Indonesia 22 percent, and China 12 percent. Other suppliers included India, Malaysia, and Russia. For all of 1995, imports were 33,200 tonnes.

Imports of tin in other forms, primarily alloys, waste, and scrap were 1,820 tonnes in June 1996, up almost 8 percent from May. For January-June 1996 imports were 11,800 tonnes, while for all of 1995 they were 29,800 tonnes.

U.S. exports of tin in June 1996 were 302 tonnes, down from 346 tonnes in May 1996. For January-June 1996, exports were 2,370 tonnes, while for all of 1995 they were 2,790 tonnes.

U.S. consumption of tin in July 1996 was 3,920 tonnes, down 2 percent from June. January-June 1996 consumption was 27,400 tonnes while for all of 1995 it was 44,800 tonnes.

### *Futures Markets*

Tin futures are traded on the London Metals Exchange (LME) and on the Kuala Lumpur Commodity Exchange (KLCE). Options are traded on the LME.

**World Mine Production of Tin** In Metric Tons (Contained Tin)

| Year | Australia | Bolivia | Brazil | China | Indonesia | Malaysia | Nigeria | Peru | Portugal | Russia[3] | South Africa | Thailand | United Kingdom | Zaire | Zimbabwe | World Total |
|---|---|---|---|---|---|---|---|---|---|---|---|---|---|---|---|---|
| 1990 | 7,377 | 17,249 | 39,149 | 42,000 | 30,200 | 28,468 | 192 | 5,134 | 4,780 | 15,000 | 1,140 | 14,635 | 3,400 | 2,221 | 1,120 | 221,000 |
| 1991 | 5,700 | 16,830 | 29,253 | 42,100 | 30,061 | 20,710 | 217 | 6,559 | 8,330 | 13,500 | 1,042 | 14,937 | 2,330 | 1,522 | 1,060 | 201,000 |
| 1992 | 6,610 | 16,516 | 27,500 | 43,800 | 29,400 | 14,339 | 186 | 9,680 | 6,560 | 6,000 | 582 | 11,484 | 2,040 | 1,020 | 950 | 182,000 |
| 1993 | 8,057 | 18,634 | 26,500 | 49,100 | 29,000 | 10,384 | 400 | 14,310 | 10,100 | 13,100 | 450 | 6,363 | 2,232 | 700 | 800 | 195,000 |
| 1994[1] | 7,100 | 16,027 | 16,800 | 54,100 | 30,610 | 6,458 | 185 | 20,075 | 7,637 | 10,460 | ------ | 3,926 | 1,922 | 1,000 | 82 | 182,000 |
| 1995[2] | 8,175 | 14,419 | 16,800 | 52,000 | 38,378 | 6,402 | 185 | 22,331 | 8,000 | 9,000 | ------ | 3,000 | 2,000 | 1,000 | ------ | 187,000 |

[1] Preliminary. [2] Estimate. [3] Formerly part of the U.S.S.R.; data not reported separately until 1992. *Source: U.S. Geological Survey*

**World Smelter Primary Production of Tin** In Metric Tons

| Year | Australia | Bolivia | Brazil | China | Indonesia | Japan | Malaysia | Mexico | Russia[2] | South Africa | Spain | Thailand | United Kingdom | Zimbabwe | World Total |
|---|---|---|---|---|---|---|---|---|---|---|---|---|---|---|---|
| 1990 | 312 | 12,567 | 37,580 | 35,000 | 30,389 | 816 | 49,067 | 5,004 | 16,000 | 1,140 | 600 | 15,512 | 6,100 | 838 | 246,000 |
| 1991 | 268 | 14,663 | 25,776 | 36,400 | 30,415 | 716 | 42,722 | 2,262 | 13,000 | 1,042 | 600 | 11,255 | 1,661 | 796 | 205,000 |
| 1992 | 240 | 14,393 | 27,000 | 39,600 | 31,915 | 821 | 45,598 | 2,590 | 6,000 | 592 | 600 | 10,679 | ------ | 716 | 195,000 |
| 1993 | 245 | 14,541 | 26,900 | 52,000 | 30,415 | 804 | 39,984 | 1,640 | 13,400 | 452 | 500 | 8,099 | ------ | 657 | 202,000 |
| 1994 | 200 | 15,285 | 20,400 | 67,800 | 31,100 | 706 | 38,119 | 768 | 11,500 | 43 | 700 | 7,759 | ------ | 82 | 207,000 |
| 1995[1] | 200 | 17,709 | 20,000 | 60,700 | 38,628 | 630 | 39,454 | 770 | 9,500 | 40 | 700 | 8,243 | ------ | ------ | 209,000 |

[8] Preliminary. [2] Formerly part of the U.S.S.R.; data not reported separately until 1992. *Source: U.S. Geological Survey*

## Tin Foreign Trade of the United States In Metric Tons

| | | Imports (For Consumption) | | | | | | | | | | | | | | |
|---|---|---|---|---|---|---|---|---|---|---|---|---|---|---|---|---|
| | | Concentrates[2] (Ore) | | | Unwrought Tin Metal | | | | | | | | | | | |
| Year | Exports (Metal) | Total All Ore | Bolivia | Peru | Total All Metal | Australia | Belgium | Bolivia | Brazil | China | Indonesia | Malaysia | Nigeria | Singapore | Thailand | United Kingdom |
| 1981 | 2,361 | 232 | ----- | 232 | 45,874 | 552 | ----- | 8,277 | 1,129 | 2,032 | 7,096 | 13,163 | 520 | 656 | 11,967 | 46 |
| 1982 | 5,769 | 1,961 | 192 | 1,416 | 27,939 | 334 | 10 | 4,340 | 2,409 | 2,632 | 5,744 | 2,364 | 124 | 600 | 9,116 | 55 |
| 1983 | 1,340 | 969 | 257 | 341 | 34,048 | 390 | 45 | 5,739 | 5,604 | 1,938 | 6,004 | 4,704 | 265 | 1,029 | 7,436 | 18 |
| 1984 | 1,429 | 3,272 | 271 | 2,502 | 41,224 | 288 | 137 | 5,438 | 10,220 | 1,640 | 4,985 | 6,622 | 60 | 781 | 9,531 | 583 |
| 1985 | 1,478 | 1,616 | 22 | 1,506 | 33,830 | 266 | ----- | 1,815 | 11,021 | 4,513 | 4,586 | 379 | ----- | 1,886 | 6,373 | 48 |
| 1986 | 1,547 | 3,936 | 259 | 3,676 | 35,768 | 94 | ----- | 4,893 | 9,456 | 2,955 | 4,149 | 6,230 | ----- | 691 | 1,901 | 730 |
| 1987 | 1,318 | 2,953 | 732 | 2,165 | 41,150 | 1,406 | 302 | 3,476 | 13,089 | 8,044 | 4,001 | 4,959 | 79 | 743 | 1,460 | 467 |
| 1988 | 1,209 | 2,837 | 923 | 1,914 | 43,493 | 1,342 | ----- | 3,926 | 16,213 | 6,223 | 5,334 | 5,317 | 41 | 1,342 | 670 | 1,354 |
| 1989 | 904 | 216 | ----- | 149 | 33,988 | 1,420 | ----- | 4,795 | 10,572 | 4,793 | 5,162 | 2,392 | ----- | 456 | 180 | 391 |
| 1990 | 658 | ----- | ----- | ----- | 33,810 | 1,660 | ----- | 8,472 | 6,535 | 4,339 | 4,695 | 3,873 | ----- | 40 | 60 | 227 |
| 1991 | 970 | 1 | 1 | ----- | 29,102 | 1,105 | 221 | 8,912 | 4,489 | 5,281 | 4,425 | 1,751 | ----- | 100 | ----- | 344 |
| 1992 | 1,888 | ----- | ----- | ----- | 27,314 | 300 | 1 | 4,623 | 8,167 | 5,389 | 3,854 | 2,799 | ----- | 320 | 427 | ----- |
| 1993 | 2,598 | ----- | ----- | ----- | 33,682 | ----- | 1 | 8,027 | 11,366 | 4,202 | 5,678 | 846 | ----- | 220 | ----- | 6 |
| 1994 | 2,560 | ----- | ----- | ----- | 32,400 | ----- | 3 | 7,260 | 9,990 | 3,230 | 6,620 | 1,390 | ----- | 142 | ----- | 666 |
| 1995[1] | 2,790 | ----- | ----- | ----- | 33,200 | ----- | ----- | 6,630 | 8,070 | 5,610 | 7,230 | 3,810 | ----- | 40 | ----- | 97 |

[1] Preliminary. [2] Tin content. *Source: U.S. Geological Survey (USGS)*

## United States Tin (Pig) Consumption (Total) In Metric Tons

| Year | Jan. | Feb. | Mar. | Apr. | May | June | July | Aug. | Sept. | Oct. | Nov. | Dec. | Total |
|---|---|---|---|---|---|---|---|---|---|---|---|---|---|
| 1981 | 4,300 | 4,400 | 4,100 | 4,600 | 4,400 | 4,350 | 3,900 | 4,200 | 3,950 | 3,900 | 3,400 | 2,950 | 54,373 |
| 1982 | 3,400 | 3,300 | 3,750 | 5,100 | 5,000 | 5,100 | 4,900 | 4,700 | 4,700 | 4,600 | 4,500 | 4,400 | 53,450 |
| 1983 | 4,400 | 4,700 | 4,900 | 4,700 | 4,700 | 4,800 | 4,300 | 4,600 | 4,700 | 4,800 | 4,400 | 4,800 | 55,800 |
| 1984 | 4,600 | 4,300 | 5,300 | 3,900 | 4,500 | 4,400 | 4,100 | 4,400 | 4,100 | 4,000 | 3,300 | 3,500 | 50,400 |
| 1985 | 4,000 | 3,900 | 4,600 | 4,500 | 4,600 | 4,400 | 4,200 | 4,400 | 4,300 | 4,500 | 4,200 | 4,000 | 51,600 |
| 1986 | 4,300 | 4,000 | 4,200 | 4,500 | 4,400 | 4,400 | 4,100 | 4,100 | 4,000 | 4,300 | 3,900 | 3,900 | 50,100 |
| 1987 | 4,100 | 3,900 | 4,200 | 4,700 | 4,300 | 4,200 | 4,400 | 4,400 | 4,400 | 4,300 | 4,600 | 4,400 | 44,219 |
| 1988 | 4,600 | 4,700 | 4,800 | 4,700 | 5,300 | 5,600 | 5,300 | 5,300 | 5,500 | 5,600 | 4,900 | 4,900 | 45,073 |
| 1989 | 4,800 | 4,700 | 4,300 | 4,500 | 4,500 | 4,100 | 4,000 | 4,200 | 4,100 | 4,300 | 4,000 | 3,300 | 46,371 |
| 1990 | 4,000 | 4,000 | 4,200 | 4,100 | 4,200 | 4,100 | 4,100 | 4,300 | 4,100 | 4,100 | 4,200 | 3,900 | 44,363 |
| 1991 | 4,100 | 3,900 | 4,100 | 4,300 | 4,100 | 4,200 | 3,900 | 4,100 | 4,000 | 4,300 | 4,100 | 4,000 | 49,000 |
| 1992 | 3,800 | 3,800 | 3,800 | 3,800 | 3,700 | 3,800 | 3,800 | 3,500 | 3,600 | 3,600 | 3,400 | 3,300 | 45,090 |
| 1993 | 3,400 | 3,500 | 3,600 | 3,600 | 3,500 | 3,600 | 3,500 | 3,600 | 3,500 | 3,500 | 3,500 | 3,400 | 47,107 |
| 1994 | 3,500 | 3,700 | 3,700 | 3,600 | 3,600 | 3,700 | 3,500 | 3,400 | 2,500 | 3,600 | 3,600 | 3,400 | 42,700 |
| 1995 | 3,500 | 3,600 | 3,680 | 3,726 | 3,877 | 3,833 | 3,544 | 3,895 | 3,825 | 3,823 | 3,735 | 3,770 | 44,808 |
| 1996[1] | 3,862 | 3,938 | 3,940 | 3,878 | 3,894 | 3,976 | 3,926 | 3,996 | 3,687 | 3,779 | 3,698 | | 42,574 |

[1] Preliminary. *Source: U.S Geological Survey (USGS)*

## United States Tin Stocks (Pig -- Industrial) In Metric Tons

| Year | Jan. 1 | Feb. 1 | Mar. 1 | Apr. 1 | May 1 | June 1 | July 1 | Aug. 1 | Sept. 1 | Oct. 1 | Nov. 1 | Dec. 1 |
|---|---|---|---|---|---|---|---|---|---|---|---|---|
| 1981 | 5,504 | 5,968 | 5,745 | 5,229 | 5,725 | 5,978 | 6,227 | 6,465 | 5,663 | 5,710 | 5,325 | 5,563 |
| 1982 | 5,988 | 3,872 | 3,490 | 3,829 | 5,222 | 4,953 | 4,653 | 3,888 | 2,910 | 2,940 | 2,970 | 3,437 |
| 1983 | 3,152 | 4,609 | 3,513 | 3,815 | 4,026 | 3,527 | 3,634 | 3,931 | 4,091 | 3,604 | 3,074 | 3,180 |
| 1984 | 3,020 | 2,968 | 2,268 | 2,840 | 2,646 | 3,119 | 2,795 | 2,688 | 2,837 | 2,495 | 2,512 | 2,326 |
| 1985 | 2,592 | 2,766 | 2,283 | 2,407 | 2,228 | 2,853 | 3,042 | 2,762 | 2,663 | 2,985 | 4,121 | 4,913 |
| 1986 | 5,665 | 5,310 | 4,692 | 3,097 | 4,127 | 3,987 | 4,032 | 4,166 | 4,246 | 3,497 | 3,554 | 4,681 |
| 1987 | 4,802 | 5,232 | 6,394 | 6,321 | 7,263 | 8,087 | 6,663 | 4,288 | 5,373 | 5,533 | 6,402 | 5,460 |
| 1988 | 4,428 | 4,490 | 5,989 | 5,631 | 5,868 | 6,128 | 6,456 | 5,665 | 4,350 | 4,171 | 4,371 | 4,781 |
| 1989 | 4,943 | 4,242 | 3,894 | 4,320 | 3,717 | 4,945 | 4,912 | 5,597 | 5,872 | 6,241 | 5,313 | 5,530 |
| 1990 | 6,072 | 5,975 | 5,824 | 6,401 | 4,959 | 3,298 | 3,792 | 3,592 | 3,836 | 4,762 | 4,819 | 4,829 |
| 1991 | 6,337 | 6,677 | 6,688 | 6,177 | 5,993 | 5,991 | 6,348 | 6,739 | 6,544 | 8,544 | 6,616 | 6,347 |
| 1992 | 3,024 | 3,022 | 3,369 | 2,844 | 2,877 | 2,901 | 2,651 | 3,111 | 3,321 | 3,454 | 3,654 | 3,178 |
| 1993 | 3,221 | 3,572 | 4,450 | 4,483 | 3,898 | 3,609 | 4,648 | 4,652 | 4,561 | 3,709 | 3,262 | 3,535 |
| 1994 | 3,651 | 4,635 | 3,775 | 3,967 | 3,471 | 3,470 | 3,825 | 3,027 | 2,891 | 2,980 | 2,844 | 2,908 |
| 1995 | 2,741 | 3,931 | 3,850 | 2,780 | 3,000 | 3,080 | 3,210 | 3,910 | 3,800 | 3,880 | 4,380 | 4,290 |
| 1996[1] | 4,580 | 6,000 | 5,200 | 4,390 | 4,880 | 5,590 | 5,760 | 5,640 | 4,790 | 4,580 | 4,810 | 6,810 |

[1] Preliminary. *Source: U.S. Geological Survey (USGS)*

# TIN

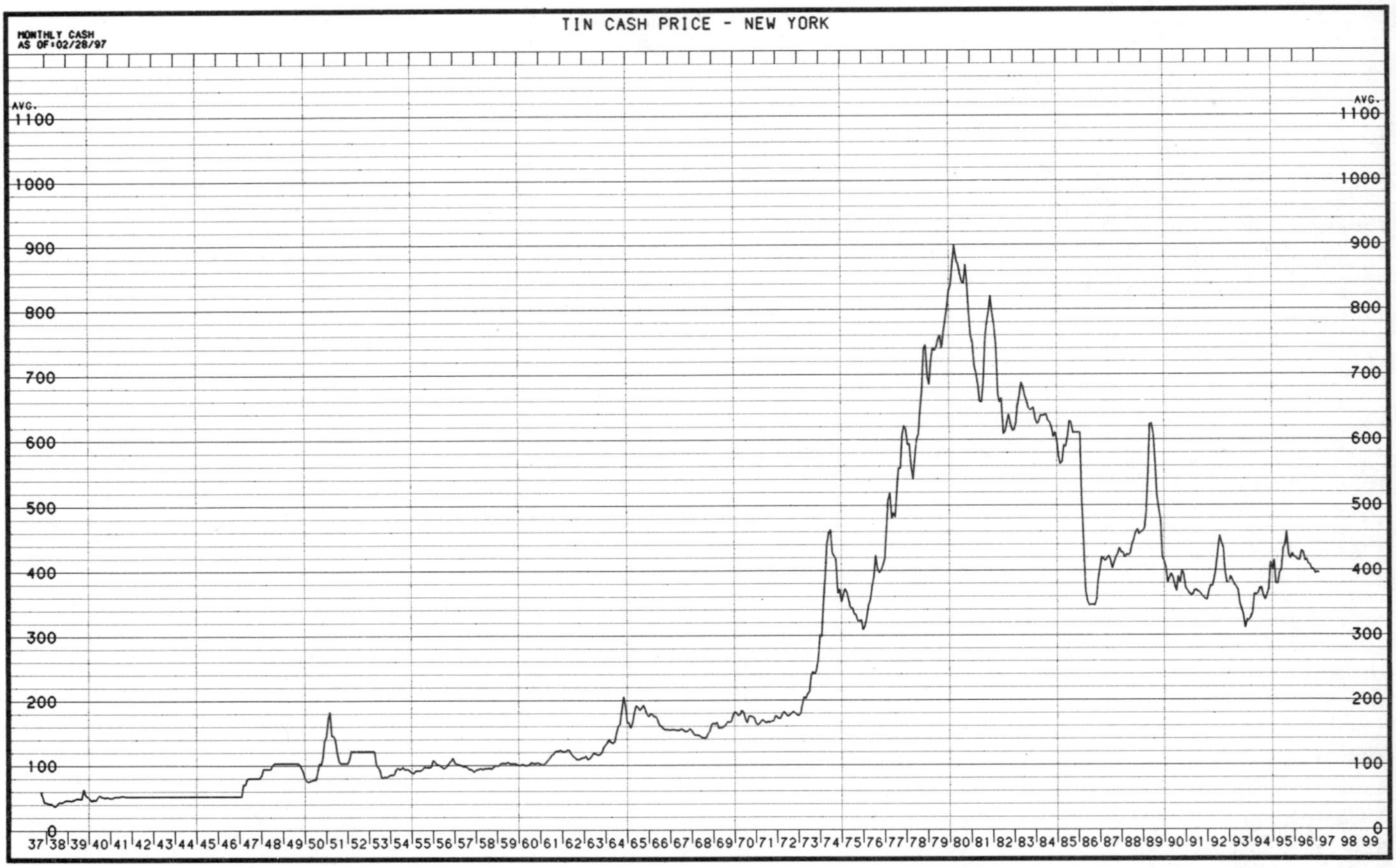


**Average Price of Ex-Dock Tin in New York** In Cents Per Pound

| Year | Jan. | Feb. | Mar. | Apr. | May | June | July | Aug. | Sept. | Oct. | Nov. | Dec. | Average |
|---|---|---|---|---|---|---|---|---|---|---|---|---|---|
| 1979 | 684.56 | 724.57 | 746.14 | 740.06 | 745.18 | 760.14 | 712.31 | 739.93 | 762.03 | 785.54 | 801.23 | 830.88 | 756.87 |
| 1980 | 836.46 | 866.39 | 900.23 | 872.21 | 861.84 | 845.19 | 836.95 | 834.61 | 861.92 | 832.92 | 788.67 | 751.36 | 840.73 |
| 1981 | 739.94 | 705.76 | 691.70 | 677.38 | 652.07 | 652.77 | 680.22 | 746.06 | 777.36 | 798.70 | 813.00 | 801.59 | 728.05 |
| 1982 | 787.41 | 749.93 | 669.51 | 649.58 | 662.35 | 643.00 | 638.00 | 636.33 | 644.33 | 627.94 | 627.93 | 630.18 | 663.88 |
| 1983[1] | 648.90 | 653.89 | 669.18 | 692.29 | 683.36 | 670.54 | 663.13 | 653.10 | 649.31 | 650.65 | 653.02 | 636.71 | 660.34 |
| 1984 | 590.60 | 592.10 | 603.40 | 605.10 | 601.70 | 602.20 | 593.50 | 594.70 | 590.20 | 578.60 | 574.40 | 566.10 | 591.05 |
| 1985 | 542.10 | 532.00 | 533.80 | 559.10 | 557.70 | 576.30 | 594.90 | 593.80 | 578.60 | 580.50 | NQ | NQ | 564.88 |
| 1986 | NQ | NQ | 350.64 | 274.98 | 265.04 | 260.28 | 261.51 | 261.26 | 260.69 | 267.48 | 292.84 | 308.26 | 280.30 |
| 1987 | 321.56 | 320.39 | 317.66 | 320.98 | 323.60 | 316.96 | 307.59 | 314.63 | 321.86 | 324.81 | 332.21 | 327.65 | 320.83 |
| 1988 | 326.68 | 321.12 | 324.79 | 323.85 | 325.28 | 337.37 | 342.18 | 351.14 | 355.20 | 347.84 | 351.10 | 352.42 | 338.25 |
| 1989 | 355.80 | 377.77 | 419.64 | 486.72 | 484.42 | 474.15 | 458.64 | 415.80 | 395.99 | 379.67 | 329.10 | 324.79 | 408.54 |
| 1990 | 317.89 | 296.28 | 302.41 | 308.97 | 307.02 | 295.86 | 288.09 | 287.48 | 279.20 | 296.11 | 292.27 | 261.82 | 295.41 |
| 1991 | 269.97 | 268.00 | 264.51 | 265.78 | 271.78 | 272.30 | 270.55 | 269.02 | 265.86 | 264.50 | 262.26 | 262.05 | 267.21 |
| 1992 | 261.30 | 267.79 | 267.52 | 277.20 | 290.05 | 313.07 | 331.10 | 322.19 | 315.66 | 291.60 | 268.54 | 271.76 | 289.81 |
| 1993 | 280.40 | 280.91 | 277.43 | 275.67 | 269.62 | 255.35 | 252.31 | 230.17 | 213.22 | 220.02 | 224.88 | 236.90 | 251.41 |
| 1994 | 249.55 | 267.55 | 261.20 | 258.49 | 277.79 | 282.43 | 276.11 | 265.35 | 279.39 | 292.17 | 325.83 | 346.21 | 281.84 |
| 1995 | 374.77 | 260.25 | 266.45 | 288.00 | 283.62 | 314.33 | 316.06 | 331.64 | 304.12 | 297.77 | 304.47 | 300.28 | 303.48 |
| 1996 | 299.55 | 297.45 | 296.68 | 308.49 | 306.71 | 296.20 | 298.47 | 291.30 | 292.13 | 285.11 | 285.87 | 280.61 | 294.88 |

[1] Data prior to 1984 are for Straits (Alloyer Price). NQ = No quote. *Source: American Metal Market*

## Tin Plate Production & Tin Recovered in the United States In Metric Tons

| Year | Tinplate Waste (Gross Weight) | Tinplate (All Forms) Gross Weight | Tin Content (Tonne) | Tin per Tonne of Plate (Kilograms) | Tin Metal | Bronze & Brass | Solder | Type Metal | Babbitt | Antimonial Lead | Chemical Compounds | Misc.[2] | Grand Total |
|---|---|---|---|---|---|---|---|---|---|---|---|---|---|
| | Tin Content of Tinplate Produced | | | | Tin Recovered from Scrap by Form of Recovery | | | | | | | | |
| 1981 | 284,505 | 3,288,662 | 13,306 | 4.0 | 1,587 | 8,894 | 3,035 | 576 | 261 | 791 | 265 | 29 | 15,438 |
| 1982 | 208,074 | 2,712,678 | 10,936 | 4.0 | 1,067 | 6,971 | 2,723 | 222 | 237 | 1,015 | 447 | 101 | 12,783 |
| 1983 | 166,186 | 2,586,810 | 9,328 | 3.6 | 1,180 | 8,517 | 3,072 | 172 | 185 | 803 | 182 | 94 | 14,205 |
| 1984 | 151,540 | 2,409,399 | 8,659 | 3.6 | 1,107 | 9,146 | 3,653 | 142 | 123 | 894 | 301 | 51 | 15,417 |
| 1985 | 146,041 | 2,215,042 | 9,321 | 4.2 | 1,302 | 8,045 | 3,565 | 122 | 88 | 791 | 186 | 10 | 14,109 |
| 1986 | 120,186 | 2,068,246 | 8,660 | 4.2 | 1,134 | 7,996 | 3,676 | 197 | 66 | 891 | W | 17 | 13,977 |
| 1987 | 141,842 | 2,302,173 | 10,357 | 4.5 | 1,353 | 10,245 | 3,765 | 66 | 77 | 623 | W | 30 | 16,159 |
| 1988 | 149,054 | 2,375,809 | 11,582 | 4.9 | 578 | 9,939 | 3,619 | 70 | 112 | 902 | W | 29 | 15,249 |
| 1989 | 153,542 | 2,263,769 | 11,764 | 5.2 | 569 | 10,305 | 3,225 | 46 | 116 | 952 | W | W | 15,213 |
| 1990 | 156,419 | 2,467,205 | 11,750 | 4.8 | 186 | 13,312 | 2,876 | 46 | 28 | 739 | W | 4 | 17,187 |
| 1991 | 166,647 | 2,468,769 | 11,482 | 4.7 | 234 | 11,719 | W | 44 | 24 | 928 | W | 2,705 | 12,949 |
| 1992 | 195,760 | 1,620,007 | 9,821 | 6.1 | 137 | 12,761 | W | 47 | 78 | 704 | W | 181 | 13,727 |
| 1993 | 196,874 | 1,625,132 | 9,945 | 6.0 | 112 | 10,670 | W | 43 | 51 | 796 | W | W | 11,672 |
| 1994[1] | 188,921 | 1,528,303 | 9,396 | 6.1 | | | | | | | | | |
| 1995[1] | 205,000 | 1,660,000 | 9,600 | 5.8 | | | | | | | | | |

[1] Preliminary. [2] Includes foil, terne metal, cable lead, and items indicated by symbol "W". W = Withheld proprietary data. *Source: U.S. Geological Survey*

## U.S. Consumption of Primary and Secondary Tin In Metric Tons

| Year | Net Import Reliance as a % of Apparent Consumption | Industry Stocks Jan. 1[2] | Net Receipts: Primary | Net Receipts: Secondary | Net Receipts: Scrap | Net Receipts: Total | Available Supply | Stocks Dec. 31 (Total Available Less Total Processed) | Total Processed | Consumed in Manufacturing Products |
|---|---|---|---|---|---|---|---|---|---|---|
| 1982 | 68 | 8,717 | 35,843 | 6,507 | 7,830 | 50,180 | 58,897 | 12,328 | 46,569 | 46,295 |
| 1983 | 73 | 7,549 | 36,494 | 5,412 | 7,435 | 49,341 | 56,890 | 11,098 | 45,792 | 45,547 |
| 1984 | 74 | 8,063 | 38,813 | 6,110 | 6,791 | 51,714 | 59,777 | 11,145 | 48,632 | 48,315 |
| 1985 | 72 | 8,430 | 38,006 | 8,904 | 7,471 | 54,381 | 62,811 | 13,928 | 48,883 | 48,669 |
| 1986 | 74 | 9,336 | 35,475 | 11,636 | 6,346 | 53,457 | 62,793 | 18,915 | 43,878 | 43,524 |
| 1987 | 74 | 9,876 | 38,401 | 11,707 | 6,635 | 56,743 | 66,619 | 21,887 | 44,731 | 44,219 |
| 1988 | 78 | 10,217 | 39,421 | 12,472 | 6,707 | 58,600 | 68,817 | 23,586 | 46,232 | 45,602 |
| 1989 | 77 | 9,242 | 37,760 | 10,901 | 8,168 | 56,829 | 66,071 | 19,184 | 46,887 | 46,463 |
| 1990 | 71 | 13,551 | 38,473 | 9,501 | 6,534 | 54,508 | 68,059 | 22,578 | 45,481 | 45,165 |
| 1991 | 74 | 12,502 | 36,126 | 1,622 | 8,370 | 46,118 | 58,620 | 13,540 | 45,080 | 44,805 |
| 1992 | 80 | 12,038 | 34,327 | 2,279 | 8,412 | 45,018 | 57,056 | 11,669 | 45,387 | 45,120 |
| 1993 | 84 | 8,556 | 37,700 | 3,280 | 8,768 | 49,700 | 58,300 | 11,566 | 46,700 | 46,600 |
| 1994 | 83 | 9,540 | 35,400 | 4,210 | 4,940 | 44,500 | 54,100 | 11,600 | 42,500 | 42,200 |
| 1995[1] | 84 | 8,480 | 39,300 | 4,100 | 6,230 | 49,600 | 58,100 | 12,100 | 45,900 | 45,800 |

[1] Preliminary. [2] Includes tin in transit to the U.S. *Source: U.S. Geological Survey*

## Consumption of Tin in the United States by Finished Products In Metric Tons (Contained Tin)

| Year | Tinplate[2] | Solder | Babbitt | Bronze & Brass | Tinning | Chemicals[3] | Tin Powder | Bar Tin & Anodes | White Metal | Other | Total | Total: Primary | Total: Secondary |
|---|---|---|---|---|---|---|---|---|---|---|---|---|---|
| 1982 | 11,134 | 13,142 | 1,915 | 4,400 | 1,887 | W | 906 | 509 | 1,177 | 11,225 | 46,295 | 33,019 | 13,276 |
| 1983 | 9,462 | 14,120 | 2,881 | 4,583 | 1,759 | W | 793 | 654 | 937 | 10,358 | 45,547 | 34,301 | 11,246 |
| 1984 | 8,825 | 17,249 | 2,684 | 4,998 | 1,748 | W | 1,057 | 526 | 958 | 11,396 | 48,315 | 37,201 | 11,114 |
| 1985 | 9,321 | 18,621 | 1,488 | 4,330 | 1,511 | W | 976 | 466 | 937 | 12,100 | 48,669 | 36,524 | 12,145 |
| 1986 | 8,660 | 15,810 | 1,324 | 3,502 | 1,437 | W | 1,002 | 449 | 1,134 | 10,204 | 43,522 | 33,324 | 10,198 |
| 1987 | 10,357 | 15,240 | 1,060 | 3,559 | 1,398 | W | W | 703 | 1,175 | 10,704 | 44,219 | 35,620 | 8,599 |
| 1988 | 11,582 | 15,288 | 926 | 3,934 | 1,406 | W | W | 557 | 1,131 | 10,777 | 45,601 | 37,529 | 8,072 |
| 1989 | 11,764 | 16,370 | 794 | 3,693 | 1,505 | W | 711 | 619 | 1,074 | 9,926 | 46,456 | 36,603 | 9,853 |
| 1990 | 11,750 | 16,443 | 763 | 3,166 | 1,707 | 6,275 | 563 | 603 | 1,045 | 2,850 | 45,165 | 36,770 | 8,395 |
| 1991 | 11,482 | 16,296 | 941 | 2,896 | 1,465 | 6,564 | 539 | 436 | 868 | 3,318 | 44,805 | 35,138 | 9,667 |
| 1992 | 9,821 | 18,461 | 916 | 2,916 | 1,275 | 6,301 | 573 | 919 | 974 | 2,964 | 45,090 | 34,983 | 10,137 |
| 1993 | 9,650 | 19,000 | 823 | 3,093 | 1,249 | 6,446 | 608 | 946 | 789 | 3,927 | 46,600 | 34,600 | 11,900 |
| 1994 | 9,480 | 15,100 | 831 | 3,080 | 1,230 | 5,740 | 625 | 1,190 | 992 | 3,990 | 42,200 | 33,700 | 8,530 |
| 1995[1] | 9,670 | 17,500 | 871 | 2,830 | 1,120 | 7,060 | 159 | 1,200 | 965 | 4,560 | 45,800 | 35,100 | 10,700 |

[1] Preliminary. [2] Includes small quantity of secondary pig tin and tin acquired in chemicals. [3] Including tin oxide. W = Withheld proprietary data.
*Source: U.S. Geological Survey*

# Titanium

Titanium's unique properties of having one-half the density of steel, excellent strength, and immunity to corrosion make it an ideal construction material for engines and airframes. Pure titanium metal is called "sponge" because of its porous cellular form. The sponge is processed to form an ingot, and the ingot is processed by mills to make plate sheet tubing. There are titanium plants in the U.S., Japan, Great Britain, China, and Russia. Other uses of titanium mill products are pollution control devices, desalination plants, chemical processing, and in tubing for power plants and oil refineries. Titanium dioxide finds use as a white pigment for exterior paints, paper production, and pigment for ink and porcelain enamels.

U.S. production of titanium ingot in the second quarter of 1996 was 13,000 tonnes, up 33 percent from the end of 1995. First half 1996 production of titanium ingots was 39,800 tonnes. Production of titanium mill products in the April-June 1996 period was 8,790 tonnes, up almost 49 percent from the same period of 1995. For the first half of 1996, mill product production was 15,900 tonnes. For all of 1995, production was 23,300 tonnes. Production statistics for titanium sponge was withheld to avoid disclosing proprietary data.

U.S. consumption of titanium sponge in the second quarter of 1996 was 6,310 tonnes, an increase of 18 percent from the second quarter of 1995. For the first half of 1996, sponge consumption was 13,000 tonnes. For all of 1995, titanium sponge consumption was 21,500 tonnes. Titanium scrap consumption in the second quarter 1996 was 6,130 tonnes, up 32 percent from the same period of 1995. First half 1996 scrap consumption was 12,200 tonnes while for all of 1995 it was 20,600 tonnes. Titanium ingot consumption in the April-June 1996 quarter was 10,100 tonnes and for the first half of 1996 it was 19,100 tonnes. For 1995, ingot consumption was 30,600 tonnes. Mill product consumption in the second quarter of 1996 was 7,210 tonnes with first half 1996 consumption at 13,200 tonnes. For all 1995, mill product consumption was 19,800 tonnes.

At the end of June 1996, U.S. government stocks of titanium sponge were 33,400 tonnes, industry stocks of sponge were 5,500 tonnes, scrap 10,100 tonnes, and ingot 3,940 tonnes.

## Average Titanium Prices in the United States

| Year | Ilmenite F.O.B. Australian Ports $ Tonne | Slag, 85% $TiO_2$ F.O.B. Richards Bay, South Africa $ Tonne | Rutile Large Lots Bulk, F.O.B. U.S. East Coast $ Tonne[3] | Rutile Bagged F.O.B. Australian Ports $ Tonne[3] | Avg. Price of Grade A Titanium Sponge, F.O.B. Shipping Point (Dollars Per Pound) | Titanium Metal Sponge (Dollars Per Pound) | Titanium Dioxide Pigments, F.O.B. U.S. Plants: Anatase (Dollars Per Pound) | Titanium Dioxide Pigments, F.O.B. U.S. Plants: Rutile (Dollars Per Pound) |
|---|---|---|---|---|---|---|---|---|
| 1985 | 38-42 | 212 | 350-360 | 371-386 | 5.70 | 3.50-4.00 | .72-.73 | .78 |
| 1986 | 47-53 | 225-230 | 355-375 | 398-422 | 4.32 | 3.90-4.30 | .75-.77 | .80-.82 |
| 1987 | 46-52 | 235-245 | 355-375 | 398-418 | 4.06 | 4.00-4.20 | .75-.77 | .80-.82 |
| 1988 | 64-77 | 250-275 | NA | 547-572 | 4.21 | 4.25-4.75 | .92-.95 | .95-.97 |
| 1989 | 67-75 | 275-300 | 540-550 | 553-632 | 5.11 | 4.80-5.30 | 1.01-1.02 | 1.04-1.05 |
| 1990 | 69-77 | 285-310 | 550-580 | 693-770 | 5.31 | 4.75 | .99 | 1.01 |
| 1991 | 68-76 | 295-325 | 606-650 | 515-545 | 5.25 | 4.75 | .99 | .99 |
| 1992 | 58-62 | 310 | 510-520 | 380-414 | 3.96 | 3.50-4.00 | .99 | .92-.95 |
| 1993 | 61-64 | 330 | NA | 370-400 | 3.75 | 3.50-4.00 | .99 | .92-.95 |
| 1994 | 74-80 | 334 | 410-430 | 450-480 | 3.96 | 3.75-4.25 | .94-.96 | .92-.94 |
| 1995[1] | 81-85 | 349 | 550-650 | 650-800 | 4.06 | 4.25-4.50 | .92-.96 | .99-1.03 |
| 1996[2] | 80-91 | 351 | 600-700 | 750-975 | NA | 4.25-4.50 | 1.06-1.08 | 1.08-1.10 |

[1] Preliminary. [2] Estimate. [3] Prices prior to 1988 are per short ton. NA = Not available. *Source: U.S. Geological Survey*

## Salient Statistics of Titanium in the United States In Metric Tons

| Year | Titanium Dioxide Pigment: Production | Titanium Dioxide Pigment: Imports[3] | Titanium Dioxide Pigment: Apparent Consumption | Ilmenite: Imports[3] | Ilmenite: Consumption | Titanium Slag: Imports[3] | Titanium Slag: Consumption | Rutile[4]: Imports[3] | Rutile[4]: Consumption | Exports of Titanium Products: Ores & Concentrates | Exports: Scrap | Exports: Dioxide & Pigments | Exports: Ingots, Billets, Etc. |
|---|---|---|---|---|---|---|---|---|---|---|---|---|---|
| 1984 | 834,889 | 193,501 | 916,198 | 409,605 | 783,391 | 209,839 | 200,858 | 180,508 | 317,902 | 8,651 | 4,109 | 106,124 | 2,071 |
| 1985[5] | 783,393 | 178,001 | 893,195 | 459,765 | 685,896 | 264,742 | 228,635 | 162,988 | 276,944 | 25,183 | 6,133 | 93,624 | 2,039 |
| 1986 | 844,274 | 183,862 | 908,055 | 422,401 | 731,436 | 328,285 | 250,677 | 158,595 | 298,601 | 4,821 | 5,809 | 104,734 | 1,922 |
| 1987 | 878,558 | 174,219 | 966,169 | 307,515 | 744,266 | 408,785 | 251,423 | 197,937 | 320,505 | 4,023 | 5,083 | 108,889 | 2,467 |
| 1988 | 926,746 | 185,468 | 991,536 | 394,170 | 679,008 | 434,641 | 300,013 | 231,124 | 352,356 | 9,368 | 5,939 | 118,422 | 2,083 |
| 1989 | 1,006,581 | 166,346 | 947,259 | 411,751 | 659,584 | 386,146 | 414,830 | 264,895 | 366,143 | 19,832 | 5,474 | 212,197 | 2,702 |
| 1990 | 978,659 | 147,592 | 925,447 | 345,907 | 688,948 | 373,623 | 390,537 | 274,605 | 369,454 | 18,765 | 5,487 | 202,288 | 2,371 |
| 1991 | 991,976 | 166,094 | 935,829 | 213,886 | 738,089 | 408,302 | 341,379 | 240,120 | 368,643 | 26,912 | 4,568 | 211,854 | 1,700 |
| 1992 | 1,137,038 | 169,260 | 999,930 | 294,585 | 684,882 | 537,118 | 539,323 | 317,399 | 460,969 | 34,665 | 2,770 | 270,422 | 1,455 |
| 1993 | 1,161,561 | 171,939 | 1,028,311 | 301,000 | 693,940 | 476,000 | 545,809 | 371,481 | 464,825 | 15,202 | 3,893 | 261,000 | 1,511 |
| 1994[1] | 1,250,000 | 176,000 | 1,090,000 | 336,000 | W | 472,000 | 583,000 | 332,000 | 510,000 | 19,000 | 4,120 | 313,000 | 1,559 |
| 1995[2] | 1,250,000 | 183,000 | 1,080,000 | 473,000 | W | 388,000 | 582,000 | 318,000 | 480,000 | 32,300 | 3,420 | 306,000 | 2,559 |

[1] Preliminary. [2] Estimate. [3] For consumption. [4] Natural and synthetic. [5] Data shown in short tons prior to 1985. W = Withheld proprietary data.
*Source: U.S. Geological Survey*

## World Production of Titanium Ilmenite Concentrates    In Thousands of Metric Tons

| Year | Australia[2] | Brazil | China | India | Malaysia | Norway | Sierra Leone | Sri Lanka | Thailand | Ukraine[3] | World Total | -- Titaniferous Slag[4] -- Canada | South Africa |
|---|---|---|---|---|---|---|---|---|---|---|---|---|---|
| 1981 | 1,478 | 17.5 | 150.0 | 179.1 | 190.4 | 727.1 | NA | 88.2 | NA | 470 | 5,266 | 837 | 408 |
| 1982 | 1,289 | 12.5 | 150.0 | 168.6 | 111.6 | 608.2 | NA | 75.3 | NA | 475 | 4,496 | 737 | 420 |
| 1983 | 1,003 | 33.6 | 154.0 | 148.2 | 245.5 | 612.8 | NA | 90.1 | NA | 480 | 4,108 | 700 | 460 |
| 1984[5] | 1,681 | 45.1 | 154.0 | 154.3 | 296.0 | 718.5 | NA | 112.5 | NA | 485 | 5,091 | 800 | 460 |
| 1985 | 1,433 | 76.4 | 140.0 | 143.0 | 314.7 | 735.8 | NA | 114.9 | 1.00 | 445 | 4,737 | 845 | 435 |
| 1986 | 1,252 | 75.5 | 140.0 | 140.0 | 414.9 | 803.6 | NA | 129.9 | 13.50 | 450 | 4,705 | 850 | 435 |
| 1987 | 1,509 | 169.3 | 140.0 | 140.0 | 509.2 | 852.3 | 5.6 | 128.5 | 27.10 | 455 | 3,937 | 925 | 650 |
| 1988 | 1,622 | 142.2 | 150.0 | 229.7 | 486.3 | 898.0 | 42.1 | 74.3 | 18.30 | 460 | 4,033 | 1,025 | 400 |
| 1989 | 1,714 | 144.2 | 150.0 | 240.7 | 533.7 | 929.8 | 62.3 | 101.4 | 17.00 | 460 | 4,353 | 1,040 | 725 |
| 1990 | 1,621 | 114.1 | 150.0 | 280.0 | 530.2 | 814.5 | 54.6 | 66.4 | 10.70 | 430 | 4,072 | 1,046 | 840 |
| 1991 | 1,381 | 69.1 | 150.0 | 312.0 | 336.3 | 625.0 | 60.4 | 60.9 | 17.10 | 400 | 3,360 | 701 | 808 |
| 1992 | 1,810 | 76.6 | 150.0 | 300.0 | 337.7 | 708.0 | 60.3 | 33.3 | 3.00 | 250 | 3,720 | 753 | 884 |
| 1993 | 1,825 | 90.6 | 155.0 | 320.0 | 289.0 | 713.0 | 62.9 | 76.9 | 20.82 | 200 | 3,750 | 653 | 892 |
| 1994 | 1,817 | 97.4 | 155.0 | 300.0 | 115.9 | 826.0 | 47.4 | 60.4 | 1.68 | 150 | 3,570 | 764 | 744 |
| 1995[1] | 2,010 | 102.0 | 160.0 | 300.0 | 151.7 | 830.0 | ----- | 60.0 | .03 | 200 | 3,810 | 815 | 990 |

[1] Preliminary. [2] Includes leucoxene. [3] Formerly part of the U.S.S.R.; data not reported separately until 1992. [4] Approximately 10% of total production is ilmenite. Beginning in 1988, 25% of Norway's ilmenite production was used to produce slag containing 75% $TiO_2$. [5] Data prior to 1985 are shown in thousands of short tons. NA = Not available. *Source: U.S. Geological Survey*

## World Production of Titanium Rutile Concentrates    In Metric Tons

| Year | Australia | Brazil | India | Sierre Leone | South Africa | Sri Lanka | Thailand | Ukraine[2] | World Total |
|---|---|---|---|---|---|---|---|---|---|
| 1981 | 254,432 | 190 | 7,397 | 55,992 | 55,000 | 14,662 | NA | 11,000 | 398,673 |
| 1982 | 243,277 | 258 | 6,374 | 52,590 | 52,000 | 7,950 | NA | 11,000 | 373,449 |
| 1983 | 180,089 | 510 | 6,100 | 79,146 | 62,000 | 8,921 | NA | 11,000 | 347,766 |
| 1984[3] | 187,860 | 454 | 6,600 | 100,641 | 62,000 | 7,129 | NA | 11,000 | 375,684 |
| 1985 | 211,615 | 713 | 6,800 | 80,611 | 55,000 | 8,558 | 110 | 10,000 | 373,407 |
| 1986 | 215,774 | 495 | 7,000 | 97,100 | 55,000 | 8,443 | 48 | 10,000 | 393,860 |
| 1987 | 246,263 | 324 | 7,000 | 113,300 | 55,000 | 7,200 | 92 | 10,000 | 439,179 |
| 1988 | 230,637 | 1,514 | 5,000 | 126,358 | 55,000 | 5,255 | 128 | 10,000 | 433,892 |
| 1989 | 243,000 | 2,613 | 9,931 | 128,198 | 60,000 | 5,589 | 150 | 10,000 | 459,331 |
| 1990 | 245,000 | 1,814 | 11,000 | 144,284 | 64,056 | 5,460 | NA | 9,500 | 481,114 |
| 1991 | 201,000 | 1,094 | 13,635 | 154,800 | 77,000 | 3,085 | 76 | 9,000 | 460,000 |
| 1992 | 183,000 | 1,800 | 10,000 | 148,990 | 84,000 | 2,741 | 281 | 5,000 | 436,000 |
| 1993 | 186,000 | 1,744 | 13,900 | 152,000 | 85,000 | 2,643 | 87 | 4,000 | 445,000 |
| 1994 | 233,000 | 1,911 | 14,000 | 137,000 | 78,000 | 2,410 | 49 | 3,000 | 469,000 |
| 1995[1] | 200,000 | 1,900 | 14,000 | ------ | 90,000 | 2,400 | ------ | 4,000 | 312,000 |

[1] Preliminary. [2] Formerly part of the U.S.S.R.; data not reported separately until 1992. [3] Data prior to 1985 are shown in short tons. NA = Not available. *Source: U.S. Geological Survey*

## World Production of Titanium Sponge Metal & U.S. Consumption of Titanium Concentrates

| | Production of Titanium (In Metric Tons) ---- Sponge Metal[2] ---- | | | | | | -- U.S. Consumption of Titanium Concentrates, by Products (In Metric Tons) -- ------ Ilmenite ($TiO_2$ Content) ----- | | | ---- Rutile ($TiO_2$ Content) ---- | | | |
|---|---|---|---|---|---|---|---|---|---|---|---|---|---|
| Year | China | Japan | Russia[3] | United Kingdom | United States | Total | Pigments | Misc. | Total | Welding Rod Coatings | Pigments | Misc. | Total |
| 1981 | 2,000 | 27,500 | 42,000 | 2,600 | 26,419 | 100,519 | 501,301 | 9,721 | 511,022 | 6,944 | 192,779 | 66,873 | 266,596 |
| 1982 | 1,500 | 18,600 | 44,000 | 2,600 | 15,600 | 82,300 | 345,618 | 6,775 | 35,293 | 5,275 | 184,403 | 35,435 | 225,113 |
| 1983 | 2,000 | 11,600 | 45,000 | 2,000 | 13,966 | 74,000 | 468,279 | 6,006 | 474,285 | 3,649 | 210,949 | 35,820 | 250,418 |
| 1984 | 2,000 | 16,938 | 46,000 | 2,500 | 24,326 | 92,000 | 492,658 | 6,319 | 498,977 | 3,911 | 231,808 | 62,920 | 298,639 |
| 1985 | 2,000 | 16,938 | 47,000 | 1,500 | 23,257 | 91,000 | 474,561 | 6,450 | 481,011 | 4,881 | 239,893 | 41,714 | 286,488 |
| 1986 | 2,000 | 18,000 | 48,000 | 1,500 | 17,500 | 87,000 | 511,070 | 1,655 | 512,725 | 7,667 | 244,178 | 57,539 | 309,384 |
| 1987[4] | 2,000 | 11,105 | 49,000 | 1,500 | 19,675 | 83,000 | 463,072 | 1,817 | 510,449 | 4,168 | 271,658 | 56,558 | 332,384 |
| 1988 | 2,000 | 16,500 | 46,000 | 1,500 | 24,000 | 88,000 | 429,736 | 590 | 429,737 | 3,737 | 262,998 | 64,641 | 331,376 |
| 1989 | 2,000 | 21,000 | 46,000 | 1,500 | 25,225 | 95,725 | 419,329 | 414 | 419,743 | 3,603 | 271,208 | 71,178 | 345,989 |
| 1990 | 2,000 | 25,630 | 47,000 | 1,500 | 24,679 | 101,000 | 445,502 | 726 | 446,228 | 4,047 | 271,637 | 71,373 | 347,057 |
| 1991 | 2,000 | 18,945 | 20,000 | 2,000 | 13,366 | 56,000 | 476,145 | 495 | 476,640 | 6,931 | 286,741 | 42,200 | 335,872 |
| 1992 | 2,000 | 14,554 | 20,000 | 2,000 | W | 38,554 | 425,876 | 647 | 426,523 | W | 405,875 | 32,553 | 438,428 |
| 1993 | 2,000 | 14,400 | 20,000 | 1,000 | 27,938 | 37,000 | 434,097 | 451 | 434,548 | W | 405,784 | 30,223 | 436,007 |
| 1994 | 2,000 | 14,400 | 12,000 | ------ | 29,510 | 33,000 | W | 637 | W | W | 460,000 | 18,500 | 478,500 |
| 1995[1] | 2,000 | 16,000 | 12,000 | ------ | ------ | 35,000 | W | 236 | W | W | 417,000 | 22,300 | 439,300 |

[1] Preliminary. [2] Unconsolidated metal in various forms. [3] Formerly part of the U.S.S.R.; data not reported separately until 1993. [4] Data prior to 1988 are shown in short tons. NA = Not available. W = Withheld proprietary data. *Source: U.S. Geological Survey*

# Tobacco

One of the most interesting developments in the U.S. tobacco market has been the shift in emphasis from the domestic market to the export market. In part this has been due to a gradual decline in cigarette consumption in the U.S. For several years U.S. cigarette use has declined, a trend unlikely to be reversed anytime soon. There have been a number of reasons cited for the decline. One has been that cigarette prices at the retail level have been increasing. The number of prohibitions and restrictions on where people can smoke continues to increase. The obvious negative health impacts of smoking as well as the declining social acceptance of cigarettes have been major contributors to the decline. As such, the per capita consumption of cigarettes has fallen to levels not seen since the early 1940's.

While U.S. cigarette production exceeds 700 billion units, exports now comprise about a third of the total. U.S. exports of cigarettes have been rising quickly as has world trade in cigarettes. In terms of production, world output of tobacco has averaged about seven million tonnes for the last few years. China is by far the world's largest producer with about 37 percent of global output. The U.S. is the next largest producer with about 10 percent followed by India with 8 percent.

The USDA estimates that world production of tobacco in 1996 was 6.3 million tonnes (dry weight), up 10 percent from the 1995 total of 5.8 million tonnes. Tobacco production in China was estimated at 2.7 million tonnes, up almost 17 percent from 1995. U.S. tobacco output in 1996 was estimated at 609,013 tonnes, up 19 percent from the previous year. India, the third largest producer, had estimated production of 451,125 tonnes, down 4 percent from 1995. Brazilian tobacco production was estimated at 348,000 tonnes, up 7 percent from 1995. Turkey produced 189,810 tonnes, up 5 percent while Zimbabwe's output was 177,726 tonnes, down 1 percent.

World exports of tobacco in 1996 were 1.7 million tonnes, down 1 percent from 1995. The major exporter of tobacco was Brazil with 14 percent of the total or 236,500 tonnes. This was down 8 percent from 1995. U.S. tobacco exports in 1996 were estimated at 210,000 tonnes, virtually unchanged from 1995. Zimbabwe was estimated to have exported 173,994 tonnes of tobacco, marginally lower than in 1995. Malawi exported 120,320 tonnes, up 21 percent from the previous year and 29 percent above 1994's level. Turkey's exports fell to 115,000 tonnes, down 10 percent from 1995. Greece exported 100,000 tonnes of tobacco, down 5 percent from 1995 and 9 percent less than in 1994.

The U.S. is the largest importer of tobacco. Imports in 1996 were estimated at 250,000 tonnes, up 26 percent from 1995, but 5 percent less than in 1994. Germany imported 208,000 tonnes of unmanufactured tobacco, down 1 percent from 1995, but 14 percent above 1994. The Russian Federation imported just over 150,000 tonnes of tobacco, up 4 percent from 1995. Japan imported 124,000 tonnes, up almost 8 percent from 1995. The United Kingdom imported 102,450 tonnes, 28 percent less than in 1995, but almost 5 percent above 1994. The Netherlands imported 89,000 tonnes, about the same as in 1994.

World tobacco consumption in 1996 was estimated at 6.9 million tonnes, almost 1 percent above the level in 1995. Between 1992 and 1996, world tobacco consumption averaged 6.9 million tonnes. China remains by far the world's largest consumer of tobacco. USDA estimated that China used 2.8 million tonnes of tobacco in 1996, about the same level as in 1995. U.S. tobacco consumption in 1996 was 725,000 tonnes, up almost 4 percent from 1995. India is the fourth largest consumer with 1996 use estimated at 445,020 tonnes, up about 2 percent from 1995. Japan's consumption in 1996 was 202,800 tonnes, up 3 percent from 1995. Indonesia consumed 195,620 tonnes of tobacco, up 8 percent from 1995. Germany consumed 179,600 tonnes, about the same level as 1995.

World tobacco stocks at the end of 1996 were 4.9 million tonnes, down 9 percent from 1995 and 24 percent less than 1994. U.S. stocks of tobacco at the end of 1996 were 1.4 million tonnes, down 6 percent from 1995. China's tobacco stocks at the end of 1996 were estimated at 867,766 tonnes, down 16 percent from 1995 and some 45 percent less than at the end of 1994. Japan's end-of-1996 tobacco stocks were 360,646 tonnes, down 2 percent from 1995. Turkey's tobacco stocks at the end of 1996 were estimated at 332,291 tonnes, down 2 percent from 1995 and 11 percent less than in 1994. Brazil's tobacco stocks have also declined. At the end of 1996, stocks were 215,500 tonnes, 20 percent less than in 1995 and 39 percent less than in 1994. Italy had stocks of 191,500 tonnes in 1996, down 8 percent from 1995 and 15 percent less than in 1994.

**World Production of Leaf Tobacco** In Thousands of Metric Tons

| Year | Brazil | Canada | China | France | Greece | India | Indonesia | Italy | Japan | Kyrgyzstan[3] | Pakistan | Philippines | Turkey | United States | Zimbabwe | World Total |
|---|---|---|---|---|---|---|---|---|---|---|---|---|---|---|---|---|
| 1987 | 410.0 | 61.4 | 1,943.0 | 33.9 | 144.0 | 460.2 | 154.0 | 162.1 | 104.4 | 296.0 | 69.0 | 79.4 | 184.7 | 539.3 | 131.5 | 6,160 |
| 1988 | 419.0 | 69.8 | 2,731.3 | 29.4 | 184.4 | 367.4 | 137.8 | 184.4 | 85.8 | 242.0 | 69.5 | 68.8 | 218.8 | 621.2 | 123.7 | 6,835 |
| 1989 | 462.0 | 75.6 | 2,830.4 | 29.2 | 197.3 | 492.8 | 146.9 | 197.3 | 74.4 | 233.2 | 71.1 | 73.3 | 269.5 | 620.2 | 135.2 | 7,111 |
| 1990 | 435.0 | 63.1 | 2,627.5 | 28.3 | 134.4 | 564.4 | 158.9 | 214.8 | 80.5 | 292.7 | 68.0 | 70.1 | 295.6 | 737.7 | 139.8 | 7,106 |
| 1991 | 422.0 | 78.7 | 3,030.7 | 29.5 | 165.7 | 555.9 | 164.9 | 193.3 | 69.9 | 250.5 | 80.8 | 82.3 | 239.4 | 754.9 | 178.1 | 7,564 |
| 1992 | 577.0 | 71.8 | 3,499.0 | 23.1 | 196.5 | 584.4 | 145.4 | 150.8 | 79.4 | 18.2 | 108.0 | 114.9 | 331.8 | 780.9 | 211.4 | 8,293 |
| 1993 | 608.0 | 86.1 | 3,451.0 | 25.8 | 148.0 | 580.6 | 152.8 | 135.7 | 67.4 | 55.6 | 106.0 | 102.5 | 338.1 | 731.9 | 235.3 | 8,300 |
| 1994 | 442.0 | 71.5 | 2,238.0 | 27.4 | 135.4 | 528.0 | 160.0 | 131.0 | 79.5 | 45.0 | 100.4 | 56.0 | 187.7 | 718.0 | 177.8 | 6,391 |
| 1995[1] | 398.0 | 79.3 | 2,314.0 | 27.4 | 131.9 | 524.5 | 171.4 | 130.0 | 78.2 | 19.0 | 80.9 | 63.7 | 206.6 | 575.4 | 209.0 | 6,508 |
| 1996[2] | 452.0 | 79.3 | 2,500.0 | 25.6 | 131.4 | 501.3 | 177.7 | 132.0 | 77.4 | 30.0 | 79.8 | 57.2 | 227.0 | 701.2 | 207.8 | 7,165 |

[1] Preliminary. [2] Estimate. [3] Formerly part of the U.S.S.R.; data not reported separately until 1992. *Source: Foreign Agricultural Service, U.S. Department of Agriculture*

## Production and Consumption of Tobacco Products in the United States

| Year | Cigarettes -Billions- | Cigars[3] -Millions- | Chewing Tobacco: Plug (Million Pounds) | Chewing Tobacco: Twist (Million Pounds) | Chewing Tobacco: Looseleaf (Million Pounds) | Chewing Tobacco: Total (Million Pounds) | Smoking Tobacco (Million Pounds) | Snuff[4] (Million Pounds) | Consumption[5] of Per Capita[6]: Cigarettes (Number) | Cigars[3] (Number) | Cigarettes (Pounds) | Cigars[3] (Pounds) | Smoking Tobacco (Pounds) | Chewing Tobacco (Pounds) | Total Products (Pounds) |
|---|---|---|---|---|---|---|---|---|---|---|---|---|---|---|---|
| 1987 | 689.4 | 2,133 | 9.9 | 1.4 | 67.3 | 78.7 | 18.0 | 46.2 | 3,197 | 31.7 | 5.50 | .52 | .27 | .89 | 6.30 |
| 1988 | 694.5 | 1,980 | 8.9 | 1.4 | 65.6 | 75.9 | 17.8 | 48.6 | 3,096 | 29.1 | 5.40 | .47 | .25 | .86 | 6.11 |
| 1989 | 677.2 | 2,010 | 8.3 | 1.3 | 64.9 | 74.5 | 17.0 | 49.7 | 2,926 | 27.9 | 4.90 | .46 | .22 | .82 | 5.67 |
| 1990 | 709.7 | 1,896 | 7.4 | 1.3 | 64.3 | 72.9 | 16.4 | 53.1 | 2,817 | 26.2 | 4.80 | .43 | .20 | .79 | 5.48 |
| 1991 | 694.5 | 1,740 | 6.7 | 1.2 | 64.3 | 72.2 | 15.7 | 54.3 | 2,713 | 24.9 | 4.70 | .41 | .19 | .79 | 5.41 |
| 1992 | 718.5 | 1,741 | 5.9 | 1.2 | 61.6 | 69.7 | 14.9 | 57.5 | 2,640 | 24.1 | 4.70 | .40 | .17 | .74 | 5.38 |
| 1993 | 661.0 | 1,795 | 5.3 | 1.1 | 58.0 | 64.4 | 13.7 | 59.1 | 2,539 | 23.9 | 4.50 | .39 | .17 | .70 | 5.12 |
| 1994 | 725.5 | 1,942 | 4.6 | 1.1 | 56.8 | 62.5 | 13.4 | 59.5 | 2,527 | 25.3 | 4.23 | .41 | .16 | .67 | 4.90 |
| 1995[1] | 746.5 | 2,058 | 4.1 | 1.1 | 57.7 | 62.9 | 12.2 | 60.2 | 2,510 | 27.6 | 4.22 | .42 | .16 | .67 | 4.91 |
| 1996[2] | 760.0 | 2,600 | 4.2 | 1.1 | 53.3 | 58.5 | 11.5 | 60.3 | 2,490 | 35.0 | 4.20 | .42 | .15 | .63 | 4.90 |

[1] Preliminary. [2] Estimate. [3] Large cigars and cigarillos. [4] Includes loose-leaf. [5] Consumption of tax-paid tobacco products. Unstemmed processing weight. [6] 18 years and older. *Source: Economic Research Service, U.S. Department of Agriculture*

## Production of Tobacco in the United States In Thousands of Pounds

| Year | Connecticut | Florida | Georgia | Indiana | Kentucky | Maryland | Massachusetts | Missouri | North Carolina | Ohio | Pennsylvania | South Carolina | Tennessee | Virginia | West Virginia | Wisconsin |
|---|---|---|---|---|---|---|---|---|---|---|---|---|---|---|---|---|
| 1987 | 2,716 | 13,804 | 72,160 | 11,070 | 304,845 | 13,338 | 653 | 3,519 | 466,592 | 12,044 | 20,700 | 94,080 | 87,291 | 76,900 | 2,592 | 8,370 |
| 1988 | 2,971 | 17,152 | 85,880 | 10,945 | 355,024 | 11,970 | 767 | 4,422 | 552,627 | 14,497 | 18,175 | 100,125 | 93,142 | 92,177 | 2,720 | 6,906 |
| 1989 | 2,793 | 17,755 | 87,200 | 13,237 | 366,551 | 8,103 | 746 | 5,450 | 541,056 | 15,925 | 17,925 | 103,680 | 79,820 | 93,814 | 1,885 | 11,248 |
| 1990 | 3,007 | 19,044 | 103,845 | 15,050 | 442,253 | 9,656 | 805 | 5,928 | 639,639 | 18,915 | 19,780 | 109,905 | 112,218 | 110,269 | 2,720 | 13,346 |
| 1991 | 2,831 | 15,312 | 80,600 | 18,920 | 479,794 | 12,900 | 830 | 6,825 | 634,655 | 22,776 | 20,765 | 111,180 | 121,524 | 116,849 | 3,420 | 15,191 |
| 1992 | 2,258 | 19,575 | 100,980 | 18,900 | 524,378 | 11,931 | 740 | 3,298 | 609,873 | 21,840 | 20,840 | 112,320 | 146,556 | 111,459 | 3,623 | 13,100 |
| 1993 | 2,533 | 18,673 | 96,320 | 17,415 | 455,080 | 12,255 | 738 | 4,760 | 608,415 | 18,900 | 18,260 | 110,760 | 139,423 | 99,544 | 3,600 | 6,643 |
| 1994 | 2,682 | 16,575 | 80,660 | 15,265 | 453,687 | 12,750 | 792 | 8,015 | 599,833 | 18,360 | 18,360 | 108,100 | 132,289 | 106,092 | 3,550 | 5,910 |
| 1995 | 3,524 | 17,676 | 84,000 | 13,601 | 328,581 | 11,475 | 918 | 5,468 | 484,599 | 15,015 | 15,685 | 105,000 | 92,907 | 81,269 | 2,600 | 6,220 |
| 1996[1] | 3,498 | 20,100 | 113,620 | 14,972 | 428,280 | 12,000 | 1,225 | 6,300 | 590,683 | 14,110 | 15,464 | 117,810 | 114,046 | 106,249 | 2,470 | 4,620 |

[1] Preliminary. *Source: Agricultural Statistics Board, U.S. Department of Agriculture*

## Salient Statistics of Tobacco in the United States

| Year | Acres Harvested 1,000 Acres | Yield Per Acre Pounds | Production Million Pounds | Farm Price ¢ Lb. | Farm Value Million $ | Tobacco (July-June) Exports[2] (Million Pounds) | Tobacco (July-June) Imports[3] (Million Pounds) | U.S. Exports of Cigarettes (Millions) | U.S. Exports of Cigars & Cheroots (Millions) | U.S. Exports of All Tobacco | U.S. Exports of Smoking Tobacco[4] | Stocks of Tobacco[5] Various Types: All Tobacco (Million Pounds) | Fire Cured[6] (Million Pounds) | Cigar Filler[7] (Million Pounds) | Maryland (Million Pounds) |
|---|---|---|---|---|---|---|---|---|---|---|---|---|---|---|---|
| 1987 | 586.3 | 2,028 | 1,191 | 157.1 | 1,871 | 500.0 | 480.3 | 100,246 | 145 | 573 | 43.3 | 3,406 | 93.0 | 43.3 | 42.0 |
| 1988 | 634.0 | 2,160 | 1,370 | 164.6 | 2,254 | 476.7 | 394.6 | 118,499 | 87 | 555 | 43.9 | 2,909 | 79.2 | 35.1 | 37.6 |
| 1989 | 678.4 | 2,016 | 1,367 | 170.8 | 2,335 | 485.9 | 365.0 | 141,782 | 78 | 582 | 46.6 | 2,714 | 75.9 | 31.8 | 27.0 |
| 1990 | 732.3 | 2,218 | 1,625 | 173.8 | 2,827 | 487.4 | 415.0 | 164,301 | 72 | 631 | 58.0 | 2,401 | 70.2 | 26.9 | 19.3 |
| 1991 | 763.4 | 2,179 | 1,664 | 177.3 | 2,951 | 511.0 | 502.2 | 179,200 | 70 | 499 | 63.2 | 2,232 | 66.7 | 25.6 | 12.1 |
| 1992 | 784.4 | 2,195 | 1,722 | 177.7 | 3,059 | 528.8 | 881.0 | 205,600 | 76 | 574 | 59.1 | 2,280 | 61.6 | 26.7 | 9.4 |
| 1993 | 746.4 | 2,161 | 1,613 | 175.3 | 2,830 | 529.7 | 707.8 | 195,476 | 67 | 458 | 62.5 | 2,412 | 64.0 | 26.7 | 7.5 |
| 1994 | 671.1 | 2,359 | 1,583 | 177.4 | 2,779 | 442.1 | 537.5 | 220,200 | 75 | 434 | 77.0 | 2,588 | 69.7 | 24.1 | 8.4 |
| 1995 | 663.1 | 1,913 | 1,269 | 184.5 | 2,305 | 432.6 | 623.3 | 231,100 | 78 | 462 | 91.8 | 2,541 | 79.5 | 20.5 | 11.1 |
| 1996[1] | 733.9 | 2,133 | 1,565 | 192.5 | 2,938 | 623.3 | 592.0 | 260,000 | 84 | 490 | 110.4 | 2,225 | 79.3 | 17.9 | 12.4 |

[1] Preliminary. [2] Domestic. [3] For consumption. [4] In bulk. [5] Flue-cured and cigar wrapper, year beginning July1; for all other types, October 1. [6] Kentucky-Tennessee types 22-23. [7] Types 41-46. *Source: Economic Research Service, U.S. Department of Agriculture*

## Tobacco Production in the U.S., by Types In Thousands of Pounds (Farm-Sale Weight)

| Types | 11-14 | 21 | 22 | 23 | 31 | 32 | 35-36 | 37 | 41 | 41-61 | 51 | 54 | 55 | 61 |
|---|---|---|---|---|---|---|---|---|---|---|---|---|---|---|
| 1987 | 690,914 | 2,600 | 17,524 | 7,451 | 419,360 | 20,738 | 6,849 | 130 | 13,300 | 23,296 | 1,864 | 5,670 | 2,700 | 1,590 |
| 1988 | 813,212 | 2,920 | 19,804 | 8,020 | 477,208 | 18,445 | 7,415 | 127 | 11,700 | 22,372 | 1,630 | 5,016 | 1,890 | 2,108 |
| 1989 | 808,350 | 2,480 | 18,463 | 7,980 | 482,568 | 17,825 | 6,430 | 104 | 10,725 | 25,512 | 1,256 | 7,648 | 3,600 | 2,283 |
| 1990 | 939,234 | 2,762 | 22,931 | 9,285 | 597,927 | 16,316 | 7,491 | 102 | 13,120 | 30,278 | 1,160 | 9,328 | 4,018 | 2,652 |
| 1991 | 911,887 | 3,563 | 20,620 | 8,704 | 658,181 | 19,920 | 8,776 | 156 | 13,735 | 32,587 | 1,433 | 9,799 | 5,392 | 2,228 |
| 1992 | 906,025 | 2,567 | 23,736 | 10,486 | 719,552 | 18,771 | 10,332 | 124 | 14,000 | 30,098 | 1,484 | 8,460 | 4,640 | 1,514 |
| 1993 | 886,908 | 1,872 | 26,985 | 12,060 | 633,838 | 18,335 | 11,123 | 104 | 12,180 | 22,094 | 1,694 | 4,690 | 1,953 | 1,577 |
| 1994 | 869,920 | 2,403 | 31,723 | 14,205 | 612,398 | 19,770 | 11,797 | 124 | 11,340 | 20,680 | 1,808 | 4,180 | 1,686 | 1,666 |
| 1995 | 746,616 | 1,540 | 26,609 | 11,041 | 436,343 | 17,935 | 8,488 | 79 | 9,225 | 19,887 | 2,441 | 4,513 | 1,707 | 2,001 |
| 1996[1] | 910,288 | 1,870 | 29,640 | 12,612 | 565,037 | 18,080 | 9,074 | 119 | 9,384 | 18,727 | 2,678 | 3,420 | 1,200 | 2,045 |

[1] Preliminary. *Source: Agricultural Statistics Board, U.S. Department of Agriculture*

# TOBACCO

## U.S. Exports of Unmanufactured Tobacco In Millions of Pounds (Declared Weight)

| Year | Australia | Belgium-Luxem. | Denmark | Egypt | France | Germany | Ireland | Italy | Japan | Nether-lands | Norway | Sweden | Switzer-land | Thailand | United Kingdom | Total U.S. Exports |
|---|---|---|---|---|---|---|---|---|---|---|---|---|---|---|---|---|
| 1986 | 11.7 | 10.1 | 14.5 | 46.5 | 8.4 | 82.7 | 3.4 | 22.5 | 83.2 | 31.2 | 4.3 | 10.2 | 11.5 | 13.0 | 21.8 | 477.5 |
| 1987 | 8.5 | 8.2 | 15.6 | 11.0 | 6.7 | 69.3 | 1.2 | 22.4 | 105.4 | 32.1 | 3.3 | 8.0 | 12.6 | 7.5 | 16.7 | 430.0 |
| 1988 | 9.0 | 9.7 | 16.4 | 15.7 | 5.7 | 87.2 | 2.0 | 32.4 | 70.4 | 41.0 | 3.7 | 12.0 | 15.5 | 13.5 | 19.6 | 481.8 |
| 1989 | 6.2 | 12.3 | 13.8 | .4 | 4.8 | 75.4 | 1.3 | 17.1 | 105.3 | 43.2 | 3.6 | 8.3 | 10.4 | 15.7 | 18.4 | 485.9 |
| 1990 | 8.3 | 12.4 | 15.1 | .5 | 5.7 | 75.9 | 1.6 | 19.3 | 106.5 | 45.3 | 3.4 | 9.5 | 13.3 | 22.2 | 20.5 | 492.5 |
| 1991 | 7.7 | 11.0 | 14.8 | 4.6 | 6.5 | 82.8 | 4.3 | 19.9 | 83.1 | 42.8 | 3.5 | 8.3 | 14.8 | 19.5 | 18.9 | 499.3 |
| 1992 | 6.9 | 21.4 | 15.6 | .2 | 4.2 | 93.3 | 2.5 | 19.0 | 131.0 | 49.9 | 3.4 | 8.8 | 7.5 | 16.9 | 24.3 | 574.4 |
| 1993 | 5.7 | 12.8 | 15.5 | 7.8 | 4.3 | 52.1 | 2.4 | 7.3 | 124.7 | 38.1 | 3.8 | 8.1 | 6.1 | 17.8 | 20.8 | 458.0 |
| 1994 | 6.4 | 12.3 | 14.9 | .3 | 3.1 | 54.1 | 1.3 | 11.3 | 126.2 | 30.9 | 1.6 | 7.3 | 6.0 | 19.0 | 14.7 | 433.9 |
| 1995[1] | 4.8 | 17.9 | 14.6 | 6.0 | 3.9 | 70.7 | 2.6 | 14.8 | 106.9 | 39.2 | 1.7 | 3.0 | 14.4 | 19.0 | 14.2 | 461.8 |
| 1996[2] | 5.6 | 40.1 | 15.1 | .4 | 3.2 | 60.3 | .5 | 17.5 | 88.7 | 40.4 | 2.8 | 3.7 | 14.9 | 15.9 | 34.4 | 490.1 |

[1] Preliminary. *Source: Economic Research Service, U.S. Department of Agriculture*

## U.S. Salient Statistics for Flue-Cured Tobacco (Types 11-14) In Millions of Pounds

| Crop Year | Acres Harvested 1,000 | Yield Per Acre Pounds | Mar-ketings | Stocks July 1 | Total Supply | Exports | Domestic Disap-pearance | Total Disap-pearance | Farm Price ¢ Lb. | Placed Under Gov't Loan Mil. Lb. | Price Support Level ¢ Lb. | Loan Stocks Nov. 30 | Loan Stocks Uncom-mitted |
|---|---|---|---|---|---|---|---|---|---|---|---|---|---|
| 1986-7 | 308.3 | 2,099 | 667 | 1,958 | 2,625 | 393 | 480 | 873 | 152.7 | 55.5 | 143.8 | 752.9 | 475.9 |
| 1987-8 | 324.6 | 2,129 | 683 | 1,752 | 2,435 | 385 | 537 | 922 | 158.7 | 24.8 | 143.5 | 630.4 | 397.7 |
| 1988-9 | 366.4 | 2,219 | 796 | 1,513 | 2,309 | 363 | 522 | 885 | 161.3 | 15.2 | 144.2 | 421.9 | 328.4 |
| 1989-90 | 390.7 | 2,069 | 838 | 1,424 | 2,262 | 387 | 567 | 954 | 167.4 | 28.4 | 146.8 | 314.5 | 218.2 |
| 1990-1 | 416.9 | 2,253 | 920 | 1,308 | 2,228 | 403 | 609 | 1,012 | 167.3 | 74.4 | 148.8 | 226.4 | 223.8 |
| 1991-2 | 402.6 | 2,265 | 882 | 1,216 | 2,098 | 403 | 472 | 875 | 172.3 | 49.9 | 152.8 | 153.7 | 174.5 |
| 1992-3 | 401.5 | 2,257 | 901 | 1,223 | 2,124 | 420 | 509 | 929 | 172.6 | 81.8 | 156.0 | 223.6 | 129.0 |
| 1993-4 | 400.1 | 2,217 | 892 | 1,195 | 2,087 | 359 | 433 | 792 | 168.1 | 204.9 | 157.7 | 330.5 | 317.5 |
| 1994-5 | 359.5 | 2,420 | 807 | 1,295 | 2,102 | 346 | 569 | 915 | 169.8 | 97.7 | 158.3 | 298.5 | 396.5 |
| 1995-6[1] | 386.2 | 1,933 | 854 | 1,187 | 2,041 | 345 | 531 | 875 | 179.4 | 12.0 | 159.7 | 157.6 | 160.4 |
| 1996-7[2] | 414.8 | 2,130 | 897 | 1,166 | 2,064 | 340 | 550 | 890 | 183.7 | | 160.1 | 181.0 | 100.4 |

[1] Preliminary. [2] Estimate. *Source: Economic Research Service, U.S. Department of Agriculture*

## U.S. Salient Statistics for Burley Tobacco (Type 31) In Millions of Pounds

| Crop Year | Acres Harvested 1,000 | Yield Per Acre Pounds | Mar-ketings | Stocks Oct. 1 | Total Supply | Exports | Domestic Disap-pearance | Total Disap-pearance | Farm Price ¢ Lb. | Gross Sales[3] | Price Support Level ¢ Lb. | Loan Stocks Nov. 30 | Loan Stocks Uncom-mitted |
|---|---|---|---|---|---|---|---|---|---|---|---|---|---|
| 1986-7 | 210.7 | 1,936 | 420 | 1,426 | 1,846 | 165 | 402 | 567 | 156.5 | 409.9 | 148.8 | 544.0 | 479.6 |
| 1987-8 | 215.9 | 1,943 | 428 | 1,279 | 1,706 | 157 | 478 | 635 | 156.3 | 374.2 | 148.8 | 332.9 | 231.0 |
| 1988-9 | 226.4 | 2,109 | 468 | 1,073 | 1,541 | 164 | 414 | 578 | 161.0 | 351.5 | 150.0 | 243.4 | 117.7 |
| 1989-90 | 244.4 | 1,975 | 498 | 963 | 1,461 | 169 | 446 | 614 | 167.2 | 398.1 | 153.2 | 314.5 | 91.6 |
| 1990-1 | 270.6 | 2,204 | 592 | 847 | 1,439 | 199 | 475 | 674 | 175.3 | 467.8 | 155.8 | 226.4 | 52.0 |
| 1991-2 | 312.0 | 2,110 | 657 | 765 | 1,422 | 209 | 407 | 616 | 178.8 | 501.5 | 158.4 | 62.3 | 32.8 |
| 1992-3 | 332.7 | 2,163 | 700 | 807 | 1,507 | 183 | 385 | 568 | 181.5 | 502.4 | 164.9 | 131.2 | 71.7 |
| 1993-4 | 299.7 | 2,115 | 627 | 939 | 1,566 | 152 | 400 | 552 | 181.6 | 492.4 | 168.3 | 178.8 | 141.9 |
| 1994-5 | 266.3 | 2,300 | 568 | 1,014 | 1,582 | 159 | 464 | 623 | 184.1 | 455.7 | 171.4 | 345.2 | 380.8 |
| 1995-6[1] | 246.6 | 2,023 | 520 | 959 | 1,479 | 165 | 386 | 551 | 184.5 | 341.6 | 172.5 | 212.5 | 38.1 |
| 1996-7[2] | 277.0 | 2,065 | 572 | 890 | 1,463 | 165 | 405 | 570 | 192.3 | 329.7 | 173.7 | 216.8 | 70.9 |

[1] Preliminary. [2] Estimate. [3] Before Christmas holidays. *Source: Economic Research Service, U.S. Department of Agriculture*

## Exports of Tobacco from the United States (Quantity and Value) In Metric Tons

| Year | Unmanufactured Flue-Cured | Value $1,000 | Burley | Value $1,000 | Total | Value $1,000 | Manufactured | Value $1,000 |
|---|---|---|---|---|---|---|---|---|
| 1991 | 115,481 | 776,654 | 61,852 | 441,223 | 226,463 | 1,427,630 | NA | 4,574,086 |
| 1992 | 146,100 | 983,478 | 64,481 | 483,743 | 260,526 | 1,650,559 | 58,115 | 4,509,395 |
| 1993 | 111,636 | 752,646 | 51,892 | 389,964 | 207,747 | 1,306,067 | 49,669 | 4,253,286 |
| 1994 | 107,411 | 749,305 | 49,859 | 380,993 | 196,792 | 1,302,744 | 63,837 | 5,367,220 |
| 1995[1] | 123,040 | 866,208 | 47,129 | 342,588 | 209,481 | 1,399,863 | 77,135 | 5,221,487 |
| 1996[2] | 112,797 | 786,473 | 52,202 | 246,074 | 222,316 | 1,390,311 | 83,383 | 5,238,340 |

[1] Preliminary. [2] Forecast. NA = Not available. *Source: Foreign Agricultural Service, U.S. Department of Agriculture*

# Tung Oil

Tung oil is derived from the seeds of the tung tree and is used as an industrial lubricant and drying agent. The tung tree is found mainly in China who is by far the world's largest producer of tung oil with 75 percent of global output. The other large producers are Argentina and Paraguay, though they remain on a much smaller scale than China.

The major producers of tung oil, China, Paraguay, and Argentina, are also the largest exporters with minor exports coming from the countries of the European Community.

Among the major importers of tung oil are Japan, Taiwan, the U.S., and South Korea. World import demand for tung oil has averaged about 40,000 tonnes.

The USDA reported that U.S. imports of tung oil in June 1996 were 15 tonnes. This was down sharply from the June 1995 import total of 674 tonnes. During the period of October 1995 to June 1996, U.S. imports of tung oil were 3,216 tonnes. This was some 39 percent above the October-June 1994/95 imports of 2,316 tonnes.

The USDA indicated that the value of U.S. tung oil imports in June 1996 was $16,000 while in June 1995 it was $593,000. For October-June 1995/96, the value of U.S. tung oil imports was $2.97 million while in October-June 1994/95 it was $2.22 million.

## World Tung Oil Trade    In Metric Tons

| | Imports | | | | | | | | | | Exports | | | | | |
|---|---|---|---|---|---|---|---|---|---|---|---|---|---|---|---|---|
| Year | Germany | Hong Kong | Italy | Japan | Netherlands | South Korea | Taiwan | United Kingdom | United States | World Total | Argentina | China | European Union | Hong Kong | Paraguay | World Total |
| 1989 | 1,193 | 4,119 | 344 | 13,137 | 631 | 2,533 | 1,538 | 1,037 | 6,474 | 44,496 | 9,506 | 24,248 | 518 | 4,085 | 8,296 | 47,254 |
| 1990 | 1,078 | 4,176 | 149 | 12,424 | 1,095 | 3,249 | 3,152 | 924 | 4,046 | 36,590 | 8,557 | 16,069 | 402 | 4,454 | 8,347 | 38,500 |
| 1991 | 1,138 | 6,476 | 109 | 11,890 | 543 | 3,035 | 4,957 | 862 | 5,646 | 39,766 | 8,522 | 14,485 | 476 | 7,182 | 9,039 | 40,600 |
| 1992 | 1,036 | 8,509 | 178 | 13,326 | 782 | 3,722 | 6,676 | 893 | 4,996 | 44,146 | 5,808 | 20,867 | 231 | 8,174 | 4,221 | 40,269 |
| 1993 | 720 | 5,222 | 164 | 6,549 | 1,351 | 3,490 | 3,595 | 608 | 4,270 | 29,793 | 2,497 | 16,990 | 369 | 6,004 | 2,295 | 29,200 |
| 1994[1] | 912 | 7,843 | 273 | 8,628 | 1,663 | 4,294 | 7,454 | 495 | 5,401 | 42,500 | 2,415 | 30,500 | 277 | 6,476 | 4,603 | 45,100 |
| 1995[2] | 890 | 3,671 | 310 | 8,429 | 2,285 | 5,000 | 5,777 | 490 | 4,427 | 36,000 | 3,820 | 22,500 | 348 | 3,838 | 3,700 | 35,360 |

[1] Preliminary. [2] Estimate. *Source: The Oil World*

## U.S. Consumption of Tung Oil in Inedible Products    In Thousands of Pounds

| Year | Jan. | Feb. | Mar. | Apr. | May | June | July | Aug. | Sept. | Oct. | Nov. | Dec. | Total |
|---|---|---|---|---|---|---|---|---|---|---|---|---|---|
| 1989 | 4,106 | 3,360 | 3,074 | 2,717 | 2,313 | 2,508 | 2,511 | 2,512 | 2,541 | 2,845 | 2,668 | 2,510 | 33,665 |
| 1990 | 2,573 | 646 | 680 | 823 | 795 | 923 | 712 | 738 | 607 | 626 | 472 | 611 | 10,206 |
| 1991 | ---------- | 1,953 | ---------- | ---------- | 1,555 | ---------- | ---------- | 1,334 | ---------- | ---------- | 1,100 | ---------- | 5,942 |
| 1992 | 435 | 459 | 574 | 498 | 502 | 694 | 572 | 705 | 674 | 873 | 530 | 790 | 7,306 |
| 1993 | 958 | 966 | 693 | 1,041 | 833 | 1,022 | 867 | 1,427 | 1,354 | 860 | 585 | 593 | 11,199 |
| 1994 | 608 | 592 | 635 | 1,408 | 1,558 | 840 | 861 | 910 | 480 | 392 | 660 | 382 | 9,326 |
| 1995 | 427 | 503 | 976 | 1,389 | 1,437 | 1,387 | 1,886 | 2,830 | 2,549 | 2,645 | 2,455 | 2,126 | 20,610 |
| 1996[1] | 1,724 | 1,427 | 1,730 | 1,750 | 1,498 | 1,813 | 2,214 | 2,024 | 1,431 | 2,045 | 1,908 | 2,081 | 21,645 |

[1] Preliminary. *Source: Bureau of Census, U.S. Department of Commerce*

## U.S. Stocks of Tung Oil at Factories & Warehouses    In Thousands of Pounds

| Year | Jan. 1 | Feb. 1 | Mar. 1 | Apr. 1 | May 1 | June 1 | July 1 | Aug. 1 | Sept. 1 | Oct. 1 | Nov. 1 | Dec. 1 |
|---|---|---|---|---|---|---|---|---|---|---|---|---|
| 1989 | 3,739 | 3,012 | 3,867 | 3,526 | 3,225 | 3,216 | 4,836 | 3,860 | 3,640 | 5,450 | 4,649 | 5,037 |
| 1990 | 5,448 | 4,648 | 2,744 | 2,529 | 3,164 | 2,859 | 2,003 | 1,553 | 1,880 | 1,018 | 1,913 | 2,374 |
| 1991 | 1,829 | ---------- | ---------- | 2,997 | ---------- | ---------- | 1,379 | ---------- | ---------- | 963 | ---------- | ---------- |
| 1992 | 1,608 | 2,421 | 2,439 | 1,605 | 1,323 | 1,540 | 847 | 1,348 | 2,162 | 1,724 | 2,560 | 3,545 |
| 1993 | 3,122 | 2,038 | 2,390 | 2,120 | 2,966 | 1,773 | 866 | 815 | 1,596 | 1,217 | 1,635 | 1,752 |
| 1994 | 1,551 | 2,053 | 1,507 | 2,049 | 2,091 | 2,591 | 2,148 | 1,562 | 820 | 2,455 | 1,712 | 1,909 |
| 1995 | 1,764 | 1,490 | 1,055 | 3,193 | 2,554 | 2,551 | 2,369 | 2,116 | 2,038 | 2,361 | 2,210 | 2,048 |
| 1996[1] | 2,013 | 1,635 | 2,232 | 3,018 | 2,386 | 2,532 | 2,641 | 2,381 | 2,670 | 2,525 | 2,459 | 2,834 |

[1] Preliminary. *Source: Bureau of Census, U.S. Department of Commerce*

## Average Price of Tung Oil (Imported, Drums) F.O.B. New York    In Cents Per Pound

| Year | Jan. | Feb. | Mar. | Apr. | May | June | July | Aug. | Sept. | Oct. | Nov. | Dec. | Average |
|---|---|---|---|---|---|---|---|---|---|---|---|---|---|
| 1989 | 41.00 | 41.00 | 41.00 | 41.00 | 41.00 | 41.00 | 41.00 | 41.00 | 41.00 | 41.00 | 41.00 | 41.00 | 41.00 |
| 1990 | 41.00 | 41.00 | 41.00 | 59.00 | 59.00 | 58.25 | 58.00 | 58.00 | 58.00 | 55.50 | 62.00 | 70.00 | 55.06 |
| 1991 | 70.00 | 63.00 | 61.50 | 63.00 | 63.00 | 61.50 | 61.00 | 61.00 | 61.00 | 61.00 | 61.00 | 70.00 | 63.08 |
| 1992 | 70.00 | 70.00 | 70.00 | 76.00 | 82.00 | 130.00 | 130.00 | 130.00 | 132.00 | 131.50 | 132.00 | 130.00 | 106.96 |
| 1993 | 130.00 | 130.00 | 130.00 | 130.00 | 117.00 | 130.00 | 130.00 | 130.00 | 107.50 | 100.00 | 94.75 | 93.00 | 118.52 |
| 1994 | 93.00 | 79.25 | 78.00 | 78.00 | 78.00 | 78.00 | 78.00 | 78.00 | 78.00 | 74.40 | 60.00 | 60.00 | 76.05 |
| 1995 | 60.00 | 60.00 | 60.00 | 60.00 | 60.00 | 60.00 | 60.00 | 60.00 | 60.00 | 60.00 | 60.00 | 60.00 | 60.00 |
| 1996[1] | 60.00 | 60.00 | 64.00 | 64.00 | 64.00 | 64.00 | 64.00 | 64.00 | 64.00 | | | | 63.11 |

[1] Preliminary. *Source: Economic Research Service, U.S. Department of Agriculture*

# Tungsten

Tungsten has unique high-temperature properties that can be used in the production of numerous items. Among its characteristics are a high melting point, high density, good corrosion resistance, as well as good thermal and electrical conductivity properties. Nearly 60 percent of tungsten is used to produce tungsten carbide. Tungsten carbide is used for cutting tools, mining and drilling tools, dies, bearings, and armor-piercing projectiles. Nearly 25 percent of tungsten use is in unalloyed tungsten, which is formed into wire and employed in filaments for incandescent and fluorescent lamps. Tungsten is also used in fireproofing materials.

The main tungsten mine operators in the world have agreed to set up a permanent tungsten organization to stabilize prices based in Nanchang, China. To support the tungsten price, the miners agreed to discuss with governments a temporary halt to selling state tungsten reserves, including wolframite and the powdered form of tungsten.

U.S. reported consumption of tungsten concentrate in June 1996 was 489 tonnes. For the January-June 1996 period, consumption was 2,910 tonnes while for all of 1995 it was 6,320 tonnes. For January-May 1996, U.S. imports of tungsten were 1,180 tonnes. For all of 1995, concentrate imports were 4,180 tonnes. At the end of June 1996, concentrate stocks were 615 tonnes while at the end of December 1995 stocks were 631 tonnes.

U.S. reported tungsten scrap consumption in June 1996 was 205 tonnes. For the first half of 1996, scrap consumption was 1,300 tonnes. Production of ammonium paratungstate in June 1996 was 544 tonnes. Other data on production was withheld to avoid disclosing company proprietary data. Consumption of ammonium paratungstate in June 1996 was 668 tonnes. For all of 1995, consumption was 7,690 tonnes. Ammonium paratungstate stocks at the end of June 1996 were 358 tonnes.

## World Concentrate Production of Tungsten In Metric Tons (Contained Tungsten[3])

| Year | Australia | Austria | Bolivia | Brazil | Burma | China | Kazakhstan[4] | Mongolia | Peru | Portugal | Rep. of Korea | Russia[4] | World Total |
|---|---|---|---|---|---|---|---|---|---|---|---|---|---|
| 1987 | 1,150 | 1,250 | 638 | 800 | 493 | 21,000 | ------ | 1,500 | 205 | 1,207 | 2,375 | 9,200 | 42,474 |
| 1988 | 1,261 | 1,235 | 900 | 738 | 307 | 30,000 | ------ | 1,000 | 432 | 1,382 | 2,029 | 9,200 | 50,869 |
| 1989 | 1,371 | 1,517 | 1,118 | 679 | 233 | 30,200 | ------ | 600 | 970 | 1,376 | 1,701 | 9,300 | 51,038 |
| 1990 | 1,086 | 1,378 | 1,014 | 316 | 443 | 32,000 | ------ | 500 | 1,536 | 1,410 | 1,361 | 8,800 | 51,900 |
| 1991 | 237 | 1,314 | 1,065 | 223 | 356 | 31,800 | ------ | 300 | 1,232 | 971 | 780 | 8,000 | 48,200 |
| 1992 | 159 | 1,490 | 851 | 205 | 531 | 25,000 | 200 | 260 | 802 | 1,870 | 247 | 6,500 | 40,400 |
| 1993 | 23 | 104 | 287 | 245 | 524 | 21,600 | 150 | 250 | 398 | 1,280 | 200 | 8,000 | 35,100 |
| 1994[1] | 11 | ------ | 462 | 155 | 548 | 27,000 | 100 | 150 | 256 | 1,000 | ------ | 4,000 | 35,400 |
| 1995[2] | 10 | 190 | 780 | 115 | 531 | 21,000 | 100 | 200 | 260 | 500 | ------ | 5,400 | 30,600 |

[1] Preliminary. [2] Estimate. [3] Conversion factors: $WO_3$ to W, multiply by 0.7931; 60% $WO_3$ to W, multiply by 0.4758. [4] Formerly part of the U.S.S.R.; data not reported separately until 1992. *Source: U.S. Geological Survey*

## Salient Statistics of Tungsten in the U.S. In Metric Tons (Contained Tungsten)

| Year | Net Import Reliance as a % Apparent Consumption | Total Consumption | Consumption of Tungsten Products by End Uses: Steel: Tool | Steel: Stainless & Heat Assisting | Steel: Alloy Steel[3] | Superalloys | Cutting & Wear Resistant Materials | Products Made from Metal Powder | Miscellaneous | Chemical and Ceramic | Exports | Imports for Consumption | Stocks at End of Year (Concentrates): Consumers | Stocks at End of Year (Concentrates): Producers |
|---|---|---|---|---|---|---|---|---|---|---|---|---|---|---|
| 1988 | 86 | 7,832 | 317 | 73 | 77 | 279 | 4,651 | 2,066 | 748 | 84 | 172 | 8,045 | 499 | 21 |
| 1989 | 84 | 7,725 | 258 | 62 | W | 258 | 5,018 | 1,828 | 476 | 52 | 203 | 7,896 | 1,261 | 10 |
| 1990 | 81 | 5,878 | 342 | 64 | 74 | 325 | 4,985 | 2,181 | 464 | 50 | 139 | 6,420 | 1,077 | 16 |
| 1991 | 91 | 5,309 | 243 | 44 | W | 287 | 4,801 | 1,941 | 614 | 44 | 21 | 7,837 | 1,778 | 26 |
| 1992 | 86 | 4,313 | 407 | 52 | 66 | 25 | 4,211 | 1,309 | 828 | W | 38 | 2,477 | 702 | 44 |
| 1993 | 82 | 2,866 | 388 | 43 | 40 | 282 | 5,064 | 1,434 | 2 | 37 | 63 | 1,721 | 592 | 44 |
| 1994[1] | 94 | 3,630 | 529 | 20 | 19 | 300 | 5,920 | 1,200 | W | 108 | 44 | 2,960 | 756 | 44 |
| 1995[2] | 66 | 6,320 | 265 | W | 18 | 215 | 6,590 | 1,200 | 3,600 | W | 10 | 4,180 | 631 | 44 |

[1] Preliminary. [2] Estimate. [3] Other than tool. W = Withheld proprietary data. *Source: U.S. Geological Survey*

## Tungsten Prices (Monthly Average) In U.S. Dollars

| Year | Jan. | Feb. | Mar. | Apr. | May | June | July | Aug. | Sept. | Oct. | Nov. | Dec. | Average |
|---|---|---|---|---|---|---|---|---|---|---|---|---|---|
| European Market (London), 65% $WO_3$ Basis, C.I.F.[1] -- $ Per Metric Ton | | | | | | | | | | | | | |
| 1992 | 61.50 | 61.00 | 61.00 | 61.00 | 60.57 | 59.21 | 57.50 | 57.50 | 55.75 | 51.67 | 50.00 | 45.00 | 56.81 |
| 1993 | 45.00 | 42.63 | 37.50 | 36.38 | 33.94 | 33.00 | 32.44 | 27.75 | 27.89 | 32.13 | 33.00 | 33.00 | 34.56 |
| 1994 | 29.94 | 29.94 | 37.71 | 35.38 | 35.38 | 37.09 | 38.10 | 38.10 | 42.03 | 45.36 | 47.63 | 49.56 | 38.85 |
| 1995 | 56.00 | 60.00 | 64.00 | 64.00 | 65.00 | 66.00 | 67.00 | 66.00 | 66.00 | 66.00 | 66.00 | 62.50 | 64.04 |
| U.S. Spot Quotations, 65% $WO_3$, Basis C.I.F., U.S. Ports (Including Duty) -- $ Per Short Ton | | | | | | | | | | | | | |
| 1992 | 57.00 | 57.00 | 56.25 | 54.40 | 52.50 | 50.88 | 49.50 | 49.00 | 49.00 | 48.10 | 43.75 | 43.50 | 50.91 |
| 1993 | 43.50 | 43.50 | 42.00 | 40.50 | 40.50 | 40.50 | 40.50 | 35.63 | 34.00 | 34.00 | 34.00 | 34.00 | 38.55 |
| 1994 | 37.48 | 40.79 | 44.10 | 44.10 | 44.10 | 44.53 | 47.95 | 48.50 | 48.50 | 48.50 | 48.50 | 48.50 | 45.46 |
| 1995 | 44.00 | 44.00 | 44.00 | 44.00 | 55.00 | 65.00 | 65.00 | 62.50 | 60.00 | 60.00 | 60.00 | 60.00 | 55.29 |

[1] Combined wolframite and scheelite quoations. *Source: U.S. Geological Survey*

# Turkeys

U.S. turkey production rose steadily during the first half of the 1990's, from 4.50 billion pounds in 1990 to 5.42 billion in 1996. To help iron out the pronounced yearend holiday seasonality for whole birds the industry has shifted a larger proportion of retail sales to prepackaged turkey parts. The additional processing required to cut up and package turkey cuts, such as breasts and legs, has increased the supply of edible trimmings which processors sell in several forms, including mechanically deboned turkey (MDT). A promising market for MDT is the export market; also, as a relatively low-cost meat protein MDT can easily be incorporated into sausage and other meat products.

U.S. per capita ready-to-cook retail weight turkey consumption reached a record high 18.5 pounds in 1996 vs. 17.9 pounds in 1995. An increase to 18.8 pounds is forecast for 1997. In the mid 1980's, per capita use averaged about 12 pounds. The October-December quarter accounts for more than a third of total use followed by a sharp tapering off in the January-March period. Traditionally, November is the highest slaughter month with a recent average of about 25 million birds. Prices follow a similar pattern, peaking generally in the fourth quarter and trending lower during the first quarter, basis 8-16 pound hens in New York. Turkeys of 14-22 pound weight are classified as toms. However, changes in consumer food tastes that favor poultry could be altering turkey's traditional marketing and price seasonality.

Federally inspected turkey production in 1996 was estimated at a record high 5.4 billion pounds vs. 5.1 billion in 1995. Net returns to producers during 1996 were not as favorable as in 1995 due to higher feed costs and smaller increases in competing meat prices. With little improvement expected in net returns, at least early in 1997, producers are apt to hold production to about 5.5 billion pounds, still a new record high if realized.

U.S. turkey exports rose to a record high 383 million pounds in 1996 vs. 348 million pounds in 1995. Estimates for 1997 focus on a rise to 405 million pounds. In the first quarter of 1996, exports climbed 60 percent over the like 1995 period on the strength of large purchases by Russia and Poland. The Eastern European pace tapered off in the rest of 1996, but some of the slack was offset by larger shipments to Mexico, traditionally the largest export market. The bulk of low priced turkey shipments to Russia are defined as "other prepared or preserved meat, meat offal, or blood of turkey."

Wholesale turkey prices edged towards 68 cents per pound in late 1966, but the average for the year of 65 cents was about unchanged from 1995. Prices for 1997 were forecast to average in the mid 60 cent per pound range.

## Turkey Meat Production and Consumption by Selected Countries — In Thous. of Metric Tons (Ready-to-Cook)

| | Production | | | | | | | | Consumption | | | | | | | |
|---|---|---|---|---|---|---|---|---|---|---|---|---|---|---|---|---|
| Year | Canada | France | Germany | Israel | Italy | Russia | United Kingdom | United States | Canada | France | Germany | Israel | Italy | Russia | United Kingdom | United States |
| 1990 | 129 | 432 | 145 | 52 | 279 | 54 | 223 | 2,048 | 125 | 315 | 208 | 44 | 272 | 92 | 211 | 1,992 |
| 1991 | 131 | 487 | 149 | 60 | 273 | 45 | 242 | 2,088 | 126 | 342 | 240 | 46 | 265 | 75 | 236 | 2,060 |
| 1992 | 132 | 558 | 159 | 68 | 269 | 37 | 246 | 2,167 | 129 | 357 | 272 | 61 | 268 | 72 | 228 | 2,086 |
| 1993 | 128 | 532 | 169 | 77 | 266 | 35 | 252 | 2,176 | 126 | 321 | 280 | 60 | 256 | 39 | 249 | 2,090 |
| 1994 | 133 | 568 | 183 | 86 | 269 | 30 | 253 | 2,239 | 128 | 330 | 295 | 75 | 245 | 45 | 258 | 2,110 |
| 1995[1] | 141 | 650 | 206 | 85 | 294 | 25 | 272 | 2,299 | 126 | 353 | 322 | 72 | 262 | 84 | 270 | 2,133 |
| 1996[2] | 143 | 680 | 215 | 79 | 310 | 22 | 280 | 2,444 | 130 | 370 | 333 | 66 | 277 | 83 | 282 | 2,241 |
| 1997[3] | 142 | 705 | 220 | 76 | 310 | 20 | 290 | 2,465 | 134 | 380 | 338 | 65 | 277 | 81 | 291 | 2,268 |

[1] Preliminary. [2] Estimate. [3] Forecast. *Source: Foreign Agricultural Service, U.S. Department of Agriculture*

## Salient Statistics of Turkeys in the U.S.

| | | | Liveweight | | | Ready-to-Cook-Basis | | | | | | | | Wholesale Ready-to-Cook |
|---|---|---|---|---|---|---|---|---|---|---|---|---|---|---|
| | | | | | | | | | Consumption | | Production Costs | | | |
| Year | Poults Placed[3] (In Thousands) | Number Raised[4] (In Thousands) | Produced Mil. Lbs. | Price ¢ Per Lb. | Value of Production Million $ | Production (Million Pounds) | Beginning Stocks (Million Pounds) | Exports (Million Pounds) | Total (Million Pounds) | Per Capita Lbs. | Feed (Liveweight Basis) | Total (Liveweight Basis) | Production Costs | 3-Region Weighted Average Price[5] |
| 1984 | 184,238 | 171,296 | 3,384.4 | 48.9 | 1,654.9 | 2,606 | 162 | 27 | 2,611 | 11.0 | 27.50 | 41.20 | 67.60 | 74.38 |
| 1985 | 198,683 | 185,427 | 3,704.0 | 49.1 | 1,819.5 | 2,826 | 125 | 27 | 2,765 | 11.6 | 21.40 | 35.10 | 60.10 | 75.56 |
| 1986 | 225,380 | 207,232 | 4,147.2 | 47.0 | 1,948.4 | 3,171 | 150 | 27 | 3,101 | 12.9 | 21.10 | 34.80 | 59.80 | 73.00 |
| 1987 | 264,228 | 240,438 | 4,894.9 | 34.8 | 1,703.1 | 3,745 | 178 | 33 | 3,580 | 14.7 | 19.40 | 33.10 | 57.60 | 57.21 |
| 1988 | 261,406 | 242,421 | 5,059.1 | 38.6 | 1,957.3 | 3,930 | 266 | 51 | 3,844 | 15.7 | 24.60 | 38.30 | 64.20 | 60.69 |
| 1989 | 290,678 | 261,280 | 5,465.5 | 40.9 | 2,234.4 | 4,181 | 250 | 41 | 4,109 | 16.6 | 26.70 | 40.40 | 66.80 | 65.75 |
| 1990 | 304,863 | 282,450 | 6,029.6 | 39.4 | 2,378.6 | 4,567 | 236 | 54 | 4,390 | 17.6 | 23.40 | 37.10 | 62.60 | 62.35 |
| 1991 | 308,083 | 285,110 | 6,110.7 | 38.4 | 2,344.7 | 4,658 | 306 | 103 | 4,541 | 18.0 | 22.72 | 36.42 | 61.83 | 60.79 |
| 1992 | 307,823 | 288,980 | 6,333.8 | 37.7 | 2,387.7 | 4,835 | 264 | 171 | 4,599 | 18.0 | 23.06 | 36.76 | 62.25 | 60.48 |
| 1993 | 308,871 | 287,650 | 6,432.6 | 39.0 | 2,509.1 | 4,798 | 272 | 244 | 4,577 | 17.7 | 22.20 | 35.86 | 61.12 | 62.83 |
| 1994 | 317,468 | 289,025 | 6,332.4 | 40.4 | 2,643.8 | 4,937 | 249 | 280 | 4,652 | 17.8 | 24.00 | 37.70 | 63.40 | 65.90 |
| 1995[1] | 320,882 | 292,856 | 6,506.1 | 41.0 | 2,774.3 | 5,069 | 254 | 348 | 4,705 | 17.9 | 21.90 | 35.60 | 60.80 | 66.20 |
| 1996[2] | 325,375 | 301,378 | 6,933.7 | | | 5,400 | 271 | 461 | 4,910 | 18.5 | 35.00 | 48.70 | 77.10 | 67.40 |

[1] Preliminary. [2] Estimate. [3] Poults placed for slaughter by hatcheries. [4] Turkeys placed August1-July 31. [5] Regions include central, eastern and western. Central region receives twice the weight of the other regions in calculating the average. *Source: Economic Research Service, U.S. Department of Agriculture*

# TURKEYS

## U.S. Basis of Turkey-Feed Price Ratio  In Pounds[1]

| Year | Jan. | Feb. | Mar. | Apr. | May | June | July | Aug. | Sept. | Oct. | Nov. | Dec. | Average |
|---|---|---|---|---|---|---|---|---|---|---|---|---|---|
| 1985 | 7.9 | 6.5 | 6.2 | 6.1 | 6.2 | 6.6 | 7.4 | 8.5 | 9.5 | 10.8 | 10.7 | 10.6 | 8.1 |
| 1986 | 6.3 | 6.4 | 6.5 | 6.7 | 7.2 | 8.5 | 9.9 | 10.8 | 11.7 | 12.6 | 11.8 | 9.7 | 9.0 |
| 1987 | 7.9 | 8.2 | 8.0 | 7.9 | 7.3 | 7.0 | 7.1 | 7.1 | 6.8 | 6.5 | 6.9 | 7.5 | 7.3 |
| 1988 | 6.2 | 5.5 | 5.2 | 5.0 | 4.9 | 4.5 | 5.3 | 5.6 | 6.2 | 6.7 | 6.7 | 5.3 | 5.6 |
| 1989 | 4.8 | 5.3 | 5.5 | 5.9 | 6.1 | 6.3 | 6.1 | 6.6 | 6.0 | 6.4 | 6.8 | 6.5 | 6.0 |
| 1990 | 5.9 | 5.7 | 6.1 | 5.9 | 6.0 | 6.2 | 6.4 | 6.7 | 7.0 | 7.6 | 7.7 | 6.7 | 6.5 |
| 1991 | 6.0 | 6.3 | 6.4 | 6.5 | 6.7 | 6.9 | 7.2 | 7.1 | 7.0 | 6.5 | 6.4 | 6.5 | 6.6 |
| 1992 | 6.0 | 5.8 | 6.0 | 6.0 | 6.0 | 6.1 | 6.5 | 6.8 | 6.7 | 7.1 | 7.2 | 7.1 | 6.4 |
| 1993 | 6.3 | 6.4 | 6.6 | 6.5 | 6.6 | 6.7 | 6.4 | 6.4 | 6.9 | 7.2 | 6.7 | 6.1 | 6.5 |
| 1994 | 5.4 | 5.4 | 5.5 | 5.8 | 5.9 | 6.0 | 7.0 | 7.4 | 7.4 | 7.9 | 8.0 | 7.3 | 6.6 |
| 1995 | 6.7 | 6.4 | 6.5 | 6.4 | 6.3 | 6.3 | 6.0 | 6.3 | 6.4 | 6.3 | 6.5 | 5.7 | 6.3 |
| 1996[2] | 5.3 | 5.2 | 5.1 | 4.7 | 4.6 | 4.9 | 4.9 | 4.8 | 5.2 | 6.2 | 6.4 | 6.2 | 5.3 |

[1] Pounds of feed equal in value to one pound of turkey, liveweight. [2] Preliminary. *Source: Economic Research Service, U.S. Department of Agriculture*

## Average Price Received by Farmers for Turkeys in the United States (Liveweight)  In Cents Per Pounds

| Year | Jan. | Feb. | Mar. | Apr. | May | June | July | Aug. | Sept. | Oct. | Nov. | Dec. | Average |
|---|---|---|---|---|---|---|---|---|---|---|---|---|---|
| 1985 | 50.30 | 40.50 | 39.50 | 39.20 | 38.50 | 40.60 | 44.00 | 47.50 | 51.80 | 56.90 | 58.40 | 59.10 | 47.19 |
| 1986 | 35.60 | 36.30 | 36.90 | 38.10 | 40.90 | 45.90 | 49.30 | 50.90 | 51.40 | 53.00 | 51.50 | 43.00 | 44.40 |
| 1987 | 35.10 | 35.80 | 35.70 | 36.30 | 35.50 | 34.10 | 33.50 | 32.10 | 31.30 | 30.20 | 34.00 | 38.40 | 34.33 |
| 1988 | 32.30 | 29.70 | 28.40 | 28.40 | 29.80 | 32.10 | 40.40 | 42.00 | 45.40 | 48.40 | 47.90 | 38.30 | 36.93 |
| 1989 | 35.50 | 38.40 | 40.30 | 42.00 | 43.60 | 43.80 | 41.20 | 40.80 | 36.40 | 38.20 | 40.70 | 39.30 | 40.02 |
| 1990 | 35.40 | 33.70 | 36.40 | 36.60 | 38.30 | 38.70 | 39.10 | 40.20 | 40.30 | 42.50 | 42.30 | 36.90 | 38.37 |
| 1991 | 33.60 | 35.10 | 37.00 | 37.60 | 38.30 | 38.70 | 39.10 | 40.10 | 40.20 | 37.00 | 37.00 | 38.10 | 37.65 |
| 1992 | 36.30 | 35.50 | 37.00 | 37.00 | 37.70 | 37.70 | 37.90 | 37.80 | 37.50 | 38.50 | 39.40 | 39.30 | 37.63 |
| 1993 | 35.60 | 35.70 | 37.60 | 37.60 | 37.70 | 37.60 | 38.70 | 39.60 | 41.10 | 43.20 | 42.70 | 40.80 | 38.99 |
| 1994 | 37.00 | 37.30 | 38.40 | 39.20 | 39.90 | 40.30 | 40.60 | 42.10 | 43.10 | 44.50 | 44.30 | 42.20 | 40.74 |
| 1995 | 39.30 | 37.20 | 38.30 | 38.30 | 38.40 | 39.30 | 39.60 | 41.90 | 43.60 | 45.20 | 47.30 | 44.00 | 41.03 |
| 1996[1] | 40.90 | 42.40 | 41.80 | 41.90 | 43.10 | 44.70 | 45.00 | 44.40 | 43.80 | 45.10 | 45.40 | 43.60 | 43.51 |

[1] Preliminary. *Source: Economic Research Service, U.S. Department of Agriculture*

## Wholesale Price of Turkeys[1] (Hens, 8-16 Lbs.) N.Y.  In Cents Per Pound

| Year | Jan. | Feb. | Mar. | Apr. | May | June | July | Aug. | Sept. | Oct. | Nov. | Dec. | Average |
|---|---|---|---|---|---|---|---|---|---|---|---|---|---|
| 1985 | 74.05 | 65.62 | 67.04 | 64.62 | 62.64 | 68.13 | 72.84 | 78.37 | 82.37 | 90.20 | 93.11 | 86.88 | 75.49 |
| 1986 | 60.25 | 61.67 | 63.94 | 64.61 | 67.08 | 73.83 | 77.85 | 80.46 | 81.21 | 83.17 | 80.68 | 71.11 | 72.16 |
| 1987 | 55.25 | 58.47 | 60.34 | 58.33 | 55.26 | 55.72 | 56.30 | 56.14 | 56.14 | 54.73 | 60.73 | 66.45 | 57.82 |
| 1988 | 52.79 | 47.09 | 47.01 | 46.90 | 49.29 | 57.14 | 70.82 | 70.46 | 76.02 | 79.64 | 75.97 | 61.59 | 61.23 |
| 1989 | 59.03 | 62.17 | 65.71 | 68.33 | 72.08 | 72.98 | 66.40 | 62.61 | 57.88 | 67.61 | 72.45 | 72.70 | 66.66 |
| 1990 | 55.55 | 55.16 | 58.86 | 59.62 | 61.27 | 62.88 | 63.37 | 66.57 | 68.99 | 76.15 | 73.70 | 56.05 | 63.18 |
| 1991 | 53.49 | 55.76 | 59.10 | 60.32 | 62.32 | 62.68 | 63.41 | 64.66 | 64.38 | 60.52 | 63.07 | 65.18 | 61.24 |
| 1992 | 58.74 | 55.00 | 58.77 | 60.00 | 60.03 | 59.46 | 57.02 | 57.80 | 61.02 | 63.92 | 65.57 | 65.14 | 60.21 |
| 1993 | 58.05 | 56.83 | 58.41 | 58.98 | 58.81 | 58.35 | 59.76 | 63.43 | 66.73 | 71.28 | 71.76 | 68.20 | 62.55 |
| 1994 | 60.09 | 59.32 | 60.98 | 61.58 | 63.14 | 64.61 | 65.26 | 66.39 | 68.98 | 73.13 | 74.01 | 70.35 | 65.65 |
| 1995 | 60.71 | 58.54 | 60.04 | 60.05 | 60.57 | 62.76 | 64.78 | 68.52 | 72.92 | 76.73 | 80.31 | 70.35 | 66.36 |
| 1996[2] | 64.60 | 64.65 | 65.07 | 64.82 | 65.39 | 65.85 | 65.66 | 64.94 | 64.16 | 69.09 | 73.60 | 70.00 | 66.49 |

[1] Ready-to-cook. [2] Preliminary. *Source: Economic Research Service, U.S. Department of Agriculture*

## Certified Federally Inspected Turkey Slaughter in the U.S. (Ready-to-Cook Weights)  In Millions of Pounds

| Year | Jan. | Feb. | Mar. | Apr. | May | June | July | Aug. | Sept. | Oct. | Nov. | Dec. | Total |
|---|---|---|---|---|---|---|---|---|---|---|---|---|---|
| 1985 | 157.7 | 148.0 | 176.4 | 177.3 | 212.5 | 238.5 | 271.1 | 295.2 | 288.3 | 341.5 | 282.5 | 210.7 | 2,800 |
| 1986 | 187.5 | 175.0 | 193.6 | 205.2 | 236.4 | 275.8 | 307.6 | 299.4 | 331.4 | 365.8 | 307.1 | 248.2 | 3,133 |
| 1987 | 215.4 | 212.8 | 241.9 | 255.0 | 274.1 | 335.8 | 358.8 | 357.4 | 383.9 | 411.4 | 373.5 | 297.0 | 3,717 |
| 1988 | 255.7 | 266.9 | 314.0 | 276.6 | 331.3 | 373.2 | 322.4 | 377.3 | 365.8 | 395.7 | 371.7 | 272.8 | 3,923 |
| 1989 | 254.1 | 248.1 | 301.3 | 268.8 | 356.9 | 388.6 | 360.4 | 430.3 | 385.7 | 422.6 | 423.1 | 334.9 | 4,175 |
| 1990 | 334.0 | 298.3 | 351.1 | 328.4 | 384.1 | 389.2 | 395.7 | 444.0 | 382.9 | 478.4 | 446.2 | 328.6 | 4,561 |
| 1991 | 365.6 | 322.0 | 329.7 | 375.8 | 398.2 | 380.7 | 402.2 | 421.8 | 404.8 | 482.0 | 419.2 | 349.9 | 4,652 |
| 1992 | 362.9 | 331.7 | 361.3 | 385.2 | 374.2 | 435.0 | 451.8 | 411.9 | 431.3 | 467.6 | 423.0 | 393.1 | 4,829 |
| 1993 | 354.1 | 322.7 | 382.9 | 391.9 | 378.7 | 446.7 | 419.3 | 426.9 | 436.0 | 451.4 | 461.8 | 375.3 | 4,848 |
| 1994 | 347.8 | 342.0 | 400.9 | 380.6 | 415.6 | 457.9 | 405.6 | 483.6 | 447.7 | 453.6 | 453.9 | 397.5 | 4,992 |
| 1995 | 386.3 | 368.9 | 433.1 | 369.6 | 441.4 | 478.4 | 409.1 | 447.3 | 419.5 | 480.2 | 463.0 | 394.4 | 5,091 |
| 1996[1] | 412.4 | 426.5 | 418.9 | 435.0 | 483.0 | 453.5 | 485.1 | 475.9 | 436.8 | 514.0 | 465.9 | 406.0 | 5,413 |

[1] Preliminary. *Source: Economic Research Service, U.S. Department of Agriculture*

**Turkey Per Capita Consumption in the U.S.** In Pounds

| Year | Jan. | Feb. | Mar. | Apr. | May | June | July | Aug. | Sept. | Oct. | Nov. | Dec. | Total |
|---|---|---|---|---|---|---|---|---|---|---|---|---|---|
| 1986 | .7 | .7 | .9 | .7 | .8 | .9 | .9 | 1.0 | 1.1 | 1.4 | 2.5 | 1.3 | 12.9 |
| 1987 | .8 | .8 | .9 | .9 | .9 | 1.0 | 1.1 | 1.1 | 1.3 | 1.7 | 2.8 | 1.3 | 14.7 |
| 1988 | 1.0 | .9 | 1.2 | .9 | 1.2 | 1.3 | 1.1 | 1.3 | 1.4 | 1.5 | 2.6 | 1.3 | 15.7 |
| 1989 | 1.0 | 1.0 | 1.2 | .9 | 1.2 | 1.1 | 1.3 | 1.4 | 1.5 | 1.7 | 2.9 | 1.4 | 16.6 |
| 1990 | 1.2 | 1.1 | 1.2 | 1.1 | 1.3 | 1.2 | 1.3 | 1.5 | 1.4 | 1.9 | 2.9 | 1.4 | 17.6 |
| 1991 | 1.4 | 1.1 | 1.2 | 1.3 | 1.4 | 1.3 | 1.3 | 1.4 | 1.4 | 1.9 | 3.0 | 1.5 | 18.0 |
| 1992 | 1.1 | 1.1 | 1.2 | 1.3 | 1.2 | 1.3 | 1.4 | 1.4 | 1.4 | 1.8 | 3.1 | 1.6 | 18.0 |
| 1993 | 1.2 | 1.0 | 1.4 | 1.2 | 1.2 | 1.3 | 1.2 | 1.3 | 1.4 | 1.8 | 3.2 | 1.5 | 17.8 |
| 1994 | 1.2 | 1.1 | 1.3 | 1.2 | 1.3 | 1.4 | 1.3 | 1.6 | 1.5 | 1.7 | 3.0 | 1.5 | 17.8 |
| 1995 | -------- | 3.6 | -------- | -------- | 3.9 | -------- | -------- | 4.2 | -------- | -------- | 6.2 | -------- | 17.8 |
| 1996[1] | -------- | 3.7 | -------- | -------- | 4.0 | -------- | -------- | 4.6 | -------- | -------- | 6.2 | -------- | 17.9 |
| 1997[2] | -------- | 4.1 | -------- | -------- | 4.1 | -------- | -------- | 4.5 | -------- | -------- | 6.3 | -------- | 19.0 |

[1] Preliminary. [2] Estimate. *Source: Economic Research Service, U.S. Department of Agriculture (ERS-USDA)*

**Storage Stocks of Turkeys (Frozen) in the United States** In Millions of Pounds

| Year | Jan. 1 | Feb. 1 | Mar. 1 | Apr. 1 | May 1 | June 1 | July 1 | Aug. 1 | Sept. 1 | Oct. 1 | Nov. 1 | Dec. 1 |
|---|---|---|---|---|---|---|---|---|---|---|---|---|
| 1985 | 125.3 | 124.1 | 129.5 | 131.1 | 157.0 | 183.7 | 243.3 | 304.7 | 387.8 | 444.5 | 484.1 | 208.2 |
| 1986 | 150.2 | 159.2 | 163.6 | 150.5 | 188.9 | 229.5 | 297.8 | 388.1 | 449.3 | 511.6 | 543.2 | 249.0 |
| 1987 | 178.2 | 198.1 | 211.4 | 226.0 | 250.8 | 298.1 | 381.6 | 472.7 | 560.0 | 640.8 | 629.9 | 321.5 |
| 1988 | 282.4 | 281.8 | 321.5 | 339.0 | 370.7 | 410.1 | 456.8 | 496.2 | 551.9 | 572.8 | 583.3 | 303.5 |
| 1989 | 249.7 | 262.5 | 263.1 | 269.2 | 298.7 | 355.6 | 454.6 | 496.9 | 574.3 | 569.3 | 571.8 | 258.6 |
| 1990 | 235.9 | 268.4 | 276.3 | 317.9 | 354.9 | 405.6 | 481.3 | 541.7 | 593.1 | 623.6 | 625.1 | 338.4 |
| 1991 | 306.4 | 302.5 | 342.2 | 370.0 | 408.5 | 453.4 | 503.1 | 571.3 | 625.8 | 667.2 | 653.0 | 305.5 |
| 1992 | 264.1 | 325.5 | 354.1 | 392.3 | 430.2 | 486.8 | 580.1 | 662.1 | 684.2 | 734.4 | 714.7 | 320.5 |
| 1993 | 271.7 | 314.7 | 359.8 | 359.2 | 424.4 | 474.0 | 556.1 | 624.2 | 678.6 | 713.8 | 683.6 | 290.6 |
| 1994 | 249.1 | 279.8 | 304.8 | 346.5 | 399.1 | 461.4 | 539.2 | 288.1 | 623.4 | 648.6 | 636.2 | 280.7 |
| 1995 | 254.4 | 312.9 | 359.5 | 432.1 | 466.2 | 536.3 | 598.8 | 651.1 | 678.2 | 686.0 | 644.2 | 270.1 |
| 1996[1] | 271.3 | 339.2 | 423.1 | 445.4 | 514.5 | 573.1 | 664.2 | 705.9 | 723.2 | 721.0 | 659.2 | 347.8 |

[1] Preliminary. *Source: Economic Research Service, U.S. Department of Agriculture (ERS-USDA)*

**Turkey (Whole frozen) Retail Price[2] in the U.S.** In Cents Per Pound

| Year | Jan. | Feb. | Mar. | Apr. | May | June | July | Aug. | Sept. | Oct. | Nov. | Dec. | Average |
|---|---|---|---|---|---|---|---|---|---|---|---|---|---|
| 1985 | 84.00 | 75.30 | 75.90 | 73.30 | 71.80 | 75.90 | 80.40 | 84.30 | 89.50 | 97.00 | 99.80 | 95.90 | 83.59 |
| 1986 | 72.60 | 71.10 | 72.30 | 72.90 | 76.30 | 83.30 | 86.30 | 90.00 | 90.20 | 92.70 | 91.90 | 80.30 | 81.66 |
| 1987 | 63.80 | 65.80 | 67.60 | 67.00 | 65.50 | 65.00 | 64.70 | 63.30 | 64.30 | 64.30 | 68.00 | 75.70 | 66.25 |
| 1988 | 63.30 | 58.00 | 57.60 | 56.40 | 57.80 | 68.30 | 72.30 | 78.50 | 83.30 | 87.50 | 84.50 | 70.40 | 69.83 |
| 1989 | 67.60 | 66.90 | 71.90 | 75.10 | 79.40 | 80.60 | 74.40 | 71.80 | 67.80 | 73.28 | 79.80 | 79.60 | 74.02 |
| 1990 | 65.20 | 64.60 | 67.30 | 69.40 | 70.10 | 70.10 | 68.70 | 73.60 | 76.60 | 81.90 | 82.30 | 66.40 | 71.35 |
| 1991 | 62.30 | 63.06 | 66.61 | 66.78 | 69.70 | 70.00 | 70.30 | 72.20 | 72.80 | 69.10 | 70.80 | 73.90 | 68.96 |
| 1992 | 67.90 | 65.80 | 68.10 | 68.70 | 69.24 | 69.04 | 65.70 | 68.10 | 69.60 | 72.30 | 74.00 | 74.90 | 69.45 |
| 1993 | 67.85 | 67.22 | 67.94 | 68.80 | 68.40 | 68.19 | 67.08 | 72.07 | 74.91 | 78.37 | 80.08 | 75.03 | 71.33 |
| 1994 | 70.30 | 69.40 | 70.60 | 70.90 | 72.00 | 72.58 | 72.77 | 74.75 | 77.32 | 79.89 | 83.33 | 77.34 | 74.27 |
| 1995 | 69.54 | 67.08 | 68.47 | 68.62 | 70.05 | 72.49 | 74.18 | 77.77 | 81.60 | 84.89 | 86.50 | 77.50 | 74.89 |
| 1996[1] | 103.50 | 104.70 | 106.90 | 101.40 | 104.30 | 104.10 | 104.40 | 108.60 | 106.50 | 107.40 | 98.10 | 102.00 | 104.33 |

[1] Preliminary. [2] Data prior to 1996 are prices to selected retailers. *Source: Economic Research Service, U.S. Department of Agriculture (ERS-USDA)*

**Turkey (Whole) Retail-to-Consumer Price Spread in the U.S.** In Cents Per Pound

| Year | Jan. | Feb. | Mar. | Apr. | May | June | July | Aug. | Sept. | Oct. | Nov. | Dec. | Average |
|---|---|---|---|---|---|---|---|---|---|---|---|---|---|
| 1985 | 25.1 | 32.0 | 29.4 | 31.1 | 31.2 | 27.0 | 23.6 | 20.1 | 17.8 | 10.5 | 4.4 | 7.2 | 21.6 |
| 1986 | 33.7 | 36.7 | 32.5 | 31.3 | 27.1 | 19.0 | 19.3 | 19.5 | 21.7 | 20.2 | 16.2 | 21.8 | 24.9 |
| 1987 | 39.8 | 37.4 | 35.4 | 33.4 | 37.3 | 40.1 | 41.1 | 41.8 | 39.0 | 38.3 | 22.0 | 13.6 | 34.9 |
| 1988 | 29.8 | 34.9 | 33.4 | 33.0 | 35.1 | 24.6 | 23.7 | 21.0 | 17.3 | 16.5 | 14.7 | 26.7 | 25.9 |
| 1989 | 29.8 | 29.9 | 25.7 | 23.2 | 20.7 | 20.7 | 30.2 | 32.3 | 34.2 | 28.9 | 13.4 | 15.4 | 25.4 |
| 1990 | 33.7 | 33.7 | 32.1 | 27.7 | 29.8 | 29.7 | 32.1 | 27.8 | 26.7 | 23.7 | 8.8 | 29.6 | 27.9 |
| 1991 | 37.1 | 38.1 | 31.2 | 33.7 | 30.9 | 32.0 | 32.6 | 31.2 | 30.3 | 34.9 | 20.8 | 17.5 | 30.9 |
| 1992 | 28.2 | 29.2 | 27.0 | 29.4 | 29.6 | 29.5 | 33.3 | 32.5 | 31.4 | 27.2 | 15.4 | 18.1 | 27.5 |
| 1993 | 30.0 | 31.7 | 32.6 | 31.9 | 32.3 | 34.5 | 35.8 | 29.7 | 27.7 | 25.0 | 13.6 | 20.4 | 28.8 |
| 1994 | 27.5 | 29.7 | 28.1 | 25.1 | 27.1 | 28.8 | 28.7 | 27.6 | 27.1 | 25.5 | 13.9 | 20.3 | 25.8 |
| 1995 | 28.5 | 32.0 | 33.7 | 32.1 | 32.7 | 32.8 | 30.8 | 28.2 | 27.0 | 20.1 | 10.6 | 21.2 | 27.5 |
| 1996[1] | 30.4 | 30.7 | 33.6 | 28.0 | 29.3 | 28.0 | 27.9 | 32.1 | 30.3 | 28.9 | 18.0 | 26.6 | 28.7 |

[1] Preliminary. *Source: Economic Research Service, U.S. Department of Agriculture (ERS-USDA)*

# Uranium

The future of uranium dioxide use in the U.S. remains questionable due to continued public resistance to the development of new nuclear power facilities. The major uses for uranium are for power generation as well as in military weapons. Military uses for uranium are likely to continue to decline as both the U.S. and the former Soviet Union are dismantling their nuclear arsenals. Other countries, which were part of the former Soviet Union, are expected to do the same. The process of dismantling these weapons has proven to be not only technically difficult but also very expensive.

There were a number of developments in the uranium market in 1996. In late summer, a ship containing 600 tonnes of uranium hexaflouride arrived at Mutsuogawara, Japan. This completed the largest naval shipment of uranium to this northern Japanese port, marking the first time uranium was transported by sea. All other movement was by land. The uranium was headed for an enrichment plant. Additionally, Japan's electric power companies announced they would transport about 90 tonnes of unprocessed uranium from Tokyo to a uranium enrichment prototype plant.

Canada's Rio Algom announced that it was proceeding with the development of its Smith Ranch uranium project in Wyoming. It expects the mine to be in production by the summer of 1997. The deposit is estimated to contain 60 million pounds of uranium. Once on stream, the mine is expected to produce 2 million pounds of uranium per year.

After years of decline, the price of uranium has started to increase and is at the highest levels since 1987. The long decline in uranium prices has tightened supplies considerably while demand has been increasing slowly. It was reported that a number of mining companies in Australia and Canada had decided to either increase production at existing mines or reopen mines that were closed.

The Energy Information Administration reported that U.S. nuclear generating units in July 1996 produced a total of 61 net terawatthours (billion kilowatthours) of electricity, some 6 percent more than in June 1996, but some 2 percent less than in June 1995. For the year, nuclear generating units produced a total of 399 net terawatthours, up close to 3 percent from the same period in 1995. For all of 1995, nuclear electricity net generation was 673 net terawatthours. Despite the adversity the industry has seen, nuclear power generation has been on a steady increase. Electricity generated by nuclear power in 1995 was up close to 17 percent from the level of 1990.

In July 1996, the nuclear portion of the U.S. net generation of electricity was 21.1 percent. For the first seven months of 1996 it was 22.5 percent, while for all of 1995 it was 22.5 percent. Nuclear powered electricity generation has held fairly steady at between 21-23 percent for the last six years.

In July 1996, the Nuclear Regulatory Commission issued no low-power or full-power licenses to nuclear power plants. On July 31, 1996, there were 110 operable nuclear generating units in the United States. Of these units, 18 units generated at less than 25 percent of capacity. There were an additional 6 units with construction permits although construction for all 6 units was canceled or halted.

**World Production of Uranium Oxide ($U_3O_8$) Concentrate** In Short Tons (Uranium Content)

| Year | Australia | Canada | China | Czech Rep. & Slovakia | France | Gabon | Germany | India | Namibia | Niger | South Africa | Spain | United States | Former U.S.S.R. | World Total |
|---|---|---|---|---|---|---|---|---|---|---|---|---|---|---|---|
| 1987 | 4,902 | 16,127 | NA | NA | 4,377 | 1,030 | 26 | 164 | 4,590 | 3,848 | 5,219 | 322 | 6,500 | NA | 47,745 |
| 1988 | 4,580 | 15,646 | NA | NA | 4,377 | 1,194 | 58 | 194 | 4,551 | 3,845 | 5,039 | 348 | 6,500 | NA | 46,846 |
| 1989 | 4,752 | 14,855 | 1,039 | 2,989 | 4,183 | 1,157 | 4,961 | 273 | 4,000 | 3,874 | 3,810 | 229 | 6,919 | 18,849 | 75,264 |
| 1990 | 4,589 | 11,400 | 1,039 | 2,600 | 3,661 | 922 | 3,864 | 273 | 4,030 | 3,682 | 3,169 | 213 | 4,443 | 18,199 | 64,642 |
| 1991 | 4,909 | 10,609 | 1,039 | 2,340 | 3,204 | 882 | 1,569 | 260 | 3,185 | 3,853 | 2,248 | 254 | 3,975 | 13,650 | 53,458 |
| 1992 | 3,032 | 12,087 | 1,039 | 2,040 | 2,755 | 702 | 325 | 299 | 2,199 | 3,855 | 2,449 | 241 | 2,822 | 11,205 | 46,124 |
| 1993 | 2,949 | 11,990 | 1,300 | 911 | 2,220 | 769 | 195 | 260 | 2,168 | 3,786 | 2,261 | 238 | 2,587 | 10,491 | 43,027 |
| 1994[1] | 3,050 | 11,950 | NA | NA | 1,700 | 750 | NA | NA | 2,500 | 3,800 | 2,250 | NA | 1,950 | NA | 41,750 |
| 1995[2] | 3,050 | 13,600 | NA | NA | 1,250 | 800 | NA | NA | 2,600 | 3,750 | 1,850 | NA | 3,050 | NA | 42,650 |

[1] Preliminary. [2] Estimate. NA = Not available. *Source: American Bureau of Metal Statistics, Inc.*

**Month-End Uranium ($U_3O_8$) Transaction Values[1]** In Dollars Per Pound

| Year | Jan. | Feb. | Mar. | Apr. | May | June | July | Aug. | Sept. | Oct. | Nov. | Dec. | Average |
|---|---|---|---|---|---|---|---|---|---|---|---|---|---|
| 1987 | 17.35 | 16.90 | 16.95 | 17.00 | 17.20 | 17.10 | 17.30 | 17.55 | 18.20 | 18.05 | 17.80 | 17.20 | 17.38 |
| 1988 | 16.85 | 16.65 | 16.55 | 16.45 | 16.10 | 15.80 | 15.45 | 15.00 | 14.50 | 14.40 | 13.30 | 12.50 | 15.30 |
| 1989 | 12.25 | 12.00 | 11.25 | 11.00 | 10.75 | 10.45 | 9.95 | 9.80 | 9.80 | 9.65 | 9.55 | 9.40 | 10.49 |
| 1990 | 9.25 | 9.05 | 8.75 | 8.65 | 8.55 | 8.80 | 9.75 | 10.80 | 11.40 | 10.10 | 9.30 | 9.15 | 9.46 |
| 1991 | 9.40 | 9.45 | 9.35 | 9.30 | 9.30 | 9.20 | 9.15 | 8.95 | 8.70 | 8.35 | 7.45 | 7.50 | 8.84 |
| 1992 | 7.55 | 7.80 | 7.95 | 7.90 | 7.85 | 7.80 | 7.75 | 7.85 | 7.95 | 8.40 | 8.55 | 8.75 | 8.01 |
| 1993[2] | 8.80 | 8.60 | 8.80 | 9.20 | 8.70 | 8.90 | 8.20 | 8.80 | 9.05 | 8.45 | 8.60 | 8.71 | 8.74 |
| 1994 | 8.58 | 8.45 | 8.25 | 8.25 | 8.23 | 8.25 | 8.23 | 8.15 | 8.13 | 8.10 | 8.13 | 8.25 | 8.25 |
| 1995 | 8.30 | 8.45 | 8.65 | 8.78 | 9.18 | 9.48 | 9.50 | 9.83 | 9.83 | 9.83 | 9.95 | 10.05 | 9.32 |

[1] Transaction value is a weighted average price of recent natural uranium sales transactions, based on prices paid on transactions closed within the previous 3-month period for which delivery is scheduled within one year of the transaction date; at least 10 transactions involving a sum total of at least 2 million pounds of $U_3O_8$ equivalent. 2 Data beginning December 1993 represents average of Unrestricted and Restricted. *Source: American Metal Market*

## Reported Average Price Settlements for Purchases by U.S. Utilities and Domestic Suppliers In $ Per Lb.[2]

| Year of Delivery | Contract Price | Market Price[1] | Price & Cost Floor | Total | Contract & Market | Year of Delivery | Contract Price | Market Price[1] | Price & Cost Floor | Total | Contract & Market |
|---|---|---|---|---|---|---|---|---|---|---|---|
| | Averages of Reported Prices | | | | | | Averages of Reported Prices | | | | |
| 1982 | 35.36 | 21.50 | 50.98 | 41.27 | 38.37 | 1989 | 20.87 | 11.48 | 22.50 | 15.42 | 19.56 |
| 1983 | 39.90 | 24.05 | 50.67 | 36.18 | 38.21 | 1990 | 17.94 | 9.18 | 19.40 | 11.65 | 15.70 |
| 1984 | 33.60 | 16.87 | 44.71 | 31.88 | 32.65 | 1991 | 13.94 | 9.04 | 21.84 | 12.62 | 13.66 |
| 1985 | 34.74 | 15.46 | 35.62 | 27.15 | 31.43 | 1992 | 13.16 | 8.65 | 18.35 | 13.89 | 13.45 |
| 1986 | 32.58 | 16.93 | 41.06 | 27.39 | 30.01 | 1993 | 14.96 | 9.57 | 14.87 | 11.03 | 13.14 |
| 1987 | 29.16 | 17.53 | 34.34 | 22.85 | 27.37 | 1994 | 10.68 | 9.76 | 20.03 | 10.57 | 10.63 |
| 1988 | 28.20 | 16.12 | 33.52 | 21.59 | 26.15 | 1995 | 10.58 | 10.19 | 17.86 | 12.05 | 10.79 |

[1] No floor. [2] $U_3O_8$ equivalent. Note: Price excludes uranium delivered under litigation settlements. Price is given in year-of-delivery dollars.
*Source: Energy Information Adminstration, U.S. Department of Energy*

## U.S. Uranium Industry Statistics In Millions of Pounds $U_3O_8$

| Year | Production: Mine | Production: Concentrate | Concentrate Shipments | Employment – Person Years: Exploration | Mining | Milling | Processing | Total[1] | Deliveries to U.S. Utilities[2] | Avg. Price Delivered Uranium $/lb. $U_3O_8$ | Imports | Avg. Price Delivered Uranium Imports $/lb. $U_3O_8$ | Exports |
|---|---|---|---|---|---|---|---|---|---|---|---|---|---|
| 1986 | 8.3 | 13.500 | 10.641 | 162 | 954 | 513 | 490 | 2,120 | 18.9 | 30.01 | 14.4 | 20.07 | 1.6 |
| 1987 | 6.0 | 12.991 | 11.558 | 183 | 819 | 432 | 568 | 2,002 | 20.8 | 27.37 | 15.9 | 19.14 | 1.0 |
| 1988 | 9.5 | 13.130 | 12.791 | 144 | 849 | 572 | 576 | 2,141 | 17.6 | 26.15 | 17.0 | 19.03 | 4.3 |
| 1989 | 9.7 | 13.837 | 14.808 | 86 | 659 | 367 | 471 | 1,583 | 18.4 | 19.56 | 13.7 | 16.75 | 2.5 |
| 1990 | 5.9 | 8.885 | 12.957 | 73 | 664 | 304 | 293 | 1,335 | 20.5 | 15.70 | 26.6 | 12.55 | 2.4 |
| 1991 | 5.2 | 7.952 | 8.437 | 52 | 411 | 191 | 361 | 1,016 | 26.8 | 13.66 | 23.1 | 15.55 | 3.5 |
| 1992 | 1.0 | 5.645 | 6.853 | 51 | 219 | 129 | 283 | 682 | 23.4 | 13.45 | 45.4 | 11.34 | 20.9 |
| 1993 | 2.0 | 3.063 | 3.374 | 36 | 133 | 65 | 145 | 380 | 15.5 | 13.14 | 41.9 | 10.53 | 21.3 |
| 1994 | 2.5 | 3.352 | 6.319 | 41 | 157 | 105 | 149 | 980 | 38.3 | 10.40 | 36.6 | 8.95 | 35.5 |
| 1995 | 3.5 | 6.000 | 5.500 | 27 | 226 | 121 | 161 | 1,107 | 43.4 | 11.25 | 41.3 | 10.20 | 19.7 |

[1] Does not include 491 person years in 1993 and 528 person years in 1994 for employment in reclamation work. [2] From suppliers under domestic purchases.
*Source: Energy Information Administration, U.S. Department of Energy*

## Commercial and U.S. Government Stocks of Uranium, End of Year In Millions of Pounds $U_3O_8$ Equivalent

| Year | Utility: Natural Uranium | Utility: Enriched Uranium[1] | Domestic Supplier: Natural Uranium | Domestic Supplier: Enriched Uranium[1] | Total Commercial Stocks | DOE-Owned & USEC-Held: Natural Uranium | DOE-Owned & USEC-Held: Enriched Uranium |
|---|---|---|---|---|---|---|---|
| 1989 | 67.3 | 48.5 | 21.2 | 1.0 | 138.1 | 77.5 | 24.7 |
| 1990 | 61.5 | 41.2 | 22.0 | 4.4 | 129.1 | 59.8 | 32.8 |
| 1991 | 70.9 | 27.1 | 18.7 | 2.0 | 118.7 | 46.8 | 36.7 |
| 1992 | 66.5 | 25.5 | 19.1 | 6.1 | 117.3 | 45.8 | 23.1 |
| 1993 | 57.9 | 23.3 | 19.1 | 5.4 | 105.7 | 52.4 | 26.9 |
| 1994 | 42.4 | 23.0 | 17.4 | 4.1 | 86.9 | 57.2 | 28.0 |
| 1995 | 40.5 | 15.8 | 13.5 | .4 | 70.1 | 82.0 | 28.8 |

[1] Includes amount reported as $UF_6$ at enrichment suppliers. DOE = Department of Energy USEC = U.S. Energy Commission.
*Source: Energy Information Administration, U.S. Department of Energy*

# Vanadium

Vanadium is used in the production of carbon and alloy steels and plates, structural bar, and pipe steels. Vanadium finds uses in ceramics as a coloring agent, enhances strength and toughness, and can be used in tools. It is commercially important as an oxidation catalyst. Ferrovanadium is an iron alloy used in steel. Vanadium pentoxide finds use in dyeing and printing applications. Vanadium is critical in the production of aerospace titanium alloys and as a catalyst in the production of maleic anhydride and sulfuric acid. The major producers of vanadium are South Africa, Russia, and China.

U.S. consumption of all forms of vanadium in June 1996 was 540,000 kilograms. Consumption of ferrovanadium was 509,000 kilograms, up 43 percent from the month before. Consumption of vanadium oxide in June 1996 was 1,120 kilograms, the same as the previous month. Statistics on consumption of vanadium-aluminum alloy and vanadium chemicals were withheld to avoid disclosing company proprietary data. Consumption of other forms of vanadium including vanadium alloys and vanadium metal was 29,600 kilograms.

U.S. stocks of ferrovanadium at the end of June 1996 were 294,000 kilograms. Vanadium oxide stocks were 6,610 kilograms while stocks of vanadium-aluminum alloys were 9,970 kilograms. Stocks of other vanadium materials were 4,520 kilograms.

By form, U.S. consumption of vanadium in steel production in June 1996 was 504,000 kilograms. Carbon steel used 139,000 kilograms in June 1996 and for the January-June 1996 period used 889,000 kilograms. Stainless and heat-resisting steel production took 1,620 kilograms and 11,700 kilograms, respectively. Full alloy steel production took 261,000 kilograms and 594,000, respectively. High-strength low-alloy steel consumed 71,700 kilograms of vanadium and for January-June 1996 used 460,000 kilograms. Tool steel used 31,000 kilograms in June 1996 and 188,000 kilograms in the first half of 1996. Consumption of vanadium in steel production during all of 1995 was 3.88 million kilograms. Use of vanadium in other end products in June 1996 was less. Most of the statistics were withheld to avoid disclosing proprietary information. Total use of vanadium in 1995 was 4.26 million kilograms.

U.S. exports of aluminum-vanadium master alloy in January-May 1996 were 132,000 kilograms. The major markets were Canada, the United Kingdom, Mexico, and Japan. Exports of ferrovanadium for the first five months of 1996 were 222,000 kilograms, supplied primarily to Canada and Mexico. Exports of vanadium pentoxide were 122,000 kilograms, shipped primarily to Italy, the United Kingdom, and Japan. Exports of other oxides and hydroxides of vanadium were 2.38 million kilograms. Exports of vanadium metal, including waste and scrap were 87,500 kilograms.

## World Production of Vanadium by Country — In Metric Tons (Contained Vanadium)

| Year | From Ores, Concentrates and Slag: China[3] | Russia[4] | Republic of South Africa: Content of Pentoxide & Vanadate Products | Content of Vanadiferous Slag Product | Total | Total[5] | From Petroleum Residues, Ash, Spent Catalysts: Japan[6] | United States[7] | Total | World Grand Total |
|---|---|---|---|---|---|---|---|---|---|---|
| 1987 | 4,500 | 9,600 | 5,842 | 10,100 | 15,942 | 30,042 | 728 | 2,275 | 3,003 | 33,045 |
| 1988 | 4,500 | 9,600 | 6,330 | 11,300 | 17,631 | 31,731 | 728 | 2,950 | 3,678 | 35,409 |
| 1989 | 4,500 | 9,600 | 7,270 | 11,300 | 18,567 | 32,967 | 868 | 2,389 | 3,257 | 36,224 |
| 1990 | 4,500 | 9,000 | 7,100 | 10,000 | 17,106 | 33,900 | 700 | 2,308 | 3,008 | 36,900 |
| 1991 | 4,500 | 8,500 | 6,500 | 8,460 | 14,962 | 31,700 | 404 | 2,250 | 2,650 | 34,300 |
| 1992 | 4,700 | 11,000 | 6,300 | 7,730 | 14,033 | 29,900 | 245 | 1,347 | 1,590 | 31,500 |
| 1993 | 5,000 | 10,000 | 6,650 | 8,400 | 15,051 | 31,500 | 252 | 2,867 | 3,120 | 34,600 |
| 1994[1] | 5,000 | 10,000 | 6,050 | 9,600 | 15,650 | 31,700 | 252 | 2,740 | 2,990 | 34,700 |
| 1995[2] | 5,000 | 11,000 | 6,500 | 9,000 | 15,500 | 32,600 | 245 | 1,990 | 2,240 | 34,900 |

[1] Preliminary. [2] Estimate. [3] In vanadiferous slag product. [4] Formerly part of the U.S.S.R.; data not reported separately until 1992. [5] Excludes U.S. production. [6] In vanadium pentoxide products. [7] In vandium pentoxide and ferrovandium products. *Source: U.S. Geological Survey*

## Salient Statistics of Vanadium — In Metric Tons (Contained Vanadium)

| Year | Consumer & Producer Stocks, Dec. 31 | Vanadium Consumption by Uses in U.S.: Tool Steel | Cast Irons | Hign Strength, Low Alloy | Stainless & Heat Resisting | Superalloys | Carbon | Full Alloy | Total | Average $ Per Lb. $V_2O_5$ | Exports: Vanadium Pentoxide, Anhydride | Oxides & Hydroxides | Ferrovanadium | Imports: Ores, Slag, Residues | Vanadium Pentoxide, Anhydride | Oxides & Hydroxides | Ferrovanadium |
|---|---|---|---|---|---|---|---|---|---|---|---|---|---|---|---|---|---|
| 1988 | 1,266 | 481 | 20 | 1,339 | 41 | 9 | 1,259 | 887 | 4,834 | 3.40 | 620 | ----- | 462 | 2,025 | 219 | ----- | 108 |
| 1989 | 1,736 | 420 | 18 | 1,225 | 96 | 38 | 1,103 | 898 | 4,646 | 6.17 | 1,171 | 1,080 | 399 | 4,210 | 133 | 106 | 527 |
| 1990 | 1,082 | 421 | 18 | 1,122 | 38 | 42 | 994 | 814 | 4,081 | 4.21 | 819 | 976 | 271 | 3,826 | 83 | 217 | 244 |
| 1991 | 935 | 242 | 15 | 919 | 37 | 14 | 919 | 739 | 3,293 | 2.85 | 700 | 1,110 | 94 | 882 | 133 | 110 | 420 |
| 1992 | 1,084 | 453 | 17 | 989 | 28 | 13 | 1,262 | 828 | 4,079 | 2.28 | 26 | 1,113 | 213 | 838 | 206 | 103 | 592 |
| 1993 | 900 | 373 | 21 | 981 | 33 | 13 | 1,413 | 789 | 3,973 | 1.45 | 126 | 895 | 219 | 1,454 | 70 | 19 | 1,630 |
| 1994[1] | 1,000 | 424 | 31 | 979 | 26 | 16 | 1,680 | 777 | 4,290 | 1.55 | 335 | 1,050 | 374 | 1,900 | 294 | 3 | 1,910 |
| 1995[2] | 438 | 443 | 40 | 1,070 | 32 | 20 | 1,870 | 833 | 4,640 | 4.63 | 229 | 1,010 | 340 | 1,900 | 547 | 36 | 1,950 |

[1] Preliminary. [2] Estimate. W = Withheld proprietary data. *Source: U.S. Geological Survey*

# Vegetables

In the first half of 1996, the USDA reported that wholesale prices for processed vegetables averaged about 4 percent higher than a year earlier. The 1996 contract average for the five leading processing vegetables (tomatoes, sweetcorn, snapbeans, green peas, and cucumbers) was estimated to have fallen 7 percent to 1.42 million acres. Acreage was down for each vegetable with green pea acreage down most at 18 percent. Cool, wet weather delayed planting in many areas and some snap bean and sweet-corn acreage was flooded out in the Midwest.

The initial estimate by USDA of 1996 contract production for green peas showed a 16 percent decline from 1995 to 412,690 short tons. Yields were up slightly though there was an 18 percent decline in harvested acreage. Favorable growing conditions in California leading to higher yields were expected to boost 1996 U.S. processing tomato production 8 percent to a record high 12 million short tons.

U.S. potato production declined 5 percent in 1995 to 442 million hundredweight. The fall-season potato crop totaled 402 million cwt., down 6 percent from the previous season. Shipments of fresh potatoes fell 3 percent in 1995. Processing use in the 1995/96 marketing year is expected to reach record highs as demand for products like frozen french fries remains strong. In the fall of 1996, summer- and fall-season U.S. potato growers were expected to harvest a modern day record-large area. The 1995 sweet potato crop was estimated at 12.9 million cwt., down 4 percent from 1994. For 1996, sweet potato acreage was expected to be 3 percent higher. With yields close to trend, 1996 sweet potato production could be between 1 and 4 percent higher.

## Commercial and Fresh Vegetables: Index of Prices Received by U.S. Growers

| Year | Jan. | Feb. | Mar. | Apr. | May | June | July | Aug. | Sept. | Oct. | Nov. | Dec. | Annual |
|---|---|---|---|---|---|---|---|---|---|---|---|---|---|
| | | | | | | Commercial[1] | 1990-92 = 100 | | | | | | |
| 1990 | 135 | 122 | 92 | 81 | 89 | 89 | 94 | 98 | 102 | 111 | 114 | 100 | 102 |
| 1991 | 95 | 84 | 114 | 107 | 131 | 109 | 91 | 88 | 90 | 88 | 109 | 88 | 100 |
| 1992 | 97 | 118 | 144 | 106 | 93 | 94 | 102 | 113 | 115 | 125 | 109 | 121 | 111 |
| 1993 | 119 | 125 | 108 | 164 | 126 | 100 | 105 | 109 | 112 | 95 | 102 | 124 | 116 |
| 1994 | 113 | 109 | 92 | 87 | 98 | 104 | 98 | 95 | 104 | 117 | 123 | 163 | 109 |
| 1995 | 118 | 108 | 147 | 173 | 158 | 122 | 93 | 98 | 115 | 101 | 102 | 93 | 119 |
| 1996[2] | 106 | 93 | 144 | 119 | 100 | 113 | 93 | 97 | 99 | 107 | | | 107 |
| | | | | | | Fresh[3] | 1982 = 100 | | | | | | |
| 1990 | 164.0 | 203.2 | 136.6 | 74.8 | 78.0 | 83.7 | 93.3 | 79.0 | 79.4 | 96.2 | 117.7 | 87.2 | 107.8 |
| 1991 | 89.3 | 87.3 | 88.4 | 112.8 | 157.0 | 138.0 | 102.0 | 82.6 | 81.8 | 73.5 | 113.1 | 76.1 | 100.2 |
| 1992 | 117.5 | 154.7 | 147.9 | 99.7 | 89.9 | 81.3 | 85.5 | 114.8 | 115.1 | 149.4 | 108.2 | 133.4 | 116.5 |
| 1993 | 128.8 | 125.8 | 117.4 | 178.5 | 163.5 | 80.7 | 98.4 | 110.5 | 117.0 | 89.5 | 141.1 | 167.0 | 126.5 |
| 1994 | 146.3 | 99.3 | 96.1 | 91.4 | 91.2 | 94.9 | 104.8 | 95.7 | 107.1 | 113.8 | 128.1 | 244.7 | 117.8 |
| 1995 | 163.5 | 149.2 | 159.2 | 199.1 | 167.2 | 127.2 | 107.3 | 94.8 | 152.9 | 116.0 | 115.8 | 125.5 | 139.8 |
| 1996[2] | 133.9 | 119.4 | 202.5 | 155.6 | 108.2 | 96.6 | 108.8 | 97.2 | 91.3 | 106.0 | 131.5 | 99.3 | 120.9 |

Indexes are not seasonally adjusted. [1] Includes fresh and processing vegetable. [2] Preliminary. [3] Producer Price Index (0113-02).
*Source: National Agricultural Statistics Service, U.S. Department of Agriculture*

## U.S. Processed Vegetables: Monthly Producer Price Index 1982 = 100

| Year | Jan. | Feb. | Mar. | Apr. | May | June | July | Aug. | Sept. | Oct. | Nov. | Dec. | Annual |
|---|---|---|---|---|---|---|---|---|---|---|---|---|---|
| | | | | | | Canned[1] (0244) | | | | | | | |
| 1990 | 117.9 | 117.8 | 118.0 | 118.8 | 118.2 | 118.5 | 116.5 | 115.2 | 115.4 | 114.4 | 114.9 | 114.0 | 116.6 |
| 1991 | 114.8 | 114.8 | 115.1 | 113.8 | 114.0 | 113.3 | 114.0 | 112.2 | 110.9 | 111.2 | 110.1 | 109.8 | 112.8 |
| 1992 | 110.3 | 109.7 | 109.3 | 108.9 | 109.8 | 109.4 | 109.5 | 109.6 | 109.2 | 109.1 | 109.5 | 109.8 | 109.5 |
| 1993 | 110.1 | 109.8 | 109.7 | 109.1 | 108.8 | 109.9 | 111.1 | 109.6 | 110.4 | 111.5 | 112.3 | 112.6 | 110.4 |
| 1994 | 113.1 | 116.1 | 116.8 | 116.5 | 117.9 | 118.0 | 118.9 | 118.1 | 116.0 | 116.0 | 114.2 | 113.1 | 116.2 |
| 1995 | 112.6 | 114.3 | 114.9 | 113.1 | 117.6 | 117.4 | 118.2 | 117.5 | 117.6 | 117.8 | 118.4 | 119.6 | 116.6 |
| 1996[2] | 120.0 | 119.8 | 120.0 | 120.4 | 120.8 | 121.0 | 122.6 | 122.1 | 121.9 | 121.6 | 121.8 | 121.7 | 121.1 |
| | | | | | | Frozen (0245) | | | | | | | |
| 1990 | 117.6 | 117.9 | 118.4 | 118.9 | 120.1 | 117.6 | 118.1 | 118.3 | 118.5 | 118.6 | 118.6 | 119.0 | 118.5 |
| 1991 | 118.4 | 118.5 | 118.3 | 117.9 | 118.1 | 117.5 | 117.8 | 117.2 | 117.4 | 116.6 | 116.5 | 116.8 | 117.6 |
| 1992 | 116.6 | 116.1 | 116.2 | 116.4 | 116.3 | 115.5 | 115.4 | 115.4 | 116.7 | 116.3 | 117.5 | 118.0 | 116.4 |
| 1993 | 118.0 | 118.0 | 117.9 | 118.7 | 119.9 | 121.1 | 121.3 | 122.1 | 122.6 | 123.2 | 123.7 | 125.4 | 121.0 |
| 1994 | 125.5 | 126.1 | 126.1 | 126.4 | 126.9 | 127.0 | 126.4 | 126.4 | 125.2 | 124.9 | 124.7 | 125.0 | 125.9 |
| 1995 | 125.1 | 124.8 | 124.9 | 124.9 | 124.2 | 123.6 | 123.2 | 123.6 | 124.4 | 124.6 | 123.7 | 124.0 | 124.3 |
| 1996[2] | 125.1 | 124.8 | 124.7 | 124.9 | 125.0 | 125.4 | 125.5 | 125.8 | 126.0 | 125.9 | 125.7 | 126.0 | 125.4 |

[1] Includes canned vegetables and juices, including hominy and mushrooms. [2] Preliminary. *Source: Bureau of Labor Statistics, U.S. Department of Labor*

# VEGETABLES

## U.S. Per Capita Use of Selected Commercially Produced Fresh and Processing Vegetables

Pounds, Farm Weight Basis

| Crop | 1986 | 1987 | 1988 | 1989 | 1990 | 1991 | 1992 | 1993 | 1994 | 1995[9] | 1996[10] |
|---|---|---|---|---|---|---|---|---|---|---|---|
| Asparagus, all | .7 | 1.0 | 1.0 | 1.0 | 1.0 | 1.0 | 1.0 | 1.0 | .9 | 1.0 | 1.0 |
| Fresh | .3 | .6 | .6 | .6 | .6 | .6 | .6 | .6 | .6 | .6 | .6 |
| Canning | .3 | .3 | .3 | .3 | .3 | .3 | .3 | .3 | .2 | .3 | .3 |
| Freezing | .1 | .1 | .1 | .1 | .1 | .1 | .1 | .1 | .1 | .1 | .1 |
| Snap Beans, all | 6.7 | 6.7 | 6.7 | 7.1 | 6.7 | 7.0 | 7.2 | 7.3 | 7.4 | 6.9 | 7.0 |
| Fresh | 1.3 | 1.2 | 1.2 | 1.2 | 1.1 | 1.1 | 1.5 | 1.5 | 1.6 | 1.6 | 1.6 |
| Canning | 3.9 | 3.8 | 3.8 | 3.9 | 3.7 | 4.1 | 4.0 | 4.0 | 3.8 | 3.6 | 3.7 |
| Freezing | 1.5 | 1.7 | 1.7 | 2.0 | 1.9 | 1.8 | 1.7 | 1.8 | 2.0 | 1.7 | 1.7 |
| Broccoli, all[1] | 4.7 | 5.3 | 6.2 | 6.0 | 5.6 | 5.4 | 5.8 | 5.2 | 5.7 | 5.5 | 5.7 |
| Fresh | 3.0 | 3.1 | 3.8 | 3.8 | 3.4 | 3.1 | 3.4 | 2.9 | 3.4 | 3.2 | 3.3 |
| Freezing | 1.7 | 2.2 | 2.4 | 2.2 | 2.2 | 2.3 | 2.4 | 2.3 | 2.3 | 2.3 | 2.4 |
| Carrots, all[2] | 9.3 | 11.3 | 10.4 | 11.5 | 11.9 | 11.2 | 12.3 | 12.0 | 13.7 | 14.1 | 13.8 |
| Fresh | 6.5 | 8.3 | 7.1 | 8.1 | 8.3 | 7.7 | 8.3 | 8.2 | 9.6 | 10.1 | 9.8 |
| Canning | 1.0 | .9 | 1.0 | .9 | 1.3 | 1.1 | 1.7 | 1.0 | 1.3 | 1.5 | 1.3 |
| Freezing | 1.8 | 2.1 | 2.3 | 2.5 | 2.3 | 2.4 | 2.3 | 2.8 | 2.8 | 2.5 | 2.7 |
| Cauliflower, all[1] | 3.1 | 3.0 | 3.1 | 3.1 | 3.0 | 2.6 | 2.5 | 2.4 | 2.2 | 1.9 | 2.2 |
| Fresh | 2.2 | 2.1 | 2.2 | 2.3 | 2.2 | 2.0 | 1.8 | 1.7 | 1.6 | 1.3 | 1.5 |
| Freezing | .9 | .9 | .9 | .8 | .8 | .6 | .7 | .7 | .6 | .6 | .7 |
| Celery, fresh | 6.6 | 6.6 | 7.2 | 7.5 | 7.2 | 6.8 | 7.4 | 7.1 | 6.8 | 6.4 | 6.7 |
| Sweet Corn, all[3] | 25.8 | 24.7 | 24.9 | 24.4 | 26.3 | 26.4 | 27.8 | 28.0 | 27.6 | 28.8 | 28.4 |
| Fresh | 6.1 | 6.3 | 5.8 | 6.5 | 6.7 | 5.9 | 6.9 | 7.0 | 8.2 | 7.8 | 7.7 |
| Canning | 12.1 | 10.6 | 10.4 | 9.5 | 11.0 | 11.1 | 11.9 | 11.2 | 10.2 | 10.5 | 10.6 |
| Freezing | 7.6 | 7.8 | 8.7 | 8.4 | 8.6 | 9.4 | 9.0 | 9.8 | 9.2 | 10.5 | 10.1 |
| Cucumbers, all | 9.9 | 10.6 | 10.1 | 10.0 | 9.7 | 9.7 | 9.6 | 9.7 | 10.1 | 10.6 | 10.4 |
| Fresh | 4.6 | 5.1 | 4.8 | 4.8 | 4.7 | 4.6 | 5.0 | 5.3 | 5.4 | 5.6 | 5.6 |
| Pickles | 5.3 | 5.5 | 5.3 | 5.2 | 5.0 | 5.1 | 4.6 | 4.4 | 4.7 | 5.0 | 4.8 |
| Melons | 24.6 | 24.3 | 23.8 | 26.5 | 24.6 | 23.4 | 25.4 | 25.0 | 25.8 | 28.2 | 27.9 |
| Watermelon | 12.8 | 13.0 | 13.5 | 13.6 | 13.3 | 12.8 | 14.8 | 14.6 | 15.4 | 15.9 | 16.0 |
| Cantaloupe | 9.4 | 9.1 | 7.9 | 10.4 | 9.2 | 8.7 | 8.5 | 8.7 | 8.6 | 9.9 | 9.4 |
| Honeydew | 2.4 | 2.2 | 2.4 | 2.5 | 2.1 | 1.9 | 2.1 | 1.7 | 1.8 | 2.4 | 2.5 |
| Lettuce, Head | 21.9 | 25.7 | 27.0 | 28.8 | 27.8 | 26.1 | 25.9 | 24.6 | 24.3 | 21.6 | 21.4 |
| Onions, all | 15.6 | 14.9 | 16.2 | 16.4 | 17.1 | 17.3 | 17.6 | 18.5 | 17.5 | 19.0 | 18.5 |
| Fresh | 13.7 | 13.4 | 14.5 | 14.8 | 15.1 | 15.7 | 16.2 | 16.5 | 16.5 | 17.7 | 17.4 |
| Green peas, all[4] | 4.1 | 3.7 | 3.7 | 3.7 | 4.2 | 4.2 | 4.1 | 3.5 | 3.7 | 3.7 | 3.7 |
| Canning | 2.2 | 2.0 | 1.8 | 1.7 | 2.0 | 1.9 | 2.1 | 1.6 | 1.5 | 1.6 | 1.6 |
| Freezing | 1.9 | 1.7 | 1.9 | 2.0 | 2.2 | 2.3 | 2.0 | 1.9 | 2.2 | 2.1 | 2.1 |
| Tomatoes, all | 79.5 | 81.0 | 78.1 | 86.2 | 90.9 | 92.8 | 89.2 | 92.4 | 89.7 | 92.1 | 95.3 |
| Fresh | 15.9 | 15.8 | 16.8 | 16.8 | 15.5 | 15.4 | 15.5 | 16.0 | 16.1 | 16.6 | 16.8 |
| Canning | 63.6 | 65.2 | 61.3 | 69.4 | 75.4 | 77.4 | 73.7 | 76.4 | 73.6 | 75.5 | 78.5 |
| Subtotal, all[8] | 239.9 | 247.2 | 249.4 | 263.7 | 268.0 | 267.1 | 271.5 | 273.9 | 272.1 | 275.9 | 278.8 |
| Fresh | 125.7 | 132.4 | 135.5 | 142.6 | 138.5 | 134.3 | 141.5 | 141.7 | 145.8 | 146.0 | 146.7 |
| Canning | 95.6 | 95.5 | 91.3 | 98.7 | 107.2 | 109.7 | 108.0 | 108.0 | 103.2 | 106.1 | 108.9 |
| Freezing | 18.6 | 19.3 | 20.9 | 20.8 | 20.3 | 21.5 | 20.6 | 22.2 | 22.0 | 22.5 | 23.0 |
| Potatoes, all | 126.0 | 126.0 | 122.4 | 127.1 | 127.6 | 130.4 | 132.4 | 136.9 | 140.7 | 140.2 | 140.4 |
| Fresh | 48.8 | 47.9 | 49.6 | 50.0 | 45.7 | 46.4 | 48.9 | 49.7 | 49.1 | 49.2 | 48.5 |
| Processing | 77.2 | 78.1 | 72.8 | 77.1 | 81.9 | 84.0 | 83.5 | 87.2 | 91.6 | 91.0 | 91.9 |
| Sweetpotatoes, all | 4.4 | 4.4 | 4.1 | 4.1 | 4.6 | 4.0 | 4.3 | 3.9 | 4.7 | 4.5 | 4.4 |
| Total, all items | 382.8 | 387.1 | 386.9 | 404.7 | 411.1 | 413.0 | 420.1 | 426.2 | 429.3 | 432.6 | 435.1 |

[1] All production for processing broccoli and cauliflower is for freezing. [2] Industry allocation suggests that 27% of processing carrot production is for canning and 73% is for freezing. [3] On-cob basis. [4] In-shell basis. [5] Includes artichokes, brussel sprouts, eggplant, endive/excarole, garlic, radishes and spinach. [6] Includes beets, chile peppers and spinach. [7] Includes green lima beans, spinach and miscellaneous freezing vegetables. [8] Fresch, canning and freezing data do not add to the total because onions are for dehydrating are included in total. [9] Preliminary. [10] Forecast. *Source: Economic Research Service, U.S. Department of Agriculture*

## Fresh Vegetables: Average Prices Received by U.S. Growers   Dollars Per Cwt.

| Year | Jan. | Feb. | Mar. | Apr. | May | June | July | Aug. | Sept. | Oct. | Nov. | Dec. | Season Average |
|---|---|---|---|---|---|---|---|---|---|---|---|---|---|
| | | | | | | Broccoli | | | | | | | |
| 1994 | 23.50 | 21.40 | 19.50 | 21.80 | 27.10 | 21.10 | 21.60 | 18.50 | 38.60 | 37.00 | 57.70 | 46.00 | 27.40 |
| 1995 | 23.70 | 33.30 | 53.40 | 33.00 | 25.50 | 26.30 | 18.50 | 30.30 | 26.70 | 22.60 | 22.00 | 26.90 | 31.40 |
| 1996[1] | 34.50 | 21.70 | 30.60 | 25.20 | 28.20 | 30.60 | 21.80 | 21.40 | 23.90 | 23.00 | | | 26.09 |
| | | | | | | Carrots | | | | | | | |
| 1994 | 10.70 | 10.50 | 11.50 | 10.30 | 12.10 | 12.10 | 13.60 | 16.40 | 15.30 | 15.50 | 15.10 | 15.60 | 12.10 |
| 1995 | 19.20 | 16.90 | 18.90 | 19.80 | 19.30 | 15.30 | 14.80 | 15.50 | 15.90 | 15.10 | 15.10 | 15.40 | 15.30 |
| 1996[1] | 12.70 | 13.80 | 15.70 | 15.80 | 12.10 | 11.00 | 10.70 | 14.70 | 12.30 | 11.30 | | | 13.01 |
| | | | | | | Cauliflower | | | | | | | |
| 1994 | 24.80 | 24.90 | 23.10 | 20.80 | 32.30 | 29.10 | 32.00 | 24.20 | 34.20 | 31.30 | 42.50 | 30.10 | 28.90 |
| 1995 | 32.00 | 33.80 | 53.80 | 68.30 | 47.70 | 37.60 | 26.90 | 29.30 | 22.00 | 23.50 | 31.10 | 34.10 | 34.90 |
| 1996[1] | 33.10 | 31.50 | 54.20 | 37.90 | 37.70 | 35.70 | 22.50 | 26.80 | 22.60 | 21.80 | | | 32.38 |
| | | | | | | Celery | | | | | | | |
| 1994 | 11.40 | 8.85 | 7.78 | 8.34 | 13.50 | 8.92 | 12.40 | 14.90 | 12.60 | 12.00 | 13.90 | 25.50 | 12.50 |
| 1995 | 24.40 | 25.80 | 20.30 | 31.30 | 24.20 | 14.60 | 11.50 | 11.10 | 16.20 | 13.10 | 12.90 | 11.40 | 16.20 |
| 1996[1] | 7.95 | 8.46 | 12.20 | 11.60 | 8.90 | 11.50 | 10.80 | 9.94 | 11.50 | 9.21 | | | 10.21 |
| | | | | | | Corn, Sweet | | | | | | | |
| 1994 | 26.80 | 17.60 | 26.40 | 17.90 | 22.00 | 22.40 | 19.00 | 14.40 | 15.60 | 21.30 | 21.50 | 35.10 | 17.20 |
| 1995 | 25.00 | 44.70 | 27.80 | 16.70 | 24.80 | 18.90 | 17.70 | 15.50 | 16.30 | 17.90 | 24.00 | 24.80 | 18.30 |
| 1996[1] | 37.10 | 24.10 | 29.40 | 21.00 | 15.70 | 12.60 | 18.80 | 18.40 | 17.10 | 17.30 | | | 21.15 |
| | | | | | | Lettuce, Head | | | | | | | |
| 1994 | 8.05 | 11.60 | 9.69 | 11.60 | 11.40 | 13.90 | 10.40 | 11.00 | 17.00 | 22.30 | 22.10 | 37.50 | 13.30 |
| 1995 | 13.40 | 9.30 | 27.30 | 48.50 | 48.20 | 15.70 | 12.80 | 15.20 | 25.60 | 15.10 | 12.50 | 11.60 | 23.10 |
| 1996[1] | 17.30 | 9.13 | 17.20 | 13.20 | 13.20 | 15.10 | 12.00 | 12.60 | 13.60 | 16.50 | | | 13.98 |
| | | | | | | Tomatoes | | | | | | | |
| 1994 | 41.50 | 19.30 | 24.50 | 16.50 | 20.70 | 30.70 | 28.20 | 29.20 | 23.20 | 28.30 | 30.90 | 37.20 | 27.50 |
| 1995 | 41.60 | 27.00 | 37.10 | 20.50 | 16.70 | 34.20 | 20.60 | 15.60 | 18.70 | 22.10 | 32.80 | 24.90 | 26.00 |
| 1996[1] | 18.80 | 33.10 | 81.70 | 50.50 | 24.40 | 24.10 | 25.00 | 21.40 | 23.70 | 29.60 | | | 33.23 |

[1] Preliminary. *Source: National Agricultural Statistics Service, U.S. Department of Agriculture*

## Frozen Vegetables: January 1 & July 1 Cold Storage Holdings   In Thousands of Pounds

| Crop | 1992 July 1 | 1993 Jan. 1 | 1993 July 1 | 1994 Jan. 1 | 1994 July 1 | 1995 Jan. 1 | 1995 July 1 | 1996 Jan. 1 | 1996 July 1 | 1997[1] Jan. 1 |
|---|---|---|---|---|---|---|---|---|---|---|
| Asparagus | 17,597 | 7,791 | 22,307 | 14,782 | 19,175 | 9,808 | 15,493 | 9,689 | 14,001 | 8,353 |
| Lima Beans | 49,264 | 65,047 | 26,164 | 49,594 | 24,093 | 59,440 | 29,783 | 60,208 | 33,350 | 59,245 |
| Snap Beans | 116,360 | 190,465 | 73,907 | 184,418 | 71,457 | 244,681 | 87,436 | 224,297 | 80,224 | 179,727 |
| Broccoli | 150,460 | 143,486 | 194,061 | 134,774 | 152,312 | 109,076 | 110,075 | 136,850 | 150,883 | 120,971 |
| Brussels sprouts | 13,000 | 26,467 | 12,029 | 34,338 | 20,166 | 30,191 | 18,181 | 18,883 | 9,533 | 16,314 |
| Carrots | 99,743 | 254,040 | 176,830 | 260,993 | 165,748 | 271,244 | 176,054 | 307,645 | 177,248 | 281,791 |
| Cauliflower | 40,636 | 71,135 | 32,461 | 60,683 | 40,077 | 77,243 | 49,561 | 65,008 | 38,355 | 54,618 |
| Corn, Sweet[2] | 285,023 | 489,019 | 239,379 | 493,411 | 119,206 | 645,985 | 199,148 | 648,994 | 215,553 | 645,424 |
| Mixed vegetables | 53,945 | 47,721 | 42,013 | 44,916 | 51,737 | 58,272 | 59,414 | 60,492 | 67,031 | 54,208 |
| Okra | 33,548 | 44,679 | 18,387 | 16,341 | 31,799 | 62,491 | 43,367 | 39,954 | 23,902 | 28,576 |
| Onions | 27,829 | 34,230 | 24,787 | 36,101 | 31,296 | 51,244 | 42,810 | 48,761 | 38,342 | 40,521 |
| Black-eyed peas | 7,323 | 12,559 | 4,636 | 9,605 | 3,159 | 13,157 | 3,145 | 9,994 | 3,529 | 9,795 |
| Green peas | 229,461 | 305,164 | 177,245 | 261,338 | 218,032 | 260,487 | 219,669 | 281,349 | 163,293 | 208,357 |
| Peas and carrots | 8,228 | 6,921 | 7,506 | 15,363 | 14,063 | 9,329 | 9,034 | 10,401 | 8,340 | 6,731 |
| Spinach | 83,863 | 56,182 | 79,337 | 47,159 | 120,542 | 70,010 | 100,274 | 68,940 | 86,281 | 47,868 |
| Squash | 43,597 | 54,708 | 40,941 | 61,679 | 53,763 | 64,533 | 39,494 | 57,785 | 44,785 | 58,749 |
| Southern greens | 21,458 | 27,173 | 22,251 | 31,786 | 29,194 | 29,993 | 30,079 | 21,659 | 32,363 | 26,936 |
| Other vegetables | 216,709 | 295,028 | 211,523 | 258,611 | 238,554 | 241,252 | 189,124 | 319,519 | 235,880 | 314,640 |
| Total | 1,498,044 | 2,300,040 | 1,405,764 | 2,015,892 | 1,404,373 | 2,288,336 | 1,422,141 | 2,390,428 | 1,422,893 | 2,185,704 |
| Potatoes | 1,131,381 | 963,167 | 989,818 | 1,006,416 | 1,099,850 | 1,083,747 | 1,116,454 | 1,123,744 | 1,057,470 | 1,098,421 |
| Grand total | 2,629,425 | 3,263,207 | 2,395,582 | 3,022,308 | 2,504,223 | 3,372,083 | 2,538,595 | 3,514,172 | 2,480,363 | 3,284,125 |

[1] Preliminary. [2] Cut-basis with cob corn converted to cut-basis using a factor of 0.4706. *Source: National Agricultural Statistics Service, U.S. Department of Agriculture*

# Wheat

World wheat production in 1996/97 of a near record large 577 million metric tons trailed initial estimates but still topped the 537 million in 1995/96, and compares with the record high 588 million in 1990/91. For the first time in four years production exceeded world usage permitting some rebuilding of severely depleted reserves. World consumption was forecast at a record high 572 million tons, up 20 million from 1995/96 and a 1991/95 average of about 554 million. Despite the 40 million ton gain in production the projected 1996/97 carryover of nearly 111 million tons (up from 103 million) is among the lowest of the past twenty years, and the world stocks-to-usage ratio of about 19.4 percent one of the lowest in thirty years.

Since the late 1980's, China has been the world's largest wheat producer accounting for nearly 20 percent of global production, a record large 109 million tons in 1996/97 vs. 102 million in 1995/96. Both China's wheat acreage and average yield have been trending higher. China's 1996/97 wheat consumption was forecast marginally higher than the record 113 million tons in 1995/96, but China's large crop may hold imports to about 8 million tons from the 12 million taken in 1995/96. However, China's import needs have little consistency as their wheat inventory is generally unknown. A second unknown is the government's willingness to utilize carryover supplies. What does appear more certain is that China's import needs are very price sensitive and world prices can quickly strengthen on talk, real or otherwise, of Chinese buying which in turn brakes their interest.

The persistent decline during the first half of the 1990's in the former USSR's wheat production may have finally been slowed in 1996/97. Production in the key republics were forecast at: Russia, 37 million tons vs. 30 million in 1995/96; Kazakstan at 10 million vs. 6.5 million; and the Ukraine at 15 million vs. 16.3 million, respectively. The Russian Federation, once the world's largest importer, now trails a number of countries. Russia's 1996/97 imports of only 2.5 million tons compares with 14 million tons early in the 1990's. Russia's chronic lack of foreign exchange and credit lines accounts for the drop in imports. Consumption among the Russian republics has also dropped with Russia's use estimated at 37.1 million tons in 1996/97 vs. 38.7 million in 1995/96, and more than 50 million tons on average in the early 1990's. The Ukraine's use of 17 million tons is a shade higher than in 1995/96, but trails the early 1990's average of more than 20 million tons.

The 1996/97 world wheat trade is forecast at 93 million tons, higher than expected due to a 2 million ton increase in feed wheat by South Korea at the expense of corn, but total trade would still lag 1995/96 by about 1.2 million tons. With about 28 million tons, or 63 percent, of the 1996/97 world production increase concentrated in the five largest exporting nations, keen price competition was expected among the exporters to maintain their market share. However, only the U.S., the world's largest exporter, is expected to see a drop; to 25 million tons from 33.6 million in 1995/96. Canadian 1996/97 exports were forecast at 20 million tons vs. 16.2 million in 1995/96; and EU exports of 14 million compare with 12.5 million, respectively. Importing nations are scattered, among those taking at least 5 million tons in 1996/97 were Brazil, China, Egypt, and Japan.

The U.S. 1996 wheat crop of 2.28 billion bushels compares with 2.18 million in 1995/96. The increase reflected a higher average yield, 36.3 bushels per acre vs. 35.8 the previous year, and planted acreage of 75.6 million acres vs. 69.1 million, respectively. Winter wheat accounts for more than half of U.S. production, 1.5 billion bushels in 1996/97 vs. 1.5 billion in 1995/965; Kansas is the largest winter wheat producing state and North Dakota generally the largest spring wheat and durum producing state. The 1996/97 durum wheat crop of 116 million bushels compares with 102 million in 1995/96; other spring wheat production was put at 688 million bushels vs. 536 million. Generally, durum wheat has the lowest yield per acre.

The U.S. imports some wheat, mostly from Canada. Carryin stocks as of June 1, 1996 of 376 million bushels, the lowest since 1983/84, compares with 507 million a year earlier. The U.S. wheat supply for 1996/97 of 2.73 billion bushels compares with 2.76 billion in 1995/96. Total usage in 1996/97 of 2.29 billion bushels compares with 2.38 billion in 1995/96 when exports accounted for one-half of total disappearance. Food use takes about two-thirds of domestic usage, feed about 20 percent, and seed the balance. If the 1996/97 supply/demand estimates are realized, ending stocks on May 31, 1997 would rise to at least 435 million bushels, boosting the stock to use ratio to 19 percent vs. 16 percent a year earlier. This ratio is often used to forecast prices; the smaller it is the greater the likelihood for higher prices as the crop year progresses.

The 1996/97 average price received by farmers was forecast to range from $4.10 to $4.70 a bushel vs. $4.55 in 1995/96.

### *Futures Markets*

Wheat futures and options are traded on the London Commodity Exchange (LCE), the Chicago Board of Trade (CBOT), the Kansas City Board of Trade (KCBT), the Minneapolis Grain Exchange (MGE), and the Mid America Commodity Exchange (MidAm). Feed wheat futures and options are traded on the Winnipeg Commodity Exchange (WCE).

## World Production of Wheat   In Thousands of Metric Tons

| Crop Year | Argentina | Australia | Canada | China | France | Germany | India | Italy | Pakistan | Russia[4] | Spain | Turkey | United Kingdom | United States | World Total |
|---|---|---|---|---|---|---|---|---|---|---|---|---|---|---|---|
| 1986-7 | 9,000 | 16,700 | 31,850 | 90,295 | 26,500 | 10,406 | 46,885 | 9,070 | 13,922 | 92,306 | 4,292 | 14,000 | 13,900 | 56,793 | 529,419 |
| 1987-8 | 8,800 | 12,442 | 25,950 | 85,840 | 27,234 | 9,932 | 44,323 | 9,381 | 12,020 | 83,312 | 5,768 | 13,000 | 11,940 | 57,362 | 502,300 |
| 1988-9 | 8,400 | 14,060 | 15,995 | 85,432 | 29,660 | 11,922 | 46,169 | 7,952 | 12,675 | 84,445 | 6,173 | 16,000 | 11,750 | 49,320 | 500,300 |
| 1989-90 | 10,150 | 14,214 | 24,796 | 90,807 | 32,100 | 14,482 | 54,110 | 7,413 | 14,419 | 87,151 | 5,200 | 12,500 | 14,030 | 55,428 | 533,001 |
| 1990-1 | 10,900 | 15,066 | 32,098 | 98,229 | 33,600 | 15,242 | 49,850 | 8,108 | 14,429 | 49,596 | 4,759 | 16,000 | 14,000 | 74,292 | 587,995 |
| 1991-2 | 9,880 | 10,557 | 31,946 | 96,000 | 34,594 | 16,610 | 55,134 | 9,416 | 14,565 | 38,900 | 5,000 | 16,500 | 14,400 | 53,891 | 542,132 |
| 1992-3 | 9,800 | 16,184 | 29,871 | 101,590 | 32,777 | 15,542 | 55,690 | 8,938 | 15,684 | 46,170 | 4,356 | 15,500 | 14,000 | 67,135 | 561,807 |
| 1993-4 | 9,700 | 16,479 | 27,232 | 106,390 | 29,630 | 15,767 | 57,210 | 7,851 | 16,157 | 43,500 | 5,000 | 16,500 | 12,900 | 65,220 | 559,216 |
| 1994-5[1] | 11,300 | 8,903 | 23,122 | 99,300 | 30,550 | 16,480 | 59,840 | 7,800 | 15,212 | 32,100 | 4,311 | 14,700 | 13,310 | 63,167 | 524,580 |
| 1995-6[2] | 9,200 | 16,975 | 25,037 | 102,215 | 30,860 | 17,760 | 65,470 | | 17,002 | 30,100 | | 15,500 | 14,310 | 69,400 | 536,769 |
| 1996-7[3] | 15,500 | 23,100 | 30,500 | 109,000 | 35,800 | 18,900 | 62,620 | | 16,907 | 34,900 | | 16,500 | 16,040 | 62,099 | 581,039 |

[1] Preliminary. [2] Estimate. [3] Forecast. [4] Formerly part of the U.S.S.R.; data not reported separately until 1990-91. *Source: Foreign Agricultural Service, U.S. Department of Agriculture*

## World Wheat Supply & Demand   In Millions of Metric Tons/Hectares

| Crop Year | Area Harvested | Yield | Production | World Trade | Utilization Total | Ending Stocks | Stocks as % of Utilization |
|---|---|---|---|---|---|---|---|
| 1987-8 | 219.7 | 2.26 | 496.0 | 115.6 | 527.4 | 147.7 | 28.0 |
| 1988-9 | 217.4 | 2.28 | 495.0 | 104.3 | 524.3 | 118.4 | 22.6 |
| 1989-90 | 225.8 | 2.36 | 533.2 | 103.9 | 532.7 | 118.9 | 22.3 |
| 1990-1 | 231.4 | 2.54 | 588.0 | 101.0 | 561.5 | 145.4 | 25.9 |
| 1991-2 | 222.5 | 2.44 | 542.1 | 110.8 | 554.7 | 132.8 | 23.9 |
| 1992-3 | 223.1 | 2.52 | 561.8 | 112.7 | 549.9 | 144.8 | 26.3 |
| 1993-4 | 222.3 | 2.52 | 559.2 | 100.2 | 561.9 | 142.1 | 25.3 |
| 1994-5[1] | 215.2 | 2.44 | 524.6 | 96.5 | 548.7 | 118.0 | 21.5 |
| 1995-6[2] | 219.6 | 2.44 | 536.8 | 93.2 | 551.0 | 103.7 | 18.8 |
| 1996-7[3] | 230.0 | 2.52 | 581.0 | 90.9 | 572.8 | 111.9 | 19.5 |

[1] Preliminary. [2] Estimate. [3] Forecast. *Source: Foreign Agricultural Service, U.S. Department of Agriculture*

## Salient Statistics of Wheat in the United States

| Crop Year | Planting Intentions | Acreage Harvested: Winter | Spring | All | Average - All Yield Per Acre | Value of Production | Foreign Trade[5]: Domestic Exports[2] | Imports[3] | Per Capita[4] Consumption: Flour | Cereal |
|---|---|---|---|---|---|---|---|---|---|---|
| | 1,000 Acres | | | | in Bushels | $1,000 | Millions of Bushels | | In Pounds | |
| 1988-9 | 65,529 | 39,800 | 13,389 | 53,189 | 34.1 | 6,683,999 | 1,414.9 | 22.7 | 130.0 | 3.8 |
| 1989-90 | 76,615 | 41,509 | 20,680 | 62,189 | 32.7 | 7,542,464 | 1,232.0 | 22.5 | 129.6 | 4.0 |
| 1990-1 | 77,041 | 49,721 | 19,382 | 69,103 | 39.5 | 7,184,427 | 1,069.5 | 36.4 | 135.8 | 4.3 |
| 1991-2 | 69,881 | 39,506 | 18,297 | 57,803 | 34.3 | 5,956,642 | 1,282.3 | 40.7 | 136.5 | 4.5 |
| 1992-3 | 72,219 | 42,123 | 20,638 | 62,761 | 39.3 | 7,978,911 | 1,353.6 | 70.0 | 138.3 | 4.7 |
| 1993-4 | 72,168 | 43,811 | 18,901 | 62,712 | 38.2 | 7,647,527 | 1,227.8 | 108.9 | 143.0 | 5.0 |
| 1994-5 | 70,349 | 41,335 | 20,415 | 61,770 | 37.6 | 7,968,237 | 1,188.3 | 91.9 | 144.0 | 5.2 |
| 1995-6[1] | 69,132 | 40,972 | 19,973 | 60,945 | 35.8 | 9,787,213 | 1,241.1 | 67.9 | | |
| 1996-7[1] | 75,639 | 39,709 | 23,141 | 62,850 | 36.3 | 9,763,670 | 950.0 | 80.0 | | |

[1] Preliminary. [2] Includes flour milled from imported wheat. [3] Total wheat, flour & other products. [4] Civilian only. [5] Year beginning June.
*Source: Economic Research Service, U.S. Department of Agriculture*

## Supply and Distribution of Wheat in the United States   In Millions of Bushels

| Crop Year Beginning June | Supply: Stocks, June 1: On Farms | Mills, Elevators[3] | Total Stocks | Production | Imports[4] | Total Supply | Domestic Disappearance: Food | Seed | Feed & Residual[5] | Total | Exports[4] | Total Disappearance |
|---|---|---|---|---|---|---|---|---|---|---|---|---|
| 1988-9 | 525.0 | 735.8 | 1,260.8 | 1,812.2 | 22.7 | 3,096.0 | 725.8 | 103.0 | 150.5 | 979.2 | 1,414.9 | 2,394.0 |
| 1989-90 | 289.0 | 412.6 | 701.6 | 2,036.6 | 22.5 | 2,761.0 | 748.9 | 104.3 | 139.1 | 992.3 | 1,232.0 | 2,224.0 |
| 1990-1 | 212.5 | 324.0 | 536.5 | 2,729.8 | 36.4 | 3,303.0 | 789.8 | 92.9 | 482.1 | 1,365.1 | 1,069.5 | 2,435.0 |
| 1991-2 | 341.2 | 524.7 | 868.1 | 1,980.1 | 40.7 | 2,889.0 | 789.5 | 97.7 | 244.5 | 1,131.6 | 1,282.3 | 2,414.0 |
| 1992-3 | 144.6 | 327.2 | 475.0 | 2,466.8 | 70.0 | 3,011.8 | 834.8 | 99.1 | 193.6 | 1,127.5 | 1,353.6 | 2,481.2 |
| 1993-4 | 183.8 | 345.3 | 530.7 | 2,396.4 | 108.8 | 3,035.9 | 871.7 | 96.3 | 271.7 | 1,239.7 | 1,227.8 | 2,467.4 |
| 1994-5 | 175.3 | 393.2 | 568.5 | 2,321.0 | 91.9 | 2,981.4 | 852.9 | 89.2 | 344.4 | 1,286.5 | 1,188.3 | 2,474.8 |
| 1995-6[1] | 163.4 | 343.2 | 506.6 | 2,182.6 | 67.9 | 2,757.1 | 883.8 | 104.1 | 152.1 | 1,140.0 | 1,241.1 | 2,381.1 |
| 1996-7[2] | 74.6 | 300.2 | 374.8 | 2,281.8 | 80.0 | 2,737.8 | 910.0 | 104.0 | 300.0 | 1,314.0 | 950.0 | 2,264.0 |

[1] Preliminary. [2] Estimate. [3] Also warehouses and all off-farm storage not otherwise disignated, including flour mills. [4] Imports & exports are for wheat, including flour & other products in terms of wheat. [5] Mostly feed use. *Source: Economic Research Service, U.S. Department of Agriculture*

# WHEAT

## Stocks, Production and Exports of Wheat by Class In Millions of Bushels

| Year Beginning June | Hard Spring June 1 Stocks | Hard Spring Pro-duction | Hard Spring Exports[3] | Durum[2] June 1 Stocks | Durum[2] Pro-duction | Durum[2] Exports[3] | Hard Winter June 1 Stocks | Hard Winter Pro-duction | Hard Winter Exports[3] | Soft Red Winter June 1 Stocks | Soft Red Winter Pro-duction | Soft Red Winter Exports[3] | White June 1 Stocks | White Pro-duction | White Exports[3] |
|---|---|---|---|---|---|---|---|---|---|---|---|---|---|---|---|
| 1988-9 | 402 | 181 | 194 | 83 | 45 | 20 | 567 | 882 | 639 | 75 | 473 | 315 | 135 | 232 | 247 |
| 1989-90 | 219 | 433 | 280 | 60 | 92 | 55 | 302 | 711 | 359 | 39 | 549 | 345 | 81 | 251 | 193 |
| 1990-1 | 155 | 555 | 201 | 50 | 122 | 53 | 215 | 1,196 | 369 | 32 | 344 | 230 | 85 | 313 | 216 |
| 1991-2 | 279 | 431 | 380 | 62 | 104 | 45 | 360 | 901 | 559 | 80 | 325 | 105 | 87 | 219 | 193 |
| 1992-3 | 131 | 707 | 438 | 55 | 100 | 47 | 194 | 967 | 464 | 41 | 427 | 210 | 54 | 266 | 195 |
| 1993-4 | 171 | 512 | 266 | 49 | 70 | 54 | 204 | 1,066 | 486 | 43 | 401 | 173 | 64 | 347 | 249 |
| 1994-5 | 201 | 515 | 292 | 28 | 97 | 40 | 227 | 971 | 422 | 45 | 434 | 212 | 67 | 304 | 222 |
| 1995-6[1] | 193 | 475 | 330 | 26 | 102 | 39 | 194 | 825 | 384 | 37 | 456 | 250 | 57 | 325 | 238 |
| 1996-7[1] | 106 | 627 | 275 | 26 | 116 | 35 | 154 | 762 | 280 | 35 | 422 | 140 | 55 | 355 | 220 |

[1] Preliminary. [2] Includes "Red Durum." [3] Includes flour made from U.S. wheat & shipments to territories. [4] Estimate.
*Source: Economic Research Service, U.S. Department of Agriculture*

## Seeded Acreage, Yield and Production of Wheat in the United States

| Year | Seeded Acreage--1,000 Acres Winter | Other Spring | Durum | All | Yield Per Harvested Acre (Bushels) Winter | Other Spring | Durum | All | Production (1,000,000 Bushels) Winter | Other Spring | Durum | All |
|---|---|---|---|---|---|---|---|---|---|---|---|---|
| 1988 | 48,800 | 13,393 | 3,336 | 65,529 | 39.2 | 19.5 | 15.7 | 34.1 | 1,561.9 | 205.5 | 44.8 | 1,812.2 |
| 1989 | 55,091 | 17,733 | 3,791 | 76,615 | 35.0 | 28.8 | 25.1 | 32.7 | 1,454.6 | 489.7 | 92.2 | 2,036.6 |
| 1990 | 56,748 | 16,723 | 3,570 | 77,041 | 40.7 | 36.7 | 34.9 | 39.5 | 2,024.2 | 583.1 | 122.4 | 2,729.8 |
| 1991 | 51,024 | 15,604 | 3,253 | 69,881 | 34.7 | 33.4 | 32.5 | 34.3 | 1,371.6 | 504.6 | 104.0 | 1,980.1 |
| 1992 | 50,922 | 18,750 | 2,547 | 72,219 | 38.2 | 41.8 | 39.7 | 39.3 | 1,609.3 | 757.6 | 99.9 | 2,466.8 |
| 1993 | 51,587 | 18,340 | 2,241 | 72,168 | 40.2 | 33.7 | 33.6 | 38.2 | 1,760.1 | 565.8 | 70.5 | 2,396.4 |
| 1994 | 49,197 | 18,329 | 2,823 | 70,349 | 40.2 | 31.8 | 35.6 | 37.6 | 1,661.9 | 562.3 | 96.7 | 2,321.0 |
| 1995 | 48,726 | 17,015 | 3,436 | 69,177 | 39.4 | 30.2 | 30.5 | 35.8 | 1,547.3 | 535.9 | 102.3 | 2,185.5 |
| 1996[1] | 52,006 | 17,487 | 3,615 | 73,108 | 36.5 | 33.6 | 32.7 | 36.3 | 1,539.0 | 627.0 | 116.0 | 2,282.0 |

[1] Preliminary. *Source: Economic Research Service, U.S. Department of Agriculture*

## Production of Winter Wheat in the United States In Thousands of Bushels

| Year | Colorado | Idaho | Illinois | Indiana | Kansas | Mich-igan | Missouri | Montana | Neb-raska | Ohio | Okla-homa | Oregon | South Dakota | Tenn-essee | Texas | Wash-ington |
|---|---|---|---|---|---|---|---|---|---|---|---|---|---|---|---|---|
| 1986 | 92,800 | 51,850 | 36,080 | 30,100 | 336,600 | 30,600 | 18,810 | 64,000 | 76,000 | 48,300 | 150,800 | 53,940 | 57,600 | 10,725 | 120,000 | 102,900 |
| 1987 | 93,750 | 60,000 | 56,050 | 34,800 | 366,300 | 19,200 | 35,420 | 79,200 | 85,800 | 46,400 | 129,600 | 49,500 | 55,080 | 14,350 | 100,800 | 104,025 |
| 1988 | 75,900 | 50,820 | 67,500 | 35,000 | 323,000 | 26,040 | 75,950 | 39,900 | 72,000 | 46,000 | 172,800 | 46,860 | 21,590 | 21,500 | 89,600 | 108,500 |
| 1989 | 57,200 | 56,700 | 105,020 | 51,920 | 213,600 | 33,920 | 86,950 | 54,000 | 55,350 | 62,730 | 153,900 | 48,900 | 35,100 | 18,900 | 60,000 | 68,900 |
| 1990 | 84,150 | 69,000 | 91,200 | 50,440 | 472,000 | 41,250 | 76,000 | 87,500 | 85,500 | 79,650 | 201,600 | 54,600 | 57,600 | 17,640 | 130,200 | 138,600 |
| 1991 | 71,300 | 49,000 | 44,800 | 28,800 | 363,000 | 24,080 | 48,000 | 76,000 | 67,200 | 52,920 | 135,000 | 41,600 | 45,500 | 7,680 | 84,000 | 40,600 |
| 1992 | 70,500 | 55,250 | 62,100 | 25,000 | 363,800 | 35,280 | 64,800 | 65,250 | 55,500 | 59,095 | 168,150 | 42,900 | 33,600 | 13,440 | 129,200 | 102,000 |
| 1993 | 94,350 | 67,150 | 68,200 | 34,840 | 388,500 | 22,140 | 53,200 | 102,900 | 73,500 | 52,520 | 156,600 | 61,060 | 56,550 | 13,940 | 118,400 | 162,500 |
| 1994 | 76,500 | 56,880 | 50,400 | 38,430 | 433,200 | 30,740 | 50,400 | 64,750 | 71,400 | 68,440 | 143,100 | 55,680 | 43,200 | 15,000 | 75,400 | 124,200 |
| 1995 | 102,600 | 58,520 | 68,110 | 39,600 | 286,000 | 37,200 | 47,970 | 54,800 | 86,100 | 73,810 | 109,200 | 57,750 | 56,240 | 15,980 | 75,600 | 133,300 |
| 1996[1] | 70,400 | 68,800 | 41,800 | 27,360 | 255,200 | 23,940 | 48,750 | 63,360 | 73,500 | 51,870 | 93,100 | 61,200 | 55,300 | 17,600 | 75,400 | 164,500 |

[1] Preliminary. *Source: Crop Reporting Board, U.S. Department of Agriculture*

## United States Official Winter Wheat Crop Production Reports In Thousands of Bushels

| Crop Year | May 1 | June 1 | July 1 | August 1 | September 1 | Current December | Final |
|---|---|---|---|---|---|---|---|
| 1986-7 | 1,603,127 | 1,578,277 | 1,553,026 | 1,532,526 | 1,532,526 | 1,519,143 | 1,520,433 |
| 1987-8 | 1,549,344 | 1,577,489 | 1,574,439 | 2,125,097 | 2,114,492 | 1,565,176 | 1,565,381 |
| 1988-9 | 1,620,257 | 1,570,417 | 1,568,052 | 1,554,812 | 1,560,970 | 1,561,145 | 1,561,910 |
| 1989-90 | 1,430,148 | 1,407,898 | 1,461,924 | 1,466,049 | 1,451,746 | 1,453,842 | 1,454,642 |
| 1990-1 | 2,091,614 | 2,089,234 | 2,035,087 | 2,054,287 | 2,036,059 | ---------- | 2,030,874 |
| 1991-2 | 1,495,943 | 1,449,418 | 1,361,316 | 1,371,946 | 1,372,182 | ---------- | 1,372,617 |
| 1992-3 | 1,618,017 | 1,618,017 | 1,573,901 | 1,600,931 | NA | ---------- | 1,609,284 |
| 1993-4 | 1,807,657 | 1,824,062 | 1,821,345 | 1,788,005 | 1,788,005 | ---------- | 1,760,143 |
| 1994-5 | 1,657,938 | 1,674,563 | 1,658,426 | 1,670,436 | 1,670,436 | ---------- | 1,661,043 |
| 1995-6 | 1,638,211 | 1,608,396 | 1,529,950 | 1,552,230 | 1,552,230 | ---------- | 1,544,653 |
| 1996-7[1] | 1,363,851 | 1,369,861 | 1,484,836 | 1,494,716 | NA | ---------- | 1,478,048 |

[1] Preliminary. NA = Not available. *Source: Crop Reporting Board, U.S. Department of Agriculture*

# Wheat

## Production of All Spring Wheat in the United States In Thousands of Bushels

| | Durum Wheat | | | | | | | Other Spring Wheat | | | | | | | | | |
|---|---|---|---|---|---|---|---|---|---|---|---|---|---|---|---|---|---|
| Year | Arizona | California | Minnesota | Montana | North Dakota | South Dakota | Total Durum | Colorado | Idaho | Minnesota | Montana | North Dakota | Oregon | South Dakota | Utah | Washington | Total Other |
| 1987 | 3,825 | 5,130 | 1,218 | 5,320 | 74,100 | 3,024 | 92,617 | 3,630 | 25,500 | 98,400 | 66,700 | 189,100 | 3,420 | 48,600 | 1,653 | 10,260 | 449,687 |
| 1988 | 4,300 | 5,605 | 840 | 2,070 | 31,200 | 816 | 44,831 | 3,640 | 24,700 | 49,450 | 18,000 | 70,500 | 4,940 | 15,600 | 1,188 | 16,120 | 205,460 |
| 1989 | 7,560 | 8,715 | 1,044 | 6,030 | 66,000 | 2,880 | 92,229 | 4,900 | 34,720 | 96,900 | 85,000 | 174,000 | 4,935 | 45,100 | 990 | 41,710 | 489,747 |
| 1990 | 4,136 | 5,346 | 1,320 | 4,465 | 103,700 | 3,204 | 122,171 | 2,800 | 30,600 | 134,750 | 53,900 | 277,200 | 3,016 | 67,200 | 1,170 | 11,480 | 583,124 |
| 1991 | 3,705 | 3,360 | 960 | 5,907 | 88,350 | 1,675 | 103,957 | 2,700 | 32,660 | 64,170 | 81,600 | 212,350 | 2,300 | 49,000 | 1,127 | 58,000 | 504,565 |
| 1992 | 3,740 | 5,115 | 470 | 4,851 | 81,700 | 990 | 99,906 | 3,619 | 44,840 | 137,500 | 79,050 | 382,200 | 4,900 | 85,000 | 1,056 | 17,640 | 757,608 |
| 1993 | 4,500 | 3,800 | 240 | 3,534 | 57,970 | 432 | 70,476 | 2,640 | 43,200 | 69,750 | 99,900 | 274,350 | 3,900 | 54,540 | 1,225 | 15,080 | 565,821 |
| 1994 | 8,554 | 5,605 | 275 | 5,340 | 76,375 | 598 | 96,747 | 3,234 | 43,400 | 70,000 | 100,500 | 278,775 | 2,900 | 51,480 | 1,012 | 9,800 | 562,291 |
| 1995 | 8,514 | 6,800 | 360 | 7,950 | 77,760 | 896 | 102,280 | 2,660 | 44,800 | 70,400 | 133,000 | 221,400 | 5,928 | 33,600 | 1,950 | 20,470 | 535,658 |
| 1996[1] | 14,760 | 13,800 | 430 | 6,750 | 79,380 | 720 | 115,840 | 5,100 | 50,400 | 100,800 | 106,600 | 313,500 | 6,405 | 83,250 | 1,680 | 18,170 | 687,875 |

[1] Preliminary. *Source: Crop Reporting Board, U.S. Department of Agriculture*

## Average Wheat Farm Prices for Leading Classes in the U.S. In Dollars Per Bushel

| Year | June | July | Aug. | Sept. | Oct. | Nov. | Dec. | Jan. | Feb. | Mar. | Apr. | May | Average |
|---|---|---|---|---|---|---|---|---|---|---|---|---|---|
| | | | | | | Winter Wheat | | | | | | | |
| 1994-5 | 3.09 | 2.99 | 3.23 | 3.57 | 3.79 | 3.76 | 3.75 | 3.67 | 3.61 | 3.47 | 3.45 | 3.65 | 3.50 |
| 1995-6 | 3.77 | 4.05 | 4.22 | 4.47 | 4.70 | 4.78 | 4.88 | 4.80 | 5.01 | 5.06 | 5.39 | 5.81 | 4.75 |
| 1996-7[1] | 5.14 | 4.67 | 4.52 | 4.28 | 4.07 | 4.05 | 4.04 | 4.02 | 3.89 | | | | 4.30 |
| | | | | | | Durum Wheat | | | | | | | |
| 1994-5 | 4.59 | 4.32 | 4.30 | 4.51 | 4.89 | 4.88 | 4.67 | 4.61 | 4.68 | 4.61 | 4.48 | 4.82 | 4.61 |
| 1995-6 | 5.20 | 5.29 | 5.33 | 5.87 | 5.80 | 5.78 | 5.75 | 5.66 | 5.72 | 5.73 | 5.63 | 5.62 | 5.62 |
| 1996-7[1] | 5.58 | 5.13 | 5.03 | 4.69 | 4.78 | 4.56 | 4.59 | 4.47 | 4.45 | | | | 4.81 |
| | | | | | | Other Spring Wheat | | | | | | | |
| 1994-5 | 3.51 | 3.28 | 3.19 | 3.38 | 3.52 | 3.51 | 3.56 | 3.50 | 3.40 | 3.38 | 3.34 | 3.53 | 3.43 |
| 1995-6 | 3.78 | 4.26 | 4.19 | 4.27 | 4.45 | 4.61 | 4.72 | 4.66 | 4.81 | 4.88 | 5.21 | 5.67 | 4.63 |
| 1996-7[1] | 5.48 | 5.30 | 4.63 | 4.41 | 4.23 | 4.11 | 4.01 | 3.95 | 3.83 | | | | 4.44 |

[1] Preliminary. *Source: Agricultural Statistics Board, U.S. Department of Agriculture*

## United States Grindings of Wheat by Mills In Millions of Bushels (60 Pounds Each)

| Year | July | Aug. | Sept. | Oct. | Nov. | Dec. | Jan. | Feb. | Mar. | Apr. | May | June | Total |
|---|---|---|---|---|---|---|---|---|---|---|---|---|---|
| 1987-8 | 62.3 | 66.3 | 65.8 | 69.5 | 66.7 | 62.5 | 59.6 | 58.4 | 61.2 | 58.0 | 65.7 | 63.8 | 759.8 |
| 1988-9 | 63.6 | 70.0 | 66.0 | 70.0 | 69.7 | 63.8 | 65.0 | 60.8 | 60.4 | 60.7 | 64.7 | 59.6 | 773.3 |
| 1989-90 | 58.5 | 70.6 | 63.6 | 67.4 | 65.1 | 58.7 | 63.4 | 64.0 | 66.7 | 61.6 | 63.6 | 60.6 | 763.8 |
| 1990-1 | 62.3 | 73.2 | 65.7 | 74.9 | 73.9 | 64.3 | 66.7 | 65.2 | 63.2 | 67.6 | 69.9 | 60.9 | 807.8 |
| 1991-2 | 65.3 | 71.2 | 67.7 | 72.2 | 73.5 | 65.6 | 65.7 | 66.0 | 65.6 | 67.3 | 67.0 | 67.2 | 814.3 |
| 1992-3 | 70.0 | 77.3 | 71.9 | 77.9 | 71.9 | 65.5 | 68.1 | 70.0 | 76.2 | 72.0 | 69.6 | 67.9 | 858.2 |
| 1993-4 | 69.2 | 75.2 | 74.1 | 75.8 | 77.0 | 76.3 | 70.0 | 68.3 | 81.1 | 73.0 | 73.0 | 70.6 | 883.8 |
| 1994-5 | 68.9 | 78.7 | 76.3 | 77.9 | 75.9 | 71.1 | 69.0 | 65.2 | 76.9 | 66.6 | 74.7 | 71.9 | 873.1 |
| 1995-6 | 69.8 | 77.8 | 74.2 | 78.4 | 74.8 | 70.0 | 70.3 | 72.6 | 72.4 | 69.6 | 72.8 | 67.9 | 870.5 |
| 1996-7[1] | 73.9 | 77.7 | 75.5 | 83.1 | 74.0 | 71.6 | | | | | | | 455.9 |

[1] Preliminary. *Source: Bureau of Census, U.S. Department of Commerce*

## Comparative Average Cash Wheat Prices In Dollars Per Bushel

| | | | | | Minneapolis | | | | | Export Prices[2] (U.S. $ per Metric Ton) | | | | |
|---|---|---|---|---|---|---|---|---|---|---|---|---|---|---|
| Crop Year Beginning June | Received by U.S. Farmers | No. 2 Soft Red Winter Chicago | No. 1 Hard Red Ordinary Protein Kansas City | No. 2 Soft Red Winter St. Louis | No. 1 Dark Northern Spring 14% | No. 1 Hard Amber Durum | No. 1 Soft White Portland Oregon | No. 2 Western White Pacific N.W. | No. 2 Soft White Toledo | Australian Standard Wheat | Canada Vancouver No. 1 CWRS 13 1/2 % | Argentina F.O.B. B.A. | U.S. Gulf No. 2 H.W. | Rotterdam C.I.F. U.S. No. 2 Hard Winter |
| 1987-8 | 2.57 | 2.89 | 2.96 | 2.95 | 3.15 | 4.13 | 3.06 | 2.74 | 2.94 | 115 | 134 | 89 | 114 | 141 |
| 1988-9 | 3.72 | 4.00 | 4.17 | 4.08 | 4.36 | 5.53 | 4.53 | 4.13 | 3.90 | 150 | 177 | 125 | 146 | 176 |
| 1989-90 | 3.72 | 3.92 | 4.22 | 3.94 | 4.16 | 4.25 | 4.28 | 3.88 | 3.80 | 176 | 202 | 151 | 171 | 190 |
| 1990-1 | 2.61 | 2.74 | 2.94 | 2.81 | 3.06 | 3.48 | 3.16 | 2.75 | 2.59 | 144 | 158 | 107 | 137 | 164 |
| 1991-2 | 3.00 | 3.49 | 3.77 | 3.32 | 3.82 | 3.61 | 4.11 | 3.66 | 3.41 | 137 | 141 | 99 | 129 | 154 |
| 1992-3 | 3.24 | 3.49 | 3.67 | 3.54 | 3.91 | 3.88 | 4.11 | 3.69 | 3.18 | 165 | 177 | 122 | 152 | 173 |
| 1993-4 | 3.26 | 3.20 | 3.60 | 3.23 | 5.02 | 5.76 | 3.53 | 3.12 | 3.16 | 154 | 192 | 131 | 141 | 200 |
| 1994-5 | 3.45 | 3.62 | 3.97 | 3.62 | 4.26 | 5.98 | 4.16 | 3.75 | 3.37 | 162 | 199 | NA | 150 | 210 |
| 1995-6[1] | 4.55 | 4.78 | 5.49 | 4.82 | 5.72 | 7.03 | 5.27 | 4.43 | 4.41 | 198 | 204 | NA | 177 | 221 |

[1] Preliminary. [2] Calendar year. NA = Not available. *Source: Economic Research Service, U.S. Department of Agriculture*

# Wheat

## Wheat Government Loan Program Data in the United States — Loan Rates (Cents Per Bushel)

| Crop Year Beginning June | National Average[3] | Target Rate | Farm Loan Prices: Corn Belt (Soft Red Winter) | Central & Southern Plains (Hard Winter) | Northern Plains (Spring & Durum) | Pacific Northwest (White) | Placed Under Loan | % of Production | Acquired by CCC Under Program | Stocks Ending May 31: Total Stocks | Total CCC Stocks | Outstanding: CCC Loans | Farmer-Owned Reserve | "Free" |
|---|---|---|---|---|---|---|---|---|---|---|---|---|---|---|
| | | | | | | | Millions of Bushels | | | | | | | |
| 1988-9 | 221 | 423 | 233 | 221 | 221 | 232 | 106 | 5.8 | 45 | 702 | 191 | 19 | 287 | 205 |
| 1989-90 | 206 | 410 | 214 | 204 | 206 | 217 | 113 | 5.6 | 62 | 536 | 117 | 30 | 144 | 245 |
| 1990-1 | 195 | 400 | 200 | 194 | 195 | 206 | 405 | 14.8 | 90 | 868 | 163 | 217 | 14 | 474 |
| 1991-2 | 204 | 400 | 209 | 200 | 204 | 214 | 143 | 7.2 | 1 | 475 | 152 | 20 | 50 | 273 |
| 1992-3 | 221 | 400 | 232 | 220 | 221 | 237 | 240 | 9.8 | .1 | 531 | 150 | 47 | 28 | 353 |
| 1993-4 | 245 | 400 | 251 | 243 | 245 | 269 | 258 | 14.7 | .3 | 569 | 150 | 67 | 6 | 413 |
| 1994-5[1] | 258 | 400 | 253 | 257 | 258 | 271 | 231 | 10.0 | 0 | 507 | 142 | 64 | 0 | 365 |
| 1995-6[2] | 258 | 400 | 254 | 258 | 258 | 276 | 114 | 4.7 | 0 | 376 | 118 | NA | 0 | 254 |
| 1996-7[2] | 258 | NA | | | | | 185 | 8.1 | 0 | 474 | 95 | NA | 0 | 364 |

[1] Preliminary. [2] Estimate. [3] The national average loan rate at the farm as a percentage of the parity-priced wheat at the beginning of the marketing year. NA = Not avaliable. *Source: Agricultural Marketing Service, U.S. Department of Agriculture*

## Exports of Wheat (Only)[2] from the United States — In Thousands of Bushels

| Year | June | July | Aug. | Sept. | Oct. | Nov. | Dec. | Jan. | Feb. | Mar. | Apr. | May | Total |
|---|---|---|---|---|---|---|---|---|---|---|---|---|---|
| 1988-9 | 121,842 | 111,498 | 107,562 | 127,564 | 93,153 | 93,309 | 100,149 | 115,846 | 127,060 | 141,780 | 115,916 | 90,658 | 1,346,336 |
| 1989-90 | 90,490 | 137,933 | 131,176 | 150,697 | 89,336 | 68,664 | 81,813 | 78,343 | 87,647 | 104,903 | 84,576 | 71,572 | 1,177,152 |
| 1990-1 | 88,235 | 80,831 | 93,617 | 107,786 | 84,488 | 76,800 | 56,444 | 66,473 | 91,313 | 112,809 | 88,526 | 81,760 | 1,029,072 |
| 1991-2 | 59,167 | 79,319 | 97,794 | 94,991 | 124,155 | 136,385 | 112,771 | 132,413 | 115,126 | 103,024 | 116,850 | 59,764 | 1,231,759 |
| 1992-3 | 75,045 | 96,382 | 99,290 | 92,723 | 132,232 | 108,235 | 111,389 | 111,584 | 118,607 | 118,782 | 126,845 | 104,540 | 1,295,653 |
| 1993-4 | 85,874 | 103,836 | 100,516 | 104,732 | 100,618 | 112,667 | 121,900 | 109,389 | 87,250 | 96,873 | 71,575 | 82,838 | 1,178,068 |
| 1994-5 | 73,364 | 66,314 | 103,941 | 117,555 | 101,450 | 107,549 | 104,139 | 93,735 | 97,478 | 98,876 | 85,251 | 75,006 | 1,124,658 |
| 1995-6 | 78,355 | 88,649 | 119,797 | 131,424 | 117,679 | 105,535 | 99,175 | 96,085 | 91,876 | 108,800 | 90,373 | 78,303 | 1,206,051 |
| 1996-7[1] | 73,715 | 108,437 | 145,840 | 125,910 | 98,302 | 75,245 | 50,979 | | | | | | 678,428 |

[1] Preliminary.. [2] Grains. *Source: Economic Research Service, U.S. Department of Agriculture*

## United States Wheat and Flour Imports and Exports — In Thousands of Bushels

| Crop Year Beginning June | Imports: Wheat: Suitable for Milling | Unfit for Human Consumption | Grain | Flour & Products[2] | Total | Exports: P.L. 480 | Foreign Donations Sec. 416 | Aid[3] | Total concessional | CCC Export Credit | Export Enhancement Program | Total U.S. Wheat Exports |
|---|---|---|---|---|---|---|---|---|---|---|---|---|
| | | | -- Wheat Equivalent --- | | | In Thousands of Metric Tons | | | | | | |
| 1987-8 | 9,020 | 969 | 9,989 | 6,097 | 16,086 | 3,321 | 1,186 | 292 | 4,799 | 9,273 | 26,679 | 40,523 |
| 1988-9 | 15,870 | NA | 15,870 | 6,798 | 22,668 | 3,020 | 137 | 806 | 3,963 | 8,897 | 17,906 | 37,660 |
| 1989-90 | 13,548 | NA | 12,583 | 9,884 | 22,467 | 2,985 | 0 | 28 | 3,065 | 7,759 | 12,806 | 28,064 |
| 1990-1 | 25,540 | NA | 25,574 | 10,832 | 36,407 | 2,975 | 0 | 0 | 3,159 | 8,339 | 15,150 | 26,792 |
| 1991-2 | 30,924 | NA | 31,019 | 9,675 | 40,694 | 2,286 | 0 | 0 | 2,416 | 13,334 | 21,111 | 34,322 |
| 1992-3 | 56,859 | NA | 56,859 | 13,142 | 70,001 | 2,043 | 890 | 0 | 4,001 | 8,538 | 21,806 | 36,081 |
| 1993-4[1] | 91,287 | NA | 91,288 | 17,529 | 108,817 | 2,801 | 0 | 0 | 3,527 | 5,874 | 18,157 | 31,145 |
| 1994-5[1] | | | 70,562 | 21,386 | 91,946 | 1,491 | 0 | 0 | 1,948 | 4,202 | 18,073 | 32,088 |

[1] Preliminary. [2] Includes macaroni, semolina & similar products. [3] Shipments mostly under the Commodity Import Program, financed with foreign aid funds. NA = Not available. *Source: Economic Research Service, U.S. Department of Agriculture*

## Wheat Stocks in the United States — In Millions of Bushels

| Year | On Farms: Mar. 1 | June 1 | Sept. 1 | Dec. 1 | Off Farms: Mar. 1 | June 1 | Sept. 1 | Dec. 1 | Total Stocks: Mar. 1 | June 1 | Sept. 1 | Dec. 1 |
|---|---|---|---|---|---|---|---|---|---|---|---|---|
| 1988 | 748.0 | 525.0 | 798.0 | 620.0 | 1,175.5 | 735.8 | 1,455.6 | 1,095.9 | 1,923.5 | 1,260.8 | 2,253.6 | 1,715.9 |
| 1989 | 463.0 | 289.0 | 832.0 | 592.0 | 764.7 | 412.6 | 1,086.0 | 830.5 | 1,227.7 | 701.6 | 1,918.0 | 1,422.5 |
| 1990 | 376.0 | 212.5 | 1,000.0 | 763.2 | 567.1 | 324.0 | 1,409.5 | 1,144.8 | 943.1 | 536.5 | 2,409.5 | 1,909.5 |
| 1991 | 532.9 | 341.2 | 828.0 | 564.8 | 863.3 | 524.7 | 1,212.7 | 877.3 | 1,396.3 | 865.9 | 2,040.7 | 1,442.1 |
| 1992 | 275.6 | 144.6 | 979.4 | 672.0 | 611.7 | 327.2 | 1,128.2 | 918.5 | 887.2 | 471.9 | 2,107.6 | 1,590.5 |
| 1993 | 378.0 | 183.8 | 987.0 | 653.1 | 670.3 | 346.8 | 1,145.6 | 932.6 | 1,048.3 | 530.7 | 2,132.6 | 1,585.7 |
| 1994 | 363.2 | 175.3 | 859.8 | 575.6 | 664.8 | 393.2 | 1,209.7 | 920.6 | 1,028.0 | 568.5 | 2,069.5 | 1,491.1 |
| 1995 | 335.3 | 163.4 | 743.6 | 477.0 | 633.8 | 343.2 | 1,137.5 | 861.3 | 969.1 | 506.6 | 1,881.1 | 1,338.3 |
| 1996[1] | 220.6 | 74.6 | 825.5 | 584.2 | 602.9 | 301.4 | 898.3 | 635.2 | 823.5 | 376.0 | 1,723.8 | 1,219.4 |

[1] Preliminary. *Source: Crop Reporting Board, U.S. Department of Agriculture*

## Wheat Supply and Distribution in Canada, Australia and Argentina In Millions of Metric Tons

| Crop Year | Canada (Year Beginning Aug. 1) Supply: Stocks Aug. 1 | New Crop | Total Supply | Disappearance: Domestic | Exports[3] | Australia (Year Beginning Oct. 1) Supply: Stocks Oct. 1 | New Crop | Total Supply | Disappearance: Domestic | Exports[3] | Argentina (Year Beginning Dec. 1) Supply: Stocks Dec. 1 | New Crop | Total Supply | Disappearance: Domestic | Exports[3] |
|---|---|---|---|---|---|---|---|---|---|---|---|---|---|---|---|
| 1985-6 | 7.6 | 24.3 | 31.9 | 5.6 | 17.7 | 8.6 | 16.2 | 24.8 | 2.9 | 16.0 | .5 | 8.5 | 9.0 | 4.4 | 4.3 |
| 1986-7 | 8.6 | 31.4 | 40.0 | 6.4 | 20.8 | 5.9 | 16.1 | 22.0 | 2.7 | 15.6 | .3 | 8.9 | 9.2 | 4.5 | 4.4 |
| 1987-8 | 12.7 | 25.9 | 38.7 | 7.9 | 23.5 | 3.8 | 12.4 | 16.1 | 3.5 | 9.9 | .2 | 8.8 | 9.0 | 4.5 | 3.7 |
| 1988-9 | 7.3 | 15.9 | 23.2 | 5.8 | 12.4 | 2.8 | 14.1 | 16.8 | 2.9 | 11.3 | .8 | 8.4 | 9.2 | 4.7 | 4.0 |
| 1989-90 | 5.0 | 24.8 | 29.8 | 6.5 | 16.9 | 2.6 | 14.2 | 16.8 | 3.0 | 10.8 | .5 | 10.2 | 10.7 | 4.5 | 6.1 |
| 1990-1 | 6.4 | 32.1 | 38.5 | 6.5 | 20.5 | 3.0 | 15.1 | 18.1 | 3.5 | 11.7 | 0 | 10.9 | 10.9 | 4.5 | 4.8 |
| 1991-2 | 10.3 | 31.9 | 42.3 | 7.8 | 24.5 | 2.8 | 10.6 | 13.4 | 3.4 | 7.1 | .8 | 9.9 | 10.7 | 4.6 | 5.8 |
| 1992-3 | 10.1 | 29.9 | 40.1 | 8.1 | 19.7 | 2.9 | 16.2 | 19.1 | 4.2 | 9.9 | .3 | 9.8 | 10.1 | 4.3 | 5.9 |
| 1993-4 | 12.2 | 27.2 | 39.4 | 9.3 | 19.1 | 5.0 | 16.5 | 21.5 | 4.1 | 13.7 | 0 | 9.7 | 9.7 | 4.3 | 5.0 |
| 1994-5 | 11.1 | 23.1 | 34.2 | 7.8 | 20.9 | 3.7 | 8.9 | 12.7 | 3.9 | 6.3 | .4 | 11.3 | 11.7 | 4.3 | 7.3 |
| 1995-6[1] | 5.7 | 25.0 | 30.7 | 8.2 | 16.9 | 2.4 | 17.0 | 19.4 | 3.6 | 13.3 | .1 | 9.2 | 9.3 | 4.3 | 5.0 |
| 1996-7[2] | 6.6 | 30.5 | 37.1 | 9.2 | 16.0 | 2.4 | 23.1 | 25.5 | 4.5 | 16.5 | .1 | 15.5 | 15.6 | 4.4 | 11.0 |

[1] Preliminary. [2] Forecast. [3] Including flour. *Source: Foreign Agricultural Service, U.S. Department of Agriculture*

## United States Wheat Quarterly Supply and Disappearance In Millions of Bushels

| Crop Year Beginning June 1 | Supply: Beginning Stocks | Production | Imports[3] | Total Supply | Disappearance: Domestic Use: Food | Seed | Feed & Residual[7] | Total | Exports[3] | Total Disap-pearance | Ending Stocks: Gov't Owned[4] | Privately Owned[5] | Total Stocks |
|---|---|---|---|---|---|---|---|---|---|---|---|---|---|
| 1989-90 | 701.6 | 2,036.6 | 23.4 | 2,761.0 | 748.9 | 104.3 | 139.1 | 992.3 | 1,232.0 | 2,224.3 | 116.6 | 419.9 | 536.5 |
| June-Aug. | 701.6 | 2,036.6 | 5.9 | 2,744.0 | 190.7 | 1.7 | 264.9 | 457.4 | 368.7 | 826.1 | 167.9 | 1,750.1 | 1,918.0 |
| Sept.-Nov. | 1,918.0 | --------- | 7.1 | 1,925.0 | 191.7 | 70.3 | -87.8 | 174.1 | 328.6 | 502.7 | 154.5 | 1,268.0 | 1,422.5 |
| Dec.-Feb. | 1,423.0 | --------- | 4.7 | 1,427.0 | 184.3 | 2.7 | 37.4 | 224.4 | 259.6 | 484.0 | 136.5 | 806.6 | 943.1 |
| Mar.-May | 943.1 | --------- | 5.8 | 948.0 | 182.2 | 29.6 | -75.4 | 136.4 | 275.1 | 411.5 | 116.6 | 419.9 | 536.5 |
| 1990-1 | 536.5 | 2,729.8 | 36.4 | 3,303.0 | 789.8 | 92.9 | 482.4 | 1,365.1 | 1,069.5 | 2,434.5 | 162.7 | 705.4 | 868.1 |
| June-Aug. | 536.5 | 2,729.8 | 8.0 | 3,274.0 | 194.1 | 1.7 | 399.7 | 595.5 | 267.7 | 863.1 | 104.6 | 2,306.5 | 2,411.1 |
| Sept.-Nov. | 2,409.5 | --------- | 13.4 | 2,425.0 | 210.6 | 62.9 | -38.3 | 235.2 | 279.4 | 514.5 | 129.9 | 1,780.0 | 1,909.9 |
| Dec.-Feb. | 1,908.0 | --------- | 7.8 | 1,918.0 | 191.0 | 2.1 | 101.5 | 294.6 | 225.5 | 520.0 | 152.5 | 1,245.2 | 1,397.7 |
| Mar.-May | 1,396.0 | --------- | 7.2 | 1,405.0 | 194.1 | 26.3 | 19.5 | 239.9 | 296.9 | 536.8 | 162.7 | 705.4 | 868.1 |
| 1991-2 | 868.1 | 1,980.1 | 40.7 | 2,889.0 | 789.5 | 97.2 | 244.5 | 1,131.6 | 1,282.3 | 2,413.9 | 152.0 | 323.0 | 475.0 |
| June-Aug. | 868.1 | 1,980.1 | 7.8 | 2,856.0 | 189.4 | 1.2 | 359.1 | 549.6 | 251.7 | 801.3 | 162.8 | 1,891.9 | 2,054.7 |
| Sept.-Nov. | 2,054.7 | --------- | 7.3 | 2,062.0 | 213.0 | 62.2 | -26.9 | 248.3 | 365.9 | 614.2 | 160.7 | 1,287.1 | 1,447.8 |
| Dec.-Feb. | 1,447.8 | --------- | 10.7 | 1,459.0 | 192.9 | 2.4 | -0.5 | 194.8 | 371.7 | 566.5 | 156.9 | 735.1 | 892.0 |
| Mar.-May | 892.0 | --------- | 14.9 | 907.0 | 194.2 | 31.9 | -87.3 | 138.9 | 293.0 | 431.9 | 152.0 | 323.0 | 475.0 |
| 1992-3 | 475.0 | 2,466.8 | 70.0 | 3,012.0 | 834.3 | 99.1 | 194.2 | 1,127.6 | 1,353.6 | 2,481.2 | 150.0 | 380.7 | 530.7 |
| June-Aug. | 475.0 | 2,466.8 | 20.1 | 2,962.0 | 212.1 | 1.4 | 345.3 | 558.8 | 282.6 | 841.4 | 151.6 | 1,969.0 | 2,120.6 |
| Sept.-Nov. | 2,120.6 | --------- | 16.4 | 2,137.0 | 218.8 | 63.4 | -81.9 | 200.3 | 345.0 | 545.3 | 151.1 | 1,440.6 | 1,591.7 |
| Dec.-Feb. | 1,591.7 | --------- | 17.4 | 1,609.0 | 196.7 | 2.6 | 5.2 | 204.5 | 356.3 | 560.8 | 150.4 | 897.9 | 1,048.3 |
| Mar.-May | 1,048.3 | --------- | 16.1 | 1,064.0 | 206.7 | 31.7 | -74.4 | 164.0 | 369.7 | 533.7 | 150.0 | 380.7 | 530.7 |
| 1993-4 | 530.7 | 2,396.4 | 108.8 | 3,035.9 | 871.7 | 96.3 | 271.7 | 1,239.7 | 1,227.8 | 2,467.4 | 150.3 | 418.2 | 568.5 |
| June-Aug. | 530.7 | 2,396.4 | 14.6 | 2,941.7 | 211.3 | 1.3 | 295.8 | 508.4 | 300.7 | 809.1 | 149.9 | 1,982.7 | 2,132.6 |
| Sept.-Nov. | 2,132.6 | --------- | 30.1 | 2,162.7 | 225.3 | 60.9 | -38.5 | 247.7 | 329.2 | 577.0 | 150.3 | 1,435.4 | 1,585.7 |
| Dec.-Feb. | 1,585.7 | --------- | 26.9 | 1,612.6 | 211.0 | 2.3 | 39.0 | 252.3 | 332.3 | 584.6 | 150.4 | 877.6 | 1,028.0 |
| Mar.-May | 1,028.0 | --------- | 37.2 | 1,065.2 | 224.1 | 31.8 | -24.7 | 231.2 | 265.5 | 496.7 | 150.3 | 418.2 | 568.5 |
| 1994-5 | 568.5 | 2,321.0 | 92.0 | 2,981.4 | 852.5 | 89.2 | 344.9 | 1,286.6 | 1,188.3 | 2,474.9 | 142.1 | 364.5 | 506.6 |
| June-Aug. | 568.5 | 2,321.0 | 30.7 | 2,920.2 | 213.2 | 1.6 | 376.3 | 591.1 | 259.6 | 850.7 | 146.4 | 1,923.1 | 2,069.5 |
| Sept.-Nov. | 2,069.5 | --------- | 21.4 | 2,090.9 | 229.3 | 61.1 | -28.8 | 261.6 | 338.2 | 599.8 | 142.8 | 1,348.3 | 1,491.1 |
| Dec.-Feb. | 1,491.1 | --------- | 17.7 | 1,508.8 | 201.5 | 2.2 | 25.6 | 229.3 | 310.4 | 539.7 | 142.3 | 826.8 | 969.1 |
| Mar.-May | 969.1 | --------- | 22.2 | 991.2 | 208.5 | 24.3 | -28.2 | 204.6 | 280.1 | 484.7 | 142.1 | 364.5 | 506.6 |
| 1995-6[1] | 506.6 | 2,183.0 | 68.0 | 2,757.0 | 883.0 | 104.0 | 152.0 | 1,139.0 | 1,240.3 | 2,379.3 | 118.0 | 258.0 | 376.0 |
| June-Aug. | 506.6 | 2,183.0 | 22.7 | 2,712.0 | 215.0 | 8.0 | 305.0 | 528.0 | 302.5 | 830.5 | 141.5 | 1,739.6 | 1,881.1 |
| Sept.-Nov. | 1,881.1 | --------- | 16.3 | 1,897.0 | 232.0 | 65.0 | -99.0 | 198.0 | 360.8 | 558.8 | 141.2 | 1,197.1 | 1,338.3 |
| Dec.-Feb. | 1,337.9 | --------- | 12.0 | 1,350.0 | 216.0 | 3.0 | 13.0 | 232.0 | 294.0 | 526.0 | 137.5 | 686.0 | 823.5 |
| Mar.-May | 823.0 | --------- | 17.0 | 841.0 | 220.0 | 28.0 | -67.0 | 181.0 | 283.0 | 464.0 | 118.2 | 257.8 | 376.0 |
| 1996-7[2] | 376.0 | 2,282.0 | 36.0 | 2,673.0 | 460.0 | 69.0 | 303.0 | 832.0 | 334.0 | 1,166.0 | 95.0 | 378.8 | 473.8 |
| June-Aug. | 376.0 | 2,282.0 | 15.0 | 2,673.0 | 225.0 | 9.0 | 381.0 | 615.0 | 334.0 | 949.0 | 109.5 | 1,614.7 | 1,724.2 |
| Sept.-Nov. | 1,724.0 | --------- | 21.0 | 1,745.0 | 235.0 | 60.0 | -78.0 | 217.0 | 308.0 | 525.0 | 96.1 | 1,123.3 | 1,219.4 |

[1] Preliminary. [2] Forecast. [3] Imports & exports include flour and other products expressed in wheat equivalent. [4] Uncommitted, Government only. [5] Includes total loans. [6] Includes alcoholic beverages. *Source: Economic Research Service, U.S. Department of Agriculture*

**Average Price of No. 2 Soft Red Winter (30 Days) Wheat at Chicago** In Dollars Per Bushel

| Year | June | July | Aug. | Sept. | Oct. | Nov. | Dec. | Jan. | Feb. | Mar. | Apr. | May | Average |
|---|---|---|---|---|---|---|---|---|---|---|---|---|---|
| 1983-4 | 3.53 | 3.59 | 3.71 | 3.62 | 3.56 | 3.42 | 3.55 | 3.47 | 3.34 | 3.57 | 3.65 | 3.65 | 3.56 |
| 1984-5 | 3.51 | 3.44 | 3.49 | 3.47 | 3.51 | 3.62 | 3.49 | 3.51 | 3.55 | 3.58 | 3.63 | 3.34 | 3.51 |
| 1985-6 | 3.27 | 3.09 | 2.87 | 2.83 | 3.04 | 3.33 | 3.46 | 3.34 | 3.37 | 3.40 | 3.39 | 3.25 | 3.22 |
| 1986-7 | 2.52 | 2.58 | 2.44 | 2.36 | 2.57 | 2.73 | 2.76 | 2.87 | 2.91 | 3.11 | 3.16 | 3.08 | 2.76 |
| 1987-8 | 2.63 | 2.54 | 2.61 | 2.77 | 2.82 | 2.80 | 3.00 | 3.23 | 3.23 | 2.94 | 3.02 | 3.13 | 2.89 |
| 1988-9 | 3.56 | 3.52 | 3.61 | 3.84 | 4.07 | 4.09 | 4.25 | 4.39 | 4.30 | 4.31 | 4.04 | 4.07 | 4.00 |
| 1989-90 | 3.87 | 3.92 | 3.94 | 3.93 | 4.07 | 4.07 | 4.13 | 4.03 | 3.92 | 3.61 | 3.83 | 3.71 | 3.92 |
| 1990-1 | 3.26 | 3.04 | 2.83 | 2.62 | 2.62 | 2.41 | 2.52 | 2.50 | 2.53 | 2.76 | 2.80 | 2.83 | 2.73 |
| 1991-2 | 2.86 | 2.79 | 2.97 | 3.24 | 3.50 | 3.57 | 3.79 | 4.12 | 4.15 | 3.71 | 3.53 | 3.68 | 3.49 |
| 1992-3 | 3.60 | 3.39 | 3.09 | 3.24 | 3.39 | 3.60 | 3.59 | 3.77 | 3.67 | 3.58 | 3.72 | 3.19 | 3.49 |
| 1993-4 | 2.82 | 3.03 | 3.12 | 2.99 | 3.02 | 3.29 | 3.53 | 3.67 | 3.48 | 3.20 | 3.15 | 3.15 | 3.20 |
| 1994-5 | 3.21 | 3.14 | 3.34 | 3.63 | 3.97 | 3.85 | 3.99 | 3.88 | 3.74 | 3.49 | 3.51 | 3.64 | 3.62 |
| 1995-6 | 3.94 | NQ | 4.26 | 4.55 | NQ | 4.97 | 5.13 | 5.02 | NQ | NQ | NQ | 5.59 | 4.78 |
| 1996-7[1] | 4.91 | 4.64 | 4.71 | 4.61 | NQ | NQ | NQ | NQ | | | | | 4.72 |

NQ = No quote. *Source: Agricultural Marketing Service, U.S. Department of Agriculture*

**Stocks of Wheat Flour Held by Mills in the United States** In Thousands of Sacks (100 Pounds Each)

| Year | Jan. 1 | April 1 | July 1 | Oct. 1 | Year | Jan. 1 | April 1 | July 1 | Oct. 1 |
|---|---|---|---|---|---|---|---|---|---|
| 1983 | 4,276 | 3,760 | 3,490 | 3,599 | 1990 | 5,207 | 5,072 | 5,818 | 7,980 |
| 1984 | 3,805 | 3,780 | 3,763 | 3,833 | 1991 | 8,051 | 5,474 | 8,115 | 6,336 |
| 1985 | 4,230 | 4,363 | 5,040 | 5,052 | 1992 | 5,660 | 5,210 | 5,841 | 5,864 |
| 1986 | 4,847 | 4,740 | 5,141 | 5,101 | 1993 | 5,487 | 4,863 | 6,197 | 5,882 |
| 1987 | 5,228 | 4,900 | 5,581 | 5,258 | 1994 | 5,611 | 5,904 | 5,834 | 6,020 |
| 1988 | 5,858 | 4,508 | 4,822 | 5,303 | 1995 | 7,060 | 6,496 | 6,312 | 6,582 |
| 1989 | 4,800 | 4,423 | 5,116 | 5,489 | 1996[1] | 6,869 | 6,516 | 5,819 | 5,758 |

[1] Preliminary. *Source: U.S. Department of Commerce*

## Commercial Stocks of Domestic Wheat[1] in the United States, at First of Month   In Millions of Bushels

| Year | July | Aug. | Sept. | Oct. | Nov. | Dec. | Jan. | Feb. | Mar. | Apr. | May | June |
|---|---|---|---|---|---|---|---|---|---|---|---|---|
| 1986-7 | 437.5 | 483.7 | 494.7 | 475.9 | 472.7 | 445.0 | 435.0 | 420.0 | 410.1 | 393.3 | 381.1 | 366.8 |
| 1987-8 | 417.8 | 436.5 | 443.7 | 451.9 | 439.9 | 421.4 | 387.1 | 361.1 | 302.6 | 261.2 | 235.6 | 203.7 |
| 1988-9 | 291.6 | 334.2 | 342.4 | 340.8 | 331.1 | 297.2 | 293.7 | 266.5 | 213.3 | 181.1 | 150.1 | 114.4 |
| 1989-90 | 130.5 | 171.6 | 211.7 | 211.8 | 196.0 | 180.2 | 164.2 | 150.4 | 127.9 | 109.7 | 87.2 | 77.8 |
| 1990-1 | 121.8 | 212.7 | 289.7 | 290.2 | 284.6 | 264.8 | 243.7 | 237.7 | ------ | ------ | 174.5 | 174.5 |
| 1991-2 | 244.8 | 275.5 | 296.9 | 308.2 | 271.0 | 264.8 | 249.8 | 227.0 | 205.2 | 180.7 | 170.9 | 209.1 |
| 1992-3 | 269.6 | 290.5 | 202.5 | 228.2 | 231.9 | 202.7 | 185.5 | 169.5 | 153.3 | 132.6 | 112.9 | 87.0 |
| 1993-4 | 102.9 | 145.1 | 171.8 | 194.9 | 199.3 | 174.9 | 169.5 | 168.3 | 162.2 | 143.8 | 127.3 | 111.3 |
| 1994-5 | 145.7 | 203.9 | 243.0 | 269.7 | 268.6 | 238.2 | 199.5 | 181.0 | 162.5 | 150.2 | 108.7 | 91.8 |
| 1995-6 | 92.3 | 161.7 | 201.1 | 234.3 | 228.3 | 200.2 | 178.7 | 170.8 | 156.6 | 137.7 | 107.6 | 87.2 |
| 1996-7 | 86.3 | 112.9 | 128.0 | 145.3 | 117.2 | 94.9 | 89.0 | 80.4 | 77.0 | | | |

[1] Domestic wheat in storage in public and private elevators in 39 markets and wheat afloat in vessels or barges at lake and seaboard ports, the first Saturday of the month. *Source: Livestock Division, U.S. Department of Agriculture*

## Average Open Interest of All Wheat Futures Contracts at Chicago & Kansas City   In Thousands of Bushels

| | Chicago[1] | | | | | | | | | | | | Kansas City[2] |
|---|---|---|---|---|---|---|---|---|---|---|---|---|---|
| Year | Jan. | Feb. | Mar. | Apr. | May | June | July | Aug. | Sept. | Oct. | Nov. | Dec. | Jan. |
| 1987 | 128,805 | 137,113 | 147,187 | 154,030 | 160,892 | 175,160 | 176,293 | 200,085 | 199,244 | 194,362 | 163,349 | 152,801 | 66,850 |
| 1988 | 192,824 | 209,322 | 206,533 | 217,011 | 209,546 | 283,122 | 283,710 | 280,121 | 342,077 | 372,677 | 348,955 | 313,480 | 112,972 |
| 1989 | 334,519 | 315,770 | 323,343 | 308,643 | 301,955 | 349,492 | 335,590 | 327,315 | 307,555 | 261,229 | 260,113 | 270,586 | 156,530 |
| 1990 | 271,124 | 281,973 | 284,920 | 257,741 | 283,120 | 319,096 | 322,882 | 298,960 | 286,186 | 291,155 | 279,248 | 235,303 | 142,888 |
| 1991 | 242,983 | 257,602 | 279,608 | 268,339 | 265,149 | 294,983 | 274,730 | 261,417 | 276,101 | 306,286 | 288,394 | 259,224 | 128,872 |
| 1992 | 307,419 | 350,761 | 294,787 | 268,528 | 254,891 | 251,702 | 300,579 | 310,357 | 250,467 | 272,821 | 288,463 | 246,317 | 177,990 |
| 1993 | 251,644 | 239,291 | 224,427 | 241,772 | 256,763 | 279,143 | 293,523 | 321,674 | 293,017 | 307,481 | 314,383 | 252,615 | 148,971 |
| 1994 | 269,558 | 240,064 | 225,548 | 237,148 | 222,762 | 273,110 | 285,754 | 326,938 | 365,999 | 392,094 | 354,076 | 335,752 | 196,237 |
| 1995 | 333,575 | 338,842 | 279,865 | 278,059 | 339,373 | 451,038 | 506,753 | 454,001 | 457,527 | 519,934 | 512,376 | 497,108 | 197,235 |
| 1996 | 513,591 | 524,036 | 456,890 | 491,299 | 466,888 | 406,056 | 346,110 | 330,642 | 327,807 | 328,193 | 304,052 | 292,663 | 218,634 |

[1] Chicago Board of Trade (CBT). [2] Kansas City Board of Trade (KCBT). *Source: Commodity Futures Trading Commission*

# WHEAT

## Average Price of No. 1 Hard Red Winter (Ordinary Protein) Wheat, at Kansas City In Cents Per Bushel

| Year | June | July | Aug. | Sept. | Oct. | Nov. | Dec. | Jan. | Feb. | Mar. | Apr. | May | Average |
|---|---|---|---|---|---|---|---|---|---|---|---|---|---|
| 1989-90 | 444 | 428 | 424 | 418 | 428 | 436 | 439 | 430 | 413 | 404 | 413 | 391 | 422 |
| 1990-1 | 360 | 311 | 289 | 282 | 281 | 278 | 278 | 271 | 277 | 294 | 298 | 304 | 294 |
| 1991-2 | 299 | 291 | 310 | 331 | 364 | 376 | 406 | 466 | 451 | 433 | 402 | 390 | 377 |
| 1992-3 | 391 | 352 | 327 | 356 | 360 | 378 | 381 | 397 | 375 | 374 | 359 | 351 | 367 |
| 1993-4 | 333 | 338 | 334 | 337 | 352 | 339 | 415 | 400 | 380 | 364 | 363 | 365 | 360 |
| 1994-5 | 360 | 348 | 370 | 405 | 431 | 424 | 427 | 406 | 398 | 387 | 386 | 422 | 397 |
| 1995-6 | 472 | 498 | 476 | 500 | 528 | 534 | 551 | 540 | 567 | 563 | 660 | 702 | 549 |
| 1996-7 | 612 | 534 | 501 | 470 | 476 | 478 | 470 | 540 | | | | | 510 |

*Source: Economic Research Service, U.S. Department of Agriculture*

## Average Price of No. 1 Dark Northern Spring Wheat at Minneapolis (14% Protein) In Cents Per Bushel

| Year | June | July | Aug. | Sept. | Oct. | Nov. | Dec. | Jan. | Feb. | Mar. | Apr. | May | Average |
|---|---|---|---|---|---|---|---|---|---|---|---|---|---|
| 1989-90 | 441 | 436 | 418 | 408 | 411 | 412 | 423 | 421 | 406 | 396 | 408 | 409 | 416 |
| 1990-1 | 396 | 356 | 305 | 284 | 285 | 280 | 282 | 283 | 285 | 300 | 307 | 310 | 306 |
| 1991-2 | 304 | 294 | 310 | 321 | 368 | 378 | 411 | 436 | 456 | 436 | 428 | 444 | 382 |
| 1992-3 | 442 | 404 | 365 | 379 | 385 | 394 | 388 | 405 | 387 | 387 | 380 | 371 | 391 |
| 1993-4 | 396 | 480 | 488 | 490 | 517 | 550 | 545 | 532 | 529 | 494 | 499 | 505 | 502 |
| 1994-5 | 420 | 414 | 400 | 427 | 440 | 441 | 437 | 421 | 409 | 411 | 430 | 461 | 426 |
| 1995-6 | 489 | 552 | 506 | 527 | 552 | 563 | 580 | 562 | 582 | 581 | 653 | 714 | 572 |
| 1996-7 | 673 | 604 | 529 | 463 | 469 | 464 | 451 | 462 | | | | | 514 |

*Source: Economic Research Service, U.S. Department of Agriculture*

## Average Price[1] Received by Farmers for Wheat in the U.S. In Cents Per Bushel

| Year | June | July | Aug. | Sept. | Oct. | Nov. | Dec. | Jan. | Feb. | Mar. | Apr. | May | Average[2] |
|---|---|---|---|---|---|---|---|---|---|---|---|---|---|
| 1989-90 | 385 | 378 | 374 | 372 | 375 | 372 | 379 | 371 | 356 | 348 | 349 | 340 | 372 |
| 1990-1 | 308 | 279 | 258 | 246 | 243 | 239 | 240 | 242 | 243 | 253 | 260 | 264 | 255 |
| 1991-2 | 255 | 250 | 263 | 280 | 307 | 325 | 344 | 354 | 378 | 372 | 365 | 364 | 300 |
| 1992-3 | 343 | 315 | 301 | 320 | 321 | 329 | 331 | 337 | 333 | 330 | 326 | 311 | 324 |
| 1993-4 | 284 | 285 | 296 | 310 | 325 | 347 | 363 | 358 | 360 | 370 | 356 | 343 | 326 |
| 1994-5 | 321 | 304 | 325 | 357 | 376 | 375 | 374 | 369 | 361 | 352 | 349 | 366 | 352 |
| 1995-6 | 384 | 410 | 426 | 453 | 472 | 481 | 488 | 483 | 498 | 507 | 532 | 573 | 476 |
| 1996-7 | 526 | 473 | 458 | 437 | 418 | 414 | 406 | 403 | 391 | | | | 436 |

[1] Weighted average by sales. [2] Includes an allownace for unredeemed loans at average loan value. *Source: Economic Research Service, U.S. Department of Agriculture*

## Average Producer Price Index of Wheat Flour (Spring[1]) June 1983 = 100

| Year | July | Aug. | Sept. | Oct. | Nov. | Dec. | Jan. | Feb. | Mar. | Apr. | May | June | Average |
|---|---|---|---|---|---|---|---|---|---|---|---|---|---|
| 1989-90 | 112.1 | 110.7 | 109.5 | 108.5 | 108.7 | 109.6 | 109.4 | 109.0 | 106.9 | 108.8 | 107.9 | 106.0 | 100.2 |
| 1990-1 | 99.7 | 93.4 | 92.0 | 91.2 | 89.4 | 89.8 | 88.7 | 90.2 | 92.0 | 93.0 | 94.0 | 93.0 | 94.5 |
| 1991-2 | 91.3 | 94.1 | 96.3 | 100.1 | 97.5 | 102.7 | 109.7 | 116.4 | 111.5 | 110.3 | 109.2 | 111.0 | 107.3 |
| 1992-3 | 104.9 | 99.6 | 104.1 | 104.4 | 104.7 | 103.5 | 107.5 | 108.1 | 107.2 | 108.4 | 105.2 | 104.7 | 105.2 |
| 1993-4 | 103.7 | 107.2 | 102.1 | 107.3 | 108.4 | 112.5 | 111.8 | 110.5 | 109.9 | 107.9 | 109.0 | 106.4 | 108.1 |
| 1994-5 | 100.8 | 101.2 | 109.2 | 112.0 | 111.2 | 111.4 | 110.7 | 108.7 | 107.4 | 109.8 | 113.5 | 118.6 | 109.5 |
| 1995-6 | 125.2 | 126.7 | 129.5 | 132.6 | 132.3 | 133.5 | 130.4 | 138.0 | 136.6 | 137.6 | 160.1 | 146.8 | 135.8 |
| 1996-7[2] | 138.0 | 127.0 | 126.1 | 124.2 | 120.1 | 121.1 | | | | | | | 126.1 |

[1] Standard patent. [2] Preliminary. *Source: Bureau of Labor Statistics, U.S. Department of Commerce (0212-0301)*

## World Wheat Flour Production (Monthly Average) In Thousands of Metric Tons

| Year | Australia[3] | France | Germany | Hungary | India | Japan | Kazakhstan | Rep. of Korea | Mexico | Poland | Russia | Sweden | Turkey | United Kingdom | Yugoslavia |
|---|---|---|---|---|---|---|---|---|---|---|---|---|---|---|---|
| 1989 | 109.0 | 435.6 | 280.0 | 102.2 | 391.3 | 378.4 | 164.0 | 134.5 | 207.0 | 241.1 | NA | 40.1 | 136.4 | 333.0 | 193.4 |
| 1990 | 114.9 | 442.7 | 218.1 | 102.4 | 394.3 | 374.3 | 163.5 | 134.7 | 209.4 | 150.6 | NA | 41.0 | 112.9 | 328.0 | 175.5 |
| 1991 | 112.7 | 464.8 | 341.1 | 97.7 | 398.0 | 390.3 | 167.8 | 130.4 | 207.3 | 128.6 | NA | 47.7 | 111.1 | 326.0 | 160.4 |
| 1992 | 113.9 | 465.2 | 327.0 | 106.9 | 400.0 | NA | 161.0 | 129.4 | 223.3 | 167.1 | NA | 44.6 | 112.2 | NA | NA |
| 1993 | 116.3 | 480.6 | 336.4 | 75.0 | 399.4 | 367.6 | 155.3 | 129.5 | 214.0 | 113.4 | 449.5 | 44.8 | 122.1 | 327.3 | 82.0 |
| 1994 | 116.9 | 470.8 | 378.8 | 62.9 | 400.0 | 387.2 | 157.0 | 132.6 | 219.8 | 150.5 | 348.0 | 45.2 | 104.9 | 333.9 | 65.0 |
| 1995[1] | 112.6 | 473.1 | 382.3 | 84.0 | 400.0 | 389.3 | 111.0 | 139.9 | 210.7 | 156.9 | 274.6 | | 119.7 | 340.6 | 81.6 |
| 1996[2] | 120.4 | | 384.4 | 74.2 | 400.0 | 383.1 | 108.9 | 140.3 | 126.0 | 111.5 | 282.6 | | 120.0 | 349.9 | 66.3 |

[1] Preliminary. [2] Estimate. NA = Not available. *Source: United Nations*

## United States Wheat Flour Production In Millions of Sacks (100 Pounds Each)

| Year | July | Aug. | Sept. | Oct. | Nov. | Dec. | Jan. | Feb. | Mar. | Apr. | May | June | Total |
|---|---|---|---|---|---|---|---|---|---|---|---|---|---|
| 1988-9 | 28.5 | 31.4 | 29.4 | 31.3 | 31.1 | 28.5 | 29.1 | 27.1 | 27.0 | 27.2 | 28.6 | 26.6 | 345.8 |
| 1989-90 | 26.6 | 32.3 | 29.8 | 31.8 | 30.0 | 27.8 | 27.9 | 28.0 | 29.2 | 27.0 | 27.6 | 26.7 | 354.3 |
| 1990-1 | 27.7 | 33.7 | 29.9 | 32.2 | 32.7 | 29.1 | 29.4 | 29.5 | 29.5 | 29.4 | 29.2 | 29.1 | 362.3 |
| 1991-2 | 29.2 | 31.8 | 30.1 | 32.2 | 32.7 | 29.2 | 29.3 | 29.3 | 29.4 | 30.0 | 29.8 | 29.8 | 363.0 |
| 1992-3 | 31.1 | 34.2 | 31.9 | 34.6 | 32.2 | 29.2 | 30.6 | 31.3 | 34.1 | 32.0 | 31.0 | 30.3 | 382.4 |
| 1993-4 | 30.7 | 33.3 | 32.9 | 33.5 | 34.0 | 33.8 | 30.9 | 30.2 | 35.9 | 32.3 | 32.2 | 31.1 | 390.8 |
| 1994-5 | 30.5 | 34.9 | 34.2 | 35.0 | 33.7 | 31.7 | 30.9 | 29.4 | 34.5 | 29.9 | 33.5 | 32.3 | 390.4 |
| 1995-6[1] | 31.0 | 34.5 | 33.0 | 35.1 | 33.4 | 31.2 | 31.5 | 32.2 | 32.1 | 31.1 | 33.1 | 30.5 | 388.7 |
| 1996-7[1] | 33.8 | 35.5 | 34.6 | 37.3 | 32.8 | 31.8 | | | | | | | 205.7 |

[1] Preliminary. *Source: Bureau of Census, U.S. Department of Commerce*

## United States Wheat Flour Exports (Grain Equivalent[2]) In Thousands of Bushels

| Year | June | July | Aug. | Sept. | Oct. | Nov. | Dec. | Jan. | Feb. | Mar. | Apr. | May | Total |
|---|---|---|---|---|---|---|---|---|---|---|---|---|---|
| 1988-9 | 7,036 | 6,400 | 6,002 | 2,402 | 7,908 | 3,368 | 6,086 | 4,108 | 6,040 | 3,974 | 6,469 | 5,205 | 64,998 |
| 1989-90 | 907 | 1,897 | 5,775 | 8,917 | 3,579 | 6,817 | 3,606 | 4,943 | 3,124 | 4,466 | 6,132 | 3,287 | 53,450 |
| 1990-1 | 1,035 | 2,207 | 2,785 | 1,464 | 3,303 | 3,407 | 4,480 | 2,698 | 3,809 | 6,301 | 3,719 | 3,525 | 38,733 |
| 1991-2 | 5,582 | 5,362 | 4,207 | 3,743 | 1,179 | 2,222 | 3,140 | 2,549 | 5,549 | 4,630 | 3,771 | 4,579 | 46,514 |
| 1992-3 | 3,257 | 5,284 | 2,856 | 2,325 | 3,840 | 4,641 | 3,903 | 2,325 | 7,744 | 5,832 | 7,499 | 5,285 | 54,791 |
| 1993-4 | 4,408 | 3,793 | 1,811 | 3,642 | 3,840 | 3,416 | 3,170 | 5,838 | 4,390 | 6,099 | 4,198 | 3,368 | 47,973 |
| 1994-5 | 2,922 | 6,824 | 5,636 | 3,407 | 3,105 | 4,721 | 4,734 | 2,805 | 7,085 | 7,617 | 6,945 | 6,005 | 61,806 |
| 1995-6[1] | 2,822 | 5,018 | 7,520 | 2,249 | 2,080 | 1,221 | 3,458 | 808 | 2,537 | 1,230 | 2,415 | 1,830 | 33,188 |
| 1996-7[1] | 2,005 | 2,008 | 1,669 | 3,133 | 2,496 | 2,748 | 2,240 | | | | | | 16,299 |

[1] Preliminary. [2] Includes meal, groats and durum. *Source: Economic Research Service, U.S. Department of Agriculture*

## Supply and Distribution of Wheat Flour in the United States

| Year | Wheat Ground 1,000 Bu. | Milfeed Production 1,000 Tons | Flour Production[3] | Flour & Product Imports[2] | Total Supply | Exports: Flour | Exports: Products[2] | Domestic Disappearance | Total Population July 1 Millions | Per Capita Disappearance Pounds |
|---|---|---|---|---|---|---|---|---|---|---|
| | | | 1,000 Cwt. | | | | | | | |
| 1988 | 769,699 | 6,163 | 344,154 | 2,727 | 346,881 | 24,097 | 185 | 322,599 | 245.0 | 132 |
| 1989 | 761,021 | 6,072 | 342,762 | 3,337 | 346,099 | 25,265 | 180 | 320,654 | 247.3 | 130 |
| 1990 | 788,186 | 6,109 | 354,348 | 3,623 | 357,971 | 18,872 | 273 | 338,826 | 249.9 | 136 |
| 1991 | 808,966 | 6,436 | 362,311 | 4,070 | 366,381 | 20,044 | 440 | 345,897 | 252.6 | 137 |
| 1992 | 833,339 | 6,707 | 370,829 | 5,037 | 375,866 | 20,711 | 619 | 354,536 | 255.4 | 139 |
| 1993 | 871,408 | 6,963 | 387,419 | 6,233 | 393,652 | 23,241 | 548 | 369,863 | 258.1 | 143 |
| 1994 | 884,707 | 7,186 | 392,519 | 9,048 | 401,567 | 24,234 | 733 | 376,599 | 260.7 | 144 |
| 1995 | 869,296 | 7,144 | 388,689 | 9,306 | 397,955 | 24,343 | 716 | 372,936 | 263.0 | 142 |
| 1996[1] | 881,526 | 7,166 | 396,176 | 8,954 | 405,130 | 11,153 | 776 | 393,201 | 265.4 | 148 |

[1] Preliminary. [2] Import and exports of macaroni and noodle products (flour equivalent), reporting methods changed in 1990. [3] Commercial production of wheat flour, whole wheat, industrial and durum flour and farina reported by Bureau of Census. *Source: Economic Research Service, U.S. Department of Agriculture*

## Wheat and Flour -- Price Relationship at Milling Centers In Dollars

| Crop Year (June-May) | At Kansas City: Cost of Wheat to Produce 100 lb. Flour[1] | Wholesale Price of: Bakery Flour 100 lb. Flour[2] | By-Products Obtained 100 lb. Flour[3] | Total Products: Actual | Total Products: Over Cost of Wheat | At Minneapolis: Cost of Wheat to Produce 100 lb. Flour[1] | Wholesale Price of: Bakery Flour 100 lb. Flour[2] | By-Products Obtained 100 lb. Flour[3] | Total Products: Actual | Total Products: Over Cost of Wheat |
|---|---|---|---|---|---|---|---|---|---|---|
| 1988-9 | 9.62 | 10.21 | 1.68 | 11.89 | 2.27 | 9.94 | 10.39 | 1.62 | 12.01 | 2.07 |
| 1989-90 | 9.58 | 10.41 | 1.45 | 11.86 | 2.28 | 9.48 | 10.00 | 1.36 | 11.36 | 1.89 |
| 1990-1 | 6.86 | 7.78 | 1.29 | 9.07 | 2.21 | 6.98 | 7.73 | 1.21 | 8.94 | 1.96 |
| 1991-2 | 8.58 | 9.53 | 1.26 | 10.79 | 2.21 | 8.71 | 9.39 | 1.16 | 10.55 | 1.84 |
| 1992-3 | 8.53 | 9.65 | 1.28 | 10.93 | 2.40 | 8.91 | 10.12 | 1.15 | 11.27 | 2.37 |
| 1993-4 | 10.03 | 10.34 | 1.46 | 11.79 | 1.77 | 11.45 | 12.50 | 1.28 | 13.77 | 2.33 |
| 1994-5 | 9.25 | 10.50 | 1.21 | 11.71 | 2.46 | 9.71 | 11.01 | 1.04 | 12.05 | 2.34 |
| 1995-6 | 12.97 | 13.35 | 1.93 | 15.28 | 2.31 | 13.04 | 13.03 | 1.68 | 14.71 | 1.67 |
| 1996-7 I | 12.61 | 13.35 | 2.19 | 15.54 | 2.93 | 13.73 | 13.98 | 2.23 | 16.21 | 2.49 |
| II | 10.82 | 11.30 | 1.96 | 13.26 | 2.44 | 10.61 | 10.88 | 1.91 | 12.79 | 2.19 |
| Dec.[4] | 10.76 | 11.10 | 2.08 | 13.18 | 2.42 | 10.28 | 10.10 | 1.97 | 12.07 | 1.79 |
| Jan.[4] | 10.56 | 11.15 | 1.90 | 13.05 | 2.49 | 10.53 | 10.90 | 1.67 | 12.57 | 2.04 |

[1] Based on 73% extraction rate, cost of 2.28 bushels: at Kansas City, No. 1 hard winter, 13 % protein; and at Minneapolis, No. 1 dark northern spring, 14% protein. [2] Quoted as mid-month bakers' standard patent at Kansas City and spring standard patent at Minneapolis, bulk basis. [3] Assumed 50-50 millfeed distribution between bran and shorts or middlings, bulk basis. *Source: Agaricultural Marketing Service, U.S. Department of Agriculture*

# Wool

World wool production (greasy) was estimated at 5.5 billion pounds (3.2 billion, clean) in 1995/96 vs. 5.9 billion in 1994/95, and a 7 billion pound average in the early 1990's. Consumption in 1995/96 of 3.3 billion pounds (clean) compares with 3.5 billion in 1994/95, and about 3.9 billion in the late 1980's. The decline largely reflects a steady contraction in world sheep numbers, to 1 billion head in 1995/96 from an average of 1.1 billion head in the late 1980's. Except for China, the sheep flock has been contracting worldwide. In Australia, the world largest wool producer, sheep numbers fell from 163 million head in 1990/91 to 122 million in 1995/96, and wool production (clean) dropped from 1,541 million pounds to 983 million pounds. Changing consumer attitudes have had an adverse effect on wool demand with casual fashions using more cotton and manmade fibers.

In New Zealand, the second largest producer, 1995/96 production of 438 million pounds compares with 470 million in 1994/95 from a sheep herd of 48 million head, the lowest in 34 years. China's sheep inventory is now the world's largest, 133 million head in 1995/96 vs. 118 million in 1994/95, producing 304 million pounds (clean) in 1995/96 vs. 287 million in 1994/95. Russia's herd dropped to 82 million head in 1995/96 from 135 million in 1990/91, producing only 284 million pounds of wool in 1995/96 vs. 381 million pounds in 1994/95. U.S. greasy wool production is insignificant; 56.2 million pounds in 1996 vs. 63.3 million in 1995.

World wool export/imports slipped in 1995/96. Exports (greasy) of 2.6 billion pounds compare with 3.0 billion in 1994/95. Australia exported 1.2 billion pounds and New Zealand 432 million pounds, the lowest totals in years.

Importing nations are numerous but China has been number one since 1993/94 when 408 million pounds were imported, followed by 553 million in 1995/95, and 494 million in 1995/96. Japan, the U.K., Italy, and France import around 200 million pounds each. The former USSR's imports have dropped dramatically each year, from 115 million pounds in 1990/91 to only 4 million pounds in 1995/96. U.S. imports fell to 88 million pounds in 1995/96 from 93 million in 1994/95. Australian wool accounts for most of U.S.imports.

Global wool prices are a function of origin and grade. South African wool prices were almost three times higher than Australian prices in 1995/96, while the latter were moderately higher than New Zealand's prices. The U.S. farm price for greasy shorn wool in 1995 of $1.04 per pound compares with $0.78 in 1994. The U.S. average for Australian grade 64 wool in 1995 of $2.81 per pound compares with $2.43 in 1994.

### *Futures Markets*

Wool futures are traded on the Sydney Futures Exchange (SFE), the Nagoya Textile Exchange, the Osaka Textile Exchange, the Tokyo Commodity Exchange (TOCOM), and the New Zealand Futures & Options Exchange Ltd. (NZFOE).

**World Production of Wool** In Metric Tons-Degreased

| Year | Argentina | Australia | China | Kazakhstan[3] | New Zealand | Pakistan | Romania | Russia[3] | South Africa | United Kingdom | United States | Uruguay | World Total |
|---|---|---|---|---|---|---|---|---|---|---|---|---|---|
| 1987 | 73,311 | 573,200 | 124,800 | ------ | 308,400 | 31,400 | 25,640 | 273,000 | 45,000 | 44,466 | 20,560 | 55,000 | 1,932,887 |
| 1988 | 81,200 | 546,585 | 112,000 | ------ | 310,100 | 32,450 | 28,000 | 286,800 | 46,200 | 47,000 | 21,660 | 54,000 | 1,931,251 |
| 1989 | 87,600 | 622,000 | 120,111 | ------ | 302,800 | 34,800 | 20,900 | 284,400 | 46,500 | 52,765 | 21,665 | 60,000 | 2,011,693 |
| 1990 | 85,800 | 724,000 | 122,400 | 64,750 | 233,000 | 28,200 | 26,500 | 136,050 | 49,500 | 53,358 | 21,140 | 58,100 | 2,029,209 |
| 1991 | 75,400 | 699,000 | 123,000 | 62,640 | 227,000 | 28,900 | 19,196 | 122,700 | 51,000 | 51,055 | 20,830 | 56,500 | 1,953,339 |
| 1992 | 74,200 | 574,000 | 121,500 | 63,000 | 221,000 | 29,600 | 16,800 | 107,400 | 48,500 | 50,876 | 19,980 | 50,700 | 1,780,613 |
| 1993[1] | 58,000 | 557,000 | 122,000 | 60,000 | 193,000 | 30,400 | 15,600 | 95,000 | 45,000 | 48,693 | 20,220 | 49,410 | 1,679,305 |
| 1994[2] | 51,000 | 581,800 | 132,600 | 60,100 | 204,600 | 31,000 | 16,900 | 87,000 | 45,000 | 50,300 | 16,500 | 49,800 | 1,713,471 |

[1] Preliminary. [2] Estimate. [3] Formerly part of the U.S.S.R.; data not reported separately until 1990. *Source: Food and Agriculture Organization of the United Nations*

**Wool Goods[1] Production in the United States** In Millions of Yards

| Year | First Quarter | Second Quarter | Third Quarter | Fourth Quarter | Total Year | Year | First Quarter | Second Quarter | Third Quarter | Fourth Quarter | Total Year |
|---|---|---|---|---|---|---|---|---|---|---|---|
| 1987 | 48.0 | 45.9 | 36.0 | 40.9 | 168.9 | 1992 | 45.7 | 47.2 | 43.9 | 39.5 | 176.3 |
| 1988 | 50.6 | 53.0 | 43.0 | 43.9 | 190.5 | 1993 | 48.4 | 48.9 | 43.9 | 42.8 | 184.0 |
| 1989 | 48.3 | 50.9 | 40.1 | 37.0 | 176.3 | 1994 | 49.1 | 51.1 | 39.4 | 39.0 | 178.6 |
| 1990 | 38.0 | 38.7 | 32.6 | 31.4 | 140.7 | 1995 | 46.8 | 45.9 | 35.2 | 34.3 | 162.2 |
| 1991 | 38.0 | 48.7 | 41.4 | 41.5 | 169.6 | 1996[2] | 44.2 | 43.5 | 30.5 | 32.5 | 150.7 |

[1] Woolen and worsted woven goods, except woven felts. [2] Preliminary. *Source: Bureau of Census, U.S. Department of Commerce*

**Consumption of Apparel Wool in the United States** In Millions of Pounds--Clean Basis

| Year | Jan. | Feb. | Mar. | Apr. | May | June | July | Aug. | Sept. | Oct. | Nov. | Dec. | Total |
|---|---|---|---|---|---|---|---|---|---|---|---|---|---|
| 1991 | ---------- | 31.6 | ---------- | ---------- | 37.1 | ---------- | ---------- | 34.6 | ---------- | ---------- | 33.9 | ---------- | 137.2 |
| 1992 | ---------- | 36.4 | ---------- | ---------- | 35.1 | ---------- | ---------- | 33.6 | ---------- | ---------- | 31.1 | ---------- | 136.1 |
| 1993 | ---------- | 35.5 | ---------- | ---------- | 35.9 | ---------- | ---------- | 35.5 | ---------- | ---------- | 34.4 | ---------- | 141.4 |
| 1994 | ---------- | 36.3 | ---------- | ---------- | 35.6 | ---------- | ---------- | 32.7 | ---------- | ---------- | 34.0 | ---------- | 138.6 |
| 1995 | ---------- | 36.3 | ---------- | ---------- | 35.5 | ---------- | ---------- | 29.4 | ---------- | ---------- | 28.1 | ---------- | 129.3 |
| 1996[1] | ---------- | 33.7 | ---------- | ---------- | 31.0 | ---------- | ---------- | 23.5 | ---------- | ---------- | 23.2 | ---------- | 111.4 |

[1] Preliminary. *Source: Bureau of Census, U.S. Department of Commerce*

## Salient Statistics of Wool in the United States

| Year | Sheep & Lambs Shorn[4] 1,000 | Weight per Fleece Lbs. | Shorn Wool Production 1,000 Lbs | Price per Lb. | Value of Production 1,000 $ | --- Shorn Wool --- Support | Payment Rate | Total Wool Production | Domestic Production | Exports Domestic Wool | Dutiable Imports for Consump.[3] 48s&Finer | Total New Supply[2] | Duty Free Imports (Not Finer than 46's) | Mill Consumption Apparel | Carpet |
|---|---|---|---|---|---|---|---|---|---|---|---|---|---|---|---|
| | | | | | | ----- ¢ Per Lb. ----- | | ------ Raw Wool (Clean Content) ------ Thousands of Pounds | | | | | | | |
| 1987 | 10,922 | 7.75 | 84,450 | 91.7 | 77,009 | 181 | 89.3 | 84,450 | 44,590 | 1,037 | 74,054 | 148,673 | 31,066 | 129,677 | 13,092 |
| 1988 | 11,531 | 7.76 | 89,482 | 138.0 | 124,993 | 178 | 40.0 | 89,482 | 47,246 | 1,247 | 72,324 | 142,740 | 24,417 | 117,069 | 15,633 |
| 1989 | 11,314 | 7.89 | 89,220 | 124.0 | 110,537 | 177 | 53.0 | 89,220 | 47,108 | 1,188 | 77,003 | 152,860 | 29,889 | 120,534 | 14,122 |
| 1990 | 11,222 | 7.84 | 88,033 | 80.0 | 69,534 | 182 | 102.0 | 88,033 | 46,481 | 2,736 | 50,328 | 115,461 | 21,355 | 120,622 | 12,124 |
| 1991 | 11,009 | 7.97 | 87,740 | 55.0 | 47,178 | 188 | 133.0 | 87,740 | 46,327 | 3,867 | 68,242 | 128,916 | 18,166 | 137,187 | 14,352 |
| 1992 | 10,521 | 7.88 | 82,943 | 74.0 | 60,162 | 197 | 123.0 | 82,819 | 43,728 | 3,413 | 65,457 | 129,599 | 23,802 | 136,143 | 14,695 |
| 1993 | 9,976 | 7.77 | 77,535 | 51.0 | 39,077 | 204 | 153.0 | 77,319 | 40,824 | 2,529 | 76,001 | 138,606 | 21,876 | 141,380 | 15,431 |
| 1994 | 8,882 | 7.73 | 68,643 | 78.0 | 52,419 | 209 | 131.0 | | 36,500 | 2,900 | 64,889 | | 24,645 | 138,563 | 14,739 |
| 1995[1] | 8,100 | 7.80 | 63,300 | 104.0 | | 212 | | | 33,600 | 6,000 | 63,781 | | 25,039 | 129,299 | 12,667 |

[1] Preliminary. [2] Production minus exports plus imports; stocks not taken into consideration. [3] Appearal wool includes all dutiable wool; carpet wool includes all duty-free wool. [4] Includes sheep shorn at commercial feeding yards. *Source: Economic Research Service, U.S. Department of Agriculture*

## Shorn Wool Prices

| Year | U.S. Farm Price Shorn Wool Greasy Basis[1] ¢ per Lb. | Australian Offering Price, Clean[2]: Grade 70's Type 61 | Grade 64's Type 63 | Grade 64/70's Type 62 | Grade 60/62's Type 64A | Grade 58's-56's 433-34 | Market Indicator[3] Cents/Kg. | Graded Territory Shorn Wool, Clean Basis[4]: 64's Staple 2 3/4' & up | 60's Staple 3" & up | 58's Staple 3 1/4" & up | 56's Staple 3 1/4" & up | 54's Staple 3 1/2" & up |
|---|---|---|---|---|---|---|---|---|---|---|---|---|
| | | ---- Dollars per Pound ---- | | | | | | ---- Dollars per Pound ---- | | | | |
| 1987 | 91.70 | 4.35 | 3.14 | 2.76 | 2.37 | 2.11 | 626 | 2.28 | 1.97 | 1.75 | 1.60 | 1.47 |
| 1988 | 138.00 | 7.43 | 4.77 | 4.16 | 3.62 | 3.08 | 1,003 | 3.47 | 2.78 | 2.39 | 2.08 | 1.90 |
| 1989 | 124.00 | 5.82 | 4.21 | 3.86 | 3.44 | 2.81 | 990 | 3.14 | 2.61 | 2.06 | 2.04 | 1.91 |
| 1990 | 80.00 | 4.76 | 3.60 | 3.26 | 2.87 | 2.46 | 870 | 2.06 | 1.66 | 1.45 | 1.30 | 1.18 |
| 1991 | 55.00 | 3.56 | 2.32 | 2.02 | 1.87 | 1.68 | 627 | 1.58 | 1.31 | 1.14 | 1.03 | .93 |
| 1992 | 74.00 | 2.58 | 2.32 | 2.17 | 2.10 | 1.94 | 557 | 1.81 | 1.61 | 1.47 | 1.35 | 1.23 |
| 1993 | 51.00 | 2.08 | 1.70 | 1.84 | 1.49 | 1.44 | 488 | 1.37 | 1.13 | 1.05 | .99 | .94 |
| 1994 | 78.00 | 3.72 | 2.43 | 3.01 | 1.96 | 1.86 | 547 | 2.12 | 1.50 | 1.26 | 1.27 | 1.21 |
| 1995 | 104.00 | 3.22 | 2.81 | 3.01 | 2.49 | 2.39 | 798 | 2.49 | 1.93 | 1.77 | 1.63 | 1.53 |

[1] Annual weighted average. [2] F.O.B. Australian Wool Corporation South Carolina warehouse in bond. [3] Index of prices of all wool sold in Australia for the crop year July-June. [4] Wool principally produced in Texas and Rocky Mountain States. *Source: Economic Research Service, U.S. Department of Agriculture*

## Average Wool Prices[1]--Australian--64's, Type 62, Duty Paid--U.S. Mills    In Cents Per Pound

| Year | Jan. | Feb. | Mar. | Apr. | May | June | July | Aug. | Sept. | Oct. | Nov. | Dec. | Average |
|---|---|---|---|---|---|---|---|---|---|---|---|---|---|
| 1987 | 252 | 259 | 288 | 325 | 327 | 335 | 332 | 373 | 341 | 348 | 347 | 356 | 324 |
| 1988 | 391 | 468 | 496 | 564 | 564 | 513 | 489 | 467 | 461 | 488 | 472 | 475 | 487 |
| 1989 | 511 | 484 | 454 | 429 | 414 | 403 | 405 | 410 | 414 | 417 | 417 | 420 | 431 |
| 1990 | 417 | 404 | 403 | 414 | 406 | 342 | 338 | 352 | 355 | 343 | 332 | 332 | 370 |
| 1991 | 334 | 335 | 209 | 221 | 271 | 286 | NA | 248 | 229 | 215 | 274 | 270 | 242 |
| 1992 | 259 | 270 | 277 | 264 | 268 | 246 | NA | 224 | 210 | 192 | 195 | 193 | 236 |
| 1993 | 186 | 176 | 170 | 158 | 179 | 169 | 167 | 154 | 153 | 171 | 175 | 176 | 170 |
| 1994 | 204 | 216 | 205 | 223 | 249 | 258 | 243 | 248 | 259 | 256 | 273 | 297 | 244 |
| 1995 | 281 | 297 | 302 | 302 | 307 | 308 | 292 | 284 | 266 | 236 | 242 | 237 | 280 |
| 1996 | 240 | 237 | 238 | 234 | 242 | 245 | 236 | 234 | 228 | 220 | 225 | 232 | 234 |

[1] Raw, clean basis. NA = Not available. *Source: Economic Research Service, U.S. Department of Agriculture*

## Average Wool Prices--Domestic[1]--Graded Territory, 64's, Staple 2 3/4 & Up--U.S. Mills    In Cents Per Pound

| Year | Jan. | Feb. | Mar. | Apr. | May | June | July | Aug. | Sept. | Oct. | Nov. | Dec. | Average |
|---|---|---|---|---|---|---|---|---|---|---|---|---|---|
| 1987 | 193 | 202 | 216 | 260 | 270 | 270 | 270 | 300 | 295 | 300 | 300 | 300 | 265 |
| 1988 | 315 | 397 | 435 | 453 | 463 | 460 | 450 | 450 | 450 | 463 | 475 | 450 | 438 |
| 1989 | 450 | 438 | 410 | 375 | 375 | 365 | 350 | 350 | 350 | 350 | 333 | 300 | 370 |
| 1990 | 294 | 287 | 287 | 284 | 275 | 257 | 242 | 235 | 235 | 235 | 225 | 220 | 256 |
| 1991 | 217 | 210 | 163 | 167 | 203 | 230 | 230 | 167 | 156 | 148 | 148 | 155 | 158 |
| 1992 | 163 | 203 | 195 | 196 | 199 | 218 | 210 | 188 | 210 | 193 | 168 | 168 | 193 |
| 1993 | 158 | 148 | 132 | 127 | 135 | 140 | 138 | 140 | 130 | 129 | 133 | 133 | 124 |
| 1994 | 140 | 150 | 170 | 201 | 226 | 230 | 230 | 235 | 250 | 238 | 238 | 252 | 213 |
| 1995 | 245 | 252 | 265 | 288 | 295 | 285 | 261 | 250 | 235 | 185 | 208 | 192 | 247 |
| 1996 | 188 | 192 | 197 | 197 | 195 | 192 | 192 | 192 | 192 | 192 | 190 | 190 | 192 |

[1] Raw, shorn, clean basis. *Source: Economic Research Service, U.S. Department of Agriculture*

# WOOL

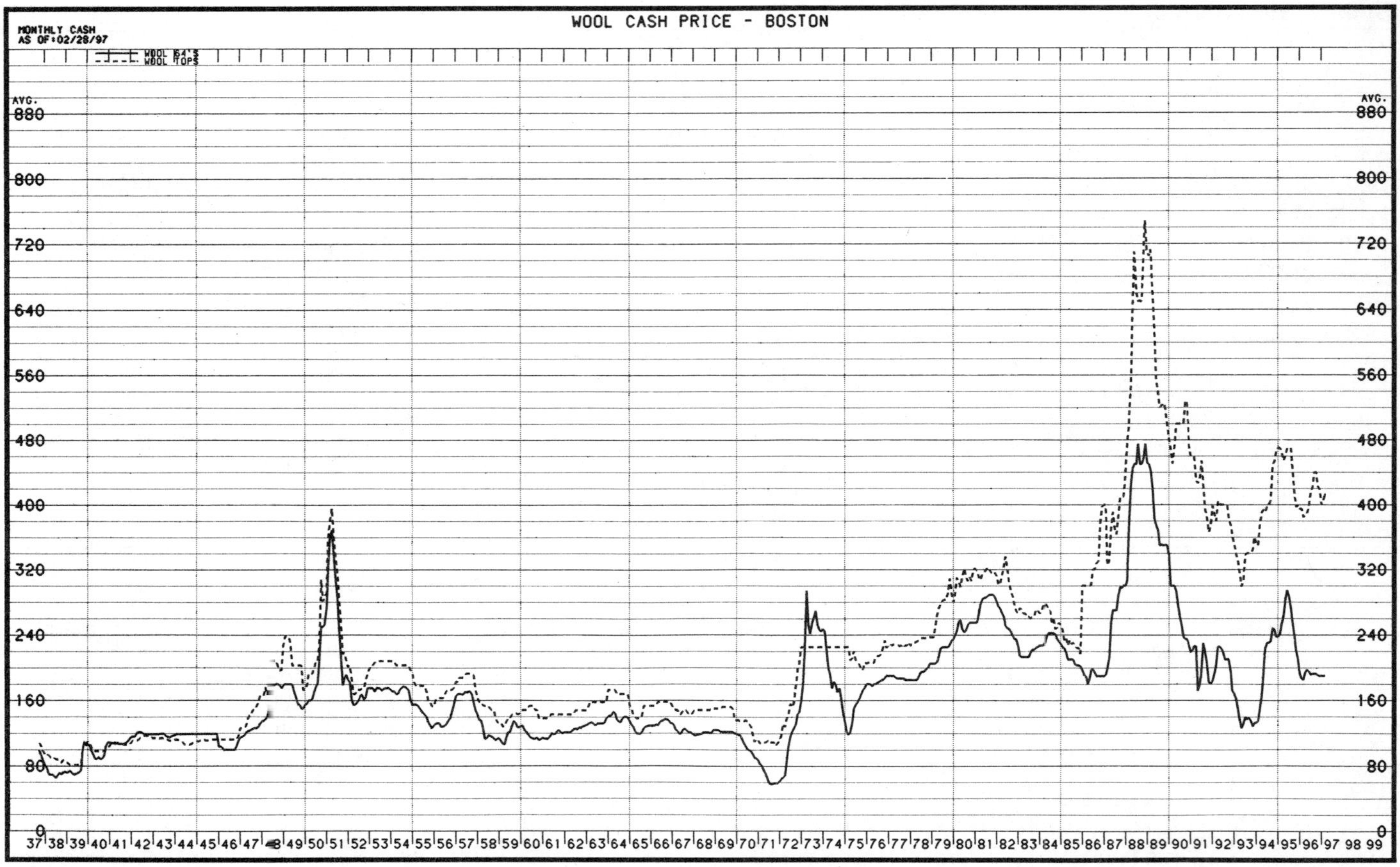


## Wool: Mill Consumption, by Grades in the U.S., Scoured Basis In Thousands of Pounds

| | Apparel Wool[1] | | | | | | | |
|---|---|---|---|---|---|---|---|---|
| | Woolen System | | | Worsted System | | | | |
| Year | 60's & Finer | Coarser Than 60's | Total | 60's & Finer | Coarser Than 60's | Total | All Total | Carpet Wool[2] |
| 1985 | 28,046 | 27,694 | 55,740 | 33,646 | 16,665 | 50,311 | 106,051 | 10,562 |
| 1986 | 34,122 | 32,167 | 66,289 | 41,719 | 18,760 | 60,479 | 126,768 | 9,960 |
| 1987 | 32,401 | 28,613 | 61,014 | 53,814 | 14,849 | 68,663 | 129,677 | 13,092 |
| 1988 | 23,769 | 20,876 | 44,645 | 54,553 | 17,871 | 72,424 | 117,069 | 15,633 |
| 1989 | 24,123 | 21,803 | 45,935 | 56,065 | 18,534 | 74,599 | 120,534 | 14,122 |
| 1990 | 26,173 | 24,941 | 51,114 | 50,630 | 18,878 | 69,508 | 120,622 | 12,124 |
| 1991 | 31,961 | 26,599 | 58,560 | 56,521 | 22,106 | 78,627 | 137,187 | 14,352 |
| 1992 | 33,878 | 25,600 | 59,478 | 58,495 | 18,170 | 76,665 | 136,143 | 14,695 |
| 1993 | 40,895 | 26,624 | 67,519 | 58,834 | 15,027 | 73,861 | 141,380 | 15,431 |
| 1994[3] | 35,960 | 26,038 | 61,998 | 59,599 | 16,966 | 76,565 | 138,563 | 14,739 |
| 1995[4] | 30,211 | 27,089 | 57,300 | 54,980 | 17,019 | 71,999 | 129,299 | 12,667 |

[1] Domestic & duty-paid foreign. [2] Duty-free foreign. [3] Preliminary. [4] Estimate. *Source: Economic Research Service, U.S. Department of Agriculture*

## United States Imports[1] of Unmanufactured Wool (Clean Yield) In Millions of Pounds

| Year | Jan. | Feb. | Mar. | Apr. | May | June | July | Aug. | Sept. | Oct. | Nov. | Dec. | Total |
|---|---|---|---|---|---|---|---|---|---|---|---|---|---|
| 1985 | 10.7 | 5.8 | 6.0 | 5.7 | 7.1 | 4.9 | 7.3 | 4.5 | 6.9 | 7.1 | 5.5 | 8.0 | 79.5 |
| 1986 | 10.2 | 8.8 | 7.6 | 7.5 | 8.0 | 8.6 | 7.8 | 6.3 | 7.0 | 5.0 | 9.2 | 10.8 | 97.0 |
| 1987 | 8.6 | 8.2 | 9.5 | 8.7 | 13.4 | 8.9 | 8.6 | 8.4 | 6.7 | 7.0 | 8.2 | 9.0 | 105.1 |
| 1988 | 12.0 | 12.7 | 8.8 | 9.1 | 8.6 | 7.4 | 7.7 | 5.0 | 3.3 | 6.7 | 8.6 | 6.7 | 96.7 |
| 1989 | 8.7 | 11.3 | 9.0 | 13.1 | 10.3 | 8.3 | 10.0 | 6.9 | 3.9 | 10.4 | 5.1 | 9.8 | 106.9 |
| 1990 | 7.3 | 9.2 | 4.7 | 8.2 | 5.0 | 4.8 | 3.4 | 5.5 | 5.0 | 6.9 | 7.5 | 4.2 | 71.7 |
| 1991 | 10.7 | 6.9 | 5.4 | 5.5 | 7.3 | 8.1 | 9.2 | 7.0 | 4.4 | 7.8 | 5.1 | 9.0 | 86.5 |
| 1992 | 10.2 | 8.1 | 7.3 | 10.6 | 8.8 | 6.2 | 6.9 | 5.0 | 3.9 | 5.5 | 9.1 | 7.8 | 89.3 |
| 1993 | 7.8 | 8.7 | 8.5 | 9.3 | 11.0 | 9.6 | 9.7 | 8.7 | 5.7 | 7.7 | 7.2 | 8.4 | 100.3 |
| 1994 | 10.0 | 7.7 | 7.7 | 12.7 | 7.5 | 7.7 | 6.9 | 6.5 | 4.1 | 5.7 | 8.1 | 7.0 | 91.7 |
| 1995 | 10.4 | 7.7 | 10.8 | 6.0 | 11.5 | 5.2 | 7.3 | 7.3 | 4.9 | 7.9 | 7.7 | 4.1 | 90.6 |
| 1996[2] | 9.6 | 9.1 | 8.8 | 5.6 | 7.0 | 5.9 | 5.3 | 6.6 | 3.1 | 4.6 | 4.6 | 5.1 | 75.3 |

[1] Data are imports for consumption. [2] Preliminary. *Source: Economic Research Service, U.S. Department of Agriculture*

# Zinc

Zinc is utilized as a protective coating on other metals, such as iron or steel, in a process known as galvanizing. Zinc also has use as an alloy with copper to make brass and as an alloying compound with aluminum and magnesium.

At a conference of the International Lead and Zinc Study Group representatives from China commented on their zinc industry. It was indicated that China expects its annual zinc demand to reach 900,000 tonnes by the year 2000, and 1.2 million tonnes by the year 2010. The increase was being supported by an increase in the use of zinc for galvanizing. Presently that process consumes 25 percent of zinc metal. It was noted that while current mines in China are seeing reduced output, the development of a new deposit in Yunnan will make up for the decline in production at other mines. Despite some consolidation among larger mine operations, small mining and smelting operations still account for more than half of Chinese output of zinc concentrates according to Platt's Metals Week.

The U.S. Geological Survey reported that U.S. mine production of recoverable zinc in the January-June 1996 period was 297,000 tonnes, down 2 percent from the same period in 1995. In June 1996, mine production of recoverable zinc was 49,800 tonnes, down 2 percent from May. 1995 mine production was 302,000 tonnes. Smelter production of slab zinc in the first half of 1996 was 181,000 tonnes, down 3 percent from the same period in 1995. Smelter production in June 1996 was 30,600 tonnes, up 2 percent from May. 1995 smelter production of zinc was 363,000 tonnes. Zinc oxide production (gross weight) in the January-June 1996 period was 67,900 tonnes, up 5 percent from the same period in 1995. June 1996 production of zinc oxide was 11,600 tonnes, the same as in May. For all of 1995, oxide production was 130,000 tonnes.

U.S. reported consumption of slab zinc in the first half of 1996 was 304,000 tonnes, down 11 percent from the same period of 1995. Consumption in June 1996 was 49,800 tonnes, down 4 percent from May 1996 and 14 percent less than in June 1995. For all of 1995, consumption of slab zinc was 638,000 tonnes. Consumption of zinc ores in January-June 1996 was 1,200 tonnes, the same as the year before. Consumption in June was 200 tonnes, unchanged from the previous month and a year ago. For all of 1995, zinc ore consumption was 2,400 tonnes.

U.S. consumption of zinc-base scrap was estimated at 60,000 tonnes for the first half of 1996, the same amount as a year earlier. In June 1996, scrap consumption was 10,000 tonnes. For all of 1995 it was 120,000 tonnes. Copper-based scrap consumption in the first half 1996 was 66,000 tonnes (recoverable zinc content), the same level as a year earlier. June 1996 consumption was 11,000 tonnes. For 1995, copper-based scrap consumption was 132,000 tonnes. There were minor amounts of aluminum and magnesium-based scrap consumption. Apparent consumption of zinc metal in January-June 1996 was 587,000 tonnes, down 12 percent from 1995. For all of 1995, zinc metal consumption was 1.24 million tonnes.

U.S. stocks of slab zinc at the end of June 1996 were 49,800 tonnes, down 5 percent from stocks at the end of May. A year earlier, stocks were 60,500 tonnes. U.S. imports of slap zinc in January-May 1996 were 331,000 tonnes.

### *Futures Markets*

Zinc futures and options are traded on the London Metal Exchange (LME).

**Salient Statistics of Zinc in the United States** In Metric Tons

| | Slab Zinc Production | | | Imports for Consumption | | Exports | | Consumption | | | Net Import | High-Grade, |
|---|---|---|---|---|---|---|---|---|---|---|---|---|
| Year | Primary | Secondary | Mine Production (Recovered) | Slab Zinc | Ore (Zinc Content) | Slab Zinc | Ore (Zinc Content) | Slab Zinc[3] | Consumed as Ore | All Classes[4] | as a % of Consumption | Price ¢ Per Lb. |
| 1981 | 346,563 | 50,192 | 312,418 | 612,007 | 245,710 | 323 | 54,232 | 840,875 | 60,643 | 1,189,369 | 65 | 44.56 |
| 1982 | 228,176 | 74,288 | 303,160 | 456,233 | 66,809 | 341 | 77,289 | 795,000 | 35,515 | 1,038,600 | 58 | 38.47 |
| 1983 | 235,694 | 69,390 | 275,294 | 617,679 | 63,156 | 427 | 60,168 | 933,000 | 36,912 | 1,246,300 | 65 | 41.39 |
| 1984 | 253,432 | 78,113 | 252,768 | 639,228 | 86,172 | 760 | 30,579 | 980,000 | 45,487 | 1,344,000 | 68 | 48.60 |
| 1985 | 261,209 | 72,563 | 226,545 | 610,900 | 90,186 | 1,011 | 23,264 | 961,000 | 39,886 | 1,257,000 | 70 | 40.37 |
| 1986 | 253,369 | 62,912 | 202,983 | 665,126 | 75,786 | 1,938 | 3,269 | 999,000 | 19,236 | 1,274,000 | 73 | 38.00 |
| 1987 | 261,345 | 82,589 | 216,327 | 705,985 | 46,464 | 1,082 | 16,921 | 1,052,000 | 2,536 | 1,324,000 | 69 | 41.92 |
| 1988 | 241,294 | 88,492 | 244,314 | 748,130 | 62,966 | 482 | 33,590 | 1,089,000 | 2,412 | 1,340,000 | 70 | 60.20 |
| 1989 | 260,305 | 97,904 | 275,883 | 711,554 | 40,974 | 5,532 | 78,877 | 1,060,000 | 2,107 | 1,311,000 | 61 | 82.02 |
| 1990 | 262,704 | 95,708 | 515,355 | 631,742 | 46,684 | 1,238 | 220,446 | 992,000 | 2,178 | 1,240,000 | 41 | 74.59 |
| 1991 | 253,276 | 124,078 | 517,804 | 549,137 | 45,419 | 1,253 | 381,416 | 933,000 | 2,098 | 1,165,000 | 24 | 52.77 |
| 1992 | 272,000 | 128,000 | 523,430 | 644,482 | 44,523 | 565 | 307,114 | 1,050,000 | 2,400 | 1,290,000 | 30 | 58.38 |
| 1993 | 240,000 | 141,000 | 488,374 | 723,563 | 33,093 | 1,410 | 311,278 | 1,120,000 | 2,200 | 1,340,000 | 45 | 46.15 |
| 1994[1] | 216,600 | 139,000 | 570,000 | 793,000 | 27,374 | 6,310 | 389,000 | 1,180,000 | 2,400 | 1,400,000 | 30 | 49.26 |
| 1995[2] | 221,840 | 131,000 | 614,000 | 856,000 | 10,300 | 3,080 | 424,000 | 1,240,000 | 2,400 | 1,460,000 | 30 | 55.83 |

[1] Preliminary. [2] Estimate. [3] Data through 1981 are reported consumption of slab zinc; 1982 forward, data are apparent consumption of slab zinc.
[4] Based on apparent consumption of slab zinc plus zinc content of ores and concentrates and secondary materials used to make zinc dust and chemicals.
*Source: U.S. Geological Survey*

# ZINC

## World Smelter Production of Zinc[3] In Thousands of Metric Tons

| Year | Australia | Belgium | Canada | France | Germany | Italy | Japan | Kazak-hstan[4] | Mexico | Norway | Peru | Poland | Spain | United Kingdom | United State | World Total |
|---|---|---|---|---|---|---|---|---|---|---|---|---|---|---|---|---|
| 1989 | 296.5 | 306.0 | 669.7 | 265.8 | 372.0 | 259.5 | 714.7 | 977.0 | 193.3 | 120.4 | 126.7 | 163.7 | 246.4 | 79.8 | 358.2 | 7,245 |
| 1990 | 308.5 | 356.5 | 591.8 | 263.1 | 350.3 | 264.4 | 731.6 | 890.0 | 199.3 | 125.1 | 120.6 | 132.2 | 252.7 | 93.3 | 358.4 | 7,178 |
| 1991 | 326.5 | 385.1 | 660.6 | 299.6 | 345.7 | 263.8 | 778.7 | 800.0 | 189.1 | 124.9 | 154.6 | 126.0 | 262.2 | 100.7 | 375.8 | 7,310 |
| 1992 | 338.0 | 310.6 | 671.7 | 319.0 | 383.1 | 253.0 | 780.6 | 250.0 | 151.6 | 127.6 | 138.0 | 134.6 | 365.9 | 96.8 | 399.5 | 7,230 |
| 1993 | 321.0 | 299.6 | 659.9 | 310.0 | 380.9 | 254.0 | 744.5 | 260.0 | 209.9 | 129.2 | 165.4 | 149.0 | 327.6 | 102.4 | 382.0 | 7,400 |
| 1994[1] | 328.0 | 306.2 | 691.0 | 310.0 | 359.9 | 242.0 | 713.3 | 200.0 | 209.2 | 131.9 | 165.0 | 158.0 | 300.6 | 101.3 | 356.0 | 7,370 |
| 1995[2] | 337.0 | 300.0 | 720.1 | 306.0 | 360.0 | 250.0 | 716.9 | 200.0 | 222.7 | 130.0 | 165.0 | 155.0 | 325.0 | 100.0 | 363.0 | 7,480 |

[1] Preliminary. [2] Estimate. [3] Secondary metal included. [4] Formerly part of the U.S.S.R.; data not reported separately until 1992.
*Source: U.S. Geological Survey*

## Consumption (Reported) of Slab Zinc in the United States by Industries and Grades In Metric Tons

| | | By Industries | | | | | By Grades | | | |
|---|---|---|---|---|---|---|---|---|---|---|
| Year | Total | Gal-vanizers | Brass Products | Zinc-Base Alloy[3] | Zinc Oxide | Other | Special High Grade | High Grade | Remelt and Other | Prime Western |
| 1989 | 884,655 | 444,603 | 95,798 | 189,690 | 70,417 | 84,147 | 458,020 | 120,433 | 94,340 | 214,410 |
| 1990 | 801,969 | 388,421 | 104,276 | 171,771 | 67,532 | 69,969 | 445,427 | 92,424 | 78,265 | 210,373 |
| 1991 | 764,038 | 364,629 | 97,952 | 169,883 | 64,035 | 67,539 | 421,316 | 91,468 | 57,786 | 189,930 |
| 1992 | 814,228 | 396,480 | 112,990 | 165,598 | 71,224 | 67,936 | 414,661 | 119,660 | 56,185 | 223,723 |
| 1993 | 1,035,000 | 532,400 | 139,500 | 222,000 | 63,448 | 141,100 | 403,696 | 116,500 | 71,202 | 182,309 |
| 1994[1] | 859,000 | 395,000 | 107,000 | 196,000 | 68,300 | 92,400 | 486,000 | 112,000 | 68,400 | 192,000 |
| 1995[2] | 1,240,000 | 390,000 | 91,500 | 194,000 | 70,900 | 90,800 | 135,000 | 98,200 | 54,400 | 251,000 |

[1] Preliminary. [2] Estimate. [3] Die casters. *Source: U.S. Geological Survey*

## Zinc Foreign Trade of the United States In Metric Tons

| | Imported for Consumption | | | | | | | Zinc Ore & Manufactures Exported: Blocks, Pigs, Anodes, etc. | | Wrought & Alloys | | | | |
|---|---|---|---|---|---|---|---|---|---|---|---|---|---|---|
| Year | Ores[1] | Blocks, Pigs, Slabs | Sheets, Plates, Other | Waste & Scrap | Dross, Ashes, Fume | Dust, Powder & Flakes | Total Value $1,000 | Un-wrought | Un-wrought Alloys | Sheets, Plates & Strips | Angles, Bars, Rods, etc. | Waste & Scrap | Dust (Blue Powder) | Zinc Ore & Con-centrates |
| 1989 | 40,974 | 711,554 | 3,066 | 9,367 | 9,031 | 7,253 | 1,241,659 | 5,532 | 2,423 | 16,515 | 2,653 | 108,086 | 8,137 | 78,877 |
| 1990 | 46,684 | 631,742 | 929 | 31,720 | 6,411 | 8,834 | 1,049,940 | 1,238 | 4,566 | 11,881 | 3,731 | 109,316 | 8,701 | 220,446 |
| 1991 | 45,419 | 549,137 | 539 | 31,596 | 6,483 | 15,424 | 687,879 | 1,253 | 4,224 | 10,385 | 6,151 | 96,314 | 5,737 | 381,416 |
| 1992 | 44,523 | 644,482 | 171 | 31,176 | 11,813 | 17,051 | 910,289 | ----- 5,886 ---- | | NA | NA | 82,088 | 5,889 | 307,114 |
| 1993 | 33,093 | 723,563 | 136 | 38,079 | 11,862 | 16,218 | 799,999 | ----- 8,765 ---- | | NA | NA | 46,385 | 6,727 | 311,278 |
| 1994[2] | 27,374 | 793,482 | 475 | 51,676 | 12,152 | 11,954 | 878,100 | ---- 13,220 ---- | | NA | NA | 58,297 | 6,603 | 389,488 |
| 1995[3] | 10,300 | 856,000 | 332 | 42,300 | 10,900 | 11,700 | 1,018,620 | NA | | NA | NA | 55,900 | 8,840 | 424,000 |

[1] Zinc content. [2] Preliminary. [3] Estimate. NA = Not available. *Source: U.S. Geological Survey*

## U.S. Mine Production of Recoverable Zinc In Thousands of Metric Tons

| Year | Jan. | Feb. | Mar. | Apr. | May | June | July | Aug. | Sept. | Oct. | Nov. | Dec. | Total |
|---|---|---|---|---|---|---|---|---|---|---|---|---|---|
| 1989 | 22.2 | 20.8 | 22.9 | 22.4 | 23.4 | 24.3 | 20.8 | 25.3 | 23.1 | 25.1 | 22.8 | 20.9 | 275.9 |
| 1990 | 26.9 | 24.8 | 26.4 | 26.2 | 27.9 | 45.6 | 50.7 | 57.1 | 44.7 | 42.7 | 40.4 | 43.6 | 515.4 |
| 1991 | 45.5 | 41.9 | 43.8 | 45.5 | 49.4 | 36.9 | 43.0 | 47.4 | 49.5 | 39.0 | 33.4 | 38.0 | 517.8 |
| 1992 | 41.5 | 48.8 | 47.7 | 40.3 | 40.7 | 40.4 | 46.2 | 49.1 | 47.6 | 36.2 | 40.4 | 42.2 | 520.1 |
| 1993 | 48.0 | 42.5 | 46.4 | 39.5 | 43.0 | 40.7 | 33.5 | 32.1 | 35.9 | 41.8 | 41.4 | 43.4 | 488.3 |
| 1994 | 43.2 | 40.2 | 48.4 | 44.0 | 47.9 | 47.1 | 52.5 | 47.1 | 50.1 | 41.6 | 46.0 | 48.0 | 557.0 |
| 1995 | 49.8 | 48.1 | 52.8 | 45.6 | 54.5 | 50.0 | 50.2 | 55.0 | 48.1 | 52.0 | 47.8 | 48.1 | 601.0 |
| 1996[1] | 52.4 | 48.9 | 49.7 | 45.5 | 50.7 | 49.9 | 53.7 | 48.0 | 46.8 | 46.0 | 40.8 | 42.8 | 575.2 |

[1] Preliminary. *Source: U.S. Geological Survey*

## U.S. Consumption of Slab Zinc by Fabricators In Thousands of Metric Tons

| Year | Jan. | Feb. | Mar. | Apr. | May | June | July | Aug. | Sept. | Oct. | Nov. | Dec. | Total |
|---|---|---|---|---|---|---|---|---|---|---|---|---|---|
| 1989 | 90.0 | 81.4 | 96.0 | 81.6 | 97.0 | 82.1 | 76.1 | 101.2 | 81.2 | 92.0 | 92.7 | 78.0 | 1,060.0 |
| 1990 | 82.4 | 79.2 | 88.0 | 74.0 | 79.4 | 91.0 | 102.8 | 100.0 | 73.0 | 86.0 | 73.0 | 67.1 | 826.5 |
| 1991 | 80.0 | 69.0 | 65.9 | 67.8 | 68.3 | 68.8 | 73.6 | 78.0 | 79.3 | 85.9 | 84.2 | 82.0 | 764.0 |
| 1992 | 93.8 | 77.2 | 85.0 | 89.9 | 76.0 | 76.9 | 47.2 | 53.8 | 52.2 | 53.5 | 50.3 | 47.6 | 814.2 |
| 1993 | 50.9 | 49.2 | 55.8 | 59.2 | 60.8 | 55.7 | 44.6 | 49.1 | 47.0 | 52.7 | 50.9 | 51.0 | 774.0 |
| 1994 | 50.8 | 53.7 | 55.7 | 58.5 | 58.7 | 52.7 | 48.0 | 53.2 | 53.6 | 53.9 | 52.5 | 45.0 | 623.0 |
| 1995 | 51.3 | 57.8 | 56.3 | 57.9 | 53.4 | 56.9 | 44.0 | 44.0 | 52.5 | 52.0 | 50.2 | 48.5 | 624.8 |
| 1996[1] | 50.1 | 50.3 | 52.2 | 49.7 | 50.3 | 55.1 | 48.9 | 53.0 | 52.5 | 56.3 | 54.3 | 53.5 | 626.2 |

[1] Preliminary. *Source: U.S. Geological Survey*

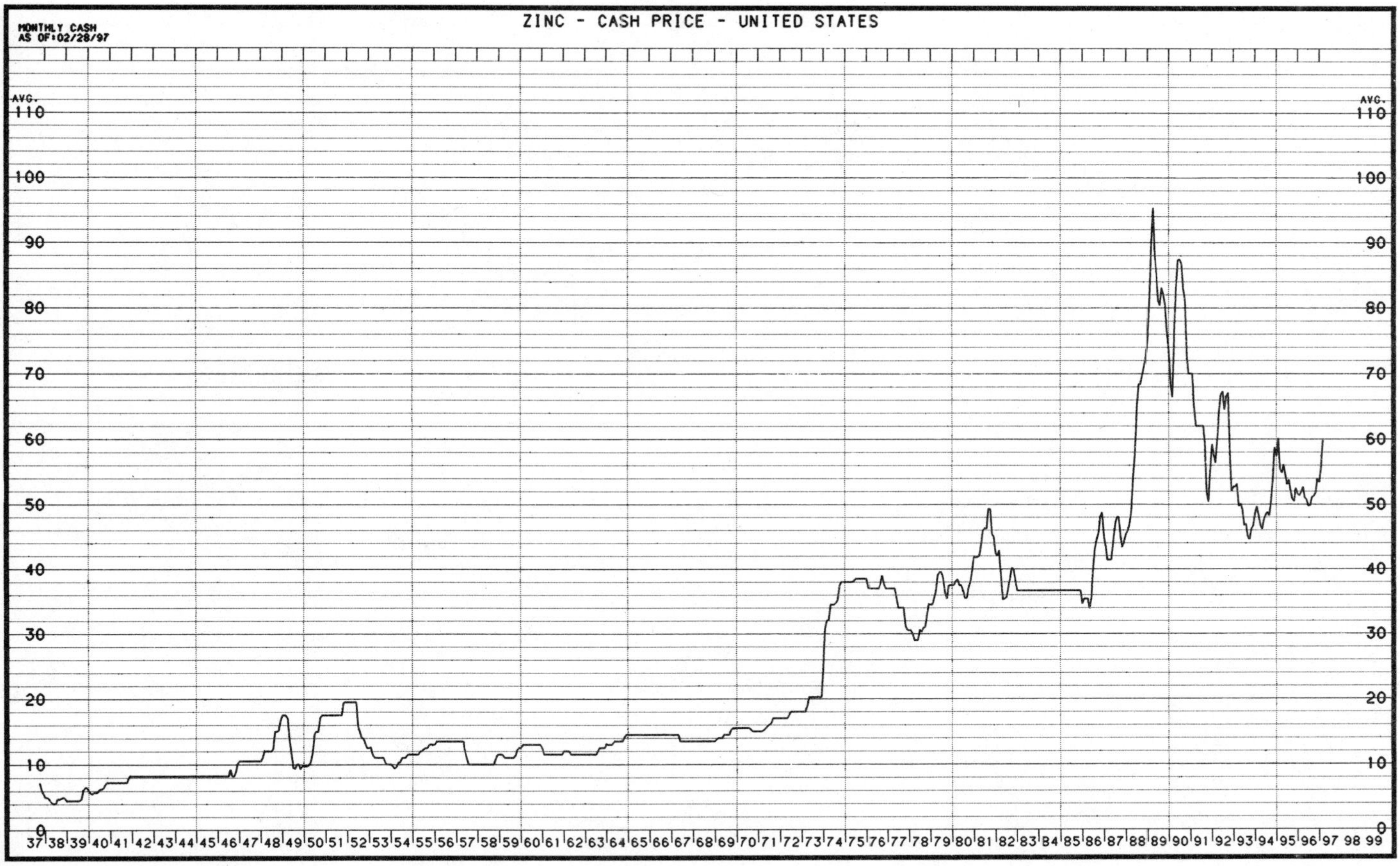


**Average Price of Zinc, Prime Western Slab (Delivered U.S. Basis)** In Cents Per Pound

| Year | Jan. | Feb. | Mar. | Apr. | May | June | July | Aug. | Sept. | Oct. | Nov. | Dec. | Average |
|---|---|---|---|---|---|---|---|---|---|---|---|---|---|
| 1987 | 43.33 | 41.38 | 41.38 | 41.38 | 44.15 | 46.92 | 48.00 | 48.00 | 44.87 | 43.38 | 44.10 | 45.38 | 44.36 |
| 1988 | 45.90 | 46.93 | 49.36 | 54.14 | 57.74 | 65.08 | 68.38 | 68.38 | 69.88 | 71.07 | 72.54 | 75.37 | 62.07 |
| 1989 | 81.58 | 89.01 | 95.38 | 87.76 | 85.38 | 81.06 | 80.38 | 83.26 | 81.88 | 80.31 | 76.57 | 73.38 | 83.00 |
| 1990 | 71.33 | 66.47 | 77.37 | 83.12 | 87.38 | 87.38 | 86.54 | 82.45 | 81.00 | 72.30 | 70.00 | 70.00 | 77.95 |
| 1991 | 70.00 | 64.53 | 62.00 | 62.00 | 62.00 | 62.00 | 62.00 | NQ | NQ | 50.44 | 54.85 | 59.22 | 60.90 |
| 1992 | 57.62 | 56.40 | 60.19 | 64.12 | 66.83 | 67.29 | 64.57 | 66.47 | 67.12 | 57.84 | 52.16 | 52.71 | 61.11 |
| 1993 | 52.70 | 53.18 | 49.72 | 50.07 | 49.27 | 46.75 | 46.90 | 45.08 | 44.54 | 46.21 | 46.54 | 48.69 | 48.30 |
| 1994 | 49.64 | 48.29 | 46.70 | 46.16 | 47.66 | 48.42 | 48.81 | 48.26 | 50.55 | 53.81 | 58.64 | 57.41 | 50.36 |
| 1995 | 60.11 | 55.44 | 54.84 | 56.08 | 54.61 | 53.08 | 53.75 | 52.00 | 50.77 | 50.42 | 52.52 | 51.60 | 53.77 |
| 1996 | 51.35 | 51.86 | 52.66 | 51.03 | 50.76 | 49.75 | 49.86 | 51.22 | 51.11 | 51.76 | 53.81 | 53.78 | 51.58 |

NQ = No quote. *Source: American Metal Market*

DATE DUE

| | | | |
|---|---|---|---|
| | | | |
| | | | |
| | | | |
| | | | |
| | | | |
| | | | |
| | | | |
| | | | |
| | | | |
| | | | |
| | | | |
| | | | |
| | | | |
| | | | |
| | | | |
| | | | |